Encyclopedia of
BILINGUAL EDUCATION

Editorial Board

Encyclopedia of
BILINGUAL EDUCATION

1

JOSUÉ M. GONZÁLEZ
Arizona State University

Editor

Los Angeles • London • New Delhi • Singapore

A SAGE Reference Publication

For information:

 SAGE Publications, Inc.
2455 Teller Road
Thousand Oaks, California 91320
E-mail: order@sagepub.com

SAGE Publications Ltd.
1 Oliver's Yard
55 City Road
London EC1Y 1SP
United Kingdom

SAGE Publications India Pvt. Ltd.
B 1/I 1 Mohan Cooperative Industrial Area
Mathura Road, New Delhi 110 044
India

SAGE Publications Asia-Pacific Pte. Ltd.
33 Pekin Street #02-01
Far East Square
Singapore 048763

Printed in the United States of America.

Library of Congress Cataloging-in-Publication Data

Encyclopedia of bilingual education / editor, Josué M. González.
    p. cm.
"A SAGE reference publication."
Includes bibliographical references and index.
ISBN 978-1-4129-3720-7 (cloth)
    1. Education, Bilingual–Encyclopedias. I. González, Josué M., 1941-

LC3707.E52 2008
370.117'503--dc22   2008001111

08   09   10   11   12   10 9 8 7 6 5 4 3 2 1

Publisher:	Rolf A. Janke
Acquisitions Editor:	Diane McDaniel
Developmental Editors:	Sanford Robinson, Sara Tauber
Reference Systems Manager:	Leticia Gutierrez
Production Editor:	Kate Schroeder
Copyeditors:	Carla Freeman, Robin Gold
Typesetter:	C&M Digitals (P) Ltd.
Proofreaders:	Anne Rogers, Penny Sippel
Indexer:	Kathleen Paparchontis
Cover Designer:	Michelle Lee Kenny
Marketing Manager:	Amberlyn Erzinger

Contents

List of Entries

Reader's Guide

Family, Communities, and Society

Accommodation Theory, Second-Language
Americanization and Its Critics
Attitudes Toward Language Diversity
Benefits of Bilingualism and Heritage Languages
Bilingual Education in the Press
Easy and Difficult Languages
English in the World
English-Only Organizations
Heritage Languages in Families
Hidden Curriculum
Hispanic Population Growth
Home/School Relations
Immigration and Language Policy
Language Brokering
Language Loyalty
Language Restrictionism
Nationality–Culture Myth
One Person-One Language (OPOL)
Peer Pressure and Language Learning
Raising Bilingual Children
Spanish, Decline in use
Spanish, the Second National Language
Spanish Loan Words in U.S. English
Transnational Students
Views of Language Difference

History

Americanization and Its Critics
Boarding Schools and Native Languages
Defense Language Institute
Early Bilingual Programs, 1960s
Early Immigrants and English Language Learning
Equity Struggles and Educational Reform

German Language Education
German Language in U.S. History
Languages in Colonial Schools, Eastern
Languages in Colonial Schools, Western
Latino Civil Rights Movement
National Education Association
 Tucson Symposium
Nationalization of Languages
Navajo Code Talkers
President's Commission on Foreign Language and
 International Studies
Puerto Rico School Language Policies
Southeast Asian Refugees
St. Lambert Immersion Study
Vietnamese Immigration

Instructional Designs

Additive and Subtractive Programs
Biculturalism
Bilingual Charter Schools
Bilingual Special Education
Costs of Bilingual Education
Deaf Bilingual Education
Designation and Redesignation of English
 Language Learners
Dual-Language Programs
English as a Second Language Approaches
English Immersion
English or Content Instruction
Gifted and Talented Bilinguals
Heritage Language Education
Indigenous Language Revitalization
Indigenous Languages as Second Languages
Literacy and Biliteracy
Multicultural Education

Languages and Linguistics

People and Organizations

Policy Evolution

About the Editor

Josué M. González is Professor of Education at the Mary Lou Fulton College of Education at Arizona State University, in the division of Educational Leadership and Policy Studies. He is also the director of the Southwest Center for Education Equity and Language Diversity at ASU. Dr. González received an EdD in Educational Leadership from the University of Massachusetts at Amherst in 1974. Known internationally for his work, Professor González was an early innovator in bilingual and dual-language education. As early as 1967, he wrote curriculum materials and designed programs at all levels, from elementary to graduate school. He has written extensively in that field and has lectured widely. He has helped train future teachers and other school leaders and has held faculty appointments at Chicago State University, Southern Methodist University in Dallas, and Teachers College in New York City. He has also held adjunct appointments at Roosevelt University in Chicago and George Mason University in Virginia.

When the U.S. Department of Education was organized by President Jimmy Carter, Dr. González was appointed the first director of the Office of Bilingual Education and Minority Languages Affairs under the nation's first Secretary of Education, Shirley Hufstedler. He was president of the National Association for Bilingual Education (NABE) from 1986 to 1987 and has served on several advisory committees and commissions. From 1999 until 2006, Dr. González was coeditor of the nation's premier professional journal in the field, the *Bilingual Research Journal*.

Contributors

Hamsa Aburumuh
University of Texas at San Antonio

Jorge A. Aguilar
Arizona State University

Alfredo J. Artiles
Arizona State University

Lani Asturias
Arizona State University

Diane August
Center for Applied Linguistics

Colin Baker
University of Wales, Bangor

María V. Balderrama
California State University, San Bernardino

Donald Jeffrey Bale
Michigan State University

Andy Barss
University of Arizona

Coni Batlle
National Puerto Rican Forum (ret.)

Alfredo H. Benavides
Texas Tech University

William Black
University of South Florida

María Estela Brisk
Boston College

Valentina Canese
Arizona State University

Mario J. Castro
Arizona State University

Ellina Chernobilsky
Rutgers University

Donna Christian
Center for Applied Linguistics

James Cohen
Arizona State University

Debra L. Cole
Teachers College, Columbia University

Mary Carol Combs
University of Arizona

Albert Cortéz
Intercultural Development Research Association

Cathy A. Coulter
Arizona State University

James Crawford
Institute for Language and Education Policy

Kimberley K. Cuero
University of Texas at San Antonio

Irene Cuyun
National Council of La Raza

María de la Luz Reyes
University of Colorado, Boulder

William G. Demmert
Western Washington University

Barbara J. Dray
Buffalo State College

Jacqueline Castillo Duvivier
National Council of La Raza

J. David Edwards
*Joint National Committee for Languages and
National Council for Languages and International
  Studies*

Lucila D. Ek
University of Texas at San Antonio

Kathy Escamilla
University of Colorado, Boulder

Alberto Esquinca
University of Texas at El Paso

Carol Evans
University of Arizona

Christian Faltis
Arizona Sate University

Barbara Marie Flores
California State University, San Bernardino

Belinda Bustos Flores
University of Texas at San Antonio

David E. Freeman
University of Texas at Brownsville

Yvonne S. Freeman
University of Texas at Brownsville

Eugene E. García
Arizona State University

Ofelia García
Teachers College, Columbia University

Heriberto Godina
University of Texas at El Paso

Gustavo González
Texas A&M University

Virginia Gonzalez
University of Cincinnati

Josué M. González
Arizona State University

Minerva Gorena
George Washington University

Margo Gottlieb
Illinois Resource Center and WIDA Consortium

Paul E. Green
University of California, Riverside

Toni Griego Jones
University of Arizona

Norma A. Guzmán
University of Texas at San Antonio

Stella K. Hadjistassou
Arizona State University

Kenji Hakuta
Stanford University

John J. Halcón
California State University, San Marcos

Holly Hansen-Thomas
Binghamton University

Timothy Hogan
Arizona Center for Law in the Public Interest

Paquita B. Holland
District of Columbia Public Schools (ret.)

Susan Hopewell
University of Colorado, Boulder

Nancy H. Hornberger
University of Pennsylvania

Sarah Hudelson
Arizona State University

Mary Esther Soto Huerta
Texas State University, San Marcos

Li-Ching Hung
Mississippi State University

Julian Jefferies
Boston College

Bryant T. Jensen
Arizona State University

Li Jia
University of Texas at San Antonio

Margarita Jiménez-Silva
Arizona State University

Eric Johnson
Arizona State University

Faryl Kander
Arizona State University

Deborah Kennedy
Center for Applied Linguistics

Hye Jong Kim
Arizona State University

Kathleen King
Arizona State University

Jo Anne Kleifgen
Teachers College, Columbia University

Janette Kettmann Klingner
University of Colorado, Boulder

Michelle Kuamoo
*National Clearinghouse for English Language
  Acquisition*

Ha Lam
Arizona State University

Juliet Langman
University of Texas at San Antonio

Jin Sook Lee
University of California, Santa Barbara

Mengying Li
Arizona State University

Na Liu
Arizona State University

Amalia Humada Ludeke
New Mexico State University

Jeff MacSwan
Arizona State University

Kate Mahoney
State University of New York, Fredonia

Nancy Sebastian Maldonado
Lehman College, City University of New York

Paul E. Martínez
New Mexico Highlands University

Leah M. Mason
Teachers College, Columbia University

Julie Renee Maxwell-Jolly
University of California, Davis

Kara T. McAlister
Arizona State University

Teresa L. McCarty
Arizona State University

Geri McDonough Bell
Phoenix Union High School District

Grace P. McField
California State University, San Marcos

Scott McGinnis
Defense Language Institute

Kate Menken
City College of New York

Betty M. Merchant
University of Texas at San Antonio

Eva Midobuche
Texas Tech University

Robert D. Milk
University of Texas at San Antonio

María Robledo Montecel
Intercultural Development Research Association

Sarah Catherine Moore
Arizona State University

Jill Kerper Mora
San Diego State University

Judith H. Munter
University of Texas at El Paso

Janet L. Nicol
University of Arizona

Silvia C. Noguerón
Arizona State University

Alberto M. Ochoa
San Diego State University

Carlos J. Ovando
Arizona State University

Chanyoung Park
Arizona State University

Gregory Pearson
George Washington University

Bertha Pérez
University of Texas at San Antonio

John Petrovic
University of Alabama

Alicia Pousada
University of Puerto Rico

Chang Pu
University of Texas at San Antonio

Victor R. Quiñones Guerra
Teachers College, Columbia University

Luis Xavier Rangel-Ortiz
University of Texas at San Antonio

Iliana Reyes
University of Arizona

Luis O. Reyes
Lehman College, City University of New York

Roger L. Rice
*Multicultural Education
   Training and Advocacy, Inc.*

Ana Roca
Florida International University

M. Victoria Rodriguez
Lehman College, City University of New York

Mariela A. Rodríguez
University of Texas at San Antonio

Rodolfo Rodríguez
University of North Texas

Kellie Rolstad
Arizona State University

Mary Eunice Romero-Little
Arizona State University

Peter D. Roos
*Multicultural Education Training and
   Advocacy, Inc. (ret.)*

Irma Rosas
University of Texas at San Antonio

Stefan M. Rosenzweig
California State University, Long Beach

Olga Gloria Rubio
California State University, Long Beach

Richard Ruiz
University of Arizona

Malena Salazar
University of Texas at San Antonio

María Teresa Sánchez
Education Development Center, Inc.

Patricia Sánchez
University of Texas at San Antonio

Guadalupe San Miguel, Jr.
University of Houston

Marietta Saravia-Shore
Lehman College, City University of New York

Peter Sayer
University of Texas at San Antonio

María M. Seidner
Texas Education Agency (ret.)

Kathryn Singh
*Instituto Tecnológico y de Estudios
  Superiores de Monterrey*

Cary Stacy Smith
Mississippi State University

Howard L. Smith
University of Texas at San Antonio

Karen Smith
Arizona State University

Michaela Steele
University of Texas at San Antonio

Debra Suárez
College of Notre Dame

Koyin Sung
University of Texas at San Antonio

Elsie M. Szecsy
Arizona State University

Yun Teng
Arizona State University

Josefina V. Tinajero
University of Texas at El Paso

Roberto Tinajero II
University of Texas at El Paso

Robert Toonkel
U.S. English, Inc.

Rudolph C. Troike
University of Arizona

Armando L. Trujillo
University of Texas at San Antonio

Pei Ju Tsai
Columbia University

G. Richard Tucker
Carnegie Mellon University

Guadalupe Valdés
Stanford University

Abelardo Villarreal
Intercultural Development Research Association

Dennis Viri
Arizona State University

Larisa Warhol
Arizona State University

Miku Watanabe
Arizona State University

Terrence G. Wiley
Arizona State University

Wayne E. Wright
University of Texas at San Antonio

Hsiaoping Wu
University of Texas at San Antonio

Nancy F. Zelasko
George Washington University

Jingning Zhang
Arizona State University

Introduction

An appropriate way to open an encyclopedia of bilingual education is to define the term in brief. The simplest definition is that *bilingual education is the use of two languages in the teaching of curriculum content in K–12 schools*. This definition is most germane to the United States, the country that is the focus of this encyclopedia. Other nations and cultures define bilingual education differently. There is an important difference to keep in mind relative to bilingual education on the one hand and the study of foreign languages as school subjects on the other. In bilingual education, two languages are used for instruction, and the goal is academic success in and through the two languages. The traditional model of foreign-language study places the emphasis on the acquisition of the languages themselves. Several entries in this encyclopedia describe emerging efforts to bring these two segments of the language-teaching world into a more unified effort.

Design of the Project

The task of assembling this encyclopedia of bilingual education in the United States was complex because the material does not come from a single discipline. It is embedded in several domains of knowledge: applied linguistics, politics, civil rights, various versions of historical events, and of course, classroom instruction. Procedurally, with the help of a small but enthusiastic editorial board and doctoral students, we began by developing an initial list of headwords that encompassed a cross section of relevant information from all of these fields and others. The result was a listing of over 300 discrete topics. We then organized the topics into several categories focused on the following:

- Family, Communities, and Society
- History
- Instructional Designs
- Languages and Linguistics
- People and Organizations
- Policy Evolution
- Related Social Sciences
- Teaching and Learning

In the front matter of the encyclopedia, readers will find a List of Entries, with all topics organized alphabetically, as well as a Reader's Guide, with topics organized by category.

A work of this type requires a huge storehouse of knowledge and experience and a common desire to package information in particular ways. An important function of the general editor is to search for and mobilize those who have the knowledge and convince them to share it in this way. Although most of the contributors are university people, they all agreed to dispense with the academic writing style they commonly use and instead employ a style intended to communicate the information to a wide readership. Having worked for more than 40 years in this field, I had personally experienced many of the trends and events on the initial list. I had also met many of the people who helped to shape the field from the beginning. More recently, I have been privileged to be part of the faculty of the Mary Lou Fulton College of Education at Arizona State University (ASU), home to an exquisite cadre of experts on literacy, English as a second language, policy, and bilingual education. I called on these friends and colleagues to pitch in, and they did so with gusto.

After an initial schema was put on paper outlining the corpus of work by category and title, the list was circulated to colleagues around the country who made suggestions for additions, deletions, and alternative ways of parsing and organizing the topics. Most of these reviewers were pleased to critique the list and volunteered themselves or others to prepare entries.

With this high level of help and support, locating contributors to write the entries was not difficult.

Contributors

The editorial board and I made a decision early on that we wanted this work to be a mix of contributions by seasoned scholars and researchers on the one hand and, on the other, promising doctoral students who might someday be listed as leading scholars themselves. We wanted the work of writing and rewriting to be another learning experience for these junior colleagues. We often paired up a senior person with one of his or her graduate students to review the entry and early drafts. Several contributors commented that the process felt somewhat like a "handing off" by senior people to those who will follow them in this work. The high quality of the results validates this intergenerational approach.

More than 150 authors wrote for the project. I thank them all for their diligent work and for helping us bring in the project on schedule. The graduate students and their mentors alike approached the task of preparing entries with enthusiasm. Several told us of their desire to portray the often controversial topics evenhandedly. Recognizing that loose rhetoric has clouded some aspects of bilingual education over the years, faculty members and editorial board members worked with entry writers to avoid the conceptual traps, assumptions, and easy generalizations that sometimes plague a complex and controversial field such as this. Drafts were reviewed with a view to shaping the entries so as to be helpful to a wide array of users.

Purpose and Content

As general editor, I often asked writers to picture who might use the book and under what circumstances. Imagine, I suggested, a young journalist rushing breathlessly to the reference librarian's desk and asking the best starting point to learn about some aspect of bilingual education in order to complete a story on deadline. The librarian suggests our encyclopedia for its design because, more or less uniformly, the entries give enough information, in a compact way, to allow this user to draft an outline for his assignment. The lists of Further Readings at the end of each entry allow the user to dig deeper into specific subtopics as needed. In effect, the Further Readings serve the user as a vertical expansion of the first entry they consult. The cross-references allow for an equivalent horizontal articulation by listing other entries in the book the user might find valuable. By reading two or three additional entries from among those listed in the cross-references, our young journalist would be able to draft his story. Finally, by selecting from the recommended readings, an in-depth look is possible within a short time.

Most of the entries in this encyclopedia are straightforward informational pieces without editorial comment. Other entries would be of little interest, and hardly credible, if they did not reflect the fact that the field of bilingual education is dynamic, controversial, and subject to multiple perceptions of reality. Ignoring these aspects of the field would be a disservice to the end user. We chose to take note of these dynamics and point out where they live: in schools, research centers, legislative bodies, advocacy organizations, and families.

Nature of the Work

This encyclopedia was not designed to push the envelope of new knowledge. We leave that function to the academic journals and scholarly books in which research and new insights are usually reported. The function of this encyclopedia is to collect and synthesize the knowledge base that is already well accepted and that has been well researched both in the United States and abroad. A handful of entries, however, go beyond the requirements of mere information giving. A small number of distinguished specialists in the field were invited to prepare entries that combine information with expert opinion or advocacy positions. The result is a group of very special entries that round out the history and current status of bilingual education in the United States with commentary on particular contexts, situations, and developments. We believe these additions to the informational content of most entries may help the reader reflect on the matrix in which bilingual education is embedded. These items are identified with a note accompanying the entries.

Readers are reminded that this work is a compendium of information on bilingual education and related topics *in the United States*. While bilingual education in this country is not completely unique, the context in which it has evolved does reflect an "American way" of thinking about languages and education and the relationship between the two. I made the judgment that greater clarity and focus on the U.S. context might be gained through an international perspective. In particular, the entries by Colin Baker, Ofelia García, Betty Merchant and Michaela Steele, and Richard Ruiz provide such international insights, while keeping a sharp focus on the U.S. context.

Readers should also understand how topics may be presented elsewhere. The encyclopedia contains many Spanish words and proper names, some of which require diacritical markings such as the acute accent over vowels. The ñ also makes an appearance in various places. In Spanish, these are conventions of spelling and so we have followed them here. In English, however, they may not be used consistently and create problems in Internet searches. If a search for accented words on the Internet or in a digital database fails to return results, repeat the search without the accents or type *n* instead of *ñ* as needed. Our apologies, but this is the state of the art at the moment.

Acknowledgments

There were many persons at Arizona State University and elsewhere who contributed in important ways to the content, spirit, and logic of this project. I am especially appreciative of the work of the editorial board. Terrence Wiley, Wayne Wright, and Nancy Zelasko were superb collaborators. The simple but honest explanation of their contributions is that the work would have never been done without their keen understanding of the task and its possibilities, as well as their willingness to write, edit, recruit authors, and gently berate those who took too long to complete assignments.

Even with wonderful Internet researchers willing to help, the task of checking all facts and citations in over 300 entries is daunting. That was my responsibility. If any facts got by me with less than total accuracy, it was my omission and not that of the authors.

In the Southwest Center for Education Equity and Language Diversity, where I work, several persons deserve special mention for their work behind the scenes. Silvia Noguerón and Gerda de Klerk shared the job of managing editors, responsible for the flow and early reading of entries. By the time the project approached completion, Silvia had become a trusted editor in English, her own second language. Pauline Stark, my administrative associate, demonstrated that she can also do a mean job of proofreading and tightening up of loose text. In her usual quiet way, Elsie Szecsy periodically asked how she could help. She would usually walk away with additional work, which she completed efficiently. Lani Asturias left before the project was complete, but during her stay served as the Internet connection, doing biographic and bibliographic fact-checking. Ha Lam went away to join her husband in Alaska, but not before writing and editing an important set of entries. My debt of gratitude to these fine coworkers is enormous.

I was especially pleased that in a work devoted to bilingual education, speakers of many languages were involved. In the Center alone we had representation from native speakers of Afrikaans, Chinese, Korean, Spanish, and Tagalog. The blending of accents was a daily reminder that bilingual education exists because the United States has become a microcosm of the linguistic world. Among our faculty colleagues, languages too numerous to name were represented. Most important, it was the delight that everyone took in this polyglot place that made us smile as we worked. A special note of gratitude is owed to our interim Dean of Education, Sarah Hudelson, who not only supported the project in every way possible; she also rolled up her own sleeves to write important entries.

Finally, I wish to acknowledge the facilitating role played by the Sage reference staff every step of the way, from our first contact with the acquisitions editor, Diane McDaniel; to developmental editors Sara Tauber and Sanford Robinson; our technology specialist, Leticia Gutiérrez; reference systems coordinator Laura Notton; the books production team, led by Kate Schroeder; and the copyediting team, Carla Freeman and Robin Gold. They are outstanding professionals, ever ready to help a beleaguered editor. For that, I humbly thank them.

Josué M. González

ACADEMIC ENGLISH

One of the goals of bilingual education in the United States is to support the learning of English by students who come from homes where other languages are spoken. A concern with student performance in mainstream classes following their transfer from bilingual education programs has prompted educators to focus on the types of English skills needed for success in academic work in which the home language is no longer used. This variety of English has been labeled *academic English.* The context in which academic English is used and the features of the text define the form that academic writing will take. This entry briefly explains both text and context and discusses broader implications of academic English for education programs.

In the view of the public, academic English is often regarded as the "best" form of that language and therefore the form schools should concentrate on developing in students. Professionals of various disciplines tend to define academic English relative to the language requirements of a particular discipline. Often, English as a Second Language (ESL) teachers working with English language learners and English educators who teach native speakers of English have different goals for academic English. This distinction exemplifies how academic English is defined differently in various contexts.

Background

An increasing focus on academic English can be traced historically to the mid-19th century, when books and other printed materials first became widely available. Newspapers and scientific tracts called for different forms of the language for different purposes. Looking at the history of the functions of writing in America, Shirley Brice Heath observed a shift from the simple conversational style used during the colonial period toward a growing attention to form near the middle of the 19th century. One aspect of this shift was a change in grammatical person. Whereas writers were once encouraged to use the first person and emphasize an equality of status between readers and writers, following the colonial period, a more impersonal writing style emerged. This new form was characterized by more prescribed and formal criteria.

Michael A. K. Halliday and James Martin believe that some of the features of academic English that developed at this time are related to the evolution of a new language of science employed by scientists in writing about their particular disciplines. Apart from new lexical terms to accommodate new knowledge, scientists unconsciously used grammatical resources, such as the construction of nominal groups and clauses, in order to build a new form of reasoned argument. This process has come to be represented in the grammar of the English language through a set of grammatical features that are often substantially different from those of everyday language. The instructional implications are also numerous. James Cummins, for example, has theorized that increasing the number of Latin-based terms in the language of the classroom may increase student performance in academic English because Latin-based words are more numerous in academic English than are words derived from other tongues. The latter, he believes, are more common in everyday language.

A Question of Context

Academic English constitutes one portion of the language capital of bilingual students. Everyday heritage language and academic heritage language, along with everyday English, are also present in various degrees in the overall repertoire that students use to different degrees, depending on the type of education they have received and the life experiences they have had outside the context of American schools. These languages and forms of language, also known as *registers,* a variety of language typically used in a specific type of communicative setting, enjoy different status in society. The standard forms of the language are usually considered "better" or more appropriate for school use, even though in linguistic terms they include the same basic features of language as everyday language forms. In English-speaking countries, English naturally enjoys a higher status than other languages. Thus, in an English-speaking society, standard English, the social version of academic English, enjoys the most prestige. With this prestige comes the perception that academic English belongs to the more privileged classes. Working-class students from lower-socioeconomic backgrounds often consider academic English the language of "rich" people and therefore do not appropriate it for their social circles. These differences are not unique to the United States. These different forms or registers of language are present in all societies. They emerge as a way to define the identity of a group and distinguish insiders from outsiders, or they are the result of new knowledge that needs expression in particular ways.

Although academic English has been described as decontextualized language, Mary Schleppegrell argues that its use is very dependent on context. For example, public speaking to demonstrate authority in the subject and writing in various disciplines require different varieties of academic English. Academic English is part of the linguistic repertoire students need to function in school when reporting knowledge and producing and reading academic text. Not all school contexts require academic English, however; when students discuss material in groups or chat with their friends during lunch, everyday language is perfectly acceptable.

The Text

Academic English presents a range of features that go against the common sense of everyday language. It is more abstract, less dependent on the context of the interaction, and contains domain-specific vocabulary, features that can make the learner feel excluded and even alienated from the subject matter. When teachers begin to focus on these difficulties, they usually think of the problem in terms of vocabulary. Although new lexical terms are a part of the challenge, the relationship between these technical terms may involve grammatical structures new to students.

One of the features of academic English that appears in all disciplines has been called *grammatical metaphor* by some linguists. As defined by Halliday and Martin, this means that one grammatical class is substituted for by another or one grammatical structure is substituted by another. The most common of these is to turn verbs (processes) into nouns (things) in order to condense information. In technical terms, it is called *nominalization.* For example, the sentence

> More people demand more goods, so then the prices will rise, because there won't be enough goods

contains three clauses, each of which has a verb *(demand, will, won't be).* But if we rephrase the sentence, the idea is presented in one clause with one verb *(will result):*

An increase in demand	will result	in high prices because of a lack of goods
(Nominal clause)	(Verb)	(Nominal clause)

In this example, two verbs, or processes, have been transformed into nouns. This condensation of the language allows the author to "pack" more information in the clauses, a consistent feature of academic language. Other features of academic English include use of complete sentences, being explicit, using the third person rather than the first, and using verb tenses to indicate different kinds of functions. For example, a historical account requires past tense *(The civil rights movement emerged in the 1950s),* whereas a historical analysis requires the present *(Movements such as the civil rights require leadership).* It is important to note that academic English is not a fixed form of language, but varies according to whether it is oral or written and according to the specific discipline, and it changes over time.

Students need to know that writing takes on different forms depending on the purpose, and students often need practice in distinguishing the genres required of them in each discipline. When writing a procedure in a science class, for instance, students have to be aware that sentences in this genre of writing must be in the imperative mood and personal pronouns have to be avoided. For example, a fourth-grade student wrote the following procedure in a state exam sample, the Massachusetts Comprehensive Assessment Scale:

> Step 1: He will get a plant.
>
> Step 2: He will get Super Grow and put it on his tomato plant.
>
> Step 3: He will sit there and watch it grow. Then he will show it to people.

In this instance, the use of the future tense, typical of predictions more than of procedures, resulted in a lower score for the student who was being tested, although grammaticality was not an issue.

The language to build concepts in the academic English of mathematics contains vocabulary that is a challenge to students, because words that they might already know (e.g., *sum, borrow, product*) take on technical meanings. More important, the academic language of math is heavily dependent on the grammatical patterning of words. At the phrase level, the relationships between clauses need to be understood in order to make sense of mathematical word problems such as the following:

> Write an equation that expresses *f,* Joey's total miles traveled from Boston, as a function of *m,* the number of miles traveled.

Teachers should explicitly talk to students about the ways in which grammar is constructing the meaning of this sentence. The technical description of this is that the second and fourth clauses are appositions helping to define the last element in the first *(f)* and third *(m)* clauses. A different relationship is established between the first and third clauses, where the last is a continuation of the first. Understanding these relationships is of utmost importance in order to understand what is being asked.

Implications for Bilingual Education

Assuming that the learning acquisition (versus learning) hypothesis holds true, individuals socialized to the different forms of English and/or a heritage language have a general understanding of these various forms of

language and when it is appropriate to use them. Some bilingual children, however, may be socialized only to the everyday form of their heritage language and/or English. Academic language may not be part of their language development experience. In short, the student must not only learn English; he or she must also learn academic English, a more complex task that usually takes place in the classroom and is not practiced on the street or the playground. This can become a problem that is often not easy to detect until the child begins to do extensive writing in class. Schools then must explicitly present academic English, relate it to their own linguistic repertoire, and create authentic situations for use of the academic variety.

Students who do not experience this language in their daily social environments need not only to experience it in the classroom but also to be convinced that they have the ability and the right to acquire it without feeling that to do so, they have to abandon their familiar forms of language or disregard their social identities. Teachers should allow students to use their everyday language when discussing matters in class among themselves and also support the use of academic English when students are doing class presentations. For example, one teacher regularly assigned students to develop PowerPoint presentations of their group work to share with the rest of the class. Such an activity required students to consider not only the content but also the language of the presentation. Written reports are also good contexts in which to practice the written form of academic English. Pauline Gibbons argues that presenting all the various forms of language in the classroom context helps students develop academic language as well as understand the differences between the forms.

Academic English is part of the linguistic repertoire that successful students need to develop, not because it is "better" than their language or other forms of English, but because students should have it available for use when they need it. Various disciplines depend on their own forms of academic language to express particular meanings and specialized knowledge, and teachers need to know the structures of these differing academic languages in order to make them explicit to students. Yet academic language is sometimes made more difficult than necessary, as when authors try to inflate the value of their writing by deliberately making it sound highbrow and overly intellectual. It is important, therefore, to determine whether the purported difficulty of a text is in fact required by the nature of the communication. Teachers and students alike need to take a critical stance with respect to academic English: to teach it and learn it but also to be able to identify its proper uses as well as its pitfalls.

María Estela Brisk and Julian Jefferies

See also BICS/CALP Theory; Discourse Analysis; Ebonics; English Immersion; Language Registers; Languages, Learned or Acquired

Further Readings

Baker, C., & Hornberger, N. H. (Eds.). (2001). *An introductory reader to the writings of Jim Cummins.* Clevedon, UK: Multilingual Matters.

Gibbons, P. (2002). *Scaffolding language, scaffolding learning: Teaching second language learners in the mainstream classroom.* Portsmouth, NH: Heinemann.

Halliday, M. A. K., & Martin, J. (1993). *Writing science: Literacy and discursive power.* London: Falmer Press.

Heath, S. B. (1981). Toward an ethnohistory of writing in American education. In M. F. Whiteman (Ed.), *Writing: The nature, development, and teaching of written communication* (pp. 25–45). Hillsdale, NJ: Lawrence Erlbaum.

Schleppegrell, M. J. (2004). *The language of schooling: A functional linguistics perspective.* Mahwah, NJ: Lawrence Erlbaum.

Valdés, G. (2004). Between support and marginalization: The development of academic language in linguistic minority children. *Bilingual Education and Bilingualism, 7,* 102–132.

Web Sites

Massachusetts Comprehensive Assessment Scale: http://www.doe.mass.edu/mcas/student

ACADEMIC LANGUAGE

See BICS/CALP THEORY

ACCENTS AND THEIR MEANING

As commonly understood, a person's *accent* refers to the way he or she pronounces words, phrases, and other linguistic features of a language in which such pronunciations differ substantially from what a native speaker of that country or culture might say. Accents are actually features of speech rather than language, but this distinction is rarely made by the general public. Hence, accents are usually considered part of the phonology of a language, a subfield of linguistics that is concerned with the study of the sounds of speech.

Rossina Lippi-Green distinguishes two different kinds of accents: first-language and second-language accents. *First-language accents* are associated with native speakers of a language and the different regional varieties that a particular language might have. In this case, the way some people sound may vary depending on the geographical area from which they and their families come. Some people use accents for their social, professional, and economic advantage. First-language accents are also associated with race, gender, ethnicity, socioeconomic status, income, and religion. These factors often shape social identity and determine the language and accent that people choose to use. Sometimes there is little choice involved. *Second-language accents* are those associated with nonnative learners/speakers of a language, such that their accents often influence the pronunciation of a nonnative or second language. For instance, a Mexican person's Spanish language phonology will influence his or her pronunciation in English language, and an English person's English language phonology will influence his or her pronunciation in Spanish.

Accents and Power Relations

People naturally have different ways of talking and saying things, though a given instance may or may not constitute a genuine accent. Speech accommodation studies conducted by Leslie M. Beebe and Howard Giles suggest that some people have attitudes about the particular way others speak, regardless of who the speaker may be. Research by critical race theorist Mari J. Matsuda suggests that the way people speak is often judged by others to measure their social, cultural, political, or economic orientation. She maintains that accents are used to create hierarchies of power in the social structure of a community and to determine a person's social standing in a particular nation or region. Matsuda claims that the judgments that are made about a person's speech go beyond the issue of linguistic competence and represent attitudes and beliefs about the person's social, cultural, political, and economic individuality.

Language constitutes an important part of people's identity, and the way people sound when they speak is an important component of their sense of belonging to a given time and space. It may not be an exaggeration to suggest that everybody speaks with an accent; what may sound "funny" or "strange" to one person may sound normal to another depending on the national, regional, and cultural context in which speech takes place. In the same way, acceptance of accents is relative to the context and the culture in which those accents are most often heard. According to the principles of cultural relativism as discussed by the anthropologist Franz Boas, an individual's behavior, beliefs, and language make sense only if interpreted in the context of that individual's culture.

U.S. culture, including language and accents, has been largely shaped by interactions of the cultures of countries that colonized various regions of the United States. Early on, English, French, and Spanish cultures were the most influential, but subsequent groups of immigrants from other countries became equally as influential. The settlers interacted and mixed with non-English-speaking immigrants from other nations, and those unions developed and spread diverse accents across the United States. Immigrants from the same country of origin often tended to cluster in specific geographic areas and thus contributed to the development of regional accents.

Language and accents are always changing because of social, cultural, political, and economic influences, such as globalization and the transnationalism of the 21st century. In the United States, however, the myth persists of a nonaccented, standard English. According to Lippi-Green, this relates to the way myths function to control people with superstition and fear. A standard view of English ignores the region, country, level of education, culture, religion, and socioeconomic class of the people who speak it. Standard English is understood as a uniform vocabulary, spelling, grammar, and pronunciation, often identified as "educated English." It is actually not any of those things.

There is really no homogeneous or generic English accent, yet many people associate regional and national accents with negative stereotypes and bias constructs. Language teachers sometimes contribute to reinforcing these stereotypes by portraying "nonstandard" regional and national accents as belonging to categories of inferiority and superiority. In business communities, people may adjust their accents in order to fit into the socially prescribed speech of a particular environment in which accents can be a burden or an advantage. For example, a person from the southern United States desiring to work in a law firm in New York City may adjust his or her accent in order to fit into the cultural context of New York City, as well as that of a corporate law firm.

Accents and Education

In the educational context, accents play an important role. During the critical years of identity formation, children pay much attention to what their peers and others think about the way they speak. Children tend to imitate and adopt the way their peers speak and to label other students according to their national or regional accents. Students' accents are often associated with certain stereotypes and function to establish and justify status or privilege. Some parents do not want their children to socialize with children who have regional or national accents different from their own. It is not unusual for these assumptions to emerge on the basis of beliefs concerning the higher or lower status of a given form of English. Some students feel intimidated about speaking because their accents are associated with culturally stigmatized groups. Within racially and culturally diverse groups, some members are looked down on for adopting mainstream accents and language varieties (which include not only accents but also vocabulary and grammatical structures) that are not part of the subculture of that particular group; such is the case with some speakers of African American vernacular. Alexander Guiora examined the relationship between a person's pronunciation of a second language and the degree of social approval the person experiences. He concluded that accents were not related to intelligence or learning abilities. Despite evidence indicating that accents will inevitably vary, English language learners must continue to face the myth that speaking with a standard accent is not only desirable but also perhaps the only way to succeed.

Luis Xavier Rangel-Ortiz

See also Cultural Deficit and Cultural Mismatch Theories; Ebonics; Language and Identity; Social Class and Language Status; Status Differences Among Languages

Further Readings

Beebe, L., & Giles, H. (1984). Speech-accommodation theories: A discussion in terms of second-language acquisition. *International Journal of the Sociology of Language, 46,* 5–32.

Boas, F. (1938). *The mind of primitive man* (Rev. ed.). New York: Macmillan.

Fairclough, N. (1992). *Language and power.* London: Langman.

Guiora, A. (1983). Language and concept formation: A cross-lingual analysis. *Behavior Science Research, 18,* 228–256.

Lippi-Green, R. (1997). *English with an accent: Language, ideology, and discrimination in the United States.* New York: Routledge.

Matsuda, M. J. (1991). Voices of America: Accent, antidiscrimination law, and jurisprudence for the last reconstruction. *Yale Law Journal, 100,* 1329–1406.

ACCOMMODATION THEORY, SECOND-LANGUAGE

The theory of linguistic accommodation was first discussed in the 1960s by Howard Giles and his colleagues. A social psychologist rather than a linguist, Giles declared that the foundation of accommodation theory lay in social psychological research on similarity attraction. He claimed, in essence, that because people both need and desire approval, it is common for individuals to induce others to evaluate them in a more positive light by reducing the dissimilarities between themselves and others. This results in speech accommodation, with a high probability that individuals are willing to adjust their speech behavior for the potential rewards that may accrue. Thus, according to the theory, when we talk with others, we unconsciously change our speech styles toward the styles our interlocutors use or admire.

Accommodation occurs in a wide variety of communication behaviors, including the speaker's accent, grammar, and vocabulary. Giles stated that accommodation may take place at the following levels when speakers compare their own speech with that of an interlocutor: speed of delivery (the speed at which one talks), pitch range (how high or low in frequency one's voice is), phonological variables (sounds used by the speaker), and vocabulary (the choice of words used). Accommodation differs according to the status of speaker and listener and is associated with power. For English language learners (ELLs), a primary reason for accommodation depends on the extent to which ELLs and immigrants want to be accepted into their host communities. If an individual moves to a new country and works at a new company, he or she would likely have a high need for social approval; thus, speaking style would be important.

Accommodation theory uses a social-psychological perspective to shed light on the relationship between social/situational factors and second-language (L2) use. It examines what social factors motivate the use of psycholinguistic choices. Studies regarding L2 learning have demonstrated that learners are sensitive to their interlocutors. For instance, ELLs tend to adapt their speech to their interlocutors by using more phonological variants. As a result, ELLs are likely to be more hesitant and briefer when addressing a listener with the same native language background as their own, and they are likely to be less prepared to negotiate any communication problems. Such a phenomenon occurs even during the early stages of learning, and learners seem to be aware of specific linguistic features that are seen as stereotypes about native speakers of the target language. ELLs are also more aware of their own identities as well as the conversation topic than are their native-speaker interlocutors. Native speakers are comfortable conversing in their first language, whereas ELLs tend never to forget that they are foreigners, especially when speaking a second tongue; that is, they realize that they do not sound like native speakers and therefore remain quiet during conversations. Likewise, this is true of the conversation topic. ELLs often feel they will sound "stupid" if they join a conversation with a native speaker when the topic is serious (philosophy, religion, war, etc.), and hence they might listen, but will not add to the conversation. Such sensitivity shows in their attitudes toward a certain topic, judging themselves as experts or nonexperts when comparing themselves with their native-speaker interlocutors. ELLs often report that they believe they are far too slow in speaking their L2 and that native speakers are unusually fast.

Giles stated that language is *socially diagnostic.* In other words, when an individual encounters someone speaking with a different accent or pronunciation, it is inevitable that he or she will make guesses regarding this particular speaker's nonlinguistic characteristics, such as social status, education level, or even intelligence. Generally, people observe the speed at which others talk, the length of pauses and utterances, the kind of vocabulary and syntax used, as well as intonation, voice pitch, and pronunciation. Apparently, language is not homogeneous or fixed; rather, it is multichanneled, multivariable, and capable of vast modifications from context to context by the speaker.

Accommodation theory is controversial because individuals tend, consciously or unconsciously, to seek identification with others through language. In fact, even the most trivial aspects of speech and pronunciation can take on crucial importance, and listeners often detect slight differences and afford them social significance.

A person's speaking style might change due to any number of variables. For example, when speaking to a nonnative speaker or a child, an individual might speak more slowly or use grammatically simple language. Accommodation theory, also called *accommodative process,* attempts to account for the different ways in which speakers may manipulate language to maintain integrity, distance, or identity by unconsciously modifying their language choice, tone, or speech rate to converge or diverge with others' behavior. Although accommodation theory is considered a sociolinguistic theory, it has been employed in various settings, including public speaking, songwriting, radio broadcasting, courtroom proceedings, and human-computer interaction.

The basic form of accommodation concerns communicators' efforts to make themselves more similar to the target in order to improve communication. In addition, accommodation theory has to do with how individuals adjust their behaviors to one another, either to become more alike or to exaggerate their differences.

In an L2 learning environment, accommodation occurs in a wide variety of communication behaviors, including accent, rate, loudness, vocabulary, grammar, register, and so on. ELLs may demonstrate accommodation to others but not be aware of their own behavior. Individuals change their speech patterns in various interactions for the purpose of demonstrating that they approve of the other person in the interaction. In L2 teaching based on accommodation theory, teachers of ELLs make whatever accommodations may be necessary. This component is sometimes called *culturally compatible instruction.*

Convergence and Divergence

According to accommodation theory, there are two main strategies: convergence and divergence. *Convergence* occurs when the speaker adjusts his or her normal speech to make it more similar to the interlocutor's speech or when the speaker converges toward a prestigious norm that he or she believes is favored by the interlocutor. In short, the speaker accepts the interlocutor's values and seeks to demonstrate that acceptance by his or her own linguistic behavior. Conversely, *divergence* occurs when speakers seek to alter their speech in order to make themselves linguistically different. Both convergence and divergence can take place in an upward or downward fashion. *Upward convergence* occurs when speakers adjust their speech to exhibit the norms of high-status individuals in their society. *Downward convergence* involves adjustments in the direction of the speech norms from a higher class to a lower class. For instance, a person with a PhD in physics will speak differently when explaining quantum mechanics to a high school dropout than when discussing physics with colleagues; that is, the physicist will use language in a manner designed to simplify complex concepts for his or her less educated interlocutor. Generally, upward convergence is the more common type because it is based on the universal desire for approval from those we respect and emulate. *Upward divergence* occurs when speakers emphasize the standard features of their speech, whereas *downward divergence* occurs when speakers emphasize the nonstandard features of their speech. An example of upward divergence would be two people from different classes arguing, with the individual from a higher-socioeconomic background emphasizing the standard features of his or her speech to distinguish himself or herself from the lower-class interlocutor. In the same example, the person of lower-socioeconomic status who emphasizes his or her less standard form of speech would be exhibiting downward divergence.

The causes of convergence and divergence can be complicated. One of the most well-known studies regarding accommodation theory was initiated by Giles and his colleagues. It concerned conversations between unequally ranked nurses and how convergence and divergence operated on the basis of their ability to use the English language. The results showed that when speaking to lower-ranked nurses, those with a higher status used a less standard English; likewise, when the lower-status nurses spoke to their higher-ranked colleagues, they spoke a more standard English. Moreover, people are more likely to convert their speech rates in a manner emphasizing the stereotype of their interlocutors' speech rates and their way of using language. In addition, speakers tend to switch from convergence to divergence as they reevaluate the person they speak to during the conversation.

In L2 learning, accommodation theory is connected with sociolinguistics and social psychology. From Giles's perspective, the ELL social group is seen as the in-group, and the target language (L2) social group is seen as the out-group, and the relationship between them is explained as *perceived social distance*. When members of the in-group and out-group communicate, they may or may not adopt positive linguistic distinctiveness strategies. When members emphasize solidarity with their own in-group members, they perform linguistic divergence from the out-group; however, when members are more concerned about status, they are more likely to exhibit convergence.

From an L2 learning perspective, convergence and divergence display the learner's attitude toward L2 learning, and apparently attitudes play an essential role regarding learning outcomes. In fact, Giles and his associates believe that if ELLs want to fully master the target language, they need to be engaged in frequent and long-term convergence instead of divergence. Although studies have been conducted concerning how learners' ethnicity affects their communication styles in the L2 classroom, there is no scientific evidence based on the learners' attitudes of convergence or divergence.

ELLs engage in convergence or divergence as a way to show the extent to which they accept the host culture and its communities. In others words, how ELLs define themselves in relationship to the host group is essential and influences their L2 proficiency level. Giles also believes that ELLs target language proficiency relies upon their learning motivation, which greatly impacts how learners perceive themselves in terms of their identities. Overall, accommodation theory has helped linguists understand why individuals emulate the speech patterns of their interlocutors. In an L2 situation, accommodation theory further helps to explain how ELLs vary in the way they use their L2 choice in terms of pronunciation, vocabulary, and grammatical structure.

Cary Stacy Smith and Li-Ching Hung

See also Social Class and Language Status; Status Differences Among Languages

Further Readings

Ellis, R. (2002). *The study of second language acquisition.* Oxford, UK: Oxford University Press.

Gibbons, J. (2005). Law enforcement, communication, and community. *Journal of Multilingual & Multicultural Development, 26,* 265–267.

Giles, H., & Coupland, N. (1991). *Language: Contexts and consequences.* Keynes, UK: Open University Press.

McCann, R., & Giles, H. (2006). Communication with people of different ages in the workplace: Thai and America data. *Human Communication Research, 32,* 74–108.

ACCULTURATION

In the fields of anthropology and education, the term *acculturation,* or the capacity to negotiate effectively both within and outside the primary culture and language, and the related term *assimilation* have been used extensively to describe specific types of contact between cultures. Anthropologists define *culture* as a deep, multilayered set of values, beliefs, and behaviors that pervades every aspect of every person's life on every level. In this view, culture is not an isolated portion of reality that can be learned as a set of facts or that can be used mechanistically to refer to phenomena in a given human context, including classrooms. Rather, it is learned, shared, and constantly changing as a result of evolving circumstances and events in our lives.

As a vehicle for cultural change and adaptation, acculturation is viewed as a process, voluntary or involuntary, by which an individual or group adopts one or more of another group's cultural or linguistic traits, resulting in new or blended cultural or linguistic patterns. Thus, for example, rural Mexican immigrant youth who begin wearing baseball caps and listening to heavy metal or rap music are considered to be acculturating or adjusting to contemporary U.S. culture. However, while they may quickly embrace their new nation's clothing styles and musical tastes, it will take a much longer time for their primary language patterns, gestures, facial expressions, value systems, and styles of social interaction to change. According to Sonia Nieto, an expert on bilingual/multicultural education, immigrant students often maintain a "deep culture" associated with their prior lives while they adapt to their new cultural environments in more superficial ways.

Unlike assimilation, which results in the loss of a person's original cultural or linguistic identity, acculturation involves adaptation and change. A Koyukon

Athapaskan who uses a snowmobile instead of sled dogs is still an Athapaskan Indian. It is not a set of particular traits that constitutes ethnic identity as much as whether a person considers himself or herself to be a member of a distinct group.

Acculturation is frequently an additive process, which can result in two or more identities that coexist harmoniously. The ability to function in a bicultural or even multicultural context is known as *situational ethnicity*. In today's global village, most people actually are multicultural and multilingual to some extent, especially those who live in large, complex societies.

Bilingual and multicultural educators see their goal as helping students to acculturate, rather than assimilate, for they believe that languages and cultures intersect in ways that enrich and energize society. There is persuasive evidence that bilingual schooling practices that affirm students' primary home languages and cultures tend to produce not only improved academic achievement but also happier learners who can effectively communicate with their relatives and ethnolinguistic communities, as well as with their adopted cultures.

The subtle processes involved in acculturation are often challenging and complex, but it is important for bilingual educators to understand them. Harbans Bhola, a noted international comparative educator who has written extensively on planned processes of societal change, suggests that any type of change can be set in motion by a group, an individual, an institution, or even an entire culture. It may be initiated intentionally or by chance, and the individual, group, institution, or culture may be either the initiator or the recipient of the contact that leads to the change. Power relationships and environmental dynamics can play an important role in acculturation. For example, the individual, group, institution, or culture may be receptive, neutral, or hostile to the contact, depending on factors such as the status of those who are promoting the change; the material resources and time required for the contact to occur; and the ideas, influences, and conceptual basis that are driving the process. In most cases, the direction of change is toward the more powerful entity. Individuals and groups from ostracized or marginalized cultures and languages tend to gravitate or be pulled toward allegedly more "prestigious" languages and cultures. When that happens, those individuals and groups may resist adaptation to the new culture or language and may feel alienated and out of place. When there is mutual acceptance and appreciation of each other's languages and cultures, however,

individuals undergoing acculturation tend to enjoy living in a bicultural and bilingual context.

Acculturation has never been a smooth, painless, or balanced process. Moreover, being acculturated does not necessarily mean giving equal time to both cultures and languages in terms of behavior. There may be myriad traits from one or both cultures that the person understands but does not necessarily act out, such as religious rituals or family traditions. There may be entire areas of life—for example, male-female relations—in which the individual consistently and predictably prefers one culture or the other.

Acculturation processes can be affected by a variety of factors, including ethnicity, geographical region, national origin, social class, level of education, prior schooling experience, types of contact with other cultural groups, religion, gender, age, and socialization practices at home. These variables all have a possible impact on the teaching and learning process.

Carlos J. Ovando

See also Assimilation; Biculturalism; Cultural Deficit and Cultural Mismatch Theories; Culturally Competent Teaching; Enculturation; Ethnocentrism; Language Socialization; Melting-Pot Theory

Further Readings

Bhola, H. S. (1988–1989). The CLER model of innovation diffusion, planned change, and development: A conceptual update and applications. *Knowledge in Society: The International Journal of Knowledge Transfer, 1*(4), 56–66.

Freeman, R. (2004). *Building on community bilingualism.* Philadelphia: Caslon.

Heath, S. B. (2004). Ethnography in communities: Learning the everyday life of America's subordinated youth. In J. A. Banks (Ed.), *Handbook of research on multicultural education* (2nd ed., pp. 146–162). San Francisco: Jossey-Bass.

Nieto, S. (1999). *The light in their eyes: Creating multicultural school communities.* New York: Teachers College Press.

Olsen, L. (1998). *Made in America: Immigrant students in our public schools.* New York: New York Press.

Portes, A., & Rumbaut, R. (1996). *Immigrant America* (2nd ed.). Berkeley: University of California Press.

Suárez-Orozco, C., & Suárez, M. (2001). *Children of immigration.* Cambridge, MA: Harvard University Press.

Valdés, G. (1996). *Con respeto: Bridging the distances between cultural diverse families and schools.* New York: Teachers College Press.

Valdés, G. (2001). *Learning and not learning English: Latino students in American schools.* New York: Teachers College Press.

Additive and Subtractive Programs

The terms *additive* and *subtractive bilingual education* came into use in the last quarter of the 20th century as it became apparent that substantive differences existed between two major forms of bilingual education. The terms suggested totally different aims and goals. They are commonly attributed to Wallace Lambert, who used them in a 1975 publication. In their simplest definitions, the terms relate to the linguistic objectives of the program: to provide students with an opportunity to *add a language* to their communicative skill sets or, conversely, to insist that children participating in the program *subtract their home language* from active use and concentrate all efforts on rapidly learning and refining their English skills. This simple statement of differences between program types masks important attitudes and ideas that underlie the ways in which language diversity is viewed by school people and education policymakers. In this entry, these differences are explored. Other entries in this encyclopedia delve more deeply into related topics mentioned here.

Factors Affecting the Choice: Additive or Subtractive?

The choice of either a policy aimed at fostering and enhancing the child's home language as part of the goals of bilingual education or one that seeks the opposite—abandoning home language use as quickly as possible—does not occur by chance. Such choices are rooted in underlying assumptions concerning the benefits, risks, utility, and cultural valuing of languages other than English in the wider society. Similarly, whether native speakers of English are included in these programs determines in part what the objectives of the program will be. In the main, children who are native speakers of English would not be involved in programs of subtractive bilingual education. When such children are involved, the programs are often referred to as *two-way immersion programs,* also known as *dual-immersion programs,* because the learning of the two languages occurs in both directions. This distinction does not always hold in n in other countries. Hence, the analysis below is limited to what is clearly the case in the United States.

Background and History

Whether they are additive or subtractive, programs of bilingual education are driven by operational policies and practices relative to the student population, length of the program in each language, level of proficiency students will pursue in each language, and, importantly, the language skills required of their teachers. Of the two types, subtractive programs are the least complex. In additive programs, the effort is much more complex and demands greater modification of the curriculum and staffing patterns than is the case when a subtractive choice is made. The fact that these differences have not been well described to the schools by state and federal offices has greatly contributed to the difficulties encountered in determining whether bilingual education is effective in meeting its objectives. Program success can be determined only if and when the goals are clear and the organization, operation, and resourcing of the program are in harmony with its stated goals.

At a deeper level, we can clarify the difference between additive and subtractive forms of bilingual education by examining the policy foundations of the two approaches. Subtractive bilingual education is rooted in the tradition of remedial/compensatory education. This was the operating ideology that shaped much of the federal government's involvement in education, beginning with the Elementary and Secondary Education Act (ESEA) of 1965 and the other large federal program, Head Start. From the outset, the government's involvement was based on a perceived need to remediate the inadequate background of children in poverty. There was a strong perception then, one that has many subscribers even today, that lack of school success by poor and minority children was due to the lack of a sufficiently robust cultural foundation on which to build—hence the need to remediate and compensate for lacunae in the child's cultural and family background. Congress was led down this path by the work of early education researchers such as James Coleman and Christopher Jencks, who had examined groups of children in poverty and concluded that it was not the failure of the schools that was operant, but rather the social and cultural matrix in which these children were raised.

The largest federal education program that sought to remediate and compensate for the negative effects of poverty and "cultural deprivation" in disadvantaged families was Title I of the ESEA. The degree to which

Congress was genuinely convinced that this was the best strategy for intervening in education is not clear. The ESEA came along at a time when the issue of states' rights was a major stumbling block to federal involvement in education. Many politicians who believed in states' rights and the reserved powers of the states to control their schools were still reeling from the impact of *Brown v. Board of Education* (1954) and federal pressures to desegregate. Title I of the ESEA was, in addition to a wonderful investment in children and youth, an effective way to soothe the bruises of states' rights supporters by providing unprecedented amounts of new funding to public education. It is perhaps coincidental that southern states, because of high levels of poverty, were entitled to substantial amounts of federal money. Politicians from the southern states were the most vociferous defenders of states' rights in education and keeping the federal government out of the public schools. But financial support was sorely needed in that region. It is not known what incentives and inducements, if any, may have been offered to secure the support of key congressional delegations to ensure passage of the ESEA in 1965 and the additions, amendments, and modifications that came later.

Title VII and Subtractive Bilingual Instruction

When Title VII of the ESEA (the Bilingual Education Act) came before the Congress 3 years after the original ESEA bill, the remediation and compensation model of intervention remained strong among educators and legislators alike. A review of the hearing record for the Title VII bills leaves little doubt that remedying the presumed deficits in children's backgrounds was one of the foundations of that bill. From the outset, Title VII had an eligibility criterion of poverty for those children who might participate in its programs. Poverty and a lack of English proficiency were thus linked early on as prime culprits in the lack of success these children encountered in school. Speakers at the Title VII hearings moved easily between their discussions of poverty and language barriers as if the two must be inextricably linked. The legislation and the program's operations in the U.S. Office of Education focused even more specifically on the poorest of the poor. Many programs sought to serve "the most needy," on the assumption that the most destitute of families would benefit the most from the

education interventions of the Great Society and the War on Poverty. Any hopes that bilingual education would someday rise to become a prestigious school offering were dashed by the requirement that only poor children could be involved in school programs funded by Title VII. The potential embrace by middle-class, English-speaking families that could have made the program more widely available (and accepted) was foreclosed by positioning the program as one serving chiefly poor and immigrant children.

The primary deficit to be remedied under the auspices of Title VII was lack of fluency in English and the language barrier that the home language was assumed to present to effective learning and teaching. There was little thought given in the initial programs to the idea of developing literacy in the home language as a means of gaining access to curriculum materials in the home language over a sustained period. At best, the philosophy of these early programs, which came to be known by the less harsh name of *transitional bilingual education,* was that the home language should be used sparingly and that students should stop participating in these programs as soon as possible. A. Bruce Gaarder, a scholar who studied the contours of these programs early on, reported the main characteristics of the first 76 funded programs as being clearly subtractive and remedial in nature.

A grave weakness of transitional bilingual education is that it denies the students literacy opportunities in both languages. Scholars in language learning, such as Gaarder and Joshua A. Fishman, objected to this approach, cautioning that it undermined important principles of bilingualism and would lead to failure. Fishman was especially blunt, even acerbic, in his condemnation of the remedial approach to bilingual education. In 1976, he wrote as follows:

> If a non-English Mother-tongue is conceptualized as a disease of the poor, then in true vaccine style this disease is to be attacked by the disease bacillus itself. A little bit of deadened mother tongue, introduced in slow stages in the classroom environment, will ultimately enable the patient to throw off the mother tongue entirely and to embrace all-American vim, vigor and vitality.
>
> My own evaluation is that compensatory bilingual education is not a good long-term bet, neither for language teaching nor for bilingual education per se. The multi-problem populations on whose behalf

it is espoused—underprivileged, unappreciated, alienated—cannot be aided in more than an initial palliative sense by so slender a reed as compensatory bilingual education. (p. 162)

But the idea of serving the poor and using the home language only for short periods had gained traction, and it prevailed in the initial Title VII law. In time, the poverty requirement was removed, but the transitional nature of the program remained with it throughout its history.

Launching a transitional program with the principal goal of teaching English aggressively and quickly ending the use of the home language required that some adjustments be made in schools and classrooms. Curriculum materials had to be adjusted or changed, and some portion of the teachers had to be bilingual themselves in order to provide the instructional bridge to English that the programs envisaged. However, the level of proficiency and literacy required of teachers in a subtractive program are far lower than those that would be needed by teachers in an additive program. After all, if there is no major effort made to maintain and improve the first-acquired language of the students, it is not necessary that the teachers be fully literate in that language. One result of this was that often, the distinction between a bilingual teacher and a bilingual *education* teacher was not made.

Dual-Language (Additive) Orientation

In addition to questions of language proficiency, class schedules and grouping practices had to be changed in order to create some classrooms that were to be taught bilingually while others were not. However, the changes required in subtractive programs were fewer and less demanding than those that were required in programs of additive bilingual education, in which both languages are taught for an extended period and literacy in two languages is the goal for all students. Further, in many of these programs, native-English-speaking children were to be involved alongside classmates who were English language learners. In such cases, programs required even greater planning and accommodation of divergent needs, such as when and for how long the two groups should interact to help each other learn their respective languages.

The underlying assumptions and values of additive bilingual education, now often referred to as *dual-language programs* or *two-way immersion,* are substantially different from the underlying notions of subtractive programs. Additive bilingual education is grounded in the ideas (a) that all children can and should learn more than one language as part of a liberal education, (b) that the underlying principles of multicultural education extend to language diversity, and (c) that children who already speak a home language other than English should be given opportunities to continue the formal study of that language and achieve literacy in it. Remediation and compensating for prior experiences are not used as criteria to include or exclude children from these programs. Instead of assuming that the home language is a barrier to learning English, it is seen as a communications tool that should be used and further developed because it facilitates learning.

The view of language diversity underlying programs of additive bilingual education is very different from the views of language differences on which subtractive programs are based. First, in an additive (dual-language) program, both languages are afforded the same deference, respect, and recognition in every aspect of the school. Teachers, except those whose jobs are to teach English or non-language-related courses, such as physical education, art, or music, must be bilingual and to some important degree biliterate. This is perhaps the major obstacle to the creation of dual-language programs today in almost every part of the country. Many people in the United States today are literate in languages other than English, but they have not been trained as teachers and must be retrained and certificated by the appropriate agency of the state if they are to take on that role effectively. Regrettably, most colleges and universities that train teachers for bilingual education do so under the assumption that such teachers will work in programs of a subtractive nature simply because they are the most numerous and more politically acceptable to funding agencies.

Most additive programs of bilingual education today have a strong parental involvement component, because parental choice and support are absolute requirements. In some schools of this type, parents are asked to sign a formal agreement with the school in which they agree to actively participate in school affairs. This is because many American families are not totally comfortable with the idea that at least in part their children will be educated in a language other than English. When the parents themselves speak the other language, the problem is less severe. When parents do not, it is not surprising that they often worry because they do not feel competent to gauge their children's progress in school.

In many of the developed nations of the world, families often have a number of choices as to how and in what languages their children will be educated. Often, in private schools, these choices are devoted to a solid liberal education, including the study of two or more languages. In the United States, these options are not commonly available in most communities. In large U.S. cities, limited options are available, although they tend to be expensive for most families. Examples are the United Nations School, in New York City, and the Washington International School, in the District of Columbia, both of which enroll many children of diplomatic families.

Perhaps the most ironic aspect of the additive/subtractive dichotomy is that bilingual education programs arose at least in part as an adjunct to the civil rights activism of second-generation immigrants. Today, because of the emphasis on subtractive programs, many children of immigrants are denied the opportunity to continue to develop the home language they already use, while English-speaking children who speak no other languages are encouraged to participate in additive programs of bilingual education. This situation widens the gap between the quality of education received by the two groups.

Josué M. González

See also Cultural Deficit and Cultural Mismatch Theories; Deficit-Based Education Theory; Maintenance Policy Denied; Primary-Language Support; Title VII, Elementary and Secondary Education Act, Key Historical Marker; Transitional Bilingual Education Programs; Views of Language Difference

Further Readings

Bangura, A. K., & Muo, M. (2001). *United States Congress and bilingual education.* New York: Peter Lang.

Bilingual Education Act, Pub. L. No. 90–247, 81 Stat. 816 (1968).

Brown v. Board of Education, 347 U.S. 483 (1954).

Center for Applied Linguistics. (2006). *Directory of two-way bilingual immersion programs.* Available from http://www.cal.org

Christian, D., Genesee, F., Lindholm-Leary, K., & Howard, L. (2004). *Final progress report of CREDE Project 1.2 Two-way immersion.* Santa Cruz, CA, and Washington, DC: Center for Research on Education, Diversity & Excellence/Center for Applied Linguistics.

Coleman, J. S. (1966). *Equality of educational opportunity.* Washington, DC: U.S. Department of Health, Education and Welfare, Office of Education and National Center for Educational Statistics.

Crawford, J. (1989). *Bilingual education: History, politics, theory, and practice.* Trenton, NJ: Crane.

Fishman, J. A. (1976). Bilingual education and the future of language teaching and language learning in the United States. In F. Cordasco (Ed.), *Bilingual schooling in the United States: A sourcebook for educational personnel* (pp. 160–164). New York: McGraw-Hill.

Gaarder, A. B. (1967, May). *Hearings on S. 428,* 90th Cong., 1st sess. Washington, DC: U.S. Congress, Senate, Special Subcommittee on Bilingual Education of the Committee on Labor and Public Welfare.

Gaarder, A. B. (1976). The first seventy-six bilingual education projects. In F. Cordasco (Ed.), *Bilingual schooling in the United States: A sourcebook for educational personnel* (pp. 214–225). New York: McGraw-Hill.

Howard, E. R., Sugarman, J., & Christian, D. (2003). *Trends in two-way immersion education: A review of research.* Baltimore, MD, and Washington, DC: Center for Research on the Education of Students Placed at Risk (CRESPAR)/Johns Hopkins University and Center for Applied Linguistics. Available from http://www.csos.jhu.edu

Jencks, C. (1972). *Inequality: A reassessment of the effect of family and schooling in America.* New York: Basic Books.

Lambert, W. E. (1975). Culture and language as factors in learning and education. In A. Wolfgang (Ed.), *Education of immigrant students* (pp. 55–83). Toronto: Ontario Institute for Studies in Education.

Ovando, C., & Collier, V. (1998). *Bilingual and ESL classrooms: Teaching in multicultural contexts* (2nd ed.). Boston: McGraw-Hill.

AFFECTIVE DIMENSION OF BILINGUALISM

Individuals who speak multiple languages are common in many parts of the world. The affective dimension of bilingualism refers to how bilingualism and multilingualism affect the emotional experience, expression, and representation of speakers of multiple languages and how they perceive themselves and are perceived by others. A better understanding of ways in which bilingual and multilingual individuals represent, process, perform, and experience emotions can be valuable for the fields of bilingual education and second-language acquisition. They are also an important matter for the fields of linguistics, psychology, anthropology, and communication. This suggestion was made by several scholars, such as Aneta Pavlenko, who also proposed that using the affective dimension of bilingualism and multilingualism as a unique lens provides new directions in the study of the relationship between languages and emotions. Finally, it enables researchers to put a human face on linguistic and psycholinguistic research, finding ways to bring speakers' lived experiences and concerns into the process of inquiry.

The affective dimension may include, but is not limited or restricted to, the facets of the voice of memoir, anger, humor, envy, jealousy, and shame or guilt, as discussed by Pavlenko. Michele Koven documents in her work that for some bilingual and multilinguals, the preferred language of emotional expression is the language learned in the public domain; yet other researchers, such as Edward Hall, found that the ability to express oneself emotionally, especially in the realm of humor, needs a nativelike proficiency in the language used.

Language, Culture, and the Self

Through *enculturation,* described as the process by which individuals learn their home culture, the affective dimension may be influenced by the adolescent stage of development. According to psychologist Erik Erikson, adolescence is characterized by the developmental stage of *identity versus identity confusion,* in which an individual's developmental task is to establish a meaningful sense of personal identity. As Pavlenko discovered in various studies, this search for identity, the relationship between language and self, is a more general part of the bilingual and multilingual experience; it is not restricted to late immigrant bilinguals, as is often assumed. Within this dimension, there is an ever-present tension between the perception that it is better to belong to one language and one culture and the perception of legitimacy in dual allegiances. In the affective dimension, Pavlenko noted, bilinguals and multilinguals may, in effect, have to make a choice and continually struggle between different ways of feeling and different cultural norms of expression. Multilinguals may feel strong differences in what their native culture sees as the norm for feelings

regarding particular groups of people; their new culture may, for example, judge certain norms as being unjustly prejudiced, such as the caste system in India or the treatment of women in Eastern culture, compared with Western culture.

Milton Rosenberg and Carl Hovland developed a model of how an attitude is held regarding language. Their model includes *t* variables related to cognition and behavior: The dependent variables are the affective area, and the measurable dependent variables are related to the behavior portion of attitude. The dependent variables include the emotions of love, dislike, or anxiety regarding language, its acquisition, and its use. The researchers mentioned above may not agree completely on all aspects of this model, but they agree on the premise that the three areas affect each other.

Kembor Sure and Vic Webb pointed out that a person who has been trained in his or her own native language is more likely to have a more positive self-image and that a bilingual person is more culturally and linguistically flexible and likely to have respect for other languages and their speakers. Pavlenko investigated whether bilinguals and multilinguals feel like different people when speaking different languages, whether others perceive them differently, and whether they behave differently. These questions are integral to the understanding of their self-image, and therefore the affective dimension surrounding the bilinguals/multilingual person. Authors who write in more than one language often find that what they have written in one language may seem so different from the piece written in the other that one might question the authenticity of each text. Tzvetan Todorov (cited by Pavlenko) discussed how he had changed the tenor of a conference paper due to the audience he was addressing and that audience's cultural mores and values. After leaving Bulgaria as a young man, Todorov returned 18 years later to present a paper on Bulgarian studies. Pavlenko related that after Todorov had translated his paper from French to Bulgarian, he realized that his new audience, the Bulgarians, would not understand what was being said. Todorov therefore had to change his perspective on the topic to fit this new audience and its values. Since Todorov's original paper was written for France, a larger country and power, he recognized that he had to adapt it to his new audience, a smaller country with less power.

Jean-Marc Dewaele and Pavlenko administered a Web questionnaire in which participants responded that they felt they had to act according to behavioral norms of the culture that corresponded to the language they were speaking. Some respondents in the study felt they experienced a transition from one language and culture to another and that this was a bridge to a person they might become. Dewaele and Pavlenko speculated that there seemed to be a change in the thinking, behavior, and self-perception of respondents in this study as they moved between different languages. The researchers theorized that these changes might be attributed to different semantic associations, linguistic repertoires, cultural scripts, frames of expectations, and imagery and memories activated by the respective languages.

Cultural Norms and Affect

Eva Hoffman explored the suggestion that some bilinguals' or multilinguals' emotional vocabularies—the expressive forms, emotion concepts, and terms for emotional behavior—give a certain distinctive shape to the speaker's feeling. Hoffman held that there might be a struggle in choosing between different ways of feeling and different cultural norms of expression—thus the possibility of going beyond a particular emotional world. She observed that Americans seem to believe that cheerfulness is a constant and insist upon it, yet her Polish background taught her that painful feelings are normal and can be shown in public.

Geri McDonough Bell documented the affective dimension of a bilingual high school student who shared that when writing an essay in class, there were times when he was thinking in Spanish and had a hard time finding the right word in English. He declared that he thought in both languages and considered that his creative side was in Spanish and his business side was in English. A subject in Koven's study of Portuguese/French speakers described the difference in her affective displays in the two languages in both intensity and style. She reported that she had a harder time getting angry in Portuguese than in French and was able to express herself more fully in her second language, French. Koven explained that the subject felt more cultural and vocabulary constraints in Portuguese than in French when expressing anger.

Dewaele asserted that the personality of speakers may have an affect on their language use, depending on whether the speaker is an extrovert or an introvert. Dewaele found that extroverts used colloquial words and emotion words more frequently than introverts, explaining that introverts may not be willing to risk

loss of face by using an inappropriate anger repertoire. For bilinguals, it is often easier to revert to the language of childhood or the language in which the bilingual feels more at ease and in command of the relevant vocabulary to express intense emotion.

Jeanette Altarriba argued that the cognitive dimension and cognitive methodologies should be applied to the study of the representation of words expressing emotions. Altarriba argued that emotion is a construct closely tied to the formation of memories and it was be likely that the language most tied to memories of emotion-laden events would be the language the bilingual or multilingual felt most comfortable using to express emotion. Altarriba set about differentiating between concrete, abstract, and emotion words. Because of the mental images attached to them, concrete words, such as *computer* or *sofa,* are more easily drawn upon than abstract words. According to Altarriba, abstract words are words that do not refer to an object or have a material basis and hold no emotion, such as the words *mastery* or *legitimate*. Words of emotion have an affective meaning and elicit degrees of arousal and pleasantness: *love, joy, coffin, death.* She also noted that it may be beneficial when interviewing people who are particularly emotional to conduct the interview in both the native and the non-dominant language in order to gather the most information possible.

Catherine Harris, Jean Gleason, and Ayşe Ayçiçeği reasoned that childhood provides an emotional context of learning because emotional regulation systems are developing during that time. Hence, emotion words acquired in early childhood would elicit stronger responses than emotion words acquired in middle childhood or later. This reasoning could support the finding that many of their study participants stated their ability to express themselves emotionally in their dominant language from childhood.

Translation and Emotional Experience

Robert Schrauf and Ramon Durazo-Arvisu questioned whether emotion is "lost in translation." They also asked whether the language of retrieval affects the intensity of emotional reinstatement. They stated that when an individual shares an experience in a particular language, context and word interpretation matter in the emotional meaning and intensity of such experience. Consequently, the direct translation of words often does not have the same connotation, and feeling is lost in the retelling of an experience when proper idioms or words are not used to convey the tone of the speaker. Ruth Berman and Dan Slobin claimed that languages differ in how their particular morphological, lexical, and syntactic conventions shape the expression of detail in narrative. When trying to understand idioms in another language, it may be confusing to see "sleep like a baby" in Spanish as *dormir como un lirón* ("sleep like a dormouse"). The syntax of the words *la mamá de Terry* can be translated to "Terry's mom" in English, instead of "the mother of Terry," as stated in Spanish. Eve Clark argued that some information may be retrieved from memory but not be narratively expressed because the target language does not provide for the obligatory expression of those details. False cognates—words that look similar to words in another language but do not have the same meaning—can cause problems in communication for the learner, as when he or she translates "embarrassed" as *embarazada* instead of as *avergonzada: Embarazada* translates to native speakers in some cultures as "pregnant." Peter Carruthers suggests that the minds of bilingual or multilinguals, as language processors, may label memories in a particular language. As documented previously, memories from early childhood are most closely associated with the first language learned by a person, and, as Schrauf proposed, the bilingual mind may encode and retrieve memories in either or both languages and may leave a linguistic mark on particular memories.

The research points to the importance of further inquiry into what constitutes the affective dimension, that area in which bilinguals and multilinguals find themselves acting and reacting in roles and character dependent upon the emotions elicited within varied situations. If the majority of individuals value a language, the affective motivation of speakers and learners of a particular language is greater. Understanding attitudes toward bilinguals and multilingualism is a crucial part of understanding the affective dimension.

Language as Social Capital

According to sociologist Robert Putnam, an individual's social capital (which includes social ties and social networks) affects the productivity of an individual and is related to status in society. Language is a form of social capital, and societies view languages in different ways. Some societies value the ability of the

individual to speak several languages, and others do not. In some societies and cultures, the language of the public domain has a higher status, and that of the private domain has a lower status.

Su-Hie Ting found that social groups are affected by other social group's languages in both positive and negative ways. The national language policy of a nation deems one language as having a higher status than others, whether the official language is English-only or the Bahasa Malaysia (Sarawak, Malaysia). The language having the higher status in society is part of the social capital individuals bring to their positions in society, therefore affecting their status in that society. Each culture and society contains mores and values that denote class structure within them. Su-Hie Ting found that as the status of languages diminishes, the languages often are lost due to lack of use in subsequent generations. The affective dimension influences how a person feels about himself or herself, and language plays a prominent role in this area. If the language an individual uses in daily life is seen as a deficit, the individual's feelings about himself or herself may be diminished and the individual's social status may be restricted.

Conclusion

The pendulum has swung periodically throughout history from a positive attitude toward individuals speaking more than one language to an attitude of suspicion. The prevailing perception of the merits of being bilingual or multilingual often depends on the political climate in a particular country at a given point in time and influences the way in which a speaker sees himself or herself and is seen by others.

Geri McDonough Bell

See also Home Language and Self-Esteem; Language and Identity; Social Learning; Status Differences Among Languages

Further Readings

Altarriba, J. (2003). Does *cariño* equal "liking"? A theoretical approach to conceptual nonequivalency between languages. *International Journal of Bilingualism, 7,* 305–322.

Berman, R., & Slobin, D. (1994). *Relating events in narrative: A cross-linguistic developmentals study.* Hillsdale, NJ: Lawrence Erlbaum.

Carruthers, P. (1998). Thinking in language? Evolution and a modularist possibility. In P. Carruthers & J. Boucher (Eds.), *Language and thought: Interdisciplinary perspectives* (pp. 94–114). Cambridge, UK: Cambridge University Press.

Clark, E. (2003). Languages and representations. In D. Gentner & S. Goldin-Meadow (Eds.), *Language in mind: Advances in the study of language and thought* (pp. 17–24). Cambridge: MIT Press/Bradford.

Dewaele, J.-M. (2004). The emotional force of swearwords and taboo words in the speech of multilinguals. *Journal of Multilingual and Multicultural Development, 25,* 204–222.

Erikson, E. J. (1968). *Identity: Youth and crisis.* New York: Norton.

Hall, E. (1959). *The silent language.* Garden City, NY: Doubleday.

Harris, C., Gleason, J. B., & Ayçiçeği, A. (2006). When is a first language more emotional? Psychophysiological evidence from bilingual speakers. *Bilingual Minds: Emotional Experience, Expression, and Representation, 10,* 257–283.

Hoffman, E. (1989). *Lost in translation. A life in a new language.* New York: Penguin Books.

Koven, M. (2001). Comparing bilinguals' quoted performances of self and others in tellings of the same experience in two languages. *Language in Society, 30,* 513–558.

McDonough Bell, G. (2004). *Catching the light: A journey of the heart and mind, an adolescent's acquisition of a second language.* Unpublished doctoral dissertation, Arizona State University, Tempe.

Pavlenko, A. (2006). *Bilingual minds: Emotional experience, expression, and representation.* Clevedon, UK: Multilingual Matters.

Putnam, R. D. (2000). *Bowling alone.* New York. Simon & Schuster.

Rosenberg, M. J., & Hovland, C. I. (1960). Cognitive, affective, and behavioral components of attitudes. In C. I. Hovland & M. J. Rosenberg (Eds.), *Attitude organization and change* (pp. 1–14). New Haven, CT: Yale University Press.

Schrauf, R., & Durazo-Arvisu, R. (2006). Bilingual autobiographical memory and emotion: Theory and methods. In A. Pavlenko (Ed.), *Bilingual minds: Emotional experience, expression, and representation* (pp. 284–311). Clevedon, UK: Multilingual Matters.

Sure, K., & Webb, V. (2000). Languages in competition. In V. Webb & K. Sure (Eds.), *African voices* (pp. 109–132). Oxford, UK: Oxford University Press.

Ting, S.-H. (2003). Impact of language planning on language attitudes: A case study in Sarawak. *Journal of Multilingual and Multicultural Development, 24,* 195–210.

Affective Filter

With the publication of the book *The Natural Approach* in 1983, Stephen Krashen and Tracy Terrell introduced a five-hypothesis model, known as the *monitor model,* that describes their view of the second-language acquisition process. In addition, they proposed a curricular approach designed to ensure an environment that would provide optimal conditions for language learning, known as the *natural approach.* Krashen's model continues to play an important role in second-language-learning circles, serving as the basis for many policy, program, materials, and teacher training decisions.

The *affective filter* is one of the five hypotheses that make up the larger monitor model. It proposes that learners who are anxious, unmotivated, or lacking self-confidence will experience a mental block, which will impede language from being understood and retained. Krashen explains that the *language acquisition device* (LAD) (a term originally coined by Noam Chomsky in the early 1960s), is the brain's processor of language. Krashen claims that when this affective filter is activated, it does not allow language to reach the LAD, and therefore acquisition does not occur. In language acquisition or learning processes, therefore, it is important to eliminate factors that cause the affective filter to rise. With the natural approach, Krashen and Terrell attempted to promote positive and productive classroom language learning environments. They felt that if learners felt motivated, self-confident, and anxiety free, they were more likely to acquire the target language.

The Monitor Model

Before describing the affective filter in more detail, it is necessary to examine its context: the five hypotheses proposed by Krashen. It is important to take a look at this context because all five hypotheses interact among themselves, causing implications for language teaching and learning. It is difficult to look at the affective filter in isolation without looking at how people learn, what type of input they need, and how they manage language elements.

In the first hypothesis, the author claims that there are two ways of developing competency in a second language: acquisition and learning. *Acquisition* is a natural process that involves the use of language in communicative settings, while *learning* is a more staged process that involves what Krashen calls "knowing about language." Acquisition occurs as we interact with others due to our need to communicate, while learning involves a more conscious manipulation of language elements, for example, in a classroom setting. Acquisition is more subconscious, informal, and based on feeling and depends on the openness or attitude of the person; learning is explicit and conscious, formal, and based on rules and depends on aptitude.

Second, Krashen claims that we all acquire the rules of language in a predictable or natural order. He calls this the *natural order* hypothesis. This hypothesis is based on work done in the areas of universal grammar (an innate language capacity that is programmed to recognize a universal grammar) and on morpheme acquisition studies (certain morphemes tend to appear first).

A third hypothesis in the model is the *monitor hypothesis,* referring to a process through which conscious learning is used to monitor language that goes in and out. Some speakers have strong monitors that allow them to catch errors and avoid them; or, from a different perspective, the monitors limit them because the speakers hesitate before responding. To use the monitor, the person must have enough time and knowledge of the rules and must focus on form. The *input hypothesis,* a fourth part of the model, emphasizes the need for comprehensible input. Being exposed to a language for hours, days, or even years does not mean that a person will acquire or learn it. If the language is contextualized and broken down into understandable segments, the person can obtain results.

The final part of the model is the *affective filter,* the mental block that prevents learners from retaining language that is being inputted. With a high affective filter, the learner does not seek input or produce language, owing to the fact that he or she feels inhibited or unmotivated to do so. Krashen believes that the strength of the affective filter increases with puberty. The filter determines which language model the learner will select, which part of the language the learner will pay attention to, when acquisition should stop, and how fast the language will be acquired.

Influences on the Affective Filter

The affective filter is influenced by three main factors: anxiety, self-confidence, and motivation. These complex factors are influenced by many variables, such as personality; learning conditions and opportunities outside of class; attitudes toward self and others, the target language, and culture; social class; age; and gender. If language teachers are aware of the many issues that are involved with this affective side of learning and take action, they are more likely to be able to facilitate the learning process.

Motivation is basically related to what we expect from a behavior and whether the result of that behavior has value for us. Our degree of motivation determines how much effort we put into something. Motivation can be conscious or unconscious, positive or negative. In language learning, we often speak of *integrative* and *instrumental motivation* (explained in the work by Robert Gardner), the former being the desire to fit into the target group and the latter referring to the need to perform some function or task with the language. Many linguists believe that integrative motivation is the most important, although most will agree that instrumental motivation also helps. The learner must be able to accomplish certain tasks in order to feel like part of the group; therefore, instrumental motivation is also required in order to facilitate integration. Instrumental motivation has its limitations in that it may activate the affective filter when learners perceive that they have reached their goals and do not need to exert more effort.

Self-confidence allows the learner to seek input and output opportunities and therefore to acquire a higher level of language. Students who consider themselves to be proactive, positive, businesslike, and focused tend to be better at language learning. If a language learner, for example, feels embarrassed about speaking because he fears that others will laugh at him or constantly point out his errors without focusing on his message, he will tend to avoid speaking or even writing. Issues related to self-confidence can be tied into the type of environment the student is exposed to, the attitude of the teacher and other learners, the relationship the learner has with the target culture and his own, his ability to comprehend input, and his ability to apply the rules of grammar through the monitor. All of these issues cause an individual to feel valuable and capable, or not.

When we speak of anxiety, the third major factor related to Krashen's affective filter, we need to look at a number of factors. Researchers have reached a variety of conclusions:

- There are several types of anxiety: *trait,* which is natural to the person; *state,* which is based on the moment in time; and *situational,* which is based on specific factors (as indicated in the work by Charles Spielberger).

- Anxiety can be positive or negative; sometimes it actually helps to motivate us, to get the adrenalin moving.
- There may be a negative correlation between test anxiety and accomplishment.
- Speech skills are affected more often than test-taking skills.
- A fear of rejection may cause inhibition.
- Subjects who perceive themselves as calm do better on tests.
- Traditional methods tend to cause more anxiety than the audio-lingual method.

The point here is that if students feel challenged, they might be able to participate and produce language; on the other hand, if they feel threatened and afraid, they might not.

Classroom Implications

Believing that the affective filter exists, and hence trying to keep it low, implies a particular attitude on behalf of the teacher and certain modifications within the classroom setting. Basically, these changes to the classroom environment are included in the natural approach created by Terrell and Krashen. An emphasis on speech production early in the process must be avoided or lessened. Terrell discussed stages of production ranging from the silent period to fluency. Students should be allowed a "silent period," during which they can listen to and absorb the language without having to formulate language responses themselves. This silent period mirrors the process experienced by children in their first-language acquisition process and allows students to take part more actively when they feel ready. When students begin to engage in language production, their efforts should be recognized, no matter how limited they are. Error correction needs to be avoided. Teachers who overemphasize correctness over message may contribute to the filter's "thickness." Modeling is the way to lead students to more correct usage.

The environment and type of activities should be taken into consideration when trying to lower anxiety and heighten self-confidence and motivation. There should be quiet, comfortable places for reading. Materials can include, for example, puppets, games, puzzles, role plays, and graphic organizers. Students should feel comfortable, interested, and intrigued with language learning. They should see the benefit of learning and feel that they are in a setting that nurtures their

process. A variety of activities should be embedded in context, creative and dynamic. Teachers should be positive and supportive, ensuring that students respect each other and their classmates. They should also bring different types of resources to the classroom. Comprehensible input that is aimed slightly beyond the learner's current level of skill allows the learner to advance steadily. Students should be encouraged to seek language development opportunities outside of class. The classroom environment and what happens within it can contribute to lowering the affective filter and an increase in language acquisition or learning.

Kathryn Singh

See also Comprehensible Input; Critical Period Hypothesis; Easy and Difficult Languages; Krashen, Stephen D.; Language Learning in Children and Adults; Languages, Learned or Acquired; Monitor Model

Further Readings

Barasch, R. M., & Vaughan, J. (Eds.). (1994). *Beyond the monitor model.* Boston: Heinle & Heinle.

Ellis, R. (1985). *Understanding second-language acquisition.* Oxford, UK: Oxford University Press.

Gardner, R. (2001). Integrative motivation and second-language acquisition. In Z. Dornyei & R. Schmidt (Eds.), *Motivation and second-language acquisition* (pp. 1–19). Honolulu: University of Hawai'i, Second Language Teaching and Curriculum Center.

Krashen, S. (1981). *Second-language acquisition and second-language learning.* Oxford, UK: Pergamon Press.

Krashen, S., & Terrell, T. (1983). *The natural approach: Language acquisition in the classroom.* Hayward, CA: Alemany Press.

McLaughlin, B. (1987). *Theories of second-language learning.* London: Edward Arnold.

Spielberger, C. D. (1972). *Anxiety: Current trends in theory and research.* New York: Academic Press.

AFFIRMATIVE STEPS TO ENGLISH

Prior to 1970, most teachers and education policymakers in the United States felt safe in assuming that the responsibility to learn English, at any age, lay with students and families. A socially Darwinian perspective prevailed. Immigrants who were diligent in learning English were assumed to have a better chance at attaining the "American dream." Regardless of age, those who could not, or did not, persevere in that endeavor for any reason were likely to lag behind in the competitive environment of U.S. society. The schools did not invent this notion; they merely reflected the mind-set that was common in the society they served. Most Americans accepted this belief; they had little reason to question it. Since many descended from immigrant forebears, they accepted the idea that immigrants would be welcome here provided they laid down their cultural baggage and embraced English quickly, as they imagined their ancestors had done. Learning English had quietly become a test of one's desire to become American. In 1974, the U.S. Supreme Court surprised the schools. It called for a form of affirmative action for teaching English. Schools, they said must teach English well, not merely offer it as a course.

In the 1960s, inspired by the civil rights movement, a slow change in attitudes began to take hold. Among the roles played by civil rights advocates, the teaching function was important. This function, also known as "shifting the paradigm," attempted to create alternative explanations for assumptions that had long been axiomatic to most Americans. In this instance, the issue could be recast by posing a question: Assuming that students put forth an effort to learn what is taught to them, how much responsibility do the schools have to teach English, and how well should they be required to teach it? For years, perhaps decades, questions such as these were academic exercises rarely heard outside college classrooms. By the mid-1970s, many social and ethical issues had been reformulated in this way. Americans were asking questions about their society in ways that were quite different from the ways of their parents. Legal and sociocultural institutions became more comfortable with the different perspectives that lay behind the new questions. Influenced by the progressive movement in education and the philosophies of John Dewey, Paulo Freire, and others, educators too were becoming uneasy with the prevailing assumptions concerning their own responsibilities. In 1970, two developments flatly challenged the traditional view of placing the responsibility for learning English solely on children and their families.

Parents File Suit Against the Schools

Civil rights lawsuits related to education were taking place nationwide in the 1970s. Among them, a group of Chinese-speaking families in San Francisco sued the San Francisco Unified School District. In *Lau v. Nichols* (1974), they argued that the school district had been negligent in its teaching of English to Chinese-speaking students. Like other students, they were required to study English for 12 years. Further, California schools expected their students to pass a high-stakes test in English at the conclusion of their high school careers. Because many Chinese students were unable to pass that test after 12 years of studying English, the plaintiffs charged that the schools were ineffective in their teaching of English and that this constituted a violation of Title VI of the Civil Rights Act of 1964. The lawsuit demanded that the schools take affirmative steps to teach English to Chinese youngsters and that they not limit themselves to teaching English language learners (ELLs) in the same way they taught native speakers of English. *Lau* experienced a laborious journey through the U.S. District Court for the Northern District of California, later the U.S. Court of Appeals for the Ninth Circuit, and eventually the U.S. Supreme Court.

The U.S. District Court for the Northern District of California, the court of first instance, reached its verdict on May 26, 1970, along the traditional line of thinking: The schools, the court said, had not created the language incompatibility problem and had no responsibility to resolve it. The parents had taught their children Chinese, not the schools. The school district, according to the court, was not guilty of denying educational benefits, because it offered the same curriculum to Chinese youngsters as it did to other children. The inability of such children to do the same level of work in English was unfortunate, but no one was at fault. Since the requirement of desegregation case law was to treat all children alike, the court found that no special responsibility fell on the schools with respect to teaching immigrant children. If they spoke a language other than English, the court reasoned, that was clearly a challenge for those children and their families. Legally, according to the U.S. District Court for the Northern District of California, the only responsibility of the school district was to educate Chinese children in the same way they did everyone else, including providing them with the same curriculum. As stated by the district judge,

These Chinese-speaking students—by receiving the same education made available on the same terms and conditions to the other tens of thousands of students in the San Francisco Unified School District—are legally receiving all their rights to an education and to equal educational opportunities. Their special needs, however acute, do not accord them special rights above those granted other students.

May 25th Memorandum of DHEW

Unsatisfied with the ruling, the *Lau* plaintiffs appealed to the U.S. Court of Appeals for the Ninth Circuit. While the *Lau* case proceeded through the legal system in California, another development was taking place in Washington, D.C., in the Office for Civil Rights (OCR) of the Department of Health, Education and Welfare (DHEW). Eventually, the action by DHEW and the advocacy of the Chinese parents would converge in the final outcome of the lawsuit.

After consulting with a panel of experts on the education of language minority children, OCR director Stanley J. Pottinger issued a memorandum to all school districts in the country that had reported enrollments of 5% or more of language minority students. In this memorandum, dated May 25, 1970, often referred to as "the May 25th Memorandum," Pottinger set the stage for changing the locus of responsibility in cases where a language difference existed between schools and families. The memorandum from the OCR made four salient points under authority of Title VI of the Civil Rights Act of 1964:

1. Where inability to speak and understand the English language excludes national origin-minority group children from effective participation in the educational program offered by a school district, the district must take affirmative steps to rectify the language deficiency in order to open its instructional program to these students.

2. School districts must not assign national origin-minority group students to classes for the mentally retarded on the basis of criteria which essentially measure or evaluate English language skills; nor may school districts deny national origin-minority group children access to college preparatory courses on a basis directly related to the failure of the school system to inculcate English language skills.

3. Any ability grouping or tracking system employed by the school system to deal with the special language skill needs of national origin-minority group children must be designed to meet such language skill needs as soon as possible and must not operate as an educational dead end or permanent track.

4. School districts have the responsibility to adequately notify national origin-minority group parents of school activities that are called to the attention of other parents. Such notice in order to be adequate may have to be provided in a language other than English.

The idea of requiring school districts to take "affirmative steps" to teach English began to set aside the traditional view that learning English, by whatever means, was the responsibility of immigrant children and their families. It remained to be seen whether the mandate from the OCR would be accepted by the schools and what means would be set in motion to guarantee its implementation. Pottinger's construction of Title VI of the Civil Rights Act of 1964 was important because it was later integrated, by reference, into the findings of the U.S. Supreme Court in *Lau v. Nichols*. With this action, a rapid convergence was occurring between the position of the executive branch of government and the federal judiciary.

Plaintiffs Appeal Their Case

Back in San Francisco, the U.S. Court of Appeals for the Ninth Circuit refused to rehear the *Lau* case. A three-judge panel, by a vote of 2 to 1, voted to reaffirm the finding of the lower court. So far, things stood as before: The schools were in compliance with the law so long as they taught all children the same way. Only one judge of the three-judge appellate panel dissented. The dissenter was Shirley Hufstedler, a prominent jurist who was to become the nation's first secretary of education just a few years later. Hufstedler was clear and unequivocal in her reasons for dissenting. She wrote, in part,

The majority opinion [of the panel] concedes that the children who speak no English receive no education and those who are given some help in English cannot receive the same education as their English speaking classmates. In short, discrimination is admitted. Discriminatory treatment is not constitutionally impermissible, they say, because all children are offered the same educational fare, i.e., equal treatment of unequals satisfies the demands of equal protection. The Equal Protection Clause is not so feeble. Invidious discrimination is not washed away because the able bodied and the paraplegic are given the same state to command to walk.

The policy initiative of the May 25th Memorandum and the judicial outcome of the San Francisco court case came together in May 1974, with the decision by the U.S. Supreme Court in *Lau*. The Court overturned the district and appellate court findings, remanded the case to be reviewed again at the district court level, and ordered the lower court to fashion an appropriate remedy. In rendering its findings, the Court put to rest the notion that school districts had no special responsibility for teaching English to ELLs. The finding was unequivocal:

> Under these state-imposed standards there is no equality of treatment merely by providing students with the same facilities, textbooks, teachers, and curriculum; for students who do not understand English are effectively foreclosed from any meaningful education. Basic English skills are at the very core of what these public schools teach. Imposition of a requirement that, before a child can effectively participate in the educational program, he must already have acquired those basic skills is to make a mockery of public education. We know that those who do not understand English are certain to find their classroom experiences wholly incomprehensible and in no way meaningful.

In addition, the Supreme Court reiterated the understanding that the OCR had the right to issue mandates to implement constitutional requirements. It cited the May 25th Memorandum and stated that the agency had not exceeded its legal authority by issuing that directive. Later that year, Congress joined in with the enactment of the 1974 Equal Educational Opportunity Act (EEOA). The act declared that "the failure by an education agency to take appropriate action to overcome language barriers that impede equal participation by its students in its instructional program" constituted national origin discrimination in violation of federal law. By codifying *Lau,* Congress became the third arm of government to accept the requirement that schools teach English affirmatively. The EEOA was important from the day it was enacted, but its importance grew as the power of Title VI of the Civil Rights Act of 1964 was eroded by an increasingly conservative Supreme Court in the decades that followed.

Implementing the Policy Change

Neither the EEOA nor the *Lau* decision solved the problem of getting several thousand school districts in the nation to embrace the new policy and to design and implement programs that would allow the new policy direction to take root. The OCR of the U.S. Department of Education had been reminded in *Lau* that it had the responsibility to provide direction to school districts in bringing this about, but the agency did not follow through with the clarity and directness of the May 25th Memorandum. Between 1974, the year of the *Lau* decision, and 1980, with the publication of a "Notice of Proposed Rulemaking," the OCR took less-than-decisive steps. It first issued guidelines to its regional offices on the implementation of *Lau* and subsequently a more elaborated document, "Task Force Findings Specifying Remedies Available for Correcting Past Educational Practices Ruled Unlawful Under *Lau v. Nichols.*" The agency could not decide whether to require bilingual education or the less complicated approach of intensive English programs for ELLs. School districts and state departments of education insisted on a resolution. They claimed that the regional offices of the OCR were inconsistent in what they were requiring school districts to do. Pressure mounted for the government to publish official rules for compliance in the *Federal Register,* the nation's official organ for promulgating such matters. To secure a settlement in an Alaska desegregation lawsuit (*Northwest Arctic v. Califano,* 1978), the government agreed to issue definitive rules for *Lau* compliance. The creation of a new U.S. Department of Education in 1980 caused the OCR to be split in two. One part remained in the Department of Health, Education and Welfare under its new name, Department of Human Services. The other part migrated to the newly created Department of Education. The reorganization caused additional delays in the publication of *Lau* rules.

When Shirley Hufstedler was appointed the nation's first secretary of education, *Lau* rules were on her list of priorities. Hufstedler was not hesitant to move. Her position on the issue had been clear since the appeal process in her prior role as a member of the appellate court. The long-awaited "Notice of Proposed Rulemaking" was published in the *Federal Register,* on August 8, 1980. The rules quickly became an issue in the presidential campaign then under way. Regional hearings were held at which many school administrators and policymakers spoke against their adoption, claiming the rules were overly intrusive. The presidential election in November 1980 ended these first attempts to implement the spirit of *Lau*. The

Reagan administration announced that the proposed rules would be rescinded and that new rules would be issued in the near future. Perhaps because of Mr. Reagan's campaign promise to deregulate government, no rules emerged from his administration. Enforcement was pursued on a case-by-case basis, and the promise of the *Lau* decision seemed unfulfilled, until a district court case in Texas ushered in new rules.

In the case of *Castañeda v. Pickard* (1981), in the lower Rio Grande Valley of Texas, a decision by a federal appeals court was to become the definitive interpretation of "appropriate action" and "affirmative steps." The court ruled that Congress intended school districts to address two separate, but interrelated, barriers to equal school participation. First, a district must address the need of students to learn English to enable them to participate competitively in an English-only school environment. Second, a district must take affirmative steps to ensure that a student is provided meaningful access to the school's curriculum, to prevent ELLs from falling behind other students in learning school subjects at an appropriate pace.

In the OCR's interpretation of *Castañeda* and its eventual adoption as a national guideline for schools, a four-part analytical framework emerged for assessing the legal adequacy of a school district's response to *Lau*. First, a district must have an educationally supportable theory for its curriculum plan. Second, it must provide adequate resources to ensure that the theory is implemented successfully. Third, it must have an assessment system to evaluate whether students are overcoming both problems. And, finally, if the assessments that were adopted fail to show progress, a school district must modify its program to enhance its chances of success.

It should be noted that *Castañeda* was not a Supreme Court decision, as was *Lau*. Nevertheless, over the years, its findings have assumed a comparable level of authority. The federal government, notably the OCR, has embraced it as if it were the law of the land, as have other federal court decisions.

Josué M. González

See also Civil Rights Act of 1964; *Lau v. Nichols,* Enforcement Documents; *Lau v. Nichols,* San Francisco Unified School District's Response; *Lau v. Nichols,* the Ruling

Further Readings

Castañeda v. Pickard, 648 F. 2d 989 (1981).

Lau v. Nichols, 483 F.2d 791 (9th Cir. 1973); 414 U.S. 563 (1974).

Northwest Arctic School District v. Califano, No. A-77–216 (D. Alaska Sept. 29, 1978).

Office for Civil Rights of the Department of Health, Education and Welfare. (1970). *May 25, 1970, memorandum: Identification of discrimination and denial of services on the basis of national origin,* 35 F. Reg. 11, 595.

U.S. Senate. (1970). *Hearings before the Select Committee on Equal Educational Opportunity,* U.S. Senate, Part 9B, 92nd Cong., 4716–4717.

AFRICAN AMERICAN VERNACULAR ENGLISH

See EBONICS

ALATIS, JAMES E. (1926–)

Born in Weirton, West Virginia, on July 13, 1926, James Efstathios Alatis enjoyed a distinguished and influential career in linguistics, fostering the study of foreign languages and promoting bilingual education and the teaching of English as a second language (ESL). His career has extended for over five decades. The child of Greek immigrants, Alatis has become internationally known and honored for his work with the U.S. Department of State, the U.S. Department of Education, Georgetown University, and the organization known as Teachers of English to Speakers of Other Languages (TESOL). His latest appointments were as Distinguished Professor of Linguistics and Modern Greek at Georgetown University; codirector of the National Capitol Area Language Resource Center; and dean emeritus, School of Languages and Linguistics, Georgetown University. He is also senior adviser to the dean of the Georgetown College for International Language Programs and Research and executive director emeritus of TESOL. He has also served as interim president of TESOL's International Research Foundation.

After serving in the Navy during World War II, Alatis earned a BA in political science and English from West Virginia University and an MA and PhD in

English linguistics from The Ohio State University. Raised as bilingual in English and Greek, he began his language career in 1955 as a Fulbright lecturer in linguistics and English at the University of Athens, where he also taught modern Greek to Americans and conducted field research in northern Greece. Shortly thereafter, he joined the U.S. State Department as an English Teaching and Testing Specialist. During this time, he helped in the design of the Test of English as a Foreign Language (TOEFL). He would later serve as an adviser for the Educational Testing Service's TOEFL unit. With passage of the National Defense Education Act in 1958 (NDEA), Alatis moved to the U.S. Office of Education as a specialist for language research and eventually became chief of the Language Research Section, at a time when foreign languages were a national priority.

In 1966, Alatis moved to Georgetown University to become an associate professor and associate dean of the School of Languages and Linguistics, the country's oldest and largest such school. Widely known as "the Father of TESOL," that same year, Alatis was instrumental in founding this organization and became its first executive secretary (director), a position in which he served for the next 21 years. During his stewardship, TESOL grew from an initial 337 members to an organization of over 12,000 members. Traveling with great frequency, he helped to develop over 60 affiliates in the United States and abroad. Under his watch, the *TESOL Newsletter* and *TESOL Quarterly* were created as informational and scholarly publications, and TESOL's annual convention grew to be one of the language profession's largest and most comprehensive meetings. Today, two key components of the annual convention are the James E. Alatis Plenary Session and the presentation of the Alatis Award. Not only did he write the book about TESOL's history, *Quest for Quality: The First 21 Years of TESOL,* Alatis led the association in defining the very nature of the profession.

Serving as dean of Georgetown University's School of Languages and Linguistics from 1973 to 1994, Alatis developed and nurtured some of the nation's most respected language programs, adding new programs in sociolinguistics and translation and interpretation, as well as creating a master's of arts in teaching in ESL and bilingual education. Under Alatis's leadership, Georgetown university's Language Roundtable became the premier language conference of Washington, D.C., with participants from government, business, and academia. He also served as director of the Title-VII-funded doctorate program for specialists in bilingual education.

In 1976, as executive director of TESOL, Alatis was the driving force in joining with seven of the nation's largest language associations to create the Joint National Committee for Languages (JNCL) to promote the development of national language policies in a unified manner. Four years later, following the *Report of the President's Commission on Foreign Languages and International Studies* (PCFLIS), as president of JNCL, Alatis spearheaded the effort to create the Council for Languages and Other International Studies (CLOIS, later to become the National Council for Languages and International Studies, NCLIS). Consistent with the PCFLIS recommendation that the language profession(s) establish a "Washington presence," this association became JNCL's affiliate to advocate on behalf of national language policies. JNCL/NCLIS has grown from 8 to 64 associations and has been responsible for hundreds of millions of dollars nationally in support of legislation and programs for languages and international education.

Author and editor of dozens of books and articles, Alatis has been the recipient of numerous awards, including the National Association for Bilingual Education's President's Award and Pioneer in Bilingual Education Award, the Northeast Conference Award for Distinguished Service and Leadership, and the Georgetown University President's Medal and Patrick Healey Award.

J. David Edwards

See also Teacher Preparation, Then and Now; TESOL, Inc.

Further Readings

Alatis, J. (1991). *Quest for quality: The first 21 years of TESOL.* Alexandria, VA: TESOL, Inc.

AMENDMENT 31 (COLORADO)

Amendment 31, a proposed change to the Colorado constitution, titled "English Language Education for Children in Public School," was presented to voters on November 5, 2002. Had it passed, that amendment would have constituted the most rigid and restrictive antibilingual education bill in history. Its passage would most likely have led to the demise of bilingual education and dual-language programs in the state and to the denial of parents' rights to select their preferred educational programs for their children. Further, it would have set a precedent for the establishment of equally restrictive in other states. Colorado voters soundly defeated Amendment 31 by a margin of 56% to 44%. This defeat was the final part of a Colorado saga that had begun 2 years earlier.

Prelude

In March 2000, an early version of Amendment 31 was brought to Colorado. The proposed initiative, then titled "English for the Children," was officially sponsored by Joe Chávez and Charles King; however, it was publicly championed by Colorado Congressman Tom Tancredo and former Denverite Linda Chávez, president of the Center for Equal Opportunity, a conservative Washington think tank. Proponents of this early version of Amendment 31 were hoping to get their proposal on the 2000 ballot. The first victory for opponents of the initiative in Colorado came on June 30, 2000. On this date, the Supreme Court of Colorado unanimously ruled that the initiative could not go forward because it contained language that was "deceptive" and "misleading."

This court ruling was significant for several reasons. First, the wording of the court's decision provided language that could be used in future political campaigns. Second, Colorado's initiative process allows for voter-initiated referenda to be floated only in even-numbered years, thereby giving the campaign 2 additional years to further organize and solidify its strategies. Third, the extra time also allowed opponents to plan a better defense against the initiative.

Provisions of the Amendment Proposal

Two years later, in January 2002, Rita Montero and Janine Chávez (daughter of Joe Chávez, a sponsor of the 2000 initiative) submitted Amendment 31. Amendment 31 would have required that "children who are learning English be placed in an English immersion program that is intended to last for 1 year or less and, if successful, will result in placement of such children in ordinary classrooms." As in other states,

Amendment 31 was intended to replace bilingual and English as a Second Language (ESL) programs with a 1-year "Sheltered English Immersion Program," the latter being only vaguely defined in the amendment. The amendment proposal purported to allow for parent waivers so that parents who wished could have their children continue bilingual or ESL classes. Parent waivers were to be granted to families whose children met one of three conditions: (1) They were already proficient in English; (2) they were 10 years of age or older; or (3) they had special individual needs. As with other states, Amendment 31 also included clauses to allow parents to sue schools and teachers for enforcement of the amendment, while concomitantly denying these educators the right to third-party indemnification. Parents' right to sue for enforcement or damages suffered by their children would have been granted for a period of 10 years. Finally, the amendment required that a standardized, nationally normed written test of academic subject matter be given each year to all children in Grade 2 or higher who were English language learners.

From the outset, official publications characterized Amendment 31 as having at least three major problems, including (1) a waiver process that, as critics pointed out, was not legitimate and made waivers difficult, if not impossible, to obtain; (2) legal consequences to educators that were severe and more punitive than those in any other state (including a 10-year statute of limitations); and (3) an undetermined cost to public schools that were already short of funding.

Opponents' Responses

In Colorado, the strategies to defeat Amendment 31 were multifaceted and broadly defined. "No-on-31" became the official name of the political campaign, but the strategies were much broader and went beyond the purely political. Approaches included legal tactics and challenges, and educational strategies. Within the educational component, there were specific projects to educate the state legislature, the general public, the media, the voters, and educators in general. Within the political component, there were specific activities designed to raise money and to build a broad-based, bipartisan coalition. The educational and legislative components of the campaign were focused on defending and strengthening bilingual education programs. Campaign workers used public debates, letters to the editor, and various research reports and monographs to demonstrate support for bilingual education and to educate the public about the benefits of bilingual education. From the outset, it was necessary to create a message that would appeal to all Colorado voters, to devise a strategy to get the message out across the state, and to conduct a well-organized grassroots campaign.

The campaign recruited credible and visible local leaders and political strategists. United in the effort to defeat Amendment 31 were religious, civic, educational, business, and political organizations. Bitter political rivals found themselves united in their anti–Amendment 31 stance. Thirty-six educational organizations, including school boards, took official positions against Amendment 31. In addition, a political consultant firm, Welchert and Britz, was retained to conduct research via focus groups in order to develop a message that could be used to educate voters about the need for multiple instructional program options for English language learners.

The creation and dissemination of a campaign message that appealed to all Coloradoans was critical to devising a winning strategy. The Feldman Group, a national political research firm, suggested two strategies that could potentially result in the defeat of the amendment: (1) argue that the initiative would not accomplish what it claimed and (2) focus voter attention on unintended consequences. Campaign messages reflected these suggestions and were created from research conducted on Colorado focus group interviews. Ultimately, the message focused on the unintended consequences of Amendment 31 and became known as PPC:

- *P*—Parental involvement and choice would be eliminated with this dangerous amendment.
- *P*—Punitive measures in the amendment (e.g., suing teachers) were too extreme for Colorado.
- *C*—Cost to the taxpayers would skyrocket if the amendment passed.

The message resonated well with voters from a variety of ethnic, economic, age, and political groups, and the general public found it easy to understand. It was brief, simple, and substantive.

Staying on message required substantial discipline. It involved not engaging in or responding to overtly racist comments that were leveled at opponents of Amendment 31. In addition, No-on-31 strategists refrained from framing the arguments as being about racism or linguistic restrictionism. This disciplined approach enabled the campaign to establish a record

of being civil in behavior and thoughtful in consideration of the issues. Grounded in PPC, the following basic submessages were communicated to the broad voting constituencies:

- Amendment 31 would force all school districts into a "one size fits all" instructional program for 1 year. Neither parents nor teachers would have the range of educational opportunities that were currently available in Colorado.
- The amendment would impact all students in Colorado schools, not just those who were second-language learners.
- The amendment would create segregated classrooms.
- Teachers could be fired and banned from teaching for 5 years under the amendment.
- The Colorado Supreme Court itself had previously described the waiver option as a "sham."
- The amendment would add another layer of testing for schools that already had too much testing to do.
- The amendment would create yet another unfunded mandate.

The effectiveness of this message reinforced for the public the unintended consequences of the amendment. Evidence of the effectiveness of these messages can be seen in the fact that the popular print and broadcast media used the message and its subtexts when writing and reporting stories about the amendment. Further evidence of the effectiveness of the message is found in polling data. According to the Feldman Group, in July 2002, a statewide voter survey on the English immersion initiative in Colorado found that 80% of voters supported the proposal. Three months later, in September, prior to a broad media campaign, that number had dropped to 60%. By November, only 44% of voters approved the amendment.

Funding the Campaigns

It is axiomatic that successful political campaigns require funding. The No-on-31 campaign was very successful in raising the money needed to fight the amendment. Evidence that the campaign attracted a broad-based coalition is found in the number of financial contributions it received. In contrast to the 12 individuals or groups that contributed to the Yes-on-31 campaign, the No-on-31 campaign received donations from between 800 and 1,000 different individuals and organizations. Parents and teachers held fundraisers throughout the state to piece together the financial resources needed. The largest donation was a $3.3 million donation made by Colorado heiress Pat Stryker. The money contributed to the campaign's ability to extend its already effective message to a broader voting audience. One week before the announcement of the large donation, polls revealed that support for Amendment 31 was down from 80% to 60%. Support was waning before Stryker's large donation funded a media blitz. The No-on-31 campaign had money, and more: a well-run campaign, an effective message, and grassroots support that extended across the state. Money helped, but money alone would not have been sufficient to defeat the initiative.

In contrast, the primary financial support for the Yes-on-31 campaign came from Ron Unz, a resident of California who had successfully backed similar legislation in California and Arizona. Unz loaned the campaign $350,000 to help pay lawyers to write the amendment and to defend it in the Colorado Supreme Court. This money also provided support to pay signature gatherers to get the initiative on the ballot and to support salaries of the English for the Children staff. Although the campaign garnered enough signatures to be on the ballot and initially seemed to have overwhelming public support, it did not gather large-scale institutional support. Not a single school district, educational organization, civic or religious organization, or news agency took a position in support of Amendment 31.

The Vote and Its Impact

The impact of winning a No-on-31 vote was enormously important for the morale of teachers, parents, and children in the state. In fact, the implications were important for multilingual families throughout the United States. When the vote was finally counted, Coloradoans voted down Amendment 31 by a 56% to 44% margin. Only 10 of Colorado's 64 counties voted "yes" on Amendment 31. In these 10 counties, the largest margin of support was 58% "yes" to 42% "no" (Elbert County). Most counties voting "yes" had a very slim victory of 51% to 49%. Amendment 31 was soundly defeated in historic areas of Colorado where Latino roots go back 500 years. For example, in Alamosa County, 71% of the voters voted "no"; in Costilla County, 73% of the voters voted "no"; and in

Conejos County, 73% of the voters voted "no." Contrary to the claims of Ron Unz and Rita Montero, Latino families in Colorado were not clamoring for an end to bilingual education and the establishment of English immersion programs. Colorado voters voted down Amendment 31 by a margin of 66% to 44%. Amendment 31 was also defeated in counties that are historically conservative. In El Paso County, 55% of the voters voted "no"; in Weld County, 51% of the voters voted "no"; and in Larimer County, 65% of the voters voted "no."

The defeat of Amendment 31 preserved local control and educational choice in Colorado schools. The victory was important for all Colorado families—language majority and English language learners—as it helped to protect the educational rights of language minority children and their parents. More important, however, this campaign, and the ensuing defeat, ensured Colorado's importance as a model for others throughout the United States resolved to support linguistic diversity and educational opportunity for English language learners. The No-on-31 victory seems to have discouraged Unz and his supporters from mounting similar efforts. Since the Colorado defeat, no other initiatives have been launched in other states.

The bipartisan coalitions and partnerships developed during the No-on-31 campaign remained vigilant in their efforts to protect the rights of children and their families. Shortly after the defeat of Amendment 31, Republican Representative Bob Decker announced that he would submit an English immersion bill to the state legislature in January 2003. The bill never made it out of committee, due in part to the work of Colorado Common Sense, a nonprofit organization that remained in existence to prevent further attempts to float amendments such as Amendment 31. In the summer of 2006, a legislator from Greeley, Colorado, submitted a proposal for an antibilingual education ballot initiative, known as Amendment 95, for consideration in the November election. As an English-only initiative, this amendment, too, would have sought to eliminate bilingual education in the state of Colorado. The bill's proponents raised little money, had no out-of-state support, and were unable to collect sufficient public support in the form of signatures to get the bill on the ballot. Nevertheless, the coalitions formed in support of educational diversity were prepared to join forces to defeat them. They had already begun filing legislative challenges and planning fund-raising events.

English Plus, the political arm of the campaign, disbanded in December 2002 after the campaign ended. Colorado Common Sense, the educational branch of the campaign, voted to continue its activities, including its work with the state legislature to develop measures to avoid future Unz-like initiatives in Colorado. Maintaining communication with the coalition of organizations that helped to defeat Amendment 31 was also part of the long-term strategy to ensure local control and multiple program options for students learning English. Professional education organizations, such as the Colorado Association for Bilingual Education and the Associated Directors of Bilingual Education, continued their efforts to improve the state's instruction, assessment, and policy relating to second-language learners.

Kathy Escamilla and Susan Hopewell

Portions of this entry have appeared, in a slightly different context, in: Escamilla, K., Shannon, S., Carlos, S., & García, J., 2003, Breaking the code: Colorado's defeat of the anti-bilingual education initiative (Amendment 31). *Bilingual Research Journal, 27,* 357–382. Printed with permission.

See also Chávez, Linda; English-Only Organizations; Language Restrictionism; Proposition 203 (Arizona); Proposition 227 (California); Question 2 (Massachusetts); Unz, Ron

Further Readings

Escamilla, K., Shannon, S., Carlos, S., & García, J. (2003). Breaking the code: Colorado's defeat of the anti-bilingual education initiative (Amendment 31). *Bilingual Research Journal, 27,* 357–382.

Feldman Group. (2002). *A statewide voter survey on the English immersion initiative.* Washington, DC: Author.

Unz, R. (2000, August 6; 2002, July 17, September 30, October 3). *Dear friends message.* Available from http://www.onenation.org

AMERICANIZATION AND ITS CRITICS

The concept of *Americanization* is defined by the *American Heritage Dictionary* as the assimilation into American life or culture "in form, style, or character." Throughout most of their history, public schools have performed that function in our society. They have played a major role in moving immigrant children and youth into the American way of life, another way of saying Americanization. Perhaps no one has been as clear and forthright about the perceived need to Americanize immigrant students as the educator and sociologist Elwood P. Cubberley, who, in 1909, asserted the need to disperse immigrant settlements with their foreign manners and customs and to "assimilate and amalgamate these people as part of our American race and to implant in their children, so far as can be done, the Anglo-Saxon conception of righteousness, law and order and our popular government," with the goal of instilling in immigrant children "a reverence for our democratic institutions and for those things in our national life which we as a people hold to be of abiding worth" (p. 2972).

Although Americanization is often portrayed as benign and useful, many contemporary scholars argue that this is not the case. Especially for linguistically and ethnically diverse children and families, the Americanization process may bring social and psychological conflict. Bilingual educators and proponents of multicultural education are among the strongest critics of the concept of Americanization and the underlying assimilation it implies. Some of these alternative perspectives on Americanization are examined in this entry.

Resistance and Conflict

In schools, the nature of the relationship between subordinated bicultural children and families, on one hand, and the educational system, on the other, sometimes involves resistance and conflict and, at other times, submission and acceptance. This reflects the dynamic and dialectic nature of education. Antonia Darder argues that to achieve a full understanding of the role of education, we need to regard schools as sites of both conflict and empowerment. That is, the plight of bicultural children and families within the education system is not one that is doomed to complete despair or failure. Particular school policies and practices, as well as individual and collective actions on the part of the agents (parents, students, administrators, and teachers) can promote more democratic schools in which the process of acculturation is far less traumatic.

Throughout the public education experience of immigrant and language minority youngsters, there are assumptions on the part of educators that explain the lack of success of students whose home language is not English as being rooted in an inability to assimilate into the mainstream culture, which is evidenced by their failure to learn English. Often, the relationship between bicultural families and the school system is a microreflection of societal tensions and conflicts in the areas of economic and social inequality. Issues of cultural dominance appear to take place at four levels: societal, institutional, interpersonal, and intrapersonal. To examine how education functions as a mechanism for legitimating social inequality, it is necessary to understand how these four levels of interaction create pressures to assimilate to the cultural and social norms of the majority. This occurs because an asymmetrical relationship often exists in terms of power and status between diverse families and, in the case of the public school system, a structure and tradition of dominance. The formal process of schooling is the gateway to entering the "American dream," and the price it exacts of new immigrants is often high.

Complexity of Acceptance

The Americanization process (i.e., acculturation and eventual assimilation into American life) is often dependent on being accepted or rejected by society. Gordon Allport suggests seven conditions that contribute to the process of social integration or rejection. The first condition is the heterogeneity of the society, a condition that hinders or promotes Americanization; as a society becomes more ethnically diverse, the level of tolerance toward diversity diminishes. The second condition is the degree of access to vertical mobility, which is often limited and thus diminishes acceptance. As more immigrants or less-privileged people achieve a college education, the competition for jobs becomes a threat for groups that traditionally held the preferred jobs in the past; those groups retaliate by limiting access. The third condition relates to rapid social changes that transform the job market and create tension between dominant and subordinate cultural groups, in the form of direct competition and in the reallocation of available resources. The fourth condition involves ignorance and barriers to communication, the propensity to act on the basis of stereotypes as opposed to actual interaction with people of ethnically diverse backgrounds, which often leads to social rejection. The fifth condition has to do with the size and density of the cultural group. As the size of the new group

increases, its social acceptance declines. The sixth condition takes the form of cultural devices to ensure or prove loyalty. This can happen even when no question has ever arisen about a low level of loyalty to the country. The seventh condition is the dominant society's view of differences in the ideology of cultural pluralism and assimilation, or the use of policies that promote social inclusion versus policies that demand one mode of behavior.

According to Allport, if immigrants or ethnically diverse persons can maneuver the above social conditions to the satisfaction of the dominant culture, the societal acceptance or ability to blend into American society increases. Likewise, for those persons who cannot engineer the expected social conditions because of poverty, immigration status, level of income, skin color, linguistic preference, or level of education, their acceptance into American society is low or tentative.

Tensions in the Americanization Process

The tension of Americanization becomes more visible as the cultural diversity of a school community increases and concerns are raised about underachievement, home language use, and the integration of bicultural children in the process of schooling. To explain immigrant children's underachievement, or failure to assimilate in the schooling processes, the notion of cultural deficiency or deprivation is often assumed to be operative, even when it is not spoken of using those terms. What is assumed is that the lack of Americanization, academic failure, and even poverty are due to failure by the immigrants themselves. In short, the victims are blamed.

Economists Samuel Bowles and Herbert Gintis, among others, have documented the existence of differential treatment in American public schools regarding resources, attitudes, and outcomes provided to students from lower-socioeconomic backgrounds or class. Wittingly or otherwise, schools engage in practices that favor middle- and upper-class English-speaking students, through the hidden curriculum (the "unofficial" learning that happens at schools that is not overtly taught; for example, rules of conduct) and the allocation of cultural resources. The result is an educational pipeline that is often inaccessible to low-income immigrant and ethnically diverse students. Differential educational treatment for students who are perceived as failing to assimilate, or at least to acculturate, contributes to the existing achievement gap for a large number of bicultural children. This discrepancy between bicultural and mainstream student academic success has led to a number of theories attempting to explain this phenomenon. These theories range from economic exploitation, such as (a) the economy's influence on the schools related to socializing children to fill in subordinate roles in a society based on economic needs; (b) cultural conflict and issues of power between subordinate and dominant culture groups; and (c) genetic, intelligence, and cultural inferiority and deficiencies on the part of the bicultural child. For example, the last assumption argues that immigrant bicultural families are lacking or missing important social and academic skills based on their "inferior" culture. Therefore, efforts need to be made to minimize these deficiencies. In schools, this is often promoted via compensatory education programs that are stigmatized as being remedial. In extreme cases, schools put minority children in low-status, low-prestige training programs, such as "food handling," which essentially prepares them for becoming waiters or waitresses.

Under the same scrutiny, these theories have been used to identify the role of the immigrant bicultural family in the academic achievement of students of color. While educators, such as James Banks, James Cummins, and Enrique Trueba, have focused on the strengths, possibilities, and knowledge that immigrant parents possess that benefit their children, contemporary educational and social models are still greatly influenced by the deficit-based hypothesis. Immigrant parents are blamed for their children's academic shortcomings, thus relieving the schools of their responsibility to provide an escape route out of poverty and deprivation. In sum, the prevailing discourse is about the failure of children to learn English, rather than the failure of the schools to teach that language effectively. Cummins argues that this form of discourse defines culturally diverse students and parents as inferior in various ways and therefore makes them responsible for their own school failure and inability to benefit economically.

Along with having a deficiency in knowledge, bicultural children are also viewed as having a deficiency in culture. Thus, the inability of bicultural students to succeed in school is not regarded as a problem with the education system, but rather the inability of the family to Americanize or acculturate into the dominant culture and its benefits.

Richard Valencia claims that the deficit theory operating in many schools is largely responsible for the failure of immigrant children and families to Americanize quickly enough to suit the culture of the schools. Educational deficit thinking is a way of blaming the victim that views the alleged deficiencies of poor and immigrant students and their families as being responsible for the students' academic failure, while holding blameless much of the structural inequality in schools and society. Deficit thinking can be found in the very popular "at-risk" construct that now underlies both conservative and liberal approaches to educational reform.

Formal Education and Bicultural Children

Educators experienced in working with linguistically and ethnically bicultural immigrant parents share a common desire to have their children succeed in school: progressing in the content academic areas, mastering English, and planning to attend college. These beliefs represent an interest in schooling and a legitimization of the American schooling process. Thus, despite the cultural differences, immigrant parents clearly accept the notion that in order to progress in this country, one must have a formal education.

The desire to succeed in formal education and in society generally runs across cultures as well as socioeconomic classes and groups. Yet for those who come from lower-socioeconomic groups, there is an obvious disadvantage in achieving their goal. Darder argues that American schools are grounded in the cultural capital (certain types of knowledge, attitudes, or dispositions that families regarded as having a certain status) of the dominant group and in the preparation of middle-class European American children to participate in their own culture. Hence, bicultural parents and their children often find the American schooling process completely alien to them. This frame of reference is transmitted to the parents, who are also expected to follow the parenting strategies of the dominant cultural group. Often, this can be a difficult task for bicultural parents who view schooling from a different cultural perspective.

Since many of the diverse parent populations in the United States come from Third World nations that tend to hold education and educators in very high regard, cultural norms prohibit them from questioning the school, the schooling process, and the school personnel. Consequently, they and their children are unable to navigate the industrialized schooling system, in which parent advocacy is not only expected but also demanded for student success. For parents who fail to participate in this expected American behavior of open advocacy for their children, this may be interpreted by school personnel as indifference, lack of interest, and incompetence. Hence, the children's academic shortcomings are further legitimized by a system that is culturally alien to parents who view teachers and educators as the people who know best for their children.

Diversity, Complexity, and Assimilation Pathways

In examining the complexity of assimilation and Americanization, one finds an enormous range of diversity among the immigrant populations of the United States. Immigrants reflect different kinds of attitudes, beliefs, opinions, and identities. Furthermore, while the nation's immigrant community is increasing, their socioeconomic profiles point to both promising and troubling conditions. Few immigrants come from well-to-do families in which both parents have been to high school or college. A large proportion come from working-class or poor families in which neither parent has finished high school.

As of 2006, 1 of every 5 students in public schools is either an immigrant or the child of an immigrant. Immigrant children are the fastest-growing sector of the U.S. child population. Research in the field suggests that while many immigrants today are achieving high levels of education and social mobility, there are many others who are poorly educated, semiskilled, or unskilled. Although European immigrants in the past were largely unskilled, they could rely on abundant factory jobs that allowed them to establish a foothold in the economy. Current economic changes as a result of globalization, however, have relegated the least fortunate immigrants to persistent poverty and racial segregation. A new surge of resegregation in many cities is contributing to a growing gap in educational quality between the schools attended by White students and those serving a large proportion of ethnically diverse students. Under such conditions, an inferior education compounds the persistent gap in educational attainment levels between immigrant (particularly Latino) and other students. This provides even more evidence that current conceptions of Americanization are not working in the ways they are purported to function by their advocates.

The research on immigrants also documents that social success is not necessarily found through education, the professions, or even extraordinary entrepreneurship, but rather through stable families acting collectively to achieve economic goals. The classic assimilation process that previous European immigrants underwent no longer applies to the new immigrant wave, as the U.S. economy has shifted from an industrial model of production to an informational model of mining conceptual space and information. Another salient condition that contributes to being incorporated or rejected into the fabric of American society is cultural capital. Cultural capital has to do with the general cultural background, knowledge, disposition, and skills that are passed down from one generation to the next. It includes ways of talking; modes of style, acting, and socializing; understanding expected behaviors; forms of knowledge; values; and language practices. The more cultural capital one acquires, the easier it is to blend into American society. Enrique Trueba argues that whereas Latino immigrants have often been seen as lacking the necessary cultural capital to succeed in the mainstream population, they, in fact, possess more cultural capital through their ability to master different languages and to cross racial and ethnic boundaries and through their general resiliency to endure and negotiate social, political, and economic hardships.

Immigrants from many nations come to the United States hoping that their children will realize dreams that they themselves could not achieve in their native countries. Karin Aguilar-San Juan reminds us that we are left with the task of asserting our language, culture, and race and at the same time challenging the categorization of people by language, culture, national origin, or skin color.

Alberto M. Ochoa

See also Acculturation; Assimilation; Biculturalism; Cultural Capital; Culturally Competent Teaching; Deficit-Based Education Theory; Language and Identity

Further Readings

Allport, W. G. (1954). *The nature of prejudice.* Cambridge, MA: Addison-Wesley.

Bowles, S., & Gintis, H. (1977). *Schooling in capitalist America: Educational reform and the contradictions of economic life.* New York: Basic Books.

Cubberley, E. P. (1909). *Changing conceptions of education.* Boston: Houghton Mifflin.

Cummins, J. (2000). *Language, power, and pedagogy: Bilingual children in the crossfire.* New York: Multilingual Matters.

Darder, A. (1991). *Culture and power in the classroom: A critical foundation for bicultural education.* New York: Bergin & Garvey.

Delpit, L. (1995). *Other people's children: Cultural conflict in the classroom.* New York: New Press.

Portes, A., & Rumbaut, R. (2001). *Legacies: The story of the immigrant second generation.* Berkeley: University of California Press.

Suárez-Orozco, C., & Suárez-Orozco, M. (2001). *Children of immigration.* Cambridge, MA: Harvard University Press.

Valencia, R. (Ed.). (1997). *The evolution of deficit thinking: Educational thought and practice.* London: Falmer Press.

Zou, Y., & Trueba, E. T. (Eds.). (1998). *Ethnic identity and power: Cultural contexts of political action in school and society.* New York: SUNY Press.

AMERICANIZATION BY SCHOOLING

The history of Americanization through education and schooling provides invaluable insights into the contemporary debates that surround bilingualism and bilingual education in the United States. The political and educational responses to increasing immigration at the turn of the 20th century served to delineate the ideological parameters that shape the debate to this day. Tony Johnson asserts that a certain mythology of Americanization has developed that forms the root of current ideologies about immigration and assimilation. The first assumes that past generations of immigrants willingly and rapidly sacrificed their cultural and linguistic heritage as a rite of passage in becoming Americans; the second singles out Latinos both historically and in present times as bucking this trend, thus representing a threat to cultural and national unity. A closer look at the history of Americanization in schools, however, may serve to dispel both of these loaded assumptions.

One complicating factor in such an overview is that the term *Americanization* has been used in the literature to refer both to the general approach to assimilation that characterized the period roughly from 1880 to 1950 and to a self-conscious movement that emerged at the time of World War I. Each is considered in turn in this entry.

Social and Historical Context

Johnson reports that some 35 million immigrants entered the United States between 1815 and 1915. Until the turn of the 20th century, the vast majority of these immigrants were German. Terrence Wiley documents that between 1870 and 1900, 2.8 million Germans immigrated to the United States, a number that fell dramatically in the first years of the new century. However, Johnson writes, there was a significant shift in immigration after 1885, as more people migrated from southern and eastern Europe. He also reminds us that immigration to the western United States increased at this time as people from Mexico and East Asia relocated in significant numbers. Bernard Weiss documents that immigrants to the East Coast were predominantly from Italy, Russia, Austria-Hungary, and the Balkans; and, in contrast to previous waves of immigrants, most who entered the United States after 1885 were Catholic, Eastern Orthodox, or Jewish. By 1900, this wave of immigration grew to 1 million people per year.

In addition to the shift in immigration patterns, the United States was undergoing an important transformation caused by rapid urbanization and the industrialization of the economy. Weiss maintains that among the most profound effects of this transformation was the reconceptualization of formal schooling. Past generations had considered education primarily a project of self-improvement. However, by the turn of the 20th century, formal schooling was increasingly seen as serving the needs of the community, particularly as an institution that could contribute to the solution of social problems. Not only would public schools produce workers equipped with the skills required by an industrial, urban economy, they would also provide a common experience for the considerable ethnic, linguistic, and religious diversity of immigrant children and shape them into responsible citizens. To underscore the scope of the challenge, Weiss cites a U.S. Immigration Commission report claiming that "in 1909, 57.8 percent of the children in the schools of the nation's thirty-seven largest cities were of foreign-born parentage. In New York City, the percentage was 71.5, in Chicago 67.3, and in San Francisco it was 57.8" (p. xiii). Educators, politicians, and social critics of all ideological persuasions placed great expectations on schools to forge one society out of many peoples and traditions.

Perspectives on Assimilation

Foremost among the expectations placed on schools was their central role in the process of assimilation. Weiss discusses a common distinction in sociology between different conceptions of assimilation. He defines *behavioral assimilation,* also known as *acculturation,* as a process in which individuals and groups from various ethnic backgrounds adopt the attitudes and practices of the dominant, national culture, often at the expense of their home cultures. He contrasts that to *structural assimilation,* which he defines as the way immigrants and their descendants integrate into the social groups, organizations, and institutions of the host country.

This distinction between behavioral and structural assimilation helps us to understand important differences in the response by politicians, social commentators, and activists, and educators to increasing immigration at the turn of the 20th century. If we look beneath the surface of the broad term *Americanization,* we find that it was a fairly large tent that encompassed nativists and outright racists, as well as liberal reformers sympathetic to immigrants. Terrence Wiley defines the former as those who sought to define and impose the rights of Anglo-Americans over those of immigrants. McClymer labels the latter as the "more sedate and pacific wing" of the movement. However, as Robert Carlson reminds us, even those Americanizers more sympathetic to immigrants nevertheless expected that immigrants would ultimately learn to accept dominant Anglo-Saxon attitude and behaviors. Although this entry will discuss how similar the actions of nativist and liberal Americanizers were toward immigrants, they will be treated as distinct and each group's practice will be discussed in turn.

Finally, Weiss identifies two further responses to the wave of immigration in this period, the "melting pot" metaphor and cultural pluralism, and contrasts them with the tradition of Americanization. In both cases, he describes them as more sympathetic toward immigrants, even though they were still theories of assimilation. The "melting pot" metaphor, coined by English playwright Israel Zangwill in 1908, rejected the demand on immigrants to subordinate their home cultures to dominant Anglo-Saxon mores and instead put forward the goal of forging a new, distinct American ethos from the mixture of its many peoples. By contrast, cultural pluralism envisioned ethnic minorities retaining their cultural traditions while participating in the American mainstream, although it was never clearly identified whose culture, values, and traditions would constitute that mainstream in the first place.

The Nativists and Schooling

Carlson describes in detail the nativists and their decades-long push to restrict immigration into the United States. Their efforts culminated in the passage of the Johnson-Reed Act of 1924, which established strict quotas on immigration from countries beyond northern Europe. With respect to formal education, nativism led to the outright segregation of ethnic and linguistic minority students from White students, especially in the West and Southwest. Johnson argues that the attitude of Anglo elites to Latinos and Asians paralleled the Jim Crow system developing in the South, namely, that certain races needed "special education" in vocational and technical skills. A dual system of segregated schools was established throughout the West and Southwest that prepared White students for their futures role as leaders and owners, while training Latino and Asian students for their lives as workers.

Sol Cohen includes in his 1974 collection of primary sources on the history of U.S. education an excerpt from Merton Hill's program from 1928 for Americanizing Mexican American children. Hill identified "the Mexican element" as "the greatest problem confronting Southern California today" (p. 2931). Far from setting up segregated schools for Latino students and then forgetting about them, however, Hill called on these separate schools to Americanize what he labeled "the Mexican peon" (p. 2931). Hill's plan centered on the following: teaching English, "to replace the Spanish [language] as the medium of use"; simple arithmetic; penmanship; hygiene, health, prenatal care, and parenting skills; art and music; "home-owning virtues . . . regarding thrift, saving and the value of keeping the money in the banks" (pp. 2931–2932); for boys, industrial arts; and for girls, training as domestic servants. Many of the above topics were to be taught by drill. To teach thrift, Hill recommended "successive copying of Poor Richard's sayings" (p. 2933). For gifted students, Hill described a leadership program of student government so students became familiar with American civic life.

Segregation applied to Asian students as well. Cohen reprinted a resolution by the San Francisco

School Board from 1905 reaffirming its commitment to exclude Japanese and Chinese students from school. Part of the resolution reads,

> It is the sense of the members of the Board of Education that the admission of children of Japanese or Mongolian descent as pupils to our common schools is contrary to the spirit and the letter of the law and that the co-mingling of such pupils with Caucasian children is baneful and demoralizing in the extreme. (p. 2971)

Cohen follows this resolution with an editorial from the November 6, 1906, edition of the *San Francisco Chronicle,* supporting the board's decision. The following is among the many reasons the publication cited in support of the board:

> There is also the objection to taking the time of the teachers to teach the English language to pupils. . . . It is a reasonable requirement that all pupils entering the schools shall be familiar with the language in which instruction is conducted. We deny either the legal or moral obligation to teach any foreigner to read or speak the English language. And if we choose to do that for one nationality, as a matter of grace, and not to do the same for another nationality, that is our privilege. (p. 2972)

Given such sentiments, it is little wonder that a court case against the San Francisco school system some 65 years later, *Lau v. Nichols* (1974), would lead to the Supreme Court decision that provided the strongest legal basis for bilingual education.

Americanizers and Schooling

Clearly, what drove the nativist response to immigration around the turn of the 20th century was racism. Still, chauvinist and paternalistic attitudes toward immigrants were just as integral to the cause of Americanization. In a 1987 publication, Carlson captures this tension with his description of Americanizers as activists who "were advocates of the unfair exchange. In return for an education that offered a way into the middle class, they expected the immigrant to repudiate cultural *particularism* eventually and to adopt the American civic religion" (p. 60). Johnson, in a 2002 publication, portrays the condescension inherent in Americanization as follows: "Common school

teachers served as middle class mothers for immigrant children, giving them baths, teaching them proper manners and appropriate dress, and instilling in them the values of hard work, perseverance, and thrift" (p. 152).

Formal schooling was at the heart of the Americanization process, both for immigrant youth and their parents. Descriptions of the content of the Americanization program for schooling are remarkably consistent among the various primary sources from the era. Again, San Francisco provides an excellent example of the relationship between schooling and Americanization. Cohen reprints in a 1974 publication an excerpt by Dr. Ellwood P. Cubberley, former superintendent of San Francisco schools, and his views on the education of immigrants:

> These southern and eastern Europeans are of a very different type from the north Europeans who preceded them. Illiterate, docile, lacking in self-reliance and initiative, and not possessing the Anglo-Teutonic conceptions of law, order and government, their coming has served to dilute tremendously our national stock, and to corrupt our civic life. . . . Our task is to break up these groups or settlements, to assimilate and amalgamate these people as a part of our American race, and to implant in their children, so far as can be done, the Anglo-Saxon conception of righteousness, law and order, and popular government. (p. 2162)

Even more-liberal campaigners for Americanization held fairly patronizing opinions of the immigrants on whose behalf they claimed to work. Carlson discusses what he calls the "humanitarian Americanizers," such as Jane Addams and Robert Woods, and their efforts on behalf of immigrants. Their work centered on what were known as "settlement houses," such as the famous Hull House in Chicago, in which reformers like Addams could demonstrate to immigrants the practices and customs of American home life. Carlson, in 1987, writes as follows:

> Attempts to demonstrate the "gracious living" that the middle class associated with the "higher" Anglo-Saxon civilization were common in the [settlement houses] and often led to incongruous situations. Settlement house lessons on the proper handling of the silver tea service gave immigrant women an excuse for time away from the tenements, but were hardly the most helpful use of that time. (p. 62)

Nonetheless, according to Carlson, these more liberal Americanizers saw schooling as the primary means to integrate immigrants, and they openly embraced John Dewey's ideas about education to deal with immigrant children. John McClymer discusses the contradictory ideas Dewey held about immigration and education. While Dewey was famous for his progressive notions of project-based learning and democratic education, he also viewed with suspicion the maintenance of ethnic cultures in the United States. In a speech before the National Education Association in 1916, as cited by McClymer in a 1978 publication, Dewey contrasted the "real Americanism" of "unity of feeling and aim [and] a freedom of intercourse" to the "dangerous thing" of ethnic groups trying to "live off their past" and refusing "to accept what other cultures have to offer" (p. 109). In Carlson's discussion of the link between liberal Americanizers and Deweyan education, we see how the grand ideas behind project-based learning ultimately translated in practice into limited vocational education for immigrant youth.

Three points stand out as remarkable about many primary sources that describe the goals of Americanization. First among them is the consistency in their description of what constituted a "typical Americanization program." The most important goal of Americanization was not just that students acquire English but also that English should serve to replace the home language. As one example, Selma Berrol relates the story of a New York City school district administrator, Julia Richman, and her efforts to enforce the use of English in New York schools. Although Richman herself was of German Jewish origin, she forbade the speaking of Yiddish in the schools she administered and assigned teachers to monitor the lunch hall and playground to enforce the rule even during breaks. In addition, Americanization also meant teaching American styles of dress, habits, and manners; American housekeeping and personal hygiene; and basic civics.

A second feature common to primary accounts of Americanization is the glaring absence of academics (e.g., the study of literature, the sciences, mathematics beyond simple arithmetic, etc.). The absence of academics from the Americanization program underscores the paternalistic, elitist attitude toward immigrants and their perceived aptitude. One might think that the study of the English language may have opened the door to more academic study in schools.

On the contrary, most primary accounts of English language study at the time reveal that language learning was reduced to reciting and copying lists of isolated vocabulary words.

Finally, replacing traditional habits of food and dress with American versions was paramount to Americanizers and betrays their privileging of behavioral over structural assimilation. One revealing, if humorous, example is the profound suspicion of ethnic food. Helen Varick Boswell, in 1916, called for a cadre of "domestic educators" to conduct home visits to Americanize immigrant mothers by teaching them the "preparing of American vegetables, instead of the inevitable cabbage." John McClymer cites a 1924 work about Americanization in a company town and the efforts taken by company officials to train Polish wives to stop preparing so much cabbage soup, as the "continual flow of steam from the kitchen stove" led to a dampness they found dangerous. In his account of anti-German hysteria in the wake of World War I, Wiley recounts the panic over German sausage. The *Denver Post* had warned their readers in an article that German sausages might contain ground glass and urged its readers not to eat them anymore.

Cultural Pluralism and Schooling

The literature reveals fewer examples of the direct impact that proponents of cultural pluralism had on schooling at the turn of the 20th century. However, there is much commentary from that period suggesting that a significant minority of Americans at the time rejected the chauvinism and paternalism inherent to the Americanization program. One stunning example comes from a U.S. Bureau of Education evaluation, reprinted in Cohen's collection of primary sources, of an adult Americanization program in Passaic, New Jersey, from 1920. The evaluation reveals a commitment to what nowadays would be called "student-centered instruction" and a deep respect for the knowledge and values that immigrant students bring with them to the classroom. The report sharply criticizes the disconnected nature of English lessons and uses negative attendance data to call for the use of immigrants' schedules and stated needs to drive the scheduling and topics of class.

Frank Thompson framed the issue in especially acute terms. In his 1920 work, *The Schooling of the Immigrants*, he asked whether we should assimilate immigrants by compulsion or persuasion. His argument questioned the "American values" allegedly at the heart of Americanization:

> A curious paradox seems involved in estimating the advantages of either method [of assimilation]: to democratize our newer brethren we must resort to autocratic procedures; the democratic method does not promise to democratize. But the democratic method at least has permitted the immigrant to Americanize himself. (p. 2372)

Thompson continued by identifying the central contradiction of assimilation, namely, that coerced assimilation often leads to maintenance of ethnic heritage as a form of resistance.

The Americanization Movement: 1914–1925

The work of John McClymer focuses in particular on one moment in history when Americanization emerged as a self-conscious movement. The advent of World War I produced an explosion of nativist reaction across the United States. Although the United States would not enter the war until its third year, the outbreak of war led to a generalized denouncement of past assimilation efforts. McClymer argues that the war forced native-born Americans to come to terms with the country's vast diversity; in a later work, he labels this coming of terms a *negative revolution* based on racism and reaction. This is the era when "100% Americanism" became the clarion call of the nation. War, writes McClymer, lent the Americanization crusade urgency; diversity, in the context of war, smacked of disloyalty.

To be sure, the Americanization movement was not the only reactionary development at this time. Instead, as McClymer documents, it developed alongside the 1916 presidential campaign, in which Theodore Roosevelt and Woodrow Wilson attempted to outdo each other in taking a tough stance on assimilation; the sedition and espionage prosecutions of 1916/1917; the Red Scare of 1919/1920; two anti-immigration laws passed in 1921 and 1924; the "American Plan" of anti-unionism, including the infamous Palmer Raids in 1919, which merged anti-immigrant and anti-Communist sentiment to deport thousands of immigrants suspected of radical left activism; the growth of the American Legion; the rebirth of the Ku Klux Klan; and the trial of Italian anarchists Sacco and Vanzetti.

The Americanization movement declared past efforts at assimilation a failure. To ensure success, this generation of Americanizers called for a mixture of professionalism and legislative action to finally solve the problem of assimilation. Carlson focuses on the professionalization of the movement, especially at the hands of Frances Kellor, a New York attorney he identifies as the primary propagandist of the movement. Kellor advocated reframing Americanization on a scientific basis so that the best methods of assimilation could be investigated and propagated.

McClymer's work on this era focuses on the bitter infighting among various federal agencies, especially between the Bureau of Education and the Bureau of Naturalization (itself a part of the Bureau of Labor), for control of the movement. In the end, few of the legislative proposals put forth by bureaucrats in either agency became law. However, the first textbooks on Americanization did emerge from the Bureau of Education in this era. Because Congress had given no authority to the bureau to lead Americanization efforts, the early textbooks were merely compilations of lessons from Americanization programs in adult schools across the country.

McClymer stresses that the Americanization movement of this era had no center. Frank Thompson's work from 1920 made the same claim. In an effort to identify various federal, state, and local programs, Thompson listed no fewer than five federal agencies, two agencies established in each state, and various county and municipal agencies that took on Americanization activities, including private councils of defense formed throughout the country to investigate local breaches of loyalty.

Despite the hydralike nature of the movement, the Americanizers were extremely effective in pushing their agenda. McClymer documents that by 1921, more than 30 states had Americanization laws, which led to the establishment in thousands of school systems of English and civics classes for immigrant adults. He estimates that some 1 million immigrants participated in these classes during the period of 1914 to 1925. Thousands of private employers and labor unions followed suit in leading English and civics classes for immigrants. Naturalization increasingly became synonymous with Americanization, and naturalization hearings were transformed into public ceremonies. Finally, the Fourth of July was proclaimed "Americanization Day" by groups such as the American Legion and the Sons and Daughters of the Revolution.

The impact of this generation of Americanization on schooling was threefold. First, programs for adult immigrants expanded rapidly throughout the country. For immigrant children, schooling had long been the primary site of Americanization. However, this period shifted the political dynamics of Americanization to equate learning English not just with elevating oneself to Anglo-Saxon standards. Instead, as Carlson describes, Americanization was equated with loyalty, and diversity was denounced as unpatriotic.

A final consequence of this era of Americanization was the criminalization of non-English languages across the country. Wiley recounts the most infamous case, that of German, and the various campaigns to eradicate the language. With the advent of World War I, private and parochial English-German bilingual schools closed; German was removed from the curricula in public schools; and in at least two cases (Nebraska and Iowa), laws were passed making instruction in German illegal. To get a sense of the impact of anti-German hysteria, Heinz Kloss documents that around the turn of the 20th century, some 600,000 children in the United States were receiving at least a portion of their education in German; the Americanization movement that grew with the advent of World War I essentially put an end to that. Wiley concludes that the Americanization movement was likely more effective in stigmatizing linguistic and cultural diversity than at achieving anything like assimilation. Thomas Ricento spells out one important consequence of this movement: Not until 1994 would the percentage of children (42.2%) in U.S. schools studying languages other than English reach the same level as in 1928.

Resilience and Difference

Weiss makes the critical point that the process of Americanization was not a unidirectional one. That is, despite the overwhelming pressure in the years 1885 to 1925 on ethnic and linguistic minorities to assimilate, there was not a single, monolithic response by immigrants. In some cases, certain immigrant groups seemed to embrace assimilation, engage in the "unfair exchange" identified by Carlson, and begin to experience significant social mobility. Weiss identifies, however, a growing body of research challenging the assumption that schooling was responsible for the entrance into the middle class of some immigrant groups. In other cases, there was more resilience among immigrants and an insistence, despite the odds, of

maintaining traditional values, practices, and language use. Factors that shaped immigrants' responses to assimilation included their social class backgrounds, education, and professional levels in their home countries; their aspirations and expectations for life in the United States; and dominant U.S. attitudes toward them after their arrival. Weiss concludes with two points that can serve us well in navigating debates about bilingualism and bilingual education today. The history of Americanization has left a profound mark on this contemporary debate but still needs to be researched further. Finally, a proper understanding of assimilation cannot be based simply on the dominant society's understanding of immigrants but must also place the needs, aspirations, values, and goals of immigrants themselves at the center of the research.

Donald Jeffrey Bale

See also Americanization and Its Critics; Cultural Deficit and Cultural Mismatch Theories; Deficit-Based Education Theory

Further Readings

Boswell, H. V. (1916). Promoting Americanization. *Annals of the American Academy of Political and Social Science, 64*, 204–209.

Carlson, R. A. (1987). *The Americanization syndrome: A quest for conformity.* London: Croom Helm.

Cohen, S. (1974). *Education in the United States: A documentary history* (Vols. 4–5). New York: Random House.

Cordasco, F. (1976). *Immigrant children in American schools: A classified and annotated bibliography with selected source documents.* Fairfield, NJ: Augustus M. Kelly.

Johnson, T. W. (2002). *Historical documents in American education.* Boston: Allyn & Bacon.

Herbst, J. (n.d.). *Bibliography of the history of American education, America and the urban age: Americanization and the response to immigration.* Retrieved October 22, 2007, from http://www.zzbw.uni-hannover.de/HerbstHist/Herbst41_4.htm

Kloss, H. (1998). *The American bilingual tradition.* Washington, DC, and McHenry, IL: Center for Applied Linguistics/Delta Systems. (Reprinted from *The American bilingual tradition,* by H. Kloss, 1977, Rowley, MA: Newbury House)

McClymer, J. F. (1978). The federal government and the Americanization movement, 1915–1924. *Journal of the National Archives, 10*(1), 23–41.

McClymer, J. F. (1980). *War and welfare: Social engineering in American, 1890–1925*. Westport, CT: Greenwood Press.

McClymer, J. F. (1982). The Americanization movement and the education of the foreign-born adult, 1914–1925. In B. J. Weiss (Ed.), *American education and the European immigrant: 1840–1940* (pp. 19–116). Urbana: University of Illinois Press.

Ricento, T. (2005). Problems with the "language-as-resource" discourse in the promotion of heritage languages in the U.S.A. *Journal of Sociolinguistics, 9,* 348–368.

Thompson, F. V. (1920). *Schooling of the immigrant.* New York: Harper & Brothers.

Weiss, B. J. (1982). Introduction. In B. J. Weiss (Ed.), *American education and the European immigrant: 1840–1940* (pp. xi–xxviii). Urbana: University of Illinois Press.

Wiley, T. G. (1998). The imposition of World War I era English-only policies and the fate of German in North America. In T. Ricento & B. Burnaby (Eds.), *Language policies in the United States and Canada: Myths and realities* (pp. 211–241). Mahwah, NJ: Lawrence Erlbaum.

Wiley, T. G. (2004). Language planning, language policy, and the English-only movement. In E. Finegan & J. Rickford (Eds.), *Language in the U.S.A.: Themes for the twenty-first century* (pp. 319–338). Cambridge, UK: Cambridge University Press.

ANDERSSON, THEODORE (1903–1994)

Theodore Andersson was a language professor and visionary who helped initiate the FLES (Foreign Language in Elementary Schools) movement in the 1950s and the bilingual education movement in the United States in the 1960s and 1970s. A lifelong interest in languages and cultures was awakened in his childhood; later, he earned a PhD in romance languages and literatures from Yale. Born to Swedish immigrants in New Haven, Connecticut, Andersson accompanied his mother to Dalarna, Sweden, in 1907, and they remained there with her family until his father had found work. Having arrived in Sweden a monolingual English speaker, he returned to New Haven 2 years later—just in time for first grade—speaking only Swedish. These and related events planted an appreciation of immigrants' experiences, a love of Swedish, and a spirit of internationalism. They also served throughout his life as touchstones for his work,

which was grounded in convictions about the personal, political, and educational benefits of bilingualism; the remarkable ability of children to acquire new languages; the challenge for immigrant families to maintain a heritage language; and the shamefulness of schools' disregard for students' heritage languages.

Andersson held positions at American University, Wells College, and Yale. At the end of World War II, he served as educational adviser for the State Department in international capacities: Western Europe, International Exchange (1945), and Vietnam, the Mutual Security Agency (1952). These opportunities illustrated his conviction that knowledge of foreign languages is fundamental for maintaining healthy communication among nations.

During the 1950s, Andersson argued for teaching languages earlier—in elementary school—documenting the existence of programs, interviewing participants, and writing about the necessary qualifications of teachers. In 1953, he directed the UNESCO Seminar on the Teaching of Modern Languages in Nuwara Eliya, Ceylon, and broached the topic there by adding his own session. Andersson's paper, expanded, was published as a book later that year.

In 1957, while Andersson was director of the Modern Language Association's Foreign Language Program, the Soviet Union's successful launch of *Sputnik,* the first artificial satellite, jarred the nation into concern about improving education. Andersson was a liaison for the Modern Language Association with the U.S. Office of Education and the congressional committees that assembled the 1958 National Defense Education Act.

When he moved to the University of Texas in 1957, Andersson was appalled to observe that Mexican American children from this state were stigmatized and demeaned for their Spanish instead of valued for their knowledge of a "foreign" language; and so he began sowing the seeds for bilingual education. In 1959, he intrepidly proposed to the state education agency that migrant Spanish-speaking children be taught in Spanish as well as English, but he received a chilly response. That same year, Andersson chided Spanish language professors and teachers for the prevailing academic prejudice against the Spanish spoken by Mexican Americans. In the same writing, he lauded an experimental bilingual instructional program in four local schools.

Andersson approached school districts about creating bilingual programs for Spanish-speaking children.

When experimental efforts started up in San Antonio and Laredo, Texas, he provided frequent consultation. He participated in state and national hearings, working with Senator Ralph Yarborough on the 1968 Bilingual Education Act and with Texas Senator Carlos Truán in the creation of the state law.

Chairing the Department of Romance Languages beginning in 1959 and noting the omission of a Mexican American scholar, Andersson created a position for an outstanding Texas high school Spanish teacher. Marie Esman Barker, George Blanco, and Albar Peña, whom he recruited consecutively, completed doctorates and became educational leaders in their own right.

In 1968, following the completion of a book on FLES, Andersson and Mildred Boyer conducted a yearlong study of bilingual education, visiting programs around the country featuring a variety of heritage languages. This culminated in a two-volume foundational text published in 1970 and a second edition in 1978.

Already in the 1970 volume, however, the authors lamented shortcomings of the federal law. Over the next decade, Andersson increasingly lost faith in the political will of the government and schools to provide the quality programs that would allow students to develop confident, academic proficiency in the non-English languages. As his hope for the schools waned, he turned to heritage language parents, exploring with them the process of teaching their preschool children to read in their mother tongues. Andersson created research projects for interested parents, directed doctoral theses on the topic, collected case studies, and ultimately wrote a guide for heritage language parents.

Carol Evans

See also Peña, Álbar Antonio; Zamora, Gloria

Further Readings

Andersson, T. (1969). *Foreign languages in the elementary school: A struggle against mediocrity.* Austin: University of Texas Press.

Andersson, T., & Boyer, M. (1970). *Bilingual schooling in the United States* (Vols. 1–2). Washington, DC: U.S. Government Printing Office.

Andersson, T., & Boyer, M. (1978). *Bilingual schooling in the United States.* Austin, TX: National Educational Laboratory.

Evans, C. (1995). *Scholar with a mission: The career of Theodore Andersson and his contributions to language education.* Washington, DC: National Clearinghouse for Bilingual Education.

ARIZONA PROPOSITION 203

See PROPOSITION 203 (ARIZONA)

ARMY LANGUAGE SCHOOL

See DEFENSE LANGUAGE INSTITUTE

ASPIRA CONSENT DECREE

The 1974 consent decree between the New York City Board of Education and Aspira of New York, Inc., established bilingual education as a legally enforceable entitlement for New York City's non-English-speaking Latino students. Aspira, a Puerto Rican community organization in New York City, had filed a federal lawsuit in 1972, known as *Aspira of New York, Inc. v. Board of Education,* to address what it contended was the deficient education of Spanish-speaking children in the city. The Aspira consent decree was a negotiated settlement, in lieu of continuing the suit in court. It mandated that the city's public schools provide core content instruction in Spanish for Puerto Rican limited-English-proficient students along with English as a Second Language (ESL) instruction.

Federal laws such as the Elementary and Secondary Education Act (ESEA) of 1965 and the Equal Educational Opportunities Act (EEOA) of 1974 helped to shape local and federal language policy for *English language learners* (ELLs), the term now used in lieu of *limited-English-proficient* students. The history of bilingual education was also shaped by court decisions such as the U.S. Supreme Court ruling in 1974 in *Lau v. Nichols,* by compliance plans developed pursuant to *Lau,* and by legally enforced negotiated settlements like the Aspira consent decree.

In *Lau v. Nichols,* the Supreme Court required that the San Francisco Unified School District address the English language "deficiencies" of non-English-speaking Chinese students. The Court, citing Title VI of the Civil Rights Act of 1964, declared that by providing all students with the same instruction in English, school administrators failed to provide equal educational opportunities to non-English-speaking students. In light of this federal precedent, on August 29, 1974, under the guidance of U.S. District Judge Irving Frankel, the City Board of Education and Aspira signed a legally binding consent decree. Aspira was represented in court by the Puerto Rican Legal Defense and Education Fund (PRLDEF), an organization founded in 1972 to represent the Puerto Rican community in court cases.

The consent decree required the board of education to establish a *transitional bilingual education* (TBE) program, defined as an instructional program using a student's native language to teach language arts and core subject matter while also providing ESL instruction. The goal of TBE programs is to move ELLs into English mainstream classes as soon as they have acquired sufficient English language proficiency to allow them to participate meaningfully in such settings. The agreement included language arts and other core content learning subjects (mathematics, science, and social studies) taught in Spanish, as well as ESL instruction.

A Puerto Rican Vision of Bilingual/Bicultural Education

In the years before the consent decree was signed, Puerto Rican parents and educators in New York City had faced institutional resistance to the implementation of bilingual and ESL instruction and to their demands for community participation in the governance of neighborhood schools. While the Puerto Rican community was struggling for bilingual/bicultural education programs, African Americans sought to obtain desegregated, high-quality schooling in community-controlled public schools. Encouraged by the civil rights victories of African Americans, Puerto Rican leaders created organizations like Aspira and PRLDEF and engaged in protracted negotiations with the central school board. These measures led to the 1974 consent decree compromise. Concurrently, both Puerto Rican and African American communities participated in the 1960s community control "school wars" that led to another political compromise, New York State's 1969 School Decentralization Law.

Puerto Rican community support for bilingual education in New York City had always been high. It was motivated by a dedication to cultural survival, reflective of their struggle for identity in New York City, the quintessential "melting pot" American city. Puerto Ricans embraced bilingual/bicultural education as an expression of a pluralist philosophy that respects the language and culture of their children and families. This was in direct opposition to the deficit models of education embedded in many compensatory programs of the 1960s. Puerto Rican community leaders and educators argued that their children and youth, as native-born citizens of the United States whose native language was Spanish, had a right to be taught in a language they understood and that this type of instruction should prevail until they could acquire sufficient proficiency in English to enable them to learn alongside their English-speaking peers.

A Limited Mandate

The TBE program resulting from the Aspira consent decree was a political compromise. It was something less than the developmental or maintenance bilingual program that was supported by the Puerto Rican and Latino community and that the Aspira plaintiffs had wanted. TBE was never established as a legal right for all Latino pupils, only for those whose command of English was deemed inadequate. Later commentators faulted Aspira's leaders and the PRLDEF lawyers for adopting a narrow litigation strategy; many community activists and bilingual advocates viewed the consent decree as founded on an assimilationist model of education that would lead to a deficit-based, remedial type of bilingual education. Over the years, this compromise created a rift between two groups: On one side were the bilingual professionals responsible for implementing and administering TBE and ESL instructional programs, along with grassroots education reformers; on the other side were the community leaders who continued to embrace developmental bilingual program models, including late-exit "maintenance" bilingual programs and, later, dual-language or two-way immersion programs.

Many Latino educators and community leaders also regarded the limited TBE mandate as a weakness of the consent decree because it did not address all the endemic conditions faced by the larger Latino student population. As a negotiated compromise, the decree was based on the then-reigning ideology that regarded the acquisition of English as the paramount social and educational imperative.

The board of education had insisted on keeping a smaller proportion of Latino ELLs in TBE programs. Approximately 40% of Latino students were to be included in the programs mandated by the decree. But the cutoff for ELL eligibility was set at the 20th percentile, a significantly low test score based on the Language Assessment Battery (LAB), a norm-referenced test of English proficiency. Most important, there were no new services or any changes in mainstream monolingual English instruction for most Latino students. Despite these limitations, the consent decree recognized the legitimacy of the Latino community's concerns and its interest in having Spanish as a medium of instruction.

From a Puerto Rican/Latino perspective, the historical context for bilingual education in New York City included a set of persistent conditions, many of which arguably still exist. Among these were the disproportionate Latino drop-out rate, Latino academic under-achievement, the lack of adequate and culturally appropriate guidance and support services, the discouragement of parent and community involvement, and the low representation of Puerto Ricans and Latinos in teaching and school administrator roles.

Impact of the Aspira Consent Decree

Scholars who have studied the Aspira consent decree, such as Isaura Santiago and Sandra del Valle, have analyzed the support for bilingual/bicultural education as part of a broader effort to gain an equal educational opportunity and address the high drop-out rate among minority group children. They also regard it as part of the struggle to gain greater community control of the schools. Antonia Pantoja, who founded Aspira in New York City in 1961, believed that the Puerto Rican communities of New York City, like other Latin American communities, understood that Spanish-English bilingualism and biliteracy (the ability to read and write in two languages) were indispensable tools for personal growth, community development, and sociocultural advancement. Thus, there was ample reason for the criticism of the consent decree that surfaced. Many community leaders were not satisfied with the transitional nature of the programs to be mandated by the decree.

Aspira's mission was that of helping to develop new leaders in New York among the city's high school Puerto Rican youth. As other Latino immigrants arrived in large numbers, they too were incorporated into the programs operated by Aspira in pursuit of this same goal. Biliteracy was seen as tied to academic achievement and also to ethnic awareness, self-affirmation, and an ethic of social responsibility and problem solving.

While Aspira was intended to represent non-English-speaking Puerto Rican and other Latino students, students from other ethnic and linguistic minority groups also benefited from the provisions of the consent decree, because the *Lau* compliance plan mirrored the consent decree's key elements. The fact that Spanish-speaking ELLs were separated from other ELLs as a plaintiff class in the Aspira lawsuit and that the case was pursued as a Puerto Rican/Latino community effort has had unexpected consequences over the years. The absence of non-Latino ELL plaintiffs has led many to see the issue of bilingual education in New York City primarily as a concern of the Puerto Rican community and other emerging Latino groups. In later years, the linguistic diversity of other ELL populations and their presumed differences regarding the desirability of bilingual instruction would be used by school officials to argue for more choice in instructional models, especially for English immersion options.

Shortly after signing the Aspira consent decree, the New York Board of Education also signed a separate *Lau* plan with the U.S. Justice Department's Office of Civil Rights, on September 15, 1977. This plan was required of the district because of the *Lau* decision. It effectively expanded the TBE program to serve students from other language groups whose limited command of English hindered their ability to learn in mainstream classrooms and whose home language was other than English. In 1974, Puerto Ricans made up the majority of Latino ELL students, whereas by 2006, most Latino students were Dominican and Mexican. The total ELL enrollment in New York City in 2006 stood around 141,000, two thirds of whom are Latino ELLs. The other one third represented more than 140 language communities.

In 1986, the Educational Priorities Panel reported that up to 40% of eligible ELLs were not receiving any mandated instruction. Collective advocacy efforts in 1989, however, resulted in a significant improvement of instruction for ELLs who were eligible to receive ESL or bilingual instruction. Also, in 1989, the State Board of Regents decided to raise the eligibility cutoff score on the English language proficiency assessment to the 40th percentile. As mentioned previously, the LAB, used earlier in New York City, had originally set the eligibility criterion at the 20th percentile. The State Board of Regents' narrower eligibility policy was based on evidence presented to them by bilingual education researchers. The eligibility cutoff score was revised despite opposition mounted by U.S. English, a national antibilingual education group.

The 1990s brought efforts by New York City's mayor, Rudolph Giuliani, to sunset the consent decree mandates. He succeeded only in getting Aspira to drop the decree's opt-out mechanism in favor of a mechanism allowing parents to opt their children into programs of their choice. In effect, children identified as ELLs would no longer automatically be placed in bilingual classes. Michael Bloomberg, successor to Giuliani, later saw a dramatic shift of ELL student enrollment from TBE to ESL program models.

By 2006, only 30% of New York City's ELLs participated in TBE programs, while 67% were enrolled in ESL programs. The reasons for this decline in student participation in TBE are complex, but the diminished emphasis on bilingual education in New York City mirrored what was happening in other parts of the country, such as Arizona, California, and Massachusetts. In these states, bilingual education was seen as suffering severe blows as a result of the "English for the Children" campaign. History has not yet rendered a judgment as to the severity of effects brought about by these measures.

Luis O. Reyes

See also Acculturation; Civil Rights Act of 1964; Dual-Language Programs; Early Bilingual Programs, 1960s; English for the Children Campaign; Language Socialization; *Lau v. Nichols,* the Ruling; Transitional Bilingual Education Programs

Further Readings

Aspira of New York, Inc. v. Board of Education, 394 F. Supp. 1161 (S.D.N.Y. 1975).

de Jesús, A., & Pérez, M. (in press). From community control to consent decree: Puerto Ricans organizing for education and language rights in NYC. In F. Matos-Rodríguez & X. Totti (Eds.), *Puerto Ricans in America: 30 Years of activism and change.* New York: Palgrave.

del Valle, S. (1998). Bilingual education for Puerto Ricans in New York City: From hope to compromise. *Harvard Educational Review, 68,* 193–217.

Fitzpatrick, J. P. (1987). *Puerto Rican Americans: The meaning of migration to the mainland.* Englewood Cliffs, NJ: Prentice Hall.

Latino Commission on Educational Reform. (1992). *Towards a vision for the education of Latino students: Community voices, student voices* (Vols. 1–2). Brooklyn, NY: New York City Board of Education.

Lau v. Nichols, 414 U.S. 563 (1974).

New York City Board of Education. (1958). *The Puerto Rican Study, 1953–57.* New York: Author.

Pantoja, A., & Perry, W. (1993) Cultural pluralism: A goal to be realized. In M. Moreno-Vega & C. Y. Greene (Eds.), *Voices from the battlefront: Achieving cultural equity* (pp. 135–148). Trenton, NJ: Africa World Press.

Reyes, L. O. (2006). The Aspira Consent Decree: A thirtieth-anniversary retrospective of bilingual education in New York City. *Harvard Educational Review, 76,* 369–400.

Santiago-Santiago, I. (1978). *A community's struggle for equal educational opportunity: Aspira v. Board of Education.* Princeton, NJ: Office for Minority Education, Educational Testing Service.

Santiago-Santiago, I. (1986). *Aspira v. Board of Education* revisited. *American Journal of Education, 95,* 149–199.

U.S. Commission on Civil Rights. (1976). *Puerto Ricans in the continental United States: An uncertain future.* Washington, DC: Author.

Willner, R. (1986). *Ten years of neglect: The failure to serve language-minority students in the New York public schools.* New York: Educational Priorities Panel.

ASSIMILATION

Assimilation is a voluntary or involuntary process by which individuals or groups completely take on the traits of another culture, leaving their original cultural and linguistic identities behind. The absorption of European immigrants into U.S. society and their adoption of American cultural patterns and social structures has generally been described as a process of *assimilation.* For many years, school programs in the United States strove to assimilate minority children. The process has also been called *Americanization.* The education of American Indian youth, for example, focused on enabling them to blend into the majority culture, while discouraging the retention of their tribal customs, beliefs, and languages. As late as the 20th century, many Native American children were physically removed from their families and transplanted to distant towns and villages, where they lived with White families in order to speed up this process.

The concept of assimilation continues to polarize teachers, school administrators, academics, researchers, politicians, and others with an interest in the place of schools in public life. On one side, there are those who feel strongly that in a democratic, pluralistic, and egalitarian society embedded in an interdependent world, the primary mission of public schools is to promote the intellectual, social, linguistic, and personal development of all students, whatever their background. According to this camp, public schooling should promote social justice; caring and advocacy for students, their parents, and their communities; curriculum reform; prejudice reduction; linguistic fairness; and respect for the cultures of those who differ from ourselves. The assimilation research literature suggests that culturally, linguistically, and socially responsive schooling produces students who feel less alienated and who tend to do well academically, socially, and emotionally. According to this view, students who take pride in their backgrounds and are able to maintain their original languages and cultures have a greater chance of doing well in school and society, while maintaining important intergenerational communication patterns in their homes and communities. This set of beliefs is common among bilingual educators.

On the other side are those who feel equally strongly that the public schools should continue to emphasize the assimilation of minorities into society and the modern economy by focusing on the core intellectual and cultural values of the Western world. Those who hold this position still believe in the notion of the "melting pot," our best-known assimilation metaphor. Although it was originally intended as a metaphor for leveling the sociocultural and racial playing field in the United States, the melting-pot concept has been criticized for being discriminatory in practice. (The author once asked the Black civil rights leader Jesse Jackson Jr. whether he believed in the melting pot—to which Jackson responded that in his opinion, most Blacks were stuck on the side of the pot.)

Advocates of the melting pot claim that multiculturalism lowers academic standards by establishing preferential policies for minority students for admission to colleges and universities; substituting "feel-good" learning for academic rigor by overemphasizing self-esteem gained through reverence for one's ethnicity and linguistic traditions; and dividing U.S. society by segregating students and teaching them competing ethnocentrisms through curricular approaches, such as Afrocentric education and bilingual/bicultural education. These critics believe that such programs undermine U.S. common culture by denying its Western roots, teaching the "wrong" values, and deemphasizing traditional moral authority based on Western religious principles.

Choosing to leave one's cultural and linguistic heritage behind can be a sad and difficult experience. Others in the family may not understand the decision and may not speak the new language. In addition, individuals who choose to assimilate are often accused by their original communities and other marginalized groups of having "sold out." Thus, for example, Black youngsters who are said to "act White" may be stigmatized as "Oreos": Black on the outside and White on the inside. There are also no guarantees that an individual who has chosen to cut off his or her original roots will be accepted by the dominant society if there is a history of prejudice and discrimination against individuals and groups from certain racial and cultural backgrounds.

The ideology and processes of assimilation thus have profound implications for school and society. In states such as California and Arizona, with restrictive English-only language policies, schools face tough ideological and curricular decisions regarding the use of other languages for instructional purposes. In such situations, teachers must work with students, parents, colleagues, and community members at each end of the spectrum—those who believe that schools have a duty to help students assimilate as a way of preparing them for life in the dominant society and those who believe in the value of pluralism—to strike a balance. Although the need to balance everyone's interests can be a daunting task for teachers, it can also be a valuable opportunity to learn more about opposing views in an area where great understanding is sorely needed.

Carlos J. Ovando

See also Acculturation; Biculturalism; Boarding Schools and Native Languages; Cultural Deficit and Cultural Mismatch Theories; Culturally Competent Teaching; Enculturation; Ethnocentrism; Melting-Pot Theory

Further Readings

Chávez, L. (1991). *Out of the barrio: Toward a new politics of Hispanic assimilation.* New York: Basic Books.

Ovando, C. J., Combs, M. C., & Collier, V. P. (2006). *Bilingual and ESL classrooms: Teaching in multicultural contexts* (4th ed.). Boston: McGraw-Hill.

Ovando, C. J., & McLaren, P. (Eds.). (2000). *The politics of multiculturalism and bilingual education: Students and teachers caught in the crossfire.* Boston: McGraw-Hill.

Peyton, J. K., Griffin, P., Wolfram, W., & Fasold, R. (2000). *Language in action: New studies of language in society in honor of Roger W. Shuy.* Cresskill, NJ: Hampton Press.

Ravitch, D. (1995). Politics and the schools: The case of bilingual education. In J. Noll (Ed.), *Taking sides: Clashing views on controversial educational issues* (8th ed., pp. 240–248). Guilford, CT: Dushkin. (Reprinted from *Proceedings From the American Philosophical Society, 129*[2], 1985)

Salins, P. D. (1997). *Assimilation American style: An impassioned defense of immigration and assimilation as the foundation of American greatness and the American Dream.* New York: Basic Books.

Webster, Y. O. (1997). *Against the multicultural agenda: A critical thinking alternative.* Westport, CT: Praeger.

ATTITUDES TOWARD LANGUAGE DIVERSITY

Although language diversity is not a new phenomenon in the United States, understanding contemporary attitudes toward language diversity can be a more complex undertaking than is commonly assumed. This entry describes selected factors related to people's attitudes toward language diversity and explores implications of these factors for understanding attitudes toward language diversity in education.

Attitudes represent people's internal thoughts, feelings, and behavioral tendencies in various contexts. Attitudes can predispose people to certain thoughts, feelings, and behaviors, and they can also be an outcome. For example, those with positive attitudes toward language diversity may be attracted to live in linguistically and culturally diverse settings, even though they themselves may be monolingual or struggling to become multilingual. Sometimes people develop positive attitudes toward language diversity in the course of fitting into a new community characterized by two or more languages. But a changing community, culturally and linguistically, could also have the opposite effect: negative attitudes toward those who are considered atypical. When that happens, those with negative attitudes toward the shift may move away; those who embrace it may choose to stay and be transformed by the changing environment.

An oft-quoted aphorism, attributed to linguists Joshua A. Fishman and Max Weinreich, states that a language is a dialect with an army and a navy. Tucker Childs points out that ultimately all languages are dialects. History and politics often decide which dialect will rise to a level warranting the term *language*. Those factors also decide people's attitudes toward languages, their own and those of others. One's own language may be understood to be of higher or lower status than the languages of others, whether to oneself or another or both. This differential may influence attitudes toward language diversity. The more powerful or historically significant the group, the more likely their dialect will be considered a language. From the perspective of the more or less powerful, or both, the language of the less powerful may not be a language at all, but a lower-status dialect. Despite the notion that all languages are dialects, people's attitudes toward other languages may result in giving one language a greater value and higher status than another.

Attitudes toward language diversity can be proxies for attitudes about other people, the people who speak those languages that are regarded negatively. Factors such as the nation the speakers came from, the sociopolitical relationships between the sending nation and the receiving nation, the reasons for emigration, the length of stay in the receiving nation, and the likelihood of returning to the sending nation influence people's attitudes toward language diversity. These factors shape the social order among diverse languages in contact and the ways in which people who already live in the receiving nation behave toward diverse languages, including their expectations that newcomers will learn a dominant language.

Those who ascribe to a nationalistic worldview (e.g., the long-standing notion of the United States as melting pot) whereby involuntary immigrants have historically shed their heritage to take on the identity of their new homeland may feel threatened by a voluntary influx of transnational speakers of other languages who do maintain their heritage language and culture. People with such nationalistic views may behave negatively toward the languages of the newcomers and to the newcomers themselves. Conversely, for those who live a comfortable, transnational existence, language diversity may elicit positive attitudes: language diversity is a natural part of life that is readily negotiable for people who may already be conversant in more than one language.

Language Diversity in U.S. History

Historical accounts provide insight into possible reasons for particular attitudes toward language diversity in the United States. Researchers such as Heinz Kloss and Marc Schell paint a picture of polyglotism during U.S. history. From pre-Colonial times to the dawn of the Republic, there were fewer English speakers than is generally assumed. Among the inhabitants in the pre-colonial and colonial eras and at the birth of the United States were many speakers of German and of aboriginal and African languages. Outside of the colonies, there were also speakers of French and Spanish.

Carol Schmid asserts that the founding fathers probably considered language an individual matter and did not consider diversity to be a problem to the degree it is seen to be today. Newcomers could use a heritage language as long as they did not intend to retain the language for a long time. Politically significant groups, such as the Germans, were accommodated in exchange for their loyalty to the cause of independence. In the revolutionary era, federal documents were published in English and in other languages.

Schmid further points out that the new U.S. Constitution was completely silent on the subject of official language and language diversity. Though the English and their descendants constituted less than half of the population at the time of the first census, Schmid notes that James Madison made no reference at all to language, culture, or ethnicity in his essays about diversity. In the *Second Federalist Paper,* John Jay wrote this often-quoted statement: "Providence has been pleased to give this one connected country to our united people—a people descended from the same ancestors, speaking the same language, professing the same religion, attached to the same principles of government. . . ." The same language was assumed to be English. Inexplicably, Jay overlooked the many speakers of other languages living in and around the colonies.

The ambivalence that Schmid notes among the founders has persisted throughout U.S. history and has shaped attitudes toward language variation. The struggle between the notion that foreigners are an asset to society or, alternatively, a threat when they attempt to preserve their language and cultural heritage continues to this day. This ambivalence and the consequent dialectic—rather than language diversity in itself—is at the core of associated dissension and social division that has been feared throughout U.S. history, when newcomers arrive in large numbers and preserve their language and culture in the new land. Both have been played out on numerous occasions in many public settings including schools and the workplace, and in the media. Although difficult to prove, it may well be that the fears connected with language and cultural diversity are what creates problems in the society, rather than diversity itself.

Influences Shaping Responses to Language Diversity

We know that individual listeners' attitudes toward language diversity generally parallel their attitudes toward the speakers themselves, but it can be difficult to locate the trigger for negative organizational or institutional responses to language diversity. Does a person's negative attitude toward other languages in the workplace reflect that person's distaste for other languages per se or for other things related to the speakers of the particular language at issue? For instance, might a person's negative attitude toward a particular language be a proxy for unease with changing demographics brought about by large numbers of immigrants who speak that language? Do negative attitudes about language diversity reflect distaste for the way people talk, or do they reflect distaste for the speakers themselves, who may be seen as a threat to employment or cultural norm? Rosina Lippi-Green attributes the root of negative attitudes in the United States toward languages other than English to a monoglot language ideology that favors one form of English. She maintains that the ideology is introduced in schools, promoted by the media, and institutionalized in the workplace. Consequently, many of those who deviate from this ideology and are members of groups held in disfavor by mainstream speakers of English can expect lesser educational opportunities and outcomes and similar limitations in the workplace.

Unexamined attitudes toward language diversity can have grave consequences in school. Deborah Byrnes, Gary Kiger, and Lee Manning point out that teachers' attitudes toward children's languages and dialects influence teachers' expectations of students' academic achievement. They also noted that teachers' negative attitudes toward language minority children are exacerbated by the disproportionate number of children who are found in lower socioeconomic groups. Being in poverty and not speaking English natively are thus linked in the minds of many people. An unwarranted cause-and-effect relationship is established.

Most public-school teachers have little or no formal training in teaching English as a second language and are not fluent in other languages. Teachers' frustrations over not understanding children's languages and cultures can easily turn into negative feelings that affect their academic expectations for these students. Moreover, an English-only movement can influence education policy and practice, further feeding the development of negative attitudes toward language diversity by education professionals. All of these factors, in combination, can lead to less than optimal educational outcomes for students.

Geneva Smitherman and Victor Villanueva note that although most teachers accept language diversity, acceptance is not necessarily translated into classroom practice or into the preparation of teachers by colleges and universities. In Smitherman and Villanueva's study, teachers who reported having received training in topics related to language diversity were more likely to have positive attitudes toward language differences and bi/multiculturalism. Smitherman and Villanueva also found a correlation between educational level and racial or ethnic background, and positive attitudes toward language diversity. The higher the level of education, the more likely a positive attitude toward language diversity is to exist. This finding is consistent with that of Byrnes, Kiger, and Manning, who assert that earning a graduate degree that includes training in teaching linguistically diverse children equips educators with greater sophistication in thinking about social, political, and educational issues related to language diversity and is associated with educators' positive attitudes toward language diversity. Contact with different languages without this preparation does not lead to positive attitudes.

In addition to external factors that influence responses to language diversity, Lippi-Green reports an internal factor—language insecurity—that affects one's attitudes toward one's own language in a linguistically diverse context. Demonstrating negative attitudes toward one's own language invites similar attitudes to the language and its speakers by others. To the degree that speakers of a regional variety (e.g., New York, Midwest, southern accents) are less than proud of that variety, other persons who speak other varieties of regional English may acquire the same negative attitudes. Further research into this factor may provide insight and additional questions, for example, regarding differences between German immigrants to the United States in the 19th century and today's

Spanish speakers with respect to linguistic security each demonstrated in their own languages. In the 19th century, the German language was considered a pathway to college within the German-speaking community, and English was the pathway to lesser pursuits in business and commerce. In the 21st century, with respect to Spanish, the situation is reversed. Those aspiring to a college education must speak English to be equipped to participate fully in higher education pursuits. The German-speaking community of the 19th century appeared to hold German as having equal status with English, despite pronouncements from outside that opposed this view. Neysa Luz Figueroa's study of the language attitudes of speakers of high- and low-prestige varieties of Spanish suggests that today's Spanish-speakers in the United States may not be as unanimous in their thinking about the status of their Spanish relative to other variations of Spanish used in Latin America and Spain. These attitudes among Spanish speakers bear on their attitudes toward English as well as others' attitudes toward language diversity that includes varieties of Spanish.

Attitudes toward language diversity are shaped by multiple influences rooted in personal, professional, and ethnic identity; social politics that involve skin color, immigrant status, and political economic power; and other social norms that assign different status to different languages. People's attitudes toward language diversity are shaped by their attitudes toward others and by their attitudes toward themselves with respect to the dominant language and culture. External and internal factors can confound efforts to investigate attitudes toward language diversity by particular people or groups of people at a particular point in time and in a particular setting. When any of these factors are left unexamined and omitted from analyses, they can mask how attitudes shape language ideologies to discriminate against groups of people who do not speak "normal" English in the United States.

Elsie M. Szecsy

See also Accents and Their Meaning; Languages and Power; Latino Attitudes Toward English; Transformative Teaching Model

Further Readings

Byrnes, D. A., Kiger, G., & Manning, M. L. (1997). Teachers' attitudes about language diversity. *Teaching and Teacher Education, 13*(6), 637–644.

Childs, T. (n.d.). What's the difference between a language and a dialect? In *The Five Minute Linguist*. Retrieved from the College of Charleston and the National Museum of Language, http://www.cofc.edu/linguist/archives/2005/08/whats_the_diffe.html

Figueroa, N. L. (2003). *"U.S." and "Them": A study of the language attitudes of speakers of high- and low-prestige varieties of Spanish toward "World Spanishes."* Unpublished dissertation, Purdue University, West Lafayette, Indiana.

Hamilton, A., & Rossiter, C. (Ed.). (1961). *The Federalist Papers*. New York: New American Library.

Kloss, H. (1998). *The American bilingual tradition.* Washington, DC: Center for Applied Linguistics and Delta Systems.

Lippi-Green, R. (1997). *English with an accent: Language, ideology, and discrimination in the United States*. New York: Routledge.

Schell, M. (1993). Babel in America; Or, the politics of language diversity in the United States. *Critical Inquiry, 20*(1), 103–127.

Schmid, C. (2001). *The politics of language: Conflict, identity, and cultural pluralism in comparative perspective.* New York: Oxford University Press.

Smitherman, G., & Villanueva V. (2000). *Language knowledge and awareness survey.* CCCC Language Policy Committee. National Council of Teachers of English Research Foundation and the Conference on College Communication and Composition.

Weinreich, M. (1945). YIVO and the problems of our time. *YIVO Bleter 25*(1), 13.

Audio-Lingual Method

The audio-lingual method of teaching second languages has a long history in bilingual education and English as a Second Language (ESL) instruction. It has its roots in World War II, when the U.S. military developed the army method for teaching foreign languages so that students would learn them quickly. Charles Fries, of the University of Michigan, was instrumental in developing this method, which is also sometimes referred to as the "Michigan Method." It was also widely called the "aural-oral" method, because students were to listen first before speaking. It was developed in reaction to the grammar-translation method predominant at the time, the effectiveness of which had come into question because so many students had failed to achieve foreign-language speaking and listening proficiency. The audio-lingual method became the dominant method for teaching modern foreign languages in U.S. schools from approximately 1947 to 1967 and was especially prominent during the immediate post-*Sputnik* era (late 1950s and early 1960s), when, galvanized by dramatic advances in the Soviet Union's rival aerospace program, the National Defense Education Act promoted increased attention to foreign-language teaching and learning.

Foundations and Objectives

Practitioners in the audio-lingual method for ESL and bilingual education were governed by a number of key principles:

- Language learning involves attending to form and structure.
- The aim is for linguistic competence and accuracy.
- Errors must be prevented at all costs in the course of instruction.
- Teachers must specify what language the student will use and control student interaction with the language.

The audio-lingual method is based on the structural linguistic and behavioral psychological view of language learning. Particular emphasis is laid on mastering the building blocks of language and learning rules for combining them. The theory of behaviorism assumes that (a) language learning is mechanical habit formation and language is verbal habit; (b) mistakes should be avoided, as they result in bad habits; (c) language skills are learned better when practiced orally first, then in writing; (d) analogy is an important foundation for language learning; and (e) the meanings of words can be learned best in a linguistic and cultural context, not in isolation.

The audio-lingual method adheres to the natural presentation of skills in this order: listening, speaking, reading, and writing. It places priority on the development of listening and speaking skills first, and reading and writing skills development is introduced after listening and speaking skills are mastered. The method is also based on the premise that students' native language patterns interfere with the learning of a second language and, consequently, use of the native language should be minimized and used primarily for clarifying information. Deriving from its roots in structural linguistics, the audio-lingual method emphasized the explicit presentation of grammatical structure and based the curriculum on a *contrastive analysis* of the grammar of the learners' native language and the target language.

The language learning environment should be a "cultural island," with realistic use of the target language. In this instance, *culture* is defined as the everyday behaviors and lifestyles of the speakers of the target language. For example, in a German classroom, if the lesson were on German foods, students would learn not only vocabulary about food in general but also about table manners and related customs of German speakers that make up the context in which food-related vocabulary and structures are situated. Also, because language acquisition is considered a matter of habit formation, the instructor makes generous use of positive reinforcement techniques to encourage good language habits and rapid pacing of drills to encourage overlearning of language structures so that students can answer automatically, presumably without stopping to think.

Some of the objectives of the audio-lingual method are accurate pronunciation, linguistic accuracy, quick and accurate response in speaking, and a sufficiently large vocabulary to use with grammar patterns to express oneself in practical, everyday situations. These objectives are achieved through memorization of dialogues and recombination of structures introduced through dialogues in drills. The development of a large vocabulary is of secondary consideration. Absent from the audio-lingual method's objectives are (a) an emphasis on using language or vocabulary to create meaning, (b) recognition of errors as a useful part of language learning, (c) student interaction with each other and with native speakers of the target language while using the target language, (d) attention to grammatical explanations in instruction, (e) attention to the emotional aspects of learning, (f) acknowledgment of one's native language as a foundation on which to base learning a second language, and (g) acknowledgment of what some call "large C" cultural artifacts, such as masterpieces of the culture's literature, performing arts, and visual arts.

The audio-lingual method is a teacher-centric approach. The teacher controls interaction in the target language and directs classroom language learning drills and other activities. The typical instructional procedure in the audio-lingual method begins with students listening to the teacher modeling a dialogue. Students repeat each line of the dialogue after the teacher. Certain key words or phrases may be changed

in the dialogue. Key structures from the dialogue are the basis for pattern drills of different kinds that follow. Students expand on the elements in the dialogue through substitutions in the pattern drills, which are organized in a particular sequence to lead students from simple repetition to more complex manipulations of language forms and structures. Typical drills beyond the repetition drill include backward buildup drill, chain drill, single-slot substitution drill, multiple-slot substitution drill, transformation drill, question-and-answer drill, and minimal pairs.

The backward buildup drill helps students learn accurate placement of sentence stress and pitch patterns by starting from the end of an utterance and gradually building up to the beginning of the utterance. In a chain drill, the teacher asks one student a question, and after the student answers the question, he or she asks it of another student in the class. The drill continues until everyone has answered and asked the question. Single-slot substitution drills present students with a model sentence from the dialogue and cue words that students substitute into the dialogue line. Multiple-slot substitution drills supply more than one cue word to substitute in the sentence. In a transformation drill, students transform model sentences from one form to another (for example, from affirmative to negative, from active to passive, or from statement to question). In a minimal-pairs drill, students distinguish between words that differ from each other by only one sound. By drilling the difference, it is thought that students will improve their perception of the distinction and, consequently, their pronunciation.

Critique and Current Trends

Apart from its strength in structuring instruction, the audio-lingual method has its limitations. Because the basic teaching method is repetition, students learn to reproduce many things but never create anything original or use patterns fluently in natural speech situations. Mechanical drills of the audio-lingual method have been criticized as boring at all levels and judged to be counterproductive when used beyond initial introduction to a new structure. Additional methods were needed to transition students from imitators to initiators of spoken communication, a detail that was often overlooked by teachers in the audio-lingual tradition. There was also a tendency to disregard content while manipulating language. Because the method also relied heavily on advanced technologies of the time, including reel-to-reel tape recorders, movie projectors, and language labs, the method created logistical problems for teachers in setting them up for instruction and during occasions when the equipment failed to function during instruction.

Its weaknesses notwithstanding, the audio-lingual method introduced the technological age to bilingual education, ESL, and foreign-language instructional practice, especially through the introduction of the language laboratory. Language laboratories were installed in many high schools and colleges throughout the United States in the 1960s. The National Defense Education Act of 1958 was the funding mechanism, and the impetus for increased interest in foreign language study to ensure national security came about during the post-*Sputnik,* cold-war era. Language students used the language laboratory for drill-and-practice sessions that were characteristic of the audio-lingual method's behaviorist and structural-linguistic-oriented approach to good language habit formation via imitation and memorization. The language laboratory generally consisted of rows of stations, each equipped with a headphone and a microphone. Students listened, responded, listened to their recorded responses, and compared their responses with a model response. The teacher sat at a console at the front of the room, where he or she could listen in on individual students and offer additional feedback or guidance. The audio-lingual method also introduced important language learning tools, including visual presentations and the use of visual cues to elicit language. In addition, it ushered in the use of a foreign language in the classroom by both teacher and pupil, and the language employed was of greater use for practical purposes than for understanding the great masterpieces of the target language culture in the target language.

In the 1960s, American linguistic theory began to change with linguist Noam Chomsky's rejection of structural linguistics and behaviorist learning theory and, along with them, the audio-lingual method. Chomsky maintained that language is not merely a habit structure; linguistic behavior involves innovation and creativity. Because language behavior is a creative enterprise, language learning must also draw from human creativity and not simply rely on behavioral conditioning. Students learn how to create new sentences not through imitation and repetition, but by generating them via their underlying competence.

As teachers began to recognize the limitations of the audio-lingual method, enthusiasm for it lessened, and its use waned. It was not immediately supplanted by any particular other method. There were a number of years of adaptation and experimentation with a variety of alternative methods, including total physical response (TPR), the silent way, and counseling-learning. None of these approaches achieved widespread acceptance. Various learning theories outside of the second-language teaching community, such as multiple-intelligences theory, whole language, cooperative learning, and competency-based teaching, influenced the acceptance of similarly oriented second-language teaching methods, including the communicative approach, which sought to address the limitations of relying solely on the audio-lingual method in teaching and learning second languages, including English in bilingual education settings. Vestiges of the audio-lingual method, including the aim for linguistic accuracy in second-language learning, are still evident in some bilingual education and ESL programs today, especially in programs espousing an eclectic approach that incorporates a variety of instructional methods reflective of multiple linguistic theories in teaching and learning a second language. After a long period of suppressing grammatical instruction in the communicative approach, the pendulum has begun to swing back to inclusion of grammar in the curriculum.

Elsie M. Szecsy

See also Defense Language Institute; English as a Second Language (ESL) Approaches; English Immersion; Four-Skills Language Learning Theory; Grammar-Translation Method

Further Readings

Brooks, N. (1964). *Language and language learning: Theory and practice* (2nd ed.). New York: Harcourt Brace.

Fries, C. C. (1945). *Teaching and learning English as a foreign language.* Ann Arbor: University of Michigan Press.

Larsen-Freeman, D. (1986). *Techniques and principles of language teaching.* Oxford, UK: Oxford University Press.

McDonough, S. (1981). *Psychology in foreign language teaching.* London: Allen & Irwin.

Richards, J., & Rodgers, T. (2001). *Approaches and methods in language teaching* (2nd ed.). Cambridge, UK: Cambridge University Press.

Skinner, B. (1957). *Verbal behavior.* New York: Appleton-Century-Crofts.

Stern, H. (1983). *Fundamental concepts of language teaching.* Oxford, UK: Oxford University Press.

B

BABY TALK

At birth, human infants are prepared to make the sounds of any language in the world. In their moments of quiet chortling as they awaken or before they go to sleep, it is possible to hear infants "practicing" many sounds. Most of these sounds will seem familiar, but some will strike the listener as decidedly foreign. An attentive listener may be able to detect sounds that are not used in the family's language.

Within a few weeks, the infant's repertoire of language sounds will begin to narrow. As the child hears the sounds coming from adoring family and friends who hover around her admiringly, the baby begins an involuntary process of screening out of her active repertoire all of the sounds she does not hear around her. The highly efficient computer that is her brain is programmed to conserve energy and effort. In this case, it is as if the brain "assumes" sounds that are not being heard are probably unnecessary and so the child will not continue to practice them. Slowly but surely, the infant will discard the "extra" sounds and rhythms, focusing in on only those she continues to hear from the people around her.

This is the reason experts in child development recommend that babies be spoken to in adult language rather than in "baby talk": Children will learn to speak using the accent and intonation they hear. Learning baby talk first means that, inevitably, all children must devote time to unlearning those sounds, replacing them with sounds actually used by adult members of their language community or that of their immediate caretakers.

It is important to remember two related concepts: First, baby talk does not usually result in permanent damage, and families should not worry when they hear it. The second point is that the extraneous sounds that are not continued are not lost forever. They simply become inactive. For years to come, the developing child will be able to call up the sounds associated with other languages he or she attempts to learn.

Josué M. González

See also Accents and Their Meaning; First-Language Acquisition; Interlanguage; Language Acquisition Device; Raising Bilingual Children

Further Readings

Caldas, S. J. (2006). *Raising bilingual-biliterate children in monolingual cultures.* Clevedon, UK: Multilingual Matters.
Cunningham-Andersson, U., & Andersson, S. (1999). *Growing up with two languages.* London: Routledge.

BAKER, COLIN (1949–)

Colin Baker is perhaps best known for being the author of a widely read textbook on bilingual education, *Foundations of Bilingual Education and Bilingualism,* which has undergone four editions. The book has sold over 60,000 copies and has been translated into Japanese, Spanish, Latvian, Greek, and Mandarin.

For Baker, early experience was no predictor of his later career. Born on October 1, 1949, in Danbury, a hilltop village in southeastern England, he remembers only one bilingual person in that village. She was a Belgian refugee speaking French and English, considered by villagers as "different." In elementary school, teachers and students were monolingual English speakers, matching his nuclear and extended family.

In high school, Baker learned Latin and French through the grammar-translation method. Conversational French was regarded as nonacademic and insufficient as a brain-developing activity; hence, it was largely avoided. All students were native English speakers and were required to use a prestigious variety called "the Queen's English."

Despite encouragement from his high school principal to attend a top English university, Baker's main interest was walking mountains. Having traversed the highest peaks in England, he wished to walk the higher Welsh mountains. Bangor is located very near those mountains, and Bangor University became Baker's home. The university overlooks a small city. The many surrounding villages are populated with bilinguals, with the great majority of the indigenous population speaking both Welsh and English fluently and some immigrants from England learning Welsh for employment or cultural enjoyment. University students can take some humanities subjects through the medium of Welsh, and bilingual education is predominant in all elementary and most high schools. In this context, bilingualism is a natural topic for study.

One of Baker's tutors, W. R. Jones, was a world expert on the relationship between bilingualism and IQ and on empirical studies of the effectiveness of bilingual education. Jones also taught Baker advanced statistical analysis for his PhD, although Jones' "teaching" mostly meant Baker's self-teaching. Thus, for young Baker, the foundations had been laid.

Another event was probably more influential in precipitating a lifelong interest in studying bilingualism. As a freshman, Baker sang in a church choir and fell in love with his future wife across the choir stalls. Anwen was the daughter of the pastor of that church, and her family lived their lives speaking mostly Welsh. Students were warmly welcomed to the house, and Baker found a second home. The seamless and effortless movement in that family between two languages, two literacies, and two cultures was in stark contrast to monolingual Danbury. The diversity and value-addedness of bilingualism became apparent and appealing. In years to come, it bore fruit in a thoroughly bilingual Baker household, with three children who were educated in two languages.

After teaching in high schools for 3 years, Baker returned to Bangor University as lecturer and subsequently as full professor (a personal chair of the University of Wales). In 1983, he read an early book on languages published by Multilingual Matters and decided he could do something similar on the Welsh language in Wales (*Aspects of Bilingualism in Wales,* published in 1985). The sheer enjoyment of publishing a book led to an early survey of bilingualism and bilingual education in 1988 (*Key Issues in Bilingualism and Bilingual Education*) and then, in 1992, a research book, titled *Attitudes and Language.*

Baker embarked on writing the *Foundations* book at the request of the managing director of the Multilingual Matters publishing company. Ofelia García, from New York, was appointed as academic consultant for that book and encouraged Baker to develop a more sociolinguistic and political approach to the subject.

Baker's subsequent *Encyclopedia of Bilingualism and Bilingual Education,* written with Sylvia Prys Jones, won the British Association for Applied Linguistics Book Prize Award for 1999 and the California Association for Bilingual Education's Special Recognition Award for 2000 for research/scholarly activity. The full-color encyclopedia is 758 pages, with over 2,000 references and an abundance of pictures and graphics. It was written entirely by Baker and Jones, was completed in 3 years, and is regarded as having both shaped and promoted the study of bilingual education and bilingualism. Among Baker's many other publishing achievements are editing three Multilingual Matters book series and being founding editor of the *International Journal of Bilingualism and Bilingual Education.* By 2007, the series "Bilingual Education and Bilingualism" included over 60 books.

Beyond his academic influence, Baker has been a force in shaping and implementing language policy. He held a government appointment as member of the Welsh Language Board (1997–2007), which has the responsibility in Wales for language planning and has played a major role in reversing language shift in Wales, thereby helping to preserve the Welsh language. Baker produced an overarching plan for the language with the board's chief executive. Baker's efforts both utilized and extended language planning theory. The Welsh plan regarded language acquisition planning (in homes, preschool education, and in schools) as the foundation for all language planning, with language reproduction in the family and language production through bilingual education. The policy developed a fourth form of language planning:

usage language planning, which promotes use of minority languages through government funding of youth activities that are not restricted to schools and classrooms.

In 2007, Baker and his colleagues Margaret Deuchar and Ginny Gathercole were awarded approximately $10 million to create a prestigious international, interdisciplinary research center on "Bilingualism in Theory and Practice" at Bangor University. Baker's goal is to develop new lines of research on bilingual education in terms of its structures, teaching, and learning methodologies and the outcomes of bilingual education for students and society.

Terrence G. Wiley

See also Bilingual Education as Language Policy; Cognitive Benefits of Bilingualism; Language Revival and Renewal; Raising Bilingual Children; U.S. Bilingual Education Viewed From Abroad

Further Readings

Baker, C. (1985). *Aspects of bilingualism in Wales.* Clevedon, UK: Multilingual Matters.

Baker, C. (1988). *Key issues in bilingualism and bilingual education.* Clevedon, UK: Multilingual Matters.

Baker, C. (1992). *Attitudes and language.* Clevedon, UK: Multilingual Matters.

Baker, C. (1993). *Foundations of bilingual education and bilingualism.* Clevedon, UK: Multilingual Matters.

Baker, C., & Jones, S. P. (Eds.). (1998). *Encyclopedia of bilingualism and bilingual education.* Clevedon, UK: Multilingual Matters.

BCLAD

See BILINGUAL TEACHER LICENSURE

BENEFITS OF BILINGUALISM AND HERITAGE LANGUAGES

Language competence is an essential component of personal, academic, and economic processes and success. Children of first-generation immigrants, who are raised in homes where a language other than English is spoken, grow up with a better-than-average opportunity to develop additive bilingualism, that is, proficiency in both English *and* their heritage language. In American schools, many do not realize this potential. Soon after they enter school, the expectations, pressures, and desire to assimilate into the majority culture lead immigrant children to quickly abandon their heritage language for English, as Lily Wong Fillmore and other researchers have found. Studies have also shown, repeatedly, the positive effects of high quality additive bilingualism on immigrant children's academic achievement, identity development, and family relationships. Richard Brecht and William Rivers, as well as Joshua A. Fishman, Robert Cooper, and Yehudit Rosenbaum, have documented potential benefits the national economy and security. This entry describes the benefits of retaining one's heritage language.

Heritage language speakers represent more than 175 language backgrounds in the United States. *Heritage language* refers to an immigrant, indigenous, or ancestral language that may have linguistic, ethnic, religious, cultural, or symbolic relevance for a speaker. In the literature, the term has been used synonymously with community language, native language, first language, primary language, and mother tongue although some authors make distinctions among these designations. Despite criticisms (as reported by Colin Baker and Sylvia Jones and by Nancy Hornberger) that *heritage* evokes images of the past and the old rather than images of something modern, valuable, and necessary, the term has continued to be used to reflect the broad range of connections to the diverse heritages that generations of immigrants in our nation retain. Not all heritage language speakers are the same; they differ in achieved proficiency levels, motivations, attitudes, and degrees of ethnic attachment toward the language. Indeed, some persons retain very little of their ancestral languages and are nonetheless known as heritage speakers because they retain some degree of passive knowledge of the language. Furthermore, heritage language speakers differ from traditional foreign-language learners in that they are likely to possess cultural knowledge that enables them to understand subtle nuances and to practice culturally appropriate behaviors more readily perhaps, than do those who study the same language as a foreign language. Often, however, heritage language speakers have not received formal instruction in the language and, thus, may lack the prestige or formal registers of the language, literacy skills, a highly developed vocabulary, and grammatical accuracy in the language.

Debate exists about the characteristics and linguistic profiles of heritage language speakers because of the broad diversity of life circumstances that can connect an individual to a language. Despite the uncertainties about what constitutes a heritage language speaker, a body of literature has been developing about the effects of heritage language maintenance on the growing population of immigrant children in the United States. One of society's greatest ills is low academic achievement among minority students. This is illustrated by the stark achievement gap between linguistic minority students and majority students and the high school drop-out rates, especially among Latino youth.

The Promise of Maintenance Programs

One mechanism that can overturn these unfavorable outcomes may be the expansion of heritage language maintenance programs. Studies by Carl Bankston and Min Zhou, Russell Rumberger and Kathryn Larson and Wallace Lambert have shown that heritage language maintenance alongside English language acquisition is a significant predictor of greater cognitive flexibility when compared with English monolingual students. Across grade levels, children who continue to develop reading and writing skills in their heritage language have been found to have higher grade point averages, higher standardized test scores in math and in English (see work by David Dolson, and Alejandro Portes and Lingxin Hao), lower drop-out rates and more positive attitudes toward high school (Kathryn Lindholm-Learly and Graciela Borsato; Wayne Thomas and Virginia Collier), higher educational expectations (see work by François Nielsen with Steven Lerner), and more ambitious plans for the future (see work by Homer García) than do their counterparts who have lost proficiency in their heritage language. This is especially noteworthy in families that have a tradition of literacy. The results differ somewhat among children from environments of multigenerational poverty whose families have little or no formal schooling and whose parents are illiterate in the heritage language. There is a suggestion in this regard that biliteracy

makes a greater contribution to education than does bilingualism.

At one point in the past, the prevailing theory was that maintaining one's native language was detrimental to a child's cognitive growth. Teachers were advised to tell parents that they should not speak the heritage language at home, and use only English to facilitate its development. The belief that bilingualism is detrimental for children's cognitive development has affected scores of children, interfered with generations of family relationships, and contributed to the considerable shortage of the nation's pool of proficient heritage language speakers. Researchers such as James Cummins and Kenji Hakuta argue that continued use and development of the heritage language positively contributes to the child's learning of additional languages and subject matter content because skills in the heritage language can transfer to new learning contexts.

Children with proficiency in the heritage language also tend to have greater confidence and self-esteem, and a stronger sense of group identity. Healthy development of ethnic identity is critical for their academic success and their ability to be well adjusted in this society. Because language is a salient marker of one's culture and ethnicity, an undeniable and intricate link exists between heritage language proficiency and group identity. Thus, through the heritage language, individuals can develop a more secure cultural and linguistic sense of self as well as a stronger bond with other co-ethnic members of the community.

Through frequent interactions within networks of co-ethnics, children are likely to gain access to the cultural and societal capital that is available in the community as well as develop a stronger sense of belongingness, which is often missing for minorities. Thus, when heritage language maintenance is positively associated and regarded with a sense of pride, children are better able to embrace both the home culture and the larger culture of school and society. Conversely, when a child's heritage language is seen as a source of shame or a marker of inferiority, the consequential language loss is related to negative self-image and cultural isolation. As immigrant children repeatedly experience the advantages that come from being bilingual, they are likely to perceive their linguistic abilities as resources, rather than as problems to hide. Positive self-image and cultural integration can increase their motivation toward school and reinforce their beliefs that they can succeed in their studies. Such children are more likely to stay in school, achieve academically, and become thriving members of society.

Role of Family

Another point with which most educators and researchers agree is that parental involvement and strong family relationships significantly influence children's academic success. Studies that have closely examined the quality of family interactions and relationships emphasize the necessity of heritage language maintenance for the children (see work by Portes and Hao and that of Michal Tannenbaum). In cases where English proficiency of the first-generation immigrant (i.e., the parents) may be low, elimination or significant reduction of the heritage language is likely to result in a breakdown in communication between parent and child, creating greater risks for familial isolation as well as cross-cultural and intergenerational conflict. Typically, these factors diminish parental status and authority in the eyes of their children and hinder the ability of the parents to play a guiding role in their children's academic, social, and moral pathways. In other words, inadequate maintenance of the heritage language may create a potential barrier for positive home socialization experiences. Without the ability for parents and their children to communicate openly and freely on a wide array of topics, there will be many missed opportunities for parents to influence and guide their children through critical transitions throughout their life spans and for children to seek guidance from their parents. In addition, for many children of immigrants, the primary caregivers are grandparents because the parents are often working long hours. The tremendous wealth of knowledge and shared wisdom that grandparents can offer children is lost without the heritage language with which to communicate. Researchers have widely documented that when children, parents, and grandparents dialogue with one another beyond routine minimal interactions, they are able to build stronger relationships and have closer family cohesiveness (as reported by the researchers mentioned earlier), which are critical factors for greater academic and social success. Thus, the maintenance and development of the heritage language is useful for second-generation immigrants for their own personal well-being and for that of their families.

Heritage Languages and Societal Needs

Heritage language maintenance has wider implications for our larger society. We live in a nation where multilingual speakers are needed to address the needs of more than 30 million non-English-speaking citizens, the demands of globalization, and concerns for national security. A critical shortage of translators and interpreters exists in hospitals, courts, and businesses, in addition to more than 80 governmental agencies. Moreover, U.S. military personnel are stationed across locations where more than 140 languages are spoken, and thus need language experts to assist them in implementing peacekeeping, humanitarian, and nation-building efforts. The situation is not getting any better; the number of agencies needing language experts has more than doubled during the past 15 years, and annually almost 35,000 governmental positions require foreign-language competence to fill, many of which currently go unfilled. Without the reinforcement of individuals with foreign-language expertise, economic, diplomatic, governmental, and military operations will be negatively affected.

Foreign-language education in the United States has been a low priority for several decades. The lack of incentive and motivation to learn a foreign language, ineffective language curricula and pedagogy, and limited resources and time have all contributed to low achievement outcomes among foreign-language learners. A more immediate and effective approach to addressing this critical shortage of multilingual speakers may be to actively support the learning and teaching of heritage languages. This can be done without infringing on the necessary teaching of English, the nation's first language. Heritage language speakers offer an opportune response to the linguistic needs of our nation. Because of their existing cultural and linguistic knowledge base, they are in a stronger position with proper training to develop superior levels of proficiency in a shorter time than are traditional foreign-language learners.

The irony of the linguistic reality of the United States became starkly apparent immediately following the tragedy of September 11, 2001, when the government was unable to find trained translators for Farsi and Arabic, despite the large numbers of Middle Eastern immigrants living in the country. One untapped resource in the United States is the pool of heritage language speakers. The nation's security, stability, and vitality rest on our citizens' understanding of different cultures and languages around the world. With each child who loses proficiency in his or her heritage language, society suffers another loss and another missed opportunity to develop a language expert.

Finally, maintenance of the heritage language also contributes to supporting the linguistic and cultural diversity of the nation. One language or culture cannot be labeled more or less valuable than another, and the diverse perspectives and funds of knowledge of each language community provide multiple vantage points that enrich our collective experience.

In the 19th century, most languages and cultures in the United States were European-based; today, much greater diversity exists. For example, more than 50% of the heritage language speakers in the United States speak languages from Latin America (Spanish, Portuguese, French), and another 25% are Asian or Southeast Asian languages (Chinese, Hindi, Khmer, Korean, Lao, Tagalog, Urdu, Vietnamese, Japanese) or from Africa and Oceania (Amharic, Arabic, Fijian, Hausa, Yoruba, Swahili), in addition to the 162 native American indigenous languages, many of which are down to a handful of native speakers. Thus, a national policy that views these languages as resources to be preserved and developed could contribute significantly to the nation's economic, political, educational, and technological advancements.

Jin Sook Lee and Debra Suárez

See also Cognitive Benefits of Bilingualism; Dual-Language Programs; Heritage Language Education; Paradox of Bilingualism; Spanish, Proactive Maintenance

Further Readings

Baker, C., & Jones, S. P. (1998). *Encyclopedia of bilingualism and bilingual education.* Clevedon, UK: Multilingual Matters.

Bankston, C., & Zhou, M. (1995) Effects of minority-language literacy on the academic achievement of Vietnamese youths in New Orleans. *Sociology of Education, 68*(1), 1–17.

Brecht, R. D., & Rivers, W. P. (2000). *Language and national security in the 21st century: The role of Title VI/Fulbright-Hays in supporting national language capacity.* Dubuque, IA: Kendall/Hunt.

Dolson, D. (1985). The effects of Spanish home language use on the scholastic performance of Hispanic pupils. *Journal of Multilingual and Multicultural Development 6*(2), 135–155.

Fishman, J. A., Cooper, R., & Rosenbaum, Y. (1977). English the world over: A factor in the creation of bilingualism today. In P. Hornby (Ed.), *Bilingualism: Psychological, social and educational implications* (pp. 103–109). New York: Academic Press.

García, H. (1985). Family and offspring: Language maintenance and their effects of Chicano college students' confidence and grades. In E. García & R. Padilla (Eds.), *Advances in bilingual education research* (pp. 226–243). Tucson: University of Arizona Press.

Hakuta, K. (1986). *Mirror of language: The debate on bilingualism.* New York: Basic Books.

Hornberger, N. H. (2005). Heritage/community language education: U.S. and Australian perspectives. *International Journal of Bilingual Education and Bilingualism, 8*(2–3), 101–108.

Lindholm-Leary, K. J., & Borsato, G. (2001). *Impact of two-way bilingual elementary programs on students' attitudes toward school and college.* Santa Cruz, CA: Center for Research on Education, Diversity & Excellence.

Nielsen, F., & Lerner, S. (1986). Language skills and school achievement of bilingual Hispanics. *Social Science Research, 15,* 209–240.

Peal, E., & Lambert, W. (1962). The relation of bilingualism to intelligence. *Psychological Monographs, 76*(27), 1–23.

Portes, A., & Hao, L. (2002). The price of uniformity: Language, family and personality adjustment in the immigrant second generation. *Ethnic and Racial Studies, 25*(6), 889–912.

Rumberger, R., & Larson, K. (1998). Toward explaining differences in educational achievement among Mexican American language-minority students. *Sociology of Education, 71*(1), 68–92.

Tannenbaum, M. (2005). Viewing family relations through a linguistic lens: Symbolic aspects of language maintenance in immigrant families. *Journal of Family Communication, 5*(3), 229.

Thomas, W. P., & Collier, V. P. (2002). *A national study of school effectiveness for language minority students' long-term academic achievement.* Santa Cruz, CA: Center for Research on Education, Diversity & Excellence.

Wong Fillmore, L. (1991). When learning a second language means losing the first. *Early Childhood Research Quarterly, 6,* 323–347.

BENNETT, WILLIAM J. (1943–)

William J. Bennett is a political commentator, best-selling author, and popular radio show host who has held important government positions, including chair of the National Endowment for the Humanities and secretary of education during the Reagan administration. His tenure in the Department of Education was marked by controversy over what was widely perceived as his opposition to bilingual education. He is also known for his role as "Drug Czar" under the George H. W. Bush administration and for his current status as unofficial moral authority of the Republican Party.

William John Bennett was born on July 31, 1943, in Brooklyn, New York, to a banker father and medical secretary mother. He attended Williams College in Massachusetts, where he received a BA in philosophy in 1965. He would go on to receive a PhD in political philosophy from the University of Texas at Austin in 1970, followed by a JD degree from Harvard Law School in 1971. Bennett remained mostly in higher education throughout the decade, serving as assistant to the president of Boston University from 1972 to 1976; executive director, president, and director of the National Humanities Center in North Carolina from 1976 to 1981; and associate professor at North Carolina State University and the University of North Carolina at Chapel Hill from 1979 to 1981.

During the 1980s, Bennett emerged as one of the nation's most prominent and controversial political figures. In 1981, President Reagan named Bennett, then a registered Democrat (he joined the Republican Party in 1986), as chairman of the National Endowment for the Humanities. As chairman, Bennett moved the agency in a more conservative direction, attacking multiculturalism and affirmative action. In 1985, Reagan appointed Bennett secretary of education, the beginning of a volatile tenure in the department. As secretary, Bennett advocated cuts in financial assistance for higher education, emphasized "character" education, and urged the passage of a constitutional amendment that would allow prayer in schools. He also asked for congressional enactment of a school voucher program, allowing children in failing schools to transfer to other schools.

Bennett also opened a national debate on bilingual education, claiming the high drop-out rate among English language learners (ELLs) was caused by the bilingual approach and the Title VII requirement that programs make some use of students' native languages and cultures. Bennett proposed the Bilingual Education Initiative in 1985, meant to spur "local flexibility" by allowing schools to spend federal funds on a wider variety of teaching methods rather than one prescribed method. Opponents viewed this move as a veiled attempt to push alternative instructional programs that used mostly English to instruct ELLs. Bennett pressed for changes in the 1988 version of the Bilingual Education Act that reflected his emphasis on the diversity of ELLs and approaches to their education. The rhetorical war initiated by Bennett's anti-bilingual education position, between bilingual educators who felt they were deliberately misled and federal officials who felt their motives had been maligned, would last until Bennett left office in 1988.

Bennett's time in the private sector would be brief. After leaving his post at the Department of Education, Bennett became president of the Madison Center, a public policy forum in Washington, D.C. Soon after George H. W. Bush was elected president, however, Bennett was named the nation's first director of the Office of National Drug Control Policy, or "drug czar," a position he held from 1989 to 1990.

After exiting the Bush administration, Bennett began to leave his mark on the world of political commentating, contributing numerous editorials on culture, politics, and education to newspapers and magazines, appearing on television shows, lecturing widely on moral issues, and hosting a popular syndicated radio program, *Bill Bennett's Morning in America*. He became a best-selling author of numerous books, including *The Book of Virtues* and *The Children's Book of Virtues,* the latter adapted to a highly popular children's animated series on public television in the United States and in the United Kingdom. During this period, Bennett was also a partner at a law firm and served as national cochairman of the Partnership for a Drug-Free America. In 1993, he also cofounded Empower America, an organization that speaks out on conservative social issues and policies, and cofounded and served as chairman of K12, Inc., a company that designs home-based learning programs.

Persons who offer moral instruction to the public can expect full media exposure should any of their own errors or imperfections come to light. In 2003, it was reported in several newspapers that Bennett had lost millions of dollars in Las Vegas and Atlantic City casinos over the previous decade. Bennett never disclosed how much he had lost but revealed that he had gambled large sums of money and said his betting days were over. Bennett made headlines again in 2005, when he made controversial statements about race and crime on his radio program. Critics across the political spectrum denounced his remarks as insensitive, but Bennett replied that he was misunderstood.

The recipient of numerous honorary degrees for his years as a public servant and conservative spokesman, Bennett continues to influence America's political and social landscape. In addition to his radio, writing, and speaking duties, he currently serves as Distinguished Fellow at the Heritage Foundation and as the Washington Fellow of the Claremont Institute, both conservative think tanks, and is chair of the organization Americans for Victory over Terrorism.

Gregory Pearson

See also Bilingual Education as Language Policy; English as a Second Language (ESL) Approaches; English Immersion; Views of Bilingual Education; Appendix A

Further Readings

Bill Bennett's Morning in America. (n.d.). *Biography.* Available from http://www.bennettmornings.com

CNN. (2003, May 5). *GOP moralist Bennett gives up gambling.* Retrieved October 23, 2007, from http://www.cnn.com/2003/ALLPOLITICS/05/05/bennett.gambling/index.html

CNN. (2005, September 30). *Bennett under fire for remarks on Blacks, crime.* Retrieved October 23, 2007, from http://www.cnn.com/2005/POLITICS/09/30/bennett.comments

Crawford, J. (1995). *Bilingual education: History, politics, theory, and practice.* Los Angeles: Bilingual Educational Services.

Grossman, M. (2003). William John Bennett, 1943– . In *Encyclopedia of the United States Cabinet* (Vol. 1, pp. 241–242). Santa Barbara, CA: ABC-CLIO.

Sobel, R., & Sicilia, D. B. (Eds.). (2003). William John Bennett. In *The United States executive branch: A biographical directory of heads of state and cabinet officials* (pp. 38–39).Westport, CT: Greenwood Press.

Stewner-Manzanares, G. (1988). The Bilingual Education Act: Twenty years later. *New Focus, 6.* Washington, DC: National Clearinghouse for English Language Acquisition. Retrieved October 23, 2007, from http://www.ncela.gwu.edu/pubs/classics/focus/06bea.htm

BERNAL, JOE J. (1927–)

Joe J. Bernal, a civil rights leader and community activist who played a key role in establishing bilingual education in Texas, was born in San Antonio, Texas, into a family of nine children. He graduated from Lanier High School in the heart of San Antonio's *barrio* in 1944. Following his service in the armed forces during World War II, he returned to San Antonio in 1946, where, through the G.I. Bill, he completed a BA at Trinity University and earned an MEd from Our Lady of the Lake University. He later completed a PhD in cultural foundations of education at the University of Texas at Austin.

For 14 years (1950–1964), Bernal worked as a classroom teacher in three South Texas school districts, an experience through which he became painfully aware of the intense discrimination experienced by Mexican American children in Texas public schools. He then worked for 10 years in the area of social services, first as a family and youth counselor for a United Way Agency and then as executive director for a community center. Bernal later served as executive director for the Commission for Mexican Affairs at the Archdiocese of San Antonio.

Ultimately, Bernal's dissatisfaction with the appalling state of affairs in the Texas public education system, combined with a strong desire to improve conditions for his community, led him into a political career through which he became known for his passionate struggle on behalf of minorities, seeking social justice and equal educational opportunity. In 1964, Bernal was elected to the Texas House of Representatives, where he served one term before being elected in 1966 as Texas's only Latino senator. During his 6 years in the Texas State Senate (1966–1972), Bernal authored many groundbreaking bills, including the state's first bilingual law in 1969, which, in permitting native-language instruction to occur when pedagogically justifiable, had the effect of repealing existing penal code penalties for teachers using a language other than English in the classroom. During his tenure in the Texas Senate, Bernal was primary author for a number of landmark education bills, such as creating free statewide kindergarten programs, providing teachers a 45-minute planning time period, and establishing the University of Texas at San Antonio. He was also responsible for backing legislation that added dental and nursing schools to the University of

Texas Health Science Center at San Antonio. His legislative contributions extend beyond education, with notable social justice achievements that include authorization of the first minimum-wage law and expunging from state statute all laws supporting segregation of the races.

Following his career as an elected public official, Bernal continued his advocacy efforts on behalf of the Mexican American community through various avenues. He first worked as a researcher and trainer for the Intercultural Development Research Association, focusing on Mexican American educational issues, and later served in the Carter administration as regional director of ACTION, a federal agency that coordinated volunteer activities in Texas and four neighboring states.

Bernal's substantial contributions to bilingual education have extended far beyond his early legislative achievements. For 7 years, he served as an executive board member for the National Association for Bilingual Education, and for 2 years, he served on the executive board of the Texas Association for Bilingual Education as legislative chair. As a founding board member of the Mexican American Legal Defense and Educational Fund (MALDEF), Bernal ensured that bilingual education remain a core agenda item intricately connected to struggles for obtaining equal educational opportunity for language minority students. As the founding chair of Mexican American Democrats of Texas, he led ongoing efforts to address weaknesses in the Texas bilingual education law and to strengthen key eligibility and accountability provisions in the law.

Following his early legislative and legal advocacy efforts, Bernal returned to his initial career as a professional educator, serving in leadership positions in two public school districts, where he guided implementation of bilingual education programs. From 1982 to 1987, he served as principal of an elementary school in the Edgewood Independent School District that, despite being situated in the lowest-income census tract in San Antonio, gained recognition for strong academic gains by students, earning a citation by the Texas Education Agency in 1986 as an exemplary bilingual education school. Bernal continued his role as instructional leader from 1987 to 1992, serving as assistant superintendent for instructional services for the Harlandale Independent School District in San Antonio, where he led efforts to strengthen implementation of bilingual education programs in the district. From 1992 to 2003, he taught a bilingual education foundations course for preservice teachers,

as an adjunct professor in the Division of Bicultural-Bilingual Studies at the University of Texas at San Antonio. Bernal returned to public service from 1996 to 2006 as an elected member of the State Board of Education, where he continued to work on public education issues affecting underrepresented groups in the state.

In recognition of his many achievements on behalf of language minority education and the Mexican American community, Bernal has received numerous awards from professional associations, business groups, unions, and civil rights organizations. His personal papers and publications, covering 40 years of community advocacy and public service, are held at the Benson Latin American Collection at the University of Texas at Austin.

Robert D. Milk

See also Texas Legislation (HB 103 and SB 121)

Further Readings

Bernal, J. J. (1994). A historical perspective of bilingual education in Texas. In R. Rodríguez, N. Ramos, & J. Ruiz-Escalante (Eds.), *Compendium of readings in bilingual education: Issues and practices* (pp. 294–300). San Antonio: Texas Association for Bilingual Education.

Joe J. Bernal Papers. (n.d.). Benson Latin American Collection, University of Texas Libraries, University of Texas at Austin.

Best English to Learn

When discussing the educational needs of English language learners (ELLs), one of the topics frequently discussed is the kind or variety of English such individuals need to learn to be successful in an English-speaking society. This is not an issue that pertains only to students who speak a language other than English, although for them, the stakes may be somewhat higher. It is not always the case that students of English should learn the same form of English they will use with classmates or on the street.

Most teachers will intuitively choose standard or "correct" language as the most appropriate to teach, although the reasons may be different from those discussed in this entry. Guadalupe Valdés, a scholar concerned with the education of linguistic minorities, mentions that the "standard English" ideology informs debates on the kind of English taught at school to the student population. This refers to the teaching of a standard variety of English and discouraging the use of other types of English that may be regarded as "incorrect," "inferior," or "improper." This entry reviews some concepts in sociolinguistics and other social sciences for a better understanding of the concept of "standard" English and how and why it is often chosen for classroom instruction.

Dialects and the Notion of Standard English

According to British sociolinguist Peter Trudgill, the term *dialect* usually refers to diversity in the varieties of a language in which vocabulary, grammar, and pronunciation may change. For example, British and American English are two different dialects, with differences in lexical items (e.g., *lift/elevator, petrol/ gasoline, bonnet/hood*), syntax (the past tense of the verb *to learn: learned/learnt*), and phonology (pronunciation). Dialects are found in other languages, such as the Spanish dialect used in Mexico compared with the Spanish dialect of Argentina, in which features such as verb conjugations and some word meanings differ. Trudgill also compares the concept of dialect with *accent,* explaining that the latter merely refers to differences in pronunciation within a language. Linguist Rosina Lippi-Green explains that geographical location is often used as a boundary to mark different accents (e.g., a Chicago accent), but other features may be used to mark boundaries as well, such as social class, gender, or race. These may also mark different dialects, provided there is variation in other language components, such as different vocabulary or syntax.

In the historical study of dialects, or *language varieties,* a more neutral term, as Trudgill explains, two approaches in linguistics have existed historically: (1) *prescriptivism,* a view that favors a certain dialect to be used and "prescribed," a standard form of language, and (2) *descriptivism,* a view that focuses on diversity in language and the description of language without placing a higher value on one variety over another. David Crystal has written that grammarians in Europe studied languages from a prescriptive perspective in the 18th century, in an attempt to label language use as correct or incorrect, establishing

grammar rules. He highlights the role of language academies in keeping the use of language "pure," such as in the case of France, Spain, or Italy. The notion of a standard language to be prescribed implies aspects of power that are not intrinsic to the linguistic structures. They have to do with conferring legitimacy on the language variety spoken by dominant groups in a society, as sociologist Pierre Bourdieu explains. In the case of English, Trudgill explains that the variety known as "standard" was used by the upper classes and became the model to emulate. Standard English, he stresses, is one dialect out of many, the dialect associated with educated and powerful people.

Lippi-Green, in her book *English With an Accent,* regards the notion of a standard language as a myth. She argues that the ideology supporting the existence of a standard language emphasizes the ideal of a homogenous language form and its role in a nation-state, allowing a certain group to control language variation. She also notes that it allows for other dialects to be labeled as "nonstandard" or "substandard." Sociolinguist William Labov conducted several studies analyzing dialects that were categorized as nonstandard, establishing that they were not to be regarded as inferior to the standard dialect: He argues that they are language systems that are different but closely related, with functional grammatical processes of their own. For example, in African American Vernacular English (also known as Ebonics), the form *be* signals habitual general conditions, as in the example Labov gives: "He always be foolin' around." It should not be seen as a mistake when compared with standard English and the use of *is* or *am.* The use of *be* is a syntax rule that is valid and consistent in this particular dialect. Other English varieties, such as Spanglish in the United States or Indian English, have been analyzed similarly, as in the work of Shana Poplack and Braj Kachru, respectively. Not only are these varieties rule governed, they also play a significant role as identity markers for their language communities.

Varieties of English in the Classroom

In his book *The Study of Nonstandard English,* Labov emphasizes the educational disadvantage of Black and Spanish-speaking students in urban areas. He stresses the need to understand English varieties used by these communities—in the latter, what he called

"Spanish-influenced English"—since using them was the best way of communication with these children and young people. Not only is this knowledge important to build bridges between speech communities; favoring and accepting standard English as the only "correct" variety works to reproduce and strengthen its dominant status in society, a role that the educational system has supported historically.

Sociolinguist James Gee addresses the impact of not mastering the ways to use language favored at school for linguistic and culturally diverse students. He gives the examples of African American students whose ways to use narratives in which they have been socialized at home are not valued when brought up at school. He stresses their disadvantage compared with children who have been exposed to academic language before starting school, as part of their socialization at home. For educators, this scenario demands ways to build bridges for students whose first encounter with different ways to use language happens at school. Courtney Cazden, a scholar whose work addresses the functions of classroom discourse, analyzes this dilemma faced by many teachers in negotiating language attitudes held by students and teachers. She recommends the contrast of dialect forms and the conceptualization of the use of "proper" language as a practical and political matter, instead of a judgment of what is right or wrong—hence considering the convenience of language features appropriate for a particular audience but also questioning and reflecting on the power issues attached to the hierarchical status of standard varieties.

In a 1988 classic article published in the *Harvard Educational Review,* the renowned educator Lisa Delpit stressed the need for every student to learn the "codes of power" (ways of talking, writing, or interacting, for example). She suggests when addressing language varieties that students need to learn the variety of power and that schools should take the responsibility to assist them in this process. However, it is necessary to analyze how the codes of power are arbitrary: not better because of intrinsic features, but due to the power associated with them. She described the case of a Native Alaskan teacher who addressed the differences between the "village English" the students spoke in their community and the "formal English" they needed to communicate with those whom she labeled "people who only knew one variety."

Bob Fecho, Bette Davis, and Renee Moore also stressed the need to involve their students in academic issues analyzing the social and political nature of language. In their work with African American students, they explored their "switch" to standard English for particular written tasks and discussed with them the implications of appropriating a standard variety for certain audiences and purposes—for example, how using standard English did not necessarily imply adopting White values. They also questioned and rejected the idea that standard English was a "universal" language or that using this dialect signaled superior intelligence.

Whether students are speakers of different varieties of English or languages other than English, the concept of a standard language and its implications should be part of conversations with them about the social, cultural, and political aspects of language. The acknowledgment of different language varieties, their use, and their role in the identity of speech communities play a crucial role in the building of bridges between home and school language practices; but opportunities to analyze, discuss, and be apprenticed to the language variety of power are also instrumental for linguistic minorities to understand the role of standard English in academic environments. At a global scale, where English is taught and widely used as an international language, similar conversations should take place between nations and societies. Different varieties of English are used and appropriated for specific purposes outside the United States, England, Canada, or Australia. Situating the role and power of standard English among other varieties may allow for critical use and understanding for language learners, as opposed to the imposition of a "right" type of English to be used.

Returning to the question of what is the best type of English to teach and learn, and based on the perspectives summarized above, it could be argued that teaching standard English may well be the best choice, but *knowing why* we choose to teach standard English is equally important for students and teachers alike. It is also important for students to understand that the existence of nonstandard forms is a natural phenomenon in all languages and that it is important to value them and the people who speak them. Similarly, English language learners should know that learning English is a wonderful adjunct to the language they already speak and not a substitute or more valuable language.

Silvia C. Noguerón

See also Academic English; Accents and Their Meaning; Ebonics; English, First World Language; Languages and Power; Social Class and Language Status; Spanglish; World Englishes

Further Readings

Bourdieu, P. (1991). *Language and symbolic power.* Cambridge, MA: Harvard University Press.

Cazden, C. (2001). *Classroom discourse: The language of teaching and learning* (2nd ed.). Portsmouth, NH: Heinemann.

Crystal, D. (Ed.). (1997). The prescriptive tradition. In *The Cambridge Encyclopedia of Language* (2nd ed., pp. 2–5). Cambridge, UK: Cambridge University Press.

Delpit, L. (1988). The silenced dialogue: Power and pedagogy in educating other people's children. *Harvard Educational Review, 58,* 280–298.

Fecho, B., Davis, B., & Moore, R. (2006). Exploring race, language, and culture in critical literacy classrooms. In D. Alvermann, K. Hinchman, D. Moore, S. Phelps, & D. Waff (Eds.), *Reconceptualizing the literacies in adolescents' lives* (2nd ed., pp. 187–204). Mahwah, NJ: Lawrence Erlbaum.

Gee, J. P. (2004). *Situated language and learning: A critique of traditional schooling.* New York: Routledge.

Kachru, B. (1986). *The alchemy of English: The spread, functions, and models of non-native Englishes.* Oxford, UK: Pergamon Institute of English.

Labov, W. (1970). *The study of nonstandard English.* Champaign, IL: National Council of Teachers of English.

Lippi-Green, R. (1997). *English with an accent: Language, ideology, and discrimination in the United States.* New York: Routledge.

Poplack, S. (1981). Syntactic structure and social function of codeswitching. In R. Duran (Ed.), *Latino language and communicative behavior* (pp. 169–184). Norwood, NJ: Ablex.

Trudgill, P. (2000). *Sociolinguistics: An introduction to language and society* (4th. ed.). London: Penguin.

Valdés, G. (2004). Between support and marginalisation: The development of academic language in linguistic minority children. *Bilingual Education and Bilingualism, 7,* 102–132.

"Better Chance to Learn"

See U.S. Commission on Civil Rights Report

BICS/CALP Theory

BICS (basic interpersonal communication skills) and CALP (cognitive-academic language proficiency) are acronyms frequently used in bilingual education to denote types or levels of language proficiency among minority students. Although the BICS/CALP distinction has become widespread among practitioners, it has been controversial among scholars. This entry includes the definition and origins of the BICS/CALP distinction and a summary of the criticisms leveled against this terminology.

Immigrant students often enter U.S. schools without full proficiency in English. At some point in each student's second-language development, a reclassification decision is made, from the status of a "limited English proficient" student to that of a "fluent English proficient" student. How to determine the point at which such reclassification is appropriate is an important and controversial issue. For bilingual educators, a persisting fear is that some children may give the appearance of full proficiency before they actually do know English well enough to get along in an all-English classroom, prompting teachers, administrators, and test developers to reclassify them too soon.

One approach to this problem was the BICS/CALP distinction, introduced in the 1970s by Canadian researcher James Cummins. Cummins believed that language minority children who speak English on the playground or with classmates might display a kind of surface fluency, which he called *basic interpersonal communication skills* (BICS), although they have not necessarily achieved *cognitive-academic language proficiency* (CALP). Cummins identified schooling and literacy as the means by which CALP could be achieved. In monolingual contexts, Cummins explained, the BICS/CALP distinction reflects the difference between the language virtually all 6-year-old children acquire and the proficiency developed through schooling and literacy. In a later definition of CALP, which he also termed *academic language,* Cummins described it as the ability to use spoken or written language without relying on nonlinguistic cues, such as gestures, to convey complex meanings.

Cummins reanalyzed cross-sectional language proficiency data reported in prior research by other scholars; the primary interest was to disentangle age of arrival from length of residence of immigrant children, both factors that could independently influence measures of language proficiency. Previous researchers had found that children who had arrived at 6 to 7 years of age eventually caught up to monolingual peers on grade-level norms, but later arrivals did not. Cummins noted that when grouping students by length of residence rather than age of arrival, one sees that older learners acquire academic second language skills more rapidly than younger learners. However, as Cummins noted, the measures used in the previous research tended to target academic rather than pure linguistic factors. In Cummins's analysis of the data, children required 2 to 3 years to approach native-level ability on language tests but as long as 5 years to approach grade level on academic measures. Cummins used the terms BICS and CALP to characterize these different "levels" of language proficiency observed in students.

Later, in response to criticisms that the BICS/CALP distinction created an artificial and arbitrarily delineated dichotomy, Cummins introduced a four-quadrants model of language proficiency, in which language proficiency was conceptualized along two continua, called *context embedded* and *context reduced*. Context-embedded communication, Cummins stressed, derives from interpersonal involvement in a shared reality that reduces the need for explicit linguistic elaboration of the message. Context-reduced communication, on the other hand, takes place in the absence of a shared reality, hence requiring linguistic messages to be elaborated explicitly.

Criticisms

Although the BICS/CALP distinction is deeply embedded in the bilingual teacher education literature as well as in the literature of bilingual special education, it remains a controversial idea among bilingual education researchers. In particular, Carole Edelsky, Marilyn Martin-Jones, Suzanne Romaine, Terrence Wiley, Kellie Rolstad, and Jeff MacSwan have characterized the BICS/CALP distinction as a kind of deficit theory; this is understood as an explanation of differential achievement that posits that students who fail in school do so because of inherent deficiencies related to their intellectual abilities, linguistic shortcomings, or lack of motivation to learn, typically transmitted by culture, social class, or familial socialization. Because the acquisition of a native language is an inherent human ability and because it reflects aspects of our biology and community lives, appealing to levels of native-language proficiency appears to explain school failure in terms of a presumed "low ability level" of the child in his or her own native language.

Critics have argued that the properties Cummins associates with the higher-order language of CALP are simply the language of a specific locus of cultural activity, namely, school. Rather than characterize this kind of language as more developed or complex, critics have argued that it should be characterized simply as *different*. There is no independent evidence supporting the presumption that academics are better at explaining their craft than the less schooled are at explaining theirs or that accompanying gestures are less useful to academics than to others. One might imagine a typical professor, for instance, trying to talk in detail about farming, boat building, or auto repair. Academics would typically lack knowledge of relevant vocabulary in these contexts—words that would be "low frequency" for them, but not for many others. Moreover, we might wonder why one would consider academic language to involve "complex grammatical structures," as Cummins believes, in comparison to nonacademic language. No persuasive evidence has been presented to show this. Rather, the evidence Cummins discussed showed a distinction between linguistic assessment, which he interpreted as measures of BICS, and academic achievement assessment, which he took to be measures of CALP.

In Cummins's framework, literacy is an aspect of language proficiency that develops later in life, layered atop the "basic fluency" or "species minimum" (a term borrowed from Jerome Bruner) that is BICS. A more traditional view among linguists, however, takes literacy to be a kind of technology used to represent language graphically. In this view, expertise in the use of print is no more an index of language proficiency than expertise in the use of photography is of visual acuity. Indeed, writing is a very recent human invention, which became widespread and publicly accessible only about 500 years ago with the advent of moveable type, and has been rejected by some societies as unimportant. By contrast, language existed long before the technology of writing and exists in all human societies today. But given Cummins's conception of language proficiency, critics have contended, we are led inescapably to the conclusion that societies that do not use writing systems have relatively "low language proficiency," restricted only to BICS, in contrast to the "highly proficient" language abilities represented in the academy in literate societies.

Hence, rather than viewing CALP (or literacy and related elements of academic achievement) as an aspect of language development, it might make more sense to view academic achievement in language-related domains as specific to the cultural setting of schools, and mastery of them simply as mastery of a domain of cultural knowledge. This permits us to view language growth independently from growth in academic subjects.

For Cummins, the BICS/CALP distinction is specifically related not only to children's developing second language but also to their first language. The association of the BICS/CALP distinction with a child's native language arguably makes the distinction reminiscent of classical *prescriptivism,* the view that some varieties of language are inherently superior to others. However, second-language learners exhibit errors of a sort that school-aged children do not exhibit in their native languages.

Unlike school-aged first-language speakers, second-language learners have developed only partial knowledge of the structure of their target language and exhibit substantial and consistent errors associated with tense, case, grammatical agreement, word order, phonology, and other aspects of structure. Moreover, whereas all normal human beings acquire the language of their speech communities effortlessly and without instruction, second-language acquisition often meets with only partial success and frequently depends on considerable effort and purposely structured input. Evidence suggests, too, that second-language development proceeds with considerable variation in rate and ultimate attainment, whereas native speakers exhibit remarkable uniformity in these respects. Because second-language teaching typically occurs at school, in a context that is outside of children's home language communities, describing a child as having limited ability in a second language does not suggest inherent deficiencies related to the child's genetic makeup, culture, class, or familial socialization, and therefore it should not be viewed from a deficit approach. The second language is specifically not a part of the child's home culture and environment. Thus, limiting the notion of CALP to the second language only, while still seen by many as theoretically dubious, would not spark charges of prescriptivism and deficit psychology.

In sum, critics have argued that notions of language proficiency, in the context of linguistic minority education, crucially must distinguish between language ability and academic achievement and that blending these constructs in the context of native-language ability, in particular, leads to unintended conceptual consequences. Furthermore, distinguishing between first- and second-language development allows us to clarify that the BICS/CALP distinction implies deficiencies inherent in the child's community only when applied to the first-language context.

SLIC: An Alternative View

Separating achievement and language as distinct psychological constructs allows us to contrast the learning situation of majority language (children in the U.S. who already know English) and minority language children in school. While majority language children have the single objective of mastering academic content (math, social studies, science, reading, etc.) in school, language minority children have two objectives they must meet to be academically successful. Like majority language children, they must master academic content; but unlike children in the majority, they must also learn the language of instruction at school. Bilingual instruction allows these children and youth to keep up academically while they take the time needed to master English. Also, in the course of developing children's knowledge of school subjects, bilingual education provides background knowledge that serves as a context for children to better understand the presentation of new academic subject matter in the second language and also helps them make inferences about the meaning of new words and grammatical structures they encounter in the new language.

An alternative to the BICS/CALP distinction was introduced by Kellie Rolstad and Jeff MacSwan in an effort to avoid some of these pitfalls. They argued that once children have learned English sufficiently well to understand content through all-English instruction, they have developed *second-language instructional competence* (SLIC). Unlike CALP, SLIC does not apply to native-language development and does not ascribe any special status to the language of school. Also, while CALP appears to equate cognitive and academic development, SLIC simply denotes the stage of second-language development in which the learner is able to understand instruction and perform grade-level school activities using the second language alone, in the local educational setting. Children who have not yet developed SLIC are not considered cognitively less developed; they simply have not yet learned enough of the second language to effectively learn through it. The SLIC concept thus avoids the implication that a child is deficient and still allows us to stress the need for children to continue to receive interesting, cognitively challenging instruction that they can understand during the time needed to achieve second-language competence.

There is little doubt that James Cummins's BICS/CALP theory has been a useful tool for practitioners in assessing where their students are in their linguistic development. At base, however, the construct remains a theory with little empirical evidence of its existence. This does not invalidate the contribution; several other important theories have remained unproven while serving as important bases on which to build additional research. Nonetheless, while critics have applauded the original intent of the BICS/CALP distinction, they have argued that certain refinements are needed to avoid some unintended negative consequences. By distinguishing between academic achievement and language ability and between first- and second-language development in school-aged children, we might be better able to characterize the language situation of linguistic minorities and their achievement in school.

Kellie Rolstad and Jeff MacSwan

See also Academic English; Designation and Redesignation of English Language Learners; First-Language Acquisition; Measuring Language Proficiency; Second-Language Acquisition; Semilingualism

Further Readings

Crystal, D. (1986). The prescriptive tradition. In D. Crystal (Ed.), *The Cambridge Encyclopedia of Language* (pp. 2–5). Cambridge, UK: Cambridge University Press.

Cummins, J. (1981). The role of primary language development in promoting educational success for language minority students. In C. Leyba (Ed.), *Schooling and language minority students: A theoretical framework* (pp. 3–49). Sacramento: California State Department of Education.

Cummins, J. (2000). *Language, power, and pedagogy: Bilingual children in the crossfire.* Clevedon, UK: Multilingual Matters.

Edelsky, C., Hudelson, S., Flores, B., Barkin, F., Altweger, J., & Jilbert, K. (1983). Semilingualism and language deficit. *Applied Linguistics, 4,* 1–22.

MacSwan, J. (2000). The threshold hypothesis, semilingualism, and other contributions to a deficit view of linguistic minorities. *Hispanic Journal of Behavioral Sciences, 20,* 3–45.

MacSwan, J., & Rolstad, K. (2003). Linguistic diversity, schooling, and social class: Rethinking our conception of language proficiency in language minority education. In C. B. Paulston & R. Tucker (Eds.), *Sociolinguistics: The essential readings* (pp. 329–340). Oxford, UK: Blackwell.

Valencia, R. (1997). Introduction. In R. Valencia (Ed.), *The evolution of deficit thinking: Educational thought and practice* (pp. ix–xvii). London: Falmer Press.

Wiley, T. G. (2005). *Literacy and language diversity in the United States* (2nd ed.). Washington, DC, and McHenry, IL: Center for Applied Linguistics/Delta Systems.

BICULTURALISM

Biculturalism is the ability to effectively navigate day-to-day life in two different social groups and to do so with the anticipated result of being accepted by the cultural group that is not one's own. As human beings live and work in shared spaces, their common experiences produce a set of values and behavioral standards, communicative and cognitive codes, as well as worldviews and beliefs. Taken together, these are the elements of culture—a dynamic, shared, interwoven system of ideas and actions that mediate our choices, values, and actions in our day-to-day lives. Unlike human emotions (e.g., love, hate), which are static and universal, culture is dynamic because it changes with time and space as well as membership. *Biculturalism* refers to the necessary knowledge, skills, and beliefs that individuals can access to participate within their own and another cultural group.

Societal Biculturalism

At the state or macrolevel, *biculturalism* suggests that two cultures merit formal recognition. According to Carol Ware, the term first appeared in *The Cultural Approach to History* and subsequently in journal articles of the 1950s that discussed struggles between Canadian Francophones and Anglophones. After a national or ethnic conflict in which neither faction completely conquers or overpowers the other, a process ensues to accommodate the two opposing ways of existence. One way this is accomplished is through language policy. Such policies create official domains for language use or diglossia. In colonized countries like India, with dozens of local languages, the end of British colonial control presented the opportunity for language planning and the creation of an official (de jure) language policy. This excerpt from the Constitution of India (November 26, 1949) is an example:

> 345. Official language or languages of a State.— Subject to the provisions of articles 346 and 347, the Legislature of a State may by law adopt any one or more of the languages in use in the State or Hindi as the language or languages to be used for all or any of the official purposes of that State . . . Provided that, until the Legislature of the State otherwise provides by law, the English language shall continue to be used for those official purposes within the State.

In the absence of an official policy, groups of language speakers often create a de facto language policy to demarcate the accepted domains for a particular language. While the possibility exists to use either of one's available languages in a given domain, there is an implicit understanding shared by members of the bicultural society that one language is more appropriate than the other. Such domains include religious activity, education, family interactions, government correspondence, and banking transactions.

Societal biculturalism can also be seen through religious practices. At times, the beliefs of a recently arriving group may violate the norms and traditions of those who lived there before. The case of American Indians is an illustrative example. Federal laws and policies of the United States frequently violated the beliefs and religious practices of the various native groups. Such policies prohibited access to sacred native religious sites or sanctioned the possession of animal-derived sacred objects. Outsiders were able to desecrate sacred native burial sites with impunity. In 1978, the U.S. Congress passed the American Indian Religious Freedom Act (AIRFA) to provide some protection for the religious practices that were an integral part of American Indian culture. The act reads in part:

> Henceforth it shall be the policy of the United States to protect and preserve for American Indians their inherent right to freedom to believe, express, and exercise the traditional religions of the American Indian, Eskimo, Aleut, and Native Hawaiians,

including but not limited to access to sites, use and possession of sacred objects, and the freedom to worship through ceremonial and traditional rites.

Outside the United States, examples of bicultural societies are Hong Kong, Hawai'i, New Zealand, Catalonia (Spain), the Philippines, and Belgium.

Individual Biculturalism

Some scholars liken biculturalism to assimilation and acculturation. While all three refer to a transformation in cultural patterns, biculturalism suggests that the change occurs without extensive loss of the ancestral culture, as described by Raymond Buriel. Usually, anthropologists and other scholars see culture as transmitted from one generation to another. In contrast, biculturalism, as a rule, is not inherited, but acquired through meaningful experiences with a culture other than the one in which a person was raised. Virginia Gonzalez, Thomas Yawkey, and Liliana Minaya-Rowe explain how immigrants learn how to bridge the use of their first and second languages in different cultural contexts and, in doing so, achieving a level of biculturalism. This process, they explain, results in the creation of a new bicultural or transcultural identity that differs from both the mainstream and minority identities. These authors describe the different possibilities for biculturalism and transculturalism: balancing the "old self" and the enactment of the "new self" or transforming to a "hybrid self."

In earlier studies, biculturalism was considered to be a necessary place along the continuum toward acculturation and assimilation. Some research studies indicate that biculturalism exists in its own, identifiable space. Conceptual models argue against a unidirectional conception of cultural change or the "either/or" conception of acculturation. In previous generations, it was widely believed that immigrants and minority group members needed to assimilate to the new culture in order to be successful in the dominant society. Research has shown that this is not the case, although some amount of acculturation or adaptation may be necessary.

Dual Frame of Reference

Biculturalism is concomitant with a dual frame of reference. Bicultural individuals possess significant knowledge and skills about more than one culture and have a strong desire to function appropriately in both.

They have a dual framework within which to interpret the actions of others and double set of values and standards by which to evaluate their own behaviors. Such individuals exist in a space with two cultural influences, internal and external, on their lives. For this reason, biculturalism is better understood as a state of mind, a part of one's being, or one's identity.

Educational Considerations

Most children from immigrant families and those from dominated cultures (e.g., Latino, African American) usually learn to live within the cultural constraints of their communities while learning to negotiate the culture(s) of the public schools. Often, the values and beliefs of the school culture (as seen through the official curriculum) are at odds with the students' (minority) home culture. Angela Valenzuela reports that bicultural students, especially from segregated, low-income, urban communities, face the derogation of their family cultures and histories.

Despite the hurdles created by schools and the broader society, some students who are able to maintain strong cultural and linguistic ties to their ancestral groups while acquiring mainstream cultural capital have greater academic success than their monolingual (monocultural) peers in U.S. schools. At the same time, children find it challenging to balance two cultural worlds. Students battle with conflicting expectations between their home culture and mainstream culture. They struggle for acceptance by peer groups. Oddly, they may experience racialization, exclusion, and even rejection by family members after achieving academic success, simply because this suggests a pattern of values and behavior that comes from outside the group itself.

Howard L. Smith

See also Acculturation; Assimilation; Culturally Competent Teaching; Enculturation; Hidden Curriculum; Social Bilingualism

Further Readings

American Indian Religious Freedom Act, 42 U.S.C. (1996).

Buriel, R. (1993). Acculturation, respect for cultural differences, and biculturalism among three generations of Mexican American and Euro-American school children. *Journal of Genetic Psychology, 154*, 531–543.

Gonzalez, V., Yawkey, T., & Minaya-Rowe, L. (2006). *English as a Second Language (ESL) teaching and learning: Pre-K–12 classroom applications for students' academic achievement and development.* Boston: Pearson/AB Longman.

Valenzuela, A. (1999). *Subtractive schooling: U.S.-Mexican youth and the politics of caring.* New York: SUNY Press.

Ware, C. G. (Ed.). (1940). *The cultural approach to history.* New York: Columbia University Press.

Web Sites

Constitution of India: http://indiacode.nic.in/coiweb/welcome.html

BILINGUAL CHARTER SCHOOLS

Since the enactment of the first charter school law in 1991, the development of charter schools (sometimes called "public schools of choice") throughout the United States has become widespread. The chief intent was to allow for the creation of legally and financially autonomous nonsectarian public schools—free from state laws and school district regulations—that would operate as private businesses accountable to children and their parents for the academic success of students. Most charter schools, as stated in individual state laws, exist as contracts that a development team enters into with an authorized entity. Generally, development teams consist of educators, parents, and concerned community members who request permission from a school district or county or state education agency to operate an autonomous public school. The contract, or charter, establishes the goals and vision of the school, and the authorizing entity grants permission for the school to operate for a specified time based on its meeting the goals set forth. Charter schools tend to be small and personalized, on average serving 250 to 300 students, and are licensed to operate for periods of 3 to 5 years before seeking renewal. Their autonomy empowers them to offer an education they believe will garner high academic results for the students they serve.

As of 2007, there were some 4,000 charter schools in 40 states plus the District of Columbia serving an estimated 1.2 million students, and the demand is growing. Public interest in and support for these schools has intensified, and financial backing from organizations like the Bill & Melinda Gates Foundation and the Walton Family Foundation have been crucial for meeting the additional expenses not covered by public funds. Scrutiny has intensified as well, especially as the first graduating classes emerge, and a greater number of independent think tanks engage in achievement studies.

The momentum behind charter schools has given rise to a dynamic education reform movement, which aims to demonstrate that basic business principles can create environments that promote successful academic institutions. For instance, with the same dollar allotment per student that traditional public schools receive, charter schools can promote creativity and innovation in educational programs that serve students of diverse backgrounds and of low-socioeconomic levels. In other words, students with the greatest need and with the least opportunities for quality educational experiences have choices not available through the traditional public school system.

The capitalist ideals of supply and demand, specialization, competition, and freedom of choice foster the development of charter schools that are compelled to implement the necessary methods to remain in business. Charter schools, although able to operate with relative flexibility, must serve the needs of parents and students while being held accountable, like any other public school, for student achievement. Ultimately, a charter school must meet the required standards of academic rigor and excellence, or it will be shut down. Several studies of existing charter schools have shown mixed results; however, for those students with the greatest need, gains have been steady and positive.

Considering all of these factors (flexibility, competition, innovation, and diverse student population), charter schools are a natural vehicle for bilingual education. In some instances, charter schools are the only vehicle for bilingual education, especially in states such as California and Arizona, where Propositions 227 and 203, respectively, abolished the right of families to enroll their children in this type of educational program. Although bilingual education in the context of charter schools is generally viewed as a tool that aids in achieving rigorous educational outcomes for English language learners as well as native English speakers, it is also viewed as ensuring equal access to opportunity and fostering positive cultural identity and self-esteem, which can be linked to academic success. In this latter capacity, bilingual charter schools offer an opportunity for students to actively pursue a meaningful connection with a culture or heritage through language maintenance and development. Although bilingual education has been at the center of heated political discussions, when linked to charter schools, it can be consistent with the concepts of parental choice, freedom from overregulation, and innovation. There are numerous bilingual charter schools in the United States today, serving as testing grounds for finding out whether this methodology works or where and with whom it may work better.

A wide array of bilingual programs exists; however, a common model employed with emerging success by charter schools is two-way, dual-language immersion. This model combines students of the same age or grade level who are native speakers of different languages, with the goal of the children becoming fluent in more than one language. This model is most effective when the number of students in each group is evenly distributed and the proper supports are readily available, such as bilingual teachers, assistants, books, and other materials. Two charter schools exemplify this model: District of Columbia Bilingual Public Charter School, in Washington, D.C., and El Sol Santa Ana Science and Arts Academy Charter School, in Santa Ana, California. Each offers students a dual-language immersion model in Spanish and English and a culturally based education anchored in program enhancements, including the arts, an extended day and year, and additional family support services. Although these are relatively new schools, each having been in operation for no more than a few years, as of 2006, they have embraced bilingual education as their program of choice and offer it in response to the needs and demands of their communities.

Because of the flexibility of charter schools, opportunities exist to implement a well-resourced, high-quality bilingual education model that is effective without the bureaucratic constraints or limitations that can result in diluted and less-effective renditions of the model. By promoting academic success through innovative language and cultural methods in a flexible and accountable structure, bilingual programs in charter schools can have the potential to advance the academic attainment of students when properly resourced and implemented.

Below are descriptions of two schools implementing bilingual education models, profiling each school's philosophy and instructional plan for promoting both academic achievement and bilingualism.

District of Columbia Bilingual Public Charter School

The District of Columbia Bilingual Public Charter School (DC Bilingual) is located in Washington, D.C., and enrolls students from pre-K to Grade 2. According to the National Center for Education Statistics, for the 2005–2006 school year, 75% of the students were of Hispanic descent.

As mentioned on their Web site, DC Bilingual first opened its doors in September 2004 and shares a similar philosophy of a parent organization named Centro Nía. The initial enrollment consisted of 122 students in early pre-K through kindergarten. The mission of DC Bilingual involves the implementation of a dual-language program, with the goal of promoting bilingualism and biliteracy skills. DC Bilingual's philosophy of learning conceptualizes it as a process that focuses on students' interaction with their peers, teachers, school staff, and home community. The school's curriculum model promotes the use of English and Spanish during instruction throughout the school day. Students are grouped according to their dominant languages for literacy instruction, but mixed grouping occurs during other school subjects (e.g., math, science, social studies), as reported on the school's Web site.

El Sol Santa Ana Science and Arts Academy Charter School

El Sol Santa Ana Science and Arts Academy Charter School is located in Santa Ana, California, and is part of the Santa Ana Unified School District. It enrolled students from kindergarten through sixth grade in 2005 and expanded to eighth grade in 2007. According to the California Department of Education, 93.8% of the school's total student population was Hispanic in the 2005–2006 school year. As of 2007, the school had been in operation for 5 years, and the charter was renewed for an additional 5 years, as reported in a message from the principal, Diana Clearwater. El Sol emphasizes and implements a dual-language immersion program in Spanish and English. As noted on its Web page, El Sol's mission involves the preparation of students for high school and higher-education entrance and the promotion of a culture of kindness, creativity, courage, and honesty.

Involvement of parents and the community is embraced at this institution. In addition, the school values the multicultural heritage its students bring and encourages those skills important for a "global citizenship." Values promoted at El Sol include ethics, integrity, social responsibility, and positive identity, as described in the school's Web site. Its educational focus prepares students to enter high school with competent literacy and math and science skills, including abilities in the arts as well.

Conclusion

The two schools described above are exemplary models of early-design bilingual charter schools. These schools adhere closely to the program quality criteria for high-quality bilingual schools. They demonstrate that given the autonomy allowed in the charter schools system, support and maintenance of bilingual instruction through charter schools may be a viable option for culturally and linguistically diverse student populations and communities.

Jacqueline Castillo Duvivier
and Irene Cuyun

See also Culturally Competent Teaching; Dual-Language Programs; Multicultural Education; Oyster Bilingual School; Program Quality Indicators; Proposition 203 (Arizona), Impact of; Proposition 227 (California), Impact of

Further Readings

Center for Education Reform. (2006). *Getting the word out: Charter schools do succeed: A guide for charter school activists provided by the Center for Education Reform.* Available from http://www.edreform.com/_upload/CER_Charter_kit2006.pdf

Cortéz, J. D., & Montecel, R. M. (2002). Successful bilingual education programs: Development and dissemination of criteria to identify promising and exemplary practices in bilingual education at the national level. *Bilingual Research Journal, 26,* 1–22.

Detrich, R., Durrett, D., & Phillips, R. (2002). *Dynamic debate: Determining the evolving impact of charter schools.* North Central Regional Educational Laboratory. Available from http://www.ncrel.org

Godard, T. M., & Hassel, B. C. (2006). *Charter school achievement: What we know.* Washington, DC: National Alliance for Public Charter Schools. Retrieved October 23, 2007, from http://www.publiccharters.org/content/publication/detail/1363

Menken, K., & National Council of La Raza. (2000). *A descriptive study of charter schools serving limited*

English proficient studies. Washington, DC: National Clearinghouse for Bilingual Education.

Moore, T. O. (2006). *Charter schools defined.* Fort Collins, CO: Edspresso.

Mulholland, L. A. (1996). *Charter schools: The reform and the research.* Tempe, AZ: Morrison Institute for Public Policy.

Ovando, C. J. (2003). Bilingual education in the United States: Historical development and current issues. *Bilingual Research Journal, 27,* 1–24.

Public School Review. (n.d.). *What is a charter school?* Retrieved from http://www.publicschoolreview.com/charter-schools.php

Zavislak, A. (2002). Where did charter schools come from? *National Charter School Clearinghouse News, 1*(5). Retrieved from http://www.ncsc.info/newsletter/May_2002/history.htm

Web Sites

California Department of Education, Data and Statistics: http://www.cde.ca.gov/ds

DC Bilingual Public Charter School: http://www.dcbilingual.org

El Sol Science and Arts Academy: http://www.elsolacademy.org

National Center for Education Statistics: http://nces.ed.gov

U.S. Charter Schools: http://www.uscharterschools.org

BILINGUAL EDUCATION ACT

See TITLE VII, ELEMENTARY AND SECONDARY EDUCATION ACT, KEY HISTORICAL MARKER; APPENDIX B

BILINGUAL EDUCATION AS LANGUAGE POLICY

Language policy and language planning are two areas of applied linguistics that are intended to be used hand in hand to assess communication problems in education and society. Unfortunately, language planning and policies have sometimes been used in ways that have actually increased communication problems, such as when, for example, their effect has been to suppress communication in particular languages or when policies to promote mainstream education in the United States only in the English language have been poorly planned or poorly implemented. The implementation of language policies usually requires a formal plan of action based on guiding principles designed to promote, accommodate, maintain, protect, or restrict the use of languages in education or society. Although formal language policies imply planning, much of the debate and implementation of policy related to bilingual education in the United States have occurred without extensive language planning.

Language acquisition planning is a form of language planning used to determine which language(s) or language varieties are promoted through schools. Bilingual education, in the broadest sense, falls under this form of planning because of the importance of formal education in determining the status and spread of languages. Traditionally, language planning also involves *corpus planning,* which deals largely with issues of selection of vocabulary, grammar, and standardization. Corpus planning typically has been more of an issue for debate among publishers and stylists, but it can also involve issues related to the identification and selection of a standard variety or varieties of language. In the early history of the United States, the lexicographer Noah Webster exerted tremendous influence on English spelling, word choice, and grammar—largely through his personal authority as a publisher. Webster was also determined to promote a distinctly "American" form of English and went to lengths to ensure that some spellings would deviate from those used by the British.

When dealing with the choice of dialects and languages, whether for use in dictionaries or school curricula, language planning also invariably involves *status planning,* which attempts to reconcile choices about which varieties are to be used, and it involves attitudes about them. Obviously, the choice of one language or variety over another has social and political implications for those who are relegated to the minority. In the early 19th century, Noah Webster also was on a personal mission to eradicate regional dialects. In recent years, there has been debate over whether social dialects, such as Ebonics (also known as African American Vernacular) or Hawaiian Creole, should be considered in instruction for the promotion of standard English. Some linguists have argued that these home and community varieties of language are rule-governed varieties that need to be considered when planning instruction for those children who speak them. Unfortunately, attempts to consider home language varieties have been misconstrued as attempts to promote them. This misperception has largely resulted from a misplaced concern over the status of one or more languages. Most experts on language acquisition believe that it is necessary to acknowledge the language varieties children bring to school in order to facilitate the acquisition of standard English but do not advocate for promoting them as varieties of wider communication. Others, however, have noted their influence on popular culture.

Formal language planning and policy prescription typically are carried out by governmental agencies or schools that have the authority to prescribe and impose rules, regulations, and guidelines in order to shape or control language behavior. Beyond formal planning, however, informal practices often have the force of policy. Thus, in addition to formal policy, those implicit, tacit, or covert prescriptions that affect language behavior should also be considered as de facto policies.

The absence of translation or appropriate curricular materials, for example, for speakers of languages other than English can exclude access to schools or needed services, whether or not there is an official policy regarding translation. The decision to promote one or more common or official languages may have a detrimental impact on the status and maintenance of others and may generate unintended consequences. In Canada, for example, the failure to seriously implement French-English bilingual policies during the 1970s helped, some observers say, to fuel the Québec separatist movement. The mere existence of a policy does not mean that it has been well planned or well implemented.

In the United States, the debate over bilingual education has occurred in the absence of serious language planning. The debate has largely been framed by opponents of a federal policy that has allowed for limited use of bilingual education as a strategy for promoting English language use and immigrant assimilation. Within this context, and often without apparent regard for facts, some opponents have maligned bilingual education as a "failed policy" and blamed it for students' low academic achievement, although the majority of eligible students have never been enrolled in bilingual programs. Further complicating matters is the fact that the media have not often provided the public with an opportunity to understand the positive benefits of bilingual education as a way to add to the nation's language resources. Proponents have championed it as an important policy alternative to English monolingual education that has the potential to enhance the language resources of students and the country itself. Regrettably, much of the debate over bilingual education has resulted in an ambiguous discourse about the "bilingual" label, without clear definitions of policies, program goals and types, or benefits to society as a whole.

Types of Bilingual Education Policies

With specific reference to bilingual education in the United States, the question arises as to what extent bilingual education has reflected a formal policy or set of policies. To address this question, it is useful to think of the ways in which bilingual education policies can be analyzed in terms of language aims and goals. Bilingual education policies may, for example, be designed to (a) promote English and one or more additional languages; (b) accommodate speakers of minority languages in English-only instruction; (c) restrict the use of some languages, as in the case of German during World War I; or (d) repress or even eradicate languages, as during the late 19th century, when American Indian boarding schools were used for that purpose.

Among additional factors to consider, Colin Baker, for example, suggests (a) the type of program, (b) type of child, (c) language(s) to be used in the classroom, (d) broader societal aims or goals, and (e) the language and literacy aims or goals. Baker's classification scheme (see Table 1) also juxtaposes types of bilingual education into two broad categories: *weak forms,* or those that promote monolingualism and/or limited bilingualism, and *strong forms,* or those that promote bilingualism and biliteracy.

Identifying policies associated with specific types of programs is useful because the bilingual education label has been too elastic and ambiguous. Federally sponsored transitional bilingual education (TBE) programs, for example, have typically fallen under the former *weak* category. Voluntary programs, such as two-way or dual-language programs, more typically offered through elite schools, have typically fallen under the *strong* category. Under Title VII, TBE, submersion, also known as *structured English immersion* and *structured English immersion with English as a Second Language (ESL) pull-out,* was the most common approach. The latter two types of programs did

Table 1   A Typology of Bilingual Education

Weak Forms for Promoting Bilingualism and/or Biliteracy

Policy Aim for Languages Other Than English	Type of Program	Typical Child	Language of the Classroom	Societal and Educational Aim	Language and/or Literacy Aim
Restrictive	Submersion (structured immersion)	Language minority	Majority language	Assimilation	Monolingualism
Restrictive	Submersion (with pull-out ESL)	Language minority	Majority language	Assimilation	Monolingualism
Repressive	Segregationist	Language minority	Minority language (forced, no choice)	Apartheid	Monolingualism
Accommodation-oriented	Transitional	Language minority	Moves from minority to majority language	Assimilation	Relative monolingualism
Weakly promotion-oriented	Majority language plus foreign language	Language majority	Majority language with L2/FL lessons	Limited enrichment	Limited bilingualism
Promotion-oriented (but it excludes access to dominant language)	Separatist	Language minority	Minority language (out of choice)	Detachment/autonomy	Limited bilingualism

Strong Forms of Education for Promoting Bilingualism and/or Biliteracy

Type of Policy Relative HL/CL	Type of Program	Typical Child	Language of the Classroom	Societal and Educational Aim	Language and/or Literacy Aim
Promotion-oriented	Immersion	Language majority	Bilingual with initial emphasis on L2	Pluralism and enrichment	Bilingualism and biliteracy
Promotion-oriented	Maintenance/heritage language	Language minority	Bilingual with emphasis on L1	Maintenance/pluralism and enrichment	Bilingualism and biliteracy
Promotion-oriented	Two-way/dual-language	Mixed language minority and majority	Minority and majority languages	Maintenance/pluralism and enrichment	Bilingualism and biliteracy
Promotion-oriented	Mainstream bilingual	Language majority	Two majority languages	Maintenance/pluralism and enrichment	Bilingualism and biliteracy

Sources: Adapted from Baker (1996, p. 172); Kloss (1998).

Note: L1 = First Language; L2 = Second Language; FL = Foreign Language; HL = Home Language; CL = Community Language.

not involve the use of the primary language of the home. Nevertheless, because students enrolled were speakers of minority languages, these programs were often depicted as being bilingual, thus adding to the public's confusion over the types of programs in which the children were actually enrolled.

As noted in the opening definition, language planning and policies are typically intended to solve communication problems. If programs are evaluated to this end based on their goals, it is clear, critics say, that many of the programs that wear the bilingual label have neither been well-informed by language planning nor clearly connected to the goal of solving communication problems of language minority students. Structured English immersion (SEI), for example, as required in several states that have restricted bilingual education, draws more from political mandates than from any clearly articulated body of research on language acquisition. It is not clear that many SEI programs require any extensive knowledge or training that would distinguish them from failed, unplanned, "sink or swim" English-only programs of the past.

In the United States, most politicized discussions of bilingual education policy have focused on language minority children. Frequently, their backgrounds in languages other than English are assumed to be the cause of their educational deficiencies. Title VII policies were largely predicated on this view, even though advocates of bilingual education tend to see minority languages as personal and societal resources rather than as detriments. At best, the deficit view has tended to result in policies aimed only at accommodating children from home backgrounds in which languages other than English were spoken and lower expectations for their academic achievement were accepted. Under the No Child Left Behind Act (NCLB) of 2001, there has been much fanfare regarding the need to promote higher expectations for all children. Nevertheless, as critics have pointed out, NCLB has provided no clear direction on how to promote equitable programs and meaningful assessment of language minority children. Thus, NCLB has left language minority children in a policy limbo. The primary debate has been over whether to assess children through English and how quickly to do so, although it has been widely recognized that most language minority children will not perform well on tests administered in English when these children have not had sufficient time to develop English and academic skills. Proponents of NCLB have countered that all children must be held to high standards to ensure

accountability. A possible danger in this scenario is that high standards, along with underfunded and poorly planned programs, fail to result in the level playing field needed for high achievement.

Again, a negative note in the history of federally supported bilingual education is that even as opponents of bilingual decried the "failure" of bilingual education, the vast majority of children eligible for Title VII services were not receiving instruction in their home languages and often received no specially designed instruction to develop the English language skills needed for advanced academic instruction. In some states restricting bilingual education, such as in California even prior to the passage of its Proposition 227, teachers in so-called bilingual programs often did not speak the home language of many children. Again, these programs were labeled "bilingual" merely because the children came from homes where languages other than English were taught. Thus, based on the erroneous assumption that children in "bilingual" programs were receiving instruction in languages other than English, rather than in English alone, bilingual education policies were blamed when language minorities underperformed on standardized tests in English.

Bilingual Education Policy and Societal Aims

Given the prevalence of Spanish as the second major language in the United States and because of the misconception that federal bilingual education policies were designed to promote the minority language of the home, Title VII and TBE programs were criticized as being "Spanish-only" programs designed to promote Spanish rather than English. These misperceptions also fueled the baseless fear that the English language was somehow being threatened by the presence of bilingual programs.

Fears of minorities' alleged unwillingness to learn English have done much to preclude any serious, well-informed debate about the value of bilingualism for the monolingual majority, particularly in the much-acclaimed age of globalization. Over a quarter century ago, the late Senator Paul Simon decried what he saw as the "foreign-language crisis" in the United States, in his popular book *The Tongue-Tied Americans*. More recently, the idea that minority languages might legitimately serve as national resources was recast under the label of *heritage* languages and has been championed largely within the context of national security and the need for languages other than English to promote economic competitiveness in the global economy. Meanwhile, with the possible exception of students studying Spanish, the portion of the "educated" population that studies "foreign" languages has dramatically declined over the past several decades. From a policy perspective, the deficit framing of bilingual education under Title VII and the lack of emphasis on it and foreign-language education under NCLB has done little, critics say, to advance the societal aim of promoting a more linguistically adept population in the United States.

Bilingual Education Policy and Language and Literacy Aims

The primary differentiation among bilingual education policies and programs relates to the aim of promoting bilingualism and biliteracy. So-called mainstream bilingual programs, or immersion programs, hold this aim for majority language children. Often, such programs are those of choice for parents who can afford to provide their children with an elite education. Thus, unlike federally supported Title VII programs, which no longer exist, there has been no stigma of deficiency associated with these programs. There have been some attempts to combine biliteracy and bilingualism as a goal for both majority and minority children. To date, the most successful programs have fallen under the label of "two-way" or "dual immersion." From a policy standpoint, these programs help to promote the status of minority languages; however, this is not always achieved when languages other than English are presented as "foreign" rather than as living community languages of the United States and the world. There has also been some concern that students in such programs can be differentially positioned based on the perceived status of their languages. For example, concerns have been raised that Spanish-speaking students of lower socioeconomic status may be "servicing" language majority English-speaking children by providing them with native-speaker modeling of the target language. In other words, in the programs' implementation, the needs of children of the majority are addressed, but not those of minorities. Given the status differential between English and Spanish, there is a need for programmatic policies that are designed to ensure that students are treated equitably. For extensive reviews and recommendations on effective dual-language

models of instruction, readers are referred to the resources provided by the Web site of the Center for Applied Linguistics.

Beyond Deficit-Based Bilingual Education Language Policies

A review of federal bilingual education policy in the United States indicates that there is substantial room for improvement if biliteracy and bilingualism are valued as educational aims for both language minority children and the general population. There is a need to consider policies that promote both the individual and societal benefits of bilingualism. Such policies also need to ensure that language minority students have adequate access to a quality education that includes the development of English for successful participation in school and society.

Moving beyond policies that merely aim to accommodate immigrant and indigenous language minority students, many believe that there is a need to develop and implement policies that value community languages and expand national language resources. Such policies need to recognize the linguistic reality of a country in which nearly 1 out of 6 people speak languages in addition to English. Constructive language policies would also need to recognize that languages other than English are used daily in the linguistic life of the country. Policies based on our linguistic reality would do well to acknowledge that the United States is not only among the largest English-speaking nations in the world—rivaled only by India, a multilingual nation with millions who can speak English—but that it also has millions who can speak Spanish and numerous other indigenous and immigrant languages and that these languages can be resources for both language minority students and the nation as a whole.

Terrence G. Wiley

See also Dual-Language Programs; English Immersion; No Child Left Behind Act of 2001, Title III; Status Differences Among Languages; Title VII, Elementary and Secondary Education Act, Key Historical Marker; Transitional Bilingual Education Programs; Views of Bilingual Education

Further Readings

Baker, C. (1996). *Foundations of bilingual education and bilingualism* (2nd ed.). Philadelphia: Multilingual Matters.

Kloss, H. (1998). *The American bilingual tradition.* Washington, DC, and McHenry, IL: Center for Applied Linguistics/Delta Systems.

Simon, P. (1980). *The tongue-tied American.* New York: Continuum.

Web Sites

Center for Applied Linguistics: http://www.cal.org

BILINGUAL EDUCATION IN THE PRESS

In today's society, the distribution of information is controlled largely by the print and electronic media. Directly and indirectly, media affect the way in which people learn about their world and form opinions on the salient topics of the day, heavily influencing the process of social relations and the slant or spin applied to the news. This becomes most apparent when one analyzes the ways in which the media guide people's relationships with social institutions (e.g., educational, religious, governmental). Lacking the time and ability to interact personally with every social institution, individuals depend on the media for information about a variety of issues. Media may not always be largely responsible for public opinion, but there are many documented cases in which this has occurred.

When the bulk of collective knowledge of a given issue is determined by the news media, the press becomes a major factor in the formation of social attitudes and beliefs. According to David Fan, has it been suggested not only that media shape public views of political issues but that they also mold opinion within specific agenda items. Michael Herzfeld maintains it is no exaggeration to say that in the United States, media are a major force in society: They create as much as they reflect the events taking place in the nation. While individual, seemingly insignificant messages conveyed in the media might appear to have minimal effect, they may accrue over time and form long-term trends of public opinion that affect the outcome of public debate. This entry examines the portrayal by media of the relationship between bilingual education and immigration and provides a context for it in the broader dynamic of society and the press.

Given that media play an important role in the construction of public opinion and have the potential to directly affect the political process, it is important to understand the impact that individual media forms have and how they are consumed by the public. There are special characteristics of newspapers that help to shape public opinion. While many people elect to watch television and/or listen to the radio for their news and information, the printed format of newspapers offers specific advantages. Newspapers are not limited by time. Readers can afford to devote more time to read and review print news and editorializing and to choose when and where they will do so. This lack of time constraint also allows newspapers to present many more stories than broadcast news on radio or television. This entry focuses on print media in one state and how it influenced the public's view of a ballot initiative to abolish bilingual education in that state.

Jeffery Mondak argues that research on the media has demonstrated that newspapers outperform broadcast media in conveying information to their audiences. Apparently, newspapers are more efficient in transmitting detailed information and enable readers to learn more about topics than do broadcast media. This suggests that people who get their information from newspapers may feel better informed and that they have learned more than people who rely solely on television news. This premise is based on the assumption that newspapers make a unique contribution to the socially shared knowledge base. Mondak also asserts that it has been reported by researchers that people who rely on newspapers as their primary source for political and social information tend to have higher levels of education, prior knowledge of politics, and a stronger interest in current affairs. It is not clear whether these factors (rather than the actual influence of newspapers) cause such individuals to seek out information from various sources and participate more actively in the political process. Whatever the case, there is little question that newspapers make a contribution to the formation and/or construction of public knowledge. Issues and topics privileged by the press in some way are more likely to become the bases for political preferences and decision making by readers who rely on this source for whatever reasons.

Media and the Construction of Social Norms

David Croteau and William Hoynes maintain that these dynamics may be seen to intensify when examining the ways in which media construct images of minority communities, their problems, and the programs designed to help them. Historically, mainstream American media sources have generally chosen "Whites" as the group norm to which all other racial groups are compared. For example, "White culture" or the "White community" is not commonly singled out in the press. However, it is not unusual for the media to reference "Black culture" or the "Latino community." Absence of a racial classification in the press usually denotes "Whiteness," or the majority culture. It is implicitly the position from which all other groups are analyzed and judged. The pervasiveness of the White perspective in media is a powerful and influential feature in the formation of public opinion. In effect, this perspective emphasizes media bias without recognizing it as such. In this sense, news media may be seen exist within a socially bounded set of values and determiners of success. Teun van Dijk argues that while many messages relayed through the media are overtly polarized, there are also covert ways of casting minorities and their preferences in an unfavorable light. Van Dijk claims that some of the following prevailing commonalities have been found in studies of the news media:

- Many of the dominant topics are directly or more subtly associated with problems, difficulties, or threats to the dominant values, interests, goals, or culture.
- Ethnic events are consistently described from a White, majority point of view.
- Topics that are relevant for the ordinary daily life of ethnic groups, such as work, housing, health, education, political life, and culture, as well as discrimination in these areas, are hardly discussed in the press unless they lead to "problems" for society as a whole or when they are spectacular in some way.

These general trends apply directly to language minority concerns. Press coverage of the recent antibilingual education ballot measures in California, Arizona, Massachusetts, and Colorado reveals some insight into how information about bilingual education is circulated.

Media Images of Bilingual Education

Whereas newspapers are only one of several media resources available to researchers, recent studies have demonstrated a direct correlation between the representation of bilingual education in newspapers and public voting trends in the cases mentioned above, as claimed by Otto Santa Ana and Eric Johnson. Although such studies might effectively display how periodicals tend to project images of bilingual education to the public, one must consider the many elements that constitute a newspaper article, and their various types, in order to understand the issues clearly. From the broad perspective of readership demographics to the minute detail of the individual journalist's own perspective, the final print version of a newspaper article has been wrought by multiple influences. A specific example of this can be seen in the media coverage of the 2000 Arizona Proposition 203 campaign, also known as the "English for the Children" ballot initiative. Supporters of Proposition 203 promoted the end of bilingual education in favor of a "sheltered English immersion" approach to language minority education. Arizona media coverage surrounding this political battle reveals how newspapers communicated messages concerning bilingual education, subtly or directly.

In the months leading up to the public vote, between January 2000 and November 2000, the two largest newspapers in the state, the *East Valley Tribune* and the *Arizona Republic,* produced a combined 73 articles that directly focused on Proposition 203 and/or bilingual education. An examination of these newspaper articles reveals certain stylistic and rhetorical features that were brought to bear on this controversial issue in favor of the ballot measure. It is possible to discuss the potential influence of newspapers by looking at this specific context from multiple vantage points. Factors such as the slant of an article, the wording of a headline, the specific text in an article, and inherent variations between newspapers play a significant role in the construction of social opinion. Some brief examples of these features will demonstrate the complexity of their relationship in the portrayal of bilingual education and language minority students.

Reading an article with a critical eye allows researchers to discern whether the information is being presented in a straightforward manner or whether there is a particular slant either for or against the issue at hand. This is most obvious when comparing news stories with editorials. Articles that convey basic information (e.g., dates, times, locations) are generally straightforward or politically neutral. Even in news stories, however, journalists may include their own opinions or value-laden statements. At this point, the news article starts to take on the characteristics of an editorial even though it was slated to be a news story.

Out of the 73 articles involved in the Proposition 203 campaign, only 9, or 12%, could be considered neutral by researchers (i.e., they did not place value on either side of the debate). It was found that the remaining 64 articles had a clear slant. With a total of 48, or 66%, the vast majority of the articles took on a negative slant (i.e., denigrating the opposition's perspective). The remaining 16, or 22%, conveyed a positive message concerning either the value of bilingual education or English immersion. When the slanted articles are broken down according to their portrayal of bilingual education, it is easy to see the potential impact on public opinion: Of the 64 slanted articles identified, 41, or 64%, contained negative depictions of bilingual education.

Headlines, Text, and the Communication of Bias

Assuming that most people will not read every article in a newspaper, the communicative impact of newspaper headlines is important in capturing the reader's attention. Some headlines are able to deliver a message potent enough to grab the reader's perspective with great power. In general, editorial letters often contain the most heavily slanted headlines. It is easy to see from the headline alone that the authors of "Time to End Bilingual Education," by Johanna Haver (*Arizona Republic,* June 12, 2000, p. B7), and "Prop. 203 Gives Students Help With English, Shot at Success: My Turn," written by Jeff Flake (*Arizona Republic,* September 6, 2000, p. 4), convey strong opinions against bilingual education. Headlines like "Teaching Limited-English Pupils in Arizona: It's Just a Mess," written by Lori Baker and Kelly Pearce (*Arizona Republic,* January 20, 2000, p. A1), and "Bilingual Ed. Must Go, Arizona Voters Say in Poll: English Immersion Programs Favored," written by Robbie Sherwood and Lisa Chiu (*Arizona Republic,* September 22, 2000, p. A1), also make definite statements against bilingual education. Considering that both of the latter headlines appeared on the front page, their exposure and communicative potential may have been greater than those of the editorials. Even though these articles might contain positive information about bilingual education, when someone merely scans the headlines, they might see only the negative viewpoint

and miss out on the reasons for the conclusion stated in the headline.

Beyond the thematic slant of an article (including the headline), the text of the article may be loaded with multiple messages and images. Even though an article might have an overall positive depiction of bilingual education and/or the needs of language minority students, individual quotations might accentuate a socially negative stereotype. For example, when a journalist quotes individuals favoring the ballot initiative as saying, "'Bilingual education is an evil system of racial discrimination that has destroyed the education of countless Hispanic children in our state,'" the reader may think about bilingual education in terms of "evil" and "discrimination." When bilingual education is portrayed in a positive light, however, the significant details of how it benefits children are often missing. Daniel González, an editorial writer for the *Republic,* asserted that "scrapping bilingual education would especially hurt Hispanic and Native American children with limited English proficiency" (July 6, 2000, p. B1), but he does not explain how this might happen.

This relationship between the positive and the negative often taps into what we think of as "natural," speculate David Croteau and William Hoynes. According to this view, nature is something that we define in contrast to culture. Unlike culture, nature is understood to be beyond human control. If social structures and relationships are perceived as natural, they take on a certain degree of permanency and legitimacy that makes them seem uncontested. For example, readers may assume that it is only "natural" that the difficulties experienced by language minority students are rooted in their home language and condition, which is, in turn, aggravated by the continued use of the language via bilingual instruction. For example, according to González, Congressman Matt Salmon blamed bilingual education for the high dropout rate among Hispanic students in Arizona. The *Republic* made no mention of the fact that there is no research evidence supporting this assertion.

The Role of Editorial Choices

While that which is included or excluded from an article depends heavily on the individual journalist, the editorial staff has the ultimate say. Since different editors have different perspectives, it is common to see some variation between different newspapers. For example, the *East Valley Tribune* ran a total of 30 articles covering the bilingual education debate, 63% of which were in direct support of Proposition 203 (i.e., against bilingual education). On the other hand, only 51% of the *Arizona Republic*'s 43 articles were in support of Proposition 203.

The editorial section provides a clear lens through which to view a newspaper's political agenda. Beyond the opinion-editorial letters that are written by the public, editors and editorial staffers frequently write articles expressing their own viewpoints. During the bilingual education debate, the *Arizona Republic* published only one editorial article, "Education Dominates Mailbag" (July 1, 2000, p. B15), that did not express any opinions for or against bilingual education. The *East Valley Tribune* published two editorial articles directly opposing bilingual education: "Plugging the Bilingual Rathole" (February 2, 2000, p. A14) and "Bilingual Bunk" (August 24, 2000, p. A14). The *East Valley Tribune* includes a disclaimer on every editorial page stating that the "opinions expressed in editorials are those of the newspaper. All other opinions on this page and on the opinion 2 page are those of the authors or artists." Realizing that newspapers openly support or oppose social issues can enable readers to understand why certain articles are being published; however, many people do not think of newspapers as having a certain agenda and simply believe that what they read is factual.

Like many social issues, bilingual education receives the most attention in the press when legislation is being contested. Although newspapers do include sound information that directly supports bilingual education, such as "Facts Elude Politician's Perspective" (*East Valley Tribune,* September 13, 2000, p. 4), written by Jeff MacSwan, and "Bilingual Ed Foe Unz Used Distorted Facts" (*East Valley Tribune,* September 13, 2000, p. A19), by Stephen Krashen, readers may react differently to research-derived statistics, facts, and discoveries as presented by experts in the field of education. Many articles published in these two papers were quickly responded to by university professors and others familiar with the research literature. Aside from publishing their letters, both papers failed to publish information from research reports in favor of bilingual education.

Finally, it must be mentioned that even though there are easily identified trends in the way bilingual education is represented in the press as a whole, individual newspapers alone cannot be held responsible for the formation of social opinions. Newspapers do contribute

to the construction of social knowledge, but they also reflect certain social interests. Multiple factors drive the articles that are published; readership demographics, sponsorship, and the layout of the newspaper also contribute to the circulation size and, ultimately, the potential influence that a newspaper can have on a community's social views. Ultimately, though, it is the spread of information through everyday interpersonal interaction that reinforces social views and attitudes. Regardless of their slant, newspapers provide a platform for discussing important issues like bilingual education. It is up to the reading public how they receive such information, what they choose to do with it, and how they represent it to others.

Eric Johnson

See also Attitudes Toward Language Diversity; English for the Children Campaign; Languages and Power; Views of Language Difference

Further Readings

Croteau, D., & Hoynes, W. (1997). *Media/society: Industries, images, and audiences.* Thousand Oaks, CA: Pine Forge.

Fan, D. P. (1988). *Predictions of public opinion from the mass media: Computer content analysis and mathematical modeling.* New York: Greenwood Press.

Herzfeld, M. (2001). *Anthropology: Theoretical practice in culture and society.* Malden, MA: Blackwell.

Johnson, E. (2005). Proposition 203: A critical metaphor analysis. *Bilingual Research Journal, 29,* 69–84.

Mendoza, M., & Ayala, H. (2000, October 11). Republic editorial is wrong: Bilingual education is an utter failure, our turn. *Arizona Republic,* p. B9.

Mondak, J. J. (1995). *Nothing to read: Newspapers and elections in a social experiment.* Ann Arbor: University of Michigan Press.

Santa Ana, O. (2002). *Brown tide rising. Metaphos of Latinos in contemporary American public discourse.* Austin: University of Texas Press.

van Dijk, T. (1987). *Communicating racism: Ethnic prejudice in thought and talk.* London: Sage.

BILINGUALISM IN HOLISTIC PERSPECTIVE

Worldwide, most people speak two or more languages, simply because multiple languages are used in their environments. Researchers and educators in the field of bilingualism and bilingual education have been interested in defining what *bilingual* means and how a bilingual person's competences can be measured. Among the several views of bilingualism, two have predominated in the field: the fractional and the holistic perspectives. The *fractional* view describes bilinguals as being the equivalent of two monolinguals in one person. This view considers bilinguals as developing parallel linguistic competence in both languages simultaneously, and studies following this perspective often compare bilinguals with monolinguals. The *holistic* view, proposed by François Grosjean, argues that each bilingual is a unique individual who integrates knowledge of and from both languages to create something more than two languages that function independently of each other. This view holds that the total of the two languages is greater than their sum, because the two languages interact with each other to increase the functionality of each. Both perspectives describe as ideal the development of *balanced* bilingual competence in speaking, thinking, reading, and writing, meaning equivalent fluency in the two languages.

Biligualism in Social Context

Balanced bilingualism is a concept that is not easily achievable; instead, bilingualism must be understood as a continuum in which language ability changes constantly in relation to the individual's social, educational, and linguistic contexts. In addition, bilingualism may be described as simultaneous or sequential. *Simultaneous bilinguals* grow up learning two languages in their environments from infancy. *Sequential bilinguals* develop mastery, or at least some proficiency, in their native languages before acquiring a second language.

Bilingualism emerges when two different language communities come into sustained contact. Language contact in different communities creates a variety of bilingual discourses that meet the needs of the members of those specific communities. Bilingualism is more valuable when some members of each language group are not bilingual. Logically, if everyone in a particular space were bilingual, there would no longer be a need for anyone to know both languages purely for communicative purposes. Some communities and countries have a policy of official acceptance of bilingualism, and, consequently, both languages are taught and have fairly equal status in society. For example, Belgium has an official policy of bilingualism in French and Flemish, not only on paper but also in practice. Thus, in the school and community, people receive training and motivation to learn both languages and use them in the public sphere.

In some countries, majority language speakers generally associate their language with nationalism and label the widespread use of other languages as a problem rather than an asset. An example of this dynamic in the United States is the so-called English-only laws that restrict the use of languages other than English in public schools. As critics have pointed out, such laws are motivated by political and ideological considerations rather than sound pedagogical theory or societal benefit. They have little if anything to do with what constitutes a good education or an adequate linguistic preparation for the future.

Research Findings

The research in this field shows that the child's native language is a good foundation on which to build the second language. In addition, it has been shown that English-only policies often have unrecognized impact beyond education when speakers of other languages absorb negative attitudes toward their home language (or varieties of their home language) and culture that are prevalent in mainstream society. The effects of these attitudes are apparent in that historically, immigrant families in the United States have tended to preserve their native languages as an important part of their cultures. Immigrants traditionally have been bilingual for two or three generations after immigrating but eventually abandon the immigrant language altogether. Today, immigrants evidence a stronger preference for speaking English and less motivation for preserving their native languages, so that the shift to English monolingualism occurs more rapidly, in most cases in two generations. In this context, English-only rules seem to be unnecessary since there is no threat to the English language posed by the new immigrants and their linguistic orientations. Ironically, while English-only campaigns in the public schools promote having minority children abandon their home languages and make the transition to English as soon as possible, private corporations that now tend to operate in several countries at once regard second languages as a valuable job skill that increases a firm's competitiveness in the international marketplace.

It is important to note that in addition to its purely communicative value, bilingualism has social, psychological, and cognitive benefits. In terms of their social communicative competence, bilinguals are able to maintain family communication and interaction across generations; psychologically, the identity of belonging to a particular language and culture group can increase bilinguals' self-esteem as well as the cohesion of their families. In terms of cognitive competence, studies have shown that young bilingual children have greater semantic flexibility than their monolingual peers in specific tasks such as object labeling. The findings of various studies differ on whether some cognitive benefits (e.g., metalinguistic awareness) may be temporary rather than permanent, adding to the existing societal ambivalence about whether the effort to maintain or develop bilingual competence is worthwhile. This ambivalence is due in large part to the fact that the researchers have not controlled for the effect of partial bilingualism as opposed to full mastery of both languages. There are indications in the research that fully bilingual and biliterate individuals benefit more from being bilingual than persons who are haphazardly or informally bilingual. Even if there is no easy answer to this question, however, there is no harm in a child's being able to communicate with members of his or her family in their first language.

Bilingualism as Social and Cultural Experience

For whom is it most important to develop communicative competence in two languages, and why? Bilingualism develops when people participate in day-to-day activities that require them to use two languages. For example, it may be an asset to be able to address family members in the native language but be able to use the second language when necessary in the broader community. Beyond the linguistic competence aspect of bilingualism, it is also necessary to consider sociocultural and political aspects. Bilingualism is more than just speaking two languages. Specifically, when people, children, and adults become bicultural through diverse sociocultural experiences, this affects their levels of bilingualism. For bilinguals who live in the linguistic borderlands, whether geographically or ideologically, a primary goal is to develop and maintain their bicultural identities through preserving their customs, values, and ways of speaking among members of their communities. Bilinguals who grow up in these borderlands develop a bicultural worldview and identity that governs when, with whom, and where

they use each of their languages. From a negative perspective, the bilingual may be viewed as being "caught" between two languages and two cultures, proficient in neither. From a borderlands perspective, in contrast, the bilingual can be viewed as the creator of hybrid spaces where experiences and knowledge in two languages and cultures contribute to his or her abilities to negotiate the social, political, and economic environment.

The languages people speak influence the cultural values they acquire as part of their bilingual worlds. Each language one learns brings with it a set of values, beliefs, and attitudes that belong to the members of a language community at a given time. Among immigrant communities, therefore, language is seen as a symbol and instrument of group identity. Moreover, the relationship between language and group identity varies as a function of the power relations between the different groups in a particular society. Children who attend schools in areas where their languages are not valued and validated tend to learn early that the language of school is the one that holds power; as a result, they typically become dominant in this second language, since most of their spoken and written instruction occurs in that language. In general, this type of ethnocentric environment leads to a form of subtractive bilingualism in which bilingual children and youth feel continual pressure to assimilate by using their native languages less and less. Children in such a situation may become either passive first-language bilinguals, able to understand but not use their native languages, or reluctant monolinguals in the majority language. When one's native language is devalued (as, for example, with indigenous languages) and speaking the majority language is key to achieving economic and social success in the mainstream society, there is little motivation to retain one's first language. This is why speakers of low-status languages typically do not resist the pressure to assimilate linguistically and culturally into the dominant society, which typically leads to rapid loss of bilingualism.

Code Switching

When individuals succeed in becoming fluent bilinguals, their sociopsycholinguistic competences in the two languages overlap, creating a hybrid. One instance in which this hybrid competency manifests itself is when speakers use both languages in the same conversation, a phenomenon known as *code switching.* Historically, and to some extent even today, critics have described code switching pejoratively as reflecting an inability to speak either language properly (hence leading to epithets such as "Chinglish," "Spanglish," or "Portuñol," a mixture of Portuguese and Spanish). Even parents who are raising bilingual children have expressed concern that mixing the two languages may have negative educational consequences. There is no evidence, however, that code switching has negative effects on children's cognitive or linguistic development. Instead, research has identified code switching and borrowing as instruments that competent bilingual speakers use deliberately as symbols of group identity. They may switch from one language to the other for pragmatic reasons, for example, to subtly convey their attitudes toward the topics under discussion. Or, they may engage in code switching purely for fun, as is common with teenagers in many cultures.

Policy Implications

The experience of becoming bilingual has effects not only at the individual level but also at the levels of family, community, and society. The circumstances of linguistic and biliteracy acquisition are in many ways unique to each individual child, because he or she is able to draw from two sets of linguistic and cultural resources. In terms of educational policy, it is not enough for teachers, educators, and policymakers to consider only the linguistic aspect of bilingualism. A comprehensive understanding of how children become bilingual, how they acquire a second language, and how they use each of the two languages in similar or different ways must incorporate knowledge of how social, cultural, and linguistic factors interact and influence their sociopsycholinguistic development.

Iliana Reyes

See also Attitudes Toward Language Diversity; Code Switching; Language and Identity; Language Education Policy in Global Perspective; Maintenance Policy Denied; Metalinguistic Awareness; Status Differences Among Languages; U.S. Bilingual Education Viewed From Abroad; Views of Bilingual Education

Further Readings

Baker, C. (2001). *Foundations of bilingual education and bilingualism* (3rd ed.). Buffalo, NY: Multilingual Matters.

González, N. (2001). *I am my language: Discourses of women and children in the borderlands.* Tucson: University of Arizona Press.

Grosjean, F. (1982). *Life with two languages: An introduction to bilingualism.* Cambridge, MA: Harvard University Press.

Santa Ana, O. (2004). *Tongue tied: The lives of multilingual children in public school.* Oxford, UK: Rowman & Littlefield.

Bilingualism Stages

Bilingualism is not an absolute condition, especially at the societal level. In the same way that saying a person is bilingual does little to describe actual language ability, labeling a community as bilingual overlooks the diversity of experiences within bilingual and diglossic societies. Joshua A. Fishman has been active in researching bilingual communities and promoting the reversal of language shift (in which a community gradually replaces one language with another, usually more dominant language). His work is based on the premise that most minority languages will not survive without active support from the community. Fishman has developed a continuum of eight stages, called the Graded Intergenerational Disruption Scale for Threatened Languages (GIDS), which describes the functions and uses of the minority language for its speakers and communities and also offers a general guideline for language revival.

Individual Versus Societal Bilingualism

Bilingualism can be understood on two levels: individual and societal (or social). Discussions about *individual bilingualism* use the individual person as a reference point and usually focus on characteristics such as age of acquisition, level of attainment, language dominance, and ability. Often, these characteristics are largely removed from their broader social context and do not take the language community into account. *Societal bilingualism,* on the other hand, refers to the way multiple languages are used in and by a community. One example of societal bilingualism is the availability of newspapers and other print media in more than one language. Another example, common in the United States, is when the home language is a minority language different from the language used in school (i.e., the majority language, English). Societal bilingualism is frequently referred to as *diglossia,* which indicates the use of two languages within one community in which the two languages have different functions. It is important to note that not all individuals in a diglossic community are necessarily bilingual. It is possible to have two groups of monolinguals living in a community where bilingualism is rare, such as in modern Switzerland.

In understanding diglossia and societal bilingualism, it is useful to examine what is meant by majority and minority languages, which are also sometimes referred to as high (status) and low (status) languages. The *majority language* is the language spoken by the majority of the population, but, more important, it is the language with the most social, economic, and political prestige. The majority language is also frequently seen by speakers of both the majority and minority languages as the key to educational and economic success. This perception can contribute to the loss of the minority language among bilinguals. A *minority language,* then, is a language that is less prestigious and has fewer political and economic uses than the majority language. The minority language is generally seen by majority language speakers as "less valuable" than the majority language, an idea that may be internalized by speakers of minority languages. However, a minority language can also serve as a symbol of identity and a source of pride for its speakers, who may claim their right to speak and maintain the minority language. In the context of the United States, the majority language is English, and minority languages are the languages of immigrant communities, such as Spanish or Yiddish, and Native American groups, such as Navajo or Yaqui.

Individual and Group Rights in the United States

Within the discussion of societal bilingualism, it is also useful to briefly visit the ideas of individual and group rights. While the United States has a long history of emphasizing individual rights, group rights have also been repeatedly recognized. For example, freedom of speech and religion are individual rights that are guaranteed by the Bill of Rights, but the Americans with Disabilities Act recognizes a particular group of people and grants them specific rights. Similarly, many laws recognize children as a group. In these cases, membership in a group guarantees certain

rights beyond those of the individual. In the case of language maintenance, some minority language communities are recognized as having the right to maintain and revive the minority language, but this right does not extend to all language minority groups (e.g., Welsh in the United Kingdom and Native American languages in the United States).

Languages are not static, and their existence depends on the willingness of the speakers not only to speak the language but also to pass it on to younger generations. When fewer and fewer people speak a language, the language along with the associated culture is in danger of dying out, a process called *language shift. Language revival* is concerned with reversing language shift, and *language maintenance* refers to the prevention of language erosion or shift. These distinctions are important in terms of societal bilingualism as they reflect the processes of increasing and maintaining the use of two languages within a community.

Fishman's Graded Intergenerational Disruption Scale for Threatened Languages

In the early 1990s, Fishman developed the Graded Intergenerational Disruption Scale for Threatened Languages (GIDS), which depicts different stages of societal bilingualism from the perspective of the minority language (see Table 1) and also serves as a guideline for reversing language shift. Fishman's GIDS is meant to support bilingualism and cultural pluralism and is based on the idea that culture and language are closely intertwined. It is important to note that Stage Eight is the worse-case scenario for a minority language, and Stage One is the best-case scenario, representing cultural and linguistic pluralism. The minority language gradually moves from being obsolete to gaining social, educational, economic, and political functions.

The Eight Stages

Stage Eight

At this stage, the language is not being spoken to younger generations, and only a few members of the oldest generation still speak the language. The language has broadly fallen into disuse, as any remaining speakers tend to be isolated from each other. The language at this point has died out; it is not used in many

Table 1 Fishman's Graded Intergenerational Disruption Scale for Threatened Languages (GIDS)

Stage One	Minority language is used in the national media, higher education, and the government.
Stage Two	Local mass media is available in the minority language, along with some governmental services.
Stage Three	The minority language is used both in school and in the workplace, especially where there is interaction with majority language speakers.
Stage Four	Education is available through the school system in the minority language, and those educational programs are controlled by members of the minority language community.
Stage Five	Literacy in the minority language is common across all generations, although it is not supported through the school system.
Stage Six	The minority language is spoken by all generations and, importantly, is learned by children as a first language. The minority language is also used in the community.
Stage Seven	Speakers of the minority language belong to the older generations. Younger generations, including those of childbearing age, do not speak the minority language.
Stage Eight	The few remaining speakers of the minority language are socially isolated. At this point, it is necessary to record and research the language for future revival.

Sources: Adapted from Baker & Jones (1998); Fishman (2004).

daily interactions and is not a part of the daily lives of people who identify with the community and language. It is necessary to bring in linguists and anthropologists to record the language and collect as much information as possible in order to reconstruct the language and its community at a later time.

Stage Seven

The language is used daily by members of the older generations but is not being learned by younger generations. Although parents may be bilingual, they speak the majority language to their children rather than the minority language. Unless precautions are taken, the language will move on to Stage Eight and eventually die out. At this point, raising children in the minority language becomes necessary, and plans must be implemented that support the community in maintaining its language. However, it is not enough that children learn the minority language as a first language; they must also continue to use it throughout their lives and pass it on to their children.

Stage Six

At this crucial stage, the language is being passed on to younger generations and is used among all generations for daily interactions. Once the language is used within the family, it will also likely be used for interactions in the community, thus establishing a language community. However, the language is used largely for informal functions, such as shopping and talking to relatives, and not for more formal functions like education or government. This stage is crucial in reversing language shift because maintaining the language at this stage is largely dependent on family decisions to speak the language, which are difficult to influence.

Stage Five

The language is being used daily among all generations both at home and in the community at this stage, but more important, literacy in the minority language is also prevalent. Literacy is crucial because it raises the status of the minority language, increases the number of functions the language can serve, and allows for communication across distance and time, which enables the minority language community to communicate its own viewpoints, beliefs, and values in the media. At this point, minority language literacy development is supported largely through home and community efforts, whereas majority language literacy is developed through formal schooling.

Stage Four

During this stage, the minority language starts to move into more formal functions, possibly at the expense of the majority language. Schools are established that support minority language development, and these schools may be controlled solely through the minority language community, or they may also be partially controlled by the central majority language government.

Stage Three

At this point, the language is spoken in the home, in the community, and at school. Literacy in the minority language is widespread, and the minority language will be used in workplaces outside of the community. In previous stages, the minority language may have been used at workplaces within the community as part of daily activity, but Stage Three is important because the minority language is used in workplaces that have national and international influence and are outside the minority language community.

Stage Two

After achieving use in the workplace in Stage Three, the minority language begins to be used in lower functions of local and national government. For instance, legal services may become available in the minority language, along with health services, electoral procedures, and so on. However, the main language of the central government is still the majority language. At this stage, mass media, such as radio and television, also become available in the minority language. Not only does this increase access to the minority language and culture, but the minority language also gains some measure of prestige through mass media.

Stage One

At this final stage, many nationwide government functions are conducted in both the minority and the majority languages. Higher education is also available in the minority language, and the minority language is widely used in a variety of functions. At this point, linguistic and cultural pluralism has been achieved. It is important to realize that the minority language has not replaced the majority language, but rather the two languages share relatively equal status.

Drawbacks

Although Fishman's GIDS is comprehensive, it is not universal. Language communities have different social, political, and historical contexts and do not necessarily achieve societal bilingualism to the same degree or in the same ways. Also, the stages in GIDS are not as linear as they may appear on paper and are, in fact, overlapping and interdependent. Finally, the stages in GIDS do not address the political and social conflicts that may arise in moving from one stage to another.

Significance for Education

Within Fishman's GIDS, schools clearly play a role in language revival and maintenance. This role, however, is secondary to that of family and community. For instance, if a minority language that is supported through schooling is not used in family and community contexts, that language becomes more of a school subject than a mode of communication, such as Irish in modern-day Ireland. Schools can greatly contribute, however, to the revival and maintenance of languages that are supported in the community, especially where literacy is concerned. One example of this is the Rough Rock Demonstration School on the Navajo Reservation. According to Teresa McCarty, the development of culturally and academically appropriate literacy materials and the teaching of Navajo as a first and second language enabled the Rough Rock School not only to further language maintenance in the community but also to create another institution where Navajo is spoken. Here, the key is that of the minority language community having a legitimate measure of control over the schools, as opposed to schools in minority language communities that are controlled by the majority language community.

Kara T. McAlister

See also Fishman, Joshua A.; Indigenous Language Revitalization; Language Revival and Renewal; Language Rights in Education; Language Shift and Language Loss; Maintenance Policy Denied; Social Bilingualism

Further Readings

Baker, C., & Jones, S. P. (Eds.). (1998). *Encyclopedia of bilingualism and bilingual education*. Clevedon, UK: Multilingual Matters.

Fishman, J. A. (1991). *Reversing language shift.* Clevedon, UK: Multilingual Matters.

Fishman, J. A. (Ed.). (2000). *Can threatened languages be saved? Reversing language shift, revisited: A 21st century perspective.* Clevedon, UK: Multilingual Matters.

Fishman, J. A. (2004). Language maintenance, language shift, and reversing language shift. In T. K. Bhatia & W. C. Ritchie (Eds.), *Handbook of bilingualism* (pp. 406–436). Oxford, UK: Blackwell.

McCarty, T. L. (2002). *A place to be Navajo: Rough Rock and the struggle for self-determination in indigenous schooling.* Mahwah, NJ: Lawrence Erlbaum.

Bilingual Paraprofessionals

Paraprofessionals emerged in the 1950s out of the occupational need to provide clerical support and assist teachers in the education of children. Since then, paraprofessionals in general and bilingual paraprofessionals in particular have played an essential role in the education of culturally and linguistically diverse children. They assist teachers who may lack the necessary preparation to teach language minority students, and they act as role models to the culturally and linguistically diverse students they serve. Because many paraprofessionals eventually become teachers, they are an important source of certified teachers committed to the success of these students.

Paraprofessionals, the term used in this encyclopedia, are also known as *paraeducators, teacher aides/ assistants, instructional aides/assistants, classroom aides/assistants, educational technicians, computer lab technicians, child caregivers,* and *extracurricular activity aides.* Some of these terms clearly specify where within schools the paraprofessionals work—in libraries, media centers, computer laboratories, and so forth. In some states and in local education agencies, one or more of these terms reflects specific steps in the career ladder.

The variety of terms used to refer to this occupation explains the lack of a universal definition for this job. Most definitions, however, focus on the roles that paraprofessionals play, namely, assisting professionals in schools (e.g., teachers, speech language pathologists, counselors) and providing services to children or their parents under the supervision of certificated personnel. Bilingual paraprofessionals are usually hired to provide educational services in more than one language, usually English and another language; help students in public or private schools, either in general or special education; and assist with students who may or may not have disabilities.

The National Resource Center for Paraprofessionals (NRCP) in its seventh report, *The Employment and Preparation of Paraeducators: The State of the Art— 2003,* highlighted the difficulties of collecting data regarding the exact number of paraprofessionals working nationwide. The report estimated the number of paraprofessionals to be more than 525,000 in the year 2000. Of that number, approximately 130,000 were assigned to multilingual, Title I, and other compensatory programs.

Historical Background

The history of the hiring of paraprofessionals, as presented in the NRCP report, clearly reflects the needs of personnel in the field of education and the changes in the paraprofessional's job description that occurred over the past 50 years. Paraprofessionals became common in the 1950s, when a shortage of certified teachers and parents' efforts to develop community-based educational services for children and adults with disabilities created a need to hire teacher assistants. At this time, paraprofessionals played mainly a clerical role and performed basic routine and housekeeping tasks in classrooms.

In the 1960s and 1970s, federal legislation such as the Head Start Act; Title I, of the Elementary and Secondary Education Act; the Bilingual Education Act, also known as Title VII; and the Education for All Handicapped Act led to the creation of programs that addressed the needs of educationally and economically disadvantaged children and their families. These programs focused on young, low-income children in elementary and secondary schools; children with limited English proficiency, now often referred to as English language learners (ELLs); and children with disabilities, respectively. All of these programs provided funding for the employment and training of paraprofessionals, including bilingual paraprofessionals. Paraprofessionals hired to serve in these programs still perform clerical and monitoring tasks but also assist the teacher and other school personnel in the education of children with specific reading, writing, and math needs.

In 1983, the National Commission on Excellence in Education issued a report titled *A Nation at Risk: The Imperative for Educational Reform,* which stressed the need for improving the quality of education in the United States. This report launched a reform movement that continues today and is aimed at the preparation of a high-quality teaching force that is held accountable for the learning that occurs in schools and establishes high standards of learning for all students regardless of ability, ethnicity, race, and socioeconomic status.

In 2001, the Elementary and Secondary Education Act was reenacted and renamed the No Child Left Behind (NCLB) Act. This federal act focused on progressively decreasing—and, by 2014, closing—the achievement gap between White, African American, and Latino students. However, the shortage of certified teachers willing to serve in low-income urban and rural areas, the lack of qualified teachers in other areas, as well as the fact that most teachers lacked the preparation needed to adequately educate the increasing number of ELLs in the country, gave a boost to the hiring of paraprofessionals in general and bilingual paraprofessionals in particular.

Under NCLB, paraprofessionals hired after January 8, 2002, and working in a program supported with Title I, Part A funds, must have completed a minimum of 2 years of study at an institution of higher education or must hold an associate's degree or higher. They also must pass a formal test administered by the state or local education agency that assesses the candidates' knowledge of reading, writing, and math as well as the paraprofessionals' ability to assist in the instruction of those subjects. Bilingual paraprofessionals who serve only as translators or implementers of activities with parents must be proficient in English and another language and need a high school diploma or its recognized equivalent. For other paraprofessional positions, the minimum qualification is a high school diploma or recognized equivalent; some require college credits or an associate's degree. Few states have policies regulating the paraprofessionals' hiring qualifications and professional development. In fact, when the regulations are in place, they are nonbinding to the local educational agencies that hired the paraprofessionals. To improve this situation, the NRCP report advocates for collaboration between states, local education agencies, schools, unions, and institutions of higher education. It also suggests three different levels of responsibility for paraprofessionals, the knowledge and skills that should be required for each level, as well as the need for preparing teachers to work with and supervise paraprofessionals.

Current Research

The research on paraprofessionals reveals that often, bilingual paraprofessionals share the same socioeconomic status, culture, language and educational experiences of many ELLs in the schools. Their intimate understanding of these students' cultural backgrounds, families, and communities, as well as the students' educational needs, contributes to warm and caring relationships between students, parents, and paraprofessionals, relationships that facilitate learning. In addition, bilingual paraprofessionals play an indispensable role as brokers of the new culture and language for culturally and linguistically diverse students and their parents; they serve as the bridge between children and their families, and teachers and administrators. As a result, bilingual paraprofessionals end up assuming many different roles and responsibilities. These include translating for parents and school personnel, assisting teachers who are monolingual speakers of English in the instruction and assessment of students not yet proficient in that language, and clerical tasks. This situation sometimes results in bilingual paraprofessionals complaining about a job that lacks the prestige and remuneration attached to performing instructional tasks in two languages, often with little or no training. Scholars and children's advocates often highlight the contradiction of having ELLs and students with special needs, who need highly trained professionals, served by bilingual paraprofessionals who often have a high school diploma or the equivalent and are not systematically trained before or after being hired to perform the many demanding tasks involved in teaching.

Paraeducator-to-Teacher Programs

Paraprofessionals' rich experiences in the classrooms, coupled with the shortage of certified teachers and the disproportionate number of White teachers serving an increasing number of ethnically and racially diverse students, led to the consideration that paraprofessionals in general, and bilingual paraprofessionals in particular, are natural candidates to become teachers.

David Haselkorn and Elizabeth Fideler conducted a survey aimed at understanding the programs, called "paraeducator-to-teacher" programs, that prepare paraprofessionals to become teachers. These programs, although available in most states, are more prevalent in states with high percentages of culturally and linguistically diverse students, such as California, New York, and Texas. The characteristics of paraprofessionals interested in becoming teachers reflect the general population of paraeducators. They are often women with families who live in the neighborhoods where they work; are members of a minority group, with low-socioeconomic status (given the low salaries of paraprofessionals); and have years of experience in classrooms that they or their children may have attended, and therefore they are prepared to navigate the school system in at least two languages. As a result of their life and work experiences, paraprofessionals have a very good grasp of their students' cultures and needs and are committed to their success. All paraeducator-to-teacher programs reported having more than one objective, but the main and common purpose of all programs was to build on the strengths of these nontraditional teacher candidates and help them become certified teachers or certified bilingual teachers. The characteristics of these teacher education programs vary. Some use mainstream teacher education programs that are available to traditional students but also accommodate the paraprofessionals' needs by providing flexible admissions, requirements, and schedules, credit for life experience, and on-the-job training. In addition, waivers are granted for the student teaching requirement in cases where the paraprofessional has worked successfully for a number of years under supervision. A few program initiatives address the shortage of certified teachers by allowing paraprofessionals to teach while working on a bachelor's degree. Virtually all programs address the academic, economic, and personal needs of the participants.

Academic issues are usually addressed by providing advisement, tutoring, and workshops that help paraprofessionals maintain an appropriate grade point average and pass the required state teacher certification tests. Financial support is offered by providing stipends, laptop computers, printers, and money for books and courses. Personal needs are addressed through the creation of support groups, run by the director or the coordinator of the program, and by encouraging paraprofessionals to bond with other colleagues with whom they can take courses.

Beatriz Chu Clewell and Ana Maria Villegas conducted a survey called the "Evaluation of the DeWitt Wallace–Reader's Digest Fund's Pathways to Teaching Careers Program" and concluded that paraeducator-to-teacher program graduates (a) have a lower rate of attrition than teachers from traditional teacher education programs, (b) are often members of minority groups that are not well represented in the teaching profession,

(c) are more likely to serve in high-need schools in urban or rural areas that serve minority students who live in poverty, and (d) are highly successful in these schools.

M. Victoria Rodríguez

See also Bilingual Teacher Licensure; Credentialing Foreign-Trained Teachers; Culturally Competent Teaching; Teacher Qualifications; U.S. Census Language Data

Further Readings

Clewell, B. C., & Villegas, A. M. (2001). *Evaluation of the Dewitt Wallace-Reader's Digest Fund's Pathways to Teaching Careers Program.* Retrieved October 23, 2007, from http//.www.urban.org/url.cfm?id=410601

Ernst-Slavit, G., & Wenger, K. J. (2006). Teaching in the margins: The multifaceted work and struggles of bilingual paraeducators. *Anthropology & Education Quarterly, 37,* 62–82.

Haselkorn, D., & Fideler, E. (1996). *Breaking the class ceiling: Paraeducator pathways to teaching.* Belmont, MA: Recruiting New Teachers.

Monzo, L. D., & Rueda, R. S. (2001). *Sociocultural factors in social relationship: Examining Latino teachers' and paraeducators' interactions with Latino students.* Santa Cruz: University of California, Santa Cruz, Center for Research on Education, Diversity & Excellence.

National Commission on Excellence in Education. (1983). *A nation at risk: The imperative for educational reform.* Retrieved from http://www.ed.gov/pubs/NatAtRisk/index.html

Pickett, A. L., & Gerlach, K. (1997). *Supervising paraeducators in school settings: A team approach.* Austin, TX: Pro-Ed.

Pickett, A. L., Likins, M., & Wallace, T. (2004). *The employment and preparation of paraeducators: The state of the art, 2003.* New York: National Resource Center for Paraprofessionals in Education and Related Human Services. Retrieved March 20, 2007, from http://www.nrcpara.org/report

Waldschmidt, E. D. (2002). Bilingual interns' barriers to becoming teachers: At what cost do we diversify the teaching force? *Bilingual Research Journal, 26,* 537–561.

BILINGUAL SPECIAL EDUCATION

Bilingual special education is defined by Julia de Valenzuela, Leonard Baca, and Elena Baca as the instances in which student participation in an individually designed, special education program is conducted in both the student's native language and English; in such a program, the student's home culture is also considered, framed in an inclusive environment. Special education is an interdisciplinary field that addresses the educational needs of English language learners with disabilities. The majority of this population is Latino, which is now the largest minority group in the nation's schools. This is a small field, partly because of limited understanding of the needs and developmental trajectories of this population but also because of a lack of programmatic research. A significant personnel shortage has been documented for years, as described by Leonard Baca and Hermes Cervantes. In the seminal text *The Bilingual Special Education Interface,* de Valenzuela, Baca, and Baca argue for a bilingual-special education interface as a way to address the limitations of fragmented and separate general, bilingual, and special education services. They recommend the seamless integration of these programs so that the needs of this population are addressed by various groups of professionals in general education.

The convergence of several contemporary reform movements is blurring the boundaries of these systems, though in rather complex ways. First, a growing anti-immigrant and antibilingual discourse has strengthened movements to curtail services for this population in some states. This situation has increased the pressure on general education, since English language learners (ELLs) are being educated in programs that offer few linguistic supports. General education is also absorbing this population at a time when federal accountability policies require states and districts to report high performance levels as measured by standardized achievement tests. This is an important challenge because ELLs have traditionally performed poorly in such measures. It is not clear how general education will address the need of these learners.

Because of the lack of specialized resources and the scarcity of qualified personnel in general education, it has been suggested that districts with significant ELL enrollment will likely place these students in special education; in fact, research conducted in California by Alfredo Artiles, Robert Rueda, Jesús Salazar, and Ignacio Higareda suggests that ELLs are disproportionately placed in disability programs. Historically, the so-called subjective disabilities have been overpopulated at the national level by ethnic minority students, particularly African American and American Indian learners, as explained by Suzanne

Donovan and Christopher Cross. These categories include learning disabilities (LD), mild mental retardation (MMR), and emotional/behavioral disorders (E/BD). ELL overrepresentation has been reported in the past two decades, as Alba Ortiz and James Yates report in their chapter in *English Language Learners With Special Needs.* It is interesting that although general educators may be using disability diagnoses as a means to cope with the aforementioned contemporary reforms, special education is transforming its identity as a result of the inclusive education movement and preventive approaches. Indeed, more students with disabilities are being educated in general education classrooms, though it has been reported by Daniel Losen and Gary Orfield that ethnic minority students are placed in more segregated settings than are their White counterparts. In turn, preventive models such as "response to intervention" (RTI) promise to identify and treat early (i.e., while the student is still in a general education environment).

These new trends are creating unique and unprecedented conditions for the education of ELLs. This entry addresses the legal background of the special education programs geared toward culturally and linguistically diverse students designated as ELLs and the implications for assessment, curriculum planning, and the nature of inclusive education programs for those students.

Legal Background

Special education laws have had a substantial impact on bilingual special education. The Individuals with Disabilities Education Act (IDEA), originally passed in 1975 and reauthorized in 2004, governs special education services in public schools. The law protects the rights of students with disabilities and their families and tries to ensure that ELLs are assessed fairly. The law includes numerous provisions outlined below.

1. *Informed consent.* Schools must obtain written informed consent from parents or guardians to evaluate a student. Parents must be fully informed of their rights, any records to be released and to whom, and the nature and purpose of the evaluation. Parents or guardians must be informed in their native language or primary mode of communication.

2. *Multidisciplinary team.* Students should be assessed by a team of professionals with varied areas of

expertise according to the student's individuals needs. The team should include at least one general education teacher and one special education teacher. For ELLs, the team should include someone with expertise in the language acquisition process.

3. *Comprehensive evaluation.* Before an initial placement, the multidisciplinary team must conduct a complete assessment in all areas of suspected disability. No single procedure can be used as the sole criterion for determining an appropriate educational program for a child. Alternative procedures should be used when standardized tests are not considered appropriate (e.g., with culturally and linguistically diverse students). A comprehensive evaluation should include an analysis of the instructional setting and the child's instructional history.

4. *Exclusionary criteria.* A student should not be labeled if the academic struggles are primarily the result of environmental, cultural, or economic disadvantage. IDEA 2004 adds that a child should not be found to have a disability if the determinant factor is poor instruction in reading or math, or limited English proficiency.

5. *Nondiscriminatory assessment.* Assessments should be (a) selected and administered so as not to be racially or culturally discriminatory; (b) provided and administered in the child's native language or other mode of communication and in the form most likely to yield accurate information on what the child knows and can do academically, developmentally, and functionally, unless it is clearly not feasible; (c) used for the purposes for which the assessments are valid and reliable; (d) administered by trained and knowledgeable personnel; and (e) administered in accordance with any instructions provided by the producer of the assessments.

Students with LDs represent about half of the special education population. IDEA 2004 includes major changes in how students should be identified as having LD (see above). States must permit the use of a process based on the child's response to research-based interventions. Multidisciplinary teams (MDT) must establish that the child was provided appropriate instruction in regular education settings, delivered by qualified personnel. Districts may now use 15% of the funds previously allocated for special education to provide students with early intervention. States must

report the number and percentages of children with disabilities by limited-English-proficiency status and gender, in addition to race, ethnicity, and disability categories. This additional record keeping will make it easier to learn more about subpopulations of ELLs identified with disabilities.

Assessment and Identification

Traditional tests have been demonstrated to be inappropriate for the assessment of ELLs. Richard Figueroa, Eugene García, and others have documented the challenges associated with test reliability and validity when tests that were not normed with ELL samples are used to assess these students. There is also considerable evidence of poor validity and reliability of tests translated prior to or during administration, a common practice in the assessment of bilingual students. The use of traditional assessment procedures that include norm-referenced tests may not be appropriate, and, instead, the assessment process must be conceptualized holistically and include the following components:

- *Preventive measures* include the adaptation of educational environments that recognize and support the potential for all students to learn, as well as utilize instructional and disciplinary approaches considered empirically valid for use with ELLs. Such measures include well-implemented bilingual and English as a Second Language programs.
- The *intervention measures* of diagnostic teaching and behavior management aim to locate the source of the ELLs' difficulties through the use of informal assessment and family input, as well as collaboration with those who have expertise in language acquisition. These data are then utilized in the provision of instruction and supports that are empirically validated for ELLs.
- *Eligibility assessment* for ELLs ensures that appropriate assessment personnel and measures are utilized following thorough review of student records; contextualized observations and less formalized testing of ELLs are implicated by assessors who have the technical knowledge and skills, as well as the cultural and linguistic awareness, to conduct bilingual assessments. Bilingual assessments must include equivalent instruments and procedures in the students' native language and English.
- Finally, *eligibility determination* for ELLs entails that MDTs include administrative, appraisal, and

instruction representatives, parent and family members, advocates and interpreters, and an expert in cultural/linguistic diversity. Ortiz and Yates explain that the MDT must rule out factors other than disability as source of difficulty, and assessment results should be reported in the student's native language and English in aggregate, complete with a description of the nature of assessments, as well as how items were administered (e.g., with interpreter, translated during administration, if items missed in English were administered in native language, etc.). Eligibility criteria for all special education categories being considered must be applied to both languages measured.

Curriculum, Planning, and Instructional Considerations

Bilingual special education programs incorporate supportive, culturally responsive learning environments as well as validated instructional practices. Optimal programs incorporate students' home cultures and include native-language instruction and a focus on English language development in addition to validated practices in literacy and the content areas. It is a heightened focus on language and cultural practices that makes bilingual special education distinct from generic special education.

Culturally Responsive Learning Environments

School climates that foster success are caring communities based on the philosophy that all students can learn. Such schools accommodate individual differences in a positive manner. Norma López-Reyna and Alba Ortiz characterize them by (a) strong administrative leadership; (b) high expectations; (c) nurturing, supportive environment and a challenging, appropriate curriculum and instruction; (d) a safe and orderly environment; and (e) ongoing, systematic evaluation of student progress.

Linguistic Support

Successful programs are those in which language development is a central focus, whether in students' native language or English. Students receive frequent opportunities to use language in an environment that promotes active engagement. Instruction focuses on higher-order thinking and active problem solving.

Teachers preteach and reinforce key terms, as explained by Marilyn Rousseau and Brian Tam, using visuals, graphic organizers, and realia to bring words to life and make them meaningful for students, as explained by Elba Reyes and Candace Bos. They help students make connections within and across the curriculum and to their own prior knowledge and experiences, as Mack Burke, Shanna Hagan, and Bonnie Grossen explain. Ideally, teachers provide students with multiple and varied opportunities to review and apply previously learned concepts.

Curricular Modifications

Baca and de Valenzuela describe modifications to make the curriculum more accessible to ELLs. These modifications are changes in content, pedagogy, and classroom instructional settings to meet the needs of individual students. For example, modifications may include adjusting the method of presentation, developing supplemental materials, tape-recording directions, providing alternative response formats, requiring fewer or shorter responses or assignments, outlining material, or breaking tasks into subtasks, as John J. Hoover and Catherine Collier explain in their chapter in *The Bilingual Special Education Interface*. Adaptations of content might also include the provision of native-language instruction and/or materials (see Table 1).

Validated Instructional Practices

Numerous instructional approaches have been found to be promising for ELLs with disabilities.

Table 1   Suggestions for Curricular Modifications

1. The curriculum should emphasize enrichment rather than remedial activities.

2. Interactive and experiential pedagogical models should be used.

3. Language development must be emphasized across the curriculum.

4. Students' unique linguistic, cultural, and experiential backgrounds should be integrated into the curriculum.

5. Parental and community involvement in this process should be encouraged.

Source: Adapted from Baca & de Valenzuela (1994).

Sharon Vaughn and her colleagues found that some effective early interventions for ELLs who struggle with reading have been provided in the students' native language and in English. These have included focused reading interventions coupled with language development activities, such as the use of repetitive language, modeling, gesturing, visuals, and explicit instruction in English language usage, as explained in the work of Sylvia Linan-Thompson, Sharon Vaughn, Peggy Hickman-Davis, and Kamiar Kouzekanani.

Instructional approaches that promote reading comprehension and content learning include graphic organizers, as described by Bos, Adela Allen, and David Scanlon; modified reciprocal teaching and collaborative strategic reading, as explained by Janette Klingner and Vaughn; and classwide peer tutoring, as proposed by Carmen Arreaga-Mayer and Charles Greenwood.

Planning

Baca and Hermes Cervantes recommend several steps for developing a comprehensive bilingual special education curriculum. The planning process should involve the parents, the general education teacher, the bilingual teacher, and the special education teacher and follow the steps outlined in Table 2.

Table 2   Planning for ELLs With Special Needs

1. Meet as a team to begin the planning process; outline planning steps.

2. Become familiar with the culture and language background of the child as well as his or her education needs.

3. Prepare an individual instructional plan with short- and long-term objectives and goals.

4. Develop individualized lessons and materials appropriate to the child's exceptionality.

5. Modify individualized lessons and materials to match the child's needs.

6. Refer to resource people for assistance and cooperation in instruction; coordinate services.

7. Evaluate the child's ongoing progress and develop a new individualized education program (IEP), lessons, and materials as needed.

Source: Adapted from Baca & de Valenzuela (1994).

Considerations for Inclusive Education Programs

Inclusive education offers students many benefits, including access to the general education curriculum and opportunities to interact with their nondisabled peers in ways not possible with other models. The general education teacher (who may or may not be a bilingual teacher) remains responsible for the student, with support from others. Inclusion is a schoolwide approach to education that relies in part on collaborative models in which general and special education teachers coteach or the special education teacher might serve as a consultant. When the student is an ELL and neither teacher is bilingual or an expert in language development, it becomes essential to add a third collaborator who has this expertise.

ELL students with disabilities who receive support in general education classrooms need curricular modifications and supplemental materials to support their learning needs and allow them to participate as fully as possible in classroom activities.

Family and Community Participation

De Valenzuela, Baca, and Baca provide a three-part rationale for promoting family and community participation in the education of ELLs: (a) parental involvement in special education, which is required by law; (b) differences between the cultural and linguistic backgrounds of school personnel and the student body and the disproportionate representation of minority students in special programs; and (c) evidence of the positive correlation between academic achievement and family involvement.

Nancy Cloud has dedicated much of her work to developing specific guidelines on how to provide opportunities for parents and community members of ELLs with special needs. In her chapter in *English Language Learners With Special Needs,* she mentions considerations must be made that are related to the family's level of acculturation and attitude/acceptance of their child. In addition, the language of the family must be accommodated for; trained translators or bilingual educators must be involved in all family correspondence between the school and the home. Educators need to understand the family's perceptions of schooling, as well as their knowledge and comfort with the school environment and infrastructure.

The special education process is potentially confusing for all parents and families, including ELLs and their families. Careful attention must be given to the way each step of the process is presented and explained. There are specific considerations to be made related to meetings and paperwork for bilingual special education students, including the language of oral and written communication both prior to and at all special education meetings, and the need to determine goals and concerns of parents and family's before options are presented at eligibility determination and individualized education program meetings.

Finally, there are many misconceptions about the involvement of parents and families of ELLs in their children's education. However, research from the National Center for Education Statistics in 1995 shows similar patterns for minority and nonminority parents' involvement in their eighth-grade students' education. Educators need to be aware of and challenge their own biases that shape interpretation of different levels and types of parent and family involvement in their children's education. A useful principle is to consider that different communities and families have different norms pertaining to family involvement in the school setting.

*Alfredo J. Artiles, Janette Kettmann Klingner,
and Kathleen King*

Authors' Note: The authors acknowledge the support of the National Center for Culturally Responsive Educational Systems (NCCRESt, at http//:www.nccrest.org, under grant number H326E020003, awarded by the U.S. Department of Education's Office of Special Education Programs. Endorsement of the ideas presented in this article by the funding agency should not be inferred.

See also Culturally Competent Teaching; Multicultural Education; Transformative Teaching Model

Further Readings

Arreaga-Mayer, C., & Greenwood, C. R. (1986). Environmental variables affecting the school achievement of culturally and linguistically different learners: An instructional perspective. *Journal of the National Association of Bilingual Education, 10*(2), 113–135.

Artiles, A., & Ortiz, A. (Eds.). (2002). *English language learners with special needs: Identification, placement, and instruction.* Washington, DC: Center for Applied Linguistics.

Artiles, A., Rueda, R., Salazar, J., & Higareda, I. (2005). Within-group diversity in minority disproportionate representation: English Language Learners in urban school districts. *Exceptional Children, 71,* 283–300.

Baca, L., & Cervantes, H. (Eds.) (2004). *The bilingual special education interface.* Columbus, OH: Merrill.

Baca, L., & de Valenzuela, J. S. (1994, Fall). Reconstructing the bilingual special education interface. *NCBE Program Information Guide Series, 20.* Available from http://www.ncela.gwu.edu/pubs/pigs

Burke, M., Hagan, S., & Grossen, B. (1998). What curricular design and strategies accommodate diverse learners? *Teaching Exceptional Children, 31*(1), 34–48.

de Valenzuela, J. S., Baca, L., & Baca, E. (2004). Family involvement in bilingual special education: Challenging the norm. In L. Baca & H. Cervantes (Eds.), *The bilingual special education interface* (pp. 360–381). Columbus, OH: Merrill.

Donovan, S., & Cross, C. (Eds.). (2002). *Minority students in special and gifted education.* Washington, DC: National Academy Press.

Figueroa, R. A., & García, E. (1994). Issues in testing students from culturally and linguistically diverse backgrounds. *Multicultural Education, 2*(1), 10–19.

Harris-Murri, N. J. (2006). *Living the dream in the promised land: Features of highly successful schools that serve students of color.* Denver, CO: National Center for Culturally Responsive Educational Systems.

Individuals with Disabilities Education Improvement Act of 2004, H.R. 1350, 108th Cong (2004). Available from http://nasponline.org/advocacy/IDEA2004.pdf

Klingner, J. K., & Vaughn, S. (1996). Reciprocal teaching of reading comprehension strategies for students with learning disabilities who use English as a second language. *Elementary School Journal, 93,* 275–293.

Linan-Thompson, S., Vaughn, S., Hickman-Davis, P., & Kouzekanani, K. (2003). Effectiveness of supplemental reading instruction for second-grade English language learners with reading difficulties. *Elementary School Journal, 103,* 221–238.

López-Reyna, N. A. (1996). The importance of meaningful contexts in bilingual special education: Moving to whole language. *Learning Disabilities Research & Practice, 11,* 120–131.

Losen, D., & Orfield, G. (Eds.). (2002). *Racial inequity in special education.* Cambridge, MA: Harvard Education Press.

National Center for Education Statistics. (1995). *The educational progress of Hispanic students.* Washington, DC: U.S. Department of Education, Office of Educational Research and Improvement.

Ortiz, A. A., & Yates, J. (2001). *English language learners with special needs: Effective instructional strategies.* Washington, DC: ERIC Education Reports.

Reyes, E., & Bos, C. (1998). Interactive semantic mapping and charting: Enhancing content area learning for language minority students. In R. Gersten & R. Jiménez (Eds.), *Promoting learning for culturally and linguistically diverse students: Classroom applications from contemporary research* (pp. 133–152). Belmont, CA: Wadsworth.

Rousseau, M. K., & Tam, B. K. Y. (1993). Increasing reading proficiency of language minority students with speech and language impairments. *Education and Treatment of Children, 16,* 254–271.

Vaughn, S., Mathes, P. G., Linan-Thompson, S., & Francis, D. J. (2005). Teaching English language learners at risk for reading disabilities to read: Putting research to practice. *Learning Disabilities Research & Practice, 20,* 58–67.

Willig, A., Swedo, J., & Ortiz, A. (1987). *Characteristics of teaching strategies which result in high task engagement for exceptional limited English proficient students.* Austin: University of Texas at Austin, Handicapped Minority Research Institute on Language Proficiency.

BILINGUAL TEACHER LICENSURE

The current state of bilingual teacher licensure and its history reflect the ongoing tension between the changing demographics of the public schools, the scholarly and research base for educating immigrant students, and national- and state-level shifts in policies governing the education of limited-English-proficient students, more aptly termed *English language learners* (ELLs). As the number of immigrant students in American public schools has increased, the definition of what constitutes a highly qualified teacher of students who speak languages other than English in the home has changed and evolved. It has done so through a growing body of research on teacher effectiveness and years of practical experience in the implementation of specialized programs of instruction for these students in schools throughout the nation. The No Child Left Behind Act of 2001 required that all students in the United States have a "highly qualified" teacher in the classroom, but the law did not define the qualifications needed for teachers to promote the academic and linguistic growth of students who are learning English. This responsibility was left up to the states acting through their licensure agencies and to institutions of higher education that offer teacher education programs.

A definition of highly qualified bilingual teachers is discernible in the scholarly research literature and is reflected in licensure policies in many states. However, the realities and practicalities of how to prepare and accredit bilingual teachers are often at odds with the theoretical and research base. The tensions between theory, research, and practice prompt the following questions and issues regarding bilingual teacher licensure: What areas of knowledge, skills, and attitudes are necessary for bilingual teachers to possess in order to be highly qualified to teach ELLs? Is there a common core of competencies that bilingual teachers share with all highly qualified teachers? If so, should bilingual teacher licensure be an "add-on" to a basic credential? If not, then should bilingual teachers be certified through different programs based on a different or separate set of standards and requirements? What level of proficiency in students' primary or native languages should bilingual teachers achieve to be effective teachers of ELLs?

History of Bilingual Teacher Licensure

The history of bilingual teacher licensure began in 1968 with passage of the Bilingual Education Act. The federal government played an important role in the development of bilingual teacher education programs during the 1970s and 1980s. Under Title VII of the Elementary and Secondary Education Act, a concerted effort at capacity building was made for preparing bilingual teachers through funding of scholarships and stipends for bilingual teacher candidates and teacher educators. Title VII was extended in 1994 but expired in 2002, to be replaced by the No Child Left Behind legislation that redefined the federal government's role in educating ELLs.

The states with large immigrant populations and those that passed laws mandating the implementation of bilingual programs (such as Illinois, Massachusetts, Texas, and California) have had licensure requirements for bilingual education teachers in place since the mid-1970s. The year 1974 marked the codification into law of the rights to equal educational opportunities for ELLs, based on the Supreme Court decision in the *Lau v. Nichols* case. The Equal Educational Opportunity Act of 1974 (EEOA) codified *Lau* and made an even stronger statement by adding the weight of the legislative branch of government to the already powerful voice of the U.S. Supreme Court. Since that time, there has been an emerging consensus in teacher education and academic communities as to the competencies or skills that were required for effective bilingual teaching. These were articulated as "guidelines" for bilingual teacher preparation programs by the Center for Applied Linguistics in 1974. Over time, organization and state licensure agencies developed and refined criteria for certification of bilingual teachers and outlined bilingual teacher education program standards and requirements.

Several federal and state court cases over the years since the *Lau v. Nichols* decision established the requirements for programs for ELLs. In 1981, *Castañeda v. Pickard* outlined a three-pronged test for programs that adequately meet the needs of language minority students, as James Crawford explains. This Texas case set the standards for determining what constituted "appropriate action" on the part of school districts to address the educational rights of students learning English. The court determined that under the provisions of the EEOA, programs had to meet three criteria: Programs for ELLs had to (1) be based on a pedagogically sound plan, (2) have sufficient qualified teachers to implement the program, and (3) have a system to evaluate the program's effectiveness in educating limited-English-proficient students. Scholars such as Diane August and Kenji Hakuta, and María Robledo Montecel and Josie D. Cortéz mention that these requirements were based on recognition of the interrelationship between effective program implementation and the qualifications in academic knowledge, instructional skills, and language proficiency of bilingual teachers.

Knowledge Base for Teaching ELLs

Efforts to establish teacher certification programs became more intense and focused in the late 1980s and early 1990s because of the growing population of immigrant students, primarily from Mexico and Latin America. Kate Menken and Beth Antunez documented in 2001 that 38 states had credential requirements for teachers of students with limited English proficiency, while 95 institutions of higher education had bilingual teacher education programs. States with the greatest number of bilingual teacher education programs were California, New York, and Texas. Although universities varied in the types of degrees in bilingual teaching offered and course and program requirements, there was a common core of standards

and competencies in the preparation of teachers for bilingual instruction. Menken and Antunez reported that this knowledge base included three main categories of coursework and certification requirements for bilingual teacher licensure in all states: (1) pedagogical knowledge, (2) linguistic knowledge, and (3) knowledge of cultural and linguistic diversity.

In addition to states' requirements for bilingual teacher licensure, a number of organizations have established standards for teacher preparation and professional development. These include the National Association for Bilingual Education (NABE) publication in 1992, *Standards for the Preparation of Bilingual/Multicultural Teachers;* the National Board for Professional Teaching Standards (NBPTS) publication in 1998, *English as a New Language Standards;* the Center for Research on Education, Diversity & Excellence (CREDE) publication in 1998, *Standards for Effective Teaching Practice;* as well as the Teachers of English to Speakers of Other Languages (TESOL) publication in 2002, *Pre-K–12 ESL Teacher Education Standards.*

The foundation for bilingual teaching is a body of theory and philosophy of second-language acquisition that preserves and promotes children's ethnic identities and cultural integrity. The pedagogical basis for bilingual education is widely accepted by second-language educators and supported by a large body of research and evaluation studies, as noted by Diane August and Kenji Hakuta. Underlying successful bilingual education is the principle of the interdependent relationship between language development and cognitive academic skills. Stephen Krashen points out that research into second-language acquisition processes in academic settings has established that learning takes place when language and concepts are linked in meaningful ways, so that they produce growth in knowledge and competency in using the language to communicate knowledge and ideas. Therefore, bilingual teachers must be knowledgeable in how to design effective instruction to make linkages between linguistic and conceptual development, as well as between learning in the students' primary language and English, as reported by Carmen Zúñiga-Hill and Ruth Helen Yopp.

Three-Tiered Approach to ELL Teacher Licensure

Teacher education programs and licensure policies have responded to the growing ELL population in classrooms in which bilingual teachers are not available. Non-bilingual-certified teachers provide specialized instruction to ELLs through various models and programs of English-only instruction, including English as a Second Language (ESL) programs, structured English immersion, and mainstream programs. Patricia Gándara and Russell Rumberger reported in 2005 that more than half (55%) of the teachers of ELLs in California taught students through resource models and pull-out instructional services. Teachers of ELLs utilized knowledge from the disciplines of linguistics and second-language (L2) acquisition and the relationship between language and academic development. They used this knowledge to identify and select appropriate teaching strategies to address learners' developing knowledge of English and growth in literacy and content knowledge.

To address the growing population of ELLs, both historically and practically, teacher education programs have developed what can be characterized as a three-tiered approach. Based on a set of generic teaching competencies that all teachers possess, credential programs have focused on "emphasis" credentials to address the particular knowledge, skills, and abilities of nonbilingual and bilingual teachers of ELLs, as indicated by Josué González and Linda Darling-Hammond. (See Table 1 for a description of the components of three levels of expertise that are addressed in teacher preparation programs.) California's licensure structure is an example of the implementation of this conceptualization of teacher competencies for educating ELLs.

Table 1 A Three-Tiered Analysis of EL/Bilingual Teacher Competencies

Effective Generic Teaching	*Effective CLAD Teaching*	*Effective Bilingual Teaching*
1. Careful and thorough lesson planning based on an understanding of a coherent and sequenced progression of the curriculum according to state and local school district frameworks and standards.	1.1. Lesson planning based on a selection of subsets of vocabulary, concepts, skills, and processes so that L2 learners are not overwhelmed with academic content, but are still challenged and engaged. 1.2. Ability to plan the curriculum around themes or "essential questions" so that L2 learners can make connections between each lesson and the overall curriculum and standards, while also being provided multiple exposures and vehicles to comprehend the content.	1.3. Lesson planning in students' L1 builds linguistic and conceptual knowledge based on the principle that new knowledge is introduced in the known language (L1) and new language is introduced and linked to the known concepts, usually learned in L1. 1.4. Bilingual teachers plan for cross-linguistic transfer of learning, including contrastive analysis of L1 and L2 language structures, to maximize metalinguistic knowledge stemming from proficiency in two different language systems.
2. Clear presentations and delivery of content based on important ideas, principles, and concepts.	2.1. Careful attention to modeling and scaffolding learning to provide a structure for L2 learners in order to sort out important ideas and reduce the "language load" for different levels of English proficiency, based on the need for comprehensible input.	2.2. Planning for systematic and consistent use of L1 and L2 as mediums of instruction and language support for learning, without resorting to concurrent translation that could diminish conceptual learning and/or the level of challenge in L2 learning.
3. Differentiated teaching to meet individual students' needs.	3.1. Differentiate instruction according to each student's language proficiency by adjusting the focus of instruction and the level of difficulty (complexity, abstraction, reading level, etc.) of the content.	3.3. Use whole-group and skills-group instruction according to language dominance and proficiency to ensure that students work at the appropriate level of challenge and complexity in both L1 and L2.

(Continued)

Table 1 (Continued)

Effective Generic Teaching	Effective CLAD Teaching	Effective Bilingual Teaching
	3.2. Knowledge of when language should be the focus of the lesson rather than the content and when the content should be the focus, with modifications and adjustments to the language used in instruction and students' tasks.	3.4. Distinguish between challenges to students' learning based on their lack of language proficiency to express their knowledge of content and when the concepts or content knowledge needs to be developed through language that students have mastered (either L1 or L2).
4. Design of appropriate learning activities and instructional materials.	4.1. Knowledge of how to modify and adapt textbooks and other reading materials through processes such as summarizing, paraphrasing, outlining, etc., to use instead of, or in preparation for, work with grade-level textbooks.	4.2. Knowledge of effective grouping patterns according to students' dominant language and L2 proficiency. 4.3. Selection and adaptation of L1 and L2 materials and texts for grade-level instruction in L1 and developmentally appropriate materials in L1.
5. Providing ample opportunities for students to practice and apply their learning.	5.1. Awareness that L2 learners need to practice their language skills in interactions with the teacher and with each other, before they are expected to read and write independently using that same language. 5.2. Careful selection of authentic tasks that encourage use of language for communicating for specific purposes. 5.3. Avoidance of artificial and excessively abstract and complex language tasks.	5.4. Knowledge of cross-linguistic transfer theory and the connections between students' academic knowledge and their growth in L2 proficiency. 5.5. Ability to develop critical thinking skills in L1 and to present increasingly challenging content material in L2 as students' proficiency increases. 5.6. Ability to determine what content needs to be introduced, practiced, and assessed in either L1 or L2 at points in time in the curriculum.
6. Setting high expectations for student performance and achievement.	6.1. Knowledge of what is reasonable and realistic to expect of L2 students as their language skills develop over time, according to the characteristics of the stages of L2 acquisition. 6.2. Ability to find alternative ways for L2 students to express and demonstrate their content knowledge without being hindered by limited proficiency.	6.3. Knowledge of the benefits of bilingualism and the expectation that students become fully bilingual and biliterate. 6.4. Knowledge of bilingual language use in the students' homes and community and affirmation of the use of two or more languages as a resource. 6.5. Expectations that students will become fully linguistically and culturally integrated into society as bilingual individuals.

Effective Generic Teaching	Effective CLAD Teaching	Effective Bilingual Teaching
7. Ongoing assessment and adjustment of curriculum according to students' learning.	7.1. Knowledge of standardized and observation-based language assessment procedures, scoring, and interpretation.	7.4. Knowledge of language assessment in determining language dominance and acquisition in bilingual development.
	7.2. Knowledge of the features of language to observe through reading assessments, such as running records, informal reading inventories, and miscue analysis	7.5. Knowledge of biliteracy development and the cross-linguistic transfer of reading skills and strategies from L1 to L2.
	7.3. Skill in the analysis of L2 students' writing for patterns of errors based on cross-linguistic transfer and/or language development.	7.6. Knowledge of comparative and contrastive linguistics between L1 and L2 and didactic strategies for presenting these concepts to facilitate bilingual and biliteracy development.
8. Integration of the language arts (listening, speaking, reading, and writing) in teaching and in planning students' performance tasks and activities.	8.1. Adjustment of the focus of reading/language arts instruction according to the proficiency level of each students (4x4 model)	8.5. Ability to differentiate instruction through thematic teaching and to coordinate content presentation and learning tasks in L1 and L2, according to a theoretically sound model of dual-language instruction.
	8.2. Attention to the "buildup" steps required to prepare L2 learners for the more abstract and complex tasks of reading and writing.	8.6. Ability to assess students' readiness for transition into greater amounts and higher levels of L2 instruction in transitional bilingual education programs.
	8.3. Knowledge of the importance of a meaning-based approach to literacy instruction.	8.7. Ability to assess students' L1 language maintenance needs and sustain their linguistic and cognitive development as bilinguals.
	8.4. Awareness of the concept of interlanguage and how to identify the possible origins of linguistic errors.	
9. Effective classroom management and creation of a positive classroom environment.	9.1. Awareness of self as a "cultural mediator" and "interpreter" with openness to learning from and about L2 students and their cultural backgrounds.	9.4. Deep knowledge of students' culture and role modeling of positive aspects of bilingual and biculturalism.
	9.2. Awareness of cultural factors in children's learning styles and preferences that impinge on motivation to learn and interact with the teacher and their peers.	9.5. Creation of a classroom environment that affirms use of L1 and L2 for all functions and levels of classroom interaction and academic study.
	9.3. Knowledge of flexible and varied patterns of grouping to meet individual needs of L2 students according to their levels of language proficiency and mastery of content.	

(Continued)

Table 1 (Continued)

Effective Generic Teaching	Effective CLAD Teaching	Effective Bilingual Teaching
10. Knowledge of grade-level programs and how his or her teaching fits into the larger curriculum plan and progression for a particular group of students.	10.1. Knowledge of the goals and objectives of the designated language minority student program (transitional bilingual education, structured English immersion, etc.) and what responsibilities he or she has for L2 students' long-range progress.	10.4. Knowledge of the goals, objectives, and structures of models of dual-language instruction and their means of implementation across grade levels and subject areas.
	10.2. Knowledge of the legal boundaries under which teachers operate in instructing L2 learners and where to go for clarification of policies and procedures.	10.5. Ability to create a coherent and progressive scope and sequence of learning language, literacy, and academic content with appropriate time frames and academic goals for instruction in L1 and L2.
	10.3. Awareness of shared decision-making processes and opportunities for collaboration in his or her role and responsibilities in educating language minority students.	10.6. Knowledge of the limitations and benefits of various forms of language and academic achievement tests and assessments in planning students' entry into, progress in, and/or exit from L1 and L2 programs.

The California Model

In 1992, the California Commission on Teacher Credentialing (CCTC) established a new system for preparing teachers for linguistically and culturally diverse student populations to respond to these changing demographics, as reported by Priscilla H. Walton and Robert Carlson. Two categories of teaching credentials were created to prepare bilingual and monolingual teachers for instruction with ELL students: The Bilingual Cross-Cultural Language and Academic Development (BCLAD) emphasis credential, authorizing teachers to provide instruction in students' native languages in bilingual education classrooms, and the Cross-Cultural Language and Academic Development (CLAD) credential, authorizing nonbilingual teachers to provide English language development and specialized content area instruction for ELLs. The CCTC also established a structure for teachers who held a basic credential to add CLAD or BCLAD certification through additional university courses and/or state examinations. The BCLAD/CLAD system designated six domains of required knowledge. CLAD certification candidates were required to demonstrate competencies in Domains 1 through 3, while bilingual candidates are required to demonstrate mastery of all six domains:

1. Language structure and first- and second-language development

2. Methodology of bilingual, English language development, and content instruction

3. Culture and cultural diversity

4. Methodology for primary-language instruction

5. The culture of emphasis

6. The language of emphasis

The CLAD credential was originally designed to qualify nonbilingual teachers for teaching assignments with ELL students who had completed and transitioned out of bilingual education programs or who were in classrooms where certified bilingual teachers were not available. However, with passage of Proposition 227 in 1998, which restricted bilingual education programs in California schools, the focus of the CLAD credential shifted to qualifying teachers for the implementation of "structured English immersion" programs of short duration according to the provisions of the new law. Simultaneously, the number of students enrolled in dual-immersion or two-way bilingual programs grew, increasing the demand for bilingual teachers to staff these programs (which served 13,000 students in 2006, according to a CCTC report). In 2002, teacher education reform legislation resulted in the elimination of the CLAD credential as an "add-on" of specific coursework and content to the basic teaching credentials. In 2006, the CCTC changed the name of the certification to California Teachers of English Learners (CTEL) and approved a new and expanded set of standards as a knowledge base for coursework and testing, as described by CCTC in 2006.

The California BCLAD/CLAD and CTEL requirements share a common core of competencies for teaching ELLs in three domains of knowledge: Language structure and language development, second-language methodology, and culture and cultural diversity. In addition to the multicultural and linguistic core courses for the CLAD, bilingual BCLAD teachers are prepared in methodology for primary-language instruction, the culture of emphasis, and must demonstrate proficiency in the students' primary language. In many universities in California, programs for certifying bilingual teachers are housed in separate departments within a college of education, while, in others, the programs are combined but with different course requirements within the same department, as explained by Walton and Carlson. Both nonbilingual and bilingual certified teachers are required to complete coursework in foundations of bilingual education and second-language teaching methodology. Required courses cover the legal requirements of limited-English-proficient student education, program models for ELLs, language assessment, and instructional strategies for developing language, literacy, and content knowledge. Teacher candidates complete methods courses emphasizing specially designed academic instruction in English and English language development, as well as courses in theories of second-language acquisition, as Menken and Antunez indicate.

Conclusion

State licensure policies for bilingual teachers reflect a common knowledge base about what knowledge, skills, and abilities are required for effective bilingual program implementation and classroom teaching. In California, as elsewhere, state agencies and institutions of higher education continue to refine and augment the knowledge and research bases for teacher certification. This expanded knowledge has been applied in teacher education and credentialing programs for enhancing the effectiveness of teachers who work with ELLs in various types of programs. Policy initiatives that increase the rigor of testing and academic demands for earning bilingual teaching certification are responses to changes in federal and state laws and policies regarding the education of ELLs and the demand for teachers with bilingual teaching skills. As the research evidence supporting effective bilingual teaching practices expands, programs and licensure regulations for certifying bilingual teachers will benefit.

Jill Kerper Mora

See also Teacher Certification by States; Teacher Preparation, Then and Now

Further Readings

August, D., & Hakuta, K. (Eds.). (1997). *Improving schooling for language minority children: A research agenda.* Washington, DC: National Academy Press.

California Commission on Teacher Credentialing. (2006). *Proposed standards for California Teachers of English Learners Certificate Program: Knowledge, skills, and abilities for the California Teacher of English Learners (CTEL) Examination.* Sacramento: California Commission on Teacher Credentialing Professional Services Division.

Center for Applied Linguistics. (1974). *Guidelines for the preparation and certification of teachers of bilingual-bicultural education in the United States of America.* Arlington, VA: Center for Applied Linguistics.

Crawford, J. (2004). *Educating English learners: Language diversity in the classroom* (5th. ed.). Los Angeles: Bilingual Educational Services.

Gándara, P., & Rumburger, R. (2006). *Resource needs for California's English learners.* Santa Barbara: University of California Linguistic Minority Research Center. Available from http:// lmri.ucsb.edu/publications/ 07_gandara-rumberger.pdf

González, J. M., & Darling-Hammond, L. (1997). *New concepts for new challenges: Professional development for teachers of immigrant youth.* McHenry, IL: Center for Applied Linguistics.

Krashen, S. D. (1999). *Condemned without a trial: Bogus arguments against bilingual education*. Portsmouth, NH: Heinemann.

Menken, K., & Antunez, B. (2001). *An overview of the preparation and certification of teachers working with limited English proficient (LEP) students*. Washington, DC: National Clearinghouse for Bilingual Education. (ERIC Reproduction Service Document No. ED455231)

Midobuche, E. (1999). *Certification and endorsement of bilingual education teachers: A comparison state licensure requirements* In J. M. González (Ed.), CBER occasional papers in bilingual education policy (pp. 1–62). Tempe: Arizona State University, Intercultural Development Research Association.

Montecel, M. R., & Cortéz, J. D. (2002). Successful bilingual education programs: Development and the dissemination of criteria to identify promising and exemplary practices in bilingual education at the national level. *Bilingual Research Journal, 25*, 1–22.

Mora, J. K. (2000). Staying the course in times of change: Preparing teachers for linguistically diverse classrooms. *Journal of Teacher Education, 51*, 345–357.

National Association for Bilingual Education. (1992). *Professional standards for the preparation of bilingual/multicultural teachers*. Washington, DC: National Association for Bilingual Education.

National Board for Professional Teaching Standards. (2007). *English as a new language standards*. Available from http://www.nbpts.org/the_standards/standards_by_cert?ID =22&x=38&y=8

Teachers of English to Speakers of Other Languages. (2002). *ESL Standards for Pre-K–12 Students*. Alexandria, VA: TESOL.

Tharp, R. G. (1999). *Effective teaching: How the standards came to be*. Berkeley, CA: Center for Research on Education, Diversity & Excellence. Retrieved from http://crede.berkeley.edu/standards/development.shtml

Walton, P. H., & Carlson, R. E. (1997). Responding to social change: California's new standards for teacher credentialing. In J. E. King, E. R. Hollins, & W. C. Hayman (Eds.), *Preparing teachers for cultural diversity* (pp. 222–239). New York: Teachers College Press.

Zúñiga-Hill, C., & Yopp, R. H. (1996). Practices of exemplary elementary school teachers of second language learners. *Teacher Education Quarterly, 23*(1), 83–97.

Black English

See Ebonics

Boarding Schools and Native Languages

The history of American Indians/Alaska Natives and their experience with boarding schools is highly complex and has created a legacy that profoundly affects their lives today. It is widely recognized that an explicit mission of the boarding schools was to aggressively replace native languages and cultures with a dominant culture and language. The pursuit of this mission, coupled with the systematic maltreatment of native children during the boarding school era, contributed to many of the psychosocial ills that persist in American Indian/Alaska Native communities today. However, the boarding school experience also unintentionally invigorated its own form of cultural resiliency among native people. Though boarding schools were a direct assault against native being and identity, the lived experience is now woven integrally into the fabric of American Indian/Alaska Native identity and serves, ironically, as a driving force in the present-day political, cultural, and linguistic self-determination of native people throughout the United States.

Boarding schools for American Indians and Alaska Natives exist to this day, although they are not as prevalent as in the past. Attendance is voluntary, and most schools now work closely with surrounding American Indian/Alaska Native groups, employing tribal members as staff who reflect, and at times even integrate, the cultures and languages of American Indian/Alaska Native students as part of their educational programming.

Foundation of the Boarding School Movement

The boarding school movement was conceived in the late 1800s and was intended to be a social reform, based in a belief that with proper education and treatment, American Indians/Alaska Natives could be assimilated into mainstream society and transformed into productive, useful citizens. The movement gained impetus after the Civil War with the establishment of Carlisle Indian School in Pennsylvania in 1879, founded by Captain Richard Henry Pratt, whose dictum was "Kill the Indian and save the man." To attend the school, native children were sent, in many cases, hundreds of miles away from family, language, and native ways. Carlisle imposed a military-style regimen designed to divest young Indian boys and girls of not only their cultures and languages but also their native physical appearance. The school proudly published "before" and "after" photos, boasting of the complete transformation of Indian youth from "savages" into "civilized" people.

The reform, offered through the agency of the Indian boarding school, was also an outgrowth of the new "peace policy" instituted by President Ulysses S. Grant, which placed the Bureau of Indian Affairs under the direct influence of various religious denominations. Between 1870 and 1930, the federal government and all of the major religious groups established and operated more than 150 on- and off-reservation boarding schools. Because many tribes were being removed from their traditional lands, a key role of this growing wave of boarding schools, besides direct assimilation of American Indian/Alaska Native people into the dominant culture, was to prepare a new generation of Indians for farming and private land ownership. The model created by Pratt at Carlisle became the cornerstone of most Indian boarding schools. Besides facilitating Indian removal from reservation settings and converting them to Christianity, the schools placed a heavy emphasis on manual labor, industrial and domestic training, and farming, as well as learning the English language. The dominant society work ethic was modeled with the "outing system," which placed American Indian/Alaska Native students in work settings outside of the boarding school. Both government officials and church leaders favored boarding schools over day schools because the process of "civilizing" the students and converting them into sedentary farmers was easier when the influences of tribal life and indigenous culture and language were absent.

Mandatory education for Indian children became law in 1893, and government agents on the reservations were instructed on how to enforce the new federal regulations. If parents refused to send their children to school, the authorities could withhold subsidies or rations or have resisters prosecuted. In the Hopi communities in Arizona, for example, parents and community leaders tried to hide their children from the government agents or outright refused to allow their children to be taken. Subsequently, a number of Hopi community leaders were tried in federal courts and imprisoned at Alcatraz. Most former

boarding school students recall the loneliness and fear they experienced because of this early separation from family and community. Once their children were enrolled in a distant school, parents lost control over decisions that affected them.

Language Policy

The keystone element of the boarding schools' assimilation mission was to induce mastery of the English language at the expense of native languages. A strategy of the boarding schools in accomplishing this was to mix children from different language groups so there were less opportunities to speak with other speakers of a native language that might be shared in common. The use of native languages was strictly prohibited by the Bureau of Indian Affairs, as was the exercise of any spiritual practices other than Christianity. In 1887, Commissioner of Indian Affairs J. D. C. Atkins declared the preeminence of both the English language and national culture not only in relationship to American Indians, but to all races:

> I expressed very decidedly the idea that Indians should be taught in the English language only. . . . There is not an Indian pupil whose tuition and maintenance is paid by the United States Government who is permitted to study any other language other than our own vernacular—the language of the greatest, most powerful, and enterprising nationalities under the sun. The English language as taught in America is good enough for all her people of all races. (p. xxi)

Students who were caught using their native languages among themselves suffered various punishments. Many former students who are elders today remember forced mouthwashing with bars of pungent brown soap.

Criticism and Reform

In 1928, a report titled "The Problem of the Indian Administration," otherwise known as the "Meriam Report," was produced at the direction of the Indian commission. This report was highly critical of government Indian policy with regard to education. The poor quality of personnel, inadequate salaries, unqualified teachers and almost nonexistent health care were some of the criticisms documented in the report. Publication of the report prompted the initiation of a movement to replace boarding schools with day schools closer to where native people lived. Critics of the boarding schools and their curricula argued that the educational programs in boarding schools assumed a transition to the workforce with an European American tradition; however, for those students who returned to their reservations, such programs were irrelevant.

The shuttering of boarding schools accelerated when John Collier was appointed commissioner of Indian Affairs in 1933. The passage of the Indian Reorganization Act in 1934 and Collier's commitment to fostering reforms in Indian policy significantly reduced the Indian boarding school population by the end of World War II. Community day schools, state-supported public schools, and nonresidential parochial schools were the dominant education institutions for American Indian children by the mid-1950s.

The reformers who encouraged the idea of education as a tool for assimilation also realized that the desired end had not materialized. Some students returned to their homes and to their tribal ways, and others, although not returning completely to their old ways, became in a sense "bicultural." Those who so strongly supported Indian education as an assimilative process viewed neither of these situations as successful assimilation. In the long run, the policy of forced assimilation had failed. Native American cultures and languages had survived, though the latter had considerably diminished for many tribal groups. The misguided efforts of the reformers had produced more negative than positive effects on the daily lives of native children and their communities.

Recent Studies and Current Issues

In the past decade, the study of American Indian boarding schools has grown into one of the richest areas of American Indian historical scholarship. The best of this scholarship has moved beyond an examination of the federal policies that drove boarding school education to consider the experiences of American Indian children within the schools and the responses of native students and parents to school policies, programs, and curricula. Recent studies by David Wallace Adams, Brenda Child, Matthew Sakiestewa Gilbert, Esther Burnett Horne, Sally Hyer, K. Tsianina Lomawaima, and Sally McBeth have used archival research, oral interviews, and photographs to consider the history of boarding schools from American Indian/Alaska Native perspectives. In doing so, they have begun to uncover the meaning and long-term implications of boarding school education for native children, families, and communities, past and present.

By highlighting native people's resistance to cultural assimilation and institutional control, these studies of Indian boarding schools illuminate the gulf between the intentions of federal assimilation policy and its ultimate results. In fact, far from eradicating traditional cultures, boarding school experiences actually facilitated cultural persistence and invigoration in a number of unintended ways. In *Education for Extinction,* Adams argues that the friendships students forged across tribal lines contributed to a pan-Indian identity that encouraged native people to work together for political and cultural self-determination in the 20th century. In *They Called It Prairie Light,* Lomawaima adds that interacting with children from other cultural traditions also worked to reinforce students' own unique tribal identities and encouraged them to maintain distinct cultural practices.

The pan-Indianism that grew out of the boarding school experience did tend to reinforce the English language as a common medium of communication among students from various tribes. This, along with punishment for speaking tribal languages with fellow speakers, also prompted the increased use of English by Native Americans amongst themselves when boarding school students returned home. The boarding school experience also imbued a sense among many of those who returned to the reservation that the "old ways" and tribal language were relics of the past. To many returnees, Natives dressing traditionally and speaking tribal languages were perceived as throwbacks when compared with the lifestyle of a "modern" Indian. Also, as language use began to shift in many American/Alaska Native communities, the change was slow, incremental, and not readily observable. Only after considerable language loss had occurred did communities began taking notice, especially in settings where the native language was integral to ceremony, ritual, and the transmission of traditional knowledge. For these reasons, tribal languages became more reduced in their domains of daily use, especially when coupled with increased reliance on literacy, which in almost all cases existed only in English.

As native people are aware of the legacy of the boarding schools and the effects it has had on them, the issue of language loss has become a particular focal point of concern. According to the Indigenous Language Institute, of the more than 300 languages spoken in the United States at the time of European contact, only 175 remain, and many of those have just a few speakers left. The U.S. government has acknowledged its role in this massive loss of native language through the agency of boarding schools and has offered congressional redress. The most recent iteration of federal law, the Esther Martinez Native American Languages Preservation Act of 2006, authorizes funding for language nests, language survival schools, and language restoration programs. The Administration for Native Americans, within the U.S. Department of Health and Human Services, also supports large-scale language preservation and revitalization programs. Many tribes, tribal schools, and native organizations throughout Alaska, Hawai'i, and the mainland United States also operate their own language revitalization or maintenance programs utilizing their own resources.

Dennis Viri

See also Americanization by Schooling; Indigenous Language Revitalization; Native American Languages, Legal Support for

Further Readings

Adams, D. W. (1995). *Education for extinction: American Indians and the boarding school experience, 1875–1928.* Lawrence: University Press of Kansas.

Atkins, J. D. C. (1887). *Annual report of the Commissioner of Indian Affairs to the secretary of the interior for the year 1887.* Washington, DC: Government Printing Office.

Child, B. J. (1998). *Boarding school seasons: American Indian families, 1900–1940.* Lincoln: University of Nebraska Press.

Coleman, M. (1993). *American Indian children at school, 1850–1930.* Jackson: University Press of Mississippi.

Ellis, C. (1996). *To change them forever: Indian education at the Rainy Mountain Boarding School, 1893–1920.* Norman: University of Oklahoma Press.

Gilbert, M. (2005). The "Hopi followers": Chief Tawaquaptews and Hopi student advancement at Sherman Institute, 1906–1909. *Journal of American Indian Education, 44*(2), 1–23.

Horne, E. B., & McBeth, S. (1998). *Essie's story: The life and legacy of a Shoshone teacher.* Lincoln: University of Nebraska Press.

Hyer, S. (1990). *One house, one voice, one heart: Native American education at the Santa Fe Indian School.* Santa Fe: Museum of New Mexico Press.

Lomawaima, K. T. (1994). *They called it prairie light: The story of Chilocco Indian School.* Lincoln: University of Nebraska Press.

Meriam, L. (1928). *The problem of Indian administration.* Baltimore: Johns Hopkins University Press.

Web Sites

Indigenous Language Institute: http://www.indigenous-language.org

BOURNE, RANDOLPH S. (1886–1918)

On occasion, one encounters a person from the past whose ideas resonate strongly in the present. One such person is Randolph S. Bourne, whose ideas about immigration, education, and culture offer much to the field of bilingual education even though he did not address that subject directly.

Bourne was born in 1886, in Bloomfield, New Jersey, at a time when unrest and conflict existed between those deeply rooted in the United States since colonial times and large numbers of new immigrants entering the country through the port of New York.

Bourne's mother's side of the family was aristocratic. His father, son of a pastor, was an unsuccessful businessman, whom his mother ultimately left when Randolph was a child. Randolph, diminutive in size, had a number of physical deformities, including a double curvature of the spine brought about by disease and a facial disfiguration caused by a birth injury. He began to read at the age of 2 and was a precocious student. In 1902, he was admitted to Princeton but left for financial reasons. By 1909, he had saved up enough money to attend Columbia University, where his professors included John Dewey and Charles Beard. He was an editor for the *New Republic,* and 300 of his pieces were published in this and a number of other journals. Bourne died at the age of 32 from the flu during the influenza epidemic of 1918.

Bourne was an early critic of the "melting pot" theory and the assumption that immigrant speakers of other languages should be forcibly assimilated into an Anglo-Saxon tradition that is unquestioningly labeled

"American." He also pointed out that Anglo-Saxons were the nation's first immigrants and did not arrive expecting to assimilate into the indigenous culture of the people already living on the continent. Bourne viewed the American culture as a federation of cultures and the United States as a "trans-nation"—a weaving back and forth with other lands—rather than a nation. According to Bourne, newcomers were integral in the building of this "trans-nation," both literally and figuratively. He asked where the English and the country would be were it not for the large German, Scandinavian, and eastern European immigrant labor pool. He also called for a departure from Americanizing America through sentimentalizing its history.

Bourne contrasted the "melting pot" with what he called a "cooperation of cultures." He maintained that the notion of the former favored the nativist element in the United States at the time and the latter notion favored immigrants. The effect of the melting pot was to obliterate distinctive languages and cultures in favor of a homogenous mass. He spoke against Americanization that imitated European nationalism, which was not working well at the time in Europe. He called for an Americanism that was conscious of cultural difference and without universal like-mindedness or undesirable overdependence on imported political structures from immigrant homelands. He cited the Jewish people in the United States as an example of a group that had linguistic and cultural ties to a homeland, but not necessarily political ones as, in contrast with the Germans and the English, who reproduced obsolete versions of their homeland political systems in the new country.

Bourne viewed education as life itself and schools as learning communities. He cautioned against school systems as institutions that did little more than abolish illiteracy and prepare the more fortunate for college or a higher education that functioned more as a business enterprise than as a community of scholarship. Bourne also cautioned against the school as an institution that overshadowed other institutions or that towered above or oppressed the communities it served. For Bourne, the purpose of education and schooling was to cultivate imagination and creativity; when they serve another purpose to the exclusion of this one, they are not educating or schooling.

The political landscape since the early 20th century has changed enormously, but the field of bilingual and multicultural education is well served by remembering Bourne's contributions to the discourse about linguistic and cultural diversity, immigration, and education. His visionary ideas continue to influence our thinking about language and cultural difference and prompt reflection on educational policy involving teaching and learning in more than one language well into the 21st century.

Elsie M. Szecsy

See also Americanization and Its Critics; Americanization by Schooling; Assimilation; Melting-Pot Theory

Further Readings

Bourne, R. S. (1916, August). Education as living. *New Republic, 8,* 10–12.

Bourne, R. S. (1916). The Jew and trans-national America. *Menorah Journal, 2,* 277–284.

Bourne, R. S. (1916, July). Trans-national America. *Atlantic Monthly, 118,* 86–97.

Bourne, R. S. (1917). The idea of a university. *The Dial, 63,* 509–510.

Resek, C. (Ed.). (1999). *Randolph S. Bourne, war, and the intellectuals: Collected essays, 1915–1919.* Indianapolis, IN: Hackett.

BRAIN RESEARCH

The study of language and the brain has a long history, beginning with reports in the 1800s of language impairment *aphasia,* meaning a loss or impairment of the power to use or comprehend words, usually resulting from brain damage. These early cases demonstrated that damage to different areas of the left hemisphere of the brain produced different types of language deficit (see Figure 1). Lesions to the temporal lobe, specifically *Wernicke's area,* compromise the ability to understand language and the ability to speak clearly. Lesions to the frontal cortex, *Broca's area,* prevent a person from producing speech. For example, a person with a lesion in this area has the ability to understand language, but words are not properly formed, and speech is slow and slurred.

Initially, these correlations were established postmortem. However, with the advent of the computed tomography (CT) scan in the 1970s, it became possible to examine brain damage in living patients and to explore changes in brain structure as a patient recovered.

During the past 15 years, there has been a marked increase in the availability of brain imaging techniques to language scientists. These techniques have made it possible, for the first time, to study brain activity correlated with language learning and processing in unimpaired subjects and in some cases to examine this activity within a short time frame. Two of these techniques have been put to relatively greater use than others, and these will be the focus of this entry.

With respect to bilingualism, imaging studies permit systematic exploration of ideas stemming from earlier reports; these indicated that seizure disorders, stroke, and other injuries, along with localized electrical stimulation during brain surgery, can affect one language and leave others unaffected in a bilingual or multilingual individual. Further, imaging studies open a new window into the perennial questions of how the age of learning a second language (L2) and degree of achieved fluency influence the way the L2 is represented in the person's mind and brain. One must be cautious when interpreting results that explore the localization of language in bilinguals, since there is some variation (particularly in localization and lateralization) even across monolinguals. However, mounting evidence shows that second languages learned relatively late, or not learned fluently, are physically represented in somewhat different regions of the brain than the first language (L1) is and are processed in a different time frame.

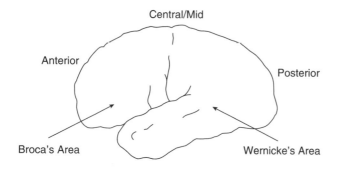

Figure 1   Left Hemisphere of Brain, With Approximate Locations of Broca's Area and Wernicke's Area

Magnetic Resonance Imaging (MRI)

The first imaging technique discussed here is functional magnetic resonance imaging. The general technique of magnetic resonance imaging (MRI) surrounds a region of the body with a high-intensity magnetic field and beams radio waves through it, creating high-resolution topographic images of tissue. Functional MRI measures changes in the metabolic activity (including blood flow and oxygenation) of specific portions of the brain during a specified activity, such as language use. Functional MRI is the technique of choice when the critical issue is localization of function within the brain; it can discriminate between small regions less than a millimeter apart in the brain. The temporal resolution of functional MRI is not as great as with event-related potentials (ERP), described below, restricting the range of questions that can be asked about the time course of information retrieval and processing. Functional MRI can produce a new image of the brain and the changes in it once every second.

In a classic study by Karl Kim, Joy Hirsch, and colleagues, results showed that there is an anatomical difference between subjects who became bilingual at an early and a late age in one of the two brain regions classically associated with language. In a silent recitation task, both groups showed activity of the same region of Wernicke's area in both languages. However, late bilinguals showed activation of different, adjacent, parts of Broca's area, depending on which of their two languages they used. Early bilinguals showed no such spatial separation. The authors suggest that Broca's area, implicated in the production and control of speech, may represent the speech properties of both languages in an early bilingual in a combined fashion. However, in a late though very fluent bilingual subject, the representation of L1 in Broca's area may be fixed and unchangeable, forcing speech information for L2 to be represented in a different anatomical position. Various possibilities exist to explain this occurrence. For example, it might be that there are physical aspects to the well-known critical period effect: Perhaps one portion of Broca's area is informationally frozen at some age-determined developmental stage. Alternatively, it could be that the mode of learning for a late bilingual—explicit instruction in a formal setting—influences the way speech information is structurally encoded. Since Wernicke's area is associated with more abstract aspects of language, including planning, semantic organization, and overall comprehension, it might not be subject to these influencing factors.

Event-Related Potentials (ERP)

The second imaging technique is based on electroencephalogram (EEG) recordings of brain activity, measured at various scalp locations. Language scientists have used this technique to determine brainwave responses to language stimuli; these responses are averaged across language stimuli (e.g., a set of sentences of one type versus a set of sentences of another type) and also averaged over a number of participants. Electrical activity may be tracked over the course of a sentence, word by word, as the sentence unfolds. The resulting electrical fluctuations are referred to as *event-related potentials* (ERPs): brainwave responses that are tied to stimulus events. ERP recordings are typically described in terms of electrode site on the scalp, polarity (negative versus positive fluctuations in the electrical charge), and timing with respect to a stimulus. Overall, ERP has been the technique of choice when the focus of the research question has been on issues of timing and functional MRI has been used to examine localization of function.

Within the ERP literature on language comprehension in monolinguals, a number of brainwave patterns or components have been identified. Next, we discuss three of these, in order of the timing of their appearance with respect to a stimulus, and provide an interpretation of each (though different interpretations have been offered in the literature and the descriptions here are certainly not uncontroversial).

One component is a *left-anterior negativity* (LAN): a negative wave at anterior electrode sites in the left hemisphere. In an early study, Helen Neville and colleagues reported left-anterior negativity as early as 125 milliseconds, after the point where a sentence became ungrammatical, for example, the underlined word in (1b) compared with the same word in (1a):

(1a) The scientist criticized Max's proof *of* the
       theorem.

(1b) The scientist criticized Max's *of* proof the
       theorem.

Left-anterior negativity has also been observed within the 300- to 500-millisecond window. Both the earlier and later variants of this effect appear to be associated with ungrammaticality.

Another component, reported by Marta Kutas, Steven Hillyard, and others, is called the "N400": a relatively negative wave that peaks approximately 400 milliseconds after the presentation of a stimulus. This component appears bilaterally (both hemispheres) over more mid- and posterior sites and correlates with a difficulty integrating the meaning of a word into that of its sentence. In the initial report, Kutas and Hillyard compared ERP responses with the final word (italicized) in sentences like the following:

(2a) He spread the warm bread with *jam.*

(2b) He spread the warm bread with *socks.*

A third component is the "P600," a relatively positive wave at 600 milliseconds poststimulus onset, with a broad distribution (bilateral, mid-, and posterior sites). This has been characterized as reflecting comprehension revision processes following a disruption of sentence form (or syntax), as in (1b).

An interesting and natural extension of this research is to test people in their L2s to determine whether or not they show the same brainwave patterns. At this juncture, it is important to address two critical distinctions. One is the distinction between (a) knowledge of a language, including vocabulary and grammatical rules, and (b) the comprehension of sentences as they unfold temporally. It is quite possible to know about grammatical rules and at the same time not be able to apply them within the short time frame required by spoken language. Likewise, one may know many words in a L2 but not be able to retrieve their meaning or integrate them within the few seconds it takes for a sentence to be presented.

A second distinction has to do with the type of participant tested, whether this person is (a) an early bilingual, someone who grew up with two languages and uses them on a daily basis, or (b) a late bilingual, someone who learned the language after puberty and is more or less fluent. Both of the brain imaging techniques described here have been used to examine early and late bilinguals. But because of the properties of these two imaging techniques, the ERP technology has been used primarily to test language comprehension processes, rather than knowledge per se, and functional MRI has been used to examine the localization of the two languages in the brain. ERP findings for comprehension of a second or nondominant language are described in terms of the type-of-sentence anomaly.

In terms of the semantic aspects, the N400 effect, which correlates with semantic anomaly or integration difficulty, has been observed in second-language learners. This wave peaks earlier for monolinguals and bilinguals presented with their dominant language than it does for bilinguals in their nondominant language. This suggests that comprehension of a second (non-dominant) language may be less efficient, or less automatic, than the processing of a first/dominant language. One would expect this of novice learners, but this appears to be true even of highly proficient users of a second language.

Referring to the syntactic aspects, a number of investigators have found that ungrammaticality produces no very early effect (the N125), even in people who started learning an L2 before the age of 3. The later LAN has been observed, although not always with the same scalp distribution. The P600 effect, indicative of sentence revision, or reanalysis, has been reported for the nondominant language in people who acquired the L2 before puberty.

Overall, the ERP findings suggest that syntactic processing of a second (nondominant) language may not be carried out in the same way as an L1. Semantic processing, on the other hand, may operate similarly in a dominant and nondominant language, but simply be less efficient.

Janet L. Nicol and Andy Barss

See also Critical Period Hypothesis; Language Acquisition Device; Languages, Learned or Acquired; Learning a Language, Best Age; Linguistics, an Overview

Further Readings

Ardal, S., Donald, M. W., Meuter, R., Muldrew, S., & Luce, M. (1990). Brain responses to semantic incongruity in bilinguals. *Brain and Language, 39,* 187–205.

Golestani, N., Alario, F.-X., Meriaux, S., Le Bihan, D., Dehaene, S., & Pallier, C. (2006). Syntax production in bilinguals. *Neuropsychologia, 44,* 1029–1040.

Hahne, A., & Friederici, A. D. (2001). Processing a second language: Late learners' comprehension mechanisms as revealed by event-related brain potentials. *Bilingualism: Language and Cognition, 4,* 123–141.

Kim, K., Relkin, N., Lee, K.-M., & Hirsch, J. (1997). Distinct cortical areas associated with native and second languages. *Nature, 388,* 171–174.

Kluender, R., & Kutas, M. (1993). Bridging the gap: Evidence from ERPs on the processing of unbounded dependencies. *Journal of Cognitive Neuroscience, 5,* 196–214.

Kutas, M., & Hillyard, S. A. (1980). Reading senseless sentences: Brain potentials reflect semantic incongruity. *Science, 207,* 203–205.

Moreno, E. M., & Kutas, M. (2005). Processing semantic anomalies in two languages: An electrophysiological exploration in both languages of Spanish-English bilinguals. *Cognitive Brain Research, 22,* 205–220.

Neville, H. J., Nicol, J. L., Barss, A., Forster, K. I., & Garrett, M. F. (1991). Syntactically based sentence processing classes: Evidence from event-related brain potentials. *Journal of Cognitive Neuroscience, 3,* 151–165.

Weber-Fox, C., & Neville, H. (1996). Maturational constraints on functional specializations for language processing: ERP and behavioral evidence in bilingual speakers. *Journal of Cognitive Neuroscience, 8,* 231–256.

CAL

See CENTER FOR APPLIED LINGUISTICS, INITIAL FOCUS; CENTER FOR APPLIED LINGUISTICS, RECENT FOCUS

CALIFORNIA PROPOSITION 227

See PROPOSITION 227 (CALIFORNIA)

CANADIAN AND U.S. LANGUAGE POLICIES

In the protracted debate about how best to create a nation of fluent English speakers in the United States, Canada serves both as a model of successful language immersion programs and as a cautionary tale with respect to the social, political, and economic dynamics that many Americans associate with the Canadian language strife in Québec. Although the histories of both Canada and the United States testify to the many languages of the native inhabitants of these lands, as well as to the multiple and varied languages of those who immigrated to these countries, the linguistic philosophy and policies of these nations have diverged significantly from the beginning.

According to the Canada Public Service Agency, prior to the Official Languages Act of 1969, English served as the official language of the Canadian government, the economy, and the educational system. Passage of the act identified English and French as the nation's two official languages and required all federal institutions to serve the public in the official language of their choice. Another significant piece of national language legislation was the 1982 Charter of Rights and Freedoms, which reaffirmed the equality of English and French with respect to their use in the Canadian Parliament and Government. In 1988, the Official Languages Act was revised to provide additional support for the language guarantees articulated in the Charter. That same year, the Canadian government adopted the Official Languages Regulations, Communications With and Services to the Public, which specified the situations in which federal offices were required to provide services in both official languages to Canadian citizens.

At the beginning of the new century, in January 2001, the Speech from the Throne, delivered by the Right Honourable Adrienne Clarkson, Governor General of Canada, affirmed the country's commitment to linguistic duality. Three months later, the Canadian prime minister, the Right Honourable Jean Chrétien, again called attention to the need for coordinated language policies and emphasized the importance of protecting the dual-language heritage of the nation. According to a Government of Canada Web site, in September 2002, Governor General Clarkson's Speech from the Throne affirmed that "linguistic duality is at the heart of our collective identity." Consistent with the tenets of this speech, the 2003 Action Plan for Official Languages was organized around three tenets: (1) Linguistic duality is part of our heritage, (2) linguistic duality is an asset for our future, and (3) the federal policy on official languages needs to be enhanced. The third revision of the Official Languages Act occurred in 2005. It further clarified the rights and obligations stipulated in the 1982 Charter of Rights and Freedoms. While current policies confirm the equality of French and English as the official governmental languages of Canada and acknowledge French as the official provincial language of Québec, these policies also proclaim the right of all citizens to receive education, government, and health services in the official language of their choice.

Whereas the language legislation in Canada has been quite consistent with respect to the establishment and protection of both English and French as the official national languages, James Crawford asserts that American efforts have focused largely on the state-level prohibition of particular languages. Examples include California's early revision of its state constitution in 1879, for the purposes of eliminating Spanish language rights and the various state bans on the public use of the German language during World War I. All attempts to mandate English as the sole official language of the United States have so far failed. These include a bill attempting to designate "American" as the national language in 1923 and the English Language Constitutional Amendment proposed in 1981 by the late Senator S. I. Hayakawa. Today, almost every new Congress is faced with at least one attempt to revisit the subject. Frustrated by the failure of these legislative proposals, members of the English-only movement have formed organizations to lobby more strongly for them. They have focused their attention on making English the official language of government agencies. A bill of this sort was approved by the House of Representatives in 1996 but was rejected by the Senate.

Much of the advocacy for designating English as the official language has now turned to the states. U.S. English, Inc., attests that some 30 states have designated English as their official language, with almost half of this legislation being enacted after 1990.

Although the operant language policies in the two neighboring countries are vastly different, it should be acknowledged that there are equally different contexts with respect to the historical, social, political, and economic circumstances that frame the language policy dynamics. Understanding these differences helps shed light on the U.S. debate about how best to transform non-English-speaking populations into fluent English speakers who are willing to abandon their respective heritage languages. According to John Petrovic, three of the differences between these countries are especially relevant to the language debate. First, the United States has traditionally promoted the idea of a single national identity, while Canada has maintained two nations with distinct cultures, religions, and languages from the outset. This dual national identity has helped preserve the use of French as an important language even though it predominates in only one province, albeit the largest in population. In addition, the language demographic distribution in Canada has remained fairly stable over the years, with the majority of the French-speaking population residing in Québec province. This shared heritage has resulted in a unified, although geographically separate, sense of purpose; this is uncommon in the United States, given not only the variety of native languages spoken by immigrant students but also the number of different cultural backgrounds represented in the early history of the country. For example, while the land purchased from France, known as the Louisiana Territory, was huge, it was sparsely populated and few French speakers lived outside of the city of New Orleans. Similarly, whereas half of Mexico was annexed by the United States in 1848, that vast expanse was also sparsely populated by Spanish speakers.

Second, in Canada, French speakers rarely experience a language shift, continuing to use their native language throughout life. Unlike the United States, where English is the chief language of communication and second-generation immigrants quickly lose their native-language skills, French-speaking Canadians enjoy both social and economic support for their native language. In the province of Québec, all official business is conducted in French. Schools and universities offer a complete education in both languages, sometimes in the same institution and sometimes in separate ones. As a consequence, throughout Canada, individuals who are fluent in both French and English are at an advantage in both the economic and political arenas.

This means, among other things, that in Canada, bilingualism pays off; in the United States, the rewards for bilingualism are fewer and far less tangible. Petrovic points out that in contrast to the French language in Canada, the Spanish language is not necessarily a pathway to higher-paying jobs in the United States. In fact, higher-paying positions are not usually associated with speaking Spanish, since many native Spanish speakers are employed in the service, agricultural, and construction industries. Unlike their U.S. counterparts, Canadians who speak French are in demand for management and other upper-level positions.

Despite these differences, much of the American discussion about how best to produce fluent English speakers has focused on language immersion programs in Canada, which are targeted mainly to minority English speakers in the province of Québec. Research by Adel Safty points out, however, that this comparison is problematic for several reasons: (a) the majority of the English-speaking children participating in these language immersion programs are middle-class children who are not at risk of school failure; and (b) the proportion of time in which French is the language of instruction declines throughout the first few years of the immersion program, with the students receiving 50% of their instruction in English by fifth grade, increasing to 80% at the secondary level. Further, although English-speaking children are considered a language minority in Québec, they are not considered so at the national level, where English enjoys the same status as French in the Canadian government.

Safty contends that in contrast to Québec, language immersion programs in the United States have tended to provide the majority of instruction in English, for the purposes of enabling predominantly minority children to master English as a means of cultural assimilation, while ignoring the development of the non-English-speaker's home language. Perhaps most important, this instruction occurs within a U.S. national context in which unaccented spoken English is strongly equated with American patriotism. Within this context, multilingualism is viewed neither as an individual nor a societal asset. This attitude, increasingly prevalent in recent years, bears a remarkable resemblance to that expressed in 1926 by President Theodore Roosevelt:

> We have room for but one language here, and that is the English language, for we intend to see that the crucible turns our people out as Americans, of American nationality, and not as dwellers in a polyglot boarding house.

While such a restrictive view of linguistic democracy is not held by all Americans, in the absence of a federal policy supportive of language diversity, grassroots groups continue to organize their efforts toward establishing English as the sole official language of the U.S. government. A very different view of language diversity is articulated in the 2003 Canadian Action Plan for Official Languages, as found on the government of Canada Web site: "Canada must build on its linguistic duality and the international nature of its two official languages more than ever. That gives it a substantial competitive edge."

As both Canada and the United States continue to experience the increased migration of linguistically diverse groups, the attitudes and beliefs about the relative value of bilingualism, and increasingly that of multilingualism, will play an important role. They will not only shape each country's internal political/social/economic environment but will also determine the extent to which its citizens are equipped with the linguistic skills they need to succeed in a global, increasingly competitive, and linguistically diverse environment.

Betty M. Merchant and Michaela Steele

See also Additive and Subtractive Programs; Heritage Language Education; Language Education Policy in Global Perspective; Maintenance Policy Denied; St. Lambert Immersion Study; U.S. Bilingual Education Viewed From Abroad

Further Readings

Canadian Public Service Agency. (2006). *Annual report on official languages 2005–06.* Retrieved October 27, 2007, from http://www.psagency-agencefp.gc.ca/reports-rapports/ol-lo/arol-ralo05-06_e.asp

Crawford, J. (1997). *Issues in U.S. language policy: The official English question.* Retrieved from http://ourworld.compuserve.com/homepages/jwcrawford/question.htm

Government of Canada. (2002, September). *Speech from the throne.* Retrieved October 27, 2007, from http://www.gnb.ca/cnb/promos/throne-2002/index-e.asp

Government of Canada. (2003). *Action plan for official languages.* Available from http://www.pco-bcp.gc.ca/olo/index.asp?lang=eng&page=action

Petrovic, J. (1997). Balkanization, bilingualism, and comparison of language situations at home and abroad. *Bilingual Research Journal, 21,* 233–327.

Roosevelt, T. (1926). *The works of Theodore Roosevelt* (Vol. 24, Memorial ed.). New York: Scribner's.

Safty, A. (1992). French immersion as bilingual education: New inquiry directions. *Canadian Ethnic Studies, 1*(2), 60–76.

Web Sites

U.S. English, Inc.: http://www.us-english.org/inc

CANADIAN BILINGUAL STUDY

See ST. LAMBERT IMMERSION STUDY

CÁRDENAS, JOSÉ A. (1930–)

A professional educator since 1950, José A. Cárdenas has never been a person of ordinary consequence. He has served as superintendent of an urban school district, chair of the education department at an institution of higher education, director of a research and development center, and at all levels of the educational professional hierarchy.

Born in Laredo, Texas, on October 16, 1930, Cárdenas earned an EdD from the University of Texas at Austin (1966), an MEd from Our Lady of the Lake University in San Antonio (1955), and a BA from the University of Texas at Austin (1950). He also served in the U.S. Army infantry as a radio operation instructor from 1951 to 1953.

When Cárdenas was named in 1955 as vice principal of Edgewood High School in San Antonio, he became the first Hispanic administrator serving the district. In 1969, he was appointed superintendent of the Edgewood School District, thus becoming the first Hispanic school superintendent in the city of San Antonio and Bexar County. He established the first districtwide, non–Head Start early childhood education program for all 3-, 4- and 5-year-old children in that district. From 1961 to 1967, Cárdenas served as associate professor and chair of the Department of Education at St. Mary's University in San Antonio. In the late 1960s, he directed research on migrant education at the Southwest Educational Development Laboratory. And, later, in 1990 to 1991, he was a visiting professor at the University of Texas at San Antonio in educational leadership. He served as a guest lecturer, consultant, and conference participant at more than 70 colleges and universities throughout the country.

As a classroom teacher, Cárdenas worked in multicultural settings with very limited resources. Later, as a school superintendent, he recognized the systemic barriers to providing the excellent education he envisioned. Although most of his peers apparently saw no such problem or felt the injustices to children were unsolvable, Cárdenas dedicated his life's work to making his vision a reality.

In 1973, Cárdenas founded the Intercultural Development Research Association (IDRA), a nonprofit research and public education organization dedicated to creating schools that work for all children. Today, IDRA continues its work as a nationally recognized research, policy, and training and technical assistance organization in bilingual and multicultural education, school finance equity, early childhood education, community involvement programs, and the design of culturally responsive technology-infused instructional programs.

After testifying in the landmark *Lau v. Nichols* (1974) case, Cárdenas assisted in the development of the "*Lau* Remedies" by the Office for Civil Rights. This document contained the first guidance provided by the Office for Civil Rights of the U.S. Department of Education for schools serving language minority populations. Its purpose was to help school districts come into compliance with the Supreme Court decision and Title VI of the Civil Rights Act of 1964.

Throughout his 5-decade career, Cárdenas was a key leader in developing litigation strategy and serving as an expert witness in more than 70 important court cases focused on services to minority and language minority students, such as *Keyes v. School District No. 1, Denver* (1973), and *Castañeda v. Pickard* (1981). He was one of the key people involved with Senator Ralph Yarborough in helping create and fund federal legislation for children who were limited English proficient: Title VII of the Elementary and Secondary Education Act.

Cárdenas was instrumental in developing the bilingual-education-related strategies that included the litigation known as the *United States v. Texas* (1970), which resulted in a court order leading to the foundation for SB 477, the Texas Bilingual Education Act. His role in the formation of that law, which is still in effect today, led to its being considered the strongest state bilingual education law in the country. In the mid-1970s, Cárdenas led a research effort to examine the funding levels needed for effective implementation of bilingual education, finding that most bilingual education programs suffer from grossly inadequate funding.

Numerous state and national organizations have honored Cárdenas for his commitment and contributions.

He was the U.S. commissioner for the International Year of the Child in 1978 and was a Special National Award recipient of the Human Rights Award given by the National Education Association in 1972. He was cited as Educator of the Year in 1980 by the Texas Association for Bilingual Education. He received the National Association for Bilingual Education Special Recognition Award in 1982 and was honored as a National Association for Bilingual Education (NABE) Texas Pioneer in Bilingual Education in 1993.

Cárdenas has authored several books, including *Multicultural Education: A Generation of Advocacy,* a historical overview of the most significant issues in multicultural education. In *Texas School Finance Reform: An IDRA Perspective,* Cárdenas documents the 28-year history of school finance in Texas. His most recent book, *My Spanish-Speaking Left Foot,* depicts the cultural influence of Mexico and the Spanish-speaking world for a Mexican American. His writings, recollections, and impressions are archived in the Benson Latin American Collection at the University of Texas at Austin.

María Robledo Montecel

See also Federal Court Decisions and Legislation; *Lau v. Nichols,* the Ruling; Multicultural Education, Training, and Advocacy (META); Texas Legislation (HB 103 and SB 121)

Further Readings

Cárdenas, J. A. (1995). *Multicultural education: A generation of advocacy.* Boston: Simon & Schuster.
Cárdenas, J. A. (1997). *Texas school finance reform: An IDRA perspective.* San Antonio, TX: Intercultural Development Research Association.
Castañeda v. Pickard, 648 F. 2d 989 (1981).
Keyes v. School District No. 1, Denver, CO, 413 U.S. 189 (1973).
Lau v. Nichols, 414 U.S. 563 (1974).
United States v. Texas, 321 F. Supp. 1043 (E.D. Tex. 1970).

CASTAÑEDA THREE-PART TEST

In the historic Supreme Court case of *Lau v. Nichols,* decided in 1974, a group of non-English-speaking students and parents of Chinese ancestry filed a class action suit against the San Francisco Unified School District (SFUSD), claiming that they had been denied a meaningful opportunity to participate in the public educational program in violation of Title VI of the Civil Rights Act of 1964 and the Fourteenth Amendment. Title VI banned discrimination based on race, color, or national origin in any program receiving federal financial assistance. On appeal, the U.S. Supreme Court decided in favor of the plaintiffs:

> Basic English skills are at the very core of what these public schools teach. Imposition of a requirement that, before a child can effectively participate in the educational program, he must already have acquired those basic skills is to make a mockery of public education. We know that those who do not understand English are certain to find their classroom experiences wholly incomprehensible and in no way meaningful. (*Lau v. Nichols,* 1974)

The ruling did not specify any specific remedy because no specific remedy had been requested by the plaintiffs. The court noted that "no remedy is urged upon us."

As a result of the *Lau v. Nichols* decision, Congress took various actions. They passed the Equal Educational Opportunity Act (EEOA) in 1974, which prohibits denial of equal access and deliberate segregation and requires districts to take actions to remedy language barriers. By codifying the language of the *Lau* decision into law, Congress ensured that the ruling of the court would endure. In addition, the legislators passed amendments to the Bilingual Education Act, which provided federal funding for bilingual programs at a higher level than before. In 1975, the Office of Civil Rights (OCR) issued the "*Lau* Remedies," which specified procedures for identifying limited-English-proficient (LEP) students, provided guidelines for determining which type of program was needed to meet students' needs, set program exit guidelines (also known as *reclassification*), and established standards for teachers in terms of the profile and training they should have. The *Lau* Remedies were used for several years by the OCR of the U.S. Department of Education in conducting *Lau* compliance reviews. But the remedies were an administrative solution that needed more power behind them.

Castañeda v. Pickard

An important complement to the *Lau* decision came in 1981 in the form of yet another court case, *Castañeda v. Pickard.* In that case, the plaintiffs charged a school district in Raymondville, Texas, with discrimination. They claimed that the district used ability grouping in a way that segregated and created learning obstacles for LEP students. They also said that the hiring of Mexican American faculty and administrators was not representative of the population in the district (close to 90% Mexican American). The district was accused, in addition, of not providing students with adequate bilingual education to overcome the linguistic barriers that prevented them from fully benefiting from the regular instructional program. Finally, the plaintiffs claimed that the use of standardized tests in English to measure progress was not an appropriate way to demonstrate academic growth. The court ruled that the district should not mix the concept of intelligence with language abilities and should not use "low" as a designator of English proficiency. The court held that ability grouping was beneficial sometimes and that it was not illegal per se. It also ruled that a focus on the English language in the early years of schooling was appropriate and that there were appropriate measures, such as learning centers, to assist students with academic matters in the district. The school district was asked to look at testing procedures and hiring practices. An interesting point about this case is that the plaintiffs sued for violation of both Title VI and the EEOA, which had codified *Lau.*

The appellate court in *Castañeda* took the step that had not been taken in *Lau:* to describe in broad terms the qualities of an appropriate program that would satisfy *Lau,* Title VI of the Civil Rights Act of 1964, and the EEOA. To facilitate decisions regarding appropriateness in the future, the Fifth Circuit Court ruled that districts must apply a three-pronged test:

1. The instructional program implemented must be based on sound theory.

2. The program should be implemented with appropriate practices, staffing, and resources.

3. There should be evaluation and evidence of effectiveness.

Implicit here is the additional point that if the program is not effective, the district should be willing and able to modify it. The court then proceeded to use its own three-part test to assess the claims of the plaintiffs in *Castañeda v. Pickard.* It ruled that the district passed Test #1. In terms of Test #2, it determined that the curriculum was fair and that the assistance to students was provided (it could be provided either simultaneously with their language program or after), but the court was concerned with staffing based on the fact that teachers had very limited Spanish levels and training in bilingual methodology. The court felt that limitations in teachers could provoke limitations in terms of program effectiveness. The district was ordered to examine its hiring practices to be sure that they were not discriminatory and to remedy them if they were. The court asked for teachers' teaching abilities to be improved. Also, related to Test #2, the court found that the district inappropriately used English language standardized tests, claiming that students should be tested in their primary or home languages. As a result of this important court case and the realization by the court that some sort of guideline was needed, the three-part test was born and subsequently adopted by OCR for use nationwide.

OCR's Interpretation of the Three-Part Test

First Prong

In the first prong of the three-part test, the program implemented by the school or district must be recognized as sound by some experts in the field or seen as a legitimate experimental strategy. This part of the test is somewhat difficult because one can usually find an expert somewhere who is willing to defend his or her theory. The courts have consistently held that they are not theoretical or curricular experts and that they must leave this judgment up to school districts to decide, which leaves the question of "soundness" up in the air. In a 1998 court case that challenged Proposition 227 in California, for example, it was determined that the approach, which allows students 1 year to achieve sufficient English to transfer into the regular instructional program, could be supported by at least one expert, although the attorneys involved with the case claimed that the majority of experts would not agree with that claim.

In the case of *Guadalupe Organization v. Tempe Elementary School District,* decided in 1972, it was determined that a maintenance bilingual program was not required in order to show "appropriate action to overcome language barriers that impede equal participation." Another case, *Teresa P. v. Berkeley Unified School District,* decided in 1989 in California, showed that credentialed teachers showed little difference in results from those without credentials. It was determined that students could be taught effectively by monolingual English teachers. The "soundness" of the program usually depends on which experts are consulted. In this regard, then, the first of the three-part tests remains somewhat unspecific.

Second Prong

In the second prong of the three-part test, programs and practices used by the district should be reasonably calculated to implement the theory effectively. This means ideally, but not always realistically, that the program must be staffed by teachers who understand both languages and who are able to select and use appropriate methods. The courts have made it clear that program effectiveness is diluted (and possibly leads to violation of Title VI, if teachers are not qualified). Districts should have appropriate selection and training procedures. Teachers need to have credentials or show evidence of working toward them. For example, in the case of *Serna v. Portales,* decided in 1974, a school district in New Mexico was charged with discrimination because it failed to hire Mexican American teachers or administrators and because students did not reach achievement levels attained by Anglo counterparts. The students were almost a full grade level behind another school; there were more dropouts; and the level of disparity in achievement levels increased as the students got older. It was determined that the district was violating Title VI. There should be both entrance and exit criteria for students involved in programs, leading eventually toward their meaningful participation in the English program. This means that students should be able to keep up with non-LEP peers, participate successfully in curriculum without simplified materials, and have retention and drop-out rates that are similar to non-LEP students. The program should have sufficient resources and materials.

In *Cintrón v. Brentwood Union Free School District,* decided in 1978, the issue involved was the reduction in bilingual staffing and, as a result, the proposal of an English as a Second Language (ESL) support center, which was found to be unacceptable by the courts. Districts must provide support despite resources available to them. In *Ríos v. Read,* decided in1978, in New York, a group of Puerto Rican students and their parents accused their district of employing teachers with a lack of language skills and methods and also mentioned a lack of textbooks. In *Keyes v. School District No. 1, Denver,* decided in 1983, in the Denver public schools, teachers were hired as bilingual teachers based on an interview and not on a test. Over the years, it has become clear that having a program that is based on sound theory is not enough if the resources to effectively implement that program are not present.

Third Prong

As part of the third prong, the program should succeed after a legitimate trial in producing results indicating that students' language barriers are actually being overcome based on goals the district has established or, alternatively, that participants overcome their language barriers sufficiently well and promptly to participate meaningfully in programs serving all other students. Attorney Peter Roos, who has worked on several relevant cases, suggests that a fourth part to the test is implicit: that the district adjust the program if it is not working effectively.

Monitoring Compliance

Who monitors compliance in terms of services to LEP students and their families, and how do they do it? The OCR of the U.S. Department of Education is the main monitoring agent. When there is reason to believe that the district may not be providing the right services, the OCR may step in and investigate and, then, based on their ruling, determine remedies that are required. The OCR bases their actions and decisions on what has been previously agreed upon in the Civil Rights Act of 1964, the OCR memorandums of 1970 and 1985, the *Lau* Remedies, and the 1991 Policy Update on Schools' Obligations Toward National Origin Minority Students With Limited-English Proficiency. The 1970 "May 25th Memorandum" and the procedures followed by OCR in its monitoring work are discussed in some detail in other entries in this encyclopedia.

The 1985 memorandum emphasized the following: Determining the need for an alternative language program and the adequacy of that program, a written compliance agreement is required only with a violation of Title VI; national origin minorities whose only language is English are not included in the requirements for service; and districts may use methods that have proven to be successful or are sound, providing a certain degree of flexibility.

The literature in this field contains both praise and criticism for the work of the OCR in compliance monitoring and recommendations. Some of the issues and implications concerning the use of the *Lau* remedies and the three-part test for compliance are as follows. One of the first issues involves defining "appropriate action." Another factor is the burden of proof placed on the plaintiff to show that the district does not meet the test. The debate regarding intentional versus non-intentional discrimination often arises and is linked to new interpretations by the U.S. Supreme Court of Title VI of the Civil Rights Act of 1964 that are still in flux. Other areas of difficulty are (a) numbers of students and their distribution by language, (b) availability of resources, (c) primary-language materials, (d) teacher qualifications, (e) ability to hire bilingual assistants, (f) involvement of parents, (g) pressures to teach English quickly, (h) academic content, (i) access to programs for gifted students, (j) misplacement in special education, (k) the demand to measure academic achievement using English standardized tests, and (1) legislation (such as Proposition 227 in California) or court rulings.

Kathryn Singh

See also Affirmative Steps to English; Civil Rights Act of 1964; *Lau v. Nichols,* Enforcement Documents; *Lau v. Nichols,* the Ruling; Office for Civil Rights, U.S. Department of Education

Further Readings

Castañeda v. Pickard, 648 F.2d 989 (5th Cir. 1981).

Cintrón v. Brentwood Union Free School District, 455 F. Supp. 57 (EDNY 1978).

Guadalupe Organization v. Tempe Elementary School District No. 3, No. CIV 71–435, Phoenix (D. Arizona, January 24, 1972).

Haas, E. (2005). The Equal Educational Opportunity Act 30 years later: Time to revisit "appropriate action" for assisting English language learners. *Journal of Law and Education, 34,* 361–388.

Keyes v. School District No.1, Denver, CO, 576 F. Supp. 503 (D. Colorado, 1983).

Lau v. Nichols, 414 U.S. 563 (1974).

Office for Civil Rights. (1970, May 25). *Memorandum: Identification of discrimination and denial of services on the basis of national origin,* 35 F. Reg. 11, 595. Retrieved February 1, 2008, from http://www.ed.gov/about/offices/list/ocr/docs/lau1970.html

Office for Civil Rights. (1985, December 3). *Memorandum: The Office for Civil Rights' Title VI language minority compliance procedures.* Retrieved February 1, 2008, from http://www.ed.gov/about/offices/list/ocr/docs/lau1990_and_1985.html

Office for Civil Rights. (1991, September 27). *Memorandum: Policy update on schools' obligations toward national origin minority students with limited-English proficiency (LEP students).* Retrieved February 1, 2008, from http://www.ed.gov/about/offices/list/ocr/docs/lau1991.html

Ríos v. Read, 480 F. Supp. (1978).

Roos, P. (2007). Getting back on the horse: Reviving bilingual education key issues for policy makers. *International Multilingual Research Journal, 1*(1), 15–31.

Serna v. Portales Municipal Schools, 499 F.2d 1147 (10th Cir. 1974).

Valeria G. v. Wilson, 12 F. Supp.2d 1007 (N.D. Cal. 1998).

CASTRO FEINBERG, ROSA (1939–)

Rosa Castro Feinberg, born on January 1, 1939, in New York City, has been a lifelong advocate for children, immigrants, and minority language learners in the United States. Upon election in 1986 to the Dade County, Florida, school board, she became the first Hispanic woman to be elected to a countywide office in that jurisdiction and served on the board with distinction for 10 years.

Castro Feinberg earned her MSc degree in curriculum and supervision from Florida State University and her PhD in Educational Administration from the University of Miami. She began her career as a language teacher. While teaching English as a Second Language (ESL) at the junior high school level and Spanish-S (Spanish for Spanish speakers), she secured donated equipment and conducted a field trial that resulted in the district's purchase of its first wireless language laboratory for English language learners. As a graduate student at the University of Miami, Castro Feinberg had collected and analyzed data that led the school system to initiate programs for English language learners whose first language was Haitian Creole.

Castro Feinberg later served as education chairperson for the Spanish American League Against Discrimination (SALAD), where she wrote a primer for advocates that led to the mobilization of resistance to restrictionist language legislation and the creation of the national English Plus Clearinghouse.

As the director of the University of Miami Lau Center, acting as third-party adviser at the request of both the State Education Agency and a community coalition led by the Multicultural Education Training Associates (META), Castro Feinberg was influential in bringing about statewide changes in legislation and regulations protecting the rights of all language minority students in Florida to learn English and other subjects. She also promoted the establishment of the principle that those who teach any subject to English language learners, in any language, must be appropriately prepared and credentialed for that assignment.

As a Dade County School Board Member, Castro Feinberg provided leadership resulting in expansion of foreign, heritage language, and biliteracy education, benefiting over 300,000 students in the country's fourth-largest school district. She also helped eliminate corporal punishment in Miami-Dade Schools and helped bring about single-member districting in school board elections, thereby ensuring that Hispanics would serve on the board. For 8 of the 10 years that Castro Feinberg served on the Dade County School Board, she was the only Hispanic member.

As a member of Florida's Postsecondary Education Planning Commission, Castro Feinberg was instrumental in the commission's authorization of a Pharmacy School at Florida Agricultural and Mechanical University, the state's historically Black university. As a faculty member at Florida International University (FIU), Castro Feinberg organized a statewide electronic mailing list for second-language educators under the auspices of the Sunshine State Teachers of English to Speakers of Other Languages (TESOL) Advocacy Committee. She has published numerous articles, reports, and monographs on bilingual education and related areas of administration and teacher training and has given numerous invited testimonies at government public hearings on language and education issues.

After her retirement in 2002, the United Faculty of Florida/Florida International University Chapter (UFF/FIU) Executive Committee approved Castro Feinberg's proposal for sponsorship of an information and referral service for immigrants and other newcomers. The West Dade Regional Library agreed to collaborate with the project as the service site and with public information support. With 50,000 immigrants entering Miami-Dade County every year, its population is among the most diverse in the nation, and the city of Miami has the highest percentage of immigrants of any large city worldwide. The first goal of this project is to serve the community by providing information to recent arrivals about existing resources and to tap FIU faculty expertise for help with problems for which there is no ready solution. The service is a volunteer operation, requiring no funds for its continuation.

Rosa Castro Feinberg's ongoing research interests include the formation and development of bilingual universities in areas such as South Florida and immigrant access to adequate health care.

Ana Roca

See also Immigration and Language Policy; Multicultural Education, Training, and Advocacy (META); Teacher Preparation, Then and Now

Further Readings

Castro Feinberg, R. (2002). *Bilingual education: A reference handbook.* Santa Barbara, CA: ABC-CLIO.

CENTER FOR APPLIED LINGUISTICS, INITIAL FOCUS

The Center for Applied Linguistics (CAL) was established in Washington, D.C., in 1959, at the height of the cold war, in response to the recognized need for a national center for information on languages, language resources, and applied linguistics. With support from the Ford Foundation, CAL was originally created under the aegis of the Modern Language Association. Over time, its sphere of activities grew to worldwide dimensions, and it was decided in 1965 to make it an independent organization. For its founders and staff, the center represented the belief that a better understanding of language through linguistics can contribute to making this a better and more humane world.

Early Years

The founding director of CAL, Charles Ferguson, was an intellectual leader in the emerging field of sociolinguistics. The early years of the center focused heavily on the teaching of foreign languages in the United

States and the teaching of English internationally, as well as on language planning issues in the use of vernacular languages for education in newly decolonized nations. The civil rights movement of the late 1960s saw CAL take the lead in research on African American Vernacular English and on the significance of language differences in schools undergoing desegregation.

CAL for many years sponsored the National Advisory Council on Teaching English as a Foreign Language (NACTEFL), a group of leaders in the field who met annually to hear reports on the work of various federal agencies involved in the teaching of English and to make policy recommendations in response. A NACTEFL recommendation for a survey of English teaching in the government's Bureau of Indian Affairs (BIA) schools led to a planning conference for the first Navajo bilingual kindergarten program in BIA schools beginning in 1969. A measure of the impact of CAL on BIA language education policy is that of 28 recommendations made to the bureau from 1967 to 1969, 75% were adopted.

An early contribution to bilingual education came through a commission from the ERIC Clearinghouse for Languages and Linguistics, then housed at CAL, to Muriel R. Saville and Rudolph C. Troike to prepare a *Handbook for Bilingual Education* (1971), which became a popular text in bilingual teacher preparation programs. With the appointment of Troike as director/president of CAL in 1972, bilingual education and minority language issues in the United States became CAL's top priority and remained so throughout his tenure to 1977. During this period, a number of new staff members were added to CAL to head up the initiatives in bilingual education. In addition, the Board of Trustees was diversified to include members familiar with minority language issues. These new members included prominent professionals in that field: Charlotte Brooks. Courtney Cazden, Arnulfo Oliveira, Christina Bratt Paulston, Dillon Platero, and Oscar García-Rivera.

Setting Guidelines for Bilingual Education

When Senator Edward Kennedy's (D-Mass.) staff began planning for the 1974 reauthorization of the Bilingual Education Act of 1968 (Title VII, Elementary and Secondary Education Act), CAL brought together a group of leaders in the field to define a set of priorities for needed changes and new initiatives, most of which were adopted in the final legislation. In particular, these included funding for teacher training programs and PhD programs, and support for research and information dissemination activities.

Concerned that the availability of federal funds would not guarantee high-quality programs of teacher education because some institutions simply relabeled existing courses or program titles to qualify for funds, and with an obvious lack of criteria for judging the adequacy of applications, CAL convened a working group of experts, including state and large city bilingual program directors, to develop a set of guidelines for the certification of teachers in bilingual education programs. These guidelines, which were published and widely disseminated by CAL, became the basis for certification requirements in a number of states. In addition, the guidelines were subsequently adopted in large part by the U.S. Office of Bilingual Education.

CAL drew on its long-established international connections to organize the First Inter-American Conference on Bilingual Education. This event was held in Mexico City under cosponsorship of the Secretaría de Educación Pública. The conference was attended by representatives of eight countries, and the proceedings were published by CAL.

The work of CAL with American Indian groups also expanded considerably during this period with the creation of an Indian Education Program division, headed by William Leap. One activity was providing logistic support for the annual Native American Bilingual Education Conference (NAIBEC). Recognizing the unique linguistic and pedagogical needs of bilingual programs for Native Americans, CAL in 1973 worked with the BIA to convene leading specialists, including representatives from a number of American Indian groups, to formulate suggested language policy guidelines for American Indian tribes. CAL also secured support and collaborated with the University of Colorado for a series of summer institutes to provide advanced training for teachers in Indian bilingual programs. In addition, CAL provided financial support to launch the *Navajo Language Review,* edited by Paul Platero.

The year 1974 was a landmark year for bilingual education, due in part, to the U.S. Supreme Court *Lau v. Nichols* decision, which found that the San Francisco schools were failing to offer a meaningful education to English language learners by providing them the same materials and curricula as native

English speakers. The San Francisco Unified School District SFUSD requested that the Center for Applied Linguistics send a team to work with the schools and a community advisory committee to develop a master plan to respond to the decision. Although the Supreme Court had avoided prescribing a specific remedy, CAL's plan, which adopted bilingual education as the most appropriate response, was accepted by the appellate court and indirectly influenced the interpretation of the *Lau* decision by the Office for Civil Rights as requiring bilingual education under certain circumstances. Although this requirement proved controversial, CAL played a central role in the evolution of official federal policy in this arena.

Concerned about the need for dissemination of research information to the field, CAL initiated the publication of a series of papers in bilingual education in 1975 and published the first book collection of papers on Mexican American Spanish and a research bibliography of linguistic work on the language of U.S. Spanish speakers.

CAL also played a significant role in the development of long-term plans for research and information dissemination, as authorized in the 1974 Title VII legislation. CAL worked closely with the staff of the National Institute of Education in the design of the National Center for Bilingual Research, and after the contract was awarded to the Southwest Educational Research Laboratory, CAL, with its long experience in information clearinghouse activities, formulated the design for the National Clearinghouse for Bilingual Education (NCBE, now known as NCELA). When the project was designated as a minority business procurement, CAL became a partner with InterAmerica Associates, which served as prime contractor for the project. Rudolph Troike became deputy director of the Clearinghouse, and Joel Gómez became director. NCBE for a number of years served as an important central coordinating hub for cooperation and information dissemination throughout the country among various units involved in bilingual education.

Anticipating the need for informed discussion leading to the 1978 reauthorization of the Bilingual Education Act, CAL, with support from the Carnegie Foundation, commissioned state-of-the-art review papers of relevant knowledge in social sciences, linguistics, law, and education and convened a series of conferences in 1976 to 1977 bringing together researchers and concerned federal policymakers. Leann Parker coordinated the conferences and edited

the resulting series of five volumes, which provided a still-valuable conspectus of the state of research knowledge.

In other directions, when the U.S. Census Bureau, together with the National Center for Education Statistics in the Department of Education, was tasked to conduct a nationwide survey to determine the need for bilingual education, CAL was awarded a large project, directed by Walter Stolz, to develop a proxy measure of English language proficiency (MELP) for use in the 1976 Survey of Income and Education. The results of the survey became the basis for appropriations under the 1978 reauthorization of Title VII. CAL also conducted research on criteria for the evaluation of bilingual education programs and carried out a feasibility study for the international assessment of bilingual programs (which ultimately influenced the design of the highly successful national bilingual educational program in Guatemala). CAL staff also had extensive input into the U.S. Commission on Civil Rights' influential 1975 report on bilingual education, *A Better Chance to Learn.* On the international front, CAL's director twice served as U.S. representative to United Nations Educational Scientific and Cultural Organization (UNESCO) conferences in Paris on minority languages in education.

In the institutionally isolated area of bilingual vocational education, CAL worked closely with the Department of Labor on developing guidelines for successful programs. Mary Galván, a former president of the Teachers of English to Speakers of Other Languages (TESOL) organization, took a major role in this work.

CAL was also active in responding to misinformation about bilingual education. In 1978, when an official of the Department of Education called a press conference to announce the somewhat negative findings of an evaluation of bilingual program effectiveness, a CAL staff member, Tracy Gray, obtained the report the night before and wrote a critical analysis exposing flaws in the study. Her analysis was given to media representatives as they emerged from the press conference, and most newspapers reporting on the study acknowledged that the results had been seriously questioned by CAL.

The fall of Saigon, Vietnam, in 1975, brought CAL to the forefront of national efforts to deal with educational aspects of the resulting refugee crisis. Literally overnight, utilizing its own resources, CAL established the National Indochinese Clearinghouse (NIC) and recruited a national network of consultants with relevant expertise. NIC staff provided guidance to government and school officials across the United States and produced resource materials to meet the needs of the refugees and those working with them. A toll-free telephone "hotline" was established, and the staff answered 11,000 inquiries and sent out 45,000 pieces of material in just 4 months. The National Institute of Education commissioned CAL to provide packets of its publications for distribution to thousands of schools in the United States. Even the Australian government requested copies of CAL materials to distribute to schools there. CAL continued to fund the Clearinghouse for 6 months before the U.S. government began providing support.

Strengthening Bilingual Programs

Given its long history as a respected autonomous professional organization, the Center for Applied Linguistics was able to serve as an independent national voice advocating for bilingual education. Research evidence clearly demonstrates that quality bilingual education is the most effective approach available for nonnative speakers of the school language. However, from the beginning of the Bilingual Education Act, lack of quality in bilingual programs was a significant threat to the success of this great educational experiment, since the purpose of bilingual education was seen generally as being compensatory instruction for ethnic minority children from poverty backgrounds (designed to transition them out of their native languages as quickly as possible and into regular English-medium instruction). Therefore, the thrust of most of CAL's work in bilingual education was aimed at strengthening the quality of programs through the establishment of higher standards for teacher training and teacher qualifications and the improvement of curriculum, materials, methods, and evaluation criteria and procedures. CAL contributed to this process by providing the public with feedback from research and informing policy decision making.

Rudolph C. Troike

See also Center for Applied Linguistics, Recent Focus; *Lau v. Nichols,* San Francisco Unified School District's Response; National Clearinghouse for Bilingual Education; Saville-Troike, Muriel; Title VII, Elementary and Secondary Education Act, Key Historical Marker; Troike, Rudolph, C., Jr.

Further Readings

Center for Applied Linguistics. (1977). *Bilingual education: Current perspectives* (Vols. 1–5). Arlington, VA: Center for Applied Linguistics.

Hernández-Chávez, E., Cohen, A., & Beltramo, A. (1975). *El lenguaje de los Chicanos: Regional and social characteristics of language used by Mexican-Americans.* Arlington, VA: Center for Applied Linguistics.

Saville, M. R., & Troike, R. C. (1971). *Handbook for bilingual education.* Washington, DC: Teachers of English to Speakers of Other Languages.

Troike, R. C., & Modiano, N. (1975). *Proceedings of the First Inter-American Conference on Bilingual Education.* Arlington, VA: Center for Applied Linguistics.

CENTER FOR APPLIED LINGUISTICS, RECENT FOCUS

From its founding to the present day, the Center for Applied Linguistics (CAL) has been a source of research, resources, and services to advance the practice of language education, to address issues related to linguistic and cultural diversity, and to inform policy on language-related topics. The improvement of education for language learners of all ages remains a prominent part of CAL's broader mission. Since the late 1960s, when demographic changes brought bilingual education into prominence, CAL has worked to build and disseminate knowledge related to bilingualism and bilingual education in the United States and abroad.

With the passage of the Bilingual Education Act in 1968 and the Supreme Court decision in *Lau v. Nichols* in 1974, bilingual education as an alternative model for teaching English language learners (ELLs) became more widely utilized. However, as policies were formulated to require bilingual education under certain circumstances, the perception of the program as a remedial compensatory approach also became more prevalent. The emphasis on *transitioning* from bilingual education to English-only instruction became stronger; bilingual programs were cast as remedial programs with the goal of teaching students English as quickly as possible, since the presence of a language other than English was regarded as a barrier to be overcome. This was assumed to occur when such students were able to move into regular (English-medium) classrooms. The possible goal of developing proficiency in two languages (native language and

English) through bilingual education was less often considered by educational decision makers.

Consistent with its mission, CAL's orientation has consistently been toward *additive bilingualism*. In policy and practice, in education and beyond, the recommended goal is to foster the full development of the native language, whether it be English or another language, as embodied in the goals of two-way immersion education described below. CAL's president from 1978 to 1991, G. Richard Tucker, advanced the notion of a *language-competent society* in the United States, in which everyone would be highly proficient in English and at least one other language, and led the organization in efforts to advance that goal. One impediment to this work was the growing strength of campaigns to make English the official and sole language of the nation and various states and to eliminate bilingual education. In response to this scenario, CAL joined forces with the National Immigration Forum, the Joint National Committee on Languages (JNCL), and other professional organizations to establish the English Plus Information Clearinghouse (EPIC). EPIC's mandate was to gather and disseminate resources and experiences that could be helpful to groups working against English-only initiatives.

More recently, CAL has worked with partners, particularly the National Foreign Language Center at the University of Maryland, on the Heritage Language Initiative to promote the maintenance and development of heritage languages in the United States (languages other than English used in immigrant and indigenous communities around the country). Bilingual programs in schools and communities are key elements of this movement. In 1999 and 2002, CAL and its partner organizations organized and sponsored two national conferences on heritage languages and produced proceedings from the conferences. They also launched the Alliance for the Advancement of Heritage Languages in order to continue to collect and disseminate resources for the field, including profiles of heritage language programs.

Bilingual education is also relevant beyond the borders of the United States, and CAL has sought to contribute positively to the improvement of the education of second languages worldwide. In 2004, for example, CAL published a report titled "Expanding Educational Opportunity in Linguistically Diverse Societies," which profiled programs in 13 countries where a key element was instruction in the mother tongue. The current global Education for All effort has not yet focused on language, despite the United Nations Educational

Scientific and Cultural Organization (UNESCO) argument for the use of the mother tongue in primary instruction, and CAL's efforts are directed at informing international and national educational institutions about this issue.

Throughout CAL's history, the education of ethnic and linguistic minorities has been a constant concern. In its research, resources, and services, CAL has sought to integrate a better understanding of language and culture to improve learning opportunities and language development for these students. These efforts are described in the next section, along with CAL's involvement with the development and implementation of two-way immersion bilingual education.

Research

Central to CAL's mission is the conduct of research that applies directly to the improvement of practice. As a partner in a series of federally funded research centers, CAL has sustained a program of research that has informed educational practice for ELLs in the United States. CAL's work with UCLA on the Center for Language Education and Research (CLEAR), 1985 to 1989, focused on integrating language and content instruction for ELLs and bringing together bilingual and foreign-language program models in a form of what is now called *dual-language education*. This research was carried forward at the University of California, Santa Cruz, in two subsequent collaborative efforts: the National Center for Research on Cultural Diversity and Second Language Learning (NCRCDSLL), from 1990 to 1995, succeeded by the Center for Research on Education, Diversity & Excellence (CREDE), from 1996 to 2004. Major studies of newcomer programs and two-way immersion education documented current practice and examined features that make those approaches effective program alternatives for ELLs. One of the major products of CREDE was a review of research, published in 2006, on language learning and academic achievement of ELLs. Among its findings was a generally positive relationship between primary-language instruction and academic success. In addition, the Sheltered Instruction Observation Protocol (SIOP) approach, a model of sheltered instruction that promotes both content and language learning through a second language, was developed in collaboration with researchers at California State University Long Beach.

Another long-term program of research, starting in the mid-1990s, has focused on literacy learning.

A series of studies examined cross-language literacy transfer for Spanish-speaking students learning to read in Spanish or English. The findings included evidence that Spanish skills predict reading ability in English for students who receive formal reading instruction in Spanish, pointing to advantages for students learning to read in their native languages. Other studies in the program examined the factors that influence English literacy development among native Spanish speakers, including type of educational program. In a complementary effort, CAL managed the work of the National Literacy Panel on Language Minority Children and Youth, a comprehensive synthesis of the literature on literacy development in this population. The report, published in 2006, pointed to the benefit of oral proficiency and literacy in the first language, among other important findings relevant to bilingual education policy and practice.

Resources and Services

CAL's mission is strongly oriented toward action, applying what is known from research to provide quality resources and services for practitioners and policymakers, in bilingual education and many other areas. For over 30 years, CAL operated the Education Resource Information Center Clearinghouse on Languages and Linguistics (ERIC/CLL) (one in a network formerly funded by the U.S. Department of Education), a valued source of information presented in accessible formats for nonspecialist consumers. ERIC/CLL responded to concerns in the field by producing digests (such as *Ten Common Fallacies About Bilingual Education,* by James Crawford, published in 1998), annotated bibliographies, and professional reference books. Among the titles most relevant to bilingual education was the 1997 reissuing of the landmark work by Heinz Kloss, *The American Bilingual Tradition.* CAL partnered with The George Washington University for several years in the operation of the National Clearinghouse on Bilingual Education (currently known as the National Clearinghouse for English Language Acquisition and Language Instruction Educational Programs), focusing primarily on publications. CAL also brought its dissemination expertise to the research centers with which it worked, producing research reports and educational practice reports, along with a newsletter and other occasional publications, for NCRCDSLL and CREDE.

In recent years, increasing use of technology has led to much broader dissemination of information through the World Wide Web. CAL's Web site provides easy access for teachers, researchers, policymakers, and the general public to accurate and comprehensible information about language-related topics, including bilingual education. The site includes professional reference materials, databases and directories, research reports, and links to a broad network of information and tools.

In addition to making resources available, CAL offers services to district and state education agencies, schools, and communities in the form of professional development, technical assistance, and program evaluations and reviews.

Two-Way Immersion Education (TWI)

A cornerstone of CAL's involvement in bilingual education since the mid-1980s has been its work on *two-way immersion* (TWI). Two-way immersion is a form of dual-language education that integrates students from English and non-English-language backgrounds, delivers instruction in both languages, and aims to develop bilingualism as well as academic achievement. CAL was among the early leaders in the development of the model, through research, resources, services, and policy guidance. CAL began to collect information about two-way immersion programs across the country in 1990, building on the directory assembled by Kathryn Lindholm-Leary for CLEAR, and eventually made the *Directory of Two-Way Bilingual Immersion Programs in the U.S.* easily accessible via the Web. The directory has become a key reference for bilingual programs, policymakers, and the media as a profile of the practice of two-way immersion.

As TWI programs proliferated, CAL continued to lead the field by setting basic standards for two-way immersion as criteria required for a program to be listed in the directory and by organizing a national effort to develop *Guiding Principles for Dual-Language Education* in 2003. These activities were informed by a long-term (and ongoing) program of research. Early studies focused on developing program profiles to define how the model works. Later research examined the impact of the TWI model on student achievement with a large-scale, longitudinal study of language and literacy development in elementary students in TWI programs. CAL researchers also conducted a longitudinal study of spelling development of native-English- and native-Spanish-speaking children in two-way immersion and mainstream English programs. These two studies found that students from both language backgrounds improved their literacy skills over time and scored as well or better than their peers in non-TWI programs and that native Spanish speakers tended to develop more balanced bilingualism than native English speakers, whose Spanish is weaker than their English.

The availability of key resources and accurate information has been an important factor in the growth and success of TWI programs, and CAL has sought to fill those needs. Information is disseminated through its Web site, e-mail bulletins, print and online publications, and presentations at meetings, workshops, and conferences. CAL is often a source for print and broadcast media on this topic and received the 2-WAY California Association for Bilingual Education "Promoting Bilingualism" award in July 2006 for its work. In collaboration with practitioners and other researchers, CAL has developed a variety of resources for program implementation, such as the *Dual-Language Program Planner* and the *Guiding Principles for Dual-Language Education.* In the field of teacher professional development, CAL developed the *Two-Way Immersion Toolkit* and the *Two-Way Immersion Observation Protocol* (TWIOP), an adapted version of the SIOP.

Donna Christian

See also Castro Feinberg, Rosa; Center for Applied Linguistics, Initial Focus; Christian, Donna; Dual-Language Programs; Heritage Language Education; National Literacy Panel; Newcomer Programs; SIOP

Further Readings

August, D., & Shanahan, T. (2006). *Executive summary: Developing literacy in second-language learners: Report of the National Literacy Panel on language-minority children and youth.* Mahwah, NJ: Lawrence Erlbaum. Available from http://www.cal.org/projects/archive/natlitpanel.html

Christian, D., & Genesee, F. (2001). *Bilingual education.* Alexandria, VA: TESOL.

Dutcher, N. (2004). *Expanding educational opportunity in linguistically diverse societies.* Washington, DC: Center for Applied Linguistics. Available from http://www.cal.org/resources/pubs/fordreport_040501.pdf

Genesee, F., Lindholm-Leary, K., Saunders, W., & Christian, D. (Eds.). (2006). *Educating English language learners: A synthesis of research evidence.* New York: Cambridge University Press.

Howard, E., & Sugarman, J. (2007). *Realizing the vision of two-way immersion: Fostering effective programs and classrooms.* McHenry, IL: Center for Applied Linguistics and Delta Systems.

Howard, E., Sugarman, J., Lindholm-Leary, K., Christian, D., & Rogers, D. (2004). *Guiding principles for dual language education.* Available from http://www.cal.org/twi/guidingprinciples.htm

Kloss, H. (1997). *The American bilingual tradition* (2nd ed.). McHenry, IL: Center for Applied Linguistics and Delta Systems.

Peyton, J., Ranard, D., & McGinnis, S. (2001). *Heritage languages in America: Preserving a national resource.* McHenry, IL: Center for Applied Linguistics and Delta Systems.

Tucker, G. R. (1986). Developing a language-competent American society. In D. Tannen & J. E. Alatis (Ed.), *Georgetown University roundtable on languages and linguistics 1985* (pp. 264–274). Washington, DC: Georgetown University Press.

Web Sites

Center for Applied Linguistics: http://www.cal.org

National Clearinghouse for English Language Acquisition and Language Instruction Educational Programs: http://www.ncela.gwu.edu

CHACÓN-MOSCONE LEGISLATION

In 1976, California assemblyman Peter Chacón and state senator George R. Moscone introduced Assembly Bill 1329: The Chacón-Moscone Bilingual Bicultural Education Act, making bilingual education mandatory in California. With support from a broad constituency, and after much debate in the state legislature, the bill became law. AB-1329 required that all limited- and non-English-speaking children enrolled in California's public schools receive instruction in a language they understand and that school districts provide them access to a standard curriculum. The act also mandated that the state provide federal, state, and local dollars to pay for these services. For a decade, the Chacón-Moscone bill (as it came to be known) was the most progressive, single most important bilingual legislation in the country.

Pre-Chacón-Moscone

The political climate of the country in the late 1960s and early 1970s was ripe for the Chacón-Moscone bill. Minority groups involved in the civil rights movement pressed for their rights, as well as educational and economic opportunities. President Lyndon B. Johnson's "War on Poverty" recognized that minority communities, particularly African Americans and Hispanics, were economically disadvantaged and needed federal support to provide their children with equal educational opportunities. Head Start programs targeted instruction to children from these communities and opened the door to the use of Spanish language instruction.

At the federal level, the Civil Rights Act of 1964 and the Elementary and Secondary Education Act of 1965 (ESEA) laid a foundation for legislation that transformed public education and ushered in a new era of bilingual education across the country, including California. Title VI banned discrimination on the basis of race, color, creed, or national origin; declared a strong legislative policy against discrimination in public schools and colleges; and prohibited discrimination in all federally funded programs. The ESEA sparked a flurry of reforms, pouring in over $11 billion per year to state educational agencies (SEAs), marking the most significant federal intervention in the history of American education. Until then, little had been done to ameliorate low academic performance among poor, immigrant, and non-English-speaking children in public schools. Congress passed Title VII of ESEA in 1968, the Bilingual Education Act, funding the first 68 bilingual education programs in the nation.

In 1972, the Massachusetts legislature passed the Transitional Bilingual Education Act, the first state-approved bilingual legislation in the nation, mandating bilingual education programs in all school districts with 20 or more children from the same non-English-language background. It would be the first of only nine states to require bilingual instruction in all school districts. In California, Assembly Bill 2284, the Chacón Discretionary Bilingual Education Act of 1972, became the state's first bilingual education bill. The Chacón bill allowed bilingual programs in all school districts with limited- and non-English-speaking children. California did not mandate bilingual education; instead, it permitted school boards broad discretion to address the educational needs of limited- and non-English-speaking children, allowing them to compete for available but limited program development dollars.

Nationally, in 1974, the U.S. Supreme Court ruled in favor of Chinese American plaintiffs in the *Lau v. Nichols* case, a class action suit against the San Francisco Unified School District alleging discrimination against non-English-speaking students. The *Lau v. Nichols* decision, decided on Title VI of the Civil Rights Act, was the most important Supreme Court decision to affect public education since *Brown v. Board of Education* (1954), 20 years earlier. The *Lau* decision did not specifically mandate bilingual education, but proposed such programs, among others, as viable options to remedy discrimination in public schools.

By 1975, several precedent-setting court cases around the country recognized the civil rights of bilingual children, mandating bilingual education as a remedy. *Aspira v. Board of Education of the City of New York* (1973) called for a consent decree for obligatory bilingual education for all New York City children who needed it. In *Serna v. Portales Municipal Schools* (1974), the 10th Circuit Court of Appeals rejected the school district's appeal, finding violations of the students' Title VI civil rights, and ordered Portales Municipal Schools to implement bilingual and bicultural instruction; to assess language minority students' achievement; and to recruit and hire bilingual teachers and school personnel. *Keyes v. School District No. 1, Denver* (1973), was a school desegregation case. The U.S. Supreme Court found that the district had violated the Equal Protection Clause of the Fourteenth Amendment and ruled in favor of the plaintiffs. The district accepted a plan for bilingual and bicultural education presented by the Congress of Hispanic Educators.

In 1975, the Department of Health, Education and Welfare and U.S. Office of Civil Rights (OCR) officials drew up the *"Lau* Remedies" to provide specific guidelines for school districts to establish educational programs to ensure compliance with the *Lau v. Nichols* decision. The *Lau* Remedies required that school districts provide programs of sound design, appropriateness of staff, and adequacy of resources. This was interpreted to mean bilingual and bicultural programs for limited- and non-English-speaking children.

Chacón-Moscone Bill of 1976

By 1976, in an era of expanding civil rights, it was the combined effect of federal legislation, U.S. Supreme Court decisions, and state mandates that reformed educational policy—and ultimately benefited limited- and non-English-speaking children. Assemblyman Peter Chacón, recognized today as the father of bilingual education in California, and State Senator George Moscone joined forces to push for Assembly Bill 1329, the Chacón-Moscone Bilingual Bicultural Education Act. The Chacón-Moscone bill called for flexible bilingual program alternatives that ranged from transitional bilingual education to full-maintenance bilingual programs. Chacón-Moscone recognized and clearly articulated that mastery of English was absolutely critical for limited- and non-English-speaking children to benefit from equal educational opportunity. Significantly, it also reiterated the notion that English-only instruction was only one of several pedagogical approaches, but certainly not the only appropriate one for limited- and non-English-speaking children. The Chacón-Moscone bill also required that California provide supplemental financial support to schools to implement these programs.

The Chacón-Moscone bill mirrored the ideal programs suggested in the *Lau* Remedies. The legislation allowed for a broad range of flexibility in instructional programs to accommodate the range of diversity in public schools, recognizing the importance of the child's level of education and accommodating the skills each child brought to their respective classrooms. The following were among the instructional programs included:

1. Basic bilingual education programs, which built on students' language skills, with daily instruction leading to English acquisition, including structured English language development and primary-language development with basic skills instruction in subject matter content until the transfer to English was made. The amount of English language instruction increased as the skills levels of English increased.

2. Bilingual-bicultural education programs, which provided instruction in two languages, one of which was English. The purpose was to achieve competence in both languages. This was achieved by providing daily instruction in English language development, including listening and speaking skills. Formal reading and writing skills in English were to be introduced as appropriate criteria were met. Daily instruction also included primary-language development, reading instruction in the primary language, selected subjects taught in the primary language, and development of an understanding of the history and culture of the United States and California and the customs, cultures, and values of the pupils being taught.

3. Experimental bilingual programs, which included innovative programs and planned variation programs. In the former, schools were encouraged to experiment with new approaches, including team teaching and other acceptable programs of instruction, to expand children's learning experiences. In the latter, the focus was on the development of appropriate instruction for those children whose English language skills were superior to their language skills in their primary language.

4. Secondary-level language development programs were Grades-7-to-12 programs of prescriptive English language development, including listening and speaking skills and linguistic and grammatical structures. Instruction was based on a diagnosis of the child's English language skills. All instruction was to be done in English. In addition, however, secondary-language development programs were to provide primary-language instruction to sustain academic achievement in the content areas required for high school graduation. The legislation provided for either a certified bilingual/cross-cultural teacher or a language development specialist, as verified in writing by the school district that the teacher was competent to teach English as a Second Language (ESL). School districts that offered such programs were not required to provide individualized learning programs (ILPs) for their students, but were required to maintain records that documented parental notices and continuous evaluation of pupil needs and services provided.

5. Secondary-level individual learning programs were individualized instructional programs designed to meet the needs of limited-English-proficient students and to build on their language skills to develop proficiency in English. They included elementary-level ILPs, any program of instruction in which basic bilingual education programs, bilingual-bicultural education programs, or experimental bilingual programs were individualized to meet the educational needs of limited- or non-English-speaking children. It was the clearly stated goal of all such programs to teach the child English. In sum, program alternatives varied widely and offered every district viable options to comply with Chacón-Moscone.

Attack on Chacón-Moscone

The Chacón-Moscone bill was recognized as the most progressive bilingual legislation of its time, a model to emulate. Other states subsequently modified their own bilingual legislation to include similar provisions in their programs. It was the first bill to require state certification of bilingual teachers, better training for nonbilingual teachers, and a fundamental understanding of the children's languages and cultures for all teachers who worked with limited- or non-English-speaking children. All bilingual teachers were expected to be proficient in the children's languages, and all teachers were to receive training in bilingual methodologies. These requirements would become a bone of contention for opponents of bilingual education.

School administrators balked at the teacher requirements, charging that it was impossible to fulfill these provisions. Hiring trained bilingual teachers was a challenge for public schools. Even with a large Latino population in California, teachers from Spanish-speaking backgrounds made up less than 5% of the teaching force at the time, both at the state and national levels. Even worse, the task of identifying and training a sufficient number of bilingual teachers for Mandarin, Cantonese, Vietnamese, Tagalog, and other languages was significantly more daunting. Complaints against these requirements swelled among associations of school administrators and nonbilingual teachers. Bilingual education soon became anathema to its opponents.

Within a year of its inception, opposition to bilingual education in California would grow steadily for the next decade. Opponents charged that bilingual programs and bicultural education were overly prescriptive, unwieldy, and inflexible. Many disputed the cost of bilingual programs and argued that the legislation expected too much from teachers. Nonbilingual teachers objected to retraining already certified teachers; and bilingual programs met with stiff resistance from the California Teacher's Association. School administrators railed against the legislation's record-keeping provisions, wanting the supplemental dollars guaranteed by the legislation but opposing restrictions on its use. Critics began to question the integrity of bilingual program leaders, charging that bilingual education was nothing more than a job program for Chicano educators. Some went so far as to brand bilingual education and educators as "un-American."

The publication in 1977 of Noel Epstein's highly influential book *Language, Ethnicity, and the Schools: Policy Alternatives for Bilingual-Bicultural Education* ushered even harsher criticism. A national education writer for the *Washington Post,* Epstein questioned whether teaching ethnic languages and cultures was an appropriate role for the federal government and, by extension, the appropriate role of public education. Epstein was successful in reframing the question, asking whether it was the nation's responsibility to provide equal educational opportunity for all its children and whether the nation had any responsibility in teaching and maintaining non-English languages and cultures. Other critics maintained that the fundamental purpose of bilingual programs was to help students become competent in English and that English should be the sole language of instruction throughout the country. Implicit in this new position was the charge that bilingual programs did not teach English. Critics targeted maintenance bilingual programs, publicly called for a speedy transition away from them, first to transitional programs and then to English-only programs. Ultimately, Epstein's book would have devastating consequences on bilingual programs nationwide.

Reeling from the controversy ignited by the Chacón-Moscone bill, the California legislature moved to amend it in 1980. With waning public support for bilingual education throughout California and across the nation, Assemblyman Chacón and Senator Moscone introduced AB 507, the Bilingual Reform and Improvement Act, a significant revision of AB 1329. The compromise legislation was intended to thwart its critics, while strengthening and preserving its more progressive elements. AB 507 deemphasized bilingual education and expanded ESL and English-only instruction.

Sensing a changing mood in the country, the opposition pushed, unsuccessfully, for legislation at the federal level to eliminate bilingual education altogether and to declare English the official language of the country. Many states followed suit. The anti-immigration climate of 1987 provided its critics even more reasons to attack the Chacón-Moscone bill, charging that bilingual education was primarily an educational program for illegal immigrants and too costly for taxpayers.

In 1987, Governor George Deukmejian, a staunch opponent of bilingual education, refused to sign renewal legislation for bilingual education. Instead, he allowed it to sunset, effectively cutting off financial support for state-funded bilingual education. The legislative mandate for bilingual education in California was severely weakened. Several attempts were made to reintroduce more moderate bilingual legislation, but the state legislature refused to consider it. A decade later, in 1998, Proposition 227, the English for the Children Initiative, effectively eliminated all bilingual education from California's public schools, replacing bilingual programs with English-only instruction.

In an ironic reversal, AB 1329, the Chacón-Moscone Bilingual Bicultural Education Act of 1976, became a catalyst for instigating a nationwide English-only movement, launching continued attempts to make English the official language of the country, and, by association, for fueling anti-illegal immigration debates.

John J. Halcón

See also English for the Children Campaign; English-Only Organizations; Epstein, Noel; *Lau v. Nichols,* San Francisco Unified School District's Response; *Lau v. Nichols,* the Ruling; Proposition 227 (California); Title VII, Elementary and Secondary Education Act, Key Historical Marker

Further Readings

Aspira of New York, Inc. v. Board of Education, 394 F. Supp. 1161 (S.D.N.Y. 1975)

Biegel, S., & Slayton, J. (1997). *Access to equal educational opportunity.* Los Angeles: UCLA Graduate School of Education. Retrieved from http://www.gseis.ucla.edu/gseisdoc/study/equa12.html

Brown v. Board of Education, 347 U.S. 483 (1954).

Crawford, J. (1999). *Bilingual education: History, politics, theory, and practice* (4th ed.). Los Angeles: Bilingual Educational Services.

Epstein, N. (1977). *Language, ethnicity, and the schools: Policy alternatives for bilingual-bicultural education.* Washington, DC: Institute for Educational Leadership.

Escamilla, K. (1989). *A brief history of bilingual education in Spanish.* (ERIC Document Reproduction Service No. ED308055). Retrieved from http://www.ericdigests.org/pre-9211/brief.htm

H. R. 7152, The Civil Rights Act of 1964. Pub L. No. 88–352. Retrieved from http://www.ourdocuments.gov/doc.php?doc=97&page=transcript

Keyes v. School District No. 1, Denver, CO, 413 U.S. 921 (1973).

Lau v. Nichols, 414 U.S. 563 (1974). Available from http://www.nabe.org/documents/policy_legislation/LauvNichols.pdf

Lyons, J. (1988). *Legal responsibilities of education agencies serving national origin language minority students.* Chevy Chase, MD: Mid-Atlantic Equity Center. Retrieved from http://www.maec.org/lyons/4.html

Office for Civil Rights. (1975). *Task-force findings specifying remedies available for eliminating past educational practices ruled unlawful under Lau v. Nichols.* Retrieved from http://www.stanford.edu/~kenro/LAU/LauRemedies.htm

Serna v. Portales Municipal Schools–New Mexico (1973).

CHÁVEZ, LINDA (1947–)

Linda Chávez is a former Reagan administration official and former president of the U.S. English organization. She is a nationally syndicated columnist, talk radio show host, and television commentator. Chávez is a controversial figure in the U.S. Hispanic community for her conservative views on immigration, affirmative action, and bilingual education.

Chávez was born in Albuquerque, New Mexico, on June 17, 1947, to an Irish-English-American mother and a Spanish American father. When she was 9 years old, her family moved to Denver, Colorado. She attended Catholic school there during her primary years and, later, the University of Colorado at Boulder, where she graduated with a BA in English in 1970. She later enrolled in the University of California–Los Angeles English and Irish Literature PhD program. While at UCLA, Chávez was asked to teach a Chicano literature course. Reluctant to add Chicano works to the course syllabus, Chávez was frequently harassed, along with her family, by her students and other militant campus Chicanos. She left the program in 1972 and relocated to Washington, D.C.

In Washington, Chávez began working for the Democratic National Committee, later assisted Congressman Don Edwards on civil rights issues, and in 1974 became a lobbyist for the National Education Association (NEA). Refusing to be pigeonholed as a lobbyist for Latino interests, however, Chávez left NEA for the more conservative American Federation of Teachers (AFT) in 1975. She served as the organization's assistant director of legislation for 2 years, then director of research and editor of its quarterly, *American Educator.* Over the next 6 years, she would pen numerous articles espousing traditional values in American schools and what she saw as the negative impact of quotas and bilingual education. Conservatives in Washington took notice of her political stance. She was invited to become a consultant to the Reagan administration in 1981 while still serving at AFT.

In 1983, President Reagan appointed Chávez to become the first female staff director of the U.S. Commission on Civil Rights. Her controversial tenure at that agency was marked by her advocating the reversal of traditional civil rights measures, including racial hiring quotas, and her views of the negative effects of affirmative action. In 1985, she was appointed director of the White House Office of Public Liaison, making her the highest-ranking woman in the Reagan White House team. She became a full-fledged Republican later that year. Embarking on a political career of her own, Chávez left the Reagan administration in 1986 to campaign for a U.S. Senate seat in Maryland on a conservative Republican platform. However, she was criticized for changing her party affiliation, her recent Maryland residency, and what some called mudslinging tactics against her opponent, Democrat Barbara Mikulski. Chávez lost the race.

Chávez left politics in 1987 to become president of U.S. English, the controversial nonprofit organization created by Senator S. I. Hayakawa to lobby for making English the official language of the country. She resigned in 1988, however, following the disclosure of an anti-Hispanic and anti-Catholic memo written by one of the organization's founders, John Tanton. After leaving U.S. English, Chávez became the John M. Olin Fellow at the Manhattan Institute for Policy Research, a conservative think tank in Washington, D.C. In the early 1990s, she became director of the institute's Center for the New American Community, which studies the impact of multiculturalism on U.S culture.

During the 1990s, Chávez became a noted print, radio, and television political commentator. Contributing pieces to a wide range of newspapers, magazines, and books, she wrote extensively on Latino topics and on what she perceived as the negative outcome of various governmental programs. During this period, Chávez also received a number of appointments, serving as chair of the National Commission on Migrant Education from 1988 to 1992, followed by a 4-year term as U.S. Expert to the United Nations Subcommission on the Prevention of Discrimination and Protection of Minorities. Her efforts did not go unnoticed, and in 2000, the Library of Congress honored Chávez as a "living legend" for her contributions to America's cultural and historical legacy.

In 2001, Chávez's reputation as a conservative Hispanic attracted the attention of President George W. Bush, who selected her to be his Secretary of Labor. During the confirmation process, however, it was revealed that Chávez had housed and provided money to an illegal immigrant during the early 1990s. Amid a firestorm of opposition and media scrutiny, she withdrew her name from consideration.

Since 2006, Chávez has served as chairman of the Center for Equal Opportunity, a conservative, nonprofit public policy research organization she founded in 1995. She is president of Stop Union Political Abuse, a nonprofit grassroots organization; chairs the Latino Alliance, a federally registered political action committee; is a political commentator on the Fox News Channel; and is a nationally syndicated columnist and talk radio show host.

Gregory Pearson

See also Bilingual Education in the Press; English for the Children Campaign; English-Only Organizations; Latino Attitudes Toward English; Official English Legislation, Favored; Views of Bilingual Education; Views of Language Difference

Further Readings

Chávez, L. (2002). *An unlikely conservative: The transformation of an ex-liberal (Or how I became the most hated Hispanic in America).* New York: Basic Books.

Center for Equal Opportunity. (n.d.). *Linda Chávez.* Available from http://www.ceousa.org

CNN.com. (2001, January 9). *Retribution sank nomination, Chávez says.* Retrieved February 1, 2008, from http://transcripts.cnn.com/2001/ALLPOLITICS/stories/01/09/bush.wrap

Meier, M. S., & Gutiérrez, M. (2003). Linda Chávez, 1947– . In *The Mexican American experience: An encyclopedia.* Westport, CT: Greenwood.

Novas, H. (1995). Linda Chávez, 1947– . In *The Hispanic 100: A ranking of the Latino men and women who have most influenced American thought and culture.* Secaucus, NJ: Citadel.

Oboler, S., & González, D. J. (2005). Linda Chávez. In *The Oxford encyclopedia of Latinos and Latinas in the United States.* New York: Oxford University Press.

Schulz, J. D. (Ed.). (2000). Linda Chávez. In *Encyclopedia of minorities in American politics.* Phoenix, AZ: Oryx.

CHINESE IN THE UNITED STATES

According to historical linguists, Sino-Tibetan Chinese is more like a language family than a single language made up of a number of regional dialects.

However, Chinese people often prefer to use the generic term *Chinese* when collectively referring to the various languages used in the country. This entry will adhere to that convention except as otherwise noted.

Usually, the Chinese language can be disaggregated into seven major dialect groups, called *Fangyan:* Mandarin, Wu, Gan, Xiang, Hakka, Yue, and Min. The northern varieties of Chinese are known as the Mandarin dialects. These dialects are spoken by more than two thirds of the Chinese people. Almost all of the Mandarin dialects are mutually intelligible. Cantonese, which is widely used in Hong Kong and the Guangdong province, falls under the Yue dialect group. In 1956, Mandarin Chinese was adopted as the official language of the People's Republic of China (PRC).

After the founding of the PRC in 1949, the country faced the problem of a very low literacy rate. To eliminate mass illiteracy, the government actively supported the simplification of Chinese traditional characters. Currently, simplified Chinese characters have been adopted in the PRC and Singapore, although in Taiwan, traditional characters are still widely used. In Chinese instruction overseas, both traditional and simplified Chinese characters are taught, depending on whether the textbooks were published in Taiwan or the PRC.

The Chinese people and their various languages have a long history in the United States. According to the decennial census, conducted in April 2000, the Chinese immigrant population in the United States exceeded 2 million persons, thus making up 0.8% of the total population. This group has been growing rapidly and constitutes a significant ethnic and linguistic group. Many of the children of recent immigrants, especially in New York and California, participate in bilingual education programs.

The history of Chinese immigration to the United States occurred in three major waves. The first wave of immigration started in the mid-19th century but was stopped by the Chinese Exclusion Act of 1882. This U.S. federal law arose from fears that too many Chinese immigrants would somehow damage the fabric of American culture. Public sentiment against Chinese immigrants of the times was similar to what is now being expressed against Spanish-speaking immigrants, especially Mexicans. A large proportion of Chinese immigrants from the first wave were poor peasants from Guangdong Province (Canton). Most of them spoke Cantonese.

The second wave of immigration started in the mid-20th century but decreased during the 1970s. This group of immigrants included anti-Communists from mainland China, bureaucrats, businessmen, and intellectuals, as well as some professionals from Taiwan and Hong Kong. The immigrants from mainland China and Taiwan spoke mostly Mandarin, and those from Hong Kong spoke Cantonese; both groups continued to use traditional Chinese characters as a means of communication. As social and political conditions in the PRC began to stabilize, the second wave of immigrants decreased considerably.

The third wave of immigration started in the last decades of the 20th century and continues today. The immigrants were composed of mainland Chinese from various socioeconomic backgrounds, with professionals as the most represented group. They spoke mainly Mandarin and used simplified Chinese characters to communicate. Part of the motivation to emigrate, specifically from Hong Kong, was the change in the political status of this territory, which was associated with the turnover of political control to the PRC.

The Chinese population in the United States has been characterized by a steady and fast growth over the past 40 years. The U.S. Census of 2000 indicated that the total Chinese population had grown from 435,000 in 1970 to over 2 million. It is estimated that a large portion of the Chinese population in the United States lives in the West and about 30% lives in the Northeast. California and New York are the states with the first- and second-largest Chinese immigrant communities, hosting about 40% and 18% of the total Chinese population, respectively.

Language has been a huge issue for Chinese immigrants in the United States. In 2000, the U.S. Census reported that nearly half the Chinese in the United States did not speak English at home or spoke English "less than very well." According to this source, Chinese persons did less well in speaking English when compared with other Asian groups. Despite the language disadvantage, 48.1% of Chinese in the United States had at least a bachelor's degree by 2000, although the place where they received their tertiary education was not reported. About one quarter of the Chinese population in the United States had less than a high school diploma.

An important historical feature of Chinese immigrants has been the phenomenon of Chinese community schools, where Chinese language, calligraphy, and culture are taught to the young. No matter how hard they have had to struggle to survive in the United

States to learn English, Chinese immigrants traditionally never stop urging their children to maintain their heritage language. In addition to immersing children in Chinese at home, many parents urge their children to attend Chinese language schools after regular school hours. Although Chinese immigrants come from different dialect backgrounds, when referring to Chinese heritage language in the United States, they normally mean Mandarin.

Most Chinese language schools are nonprofit schools, which are operated by parents and open on weekends or after regular school hours. The funding generally comes from tuition and fund-raising. Parents and communities provide great human resources to Chinese language schools, including instructors and staff. With more than 100 years of history, Chinese language schools have evolved into an organized and influential educational force that plays a significant role in Chinese language and culture preservation.

At the present time, Chinese programs target both nonheritage language learners and heritage learners. In many places, heritage learners are fewer than those who wish to learn Chinese as a foreign language. The growing interest in learning Chinese as a foreign language is not directly related to maintaining Chinese as a heritage language or as a language used in bilingual education, as that concept is defined in the United States. Overall, the Chinese language appears to enjoy an increased popularity that is likely to continue in the future. An important historical shift is that Chinese is now associated with higher-economic and social value than was the case in previous decades. This is motivating more heritage learners to maintain the language via public and private programs in which Chinese is taught and, collaterally, attracting nonheritage learners to learn Chinese.

Na Liu, Mengying Li, and Yun Teng

See also Chinese Language Study, Prospects; Heritage Language Education; Status Differences Among Languages

Further Readings

Chang, I. (2003). *The Chinese in America.* New York: Penguin.

College Board. (2004). *AP Chinese Q&A.* Available from http://www.collegeboard.com/prod_downloads/about/news_info/ap/qanda_english.pdf

Guo, L. (2004). Between Putonghua and Chinese dialects. In M. Zhou & H. Sun (Eds.), *Language policy in the People's Republic of China: Theory and practice since 1949* (pp. 45–53). Norwell, MA: Kluwer Academic.

Norman, J. (1988). *Chinese.* Cambridge, UK: Cambridge University Press.

Ramsey, S. R. (1987). *The languages of China.* Princeton, NJ: Princeton University Press.

U.S. Census Bureau. (2000). *Census 2000 summary file 2 (SF 2) 100-percent data.* Available from http://factfinder.census.gov

Wang, X. Y. (Ed.). (1996). *A view from within: A case study of Chinese heritage community language schools in the United States.* Washington, DC: National Foreign Language Center.

Wong, S. C., & Lopez, M. G. (2000). English language learners of Chinese background. In S. L. McKay & S. C. Wong (Eds.), *New immigrants in the United States: Readings for second-language learners* (pp. 263–305). Cambridge, UK: Cambridge University Press.

CHINESE LANGUAGE STUDY, PROSPECTS

There is little question that the future prospects for Chinese language study in the United States are brighter than they have ever been. On a regular basis, articles in the widest possible range of press and media outlets speak of the 21st century as being "the Chinese century" in the areas of economics, politics, and technology. This scenario parallels earlier trends for the Russian language in the post-*Sputnik* years and the Japanese language during the 1980s. Russian and Japanese did not receive an impetus by government agencies, but the picture for Chinese seems brighter.

Many U.S. leaders recognize that for the United States to maintain its place among the world's superpowers, a deeper understanding of the language and culture of this country's greatest trade partner, China, is essential. Equally important is the recognition that for Chinese, a complex language with multiple dialects and varieties, the U.S. higher-education system alone cannot bring students to truly professional levels of language proficiency. This perception has yielded tangible results in the form of local, state, and federal economic incentive programs for developing long sequences of instruction in Chinese language and culture beginning at the elementary school level. The Chinese K–16 Pipeline Project, sponsored by the National Security Education Program (NSEP), is one example of a locally based program. In addition, the creation of an Advanced Placement (AP) Chinese course and examination by the College Board, which began during the fall 2006 academic year, provides the potential for facilitating programmatic articulation both horizontally, among a wide core group of secondary schools, and vertically, between those secondary schools and the colleges and universities their students will subsequently attend. Given such conditions, one might be justifiably optimistic about the potential for a broadly based, well-articulated system to support and enhance Chinese language teaching.

Educational System Stakeholders

A potentially negative force in achieving momentum for moving in this direction is the existing system, or systems, that support Chinese language education in the United States. More specifically, it is the existence of a large and loose network of what have been alternately called Chinese "community schools," "heritage language schools," and "Saturday schools," the latter designation based on the frequent need to hold classes on a Saturday, when either a public school building or church would be most readily available.

Originally established in the San Francisco Bay area during the early years of the 20th century, these community-based programs' principal initial purpose was the preservation of Chinese customs and traditions among immigrant populations, with much emphasis on cultural awareness and a true education *in the language,* as opposed to taking classes in Chinese. Beginning in the 1950s, regionally based interaction and communication among these individual schools led to the formal creation of a number of community school organizations, in some cases preceding the establishment of the more mainstream college- and university-professor-based Chinese teacher organizations. The Chinese language teaching architecture is unique among all foreign-language educational systems in the United States. In support of teachers and learners of Chinese, four separate associations in three distinct institutional settings currently exist. For instance, the Chinese Language Teachers Association (CLTA), which serves mostly colleges and universities, includes among its members representatives from all major Chinese language teaching constituencies within the United States: K–12, community/heritage schools, and higher education. It is first and foremost an organization of tertiary-level teachers. Teachers at

the primary and secondary school levels rely on the Chinese Language Association of Secondary Elementary Schools (CLASS) as their forum. CLASS was established in 1987 in reaction to CLTA's relative inability, and in some cases unwillingness, to respond to the needs of the precollegiate teaching and learning community.

Unique to the architecture of the foreign-language field in the United States are the National Council of Associations of Chinese Language Schools (NCACLS) and the Chinese Schools Association in the United States (CSAUS). Both organizations were established in 1994, in partial response to the establishment of the Scholastic Achievement Test (SAT) II, Chinese with a listening section. NCACLS and CSAUS differ from CLTA and CLASS in that they are not individual membership organizations, but rather organizations of organizations. For example, NCACLS is a council of 15 regional Chinese community school organizations with primary connections to immigrant populations from Taiwan, and CSAUS is a single national organization with members consisting of individual schools, whose volunteer teaching and administrative staffs are largely immigrants or descendants of immigrants from the People's Republic of China.

Beyond the complexity of the structure of the foreign-language field are the quantitative comparisons among these sectors in light of the conventional patterns of less commonly taught language such as Chinese, which finds its greatest institutional and instructional stronghold at the college/university setting. It is, in fact, quite the opposite, as revealed in the following data from the year 2002, the last year when comparable data compilations or estimates were available for all three institutional levels. According to a fall 2002 survey of foreign-language enrollments at U.S. institutions of higher education conducted by the Modern Language Association, Chinese courses had 34,153 students enrolled nationwide, and, in 2002, Chinese was the seventh most commonly studied language in American colleges and universities. Results indicated an enrollment increase of 20% since the last survey was taken in 1998.

A report on 2001/2002 Chinese enrollments at the precollegiate level conducted by the Secondary School Chinese Language Center (SSCLC) at Princeton University, in January 2002, presented statistics for that final year. These statistics revealed that the United States had 203 schools in 31 states that offered Chinese language classes, with a total student enrollment of

23,900. Grades 9 to 12 had 12,660 students; Grades 7 and 8 had 3,579 students; and kindergarten through Grade 6 had 7,661 students enrolled in Chinese classes.

According to the NCACLS Web site in 2002, student enrollment at NCACLS-affiliated Chinese community schools was estimated to be around 100,000. During the same time frame in 2002, CSAUS also reported student enrollment of approximately 60,000. With no claims being made for instructional program comparability across sectors, these data confirm that at least 70% of students studying Chinese in the United States in 2002 were doing so in community school settings. And while comprehensive surveys for K–12 and higher education have not yet been conducted, there is every indication that those percentages have not shifted significantly since 2002.

Extra-Educational Systemic Stakeholders

Further complicating the pattern of organizational support for Chinese language education in the 21st century is the emergence of new stakeholders interested in the development of Chinese language programs. During the last two decades of the 20th century, a number of primarily Washington, D.C.–based, nongovernmental organizations provided professional and material developmental support to the Chinese language field. Most notably, the Center for Applied Linguistics provided a series of Chinese proficiency tests. In addition, the National Foreign Language Center (NFLC) supported the establishment of both CLASS and NCACLS and secured a 3-year grant for a Chinese Language Field Initiative funded by the Henry Luce Foundation. The latter venture is the first and only instance in which K–12, college, university, and heritage language institutional representatives have been brought together to develop a comprehensive design for the emerging Chinese language field.

A more recent addition to the total Chinese-dedicated, domestic nongovernmental community has been the Asia Society. In 2006, it created a position for an executive director for Chinese Language Initiatives, wrote a handbook laying out the basics for designing a Chinese language program at the precollegiate level, and produced two monographs on the topic of expanding Chinese language field capacity in the United States. The College Board was influential in helping expand the Chinese language field by developing the Chinese AP course and examination.

This places them very much within the realm of major stakeholders.

Foreign Governmental Organizations

Beyond American shores, there is no more critical player than the Office of Chinese Language Council International, formerly known as the National Office for Teaching Chinese as a Foreign Language; it is also commonly referred to as the "Hanban," the acronymic shorthand of its full title. Essentially, this addition of the Ministry of Education for the People's Republic of China expands their global role to all aspects of promoting Chinese language education and extends from freely provided textbooks to the establishment of over 100 Confucius Institutes dedicated to the mission of Chinese language instruction. It may well rival and potentially surpass comparable models, such as the Alliance Française (French) and the Goethe Institute (German). In short, the stakeholders are many, but more extensive coordination is needed.

Bilingual Education Within the Chinese Language Field

What makes the community or heritage school community so significant within the context of bilingual education are the actors involved: students and even teachers who reside within not just those instructional settings, but within all Chinese language learning programs in the United States. They are representative of the vast continuum of what may be termed the *bilingual student*. Despite the inherent difficulty in defining just what a second-language learner of any language is, Chinese included, one can minimally identify three key constituencies that may prove to be major components within the Chinese language learning community in the United States for the 21st century.

For those teachers working in all Chinese language instructional settings in the United States today, the term *native listener* has become an increasingly prevalent label for students who are nonliterate (sometimes *preliterate*) and those who are nonfunctional speakers of the language, but who, by virtue of being exposed on a daily basis to the language, possess extraordinary receptive skills.

It should be pointed out that different forms of Chinese predominate in different parts of the People's Republic of China. A significant population of young men and women are aurally and orally proficient in a non-Mandarin dialect and are fully literate, by virtue of having received a full secondary-level precollegiate education. They are readers and writers of the Chinese script, but do not have sufficient Mandarin listening and speaking skills to function in the lingua franca. This diverse group first came to the attention of Western educators in 1997, when the initial tide of emigrants from Hong Kong left in anticipation of the impending change in the political and economic status of the city.

Another aspect of the development of the Chinese language educational field has been seen in the rise of programs in community schools specifically tailored to a growing social phenomenon of programs for students of non-Chinese-speaking parents, more recently termed as outreach to families with children from China. The change in terminology is particularly significant in that it represents a growth in the target constituency to include not just adoptive children, but also their generally non-Chinese-speaking adoptive parents. Such programs may over time ultimately provide experiential lessons in and models for how to most effectively teach both second- and foreign-language learners of Chinese and the wide range of iterations of Chinese heritage language learners.

Finally, the field of Chinese language teaching must grapple with the wide variety of languages and dialects that prevail in China today. Since some of these languages are aurally distinct, although they use the same writing system, there are challenges in this regard that do not exist among other language families.

Scott McGinnis

See also Chinese in the United States; Center for Applied Linguistics, Recent Focus; Heritage Language Education; Modern Languages in Schools and Colleges

Further Readings

Brecht, R., & Walton, A. R. (1994). National strategic planning the less commonly taught languages. *Annals of the American Academy of Political and Social Science, 532,* 190–212.

McGinnis, S. (2005, February). *Statistics on Chinese language enrollment.* Retrieved October 27, 2007, from http://clta.osu.edu/flyers/enrollment_stats.htm

McGinnis, S. (in press). From mirror to compass: Chinese as a heritage language education in the United States. In D. M. Brinton & O. Kagan (Eds.), *Heritage language acquisition: A new field emerging.* Mahwah, NJ: Lawrence Erlbaum.

Peyton, J. K., Ranard, D. A., & McGinnis, S. (2001). *Heritage languages in America: Preserving a national resource.* Washington, DC: Center for Applied Linguistics/Delta Systems.

Stewart, V., & Wang, S. (2005). *Expanding Chinese language capacity in the United States.* New York: Asia Society.

Walton, A. R. (1996). Reinventing language fields: The Chinese case. In S. McGinnis (Ed.), *Chinese pedagogy: An emerging field* (pp. 29–79). Columbus, OH: Foreign Language Publications.

CHRISTIAN, DONNA (1949–)

Donna Christian, president of the Center for Applied Linguistics (CAL) since 1994, was born in Schenectady, New York, on November 14, 1949. Following graduation from St. Lawrence University, from which she earned a BS degree in mathematics in 1971, she moved to Washington, D.C., to attend Georgetown University. There, in 1973, she completed an MA degree in applied linguistics, with a minor in French, and in 1978, a PhD in sociolinguistics, with specialization in language variation and minors in applied linguistics and theoretical linguistics.

Christian began her career at CAL in 1974. CAL is a private, nonprofit organization that works to promote and improve the teaching and learning of languages, serves as a resource on issues related to language and culture, and conducts research on critical topics in those areas. As a research associate there, Christian participated in studies funded by the U.S. Department of Education and privately supported studies on the relationship between linguistic diversity and access to education. In 1979, she took a leave of absence from CAL to serve as a Fulbright Senior Lecturer in Linguistics at Adam Mickiewicz University in Poznan, Poland, for 2 years.

After returning to CAL, Christian served as associate director, director of the Research Division, and director of the English Language and Multicultural Education Division. During this time, she served as a member of the Stanford Working Group on Federal Education Programs for Limited-English-Proficient Students, chaired by Kenji Hakuta, which advised on reauthorization of the Bilingual Education Act. She also served as associate director of the National Clearinghouse for Bilingual Education, coordinated

CAL's work for the UCLA-based Center for Language Education and Research, and codirected an evaluation of the bilingual program in the Red Clay Consolidated School District (Wilmington, Delaware). Christian's professional life during this time included a number of adjunct faculty appointments at nearby universities, including the University of Virginia School of Education, Northern Virginia Center; the Georgetown University Linguistics Department; and the George Washington University School of Education, where she taught courses in sociolinguistics and education geared to the professional preparation of teachers of English language learners.

Under Christian's leadership, CAL has conducted pivotal work in the development of two-way immersion as an effective means of promoting bilingualism. Two-way immersion programs integrate language minority and language majority students, providing instruction in both English and the native language of the language minority students. The structure of these programs varies, but they all integrate students for most content instruction and provide this instruction in the non-English language for a significant portion of the school day. In addition to supporting bilingualism and biliteracy, these programs strive to promote grade-level academic achievement and positive cross-cultural attitudes and behaviors in all students. Beginning in the 1980s, Christian directed a series of projects on two-way immersion education, including an extended research program under the auspices of three federally funded research centers: the Center for Language Education and Research at UCLA and, at the University of California, Santa Cruz, the National Center for Research on Cultural Diversity and Second Language Learning and the Center for Research on Education, Diversity & Excellence. Her extensive work laid the foundation for CAL's ongoing research, professional development, and preparation of resources for educators in this area.

Since her appointment as CAL's president, Christian has played an advisory role on many of CAL's activities related to bilingualism, including the biliteracy research program on Developing Literacy in Spanish Speakers and the National Literacy Panel on Language Minority Children and Youth, both federally funded initiatives. Christian's contributions to the field of bilingual education also include numerous publications on the effectiveness of two-way education and the development of two-way immersion programs. In addition, during Christian's tenure as president, CAL has expanded its resource offerings in bilingualism with new professional development resources for teachers and a series of how-to publications on two-way immersion programs.

Christian is frequently asked to consult outside of CAL on issues of research, policy, and practice, and she has advised government policymakers on current language learning research and encouraged them to formulate language education policies with input from the field of applied linguistics. She currently serves on the editorial boards of the *International Journal of Bilingual Education and Bilingualism* and the *Heritage Language Journal* and on the board of directors of the International Research Foundation on English Language Education (TIRF) and the Advisory Board of the Hispanic Family Literacy Institute (National Center for Family Literacy).

In recognition of her contributions to the field of bilingual education, in 2006, Christian received the Promoting Bilingualism award from 2wayCABE, an affiliate of the California Association of Bilingual Education. The certificate acknowledges Christian's promotion of substantive research and program development in two-way immersion and her advocacy of bilingualism and biliteracy throughout the United States.

Deborah Kennedy

See also Center for Applied Linguistics, Initial Focus; Center for Applied Linguistics, Recent Focus; Hakuta, Kenji; LaFontaine, Hernán; National Clearinghouse for Bilingual Education; National Literacy Panel; Stanford Working Group

Further Readings

Christian, D., & Genesee, F. (Eds.). (2001). *Bilingual education*. Alexandria, VA: TESOL.

Christian, D., & Howard, L. (2003). *Two-way immersion 101: Designing and implementing a two-way immersion education program at the elementary level*. Santa Cruz: University of California, Santa Cruz, Center for Research on Education, Diversity & Excellence, and Center for Applied Linguistics.

Christian, D., Howard, E., & Sugarman, J. (2003). *Trends in two-way immersion education: A review of the research* (Report No. 63). Baltimore: Center for Research on the Education of Students Placed at Risk.

Christian, D., Howard, L., Lindholm-Leary, K., Sugarman, J., & Rogers, D. (2005). *Guiding principles for dual-language education*. National Clearinghouse for English Language Acquisition/Center for Applied Linguistics. Available from http://www.cal.org/twi/guidingprinciples.htm

Civil Rights Act of 1964

The Civil Rights Act of 1964 outlaws "national origin discrimination" by public entities that receive federal financial assistance. In part, the bar against national origin discrimination has been construed as a bar against language discrimination. The act is the U.S. government's primary tool to ensure that states and school districts receiving federal funds meet the needs of English learners in schools.

Historically, the Civil Rights Act of 1964, specifically Title VI of the law, was of assistance to private individuals subjected to language discrimination. It is of less moment to private parties today due to the passage in 1974 of the Equal Educational Opportunity Act (EEOA), which mandates school districts to meet the needs of students with limited English proficiency, and the U.S. Supreme Court's *Alexander v. Sandoval* (2001) decision, discussed here, which requires private litigants to prove intentional discrimination. The EEOA specifically allows private enforcement and does not require proof of intentional discrimination. Thus, EEOA has become the principal means for private enforcement of the rights of limited-English-proficient (LEP) students.

Historical Background

The Civil Rights Act of 1964 has its genesis in the civil rights movement that enveloped the nation, particularly the South, in the years following the U.S. Supreme Court's decision in *Brown v. Board of Education* (1954) desegregating U.S. public elementary schools. That decision produced massive opposition from Whites in the South and racial violence aimed against Blacks and their supporters. Bombings and lynchings in the South were met by massive civil disobedience as hundreds of "Freedom Riders" joined southern Blacks in attempts to register voters and desegregate businesses, public transportation, swimming pools, and all institutions of the segregated South and, later, of the large urban centers of the North. Lacking political clout, Blacks flooded the federal courts with lawsuits to enforce *Brown* and to utilize *Brown* to end all forms of racial segregation, including public accommodations. Some of that litigation was successful. However, America's schools overwhelmingly remained segregated.

In August 1963, the civil rights movement, joined by church congregations, women's groups, and labor unions, conducted a massive march on Washington. Through all of this strife, the federal government continued to fund segregated entities throughout the country. A major demand of the protests was an end to this federal support of segregation.

Title VI of the Civil Rights Act of 1964 was the formal entrance of the U.S. Congress into the civil rights struggle that defined the United States in the 1960s. The law had seven titles:

I. Voting rights protections

II. Equal access to public accommodations

III. Authorization for the U.S. Attorney General to initiate school desegregation suits.

IV. The establishment of a federal Community Relations Service to stop racial violence.

V. Extension of the law creating the U.S. Commission on Civil Rights

VI. Prohibiting federal funding to programs that discriminated on the basis of race, color, or national origin

VII. The establishment of a commission on equal employment opportunities

The Black struggle for civil rights spread to other groups, including women, people with disabilities, and language minorities. With respect to language minorities, a demand for an equal educational opportunity was paramount. Segregation had been challenged by the Latino community as far back as the 1940s, with the successful case of *Méndez v. Westminster School District* (1946) in California. Even when schools were desegregated, however, Latinos, Asians, and other language minorities struggled for culturally appropriate curricula and for comprehensible instruction.

Title VI and Its Effects

Title VI of the Civil Rights Act of 1964 provides as follows:

No person in the United States shall, on the ground of race, color or national origin, be excluded from participation in, be denied the benefits of, or be subjected to discrimination under any program or activity receiving Federal financial assistance.

The concept was a simple one; taxpayer money should not be used to further discrimination against any persons who paid such taxes.

Because most state education agencies (SEAs) and local school districts or education agencies (LEAs) receive federal funds, they may not discriminate on the basis of race, color, or national origin. The agency charged by Congress with enforcing this law, the Office for Civil Rights (OCR) in the U.S. Department of Education, has interpreted the phrase *national origin* to include LEP students, and this interpretation has been accepted in numerous court cases.

Title VI was not self-enforcing. Rather, the U.S. Department of Health, Education and Welfare (DHEW) was charged with the task of law enforcement, a task that has fallen on its successor, the OCR. Title VI contained a detailed enforcement mechanism, a political compromise that made it extremely difficult to terminate federal assistance. Those administering the law had discretion as to whether to act at all. Over the years, the vigor with which Title VI has been enforced has waxed and waned, depending on the will of the executive branch.

According to its provisions, all rules for the enforcement of Title VI were to be approved by the president of the United States. This task is often delegated by the president to the Office of Management and Budget, ostensibly because that unit is most knowledgeable about cost implications on the agencies affected. Attempts to seek "voluntary compliance" prior to fund termination were made mandatory. No funds could be terminated without notice and a full hearing, similar to a court proceeding before a federal administrative law judge. If a decision was made to terminate funds, a written report to Congress had to be made. Finally, the allegedly discriminating agency could seek an appeal to a federal court. These provisions of Title VI have made it less than practical to withdraw funds from any offending agency of government. The process is simply too cumbersome and subject to the political winds blowing at any particular moment. Nonetheless, Title VI has played an important role in litigation affecting English language learners (ELLs) at all levels.

It is important to consider the political context for the enactment of the Civil Rights Act of 1964. In 1965, Congress passed the Elementary and Secondary Education Act. Title VII of the act, added in 1968, was the federal government's first attempt to specifically meet the needs of LEP students by providing monies to fund programs and to provide teacher training, books, and parental involvement. The 1960s also are noted for the "War on Poverty" and its legal services component. For the first time, attorneys could assist LEP students in securing their rights in federally funded programs. Finally, the era was marked by immigration reforms aimed at eliminating discriminatory preferences based on race and place of birth. Restrictions on immigration from Asia were also abolished.

On May 25, 1970, DHEW issued guidance to school districts that explicitly interpreted the requirements of Title VI of the Civil Rights Act of 1964 with respect to English language learners. (The U.S. Department of Education did not yet exist.) In a widely circulated memorandum, Stanley Pottinger, director of the Office for Civil Rights in DHEW, wrote as follows:

> Where the inability to speak or understand the English language excludes national origin–minority group children from effective participation in the education program offered by a school district, the district must take affirmative steps to rectify the language deficiency in order to open its instructional program to these students.

The memorandum further prohibited schools from misclassifying students who needed language instruction by placing them in classrooms for the mentally retarded. Ability grouping could be used to enhance language education but could not become permanent dead ends. The memorandum went on to inform school districts that they have the responsibility to adequately notify LEP parents of school activities that are called to the attention of other parents. Such notice, in order to be adequate, may have to be provided in a language other than English. That provision of compliance practice is still in effect.

Lau v. Nichols and the Lau Remedies

Opposition and/or inattention to the law and subsequent regulations led to litigation, around the U.S. Chinese students who were denied special programming and went to court in San Francisco, arguing that their rights under Title VI of the Civil Rights Act were being violated. In *Lau v. Nichols* (1974), a unanimous U.S. Supreme Court agreed with the students and held that "there is no equality of treatment merely by providing students with the same facilities, textbooks, teachers and curriculum," for students who do not understand English are "effectively foreclosed from any meaningful education." Classroom experiences for these students would be "wholly incomprehensible and in no way meaningful."

The Supreme Court decision in *Lau* did not determine a remedy for the violation of the student's rights. Rather, the Court noted that this was the responsibility of the federal executive branch, in this case the OCR in the U.S. Department of Education. The Court avoided passing on the merits of the bilingual education versus English as a second language (ESL) controversy. It did, however, validate the May 25th memo issued by DHEW. As a direct result of the decision, the San Francisco Unified School District adopted a transitional bilingual education master plan approved by the federal district court.

Congress quickly codified *Lau* by passing the Equal Educational Opportunity Act (EEOA) of 1974. The statute provides as follows:

> No state shall deny equal educational opportunity to an individual on account of his or her race, color, sex or national origin, by . . . (f) the failure of an educational agency to take *appropriate* action to overcome language barriers that impede equal participation by its students in its instructional programs. (emphasis added)

These two pieces of legislation, Title VI and the EEOA, were subsequently utilized in tandem in further litigation to improve the education of LEP students in particular cases where litigation was appropriate.

Neither EEOA nor Title VI defined what constitutes "appropriate action." Language minority parents and students frequently demanded bilingual-bicultural maintenance programs or, at the very least, primary-language instruction in the subject matters. This was urged to prevent students from falling behind in other subjects while learning English. Schools generally decided to offer much less: ESL programs conducted in English, with bilingual paraprofessionals assisting in content areas (math, science, social studies) when paraprofessionals or teachers aides were available. Frustrated parents continued their struggle in the courts and in Washington.

In August 1975, DHEW issued policy guidelines titled "Task Force Findings Specifying Remedies Available for Eliminating Past Educational Practices Ruled Unlawful" under *Lau v. Nichols*. The document,

popularly referred to as the "*Lau* Remedies," was never published in the *Federal Register*, and thus the Remedies did not become regulations. They did, however, guide DHEW (and subsequently Department of Education) staff in their efforts to assist language minority students.

The *Lau* Remedies for the first time detailed certain components of an "appropriate" program for language minority students. In keeping with explicit language in the decision, the Remedies went further than the Court decision in *Lau*, requiring districts to educate students in their primary language when it was their strongest language and until they could compete in English-only settings. For the first time, districts were required to identify students in need of a program, evaluate students' proficiency in English, determine an appropriate instructional program, determine when students were ready to be transferred into the mainstream program, and determine teacher qualifications. Pursuant to these remedies, DHEW conducted hundreds of reviews and negotiated plans with districts to meet the needs of LEP students. The federal courts were also kept busy at the task of fleshing out the requirements of the law. Most of these plans required a level of native-language instruction for LEP students. State legislatures were also active during the 1970s in passing laws, some of which mandated limited bilingual education programs. At the peak of this stage of civil rights protection, 16 states passed laws or enacted regulations requiring some form of bilingual education in their schools.

In 1980, the new U.S. Department of Education sought to refine the *Lau* Remedies and to turn them into regulations that would be binding on all school districts across the country. Formally known as a "Notice of Proposed Rulemaking," the proposed *Lau* regulations and their interpretation of Title VI of the Civil Rights Act of 1964 were considered by many to be overly prescriptive given the great diversity of students and differing needs and abilities of different schools, states, and regions. Before the new administration took office, the proposed *Lau* regulations were withdrawn. Since that time, the OCR in the U.S. Department of Education has utilized internal memoranda and other policy documents to evaluate school district compliance under Title VI.

Today, without the benefit of published regulations and often relying on the EEOA as well as Title VI, the OCR looks at identification, assessment, programming, exit criteria, teacher qualifications, evaluation, prohibitions against segregation, and the like to determine whether the district is upholding its obligations under *Lau*. Theoretically, all school programs and activities, including gifted and talented programs, should be equally accessed by LEP students. Students with disabilities who are also LEP fare best under the policies, since they have a whole body of additional disability law to protect them. School districts at the time of this writing are allowed considerable discretion by the OCR in how these children are served.

The *Castañeda* Standard

In evaluating whether a district program meets Title VI, the OCR often follows a case decided under the EEOC. In the case of *Castañeda v. Pickard* (1981), the court set out a three-pronged test to determine whether LEP student rights were being violated. This test is discussed elsewhere in this encyclopedia. It is important to point out, however, that the *Castañeda* court made a few other critical rulings that have contributed to broaden the definition of protection offered by the Civil Rights Act of 1964. First, LEP students must be provided not only the opportunity to learn English but also the opportunity to have access to the school district's entire educational program. Thus, the adequacy of a district's response is measured by determining how each of the three responsibilities is addressed, using the three prongs as a guideline. Second, the court left the following open to the district,

> The sequence and manner in which LEP students tackle this dual challenge so long as the schools design programs which are reasonably calculated to enable these students to attain parity of participation within a reasonable length of time after they enter the school system.

Although decided under the EEOA, the *Castañeda* standard has been adopted by the federal government pursuant to Title VI as its rule for enforcement. Individuals can invoke Title VI by filing a complaint with the U.S. Department of Education. The individual can be a parent, student, teacher, or advocacy organization; indeed, anyone can file a complaint. This need not be a formal process and may be done in a parent's home language. Complaints can be filed online or simply by a letter setting forth the contentions that a school or district is not providing an adequate program to LEP students. This is sufficient

to trigger OCR review. The greater the detail, the larger the number of complainants involved; or the involvement of advocacy organizations often enhances the likelihood of the OCR taking the complaint seriously. While the ultimate remedy of fund cutoff is theoretically possible, this remedy is rarely invoked. Rather, many complaints lead to a negotiated settlement that can, if adequately monitored, result in improved services. Individuals may also file complaints with the SEA.

Remedies under Title VI (or the EEOA) often address identification issues, premature reclassification, teacher qualifications, resources, adequacy of ESL, and access to the curriculum as set forth in *Castañeda*. While the failure to provide native-language instruction or bilingual programming has not in recent years been found to be a cause per se of a Title VI violation, it may become part of a remedy. Some advocates believe that in certain circumstances, a court might find the failure to deliver such programming to be an affirmative legal failure, but no court has found as such since the early 1980s.

Other Cases

Finally, in a series of cases, federal courts have held that "federal law imposes requirements on the State Agency to ensure that plaintiff's language deficiencies are addressed" (e.g., *Idaho Migrant Council v. Board of Education,* 1981, and *Gómez v. Illinois State Board of Education,* 1987). All of these cases have relied to some degree partially or totally on the protection afforded by the Civil Rights Act and the EEOA. It is also worth noting that the OCR, which enforces Title VI (but not the EEOA), has nonetheless adopted the state agency accountability standards of *Castañeda* and has issued a variety of documents over the years to clarify their interpretation of the nexus between these two laws. The last policy update occurred in 1991. These documents, like the *Lau* Remedies, have not been formalized into regulations, but are still relied on by the OCR.

By means of these legal tools, many derived from precedents in interpreting Title VI of the Civil Rights Act, advocates have negotiated a number of important court agreements expending protections for LEP students. For example, *LULAC v. Florida Board of Education* (1990) defines rights for Florida's massive LEP population. Similarly, *El Comité de Padres v. Honig* (1995) requires the state of California to monitor and enforce the state's laws regarding LEP students.

Conclusion

It should be noted that the future of Title VI of the Civil Rights Act of 1964 is uncertain. A recent U.S. Supreme Court decision prohibits the private enforcement of Title VI. In *Alexander v. Sandoval* (2001), the Court held that Title VI does not permit individuals to sue to stop practices that appear neutral on their face but have the effect of discriminating by creating a "disparate impact" on minorities. This ruling flew in the face of hundreds of suits previously allowed by the federal courts in the education area, along with a host of other issues including environmental racism. Post-*Sandoval*, only the U.S. government can file such suits. Individual suits will be allowed only if the plaintiffs can prove intentional discrimination, a very difficult standard to meet.

In the future, the close nexus between EEOA and Title VI of the Civil Rights Act of 1964 may be altered. *Sandoval* does not apply to actions brought under the EEOA, nor does it prohibit state court actions. States such as California have passed their own versions of Title VI. However, there has been very little notable state court action on this issue, and it remains to be seen whether state court action can fill in the void. Congress has been presented with bills to overrule *Sandoval* but has yet to act and allow private rights of action. However, while access to the courts may be curtailed in light of *Sandoval*, complaints by individuals can still be filed with the OCR in the U.S. Department of Education. The OCR can also initiate its own enforcement activities and investigate school districts without the filing of a complaint.

Stefan M. Rosenzweig

Author's Note: The author wishes to thank Peter D. Roos, Esq., for valuable editorial assistance.

Editor's Note: Because they are often used in tandem, this entry on the Civil Rights Act of 1964 should be read in conjunction with the entry on the Equal Educational Opportunity Act of 1974.

See also Equal Educational Opportunity Act of 1974; *Lau v. Nichols,* Enforcement Documents; *Lau v. Nichols,* the Ruling; Office for Civil Rights, U.S. Department of Education

Further Readings

Alexander v. Sandoval, 532 U.S. 275 (2001).
Brown v. Board of Education, 347 U.S. 483 (1954).
Castañeda v. Pickard, 648 F.2d 989 (5th Cir. 1981).
Civil Rights Act of 1964, Pub. L. No. 88–352 (1964).
Crawford, J. (2005). *Bilingual education: History, politics, theory, and practice* (4th ed.). Los Angeles: Bilingual Education Services.
El Comité de Padres v. Honig, No. 281824 (Superior Ct. Sacramento County, 1995).
Equal Educational Opportunity Act, 20 U.S. C. 1701–1720 (1974).
Gómez v. Illinois State Board of Education, 811 F.2d 1030 (7th Cir. 1987).
Halpern, S. C. (1995). On the limits of the law: *The ironic legacy of Title VI of the 1964 Civil Rights Act.* Baltimore: John Hopkins University Press.
Idaho Migrant Council v. Board of Education, 647 F.2d 69 (9th Cir. 1981).
Lau v. Nichols, 414 U.S. 563 (1974).
LULAC v. Florida Board of Education, C.A. # 90–1913-M (S.D. Fla. 1990).
Méndez v. Westminster School District, 64 F. Supp. 544 (S.D. Cal. 1946).
U.S. Department of Education, Office of Civil Rights. Customer service standards for the case resolution process. Retrieved February 1, 2008, from http://www.ed.gov/about/offices/list/ocr/customerservice.html

---

CLAD/BCLAD

See Bilingual Teacher Licensure

Classroom Discourse

Oral communication is an essential component of schooling, without a doubt the single most important vehicle of interaction between teacher and students, as well as among students, as they discuss concepts and ideas. It is also the principal way through which learning is demonstrated. For this reason, the spoken word, or speech, is generally considered to be the most important mediator of student learning. The study of classroom discourse is concerned with the use of oral communication in educational processes. Courtney Cazden points out that whereas the word *discourse* is used to refer more generally about "talk," it is also used to refer to communication that is socially positioned involving systems of shared meanings and social practices. In this sense, discourse is always ideological, as it reflects the values, beliefs, and social practices of the community or institution in which it occurs. At the same time, certain types of discourse (e.g., academic discourse) can privilege certain types of students (e.g., White, middle class), while leaving other students who belong to different cultures and linguistic communities at a disadvantage.

As a mediator in student learning, discourse not only allows students access to knowledge but also interacts with students' own subject knowledge and cultural knowledge and acts as a tool for coconstructing meaning and learning with teachers and fellow students. In this sense, discourse may act as a scaffold that allows knowledge to be constructed in the classroom community with the aid of the teacher or peers, to be appropriated by individual students. By repeatedly participating in activities mediated by discourse, students become participants in different social contexts, including the classroom.

Research Findings

Early research in classroom discourse was concerned with the structure of classroom communication. Different types of participant structures, or ways in which turns are allocated in an interaction, were noted by Susan Philips, including (1) teacher/whole group, (2) teacher/small group, (3) students working independently, and (4) students interacting in small groups. The first of the four, in which the teacher addresses the group as a whole, is the dominant structure, and, consequently, classroom communication is dominated by teacher talk, which in this case refers to all the utterances produced by the teacher. Teachers initiate interaction at significantly higher rates than students. Research in classroom interaction, including Cazden's and Hugh Mehan's, has documented that roughly two thirds of all utterances in classroom interaction are produced by the teacher.

The most documented and most common form of talk in classroom interaction is a three-turn sequence referred to as *initiation-response-evaluation* (IRE) or *initiation-response-feedback* (IRF). This type of interaction has been considered somewhat of a norm or the "default pattern" in classroom communication. It is characterized by the teacher asking a question or giving a prompt, students responding, and the teacher giving an evaluation, feedback, or follow-up. This pattern of interaction is most noticeable during teacher-led activities in which the teacher controls both the topic of conversation and the allocation of turns. In this type of interaction, there is usually an expected answer, or at least a range of satisfactory answers, to which the teacher responds. When the response is not satisfactory, the sequence takes an extended form until reaching closure by the teacher giving a satisfactory evaluation. Mehan documented this type of interaction and observed that teachers prompt replies, repeat, and simplify elicitations until accepting students' responses and reaching a satisfactory conclusion to the interaction.

Mehan also described classroom lessons as being hierarchically structured, with the IRE sequence at the base, forming *topically related sets,* chunks of conversation linked by a common theme or topic, which in turn form *phases,* which constitute a *lesson.* In this structure, the teacher is seen as an orchestrator of classroom discourse, most of the time having control of both the topic of interaction and how this interaction is conducted. However, students are active participants and play a critical role in the successful orchestration of lessons. They work together with teachers in providing responses and demonstrating communicative competence in this type of discourse. Improvisation also plays a part as participants, both teachers and students, adapt to the variations in the complex environment called *classroom.*

Although this triadic form of interaction is prevalent in classroom discourse, researchers such as Philips and Cazden observed variations as teachers or students engaged in *narrative discourse,* which is more monologic in nature. Narratives involve a sequence of events, and the speaker is allowed a much longer turn; responses serve the purpose of clarification rather than evaluation. These include stories, reports, descriptions, and explanations. Unlike everyday storytelling, however, school narratives are subject to the control of the teacher, whose responses usually relate to the appropriateness of topic and/or way to talk about it. Cazden observed two types of narratives during sharing time, which she labeled as *topic centered* and *episodic.* While topic-centered stories revolve around one main topic and have a clear beginning and end, episodic stories move from one event to another; and shifting scenes last longer in episodic than in topic-centered stories. These represent two different cultural models of what stories should look like. Cazden reported that teachers value the first kind, while not always understanding the second. Cultural differences in how to construct stories may conflict with mainstream teachers' views of how narrative should take place in the classroom. Researcher Shirley Brice Heath observed a "mismatch" between students' "ways with words" and teachers' expectations when students did not come from White middle-class backgrounds.

Cazden also notes other variations in classroom discourse, which involve change in participant structure, the purpose of talk, the medium of interaction, and, as noted previously, cultural differences among students. When teachers interact with only some of the students in small groups or one-on-one during conferences or when students ask for help, interactions take a different form and in many instances diverge from the IRE pattern. Other factors that allow for variations in lesson structure depend on how speaking rights are distributed and whether students have the opportunity of self-selecting as opposed to being selected by the teacher. When students address each other directly instead of the teacher being the addressee of their responses, other structures in conversation are observed. This also happens when teachers make an effort to move from questioning students to using declarative statements, reflective statements, or invitations to elaborate or remain silent, allowing students more time to respond and to elaborate on their own responses. Whether instruction is carried out in real time or through electronic media has an important impact in the structure of participation, as there is a lapse in time that allows for more elaboration. Electronic media also allows for simultaneous participation and the occurrence of multiple conversations or threads.

Importance of Cultural Factors

Cultural differences make up one of the most important factors in how interaction occurs in the classroom, as this involves the participants and their perceptions and cultural expectations of a given event. Cultural differences are also among the most difficult factors of interactions to identify and track. As with many other human behaviors, patterns of teacher-student interaction are culturally based and certain patterns cannot be considered "natural" in any sense. What is expected from students in one culture may be completely inappropriate in another. The demands of classroom discourse are new to all children, such as being in large groups, segregated by age, and differences in cultural understandings regarding participation in a given event

may interfere with how lessons are conducted. In the United States, while students from White, middle-class families come to school with a set of understandings that may be finely attuned to the school culture, students from other cultural and linguistic backgrounds have historically had problems in adapting to the communicative expectations of their classrooms.

Children who come from diverse sociocultural and linguistic backgrounds often bring with them a different set of communicative expectations and interaction rules. Unlike mainstream children who are familiar with patterns of interaction that include cross-examination and tasks similar to what they encounter in schools, minority children bring to school a different set of cultural experiences. Heath, in her famous study of three communities in Appalachia, found that the "ways with words" of the three communities were very different, including narrative styles, organization of communication between infants and caregivers, participant structures, and communicative competence. Other researchers, like Philips and Ron and Suzanne Scollon, who have worked with Native American communities, observed different patterns of community activity and communication styles, including cultural assumptions, orientation to tasks, participation and roles in interaction, right to speak, wait-time, turn allocation, addressing the group rather than individual, and the presentation of the self. These cultural and communicative differences have been shown to have an important impact on how minority students and their communicative competences are perceived by teachers and the educational system. In many cases, different cultural and linguistic backgrounds entail a differential treatment and differential access to literacy. These students fail to respond to school situations such as tests that are frequently administered under conditions that seem unfamiliar and at times threatening. When instructional and elicitation conditions are changed, there is often a radical improvement in student response.

Linguistically diverse students also come to school with a range of communicative competences that in many instances include the use of multiple languages. Bilingual/multilingual discourse includes the alternate use of more than one language in the form of code switching or code mixing. While scholars disagree strongly, many teachers still regard code switching as an aberration that interferes with the use of standard language. Bilingual and bidialectic students also bring distinct ways of pronouncing and enunciating words and sentences that include different sets of homophones and hypercorrections. While these differences in language and ways of communicating may or may not have implications for literacy instruction, they have a significant influence on a teacher's expectations and, consequently, on the learning environment. For example, many times teachers focus on form instead of meaning when confronted with language that differs from the standard norm. However, researchers such as Heath and Ana Celia Zentella have shown that all dialects and bilingual ways of communicating, including code switching, are rule governed and culturally appropriate to those who use them; hence the importance of understanding code alteration and its meaning in everyday interaction. Looking at communicative competence as knowledge not only of grammatical structure but also of the relationship between form and functions of language, which are embedded through language use in social life, and conceptualizing language in terms of difference rather than deficit are important steps in recognizing the linguistic and cultural competences and resources that students bring to classroom interaction. This involves a shift from students simply assimilating the type of language favored in the classroom and focusing on appropriateness to a more active student role in acquiring or appropriating certain language forms for their own "benefit" or use.

Discourse and Dialogue

Allowing for a variety of communicative and instructional patterns that range from more monologic and teacher centered to a dialogue between students and teacher enhances students' opportunities to display their communicative competences and become active members of the classroom community. This is especially important when considering discourse as an integral part of speakers' identities and cultural construction of reality. Discourse both relates to and defines such reality, reflecting and playing a crucial role in the formation of participants' identities as members of a community of practice. As children take control of new ways of talking, thinking, and being, discourse becomes a mediator in the formation of their identities as "students." Furthermore, different types of discourses, including oral and written forms, are becoming increasingly important in today's information society. Providing opportunities for students to learn these new forms of discourse, which integrate

information technology, may provide more equitable opportunities for them and improve their linguistic and cultural competences as they become members of a globalized society. However, given the current focus on standardization and accountability and the widespread use of scripted curricula, making space for this variation in classroom discourse becomes increasingly more difficult for both teachers and students.

Valentina Canese

See also BICS/CALP Theory; Code Switching; Discourse Analysis; Language and Identity; Social Learning; Vygotsky and Language Learning

Further Readings

Cazden, C. B. (2001). *Classroom discourse: The language of teaching and learning* (2nd ed.). Westport, CT: Heinemann.

Cazden, C. B., John, V. P., & Hymes, D. (Eds.). (1972). *Functions of language in the classroom.* New York: Teachers College Press.

Heath, S. B. (1983). *Ways with words: Language, life, and work in communities and classrooms.* Cambridge, UK: Cambridge University Press.

Hicks, D. (Ed.). (1996). *Discourse, learning, and schooling.* Cambridge, UK: Cambridge University Press.

Mehan, H. (1979). *Learning lessons.* Cambridge, MA: Harvard University Press.

Philips, S. (1983). *The invisible culture: Communication in classroom and community on the Warm Springs Reservation.* New York: Longman.

Scollon, R., & Scollon, S. (1981). *Narrative, literacy, and face in interethnic communication.* Norwood, NJ: Ablex.

Zentella, A. C. (1997). *Growing up bilingual: Puerto Rican children in New York.* Malden, MA: Blackwell.

CLASSROOM LANGUAGE

See BICS/CALP THEORY

CODE SWITCHING

Spanglish, Franglais, Konglish, mix-mix, and *pocho* are examples of the generally pejorative labels for alternation between languages, formally known by linguists as *code switching,* probably the most misunderstood and unjustifiably maligned form of bilingual behavior in the world. As demonstrated by researchers studying the phenomenon for the past half century, however, code switching is really a most remarkable ability, worthy to be admired rather than disrespected and criticized. This entry presents what is known about code switching, a skill that has already yielded insights into children's behavior in the process of acquiring two or more languages.

Common Misunderstandings About Code Switching

The mistaken idea that code switchers are somehow confused between their two (or more) languages comes primarily from monolinguals who are unable to conceive how anyone could switch languages so effortlessly. Their monolingual brains are unable to process the rapid alternation between languages, and they erroneously imagine that the code-switching speakers are unable to keep their languages separate. This popular misconception was explained by a Texas professor of Spanish who responded to a complaint that code switchers were confusing their languages: "When the students are in my class, they speak only Spanish, and in their other classes they speak only English. But when they get together in the cafeteria for lunch, they freely code-switch with one another."

Others—equally uninformed about the nature of language—object to code switching because they see it as threatening the supposed purity of their language, although with respect to language, the notion of purity has no basis in fact. The Spanish professor's response likewise debunks this concern, since code switchers can and do separate their languages when this is called for and code-switch with peers when the context is appropriate.

The Nature of Code Switching

It should be clarified at the outset that the term *code* as used here does not imply something secret, but reflects the idea that a language *encodes* information in symbolic form and that different languages can therefore be seen as different codes. For instance, the animal referred to in English by the term *horse* is labeled *caballo* in Spanish, *cheval* in French, *Pferd* in German, and *ma* in Chinese, all encoding the same referent. Information may be encoded grammatically in different ways as well. English, for example, indicates that a noun is the object of a verb simply by placing it after the verb, as in *John hit the ball,* whereas in Russian or German, this would be shown by means of an accusative-case suffix on the noun or noun phrase (just as English changes the pronoun *he* to *him*). In English, questions are formed by moving the first auxiliary verb (or *do* if there isn't one) to the beginning of the sentence, as in *Is he coming?* whereas in Chinese, Korean, or Vietnamese, the question would be indicated simply by placing a question particle (e.g., *ma* in Chinese, *kka* in Korean) at the end of the sentence.

Code switching is usually divided into two types: *intersentential,* switching between sentences, or *intrasentential,* switching within sentences. The former is less remarkable, since it involves no grammatical interaction between the respective languages. Most research on the grammar of code switching has focused on the intrasentential type. (Somewhat confusingly, many European researchers reserve the label *code switching* for the first type and use *code mixing* for the second; however, it is important to recognize that this usage does not imply that code switching is just a random or mixed-up alternation between languages.)

Whereas only fluent bilinguals can code-switch within sentences, not all fluent bilinguals are able to do this, since it is a skill that comes from practice in communicating with other code switchers. Many bilinguals can change from using one language for a whole discourse to another for a different discourse but cannot switch from one language to another within a single sentence.

There has been a huge growth of research on code switching in the past 20 years, with several thousand articles and a number of books published on the subject. A recent Google search yielded no fewer than 365,000 hits. Researchers have generally considered code switching from one of three perspectives: sociolinguistic, grammatical, or psycholinguistic, corresponding to these questions: "Why do people code-switch?" "What do they do when they code-switch?" and "How do they code-switch?" We will discuss each of these in turn.

Why Do People Code-Switch?

Most fluent code switching occurs unconsciously, and speakers are often surprised when told that they have been switching. The reasons for switching are various. As suggested in the opening anecdote above, close acquaintances may code-switch simply because it signals personal solidarity or because it is emblematic of bicultural group membership. Austrians schooled before World War II used both Austrian German and school ("High") German *(Hochdeutsch)* only in separate discourses, whereas those who were schooled after the war often code-switched, partly as a marker of social identity. People who are close friends or who share numerous experiences may feel more comfortable using their languages interchangeably with one another.

Switching is often triggered by the topic being discussed. Friends discussing their experiences in school may unconsciously switch to the school language or intersperse vocabulary relevant to the school context for which they may have no native-language equivalent. Although it is convenient to think of words as having neutrally equivalent meanings, as *horse/caballo/cheval/Pferd/ma,* mentioned above, particular words in one language may evoke emotional or experiential associations that trigger a switch into that language. For a person reared on a ranch among *caballos,* English *horse* may seem a sterile book word. While discussion of home topics might be predominantly in the first language, a recounting of a hospital visit, for example, might trigger more use of English.

Genuine code switching involves more than just the substitution of one word for another, however, as discussed in the next section. If a speaker happens not to know a term in his or her native language and knows it only in the second language, the use of this term is more accurately a case of *borrowing* to fill what linguists would call a "lexical gap" in the first language. A non-English speaker living in the United States who had never experienced a four-lane divided highway in his native country might not have a ready term for it and so might refer to the *freeway* or *expressway* even in the middle of an otherwise non-English sentence.

Grammar of Code Switching

It is never the case that "anything goes" in code switching, but research has shown that there are always grammatical factors at work that limit the possibilities. Fluent bilinguals who code-switch are generally in close agreement as to what constitutes a grammatical versus an ungrammatical switch. Rosario Gingràs found, for example, the following percentages of agreement on the acceptability of Spanish-English code-switched sentences (note that adjectives

in Spanish usually follow nouns, whereas in English, they precede nouns; here *el* = "the"; *hombre* = "man"; *viejo* = "old"; and *enojado* = "angry"):

El	old	man	*está enojado.*	(94%)
The *hombre viejo*			is angry.	(90%)
El	man	old	*está enojado.*	(0.5%)
El	*hombre* old		*está enojado.*	(0.0%)

Several generalizations emerge from these examples that apply to many other language pairs as well. One of the best known of these is what Shana Poplack called the "equivalence constraint," which says that if two languages differ in their word order, it will be ungrammatical to switch at a point that would violate either of their respective grammars. English adjectives precede the noun they modify, whereas Spanish adjectives usually follow the noun. Speakers strongly reject a switch into English that would place the adjective after the noun, even if all the rest of the sentence is in Spanish, since this would violate English grammar. The equivalence constraint explains why it is difficult for Korean speakers to code-switch into English (apart from the insertion of individual nouns), since the basic word order in Korean is subject-object-verb, whereas in English it is subject-verb-object; postpositions in Korean follow nouns, whereas corresponding prepositions in English precede nouns; and relative clauses in Korean precede nouns, whereas they follow nouns in English.

A number of highly specific constraints on code switching have appeared in the literature and have been confirmed in a variety of studies on various language pairs. These include not switching in the following instances:

1. Between auxiliary (helping) verbs

2. Around negatives and "WH-question" constituents

3. Between attached pronoun forms and the words they modify

However, some constraints or lack thereof seem to be specific to particular languages or language pairs. For instance, Hindi speakers rarely switch following subjects, whereas this is common in Spanish/English switching.

In addition to purely grammatical restrictions or "rules" on possible code switching, there is an additional intriguing constraint having to do with the sociocultural status relations of the languages involved. For language pairs such as Japanese and English, which speakers perceive as having sociolinguistic parity, switching in either direction seems equally possible. However, for situations in which one language has a higher perceived social status than the other, switching tends to be asymmetrical—occurring only from the lower language to the higher language. This restriction was first noted for Swedish/English switching among Swedish Americans, but it has been observed frequently in former colonial situations in India and Africa and among Mexican Americans in the United States. The interesting puzzle here is what—in the nature of neurological storage, access, speech production, and control mechanisms—within the brain permits shifting to the socially dominant language channel from the less prestigious language channel but inhibits it in the opposite direction.

There is an extensive technical literature on proposed grammatical bases for various constraints, and considerable theoretical disagreement. It is overwhelmingly clear from all of the data, however, that switching is not random, but is governed by grammatical regularities in and between the languages involved.

Psycholinguistics of Code Switching

How the brains of code switchers manage two languages simultaneously is only beginning to be understood, and the better it is understood, the more this remarkable ability is appreciated. The study of code switching can provide a unique "window into the brain" to allow us to analyze how online processing of language actually takes place.

For speakers in code-switching mode, the evidence shows that the brain is in fact encoding the same message simultaneously in both languages, in parallel channels. In the past, it was assumed that this was impossible and that only one channel could be involved in language production. However, recent psycholinguistic research on bilinguals has demonstrated that when a bilingual person hears or reads a word in one language, the corresponding expression in the other language is at least partially activated. In other words, even when a bilingual appears to be operating solely in one language, the brain storage for the other language is still at least passively involved.

Evidence for the parallel-channel processing model comes from several types of data. First, code switching usually occurs in a smooth, seamless flow of speech, which in most instances shows no indication of time lapse such as might be expected if one or another system were being alternately started up and shut down.

The second type of evidence shows that grammatical agreement crosses languages, even when one language may not show evidence of it. For example, in

The old *man* está enojado,

the predicate adjective, *enojado* ("angry" in Spanish) shows obligatory "masculine" gender agreement with the final "o," even though the spoken subject *the old man* is in English. Thus, even though the subject is actually uttered in English, which requires no gender agreement on adjectives, the Spanish channel processor is giving evidence that it is generating a parallel, but unuttered, subject that is determining the agreement selection. Similar examples are found in other languages.

The third kind of evidence for parallel-channel processing, from research conducted by Erica McClure and Miwa Nishimura, lies in examples from various languages of linguistic *doublings* or *overlappings* which sometimes occur in code switches. The following examples show utterances in English, where the speakers switched to another language (Spanish, Japanese and Korean), in which the content of the switch repeats the meaning in English. Each example is followed, by a literal translation of the text in italics, below, in brackets:

I can't do it ¡*No puedo!*

[not–can, 1st person]
(Spanish: McClure, 1977)

We bought about two pounds *gurai kattekita no.*

[about–bought]
(Japanese: Nishimura, 1985)

These examples show that whole structures already assembled in one language can be switched from one channel to the other or the switch may occur around a word (typically a noun) and the performance of the sentence can proceed along the other language track.

Child Bilingualism and Code Switching

In many areas of the world, it is considered normal for children to grow up speaking two or more languages, and multilingualism is taken for granted. In places like Indonesia and West Africa, it is commonplace for people to speak three or four languages and understand several more. However, in the United States, social and institutional forces for the use of English are so powerful and pervasive that it is difficult for children to maintain and adequately develop a heritage language. If the home language is retained at all, it is likely to be restricted in use to close personal contexts and not fully developed for literacy and formal public cultural contexts.

Research indicates that very young children initially do not recognize the differences between languages and therefore merge them in a single linguistic store in the brain. However, gradually, beyond the age of 3 or even earlier, they begin to sort them out on the basis of who speaks what. Thus, German may be "father's language," or Korean may be "grandmother's language," and the child will separate the codes in his or her brain for communicating with particular individuals. There is no evidence whatsoever to suggest that beyond the very initial stages of language learning, children ever confuse different languages. A good example is that of a 6-year-old girl in Texas, the daughter of deaf Hispanic parents, who had learned sign language to communicate with them, Spanish to communicate with her hearing grandmother and neighborhood playmates, and English for other playmates and for school; she also regularly served as an interpreter for her parents with speakers of both English and Spanish.

The usual advice given to parents who are themselves bilingual or who are dominant in different languages is to try to adhere to a "one person, one language" strategy, so that children more quickly distinguish the languages they hear and associate them with different speakers. However, this is difficult to maintain in practice, though it is probably helpful to the extent that it can be carried out. Thousands or even millions of competent adult bilinguals have grown up in homes where code switching was common, and there is no evidence that this has had any negative effect on their command of their respective languages.

Conversely, introducing the national language too early when it is not the language of the home (as in programs like Head Start) is likely to interfere with the full development of the native heritage language and create permanent cognitive impairment. The disruptive effects of early introduction of English, for example, is shown by the fact that children in the United States with Mexican backgrounds who attend school through the second grade in Mexico do better academically by the time they reach the sixth grade than their younger siblings who begin school in the United States and have had more exposure to English but less to Spanish.

The fact that code switching is a particular skill is supported by research on the acquisition of code-switching ability by children. The evidence for this comes from the fact that young children learning two or more languages may make a number of switches that would be "ungrammatical" in adult speech before they fully develop the skill to simultaneously manage two discrete linguistic systems. Encouraging code switching as a pedagogical and parenting strategy may therefore actually contribute to the development of both languages, though care should be taken that one language does not come to dominate and inhibit the development of the other. This consideration is particularly important where the heritage language lacks the social status or community reinforcement of the ambient national language.

Conclusion

Until such time as we develop tools to examine language processing in the brain at the level of neurons or molecules, the study of code switching will continue to offer one of the best opportunities to observe the ongoing process of sentence production in real time and constitutes the next best thing to being able to see inside the brain itself. Unfortunately, as we have discussed, popular misunderstanding of the phenomenon has led to negative attitudes toward the practice; consequently, labels such as *Spanglish* (which was even the title of a motion picture), *pocho,* and *mix-mix* (in the Philippines) may be associated with a deficit view of code switching. Code switching needs to be seen as the remarkable mental feat that it is and its users recognized for their linguistic skill. Far from being criticized due to ignorance, code switchers should be celebrated for their competence.

Rudolph C. Troike

See also Discourse Analysis; Language Acquisition Device; One Person-One Language (OPOL); Second-Language

Acquisition; Spanglish; Status Differences Among Languages

Further Readings

Gingràs, R. (1974). Problems in the description of Spanish-English intrasentential code-switching. In G. Bills (Ed.), *Southwest areal linguistics* (pp. 167–174). San Diego: University of California at San Diego, Institute for Cultural Pluralism.

Jacobson, R. (Ed.). (2001). *Codeswitching worldwide II.* Berlin and New York: Mouton de Gruyter.

McClure, E. (1977). Aspects of code switching in the discourse of bilingual Mexican-American children. In M. Saville-Troike (Ed.), *Linguistics and anthropology* (pp. 93–115). Washington, DC: Georgetown University.

Meyers-Scotton, C. (1993). *Duelling languages: Grammatical structure in codeswitching.* Oxford, UK: Oxford University Press.

Nishimura, M. (1985). *Intrasentential code-switching in Japanese and English.* Unpublished doctoral dissertation, University of Pennsylvania, Philadelphia.

Park, J., Troike, R. C., & Park, M. (1989). *Constraints in Korean/English code-switching: A preliminary study.* Paper presented at the 9th Second Language Research Forum, University of California, Los Angeles.

Poplack, S. (1980). Sometimes I'll start a sentence in Spanish y termino en español: Toward a typology of code-switching. *Linguistics, 18,* 581–618.

COGNATES, TRUE AND FALSE

People learning a new language often rely on their knowledge of their native language as they attempt to communicate, especially when the two languages are related and have many words that look or sound alike. This is a useful strategy, but it can backfire, as many language students know. Some cases can be humorous and provide listeners with a good laugh or at least a stifled one. A well-known example concerns a young unmarried woman who studied some Spanish to use when visiting Spain. The first night in Spain, at a formal dinner, she is asked to give a short speech. She rises and begins by explaining that she is *embarazada* that her Spanish is not better. Some of the guests who knew some English laughed, guessing her faux pas. Only later did a sympathetic friend explain that the Spanish word she used means *pregnant,* not *embarrassed,* as she had intended.

This story illustrates the problems false cognates can cause. False cognates, such as *embarazada* and *embarrassed,* are words from two languages that look alike but come from different roots and have completely different meanings. When language learners, like the woman in the story, try to draw on the surface similarity to fill a gap in their vocabulary, the results can indeed be *embarrassing.*

Even though false cognates can cause communication problems for language learners, they can be an important resource to draw on for building a wider vocabulary in the new language. Cognates are words derived from the same root or, literally, words that are born together (from the Latin *co,* meaning *with* or *together,* and *gnatus,* meaning *born*). English language learners must draw on all available resources, including cognates, because they face a formidable task in acquiring English vocabulary.

Michael Graves cites studies showing that native-English-speaking third graders have a reading vocabulary of about 10,000 words. The average 12th-grade student's reading vocabulary is nearly 40,000 words. This means that children acquire about 3,000 words each year. Much of this vocabulary is acquired through reading. As they read, students infer word meanings from context. Estimates of the number of words students learn from context vary. However, middle-grade students learn somewhere between 800 and 8,000 words annually simply from reading. School texts contain more words than does oral language that form part of the academic vocabulary students need to succeed academically. Students who read more acquire more of these words. It is a clear case of the rich getting richer.

Many English language learners start third grade with far fewer than 10,000 words. Because they have more limited vocabularies, they do not read nearly as much in English as do their native English-speaking classmates. Since reading is a major source of vocabulary acquisition, English learners do not acquire as many words from reading as their native English-speaking peers. As a result, rather than catching up, they may actually fall further behind each year. However, when teachers read to English learners and provide time and encouragement for bilingual students to read, vocabulary growth is accelerated. Further, teachers of English learners can help their students acquire English vocabulary as they infer word meanings by looking for cognates.

As a cautionary note, there are some cognates whose meanings have drifted far apart. An international student from Mexico might say she plans to *inscribe* at a university in the United States, when she actually plans to *register.* Her choice of words is understandable, since the Spanish word *inscribir* means *register.* While the Spanish *inscribir* and the English *inscribe* come from the same Latin roots and are related, the meanings in the two languages are very different. A jeweler might *inscribe* a spouse's name on a wedding band, but one cannot *inscribe* at the local college. Nevertheless, many cognates retain similar meanings.

Often, people think of the benefits of instruction in cognates for native Spanish speakers, since Spanish and English have so many cognates. However, other languages, especially those from the Indo-European language family, share cognates with English. The authors became aware of this when they were living and teaching in Lithuania. Among the food items they once purchased was a box of breakfast cereal. They noticed that on the side panel, the company had listed the ingredients in several different languages. Many of the words for basic ingredients, such as *sugar, honey,* and *salt* showed remarkable similarity across a range of languages, at least in the written form. The company listed the ingredients in the following languages: German, Romanian, Lithuanian, Latvian, Polish, Czech, Croatian, Slovakian, Slovenian, Yugoslavian, Estonian, and Hungarian. Ingredients were also listed in Russian and Bulgarian, but these were written in Cyrillic script. In the latter cases, students would have more difficulty noticing cognates across different writing systems unless they heard them spoken rather than try to read them. Table 1 lists the words for *sugar, honey,* and *salt.*

It is interesting to note that not all of these languages are members of the Indo-European language family. Both Estonian and Hungarian belong to the Uralic language family. Even though these languages are not related to the others, the names for the ingredients are remarkably similar. The word for *sugar* is similar in all the languages. Despite the fact that some spell the word with *s,* some with *z,* and others with *c,* those letters probably all represent similar sounds. The words for *honey* are also similar except for the German *Honig,* which is close to the English word. The other languages have a word like the English word *mead,* which is a drink made with honey. Finally, all the words for *salt* start with *s,* and most of them include an *l.* This brief comparison of basic words across a range of languages suggests that students from a number of language backgrounds could

Table 1   Translations of the Words *Sugar, Honey,* and *Salt* Across Languages

Language	Example 1	Example 2	Example 3
English	sugar	honey	salt
German	Zucker	Honig	Salz
Romanian	zahăr	miere	sare
Lithuanian	cukrus	medus	druska
Latvian	cukurs	medus	sáls
Polish	cukier	miód	sól
Czech	cukr	med	sůl
Croatian	šećer	med	sol
Slovakian	cukor	med	sol'
Slovenian	sladkor	med	sol
Yugoslavian	secer	med	so
Estonian	suhkur	mesi	sool
Hungarian	cukor	méz	só

benefit from cognate identification and study. This can be done as a fun activity rather than as a dull exercise in linguistics.

James Cummins's studies have established that what a person knows in one language can transfer to a second language because there is a common underlying proficiency. Cummins cites research that shows an interdependence among the concepts, skills, and linguistic knowledge in two languages. As a result, vocabulary knowledge transfers across languages. Since words may be thought of as labels for concepts, if a student knows a concept in the first language, the student more easily acquires the vocabulary for that concept in a second language. If the two languages are related, the words used to express a concept may look and sound alike. Since many words that make up academic English have Latin roots, students who speak a Latinate language, such as Spanish or French, already know related words. By accessing these cognates, English learners can rapidly increase their academic English vocabularies.

Table 2 lists some English-Spanish cognates from social studies and science.

More than 80% of the limited-English students in U.S. schools are native Spanish speakers, and

Table 2 Social Studies and Science Cognates in English and Spanish

Social Studies		Science	
English	Spanish	English	Spanish
civilization	civilización	geography	geografía
history	historia	biology	biología
past	pasado	analysis	análisis
pioneer	pionero	diagram	diagrama
colonial	colonial	experiment	experimento
diary	diario	formula	fórmula

between 20% and 30% of the English words in school texts have Spanish cognates. For these reasons, it is especially helpful to teach native Spanish speakers to identify and use cognates.

Teachers can help students access cognates by engaging them in activities that increase their awareness of similar words across languages. Joan Williams lists several strategies teachers can use. For example, a teacher might begin by putting book pages on an overhead transparency and having students find cognates. Students could work in pairs to identify cognates. The teacher could also create a cognate wall. Pairs of students could add the cognates they find to the wall. This activity could extend throughout a unit of study, and students could list as many cognates as possible related to the topic. Further, the class could develop a cognate dictionary, using the words from the cognate wall.

A similar exercise can provide students with some lighthearted moments by identifying false cognates. They would no doubt find it interesting to know that a *tuna* in English is a type of fish, while in Mexican Spanish it is the fruit of a cactus and in Spain it is the name of a roaming group of minstrel singers.

Timothy Rodríguez suggests that once students identify cognates, they can work together to categorize them. This is an excellent activity to raise word consciousness and increase the important academic skill of categorization. Rodríguez's students found several ways to classify Spanish-English cognates. For example, some, like *colonial* have the same spelling. Others, like *civilization* and *civilización,* have a predictable variation in spelling. The derivational suffix *-tion* in English is almost always spelled *-ción* in Spanish. This is a great spelling lesson learned quickly. Other cognates like *sport* and *deporte* have the same root. Some

cognates share only one of the meanings of the word. An example is that *letter* in English can refer to a letter of the alphabet or a business letter, but in Spanish, the cognate *letra* means only a letter of the alphabet. As students collect cognates, they can categorize them. This exercise helps make them more aware of the different cognates that exist. Students can then apply their knowledge of cognates to academic English reading.

Although drawing on false cognates can lead to embarrassing moments, accessing true cognates can boost vocabulary acquisition for many English language learners. Teachers should take advantage of this valuable resource to help English learners build academic language proficiency in English.

Yvonne S. Freeman and David E. Freeman

See also Grammar-Translation Method; Indo-European Languages; Spanish Loan Words in U.S. English

Further Readings

Cummins, J. (2000). *Language, power, and pedagogy: Bilingual children in the crossfire.* Tonawanda, NY: Multilingual Matters.

Nash, R. (1990). *NTC's Dictionary of Spanish cognates thematically organized.* Chicago: NTC Publishing Group.

Rodríguez, T. A. (2001). From the known to the unknown: Using cognates to teach English to Spanish-speaking literates. *Reading Teacher, 54,* 744–746.

Williams, J. (2001). Classroom conversations: Opportunities to learn for ESL students in mainstream classrooms. *Reading Teacher, 54,* 750–757.

COGNITIVE BENEFITS OF BILINGUALISM

This entry focuses on how bilinguals differ from individuals who speak only one language in performing a variety of simple cognitive tasks. It explores the intersection of linguistic and cognitive skills, along with factors that should be considered in studies comparing bilingual and monolingual subjects, notably students.

Researchers have found that some of the cognitive advantages of being bilingual include enhanced cognitive functioning, a greater number of cognitive pathways, and enhanced memory and brain plasticity. Andrea Mechelli and her collaborators explain that *brain plasticity* refers to the ability of the brain to functionally change and that learning a second language helps build density in the gray matter of the brain. The findings of their study provide evidence of the impact of second-language acquisition on the structure of the human brain.

A comparison of grammar, sentence structure, and word usage of two distinct languages and the inherent complexities of the cognitive process has found that bilinguals have a greater understanding of the intricacy of language. The higher the degree of bilingualism, the more cognitive benefits accrue to the individual. It is worth noting that not all bilinguals have these advantages, especially those with underdeveloped skills in two languages. The more bilingual the person is, the more noticeable are the advantages.

In addition, bilingualism has been found to foster classification skills, concept formation, analogical reasoning, visual-spatial skills, and creativity and has other cognitive gains. The ability to know two or more words for one object or idea may provide an added cognitive flexibility. If a word in one language can mean two or more different things, bilinguals, who are able to bridge the first language to the second language, are thereby provided with an added dimension to the word. To illustrate this, Colin Baker provides an example using the Welsh word *ysgol,* which means both *school* and *ladder* in Welsh and provides the bilingual with the added dimension in English of *school as a ladder.* Knowing two languages opens up a bilingual's mind to ways in which to differentiate concepts and enhance and expand meaning. Bilingual persons experience two different ways in which to conceive and think about an idea or concept; hence, their thought process broadens. Ellen Bialystok found that compared with monolingual children, bilingual children can count words in a sentence, which is a difficult task for children at a young age. Young bilinguals appear to have a deeper processing ability, which helps them to understand that words can be isolated from sentences. This understanding of the identity of words helps them understand parts of speech and the intertwining of words to make meaning. Bilinguals have also been shown to be more analytical regarding the structure of language. It is this metalinguistic awareness that is so important for children's reading skills.

Luis Moll has defined two types of cognitive structures: (a) structures of explanation and (b) structures for cognitive activity. Structures of explanation aid a person in the organization of perception in new ways. The structures for cognitive activity operate on the level of cognitive process. As second-language learners are learning and using a new language, they are relying on both the structures of explanation and the structures for cognitive activity they already have acquired in their first language. Both operate on the level of cognitive processes, which contain the structures for memorization and recall that are so important for building a solid base for the new language.

This is the area of the brain where context cluing and the formation of concept mapping take place, in order to relate what has been learned to the actual production of language in the areas of reading, writing, and oral construction. As the two learned languages intertwine, the brain enables the speaker to draw on what has been learned in both languages, therefore giving the bilingual a broader basis for problem solving and critical thinking. Knowing more than one language gives bilinguals more information and knowledge to draw from. Consequently, they are able to analyze the information obtained and use either deductive thought processing or inductive reasoning to or build upon a concept.

According to Ron and Suzanne Scollon, people use cognitive schemas to do things to communicate and socially interact in a language and culture. A person learning his or first language develops cognitive schemas for that culture and social environment. As this same person learns a second language, other cognitive schemas must be learned. Also, second-language learning builds new neural pathways, according to Fred Genesee. The brain develops this new knowledge by building new neural pathways, then "rewires" itself and prepares for more information input, which includes finer problem-solving and critical thinking skills and an increase in the creative process.

Strategies to Enhance Bilinguals' Cognitive Skills

Teachers of second-language learners are encouraged to use strategies that help develop reflective and problem-oriented teaching styles. Language learning helps to develop problem-solving and critical thinking techniques and enhances bilinguals' skills already in place. Josué M. González and Linda Darling-Hammond point out that cognitive mapping and conceptual scaffolding are areas in which the brain is able to make new connections and create ways to conceptualize relationships between words and abstract ideas. Through the use of cognitive coaching, teachers are able to help second-language learners understand the constructs and similarities between their native language and their new language. Edward Pajak explains that cognitive coaching is driven by four assumptions: (1) that all forms of behavior are influenced by a person's perceptions; (2) that teaching is a decision-making process during all stages of instruction; (3) that to change behavior, there should be some form of alteration of the mind; and (4) human beings' intellectual abilities grow throughout a person's lifetime.

The interaction between teacher and language learner can be a powerful tool to help students acquire strong problem-solving and critical thinking skills in the area of language development by someone who models reflective thinking. According to Pajak, these techniques rearrange and restructure mental processes among the participants, regardless of whether they are teachers or students.

Conceptual scaffolding in learning allows and encourages the building of ideas and concepts upon a framework so that each new idea or concept emerges from a prior one. Previous knowledge a person has in his or her first language is built upon with each new piece of knowledge learned in the second language. Thus, immigrant students who possess essential skills (i.e., in reading, writing, comprehension, and mathematics) in their native languages will have an advantage when learning a new language, particularly in those subject areas needed for school or in the workplace. this framework. This framework the learner uses to add new pieces of information learned (such as vocabulary, grammar, and cultural knowledge) is the very basis for the learner to make connections and comparisons and build on bilingual skills. This precept is one that bilingual educators use to encourage language learners to draw on a base of understanding in their native language in order to build a second language and transfer this new knowledge to their everyday lives at home, in the community, and in the workplace.

In the field of bilingual education, it is common knowledge that a second language is acquired through both subconscious and conscious learning. It is therefore thought that learning both in a simulated environment (the classroom) and in an authentic environment (the world outside the classroom) are integral to the sound acquisition of a second language.

Colin Baker distinguishes between "paper and pencil" intelligence and the wider scope of intelligence.

So much of what society deems intelligence is measured by tests or the "paper and pencil realm" of intelligence. Baker emphasizes that the language in which the testing is conducted (i.e., whether it is the stronger and more dominant language of the individual) is an important factor in testing. Based on his research, Baker found that areas of mental activity other than the intelligence quotient (IQ) needed to be investigated in order to further delve into cognitive functioning among multilinguals. As Baker explains, IQ testing has to do with convergent thinking and deals with only one correct answer. Divergent thinking, Baker proposes, should be another style to investigate in the realm of testing because divergent thinking involves imagination and creativity, like finding more than one correct answer to a problem—more of a multiple questioning, which can be used to discover other avenues of looking at a question by asking more questions. In the Ellis Torrance Test of Creative Thinking, Torrance analyzed answers to the "uses of an object" (e.g., unusual uses of cardboard boxes or tin cans) in four categories: fluency, flexibility, originality, and elaboration. Baker summarizes that in the areas of scoring for these categories, the question to be asked is this: Does the ability to speak more than one language add to cognitive abilities due to the increased fluency, flexibility, originality, and elaboration in thinking?

James Cummins found that these four areas (fluency, flexibility, originality, and elaboration) differed depending on whether the bilinguals tested were balanced (equally fluent in both languages) or nonbalanced. Balanced bilinguals did better in the categories of fluency and flexibility scales of verbal divergence but not as high on originality of thought. As reported by Baker, Cummins proposes the notion of a threshold level of language competence; he asserts that bilingual children should attain this level in both of their languages. If that is not the case, there might be cognitive deficits. Hence, such competence should be attained for them to benefit from cognitive growth as an influence of bilingualism. Bialystok, as reported previously, found through research that bilingual children were superior to monolinguals on measures of cognitive control of linguistic processes. This is to say that the children could differentiate, for example, the semantic (order of words) structure of a sentence for its grammatical correctness.

Baker admits that there are limitations to this research, such as the matching of groups; comparing bilinguals and multilinguals needs to match all variables, not just language, including social status, cultural background, level of fluency in each language, and educational background. Baker asserts that future research needs to address the following issues:

1. Match monolingual and bilingual groups on all variables other than language.

2. Possibly focus on other types of bilinguals, not just balanced bilinguals.

3. Investigate the cause-and-effect relationship of bilingualism. Does bilingualism come first and cause cognitive benefits, or do cognitive abilities enhance language learning, or do cognitive development and language learning work hand in hand?

4. Ask whether all children benefit from bilingualism or just certain children, depending on social class or cognitive ability level.

5. Consider the hopes and ideologies of the researcher; for example, Kenji Hakuta impels us to consider the rationale behind methods used by researchers.

6. Consider whether the cognitive effects found are temporary or permanent.

Cultural diversity and learning styles must also be discussed when exploring the cognitive benefits of bilingualism. All cultures do not problem solve or critically think in the same manner. Teachers frequently ask single-answer or closed-ended questions instead of open-ended questions that involve more complex problem-solving skills. Their emphasis may be on details, building the whole from the parts and moving from the specific to the general. Yet many cultures are more oriented to inductive thinking (working from the specific observation and building upon it) rather than deductive thinking (working from the broader generalization to the specific) and more interactive and communal in constructing critical thinking skills. Social interaction, group activity, and active participation in a meaningful environment are integral components to teaching second-language learners.

In the cognitive realm, a learner's particular style, the process he or she uses for problem solving and for demonstrating what is known and can be accomplished, is essential knowledge for an educator to progress in instruction and the facilitation of learning for an individual. When a person interacts with new ideas, situations, people, and information, there are several different areas of involvement. According to Pat Guild and Stephen Garger, these include *cognition* (ways of knowing), *conceptualizing* (formulating ideas and thoughts), *affective reacting* (feeling and valuing), and *acting* (exhibiting some kind of behavior). These areas of involvement are magnified and become twofold for multilinguals because they bring different former knowledge from their native languages, including culture, communication, comparisons, connections, and communities, and therefore must learn to function well in these areas in multiple languages.

Cognitive development is stimulated by cognitive conflict or sociocognitive conflict, as Genesee explains. This conflict is derived from social interaction between peers who have different perspectives of a problem. Peer collaboration on a project is beneficial to a person's cognitive development, and the ability to look at a problem from two different languages with different ways of reasoning, both inductive and deductive, brings yet another dimension to the problem or situation. This is what research by Genesee and others refers to when they say that through the learning process, in the acquisition of another language, one's cognitive abilities change and grow through the construction and development of new neuron pathways and the "rewiring" of the brain. When paired with a bilingual partner, monolingual children gained new insight into the workings of a bilingual mind; in this way, the ability to view problems or challenges from a different linguistic perspective becomes highly valuable. Children who were paired with more competent partners were led to higher levels of thinking.

Cognitive connections in the brain are made between the first language and subsequent languages. As Baker explains, the bilingual person experiences two different ways in which to conceive and think about an idea or concept, allowing the thought process to broaden. Cognitive skills can be developed, and through the use of different teaching strategies and techniques, such as cooperative learning, cognitive mapping, and cognitive coaching, educators can facilitate bilingual students' learning by connecting their native languages to subsequently acquired languages.

Geri McDonough Bell

See also BICS/CALP Theory; Brain Research; Metalinguistic Awareness; Underlying Linguistic Proficiencies

Further Readings

Baker, C. (1993). *Foundations of bilingual education and bilingualism.* Clevedon, UK: Multilingual Matters.

Bialystok, E. (1992). Attentional control in children's metalinguistic performance and measures of field independence. *Developmental Psychology, 28,* 654–664.

Cummins, J. (1975). *Empowering culturally and linguistically diverse students with learning problems.* Retrieved from http://www.ericdigests.org/pre-9220/problems.htm

Gay, G. (2000). *Culturally responsive teaching, theory, research, and practice.* New York: Teachers College Press.

Genesee, F. (2000). *Brain research implications for second language learning.* Retrieved February 1, 2008, from http://www.cal.org/resources/digest/0012brain.html

González, J., & Darling-Hammond L. (1997). *New concepts for new challenges: Professional development for teachers of immigrant youth.* McHenry, IL: Center for Applied Linguistics/Delta Systems.

Gonzalez, V. (1999). *Language and cognitive development in second language learning: Educational implications for children and adults.* Boston: Allyn & Bacon.

Guild, P., & Garger, S. (1985). *Marching to different drummers.* Alexandria, VA: Association for Supervision and Curriculum Development.

Hakuta, K. (1986). *Mirror of language: The debate on bilingualism.* New York: Basic Books.

Mechelli, A., Drimon, J. T., Noppeney, U., O'Doherty, J., Ashburner, J., Frackowiak, R., et al. (2004). Neurolinguistics: Structural plasticity in the bilingual brain. *Nature, 431,* 757. Abstract retrieved from http://www.nature.com/nature/journal/v431/n7010/abs/431757a.html

Moll, L. (1999). *Vygotsky and education: Instructional implications and applications of sociohistorical psychology.* Cambridge, UK: Cambridge University Press.

Pajak, E. (1993). *Approaches to clinical supervision: Alternatives for improving instruction.* Norwood, MA: Christopher-Gordon.

Scollon, R., & Scollon, S. W. (2001). *Intercultural communication.* Malden, MA: Blackwell.

COLLIER, VIRGINIA P. (1941–)

Virginia P. Collier was born in Greenup, Illinois, in November 1941. During her childhood, she spent 5 years in Mexico and Central America, and from age 12 on, she served as assistant to her father (a professor of Central American history at the University of North Carolina, Greensboro), conducting research in the libraries and archives of Guatemala City, San Salvador, Tegucigalpa, Managua, and San Jose.

Collier is professor emerita of bilingual/multicultural/ESL education at George Mason University in Fairfax, Virginia. She is best known for her work with senior researcher Wayne Thomas, conducting longitudinal research on school effectiveness for linguistically and culturally diverse students, working with many school districts in all regions of the United States over the past 22 years. Their award-winning national research studies have had a substantial impact on school policies throughout the world. She is coauthor with Carlos J. Ovando and Mary Carol Combs of a popular book for teachers, *Bilingual and ESL Classrooms: Teaching in Multicultural Contexts,* a well-known, comprehensive text on research, policy, and effective practices for serving students of culturally and linguistically diverse backgrounds. In addition, Collier has over 70 other publications in the field of language minority education, including her popular monograph *Promoting Academic Success for ESL Students.*

In her collaborative work with Wayne Thomas, Collier has contributed new theoretical perspectives for the field of bilingual/multicultural education. The research partners are well-known for developing the *prism model,* a theory and guide to empirical research. This model makes predictions about program effectiveness from a theoretical perspective. Collier and Thomas have tested the prism model by collecting and analyzing program effectiveness data, and they have refined the model on the basis of empirical findings. They have also developed unique theoretical perspectives on analyses of longitudinal student data, to demonstrate the importance of following English learners' achievement over long periods of time. By following individual student progress over 5 to 6 years at minimum (instead of the typical 1 to 2 years), they have shown that the typical short-term finding of "no significant difference across programs" has misled the field and policymakers; in fact, long-term findings yield extremely significant differences among school programs. Importantly, they have found with consistency in each of their research studies that only high-quality bilingual schooling has the potential to close the academic achievement gap. By introducing degree of gap closure as the primary measure of program success, rather than pre-post score differences among groups, they have shown that English-only and transitional bilingual programs of short duration close only about half of the achievement gap, whereas high-quality long-term bilingual programs close all of the gap after 5 to 6 years of schooling through two languages.

After 24 years of teaching and conducting research, Collier retired from her position as professor of bilingual/multicultural/ESL education at George Mason University in 2005. During her association with George Mason, she served as research professor; associate director of degree programs for master's and doctoral students in bilingual/ESL education; director of the program for English as a Second Language (ESL) teachers; and instructor of graduate courses in methods, second-language acquisition, curriculum development, research, and policy in bilingual/multicultural/ESL and foreign-language education. In 1989, she received the Distinguished Faculty Award from George Mason University for excellence in teaching, scholarship, and service.

Proficient in Spanish and English, Collier has served the field of bilingual/multicultural/ESL education for 38 years as parent, teacher, researcher, teacher educator, and doctoral mentor. Her educational background includes a PhD (1980) from the University of Southern California, with specialization in intercultural education, bilingual education and linguistics; an MA with distinction (1973) from American University, with specialization in Hispanic literature and English linguistics, and a BA (1963) from the University of North Carolina, Chapel Hill, with specialization in Spanish and Latin American studies.

Collier has served as keynote and featured speaker at national and international conferences in North America and Europe. She has received prestigious research grants, including a research grant (1996–2002) from the Center for Research on Education, Diversity & Excellence (CREDE) and the Office of Educational Research and Improvement (OERI), U.S. Department of Education; Field-Initiated Studies Grant (1991–1992), U.S. Department of Education; a study grant from the government of Sweden (1982) to conduct research on the education of immigrants in Sweden; and an award (1981) for one of the top 10 dissertations in bilingual education, recognized by the National Advisory Council on Bilingual Education, U.S. Department of Education. Since 1988, both Wayne Thomas and Virginia Collier have been regularly interviewed by the popular media, with 153 published newspaper articles and interviews on television and radio in the United States and abroad, reporting on their continuing research findings.

Judith H. Munter and Josefina V. Tinajero

See also Dual-Language Programs; Measuring Language Proficiency; Program Effectiveness Research

Further Readings

Collier, V. P. (2004). Teaching multilingual children (abridged versions of "Teaching" and "Language" chapters from C. J. Ovando, V. Collier, & M. Combs, 2003). In O. Santa Ana (Ed.), *Tongue-tied: The lives of multilingual children in public education* (pp. 222–235). Lanham, MD: Rowman & Littlefield.

Collier, V. P., & Thomas, W. P. (2004). The astounding effectiveness of dual-language education for all. *NABE Journal of Research and Practice, 2,* 1–20.

Collier, V. P., & Thomas, W. P. (2007). Predicting second-language academic success in English using the prism model. In C. Davison & J. Cummins (Eds.), *International handbook of English language teaching* (pp. 333–348). New York: Springer.

Collier, V. P., Thomas, W. P., & Tinajero, J. (2006). From remediation to enrichment: Transforming Texas schools through dual language education. *Texas Association for Bilingual Education Journal, 9*(1), 23–34.

Ovando, C. J., Combs, M. C., & Collier, V. P. (2006). *Bilingual and ESL classrooms: Teaching in multicultural contexts* (4th ed.). New York: McGraw-Hill.

Thomas, W. P., & Collier, V. P. (2000). Accelerated schooling for all students: Research findings on education in multilingual communities. In S. Shaw (Ed.), *Intercultural education in European classrooms* (pp. 15–35). Stoke on Trent, UK: Trentham Books.

Thomas, W. P., & Collier, V. P. (2002). *A national study of school effectiveness for language minority students' long-term academic achievement.* Santa Cruz: University of California, Santa Cruz, Center for Research on Education, Diversity & Excellence. Available from http://www.crede.berkeley.edu/research/llaa/1.1_final.html

Thomas, W. P., & Collier, V. P. (2003). *A national study of school effectiveness for language minority students' long-term academic achievement* (CREDE Research Brief #10). Santa Cruz: University of California, Santa Cruz, Center for Research on Education, Diversity & Excellence.

Thomas, W. P., & Collier, V. P. (2005). *Thomas and Collier selected research sources on the Internet.* Retrieved February 1, 2008, from http://www.thomasandcollier.com/archive.htm

COMMUNICATIVE APPROACH

The communicative approach to language learning ushered in the beginning of learner-centeredness in language learning. Previously, in the mid-20th century, language teachers followed highly prescriptive methods, and language learning was understood to be primarily a matter of habit formation around various grammatical structures. That approach to language teaching and learning is described elsewhere in this encyclopedia.

The communicative approach can be *strong* or *weak*. The weak version stresses the importance of language learners to use the target language for communicative purposes. The strong version stresses that language is acquired through communication. The weak version has to do with learning to use the target language; the strong version has to do with using the target language to learn it.

In the 1960s, American linguistic theory began to change. Some of these changes stemmed from Noam Chomsky's assertion that to know a language is not simply habit formation and learning and applying rules of grammar. Knowing a language, according to the new thinking, also involves innovation and creativity. The communicative approach also drew from the works of Dell Hymes, John Gumperz, and other sociolinguists who questioned the competence-performance distinction and advanced the idea of language usage in social settings for communicative purposes. In Great Britain, the communicative approach developed slightly differently, partially from the concepts of language notions and functions and partially from concepts related to task-based learning. Language learning within these understandings became more a matter of developing students' proficiency in communicating meaning and less one of replicating structurally accurate language through rote exercises with little or no meaning.

The communicative approach arrived at a time when the field of language teaching appeared ready for a new approach because the winds of change were prevailing in the general educational community. During this period, there was increased interest in cooperative learning methods, multiple-intelligences theory, authentic assessment, and other learner-centered approaches to teaching and learning across the curricula. Traditional language learning methods such as the audio-lingual method went out of favor, and the communicative approach offered a humane, less dreary way to learn.

The communicative approach is considered an approach, not a method, because there is no single universally accepted linguistic theory, learning theory, or instructional model that all teachers and learners follow. Instead, language teaching procedures and syllabi are grounded in broad theoretical concepts and beliefs about language acquisition. Because of this theoretical breadth, the communicative approach has been accessible to practitioners from a variety of traditions. Many have been able to identify with it and interpret it in different ways.

Since its emergence in the late 1970s and early 1980s, the communicative approach has gone through a number of phases. The first phase reorganized the teaching syllabus from one based on structure to one based on communicating meaning. In the second phase, attention was paid to analyzing learner needs and making that analysis an essential component of the approach. In the third phase, the focus was on developing interactive, group-oriented learning activities.

Beliefs and Principles

Adherents of the communicative approach follow a number of complementary beliefs and principles that guide a variety of curricular and instructional practices: (a) Learners learn a language by using it to communicate, (b) authentic and meaningful communication should be the goal of classroom activities, (c) fluency is an important dimension of communication, (d) communication involves the integration of different language skills, and (e) learning is a process of creative construction and involves trial and error.

Additional concepts that shape the communicative view of language are that (a) language is a system for the expression of meaning, (b) the primary function of language is to allow interaction and communication, (c) language structure reflects communicative use, and (d) units of language include not only grammar and structure but also communicative meaning as exemplified through discourse. Various linguistic theorists represent important concepts as they relate to the communicative approach. Each concept complements and extends the next and lends texture and depth to the description of the communicative approach, which, in turn, guides any of a number of ways in which the approach is manifest in practice. Language conveys meaning in the communicative approach. Given this understanding of language, communicative teachers aim to make communicative competence the goal of language teaching and to develop procedures for teaching the four language skills (i.e., listening, speaking, reading, and writing) that acknowledge the interdependence of language and communication.

Important features of communicative teaching include the following:

- Meaning is the primary focus.
- Dialogues illustrate communicative functions but are not memorized as a way to absorb patterns.
- Language learning is learning to communicate.
- Drilling is permitted, but it is peripheral.
- Comprehensible pronunciation is sought.
- Judicious use of the home language is permitted.
- Translation is permitted when needed and when there is a benefit.
- Communicative competence (not linguistic competence) is the desired goal.
- Mistakes are necessary to learning.
- Students are expected to interact with other people.
- The teacher cannot know exactly what language forms and structures the students will use.

A person who develops good communicative competence acquires both knowledge and ability to use language to determine (a) practical feasibility (Can it be done?), (b) feasibility with respect to available means of implementation (How can it be done?), (c) appropriateness to context (Is it appropriate to do?), or (d) actuality and what is entailed to do or accomplish something (What was done?).

There are four dimensions of communicative competence: grammatical competence, sociolinguistic competence, discourse competence, and strategic competence. *Grammatical competence* is linguistic competence, or grammatical and lexical capacity. *Sociolinguistic competence* refers to the relationship between the social context in which the communication takes place and the communicative purpose of the interaction. *Discourse competence* refers to the interconnectedness of message elements in discourse to communicate meaning. *Strategic competence* refers to coping strategies communicators use to initiate, terminate, maintain, repair, or redirect communication. In this view, therefore, there is no single measure of proficiency or fluency; all four measures should be taken and reported as necessary.

Practices and Roles

Though its linguistic theoretical base is deep, little emphasis is placed on any particular learning theory in the communicative approach. Elements of learning theory must be extrapolated from communicative language teaching practices. One such element is that activities that promote real communication also promote learning. A second is that activities that use language to carry out meaningful tasks promote learning. A third element is that language that is meaningful to the learner promotes learning. Finally, acquisition of communicative competence is skill development, which acknowledges that practice is a means toward developing communicative skills.

It is difficult to describe a particular procedure that all lessons in the communicative approach employ, because many procedures are compatible with its beliefs and principles and no particular learning theory is embraced to the exclusion of others. Nonetheless, activities should enable learners to attain the communicative objectives of the curriculum; engage learners in communication; and require information sharing, negotiation of meaning, and interaction. These goals are achieved through a number of generally accepted teaching practices, including (a) exploiting real-life language in the classroom, (b) constantly using the target language, (c) encouraging student learning in the affective domain, (d) tolerating linguistic errors because accuracy is less important than fluency, (e) arranging instruction to encourage cooperative learning relationships between students, and (f) eliciting the understanding of grammar and vocabulary as an outgrowth of the range of functional and situational contexts that are a part of the lesson itself.

The communicative approach balances the role of the teacher, learners, and instructional materials and the relationships among them differently from traditional methods. The learner is seen as a negotiator between self, the learning process, the object of learning, and other learners. Failed communication is shared between speaker and listener and is something from which to learn. Successful communication is a joint accomplishment. The teacher serves multiple roles: facilitator and independent participant in the learning-teaching group. The teacher organizes resources and is also a resource. The teacher also guides classroom procedures and activities. Finally, the teacher is a researcher and contributor to students' learning. Additional teacher roles are needs analyst, counselor, and group process manager. Instructional materials are used to promote communicative language use and may be text-based, task-based, or realia. *Text-based materials* may weave communicative activities into a structurally organized textbook. *Task-based materials* are typically one-of-a-kind resources that encourage pair communication and student interaction. *Realia* are authentic, real-life materials, such as signs, magazines, maps, pictures, or charts, around which communicative activities can be built.

Some suggest that instructional and classroom management arrangements in the communicative approach have much in common with predecessor methods, such as the audio-lingual method. The communicative approach does not reject traditional methods; it reinterprets and extends them into a more cohesive whole. Teaching points may continue to be introduced via dialogues that resemble dialogues from the audio-lingual method. What distinguishes communicative dialogues from audio-lingual dialogues is how they are used. Instructional arrangements in the communicative approach contextualize the teaching points introduced via dialogues by drawing from them in role play or simulation activities. However, there is disagreement about the level of control learners need over language skills before they can apply them to communicative tasks. Some maintain that learners must first have control over language skills before applying them to communicative tasks; others advocate for learner engagement in communicative tasks from the beginning of instruction.

Its strengths notwithstanding, the communicative approach surfaced a number of criticisms. For instance, in countries with educational traditions from different those in the United States and Great Britain, where the communicative approach is rooted, the communicative approach may be less successful because teacher and learner role expectations in the approach may not be culturally universal. Also, when teacher and learner role expectations are culturally appropriate, teachers may be underprepared for the additional expectations beyond content knowledge that are integral to the communicative approach, especially group process management and instructional materials development. Also, because of a lack of a learning theory common to all and consequent instructional models, it is difficult for teachers to learn how to use the approach in classrooms. Finally, without a structural foundation and minimal

attention paid to pointing out errors, language learners are at greater risk for replicating each other's errors, which can lead in rare cases to the formation of a classroom dialect. Because evaluators focus on communication, learners may never achieve learning the second language completely, because it is more difficult, in this approach, to learn to recognize one's own errors.

Contributions to Bilingual Education Practice

The communicative approach initiated the post-method era of language teaching, which subsequently included other learner-centered approaches, such as multiple intelligences, the natural approach, competency-based language teaching, and cooperative language learning. *Approaches* have in common a set of theories and beliefs about language and language learning from which principles for teaching a language are derived. None leads to a specific set of prescriptions for teaching a language, and teachers have latitude in how to apply these principles in classroom practice. In contrast, *methods* are specific instructional designs or systems based on a specific theory of language and language learning. Examples include the audio-lingual and grammar-translation methods, Total Physical Response, Suggestopedia, Counseling-Learning, and the Silent Way. Each contains detailed specifications of content, teaching procedures, and learner and teacher roles, and they allow for little individual variation in applying these specifications. Teachers must learn the method and apply it according to the rules.

Approaches have long shelf lives because their flexibility allows for continuous revision, and methods have short shelf lives because their specificity does not permit revision. When considered in conjunction with its methodological predecessors, the communicative approach complements methods such as the audio-lingual and grammar-translation methods by offering an environment that extends the reach of mastering structure as an end in itself to a means to the greater end of fluent communication.

Elsie M. Szecsy

See also Audio-Lingual Method; Grammar-Translation Method; Language Defined; Languages, Learned or Acquired; Literacy and Biliteracy; Natural Approach

Further Readings

Canale, M., & Swain, M. (1980). Theoretical bases of communicative approaches to second language teaching and testing. *Applied Linguistics, 1,* 1–47.

Chomsky, N. (1965). *Aspects of the theory of syntax.* Cambridge: MIT Press.

Gumperz, J. (1982). *Discourse strategies.* New York: Cambridge University Press.

Gumperz, J., & Hymes, D. (1986). *Directions in sociolinguistics: The ethnography of communication.* New York: Blackwell.

Hymes, D. (1996). *Ethnography, linguistics, narrative inequality: Toward an understanding of voice.* London: Taylor & Francis.

Littlewood, W. (1981). *Communicative language teaching.* New York: Cambridge University Press.

Richards, J., & Rodgers, T. (2001). *Approaches and methods in language teaching* (2nd ed.). New York: Cambridge University Press.

Savignon, S. (1972). Teaching for communicative competence: A research report. *Audiovisual Language Journal, 10,* 153–162.

Savignon, S. (1991). Communicative language teaching: State of the art. *TESOL Quarterly, 25,* 261–277.

COMMUNITIES OF PRACTICE

Although the term *communities of practice* is sometimes used to refer, somewhat generically, to learning communities or learning groups, it also refers to the social learning theory posited by educational theorists Jean Lave and Étienne Wenger. In the late 1980s, they developed the concept of communities of practice to explain how people develop new knowledge in real-life situations. This theory, which has been applied in research on bilingual education and second-language learning, is based on the notions of situated learning, social interaction, apprenticeship, and identity. Communities of practice in bilingual classrooms promote social interaction, group learning, and a shared knowledge of the cultures, norms, activities, and discourses that make up the situated experience of a second-language learner in school.

Language Learning and Communities of Practice

More than just a general group of learners, a community of practice is a cohesive aggregate of participants whose participation is guided by more experienced community members as they travel along the developmental path of language and school learning. Bilingual children in school must learn at least one language (in immersion programs) and often two (in the case of maintenance bilingual programs) and, at the same time, grade-level academic content. Their socialization to the target language(s) and to school is facilitated by their interactions within communities of practice.

Communities of practice in bilingual classrooms emphasize the dynamic social component of learning and highlight collaboration and cooperation between students who are learning language and academic content at the same time. In the classroom, incorporation of ideas drawn from communities of practice benefits bilingual students by providing a community network within which learners can participate to gain linguistic and content knowledge. As learning theory, the community of practice concept is used to understand how bilinguals engage and interact in communities to learn language and content.

Lave and Wenger's initial notion of developing new knowledge in real-life situations has since been expanded to include traditional venues for learning, such as school classrooms. As a social theory of learning, the community-of-practice perspective provides a way to view how members of a particular community work in concert to learn and create knowledge within a particular practice. Community of practice differs from other social theories of learning in that it highlights the contextual nature of learning (it is situated in particular settings, such as a classroom). Other notions specific to the theory include apprenticeship (old-timers socialize newcomers) and participation as a developmental trajectory (one moves from a legitimate peripheral participant to a full participant in the learning practice). This theory was not designed specifically with language learning at its core; rather, it is a theory of learning that incorporates language.

Wenger defines a *practice* as something that includes the rules and procedures, language and tools, forms and documents, symbols and visual images, and roles and responsibilities that members of the practice are responsible for knowing and taking on. The overall social environment, artifacts, and tasks and activities in which members participate thus represent a social practice. The practice in a bilingual or second-language classroom is what teachers and students do on a daily basis to promote language and content learning. Activities such as morning message or daily reviews in both languages are part of the class practice. Within the community-of-practice model, novices or "newcomers" becoming socialized to the common learning practices of a particular situation, such as first- and second-language learning in school, work with experts, or "old-timers," to gain access to accepted practices.

In communities of practice, people learn through the process of participating in particular communities and their day-to-day work. Broadly defined, a *community of practice* is a group of individuals working together toward a common goal whose shared knowledge and common interest facilitate their learning and, ultimately, acquisition of the common goal. In the case of many bilingual students in school, their common goal is acquisition of two languages, usually the majority and minority languages spoken in their larger community. Within a community of practice, learning is a social endeavor in which community members come together based on shared interest and engagement (all learning two languages) and all members are engaged in a common practice—becoming bilingual. A community of practice in a bilingual classroom can consist of students from the same linguistic background, such as Spanish speakers in a transitional bilingual class. It can also be made up of learners from varied languages, as in dual-language programs.

Bilingual Education as Practice

The relationship of the communities-of-practice model to bilingual education is twofold. It is employed as a learning theory in educational research, commonly used in research on bilingual learners, and as a concept synonymous with the idea of a *learning community*. As a learning theory, communities of practice view learning as a social process, rather than an individual one. Since the inception of the term *communities of practice* in the late 1980s, community-based learning has grown tremendously in popularity and has penetrated the fields of bilingual education and second-language acquisition in research and in education generally.

Its usefulness notwithstanding, the term *community of learners* was singled out in 2006 by the Lake Superior State University in its annual superlative list of terms new to the English lexicon as a highly overused expression. The fact that this otherwise undesirable label has been bestowed upon the term suggests that learning communities are now ubiquitous in educational settings.

Three characteristics must be in place to establish a community of practice: *mutual engagement,* a *joint enterprise* such as a task or activity, and a *shared repertoire of negotiable resources*. Within the community of practice in the bilingual classroom, students are mutually engaged in a common task or, more specifically, a joint enterprise, such as a classroom assignment or a 6-week theme-based project. The shared repertoire of negotiable resources includes language and specific ways of using language in certain communities, as well as the various tools, routines, stories, and genres that are used in particular practices. In a bilingual classroom in the United States, the shared repertoire consists not only of the target languages being used by the teacher and the students (e.g., Spanish and English, or Cantonese and English) but also the academic and social communicative competence (including lexicon, grammatical structure, semantics, pragmatics) in the languages being studied.

It is not necessary that members in a community of practice hail from a homogeneous background. In the same way that a bilingual classroom consists of highly heterogeneous populations, in terms of language proficiency, ethnicity, nationality, and level of education, a community of practice represents a diverse community of members. It is also important to note that communities of practice may or may not be intentionally created communities; some simply develop organically, while others are consciously created.

A classroom is an example of a heterogeneous community that has a joint goal, shared repertoire, and mutual engagement in academic and social endeavors. In a classroom, all students are expected to carry out a common, negotiated enterprise, such as the learning of a particular content area subject, for example, math or social studies. The shared repertoire is particularly important in a classroom of language learners because it refers not just to common registers and discourse about the content area or topic the students are learning but also to the shared understandings of the activities and artifacts involved in the overall practice. As students work collectively on a common enterprise, they continue to develop the shared resources that form a part of their practice. For example, fourth-grade students in a writing workshop in English know the parts of the writing process and how to carry it out, and they know that in the prewriting, or drafting phase, a "sloppy copy" is an acceptable product. All of these aspects of the class are part of the shared repertoire and joint enterprise and serve as part of the classroom practice.

Within the community-of-practice theoretical framework, the term *legitimate peripheral participation* describes the process of how newcomers shift from the periphery of the community to the center, to become full participants in the community of learners. *Legitimate* is used in this phrase to give credibility to the status of the novices in terms of their engagement and membership in the community, despite the fact that they have not yet become masters of the community's knowledge. In a transitional bilingual classroom, a recent immigrant with limited proficiency in the majority language would be considered a legitimate peripheral participant. In a Mandarin Chinese and English two-way bilingual classroom, the monolingual Anglophone child could also be a legitimate peripheral participant—until he or she gains enough proficiency in Mandarin Chinese to be considered fluent. This shift from legitimate peripheral participation to full participation (and fluency in the target language) reflects one's learning. However, the movement from the periphery to the center of participation is not a unidirectional trajectory. The dynamic experienced by learners is characterized by multiple shifts in identity as they move along an often uneven path of learning.

The concept of *identity* is central to community of practice. As members progress from legitimate peripheral participants to full participants in a community, their identities shift and transform. According to the authors of the framework, identity is the "negotiated experience" that is coconstructed by the learner and the community members with whom he or she engages in a learning situation. A participant in the process of learning works to develop the many varied and competent identities that are necessary for appropriate participation in a particular situation or practice. For a language learner to be successful in school, a student must know how to negotiate academic situations in whichever language he or she is addressed. For example, in a bilingual classroom, a student learns to play myriad academic and social roles, including scientist, helper, mathematician, group member, and teacher's pet—in two or more languages. The bilingual student's identity changes and develops as he or she interacts with bilingual interlocutors, texts, and resources to gain new knowledge about language and content.

School-based ethnographic research that relies on the community-of-practice concept has been conducted with bilingual students from a variety of language minority backgrounds, including Spanish, Japanese, Chinese, Polish, and Punjabi. Although the community-of-practice framework is widely employed in research studies of language minority students, some researchers have criticized it for being too simplistic a theory to explain language learning. They claim the framework does not take into account the complex social aspects of learning in school. Bilinguals in schools, including those who have successfully exited bilingual or second-language support programs, are often relegated to the margins of the greater educational society, with little hope of becoming legitimate participants in the classroom or educational community. Further, since the community of practice views learning as a group endeavor rather than as a traditional teacher-student classroom relationship, some researchers maintain that the framework is not compatible with classroom learning. Nevertheless, the community-of-practice framework is heavily utilized as a foundational theory in understanding how bilinguals learn their first and second languages in schools.

Sometimes called *learning communities, learning networks,* or *communities of learners,* communities of practice are created (often purposefully and intentionally) in bilingual and English as a Second Language (ESL) classrooms. In bilingual classes, children naturally form communities of practice that share expectations of learning, interaction with each other, and a bond that includes the understanding of what it is like to be a learner in a bilingual classroom. Students share an understanding of how their teachers will use both languages in class—be it Spanish in math class and English in social studies, or translation in each class. They also understand as a classroom community when and where to talk science, math, or music and in which target language they are studying.

Outside and Inside the Classroom

Communities of practice are also created in in-service and pre-service teacher education for second-language learning. Practitioners are encouraged to work in teams or communities to better serve the needs of students learning two languages. Communities of practice can thus include not only students but also teachers, administrators, parents, and other community members. In two-way bilingual programs, for example, there is an emphasis on creating community between members of both language groups. Often, bilingual community members, such as politicians, local celebrities, and family members of students, are encouraged to participate in school practices and activities (such as science fairs or holiday celebrations) that work to create a cohesive and supportive school environment. At both the elementary and secondary levels, the push to create communities of practice is strong and is growing ever stronger. This emphasis on communities of practice is seen in many recently published pedagogical texts that promote the development of learning communities within schools; in professional journals, such as TESOL's (Teachers of English to Speakers of Other Languages) practitioner publication, *Essential Teacher,* which includes several regular columns under the heading "Communities of Practice"; at conferences for researchers and educators, such as NABE (National Association for Bilingual Education) and AERA (American Educational Research Association); and in schools and classrooms themselves.

Holly Hansen-Thomas

See also Classroom Discourse; Language Socialization; School Leader's Role; Situated Learning; Social Learning; Vygotsky and Language Learning

Further Readings

Kanno, Y. (1999). Comments on Kelleen Toohey's "Breaking them up, taking them away: ESL students in Grade 1": The use of community-of-practice perspective in language minority research. *TESOL Quarterly, 33,* 126–136.

Lave, J. (1991). Situating learning in communities of practice. In L. Resnick, J. Levine, & S. Teasley (Eds.), *Perspectives on socially shared cognition* (pp. 63–84). Washington, DC: American Psychological Association.

Lave, J., & Wenger, É. (1991). *Situated learning: Legitimate peripheral participation.* Cambridge, UK: Cambridge University Press.

Toohey, K. (2000). *Learning English at school: Identity, social relations, and classroom practice.* Clevedon, UK: Multilingual Matters.

Wenger, É. (1998). *Communities of practice: Learning, meaning, and identity.* Cambridge, UK: Cambridge University Press.

COMPOUND AND COORDINATE BILINGUALISM

How do bilinguals organize meaning associated with their two languages? Do some bilinguals live in and express two different worlds of meaning, while others draw on the meaning system imposed by the language they learned first in order to produce their second language? Does how they became bilingual affect the way they are able to express meaning in their two languages? These questions were addressed in the early 1950s, first by Uriel Weinreich and then by Susan Ervin and Charles Osgood, who proposed a distinction between *coordinate* and *compound bilingualism.*

Weinreich was interested in describing how bilingualism develops when speakers from two different languages come into contact and speakers from one of the groups attempt to learn the language of the other group. Weinreich distinguished among three types of bilinguals, based on the relationship among *signs* (concrete objects), *signifiers* (the words used to denote them), and *signified* (the representation of meaning associated with the words). In this view, Type A bilinguals have an independent word and meaning system. In other words, for this type of bilingual, signifiers used in Language A have a meaning that is independent from the meaning of the same signifiers in Language B. For example, a Type A bilingual would associate a particular meaning for the signifier *pencil* in English and another meaning for the same signifier, *lápiz,* in Spanish. For bilinguals of this type, the two meanings are associated with language-specific information, because the meanings were constructed not only from information processes occurring in each language but also as a result of formations that were built up from separate experiences that shaped the meaning of the words within specific contexts.

According to Weinreich, Type B bilinguals have a single meaning system for words in the two languages. This means that any new words the learner acquires are necessarily tied to the meaning those words already have in the learner's first language. Accordingly, *pencil* and *lápiz* are separate words, but their underlying meaning is the same across the two languages. The reason for this is because Type B bilinguals acquire their second language in the same contexts as they acquired their first language.

Weinreich also proposed a Type C bilingual, who in the early stages of learning a second language translates every new word using the meaning system of the first language. As in Type B bilingualism, the meaning of any new word remains the same as in the first language (*pencil* as an object for writing, drawing, etc.), with no meaningful association between the signifier *lápiz* and what a *pencil* signifies in Spanish. The difference between Type B and Type C is essentially strategic. Type C bilinguals necessarily translate from their first language to the new language in order to learn it, while Type B bilinguals build up proficiency in their two languages using one meaning system.

Ervin and Osgood collapsed Weinreich's three-part system into two main categories, called *coordinate* and *compound* bilinguals, with Weinreich's Type A representing the former and Types B and Type C combined to form the latter. For them, the two languages of a coordinate bilingual correspond to two independent meaning (signifying) systems. A compound bilingual, in contrast, has one meaning system for the two languages. The added value of Ervin and Osgood's work was that it considered how an individual might become one type or the other, an extension of the original idea that has generated popular as well as academic interest ever since. To wit, Ervin and Osgood hypothesized that the difference between compound and coordinate bilingualism could be explained in terms of the contexts in which an individual acquired the second language. Moreover, while Weinreich talked mainly about adult bilinguals who were also literate in their first language, Ervin and Osgood were interested in child bilingualism as well as bilingualism in adulthood. For them, *compound bilingualism* was the result of individuals having learned the second language while constantly relying on their first language or of learners growing up with the two languages in their daily lives. For adult learners, it mattered not whether the second language was learned in school or in a foreign country. What was important was the existence of one meaning system, regardless of when or under what conditions bilingualism was acquired.

Ervin and Osgood argued that *coordinate bilinguals* were distinct from compound bilinguals, not only because the meaning system of the two languages was language-specific but also because the conditions under which they learned the two languages enabled learners to develop separate meaning systems. Coordinate bilinguals, they asserted, do not learn by translating from one language to another or by relying on what words mean in the other language. Rather, coordinate bilinguals develop because they learned their two languages in different contexts. By *contexts,* they mean separate domains, such as home, school, religion, recreation, education, and work. These domains can exist either in the same geographic environment or in different places. For example, children who grow up using their two languages for separate purposes in different domains as well as children who

grow up learning one language in one country and a second one in another country are both likely to develop into coordinate bilinguals.

Problems With the Compound-Coordinate Distinction

As with any concept, it is important to examine the compound-coordinate distinction against the background of the period in which it was created. In the 1950s, language was viewed as a habit that was formed through the reinforcement of correct forms. Semantics, the study of word meanings, was in its infancy. As linguistics became more sophisticated and researchers began testing the Ervin and Osgood hypothesis, several problems emerged, leading to an almost complete rejection of the distinction. Karl Diller pointed out that the terms *compound* and *coordinate* are poorly defined and often contradictory and no experimental evidence supports the basic distinction. Since the original work was done at the word level, once Ervin and Osgood extended the meaning of the two kinds of bilingualism to include how they were developed, new questions arose that began to erode confidence in the distinction. For example, if a child grows up speaking English to his father and other family members and Spanish to his mother and her family, becoming equally proficient in the two languages over time and into adulthood, is this person a compound or coordinate bilingual? According to Ervin and Osgood's definition, he would be compound; according to Nelson Brooks, however, he would be coordinate, a "true" bilingual, who has high proficiency in two languages with highly developed meaning systems in both. Ervin and Osgood addressed this issue in their original work by suggesting that there may be two types of compound bilinguals: those who rely on their first language to build a meaning system and those who rely on both of their languages, but with neither language having prominence. Over time, it became clear that the original distinction was more like a continuum, with no sharp differences between the two concepts.

As Diller also pointed out, compound bilinguals, as defined by Ervin and Osgood, should be better translators than coordinate bilinguals, because many in this category learned their second language through translation techniques. However, Wallace Lambert found no difference between compound and coordinate bilinguals in their abilities to translate from one language to the other. Another difficulty Diller alluded to is the claim that compound bilinguals have merged linguistic systems. This may be a possibility for beginning language learners and children who acquire two languages in childhood but not for highly proficient compound bilinguals, because a merged linguistic system would always cause interference from one language to the other. In other words, once a bilingual becomes highly proficient in two languages, regardless of the route, the original distinction no longer serves any purpose.

A Distinction Persisting in New Forms

Like many of the concepts developed in the 1950s to capture variation among bilinguals, the compound and coordinate bilingualism categories have remained alive despite serious doubts about their validity and usefulness. One of the reasons the distinction has persisted is because it became attached to bilingual behaviors that were hinted at in the original work. For example, compound bilingualism became associated with code-switching behaviors among bilinguals who grew up in the United States, acquiring two languages simultaneously and using them for similar purposes within various cultural settings. Bilinguals of this type, it was argued by Joshua A. Fishman, would eventually shift to the dominant language, namely, English. To avoid language shift and language loss, Fishman argued that bilinguals needed to develop diglossia or social bilingualism, the functional distribution of two languages into separate domains of use, much like what coordinate bilinguals do when they grow up speaking one language in one country (or social context) and a second language in another country (or social context). Bilingualism without diglossia, akin to compound bilingualism without separate places in which the meaning systems of the two languages live separate lives, was considered to be a weaker type of bilingualism that was bound to atrophy over time.

Code switching and code mixing, sometimes referred to as *intersentential* and *intrasentential* code switching, respectively, were also perceived by many language purists as incomplete systems or interlanguages that were neither fully one language or the other and thus inferior to "pure" languages. This perspective, along with the idea that diglossia was a necessary condition for the development of bilinguals who did not mix their two languages, harkens back to the 1950s claim by Ervin and Osgood, and later Lambert, that coordinate bilinguals

were the only "true" bilinguals; compound bilinguals, relying on a single meaning system, were not "true" bilinguals because they either mixed their two languages or relied on translation for expressing meaning in the second language. It was not until the 1980s and 1990s that ethnographers, who lived and studied communities populated by bilinguals who learned and used two languages in their daily lives, found that code switching and diglossia, like their predecessors' compound and coordinate bilingualism, were much more complex than the earlier research had assumed.

Despite many problems with the distinction between compound and coordinate bilingualism and its offshoots, some researchers continue to use the concepts to study bilingual autobiographical memory and bilingual long-term memory. Moreover, the distinction continues to be mentioned as a way to understand bilingualism, with little or no critique of its usefulness or validity as a construction of bilingual realities.

Christian Faltis

See also Bilingualism Stages; Brain Research; Concurrent Translation Method; Contrastive Analysis; First-Language Acquisition; Language Dominance; Metalinguistic Awareness; Second-Language Acquisition

Further Readings

Brooks, N. (1964). *Language and language learning: Theory and practice.* New York: International Thomson.

Diller, K. (1970). "Compound" and "coordinate" bilingualism: A conceptual artifact. *Word, 26,* 254–261.

Ervin, S., & Osgood, C. (1954). Second language learning and bilingualism. *Journal of Abnormal and Social Psychology Supplement, 49,* 139–211.

Fishman, J. A. (1967). Bilingualism with and without diglossia; Diglossia with and without bilingualism. *Journal of Social Issues, 23*(2), 29–37.

Lambert, W. E. (1969). Psychological studies of the interdependencies of the bilingual's two languages. In J. Puhvel (Ed.), *Substance and structure of language* (pp. 99–126). Los Angeles: University of California Press.

Weinreich, U. (1953). *Languages in contact.* New York: Linguistic Circle of New York.

COMPREHENSIBLE INPUT

This controversial concept was developed by Stephen Krashen in the 1970s and 1980s in connection with the *input hypothesis,* which claims that the way humans acquire language is by understanding messages or by receiving *comprehensible input.* In the late 1970s, Krashen referred to comprehensible input as *intake.* About a decade earlier, S. Pit Corder had distinguished intake—language that a learner understands, takes in, and uses—from input—any stretch of language available to the learner. Krashen originally claimed that intake alone was both necessary and sufficient for second-language acquisition. His preliminary writings focused on the acquisition of grammatical structures, mainly morphemes. By the mid-1980s, he extended his claims about comprehensible input to include the acquisition of lexical items embedded in messages and the acquisition of literacy.

The input hypothesis asserts that learners become more proficient in a second language when they understand language input that includes grammatical structures slightly beyond their current proficiency levels. Messages directed to the learner that contain language structures too far beyond the learner's current proficiency do not help the learner develop greater or expanded proficiency, because they leave gaps in understanding and therefore in production. Krashen uses the expression $i + 1$ to capture the idea of language input that is "slightly beyond" the learner's current level of competence. In the expression, the term i equals the learner's current competency level, so that $i + 1$ is the next level or stage the learner is ready to acquire. Messages to the learner that contain structures that extend well beyond the learner's current proficiency level, say, $i + 5$ or $i + 9$, are by definition incomprehensible, and thus, because the learner cannot process the structures in the message, the structures will not be acquired.

Krashen (with Tracy Terrell) points out, however, that this is a theoretical and conceptual portrayal. Comprehensible input does not need to be finely tuned to each learner's $i + 1$ level to be useful for acquisition. In a classroom where language learners are at different levels of proficiency, a teacher cannot possibly adjust for all the variations in level present in the classroom. The teacher's role is to make sure that learners understand what is being communicated to them orally or in writing. If learners understand the input and there is an ample amount of it, learners are likely to receive $i + 1$ geared to their acquisition needs. This is what Krashen refers to as "casting a net" of language wide enough to ensure that there are multiple instances of the individual student's $i + 1$.

Sources for Comprehensible Input

Given the importance of comprehensible input for second-language acquisition, what are some of the ways that learners gain access to $i + 1$? According to Michael Long, there are four ways that input can be made comprehensible: (1) Some speakers, especially language teachers, caregivers, and people in continuous contact with foreigners, modify their input to learners; (2) learners use more than linguistic resources to assist comprehension; (3) speakers often orient their communication with language learners to the here and now; and (4) it is possible to modify the interactional structure of conversations between speakers and learners.

Modified Input

Teachers, caregivers, and people who interact with foreigners often modify—simplify and elaborate—to ensure meaningful communication. According to Krashen, the key characteristics of simplified input are as follows:

- Slower rate and clearer articulation, which helps learners identify word boundaries more easily and allows more processing time
- More use of high-frequency vocabulary, less slang, fewer idioms
- Syntactic simplification, shorter sentences

Modified input that simplifies language has been shown to facilitate comprehension in numerous studies. These include caregiver studies done in the 1970s by Toni Cross and in the 1990s by Catherine Snow and Charles Ferguson; research on foreigner talk done by Ferguson in the early 1970s; and studies of teacher talk in classroom settings, like those conducted by Rod Ellis, and Michael Long and Charlene Sato in the early 1980s. Another form of modified input is the use of elaborations, paraphrasing information and providing definitions of low-frequency words, when the words are introduced for the first time. As Ellis found, elaborations, used judiciously, have been shown to be helpful to learners who are at more-advanced stages of language acquisition.

When teachers modify their language to learners in these ways, they enable them to understand language that is slightly beyond their input levels and thus to acquire more advanced structures. As learners become more advanced speakers, the complexity of language addressed to them also becomes more advanced, so that modifications are adjusted to the needs of the learners.

Extralinguistic Support

A second way that learners understand language that is slightly beyond their current ability is by paying attention to extralinguistic information and using their knowledge about the world to make sense of language directed to them. *Extralinguistic information* means cues and clues about what is happening in the exchange of information as the teacher or more capable language user attempts to communicate with learners. When speakers cast a net of language, learners are able to understand much of what is being communicated because of what they already know about language (e.g., greetings, descriptions, labeling, story parts, etc.). Input to learners can also be made meaningful when the speaker uses visual supports (photos, drawings, videos), nonverbal gestures (smiles, frowns, hands, pointing), paraverbal support (whispers, sighs, expressive sounds), graphic organizers (Venn diagrams, T charts, maps), and realia (real objects that students can see, touch, and feel) that focus learners on the concrete here and now. All of these extralinguistic mechanisms provide support to the net of input that speakers cast over learners as they strive for $i + 1$.

Focus on the Here-and-Now

Especially for beginning language learners, language can be made comprehensible by linking it to ideas and expressions that the learners can literally see, touch, and feel in front of them. As Krashen and Terrell argue, the here-and-now also refers to using language that is mainly in the present tense or in the form of commands to which the learners respond physically.

Interactionally Modified Input

Another way that teachers make input comprehensible derives from the way they modify the interactional structure of conversations with learners. *Interactionally modified input* has become more widely known as *negotiation for meaning*, which, according to Long, is a process by which learners and teachers give and interpret signals regarding how much they think they understand each other. This results in adjustments to form, structure, and content of the conversation, until an acceptable level of understanding is reached.

Long argues that interactional modifications are likely to occur in two-way communicative tasks, where native speakers and language learners negotiate the meaning of what they are saying to make it more comprehensible to one another. Because the native speaker needs to exchange information with the learner, he or she must focus on learner feedback to be successful. As the learner negotiates information with the native speaker, this compels the native speaker to adjust language input until what is being said is comprehensible to the learner. Through this two-way exchange of information, learners are provided with comprehensible input that promotes language acquisition.

Situating Comprehensible Input

It is important to situate Krashen's introduction of the concept of comprehensible input historically and in terms of its epistemological framework. Comprehensible input, as the essential ingredient for second-language acquisition, is tied to several important beliefs about language acquisition that were current when Krashen first developed the concept. An important idea in Krashen's work is that language acquisition happens exclusively inside the head of the learner. This perspective comes from the belief that the mind and the way it works are separated from what happens in the world. In other words, learning is not social, but individual, and unconnected to becoming a member of a particular sociocultural group. While what happens in the world can affect whether or not people (teachers and peers) enable input to be comprehensible, acquisition is always the result of the internal processing of comprehended messages, not the result of becoming a member of a community where the language being learned is used as a tool.

Krashen developed the concept of comprehensible input at a time in the 1970s when the work of cognitive linguist Noam Chomsky, first-language psychologist Roger Brown, and child language experts Toni Cross, Elissa Newport, Lila Glietman, and Henry Glietman was at the forefront of new ideas about language acquisition. In simple terms, the prevailing belief in the late 1970s and early 1980s was that when people comprehend language, an internal language mechanism, the *language acquisition device* (LAD) processes the language. The LAD is connected internally to an innate human capacity to learn language through the universal grammar. According the *universal grammar theory,* humans have the capacity to acquire any language; the language system they acquire and become proficient in depends on the language they hear and understand most. The LAD organizes the language that is comprehended according to the rule system generated through the universal grammar. With continued language input, the LAD organizes the language so that over time, if there is sufficient language input, the person develops full competency in that language.

Linguistically, Krashen relied on Chomsky's *generative theory of language,* which he had developed in the 1960s and early 1970s. This view held that language is a generative system made up of deep- and surface-level components and that what is important to understand is how individuals acquire competency in the generative system, not how they perform language itself. For Chomsky, the deep structures of language are innately human, and they are derived from the interaction between the universal grammar and the LAD. Young children intuitively acquire certain grammatical rules that will eventually enable them to generate an infinite number of language-specific grammatical sentences. What children actually produce as a result of rules is unimportant, because if the rule is acquired, the production will be grammatically correct according to that rule system. Although Krashen did not use generative grammar theory in his work, he relied on Chomsky's basic ideas about linguistic competence, especially how children intuitively and with minimal effort acquire language structures. Moreover, like Chomsky, Krashen gave minimal importance to performance or output. In fact, a corollary of the input hypothesis is that speaking does not lead to acquisition: Its role is to generate more comprehensible input. Krashen claims that when learners speak, they encourage input because people converse with them, supplying input that is likely to be related to the topic of the conversation and, consequently, meaningful to the learner.

Krashen relied a great deal on child-language research as evidence to support the value and role of comprehensible input in language acquisition. Much of this research examined how caregivers (usually highly educated mainstream parents) interacted with infants and toddlers who were in the process of acquiring their native languages. This research found that caregiver speech to young children was syntactically simpler than adult-to-adult speech and roughly tuned to the child's current level of linguistic competence. Caregiver speech was also found to be oriented to here-and-now speech about topics, objects, and events that the child could easily perceive because they were in the immediate environment. Krashen interpreted this research as strong evidence for how simplified speech and extralinguistic support provide the child with the necessary ingredient for language acquisition.

Another belief that Krashen relied on to develop his ideas about comprehensible input was that there are two distinct ways of developing ability in a second language: consciously or subconsciously. The conscious process results in knowing about language and its rules and was at the time the most prevalent way to teach second languages. Acquisition of a second language, however, happens subconsciously, when the focus is on meaning and messages are comprehensible. For Krashen, subconscious acquisition is akin to "picking up" a language by being immersed in a setting where meaning and purpose are central. The reason people are successful at picking up a language is that many of the messages addressed to them are aimed at making meaning, in other words, comprehensible input. An important implication of the distinction between learning and acquisition is that the only way to gain proficiency in a second language is through acquisition, by receiving continuous comprehensible input. Learning is useful only as a monitor, to make corrections either before or after speaking or writing.

Problems With Comprehensible Input

The idea of comprehensible input as the essential reason for second-language acquisition is troubling to many in the field of language acquisition research, so much so that by the turn of the century, as Karen Watson-Gegeo and Sarah Nielson documented, few second-language acquisition scholars referred to comprehensible input as central to theoretical work in second-language acquisition. Accordingly, despite the substantial contribution the input hypothesis and comprehensible input have had on second-language acquisition studies, it has received strong rebukes from several researchers, who criticize the term as being atheoretical, unmeasurable, and extremely vague. Kevin Gregg argues that the input hypothesis does not stand up to conditions that any theory of second-language acquisition needs to meet. In particular, Gregg is concerned that Krashen does not adequately define the terms he uses in his writings on comprehensible input. For example, Krashen interchanges the term *language* with *grammatical structures,* when he apparently really means a particular set of grammatical morphemes. Gregg and others have also expressed concern that there is no way to measure comprehensible input.

Lydia White rejects the input hypothesis because it places too much emphasis on comprehensible input, when, for her, it is *incomprehensible input* that is crucial for second-language acquisition. If the input is comprehensible, then there is no need for learners to negotiate for meaning. White contends that comprehension difficulties provide important negative feedback to learners, enabling them to adjust their developing language based on feedback provided in the conversational repair work.

Susan Gass questions whether it is comprehensible or *comprehended* input that is responsible for second-language acquisition. For her, comprehensible input implies that the speaker controls the comprehensibility through modified input, use of extralinguistic support, and focus on the here-and-now. In comprehended input, the onus for comprehension is on the learner and the focus is on the extent to which the learner understands language addressed to him or her. So which is it, comprehensible or comprehended input that matters to second-language acquisition? Krashen argues that in order for learners to move to the next level of competency, they must process the *i + 1* they receive. It is not enough for speakers to modify their input to, or in interaction with, learners; ultimately, the learner has to comprehend the language for it to be useful for acquisition.

Merrill Swain also makes the argument that in addition to comprehensible input, learners need to produce *comprehensible output* in order to develop proficiency in a second language. Swain argues that comprehensible input may be necessary for the beginning stages of language development, but in order to develop complex syntax required for long stretches of language used in descriptions, explanations, justifications, and summaries, learners need to practice with comprehensible output. As Krashen pointed out, one of the corollaries of the input hypothesis is that speaking is the result of acquisition, not its cause. Swain argues that nudging learners to speak moves them from semantic processing to syntactic processing. When learners are forced to produce language, they may recognize the gap between what they want to produce and what they are able to, and because of this, they may pay closer attention to how native speakers use language for extended discourse. Pushed output involves providing learners with useful and consistent feedback, which encourages self-repair; this may lead to more accurate and precise language use.

Finally, there is the problem of how comprehensible input becomes intake and how intake leads to acquisition. As indicated by Eun Sun Park, most studies involving comprehensible input assume that some combination of speech modifications, extralinguistic support, a here-and-now emphasis, and negotiations for meaning involving judicious push output stimulate acquisition. However, in fact, as claimed by Long, most studies involving comprehensible input have focused on showing that language and conversational modifications promote the comprehension of input. Park argues that few studies have been able to show that comprehensible input promotes acquisition, mainly because the construct of *acquisition* has not been sufficiently explained or operationalized. Moreover, all of the research used to support the input hypothesis comes from Western settings involving mainstream middle-class, well-educated people. There are many examples of caregiver speech interaction in non-Western societies in which caregivers do not adjust their speech to young children, making no attempt to provide comprehensible input, and yet children in all of these settings acquire the language of their communities. Thus, even the supposed link between language/conversational adjustment and comprehensible input is questionable.

Current Developments

Despite the long-term debates over the role of comprehensible input in second-language acquisition, there is, as documented by Park, considerable support for the idea that when learners can negotiate comprehensible input and are also encouraged to repair their output in order for it to be more comprehensible, such "interactional contexts" are more conducive to language development than just providing comprehensible input. Moreover, as documented by second-language researchers, such as Stephen Cary, Jana Echevarria, Anne Graves, Mary Ellen Vogt, and Deborah Short, though there is little value in pursuing the role of comprehensible input as the single reason for second-language acquisition, the idea of providing language learners with lots of comprehensible input is highly regarded among classroom teachers working with language learners and native speakers together. Especially among teachers working in school settings filled with English learners where language and content are integrated, belief in the value of comprehensible input for promoting language acquisition appears to be exceptionally strong, regardless of what research has to say about its usefulness and despite the fact its theoretical basis has been judged as largely indefensible.

Christian Faltis

See also First-Language Acquisition; Krashen, Stephen D.; Language Acquisition Device; Languages, Learned or Acquired; Monitor Model; Second-Language Acquisition; SIOP; Specially Designed Academic Instruction in English

Further Readings

Cross, T. (1977). Mother's speech adjustments: The contribution of selected child listener variables. In C. Snow & C. Ferguson (Eds.), *Talking to children* (pp. 151–188). New York: Cambridge University Press.

Faltis, C. (1984). A commentary on Krashen's input hypothesis. *TESOL Quarterly, 18,* 352–357.

Ferguson, C. (1975). Towards a characterization of English foreigner talk. *Anthropological Linguistics, 17,* 1–14.

Gass, S., & Madden, C. (Eds.). *Input in second language acquisition.* Rowley, MA: Newbury House

Gregg, K. (1994). Krashen's monitor theory, acquisition theory, and theory. In R. Barasch & C. Vaughan James (Eds.), *Beyond the monitor model* (pp. 37–55). Boston: Heinle & Heinle.

Krashen, S. (1985). *The input hypothesis: Issues and implications.* New York: Longman.

Long, M. (1982). Native speaker/non-native speaker conversation in the second language classroom. In M. Long & C. Richards (Eds.), *Methodology in TESOL: A book of readings* (pp. 339–354). Rowley, MA: Newbury House.

Park, E. S. (2002). On the potential sources of comprehensible input for second language acquisition. *Working Papers in TESOL and Applied Linguistics, 2*(3), 1–21.

Snow, C., & Ferguson, C. (Eds.). (1977). *Talking to children.* New York: Cambridge University Press.

Swain, M. (1985). Communicative competence: Some roles of comprehensible input and comprehensible output in its development. In S. Gass & C. Madden (Eds.), *Input in second language acquisition* (pp. 235–252). Rowley, MA: Newbury House.

White, L. (1987). Against comprehensible input: The input hypothesis and the development of L2 competence. *Applied Linguistics, 8,* 95–110.

Concurrent Translation Method

The Concurrent Translation Method is widely used in bilingual education classrooms where teachers interchangeably use two languages during instruction. While implementing the Concurrent Translation Method, a teacher constantly alternates between the target language (e.g., English in the United States) and students' native language. Although its effectiveness has been contested, the Concurrent Translation Method remains one of the most commonly used bilingual instructional methods. As illustrated in the example on the following page, a bilingual (English/Arabic) second-grade teacher uses the Concurrent Translation Method while introducing a whole-group science lesson to native English and Arabic speakers. (Note: Arabic writing begins in a right-to-left direction.)

In bilingual classrooms, teachers may employ the Concurrent Translation Method in different ways and for different purposes. Some teachers may tend to use this method throughout the entire instructional school day, while others may use it only sparingly, depending on the context. For example, teachers may choose to use the Concurrent Translation Method when they are team teaching with a non-bilingual education teacher, because in this context, native speakers of different languages are brought together for instruction.

The intentions of the teachers who use this method are twofold. First, bilingual teachers using this method generally strive to ensure that all students comprehend fully by repeating the same information in both languages. Second, they seek to include all students during the lesson, regardless of their native language. While this method is used with the best of intentions, it has been proven to be ineffective.

Teacher: Today we are going to learn about electricity.

اليوم سنقوم بالدراسه عن الكهرباء.

[direct translation of above]

What does electricity mean to you?

ماذا تعني لكم الكهرباء ؟

[direct translation of above]

Jeremy: Like when we turn on the lights.

Huda:

تساعدنا في رؤية الأشياء في الظلام.

[It helps to see things in the dark.]

Teacher: Okay. Good thinking. So we need electricity to turn on the lights so we can see in the dark.

تفكيرُ جيد. نحن نحتاج الكهرباء لتساعدنا في تشغيل الإضاءه كي نتمكن من أن نرى في الظلام.

[direct translation of above]

Teacher: Now, let's do an experiment with our fifth-grade buddies.

الآن، لنقم بإجراء تجربه عمليه مع أصدقاءنا الطلبه في الفصل الخامس.

[direct translation of above]

Teacher: Are you ready?

هل أنتم مستعدون؟

[direct translation of above]

Although the Concurrent Translation Method is one of the most commonly used in bilingual education classrooms, the inherent drawbacks to this method seem to outweigh the benefits. According to many researchers, such as Rodolfo Jacobson, Judith Lessow-Hurley, and Robert Milk, there are several major criticisms regarding this method:

1. *Tuning Out the Nondominant Language.* Since students know that the information will eventually be provided in their dominant language, they often become accustomed to (a) not paying close attention when their nondominant language is being used and (b) overly relying on getting the information via their dominant language.

2. *Lack of High-Quality Exposure to Target Language.* One of the main premises of bilingual education is to develop proficiency in the target language. However, when the Concurrent Translation Method is overly used, the exposure to the target language is of low quality, because this method provides only a rough direct translation. Therefore, students are not required to develop critical thinking skills and

strategies in the target language. In other words, students develop a passive response when the target language is in use.

3. *Lack of Motivation for Students and Teachers.* Another criticism regarding the Concurrent Translation Method relates to one of the most important aspects of the learning process—motivation. Using concurrent translation in bilingual classrooms tends to be extremely boring for students and goes against what research suggests for motivating students and contextualizing the subject matter.

4. *Draining for the Teacher to Implement.* This method can become increasingly taxing on a teacher who is constantly trying to alternate between two languages. One way to lessen the amount of effort on the part of the teacher is to separate the languages according to the person presenting the lesson. For instance, the teacher can consistently conduct the lesson in one language while a fellow teacher or paraprofessional can conduct the instruction in the other language.

5. *Disproportionate Time Spent in Each Language.* Teachers often underestimate the amount of time the target language is used during instruction. In other words, teachers have a tendency to dedicate less time to a student's native language. One consequence of this disproportionate language use is that students may come to think of English as the more valuable language. Another consequence is that the amount of time devoted to the primary language for academic purposes will be minimized, which may affect student achievement.

6. *Random Use of Languages.* Teachers may assume that they are implementing the Concurrent Translation Method, when, in reality, they often code-switch during instruction. Lessow-Hurley contends that the most effective ways to use languages concurrently during academic instruction are after the teacher has articulated a complete thought. Although we need to recognize that code switching is linguistically complex and serves a variety of purposes (e.g., expressing group solidarity, stressing a point, etc.), much of the literature on dual-language instruction recommends that teachers separate the languages entirely or at least try to avoid code-switching in the middle of a spoken phrase, sentence, or thought.

7. *Loss of Instructional Time.* Approximately one half of instructional time is spent on directly translating the lesson. As a result, a lot of instructional time ends up being wasted, which results in less elaborated language and fewer critical connections to the content. An alternative to the Concurrent Translation Method where instructional time does not have to be lost is discussed in the next section.

Given the numerous criticisms of the Concurrent Translation Method, we may ask ourselves whether it would ever be appropriate to use such a method. Many bilingual educators and researchers, such as Rodolfo Jacobson, for example, advocate for a separation of languages either by content area or by time of day. This separation is ideal in dual-language bilingual education programs. However, many bilingual classrooms may have the need to use both languages concurrently. Therefore, two alternative methods are widely recommended in lieu of the Concurrent Translation Method: (1) the preview–review method expounded upon by Lessow-Hurley and (2) the new concurrent approach developed by Jacobson.

In the preview–review method, the two languages are used within the same lesson. However, the languages are separated according to the lesson components. Generally, teachers introduce and conclude the lesson in one language and use the other language for teaching the lesson. Teachers usually choose the primary language for the preview–review and the second language for the teaching of the content of the lesson.

Jacobson, who coined the term *New Concurrent Approach* (NCA), has studied it since the 1970s. The difference between the Concurrent Translation Method and NCA is how the pattern of language use plays out in the classroom. While the Concurrent Translation Method occurs as a direct translation, NCA provides for cognitively rich concurrent use of both languages. In other words, when teachers employ NCA, they alternate between the languages by building on the content progressively with each remark (regardless of the language being used at that specific time). In the following example, a bilingual (English-Spanish) education teacher alternates between the two languages:

Teacher: *¿Qué aprendieron durante el paseo al museo?* [What did you learn during the field trip to the museum?]

Cecilia: *Aprendimos cómo los dinosaurios vivían y qué comieron.* [We learned how the dinosaurs lived and what they ate.]

Teacher: What did you notice about the dinosaurs' teeth? *Cuéntenme algo acerca de la forma o tamaño de los dientes.* [Tell me something about the shape or size of their teeth.]

Leslie: Oh, like when the meat eaters had sharp teeth so they could eat other dinosaurs.

Alberto: *Y los que comen zacate tienen dientes planos.* [And the ones that ate grass have flat teeth.]

Teacher: *¿Tienen otras observaciones acerca de los dientes?* [Do you have any other observations about the teeth?]

In the above example, the teacher uses the two languages to build on scientific concepts, so that the students gather new information by actively attending to each language. Instead of directly translating each utterance as in the Concurrent Translation Method, the teacher purposefully alternates between the two languages. The aim is that both languages are used in a balanced manner and structured so that the students do not tune out either language.

Although the Concurrent Translation Method is widely used, greater attention to alternative methods such as the preview–review method and the New Concurrent Approach would be useful. To gauge which alternative method best would suit their classrooms, bilingual teachers must consider a variety of factors, such as instructional goals, teacher and student bilingual proficiency, and the demographic/linguistic makeup of the class.

Kimberley K. Cuero and Hamsa Aburumuh

See also Code Switching; English as a Second Language (ESL) Approaches; Primary-Language Support

Further Readings

Jacobson, R. (1995). Allocating two languages as a key feature of a bilingual methodology. In O. García & C. Baker (Eds.), *Policy and practice in bilingual education: Extending the foundations* (pp. 166–175). Clevedon, UK: Multilingual Matters.

Lessow-Hurley, J. (2005). *The foundations of dual language instruction* (4th ed.). Boston: Pearson Education.

Milk, R. (1993). Bilingual education and English as a second language: The elementary school. In M. B. Arias & U. Casanova (Eds.), *Bilingual education: Politics, practice, research* (pp. 88–112). Chicago: University of Chicago Press.

Container Theory of Language

It is not uncommon for persons unfamiliar with linguistics to suggest that the brain and speech mechanisms of children probably function better when they are unencumbered by more than one language. In this view, it is assumed that to avoid confusion, developing one language at a time is preferable to using two or more languages concurrently, especially in school classrooms. This can lead to the conclusion that bilingual education is unwise. The basis for this is the notion that the brain and the apparatus for language learning and production are similar to a one-lane road or a container with limited capacity. Parents and even school personnel are often surprised to learn that the human brain appears to have unlimited capacity to process language and that its limits, if any, are not yet known.

To understand the reasons for these false assumptions, it is necessary to understand some important features of languages, how they are learned, and their patterns of use. For many people, perhaps for most, the organs of speech production become accustomed to one language and have difficulty learning new sounds that do not exist in the mother tongue. The nuances of one's native language are learned early on by the nerves and muscles involved. In time, muscles and nerves lose the ability to make sounds that are not used in that language. The trilled "r" in Spanish is difficult for native English speakers because it does not exist in English and it is difficult for the speech organs of monolingual English speakers to produce. For native Chinese speakers, the challenge is even greater because Chinese does not contain the "r" sound at all, trilled or otherwise. Some scientists suggest that some sounds may be forgotten, because at birth, babies are capable of making the sounds of every language in the world. This seems logical. If there existed a language whose sounds could not be learned by infants, that language would quickly evolve and be replaced by a modification of that language that would not include the "impossible" sounds. What may actually happen in infancy is that children's brains keep track of sounds that are used in their environments and keep those sounds as part of their active repertoires of speech. Sounds that are not part of their native languages fade away, making it difficult to learn a second language without a distinguishable accent. It is important, however, to distinguish between speech and language.

While meaningful sounds are part of what we commonly know as *language,* they are more properly called *speech,* because they concern only the spoken version of a language, not the written form.

Accents and Communication

Accents also influence the perception of language interference in the brain. Hence, they require additional explanation. Most accents do not pose a serious problem to communication. It is possible for a brilliant scientist like Albert Einstein to speak heavily accented English and to be no less brilliant for it. Like Einstein, many Americans speak with an accent, a situation in which the sounds and inflections of the native language creep into spoken English but do not impair the person's command of the language. Usually, accents are a minor problem that can be eliminated through coaching, although most people have little need for this. Movie and stage actors quickly learn accents when they are called for by the parts they are playing. In those cases, the opposite situation obtains: The actor has a great accent but may not know the language well enough to order breakfast. For more serious problems of accents, it may be necessary to take up a sustained regimen of exercise, not unlike what must be done for little-used muscles. Severe accents tend to occur among adults but rarely last very long in children because, among the latter, the muscles and nerves involved in speech production retain the ability to utter new and unfamiliar sounds. This flexibility in the speech organs lasts into early adolescence in most cases.

The presence of an accent is not indicative of confusion between languages or of trying to do more than the brain can handle. It is simply the result of having learned only the necessary sounds for one's native language and discarding, involuntarily, all others and subsequently finding a need to produce them.

Most of the discussion above has to do with the mechanics of speech production. It has little to do with languages taking up too much space in the brain. It is also related to the efficacy of language teaching methods, a topic discussed below. Elsewhere in this encyclopedia, the core elements of language are reviewed, such as phonology, morphology, syntax, and lexicon. It is primarily in the phonology of language that an "accent" is most noticeable. Much of what we associate with interference between languages is little more than an "accent" emanating from

habits of speech rooted in the first-acquired language. They are not due to size limitations of the brain.

Why the Container Theory Is Misleading

The human brain is capable of learning and processing many languages. In fact, scientists today are not certain of the number of languages that can be learned and used by an average human. The lack of a definitive answer to this fascinating question is that the number of variables that bear on the number of languages is too large and complex to control in a laboratory setting. Whatever the maximum number of possible languages may be, it is not true that an average child can become confused by using two or three languages in school. Depending largely on the age at which a given language is learned, a discernible "accent" may be present. This does not mean that the child in question does not have a total and complete command of a language in every other respect: vocabulary, sentence construction, grammar, semantics, and so on.

This fact becomes easier to grasp when we set aside the idea that the brain is a container that holds a limited amount of language and that one language is enough to fill it. The brain has an enormous capacity to process data; and data in small and large sets make up language. Persons who speak several languages find it easier to learn additional languages. The reason is that languages inform each other in the process of learning them. Once a child understands what he or she can do with language and the process is made enjoyable, it becomes easier to figure out how to do the same thing with the other language he or she is learning. This process is part of the innate curiosity of children to explore and understand their environments. In short, our capacity for language learning is improved by experience in using language—any language.

Some linguists believe that humans have a built-in predisposition to learn languages, called *common underlying proficiency.* This capacity, according to theorists like James Cummins, facilitates the learning of new languages. If this is true, it can be argued that humans are "hardwired" to handle more than one language at a time. Language has several functions. It is, among other things, an analytical tool. Using one's native language to help understand the workings of another facilitates the learning of the second language. Learning the second language facilitates the third, and so on. For most children in schools today, this bit of science remains untested due to the lack of understanding by teachers of the processes involved.

An Alternative Metaphor: The Computer

However useful it may be in adult life, it is not usually required of children in the United States that they learn more than two languages, the language of their parents and English, the lingua franca of the wider society. Our current understanding of the brain leaves no doubt that the brain is much more than a mere container. The complexities of language can be understood only if we abandon the idea of "brain as container" and replace it with the idea of "brain as computer," with a number of processors functioning simultaneously. It is possible for one set of processors to be learning math, science, or social studies, while another set is quietly engaged in sifting and sorting the peculiarities of the second language the child is trying to learn. This multitasking capacity is unique to the human brain, a supercomputer more powerful than any electronic computer yet devised. It bears remembering that computers were invented by brains, but there is not a brain that has ever been created by a computer.

If the brain is not a container and if it can process more than one language at a time, why is it difficult for schools to teach children who come to school speaking a language other than English? The answer is that language teaching and language learning are complex phenomena that are not intuitive. The *art of teaching languages* must be preceded by a good understanding of the *science of language,* an understanding that many teachers are not given during their days as undergraduates preparing to teach. The problem here is the inadequacy of teacher education programs, rather than the inadequacies of young brains. Many immigrant children enter American schools lacking academic mastery of the language of their parents. They may not be literate in that language and therefore do not have the tools of that language to use when learning their second language, English. In their haste to teach English and prepare students for high-stakes tests, many schools overlook this handicap and push these students, prematurely, into English-only instruction. The result is an overly protracted period of mastering English. What they need is not fast-and-furious English. What is most helpful is to provide the child with ways to fill the gap that is left by incomplete academic mastery of the first language.

Academic language mastery in the first language provides the child with a useful set of tools to use in learning the second.

What Learning Theory Tells Us

Avoiding the use of a child's home language while learning English is a mistake. Learning theory suggests that learners make better progress when they use what is already known as a bridge to what they wish to learn. This is a cornerstone principle in bilingual education programs. It is compatible with the learning and language theories advanced by well-known scientists, such as Lev Vygotsky, Jean Piaget, Noam Chomsky, and others.

Regrettably, while the problem of inadequate teacher education has been known for some time, the realization that teachers must be prepared to teach English to nonnative speakers has not had a major impact on teacher education. University students who are preparing to become teachers of English in the public schools spend a good deal of time and effort learning how to teach English literature to native speakers of the language and how to express themselves properly in tests, such as the SAT writing section. During their years of preparation, teachers in training may never focus on teaching the language to immigrants and other nonnative speakers, the segment of the student population that is growing faster than any other. They also learn to teach the beaux arts of a language, its poetry, and its fiction more than its use as an instrument for learning. Much of the problem schools encounter in teaching English to English language learners is due to limits in the knowledge base of the profession, not the limitations of the bilingual brain.

Josué M. González

See also BICS/CALPS Theory; Brain Research; Languages, Learned or Acquired; Learning a Language, Best Age; Linguistics, an Overview; Raising Bilingual Children; Semilingualism; Teacher Qualifications; Underlying Linguistic Proficiencies

Further Readings

Baker, C., & Hornberger, N. H. (Eds.). (2001). *An introductory reader to the writings of Jim Cummins.* Clevedon, UK: Multilingual Matters.

Cummins, J. (1980). The entry and exit fallacy in bilingual education. *NABE Journal, 4,* 25–60.

Continua of Biliteracy

The *continua of biliteracy* model offers an ecological framework in which to situate research, teaching, and language planning in linguistically diverse settings. *Biliteracy* is defined here as any and all instances in which communication occurs in two or more languages in or around writing. Instances of biliteracy include biliterate events, actors, interactions, practices, activities, programs, sites, situations, societies, and worlds. The model or framework uses the notion of intersecting and nested continua to demonstrate the multiple and complex interrelationships between bilingualism and literacy and the importance of the contexts, media, and content through which biliteracy develops. The notion of *continuum* is intended to convey that, although one can identify points on the continuum, those points are not finite, static, or discrete. On any one biliteracy continuum there are infinitely many points; any single point is inextricably related to all other points; and all the points share fundamental commonalities. Furthermore, across the multiple intersecting and nested continua, there are many points at which connection, transfer, and reinforcement of biliteracy may occur.

The continua of biliteracy model is an ecological framework, metaphorically incorporating themes of evolution, environment, and endangerment, paralleling those in biological and environmental ecology. Specifically, an ecological view of language posits that languages (a) live and evolve in an ecosystem along with other languages *(language evolution);* (b) interact with their sociopolitical, economic, and cultural environments *(language environment);* and (c) become endangered if there is inadequate environmental support for them vis-à-vis other languages in the ecosystem *(language endangerment).* Significantly, the ecology movement is not only concerned with studying and describing those potential losses but also counteracting them.

Origins and Implications of the Framework

The initial impetus for formulating the continua of biliteracy framework was the Literacy in Two Languages project, a long-term comparative ethnographic research project in two language minority communities of Philadelphia, beginning in 1987.

Looking to scholarly literature to inform the research, Nancy H. Hornberger, the author of this entry, found very little work on biliteracy, which left the definition of the term implicit, assuming a meaning roughly glossed as reading and writing in two languages or in a second language and focusing primarily on mastery of reading and writing in two languages.

A broader theoretical common ground that emerged in considering the larger literatures on bilingualism, the teaching of second/foreign languages, literacy, and the teaching of reading/writing was that dimensions of bilingualism and literacy are traditionally characterized in terms of polar opposites, such as first versus second languages (L1 versus L2), monolingual versus bilingual individuals, or oral versus literate societies. These polar opposites turn out, under the scrutiny of research, to be only theoretical end points on what is in reality a continuum of features. This notion became the building block for the continua model of biliteracy.

Specifically, the continua framework depicts the *development* of biliteracy along intersecting first language-second language, receptive-productive, and oral-written language skills continua; through the *medium* of two (or more) languages and literacies whose linguistic structures vary from similar to dissimilar, whose scripts range from convergent to divergent, and to which the developing biliterate individual's exposure varies from simultaneous to successive; in *contexts* that encompass micro- to macrolevels and are characterized by varying mixes along the monolingual-bilingual and oral-literate continua; and with *content* that ranges from majority to minority perspectives and experiences, literary to vernacular styles and genres, and decontextualized to contextualized language texts.

The notion of continuum conveys that all points on a particular continuum are interrelated and the intersecting and nested relationships among the continua convey that all points across the continua are also interrelated. This ecological framework suggests that the more their learning contexts and contexts of use allow learners and users to draw from across the whole of each and every continuum, the greater are the chances for their full biliterate development and expression. Implicit in that suggestion is the recognition that there has usually not been attention to all points and that movement along the continua and across the intersections may well be contested. In educational policy and practice regarding biliteracy, there tends to be an implicit privileging, such that one end of each continuum is associated with more power than the other (e.g., written development over oral development). There is a need to contest the traditional power weighting by paying attention to, granting agency to, and making space for actors and practices that have traditionally been the less powerful ends of the continua.

As mentioned earlier, the original work in which the continua of biliteracy framework arose was the Literacy in Two Languages project in Philadelphia. Through participant observation, interviewing, and document collection in school and community settings in the Puerto Rican community of North Philadelphia and the Cambodian community of West Philadelphia, Hornberger, along with a group of graduate students, sought to understand biliteracy attitudes and practices in classroom and community and their fit with local, state, and national policies and programs addressing them. The continua framework proved useful in analyzing the data and drawing conclusions from the research; and by the same token, the ongoing research continually informed the evolving framework.

For example, an early paper from this project showed how *biliteracy contexts* for Puerto Rican and Cambodian students in Philadelphia in the 1980s were framed and constrained by an ecology in which national policies—such as the proposed English Language Amendment, the Bilingual Education Act renewals of 1984 and 1988, and the Immigration Reform and Control Act of 1986—emphasized English acquisition at the expense of minority language maintenance; the educational system used minority languages only to embed the more powerful English literacy; and the assimilative charm of English pulled students' biliterate development toward this language. Hornberger in collaboration with Joel Hardman published a study of adult biliteracy development in programs in this same community, in which they highlighted the inadequacy of an autonomous, cognitive-skills-based view of literacy with its emphasis on a single, standardized schooled literacy in the second language. They made the argument for the benefits of an ecologically complementary ideological, cultural practice view.

Hornberger and Cheri Micheau found that faculty and staff of two-way bilingual programs in the Puerto Rican community continually faced challenging decisions related to the *media of biliteracy,* such as (a) placement of students in English-dominant and Spanish-dominant streams, (b) distribution of English and Spanish in the program structure and the classroom, and (c) instruction and assessment in a language ecology of coexisting standard and nonstandard varieties of English and Spanish. In an ethnographic dissertation study of literacy, identity, and educational policy among Cambodian women and girls in Philadelphia, Ellen Skilton-Sylvester expanded the original continua framework to include *biliteracy content,* to account for the important role of contextualized, vernacular, and minority texts in the women's and girls' biliterate development.

Applications for Analysis and Action

Beyond these analytical uses within the ecology of languages in Philadelphia, the continua framework has been applied toward both analysis and action in a range of other ecological contexts in the United States and internationally, as illustrated in studies published in a book, *Continua of Biliteracy,* edited by Hornberger and summarized here. At the program level, Mihyon Jeon found in the continua framework a rationale for Korean-English two-way immersion program policies, while Viniti Basu contrasted the ecology of bilingual education in two schools of New Delhi, India, showing why one school is more successful in making its students proficient in their second language. At the level of multilingual classroom ecologies, Diana Schwinge analyzed via the continua how two U.S. bilingual education teachers adapted a mandated curriculum to use the available linguistic, cultural, and textual resources in their classrooms to enable students to become biliterate, while South African colleagues Carole Bloch and Neville Alexander used the continua as a model to explore ways of developing, trying out, and demonstrating workable strategies for teaching and learning multilingually in one Cape Town primary school.

Bilingual teacher professional development offers other instances of biliteracy ecology that the continua framework has been used to elucidate and shape. Comparing two groups of bilingual teacher education candidates in the Southwest, namely, Mexican normal school graduates and Latina paraprofessionals, Bertha Pérez and colleagues found the biliteracy continua dynamically present within the teacher preparation program in the acceptance of the use of English and Spanish vernaculars, which, in turn, enables the teacher education candidates to understand the local community's use of the vernacular while also providing opportunities for development of their own academic use of standard English and Spanish. Hardman and Melisa Cahnmann each used the continua framework to look closely at tensions and struggles in the classroom practice of English as a Second Language/ bilingual teachers, around the control of content in one case and the teacher's assessment and correction of students' oral and written productions in the other. Equally, the continua model has been applied to consider students' biliteracy, in a consideration of language minority student voices in rural Arkansas (Felicia Lincoln) and of biliteracy development among Latino youth in New York City (Carmen Mercado).

Other uses of the continua framework also illustrated in this publication include its application as an ecological model for considering language policy: Bloch and Alexander on South Africa's multilingual language policy, Colin Baker on the Welsh National Curriculum, and Hornberger's work looking comparatively at implementational and ideological spaces for multilingual education in South Africa, Bolivia, and Paraguay. In the United States, the continua framework has been applied in describing, analyzing, and interpreting Puerto Rican community bilingualism and heritage language education for Korean American and Chinese American learners. This work, conducted by Rebecca Freeman, Holly Pak, and Hornberger and Wang, highlights the centrality of ecology and identity in the biliterate development of heritage languages and their speakers.

Taking up themes of ideology and identity in relation to the ecology of biliteracy, a group of researchers and educators in the Pacific Islands have used the continua framework to explore the language policy/ practice connection in classrooms they characterize as *linguistic borderlands:* In these classrooms, teachers contend with postcolonial educational policies designating English as the main medium of instruction, even though the children come to school speaking Marshallese, Palauan, or Samoan. The authors, Marylin Low and her colleagues, called attention to the need for a dialogic space where community members can query which language(s) should be the medium of instruction and for what purposes. Christine Hélot applied the continua framework as a lens to elucidate ideological principles and biases underlying language education policies in France, which tend to favor prestigious bilingual education for monolingual learners and neglect the bilingualism of minority speakers; and she reported on a language awareness initiative carried out

in a small, rural primary school in a multicultural community in southern Alsace that reverses the imposed relations of power. This initiative begins to bridge the gap between prestigious bilingualism and minority bilingualism by opening the school to parents and making classrooms inclusive of all the languages and cultures of their pupils.

In New York City, Lesley Bartlett's ethnographic study of multilingual, multimodal, transnational literacy practices of Latino immigrant youth in Manhattan employed the continua of biliteracy framework in seeking to understand how academic English literacy intersects with out-of-school literacy practices of these youth and how their multiple literacies might serve as resources in school. In the Bronx, Sharon Utakis and Marianne Pita considered the transnational practices and identities of the Dominican community, arguing that the continua of biliteracy provides a framework by which to articulate policy and pedagogical changes needed to do justice to the educational needs of Dominican students, in contrast to current policy and practice that presents these students with unacceptable forced choices between Spanish and English, home community and host community, and local and global affiliations.

The potential of the continua framework as a tool teachers can use in opening up ideological spaces in the local contexts of classrooms, in turn, contributing to changes in the community and society, is a theme emerging from the above work. Reciprocally, Hornberger's consideration of community and classroom challenges faced in implementing transformative multilingual language policies in three national contexts—postapartheid South Africa's new constitution of 1993, Bolivia's National Education Reform of 1994, and Paraguay's postdictatorship education reforms of 1992—illustrates that ideological space opened up by top-down policies can contribute to the emergence of new discourses in implementational spaces at the grassroots level.

Future Directions

There remain unanswered questions about the continua framework. It has proven useful in ethnographic research and as a guide for action but has yet to be tested as a basis for experimental or survey research. Likewise, it originated as a descriptive framework and has developed as an applied lens for research but remains relatively uncharted for predictive and explanatory uses. Such uses need further exploration through continuing research and development in a wide range of settings and circumstances.

Meanwhile, the continua framework is already being put to activist, transformative uses at individual, classroom, community, and societal levels. For instance, language planners can use the continua to look closely at particular instances of biliteracy, identify contradictions between beliefs and practices or discrepancies between policy and implementation, and then use those contradictions and discrepancies to further pry open ideological and implementational spaces for biliteracy development. The model moves beyond a programmatic concern to offer an overarching conceptual tool and tangible methodological guide to address the challenges of multilingual education found everywhere in our world, a schema for understanding and intervention at micro- to macrolevels.

Basic questions about biliteracy remain: Who becomes biliterate and where, when, how, and why do they do so? What is the role of family, home, school, community, and wider society in fostering and promoting biliteracy? Perhaps the continua framework can contribute to answering such questions and thereby serve teachers, researchers, and policymakers in bringing about more optimistic and just language and literacy futures for all learners.

Nancy H. Hornberger

See also Bilingual Education as Language Policy; Critical Literacy; Hornberger, Nancy; Language and Identity; Language Education Policy in Global Perspective; Language Policy and Social Control; Literacy and Biliteracy; Views of Bilingual Education

Further Readings

Bartlett, L. (2004). *Transnational literacy practices of Latino immigrant youth: A social analysis.* Unpublished manuscript.

Freeman, R. D. (2004). *Building on community bilingualism.* Philadelphia: Caslon.

Hélot, C. (2005). Bridging the gap between prestigious bilingualism and the bilingualism of minorities: Towards an integrated perspective of multilingualism in the French education context. In M. Ó. Laoire (Ed.), *Multilingualism in educational settings* (pp. 15–32). Hohengehren, Germany: Schneider.

Hornberger, N. H. (1989). Continua of biliteracy. *Review of Educational Research, 59,* 271–296.

Hornberger, N. H. (Ed.). (2003). *Continua of biliteracy: An ecological framework for educational policy, research, and practice in multilingual settings.* Clevedon, UK: Multilingual Matters.

Hornberger, N. H. (2005). Nichols to NCLB: Local and global perspectives on U.S. language education policy. *Working Papers in Educational Linguistics, 20*(2), 1–17.

Hornberger, N. H. (2006). Voice and biliteracy in indigenous language revitalisation: Contentious educational practices in Quechua, Guarani, and Maori contexts. *Journal of Language, Identity, and Education, 5,* 277–292.

Hornberger, N. H., & Hardman, J. (1994) Literacy as cultural practice and cognitive skill: Biliteracy in a Cambodian adult ESL class and a Puerto Rican GED program. In D. Spener (Ed.), *Adult biliteracy in the United States* (pp. 147–169). Washington, DC: Center for Applied Linguistics.

Hornberger, N. H., & Micheau, C. (1993). "Getting far enough to like it": Biliteracy in the middle school. *Peabody Journal of Education, 69,* 30–53.

Hornberger, N. H., & Skilton-Sylvester, E. (2000). Revisiting the continua of biliteracy: International and critical perspectives. *Language and Education: An International Journal, 14,* 96–122.

Hornberger, N. H., & Wang, S. C. (2008). Who are our heritage language learners? Identity and biliteracy in heritage language education in the United States. In D. M. Brinton, O. Kagan, & S. Bauckus (Eds.), *Heritage language education: A new field emerging* (pp. 3–35). New York and London: Routledge.

Low, M., Penland, D., Ruluked, E., & Sataua, P. (2004). *Oral traditions and English: Language policy/practice relations in postcolonial classrooms.* Paper presented at the Annual Meeting of the American Association for Applied Linguistics, Portland, OR.

Skilton-Sylvester, E. (1997). *Inside, outside, and in-between: Identities, literacies, and educational policies in the lives of Cambodian women and girls in Philadelphia.* Unpublished doctoral dissertation, University of Pennsylvania, Philadelphia.

Utakis, S., & Pita, M. (2005). An educational policy for negotiating transnationalism: The Dominican community in New York City. In A. S. Canagarajah (Ed.), *Reclaiming the local in language policy and practice* (pp. 147–164). Mahwah, NJ: Lawrence Erlbaum.

CONTRASTIVE ANALYSIS

Contrastive analysis was developed in the mid-1940s as a hypothesis of second-language acquisition tied to a method for teaching languages. Proponents of contrastive analysis regard language as a conditioned response, a process derived from a behaviorist approach to learning. They believe that errors produced by second-language learners are the result of interference from the learner's native language. Contrastive analysis refers specifically to the process of comparing the structures of two languages with each other for the purpose of determining the degree of difference between the two languages. From this analysis, it is posited that teachers will be able to predict errors that learners of a given native language will make in learning a specific second language (L2). From this information, teachers will be able to design materials and methods that focus on the areas of greatest contrast, which are predicted to be the areas of greatest difficulty for learning. Contrastive analysis was one of the most influential approaches to teaching an L2 in the 1960s and 1970s. The audio-lingual method represents one such method that relied on the tenets of behaviorism and contrastive analysis.

Contrastive analysis is important for bilingual education, as it represents one of the first direct applications of theory to the development of methods and materials for teaching an L2. Although the theory behind contrastive analysis has fallen out of favor, many practices originally designed on the basis of it are still quite prevalent in bilingual and L2 classrooms. Contrastive analysis is seen as the precursor to the development of the field of applied linguistics, a field that holds bilingualism and bilingual education among its central foci.

Development of the Theory

Originally developed in the 1940s and 1950s, the contrastive analysis hypothesis was based on structural linguistics as well as behavioral psychology, the predominant theories of language and learning at the time. Charles Fries originally presented contrastive analysis in 1945. Later, Robert Lado, of Georgetown University, presented the contrastive analysis hypothesis. This hypothesis stems from the view of learning as the development of a new set of behaviors or habits. Language was defined in terms of language structures at the level of the sound system (phonology), the word or lexicon (morphology), and the sentence (syntax or grammar). With the structural view of language and the behavioral view of learning, the task for practitioners was to determine which habits

needed to be "undone" and which new habits needed to be formed in order to be successful in learning a second language.

The core concept of contrastive analysis is that the main source of errors and difficulty in learning the L2 occur as a result of interference, the transferring of habits from the native language to the target language. The hypothesis states that these difficulties stem from the differences that exist between languages. Given the behaviorist theory of learning, the greater the differences, the greater the learning difficulties will be. The most important task of those conducting contrastive analysis is to compare aspects of the two languages in order to predict the difficulties and errors that will occur in L2 learning. Having compared given aspects of the two languages, the instructor can ignore what is common to them, as that part of learning the two languages will proceed without much difficulty. The instructor is expected to teach and develop teaching materials that focus on the areas of difference. Those differences are then practiced through extensive repetition, the hallmark of behaviorist learning.

The contrastive analysis hypothesis had a strong and a weak version. The strong version held that it was possible to completely contrast the system of one language (grammar, lexicon, and phonology) to the language system of an L2 and design teaching materials from that comparison. The weak version of the hypothesis took its starting point from observations of actual difficulties or errors that learners displayed when learning an L2 and attempted to account for those errors on the basis of differences between the first or native language and the L2. For this version, one starts with evidence from real language data, such as from inaccurate translation, foreign accents, and common student errors in the target language.

For example, in comparing the grammar of English and Spanish, the placement of the adjective in relation to the noun is often reversed: "a sound mind" is *una mente sana* (a "mind sound"). A second example from the comparison of English and Hungarian would yield the observation that Hungarian employs postpositions while English employs prepositions: "in the house" and *a házban* (the "house in"). These examples represent areas in which the contrastive hypothesis would predict difficulties for learners of either language. That is, the new structures would have to be learned. Other areas of the language structure that are the same, such as the placement of the article (e.g., *the* and *a* in English) before the noun, would be learned automatically through positive transfer for learners of both Spanish and Hungarian, as all three languages place the article before the noun.

The application of contrastive analysis to teaching rests on the notion that students will "naturally" acquire features of the new language that are similar to their first or stronger language. Therefore, teaching time should focus on those features of the L2 that contrast with the first or stronger language. Based on these ideas, teachers, particularly in the 1960s and 1970s, were trained in contrastive analysis with the aim of analyzing and comparing grammars of the first and target languages of their students and often training their students to compare and contrast the language systems as well. The method par excellence tied to the contrastive analysis theory was the audio-lingual method, through which learners are drilled to produce correct responses and errors are immediately corrected, in order to maintain a strong emphasis on habit formation.

In its initial conceptualization, contrastive analysis focused on smaller structures of language, in particular at the level of phonology, morphology, and syntax. Later, contrastive analysis techniques were applied to broade- level features of language, such as pragmatic and discourse-level features. According to Robert Kaplan, these studies, also called *contrastive rhetoric*, focus on comparisons of pragmatic functions of language, such as politeness strategies or ways in which speakers of different languages organize narratives for different purposes, such as argument or explanation. This extension focused attention on another central source of inspiration for contrastive analysis: the study of language contact and, by extension, the relationship between language and thought as articulated in the Sapir-Whorf hypothesis—language influencing the way native speakers perceive the world.

Difficulties With Contrastive Analysis

Beginning in the 1960s, a number of problems were identified relative to the contrastive-analysis hypothesis. First, from a methodological perspective, it proved difficult to clearly outline the places in which two languages do contrast and to determine the degree of distance between them. That is, the question of how to measure difference and distance was difficult to answer. Second, in terms of errors and their relationship to language structure, empirical studies beginning in the 1960s demonstrated that many errors made by L2 learners could not be explained on the basis of structural differences between the two languages. Moreover, certain errors that contrastive analysis predicted to occur did not actually occur. Indeed, other studies began to show that learners had more difficulty in learning structures that were quite similar between the two languages, a result in direct conflict with the predictions of contrastive analysis.

In addition, studies of classroom practice showed that imitation, reinforcement, and error correction, the hallmarks of the behaviorist theory, did not seem to be central to the process of language acquisition as predicted by the contrastive analysis hypothesis. Even after years of pattern practice, some errors remained. Finally, the shift in paradigm to mentalist or cognitive models of language learning, heralded by the Chomskyan revolution in the 1960s, led to a new interpretation of language learning and the purpose of learner errors. Essentially, errors were seen not as habits transferred "incorrectly" to the second language, but rather as hypothesis-testing activities on the part of the learners as they developed new rules for organizing a developing language system. In sum, the contrastive-analysis hypothesis served as a source for empirical research ideas that ultimately proved untenable in the face of newer models of learning.

Contrastive Analysis Revisited

As with many applied areas, contrastive analysis as a practice has carried on long after its theoretical promise ended. In the classroom, practices developed on the basis of contrastive analysis are still often used and even advocated. These practices include the use of language labs for language drills, as well as teachers and students comparing elements of language structure and analyzing learners' errors. Instead of tying such activities to mechanical drills, they are tied to the cognitive notion of *noticing differences* as a cognitive strategy for focusing attention in learning particular aspects of a language.

Insights from contrastive analysis have also been fruitfully employed in machine translation software that is becoming increasingly sophisticated and that draws insights from the nature of similarities and differences in languages at the structural (sentence) level as well as the semantic (meaning) and discourse (paragraph) levels. These are translated, by means of artificial-intelligence programming and used in translation software.

Finally, Claire Kramsch and Paul Kei Matsuda believe that a reconsideration of some of the insights derived from contrastive analysis, coupled with reconsiderations of the insights of the Sapir-Whorf hypothesis and its concern with linguistic relativism, are leading to a reevaluation of the role of culture in the field of L2 teaching and learning. In this sense, contrastive analysis remains an important contribution to the field of bilingual education and L2 teaching and learning, as its insights continue to be reevaluated in the light of advances in theories in language and learning.

Juliet Langman

See also Audio-Lingual Method; Error Analysis; Interlanguage

Further Readings

Fries, C. (1945). *Teaching and learning English as a foreign language.* Ann Arbor: University of Michigan Press.

Kaplan, R. B. (1966). Cultural thought patterns in intercultural education. *Language Learning Journal, 16,* 1–20.

Kramsch, C. (2004). Language, thought, and culture. In A. Davies & C. Elder (Eds.), *Handbook of applied linguistics* (pp. 235–261). Malden: MA: Blackwell.

Matsuda, P. K. (2001). On the origin of contrastive rhetoric: A response to "The origin of contrastive rhetoric revisited" by H. G. Ying (2000), *International Journal of Applied Linguistics, 11,* 257–260.

Lado, R. (1957). *Linguistics across cultures.* Ann Arbor: University of Michigan Press.

Robinett, B. W. (1983). *Second-language learning: Contrastive analysis, error analysis, and related aspects.* Ann Arbor: University of Michigan Press.

Sridhar, S. N. (1981). Contrastive analysis, error analysis, and interlanguage: Three phases of one goal. In J. Fisiak (Ed.), *Contrastive linguistics and the language teacher* (pp. 207–241). Oxford, UK: Pergamon.

Wardhaugh, R. (1974). *Topics in applied linguistics.* Rowley: MA: Newbury House.

Willems, D., Defrancq, B., Colleman, T., & Noel, D. (Eds.). (2003). *Contrastive analysis in language: Identifying linguistic units of comparison.* New York: Palgrave MacMillan.

Costs of Bilingual Education

Educators, policymakers, and others have long struggled with issues related to the additional costs involved in educating English language learners.

These concerns increased after 1974, when the U.S. Supreme Court made it clear that a failure to provide specialized instruction to these children constituted a violation of law. Although the decision did not mandate bilingual education, it was the preferred solution in many schools and communities, including the San Francisco Unified School District, the original venue of the *Lau v. Nichols* (1974) decision. One of the most consequential results of this landmark decision was to spur state efforts to improve their programs across their respective school districts. Much of this came about through the expansion of state-level bilingual education efforts. For a time, the legal requirement that English language learners be provided appropriate instruction enhanced the development of bilingual education in the public schools.

Federal funding for bilingual programs was first provided through an amendment to the Elementary and Secondary Education Act (ESEA) of 1965. That amendment, known as Title VII, ESEA, or simply the Bilingual Education Act, provided funding for local school implementation of bilingual programs, with awards provided to schools that were successful in a competitive grant process. Funding levels depended on the amounts requested by the programs and could vary extensively, owing to the variation of bilingual education strategies being implemented. Because participation in Title VII was voluntary, it provided opportunities to pilot new bilingual education models but did not include mandates requiring states to implement bilingual programs. The *Lau* decision provided greater pressure for states with large numbers of *limited-English-proficient* (LEP) students (another label for *English language learners,* used often in policy documents) to adopt more effective instructional practices for this student population and to provide funding to support those efforts. An analysis of state requirements conducted in 1982 revealed that by then, 9 states had mandated implementation of bilingual instructional programs for LEP students. Another 16 states provided local option program implementation. Whether mandated or implemented at local option, all of these programs implied additional funding. They required information on the level of funding needed to implement an effective program.

Early Bilingual Education Cost Studies

In the early 1970s, researchers initially debated issues as basic as what actually constitutes a "bilingual education" program. In 1973, José A. Cárdenas, an expert on language minority children's education, proposed that although local variants of bilingual programs existed, the critical elements of a universal bilingual education model included the following: (a) determination of students' language dominance and fluency; (b) staffing and staff utilization; (c) specialized staff training; (d) specialized materials; (e) instructional methodologies used; (f) time and space factors, including instruction in either language, grouping, and organizational patterns for instruction; and (g) special efforts targeted on expanding community involvement.

The Intercultural Development Research Association (IDRA) conducted one of the earliest cost studies of bilingual programs in the mid 1970s. In that seminal study, the IDRA research team used a *panel of experts* methodology to identify what practitioners in the field of bilingual education considered to be critical elements of an effective bilingual education program. These included student assessment, program evaluation, supplemental curricular materials, staffing, staff development, and parent involvement. In the IDRA bilingual education cost model, only those costs unique to the implementation of the specialized program were considered. For example, the costs of providing a teacher with state-adopted English language textbooks were not included, since all students would be provided these. On the other hand, specialized costs were considered, such as the additional assessments required to determine LEP students' native language and English language proficiency for instructional placement purposes. In addition, the costs of specialized staff training and professional development, specialized materials and auditory equipment, and program evaluation were included.

IDRA researchers collected actual cost information on the various components and developed an actual dollar cost figure for program delivery. The bilingual education cost levels varied slightly depending on the grade levels involved and the number of years a program had been in existence, with newer programs reflecting slightly higher costs for startup. The funding amounts ranged from $200 to $250 per student served, in 1976 dollars. A Houston Independent School District researcher, Herbert Alston, used the same methodology to estimate bilingual education costs in the Houston School District and came within $2 of IDRA cost estimates.

The first IDRA study focused on implementing bilingual programs in Texas. Later replications of the study, by IDRA, included analyses of costs in Colorado and Utah. These later studies conducted by María del Refugio Robledo, Roberto Zárate, Michelle Guss Zamora, and José A. Cárdenas, respectively, determined that in addition to the basic costs identified in the Texas study, Colorado and Utah costs included additional resources needed to recruit and retain bilingual teachers, a resource that is more available in Texas than in other states. Costs in these two additional states reflected a similar pattern, though totals tended to vary slightly based on school finance differences among states. Whereas the Texas study was limited to kindergarten through sixth grade, the Colorado and Utah studies included middle and high school costs and were divided into startup versus maintenance costs. Results in both states reflected slightly higher costs for the upper grade levels.

RAND Corporation Cost Study

In addition to the IDRA-generated bilingual education cost estimates, other researchers have conducted bilingual education cost estimates that have taken a slightly different approach. For example, in 1981, RAND Corporation researchers assessed the actual financial outlays of school systems to implement bilingual education program variants in a number of school districts in selected states around the country. In this study, program variants examined included pull-out programs, where LEP students were removed from the regular class and provided one-on-one or small-group supplemental instruction by an additional teacher; team teaching, in which a bilingual and an English monolingual alternated instruction to a group of LEP students; and bilingual programs delivered by a bilingual teacher in a self-contained classroom environment.

The cost estimates derived from this study revealed that add-on costs in different locales ranged from $200 to $700 per student, depending on the approach used and additional staff involved in delivering the program. Given the historical lack of interstate communication regarding LEP program funding, such variations were not surprising. But the RAND study, like the IDRA study, clearly revealed the complexities involved in attempting to assign a "real world" cost estimate for providing bilingual instruction in a wide variety of environments and program models.

Later Cost Studies
of Bilingual Education

Interest in defining what constitutes an *adequate education* that fueled many education finance reform efforts in the 1990s—spurred by state-level challenges regarding the level of funding provided to local school systems—led to research studies on the cost of education, both bilingual and otherwise. The research approaches vary widely but can be generally characterized into a range of types. In its primer on cost models, the National Access Network grouped the major methodologies into the following:

1. *Professional judgment studies:* costing techniques that rely on gathering input from groups of education professionals (teachers, administrators, special program designers, etc.) on the essential components necessary for a particular type of program, followed by collection of data on the actual dollar costs of those services.

2. *Expert judgment studies:* evidence-based methods that rely on a combination of effective schools research in tandem with expert panels to define and cost out "effective" educational practices.

3. *Successful school or school district studies:* based on data on existing school operations, followed by development of costs actually experienced in those settings.

4. *Cost function (or value-added) studies:* attempt to determine, compared with an average district, how much a district would need to spend to reach a certain performance target, in light of particular student characteristics.

A survey and related analyses conducted by Bruce Baker and Paul Markham in 2002 indicated that state funding levels and approaches continued to vary widely around the country, despite an emerging recognition that funding levels should not be as disparate for reasons other than instructional model variation and state-specific factors, such as teacher salaries, and so on. In their study, Baker and Markham reported that states fund LEP-targeted instruction in a variety of ways, ranging from flat grants based on student counts to providing funding for additional personnel units in state formulas. Some states use varying student "weights" that range from 10% of regular program costs in Texas to 50% add-on funding in New Mexico. These wide variations may be due to a lack of a more robust body of studies of bilingual education funding patterns.

In a later analysis of LEP add-on funding using common core data, the authors concluded that among the 12 states whose data were reviewed, 50% provided funding considered adequate, 50% provided funding that could be defended as "rational," and 33% were considered equitable.

The Arizona Bilingual Education Cost Study

Some of the latter studies have been driven by school finance litigation challenging the adequacy level of funding provided to local school systems by their respective states. In some of the challenges, costs for "special populations" include add-on costs for serving LEP students. As part of litigation related to provision of services needed for LEP students in Arizona, a federal court judge mandated a study of add-on costs associated with providing required service for this student population in that state. The study was conducted by the National Conference of State Legislatures and relied on input from expert state and national judgment panels to identify critical program elements. The Arizona specific cost study concluded that the incremental student costs—those costs over the costs required to provide instruction to non-LEP students—ranged from $2,571 for high-need elementary schools to a low of $1,026 in additional costs for low-need high school level LEP students. As this entry is written, the Arizona legislature and the federal courts are still arguing the issue, for example, in *Flores v. Arizona* (1992), as reported elsewhere in this encyclopedia.

Conclusion

Consideration of the additional costs required to provide specialized bilingual instruction to LEP students will continue to be addressed as states struggle with a new round of legal challenges that attempt to require states to provide sufficient funding to deliver an adequate education to all students. This new round of litigation may lead to further questions regarding what is an "adequate bilingual education" and how much it costs to provide it to different pupils with different languages, different English skills, differing program models, and differing state and local school systems.

Additional research is needed on the actual costs involved in providing specialized instruction for LEP students in the United States. The early cost studies, conducted by IDRA and the RAND Corporation, were valuable contributions to the literature and provided important examples of add-on costs involving special populations. Later studies by the Education Commission of the States and Baker and Markum provided insights into how states were funding programs at the time. The Arizona cost study is one of a very few studies that have attempted to develop true estimates of the costs for providing specialized services to LEP students. Some state-level cost studies have tended to either ignore special costs involved in serving LEP students or lump these programs into "special population" estimates that group very different pupil subgroups into broad categories. Such designs have provided insufficient information to policymakers in need of good estimates in support of good policy making. More often than not, lack of comprehensive information has tended to support long-standing state practices of providing insufficient funding for these programs. The result is that today, few states have readily available bilingual education cost information to guide their decision making. Because LEP student needs may vary and program approaches result in varying costs, it is inappropriate to prescribe one uniform amount for all states serving LEP students around the country. By the same token, after allowing for state-specific and program-variant cost variations, funding for English language learners should be much more uniform across and within states.

María Robledo Montecel and Albert Cortéz

See also *Flores v. State of Arizona;* Office of Bilingual Education and Minority Language Affairs; Title VII, Elementary and Secondary Education Act, Key Historical Marker

Further Readings

Alston, H. (1977). *Estimates of personnel needed and costs of HISD bilingual education program.* Houston, TX: Houston Independent School District.

Baker, B. D., & Markham, P. L. (2002). State school funding policies and limited English proficient students. *Bilingual Research Journal, 26,* 659–680.

Cárdenas, J. A. (1997). *Texas school finance reform: An IDRA perspective.* San Antonio, TX: Intercultural Development Research Association.

Cárdenas, J. A., Bernal, J. J., & Kean, W. (1976). *Bilingual education cost analysis.* San Antonio, TX: Intercultural Development Research Association.

Carpenter-Huffman, P., & Samulon, M. (1981). *Case studies of delivery and cost of bilingual education: A RAND note.* Santa Monica, CA: RAND.

Education Commission of the States. (2007). *Recent state policies: Bilingual and ESL.* Available from http://www.ecs.org/ecs/ecscat.nsf

Flores v. Arizona, 48 F. Supp.2d 937 (D. Ariz. 1992).

Guss-Zamora, M. (1979). The cost of bilingual education: Some research findings. *Journal of the Texas Association for Bilingual Education, 1*(1), 21–33.

Guss-Zamora, M., Zárate, R., Robledo, M., & Cárdenas, J. A. (1979). *Utah: Bilingual education cost analysis.* San Antonio, TX: Intercultural Development Research Association.

McGuire, C. K. (1982). *State and federal programs for special populations.* Denver, CO: Education Commission of the States.

National Access Network. (2006). *A costing-out primer.* New York: Teachers College, Columbia University. Retrieved February 1, 2008, from http://www.schoolfunding.info/resource_center/costingoutprimer.php3

National Conference of State Legislatures. (1975). *Arizona English language learner cost study.* Washington, DC: Author.

Robledo, M., Zárate, R., Guss-Zamora, M., & Cárdenas, J. A. (1978). *Colorado: Bilingual education cost analysis.* San Antonio, TX: Intercultural Development Research Association.

CRAWFORD, JAMES (1949–)

James Crawford is among the foremost authorities on bilingual education policy in the United States. A journalist by training and consumer of academic research and literature by character, he has consistently provided astute coverage and analysis of bilingual education policies and politics for more than 20 years.

Crawford grew up in Knoxville, Tennessee, and attended Harvard College, graduating cum laude in 1971 with a bachelor's degree in English. He began his journalism career in 1979 as a newsletter editor for the Massachusetts Coalition for Occupational Safety and Health in Boston, and he soon began to contribute to publications including *The Nation, Mother Jones,*

Common Cause Magazine, Business & Society Review, In These Times, Jack Anderson Enterprises, Pacific News Service, and United Feature Syndicate.

In 1983, Crawford became the congressional editor of *Federal Times,* a weekly source of news and information about the U.S. Congress and the federal government. He joined the staff of *Education Week* in 1985 as a staff writer and Washington editor. At the newspaper, Crawford soon began to focus on bilingual education and its various dimensions—social, cultural, and political—always with an eye on the shifting public policy in that arena. He covered the issue at a period of contentious national debate about the best way to teach English language learners. This debate was largely fueled by ideological passions about language loyalty, immigration reform, and national identity. Crawford injected a healthy dose of skepticism and an interest in research and pedagogy. His reporting avoided the superficial, scattershot analysis that typified most coverage of bilingualism and bilingual education at the time. Instead, he examined the research literature in many disciplines: applied linguistics, socio- and psycholinguistics, second-language acquisition theory and teaching, contemporary and historical language and education policies, and language planning. Crawford's obvious expertise in the field and his ability to explain complex policy issues to a lay public—including research methodologies and conclusions—set him apart from other journalists. He attended numerous bilingual education conferences, academic symposia, and other venues, interviewing teachers, administrators, parents, and university researchers. Thus, he came to know the field through a relentless search for information and perspective.

During Crawford's tenure at *Education Week,* Congress went through the process of reauthorizing the Bilingual Education Act (Title VII of the Elementary and Secondary Education Act). Crawford covered the frequently rancorous House and Senate committee hearings. He wrote extensively about the ideological stances of Federal Department of Education officials and their connections to "English-only" organizations. Consequently, his investigative reporting on the reauthorization process was thorough and even muckraking. His *Education Week* articles still stand as a detailed and fascinating historical record of the federal debate about bilingual education policy during the Reagan administration.

Crawford left *Education Week* in 1987 to pursue freelance writing on bilingual education and language. He published his first book, *Bilingual Education: History, Politics, Theory, and Practice,* in 1989. Now in its 5th edition and renamed *Educating English Learners: Language Diversity in the Classroom,* the book remains one of the most widely used texts in teacher training programs. Crawford continued to write and lecture throughout the 1990s, publishing three more books and monographs: *Hold Your Tongue: Bilingualism and the Politics of "English Only"; Language Loyalties: A Source Book on the Official English Controversy; Best Evidence: Research Foundations of the Bilingual Education Act;* and *At War with Diversity: U.S. Language Policy in an Age of Anxiety.* He has also published articles in numerous anthologies and edited volumes, as well as in professional and academic journals, like the *American Journal of Sociology, Bilingual Research Journal,* and the *International Journal of the Sociology of Language.*

From 2004 to 2006, Crawford served as executive director of the National Association for Bilingual Education (NABE), the largest professional organization of bilingual educators in the United States. At NABE, he was known for his vast knowledge of and insights into government policy. Crawford's ability to navigate the political culture of Washington and Capitol Hill made him particularly effective. Under his leadership, the organization gained status as a nationally recognized voice for the rights of English language learners.

Today, James Crawford continues to serve the field as an independent writer, lecturer, and consultant, specializing in language and education policy. He is the founder and director of the Institute for Language and Education Policy, an organization that seeks to promote research-based advocacy for English language and heritage language learners.

Mary Carol Combs

See also Bilingual Education as Language Policy; Bilingual Education in the Press; National Association for Bilingual Education; Official Language Designation; Appendix E

Further Readings

Crawford, J. (1989). *Bilingual education: History, politics, theory, and practice.* Trenton, NJ: Crane.

Crawford, J. (1992). *Hold your tongue: Bilingualism and the politics of "English only."* Reading, MA: Addison-Wesley.

Crawford, J. (Ed.). (1992). *Language loyalties: A source book on the official English controversy.* Chicago: University of Chicago Press.

Crawford, J. (1995). Endangered Native American languages: What is to be done, and why? In T. Ricento & B. Burnaby (Eds.), *Language and politics in the United States and Canada: Myths and realities* (pp. 151–165). Mahwah, NJ: Lawrence Erlbaum.

Crawford, J. (1996). Seven hypotheses on language loss: Causes and cures. In G. Cantoni (Ed.), *Stabilizing indigenous languages* (pp. 51–68). Flagstaff: Northern Arizona University, Center for Excellence in Education.

Crawford, J. (1997). *Best evidence: Research foundations of the Bilingual Education Act.* Washington, DC: National Clearinghouse for Bilingual Education.

Crawford, J. (1997). California's Proposition 227: A postmortem. *Bilingual Research Journal 21*(1). Retrieved from http://brj.asu.edu/archives/1v21/articles/Issue1 Crawford.html

Crawford, J. (1998). Anatomy of the English-only movement: Social and ideological sources of language restrictionism in the United States. In D. Kibbee (Ed.), *Language legislation and linguistic rights* (pp. 96–122). Amsterdam: Benjamins.

Crawford, J. (1998). Language politics in the United States: The paradox of bilingual education. In C. J. Ovando & P. McLaren (Eds.), *The politics of multiculturalism and bilingual education: Students and teachers caught in the cross fire* (pp. 106–125). Boston: McGraw-Hill.

Crawford, J. (2000). *At war with diversity: U.S. language policy in an age of anxiety.* Clevedon, UK: Multilingual Matters.

Crawford, J. (2001). Review of *Language policy and identity politics in the United States,* by R. Schmidt. *American Journal of Sociology, 106,* 1465–1466.

Crawford, J. (2002). Comment [in response to focus article on bilingual education by Eugene García]. *International Journal of the Sociology of Language, 155/156,* 93–99.

Crawford, J. (2004). *Educating English learners: Language diversity in the classroom* (5th ed.). Los Angeles: Bilingual Educational Services.

Crawford, J. (2006). The decline of bilingual education: How to reverse a troubling trend? *International Multilingual Research Journal, 1*(1), 33–37.

Crawford, J. (in press). Loose ends in a tattered fabric: The inconsistency of language rights in the United States. In J. Magnet (Ed.), *Language rights in comparative perspective.* Markham, Canada: LexisNexis Butterworths.

Crawford, J., & Krashen, S. (in press). *English learners in American classrooms: 101 questions, 101 answers.* New York: Scholastic.

Web Sites

James Crawford's Language Policy Web Site & Emporium: http://ourworld.compuserve.com/homepages/jwcrawford

CREDENTIALING FOREIGN-TRAINED TEACHERS

There are an estimated 20,000 immigrants from Spanish-speaking countries who are professionally trained and experienced teachers but remain an unrealized source of human capital in the United States. Typically, they are underemployed and earning a minimum wage. With the rising number of language minority students in U.S. public schools and the shortage of bilingual education teachers, teachers with foreign credentials can be a viable domestic resource that can help to meet the U.S. shortage of bilingual education teachers. This entry describes efforts in this direction that have already been tried and proven successful.

Although various mechanisms exist for credentialing foreign-trained teachers, such as requiring them to pass state-mandated credentialing exams, not all such efforts have been effective in mobilizing this resource. One notable effort in credentialing foreign-trained teachers was Project Alianza, funded by the Kellogg Foundation in 1998. Because project participants already lived in the United States, the project explored the potential that *normalistas,* Mexican teachers with credentials obtained from a normal school in Mexico could contribute to the education of immigrant students, avoiding the need to recruit teachers outside the country. Project Alianza identified and selectively enrolled qualified normalistas, who held documented U.S. residency status in university teacher preparation programs of study. In this way, participants were able to address issues linked to the U.S. educational system through formal study in college classrooms and practical work in K–12 classrooms in ways similar to those required of U.S.-trained teachers.

The prototype for Project Alianza was derived from a pilot program at California State University, Long Beach (CSULB), in which 27 credentialed normalistas participated in an accredited program of study that combined the resources of CSULB and one of the campuses of Mexico's Universidad Pedagógica Nacional (UPN). This binational effort enabled the normalistas to obtain a *licenciatura* (equivalent to a bachelor's degree) through the UPN and then complete California teacher certification requirements at CSULB. Project summary outcomes indicated that of the 27 normalistas, only 4 passed all three portions of the California Basic English Skills Test (CBEST), thereby highlighting one of the problems all such programs encounter—in short, that the levels of English language proficiency acquired in Mexico are not sufficient for college-level academic work. Of the 27 normalistas, 10 were hired as fully credentialed bilingual teachers in the Los Angeles area, and the remaining participants obtained only paraprofessional positions.

During the summer of 1997, an advisory group met to retool the design for Project Alianza. The advisory group included the Intercultural Development Research Association (IDRA), the Mexican and American Solidarity Foundation, and Arizona State University (ASU) as research partners. Each Project Alianza university site was also part of the advisory group and included California State University Long Beach, Southwest Texas State University (now Texas State University), University of Texas at San Antonio (UTSA), and University of Texas Pan American (UTPA). During the second through fourth years of the project (1999–2001), additional satellite institutions were selected and mentored by the founding project institutions. These satellite institutions, in chronological order, were the University of Texas at El Paso, Texas Woman's University, Texas A&M International at Laredo, and California State University, Bakersfield.

Challenges in Credentialing Foreign-Trained Teachers

The credentialing of foreign-trained teachers tested existing university structures and curricular policies, creating a need for systemic changes. For example, admission offices were often underprepared to evaluate and validate foreign transcripts when assigning student classification and ranking (e.g., freshman, postbaccalaureate) to newly admitted normalista cohorts. Faculty and staff at all levels were challenged by the normalistas' language status as nonnative English speakers. In addition, the faculty and staff teams assigned to implement Project Alianza were tasked not only with realizing project goals but also with having to challenge institutional practices that hindered normalistas' academic progress once they had been admitted. Faculty members also discovered that the normalistas' training had emphasized the "banking" approach to teaching, contradictory to constructivist teaching approaches reflective of best practices in constructing knowledge. Beyond having to pass English language state-mandated admissions tests, normalistas also had to negotiate myriad bureaucratic processes at the institutions of higher education and degree-issuing agencies in their countries of origin, at U.S. foreign credentialing agencies, and at their respective U.S. admitting university campuses. These efforts required inordinate time and energy for normalistas and project staff alike.

Empirical studies also identified a variety of challenges that informed the Alianza coordinators and directors about normalistas' notions and their professional development needs. Interviews with potential candidates prior to the selection process revealed that many normalistas were against bilingual education because of preconceived notions that the approach had detrimental effects on the education of language minority students. They also perceived bilingual education teachers' proficiency in Spanish to be inadequate to impart competent instruction and further believed that the role of schooling was to provide instruction only in English. Some perceived that bilingual education countered American values such as patriotism to the United States, acquisition of the English language, assimilation, and acceptance into the majority society. Others were concerned that bilingual education might cause students to speak English with an accent. These insights were valuable to the pedagogical design to prepare competent bilingual education teachers. Project organizers found these beliefs to be instructive because they were not very different from the language attitudes of the general population. Because they had not experienced bilingual education in their own country or in their own studies, these Mexican teachers relied on the rhetoric they had heard and read in the media with respect to bilingual education.

New challenges emerged as the normalistas interacted with their U.S. programs of study. While normalistas were usually prepared to teach reading, science, and mathematics in Spanish, their language proficiency was not the only skill needed to teach in a bilingual education classroom. They lacked knowledge about the sociopolitical, sociocultural, and historical experiences unique to language minority students in the United States. Since the normalistas' identities had been continually affirmed in their native country, they did not have a sense of the struggle of ethnic minorities and their situated experiences within the U.S. educational system.

Programs of study were therefore designed to assist normalistas to understand the diverse teaching contexts that they would encounter. A core curriculum addressed essential knowledge about the cultural history of language minorities in the United States; the theoretical foundations of bilingual education; research on cognition, bilingualism, and biliteracy; sociocultural and sociolinguistic issues; and language loss, dialects, and attitudes toward language varieties within language minority communities. Normalistas had to learn about the influence of culture, language, and ethnicity on the social construction of identity and how these processes affect teachers' expectations of students. In addition, normalistas faced a considerable challenge in speaking and writing English at advanced levels, as required by the culture of the schools; in mastering standardized testing, including credentialing examinations; and in delivering instruction competently in English.

In terms of their native-language proficiency, normalistas possessed high oral language proficiency in Spanish; however, their writing proficiency varied, reflecting either the rigor of their program of study or their attained levels of education. Project Alianza coordinators therefore consistently monitored student academic needs and progress in order to secure the appropriate training for the normalistas.

Initial findings further indicated that normalistas were less adaptive than other teacher candidate groups in working with students who spoke language varieties of Spanish and English and were less inclined to integrate principles of multicultural education into their instruction. Once hired as certified teachers of record, principals reported that normalistas needed additional professional development in the areas of classroom management, teaching children with special needs, and inclusion practices.

Addressing the Challenges

Each Project Alianza site team relied on the binational nature of the project, turned to existing community resources and structures, and examined existing programs of study to enact changes necessary to realize project goals. One key community partnership included the Mexican Consulate as an unofficial but engaged partner. The binational nature of the project facilitated the exchange of information with this office, making the Mexican Consulate a hub for recruitment. Universities also utilized different types of media within their communities to disseminate information about the innovative program. This included the Internet, as

well as Spanish and English language newspapers, radio, and television. Universities prepared brochures to share with school districts, community agencies, county offices, and professional teacher organizations. Word of mouth was extensive, pervasive, and effective. The combined efforts of all of those involved resulted in strong responses from communities typically underserved by universities. An unplanned but welcome effect of Project Alianza was that of bringing participating universities in closer touch with immigrant communities involved in the project.

One of the project's goals was to strengthen binational ties with Mexico and to expand university students' awareness of the transnational influences on the U.S. educational system. Each university participated in a binational experience in which project coordinators selected normalistas and other teacher candidates to attend summer institutes in different cities in Mexico. The coordinating triad, U.S. universities, the Mexican American Solidarity Foundation, and Mexican normal schools *(escuelas normales)* facilitated 6-day summer institutes that provided cultural seminars about Mexico and the Mexican educational system. Seminars were held at urban, rural, private, and public schools and cultural institutions. The summer institutes culminated in a 1-day microteaching experience in which U.S. students taught in a public school with the assistance of an Mexican peer student from the *escuela normal*.

Since the acquisition of English was a priority, some universities hired a tutor of English as a Second Language (ESL) as a strategy to accelerate the acquisition of English, while other sites paired English-dominant-speaking students with normalistas as a way to increase basic interpersonal communication skills and expand their use of academic language. As the normalistas progressed through their program of study, cross-coordination with faculty members in other academic departments became a continual activity. Faculties had to be apprised of the students' particular language needs and the importance of allowing the students to study while they acquired proficiency in English. This accommodation required increased planning, modifying teaching approaches, and increasing the number of tutoring sessions.

Owing to the diversity and uniqueness of each normalista cohort, universities were charged with tailoring programs of study that met requirements unique to each site and the community it served. The cohort at

CSULB, for example, was made up of credentialed normalistas who had applied as degree-seeking students, paraprofessionals (teacher assistants), and traditional students. Each student's bilingual language proficiency was measured with a placement test. Then, the students were enrolled as a blocked cohort in a degree-seeking and teacher certification program. The students took night and weekend courses with Spanish-language-proficient faculty. The Project Alianza cohort at Southwest Texas State University (now Texas State University) was distinct and included normalistas and paraprofessionals enrolled in the teacher preparation component of an undergraduate degree program. Some of the credentialed normalistas, who possessed a command of English, pursued teacher certification through a postbaccalaureate program. In contrast, the University of Texas at Pan-American Project Alianza cohort included normalistas who already possessed a bachelor of arts degree (licenciatura). Their professional education and bilingual education coursework led to certification through a postbaccalaureate, four-semester, dual-language program that also included enrollment in summer courses.

The profile of the UTSA Project Alianza diverged from the others and included normalistas with different levels of credentials, paraprofessionals, and college-aged students. Normalistas with a bachelor of arts degree (licenciatura) in education were allowed to complete a six-semester postbaccalaureate program of study and were accepted into the project if their transcripts demonstrated a grade of B+ or better (8.5 on a 10-point system) in their programs of study. Individuals without a licenciatura were given college credit from courses completed beyond the *normal básica* (equivalent to 1 year beyond high school in the United States). These students were required to demonstrate a grade of B+ or better in their teacher preparation programs. Normalistas with only *normal básica* were accepted as first-year. degree-seeking students, having met the grade point average (GPA) requirement.

At the UTSA, all normalista applicants were screened using the Michigan Test of English Language Proficiency; only those who could demonstrate an intermediate level of English proficiency were accepted. Paraprofessionals and first-generation college students were accepted into the project if they had completed a minimum of 30 college semester hours of the core curriculum and held a minimum

2.25 GPA. The applicants were also screened informally for Spanish language proficiency during their interviews and formally through the Bilingual Prochievement Test, which assessed their listening, speaking, reading, and writing proficiencies.

Benefits of Credentialing Foreign-Trained Teachers

The implementation of Project Alianza redefined teacher preparation programs by challenging institutions of higher education to broaden their perspectives of enhancing bicultural and binational relationships. Moreover, with the success rate documented at each university, there was a change in attitude that coincided with an awareness of the social and economic potential that normalistas, as professionals with a somewhat divergent set of prior experiences, could offer U.S. schools and universities.

Empirical findings indicated that after having completed their programs of study, normalistas demonstrated competency as knowledgeable teachers of culturally and linguistically diverse students, once they had acquired the essential mediation tools stemming from their comprehension of and commitment to the philosophy of bilingual education. They were observed activating and employing children's cultural knowledge and engaging them in the construction of new knowledge and skills. In addition, the majority of the normalistas had an internal sense for control and believed all children could learn. Findings also indicated a positive main effect of "spirituality" as moral worth, a factor mediating normalistas' general teaching efficacy and personal teaching efficacy. Having a positive efficacy was viewed as influencing normalistas' perceived ability to teach and to have an impact on students. Another study revealed that rather than simply viewing teaching as a profession, the normalista perspective was one of moral commitment and vocation.

Project Alianza expanded the definition of the "college student" by having granted university admission to foreign-trained professionals acquiring English language proficiency. This resulted in requiring monolingual faculty members within and outside of teacher education programs to adapt instruction for linguistically diverse learners, which reified the circumstance of U.S. public schools at all levels. Similarly, Project Alianza offered faculty members teaching bicultural bilingual education courses increased opportunities to engage bilingual education methods and theoretical principles in their teaching and to witness the unfolding second-language acquisition of adult learners.

Conclusion

In retrospect, an added project goal providing a teacher "induction year" would have strengthened the normalistas' professional growth and supported their transition into bilingual education classrooms, probably making the process smoother. As first-year teachers in a U.S. bilingual classroom, they would have benefited from scheduled consultations with faculty and from having faculty conduct classroom observations to provide feedback, answer questions, and provide coaching as needed. This is, therefore, a recommended teacher retention strategy for future projects.

Institutions of higher education are well-advised to articulate, research, and establish a border pedagogy within their teacher preparation programs and to provide for its diffusion in public schools. This can be achieved by preparing more bicultural/bilingual education teachers to meet the academic needs of an expanding number of culturally and linguistically diverse student populations in U.S. schools. Foreign-trained educators such as normalistas are viable assets to the education of Spanish-speaking students in terms of the cultural, linguistic, academic, and professional knowledge and experience they possess. To maximize their potential as effective teachers in U.S. classrooms, foreign-trained teachers must be engaged in a comprehensive program of study that develops competency.

Belinda Bustos Flores
and Mary Esther Soto Huerta

See also Bilingual Paraprofessionals; Culturally Competent Teaching; Teacher Certification by States; Teacher Preparation, Then and Now; Teacher Qualifications

Further Readings

Cantú, L. (1999). Project Alianza: Tapping community resources for bilingual teachers. *IDRA Newsletter, 2*(2), 1–2, 8.

Clark, E. R., & Flores, B. B. (1997). Instructional snapshots in Mexico: Preservice bilingual teachers take pictures of classroom practices. *Bilingual Research Journal, 21,* 103–113.

Clark, E. R., & Flores, B. B. (2000). Report on a study of *normalistas'* ethnic identity and teaching efficacy. *NABE News 24*(1), 20–23.

Clark, E. R., & Flores, B. B. (2001). Is Spanish proficiency simply enough? An examination of *normalistas'* attitudes towards Spanish, bilingualism, and bilingual teacher pedagogy. *MEXTESOL Journal, 25*(3), 13–27.

Flores, B. B. (2001). Thinking out of the box: One university's experience with foreign-trained teachers. *Educational Policy Analysis Archives 9*(18). Retrieved February 1, 2008, from http://epaa.asu.edu/epaa/v9n18.html

Flores, B. B., & Clark, E. R. (2002). *El desarrollo de Proyecto Alianza: Lessons learned and policy implications.* Tempe: Arizona State University, Center for Bilingual Education and Research.

Flores, B. B., & Clark, E. R. (2004). A critical examination of normalistas self-conceptualization and teacher efficacy. *Hispanic Journal of Behavioral Sciences, 26,* 230–257.

Flores, B. B., Strecker, S., & Pérez, B. P (2002). Critical need for bilingual education teachers: The potentiality of *normalistas* and paraprofessionals. *Bilingual Research Journal, 26,* 687–708.

García, A. G., & González, J. M. (2000). *The views of Mexican normalista and U.S. bilingual education teachers: An exploratory study of perceptions, beliefs, and attitudes.* Tempe: Arizona State University, Center for Bilingual Education and Research.

Pérez, B. P., Flores, B. B., & Strecker, S. (2003). Biliteracy teacher education in the Southwest. In N. H. Hornberger (Ed.), *The continua of biliteracy: An ecological framework for educational policy, research, and practice in multilingual settings* (pp. 207–231). Clevedon, UK: Multilingual Matters.

Petrovic, J. E., Orozco, G., González, E., & Díaz de Cossio, R. (1999). Mexican normalista teachers as a resource for bilingual education in the United States: Connecting two models of teacher preparation. In J. M. González (Ed.), *CBER explorations in bi-national education* (Issue No. 1, pp. 1–88). Tempe: Arizona State University, Intercultural Development Research Association.

Supik, J. D. (1999). Project Alianza: A model teacher preparation and leadership development initiative: First year findings. *IDRA Newsletter, 26,* 3–6.

Vallejo, C., & García, A. G. (2001). Teacher recruitment and employment practices in selected states: Promising prospects for foreign-trained teachers. In J. M. González (Ed.), *CBER explorations in bi-national education* (Issue No. 5, pp. 1–41). Tempe: Arizona State University, Intercultural Development Research Association.

CRITICAL LANGUAGES FOR THE UNITED STATES

What is most problematic about defining *critical languages* for any government or nation is the range of stakeholders involved—academic, governmental, private sector, and others. This entry focuses on how the U.S. government has set standards for what its various components consider to be the most critical language needs for the near future until 2015.

The existence of a common priority list across federal agencies is doubtful; indeed, the terminology used for such priorities varies from unit to unit. For the Department of State, a single list of "critical languages" has been promulgated on the department Web site. In contrast, the Department of Defense has developed (for official use only; i.e., not for publication) a bipartite "Strategic Language List"; this is divided between "Immediate Investment Languages," for which there is a requirement for substantial organic capability projected through 2015, and "Stronghold Languages," which require in-house capability to be developed and/or identified. No rank ordering is being given because, again, there is no consensus-based ranking of language needs across the various federal agencies. As the experience of the late 20th and early 21st centuries has made clear, priorities shift by the decade and, indeed, sometimes even by the year or month.

Within these limitations, the following is a reasonably reliable list of critical languages for the United States in the 21st century, in alphabetical order:

1. *Arabic*—including Modern Standard Arabic (MSA) and regional dialects

2. *Chinese*—including Mandarin, Gan, Cantonese, and Wu (Shanghai)

3. *Indic*—including at least, but not necessarily limited to, Bengali, Hindi, Punjabi, and Urdu

4. *Korean*

5. *Persian*—including at least, but not necessarily limited to, Dari/Afghan, Farsi/Iranian, Kurdish, Pashto, and Tajiki

6. *Russian*

7. *Turkic*—including at least, but not necessarily limited to, Azerbaijani, Kazakh, Turkish, Turkmen, and Uzbek

Although the initial impression is that the focus of this critical languages listing is largely within the realm of the Less Commonly Taught Languages (LCTLs), many federal organizations also place a high value on the development of language and cultural communicative skills in the more commonly taught languages for their personnel. The Department of Defense includes French, Portuguese, and Spanish among its "immediate investment languages," perhaps more a recognition of the ongoing strategic value of these languages than the more short-term tactical importance of many of the LCTLs, particularly within the former Soviet republics and the Muslim sphere of influence.

In an attempt to more broadly provide support the development of a national capacity for the critical languages in particular, a major announcement was made on January 5, 2006. On that date, President George W. Bush addressed a conference of approximately 50 American university presidents to announce the introduction of the National Security Language Initiative (NSLI). NSLI is unprecedented in American history in that it is a joint project of four major federal agencies: the Department of Defense, the Department of Education, the Department of State, and the Office of the Director of National Intelligence. The initiative has three major goals: (a) expanding the number of Americans mastering critical-need languages, beginning study at an earlier age; (b) increasing the number of advanced-level speakers of foreign languages, in particular those classified as critical need; and (c) increasing the number of foreign-language teachers and necessary resources.

Were it to be fully funded, NSLI would be composed of 14 separate programs and have a total starting budget of $115 million dollars for fiscal year 2007. Some pieces of NSLI were in fact already in existence in the Department of Education with appropriated funds for fiscal year 2006, such as the Foreign Language Assistance Program (FLAP) and the National Flagship Language Initiative (NFLI). Other portions received funding for fiscal year 2007, including the Youth Exchange-Summer Language Institutes (Department of State) and STARTALK, a new national initiative in summer language education (Office of the Director of National Intelligence Programs). It remains to be seen how warmly the NSLI initiative will be received by politicians in the Congress and by succeeding administrations.

Scott McGinnis

See also National Defense Education Act of 1958

Further Readings

U.S. Department of Education. (n.d.). *National Security Language Initiative*. Retrieved from http://www.ed .gov/about/inits/ed/competitiveness/nsli/index.html

U.S. Department of State. (n.d.). *Gilman Scholarship Program*. Retrieved February 19, 2007, from http:// exchanges.state.gov/education/educationusa/ abroadgilman.htm

CRITICAL LITERACY

To understand the concept of critical literacy, it is useful to compare it to that of *literacy* in its simplest and most commonly used form, namely, the ability to read and write with a degree of understanding. In education terms, literacy is the continued development of oral language into the written word and the ability to communicate through it. Literacy includes the concept of understanding what the text purports to tell us. Critical literacy can be regarded as a step above that of simple literacy. It is an approach to developing literacy skills that contextualize the reader and the text within sociohistorical frames and the cultural and political environments of reader and text. In its broadest sense, critical literacy is also an approach to life, to language, to agency, and to the search for truths that are omitted from the text, as well as the reasons why those omissions occur. Literary criticism is one form of critical literacy, as, for example, articles in the *New York Times Book Review*. Theater critics also employ techniques of critical literacy to lay bare the meaning behind the text and the music in a performance. Many avid readers and theatergoers decide whether to read a book or attend a performance on the basis of what a trusted critic has to say about the work in question.

Critical literacy implies approaches to teaching literacy in the classroom, yet it also embodies empowerment, emancipation, and the ability of school people (teachers and students and others) to manifest change through language.

Though there are differences in how critical literacy is manifested in the classroom, in general, readers come to texts not only to gain meaning from them; texts are contextualized by the reader (who also resides within specific known contexts), who asks questions such as these: Who wrote this text and why? How does the writer benefit from this text? What are some unquestioned assumptions within this text? Who is privileged by it? As students critically examine texts, they question social roles and power structures.

Just as students question texts within the world in reading and in writing, students question the world around them. Through writing, students often find their *voice,* the basis on which they express views and opinions and give balanced weight to "facts." Often, writing becomes an act of resistance to what others wish students would value or adopt as their own. In writing, students find agency, and through this practice, students can engender change in small and big ways. Perhaps the most important change concerns the student's own willingness to question or embrace what he or she is asked to read.

In the classroom, critical literacy is not confined within the boundaries of language arts: It is a distinctive approach to teaching that resides in all content areas. Where there is language, there can be a critical stance, and where there is content, there is language. Through reading and writing, students begin to learn about the world and about themselves within the world. They may begin to look at power structures and learn to question and take action against a status quo that historically and currently oppresses marginalized populations, including language minorities.

Historical Background

Ira Shor, a leader in the area of critical literacy teaching, traces the beginnings and historical path of this field to the 20th century. Critical literacy in the United States finds its beginnings as far back as John Dewey, who was born in 1859. Dewey, like Horace Mann before him, wanted to mediate growing class divisions through mass education. Dewey found that curricular divisions between elite students and those of the working class perpetuated class divisions. Elite students received a liberal arts education, in which philosophy and utility did not meet. Working-class students, however, received basic skills and job training. Dewey envisioned a curriculum for all, based in utility and philosophy—a curriculum that would develop reflective citizens for a healthy democracy. Dewey's contributions to education have proven foundational to critical literacy, which is situated in the experiential realm. It differs greatly from the traditional study of philosophy, which is often dealt with as if the subject were external to the learner.

Along with John Dewey, the work of Lev Vygotsky and Paulo Freire, among others, has also contributed to critical literacy. Vygotsky, like Dewey, believed that learning situates itself best in experience. In his work explaining the process of learning, he proposed the idea of the *zone of proximal development* (ZPD). Vygotsky believed that there is a zone in which a student can learn through interaction with a teacher or a more capable peer who helps the learner achieve more than what would be possible without such support. With Vygotsky's ZPD, learning begins with each individual student and his or her unique potential, just as in Dewey's thinking, learning begins in experience and is built into organized reflective knowledge through both theory and practice.

The work of Dewey and Vygotsky brought learning to the experiential and individual realm, but it was largely the work of Paulo Freire that brought learning and literacy to a broader social arena. Freire was a Brazilian educationist whose work has been highly influential. Freire emphasized the role of education in transforming lives, focusing on dialogue in learning and pedagogy as liberation. He considered a good education to be inherent to the practice of democracy but only when it is done in the pursuit of truth and justice. The notion embodied in the call in the 1960s to "speak truth to power" is rooted in Freire's teachings. Freire's work brings together the fundamental elements of Dewey's and Vygotsky's and adds to them the contextual aspects of learning: the power structures and roles in which students and teachers alike reside. In Freirian constructs, it is not the teacher who gives knowledge to the students; rather, knowledge is coconstructed, and student and teacher alike learn and grow through a process that is reciprocal and mutual.

Purposes of Critical Literacy

The aims of critical literacy include those of a more traditional vein, which is to facilitate the development of literacy skills in children. Critical literacy goes beyond a notion of literacy skills as performance skills (i.e., the learner's achievement in conventional reading/writing). Teachers who use critical literacy aspire to help children create a sense of self as a reader/writer *in the world*—a knowledge of what written text accomplishes, and for whom. Further, it acknowledges a child's agency; through critical literacy, both students and teachers can become agents for social change.

While some teachers may feel a reluctance to engage in what they deem "political" education, it warrants stating that educational acts are inherently political. Teachers who fear a critical approach to teaching may not understand that teaching methods aligned with status quo ideologies can also serve to perpetuate oppressive social forces. Although that may not be a purposeful choice on the part of such teachers, it is a result of traditional teaching methodologies. Teaching is thus inherently political. Critical literacy is a means by which educators can uncover buried political assumptions and their eventual outcomes in the lives of children.

Classroom Practice

Allan Luke and Penelope Freebody are Australian educational researchers involved in the study of critical literacy. They have developed a four-tiered approach to early reading instruction, which addresses the following practices:

1. *Coding practices: Developing resources as a code breaker.* How do I crack this text? How does it work? What are its patterns and conventions? How do the sounds and marks relate, singly and in combinations?

2. *Text-meaning practices: Developing resources as a text participant.* How do the ideas represented in the text string together? What cultural resources can be brought to bear on the text? What are the cultural meanings and possible readings that can be constructed from this text?

3. *Pragmatic practices: Developing resources as text user.* How do the uses of this text shape its composition? What do I do with this text, here and now? What are others likely to do with it? What are my options and alternatives for action—that is, for responding?

4. *Critical practices: Developing resources as a text analyst and critic.* What kind of person, with what interests and values, could both write and read this naively and unproblematically? What is this text trying to do to me? In whose interests? Which positions, voices, and interests are at play? Which are the silent and absent?

These four tiers are taught simultaneously and organically, as children become readers and writers. Thus, critical practices are not an addition to optimal classroom practices. Rather, they are always included. These practices are framed within a notion of literacy as socially situated, and teaching resides in the sociological realm. The critical literacy classroom always recognizes the unique sociocultural identity of each student, as well as the ability each individual brings to become a critical interpreter of texts.

Classroom Practice: An Example

Critical literacy in the classroom is as varied as teachers' approaches. As curriculum in the critical literacy classroom most often stems from student interest, it does not lend itself to canned curriculum programs. An example of a critical literacy classroom is provided in the following vignette.

A ninth-grade U.S. history class is doing a unit on westward expansion. The basal text series includes a short, three-paragraph section on what is known in U.S. history as the "Trail of Tears." The text also includes a picture with a caption. Though the teacher is required by her school district to use that particular text and not substitute it with another, she is able to use supplemental material as well. As a part of her unit on westward expansion, the teacher asks the class to read the textbook paragraphs on the Trail of Tears and then discuss in groups the following questions:

1. Who benefits from the text as it is written?

2. Whose voice is silenced? Whose is privileged?

3. How is language used in the text? Are events glossed over or romanticized? Why?

4. Does it seem certain events or details are omitted? Why?

The teacher then provides the students with additional texts, or the students conduct research to find texts, including primary sources (such as the Indian Removal Act of 1838, journals from the period, newspaper archives) and secondary sources. The students may do research on their own, based on inquiry questions they have generated. The teacher and students alike then read and examine multiple and conflicting texts and engage in activities that contextualize the texts historically, culturally, and discursively, critically comparing texts to one another. Students are provided many choices in the direction of their explorations, reading, writing, and activities.

As students learn more about the event from various sources and perspectives, they investigate how ideologies in the different texts position various groups. They may reread texts multiple times through multiple lenses. Finally, students articulate their own views in regard to the texts. Through writing (e.g., a journal from the perspective of a Cherokee girl or boy, a letter of protest, etc.), students can find clarity in terms of their stance in regard to a given text or event. As students examine and compare texts, the classroom is full of animated discussion. In the critical literacy classroom, multiple voices are heard (not just the teacher's). The most effective critical literacy classes include a final step, and that is in supporting students in creating opportunities to take social action, for example, participating in a demonstration or writing a letter to a member of Congress.

In the bilingual classroom, texts can be read, written, and/or discussed in the students' native language. Multiple sources can be found in both languages. Opinions from students from all over the world lend richness to classroom discussions that can be conducted bilingually. Any number of teaching methodologies can be used to scaffold participation of all students, each with an important role in generating ideas and interpretations for discussion.

Critical literacy is centered in student interest and agency, and so student engagement is often higher than in more traditional classrooms. Students have a sense of investment in curriculum that is negotiated. Student involvement is thus activated and sustained in a classroom that offers both knowledge and agency.

Conclusion

Like all approaches in education, critical literacy changes and grows. Critical literacy educators continue to study the relationships between language, power, and identity in the classroom. As research about critical literacy continues, it is increasingly incorporated in various iterations as an approach to literacy instruction in the classroom.

Students in bilingual classrooms are often falsely considered to have a deficit in learning simply because they are not native speakers of English. Critical literacy approaches, on the other hand, value the diversity in perspective and interpretation that bilingual and bicultural students bring to the classroom. Bilingual students thrive on critical literacy approaches that facilitate biliteracy development, while contributing to the creation of critical citizens of our world who understand the power of language in creating social change.

Cathy A. Coulter

See also Americanization by Schooling; Assimilation; Attitudes Toward Language Diversity; Languages and Power; Language Socialization; Latino Civil Rights Movement; Literacy and Biliteracy

Further Readings

Luke, A. (2000). Critical literacy in Australia: A matter of context and standpoint. *Journal of Adolescent & Adult Literacy, 43*(5), 448–461.

Luke, A., & Freebody, P. (1997). The social practices of reading. In S. Muspratt, A. Luke, & P. Freebody (Eds.), *Constructing critical literacies* (pp. 185–225). Creskill, NJ: Hampton Press.

Freire, P. (1970). *Pedagogy of the oppressed.* New York: Seabury.

Shor, I., & Pari, C. (Eds.). (1999). *Critical literacy in action* Portsmouth, NH: Heinemann.

CRITICAL PERIOD HYPOTHESIS

A *critical period* refers to a limited time within which an event can occur. A critical period hypothesis suggests that there is a point in time after which a given transformation will not occur or will occur only after tremendous effort, if necessary stimuli are withheld. A famous example of this in the field of ethology is the research of Konrad Lorenz on the domestication of the Greylag goose. Lorenz discovered that goslings would learn the characteristics and follow the first suitable moving stimulus they saw within a critical period of 36 hours.

Neurologists first attempted to document the relationship between the development of the brain and the process of language acquisition. Wilder Penfield and Lamar Roberts first introduced the idea of a critical period in the neurolinguistic literature, with their findings that children with significant brain damage from injury or disease were better able to relearn language than were adults. Following on these findings, Eric Lenneberg argued in his seminal book *Biological Foundations of Language* that maturational aspects of the brain result in a critical period for language development. Lenneberg hypothesized that if one's language capacity is not developed prior to puberty, it can never become fully functional. Focusing on abused (and feral) children, deaf children, and children with aphasia (a form of brain injury), further classic studies found that normal acquisition of a first language stopped after puberty. It is now widely accepted that a critical period for first-language acquisition exists.

Nevertheless, given that the natural "experiments" provided by feral children and others deprived of first-language stimulation are few and far between, it is impossible to draw definite conclusions except that

provided proper language stimuli, acquisition of normal language is guaranteed for children up to the age of 6. From this age, as Stephen Pinker summarized the evidence, acquisition is steadily compromised until shortly after puberty. Acquisition of normal language after puberty would be rare, if at all possible.

Supporting Theories

There are many theories that explain the critical period hypothesis. One of these is *brain plasticity theory,* which posits that the increase in age reduces the malleability of the brain and therefore reduces the ability of the individual to acquire language. Lenneberg believed that after *lateralization*—the development of specialized functions for each side of the brain—the brain loses plasticity. He claimed that lateralization of the language function is normally completed at puberty, making postadolescent language acquisition difficult. Another theory is *imprinting.* Imprinting can be compared to the taking of a still photograph, when a specific moment (i.e., behavior) becomes fixed in time. As opposed to instinct, imprinting theory relies on the acquisition of a particular behavior through imitation during the critical period in which learning of that behavior occurs, such as Lorenz's research with the Greylag goose.

Implications for Second-Language Learning

Both of these theories can be extended to explain the more difficult process of learning a second language. Indeed, the conclusion of the existence of a critical period for first-language acquisition has led many researchers to argue that there is also a critical period for second-language learning, since some of the same general language mechanisms that seem to "shut down" for first-language acquisition must logically affect subsequent language-learning endeavors. Lenneberg, whose research and evidence was based on first-language acquisition, generates several claims regarding second-language acquisition. He argued that most people (including adults) can learn a second language, although there is a rapid increase in what he calls "language-learning blocks" after puberty, resulting in the need for a conscious and labored effort (unlike the less laborious acquisition process of prepubescent children). Lenneberg also pointed out that foreign accents are not easily overcome after puberty.

Stephen Pinker argues that the language-learning circuitry of the brain is no longer needed once the mother tongue has been learned, and so it is simply discarded, making a second language more difficult to learn. Since the brain is metabolically greedy, it must make efficient use of resources. Having neural tissue lying around waiting to learn a second language is simply inefficient. For Pinker, then, the critical period is a product of natural selection.

The natural ability of young children to learn a second language with greater ease than adults and to acquire superior levels of fluency are now widely held beliefs, and not particularly controversial. Whether these observations prove the existence of a critical period for second-language acquisition and establish the extent to which age affects one's ability to learn a second language are questions researchers continue to study, with complicated and often contradictory results.

Research Studies

Many researchers have attempted to identify a specific age or age range in which there is a marked difference in the ability to learn a second language. Since it is generally associated with biological and maturational factors, the years prior to the onset of puberty are identified as the critical period. Although there is no consensus on a more precise age range that constitutes the critical period, it has been posited to range from approximately 5 to approximately 15 years of age. Generally, regular exposure to a second language prior to the age of 5 or 6

would mimic first-language acquisition, and thus it would more accurately be a case of acquiring two first languages. Nevertheless, this supports the critical period hypothesis claim that becoming a bilingual person occurs with greater ease and efficiency in this scenario, as compared to becoming bilingual later. Thus, it might be argued that the critical period for second-language acquisition is the same as that for first-language acquisition. For example, in a frequently cited study, Jacqueline Johnson and Elissa Newport showed that immigrants to the United States performed increasingly poorly on language tasks as their age of arrival increased. Performance on their tests was linearly related to age of arrival up to puberty. After puberty, performance was low but highly variable. Johnson and Newport concluded that the effects of the first-language critical period extended to a second language too.

But do such results really confirm the existence of a critical period? In *The Age Factor in Second Language Acquisition,* David Singleton and Zsolt Lengyel concede that in general, younger is better in the long run. However, the use of the term *critical period* is often reduced to the belief that a second language must be learned early or not at all. It seems that for a second-language critical period to exist, one must demonstrate that there is an offset and flattening period. In other words, there would be evidence of a sharp decline in ultimate proficiency attained in a second language as the terminus of the critical period approaches (see Figure 1a) or a complete discontinuity (see Figure 1b).

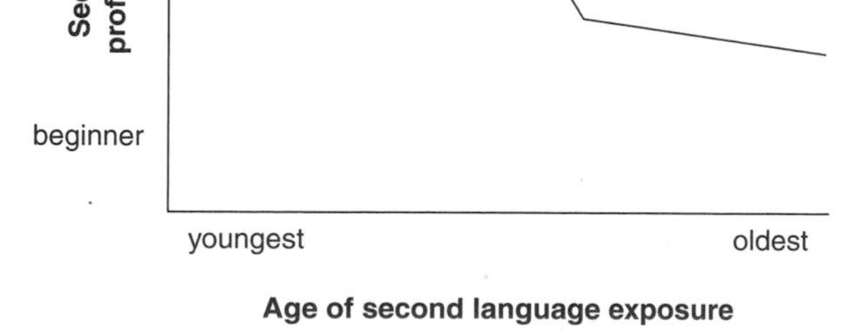

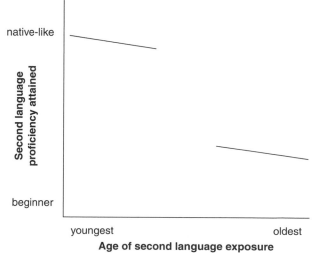

Figure 1a   Decline in Second-Language Proficiency Attained

Figure 1b   Discontinuity in Second-Language Proficiency Attained

This extreme view is simply not supported by research, and therefore many researchers in second-language learning prefer the terms *sensitive* or *optimal period*. For example, John Bruer suggests the analogy of a reservoir that gradually evaporates, as opposed to a window slamming shut. Kenji Hakuta, Ellen Bialystok, and Edward Wiley have demonstrated in their research that contrary to the predictions above, there is neither a sharp decline nor a discontinuity, but a steady decline in the degree of second-language acquisition success (see Figure 2).

Given the flat trajectory of the correlation found by Hakuta, Bialystok, and Wiley between age of exposure to, and ultimate proficiency in, a second language, their results provide evidence against both the critical and optimal periods. Their results also suggest that the "reservoir" never evaporates completely. However, because they tested the critical period ending at age 15 (the typical onset of puberty) and the other researchers have identified a much earlier critical period (5, 6, or 12 years of age), the results here have been questioned. Nevertheless, there is not enough evidence for the existence of a discontinuity, and it is still not clear whether there is a biological cause for variance in ultimate proficiency levels.

Also to be considered is the way "language" is operationalized for research purposes. For example, there may be different critical periods for different parts of language. Here, it may be useful to

distinguish between critical periods for speech and language. Generally, *speech* refers to the ability to and act of articulating the sounds necessary to language, whereas *language* refers to a system of communication involving lexicon (vocabulary) and syntax (rules or grammar). Pronunciation, an aspect of speech, is widely believed to have a critical period, whereas lexicon and syntax can be acquired well into adulthood. There are exceptions in both of these instances, nullifying the critical period as an inflexible rule and pointing more to an optimal period.

Directions for Future Research

What makes a particular period optimal is now the subject of much debate. Is this caused by physiological reasons, as per the lateralization theory? Or is it caused by experiential or environmental reasons? Karl Kim and his colleagues, for example, provide some evidence that children and adult language learners process second languages differently. Whereas the adult brain separates the two languages, using different parts for different languages, children use the same part of the brain to process both languages. Those who prefer experiential explanations of an optimal period point out that the fact that children and adults may process language differently is not necessarily a causal relationship between age and language proficiency and that there is little evidence to suggest it is. They instead point to social and experiential factors, such as confidence in one's ability and the extent to which the experience of one's first language interferes with one's perceptions of other languages.

In other words, whether or not there is a critical or optimal period and whether or not there are biological or environmental explanations, it is still the case that with sufficient instruction, training, and practice, older children and adults can become fluent in a second language, overcoming even their foreign accents. In fact, there is evidence to suggest that even though starting earlier may be better in the long run, in the initial stages of second-language learning, older children and adults are quite efficient, progressing much more rapidly than young children. This is due to the more-sophisticated skills they bring to the learning task and to the background knowledge they already possess. This also helps to explain why bilingual education programs are so effective: They foster the growth of content-area background knowledge in the

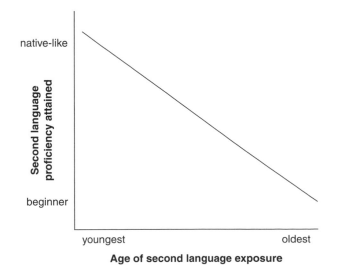

Figure 2   Steady Decline in Second-Language Proficiency Attained

first language, making instruction in the second language more comprehensible.

John Petrovic

See also Accents and Their Meaning; Compound and Coordinate Bilingualism; Learning a Language, Best Age; Underlying Linguistic Proficiencies

Further Readings

Birdsong, D. (Ed.). (1999). *Second language acquisition and the critical period hypothesis.* Mahwah, NJ: Lawrence Erlbaum.

Bruer, J. T. (2002). *The myth of the first three years.* New York: Free Press.

Hakuta, K., Bialystok, E., & Wiley, E. (2003). Critical evidence: A test of the critical-period hypothesis for second-language acquisition. *Psychological Science, 14,* 31–38.

Johnson, J. S., & Newport, E. L. (1989). Critical period effects in second language learning: The influence of maturational state on the acquisition of English as a second language. *Cognitive Psychology, 21,* 60–99.

Kim, K. H. S., Relkin, N. R., Lee, K., & Hirsch, J. (1997). Distinct cortical areas associated with native and second languages. *Nature, 388,* 171–174.

Krashen, S. D., Scarcella, R. C., & Long, M. H. (1982). *Child-adult differences in second language acquisition.* Rowley, MA: Newbury House.

Lenneberg, E. (1967). *Biological foundations of language.* New York: Wiley.

Lorenz, K. (1971). *Studies in animal and human behavior.* Cambridge, MA: Harvard University Press.

Penfield, W., & Roberts, L. (1959). *Speech and brain mechanisms.* Princeton, NJ: Princeton University Press.

Pinker, S. (1994). *The language instinct.* New York: Morrow.

Singleton, D., & Lengyel, Z. (1995). *The age factor in second language acquisition.* Clevedon, UK: Multilingual Matters.

Singleton, D., & Ryan, L. (2004). *Language acquisition: The age factor* (2nd ed.). Clevedon, UK: Multilingual Matters.

CULTURAL CAPITAL

The concept of cultural capital (sometimes referred to as *culture* capital) was originally developed by Pierre Bourdieu, a French sociologist influenced by the earlier work of Émile Durkheim and Max Weber. Cultural capital can be used to describe those cultural practices, experiences, perspectives, and knowledge that are passed along from one generation to the next and can have a significant impact on a person's encounter with a different social or cultural group. How people place a particular value or lack of value upon particular forms of cultural capital can help educators understand how and under what conditions students learn best and achieve success in school. The concept of cultural capital can thus be used to examine how the enterprise of education acts as a critical springboard, granting the potential for minorities to transcend socioeconomic class differences. However, cultural capital also serves to explain how schools regulate and even regenerate these differences through the validation of the existing or dominant social class structure. According to Bourdieu, students in school are socialized and taught in a manner that consistently perpetuates their class status. In a very basic sense, cultural capital can be thought of as "coins in your pocket," with "coins" being a metaphor for the cultural attributes a student brings to school. The currency that each student can render will correlate with positive outcomes that subsequently translate into a better education, and school success will facilitate the young person's acculturation into mainstream society. This presupposes, of course, that the school accepts the cultural "coins" of all their students and values them.

Bourdieu's theory largely revolves around four key points. First, each social class reproduces its own unique form of cultural capital. Second, schools are institutions that largely serve to add value to the cultural capital of the upper class and subtract value from the cultural capital of the lower class. Third, the notion of success in school consistently favors the upper class, and this success is later translated into tangible economic wealth. Fourth, schools act as a symbolic crossroad that officially sanctions the existing social hierarchy through their complementary academic hierarchy.

Another important dimension of Bourdieu's theory is the concept of the *habitus,* defined as the shared attitudes, beliefs, and perceptions that are rendered within one's environment. Perceptions in relation to the habitus are not individual, but are, rather, the perceptions that encompass the wider beliefs shared in a consensus among members of a particular community. For example, having a preference for attending a musical concert of either classical music or punk rock reflects particular individual dispositions and a particular habitus given those preferences; however, the habitus between classical music and punk rock reflects elements unique to the wider perception of socioeconomic status and affluence among a particular community of music listeners. The habitus can also reaffirm negative predispositions, such as how classical music is better than punk rock because it is situated within a particular perception of affluence. A more relevant example can reveal how some English language learners (ELLs) could be led to believe that pursuing a higher education is an option limited only to fluent-English-speaking White students.

Cultural Capital and Linguistic Capital

For ELLs in the United States, cultural capital can be seen in the status assigned to the language of the dominant cultural group. Schools consistently ascribe greater value to English than to any other language spoken by their students. This exemplifies how cultural capital can also be more specifically translated into *linguistic capital*. Bourdieu has observed that linguistic capital is especially influential during a student's early years of schooling and that it is probably the most important factor influencing a student's career opportunities in comparison to other factors. Thus, ELLs arriving in the United States already speaking a dialect of standard English possess some form of linguistic capital that will allow for greater success in school. Linguistic capital in conjunction with cultural capital refers to knowledge about spoken and written language, as well as the communicative competence necessary for participating effectively in different contexts. However, linguistic capital assigns a hierarchical and situational dimension to language, and it can be used to observe how language has been disproportionately perceived and privileged by the dominant cultural group.

A good example is the differentiation in the social perception of Black English, which historically has been stigmatized due to its origin in racism and slavery. However, as the work of the linguist William Labov has illustrated, Black English or African American Vernacular English (AAVE), also known as Ebonics, constitutes a legitimate dialect of English, with a phonology and semantic structure consistent with that of other varieties of English. One could argue, of course, that because Ebonics has been correlated with historically racist attitudes toward African Americans, its linguistic capital is diminished despite its linguistic validity. Shirley Brice Heath similarly observed that African American speakers of AAVE in her study spoke a dialect at home that was not privileged in the school setting and that these students encountered significant barriers for a quality education. There is reason to believe, therefore, that the negative attitudes of school people and of the students themselves may be similar with respect to certain varieties of AAVE. In short, it is possible for an African American student to internalize the same negative perceptions of his or her language as might be held by members of the dominant group in the community.

The concept of linguistic capital also has the capacity to explain the value of unique communicative practices shared among particular communities. For example, ELLs with Mexican backgrounds can also share a unique understanding of *consejos* (folk wisdom), *dichos* (proverbs), and *cuentos* (stories) that convey highly respected folk wisdom. We also know that ELLs of Mexican background can be responsible for a number of complex economic tasks in the process of translating English for their parents. Carlos Vélez-Ibañez has shown how ELLs of Mexican backgrounds can share *funds of knowledge* (skills and knowledge from students' households) that demonstrate the complex intellectual knowledge and practices of Mexican homes. Luis Moll has further interpreted how the funds-of-knowledge approach can be implemented by teachers for the culturally relevant instruction of public school students.

Thus, linguistic capital may serve to explain the various communicative practices inherent among ELLs and their families either in a positive light, acknowledging the diverse linguistic backgrounds within the school environment, or from a more negative perspective, focusing on the mismatch between the communicative practices that are valued at school and at home. Furthermore, a strict and narrow focus on the nature of linguistic capital itself falls short of explaining how these variations in capital influence the ability to succeed in school and in society. It would be a mistake to frame the scope of cultural capital as being limited to linguistic capital for ELLs, because it ignores other, less obvious practices that influence their schooling situations that cannot be explained solely by looking at the ability a student has to speak the language variety favored at school. These obstacles can also be explained through the notion of a hidden curriculum or a self-fulfilling prophecy, which can be used to examine the less explicit dynamics of the educational process—including ways of acting or speaking or holding certain attitudes toward academic institutions or authorities. As an example, parents of a minority background who regard the schoolteacher as the authority in their child's education might not display overt engagement with the school, out of respect; this behavior may be misinterpreted by the school as lack of parental involvement and interest. This mismatch between the behaviors and dispositions common among mainstream parents (the cultural capital valued at school) and those that minority parents bring may have repercussions in the child's status as a "competent" or "at-risk" student.

The Influence of Class and Gender

To deepen an understanding about cultural capital would require understanding a complex definition of culture, specifically through the intersecting influences of gender, class, race, ethnicity, and language. An understanding of class differences in relation to cultural capital has been a consistent feature in the research, but gender has grown as an important dimension. For example, one obvious difference would be the perception of masculinity through working-class role models for young males in school, as evidenced through the work of Paul Willis. He has observed how male students perceive a trajectory into factory work and criticize their education at school as an effeminate, unworthy endeavor.

Cameron McCarthy has similarly noted how problematic conceptualizations about race and ethnicity are subsequently affected by the intersections of class and gender. For example, there can be unique variations between Mexican male and female immigrants in terms of how they interpret gender roles that are echoed in school and community. Mexican male immigrants can be quite comfortable thinking that it is their inherent destiny to take up unskilled labor at the meatpacking plant or in the fields. Mexican female immigrants can be brought up thinking that it is their inherent destiny to perfect their domestic skills in preparation for marriage. However, upper- and middle-class Mexican immigrants, male and female, would have far different interpretations about the role of education in their lives. Whereas these abbreviated examples hinge upon broad generalizations, they are meant only to indicate how there can be no clean categorization of any particular ethnic group without taking into account the intersections of class and gender.

According to Bourdieu, social class is a critical component of how cultural capital is manifested in school. However, his theory has been criticized for feeding into a deficit perspective for explaining student failure, because theories of social reproduction act under the assumption that minorities are mostly destined to do poorly in school, due to the very nature of our societal structure. Students can benefit from the acknowledgment of different resources and backgrounds they bring to school and from transformative practices that allow them to gain new cultural knowledge and dispositions necessary to navigate different contexts and worldviews.

Heriberto Godina

See also Accents and Their Meaning; Ebonics; Hidden Curriculum; Languages and Power; Social Class and Language Status; Social Class and School Success; Status Differences Among Languages

Further Readings

Bourdieu, P. (1977). Cultural reproduction and social reproduction. In J. Karabel & A. H. Halsey (Eds.), *Power and ideology in education* (pp. 487–510). New York: Oxford University Press.

Bourdieu, P., & Passeron, J. (1977). *Reproduction in education, society, and culture*. London: Sage.

Heath, S. B. (1988). *Ways with words: Language, life, and work in communities and classrooms*. New York: Cambridge University Press.

Labov, W. (1982). Objectivity and commitment in linguistic science: The case of the Black English trial in Ann Arbor. *Language in Society, 11,* 165–201.

Macleod, J. (1995). *Ain't no makin' it: Aspirations and attainment in a low-income neighborhood*. San Francisco: Westview Press.

McCarthy, C. (1988). Rethinking liberal and radical perspectives on racial inequality in schooling: Making the case for nonsynchrony. *Harvard Educational Review, 58,* 265–279.

Vélez-Ibañez, C., & Greenberg, J. (1992). Formation and transformation of funds of knowledge among U.S. Mexican households. *Anthropology and Education Quarterly, 23,* 313–335.

Willis, P. (1981). *Learning to labor: How working-class kids get working-class jobs*. New York: Columbia University Press.

CULTURAL DEFICIT AND CULTURAL MISMATCH THEORIES

The principal focus of bilingual education is that of mediating language differences between students' families and schools. But language is firmly embedded in a cultural matrix. The meanings we ascribe to language differences flow from the more generalized societal views regarding the concept of *cultural differences,* a broader and deeper notion. Often, whether willfully or not, a school's conception about the meaning of cultural differences casts a strong influence on the type of language instruction it provides to students, whether or not they are English language learners.

During the last half of the 20th century, American social scientists and education researchers sought to explain the lack of school success by immigrants and minority youngsters in various ways. A strong research theme pursued in many studies was the link between a child's (or a group's) culture as a determinant factor in a lack of participation in educational institutions. This entry examines two of the most common sets of beliefs on this matter.

Cultural Deficit Theory

Adherents of cultural dysfunction as a determinant of engagement and success in school have argued that the effects of low family socioeconomic status are the result of a culture of poverty that has powerful effects across generations. They argue that this syndrome is transmitted from one poor generation to the next. It robs individuals and the groups they belong to of the ability to succeed in society or even to aspire or attempt to do so. The concept of a "culture of poverty" arose from the work of anthropologist Oscar Lewis. He observed acute multigenerational poverty and its effects in several countries and found surprising commonalities. According to Lewis, the very poor, regardless of race or ethnicity, live disintegrated lives characterized by fatalistic, violent, cynical, and unproductive attitudes and values. This situation of acute, multigenerational poverty with little hope of improvement produces an endemic dysfunction similar to what occurs in the caste systems of some societies. In caste systems, the poorest of the poor come to accept their marginality and believe they can do nothing to escape it. Long-term planning and future goals

fall victim to despair and anomie. According to the concept of culture of poverty, the poorest of the poor live for the moment and seek short-term gratification. They do not accept the idea that participating in education will bring rewards later, sometimes much later. The reason is that they do not often see this happen with people they know.

While much of Lewis's work was conducted abroad, in the United States, his findings were often applied to African Americans. Not surprisingly, the situation of immigrants and language minority groups was painted with the same conceptual brush. Among the earliest research was the study of Mexican and Mexican American peoples. Sociologist Lyle Saunders preceded Lewis by a decade. Saunders gave the following characteristics, in which he portrays significant variation between the Anglo- and Spanish-speaking ideal:

1. The Spanish American or Mexican American tends to be oriented toward the present or the immediate past. Anglos, on the other hand, are oriented toward change and progress. The Spanish-speaking people, having had until recently little contact with change, find the old and tried more attractive than the new and unfamiliar.

2. Anglos are doers and are preoccupied with success. Spanish-speaking people want "to be" rather than "to do." Life in the villages did not stimulate a drive toward success.

3. Spanish-speaking people are more inclined than Anglos toward acceptance of and resignation to whatever may come to them.

4. The Anglo has a greater preference for independence. In harmony with relations in the village culture, Spanish-speaking people accept the role of dependency as a quite natural relation.

Lewis's findings concerning Puerto Rican families in La Perla, then a San Juan slum, were similar to Saunders's findings concerning Mexicans. These perceptions about the nation's Puerto Rican and Mexican American population were important for several reasons. First, they seemed to confirm long-standing views held by non-Hispanics about Hispanics as mentioned in studies of popular literature. The second reason is that they seem to legitimize, through social science research, the use of the dominant "Anglo culture" as the normative model of being American.

Finally, they are important because these paradigms allowed educators and others to blame the victims of discrimination for their own woes. Admittedly, by the standards of contemporary social science research, these assertions about Latino culture are little more than stereotypes. It is important to remember that they, too, bore the imprimatur of social science and that many school people learned these theories during their own education.

In all of the cases mentioned above, the research focus was not on schools and education, although these ideas were seminal and easily spilled over into that field. It is unlikely that Lewis could have predicted either the excitement or the firestorm that would be produced by his work. Today, some scholars maintain that Lewis fueled a generalized rethinking of American social policy, with lingering effects in public policy that are felt to this day. His theory was used to confirm widespread fears that the growing urban underclass needed to be resocialized into psychologically stable, optimistic, hardworking citizens. With Lewis, the discourse of cultural deficits was put on the table in a serious way. His analysis became the basis of several government studies and programs that sought to help immigrants and poor people by attempting to change their native cultures and make them into something different.

Shortly after the publication of Lewis's work on the culture-of-poverty, researchers took up the theme with variations. Led by social scientists, research teams began to examine cultural deficit theory and its implications for education. Among the most important of these scholars were James Coleman and Christopher Jencks, both social scientists. They led research teams that looked into the links between family and community life and success in schools. They stopped short of blaming the culture of poverty but noted that family and community life influences school performance more than other factors. They argued that failure or success in school should be regarded more broadly as the result of the totality of influences on children's lives, not merely their experiences in the classroom.

In his seminal study *Inequality,* Jencks presented the results and interpretations of 3 years of research into various aspects of uneven conditions. He reported on a wide range of topics: (a) access to privileged schoolmates and fast classes; (b) the nature and extent of cognitive abilities; (c) the heredity/environment controversy; and, importantly, (d) the weight of economic background, race, and family background. To some degree, Jencks and his research team disputed Lewis's more simplistic cause-and-effect relationships. The Jencks team pointed out that it is not a single factor, but several, that determined success in school of the urban poor. It was Jencks's belief in the importance of family and community influences that caused him to be associated with Lewis's theory that the poor carry with them the germ of failure. According to Jencks, schools and other social institutions lack sufficient power to overcome these factors. Jencks's views were complemented by those of Coleman, who argued that the effects of poor communities on children's lives may be more powerful than the effects of the schools they attend. The collective output of these scholars brought into question how much formal schooling can hope to accomplish with poor students, and even whether they should attend school at all. Lewis's anthropological perspective and Jencks's more sociological interpretations were widely regarded as being two peas in a single conceptual pod.

In fairness to Coleman, Jencks, Lewis, and other researchers of the time, it should be noted that their ideas were presented in a context of optimistic social policy, in which the actions by government and social institutions were believed to be important factors in reversing the negative influences of the past. By emphasizing the intractability of the effects of poverty and environment, Jencks and Lewis were accused of blaming the victims for their own misfortunes and lowering the expectations for what could be done through current and prospective government programs, such as Head Start and Title I of the Elementary and Secondary Education Act of 1965, and subsequent amendments, such as Title VII, the Bilingual Education Act, which came later. The negative findings of this research did not deter advocates of these remedial programs aimed at fighting the long-term effects of poverty. To them, the studies bolstered the rationale for intervening in the distressed lives of poor children and families.

Cultural Mismatch Theory

Another explanation for the persistently high failure rate among racial and ethnic minorities also relates to a perceived lack of fit between their ethnic or racial groups, on one hand, and the overall culture of school and society, on the other. However, while the culture-of-poverty theory holds that the effects of profound multigenerational poverty are beyond the capacity of social institutions to change, adherents of the incompatibility theory, also called *cultural mismatch theory,* argued that its effects can be overcome by modifying the institutions themselves, rather than the members of the group in question. These theories recognize cultural differences among groups but place the responsibility for cultural adaptation on the institutions instead of its clients. José A. Cárdenas, a prominent Texas educator, compared the difference between the two approaches this way, in a personal communication with the author: "It's very much like trying on a pair of new shoes and, upon finding that the shoes don't fit, asking the client to change feet." An important element of this theory is that instead of assuming an intractable defeatism among the very poor, its proponents argue that cultural differences can be bridged and the cycle of poverty can be broken.

Cultural mismatch theory emphasizes microlevel sociological variables, including disparities between home and school environments, as the principal causes of school failure. Anthropologist John Ogbu has referred to these disparities as "primary cultural discontinuities" rooted in preexisting differences between immigrant and host societies. In this view, these primary cultural discontinuities cause conflict between students and schools and lead to academic failure. These twisted interactions, attributions, and labeling on the part of school staff and students result in disruptions of the teaching and learning process. Importantly, these disruptions lead to student rejections of the cultural values and academic demands of the school and, subsequently, to academic failure. Because of these cultural mismatches, minority students experience unintentional but inferior instruction in the classroom. It is a common view among scholars today that discontinuities and incompatibilities in values or beliefs exist but that students from those groups are capable of overcoming those incompatibilities and achieving success provided that the schools make curricular and methodological adaptations.

Adherents of the cultural mismatch theory propose remedies that avoid a negative valuing of the learner's cultural background and promote a proactive use of the learner's culture as part of the instructional regimen. In their proposals, there is agreement that the essential difference is in (a) designing educational programs capable of overcoming the negative effects of marginality and poverty and (b) causing social and cultural institutions to change in ways that allow entry to members of minority groups without asking them to

"change feet." In this approach, the proposed remedies are based on avoiding comparisons between the child's culture and that of more privileged members of society, especially when those comparisons result in the conclusion that the child's culture is somehow deficient. Instead, proponents of a more positive approach would employ the strengths of the learner's culture as elements that are embedded in the curriculum. In this way, minority students are given strong positive images of their own cultural groups with which to identify; and at the same time, they are exposed to the dominant culture and learn to accept and manipulate it more seamlessly. Teachers are expected to become "culturally proficient" in the learners' cultures and to use elements of those cultures that lend themselves to classroom work. Various authors have used the terms *cultural capital, culture-based curriculum,* and *funds of knowledge* to describe the cultural resources that all groups possess and that can serve to make schoolwork more relevant to students.

Today, Oscar Lewis and the culture of poverty has been largely forgotten, although remnants of his theory abound, both in research and in instructional interventions. The most common interpretation today is more neutral. The prevailing view is that cultural discontinuities or incompatibilities exist within a framework of cultural differences that can be managed and overcome through diligent work on the part of schools. Differences are merely that: differences, not deficiencies. Often, the line between theories of cultural difference, on one hand, and cultural deficit, on the other, is indistinct. The principal difference is whether the program intends to change the cultural orientation of the student or whether it seeks to create a climate of mutual accommodation through which both students and schools adjust to social and cultural changes that affect them both. Advocates of mutual cultural adaptation attribute value to the backgrounds of immigrant children. They do not regard their cultures as being deprived or impoverished, but hold that schools can and should adapt to the culture of their students, building on strengths rather than weaknesses.

The effects of poverty, however, especially profound multigenerational poverty, are not forgotten and continue to be explored. There is little doubt that socioeconomic variables often interfere with or slow down educational progress. The deepest levels of poverty create the biggest problems. This is because such poverty is a marker of lack of experience with formal schooling. Not enough is known about the factors that mediate the success of minority children from high-poverty backgrounds. Regrettably, there has been a tendency among researchers to focus almost exclusively on predictors of academic failure, not success. There is little empirical research on minority students who are academically successful and able to surmount the detrimental conditions and events that place them at risk of failure. Notwithstanding the research gaps, academics and social activists who believe in more-benign forms of cultural differences have put forward interesting proposals on how to bridge such differences. These suggestions are founded on the idea of culturally competent teaching and the recognition, by curriculum planners, of the value of children's home cultures and their value as part of the school's curriculum.

An important implication for bilingual education is how the schools deal with the home language of students learning English, since those differences can be some of the most marked contrasts between home and school. At the level of professional discourse, the notion of a "lack" or "limited" English ability has been changed. Where it has been commonplace to speak of students with "limited English proficiency" (LEP), it is now customary to refer to these same students as "English language learners" (ELLs). Perhaps a more important point is acknowledging that transitional bilingual education may send the wrong message to children and their families: the idea that the home language will be used in school only for a limited time. This may convey the idea that their language is not important enough to study throughout the grades. For that reason, the concept of "transitional bilingual education" has yielded to the more democratic form known as "dual-language immersion" and "two-way bilingual programs," in which English-speaking students learn the language of their minority classmates as the latter learn the lingua franca.

Instructional tweaks and curricular changes, however, do not suffice to challenge ideologies that are deeply rooted in cultural deficit thinking. A critical approach to professional development, one that raises awareness of the misconceptions behind these ideas, may contribute to a more insightful sense of the teacher's role in these dynamics.

Josué M. González

See also Culturally Competent Teaching; Deficit-Based Education Theory; Enculturation; Language Socialization; Multicultural Education; Nationalization of Languages; Social Class and Language Status; Social Class and School Success

Further Readings

Coleman, J. S. (1966). *Equality of educational opportunity.* Washington: U.S. Department of Health, Education and Welfare, Office of Education.

Jencks, C. (1972). *Inequality: A reassessment of the effect of family and schooling in America.* New York: Basic Books.

Lewis, O. (1959). *Anthropological essays.* New York: Random House.

Ogbu, J. (1978). *Minority education and caste: The American system in cross-cultural perspective.* New York: Academic Press.

Saunders, L. (1954). *Cultural differences and medical care: The case of the Spanish-speaking people of the Southwest.* New York: Russell Sage Foundation.

CULTURALLY COMPETENT TEACHING

How much does an individual need to know about a given cultural group to be considered culturally competent in working with students of that group? Ideas about cultural competence continue to be informed through different perspectives upon a shared definition of *culture* that includes, but is not limited to, perceptions about race, ethnicity, gender, sexual orientation, socioeconomic status, language, and dialect. Cultural competence implies sensitivity toward issues of culture in conjunction with a social service, such as the medical profession, which has begun to reassess negative assumptions related to folk healing or *curanderismo*, or with the legal profession, which has reassessed negative characterizations of minorities through critical race theory. At its most basic, cultural competence means respecting cultural differences in one's professional practice much more than it does knowing a great deal about the particulars of a given cultural group.

Cultural competence has been a fairly recent innovation with roots in health and mental health services, as reported by Terry L. Cross, Barbara J. Bazron, Karl W. Dennis, and Mareasa R. Isaacs. In education, culturally competent teaching has been discussed through the similar concepts of *culturally relevant pedagogy* and *culturally appropriate instruction*. For English language learners, culturally competent teaching would require a teacher's basic acknowledgment and respect for his or her student's home language and the cultural differences they bring to the classroom. Teachers tapping into an authentic understanding of culture would more likely benefit from successful learning experiences for their students, who would then be meaningfully integrated within their own learning community. Teachers who engage in culturally competent teaching are able to show how their instructional approaches correspond to their levels of awareness about cultural differences. Students similarly have to be understood from the perspective of cultural competence in their engagement at school. Gloria Ladson-Billings has observed how African American students are responsible for negotiating both their ties to their peer groups and the academic demands that reflect the attitudes and attributes of the dominant White culture. She argues that curricula should relate closely to the background experiences of minority students and not create a dilemma for students who may have to choose between their peer groups and academic success. Signithia Fordham and John Ogbu have similarly explained the dilemma of cultural inversion for African American students, who may view academic success as the "burden of actin' White." One way of understanding how culturally competent teaching can unfold in the classroom is to analyze where it could best be implemented.

Constructivist and Transmission Orientations

Classroom instruction can unfold from either a constructivist or transmission orientation. In a *constructivist approach,* the negotiation of meaning between the teacher and student becomes an important aspect of instruction. Culturally competent teaching can be more readily embedded within the classroom when constructivism is practiced. Some constructivist practices, such as the *funds-of-knowledge* approach, place a greater emphasis and value upon the student's background culture, which, in turn, helps the teacher and student to connect to and shape subsequent intellectual activities in and outside the classroom. Another example could include a *critical literacy* approach, as advocated by Paulo Freire, which reflects a similar constructivist approach that negotiates meaning as a trajectory that can also lend insight into an authentic interpretation of social justice. There exists considerable evidence on how shifting the curriculum focus between either a minority or majority student perspective results in differentiated outcomes. For example, Linda Spears-Bunton found that White students became

uncomfortably challenged in interpreting a shared reading of an African American text, and, conversely, African American students in the same class grew more fluent in their discussions about the reading. Previously, when the readings covered content that the White students were comfortable with, African American students had a more difficult time participating in discussion. It stands to reason that culturally competent instruction would result in a better engagement with the classroom material when background contexts and schemas can be activated from students' prior experiences, as reported by Margaret S. Steffensen, Chitra Joag-Dev, and Richard Anderson.

Culturally competent instruction can also be specifically centered around a cultural curriculum and can be exemplified through earlier efforts on instruction about African culture for African American students, as suggested by Molefi Kete Asante. Similarly, this can be done when centering instruction around Mexican ancestry for Mexican American students. It is important to recognize, however, that merely including ethnic or heritage materials in the curriculum may not be sufficient to overcome issues arising from a lack of opportunity, historical oppression, or long-term inequities. It is the *meaning* of cultural differences that must be considered, rather than the differences themselves. The latter must be handled lightly and deftly in order to prevent stereotyping. Constructivist practices seem to be a better fit for recognizing the potential that culturally competent teaching has to offer.

In contrast, a *transmission-based approach,* such as that promoted by curriculum designs such as those inherent in the No Child Left Behind Act of 2001, pushes instruction toward the other side of the continuum through the enforcement of standardized tests that resonate with a similarly standardized curriculum. Transmission instruction tends toward a generalizable quality that suggests a one-size-fits-all approach. Lisa Delpit has articulated how classrooms are a microcosm of the wider society and reflective of a *culture of power* that stigmatizes the participation of minority students, who become subordinated. This occurs when standards are defined largely by the dominant culture. For English language learners, participation in the culture of power requires not only understanding the language of the dominant culture but also understanding the pragmatic behavior implicitly used within the language sanctioned by the dominant culture. Students benefit from being explicitly taught how to navigate through the framework of a culture that may be insensitive to their conceptualizations of reality. A transmission-based approach more readily embraces an assimilative stance toward education for the culturally diverse student. Both approaches have their pitfalls and merits, and both entail considerations about how students comprehend meaning within the curriculum. Specifically, a constructivist approach moves away from the parameters defined by the culture of power and can risk diminishing a student's engagement with opportunities for social mobility; and a transmission approach infuses inauthentic interpretations of literacy for students who are basically prepared for standardized testing. Thus, culturally competent teaching can be different along different sides of this continuum and can strike a medium whereby students benefit from becoming familiar with both opportunities for upward social mobility and those that recognize the unique individual qualities that allow students a sense of belonging in the classroom.

Insights From Anthropological Research

Some seminal anthropological research has led to some unique insights for understanding how culturally competent teaching unfolds. Frederick Erickson and Gerald Mohatt determined how teachers have differed in their styles and approaches for interacting with students, with specific evidence about how social control was enforced through patterns of time and tempo of lessons with them. It should come as no surprise that teacher efficacy is a strong factor for reaching particular students, but students themselves also differ in how their background cultural knowledge predisposes them for optimal or negative experiences in the classroom. In an ethnography of the Warm Springs Indian Reservation, Susan U. Philips found how students and teachers differed in their school performance in terms of the participation structures used. Native American students became more engaged in school when instruction tapped into their sense of quiet independence that had been learned at home from their parents. Similarly, White students became more engaged when instruction mirrored more of a transmission-based approach that they expected to be a normal part of school. Thus, culturally competent teaching would also entail recognizing unique differences in the learning styles of student that emanate from home practices of interacting with members of their families and communities.

Culturally competent instruction can also go beyond whether or not the language of the classroom is English. It also entails teacher understandings of how students differ in their communicative patterns. Kathryn Hu-Pei Au studied Hawaiian school children and found that their speech patterns engaged a narrative *talk story,* which to the unperceptive teacher might be characterized as "noisy interruptions." When instruction for Hawaiian children facilitated their disposition for talk story, reading achievement increased. In another anthropological study of Puerto Rican children in New York, Ana Celia Zentella found that the use of code switching among English-Spanish speakers contained a greater complexity than had been ascertained before. Code switching could greatly enhance comprehension and could be used for a variety of school purposes. Zentella's findings helped to displace negative perceptions about the use of code switching among English language learners. One of the shared features from these anthropological studies exemplifies how culturally competent teaching seeks to bridge practices learned at home with those of the classroom. However, an important criterion for teachers validating culturally competent instruction requires not limiting these findings to categorize particular ethnic or racial groups of students, but rather understanding the *limits of essentialism.* This term, explained by Cameron McCarthy and Warren Crichlow, refers to the problematic tendency to view social groups as inherently similar entities. Teachers should look beyond the inherently limited environmental scope of previous research. In this sense, culture can be realized as a dynamic force that is in a constant state of change and can be redefined through the trajectory of time and the intersection of gender and class.

Conclusion

Returning to the original question regarding how much a teacher needs to know about a given culture in order to be a good teacher, clearly a deeper knowledge is preferable to shallow knowledge. Most of all, however, the teacher must recognize the importance of the cultural underpinnings of curriculum, any curriculum, and the fact that teaching methodologies influence the degree to which he or she becomes culturally competent. The importance of adequate teacher preparation programs focusing on culture cannot be overemphasized. The work of Ana María Villegas and Tamara

Lucas in this connection is particularly useful in shaping the content of such programs.

Heriberto Godina

See also Credentialing Foreign-Trained Teachers; Language and Identity; Multicultural Education; Ogbu, John; Teacher Qualifications

Further Readings

Asante, M. K. (1993). *Malcolm X as cultural hero and other Afrocentric essays.* Trenton, NJ: Africa World Press.

Au, K. (1980). Participation structures in a reading lesson with Hawaiian children: Analysis of a culturally appropriate instructional event. *Anthropology & Education Quarterly, 11,* 91–115.

Cross, T. L., Bazron, B. J., Dennis, K. W., & Isaacs, M. R. (1989). *Toward a culturally competent system of care.* Washington, DC: Georgetown University Child Development Center, CASSP Technical Assistance Center.

Delpit, L. (1995). *Other people's children: Cultural conflict in the classroom.* New York: New Press.

Erickson, F., & Mohatt, G. (1982). Cultural organization and participation structures in two classrooms of Indian students. In G. Spindler (Ed.), *Doing the ethnography of schooling* (pp. 131–174). New York: Holt, Rinehart & Winston.

Fordham, S., & Ogbu, J. (1986). Black students' school success: Coping with the "burden of 'actin White.'" *Urban Review, 18,* 176–206.

Freire, P. (1990). *Pedagogy of the oppressed.* New York: Continuum.

Godina, H. (2003). Mesocentrism and students of Mexican background: A community intervention for culturally relevant instruction. *Journal of Latinos and Education, 2,* 141–157.

Ladson-Billings, G. (1995). Toward a culturally relevant pedagogy. *American Educational Research Journal, 32,* 465–491.

McCarthy, C., & Crichlow, W. (1993). Introduction: Theories of identity, theories of representation, theories of race. In C. McCarthy & W. Crichlow (Eds.), *Race, identity, and representation in education* (pp. xiii–xxix). New York: Routledge.

Philips, S. U. (1983). *The invisible culture: Communication in classroom on the Warm Springs Indian Reservation.* Prospect Heights, IL: Waveland Press.

Spears-Bunton, L. (1992). Literature, literacy, and resistance to cultural domination: Views from many perspectives. In *The 41st National Reading Conference Yearbook* (pp. 393–401). Chicago: National Reading Conference.

Steffenensen, M. S., Joag-Dev, C., & Anderson, R. (1979). A cross cultural perspective on reading comprehension. *Reading Research Quarterly, 15,* 10–29.

Vélez-Ibañez, C., & Greenberg, J. (1992). Formation and transformation of funds of knowledge among U.S. Mexican households. *Anthropology and Education Quarterly, 23,* 313–335.

Villegas, A. M., & Lucas, T. (2002). *Educating culturally responsive teachers: A coherent approach.* Albany: SUNY Press.

Villegas, A. M., & Lucas, T. (2007). The culturally responsive teacher. *Educational Leadership, 64*(6), 28–33.

Zentella, A. C. (1997). *Growing up bilingual: Puerto Rican children in New York.* Malden, MA: Blackwell.

CULTURE SHOCK

Culture shock emerged in the mid-1950s as a useful concept to help explain the emotional tension, adjustment problems, and difficulties immigrants, refugees, and foreign students face at school and in their personal lives when they are thrust into new environments. In the new setting, interrelations with friends, family members, and the broader community, as well as salient linguistic, cultural, and religious values, cannot be maintained or publicly practiced by these groups, since they often differ from the values and practices of the host society. In schools, culture shock has gained some attention due to the steady rise in the number of immigrants attending U.S. schools and the considerable differences between ethnic groups and mainstream student school performance.

Kalvero Oberg postulated that culture shock reflects the level of anxiety, apprehension, and distress faced when an individual's native culture or the culture that individual was raised in is replaced by a new cultural surrounding, with its own distinct cultural and linguistic signs and symbols. This new, unaccustomed environment includes communication, cultural, and social barriers that often lead these individuals to experience acute challenges, psychological distress, and internal struggles with maintaining their identities. Although contact with the new culture might not always result in a frightful experience, exposure to unfamiliar surroundings leads them to strive to fit into this new culture, as explained by Colleen Ward and her colleagues. The problem with this adjustment is that core values and salient linguistic and social/cultural features that helped mold one's ethnocultural and social identity no longer hold the same value.

Initially, scholars such as Celia J. Falicov, Colleen Ward, Stephen Bochner, and Adrian Furnham shifted attention to immigrant children and their families' attitudes toward the host culture and their ability to build interpersonal relations with host culture members and to develop new identities and social skills to help them in the acculturation process. More recently, Alicia Núñez and Juneau M. Gary wrote that to understand the gravity of cultural shock in immigrant children, educators must take into account multiple interrelated factors, including various social, individual, psychological, and physical attributes of each individual and the way they affect the transition or gradual adaptation into a new culture. With bilingual or multilingual children, it is also critical to look closely at their personality traits, their expectations, and previous contacts with the host culture, host culture members, or institutions, as well as their parents' attitudes toward the host culture and the ways they develop coping skills to overcome culture shock.

Sequential Stages of Culture Shock

Several phases have been proposed by Oberg, Peter Adler, and other scholars to acknowledge the interrelation of psychosocial, sociocognitive, and behavioral factors that can bring about culture shock. Adler's five-stage culture shock experience, which is often cited, begins with the contact with the new culture, or what has been termed the *honeymoon stage.* For example, immigrant children and English as a Second Language (ESL) students who move to the United States are often eager to dive into this new experience and may also develop an ideal image of this new culture, expecting to gain positive and adventurous experiences. Immigrant children might express some level of trepidation, but overall they are enthusiastic about experiencing this new and linguistically rich environment. However, psychological and emotional pressure begins to build during the *disintegration stage,* in which differences between their home countries and this new society often lead to uncertainty, confusion, emotional distress, alienation, and frustration. During this stage, cross-cultural differences become more apparent to those immigrant children who have had no preschool or kindergarten experience and no linguistic and social competence to function in a new school context. These young children often feel powerless,

unable to communicate their needs or to fully participate in class, since the classroom is a new cultural and linguistic experience. They often become isolated, introverted, and emotionally distressed. Older students, especially those of high school age, are often more traumatized by these experiences, as Angela Valenzuela has reported.

This psychological and emotional distress continues into the third stage, also known as the *reintegration stage,* during which immigrant children and ESL students believe that individuals from the host culture are responsible for a good proportion of the problems encountered during this new cultural experience. They adopt a rather defensive approach, trying to protect their cultural roots and values. At the same time, they develop a deeper understanding of the sociocultural values of the host culture. Experiences and interactions with the host culture often determine whether they can resolve such conflicts and eliminate emotional distress or return to the previous stages of culture shock. Normally, these stressful experiences are eliminated during the fourth stage, the *autonomy stage,* in which students grasp the sociocultural and linguistic values of the host society and are more accepted by the host culture. These students develop a sense of self-efficacy and self-confidence about the core social and linguistic values of the host culture, but there are still instances in which they find themselves as outsiders or not fully acculturated. They adapt and embrace this new host culture and cross-cultural experience during the *interdependence stage.* This is when they acknowledge and value their multicultural personalities. That is, they value and respect both the similarities and differences between their native and new cultures and develop a deeper understanding of this cross-cultural learning experience.

In the multicultural classrooms of today, scholars postulate that it is critical to identify the causes of cultural shock in immigrant and ESL children. Increasingly, educators believe that in today's multiethnic classrooms, there is a need to acknowledge the sources of the factors that contribute to culture shock.

Psychosocial, Cognitive, and Individual Factors Leading to Culture Shock

Scholars such as Furnham and Bochner, Michael Winkelman, Gladys González-Ramos, and Manny J. González hold that culture shock should be viewed in the light of multiple interrelated personal, psychosocial, cognitive, and family reasons influencing this transitional and transforming experience. First, they call attention to *stress* not simply as an emotional or psychological response but also as a physiological or somatic reaction that immigrant children and their families face, as explained by Winkelman and Ward, Bochner, and Furnham. As immigrant children and their families leave their home countries, either voluntarily as immigrants or involuntarily as refugees, they go through considerable stress. Immigrant children are more susceptible to such stress since they are under a lot of pressure to adapt both at school and in the social setting. They are not familiar with the institutional or social environment, and they suddenly find themselves without their friends, relatives, or support systems. They are emotionally distressed, confused, and insecure in this new social setting. The level of psychological stress is even higher in immigrant children at the adolescent stage who suddenly struggle to understand the sociocultural values of the new culture but at the same time function in a school environment without the necessary linguistic, social, or cultural competence. Going through such an emotionally stressful experience sometimes creates somatic or physiological responses, since the body's immune system might be compromised, increasing the risk for illness and health problems in general. Immigrant children often feel isolated, depressed, and nervous in various social situations or in a school environment where they are required to participate in group work.

Second, the pressure of trying to understand a new culture, along with its socially accepted behavior and norms, can be overwhelming, which contributes to cognitive fatigue, as discussed by George M. Guthrie and Winkelman. Immigrant children and adolescents need to pay considerable attention to the social and linguistic dynamics arising during verbal interactions and to the nonverbal cues employed in conversation. To a higher degree than native speakers of English, a fuller cognitive involvement is necessary to understand and develop the socially accepted skills to progress in this setting. Such considerable effort to deal with the new communication and social tasks often leads immigrant children to feel "mentally tired" and withdrawn from social or school functions and activities.

Third, the social roles and public persona immigrant children adopted and displayed in their home countries is no longer considered as the norm in this new culture. As a result, immigrant children go through *role shock,* as Francis C. Byrnes and

Winkelman explain. They realize that there is a disparity between their socially embraced character and what the members of this new community believe to be acceptable public roles. In the host community, they can no longer rely on the interpersonal relations built at home with family members, relatives, and friends. They need to establish new relations with children and adults in their current host environment. However, their social skills need to adhere to the socially acceptable etiquette of the target culture. To establish these social relations, immigrant children need to adopt a socially accepted persona that might often contradict, question, or challenge the role that they maintained in their home countries or in the family, thus leading to role shock. Often, immigrant children receive little guidance in this process of adapting to the new culture. Ward and her colleagues further explain that many immigrant parents who arrive in the host country have limited proficiency in the language, while immigrant children tend to acquire language and cultural values more quickly, due to formal study in school. Hence, they often have the responsibility to act as translators for their parents. In many instances, immigrant children find themselves in social situations in which they take a more challenging social and family role, assuming more responsibilities in this new setting. Because they acquire a new and unknown role of language brokering, the relationship between such children and their parents may be altered.

Fourth, Winkelman has suggested that immigrant children also endure a *personal shock,* since they experience so many life-altering events in their efforts to acculturate or form part of the youth culture and community in which they are newly immersed. Immigrant children and adolescents lose important individuals in their lives as they acculturate. At the beginning, this separation is overwhelming, causing stress, insomnia, and reservation in creating new relationships. In addition, some studies, such as those conducted by Rosendo Urrabazo, have indicated that Mexican immigrant children may go through serious emotional hardships or traumatic events while crossing the U.S.-Mexico border, such as rape, robbery, and fear of being detained and deported. Yet such events are rarely discussed with teachers or school administrators, and, even worse, the psychological support is not available to all immigrant children who need it. In cases in which such services are available, immigrant children might not request them. Instead, if they cannot perform to the same levels as mainstream students in the class, their teachers and peers may come to believe that these students do not possess the knowledge-building skills or the desire to thrive in school. Such deficit-based thinking, however, may leave immigrant children to seek alternative ways to cope with the trauma, such as excessive eating, insomnia, lack of interest in their everyday interactions, depression, apparent disengagement from school activities, tension, and agitation, as reported by González-Ramos and González, and Falicov. Some immigrant children, and especially adolescents and adults, may even feel that the social norms and roles of this new society infringe upon their personal, cultural, religious, and moral values. Such differences may lead to value conflicts between immigrant families and their new communities and dysfunctional adult behaviors later.

Teaching Practices to Overcome Culture Shock

Culture shock, then, is a multifaceted process. The ways in which immigrant children, along with their families, respond to cultural adaptation depend on various idiosyncratic and psychological factors, the effective use of problem-solving skills, and the support received from the school, social, and family environments. School administrators and teachers can help with the process of acculturation by acknowledging the diverse ethnic, cultural, and linguistic backgrounds of immigrant children and addressing problems the children face with cultural adjustment as they are immersed in the learning culture.

Acculturation is a slow and psychologically and emotionally demanding process, often requiring effort to embrace children's ethnocultural and linguistic heritage. Through constructive lesson plans and group activities, teachers can help immigrant children become more acquainted with the social values and language of the target culture and teach them to develop problem-solving strategies and approaches to effectively deal with culture shock. Teachers can also help by broadening their knowledge of what constitutes appropriate and socially acceptable norms and values for immigrant children and by respecting their cultural, linguistic, and religious values. They can adopt practices and prepare lesson plans that are rich in cultural and linguistic context. Scholars like González-Ramos and González also recommend involving the family to discuss the levels of literacy their children developed in the native language, the kind of experiences or struggle each has experienced, and the differences in intercultural communication and prior school practices to which they were exposed. Teachers could also establish an interactive forum to foster the development of interrelations among immigrant students and open the path to understanding cultural differences and eliminating their stress. Because of the language skills of their staff, bilingual schools have an advantage in this regard, since bilingual personnel can mount and sustain such interactions with families.

In addition, the process of acculturation may be aided by teachers cooperating closely with mental health services in their school districts. Mental health support services, clinical psychologists, and school counselors are likely to have a good grasp of psychological, emotional, cultural, and linguistic issues of immigrant families and their children; their current living conditions and personal and social challenges with this community; and how these factors influence child development and performance. Such individuals can also open a dialogue with the parents and encourage helpful involvement in school for the entire family. School counselors can discuss with parents, school administrators, and teachers the psychological, academic, and intellectual needs of immigrant children. If such instrumental factors determining students' mental and psychological health are not addressed early on, even the best-designed instructional approaches might not be sufficient to ensure adequate performance in school.

Specially designed programs can provide the bases to improve interaction, teamwork, and collaboration between school, teachers, parents, and children and can also lend immigrant children a voice in dealing with institutional, social, linguistic, and academic challenges that lie ahead. Culture shock is a demanding process that may be addressed in schools with high numbers of immigrant students by adopting comprehensive programs and keeping teachers and school administrators informed about immigrant students' social, academic, and family roles in their new environments. Removing immigrant children from the safety net of their known environments may lead to puzzling behavioral and emotional problems that, if ignored, could become long-term adjustment issues. Special language-oriented programs such as bilingual education are important, but cannot be expected to resolve all such complex issues.

Stella K. Hadjistassou

See also Acculturation; Cultural Deficit and Cultural Mismatch Theories; Culturally Competent Teaching; Multicultural Education

Further Readings

Adler, P. S. (1975). The transitional experience: An alternative view of culture shock. *Journal of Humanistic Psychology, 15,* 13–23.

Bochner, S. (2003). Culture shock due to contact with unfamiliar cultures. In W. J. Lonner, D. L. Dinnel, S. A. Hayes, & D. N. Sattler (Eds.), *Online readings in psychology and culture* (Unit 8, Chap. 7). Bellingham; Western Washington University, Center for Cross Cultural Research. Retrieved February 1, 2008, from http://www.ac.wwu.edu/~culture/Bochner.htm

Byrnes, F. C. (1966). Role shock: An occupational hazard of American technical assistants abroad. *Annals of the American Academy of Political and Social Science, 368*(1), 95–108.

Falicov, C. J. (1998). *Latino families in therapy: A guide to multicultural practice.* New York: Guilford.

Furnham, A., & Bochner, S. (1986). *Culture shock: Psychological reactions to unfamiliar environments.* London: Methuen.

González-Ramos, G., & González, M. J. (2005). Mental health care of Hispanic immigrant children: A school-based approach. In M. J. González & G. González-Ramos (Eds.), *Mental health care for new Hispanic immigrants: Innovative approaches in contemporary clinical practices* (pp. 47–58). Binghamton, NY: Haworth Social Work Practice Press.

Guthrie, G. M. (1975). A behavioral analysis of culture learning. In R. W. Brislin, S. Bochner, & W. J. Lonner (Eds.), *Cross-cultural perspectives on learning* (pp. 95–115). New York: Wiley.

Nuñez, A., & Gary, J. M. (2006). *Facilitating acculturation among school-age Latino immigrant children.* Retrieved from http://www.njcounseling.org/NJCA-Journal/subpages/NunezGary.html

Oberg, K. (1958). *Culture shock and the problem of adjustment to new cultural environments.* Washington, DC: Department of State, Foreign Service Institute.

Oberg, K. (1960). Culture shock: Adjustment to new cultural environments. *Practical Anthropology, 7,* 177–182.

Pedersen, P. (1995). *The five stages of culture shock: Critical incidents around the world.* Westport, CT: Greenwood.

Urrabazo, R. (1999). Therapeutic sensitivity to the Latino spiritual soul. In M. T. Flores & G. Carey (Eds.), *Family therapy with Hispanics: Toward appreciating diversity* (pp. 205–227). Boston: Allyn & Bacon.

U.S. Census Bureau. (2007). *Hispanic heritage month 2007.* Retrieved from http://www.census.gov/Press-Release/www/releases/archives/facts_for_features_special_editions/010327.html

Valenzuela, A. (1999). *Subtractive schooling: U.S. Mexican youth and the politics of caring.* New York: State University of New York Press.

Ward, C., Bochner, S., & Furnham, A. (2001). *The psychology of culture shock* (2nd ed.). Philadelphia: Routledge.

Winkelman, M. (2002). *Cultural shock and adaptation.* Retrieved from http://www.asu.edu/clas/shesc/projects/bajaethnography/shock.htm

CUMMINS, JAMES (1949–)

James Cummins is an internationally renowned researcher and advocate in the field of language minority education. His academic work has had a significant influence on the theoretical discourse of bilingual education and bilingualism. His professional interests include research on the acquisition of conversational and academic proficiency in a second language, the efficacy of language minority education programs, as well as social justice issues and how coercive power is wielded in international arenas. Much of Cummins's research has focused on the nature of language proficiency and second-language acquisition, with particular emphasis on the social and educational barriers that limit academic success for language minority students.

Born in Ireland on July 3, 1949, and raised there, Cummins credits his academic interests partially to growing up there in the 1950s and 1960s, when school policy reflected a desire to revitalize Gaelic, the Irish language. His book *Negotiating Identities: Education for Empowerment in a Diverse Society* reflects his dual concern with interpersonal negotiation of identity between educators and students and how this process relates to the broader operation of power relations in society.

Cummins received a PhD in educational psychology from the University of Alberta in 1974. Previously, he had been awarded a bachelor of arts degree by the National University of Ireland in 1970. He has been a professor at the Ontario Institute for Studies in Education (OISE) of the University of Toronto since 1980 and recently was appointed as a Canada Research Chair at the OISE. He is well-known for his theoretical and seminal contributions during the 1970s, including a theoretical perspective on the relationship between bilingualism and thought; the influence of bilingualism on cognitive growth; linguistic interdependence; and the educational development of bilingual children.

Cummins is perhaps best known for his having introduced the distinction between *basic interpersonal communicative skills* (BICS) and *cognitive academic language proficiency* (CALP) in order to highlight some of the challenges encountered by language minority students as they attempt to catch up to their peers in academic aspects of the school language. BICS refers to conversational fluency in a language, while CALP refers to students' ability to understand and express, in both oral and written modes, concepts and ideas that are relevant to success in school—in other words, more-academic language. His work in this arena is not without controversy. In the *Encyclopedia of Language and Education*, Cummins describes the origin, rationale, and evolution of the concept together with empirical evidence of the BICS/CALP distinction. He also responds to critiques of the BICS/CALP theory.

Cummins has studied and lectured all over the world. He delivers 12 to 15 keynote/invited plenary presentations a year and more than 40 workshops to educators on topics related to language learning, bilingual education, English as a Second Language, multicultural education, special education, technology and education, and educational reform.

In 2005, Cummins was invited to deliver the Joan Pedersen Memorial Distinguished Lecture on "Diverse Futures: Rethinking the Image of the Child in Canadian Schools." He was honored in 2000 when his 1986 paper "Empowering Minority Students: A Framework for Intervention" was selected by the *Harvard Educational Review* (HER) to appear in the *HER Classics Series*. This series consists of 12 papers published in HER between 1931 and 2000 that are recognized as having made particularly notable contributions to education. In May 1997, Cummins was awarded an honorary doctorate in humane letters from the Bank Street College of Education in New York.

Cummins has written 18 books and edited 10 others. He has published 150 book chapters and written 110 refereed journal articles, which have contributed to the impact of his work on the field of language minority education. One of his most influential publications is a volume, coauthored with

Dennis Sayers, that analyzes the educational implications of the Internet, published in September 1995 as *Brave New Schools: Challenging Cultural Illiteracy Through Global Learning Networks*. His work in *Negotiating Identities: Education for Empowerment in a Diverse Society* focuses on strategies for promoting academic development among culturally diverse students. It is widely read in university courses in the field. A second edition of this book appeared in 2001. In the same year, a collection of Cummins's most important academic papers over a 30-year period were published under the title *An Introductory Reader to the Writings of Jim Cummins,* edited by Colin Baker and Nancy Hornberger.

Kate Mahoney

See also BICS/CALP Theory; Cognitive Benefits of Bilingualism; Language and Identity; Semilingualism; Underlying Linguistic Proficiencies

Further Readings

Baker, C., & Hornberger, N. H. (2001). *An introductory reader to the writings of Jim Cummins.* Clevedon, UK: Multilingual Matters.

Cummins, J. (2000). *HER Classic Reprint: Empowering minority students: A framework for intervention.* Retrieved from http://www.hepg.org/her/abstract/98

Cummins, J. (2000). *Language, power, and pedagogy: Bilingual children in the crossfire.* Clevedon, UK: Multilingual Matters.

Cummins, J. (in press). BICS and CALP: Empirical and theoretical status of the distinction. In B. Street & N. H. Hornberger (Eds.), *Encyclopedia of language and education* (2nd ed., Vol. 2). New York: Springer Science and Business Media LLC.

Cummins, J., Brown, K., & Sayers, D. (2007). *Literacy, technology, and diversity: Teaching for success in changing times.* Boston: Allyn & Bacon.

Cummins, J., & Davison, C. (Eds.). (2007). *International handbook of English language teaching* (Vol. 1). New York: Springer-Verlag.

Cummins, J., & Sayers, D. (1995). *Brave new schools: Challenging cultural illiteracy through global learning networks.* New York: St. Martin's Press.

Schecter, S., & Cummins, J. (Eds.). (2003). *Multilingual education in practice: Using diversity as a resource.* Portsmouth, NH: Heinemann.

Deaf Bilingual Education

Deaf students are often neglected in the academic and professional discourse in the bilingual education field. In policy and practice, however, bilingual education is not limited to immigrant students whose family members speak a minority language, or to students learning a new language in addition to the majority language. There are many bilingual education programs for the deaf, and the number of such programs has been growing steadily around the world. Bilingual education for the deaf differs from other programs in a major way. The languages in a bilingual education program for the deaf include a sign language and a nonsigning language (the majority spoken language of the hearing community). For example, the two languages taught at a school for the deaf in Stockholm are Swedish Sign Language and Swedish. At another school in Fremont, California, they are American Sign Language and English.

The *modality* of language for the deaf students is different from that of other bilingual students. A sign language is a linguistic system of manual/visual, rather than vocal/aural, communication. Like any vocal language, each sign language has its own phonological, morphological, syntactic, and semantic rules. If we are able to overlook the modality for a moment, it becomes clear that bilingual programs for the deaf are like other bilingual programs. Deaf students who use a sign language can be regarded to be members of a minority language group; most of them use sign language as the primary mode of communication, yet they do study and develop skills in the majority (nonsigning) language at school. This entry describes some of the challenges and concerns in the filed of deaf bilingual education.

Bilingualism Revisited

To discuss bilingual education for deaf students, it is critical to understand language use and bilingualism, and the modalities through which a language can be expressed. The term *bilingual* can mean different things for someone deaf or hearing. Different types of modal bilingualism might include knowing the following:

- Two different signed languages
- Two different nonsigned languages
- A signed language and a nonsigned language

A person may be a proficient user of Italian Sign Language and Costa Rican Sign Language, two sign languages. Another person may know French and Chinese, two nonsigning languages. And yet another person may be able to communicate in American Sign Language and English, a sign language and a nonsigning language. These are all examples of bilingual uses; only the mode of bilingual language use of the deaf community is different from that of others. A person who knows a sign language and a nonsigned language is said to be *bimodal bilingual*.

Modality is an important and controversial issue. The modality of sign languages is sign, whereas the modes of most majority languages (Spanish, English, Russian, etc.) are speech and writing. Each language has its own range of modalities. Not all vocal languages have a written form (for example, some Amerindian languages), and even some nonsigned languages do not

213

have a vocal form. For example, many people continue to write in Latin even though no one speaks it anymore. Historically, a language that can be communicated through both spoken and written modes has the most prestige and legitimacy. Several communities have attempted corpus planning (interventions to change the form of a language) to develop a writing system for their language (e.g., Quechua in Peru) to get support for their bilingual education projects. Even some signing communities are exploring the possibilities of developing writing systems for their sign languages. In a sense, for any language to be recognized and legitimized, it is necessary to have it "usable" in both writing and speaking or signing modes, even if the language is already fully functional among the members within a community.

The modality of sign languages is often the cause of controversy in the deaf education field. Educators and policymakers have questioned the effectiveness of signing in educational programs for the deaf. Signing was not recognized as a legitimate modality for years. English professor William Stokoe has been cited as the greatest agent for change in educators' views on signing. His research work in the early 1960s on signing used by deaf Americans showed specific linguistic patterns in these people's signing. Many studies that followed provided further evidence that sign languages around the world do have their own linguistic patterns. At the same time, researchers started to explore the link between sign language and language development. The amount of evidence for the importance of sign language use in the education of the deaf has been increasing ever since. In many places, signing is now deemed an acceptable modality, and recognition is given to sign languages as full-fledged languages. Despite the recognition of sign languages as true languages and the developments in sign language and deaf education studies, however, some still challenge the claim that languages in the signing mode can be effective and useful in bilingual programs.

Bilingual Education for the Deaf

In the field of deaf education, views diverge about how two different modal languages should be addressed in language planning and practice. These views can be categorized into three areas (see Table 1). Some schools do not endorse the use of sign languages and require that the classes be conducted orally. They enact policies of "oralism," which place great emphasis on the development of speech skills and education through the language of the speaking community. Such schools usually forbid or discourage the use of sign languages at school and, in some instances, even at home. Another group of educators see value in using manual communication in classes and use some manual system of communication. (These communication systems differ from sign languages in the way they use signs, and the syntax; that is, the order of the signs in the sentence, follows the order of the majority spoken or written language.) Among examples of manual systems are Signed French, Signing Exact Italian, and Cued Speech.

A third body of educators views sign languages as separate languages to be learned and developed along with the languages of speaking communities. At bilingual schools, both the sign language and the language of the speaking community are acknowledged and viewed as equally important languages in the education of the deaf. Programs that include education of both languages can also be found at schools for hearing students who learn sign language as an additional language.

Not all programs for the deaf fall neatly in these categories, which should be seen as points on a spectrum. Some programs may have overlapping characteristics. Even within a single program, one teacher might use some manual communication but another teacher might not use any at all.

Among bilingual programs for the deaf, no two programs are alike. How the two different modal languages are used and how the teaching of these languages is planned vary from school to school. At one end, a sign language is used as a medium of instruction across the curriculum but is never taught as a subject. At the other end, some schools include sign language developmental objectives and metalinguistic analysis of both languages in their curricula. The underlying principle in all bilingual models is that a sign language is deaf children's natural and visual language; signing allows them full and immediate access to information and language itself.

Bilingual education for the deaf is still in its early stages. But since its inception in the 1970s, studies have indicated conclusive results. It helps if students have sign language skills before learning a nonsigning language; leading researchers in deaf education have shown that deaf children who have a strong foundation in a sign language are more likely to have stronger skills (reading and writing) in the nonsigning language than other deaf children do. Using a sign language as the medium of instruction in class has

Table 1 General Perspectives on the Use of Modal Languages at School

	Oralism	*Manual Systems*	*Bilingualism*
Policy Stance	Mono-modal monolingualism	Bimodal monolingualism	Bimodal bilingualism
Main Medium of Instruction	Nonsigning language	Nonsigning language with manual support	Sign language
Manual Communication	Not allowed or recognized	Recognized	Recognized and encouraged
Primary Focus	Skills (especially speaking and listening) in the language of the speaking community	Skills in the language of the speaking community	Skills in both the language of the speaking community and sign language

been shown to be conducive to development of literacy skills across the curriculum. Documented case studies also indicate improvement in nonliteracy areas. Deaf students have more self-esteem and a healthier attitude toward education in bilingual programs that acknowledge their deaf identity and support the use of a sign language. Their cognitive functions appear to be stronger if they are educated at a school that supports sign language development in addition to written language development.

Even with these important developments, challenges remain. The greatest one is the growing diversity of the student population; more immigrant students and students whose relatives do not speak the majority language are entering the school system. These students need bilingual support for development in signing and nonsigning languages, and they require assistance to deal with two nonsigned languages (the majority language and the home language). In a sense, these students have "double-bilingualism" concerns that arise from their needs as deaf communicators and as immigrants. Research progress in this area is slow but steady.

Just as it is for many other bilingual communities, language planning and policy in deaf education is affected by many different factors, including perspectives on languages, language politics, budget, number of qualified bilingual teachers, national examinations or requirements for proficiency in the majority language, and pressure from the parents or caregivers for a greater focus on the majority language. Nonetheless, bilingualism continues to be a growing field within the deaf education field.

Debra L. Cole

See also Bilingual Special Education; Brain Research; Deficit-Based Education Theory; First-Language Acquisition; Linguistics, an Overview

Further Readings

Erting, L., & Pfau, J. (1997). *Becoming bilingual: Facilitating English literacy development using ASL in preschool* [Sharing Ideas paper]. Washington, DC: Gallaudet University, Laurent Clerc National Deaf Education Center. Available from http://clerccenter.gallaudet.edu/Products/Sharing-Ideas/index.html

Maher, J. (1996). *Seeing language in sign: The work of William C. Stokoe*. Washington, DC: Gallaudet University Press.

Mashie, S. (1995). *Educating deaf children bilingually.* Washington, DC: Gallaudet University, Pre-College Programs.

Nover, S., & Andrews, J. F. (1998). *Critical pedagogy in deaf education: Bilingual methodology and staff development. Year 4 (2000–2001).* Santa Fe: New Mexico School for the Deaf.

Prinz, P. M., & Strong, M. (1998). ASL proficiency and English literacy within a bilingual deaf education model of instruction. *Topics in Language Disorders, 18*(4), 47–60.

Stokoe, W. C. (1960). *Sign language structure: An outline of the visual communication systems of the American deaf.* Studies in linguistics: Occasional papers (No. 8). Buffalo, NY: Department of Anthropology and Linguistics, University of Buffalo.

Stokoe, W. C. (1978). *Sign language structures: The first linguistic analysis of American sign language.* Silver Spring, MD: Linstok Press.

DE AVILA, EDWARD (1937–)

Edward De Avila is a developmental psychologist, researcher, and educator in the field of childhood English language development and language proficiency and educational group methods with children of diverse languages. His most notable contribution, in collaboration with Sharon Duncan, PhD, is in the measurement of English proficiency. The research by De Avila and Duncan established that the single most important variable for predicting the academic success of language minority students is linguistic proficiency. De Avila is also the former president of the Linguametrics Group and past president of De Avila, Duncan and Associates. This entry describes De Avila's contribution to bilingual assessment and education.

De Avila was born in 1937 to a Mexican-born father and a mother of Irish ancestry. When asked where he was born, his reply has always been "in a little town in Northern Mexico called Los Angeles." De Avila grew up speaking Spanish, surrounded and supported by a large extended family on his father's side. He failed to complete high school; instead, he learned to be a draftsman. At work, his supervisors saw his potential and encouraged him to go to the city college. From there, he transferred to the University of California at Berkeley, where he received his BA in 1964. He completed his MA at Colorado State and obtained his PhD from York University in Toronto, Canada, in 1973. From childhood, he confronted and dealt with issues related to language, culture, family dynamics, and educational struggles and strivings. His interest in children and his pursuit of fairness and equal access to a good education for underserved and little-understood English language learners has guided much of his research and applied work. In 1966, he developed a child-friendly Piaget-driven test titled Cartoon Conservation Scales. While at Stanford University (1974–1978) as a senior research associate and visiting associate professor, he documented in *Descubrimiento* (1987) a system he developed for learning science and that he tested in bilingual cooperative learning groups in classrooms where English language learners and Spanish language learners were learning a second language from the process of interacting with one another.

De Avila is best known for the development of the English proficiency tests titled Language Assessment Scales (LAS), published in 1975, coauthored with Duncan. These sets of tests have become the benchmark for assessing English language proficiency in public and private school systems within and outside the United States. English proficiency is distinguished from English achievement in that the former is a measure of the functional level (grade level) at which the individual is speaking English. Although linguistic proficiency and academic skills are correlated, they are distinctly different. A child's English proficiency level would inform the teacher what the child is able to understand in a mainstream classroom with children of similar age. A key element of the LAS tests is the oral portion that requires the child, or adult, to spontaneously verbalize a narrative in response to a picture. Thus, an actual sample of speech is then categorized, scored, and placed in a spectrum of English proficiency.

De Avila has ventured into other venues, such as voice-activated computer software and television programming, to bring the message that bilingualism is intrinsically a cognitive asset, and to expand the knowledge and Spanish vocabulary of children and adults alike. Those who were children or had children between 1974 and 1978 might remember *Villa Alegre,* the bilingual television series for children that broadcast more than 200 shows. De Avila was its director of research and curriculum. Many language minority groups from indigenous communities in Canada, the United States, and many South Pacific islands have benefited from De Avila's direct and applied consultations about English language education and proficiency and about the ways that traditional indigenous languages may be preserved and kept alive.

Just as important have been De Avila's lifelong efforts to influence national, state, and local policies as they relate to the scope and implementation of Title I for English language learners. He has given expert testimony before Congress, state legislatures, and boards of education in numerous states and districts. More recently, he became a consultant in a California state suit that highlights the adverse affect on Spanish-speaking children of the No Child Left Behind mandated testing requirement.

During his long career in the field of education, cognitive development, and bilingualism, De Avila has also authored and coauthored numerous articles, books, and manuals. He has been a consultant to corporate, governmental, and nongovernmental organizations within and outside the United States, specializing in language and cognition, assessment of intellectual and linguistic development, and school organization and management as it relates to child performance.

De Avila's investigations into language produced some findings addressing the effects of bilingualism. One of them was that when background variables, such as familiarity with test formats, are controlled through pre-training, many ethnolinguistic differences disappear. Another was that linguistic minority children do not constitute a monolithic, homogeneous group any more than monolingual students do. De Avila and Duncan's work established that students who are proficient in two languages tend to be cognitively advanced rather than "behind," as has often been reported in the literature. This finding challenged previous research that aimed to show the deleterious effects of bilingualism.

Marietta Saravia-Shore

See also BICS/CALP Theory; Measuring Language Proficiency

Further Readings

De Avila, E. A., & Duncan, S. E. (1990). *Language Assessment Scales.* Monterey, CA: CTB/McGraw-Hill.

De Avila, E. A., Duncan, S. E., & Navarrete, C. (1987). *Finding out/Descubrimiento.* Northvale, NJ: Santillana.

DECODING

See PHONICS IN BILINGUAL EDUCATION

DEFENSE LANGUAGE INSTITUTE

The products of military research and development activities are often found, years later, in the civilian environment. The Internet is perhaps the most famous of the many devices invented by the military for its own purposes that are now used widely in civilian life. Jonas Salk developed influenza vaccines while serving in the military. Other examples include the biodegradable detergents and fire-retardant fabrics found in many households today. This entry reviews the history of the Defense Language Institute (DLI), another military enterprise with effects on civilian

life, including bilingual education and other types of language teaching. The DLI is well known for its introduction and refinement of the audio-lingual method of language teaching, first for teaching languages to soldiers, and subsequently to children and youth in schools across the nation in the late 1950s and early 1960s.

A forerunner of the DLI was a secret school to teach the Japanese language established by the U.S. Army in 1941, before U.S. involvement in World War II. Classes in the secret school began with 4 teachers and 60 students in an abandoned airplane hangar at Crissy Field in San Francisco. The students were mostly second-generation Japanese Americans from the West Coast. During the war, the Military Intelligence Service Language School (MISLS), as it came to be called, grew dramatically. West Coast Japanese Americans were moved to internment camps in 1942, and the school moved to temporary quarters at Camp Savage, Minnesota. When the school outgrew these quarters, it moved to Fort Snelling, Minnesota.

In 1946, the school moved to the Presidio of Monterey in California. There, it was renamed the Army Language School, which expanded in 1947 and 1948 to meet cold war language training requirements. Russian became the largest language program, followed by Chinese, Korean, and German. After the Korean War (1950–1953), the Army Language School became a pacesetter with the audio-lingual method and the application of educational technology such as the language laboratory.

The National Defense Education Act of 1958 (NDEA) paved the way for the Army Language School's audio-lingual method to transition to the civilian sector, by providing funding to support language teacher training. The NDEA aimed at strengthening the national defense through educational improvement efforts in science, communications technology (e.g., audio, video, television), vocational education, and foreign languages. Summer language institutes were organized under contract with institutions of higher education. The institutes included demonstration classes with junior high and senior high school students, where teachers and learners could practice new methods.

The institutes' curricula allowed students to make measurable improvement in essential criteria for effective language teaching in the audio-lingual method's structural linguistic approach—listening, speaking, reading, writing, and conducting linguistic analysis—as well as expanding participants' knowledge of the culture of the people who speak the language natively. Institutes were also expected to instruct in the use of modern classroom methodologies and in the use of new instructional materials and mechanical and electronic devices intended to assist in developing pupils' language skills. Institute students observed demonstrations of best practices and were provided with frequent opportunities for guided classroom experience with new methods and materials.

During the 1950s, the U.S. Air Force met most of its foreign-language training requirements through contract programs with universities such as Yale, Cornell, Indiana, and Syracuse. The U.S. Navy taught languages at the Naval Intelligence School in Washington, D.C. These programs were consolidated in 1963 to form the DLI. The DLI had two branches: DLI West Coast, where the Army Language School had been, and DLI East Coast where the Naval Intelligence School had been.

During the U.S. involvement in Vietnam (1965–1973), the DLI increased its language training offerings. More than 20,000 service personnel studied Vietnamese. In the 1970s, the institute's headquarters and all resident language training were consolidated and moved to the West Coast branch, which was renamed the Defense Language Institute Foreign Language Center (DLIFLC). In 1973, the U.S. Army Training and Doctrine Command (TRADOC) took administrative control. In 1976, English language training operations were moved to the U.S. Air Force, which also operated the Defense Language Institute English Language Center (DLIELC).

After the Vietnam War, the DLIFLC became an academically accredited institution (1979); the position of academic dean was reestablished in 1981. In 1981, a joint-service general officer steering committee was established to provide advice on the foreign-language program, which is currently performed by the Defense Foreign Language Program Policy Committee.

Most recently, DLIFLC foreign-language teaching methodology has become more proficiency-oriented, using team teaching and a staffing ratio that reflects fewer students per instructor. In 1994, the DLIFLC signed an agreement with Monterey Peninsula College that permits as many as 27 credit hours earned in any of the DLIFLC's basic programs to be counted toward an associate of arts degree. This agreement is one of a number of innovations in foreign-language education that continue to draw from innovative educational technologies to train and support military linguists and to support critical national requirements for language training.

The DLIFLC now provides on-campus instruction in 23 languages and several dialects. Instruction is also provided under contractual arrangements in Washington, D.C., in more than 84 languages and dialects.

Elsie M. Szecsy

See also Audio-Lingual Method; Language Study Today; National Defense Education Act of 1958; Professional Development; Teacher Preparation, Then and Now; Technology in Language Teaching and Learning

Further Readings

Department of the Army. (1979). *Army patents*. Pamphlet 27–11. Washington, DC: Author.

Finocchiaro, M., & Weiss, D. (1963). An alternative to the NDEA Institute. *The Modern Language Journal, 47*(4), 147–149.

Flemming, A. S. (1960). The philosophy and objectives of the National Defense Education Act. *Annals of the American Academy of Political and Social Science, 327,* 132–138.

Irving, E. U. (1963). An NDEA Institute's influence in changing foreign language teaching methods. *Hispania, 46*(1), 121–124.

Ulin, R. O. (1967). What makes an NDEA Institute different? *Peabody Journal of Education, 44*(6), 357–360.

Web Sites

Defense Language Institute Foreign Language Center: http://www.dliflc.edu

DEFICIT-BASED EDUCATION THEORY

As explained by Richard Valencia, deficit-based thinking (or deficit-based pedagogy) offers a theoretical basis to account for the individual, cultural, ethnic, language, and social conditions perceived to be responsible for low academic performance in African American, Native American, Latino, Appalachian, and other underprivileged children. According to this deficit-based view, when individual students from cultural, racial, and ethnic-minority backgrounds enter school, they *lack* the self-determination, genuine interest, and knowledge-building skills to achieve academic success. The major assumption, in this view, is that children of minority ethnic or racial or of White low socioeconomic backgrounds bring into the classroom what are believed to be limited oral, social, interactional, and cognitive skills. The lack of these instrumental skills for academic success places students in an asymmetrical or unequal relationship to what Basil Bernstein considers as the more intellectually and linguistically equipped children of the middle and upper classes.

Norbert Dittmar, Jeff MacSwan, and Kellie Rolstad indicate that theories of low personal and academic achievement in impoverished children are often developed based on a stark contrast with the successful striving for academic achievement of affluent children. Based on this assertion, children who are brought up in financially insecure environments lack the necessary critical social skills, linguistic competency, and cognitive abilities. In their immediate social or family environments, they do not engage in intellectual conversations with highly educated and career-oriented adults who can pass on the necessary zeal for learning. The parents or community, through everyday socialization and labor-intensive practices, immerse students into a culture that lacks the linguistic and financial resources as well as the solid knowledge to stimulate these children intellectually and to instill in them the motivation for their academic success. Hence, so the theory holds, students are raised and socialized in deficit-based communities that allegedly hinder learning experiences, and later form a strong barrier in the school setting by not equipping students with the necessary linguistic, sociocognitive, and knowledge-building skills to succeed in school (see Valencia's work for a review of these theoretical frameworks).

Other scholars, such as William Ryan, Daniel G. Solórzano, Octavio Villalpando, Leticia Oseguera, and Valencia disagree with these views. These scholars contend that the failure of these children to succeed in school has to do with the design of school programs aimed at English-speaking middle-class students, whose parents are also educated and pass on these financial advantages, secure lifestyle, and knowledge to their children. Impoverished parents have less to pass on to their children; in school, however, their children encounter a curriculum and a school culture that has not been designed to meet their academic needs. As Ryan postulates, the deficit-based theory is sometimes regarded as an attempt to "blame the victim" of inequality, rather than to assign responsibility more broadly, especially to the designers and implementers of education policies. In this entry, the pros and cons of these arguments are reviewed in greater detail.

Underpinnings of Deficit-Based Theory

The theoretical blueprint for deficit-based thinking is what has been referred to as the cultural, racial, ethnic, socioeconomic, and linguistic inferiority of lower-class children when compared and contrasted with the cognitive skills, linguistic abilities, and academic superiority of the middle and upper classes. Thus, scholars such as William McDougall, Carl Bereiter, and Siegfried Engelmann hypothesized that multiple causal factors affect children's low achievement and test performance, including genetics, eugenics, and a learner's inherent genetic code. McDougall focuses on the notion of *eugenics,* a philosophical argument encouraging a considerable increase in selective birthrates in the intellectually "superior half" of the U.S. population because, as he believes, it is threatened by the "inferior half" or children of Black and immigrant backgrounds. Richard J. Herrnstein and Charles Murray, on the other hand, assert that intelligence is an inherent or genetically derived characteristic more prominent in White than in Latino or Black children. Further, exposure to an impoverished and counterproductive environment, ineffective parenting, and limited access to resources have been identified as some of the primary causes for students' low personal and academic success. Based on these cultural, ethnic, and class-based ideas, several prominent theoretical frameworks have been introduced within the category of deficit-based thinking.

Several scholars, including Solórzano, Villalpando, and Oseguera, maintain that the often racially segregated practices of schools should be held liable for the low school performance and standardized tests of minority students. Oscar Lewis, in contrast, turned attention to what has been termed the "culture of poverty." According to the latter, children living in impoverished conditions perceive themselves as part of a socially inferior subculture. As a result, they and their parents do not view education as a way to escape poverty and oppression. They regard themselves as being locked into conditions of despair that often go back several generations. Too often, the theory holds, the poor repeat this counterproductive behavior and pass on such beliefs and practices to future generations. Such arguments have received extensive criticism for identifying as the source of all academic failure the individual child and the cultural, social, and economic conditions that exist in that child's immediate family or community. In essence, Ryan states, "blaming the victim" for the socioeconomic circumstances of the allegedly deficit-based culture or discourse community in which that child is brought up does not eliminate oppressive or discriminatory school practices. To the contrary, it helps perpetuate a socially and racially structured system.

Portraying a child's learning experiences within the immediate or extended community as deficient or inferior has further and more instrumental implications. Consider, for example, that children's language is often treated as incorrect, restricted, more limited, and socially stigmatized. An "atypical" verbal repertoire or accent has led observers to assume that children possess limited developmental, cognitive, and linguistic skills required to engage in stimulating and knowledge-building conversations and to succeed later on in college and in adult life. The immediate family of the children, especially the parents, is also held responsible for not creating environments that scaffold children's intellectual growth or stimulate their cognitive development early on. The assertion that the parents' financial constraints and their inability to cultivate the value of reading, technology, moral values, and an enriched linguistic system are also considered as deterring factors to students' achievement.

A substantial body of work, including that of Walter Miller and Daniel Moynihan, on this potentially intellectually deprived environment focused on African Americans, their perceived deficient linguistic and socialization system, their inability to move out of the ghetto, and their tendency to settle for a marginalized lifestyle. In the 1950s, 1960s, and 1970s, for example, some scholars, such as Miller, claimed that African American children exposed to poverty were immersed in a culture that promoted gang-related activities and formed a threat to the mainstream middle-class culture (see work by Arthur Pearl). Interestingly, in many cases, African American vernacular—what society or educators often perceive as aggressive, violent, and restricted discourse (the development of limited verbal knowledge)—was used as evidence to support African American children's tendency for violence, immoral, unethical, and often criminal behavior, which clashed

with the autonomous and verbally intelligent middle or upper class.

This notion of restricted discourse was particularly important because it was often perceived as a precursor for underprivileged students' low scores on verbal IQ and standardized tests, and for the development of curricula and lesson plans to enhance linguistic competence among the so-called *linguistically deprived* children. Such approaches, however, often encouraged the use of teacher-guided but unchallenging and not carefully scaffolded language activities because Black children were perceived as intellectually and academically deprived. The same line of thought also asserted that, before school, low-socioeconomic-background children had experienced limited verbal stimulation in their environments (see work by Bereiter and Engelmann). Studies conducted in this area by Bereiter, Engelmann, Jean Osborn, and Philip Reidford also claimed that 4-year-old children from an African American background did not develop the required linguistic competence to construct syntactically correct phrases or questions. In some cases, such deficit-based approaches were reinforced by considering teachers in school districts with underprivileged and low-performing students as relying on ineffective teaching approaches. Hence, the path to the enculturation of disadvantaged children into a verbally stimulating and rich discourse, often perceived as the key to academic success, was to propose new curricula or educational programs. For example, as Pearl notes, the federally supported Head Start program of 1965 and its school-based counterpart, Title I of the Elementary and Secondary Education Act, aimed, among other things, to increase funding allocated for enhancing the linguistic competency of lower-socioeconomic-status students. In short, these programs assumed that, to prepare disadvantaged youngsters for school success, they must be changed radically to compensate for the lack of a linguistically and culturally enhanced learning environment.

The limited nature and range of opportunities these children would otherwise enjoy was not the only framework guiding deficit-based ideologies; the inherent interlink between the biological-environmental factors influencing IQ tests also formed the theoretical tenets of many scholarly discussions and studies. In 1969, for example, a prominent educational psychologist, Arthur Jensen, proposed genetic factors as an underlying reason for the lower IQ scores of children of Black or lower-socioeconomic origin compared with their White peers' IQ scores. Along with this reliance on hereditary predispositions, various peda-gogical approaches were introduced. Consider, for example, the "Level I and Level II theory" in which Jensen proposed immersing lower-class White and Black children into instructional material to expose them to simple and rather rote recall strategies and techniques, or what is termed as Level I. On the other hand, Level II required more complex and abstract cognitive skills that, according to this approach, Black children showed little evidence of possessing. After this genetically related approach, several scholarly interpretations followed, including the 1987 published review of IQ intelligence in children of Mexican American or Puerto Rican descent (see work by Lloyd M. Dunn). Interestingly, the report concluded that both the environment and Mexican American or Puerto Rican students' cognitive genetic predisposition needed to be examined because they both played instrumental roles in students' lower performance.

Within this genetically oriented deficit hypothesis, Herrnstein and Murray's highly publicized and politi-cized *Bell Curve* drew attention to the "cognitive elite" or that part of the population with high intellectual competency, who were also believed to display exem-plary IQ performance and socioeconomic success. Within this hierarchy, then, for the remaining popula-tion, low IQ performance and limited cognitive skills pointed to students' inept academic endeavors and unsuccessful strivings for future success. Immigrants, African Americans, and generally individuals occupy-ing the lowest tiers of this income-determined and socially determined hierarchy were also deemed to have lower intellectual abilities, IQ scores, and, conse-quently, limited potential for socioeconomic or profes-sional achievement.

Beyond Deficit-Based Thinking

Crafting a genetically oriented stance diverted atten-tion to *deficiencies* in genetic predispositions, but Henry Garrett indicated that the focus should hinge on further exploring the *differences* between genetic, intellectual, sociocultural, and linguistic values in minority, African American, and immigrant students. The unquestionably high rate of minority and African American students encouraged to attend remedial educational or special-needs programs led scholars to propose a comparative pedagogical approach that acknowledges such differences or what is termed as "cultural-relevant pedagogy" (see work by

Tyrone C. Howard). Traditionally, educators relied on instructional practices based on mainstream ideologies or on a rather restricted approach to what constitutes performance and academic achievement. However, educators needed to expand such practices to take into consideration a much broader and polydimensional approach to what constitutes culture, ethnicity, and race, and how these influence language, identity, and school performance. Solórzano, illalpando, and Oseguera hold that it is unorthodox to expect a considerable improvement in the academic success or the number of ethnic minority and Black students attending 4-year colleges and graduate schools, unless educators develop broader notions of cultural, ethnicity, linguis-tic, and racial factors and their critical role in shaping a student's identity. Further, these scholars note that adapting "race-conscious" practices might also require a close reconsideration of admission policies and measures in 4-year colleges, such as the culturally and racially biased standardized exams that discourage ethnic minority and Black students from attending 4-year colleges. Such views, however, were highly criticized as conservative-driven ideologies, which capitalize on ethnic and racial differences but do not provide a solid practical approach or policy regarding how to overcome the low attendance rate of ethnic minority/race students in 4-year colleges.

The prospect of such deficit-oriented dynamics continuing to play a prominent role in instructional practices, especially with the large increases in immi-grant students in the United States, is unfortunate. Howard indicates that a fruitful alternative is to immerse students into "culturally relevant pedagogy"—in essence, formulating instructional material and reflec-tive activities where the object of study is not based on abstract theoretical contexts but on relevant, culturally valuable, and effective linguistic practices. Teachers must acknowledge the heterogeneity in cultural, eth-nic, racial, linguistic, and social values of the students in each classroom. Further, through constant critical evaluations, constant interactions with children's culture, and modifications of their practices, teachers should treat culture, race, and ethnicity as an inherent part of their students' competencies; such competen-cies can form powerful constructs for future academic success.

Some scholars go even further to suggest practices, such as using the students' cultural repertoire and transformative teaching that promotes high levels of teacher-family-community relationships through frequent interactions with students' home, immediate social, and community environments. Norma González, Luis Moll, and Cathy Amanti of the University of Arizona have proposed a culturally centered ethnographic program, also known as *funds of knowledge.* Instead of relying on students' performance in the classroom, teachers experienced how the child-parent and other community interactions formed a powerful source for how students cooperatively built their practical, cultural, and interactional funds of knowledge.

Observations of these sociocultural dynamics, such as the interactions, negotiation of values, reinforcement of interrelations, and children's cultural and individual experiences, help teachers gain a deeper and more conceptual understanding of students' cultural values and everyday struggles. More important, experiencing the individual and socioeconomic conditions of each family, as well as their interactional dynamics, helped teachers establish the connection between instructional material and culture. Through culturally sensitive approaches, teachers valued students' culture, and no longer treated it as an inherent liability to students' success. Teachers' outreach ventures transformed their personal perceptions of culture and students' learning experiences through more culture-driven material. Such approaches are difficult to incorporate into traditional patterns of school organization and curriculum models in wide use, but the promise they hold for bringing about genuine change in the way schools think of their students is great.

Stella K. Hadjistassou

See also Cultural Deficit and Cultural Mismatch Theories; Culturally Competent Teaching; Multicultural Education; Transformative Teaching Model

Further Readings

Bereiter, C., & Engelmann, S. (1966). *Teaching disadvantaged children in the preschool.* Englewood Cliffs, NJ: Prentice Hall.

Bereiter, C., Engelmann, S., Osborn, J., & Reidford, P. A (1966). An academically oriented preschool for culturally disadvantaged children. In F. M. Hechinger (Ed.), *Pre-school education today* (pp. 105–135). New York: Doubleday.

Bernstein, B. (1970). A sociolinguistic approach to socialization with some reference to educability. In F. Williams (Ed.), *Language and poverty* (pp. 25–61). Chicago: Markham Press.

Dittmar, N. (1976). *A critical survey of sociolinguistics: Theory and application.* New York: St. Martin's Press.

Dunn, L. M. (1987). *Bilingual Hispanic children on the U.S. mainland: A review of research on their cognitive, linguistic and scholastic development.* Circle Pines, MN: American Guidance Service.

Garrett, H. (1973). IQ and racial differences [pamphlet]. Cape Canaveral, FL: Howard Allen.

González, N., Moll, L., & Amanti, C. (Eds.). (2005). *Funds of knowledge: Theorizing practice in households, communities, and classrooms.* Mahwah, NJ: Lawrence Erlbaum.

Herrnstein, R., & Murray, C. (1994). *The bell curve: Intelligence and class structure in American life.* New York: Free Press.

Howard, T. C. (2003). Culturally-relevant pedagogy: Ingredients for critical teacher reflection. *Theory into Practice, 42*(3), 195–202.

Jensen, A. (1969). How much can we boost IQ and scholastic achievement? *Harvard Educational Review, 39,* 1–23.

Lewis, O. (1959). *Five families: Mexican case studies in the culture of poverty.* New York: Basic Books.

MacSwan, J., & Rolstad, K. (2006). How language proficiency tests mislead us about ability: Implications for English language learner placement in special education. *Teachers College Record, 108*(11), 2304–2328.

McDougall, W. (1921). *Is America safe for democracy?* New York: Scribner's.

Miller, W. (1958). Lower class culture as a generating milieu of gang delinquency. *Journal of Social Issues, 14,* 5–19.

Moynihan, D. (1965). *The Negro family: The case for national action.* Washington, DC: U.S. Government Printing Office.

Pearl, A. (1991). Systemic and institutional factors in Chicano school failure. In R. Valencia (Ed.), *Chicano school failure and success: Research and policy agendas for the 1990s* (pp. 273–320). London: Falmer.

Pearl, A. (1997). Cultural and accumulated environmental deficit models. In R. Valencia (Ed.), *The evolution of deficit thinking* (pp. 132–159). Washington, DC: Falmer.

Ryan, W. (1976). *Blaming the victim.* New York: Vintage Books.

Solórzano, D., Villalpando, O., & Oseguera, L. (2005). Educational inequities and Latina/o undergraduate students in the United States: A critical race analysis of their educational progress. *Journal of Hispanic Higher Education, 4*(3), 272–294.

Valencia, R. (Ed.). (1997). *The evolution of deficit thinking.* Washington, DC: Falmer.

Valencia, R., & Solórzano, D. (1997). Contemporary deficit thinking. In R. Valencia (Ed.), *The evolution of deficit thinking* (pp. 160–210). Washington, DC: Falmer.

DESIGNATION AND REDESIGNATION OF ENGLISH LANGUAGE LEARNERS

For the past 40 years, educators have used a categorical scheme to label linguistically and culturally diverse students through their years of schooling. Typically, though not uniformly, a three-part system has been institutionalized by states and school districts; namely, those students who (1) are non-English proficient, thus considered English language learners (ELLs), who qualify for language support services; (2) have changed their status to redesignated English language learners, once having attained English language proficiency; or (3) have been deemed English proficient, upon initial entry into a school district, and are able to participate in general education classes without language support.

Table 1 shows the relationships between these categories.

This designation system, intended to assist educators in the allocation and provision of appropriate educational services for linguistically and culturally diverse students, has been fraught with controversy. Issues include its fairness and equity, the fear that students are being denied opportunities to learn, erratic funding formulae for language support services, and the design and implementation of best practices. This entry describes the criteria associated with each of the categories, and data used in the decision-making process. The reader is cautioned that from district to

Table 1 Identifying and Redesignating English Language Learners in Illinois, Pre– and Post–No Child Left Behind (NCLB)

	Identifying English language learners	Redesignating English language learners: Monitoring annual progress	Redesignating English language learners as language minority students
Required Measures **Pre–NCLB**	Home Language Survey	Nationally norm-referenced language proficiency tool in English, grade levels K–12 (L, S, R, W)	50th percentile on a nationally norm-referenced English language proficiency test
	Nationally norm-referenced language proficiency tool in English, grade levels K–12 (L, S, R, W)	*Illinois Measure of Annual Growth in English* (IMAGE-grades 3–11; R, W), the state's English language proficiency test	
Required Measures **Post–NCLB**	Home Language Survey	*Assessing Comprehension and Communication in English State to State for English Language Learners* (ACCESS for ELLs®, grade levels K–12), the state's English language proficiency test	Composite score of English language proficiency level 4, Expanding, on ACCESS for ELLs
	WIDA-ACCESS Placement Test (W-APT), grade levels K–12 (L, S, R, W)	*Illinois Measure of Annual Growth in English* (IMAGE-grades 3–11), the state's test of academic achievement for English language learners	

district and state to state, these descriptions may vary slightly.

Eligibility Requirements for Special Services: Identifying ELLs

Historically, a national consensus has never been reached regarding the definition of *English language learners* or the counterpart legal term, *limited-English-proficient* students. The 2001 reauthorization of the Elementary and Secondary Education Act, commonly known as the No Child Left Behind Act, provides broad guidelines toward reaching a common understanding: ELLs are elementary or secondary school students, aged 3 through 21, not born in the United States or whose native language is other than English. According to Part A, Section 9101 of the act, these students' non-English home environment has significantly affected their level of English language proficiency so that their speaking, reading, writing, or understanding of English may affect "their ability to meet the State's proficient level of achievement on State assessments, or ability to successfully achieve in classrooms where the language of instruction is English."

These general descriptive criteria, provided at a federal level, produce many different interpretations across states and the outer territories of the United States. These variations in defining ELLs can be attributed to many factors. Such differences emanate from the following factors: (a) use of various language proficiency instruments, (b) the varied cut-scores of these measures, (c) state expectations of student progress and attainment of English language proficiency, (d) the amount of time (in years) allowed for language support, and (e) the financial backing states are willing to bear.

The identification of ELLs has always been within the purview of individual states. States, in turn, have frequently given latitude to school districts in the selection of instruments and criteria for determining the subset of linguistically and culturally diverse students to be classified as English language learners. In general, neither states nor districts have tended to use multiple measures to make these critical decisions.

Many districts have had flexibility in the design of Home Language Surveys. These quick screening devices, generally attached to registration forms upon students' entry into a school district, consist of a series of questions. Their purpose is to distinguish between students from linguistically and culturally diverse backgrounds and students who have never been exposed to another language or culture outside of English. Typically, family members are asked (in their native language) questions such as "Is there language other than English spoken at home?" and "Does your child speak this language?" An answer in the affirmative to either question labels a student as linguistically and culturally diverse, and hence, triggers a round of language proficiency assessments.

Before 2003, most states allowed school districts the freedom to select one of several measures of English language proficiency to ascertain which linguistically and culturally diverse students qualified as ELLs. Illinois, for example, offered a choice of four different instruments; Wisconsin, its neighbor to the north, offered a different set of four measures. However, identification and placement of ELLs has often rested on a scale created by a single instrument. A two-tiered framework that included diagnostic information useful for instruction, such as a student's literacy level, and academic achievement data, such as performance in the student's native language, were rarely implemented.

This discretionary policy resulted in huge variability in the designation/redesignation assignment of students across states and between school districts. Lack of uniform criteria for identification created discontinuity of services for this often-mobile population of students. Hypothetically, a linguistically and culturally diverse student may be considered English proficient in one district, but then move to a neighboring town and be classified as an English language learner. Additionally, the types of language support services afforded this student may also vary greatly.

The provisions of No Child Left Behind have alleviated this dilemma, to some extent; states must now administer a single English language proficiency instrument for federal accountability purposes. Even so, there remains a huge disparity from state to state in the identification of linguistically and culturally diverse students and its subgroup of ELLs. Within a specific state or school district, teacher inconsistency in scoring screening measures, particularly the productive language domains of speaking and writing, may contribute to unreliable placement decisions. Once identified and placed in a language education program, redesignation of English language learners may then rely on a different set of criteria.

Moving Along the Continuum: Redesignating ELLs

Redesignation or reclassification applies to two different situations. The first refers to ELLs' movement along the second-language acquisition continuum to a specified milestone or benchmark. This internal index corresponds to students' annual progress on their state English language proficiency test(s). Programmatically, this redesignation, attributed to students' increased English language proficiency, may result in a shift in instructional emphasis or type of language support. For example, students may no longer qualify as newcomers, or students in transitional bilingual education programs may witness the lessening of native-language support, whereas other ELLs may be introduced to specific sheltered content classes.

The second use of the term *redesignation* refers to ELLs' full attainment of English language proficiency, indicating that they have reached the threshold that ensures their meaningful participation in general education classes. Again, this criterion is often set by the state's English language proficiency test (among other factors or measures). By being "exited" from language support services, the students officially drop their designation of English language learners and assume (or resume) their language minority status. Interestingly, these two widely practiced uses of the term *redesignation* correspond to two of the three federal accountability criteria for ELLs outlined in Title III of the No Child Left Behind Act.

The issue of redesignation is as thorny as initial identification, partly because it is an expedient way to classify and sort students. Often only one data source—the state English language proficiency measure—is responsible for this determination. Few states demand the review of academic achievement data as part of their redesignation formula. California, with by far the largest population of ELLs, is one of the exceptions.

ELLs are a temporary and fluid disaggregated subgroup of students, so expectations for accountability that are not feasible for them have been set. This dilemma is compounded by states taking differing perspectives on the collection, reporting, and use of information on the students' English language proficiency and academic achievement. Educators of ELLs generally agree that today, redesignation should be based on both English language proficiency data and solid academic performance, using large-scale and classroom-based measures for both. This triangulation of data lends predictive validity and justification for shifting ELLs to the redesignation category (from *A* to *B* in Table 1). Relying on an assessment system composed of multiple data sources, multiple levels of implementation, and collected at multiple points in time lends more credibility, comprehensiveness, and confidence in data-driven decisions.

Ensuring Academic Success of ELLs

Some linguistically and culturally diverse students enter school having competently developed two or more languages. Others may have been raised with English as their primary language, such as heritage language learners. Still, other students may have been redesignated ELLs from prior years. Whatever the case, substantial numbers of students who are exposed to and may interact in a multitude of languages and cultures on a regular basis do not qualify for language support services.

Although these language minority students may exhibit English language proficiency comparable with that of native English speakers at some point, this does not preclude them from eligibility for programs of language support or home language development during the rest of their school careers. This often-itinerant student population, coupled with the ambiguity of requirements for language education programs, leads to inconsistency in the designation and redesignation process. For example, linguistically and culturally diverse students who are deemed proficient by one measure or set of criteria may be classified as ELLs when they move to another state that uses other instruments and criteria for designation purposes. In addition, it is difficult to predict the destiny of young language minority students whose literacy is not fully developed; although orally proficient in English, without strong academic language, they may struggle with increased content demands at higher grade levels.

Given the possible reauthorization of the No Child Left Behind Act at some point, Michael Kieffer, Nonie Lesaux, and Catherine Snow from the Harvard Graduate School of Education have proposed that accountability for the current subgroup of ELLs be expanded to encompass all linguistically and culturally diverse students (that is, to extend membership in the subgroup from *A* to *C* in Table 1). If so, the education community will no longer have to rely on the arbitrary demarcations that come with the designation and redesignation procedures in use today. Additionally, it will be possible to obtain a richer, more comprehensive picture of the students' range of performance. If that occurs, educators can concentrate their efforts on maximizing the language development and academic achievement of linguistically and culturally diverse students, and feel more confident that these students have been properly identified.

Margo Gottlieb

See also English Immersion; Measuring Language Proficiency; No Child Left Behind Act of 2001, Testing Requirements; Proficiency, Fluency, and Mastery

Further Readings

August, D., & Hakuta, K. (Eds.). (1997). *Improving schooling for language minority children: A research agenda.* Washington, DC: National Academy Press.

Gottlieb, M., & Nguyen, D. (2007). *Assessment and accountability in language education programs: A guide for teachers and administrators.* Philadelphia: Caslon.

Kieffer, M., Lesaux, N., & Snow, C. (2006, November). *Promises and pitfalls: Implications of No Child Left Behind for defining, assessing, and serving English language learners.* Paper presented at Measurement and Accountability Roundtable, Washington, DC.

Ragan, A., & Lesaux, N. (2006). Federal, state, and district level English language learner program entry and exit requirements: Effects on the education of language minority students. *Education Policy Analysis Archives, 14*(20). Retrieved from http://epaa.asu.edu/epaa/v14n20

DIGLOSSIA

See SOCIAL BILINGUALISM

DISCOURSE ANALYSIS

Discourse analysis is concerned with the study of language use beyond the boundaries of the sentence. The term refers to analysis of larger linguistic units such as conversations or written texts, and most discourse analysts ultimately aim to understand the relationship between language and society. The scope of discourse analysis is vast, drawing on a variety of disciplines and encompassing an array of perspectives. Within bilingual education, researchers generally have taken a sociocultural approach to analysis, building largely on the work of Dell Hymes, who pioneered the field known as the ethnography of communication. In the 1970s, several foundational volumes were published elaborating this approach, which argues that language must be studied as communication in its sociocultural context. In 1972, Hymes collaborated with John Gumperz to edit *Directions in Sociolinguistics;* in the same year, with Courtney Cazden and Vera John, Hymes proposed how this approach could be applied to classroom research in *Functions of Language in the Classroom.* In 1974, he addressed the importance of using the approach as a basis to study bilingual education in *Foundations in Sociolinguistics.* The contributions of Gumperz provide another sociocultural dimension by focusing on people's interpretation processes within discourse. His *Discourse Strategies* and *Language and Social Identity,* both published in 1982, are important to those interested in bilingual education because of the focus on interethnic discourse in various contexts. Gumperz and colleagues show that people's miscommunication can occur because of differences in communicative styles.

Researchers in bilingual education who take an ethnographic approach to discourse analysis argue that it contributes to a more fully satisfactory portrait of communicative practices in communities and classrooms where two or more languages are at play. With the increasing numbers of immigrant children entering the nation's schools, analysis of classroom discourse offers detailed descriptions of these students and their teachers engaging in learning moments sometimes effectively, sometimes inadequately, and always in a complex world of social interaction. This research approach has begun to make classroom communication, in all its complexity, better understood. Topics examined include the kinds of specialized "discourses" students must learn in school to attain academic achievement, the different communicative styles children bring from home to school, language choice in bilingual classroom situations, and the nature of communication in "mainstream" and English as a Second Language (ESL) classrooms. Beyond these descriptive analyses, researchers are also interested in the role of power in discourse. This entry focuses on studies of discourse in classrooms that include language minority students.

"Discourses" Circulating in and Through Classrooms

James Gee provides an overarching perspective on the variety of discourses that affect classrooms and argues that these discourses are associated with specific sets of values and beliefs. He makes distinctions among various discourses: Primary discourses are learned in the home (and, in the case of language minority children, in a different code), whereas secondary discourses are learned outside the home in school and elsewhere. Students must learn to work within specific secondary discourses at school for their academic performance to be considered successful. For example, as Cazden, Hugh Mehan, and others have shown, one classroom discourse structure is different from ordinary conversational structure: The teacher initiates, the student responds, and the teacher evaluates the response. This tripartite structure gives teachers control of the right to speak and to decide which students may participate, how they participate, and when. This significantly affects students who are learning through the medium of a second language; they are doubly constrained because of their limited opportunities to engage with the subject matter and their few occasions to practice speaking the target language. Research demonstrates that opening up classroom discourse structures gives students more opportunities to engage the subject matter and with one another. A shift in participation structure to student-centered, peer collaboration on learning tasks can give rise to productive discourse leading to academic achievement.

Home Versus School Discourses

When students from diverse sociocultural backgrounds engage in primary discourse practices and other forms of knowledge that do not resonate with school discourse patterns, teachers may not recognize or accept these practices as equally valuable. Effective educators design their teaching by considering what Luis Moll, Cathy Amanti, and Norma González call "funds of knowledge" that students possess. Several studies illustrate the diverse discursive resources brought into the classroom. Susan Philips's classic volume, *The Invisible Culture,* about discourse practices on the Warm Springs Indian reservation in Oregon, showed that Indian children learn discourse participation structures at home that are different from the participation structures in the school, resulting in Anglo teachers' misinterpretation of the children's turn-taking behaviors and other ways of speaking. Shirley Brice Heath demonstrated how primary discourses sometimes clash with school discourses in her ethnography of communication, *Ways With Words,* which described the home-school relationship of three speech communities in the Piedmont Carolinas.

Studies such as these prompted educational researchers to describe students' home discourse patterns to recommend improved learning opportunities (sometimes called *positive transfer*) in the classroom. For example, researchers at the Chèche Konnen Center in Massachusetts found that native speakers of Haitian Creole use certain discursive practices that are culturally congruent with the discourse of argumentation in science, thus demonstrating how the home language can be a resource for learning rather than an impediment, as is often assumed. In a similar vein, the Kamehameha Early Education Program (KEEP), a research center established to meet the needs of native Hawaiian children, has paid particular attention to children's reading development. The researchers demonstrated that these students' reading improves when the participation structure of reading lessons maintains a close fit with the discourse of talk-story, part of the Hawaiian storytelling practice. These and similar studies show that teachers can effectively draw on funds of knowledge to guide students in developing a discourse to talk about subject matter areas and about literacy.

Two Languages, One Classroom

Bilingual classrooms have been productive sites for analyzing how two languages are used to help students learn. The earliest research focused on how the two languages of instruction were allocated within the various bilingual education program models. However, discourse analysts argued that it was not enough simply to document the amount of time spent on each language; rather, the purposes for which each language was used significantly affected students' academic achievement. Thus, a major focus has been on understanding language choices in the classroom, particularly the functions of language alternation or code switching. Code switching has been one of the most prolific areas of research in bilingualism and has laid the foundation for bilingual classroom discourse studies, providing insights that are particularly important for bilingual educators. Code switching can be defined as the use of two languages within the same interaction to convey social meaning. Researchers have found that fluent bilinguals who use their two languages in this way can do so seamlessly and thereby expand their overall communicative competence. Contrary to popular belief, it is a skill that fluent bilinguals have, not a "crutch" used to make up for lack of language proficiency. Code-switching choices depend on who is participating, the topic addressed, and the social situation. Children raised bilingually develop the ability to code-switch appropriately, showing more sophisticated uses of this skill as they grow older. Ana Celia Zentella's *Growing up Bilingual* is a synthesis of two decades of the study of Puerto Rican code-switching practices in community and classroom. She found that young people code-switch for a wide variety of stylistic purposes such as choosing an expression in the language that conveys an idea more accurately.

Zentella's and others' research supports code switching in classrooms as a viable way of facilitating learning. If learning is "change of knowledge"—moving from what is already known to something new—then the learner's already-known first language is a good starting point. Teachers who are bilingual switch to the students' mother tongue as a scaffolding strategy to guide students into learning subject matter and into English language and literacy. Teachers provide procedural information, especially in content learning, to clarify or elaborate on a concept. Research has also shown the benefit of code switching in peer interaction in classrooms. As children advance their bilingual communicative competence, they become able to switch languages appropriately, deploying both languages for effective classroom communication. Peers involved in school tasks switch codes to clarify ideas, ask questions, change topics, or underscore directives. Research further shows that, in cooperative learning situations, language minority students use code switching (in addition to the discourse strategies that native-speakers of English use) while they work together to learn something new.

When the Language Game Is English

Discourse analysts have followed language minority students into ESL and "mainstream" classrooms to observe their learning experiences and have found that students use several strategies to make sense of what is happening while their English competence is still developing. Students with little or no English make use of "school scripts" for predictable, routinized classroom activities to make sense of the communication. From infancy, all children develop, as part of their set of primary discourses, frames for interpretation that are continually (re)constructed through interaction. They gain a sense of what is happening around them in recurrent events like getting dressed, taking a bath, and preparing for bed; they acquire their first language in the context of these routinized activities and then add to their repertoire of scripts when they go to school. Students draw on interpretive frames learned in the native language to interpret "what is happening" in recurrent events in the English-medium classroom. For example, language minority students in the early grades are able to figure out the structure of lessons, the rules for turn-taking in instructional interaction, and expectations for behavior, even if they don't completely understand the verbal exchange.

Another strategy students apply is the use of their native language to support learning in English-medium environments. Students who speak the same mother tongue confer among one another to check for understanding of what is being said in English. Individually, they use self-directed speech to practice the concepts presented to them in English. When called upon, preschool children have been observed to "answer" in the native language, with the teacher providing feedback in English even without discerning their words. Skilled ESL and mainstream teachers develop strategies of their own to communicate with language minority students. While the students are developing their school discourses in English, teachers accommodate their language to students' different levels of understanding, and teachers adjust their talk as students' English competence increases.

These findings illustrate ways in which participants make meaning in mainstream and ESL classrooms. However, recent English-only policies for classrooms have resulted in diminished use of the native language for scaffolding learning. Guadalupe Valdés demonstrates in *Learning and Not Learning English* that, under these English-only policies, academic discourse in ESL instruction for immigrant secondary school students does not prepare them adequately for further academic work. Other research confirms the negative consequences of such a policy: Students in these classrooms avoid English to avoid failure and embarrassment. Thus, little English is produced even though the same students speak to one another in English outside the classroom. Valdés and others have shown that, when the curriculum is prescriptive and restrictive, it is difficult for teachers to incorporate spaces for language minority students' learning.

Language, Power, and Critical Discourse Analysis

Recently, a few bilingual discourse studies have progressed beyond description toward highlighting power-wielding in classroom discourse—detecting what counts as legitimate language, who maintains control, whose language becomes marginalized, and how power relations are tested and contested. This critical focus reflects the move to analyze discourse within a broader framework of social theory. In studies of discourse and power in schools, scholars have shown how, through interaction between teachers/ counselors and students/parents, decisions are made based on locating problems within individual students, thus further marginalizing language minorities. Fredrick Erickson and Jeffrey Shultz's 1982 *The Counselor as Gatekeeper* was a precursor of Critical Discourse Analysis (CDA). Their fine-grained analysis of social interaction showed students and counselors accomplishing placement decisions through discourse, which favored some students over those less powerful.

Power relations can be reflected in the fact that languages do not have the same symbolic value within schools. School personnel, by their position of authority, possess what Pierre Bourdieu calls the "legitimate language," which puts constraints on what others may say, to whom, how, and under which circumstances. In classrooms, the home language is used to accomplish social functions such as disciplining students, whereas English is the language of academic content, assessment, and authority. Similarly, different dialects (varieties) of the home language are positioned as relatively lower in prestige and value: In Canada, Monica Heller demonstrates that judgments are not just about French versus English but which varieties of French (and their speakers) are considered valuable. Other studies show how students resist policies through discourse, refusing to speak the target language or contesting placement decisions. Still others show uses of discourse to open possibilities for change from positions of subordination to power, such as students' use of translation to reveal their competency as learners. More attention to CDA studies that demonstrate possibilities for change can expand the field productively and contribute to an equitable education for language minority students.

Jo Anne Kleifgen

See also Classroom Discourse; Code Switching; Languages and Power

Further Readings

Bourdieu, P. (1977). The economics of linguistic exchanges. *Social Science Information, 16,* 645–668.

Cazden, C., John, V. & Hymes, D. (Eds.). (1972). *Functions of language in the classroom.* New York: Teachers College Press.

Erickson, F., & Shultz, J. (1982). *The counselor as gatekeeper.* New York: Academic Press.

Gee, J. P. (1996). *Social linguistics and literacies.* London: Taylor & Francis.

Gumperz, J. (1982). *Discourse strategies.* Cambridge, UK: Cambridge University Press.

Gumperz, J. (Ed.). (1982). *Language and social identity.* Cambridge, UK: Cambridge University Press.

Gumperz, J., & Hymes, D. (Eds.). (1972). *Directions in sociolinguistics.* New York: Holt, Rinehart and Winston.

Heath, S. B. (1983). *Ways with words.* Cambridge, UK: Cambridge University Press.

Heller, M. (1996). Legitimate language in a multilingual school. *Linguistics and Education, 8,* 139–157.

Hymes, D. (1974). *Foundations in sociolinguistics.* Philadelphia: University of Pennsylvania Press.

Mehan, H. (1979). *Learning lessons: Social organization in the classroom.* Cambridge, MA: Harvard University Press.

Moll, L., Amanti, C., & González, N. (1992). Funds of knowledge for teaching: Using a qualitative approach to connect homes and classrooms. *Theory Into Practice, 31*(2), 132–141.

Philips, S. (1983). *The invisible culture.* Prospect Heights, IL: Waveland.

Valdés, G. (2001). *Learning and not learning English.* New York: Teachers College Press.

Zentella, A. C. (1997). *Growing up bilingual.* Malden, MA: Blackwell.

DUAL-LANGUAGE PROGRAMS

Dual-language programs, also known as two-way immersion programs, were developed on the basis of research by Wallace Lambert and Richard Tucker on French-English dual-language schools in Canada in the 1970s. Much success in achievement and positive attitudes toward out-group language speakers were reported from the Canadian programs for both the Anglophones (English speakers) and Francophones (French speakers) in the schools.

The first dual-language programs were developed and implemented in the United States in 1963. By 1981, fewer than 10 dual-language programs had been documented, but they grew to about 30 in the mid-1980s.

Since then, the number of programs grew to 248 by 2000, and 338 programs were operating in 29 states and Washington, D.C., by 2006. This entry describes dual-languages programs and some of the issues relating to these programs.

Key Features and Goals

According to Elizabeth Howard and Julie Sugarman's 2001 report, three features distinguish dual-language programs: (1) Language majority and language minority students are taught together for at least half of the school day; (2) both groups of students are provided both literacy and content instruction in both languages; and (3) language majority and language minority students are roughly balanced, with each group composing at least one third of the student population.

The major goals of dual-language programs are bilingualism, biliteracy, and cross-cultural awareness. Indicators of successfully attaining these goals include high proficiency in the first and second languages for both groups of students, academic achievement as indicated by grade level or higher performance for both groups of students, and positive attitudes and behaviors about other cultures.

Geographic, Language, and Student Representation

Most dual-language programs are located in California (108 programs), Texas (57 programs), and New York (28), as reported by the Center for Applied Linguistics (CAL) in 2006. Most of these programs are operated by public schools, with about a quarter of them in place at magnet and charter schools. A little over 12% of the programs are schoolwide, but the majority of the programs (nearly three quarters of the elementary programs) and all of the secondary programs are programs within schools.

Most dual-language programs are Spanish/English, with a few each in French/English, Korean/English, Japanese/English, Navajo/English, and Chinese/English. In the past, Portuguese/English and Japanese/English programs have also been in operation. A small percentage of students (as much as 5%) in about 40 programs are native speakers of a language other than the two used in the program in which they are enrolled.

On average, about half of all dual-language programs have language majority speakers comprising a mixture of ethnic backgrounds including larger groups of White and Latino students (between 10% and 20%). African American, Asian, and Native American students are generally 1–2% of the program population, reflecting proportions of the general demography in the country and in the schools for Asian and Native American students, but proportions far lower than the at-large figures for African American students. Program participants in California and New York show a distribution of various ethnic groups rather than the presence of one or two major ethnic groups, whereas Texas has a higher number of programs with a clear ethnic majority. At 35%, Texas also has the highest number of students from Latino backgrounds who are language majority speakers, compared with 10% for New York and 7% for California.

Many dual-language programs include students of low socioeconomic backgrounds. In about one third of the programs, at least half of both language majority and language minority students receive free or reduced-fee school lunches, a commonly used indicator of socioeconomic background. Generally, more language minority students participate in such subsidized lunch programs than language majority students do, and this is the case in California, Texas, and New York.

Program Types, Regional Patterns, and Grade Levels

Three different program models of dual-language programs exist. The 90–10 model introduces the minority language for about 90% of the instructional day and uses English about 10% of the day in the primary grade levels. The 80–20 model uses the minority language 80% of the day and English about 20% of the day in the primary grade levels. The 50–50 model uses the minority language and English each about 50% of the instructional day. All three models include about 50% minority language instruction and 50% English instruction by the fourth grade. A small percentage of programs separate students by language for part of the school day in the primary grades, providing different proportions of instruction in the two languages.

California has more than half of its programs using the 90–10 or the 80–20 model, whereas Texas has a rough balance between the 50–50 and the other two models (as reported by Howard, Sugarman, and Christian in 2003). New York has more than half of its programs using the 50–50 model. California has the highest percentage of programs at the middle and high school levels, with about one-fifth of the state's dual-language programs at these levels.

The language of initial literacy instruction reflects some geographical patterns as well. California has more than half of its programs introducing literacy in the minority language to both language majority and language minority students. Less than half of the Texas programs and few of the New York (only one as of 2000) programs use initial literacy instruction in the minority language.

Most programs are at the pre-kindergarten through fifth-grade level (302), and 129 sites operate programs for just pre-kindergarten through second-grade levels. There are currently 53 programs at the middle school level and 14 at the secondary level.

Research Findings

CAL has reviewed and archived the bulk of the research conducted on dual-language programs. Of primary interest to researchers and various stakeholders is the issue of student outcomes. This section highlights some outcomes on oral, reading, and writing proficiency among upper-elementary school students, reviews attitudes among secondary and middle school students who had participated in dual-language programs, and concludes with the findings of a report that reviewed the research on dual-language programs.

A longitudinal study was conducted among 484 third graders in 11 Spanish/English dual-language programs who were followed through the fifth grade, as reported by Donna Christian, Fred Genesee, Kathryn Lindholm-Leary, and Elizabeth Howard in 2004. Both native Spanish speakers and native English speakers demonstrated high oral English proficiency levels at the end of third grade, with native Spanish speakers showing a slightly lower average score. By the end of fifth grade, both groups demonstrated a high level of oral English proficiency. A similar trajectory was found for English reading, with both groups demonstrating successful reading and comprehension of grade-level passages in English. In English narrative writing, both groups demonstrated "reasonably high levels" of performance on the non-standardized assessment, with both groups not attaining maximum scores (as had been the case with oral English and English reading).

A follow-up study examined student attitudes in a sample of 142 high school students who had attended dual-language programs in elementary school (reported by Christian and her colleagues in 2004). Sixty-six percent of the students were previous English language learners (ELLs) of Hispanic backgrounds, 20% were native English speakers of Hispanic backgrounds, and 13% were native English speakers of European American backgrounds. The first group included students who had lower levels of education and economic means in the home. All students indicated the following: very positive attitudes toward school, a high value on a good education and good grades, a desire to attend college, and the benefits of being bilingual. Half of the Hispanic students who were former ELLs stated that the dual-language program kept them in school and deterred them from dropping out. The same group tended to rate the program much more favorably than did the European American students, and slightly higher than Hispanic students as a whole. Most students reported using Spanish weekly or more and rated their Spanish level to be medium.

Another follow-up study examined achievement and attitudes among 199 middle school students who had participated in a dual-language middle school program (reported by Christian and her colleagues in 2004). Fifty-two percent of the students were previous ELLs of Hispanic backgrounds, 28% were native English speakers of Hispanic backgrounds, and 16% were native English speakers of European American backgrounds. The first group of students had lower levels of education and economic means in the home than did the other two groups. All students indicated very positive attitudes toward school, a high value placed on a good education and good grades, a desire to attend college, and benefits of being bilingual. Among the three groups of students, Hispanic students who had formerly been ELLs rated themselves lower on English reading and writing than did the other groups but also rated the program much more favorably than the other groups did. Most students reported using Spanish weekly or more and rated their Spanish proficiency to be at the medium level.

Howard, Sugarman, and Christian compiled in 2003 a comprehensive review of research on dual-language programs. The review found that, on the whole, dual-language programs have maintained general consistency in program goals and aspects; have teachers who are well-prepared and have ongoing professional development opportunities; have students and parents with positive attitudes toward dual-language programs, bilingualism, and multiculturalism; and have positive student academic outcomes, with both groups of students performing as well as or better than peers on standardized achievement exams when compared with peers in alternative programs.

Issues and Challenges in the Field

A major issue in the field is the number of available bilingual teachers and staff who can teach in the dual-language programs. More than half of all dual-language schools indicated bilingual proficiency among 100% of their teaching staff, with higher proportions (more than 50%) in California, and slightly lower proportions (less than 50%) in Texas and New York. Fewer than 10% of programs reported that less than half of the teachers and staff were proficient in two languages (as reported by Howard and Sugarman in 2001).

These authors also report that concerning support staff, about a third of all dual-language programs indicated that 100% of the support staff were fully proficient in two languages. California and Texas had slightly higher proportions at 33% and 44%, respectively, and New York had a lower proportion (20%). Materials for dual-language programs, especially for the upper grades and for non-Spanish minority languages, is another ongoing issue and area of need.

Articulation to middle schools and secondary schools is another issue in the field. Most dual-language programs are at the grammar school or elementary school level, and relatively few such programs exist at the higher levels. Full biliteracy development in academic content areas at the middle and secondary levels are hampered by such circumstances.

Other challenges include ensuring equal status of both languages being taught. Given the reality of the United States, a monolingual society that engenders differential power statuses for English and non-English languages, it is often difficult to realize the ideal goals of dual-language programs. Many studies have reported on the "hidden curriculum" that operates and provides for more opportunities to use English while marginalizing the use of the minority language in dual-language programs for both academic and social purposes.

Among other aspects that need to be negotiated in the implementation of dual-language programs are the required standardized testing in English, and the English-only and antibilingual legislation or efforts in many states in the country.

Grace P. McField

See also English Immersion; Pull-Out ESL Instruction; St. Lambert Immersion Study

Further Readings

Center for Applied Linguistics. (2006). *Directory of Two-Way Bilingual Immersion Programs.* Avaialable from http://www.cal.org

Christian, D., Genesee, F., Lindholm-Leary, K., & Howard, E. R. (2004). *Final progress report of CREDE Project 1.2 Two-way immersion.* Santa Cruz, CA: Center for Research on the Education, Diversity & Excellence and Center for Applied Linguistics.

Howard, E. R. & Sugarman, J. (2001). *Two-way immersion programs: Features and statistics.* ERIC Digest EDO-FL-01–01). Washington, DC: ERIC Clearinghouse on Languages and Linguistics. Retrieved February 1, 2008, from http://www.cal.org/resources/digest/0101twi.html

Howard, E. R., Sugarman, J., & Christian, D. (2003). *Trends in two-way immersion education: A review of research.* Baltimore: Center for Research on the Education of Students Placed at Risk (CRESPAR)/Johns Hopkins University and Center for Applied Linguistics. Available from http://www.csos.jhu.edu

Lambert, W. E., & Tucker, G. R. (1982). Graduates of early French immersion. In G. Caldwell & E. Waddell (Eds.), *The English of Quebec: From majority to minority status* (pp. 259–277). Lennoxville, Québec: Institut Québécois de recherché sur la culture.

E

EARLY BILINGUAL PROGRAMS, 1960s

Prior to enactment of the Bilingual Education Act of 1968 (Title VII of the Elementary and Secondary Education Act), school districts from New York to California experimented with bilingual education programs. Significant for being the first, and the catalyst for others, was the bilingual-bicultural education program at Coral Way Elementary School, in Miami, Florida, serving primarily Cuban refugee children. Two other notable programs included one in Texas for Mexican American students at Nye Elementary School of the Laredo United Consolidated Independent School District and another for Navajo children at Rough Rock Demonstration School in Arizona. Although many bilingual programs were started prior to 1968, this entry focuses primarily on Coral Way Elementary, Nye Elementary, and Rough Rock because of their national distinction as the first new programs launched with little or no policy guidance.

Bilingual programs gained acceptance in the early 1960s as a result of wide-ranging efforts by language minority communities in lobbying legislators and educational policymakers for culturally relevant education programs. Parents and community activists argued that low academic performance and persistently high drop-out rates were the result of recalcitrant "sink or swim" linguistic policies, referring to the lack of support for language learners in English instruction. They recommended bilingual education as an alternative. Their proposals, however, were largely ignored until pressure from Cuban refugees convinced the Miami schools to launch a bilingual program there.

News of the first bilingual program at Coral Way Elementary School in Florida sparked enormous interest across the nation, and programs soon followed for Mexican Americans, Puerto Ricans, and Native Americans. Bilingual programs in Texas mushroomed in the San Antonio Independent School District, Edinburg Independent School District, and Harlandale Independent School District and in Del Rio, Zapata, Del Valle, and Corpus Christi. Elsewhere, bilingual programs emerged in Pecos, New Mexico, in 1965, and in Calexico and Marysville, California. Bilingual programs were opened in Las Cruces, New Mexico; Hoboken, New Jersey, and St. Croix, Virgin Islands. Swift implementation of bilingual programs across the country underscored the urgency for legislation at the federal level when the Bilingual Education Act became a reality in 1968.

Background

Three historically significant events converged to lay the foundation for the creation of bilingual education programs: passage of the National Defense Education Act of 1958; the Cuban Revolution in 1959; and the escalation of civil unrest among U.S. minority groups, leading to President Lyndon B. Johnson's "War on Poverty" programs and the enactment of the Civil Rights Act of 1964.

National Defense Education Act (1958)

On October 4, 1957, Americans learned that the Soviet Union had launched *Sputnik,* the first space satellite to successfully orbit the earth. Government analysts needed to provide an explanation as to why the

Soviet Union had surpassed the United States in this arena—and concluded that the Soviet system of public education was superior to that of the United States. On that assumption, Congress took immediate action to regain a competitive edge in mathematics, science, and technology development. In 1958, Congress passed the National Defense Education Act (NDEA). This act provided funds to school districts to improve instruction in math, science, and technology and to support and promote foreign-language instruction.

The NDEA funded Foreign Languages in Elementary Schools (FLES) instructional programs throughout the country, reversing a historical neglect of foreign languages at that level. FLES programs were intended to develop a large pool of American foreign-language experts to help the United States compete globally, protect its interests abroad, and communicate effectively with international leaders. Programs to improve the language proficiency of high schoolteachers were also funded. These early language education programs paved the way for English as a Second Language (ESL) classes and experimental bilingual programs for limited-English-proficient students.

The Cuban Revolution

On January 1, 1959, Fidel Castro's guerilla army succeeded in ousting dictator Fulgencio Batista from Cuba, resulting in Castro's eventual assumption of power as leader of that country. The aftermath of Castro's victory indirectly advanced the cause for bilingual education in the United States.

Initially, the United States supported Fidel Castro, but relations soured soon after the revolutionary declared himself dictator, expropriated property owned by U.S. corporations, nationalized industry and agriculture, and embraced communism as Cuba's form of government. Those actions led to a break in diplomatic relations with the United States and an imposed embargo on Cuba that continues today. Thousands of upper- and middle-class Cubans fled to the United States, where they were given refuge.

The Civil Rights Movement and the War on Poverty

Civil unrest mounted in inner cities of the United States as African Americans grew weary of poverty and blatant discrimination in voting, schooling, jobs, housing, public facilities, and transportation. Widespread dissatisfaction with living conditions in many inner cities and voter repression in the South led to the civil rights movement. Influenced by Malcolm X and Dr. Martin Luther King Jr., Black Americans and their supporters held massive demonstrations, marches, sit-ins, and protests throughout the country. As civil disorder heightened, African Americans demanded justice and equality, as well as economic and educational opportunities. Violent clashes between police and demonstrators received wide media coverage in newspapers, radio, and television. As a result, the civil rights movement widened, encompassing Chicanos and American Indians who led their own demonstrations and marches, asserting that, like Black Americans, they too were victims of years of discriminatory practices. English-only instruction and the infamous "no-Spanish-speaking rules" came under attack by Chicanos, as they made their own demands for changes in schools.

Intense pressure from civil rights activists led to the passage of the Civil Rights Act of 1964. Title VI of this act specifically banned discrimination on the basis of race, class, creed, or national origin in all government agencies receiving federal funds, including public schools. This particular provision would prove to be a key argument in the U.S. Supreme Court decision *Lau v. Nichols,* decided in 1974. In that decision, the Court ruled that English-only instruction in schools discriminated against students who did not understand the language of instruction. Further, it identified bilingual education as one of a few possible remedies to counter school discrimination against non-English-speaking students.

In addition to civil rights legislation, President Lyndon B. Johnson revealed his plan for creating a "Great Society" for all Americans. He began by declaring a "War on Poverty." The centerpiece of the War on Poverty was the Economic Opportunity Act of 1964, which created the Office of Economic Opportunity (OEO) to oversee a variety of community-based antipoverty programs, including education programs. The Elementary and Secondary Act of 1965 was amended to provide federal aid to public education. Also launched was Project Head Start, a program that specifically encouraged input from minority communities regarding the appropriateness of educational programs for younger children not yet in school. A series of legislative bills under the War-on-Poverty umbrella served to protect civil rights and expand social programs aimed at eliminating poverty and racial discrimination in the areas of education, health, inner cities, transportation, consumer protection, and the environment.

Bolstered by civil rights legislation, War-on-Poverty initiatives, and the success of the bilingual education program at Coral Way Elementary, Chicanos, Puerto Ricans, and American Indians—all victims of native-language repression—pressed for bilingual programs of their own.

Coral Way Elementary School

Anti-Communist sentiment and the cold war of the 1950s and 1960s provided strong grounds for U.S. support of refugees fleeing Fidel Castro's Communist government. Under the auspices of Operation *Pedro Pan* and in joint collaboration between the Catholic Church and the U.S. government, anti-Castro parents sent about 14,000 children to the United States before the October 1962 Cuban Missile Crisis. Cuban children were dispersed around the country wherever church groups could provide refuge and sponsorship. Many parents hoped they would soon join their children or return to Cuba after what, they believed, would be a quick defeat of Castro. This was not to be.

A majority of Cuban refugees settled in Miami-Dade County, Florida. The large influx of Spanish-speaking children in Miami's schools posed a major instructional challenge. Cuban parents feared their children might soon forget Spanish and fall behind academically during their time in the United States and hence requested bilingual programs. With support from the Ford Foundation, Dade County Public Schools initiated ESL programs for them, and, in 1961, they began "Spanish for Spanish speakers" classes to supplement bilingual programs. For its part, the federal government was willing to accommodate the refugee community as a way of welcoming their flight from communism.

In the fall of 1963, Miami-Dade County Public Schools established a full-fledged bilingual education program at Coral Way Elementary School. Credentialed teachers in the district who were bilingual were asked to teach there and to do so in Spanish as well as English. Among the early refugees, there were a number of well-educated professionals, a good number of whom had been teachers in Cuba. They were hired as paraprofessionals to support the Spanish instructional strand of the bilingual program. Teachers who had been certified in Cuba were offered the opportunity to become certified in Florida. Although the bilingual program was primarily designed for Cuban students, it also accepted native English speakers. The program at Coral Way Elementary was initiated as an enrichment program, with the goal of developing Spanish-English bilingualism for all students. Spanish speakers were taught their morning curriculum in Spanish, while English speakers received theirs in English. Languages were switched in the afternoon; that is, Cuban students were taught in English, and English speakers were taught in Spanish. For extracurricular classes and periods like art, music, physical education, and lunch, students were mixed. From the beginning, the program showed potential for success because it employed trained personnel who could deliver instruction in both languages. After only 3 years, the school reported that students were equally proficient in both languages and cultures. The Coral Way Elementary Bilingual Program continues to be successful and is often cited as a model dual-language program.

Nye Elementary School

Soon after news of the bilingual program's success at the Coral Way Elementary School, the Laredo United Consolidated Independent School District, a school district on the Texas-Mexico border, established its own bilingual program. Mexican Americans were more than ready; they had spent decades fighting for some form of bilingual education. They understood that the exclusive use of English as language of instruction posed significant problems for their children, many of whom spoke Spanish exclusively. As early as the 1930s, George I. Sánchez, psychology professor at the University of Texas at Austin, had argued that Mexican American students scored low on IQ tests because they did not understand English, the language in which the test was administered, not because they were mentally retarded. He suggested that a way to ameliorate the problem was to provide such students some form of bilingual program that would permit use of Spanish to access academic content while learning English.

Mexican American leaders and educators welcomed developments in Florida. Many school districts, particularly in South Texas, were eager for the opportunity to launch their own bilingual programs for Mexican American students. Laredo United

Consolidated Independent School District (LUCISD) was the first to launch a bilingual education program in Texas. Members of the LUCISD board of trustees, in collaboration with officials from the Texas Education Agency and professors of the Foreign Language Department at the University of Texas, designed and implemented the pioneer bilingual program at Nye Elementary School in 1964. The two-way bilingual program, in which native Spanish speakers could learn English and native English speakers could learn Spanish, began in first grade. As the first class moved up the grades, the bilingual program expanded until it reached fifth grade. The program at Nye Elementary School in Laredo blazed the trail for the proliferation of bilingual programs in the state and holds the distinction of being the first to permit Texas students the use of their native language in the classrooms and on the school grounds. It was the first instructional challenge to the rule that prohibited the use of Spanish in classrooms.

Rough Rock Demonstration School

ESL was introduced to Navajo children at Rock Point Community School in 1963–1964. In 1967, the school began a limited bilingual program for beginners that combined ESL with initial literacy in Navajo. A full-fledged bilingual instruction program, however, was established in 1966 at nearby Rough Rock Demonstration School with funds from the Office of Economic Opportunity (OEO) and the Bureau of Indian Affairs (BIA). Through a unique contract between OEO, the BIA, a locally elected Navajo school board, and a trustee board of the Navajo Tribe called DINÉ Inc. (referencing the Navajo term *Diné* ("The People") and "Demonstration in Navajo Education"), federal funds flowed directly from OEO and the BIA to the school, enabling the development of an unprecedented 3-year demonstration project. The project started in Lukachukai, Arizona. However, the grafting of a bilingual demonstration project onto an existing BIA school proved untenable, and the following year, the project moved to the new and as yet unstaffed BIA school at Rough Rock, Arizona.

The Native American community unanimously endorsed the demonstration project, making it possible for the Rough Rock Demonstration School to officially open on July 1, 1966. The BIA contributed $307,000, money it would have allocated if it had operated the school, and OEO offered an additional $329,000 for intensive experimentation and demonstration. Program innovations included (a) school-community relations and parental involvement, (b) cultural identification, (c) home and school visitation, (d) language development and ESL instruction, (e) Navajo language learning, (f) in-service training and staff orientation, (g) adult education, (h) dormitory living, (i) guidance and counseling, and (j) auxiliary services, such as evaluation, recreation, art, finances, social work, and a school library.

The Rough Rock Demonstration School achieved new levels of support for Native American children in school. The school board found creative ways to ensure support for every aspect of the project. Navajos were directly and actively involved in all aspects of school operations: running the dormitory and serving as teachers, foster parents, adult counselors, custodians, cooks, bus drivers, and laundry workers. Elders shared Navajo traditions, legends, and history with students. To allay parents' fear that the demonstration school might revive the federal government's practice of rounding up their children and sending them to boarding school for assimilation and eradication of their language, the school board established a policy stating explicitly that the children belonged to the parents and not to the school. In a departure from previous boarding school policies, students were permitted to go home on weekends or whenever their parents requested their return, fully securing parental rights over their children. This simple but clear policy yielded a positive outcome. As Navajo parents became familiar with school instructional programs, they pushed their children to stay in school. Attendance increased, and truancy declined.

Both English and Navajo were used for instruction at Rough Rock, and learning Navajo and promoting cultural identification were central to the curriculum. This policy facilitated learning Navajo culture, traditions, and history in both formal and informal settings. Teachers, parents, and elders acquainted students with Navajo etiquette, beliefs, and oral traditions. The school enjoyed enormous success and widespread support from the Native American community. In its first 3 years, thousands of people visited Rough Rock School. As a symbol of its success and importance to the community, Rough Rock is called *Diné Bi'ólta'*, "The People's School" or the "Navajos' School," a designation now shared by many Navajo schools that have followed Rough Rock's lead in exerting local education control.

Rough Rock demonstrated that given the opportunity to design an ideal school for their children and the authority to run it, Native American education by Native Americans could succeed. A remarkable fact about Rough Rock's success is that among the original seven members of the school board responsible for the unique experiment, they had completed a combined total of five years of schooling. Perhaps their own contrastive experiences with traditional Navajo education and failed federal schooling freed them to explore innovative ways to create a comprehensive education program, placing Navajo language, culture, and values at the center of the curriculum.

Navajo leaders understood that their children's success or failure in school depended largely on the social, cultural, economic, and political conditions and attitudes of the community surrounding it. In creating a comprehensive educational experiment, they tried to involve as many community members as possible in the project as a way of providing employment opportunities and boosting cultural pride among parents and the community.

In the 1980s, the school's name was changed to Rough Rock Community School, signaling that the "demonstration" had succeeded in securing local education control. Over the past 40 years, however, it has experienced declining support as the push for standardization and English-only instruction has gained momentum. Despite the current politicization of bilingual education programs, Rough Rock Community School is widely recognized for its historic demonstration and remains a crown jewel of American Indian education.

A Lost Promise

Bilingual education programs of the 1960s, such as those at Coral Way Elementary, Nye Elementary, and Rough Rock Demonstration School, offered a promise of academic success for language minority students and, in some cases, an opportunity for English-speaking youngsters to learn another language. Each program supported an additive model of bilingualism, grounded in the pedagogical principle that students' languages and cultures form the basic foundation for further learning. Just as English is considered the best medium of instruction for native English speakers, bilingual advocates believe that native-language instruction provides linguistic minority students optimal opportunities for learning academic content.

Those early bilingual programs still stand as exemplars to emulate.

It should be noted, however, that federal financial support played a key role in creating those programs. Subsequent policies for those funds tended to promote the teaching of English at the expense of the home language. In effect, the same sources of funding that created those programs may have also led to undermining their full potential in later years. Even now, federal funding continues to undergird most current bilingual programs. With diminishing financial resources and strong opposition from English-only proponents, however, it is increasingly difficult to maintain them. Changes in the level of opposition to the use of non-English languages for instruction have led to waning support for bilingual education. Those programs, though promising, suffered under a slumping economy, budgetary constraints at the national and state levels, and xenophobic fears of a largely monolingual citizenry. Given their early success, one can only wonder how those positive results might have altered the academic achievement of linguistic minority students had they continued over the past 40 years.

María de la Luz Reyes and John J. Halcón

See also Dual-Language Programs; Indigenous Language Revitalization; Language Socialization of Indigenous Children; National Defense Education Act of 1958; Oyster Bilingual School; Appendix A

Further Readings

Andersson, T., & Boyer, M. (1971). *Bilingual schooling in the United States.* Washington, DC: Government Printing Office.

Bangura, A. K., & Muo, M. (2001). *United States Congress and bilingual education.* New York: Peter Lang.

Beebe, V. N., & Mackey, W. F. (1990). *Bilingual schooling and the Miami experience.* Coral Gables, FL: University of Miami, Institute of Interamerican Studies, Graduate School of International Studies.

Roessel, R. A. (1968). An overview of the Rough Rock Demonstration School. *Journal of American Indian Education, 7*(3), 2–14.

Spolsky, B. (1973). *The development of Navajo bilingual education.* Paper presented at the Symposium on Sociolinguistics and Language Planning of the AAAS/CONACYT meeting on "Science and Man in the Americas," Mexico City. (ERIC Reproduction Service Document No. ED094 559)

EARLY IMMIGRANTS AND ENGLISH LANGUAGE LEARNING

Among the arguments made by opponents of bilingual education is this: previous generations of immigrants did not have bilingual education to help them learn English and they had little trouble doing so. If bilingual education was not needed before, the argument suggests, it is likely that modern-day immigrants can get along without it as well. A second part of this argument is the idea that bilingual instruction can become a crutch that may actually delay the acquisition of English instead of aiding it. It makes sense to these critics that concentrating on English alone will bring better and quicker results than using the home language for part of the school day. These views concerning bilingual education appear to have surface validity, but the notions on which they rest are not supported by science.

The Immigrant Experience Then and Now

There is good evidence that immigrants of the past, for example, from the early 20th or late 19th century, did not learn English quickly. In fact, many never learned it at all. Most immigrants survived and even prospered because their livelihoods often did not require literacy in English or even a strong command of the spoken language. Most immigrants lived and worked in rural areas or in urban enclaves where English was not an absolute necessity. Generally, they engaged in occupations in which acquiring a thorough knowledge of the language could occur at a more leisurely pace than what is needed today. On average, the learning of English must be done much more rapidly today. Education requirements for better employment outside the ethnic neighborhood, together with a powerful youth culture played out in English, and greater attention being focused more-effective teaching methods make the rapid learning of English a more credible scenario than its rejection or deferral.

In ethnic neighborhoods across the country, older immigrants have always used their native languages at the hearth and among friends and neighbors who belonged to the same ethnic groups. Some adults never learned English, although their children and grandchildren learned the language as a school subject. Ethnic neighborhoods are not very different today.

A stroll through Chinatown in San Francisco, 18th Street in Chicago, or the Magnolia community in Houston makes this quite clear. If it is possible for certain groups in 21st-century America to live without much contact with English-speaking Americans, we can only imagine what the situation may have been at the turn of the 20th century, when the proportion of immigrants to natives was even higher than it is today.

A study conducted by University of California professor Lily Wong Fillmore reviewed family cases in which a language gap had developed between young children and older members of the family. Among the former, only English was used, while among the older members, the home language was the only language spoken. This linguistic divide within families interferes with normal processes of intergenerational communication. It deprives children of the wit and wisdom that is often gifted by the oldest members of the family to the youngest. In addition, it makes it more difficult for the whole family to be involved in the school experiences of the young. Through bilingual education, these problems can be greatly reduced or eliminated.

The assertion that earlier immigrants learned English more quickly and perhaps more enthusiastically than do newcomers today is difficult to prove or disprove beyond a shadow of a doubt. In the highly globalized transportation and communications environment of today, it is not surprising that many immigrants are reluctant to abandon their home languages, especially within ethnic communities. In a rapidly shrinking world, languages, all languages, are simply more valuable today than they were to previous generations of immigrants. The widespread availability of television, radio, and print media in languages other than English are a testimony to this. It does not follow, however, that there is any hesitation to learn English, the lingua franca of U.S. society. Valuing a home language and holding it in high regard says little about the attitudes that may prevail about the dominant language of the society. This is undoubtedly the case in the United States, one of the homes of the most popular and widely used language on the planet.

Most immigrants that arrived here in the heyday of Ellis Island from Europe never expected to return to their countries of origin. They also never expected to use their languages for very long after their arrival. It is probably true that they were more predisposed to abandon their immigrant languages and embrace English with a high degree of resolve, born of having no other choice. Voluntarily or otherwise, many immigrants had their names changed at Ellis Island to signal their commitment to a new country they never expected to leave. Many of today's immigrants come with a different mind-set. They do not often come to the United States with little hope of ever seeing their homelands again. Indeed, many return regularly to visit relatives and to enjoy holidays with friends and family. Airline companies are well aware of this. During every holiday period, it is almost impossible to obtain bargain fares to destinations in Mexico, Asia, or Africa. Many flights are packed with families from those countries returning home to spend the holidays with their families, fully expecting to return to the United States afterward. The Mexican government has instituted a special program, *Programa Paisano*, to welcome these visitors, facilitate their entry to the country, and help them enjoy their visits.

Can Bilingual Education Become a Crutch?

Many advocates for bilingual education believe that immigrant families should have the option, at public expense, of having their children educated solely in English or in a bilingual mode in which their language of origin is maintained and further developed. Opponents claim that reducing the time spent on learning English makes it more difficult for schoolchildren who are not native speakers to learn it—in short, that bilingual education retards the learning of English instead of assisting in its acquisition.

There is no research evidence to support this position. The assumption that one language interferes with another is based on mistaken assumptions about the human brain and the nature of language. Elsewhere in this encyclopedia, the *container theory of language* is examined: the assumption that language occupies space in the brain and that languages compete with each other for the space available. The assumption that two or more languages will "crowd" each other and interfere with the development that would take place if the entire brain space were devoted to a single language is not supported by linguistic science or brain research.

There are three points to keep in mind in this connection. First, research has demonstrated clearly that languages do not compete with each other in the human brain. In childhood, while children are acquiring the basics of language, it is often the case that they are uncertain about which word belongs to what language. While this period of word identification is under way, children may in fact use a word from one language as

they are speaking another. That is because in infancy, children growing up in bilingual environments may not be aware that they are learning two languages at once. Once this process is complete, however, there is no further confusion. Children achieve clarity about the two (or more) languages in their environments, and they learn when it is most appropriate to use one or the other. The period of "interference" is nothing more than the identification and sorting out of the shared language elements. There is no research evidence that this form of interference is permanent or damaging in any way. Given the family and community acceptance of two languages as being equally worthy, the child simply learns both languages in the same amount of time it takes monolingual children to learn one. It is important to note, however, that this occurs only when the two languages in question are afforded equal value and respect in the child's social circles. Children are quick to recognize disparities in the valuing of languages in their social world. In using language, they are very much influenced by the relative value that attaches to one language or another. This is often the case in the United States, where English is more highly valued in the wider society than are immigrant languages.

The second point to remember in this regard is that the human brain has vast unused capacity for learning in general. Whether we focus on mathematics, physics, chemistry, rocket science, or French, it is unlikely that the limits of the brain's capacity for learning would be reached in most humans. Scientists who study the brain estimate that in most cases, we use only a fraction of the total capacity of the brain during our lifetimes.

Linguistic science has made great progress in understanding the nature and use of languages. Consider the case of "accents," which may be present even when an individual knows a language well. In the past, accents were often interpreted as indicators of an inferior education. Today, we know that accents are markers that point to regional differences, such as a "southern accent" or a "New York accent" in American English. The presence of an accent does not mean that a user's command of a given language is incomplete or flawed. Similarly, when immigrants learn English after puberty, an accent may mark their oral use of the language for many years, even when they achieve a thorough and well-internalized knowledge of the new language. When it comes to reading and writing a language, however, accents are not easy to detect. In addition, the phenomenon of *code switching*, discussed elsewhere in this book, is now better understood as an advanced form of language manipulation, not as inadequate mastery of two languages.

Finally, an amazing aspect of language learning is that one language can be helpful in learning another. Multilingual individuals who speak a number of languages assert that each succeeding language they have learned has been easier to learn than the last. This is because the human brain can draw analogies between what is known and what we wish to learn. We look for patterns that will make the job easier. We progress from the known to the unknown, and we find it easier to learn what lies just outside the boundaries of what we have mastered already. In short, learning one language prepares us for learning the second, and the first two make it easier to learn a third. Knowledge is transferred from one language to another with amazing ease. Once we understand the idea of modifying nouns or adjectives, for example, we test aspects of the new language to see how similar it is to the previous one. If it is similar, we apply the same rules until we find the boundaries of that transference of knowledge. We then make course corrections to the rule when we apply it in the target language. Most of this growth by testing occurs automatically, without our knowledge of being immersed in it.

How valid is the argument that early immigrants did not need bilingual education and that they were able to learn English without it? This is folk knowledge; the facts do not support this assertion from any point of view of science. It is likely that early immigrants did not have an easier time learning English, simply because they were not engulfed in it as today's immigrants are—they often lived and worked in ethnic neighborhoods in which the home language was all that was needed to carry out the functions of everyday life. Our knowledge of linguistic science and recent brain research demonstrate quite clearly that bilingual education is not likely to become a crutch that deters or defers the learning of English. It is more likely to be the case that strict punitive rules against the use of home languages in teaching will do more harm.

Immigrants at a different point in our national history may have found it easier to progress and acquire a nest egg to pass on to their children simply by working hard, building their homes with their own hands, and living in relative isolation from their countries of origin as well as their English-speaking neighbors. Today, neither of these two conditions holds true. Finding the best and most efficient ways of teaching

and learning English is much more important today given the education requirements that U.S. society demands. Evaluations of bilingual education programs suggest that bilingual instruction is helpful in this regard.

Josué M. González

See also Assimilation; Bilingualism Stages; Code Switching; Container Theory of Language; Language Shift and Language Loss; Views of Bilingual Education; Views of Language Difference; Wong Fillmore, Lily

Further Readings

Rumbaut, R., Massey, D., & Bean, F. (2006). Linguistic life expectancies: Immigrant language retention in Southern California. *Population and Development Review, 32,* 447–460.

Wong Fillmore, L. (1991). When learning a second language means losing the first. *Early Childhood Research Quarterly, 6,* 323–346.

EASY AND DIFFICULT LANGUAGES

The idea that some languages are difficult to learn while others are easy is common and widespread. Many people around the world believe it to be true. Upon reflection, however, we find that while this idea seems reasonable—all languages are not equally accessible to all learners—it has not been proven that ease of learning or difficulty is based on the language itself. As we will point out, the difficulty or ease of learning may be attributable to the learner and/or to the kind of instruction received. Although the fundamentals are not complicated, it is important to review the evidence supporting these assumptions, because they have implications both for students and teachers of all languages.

How Contrasting Language Features Influence Us

Generally, languages cannot be readily categorized as being inherently difficult or easy to learn. What constitutes a difficult language for one person or group may not be the same for another set of individuals. Languages are easy or difficult in comparison to a person's first-acquired or dominant language. The first, or home, language is the template employed by young learners—consciously or otherwise—to generalize about the way all languages should "behave." Languages that are acquired early on in a person's life are easily and deeply ingrained. For young learners, they serve as the expected pattern for languages that come later. A person who asserts that a given language is easier than another is likely to be comparing particular aspects of the target language and finding them to be similar to those in his or her "base" or first-acquired language. Similarly, when the student of a new language is bedeviled by some aspect of the new language (e.g., spelling, verb or gender usage, placement of adjectives) he or she may reach the conclusion that it is more difficult because it has a distinctly different way of implementing that particular function. For example, a person who speaks a language that uses the Roman alphabet will find that, relatively speaking, another language that uses the same alphabet is easier to learn than a language (any language) written in the Cyrillic alphabet, such as Russian. Similarly, a language that is read from left to right will be easier for Westerners than one that is written and read from right to left, as in Arabic.

However, not all languages written in the Roman alphabet are equally easy or difficult. This is because one language may be more or less similar to one's native language on other features; for example, English speakers might find the use of the subjunctive verb tense in the target language mystifying, since modern English has now abandoned the use of this tense almost completely. Many speakers of English believe that the subjunctive verb form is difficult to master, while a native speaker of a language in which the subjunctive is common (such as Spanish) will recognize that familiar verb form when learning a language such as French. Other dimensions of language may also come into play. These comparisons can be made in a number of different arenas or usage areas of language. To the untrained ear, Japanese has pronunciations of vowels and consonants similar to those in Spanish. That feature, taken alone, might lead us to believe that Japanese can be learned easily by a native speaker of Spanish. In fact, this is usually not the case. The reason is that these two languages use different writing systems, and the corpus of transportable words and phrases is very small in either direction. Theoretically, Spanish speakers listening to Japanese might be able to hear every vowel and consonant being spoken, but they might not understand a single word. Anticipating

ease of learning based solely on a single linguistic feature may lead a person to underestimate the difficulty of learning a particular language.

Factors Other Than Linguistic Differences

Isolated structures and features of a language might cause learners to believe that a given language is more difficult than another. But linguistic features and grammatical conventions are not the only factors that contribute to making a language difficult or easy to learn. There are several other factors involved. Most of these have to do with learners' dedication to the task or their ability to absorb the essential ways in which the target language works: (a) recognition of the number of words and phrases the learner can "port" from the first language to the second; (b) recognition of similarities in morphological or syntactic patterns, such as forming plurals from singular nouns; (c) willingness to attempt, boldly, to automate responses to verbal cues in a lively conversation without undue hesitation; (d) ability to assemble combinations of words and express oneself creatively in the new language; (e) progress in mastering the cognitive, emotive, and volitional function of language; and (f) ability to grasp meanings embedded in idiomatic expressions such as those encountered in jokes, songs, or word play.

These factors may be more influential than the purely linguistic features in the easy/difficult formulation. Some of the features of a language that initially appear to be difficult are not profound and can be easily overcome in the early stages of learning the new language. For instance, the placement of adjectives before or after the noun is often a problem for students who are beginning study of another language. The use of capital letters in German may seem complicated to native speakers of Spanish, a language in which relatively few words are capitalized. Assignment of the proper gender to common nouns is difficult for native speakers of English, because in English, word gender is of little relevance for sentence construction. In Latinate languages, those that derive their respective grammars from Latin, gender is important. Few native speakers mistake a masculine noun for a feminine one. Word gender may seem arbitrary to new learners, and it may take some time before they can "sort out" the rules that help explain this concept. Unless the key to such mysteries is found early on in the study of a language, the level of complexity and difficulty involved can be overestimated.

An additional point must be kept in mind to round out this discussion of the relative difficulty of learning languages. Learning a language is not a process that proceeds at a uniform level of difficulty along the road to mastery. If we frame this process as a series of stages ranging from rank beginner to the fluency associated with educated native speakers, we can assume that different languages, depending on the language used as referent, could be easy or difficult in the earlier, middle, or advanced stages. Full mastery is based on building a solid foundation of basic skills and rules and progressing to the more subtle and complex aspects of the target language. For some learners, the most difficult stages will be the most advanced, replete with subtleties and nuances. For others, it might be the initial encounter with the language that overwhelms them. We might be taken aback by hearing a native speaker communicate in what appears to be excessive speed—and the realization that we understand next to nothing. Still other learners will judge the middle levels as the most difficult, for it is here, and not effortlessly, that a language begins to be useful in communicating with others, while reminding us that we have a good distance yet to travel to achieve full mastery.

Languages in the Environment

It is important to remind ourselves that languages do not live exclusively in classrooms. They are interactive and shared phenomena that exist in a societal matrix and in many domains: business, education, entertainment, religion, and so forth. Languages exist on the street, in music, in cinema, on TV, and in work environments. The relative difficulty of learning a language is often made easier or more difficult by the student's participation, or lack of it, in the sociocultural matrix in which the language is being studied. When language students can leave the classroom and immediately use what they have learned that day, the sense of difficulty is reduced. Similarly, if students make it a habit to listen to radio and TV in the target language, they may conclude that the language in question is not as difficult as it might be if they were not embedded in the social environment of the language. Close friendships and home stays with families who are native speakers of the target language greatly diminish the sense that a language is exceptionally difficult. Languages that are studied solely in the classroom may feel difficult because there is little opportunity outside the classroom to experience them in real life. This is not to diminish the importance of good teaching and a fruitful classroom environment. The skills of teachers and sound methods of instruction no doubt influence the student's impression of a language being difficult or easy.

Linguistic Distance

Much of what we know concerning the relative ease or difficulty of learning a language can be summarized under the concept of *linguistic distance,* drawn from the field of linguistics This concept relates to the similarity or difference that exists between one's referent language, presumably the first-acquired language, and the target language, the object of one's learning efforts. Until very recently, linguistic distance was a sketchy concept that linguists could not quantify. Recently, research has begun to show interesting results in efforts to make linguistic distance measurable, hence more useful. It remains to be seen just how useful the concept may become in the future. For now, it can be reduced to a simple statement: A new language is easy or difficult to learn depending on how different it is from a language an individual already knows.

Finally, it should be stressed that much of the discussion above applies more readily to studies of "foreign" languages than it does to bilingual classrooms. In bilingual education, because the task is not merely to learn English but also to master subject content, both tasks are at play throughout the experience. One such complication is that as English language learners develop language skills, it is not easy to determine the degree to which newly acquired language skills are in the social realm ("playground" English) or whether the new skills signal a deeper knowledge, such as asking questions, explaining abstract concepts, or seeking clarification from teachers or peers ("classroom" English). Often, children who appear to be proficient in the levels of social or playground language may be quite limited in the more complex uses of classroom language.

Josué M. González

See also Academic English; Accents and Their Meaning; BICS/CALP Theory; Cognates, True and False; Contrastive Analysis; Indo-European Languages; Linguistics, an Overview; Measuring Language Proficiency; Underlying Linguistic Proficiencies

Further Readings

Chiswick, B. R., & Miller, P. W. (2004). *Linguistic distance: A quantitative measure of the distance between English and other languages* (IZA Discussion Paper No. 1246). Available from http://ftp.iza.org/dp1246.pdf

National Virtual Translation Center. (2006). *Language learning difficulty for English speakers.* Retrieved February 1, 2008, from http://www.nvtc.gov/lotw/months/november/learningExpectations.html

EBONICS

The term *Ebonics* is derived from the combination of *ebony* (black in color) and *phonics* (the association of letters to sounds in reading/writing). The concept is also referred to as Black English, Black Vernacular English, African American English, and African American Vernacular English (AAVE). The term is believed to have been coined by social psychologist Robert Williams and introduced by him at a conference in 1973. Ebonics has its roots in English and African languages. There is considerable debate over whether Ebonics constitutes a language or a dialect, or something altogether different outside the strict definitions of those two terms. While Ebonics does not figure prominently in the dialogue and policy debate on bilingual education, a summary discussion of its nature is helpful in understanding why it often appears in parallel to discussions of bilingual education but is not generally considered an integral part of it.

Although the various terms mentioned above are often used interchangeably, many scholars hold that the term was originated in order to distinguish it from past terms focusing more on English roots and influences of the language/dialect and on the low status normally ascribed to Black varieties of English. Ebonics, then, was meant to be used as a label by those interested in emphasizing the African roots of the language/dialect. It also became a useful term, early on, in discussing the possible mismatch between the language of teachers and that of their Black students. A court case in Ann Arbor, Michigan (*Martin Luther King Junior Elementary School Children v. Ann Arbor School District Board,* decided in 1979), gained attention when the court ordered that Ann Arbor teachers be instructed in the basics of Ebonics in order to better understand the language spoken by many of their students.

Ebonics is not concerned simply with word usage but also with pronunciation, word order, sentence structure, vocabulary, etymology, and notions of epistemology surrounding certain speech patterns. Interestingly, Ebonics is not spoken only by African Americans, but is spoken to various degrees by persons of diverse ethnic backgrounds. Further, not all African Americans are speakers of Ebonics.

The origin of Ebonics is directly linked to the American slave trade, in which millions of Africans were brought to the Americas and forced to learn English without formal instruction. In this situation, the speech and speech patterns of West Africa intermingled with the speech and speech patterns of English, forming a hybrid, which until recently had received scant attention at the scholarly or policy levels. As alluded to earlier, some scholars see the speech patterns of Ebonics as reminiscent of West African languages, particularly those in the Niger-Congo region, thus making English a more distant influence while placing the African languages and speech patterns at the center of Ebonics, as discussed in work by Ernest Dunn and Charles DeBose. Others, perhaps the majority of linguists, argue that English is the mother language of Ebonics, considering the centrality of English vocabulary in Ebonics. In either case, it cannot be denied that Ebonics was formed by the complex hybridization of English and West African languages and speech patterns.

Ebonics and Linguistics

Many outside the field of linguistics see Ebonics as a perverted form of standard English, as explained by Peter Trudgill and William Cosby, incorporating "bad" or "sloppy" writing, speech, and sentence structure. What one must consider is that all languages are socially constructed and are born out of particular social systems. Even standard English, which is held up as the normative language of the United States, has gone through numerous changes and mutations throughout its history. At one point in its history, English itself was seen as a low-class language of questionable parentage and fit for use only by poor and uneducated peasants. Ebonics is a similar case, as it is a complex language/dialect with varying features whose future is not yet fully defined. Whether looking at syntax, semantics, sentence structure, or lexicon, Ebonics is a collection of speech patterns in the same way any language or dialect is. At this point in its history, however, Ebonics has not reached the point of being widely sought out as a prestigious language to study and learn. Some even argue against the uniqueness of Ebonics on the basis that its speech structures fall in line with the patterns of standard English and other English dialects and are more similar to English than to any West African tongue, as explained by Stefan Martin and Walt Wolfram. In essence, Ebonics is acting no differently than all other languages, in that it has an origin, has linguistic forbearers and influences, and continues to evolve and change.

An important similarity between standard English and Ebonics is that both follow the basic word order of subject-verb-object. This similarity also serves to emphasize the historical links between English and Ebonics. Also, Martin and Wolfram explain that similar to forms of English, the central element in a phrase, which they call "the head," is found at the left. Some qualities that make Ebonics different from standard English (though they can be found in other languages and some English dialects) are pleonastic (redundant) negation, use of multiple negation (e.g., "Don't nobody go to the store"), negative inversion, and the dropping of the copula (e.g., "Where you going?"), as in Russian and some other languages. There is continued debate on which features are unique to Ebonics and which are also readily found in standard English and dialects of English.

Ebonics and Politics

Ebonics is not only a field of study for linguists; it is part of the social and political fabric of the United States. The most famous illustration of this occurred in 1996, when the Oakland, California, public schools pushed to use Ebonics in the classroom in an effort to improve the English language skills of African American students. Proponents of the plan did not want to teach Ebonics per se, but to use Ebonics as a transition to standard English, much in the same way Spanish speakers in programs are characterized as having "home language support."

Some, like (then) California School Superintendent Delaine Eastin and the Reverend Jesse Jackson, Jr. (as indicated in a PBS report), took this resolution as meaning the Oakland School District would be teaching Ebonics instead of standard English to its students, and there was some uproar over the proposal. Many found that the passed resolution was validating what they saw as "bad" English and fought against the measure.

In a response to resolutions such as the one passed by the Oakland School District, the U.S. House of Representatives submitted its own resolution, which was referred to the Committee on Education and the Workforce. The resolution stated, as cited in David J. Ramírez and colleagues' *Ebonics: The Urban Education Debate,*

> Whereas "Ebonics" is not a legitimate language: Now, therefore, be it Resolved, That it is the sense of the House of Representatives that no Federal funds should be used to pay for or support any program that is based upon the premise that "Ebonics" is a legitimate language. (p. 135)

Many protested responses such as these, finding them close-minded and even racist. The use of Ebonics in schools remains a complex social and political issue and continues to be discussed and debated at both local and national levels.

Roberto Tinajero II

See also Accents and Their Meaning; Social Class and Language Status; Status Differences Among Languages; World Englishes

Further Readings

Baugh, J. (1999). *Out of the mouths of slaves: African American language and educational malpractice.* Austin: University of Texas Press.

Cosby, W. (1997, January 10). Elements of Igno-Ebonics style. *Wall Street Journal,* p. A11.

DeBose, C., & Nicholas F. (1993). An Africanist approach to the linguistic study of Black English: Getting to the roots of tense-aspect-modality and copula systems in Afro-American. In S. S. Mufwene (Ed.), *Africanisms in Afro-American language varieties* (pp. 364–387). Athens: University of Georgia Press.

Dunn, E. F. (1976). Black-southern White dialect controversy. In D. Sears Harrison & T. Trabasso (Eds.), *Black English: A seminar* (pp. 102–122). Hillsdale, NJ: Lawrence Erlbaum.

Green, L. J. (2002). *African American English.* Cambridge, UK: Cambridge University Press.

Labov, W. (1972). *Language in the inner city: Studies in Black English Vernacular.* Philadelphia: University of Pennsylvania.

Martin Luther King Junior Elementary School Children v. Ann Arbor School District Board, 463 F. Supp. 1027 (1979).

Martin, S., & Wolfram, W. (1998). The sentence in African-American Vernacular English. In S. S. Mufwene & J. Baugh (Eds.), *African-American English: Structure, history, and use* (pp. 11–36). New York: Routledge.

McWhorter, J. H. (1998). *Word on the street: Debunking the myth of a "pure" standard English.* New York: Basic Books.

PBS. (1997). *Reading matters.* Retrieved from http://www.pbs.org/newshour/bb/education/ebonb_1-9.html

Ramírez, J., Wiley, T., De Klerk, G., Lee, E., & Wright, W. (Eds.). (2005). *Ebonics: The urban education debate.* Clevedon, UK: Multilingual Matters.

Trudgill, P. (2002). *Sociolinguistic varieties and change.* Washington, DC: Georgetown University Press.

Williams, R. (Ed.). (1975). *Ebonics: The true language of Black folks.* St. Louis, MO: Institute of Black Studies/Robert Williams and Associates.

ELL IDENTIFICATION PROCESSES

See DESIGNATION AND REDESIGNATION OF ENGLISH LANGUAGE LEARNERS

ENCULTURATION

Despite conceptual disagreement over a specific definition of culture, anthropologists tend to agree on three basic characteristics: (1) Culture is not innate or inherited genetically; it is learned; (2) culture is shared, and it has an important role in defining the social boundaries of different groups; and (3) the various facets of culture are interrelated. Enculturation is the process by which family and community members pass on the core values and behaviors of their cultures to the next generation. These new cultural recipients, in turn, become active observers of, and participants in, the way of life of their families and communities. Through a lifelong process, they pick up and internalize those core cultural and linguistic values and play an important role in passing them along to the following generation. In that sense, they become culture bearers. In addition, they also pass along any changes that those traditions have undergone during their lifetimes. In this sense, they also play an important role as culture makers.

Culture is not carried in our genes. It is through the process of enculturation that we learn to become members of our speech communities—to understand, speak, read, and write our languages—as well as to function effectively within our shared culture. Through family and community traditions, we come to know who we are and what our culture expects of us—whether we see ourselves as Chinese, Mexican, Korean, Inupiat, British, Navajo, Nicaraguan, German, French, Argentinean, South African, and so on. When a child accidentally touches a hot object and immediately withdraws his or her hand, this demonstrates a physical reflex that does not have to be taught. But whether the child's response to that unpleasant surprise is a scream of "Ay!" or "Ow!" is an artifact of culture, something transmitted through social interaction. An essential characteristic of being human is the manner in which we, both consciously and unconsciously, transmit cultural patterns to succeeding generations. A newborn infant is a clean cultural slate. Long before children enter a school classroom, however, culturally coded behavioral patterns have been learned through the process of enculturation.

Because cultural patterns are learned, they are highly variable. For example, interaction between parents and children does not follow a single pattern that is innate to all humans. In some native Hawaiian families, when children are involved in a conflict with siblings or friends, parents will discipline everyone involved rather than attempting to identify the guilty parties. Consequently, these children may learn more readily to resolve interpersonal problems within their peer groups rather than sharing them with the adults. In the classroom, however, which generally operates on the basis of a cultural system different from that in the home, teachers will probably want to know who is specifically responsible for any unacceptable behavior. Children may thereby learn different ways of interacting with each other and with adults.

Enculturation exists only in relation to a specific social grouping. Humans acquire and create culture only as members of particular identity-defining groups. Because groups tend to maintain some aspects of their identities while periodically modifying other aspects, individuals function as both cultural consumers and culture change agents. What we do with what we receive as cultural consumers and how we design and construct new connections may create some ambiguity or a lack of stability with respect to cultural processes. In other words, humans are always becoming both "a part of" and "apart from" a given cultural and linguistic context. For example, a child in her home cultural environment will learn ways to give or get information and attention that are appropriate to her ethnic group. In school, however, she may have to leave those patterns behind to some extent as she learns alternative forms of communication that are more appropriate to the classroom setting. Through such social contact with members of her own and other cultural groups, her cultural identity develops.

Although culture plays a role in defining ethnic boundaries, those boundaries are usually quite porous. To use a saying that folk singer Pete Seeger attributed to his father, "Plagiarism is basic to all culture." Throughout history, societies have always borrowed from each other without giving credit to the source. In turn, this unacknowledged appropriation has been a principal source of the constant development of cultural patterns "apart from" the original ones. This perpetual state of becoming—of new beginnings crafted on old ones—gives culture its dynamic and fascinating character.

The cultural traits of a particular group of people are largely integrated with each other to form an interrelated whole. Cultural traits are not a random hodgepodge of discrete customs with no relation to each other. To some extent, this integrated consistency derives from adaptation to the environment. For example, preindustrial hunting-and-gathering societies were characterized by low population density, a nomadic lifestyle, and limited material possessions. The subsequent development of agriculture-based societies brought higher population density, larger settled communities, and increased acquisition of material possessions. Cultural patterns tend toward a psychological integration of values and beliefs as well. Thus, childrearing practices and family living arrangements within a particular cultural group tend to reflect the same values and beliefs that the group's folktales portray. Of course, no two individuals within any cultural group are completely alike, and change is constantly occurring. Therefore, the components of a culture are not always in complete harmony with each other, but there is an adaptive tendency toward reasonable consensual agreement.

Because cultural patterns are integrated, a change in one aspect of a culture can, and probably will, affect many other aspects of that culture. Athapaskan Indians of the Yukon traditionally followed a seminomadic way of life, moving from fishing camps to hunting camps as the seasons changed. When compulsory formal schooling was introduced into remote Alaskan villages in the 1930s, however, residents were forced to end their traditional seasonal travels.

Thus, with changes in the form of education came changes in residential patterns, along with concomitant changes in subsistence patterns, the local economy, patterns of social interaction, and the loss or weakening of indigenous languages. The Micronesian islands underwent a comparable process when the introduction of Western schooling practices brought about many other changes in cultural patterns.

The above generalizations—that culture is learned, shared, and integrated—provide some grasp on the concept of enculturation, but they do not give one a comprehensive hold. Culture is learned, but most of the teaching of culture takes place without reflection, and the content is modified to some extent as it is transmitted. Culture is shared and has defined boundaries, but the members of a social group do not all share the exact same culture, and the boundaries of that culture are permeable. Components of a culture seem to be interrelated as in a system, but this system does not always seem to behave according to clear, systematic rules.

To make the understanding of enculturation even more elusive, there is the inevitable problem of bias. Because we are all culture bearers, when we study or simply observe the behavior of members of another cultural group, we are inevitably influenced by our own cultural backgrounds. We all view the world through the lenses of our own cultures and make many decisions about our observations based on our cultures, whether we are conscious of it or not. This includes instructional decisions. Those decisions may match those expected by the various expectations of diverse cultural backgrounds of our students. Teachers often try to be culturally competent in their teaching, which means finding a suitable accommodation between our actions and the cultural values.

It is important for teachers of English language learners to understand the dynamic and complex process associated with cultural and linguistic shift across generations. It is important, for example, to know that children have the capacity to both accept and modify the core values that they have received from parents and the community. But newly arrived immigrants from a particular ethnic group may not be cultural mirror images of members of the same group who have been here for generations. While it is difficult to know all the enculturation processes that affect their students, teachers can and do, in an incremental way, discover core values in their students and families and use those in designing and implementing culturally and linguistically responsive teaching. *Acculturation,* a related concept applicable to learning other cultures beyond one's own, places pressures on students to decide whether to remain close to the values imparted to them at home or to venture out into the larger society as acculturated or assimilated individuals. Knowing that culture is learned, shared, and constantly changing can be a cause for optimism. It means that teachers, students, and parents working together have the ability to modify values, attitudes, and behavioral patterns.

Carlos J. Ovando

See also Acculturation; Assimilation; Cultural Deficit and Cultural Mismatch Theories; Culturally Competent Teaching; Language Socialization; Melting-Pot Theory; Nationalization of Languages

Further Readings

Gonzales, N. A., Knight, G. P., Birman, D., & Sirolli, A. (2004). Acculturation and enculturation among Latino youths. In K. Maton, B. Ledbetter, C. Schellenbach, & A. Solarz (Eds.), *Investing in children, youth, families, and communities: Strengths-based public policies* (pp. 285–302). Washington, DC: American Psychological Association.

Masahiko, M., & Ovando, C. J. (2004). Language issues in multicultural contexts. In J. Banks & C. McGee Banks (Eds.), *Handbook of research on multicultural education* (2nd ed., pp. 567–588). San Francisco: Jossey-Bass.

Ovando, C. J., Combs, M. C., & Collier, V. P. (2006). *Bilingual and ESL classrooms: Teaching in multicultural contexts* (4th ed.). Boston: McGraw-Hill.

Robins, K., Lindsey, R., Lindsey, D., & Terrell, R. (2002). *Culturally proficient instruction: A guide for people who teach.* Thousand Oaks, CA: Corwin Press.

ENGLISH, FIRST WORLD LANGUAGE

The English language was originally propelled by the spread of the British Empire in the 19th century and, subsequently, by the expansion of the U.S. economic and political influence in the 20th century. English now extends across the globe. By the 21st century, English had become the main world language of literature, periodical publications, science, advertising, pop music, cinema, and technology. In approximately 75 countries, English is either the first language (L1) of the majority of the population or it is used extensively in important social institutions. Conservatively,

it is safe to say that there are close to 330 million L1 speakers of English in the world. If Creole varieties of English are included, the number swells to around 400 million speakers. Furthermore, it has been estimated that there are currently 430 million second-language (L2) speakers of English and an additional 750 million speakers of English as a foreign language (EFL).

While these numbers might seem staggering, an exact assessment of the actual number of people who speak and/or use English on a daily basis is impossible to attain, owing to multiple factors (e.g., skewed census data, accuracy in identifying a person's proficiency, and limited access to political records). Roughly speaking, though, there are close to 2 billion people across the globe who use English in some form or capacity, according to David Crystal in his work *English as a Global Language.*

How and why has English attained such a commanding role in the everyday lives of so many people? On a global level, English has taken many forms and is used for many different purposes. To understand the functions that English has in societies around the world, it is necessary to consider the historical influence of colonialism and the modern course of economic globalization. Categorizing societies according to the prevalence and type of English spoken allows us to understand how these processes have affected social interaction on both local and global scales. Braj Kachru has developed a framework of three concentric circles that concisely categorizes all societies that use English:

1. The *inner circle* (320–380 million speakers) includes societies in which English is the medium of public and private life and English is overwhelmingly the first language (e.g., the United Kingdom and the United States).

2. The *outer circle* (300–500 million speakers) is made up of societies in which English is either used by the state as an official language and has become part of the country's most important social institutions (although it may not be the first language of all citizens) and/or has a significant role as an additional language (e.g., India and Singapore).

3. The *expanding circle* (500 million–1 billion speakers) encompasses those states whose members recognize the importance of English for international communication, though they do not have a history of colonization by countries from the inner circle (e.g., China and Russia).

It can be suggested that although useful, Kachru's model situates the inner-circle countries as retaining the power to measure the linguistic correctness of English, despite the growing global *majority* of "nonnative" (i.e., L2 or English as a foreign language) speakers of English.

The modern intertwining of economic systems between different countries around the world has produced an increased need for cross-cultural communication. The prominence of each language and the amount of linguistic overlap between different cultural groups naturally establishes a hierarchy of languages. Periphery languages are those least used in the network, and core languages are seen as vital for connecting to the greatest number of other groups. Most experts agree that English has risen to the top as the most important language for spanning the global economic communities, and, for that reason, it is often recognized as a high-status language, perhaps the highest in the world.

Inherent in any type of linguistic hierarchy is the view of superiority and subordination. Robert Phillipson has addressed the domination and influence of English as *linguistic imperialism.* The teaching of English in countries that are politically marginalized or economically impoverished is a reflection of colonial periods when elites ruled and educated indigenous populations through the colonial language. Those in positions of power create a dependency on English and establish it as a powerful language that shapes relationships between countries and defines access to economic resources.

While the economic weight of the United States is an obvious factor in the shaping of cultural relationships, the political impact of American policies and agencies is just as far-reaching. The influence of the United States on intergovernmental organizations, like the World Bank and the International Monetary Fund (IMF), extends into the linguistic realm in profound ways. Since the United States is often the biggest contributor to these types of organizations, peripheral stipulations are often included in the workings of these entities, arguably the most powerful in the world. As a result of this influence, the IMF and the World Bank can insist that client states include English in their education systems as part of their development.

Although English clearly plays an influential role on an international level, its status in the United States is often misunderstood. As of 2006, the United States has approximately 70% of all English-native-language

speakers in the world (excluding Creole varieties, such as the variety of English spoken in Jamaica). Despite such a strong base of native speakers, many people fear that the status of English in the United States is eroding. Since the 18th century, English has always been the dominant language in the United States; no other language has even come close to surpassing it. Most concerns about the status of English have to do with the prominence of foreign immigrants. Some arguments against these concerns include the following: First, competence in English continues to be highly correlated with social status, prestige, and income in the United States. Second, when language minority individuals are able to speak English fluently, the use of a minority language is not correlated with low economic standing. Third, immigrants should not be viewed as a force that "dilutes" or diminishes the prominence of English. The life opportunities these groups provide are shaped by their intergroup differences. In addition, emphasis should not be placed on multiple ethnic inequalities whereby culture, language, class, and race are inextricably linked.

A quick glance at the 2000 U.S. Census data will help situate the prominence of English in the United States. Of the 262,375,000 people over the age of 5 identified by the 2000 decennial census, only 8.1% (21,320,407) of the total population is reported to speak English "less than very well." Hence, approximately 92% of the nation speaks English "very well." These figures, along with the role and spread of English globally, seem to contradict the claim that English is in danger of being overtaken by other languages.

Finally, it is important to note that English has become the language of choice of young people around the world. Driven largely by the dominant role that English plays on the Internet and in popular music, teenagers around the world have settled on English as the favored language in which to communicate with their peers. Music, movies, and video games help to promote English even more among the young. Even in cultures that may differ markedly from the United States in political ideology and action, a substantial proportion of young people are studying and using English more than ever.

Eric Johnson

See also Languages and Power; Native English Speakers, Redefined; Official Language Designation; Spanish, the Second National Language; U.S. Census Language Data; World Englishes

Further Readings

Crystal, D. (2004). *English as a global language.* New York: Cambridge University Press.

Kachru, B. (1985). Standards, codification, and sociolinguistic realism: The English language in the outer circle. In R. Quirk & H. Widdowson (Eds.), *English in the world: Teaching and learning the language and literatures* (pp. 11–30). Paper presented at conference, "Progress in English Studies," 1984, September 17–21, London. Cambridge, UK: Cambridge University Press.

Phillipson, R. (1992). *Linguistic imperialism.* New York: Oxford University Press.

U.S. Bureau of the Census. (2000). *Ability to speak English* (Summary file 3, QT P17). Available from http://www.census.gov/main/www/cen2000.html

ENGLISH, HOW LONG TO LEARN

Although on its surface the issue may appear simple, the question of how long it takes schoolchildren to learn English well enough to use it effectively in school is not easy to answer definitively. This entry reviews some of the research findings on the subject, with appropriate cautions as to how authoritative any type of answer may be. Consider the case of a middle-class, English-speaking child whose parents also speak English and are high school graduates. How long, typically, would it take such a child, if unburdened by unusual extraneous factors, to become academically proficient in his or her native language? The answer, of course, depends on how we define *proficiency.* The proficiency of a kindergartner is quite different from that of a second, fourth, or sixth grader. Learning and polishing language skills, even for native speakers of English, is a process fostered by parents and schools beginning at birth and continuing for 17 or 18 years if the college or university attended keeps with the normal conventions of English course taking. If the student then goes on to a college or university that keeps with the normal conventions of English course taking, he or she will be required to continue the study of his or her native language for at least 2 more years en route to a bachelor's degree.

For simplicity's sake, let us assume that a typical native speaker of English has gained a better-than-average command of English (or proficiency) by the time he or she enters middle school; that is, around the age of 10 or 11. How different is the challenge of learning English for an immigrant child; for example, a young boy who begins attending an American school in the third grade? Assuming that this child has only recently arrived in the country, he has missed 7 or 8 years of experience using English. Comparatively, native English speakers can be expected to use the language more expertly. When it comes to language learning, such a head start is difficult to make up, although it is done every day by students who participate in good programs designed to help them do so.

Some of the research in this field, such as the work of Stephen Krashen, has found that the process of learning one's first language is substantially different from learning a second or third language later on. This research argues that we acquire our first language around the hearth, where we are surrounded by and immersed in that language, often without any other. In short, the first language is not learned by studying it in school as a subject; granted, its mechanics are improved and its formal conventions examined and refined through high school and college, but the basic and essential command of the spoken language is acquired before adolescence. The immigrant child in our example did the same with his home language—Chinese, perhaps. Having come to the United States and entered a school where English is the predominant language, he must now learn English, not in the same way as his English-speaking classmates, but as a school subject. In this vastly different process, the burden of learning English is shared with teachers. Good teachers who are well versed in the art and science of language teaching will help this child reduce the time necessary to gain proficiency in English. Average and poor teachers untrained in this type of work may struggle in this process, which might have implications for the amount of time needed for this student to learn English.

After decades of research in the field, most linguists admit that there is no definite answer to the question of length of time required to learn English in the U.S. context. Language learning, beyond acquiring one's first language, is a complex process that does not occur in isolation from other skill development. Further, the variables that impinge on a child's ability to learn it are too numerous to control in a classic experimental way; current research methods may be insufficiently developed to handle the burden of numerous variables.

Acquiring the English Language

First-Language Acquisition

Although no one knows the exact length of time required by a visitor or immigrant child to acquire English, researchers agree that first- and second-language acquisition are lifelong processes that follow a similar pattern of development. The development of a complex oral language system from birth to age 5 is universal, notwithstanding physical disabilities or lack of human interaction. However, how long it takes to complete this development is dependent upon the cognitive capacity of the child. Language development at this stage is rudimentary, and speakers cannot use language in a manner as sophisticated as that of older children. Nonetheless, the base of language acquired during these years is highly important in subsequent stages of language learning and use.

Under ordinary circumstances, children aged 6 to 12 develop subtle phonological distinctions, vocabulary, semantics, syntax, formal discourse patterns, and complex aspects of pragmatics in the oral system of their first language, as Virginia Collier explains. Ordinarily, children at this age begin formal schooling and begin to add the more complex literacy skills of reading and writing to the previously acquired speaking and listening skills. Both sets of skills continue to increase across academic content areas, grade levels, and domains. First-language development should occur at the same level and rate as the cognitive capacity of the student, given no physical disabilities. Thus, it is difficult for an 8-year-old to master the science of physiology because he or she has not developed the cognitive abilities to understand the complex and abstract terminology associated with that field.

An adolescent entering college must continue to acquire enormous amounts of vocabulary across disciplines of study and develop more complex writing skills, processes that continue into adulthood. Collier describes how adults continue to acquire new subtleties in pragmatics and changes in discourse through everyday written and oral communications. It seems clear that first-language acquisition is a long process that continues throughout the life span.

Brain research has added to our understanding of how individuals acquire language. Fred Genesee explains that in early stages of learning, neural circuits are randomly activated and connections are weak or incomplete, similar to a blurry photograph. However, with more practice, exposure, and experience, the picture gains clarity and detail. The repeated exposure allows for less input to activate this network. Over time, activation and recognition become automatic, and the learner can focus on more complex tasks and skills. Genesee emphasizes the time-consuming nature of this task, which this type of research explains in detail: Time is necessary for new neural networks and connections between networks to be made, such as those between a first and second language.

Second-Language Acquisition

Second-language acquisition is an equally complex process that develops in stages, requires time and oral exposure, and is influenced by a number of external variables. Patton Tabors has proposed the *multiple container theory*, which describes how individuals acquire a second or subsequent language. He uses the metaphor of a glass filled with water to explain children's first-language acquisition. The first language is represented by one glass filled with one liquid. The second language is represented by an added second glass; it already contains liquid that, according to Tabors, represents what the child knows about the way language works. However, this second glass needs to be filled with second-language "liquid." Exposure, in Tabors's metaphor, is represented by the amount of liquid that fills each glass; hence, the glasses can be filled simultaneously, or they may contain unequal amounts of liquid.

Thus, language "liquid" amounts may differ based on language learning happening at a given time. However, the amount of language retention in either language depends on language use and exposure: If there is not enough exposure or practice with a specific language, the language liquid can "dry up" and the language will be lost. This theory also recognizes the maintenance and development of the first language.

The process of second-language acquisition is further complicated when applied to the proficiency and language mastery required to be successful in formal school settings. In school, second-language learners are expected to reach a level of both academic and language proficiency equal to that of native English speakers. And with more than 5 million English language learners (ELLs) in Grades K–12 in U.S. public schools (according to data provided by the National Clearinghouse for English Language Acquisition for the 2004/2005 school year), administrators, policymakers, parents, and educators are concerned with how long the process of second-language acquisition can take for ELLs to perform on par with native English speakers.

Research Findings: Academic Second-Language Proficiency

In the United States, public schools provide instruction in all-English classrooms. Therefore, the focus for second-language proficiency will highlight findings from typical all-English learning environments. In contrast, second-language acquisition will also highlight findings from bilingual education. All findings are based on U.S. programs.

All-English Instruction

Researchers have conducted numerous studies on second-language acquisition in academic settings. Canadian researcher James Cummins, as cited by Virginia Collier and Wayne Thomas, established the concept of different levels of language proficiency and theorized that second-language learners can reach conversational proficiency in 2 to 3 years, whereas academic language proficiency can take an additional 5 to 7 years. Collier has built on the work of Cummins to identify a pattern of second-language acquisition in U.S. schools that is consistent across student groups, home language, country of origin, socioeconomic status, and other factors. The patterns are consistent for U.S. schools where all instruction was provided in the second language, English.

The first pattern concerned level of formal schooling. Students with no formal schooling in their first language require 7 to 10 years or more to acquire academic English proficiency, according to Collier. Also, ELLs with little or no formal schooling in their first language will make fewer achievement gains from fourth grade through high school, as the academic and cognitive demands of the curriculum increase with each year. Research shows that these ELLs might achieve 6-to-8 months' gain each school year relative to their native-English-speaking-peers' achievement gain of 10 months.

The second pattern concerned age and formal school experience in the first language. ELL students aged 8 to 11 years with 2 to 5 years of formal schooling in their first language performed on par with native English speakers in 5 to 7 years. However, students who arrived before the age of 8 required 7 to

10 years or more, due to lack of formal schooling in the first language. These findings appear to support the underlying theory of transitional bilingual education, which is that the use of the home language for instruction helps children learn both English and school subjects.

Bilingual Education

In contrast to all-English instruction, students who receive instruction in both the first and second language typically score at or above grade levels in their first languages in all subject areas while they build academic proficiency in the second language. Research shows that after 4 to 7 years of quality bilingual instruction, students typically reach and surpass native English speakers' academic performance in all subject areas. This phenomenon is confusing because one would think that with two languages being learned, the student would require more time to reach academic proficiency in both languages. However, it appears that because students have attained and maintained grade-level proficiency in the first language during the 4 to 7 years it takes to acquire a second language, they are more likely to sustain their achievement over time and often outperform their monolingual peers during the secondary years of school.

Additional Considerations: External Variables

Second-language acquisition is also dependent on many external variables that can affect the amount of time required to learn English. Gilbert García lists some of them:

- *Variability among the population of ELL children and youth:* ELL children and youth come from diverse backgrounds that include country of origin, culture, and socioeconomic status.
- *Foreign-born status:* Recent statistics show that approximately 45% of ELLs are foreign-born. They enter U.S. schools at different ages, with diverse exposure to English.
- *Formal schooling in native country:* ELLs have varied formal schooling experiences and first-language development.
- *Native-born status:* Statistics show that approximately 55% of ELLs are born in the United States.

- *Range of first- and second-language development:* ELLs, whether foreign- or native-born, can enter U.S. schools with varied levels of first- and second-language proficiency.
- *Socioeconomic status:* Students who come from backgrounds of poverty often have limited language proficiency and readiness skills to be successful in school.
- *Teacher preparation:* The most significant variable for second-language acquisition is teacher preparation. Unfortunately, research shows that many U.S. educators lack formal preparation to work with second-language learners. There is a shortage of bilingual and English as a Second Language (ESL) educators in the United States.

Conclusion

Second-language acquisition has consistently been a subject for debate among policymakers. U.S. schools are now being held accountable for annual academic achievement targets that include disaggregated data on achievement by ELLs. As a result, policymakers and administrators have made the argument that second-language acquisition should (a) be on par with native English speakers within 3 years and (b) decrease the achievement gap.

Many researchers and scholars argue that these goals are not realistic or possible in all English schools, nor are they consistent with research. Research shows that ELLs in the early grades can perform on grade level with their peers within 2 to 3 years. However, this research is misleading for policymakers who anticipate that ELLs will continue to make the same gains over time. Therefore, the achievement gap is a result of three factors, cited by Thomas and Collier:

1. *Second-language acquisition does not occur in isolation from other skill development.* Native English speakers are, of course, not standing still waiting for ELLs to catch up. They continue to develop cognitively, linguistically, and academically with each school year in an "English-friendly" learning environment.

2. *The cognitive, linguistic, and academic demand across curricula and subjects continues to increase with each school year.* Subsequently, ELLs who showed impressive gains in the early grades typically make 6-to-8 months' achievement gains each year in English-only schools. Hence, it is statistically logical

that the achievement gap will continue to widen over time.

3. *There is a lack of quality bilingual programs and well-prepared teachers to meet the needs of U.S. schools.* Research indicates that students in bilingual programs reach, maintain, and surpass grade-level achievement of monolingual peers into and throughout the high school years. Further, the amount of time to acquire a second language is less (4 to 7 years) compared with English-only programs (7 to 10 years).

Research clearly supports the notion that language acquisition is a lifelong process. Perhaps the question for policymakers should not be how long it takes to learn English, but rather under what conditions, with what resources, and from which teachers does optimum English language learning occur? Answers to that question remain elusive. The legal requirement flowing from the *Lau v. Nichols* (1974) decision of the U.S. Supreme court is that children be taught English effectively and that their study of academic subjects not be allowed to lag due to inadequate English. However, several states now require that ELLs be in special English instructional programs no longer than 1 year, a time span that is grossly inadequate according to most of the relevant research.

Michelle Kuamoo

See also Academic English; BICS/CALP Theory; English in the World; Language Learning in Children and Adults; Program Effectiveness Research

Further Readings

Collier, V. (1995). Acquiring a second language for school. *Directions in Language & Education, 1*(4), 1–7.

García, G. (2000). Lessons from research: What is the length of time it takes limited English proficient students to acquire English and succeed in an all-English classroom? *Brief National Clearinghouse for Bilingual Education, 5,* 1–15.

Genesee, F. (2000). *Brain research: Implications for second language learning.* Washington, DC: ERIC Clearinghouse on Languages and Linguistics. (ERIC Reproduction Service Document No. ED447727)

Krashen, S. (1985). *The input hypothesis.* Beverly Hills, CA: Laredo.

Krashen, S., & Terrell, T. (1983). *The natural approach: Language acquisition in the classroom.* New York: Prentice Hall.

Morrison, R. (2002, September 29). The Englishing of earth: Extending English as a foreign language. *The Times* (London), p. 2.

National Clearinghouse for English Language Acquisition and Language Instruction Educational Programs. (2006). *NCELA FAQ: How many school-aged English language learners (ELLs) are there in the U.S?* Retrieved from http://www.ncela.gwu.edu/expert/faq/01leps.html

Tabors, P. (1997). *One child, two languages: A guide for preschool educators of children learning English as a second language.* Baltimore, MD: Paul H. Brookes.

Thomas, W., & Collier, V. (1997). School effectiveness for language minority students. *Resource Collection Series, National Clearinghouse for Bilingual Education, 9,* 1–96.

English as a Second Language (ESL) Approaches

In language classrooms, to meet language learners' needs and to understand why learners can benefit from certain methods, it is essential for language teachers to understand theory-based approaches. Approaches are the roots of teaching methods. As defined by Edward Anthony, language approaches are theoretically well-informed positions and beliefs about the nature of language and language learning. In other words, approaches serve as the principles of language teaching.

With English acquisition as the primary goal, English as a Second Language (ESL) instruction is also an essential element of any bilingual program. Likewise, ESL approaches can also shed light on bilingual classroom practice. This entry focuses on introducing and discussing some major approaches that have guided ESL teaching, including the grammar-based approach, communicative language teaching, the content-based approach, sheltered English instruction, the whole-language approach, the natural approach, cooperative language learning, and task-based language teaching. The work of Jack C. Richards and Theodore S. Rodgers provides a comprehensive overview of the historical development of ESL methods and approaches. Much of the discussion below draws on their frameworks and descriptions of the theories and practices associated with each of these approaches.

Grammar-Based Approach

The *grammar-based approach* addresses the structure or grammatical elements of language in order to improve language skills. In an ESL class taught through the grammar-based approach, typically, the teacher spends most of the available class time explaining grammar elements; the students are mere listeners.

The *grammar-translation method* is a practice of the grammar-based approach. Grammar is taught with extensive explanations in students' native language, and later practice is through translating sentences from the target language to the native language, or verse visa. Little attention is paid to the content of texts; rather, emphasis is on language form itself. Similarly, little attention is paid to pronunciation and active use of English.

Although to some extent, focus on form is essential for English learners, especially English beginners, the grammar-based approach has many obvious drawbacks. No class time is allocated to allow students to produce their own English sentences, and even less time is spent on English output production (spontaneous or reproductive). Students may have difficulties "relating" to the language because the classroom experience is disconnected from real life. There is often little contextualization of the grammar; thus, students memorize abstract rules in isolation. Therefore, grammar-based approaches have largely been rejected by the field, though grammar instruction is still considered by many as an essential component of ESL instruction and can be included within other approaches.

Communicative Language Teaching

Communicative language teaching (CLT) is a current recognized approach and is influenced by theories of language as communication and the functions of language (e.g., how to make a request). The emphasis of CLT is on functional communication, social interaction, and real-life language use. Addressing fluency and accuracy, this approach considers integrated components of communicative competence, including the grammatical, functional, and sociolinguistic. The major tenet of CLT is that language acquisition is achieved through using language communicatively, rather than from repetitious drills that are common in the grammar-based approach.

In an ESL class with the CLT approach, the teacher's role is that of facilitator. The teacher sets up exercises and then gives direction to the class, but the students have much more speaking opportunities than they have in a traditional ESL classroom. The classroom is stress free and student centered. In addition, teachers utilize a variety of techniques (e.g., dialogues, role plays) to get students involved and use peer tutoring, pairs, or small groups to increase class inter-action and communication-in-context practices. Class activities focus on information negotiation and infor-mation sharing as well as language functions (e.g., giving instructions) in order to help engage students in meaningful and real lifelike language use. Students can be motivated to learn by their desire to communi-cate in meaningful ways about meaningful topics.

Content-Based Approach

The *content-based approach* combines language learning with subject matter (e.g., math, science) learning in an ESL class. This approach sharply con-trasts with the traditional ESL instruction in which language skills are taught in an isolated way. The foundation of the content-based approach is the prin-ciple that language learning is more successful when students use language as a means of acquiring infor-mation. Although all students in class are second-language learners, ESL teachers make use of grade-level appropriate curricula in a content area to teach ESL students. Thus, the content-based approach can help ESL students develop both language and acade-mic knowledge. At the same time, however, ESL teachers face challenges and may need more training in various content areas.

In adopting a content-based approach, teachers are in charge of choosing a subject of interest to students. Language-focused follow-up exercises (e.g., plural versus singular in math) are included to help students draw attention to the target language skills or linguis-tic features needed to learn and talk about that subject. Teachers monitor students' English output and pro-vide immediate feedback. Teachers should differenti-ate between achievement in language skills and achievement in the subject matter when evaluating students. ESL teachers may ask this critical question: How much content best supports language learning?

Sheltered English Instruction

Sheltered instruction is a commonly used approach today. It uses English as the medium of content area instruction. The instructor can be an ESL teacher or a content-area-trained teacher to use a variety of strate-gies and techniques to make the instruction compre-hensible for ELLs. Structured immersion classrooms may include both ESL and English-proficient students. Sheltered English instruction serves as a bridge and connects the ESL instruction with the academic main-stream instruction (e.g., regular math instruction designed for English-fluent student). It provides sub-ject instructions to ESL students while emphasizing development of English language skills. In addition, all students and teachers in class socialize with cultur-ally appropriate classroom behaviors. However, this approach requires students to have already acquired some English language skills. Teachers are also required to have some appropriate training in shel-tered English instruction before teaching the class.

In sheltered English instruction, teachers create a stress-free learning environment and use multiple sources, such as physical activities, visual aids, and body language, to teach key vocabulary for concept development in subject areas. Teachers not only adopt multiple techniques to make content area materials comprehensible for ESL students but also understand ESL students' second-language-acquisition process and cultural differences. The sheltered English instruc-tion approach may include a primary language instruction component. Teachers make effective use of students' native languages in the classroom in order to make lessons taught in English more comprehensi-ble. Interactions with English-proficient students may also be incorporated in lesson to increase ESL students' opportunities of practicing English in a natural way. Sheltered English instruction is a key component in most bilingual education models, as it is used to gradually increase English content area instruction as students make the transition from native language to English language instruction.

Whole-Language Approach

Different from the phonetic approach that focuses only on fragmented language, such as phonemic awareness and phonics drills, the main characteristic of the *whole-language approach* is that language teaching should not be separated into component skills, but rather experienced as an integrated system of communication (listening, speaking, reading, and writing). Rather than focusing on language as a mechanical skill, it is taught as a connection to students' existing language and life experience. Language used in class must be meaning-ful and carry out authentic functions. Teachers who use the whole-language approach teach students to use phonics (sound-based), semantic (meaning-based), and syntactic (structural and context) cues when reading to help the students make meanings from the texts they read. In short, the whole-language approach addresses the importance of meaning and meaning making in English teaching and learning. In addition, the whole-language approach to some extent draws on an interactional perspective of language learning and advocates cooperative learning and participatory learning by using authentic language.

The four language skills are integrated in class and are improved simultaneously. Students read and write with others in class. Student-centered classroom empower students to learn according to their interests. ESL teachers adopting the whole-language approach usually use authentic literature for ESL students to develop and practice their reading skills. Writing is also for real audiences.

Natural Approach

The *natural approach* was developed by Tracy Terrell in the 1970s. This approach advocates that comprehensible language input is essential for triggering language acquisition. Terrell focuses on improving basic personal communication skills in her teaching and views communicative competence progressing through five stages: (1) the preproduction stage of aural comprehension, (2) early speech production, (3) speech emergence, (4) intermediate fluency, and (5) advanced fluency. In other words, comprehension typically precedes production, and students' progress occurs naturally.

An ESL classroom using the natural approach includes the following:

1. Students are not forced to speak English until they feel ready to do so.

2. The teacher is the source of English input and uses variety of materials and classroom activities.

3. The teacher creates a stress-free learning environment and does not correct student errors in front of the class.

4. Facilitating the interaction of students in pair or small groups to practice newly acquired structures is a major focus in class. The grammar structure should be learned in a natural order.

5. Activities incorporate a wide variety of visual aids (e.g., picture), hands-on manipulative, and realia.

6. Classes are student centered.

7. Formal grammar instruction should be kept to minimum.

The natural approach provides ample guidance and resources for ESL students at the beginner levels but has limitations in teaching advanced English learners. Moreover, since this approach allows the delay of oral production until speech emerges, it is hard to manage class activities to meet students' different speech-emerging timetables.

Cooperative Language Learning

Cooperative language learning (CLL), as its name indicates, aims at getting students involved in language learning by using cooperative activities while developing communicative competence. This approach is influenced by an interactive perspective of language learning and a theory of cooperative learning. CLL also embraces some principles of communicative language teaching. A major characteristic of CLL approach is that it can raise students' awareness of language structure, lexical items, and language functions through interactive tasks.

By using such an approach, teachers can increase students' frequency of English language use and variety of English learning practices, because the CLL approach helps develop students' critical thinking skills as they need to collaborate with their peers to design plans for their group, to challenge others' views, and to provide constructive criticism as well as alternative solutions. It fosters opportunities for students to be resources for each other. Advantages of the CLL approach include enhancing students' self-esteem and promoting students' motivation; however, some students may be unaccustomed to working collaboratively with others on academic tasks. Thus, teachers may need to give extra attention to collaborative skills, such as disagreeing politely and asking for help and explanation. Teachers may also need to be aware of factors such as different cultural expectations, individual learning styles, and personality differences that can affect the successful application of the CLL approach.

In an ESL classroom with the CLL approach, pair and small-group work are emphasized to carry out class activities and learning. Teachers use peer tutoring and peer monitoring to build up cooperation in learning. By facilitating collaboration, teachers devalue competition among students and thus decrease students' stress or fear in language learning. The classroom is student centered; teachers need to ensure that every student in groups participate in activities. Cooperative interaction usually follows a teacher-directed presentation of new material.

Task-Based Language Teaching

The *task-based language teaching* (TBLT) approach uses tasks as a core unit of instruction in language teaching. The basic premise of TBLT is that language should be learned through a set of meaningful communicative tasks that involve students in comprehending, producing, or interacting in the target language. In other words, tasks should go beyond pure practices of language skills. This approach emphasizes the meaningfulness and authenticity of language use, which also links to the communicative language teaching approach. Engaging students in task-based activities can help students contextualize and activate language learning. In short, tasks provide opportunities for language input and output.

ESL teachers working with TBLT link the curricular goals with communicative goals. Furthermore, teachers identify types of tasks (e.g., academic related, social related) that enhance learning and variables that may affect the success of task completion (e.g., English proficiency level, the complexity of the task). As Susan Feez describes, tasks adopted in a TBLT classroom can be either those that students might need to achieve in real life or that have a pedagogical purpose specific to the classroom. When evaluating students, teachers should focus on the process of completing the task instead of the product.

Conclusion

Although each of the approaches described here has its own characteristics, considerable overlaps of these approaches are commonly observed in different ESL instruction. The choice of approach naturally depends on student factors such as age and proficiency level and the availability of resources within the learning environment. Appropriate approaches to English language teaching are the keystone of teachers' choices of teaching methodology.

Chang Pu

See also Audio-Lingual Method; Communicative Approach; Grammar-Translation Method; Natural Approach; SIOP; Whole Language

Further Readings

Anthony, E. M. (1963). Approach, method, and technique. *English Language Teaching, 17,* 63–67.

Brown, D. H. (2001). *Teaching by principles: An interactive approach to language pedagogy.* New York: Addison-Wesley Longman.

Fezz, S. (1998). *Text-based syllabus design.* Sydney, Australia: National Center for English Teaching and Research.

Richards, J., & Rodgers, T. (1986). *Approaches and methods in language teaching.* Cambridge, UK: Cambridge University Press.

Terrell, T. D. (1977). A natural approach to second language acquisition and learning. *Modern Language Journal, 61,* 325–336.

ENGLISH FOR THE CHILDREN CAMPAIGN

State education agencies reported that the number of limited-English-proficient students in the nation's schools rose from 2.1 million in the 1990–1991 academic year to more than 3.7 million in 1999–2000. A congressionally mandated study found that these students received lower grades, were judged by their teachers to have lower academic abilities, and scored below their classmates on standardized tests of reading and math. Subsequent responses to these problems have run the gamut. Some policymakers have advocated bilingual education as a remedy, while others have taken the opposite view and blamed bilingual education for the inequities. The latter argue that bilingual education programs are responsible for retarding the acquisition of English by children who need desperately to have an age-appropriate command of that language. Beginning in the 1980s, sentiments against bilingual education became increasingly critical as more and more communities adopted bilingual education programs. Shortly after taking office, President Ronald Reagan announced that it was erroneous and unaligned with American concepts to have bilingual programs in order to preserve students' native languages and that such programs would not allow students to achieve enough English proficiency to participate in the job market. Many people listened. By feeding on the frustration of policymakers and the increasingly harsh rhetoric surrounding debates over these programs, proponents of

English-only instruction were able to gain support for more restrictionist language policies in the schools. By the late 1990s, many states had contributed substantial amounts of money to resolve these problems, but the number of English language learners (ELLs) did not diminish. Opposition to bilingual education became more organized and determined to curtail or eliminate these programs.

Nowhere were these issues more evident than in California. During the 1990s, California had approximately one third of the bilingual education programs in the country. With antibilingual education sentiments at an all-time high, Ron Unz started the "English for the Children" campaign, designed to dismantle bilingual education in the state.

Educated as a theoretical physicist, Unz had run unsuccessfully as a Republican candidate for governor of California in 1994. With the support of anti-bilingual activists, Unz collected more than 510,000 signed petitions from registered voters to launch a voter initiative that would end bilingual education in the public school system. The initiative went on the ballot in California in 1998. Unz, a multimillionaire software developer, vowed to dig deep into his own pockets and spend whatever it took to get the measure passed.

Benefiting from the swell of xenophobia that dominated the state's politics during that time, Unz and the English for the Children campaign constructed a platform from which to promote California's Proposition 227. According to this proposition, the bilingual education services offered in California inhibited students' English acquisition and overall educational progress. Proposition 227 was promoted as an elixir for language minority students' ailments and an alternative to bilingual education, promoting a 1-year English immersion course to prepare non-English-speaking students for mainstream classes. According to the Unz initiative, language minority students were to be placed in *sheltered English immersion* (a term coined by the English for the Children movement) for a period usually not to exceed 1 year, before being mainstreamed into the regular education classroom. As originally stated in Article 2, Section 305, of the proposition,

> All children in California public schools shall be taught English by being taught in English. In particular, this shall require that all children be placed in English language classrooms. Children who are

English learners shall be educated through sheltered English immersion during a temporary transition period not normally intended to exceed one year. Local schools shall be permitted to place in the same classroom English learners of different ages but whose degree of English proficiency is similar. Local schools shall be encouraged to mix together in the same classroom English learners from different native-language groups but with the same degree of English fluency. Once English learners have acquired a good working knowledge of English, they shall be transferred to English language mainstream classrooms.

While the initiative was harsh and heavy-handed, a waiver option allowed parents to exclude their children from the sheltered English programs and place them in bilingual programs if the child (a) already possessed good English skills, (b) was over 10 years old and the school staff thought it would benefit him or her to be in a bilingual education program, and (c) was in a special needs program. Students could be mixed by age and grade. Teachers and/or other school personnel could be sued to ensure that instruction was delivered in English. Within 1 school year, students were expected to attain a "good working knowledge of English" so that they could be transferred to a mainstream classroom with native-English-speaking children. In this context, the minority language students were expected to comprehend the subject matter in English, without any further language instruction.

Unz targeted this campaign at California's Latino communities. He capitalized on discontent with the public schools and sought to make bilingual education the scapegoat. Expensive ads promoting the initiative appeared in Spanish language media. Some advocates for immigrant rights, along with a few Asian and Latino politicians, signed on as well. Although Unz adamantly denied having any anti-immigrant motivations for promoting Proposition 227, he could not deny his ties to more overtly biased organizations. Unz's cochairperson of the initiative was Gloria Matta Tuchman, a first-grade teacher from Santa Ana who finished fifth in the 1994 race for California State Superintendent of Public Instruction. Although she was not hesitant to announce her Mexican American roots, Tuchman was reserved about her ties to the English-only movement. She joined U.S. English, an organization working to make English the official language of the country, and served as a member of its board of directors between 1989 and 1992. Another outspoken supporter of Unz and English for the Children was Linda Chávez. Chávez served as the executive director of U.S. English until a memorandum by one of its founders was made public in which he made stereotypical remarks concerning Latinos. She resigned her position on the board and later founded the Center for Equal Opportunity, which opposes bilingual education and affirmative action programs. Unz served on the board of directors of the center and worked closely with Chávez for years.

In 1998, California voters passed Proposition 227, the original English for the Children referendum. Although initially this law prohibited language minority students from receiving bilingual education services, the waiver option allowed many parents to place their children back into bilingual programs. Touting ostensibly higher testing scores after the first year of the implementation of Proposition 227 (even though children in waiver bilingual programs performed just as well, as shown in research conducted by Stephen Krashen), the English for the Children campaign moved on to Arizona.

As they had done in California, the organization leaders were able to get Proposition 203 on the November 2000 ballot in Arizona. Despite many educators, researchers, and community organizations around Arizona denouncing Proposition 203, the pro-203 community was able to reinforce its position through a well-funded and well-organized media campaign. Unz and his followers were able to accumulate enough political and social support to once again overshadow the opposition and convince the public of the initiative's ostensible integrity. Due to the large number of students who were able to opt out of the sheltered English immersion programs in California, Unz rewrote the Arizona referendum to make it more restrictive for students and parents and more punitive for educators who might stray from the guidelines.

Basing their claims on the alleged success of students in California, the Arizona brand of English for the Children was able to avoid some of the accusations of cultural insensitivity. Caught in a landslide of confusing test scores, patriotic tropes, and ethnocentric statements, the majority of the public, including many Latinos, understood the initiative as a step toward a better education for non-English-speaking students. On November 7, 2000, Arizona's voting public voted with a 64% majority to limit the

educational services that language minority students receive. The same 1-year program that was called for in California was to be offered in Arizona.

The Unz organization did a good job convincing the public that all language minority children were failing in school and that their failure was due to bilingual education. Interestingly, only 30% of students eligible for language services in Arizona were involved in true bilingual education programs. Thus, advocates of Proposition 203 successfully persuaded the voting public to support the point of view that blamed Arizona students' low achievement on a program in which the majority of students were not even involved.

After Proposition 203 became law in Arizona in 2000, Unz mounted a campaign in Massachusetts. On November 5, 2002, 70% of voters in that state approved Massachusetts's "Question 2." Aligned with Arizona's version of the law, this version of the English for the Children program dismantled Massachusetts's bilingual education programs and placed strict regulations on educators. Shifting from the original name of the instructional program as sheltered English immersion, Unz's group modified the name to *structured* English immersion, to appear more rigorous in their approach.

During the same year as the Massachusetts campaign, Unz also attempted to plant his views in Colorado. Although English for the Children had succeeded in California, Arizona, and Massachusetts, Colorado voters rejected Unz's ballot initiative in 2002. The campaign in Colorado proved unsuccessful for several reasons. During the initial attempt to get the law on the ballot in 2000, the Colorado Supreme Court declared the measure unconstitutional due to deceptive and misleading wording (mostly about the waiver process). Undeterred, its proponents regrouped and promised to return, and, in 2002, Unz was successful in getting his initiative placed on the ballot as "Amendment 31" (formally titled "English Language Education for Children in Public Schools"). During those 2 years, however, probilingual education groups (e.g., English Plus and Colorado Common Sense) were able to rally support across the state and promote their "No-on-31" campaign, as reported by Kathy Escamilla, Sheila Shannon, Silvana Carlos, and Jorge García. Instead of focusing on the benefits of bilingual education programs and promoting scientific research, opponents of English for the Children attacked the actual initiative. Ultimately, the focus of No-on-31 was narrowed down to three basic tenets, summarized as "PPC": (1) Parental involvement (P) and choice would be eliminated, (2) Punitive measures (P) in the amendment (e.g., suing educators) were considered too extreme, and (3) Cost (C) to the taxpayers would skyrocket if the amendment passed.

Opposition to the initiative came in many forms. In September 2002, the board of education of the Denver Public Schools voted unanimously to oppose Amendment 31. Pat Stryker, an education activist, donated $3.3 million to the No-on-31 cause. Parents and educators organized to raise money and distribute literature. In all, it was a successful grassroots effort that enabled the voters of Colorado to understand the implications of Amendment 31. Among the most effective arguments made against the initiative was that (a) it would create segregated classrooms, (b) it would diminish parental choice, (c) educators could be fired or banned for 5 years as a form of punishment, and (d) the amendment would require even more funding than what schools were receiving at the time. Although Unz was able to fund attorneys to write and defend the initiative, pay workers to gather the needed signatures to get the measure on the ballot, and financially support the Colorado staff of English for the Children, the measure was rejected by a margin of 56% to 44%.

Unz and his supporters managed to construct an image of their movement as defenders of children who want to learn English but are being cheated by bilingual education. Their campaign did nothing to ameliorate bilingual education's woes, such as lack of resources, disparate methodologies, and national standardization efforts. As some critics have pointed out, the movement glosses over intentions of removing languages other than English from public schools. However, the English for the Children campaign garnered the support of many well-meaning voters who did not fully understand the implications of the measure. While successful in three of the four states in which they campaigned, none of its key players were able to win enough support to return to elected politics. Tuchman, Chávez, and Unz had all run for office unsuccessfully before the initiative campaign. None of them have run for office since.

Eric Johnson

See *also* Amendment 31 (Colorado); Chávez, Linda; English Immersion; English-Only Organizations; Proposition 203 (Arizona); Proposition 227 (California); Question 2 (Massachusetts); Unz, Ron

Further Readings

Escamilla, K., Shannon, S., Carlos, S., & García, J. (2003). Breaking the code: Colorado's defeat of the anti-bilingual education initiative (Amendment 31). *Bilingual Research Journal, 27*, 357–382.

Johnson, E. (2005). Proposition 203: A critical metaphor analysis. *Bilingual Research Journal, 29*, 69–84.

Krashen, S. (2000, September 13). Bilingual ed foe used distorted facts. *East Valley Tribune*, p. A19.

Unz, R., & Tuchman, G. M. (1997). *English language education for children in public schools*. Retrieved from http://www.onenation.org/fulltext.html

ENGLISH IMMERSION

English immersion, an approach to teaching English by providing instruction solely through English, holds considerable appeal in the American imagination. Surely, the best way to learn a language is to immerse oneself in it, many believe, and the more deeply and thoroughly the immersion, the more quickly the language will be learned. Several states, such as California, Arizona, and Massachusetts, have adopted laws mandating English immersion for all children who do not know English. Many proponents of English immersion cite studies of French immersion programs in Canada to support laws mandating English immersion. But what is language immersion, and how does it work?

Immersion Programs for English-Speaking Children

Language immersion programs for English-speaking children, in which students learn a new language as they study academic subject matter through the new language and through English, have been established as highly effective. After 6 years in such a program, English-speaking children can be expected to perform at or above grade level in their academic work and can typically read, write, and speak a foreign language. In the French programs in Québec that are often cited, children receive 90% to 100% of immersion language instruction the first year, which then decreases yearly while instruction through English increases, until the proportion reaches 50/50 by fifth or sixth grade. Parents are cautioned that they must expect their children to remain in these programs for a minimum of 6 years, because learning a new language takes many years. Despite the lengthy time commitment, immersion programs appeal strongly to English-speaking parents who are eager for their children to attain fluency and literacy in another language as an educational enrichment.

English Immersion in the United States

English immersion, as it is implemented in the United States, follows a different approach. Supporters of English immersion argue that young children can learn English quickly and easily and can then turn their attention to academic learning. In California, Arizona, and Massachusetts, where English immersion has been legally mandated, children are expected to learn English within 1 year and then exit the program. When pressed for evidence to support the use of this 1-year, monolingual program model, English immersion advocates typically cite the success of the 6-year, bilingual immersion programs. Conflating these two very different programs leads to considerable confusion over the education of English language learners (ELLs).

The controversy surrounding the best ways to educate ELLs is not likely to be resolved merely by clarifying the pedagogical differences between foreign-language immersion programs and the English immersion programs as currently implemented. Nevertheless, a clear understanding of what immersion is and how it is meant to work constitutes an essential first step.

"Sink or Swim" Versus Structured Immersion

When schools provide no services to students struggling to learn English, placing them in classrooms alongside English-speaking students, some ELLs can eventually learn English and recover academically, while others cannot. Such a lack of support is termed a "sink or swim" approach and was common before the Supreme Court's *Lau v. Nichols* decision of 1974, which required schools to provide support for ELLs. Early advocates of English immersion in the United States had noticed the success of French immersion programs for English-speaking children and recognized that French immersion was not "sink or swim," but rather had a very clear structure.

To distinguish English immersion from the sink-or-swim approach, English immersion advocates Keith Baker and Adriana de Kanter insisted their approach be "structured" as well, terming it "structured immersion," and outlined three essential characteristics to which they attributed the success of immersion programs. First, they noted that teachers must understand the language spoken by their students. Second, they recognized that the curriculum and materials must be specially designed and structured for immersion students. Third, they noted that teachers must be trained to use immersion methods.

However, in laws enacted in the late 1990s mandating structured English immersion (SEI) in several states, these minimal requirements for structure were dropped. Teachers are not required to be (and typically are not) bilingual, and no special curriculum is used. When teachers are assigned to teach English learners, they are asked to undertake some minimal SEI training; but often the training consists primarily of techniques to teach English as a Second Language (ESL), rather than information on the theory or practice of immersion. Indeed, a study conducted by Wayne Wright and Daniel Choi showed that SEI teachers in Arizona who had taken an SEI training course did not know what SEI was or how it was meant to work.

The Basic Premise of English Immersion

Proponents of English immersion subscribe to the basic premise that unlike adults, children learn new languages quickly, easily, and perfectly. Unfortunately, research in language acquisition does not support this claim, with the single exception of pronunciation. If children are exposed to the new language before the onset of puberty, their chances of attaining a native-like accent are considerably greater than if they begin learning a new language at a later age. Ironically, this aptitude for accent, combined with a natural desire to fit in with their peers, can often fool adults into thinking that young English learners are proficient in English long before they truly are. It takes the typical student considerably more than a year or two to learn a new language well enough to pass academic tests given in that language, and this is true whether the students are children or adults. Still, it is widely believed that young children are better language learners than older students or adults, regardless of the research evidence.

The evidence that is often cited in support of short-term, monolingual English immersion programs is drawn largely from research on multiyear, bilingual English immersion programs, which differ dramatically from English immersion in their student populations, goals, curricula, teacher qualifications, and years of duration, among other factors.

Learning a Foreign Language Versus Learning a Second Language

SEI, popularly referred to as both *structured* and *sheltered English immersion,* differs from *foreign-language* (FL) *immersion* in important respects. One difference lies in the student population and the students' social and linguistic status vis-à-vis the immersion language in particular. Language acquisition researchers worldwide maintain the crucial distinction between (a) students who know the language of wider communication (for example, English in the United States) and are undertaking to learn another language (foreign to the wider society) and (b) students whose home language is regarded as foreign by the mainstream society and are undertaking to learn a second language, the language in use for wider communication. English-speaking children in the United States trying to learn Spanish as a foreign language, for example, have very different experiences and outcomes than Spanish-speaking children trying to learn English as their second language.

Differences in Status

FL immersion was designed as educational enrichment for children who know English, not for children whose educational futures hang on their ability to learn English. Wallace Lambert and Richard Tucker, early researchers of the French language immersion programs in Canada, explained in 1972 that while FL immersion is "additive" and beneficial for English-speaking children, this is because they learn through both languages for many years and never risk losing proficiency in their first language.

Lambert, Tucker, and other leading immersion researchers attempted to dispel many of the myths that had already sprung up regarding immersion education, warning that evidence from FL immersion could not be used in support of arguments for using English immersion in English-speaking countries. Among the reasons cited were that in FL immersion, great care is taken to ensure the new language is learned at no expense to either academic achievement or to proficiency in the student's first language; FL immersion involves specific instructional services for language learners; and FL immersion is not imposed on children by the school or government, but is actively sought by parents. However, even the most casual observation of English immersion classrooms in the United States reveals that many children are studying English at great cost to their academic achievement, many children are losing their proficiency in their first language, many children receive no specific instructional services, and English immersion is often imposed over the strong protests of parents and community.

Despite explicit and repeated warnings by immersion researchers against using English immersion (often it is *submersion*) with language minority children, several states now mandate its use. It is unlikely, however, that stakeholders, educators, policymakers, or parents understand that English immersion, in the way it has been often interpreted, is a risky intervention. Simply put, it has not been established as effective, and it has been explicitly warned against by the researchers who understand it best.

While social and linguistic status plays a role in the problems caused by English immersion, more critical still are differences in the duration, goals, and teacher qualifications between the two types of programs.

FL Immersion: A Long-Term, Bilingual Approach

Program Duration

The FL immersion model adopted in many elementary schools in Québec was created as a long-term (6 years or more) program, designed to promote bilingualism and biliteracy among English-speaking children, while supporting academic inquiry through English and the foreign language, French. Students may use English at any time, whether to request clarification or to explain their own understanding. Although in the early years, much of the instruction from the teacher is given in the new language, the teacher always understands and responds to students' use of English, often reflecting students' comments and questions back to them in the immersion language. The amount of instruction in the native language, English, remains at this level or increases yearly until it is carried out 50% of the time and students become skilled at speaking, reading, and writing in both English and the foreign language.

Program Goals

In contrast to FL immersion, no attempt is made in SEI programs to allow for the children's first-language development or to teach them literacy in two languages. Students are not permitted to study academic subjects through the language they already know, nor are teachers required to be bilingual, so students are typically unable to ask questions or understand instruction. Hence, SEI clearly constitutes an entirely different model from the long-term, bilingual FL immersion program described above. It is, moreover, a model that has been implemented without having been systematically researched because of misunderstandings of the dramatic differences between a 6-year or more program with the goals of academic excellence, bilingualism, and biliteracy and a 1-year program that strives for the quick, surface development of English only.

Teacher Qualifications

In the initial years of FL immersion, teachers must be bilingual. Simply put, teachers have been found to be most effective when they can understand the questions and concerns of their students. When students have not yet learned enough of the immersion language to phrase their questions and comments in that language, teachers must be able to understand the children's home language. It is essential that teachers be able to communicate with all students directly, even though the teachers themselves may never speak the students' language in class. In later years, as the children become more proficient in the foreign language, the teacher may be monolingual in that language. In contrast to teachers in FL immersion programs, it has been noted that many, if not most, of the teachers currently engaged in teaching SEI are not bilingual and often do not even permit other students to translate questions or comments.

Immersion teachers must also be trained to use immersion methods. Teachers must become skilled at providing an instructional context that is comprehensible to all students at all times, reducing or elaborating the linguistic demands of academic activities to suit the learners. As in any program, instructional settings should vary among whole-group, small-group, and individual activities, but an effective immersion teacher must always be cognizant of the linguistic interactions and how to best facilitate them. Sometimes students working collaboratively in small groups may be encouraged to discuss issues in their first language; at other times, they may be encouraged to use their foreign language. The skilled foreign-language teacher develops a fine-tuned sense of the appropriateness of the linguistic demands for any given setting or activity. In contrast, in many cases, children in English immersion settings have been forbidden to speak in their first language and, in some cases, have suffered verbal and physical punishment for doing so.

An Authentic English Immersion Program

Modeled properly after the FL immersion approach, English immersion would use bilingual teachers, trained in immersion methods, to engage students in a specially designed academic immersion curriculum. Student comments and questions could be phrased in either language, since teachers would understand both. Despite attempts to maintain at least 50% of instructional time in the students' home language, students' use of English would naturally outstrip their use of the home language as they develop proficiency in English, as is consistently noted in the research literature. The program would last for a minimum of 6 years, after which students would be expected to demonstrate proficiency in speaking, reading, and writing in both languages. What might students achieve in a model such as this?

In fact, two models that meet these requirements have been implemented and researched. They are *maintenance,* or developmental, bilingual education for ELLs, and *dual,* or two-way, immersion. The maintenance model, first implemented in the 1960s, has been largely replaced by *transitional* bilingual programs, not because transitional programs were found to be superior in any way, but because public opinion did not support long-term programs. If people believe that children can learn English quickly, easily, and well, they will see no need to provide young students with academic support or to ensure that they develop bilingualism and biliteracy. Transitional bilingual programs allow young children to use their home language only as a means to transition into all-English instruction, expected to occur within approximately 3 years. However, even 3 years seems unacceptably long to those who assume that English can be learned quickly and easily and who find the educational needs of ELLs inconvenient. Instead, policies and laws have been implemented requiring that students learn English within 1 year, but it can already be observed that legislating away the difficulties of learning English has not proven effective.

Parents and educators interested in ELL children developing bilingualism and academic success find it increasingly difficult to locate developmental bilingual programs, with one exception: two-way bilingual (or dual-language) immersion programs. Dual-language immersion (DI) programs have not only been maintained in the face of attacks against bilingual education but have also increased and expanded. The success of the DI model is due in large part to its effectiveness in teaching a foreign language to English-speaking children who have experienced little success in other models of foreign-language instruction.

Dual Immersion: English Immersion Plus

Dual immersion has as a goal the attainment of bilingualism by two different monolingual populations, instructed together. It integrates English speakers and English learners in such a way that all students become bilingual and biliterate. Programs vary considerably in amount and distribution of instruction through the two languages, but all aim to provide at least 50% of instruction through the target minority language and focus on teaching language through academic content. In all DI models, the ELLs, when taught in their first language, are able to fully comprehend what occurs in the classroom and are supported in their gradual acquisition of English, because the form of English immersion these children undergo meets all the requirements for authentic English immersion listed above.

Besides its potential for positively impacting school success, DI may be the most promising educational approach for promoting societal bilingualism, because it aids language minority children in maintaining their home language while at the same time teaching a second language to English-speaking children. In states in which English immersion has been mandated, DI programs have persisted, partly due to the political support garnered by English-speaking participants and because bilingual approaches that include

English-speaking children are perceived as less threatening to mainstream voters, as James Crawford and others have noted. However, federal legislation requiring earlier standardized testing has begun to push FL programs to emphasize English over FL instruction, a development that does not bode well for the future success of FL or DI programs. Furthermore, in Arizona, particularly harsh interpretations of the SEI law have considerably weakened the DI model. For example, only children who already know English can be included, so the positive dynamics created by two groups of children learning from each other are lost.

Can SEI Programs Be Improved?

Truly bilingual instruction serves children well: English learners can learn English, while using English and their first language to learn academic content, and children who already know English can add bilingualism to their educational accomplishments. Why does SEI continue to receive support among policymakers and the public? Many people believe that young children possess superior abilities to learn a second language that allow them to absorb the language quickly, easily, and painlessly. Research has uncovered no such abilities, and, in fact, studies of FL immersion programs have shown the reverse to be true. Many also believe that the success of immersion models in teaching foreign languages means that schools need do little or nothing in order for children to learn English—despite the teacher qualifications and training that are necessary and the years of study that English-speaking children are required to put into their education in order to become bilingual, biliterate, and academically successful. FL immersion programs and English immersion programs are far more different than similar, and predictions for the success of English immersion cannot be made on the basis of FL immersion success. However, assumptions about children's ability to learn English with 1 year of SEI persist, despite the efforts of immersion researchers and teachers to educate and caution educators, policymakers, the media, and the public.

Kellie Rolstad

See also Dual-Language Programs; English for the Children Campaign; Pull-Out ESL Instruction; Proposition 203 (Arizona), Impact of; Proposition 227 (California), Impact of; St. Lambert Immersion Study; Transitional Bilingual Education Programs

Further Readings

Baker, K., & de Kanter, A. (1981). *Effectiveness of bilingual education: A review of the literature* (Final draft report). Washington, DC: Department of Education Office of Planning, Budget, and Evaluation.

Christian, D., Montone, C., Lindholm, K., & Carranza, I. (1997). *Profiles in two-way bilingual education.* McHenry, IL: Delta Systems.

Genesee, J. (1984). Historical and theoretical foundations of immersion education. In R. Campbell (Ed.), *Studies on immersion education: A collection for U.S. educators* (pp. 32–57). Sacramento: California State Department of Education.

Hernández-Chávez, E. (1984). The inadequacy of English immersion education as an educational approach for language minority students in the United States. In R. Campbell (Ed.), *Studies on immersion education: A collection for U.S. educators* (pp. 144–181). Sacramento: California State Department of Education.

Lambert, W. E., & Tucker, G. R. (1972). *Bilingual education of children: The St. Lambert experiment.* Rowley, MA: Newbury House.

Lindholm-Leary, K. J. (2001). *Dual language education.* Clevedon, UK: Multilingual Matters.

Mahoney, K., MacSwan, J., & Thompson, M. (2004). The condition of English language learners in Arizona: 2004. In D. García & A. Molnar (Eds.), *The condition of pre-K–12 education in Arizona, 2004* (pp. 3.1–3.27). Tempe: Arizona State University, Education Policy Research Laboratory. Available from http://epsl.asu.edu/aepi/AEPI_2004_annual_report.htm

Rolstad, K., K. Mahoney, K., & Glass, G. V. (2005). The big picture: A meta-analysis of program effectiveness research on English language learners. *Educational Policy, 19,* 572–594.

Swain, M., & Johnson, R. K. (1997). Immersion education: A category within bilingual education. In R. K. Johnson & M. Swain (Eds.), *Immersion education: International perspectives* (pp. 1–16). New York: Cambridge University Press.

Thompson, M. S., DiCerbo, K., Mahoney, K., & MacSwan, J. (2002). ¿Éxito en California? A validity critique of language program evaluations and analysis of English learner test scores. *Education Policy Analysis Archives, 10*(7). Available from http://lmri.ucsb.edu/resources/prop227.php

Wright, W. E., & Choi, D. (2006). The impact of language and high-stakes testing policies on elementary school English language learners in Arizona. (Abstract) *Education Policy Analysis Archives, 14*(13). Retrieved from http://epaa.asu.edu/epaa/v14n13

ENGLISH IN THE WORLD

Bilingual educators in the United States give a high priority to learning English. This is an incontrovertible need. Differences arise only on whether it is necessary to coerce children to give up their native languages in order to learn English. In recent decades, the press has reported on a creeping fear that English in the United States is somehow threatened. Nothing could be further from reality. The emphasis on the teaching and learning of English is well justified, however, when we consider the importance of that language, not only in the United States but around the world. Curiously, some of the fiercest proponents of English may not know the extent to which English predominates in the world. When asked to name the countries in which English is spoken as the national language, many college students name the United States, Canada, the British Isles, and Australia. Some might even include New Zealand or some of the islands of the Caribbean. Most Americans are surprised to learn that there are quite a few countries in which English predominates and is even considered the national language. The *Oxford Dictionary Online* notes the following:

> Australia, Botswana, the Commonwealth Caribbean nations, Gambia, Ghana, Guyana, Ireland, Namibia, Uganda, Zambia, Zimbabwe, New Zealand, the United Kingdom, and the United States have English as either de facto or statutory official language. In Cameroon and Canada, English shares this status with French; and in the Nigerian states, English and the main local language are official. In Fiji, English is the official language with Fijian; in Lesotho with Sesotho; in Pakistan with Urdu; in the Philippines with Filipino; and in Swaziland with Siswati. In India, English is an associate official language (after Hindi), and in Singapore English is one of four statutory official languages. In South Africa, English is the main national language—but just one of eleven official languages.

Oxford.com also reports that the 75 countries in which English is commonly spoken have a combined population of approximately 2 billion people. Accordingly, Oxford explains that approximately 1 in 4 people in the world speaks English with a modicum of fluency. In his book *English as a Global Language,* David Crystal maintains there are 1,500 million speakers of English worldwide.

English is the second most spoken language in the world. Only the combined varieties of Chinese, taken together, have more speakers. In addition to being the de facto national language of more than a dozen countries, English is the top language used in aviation, commerce, tourism, higher education, international law, the Internet, and the media.

Some observers liken the spread of English to the growth of our galaxy. It emerged from the explosive origins and growth of the United States. As the new nation gained power and prestige, so did its language. When the United States became the sole superpower in the world, English became the language of choice for many purposes. Do other languages threaten the hegemony of English around the world? Hardly: China has no fewer than five languages, and many people do not understand each other's language. Spanish runs third in the world. It is not commonly associated with a world power and for that reason alone is not a threat to English.

Josué M. González

See also English, First World Language; Nationalization of Languages; Native English Speakers Redefined; Spanish, the Second National Language; World Englishes

Further Readings

Ask Oxford.Com. (n.d.). *Ask Oxford: How many countries in the world have English as their first language?* Retrieved from http://www.askoxford.com/globalenglish/questions/firstlang/?view=uk

Crystal, D. (2003). *English as a global language* (2nd ed.). Cambridge, UK: Cambridge University Press.

ENGLISH-ONLY ORGANIZATIONS

English-only organizations are composed of supporters who believe that English alone should be the "official" language of the United States. Most of these organizations are active in lobbying for state and federal legislation in support of English-only laws. The laws promoted by these groups usually require that English be the only medium of instruction in schools and typically require that all government and official documents be published exclusively in English. Advocates of English-only organizations believe that learning and speaking English are essential in order for immigrants to succeed and achieve the "American dream" in the United States. Although many groups are interested in English-only policies, the most notable are U.S. English, English First, the Research on English Acquisition and Development Institute (READ), the Center for Equal Opportunity (CEO), ProEnglish, and English for the Children.

Opponents of English-only organizations believe that these groups fail to recognize the linguistic, cultural, social, and ethnic experiences and resources that immigrants bring to the United States; that the contributions of immigrants and English language learners (ELLs) should not be ignored; and that by emphasizing assimilation and Americanization, the cultural heritage of immigrants is devalued. Critics who oppose English-only organizations also believe that such organizations ultimately marginalize ethnic and linguistic minorities from mainstream involvement in the United States and that in order to make English the sole official language of the country, these practices would harm rather than help immigrants. They further argue that it is the diversity of its people and cultures that makes the United States strong and that this society is best served when everyone has equal access to the rights and opportunities that are guaranteed to its members.

Historical Background

In 1911, the newly formed Immigration Commission announced findings that showed little concern over immigrants' English language knowledge upon their arrival in the United States. A few years later, however, on September 1, 1917, the National Americanization Committee—a group aimed at "Americanizing" immigrants—launched a campaign called "English First." Its purpose was to teach English to all of the nation's immigrants. The ideological distinction between the findings of the Immigration Commission in 1911 and the aim of the National Americanization Committee 6 years later speaks of the social forces that led to the dissemination of English-only ideology.

Pressure for English-only is evident throughout American history, but significant shifts toward language restrictions, aimed at immigrant communities, is most notable during and after World War I.

Although World War I ended in 1918, xenophobic sentiments against German immigrants and German Americans created anti-German language movements in communities in which German immigrants had settled. During this period, communities enacted laws that prohibited the use of the German language in schools, on public documents, during community meetings, and on other civic occasions. In one town, inhabitants were threatened with fines for speaking German on the street. In 1923, *Meyer v. Nebraska* was an important Supreme Court case related to anti-German restrictionism. In this court case, the state of Nebraska fined Robert T. Meyer for reading verses from the Bible in German to one of his students. Under Nebraska law, Meyer was initially found guilty; the case, however, was later overturned by the U.S. Supreme Court, which found the original ruling unconstitutional.

Early organizations that called themselves "English-only" were few; however, two factions emerged that harbored goals similar to those of today's English-only organizations: (1) those whose aim was restrictionist in nature and (2) those that emphasized acquiring English language proficiency.

Contemporary Activities

The civil rights movements of the 1950s and 1960s prompted an increased attention to social justice and equity that created changes in perceptions of language diversity. Judicial decisions against schools that did not support the needs of ELLs also emerged over about a 15-year period, beginning in the late 1960s through the mid-1970s. The most notable of these policies was the Bilingual Education Act of 1968, also known as Title VII of the Elementary and Secondary Education Act (ESEA). Judicial decisions subsequent to the Bilingual Education Act, such as *Lau v. Nichols* (1974) and *Serna v. Portales Municipal Schools* (1974), found that students' civil rights were being violated on the basis of language. These cases help to demonstrate that through the mid-1970s, ELLs in schools were being faulted at two levels: by being undersupported and by being segregated on the basis of linguistic and ethnic background. Recently, English-only organizations have been founded largely in response to legislation and policies aimed at fostering linguistic diversity and multilingualism, the enactment of which has seen an increase of funding for programs in support of multilingualism.

In 1981, 2 years before he founded the organization U.S. English, Senator S. I. Hayakawa introduced a bill in the U.S. Senate to make English the official language of the United States. The relationship between English-only organizations as oppositional to policies that support ELLs was demonstrated that same year in an appellate court decision, when *Castañeda v. Pickard* was handed down. The court found that programs intended to meet the needs of ELLs must adhere to a set of three criteria. Schools that did not meet each criterion were considered to be in violation of ELLs' civil rights. Legislation and momentous cases illustrate the ideological shift among both the legislators' intentions in lawmaking and the justices' interpretation of laws relative to linguistics and civil rights. The rise in number and quality of bilingual education programs appears to parallel the rise and vehemence toward antibilingual and English-only approaches to the education of ELLs.

U.S. English is the oldest and largest association dedicated to making English the "official" language of the United States. It was founded in 1983 by Senator S. I. Hayakawa of California, who served as honorary chairman from 1983 to 1990. The organization's chairman, as of 2007, is Mauro E. Mujica, a businessman and immigrant who has served U.S. English since 1993. Mujico maintains that English is the key to opportunity for immigrants and has declared that English is under attack by the government, schools, and the court system. The goal of U.S. English is to ensure that English continues to serve as an integrating force among the nation's many ethnic groups and remains a vehicle of opportunity for new Americans. The organization has three missions: (1) to help improve the teaching of English to immigrants, allowing them to enjoy the economic opportunities available in the United States; (2) to study language policy and its effects around the world, so that Americans can apply the lessons learned through the experiences of other countries to the United States; and (3) to raise public awareness through the media about the importance of English as the common language of the United States.

English First, based in Springfield, Virginia, is a nonprofit grassroots lobbying organization founded in 1986. It currently has about 150,000 members and believes that immigrants in this country must be able to speak with each other. They believe that the English language unites Americans, and they oppose to the use of tax dollars to divide Americans on the basis of language and ancestry. English First claims to be the only organization to testify against bilingual education and the only pro-English group to lead the fight against bilingual education. English First has three stated goals: (1) to make English the official language of America; (2) to eliminate what it characterizes as costly and failed programs, such as bilingual education and bilingual ballots; and (3) to give every child the opportunity to learn English while young.

The Research for English Acquisition and Development Institute (READ) was founded in 1989. It supports research in the area of effective English language learning programs, produces policy reports and briefs, and publishes an annual scholarly journal called *READ Perspectives*. The current president of READ Institute is Linda Chávez. Chávez believes that bilingual education programs keep students who do not speak English in programs that do not teach them English and, instead, try to maintain students' native languages. READ's goal is to make its findings available to those who are concerned about the education of language minority students. The mission of the organization is to support research on English language learning and schooling for language minority children and to reform bilingual education. The parent organization for READ is the Center for Equal Opportunity (CEO).

Chávez founded CEO in 1995. This organization focuses on the areas of racial preferences, immigration and assimilation, and multicultural education. CEO promotes the assimilation of immigrants into U.S. society, conducts research on the economic and social impact of immigrants in the United States, and opposes bilingual education on the basis of the belief that multiculturalists control the schools and universities. CEO has written several books to help teachers and parents learn how to oppose bilingual education programs. CEO is affiliated with the READ Institute.

ProEnglish was founded in 1994 under the name English Language Advocates, in defense of an Arizona ballot initiative to make English the state's official language. It is a nonprofit organization that promotes making English the official language of the United States. Their goals include (a) to promote the adoption of laws that declare English the official language of the United States, (b) to defend the right of states to make English the official language of government operations, (c) to end bilingual education in schools, (d) to repeal federal mandates that translate government documents into languages other than English, and (e) to

work to oppose statehood for territories that have not adopted English as their official language (such as Puerto Rico).

English for the Children was founded in 1997 by Ronald Unz, a California businessman. English for the Children began as an initiative campaign in California; its aim was to outlaw bilingual education and teach all ELLs through English immersion. Unz drafted Proposition 227 and campaigned for the measure to pass. In June 1998, the measure passed by a 61% landslide, causing the disruption and dismantling of many bilingual programs in California. This initiative helped English for the Children, which became the newest large-scale English-only organization. The 5 years following Unz's announcement of the English-only initiative sparked an outcry of Americans in support of language measures focused specifically on schools. Voters in other states, such as Arizona and Massachusetts, also mandated legislation that called for a means of teaching students English through immersion, as opposed to bilingual education.

English-Only in Education: Historical View

The most obvious example in American history of English-only enforcement in schools is that of the Native American boarding school experience. This case illustrates the country's history of forced assimilation through schooling and the relationship between Americanization and English acquisition. Indian boarding schools were the intended mechanisms through which to achieve Americanization and the "civilizing" of indigenous children, thus resulting in Native American students' loss of language, culture, and identity.

In 1879, the federal government began requiring that Native American children be taken from their parents and sent to boarding schools located hundreds of miles away. All activities in boarding schools were conducted only in English from the moment students arrived. Subjects were the same as those for White students, but Native American children were also required to study the Bible and etiquette and other Americanizing lessons. Girls were taught needlepoint, and boys played traditional American sports, such as baseball and basketball. Students were entirely forbidden from speaking their native languages and engaging in any indigenous ceremonies. For those who disobeyed the rules, extreme punishments resulted.

One of the main goals of boarding schools was to replace Native American languages with English. Overwhelmingly, this aim was achieved, and indigenous American communities across the country today are fighting to regain this loss of language. It is not possible to review the many cases of forced English-only in schools, but the Indian boarding school experience embodies the historical intentions of policies to transition children away from native languages and cultures and toward the English-speaking, American culture.

English-Only in Education: Contemporary View

Contemporary movements toward English-only in education and the organizations that support them were mentioned earlier with reference to Unz and English for the Children (both the organization and the ballot initiative). Often referred to as the "Unz initiative," the first English-only proposition passed in the United States was strongly supported by the English-only organizations listed above. Unlike the other associations that often contained a strong anti-immigrant component, the education component of English-only organizations focuses tightly on the presumed benefits and advantages of educating immigrant children solely in English.

After the passage of Proposition 227, English for the Children founded a chapter in Arizona, and, in November 2000, Proposition 203 (Arizona's English-only law) passed with about 68% of the vote. In 2002, English for the Children proposed ballot initiatives in both Massachusetts and Colorado (Question 2 and Amendment 31). While Question 2 passed in Massachusetts, Amendment 31 failed in Colorado. A key reason for this failure may be seen in the campaigning decisions made by bilingual education advocates in Colorado. Instead of trumpeting the successes of bilingual education, as had been done in California and Arizona, English Plus campaigned by feeding off anti-immigrant sentiments in the state. The advertising promoted the idea that students, mostly Spanish-speaking immigrants from non-White backgrounds, be removed from bilingual education classrooms and placed in all-English-speaking, mostly White classrooms. Essentially, English Plus of Colorado prompted voters to vote against Amendment 31 by suggesting that if bilingual education were outlawed, non-White,

Spanish-speaking children would then flood into predominantly White, English-speaking schools and classrooms.

Since the defeat of Amendment 31 in Colorado and the victories in Massachusetts, Arizona, and California, English for the Children has gone into hibernation and is no longer active. This may be due, at least in part, to the fact that its founder no longer supports the organization's paid staff. Apart from this association, other English-only groups have not focused heavily on English-only in schools, with the exception of the READ Institute, which heralds the success of English immersion for teaching English learners.

The Future of English-Only

It is difficult to foresee how English-only organizations will realign efforts toward state and federal official English policies in future political campaigns. In an era when anti-immigrant sentiment is rampant, as largely Spanish-speaking workers enter the United States, English-only organizations and movements are likely to thrive, given their oppositional nature. Recently, a key figure in READ, Rosalie Pedalino Porter, has been closely tied to decisions about how English immersion programs will be implemented in Arizona, post–Proposition 203. In 2006, READ completed a study funded by the Arizona Department of Education, which claims improved achievement rates for English learners in English immersion settings. U.S. English and ProEnglish are focusing efforts on establishing English as the official language in states and ensuring that official English legislation is upheld in courts. Throughout U.S. history, English-only organizations and movements have sprung up as immigration trends increase sharply. Whether the emphasis of these groups is official English or English-only in schools, it appears that they are largely born out of a desire for stronger control of immigrant populations, to be achieved through linguistic and cultural assimilation. Hence, the future of one is dependent on the fortunes of the other.

Sarah Catherine Moore

See also Americanization and Its Critics; Americanization by Schooling; Chávez, Linda; Hayakawa, S. I.; Official English Legislation, Favored; Official Language Designation; Tanton, John H.; Appendix E

Further Readings

Baron, D. (1990). *The English-only question: An official language for Americans?* New Haven, CT: Yale University Press.

Castañeda v. Pickard, 648 F.2d 989 (1981).

Crawford, J. (1992). *Hold your tongue: Bilingualism and the politics of "English only."* Reading, MA: Addison-Wesley.

Crawford, J. (1992). *Language loyalties: A source book on the Official English controversy.* Chicago: University of Chicago Press.

Lau v. Nichols, 414 U.S. 563 (1974).

One Nation/One California. (1997). *English for the Children.* Retrieved from http://www.onenation.org/people.html

ProEnglish. (n.d.). *Who we are: All about ProEnglish.* Retrieved from http://www.proenglish.org/main/gen-info.htm

Research on English Acquisition and Development Institute. (n.d.). *READ Institute provides first comprehensive study of program costs for non-English-speaking students.* Available from http://www.ceousa.org?READ/index.html

Right Web. (2004). *Center for equal opportunity.* Retrieved from http://rightweb.irc-online.org/profile/926.html

Serna v. Portales Municipal Schools, 499 F.2d 1147, 1154 (10th Cir. 1974).

U.S. English, Inc. (n.d.). *About U.S. English.* Retrieved from http://www.us-english.org/inc/about

ENGLISH OR CONTENT INSTRUCTION

Among earlier generations of immigrants, especially adults, it was not uncommon for English language learners (ELLs) to study and learn English first and subsequently learn other subjects and skills in English. Persons unfamiliar with the status of current language policy in the United States often ask why schools do not employ an intensive English immersion program that takes up the students' entire day until they master the language. In short, why not teach them English first, intensively and without other subjects to distract them, before they are exposed to other portions of the curriculum such as history, science, or math? The answer is in two parts. First, that such a sequence would be in violation of the spirit of the *Lau v. Nichols* (1974) decision, which is detailed elsewhere in this encyclopedia. The second is that such a plan would not comport with the education profession's current thinking on how curriculum should be organized and sequenced. This entry briefly explores both of these reasons.

In the *Lau* decision, the U.S. Supreme Court spoke directly, tersely, and unequivocally to this point:

> Basic English skills are at the very core of what these public schools teach. Imposition of a requirement that, before a child can effectively participate in the educational program he must already have acquired those basic skills is to make a mockery of public education.

The Court also noted that because California requires all graduating students to pass a test in English at the end of their high school years, the schools have a legal responsibility to teach that language effectively. In short, it is not enough to require a certain score on the English test in order to graduate; there is a concomitant requirement that the schools teach that language well. We are not privy to the justices' complete thinking on this subject, but a review of the full decision suggests that they were not willing to impose greater requirements and responsibilities on language minority children that go beyond what is imposed on native speakers of English (see Appendix C for full text of the decision.). Instead, the decision focused on the responsibility of schools, since that was the issue before the court: to what degree schools are responsible to rectify a situation they did not create themselves, a linguistic incompatibility between the school and a segment of its student body. At the appellate court review of the case, Judge Shirley Hufstedler had made this point in clear and explicit terms. She pointed out that children learn whatever language is taught to them by their parents and that neither the teaching nor the learning of the non-English language can be used to negate the responsibilities of the schools relative to the lingua franca. Hufstedler argued that students could not be blamed or punished for having learned the language taught them by their parents.

Judge Hufstedler did not prevail at that level, but her idea and attendant logic found a more hospitable climate in the subsequent appeal to the Supreme Court. The appellate court had sided with the plaintiff, the San Francisco Unified School District, by ruling that the district had not created the linguistic incompatibility and was not, therefore, responsible for correcting it. Hufstedler and the Supreme Court saw things differently: It was not the legal responsibility of families to teach English to their children before they enter school. Rather, it was the school's responsibility to develop that language at the same time they were teaching other subjects to those children. The Court made it clear that it did not wish to see any delays in the ELLs' engagement with the full curriculum, which may have resulted if children were first required to learn English.

A separate but equally important concept, derived from desegregation case law, may have also entered into the justices' thinking on the question of precedence of English. Assuming that some students in the *Lau* case were totally monolingual in Chinese, if the schools were to concentrate solely on English for a time, it would be necessary to segregate those students because their instructional program would be vastly different from that of their English-speaking classmates. Thus, a condition of instructional segregation would be created, which is not permitted under desegregation case law. Furthermore, this position recognizes the fact that learning is a social process and that students learn much from each other. This is especially true in regard to language. In mixed classrooms in which some students are fluent in English and some are not, it stands to reason that the latter students would find many more opportunities to practice the target language with other students who speak that language better then they do, and if the minority language were also being taught to the native speakers of English, they too would benefit from the presence of competent speakers in that language sitting side by side in the same classrooms. Segregating them for intensive direct instruction in English would deprive them of that opportunity.

Finally, but no less important, putting English into the category of a prerequisite to other school subjects violates contemporary thinking by education professionals regarding the structure of curriculum and the social nature of learning. Most linguists agree that in the context of schools and classrooms, language is more than a mere communicative tool. Languages are subjects that are taught in schools, but they are also the carriers of information and the means by which shared learning or social learning is based, as explained by sociocultural theory, drawing on the work by Russian psychologist Lev Vygotsky. Attempting to teach English without its cargo of subject content would entail teaching a hollow body of language that would challenge the best teachers in terms of its content. The most effective way to teach the prevailing school language is to teach it in the way it is normally used in school, with a full cargo of subject matter content.

Returning once again to the story of the adult immigrants of yesteryear, it should be acknowledged that the period during which those immigrants were denying themselves access to the benefits of mainstream America and not learning English could have been a protracted one. Because they were working and making a living for themselves and their families, it is not surprising to learn that many of them put off learning English not merely for a few months, but for a whole generation. They decided that English would be the language of their children, even though it would not be their own language. The context in which these life stories occurred is also important to consider. Many immigrants who came to the United States in the late 19th and early 20th centuries took jobs in which English was not an important requirement. Fellow immigrants who had been here longer acted as language brokers to help them negotiate those situations in which English was needed. Today, however, jobs in which English is not required are almost nonexistent. Thus, learning English cannot be long deferred. For schoolchildren and youth, the situation is even more urgent and time sensitive: Being able to learn English in a comfortable but effective way is essential in order to keep up with their classmates. In addition, learning English must be embedded in other activities aimed at gaining facility with school subjects and with the social rules of American youth at the same time they are learning the language of greater commerce. Bilingual education is the program of choice that allows comprehensible instruction and the learning of English to take place simultaneously.

Josué M. González

See also Academic English; Affirmative Steps to English; BICS/CALP Theory; *Lau v. Nichols,* the Ruling; Social Learning; Vygotsky and Language Learning; Appendix C

Further Readings

Lau v. Nichols, 483 F.2d 791 (9th Cir. 1973).

Lau v. Nichols, 414 U.S. 563 (1974).

Vygotsky, L. (1978). *Mind in society: The development of higher psychological processes.* Cambridge, MA: Harvard University Press.

EPSTEIN, NOEL (1938–)

Kalman Noel Epstein was an editor of the *Washington Post* for more than 30 years and, earlier, of the *Wall Street Journal*. He made an important contribution to the debate over bilingual education with his 1977 book, *Language, Ethnicity, and the Schools: Policy Alternatives for Bilingual-Bicultural Education*. Epstein's book highlighted the issues that school board members and some unions found controversial in the Bilingual Education Act, Title VII, of the Elementary and Secondary Education Act (ESEA). He was especially critical of government funding of bilingual bicultural maintenance programs in public schools. A maintenance bilingual program was one of the options in the Bilingual Education Act that had been reauthorized in 1974. Other options local districts could choose, and which most did, were transitional bilingual programs in which the native language was used as a bridge to learning English as a second language (ESL) as soon as possible.

Epstein coined the term *affirmative ethnicity*, defined as a policy of government-financed support and promotion of ethnic identities by protecting existing languages and cultural communities in the schools. He questioned the bicultural component of the maintenance bilingual programs, which had as their goals students learning English while maintaining their native languages and affirming their cultures—that is, becoming bilingual and bicultural. Epstein did not object to the right of groups to maintain their languages and cultures, but he posed the question as to whether it was the role of the federal government to finance students' attachments to their ethnic languages and cultures. He noted that historically, this was the role of families, religious groups, ethnic organizations, and private schools. Critics charged that, like other nativists, Epstein ignored the fact that adherents of maintenance bilingual education are supporters of the public schools. As taxpayers, they have the right to advocate for instructional programs of their choice for their children.

Epstein is credited with helping shape the U.S. policy on bilingual education. He wrote in *Language, Ethnicity, and the Schools* that two lobbying groups had expressed concerns about federally sponsored biculturalism. The National Association of School Boards at that time suggested that the legislation, Title VII of the ESEA, could be read as promoting a divisive, Canadian-style biculturalism. The United Auto Workers union was also concerned that the bicultural components of the Bilingual Education Act might lead to separation rather than integration in the schools. Epstein's 1977 book was the first to provide a broad canvas for discussing the political context for bilingual, bicultural education. He suggested that the policy had become perhaps the largest federally funded policy in the United States of an "ethnic, political wave that was sweeping the globe" (p. 4). He wrote that he had no question that bilingual-bicultural policy was largely the result of the "quest of discriminated-against minority groups, and particularly Hispanic Americans, for more power, prestige, and jobs" (p. 4).

Epstein's 2004 book, *Who's in Charge Here? The Tangled Web of School Governance and Policy*, which he edited, brings together varied perspectives on another debate: the extent of the role of the federal government in schooling. Scholars present arguments and analyses in support of either more centralization or more local decision making as a better direction for school improvement. In his introduction, Epstein noted that there were already two major competing lines of authority; local schools and districts were originally "protected" from politics by being responsible not to the mayor or governor, but to state boards of education. However, large city school systems (Chicago, New York, Boston, Philadelphia) have increasingly been taken over by mayors, to be accountable to their electorate and the federal government in meeting national standards of annual achievement testing under the No Child Left Behind Act of 2001.

Epstein was born in New York City in 1938. After earning a BS in journalism from New York University in 1961, he was a journalist and later assistant national editor of the *Wall Street Journal* until 1970. He moved to the *Washington Post* as assistant national editor from 1970 to 1971, education editor from 1973 to 1976, and managing editor of the Sunday "Opinion" section from 1971 to 1973 and 1977 to 1978. He was also editor and publisher of the *Post's National Weekly Edition* from 1986 to 1996 and has been director of Washington Post Books since 1997. He has been a scholar in residence with the Institute for Educational Leadership and journalist in residence at George Washington University. Epstein is currently a principal in Stakeholder Strategies, a communications firm that is a division of Venn Strategies, working with lobbyists and issue experts on business and government affairs.

Marietta Saravia-Shore

See also Immigration and Language Policy; Maintenance Policy Denied; Views of Bilingual Education; Views of Language Difference; Appendix D

Further Readings

Epstein, N. (1977). *Language, ethnicity, and the schools: Policy alternatives for bilingual-bicultural education.* Washington, DC: Institute for Educational Leadership.

Epstein, N. (Ed.). (2004). *Who's in charge here? The tangled web of school governance and policy.* Washington, DC: Brookings Institution Press and Education Commission of the States.

EQUAL EDUCATIONAL OPPORTUNITY ACT OF 1974

The Equal Educational Opportunity Act of 1974 (EEOA), like its close relative the Civil Rights Act of 1964, has its roots in the civil rights struggles of the 1950s and 1960s. For matters of language, Title VI of the Civil Rights Act is the most pertinent aspect of that law. It provides that "no person in the United States shall on the grounds of race, color or national origin, be excluded from participation in, be denied the benefits of, or be subjected to discrimination under any program or activity receiving Federal financial assistance." In the landmark U.S. Supreme Court decision of *Lau v. Nichols* (1974), the Court held that Chinese students who were limited in their English proficiency had been denied their rights under Title VI by a refusal to provide them with special programming. Essentially, the Court stated that "there is no equality of treatment merely by providing students with the same facilities, textbooks, teachers and curriculum," because students who do not understand English are "effectively foreclosed from any meaningful education."

The findings in *Lau* were based on the Civil Rights Act, but Congress quickly codified *Lau* in new legislation called the Equal Educational Opportunity Act of 1974. The relevant section, 1703(f), provides as follows:

No state shall deny equal educational opportunity to an individual on account of this race, color, sex or national origin, by . . . (f) the failure of an educational agency to take appropriate action to overcome language barriers that impede equal participation by its students in its instructional programs.

Ironically, many in the civil rights community opposed this legislation because it was part of an effort to stop the use of busing to achieve desegregated schools. The EEOA's companion piece of legislation was titled the "Student Transportation Moratorium Act" and was intended by President Nixon to stop school busing and preserve "neighborhood" schools.

Perhaps the most important feature of the EEOA is that it allows for private right of action, the right by an individual to bring suit against a government entity. The act clearly states that "an individual denied an equal educational opportunity . . . may institute a federal court action." The ability to file a private right of action has become critical following the U.S. Supreme Court's decision in *Alexander v. Sandoval,* in 2001, requiring private litigants to establish intentional discrimination while proceeding under Title VI of the Civil Rights Act of 1974. The attorney general of the United States is also empowered to file suits under the EEOA, a power rarely used. Most of the work of ensuring an equal educational opportunity has been generated by parents and advocacy organizations.

Neither Title VI, the *Lau* decision itself, nor the EEOA defines the meaning of "appropriate action to eliminate language barriers." Several court cases took up this task. In the late 1970s, African American students in Ann Arbor, Michigan, who spoke a vernacular of English referred to as "Black English" or "Ebonics," attempted to use the EEOA to improve their instruction in *Martin Luther King Junior Elementary School Children v. Ann Arbor School District Board* in 1978. The students succeeded in convincing the federal judge that they suffered from a "language barrier" "that impede[d] equal participation by its students in its instructional programs" (20 U.S.C. Section 1703 (f)). This case was not appealed to an appellate court and, as a consequence, has not become a precedent followed by other courts.

The case most frequently cited with respect to "appropriate action" is the *Castañeda* case. In *Castañeda v. Pickard,* decided in 1981, the court set out a three-pronged test to determine whether the rights of students with limited English proficiency (LEP) were being violated:

1. Determine whether the school district "is pursuing a program informed by an educational theory recognized as sound by some experts in the field or, at least, deemed a legitimate experimental strategy."

2. Determine whether steps are taken "to implement effectively the educational theory adopted by the school."

3. After a "legitimate trial" period, the program is to be examined for indications "that the language barriers confronting students are actually being overcome." In other words, the program must be evaluated and, if found to be failing, modified by either changing the program itself (Prong 1) or taking further steps to implement the adopted theory of instruction (Prong 2).

The *Castañeda* case had other critical components: First, that English language learners (ELLs), often termed *LEP students* in legal documents, must be provided not only the opportunity to learn English but also the opportunity to have access to the school district's entire educational program. Thus, in evaluating a school district's program, each of the three *Castañeda* prongs must be met. They must be met with respect to teaching English and with respect to teaching the entire curriculum.

Second, the court left open to the district the "sequence and manner in which LEP students tackle this dual challenge so long as the schools design programs which are reasonably calculated to enable these students to attain parity of participation within a reasonable length of time after they enter the school system." Although it was decided under 20 U.S.C. Section 1703(f), the *Castañeda* standard has been adopted by the federal government pursuant to Title VI as its rule for enforcement.

A challenge to the appropriateness of the Denver Public Schools program for LEP students utilized the *Castañeda* standard. In *Keyes v. School District No. 1, Denver,* decided in 1983, the court held that "transitional bilingual programs" designed to teach English and to provide understandable instruction in content areas while students are learning English was a sound educational theory. However, the Denver schools had failed to implement the theory by, among other things, failing to hire and train qualified teachers. The court declined to rule on the third prong of *Castañeda.*

Although the court in *Keyes* found that the evidence before it did not compel bilingual or primary-language instruction as the exclusive means to provide access to LEP students, it is possible that in the right circumstances, such a remedy might be required. First, as *Keyes* states, if a district chooses to implement such a program, it must do so in an appropriate manner. In fact, the settlement negotiated in *Keyes* was an extensive model of bilingual education. Second, it is still possible that other courts, based on a full record, could require a bilingual program for certain students. For example, a court could find that a student possessing no English language skills might require such a program or a student without English language skills who is also a student with disabilities might require some primary-language instruction. Without such a language barrier, it is unlikely that a court would allow such a remedy.

Following *Castañeda,* a series of federal court cases have held that federal law imposes requirements on state educational agencies (SEAs) to enforce the EEOA. Among the most important of these cases are *Idaho Migrant Council v. Board of Education* (decided in 1981) and *Gómez v. Illinois State Board of Education* (decided in 1987). At a minimum, the state's obligation is to set forth minimum standards for school districts in areas such as identification of LEP students, programming, and teacher qualifications and to monitor and enforce the state standards. The state must also provide resources when the district is unable to provide an appropriate program. The latter requirement is at the heart of *Flores v. Arizona.*

In 1992, *Flores v. Arizona* was filed in federal court, alleging the state's failure to appropriately teach English and to enable LEP students to acquire content skills. Eight years later, the court ruled that the state had failed to adequately fund the program. The court stated that the EEOA was being violated since the "arbitrary and capricious" LEP appropriation was ineffective in ensuring that the educational theory selected by the state could be implemented. Failure of the Arizona legislature to appropriate sufficient funds led to the court holding the state in contempt. In July 2006, the U.S. Court of Appeals for the 9th Circuit reversed an order of the District Court holding the state in civil contempt for its alleged inactions. It remains to be seen whether the aspirations of the EEOA drafters will prevail in Arizona. However, while enforcement has proven difficult in *Flores,* the requirements of state responsibility still stand.

In sum, given the recent limitations placed on private right of action under Title VI of the Civil Rights Act of 1964, the EEOA has become the primary legal tool to ensure that LEP students receive an equal educational opportunity.

Stefan M. Rosenzweig

Author's Note: The author wishes to thank Peter D. Roos, Esq., for his editorial assistance.

See also Affirmative Steps to English; *Castañeda* Three-Part Test; Civil Rights Act of 1964; Federal Court Decisions and Legislation; *Lau v. Nichols,* the Ruling

Further Readings

Alexander v. Sandoval, 534 U.S. 275 (2001).

Castañeda v. Pickard, 648 F.2d 989 (5th. Cir.1981).

Crawford, J. (1999). *Bilingual education: History, politics, theory, and practice* (4th ed.). Los Angeles: Bilingual Education Services.

Equal Educational Opportunity Act, 20 U.S. C. 1701–1720 (1974).

Flores v. Arizona, 48 F. Supp.2d 937 (D. Ariz. 1992).

Gómez v. Illinois State Board of Education, 811 F.2d 1030 (7th Cir.1987).

Idaho Migrant Council v. Board of Education, 647 F.2d 69 (9th Cir.1981).

Keyes v. School District No.1, Denver, Colorado, 576 F. Supp. 503 (D. Colorado, 1983).

Lau v. Nichols, 414 U.S. 563 (1974).

Martin Luther King Junior Elementary School Children v. Ann Arbor District, 431 F. Supp. 1324 (E.D. Mich. 1978).

Office for Civil Rights. (1990, April 6). *Memorandum. Policy regarding the treatment of national origin minority students who are limited English proficient.* Retrieved from http://www.ed.gov/about/offices/list/ocr/docs/lau1991.html

Web Sites

Office for Civil Rights:
http://www.ed.gov/about/offices/list/ocr

EQUITY STRUGGLES AND EDUCATIONAL REFORM

The struggle for improved educational opportunities for language minority children has gone through several changes in emphases and direction since the late 1960s. Language compatibility and cultural respect have been important components but by no means the only ones in the struggle for equity in education. Proponents and advocates of quality schooling for Latino students have always known that a better education would not come about merely by including the Spanish language in the curriculum, no matter how ably this inclusion was planned and executed. This entry sketches some of the changes that have occurred over a period of 40 years in this ongoing quest for quality instruction and equity in American public education.

Struggle for Quality Instruction in Recent Decades

Since the creation of Anglo-oriented public schools and the enactment of laws requiring children to attend them, activists have supported a variety of reforms to make these institutions more responsive to language minority students. One of the most important reforms they have supported has dealt with quality instruction in general and with gaining access to a differentiated curriculum geared toward meeting the diverse academic, linguistic, and cultural needs of those students in particular.

The struggle for quality instruction intensified after the 1960s. Unlike earlier decades, when the majority of educators, scholars, and policymakers were Anglos, in this period, an increasing number of them were Latino. Alongside the community activists and the practitioners in the schools, these scholars and researchers conducted research and provided the knowledge necessary for improving the schools serving Latino children. The work of these activist scholars was generally quiet and behind the scenes but no less effective for it.

In the 1960s, Latino activists involved in the education of Latino children (e.g., José Cárdenas, Frank Angel, Armando M. Rodríguez) and many others struggled for and either promoted, supported, or helped establish a variety of curricular innovations aimed at improving the low academic achievement of English language learners (ELLs) in the public schools. Among the most popular were early childhood, migrant, bilingual, and adult education programs, but by the following decade, most of them began to concentrate on bilingual education. Bilingual education, as Guadalupe San Miguel has written in *Contested Policy: The Rise and Fall of Federal Bilingual Education Policy in the United States,* is viewed as the best means for bringing about significant changes in the way the schools educated these children and developed their various linguistic, cultural, and academic interests. The emphasis of this curricular innovation was to improve academic achievement by ensuring equal access to the mainstream or standard curriculum by children with limited English proficiency, commonly referred to as "limited English proficient" (LEP) students. They are now known as "English language learners" (ELLs). Bilingual education has affected mostly children enrolled in the elementary schools.

In the mid-1980s, a new crop of Latino scholars, researchers, and practitioners emerged and played important roles in promoting school changes throughout the country. Individuals such as Carlos E. Cortés, Josué M. González, Alfredo Castañeda, Beatrice Arias, and many others worked in alliance with both older activists and a variety of minority and majority group members to improve educational opportunities for Latinos. These activist scholars expanded the discourse on Latino education and went beyond both language and bilingual education to other concerns and reforms.

For more than a decade following the passage of the federal bilingual education act of 1968, scholars had focused on language issues in the education of Latino students and on the establishment and strengthening of bilingual education throughout the country. In the 1980s, they began to systematically explore factors other than language that impacted the education of these children and to consider a variety of other curricular and institutional reforms that would benefit their learning in the schools. The publication of *Beyond Language: Social and Cultural Factors in the Schooling of Language Minority Children,* by the Evaluation, Dissemination, and Assessment Center at the California State University at Los Angeles in 1986, was indicative of this trend. In this publication,

scholars and activists argued that Latino underachievement was due to a host of social and cultural factors in addition to language. Among some of the most important social and cultural factors identified as impacting the education of Latinos were teacher attitudes toward minority groups, cultural values, parental involvement, group attitudes toward education, historical experiences, language use patterns, and self-identity. Educational programs, in order to positively impact the academic achievement of these students, the authors asserted, had to address these concerns in a systematic fashion. Effective school reform, in other words, needed to go beyond language and beyond bilingual education.

Educators and scholars not only expanded the discourse on underachievement, they also shifted the emphasis of their concerns away from ELLs in the elementary grades to secondary-school-aged students who were relatively proficient in English but still underachieving. Most of these students, as noted in the National Commission on Secondary Schooling for Hispanics report *Make Something Happen: Hispanics and Urban High School Reform* (published in 1984), attended segregated and overcrowded inner-city schools, had poor school achievement levels, were disproportionately tracked into vocational and general education programs, dropped out of school in large numbers, and had low college enrollment. They attended large, impersonal urban schools, and their needs were different from those of ELLs in the elementary grades. These students then required different types of curricular and instructional programs and more personal attention and support from adults and from school officials.

The shift and expansion of attention to underachievement in secondary schools and broader-based inequities was slow. It occurred in the context of an acrimonious debate over bilingual education and a new national concern with the quality of public education. Beginning in 1983 with a national report that noted that the nation was "at risk" because of declining academic competitiveness, this movement soon overwhelmed the equity struggles of the Latino community. The 1983 report, *A Nation at Risk,* sponsored by the National Commission on Excellence in Education, urged immediate improvement in the nation's schools and led to the emphasis on excellence or quality education, including improved standards, a more rigorous curriculum, and accountability.

Although this report called for excellence or quality education, many Latino activists and their allies raised questions about its relationship to equity concerns and sought to blend both of these movements. Peter Roos, a strong advocate of quality instruction for Latinos, for instance, analyzed the tensions between traditional views of equality and the proposed concepts of quality in an article called "Equity and Excellence," which he wrote for the National Commission on Secondary Education for Hispanics in 1984. In this article, Roos called not only for quality education, but for equity as well.

Working within this context of a national call to action, Latino and non-Latino activists pressured or compelled federal and state officials to form special committees or enact legislation to investigate and address the issue of improving the quality of education for Latino youth. Emphasis in most cases, as noted in *Make Something Happen,* was on emphasizing the devastating impact that high drop-out rates and low school achievement levels of Latino high school students were having on minority communities and on American society. Scholars and researchers also conducted investigations and research on the status and drop-out rates of Latino students in the schools, proposed recommendations to address these concerns, and encouraged local and state leaders to promote significant reforms, including curricular changes, to ensure academic success.

The nature of the struggle during the latter decades of the 20th century thus changed, without great fanfare, from one demanding access to a differentiated curriculum to one aimed at getting access to a rigorous curriculum. At the elementary level, activists and scholars interpreted this shift to mean getting access to a rigorous curriculum through quality bilingual education. At the secondary level, they focused on getting access to both a college preparatory and an accelerated curriculum made up of magnet, gifted and talented programs, and Advanced Placement classes.

Struggle for Quality Education Through Bilingual Education

Despite the multifaceted nature of these curricular struggles, the dominant theme continued to be high-quality bilingual education. This specific curricular innovation, as noted earlier, was supported for various reasons. Foremost, it continued to be viewed as the most important means for bringing about significant change in the education of linguistically and culturally distinct children, and it united all educators around a central theme in the education of Latinos: language and culture. In addition, it addressed the linguistic, cultural, and academic concerns of these children. For these and other reasons, the quest for access to a rigorous curriculum through quality bilingual education continued unabated, although the results in terms of policy change were minimal.

This struggle, although difficult and contentious, was waged on multiple fronts—in Congress, the courts, the executive branch, the streets, the schools, and the universities—and involved both Latino and non-Latino individuals and organizations working together or in coalitions. It encountered many obstacles, especially national desegregation mandates, a diversity of approaches, a declining activist federal bureaucracy, and political opposition to it by educators, Anglo parents, and conservative organizations.

The struggle for bilingual education, as noted earlier, originated in the 1960s. In the early part of the decade, Latino activists and their allies took advantage of the new social and political climate in the society to reject subtractive and ineffective schooling and to articulate oppositional ideologies, structures, and policies aimed at supporting Latino student success through significant educational reform. Most of these educators and activists focused on language as the linchpin of significant school reform. Bilingualism and bilingual education came to be viewed by many educators and activists as a viable tool for promoting comprehensive curricular, administrative, and political reforms aimed at improving Latino academic success and minority empowerment. Among the changes sought by those in support of bilingual education were the repeal of English-only laws, the use of Spanish in interactions between community groups and their schools, the hiring of minority language administrators and teachers, and the election of Latinos to local boards of education. All of these changes were needed, it was felt, to address the total linguistic, cultural, political, and academic needs of these students. These hopes served as the inspiration for the passage of the Bilingual Education Act of 1968. Once enacted, this bill became Title VII of the Elementary and Secondary Education Act (ESEA) of 1968.

Title VII, as the Bilingual Education Act came to be known, did not promote comprehensive reforms to improve the education of Latino children as many activists involved in its passage had hoped for. This bill was, in reality, a minor albeit important piece of federal legislation. It was programmatically small and both categorical in nature and compensatory in intent. Also, the policy's purpose and the program's goals were vague or undefined. During the next several decades, however, as San Miguel has noted in *Contested Policy,* Latino activists and their allies helped transform this minor voluntary piece of legislation aimed at low-income, "limited English speaking" students into a major programmatic effort reinforced by state legislation in some 15 states. Despite pervasive passive resistance or nonsupport for bilingual education, the proponents made several important changes to this policy by the late 1970s. With the support of the federal government, they transformed the voluntary character of federal bilingual education policy, established a federal preference for using native-language instructional approaches, delineated and expanded the goals of this policy, increased the bill's funding, and expanded its scope to include capacity-building activities. A decade after the enactment of Title VII, ESEA, bilingual education was mandatory throughout the country and was supported by a variety of state and local measures and funding streams.

Obstacles to Bilingual Education

Although successful in transforming bilingual education from a vague concept to implemented reality, proponents of this curricular policy experienced challenges beyond political opposition or program misunderstanding. One of the most important challenges during the 1970s was another federal mandate: desegregation policy. This policy, embodied in judicial mandates, federal legislation, and executive actions issued between 1954 and the 1970s, required the dispersal of minority students, including Latinos. Bilingual education, on the other hand, often required the concentration of ELLs in order to bring together a critical mass of teaching resources. Different Supreme Court decisions and policy statements supported both of these potentially clashing positions. The judicial basis for desegregation was the *Brown v. Board of Education* ruling in 1954, which prohibited racial segregation in education. The judicial support for bilingual education was the *Lau v. Nichols* decision of 1974, which ruled that local school districts had to take affirmative steps to overcome the language "deficiency" experienced by language minority students. Latino activists, however, did not perceive the requirement to provide special language programs to ELLs as clashing with the requirement to desegregate the public schools. They believed that bilingual education could be effectively incorporated into desegregated settings. However, a federal court in the Denver desegregation case in 1973, *Keyes v. Denver School District No.1, Denver,* shattered this illusion. It found that bilingual education was not a substitute for desegregation and had to be subordinate to a plan of school desegregation. Gradually, unimpressive results led to diminished support for desegregation among Latinos, and support for bilingual education flagged in the face of organized opposition to the concept. Fragile coalitions that had fought together for both programs weakened once there was no longer a common programmatic goal.

Although bilingual education suffered setbacks during this period, those setbacks were not always obvious to the casual observer. The prevalence and growth of bilingual education, in addition to other social, economic, and political factors, created fears and anxieties among Americans of all colors, classes, and genders and sparked a vigorous opposition. In the latter part of the 1970s, this opposition was highly disorganized and limited primarily to journalists and researchers. In the 1980s and 1990s, Republicans in the executive and legislative branches of the federal government and special interest groups, especially English-only organizations, conservative authors, and parent groups, began an open battle against bilingual education.

Two early critics of bilingual education were Keith Baker and Adriana A. de Kanter, who, in 1981, wrote *Effectiveness of Bilingual Education: A Review of the Literature.* Other notable publications were Tom Bethel's 1979 article "Why Johnny Can't Speak English"; John R. Edwards's "Critics and Criticism of Bilingual Education"; the address in 1985 by William J. Bennett, U.S. Secretary of Education, to the Association for a Better New York; and Rosalie Pedalino Porter's book *Forked Tongue: The Politics of Bilingual Education.* In "Conservative Groups Take Aim at Federal Bilingual Programs," James Crawford gives an overview of three organizations opposed to bilingual education: Save Our Schools (SOS), the Council for Inter-American Security, and U.S. English. More general studies attacking bilingualism and diversity in American life include Arthur M. Schlesinger, Jr.'s *The Disuniting of America* and William J. Bennett's

The Devaluing of America: The Fight for Our Culture and Our Children.

The opponents pursued two major strategies, one aimed at attacking the empirical basis of bilingual education and the other at repealing or modifying federal bilingual education policy. Both of these were highly contested by the proponents.

The first major strategy raised questions about the goals, effectiveness, and consequences of federal bilingual education. Opponents within and outside the federal government argued, among other things, that bilingual education was ineffective in teaching English and that English-only methods were available to accomplish this goal. They also argued that bilingual education failed to assimilate immigrant children as fast as it could, promoted Hispanic separatism and cultural apartheid, created an affirmative action program for Latinos, contributed to social divisions based on language, and led to the federal imposition of curricula at the local level by mandating one single approach to educating ELLs.

Proponents of bilingual education vigorously countered all these charges. A few of them, as in Ann Willig's report "A Meta-Analysis of Selected Studies on the Effectiveness of Bilingual Education," published in the *Review of Educational Research* in 1995, criticized the methodological flaws and conclusions of studies indicating that bilingual education programs were not effectively teaching ELLs. Some proponents argued that no significant research showing the success of English-only methods existed and concluded that findings showing the success of well-designed bilingual programs were distorted or suppressed. Many of these arguments were reflected in the U.S. General Accounting Office's report of 1987, titled *Bilingual Education: A New Look at the Research Evidence.* Still others noted that the attack against this policy was ideologically inspired or that the arguments against bilingual education were, as Stephen D. Krashen noted in 1999, in *Condemned Without a Trial*, "bogus."

In addition to attacking various aspects of bilingual education policy, opponents also sought changes in federal bilingual education funding and in the federal compliance enforcement in order to water down the programs funded with those resources. Opposition within the federal government came primarily from elected officials in the executive and legislative branches of government. The former will be referred to as *executive opponents,* the latter as *congressional opponents.*

Executive opponents, led by the president of the United States, sought to weaken federal support for bilingual education. President Ronald Reagan initiated the campaign against bilingual education in 1980. In his first term, he tried to halt the growth of bilingual education by seeking rescissions and decreased funding. During his second term, he developed a new initiative to undermine bilingual education. Reagan appointed William J. Bennett, an outspoken opponent of bilingual education, to head the Department of Education and to lead the campaign against it. Once in office, Bennett developed and implemented a coherent plan to redirect the program toward more English instruction. First, he eliminated the mandatory provisions of bilingual education by dismantling its civil rights component. Second, he downgraded the primary instrument for enforcing the *Lau v. Nichols* (1974) Supreme Court decision, the Office for Civil Rights, by reducing its enforcement budget and staff. Finally, he weakened the administration of bilingual education and tried to undo existing *Lau* agreements.

Proponents of bilingual education, especially Latino groups, opposed these changes and criticized Bennett for his shortsightedness and the negative implications his strategy could have for language minority children. Their opposition, however, had no significant impact on Bennett's efforts to undermine bilingual education.

Congressional opponents also took a variety of actions against bilingual education. Between 1980 and 2001, they introduced numerous pieces of legislation aimed at repealing the federal bilingual education law. In 1993, for instance, two bills were introduced to repeal the Bilingual Education Act, but no action, as the *Congressional Quarterly Researcher* noted in that same year, was taken on them. One of the most publicized bills aimed at eliminating the federal bilingual education bill was submitted by House Majority Whip Tom Delay (R-Tex.) in April 1998. Known as the "English for Children Act," this bill would have effectively ended federal funding for about 750 bilingual programs nationwide. This bill's provisions, as well as opposition to it by the League of United Latin American Citizens and both Gene Green and Sheila Jackson, U.S. Congressional Representatives from the Houston area, were summarized in an article written by Greg McDonald for the *Houston Chronicle* in April 1998. In many cases, opponents of bilingual education also introduced English-only bills in an effort to eliminate bilingual education policies. None of them, as San Miguel noted in *Contested Policy,* became law.

Unable to repeal bilingual education, congressional opponents sought changes in federal policy. Two key changes were made over the years and were reflected in the reauthorization of the Bilingual Education Act of 1994. One of these placed limits on the number of years ELLs could participate in bilingual programs, on the number of English-speaking children eligible to participate, and on the amount of non-English languages one could use in bilingual education. The other major change focused on redefining bilingual education policy to allow for the inclusion of non-English-language approaches.

In the first half of the 1990s, the election of President Clinton, a supporter of bilingual education, to the White House temporarily halted the opposition's efforts. His election led to the strengthening of bilingual education legislation in 1994. During the second half of the decade, following the assumption of control by Republicans of both chambers of Congress, the election of Republican George W. Bush to the White House in 2000, and the successful dismantling of bilingual education in Californian and Arizona, opponents in Congress renewed their attempts to change bilingual education policy. In 2001, a new bill was enacted that included most of the provisions that had been promoted by bilingual education opponents. This legislation, the No Child Left Behind Act of 2001, amended and reauthorized the ESEA for the next 6 years. Among its many changes, this law reauthorized the Bilingual Education Act of 1994. It became Title III of the overall bill. This title, a major overhaul of federal programs for the education of ELLs and recent immigrant students, provided more funds for their education, but it also officially repealed bilingual education and replaced it with English-only legislation. The term *bilingual education* was removed from all programs of the Department of Education, including the office that once managed Title VII. Taken together, these actions signaled an escalating lack of support for bilingual education at the federal level. Although proponents lost this particular battle, the war over bilingualism in American life was far from over. Before long, the primary arena for the continuing struggle shifted to the states, notably, those states that allow voter initiatives and referenda.

Guadalupe San Miguel, Jr.

See also Bennett, William J.; English for the Children Campaign; Improving America's Schools Act of 1994; No Child Left Behind Act of 2001, Title III; Paradox of Bilingualism; Porter, Rosalie Pedalino; Program Effectiveness Research; Roos, Peter D.; Views of Language Difference

Further Readings

Baker, K., & de Kanter, A. (1981). *Effectiveness of bilingual education: A review of the literature.* Washington, DC: U.S. Department of Education, Office of Planning, Budget, and Evaluation.

Bennett, W. (1992). *The devaluing of America: The fight for our culture and our children.* New York: Touchstone.

Bennett, W. J. (1992). Bilingual education act: A failed path. In J. Crawford (Ed.), *Language loyalties: A source book on the official English controversy* (pp. 358–363). Chicago: University of Chicago Press.

Bethel, T. (February, 1979). Why Johnny can't speak English. *Harper's Magazine,* pp. 30–33.

Bilingual Education Act, Pub. L. No. 90–247, 81 Stat. 816 (1968).

Brown v. Board of Education, 347 U.S. 483 (1954).

Crawford, J. (1986, March). Conservative groups take aim at federal bilingual programs. *Education Week, 19,* 1.

Crawford, J. (1989). *Bilingual education: History, politics, theory, and practice.* Trenton, NJ: Crane.

Crawford, J. (2000). *At war with diversity: U.S. language policy in an age of anxiety.* Buffalo, NY: Multilingual Matters.

Edwards, J. R. (1980). Critics and criticism of bilingual education. *Modern Language Journal, 64,* 409–415.

Evaluation, Dissemination, and Assessment Center. (1986). *Beyond language: Social and cultural factors in the schooling of language minority children.* Los Angeles: California State University, Evaluation, Dissemination, and Assessment Center.

González, J. M. (1979). *Towards quality in bilingual education: Bilingual education in the integrated school.* Rosslyn, VA: National Clearinghouse for Bilingual Education.

Keyes v. School District No. 1, Denver, Colorado, 413 U.S. 189 (1973).

Krashen, S. (1996). *Under attack: The case against bilingual education.* Culver City, CA: Language Education Associates.

Krashen, S. (1999). *Condemned without a trial: Bogus arguments against bilingual education.* Portsmouth, NH: Heinemann.

Lau v. Nichols, 414 U.S. 563 (1974).

McDonald, G. (1998, April 22). Delay bill would end federal support of bilingual education. *Houston Chronicle.* Retrieved from http://www.humnet.ucla.edu/humnet/linguistics/people/grads/macswan/HC2.htm

National Commission on Excellence in Education. (1983). *A nation at risk: The imperative for educational reform.* Washington, DC: Author.

No Child Left Behind Act. Pub. L. No. 107–110 (2002).

Porter, R. P. (1990). *Forked tongue: The politics of bilingual education.* New York: Basic Books.

Roos, P. D. (1984). Equity and excellence. In National Commission on Secondary Schooling for Hispanics (Ed.), *Make something happen: Hispanics and urban high school reform* (Vol. 2, pp. 75–78). Washington, DC: Hispanic Policy Development Project.

San Miguel, G., Jr. (2004). *Contested policy: The rise and fall of federal bilingual education in the United States, 1960–2001.* Denton: University of North Texas Press.

Schlesinger, A. M. (1992). *The disuniting of America.* New York: Norton.

U.S. General Accounting Office. (1987). *Bilingual education: A new look at the research evidence.* Washington DC: Author.

Willig, A. (1995). A meta-analysis of selected studies on the effectiveness of bilingual education. *Review of Educational Research, 55,* 269–317.

Worsnop, R. L. (1993, August 13). Bilingual education. *CQ Researcher, 3,* 697–720. Retrieved from http://library .cqpress.com/cqresearcher/cqresrre1993081300

ERROR ANALYSIS

Error analysis comprises a variety of linguistic analyses of the errors language learners make in producing or comprehending a new language. The two questions that guide this analysis are as follows: (1) What types of errors do they make? and (2) what are the sources of these errors? During the heyday of error analysis, it was thought that such analysis could give language teachers an idea about where learners are in the language learning process so that they could help students by focusing on areas that seemed most troublesome. Today, there is less enthusiasm concerning the benefits of error analysis, although it has particular uses as a diagnostic tool for teachers.

Error analysis is a learner-centric approach. S. Pit Corder claimed that through this approach, the developmental process of language learning could be better understood, and teachers would be able to build a syllabus meet language learners' needs. The assumption here is that each learner's mind has a built-in syllabus for language learning. To find this learner-generated sequence and adapt instruction to it is more efficient than to follow an instructor-generated sequence and impose it upon the learners, which was the method that dictated language teaching in the past. The instructor-generated

syllabus is associated with the behaviorist approach to language learning and uses a contrastive analysis method that predicts difficulties the learner would have, by comparing the linguistic structures of the target language and the native language. Using error analysis, it was expected that teachers would build a syllabus on these assumptions, without actually observing and analyzing the language being produced. Error analysis was the first important attempt to study the learner's language in itself, and thus some researchers believe it to be the beginning of the field of second-language acquisition research.

Historical Overview

The potential benefits of looking at learners' errors had not been recognized until the 1960s. In the behaviorist approach, which had been a prevailing learning theory since the 1930s, it was believed that children learned their first language by imitating and forming a habit of connecting stimulus and response. Within this framework, learning a second language was viewed as developing a new set of language habits and transferring the language habits from the first language. Contrastive analysis, therefore, was a way to predict a learner's difficulty or ease of establishing a new language habit. More similarities between the two languages meant an easier transition in learning the target language, because learners could transfer a beneficial habit from their first language to the target language. Errors were considered bad habits that needed to be prevented and could be predicted, reduced, and eventually eliminated.

In the 1960s, the behaviorist theory of language learning was challenged by the growing recognition that children acquire their first language not by imitating or being reinforced, but by playing active roles in creating their linguistic rules. Children's incorrect forms in their mother tongue during their first-language acquisition is demonstrated evidence that children set hypotheses and test them, and construct linguistic rules. This new perspective in child language acquisition had an impact on the field of second-language learning. A second-language-learner's errors began to be viewed in the same way, regarded as a window through which teachers and researchers could see what strategies a learner employs while learning a language. In this view, errors were no longer regarded as bad habits, but as the logical steps in constructing and testing rules for the new language.

Error Analysis Research

Not all errors are a focus of error analysis. In his chapter "The Significance of Learners' Errors" in the edited book *Error Analysis (1974),* Corder distinguished "errors" from "mistakes." *Mistakes* are any nonsystematic errors that language speakers make because of fatigue, slip of the tongue, or emotion. Speakers know when they have made mistakes and, if asked, can correct them easily, because they know the rules. These are also called *errors of performance.* Errors in error analysis are *errors of competence,* which are systematic and occur repeatedly. These errors show the learners' *transitional competence,* which is in the process of moving toward the competence of native speakers. They are not errors to the language learners who make them, only to the native speakers who hear them. Therefore, learners cannot correct the errors by themselves, because according to their linguistic systems, they are using the correct rules. These systematic errors of competence are the focus of error analysis. The utterances of language learners should be observed regularly by the teacher in order to differentiate errors from mistakes.

Conducting error analysis involves a few steps. First, samples of a learner's language in oral or written forms are collected. Then, errors in the sample data are carefully identified for errors that are not only overt but also covert. In this step, teachers need to be aware that even well-formed sentences may contain errors. The meaning of the sentence can be different from what the learner intended, or the learner may not know the rules but accidentally made a well-formed utterance. In some cases, the learner's utterance does not seem to have any errors in its sentence structure but may not be what a native speaker of the language would say in that context. One example given by Corder is "After an hour it was stopped." This sentence does not appear to contain any errors, but if the learner used "it" to refer to "the wind," then this sentence becomes erroneous. How can one figure out the intended meaning of the learner's utterance? The best way is to ask the learner, if necessary, in their mother tongue. This way, the researcher or teacher can make an authoritative reconstruction of the sentence in the target language by asking what a native speaker of the target language would have said to express this meaning in that context. When making an authoritative reconstruction is not possible, the intended meaning needs to be inferred by the structure of the sentence and the context of how it was written or spoken; this is called *plausible reconstruction.*

This process denotes an important difference between contrastive analysis and error analysis. While in contrastive analysis, the learner's native language and the target language are compared; in error analysis, the learner's utterance, which is also known as *interlanguage,* is compared to the target language.

The next step is to linguistically describe the nature of the error by comparing the meaning of the sentence and the structure of the sentence, for instance, comparing errors of a grammatical category such as a missing article versus errors made on a morphology level or syntactic level. Then, linguistic and psycholinguistic explanations of the error need to be made by answering how and why the learner made such an error. The different types of errors in error analysis vary among researchers in error analysis. Jack C. Richards suggests there are three kinds of errors: *interlanguage, intralingual,* and *developmental.* Interlanguage, or "language transfer," errors occur when the learner tries to apply rules from his or her mother tongue to those of the second language. Therefore, the learner's first-language background plays a part in this type of error. Contrary to the interlanguage errors, language learners show a similar pattern in making an intralingual error and a developmental error regardless of their language backgrounds. This type of error is thought to originate from the language structure itself and is found not only in the production of the second-language learner but also in the language of children who are acquiring the language as their first language. One example of intralingual errors is missing a modal auxiliary (the verb *to be*), as in the following sentence: *What you reading?* Two other researchers, Heidi C. Dulay and Marina K. Burt, categorize errors differently. Their two categories, "interference-like goofs" and "first-language developmental goofs" are similar to Richards's interlanguage and intralingual errors, respectively. The other two types are "ambiguous goofs," which can be either interference-like goofs or first-language developmental goofs, and "unique goofs," which are not found in the children's language acquisition of the target language. Because some categories of errors are unclear, generally, researchers classify errors as interlingual errors and intralingual errors.

During the 1970s, many studies were conducted in error analysis. As mentioned above, some research was done to find out the different sources of these errors. Studies on what type of error occurred more frequently were conducted, and it was concluded that intralingual errors occur more often than interlingual errors. Error analysis also brought about new ideas in teaching languages. Whereas in the behaviorist view of learning, the teachers' role was to prevent the learners from making errors and the main classroom activities were drills of the correct rules or forms, within this new perspective, correcting the errors immediately was not desirable because it could deprive the learner of the opportunity to reformulate their hypothesis about rules of the target language. It is recommended, as for an adult during child-adult conversations while a child is acquiring his or her first language, that teachers repeat what the learner said in the correct form or ask the learner in the correct form, rather than point out the incorrect form and provide the correct one immediately.

Limitations of Error Analysis

Over time, the limitations and problems of error analysis have become clear. One of the problems is the difficulty in identifying errors. As Rod Ellis mentions, dialects exist in every language. Depending on what dialect of the second language is used to compare with the learner's language production, his or her utterance can contain errors or can be errorless. How much corpus or sample of the learner's utterance is needed to decide whether the error is a real error, a mistake, or a feature of a different dialect? Another issue is whether teachers or researchers can rely on the learner's retrospective explanation of their intended meaning. Learners may lack the necessary metalinguistic knowledge to talk about their oral or written utterance. Ellis points out that there is a problem with reconstruction, as well. To conduct an error analysis, reconstruction of learners' oral or written sentences is necessary. However, in some cases, the learner's sentences can be reconstructed in different ways without losing the learner's intended meaning. Ellis gives an example of "I am worried in my mind." This utterance can be reconstructed as "I am feeling worried" or "I have a problem on my mind" as well. The description of errors will be different depending on which of these two reconstructed sentences is chosen as a correct form. It can be an error of using a wrong verb or a wrong preposition. Another limitation is the difficulty in pinpointing the source of the error. Dulay and Burt call this type of error "ambiguous goofs." For example, if a Spanish speaker produces a sentence like *Susan not can read,* this error can be referred to as interlingual, because in Spanish, the negation word comes before the verb. Yet it can be categorized as intralingual, because English-speaking children learning their first language also go through this developmental stage.

An important study that points out a critical problem in error analysis was conducted by Jacquelyn Schachter. She looked at the relative-clause production of students from four different language groups: Persian, Arabic, Chinese, and Japanese. In her study, she observed that the total number of relative clauses Persian and Arab students produced was much greater than that of Chinese and Japanese students. The percentage of errors was also higher in Persian and Arab learners than in the other two groups, although relative-clause formation of Persian and Arabic languages is similar to English compared with that of Chinese and Japanese. If one focuses only on the number or percentage of the errors in producing relative clauses, it could be concluded that Persian and Arab learners have more difficulty producing relative clauses than do Chinese and Japanese learners. However, Schachter's conclusion was that due to the difficulty, Chinese and Japanese learners avoided using relative clauses or used them very carefully, and this led to fewer errors.

Owing to the limitations and methodological issues inherent in error analysis, interest in this method has diminished. It is thought that like contrastive analysis, error analysis gives only a partial view of language learning, and it is too complicated for the average teacher, untrained in linguistics, to use.

Hye Jong Kim

See also Contrastive Analysis; Interlanguage

Further Readings

Corder, S. P. (1974). Error analysis. In J. P. B. Allen & S. Pit Corder (Eds.), *Techniques in applied linguistics* (pp. 122–154). Oxford, UK: Oxford University Press.

Corder, S. P. (1974). Idiosyncratic dialects and error analysis. In J. C. Richards (Ed.), *Error analysis: Perspectives on second language acquisition* (pp. 158–171). London: Longman.

Corder, S. P. (1974). The significance of learners' errors. In J. C. Richards (Ed.), *Error analysis: Perspectives on second language acquisition* (pp. 19–27). London: Longman.

Dulay, H. C., & Burt, M. K. (1974). You can't learn without goofing: An analysis of children's second language 'errors.' In J. C. Richards (Ed.), *Error analysis: Perspectives on second language acquisition* (pp. 95–123). London: Longman.

Ellis, R. (1985). *Understanding second language acquisition.* Oxford, UK: Oxford University Press.

Gass, S. M., & Selinker, L. (2001). *Second language acquisition: An introductory course.* Mahwah, NJ: Lawrence Erlbaum.

Richards, J. C. (Ed.). (1974). *Error analysis: Perspectives on second language acquisition.* London: Longman.

Schachter, J. (1974). An error in error analysis. *Language Learning, 24,* 205–214.

ESCAMILLA, KATHY (1949–)

Kathy Escamilla was born on April 16, 1949, in Greeley, Colorado. She earned a PhD in 1987 from UCLA in curriculum and study of schooling, with an emphasis in bilingual education, after having completed an MS in education, with an emphasis in bilingual-bicultural education at the University of Kansas (1975) and a BA in Spanish and education at the University of Colorado, Boulder (1971). Escamilla began her career as a bilingual elementary and early childhood teacher in Colorado and California. She subsequently lectured in the division of teacher education at California State University, Fullerton (1978–1982), and served as director of Bilingual Programs for the Tucson Unified School District (1983–1988). She also served as an assistant professor and research associate at the University of Arizona (1988–1990), the BUENO Center for Multicultural Education (1990–1992), and the University of Colorado, Denver (1992–1998). She is currently a professor in the School of Education at the University of Colorado, Boulder, where she has been a faculty member since 1998.

Escamilla engages in research that supports effective models of intervention for English language learners. For more than 35 years, she has explored questions related to the development of bilingualism and biliteracy for Spanish-English bilingual children in the United States. Her work challenges the assumption that language, literacy, and evaluation theories developed in monolingual contexts are appropriately applied to multilingual children. Further, her research reinforces her belief that all languages are cognitive, linguistic, and societal resources.

Escamilla's primary research interests include the following foci: language and literacy acquisition theory for bilingual children, methods of bilingual/multicultural education, sociolinguistic and sociocultural practices in classrooms and schools, and the impact of assessment on multilingual communities. She has published and lectured extensively on each of these topics. Much of her research questions the teaching of Spanish using English methodologies. Her book chapters in *The Power of Two Languages* and *The Handbook for Literacy Assessment for Bilingual Learners,* as well as articles in *Equity and Excellence in Education* and the *Bilingual Research Journal,* examine literacy instruction and assessment in bilingual programs.

Working with colleagues, Escamilla reconceptualized the English reading program Reading Recovery into Spanish. Her research in this field culminated with the publication in 1996 of *Instrumento de Observación de los Logros de la Lecto-Escritura Inicial* (Observation Instrument for Initial Reading/Writing Achievement). This program is a research-based Spanish language reading intervention designed to accelerate literacy for Spanish-speaking first-grade students. Aspects of this research were reported in peer-reviewed journal articles and two book chapters. The articles appeared in *Education and Urban Society* (1992); *NABE Conference Proceedings* (1992); and *Literacy, Teaching, and Learning* (1994, 1998). The book chapters appeared in *Research on Reading Recovery* (1997) and *Early Intervention and Early Literacy* (1998).

As coinvestigator on a 3-year project to examine assessment practices and the impact of high-stakes testing on English language learners, Escamilla examined the results of English language learners' achievement in reading, writing, and math, as measured by the Colorado Student Assessment Program (CSAP). Results indicated that students were doing well on the Spanish CSAP and that Spanish CSAP results correlated well with students' CSAP testing in English. The results of this study are reported in four monographs, from 2000, 2001, 2002, and 2003, and one article that appeared in the *Bilingual Research Journal* in 2003.

Escamilla is a member of numerous professional organizations in education and has served two terms as the president of the National Association for Bilingual Education (1993–1994, 1995–1996). She has served as a member and chair of various committees for the National Association for Bilingual Education and the American Education Research Association. She has functioned as a member of the board of editors for the *Bilingual Research Journal* and the *Literacy, Teaching, and Learning Journal.* She is currently a member of the American Educational Research Association (AERA) Spencer Review Panel for Pre-Dissertation Fellows, the American Association of Colleges of Teacher Education (AACTE) Committee on Research, and the Associated Directors of Bilingual Education (ADOBE). Escamilla participates on the Colorado Department of Education steering committee for examining issues relating to limited-English-proficient students and has been a consultant to school districts in Colorado, Texas, and California in the areas of bilingualism and biliteracy.

Kathy Escamilla and Susan Hopewell

See also Amendment 31 (Colorado); Literacy and Biliteracy; Raising Bilingual Children

Further Readings

Escamilla, K. (1999). Teaching literacy in Spanish. In J. Tinajero & R. DeVillar (Eds.), *The power of two languages 2000* (pp. 126–141). New York: MacMillan/McGraw-Hill.

Escamilla, K., & Coady, M. (2001). Assessing the writing of Spanish speaking students: Issues and suggestions. In J. Tinajero & S. Hurley (Eds.), *Literacy assessment of second language learners: Effective dual language use across the curriculum.* (pp. 43–63). Boston: Allyn & Bacon.

Escamilla, K., & Nathenson-Mejia, S. (2003). Preparing culturally responsive teachers: Using Latino children's literature in teacher education. *Equity and Excellence in Education, 36,* 238–248.

Escamilla, K., Shannon, S., Carlos, S., & García, J. (2003). Breaking the code: Colorado's defeat of the anti-bilingual education initiative (Amendment 31). *Bilingual Research Journal, 27,* 357–382. Retrieved from http://asu.edu/archive.html

Nathenson-Mejia, S., & Escamilla, K. (2003). Connecting with Latino children: Bridging gaps with children's literature. *Bilingual Research Journal, 27,* 101–116. Retrieved from http://asu.edu/archive.html

ESCOBEDO, DEBORAH (1954–)

Deborah Escobedo has been involved in litigation and administrative and legislative advocacy on education equity issues, in particular those involving the rights of language minority and immigrant children. Born on March 9, 1954, in Lynwood, California, she received her JD from Boalt Hall School of Law in 1979.

Escobedo has had extensive experience in litigating statewide issues impacting California's immigrant communities and has been either lead counsel or cocounsel on legal challenges such as *Valeria G. v. Wilson* (1998), *Angel v. Davis* (2002), *Pedro A. v. Dawson* (1994), and *Pazmiño v. California Board of Education* (2003) and to statewide antibilingual and anti-immigrant initiatives Proposition 227 and Proposition 187. In *Pazmiño v. California Board of Education,* Escobedo was lead counsel, and it was one of the first successful cases brought under the federal No Child Left Behind Act of 2001.

The *Valeria G. v. Wilson* suit was filed on June 3, 1998, the day after voters in California approved Proposition 227, a ballot measure designed to severely limit bilingual education for 1.6 million English language learners in California. *Valeria G. v. Wilson* was a class action suit filed on behalf of limited-English-proficient students, their parents, and several immigrant rights organizations. The suit charged that Proposition 227 denied language minority children equal access to educational opportunity. Both the U.S. District Court and the Ninth Circuit Court of Appeals denied the request to block the implementation of Proposition 227. However, Escobedo eloquently and prophetically stated that "the state should be the guarantor of educational opportunity for all children in California. . . . The state is willing to put these children's future at risk. We are not—and they shouldn't be" (*ACLU News,* 1998) and that the proposition "would cause immediate and profound disruption of the education of students who can least afford such disruption" (CNN, 1998).Undaunted by defeat, Escobedo has kept fighting.

The case of *Pedro A. v. Dawson* was filed after the passage of Proposition 187 in California. The goal of Proposition 187 was to prevent undocumented immigrants' access to benefits and public services, including public education. *Pedro A. v. Dawson* was filed to halt the implementation of Proposition 187 and its exclusionary provisions. Legal challenges to Proposition 187 were filed in both state and federal courts, and the proposition was declared unconstitutional at both levels. Escobedo was a major force in the successful fight against implementation of this proposition, seen by many as overtly anti-Latino.

The case of *Pazmiño v. California Board of Education* is significant for several reasons. The state of California severely restricted bilingual education with the passage of Proposition 227 in 1998. However, under certain conditions, parents and school districts maintained bilingual education programs. With the passage of No Child Left Behind in 2001 came a federal grant program aimed at helping children learn to read. This program was called "Reading First." The state of California accepted federal funds under the Reading First initiative but restricted school districts' access to Reading First monies to school districts that were teaching in English only. The *Pazmiño* case challenged the state of California's decision to provide Reading First money only to districts teaching in English, claiming that the policy excluded about 16,000 children in California who were still receiving some form of bilingual education. Many school districts, some of California's poorest, did not even apply for Reading First money because they still offered bilingual education and feared they did not qualify. In 2003, the San Francisco Superior Court ordered California to make funding from Reading First available to children who were learning to read in languages other than English and to children in bilingual programs, as well as all English programs.

Escobedo received the National Hispanic Bar Association Award for Excellence in Public Service in 1998, the San Francisco Minority Bar Coalition Unity Award in 1997, and the California La Raza lawyers Association's Cruz Reynoso Community Service Award in 1992. She has also received numerous awards from education-related organizations for her advocacy on behalf of language minority children. Escobedo is also a writer and frequently contributes to educational publications that focus on issues of race, ethnicity, language, and education.

Since 2005, Deborah Escobedo has been a staff attorney at the Youth Law Center in San Francisco. In addition to her stellar career as an attorney and advocate for language minority and immigrant students, she is involved in many civic activities in San Francisco and California. She was appointed by the San Francisco Board of Supervisors to serve on the Immigrant Rights Commission in 2005. In 2006, she was appointed to serve on California's Blue Ribbon Commission on Children in Foster Care, a committee that has been charged with helping to find secure safe and permanent homes for California's 97,000 foster children.

Kathy Escamilla and Susan Hopewell

See also Muticultural Education, Training, and Advocacy (META); No Child Left Behind Act of 2001, Title III; Proposition 227 (California); Proposition 227 (California), Impact of

Further Readings

Angel v. Davis, 307 F.3d 1036 1040 (9th Cir. 2002).

California judge won't halt bilingual education ban. (1998, July 15). CNN.com. Retrieved from http://www.cnn.com/US/9807/15/bilingual.court.fight

Pazmiño v. California Board of Education, # CPF03–502554 (Superior Ct., San Francisco County, 2003).

Pedro A. v. Dawson, No. 965089 (Superior Ct. San Francisco County 1994).

Proposition 227 appealed: Civil rights group seek trial on bilingual ed measure. (1998). *ACLU News, 62*(5). Retrieved from http://www.aclunc.org/news/print_newsletters/september-october_1998.shtml

Valeria G. v. Wilson, No. C-98–2252-CAL (N.D. Ca. 1998).

ETHNOCENTRISM

Ethnocentrism (sometimes *ethnocentricism*) is often defined as the presumption that one's own culture is superior to all others and, consequently, that other cultures should be judged by the standards and definitions of one's own. In most of the conceptual literature that examines relationships between groups, the concept of ethnocentrism is given a decidedly negative slant. Often, there is little or no distinction made between ethnocentrism and racism. At times, the difference between the two concepts is assumed to be one of degree. Positioning ethnocentrism in this way causes us to view the concept with suspicion and to assume that people who are ethnocentric have made a conscious choice to feel and behave that way. While volition may be a factor in some forms of ethnocentrism, it is not always central to the concept.

Like racism, ethnocentrism may be examined through the beliefs and actions of individuals, in culturally or ethnically defined groups of people, or in social institutions and their practices. There are important differences between these levels of analysis. To gain greater insight and build an understanding of ethnocentrism, it is helpful to know its bases and functions in human development, because this perspective cuts across many, perhaps most, ethnic cultures. Having done so, we can then extend this analysis to the institutional level and perhaps gain a better understanding of how this concept relates to school policies and practices that affect particular programs such as bilingual education.

Ethnocentrism, Good and Bad

Anthropologists say it is not unusual for members of human groups to identify their own cultures as the best in the world. It requires only a moment's reflection to understand how this might be true. Through enculturation, we acquire the patterns, paradigms, exemplars, and behavioral templates that have worked well for the group or groups with which we identify most closely. These are the patterns of thought, action, and belief that have worked well for "our own kind," however we may interpret that phrase. Many people in the world have had little or no firsthand experience with other groups. For those who know no other culture or worldview, is it surprising that they think theirs may be the best one? Not at all. The idea that one's preferred way of living and valuing is the best (or among the best) is probably the foundation of ethnocentrism and an ethnocentric outlook. Paradoxically, it is also the foundation of a healthy concept of self.

Erik Erikson, in his book *Childhood and Society,* made the case that child development occurs in stages, proceeding from the simple to the more complex. While much has been learned about his *stage theory of development* since Erikson first proposed it, the schema is still accepted among psychologists and educators as a useful framework in understanding child development. Using this concept as base, we can gain insights on how cultural differences may be reflected in later life, even when the child has taken little notice of his or her induction into a particular cultural or value system. Erikson did not set out to explain enculturation with his theory. His purpose was to explain the stages of life that he believed were benchmarks leading to healthy adulthood. He argued that human development proceeds in stages beginning at birth. In total, Erikson reported eight stages that constitute the task of an individual's growth. At each stage, there is a tension or struggle between polar opposites, which operates to create a resultant "virtue" or coping ability. When the skill(s) associated with any stage are acquired, the individual is able to move on to meet the demands of the next level. Since enculturation is a developmental task, we can assume that the requirements of one's identity or ethnic group are deeply involved in the resolution of these tensions.

Table 1 shows a summary of the stages, tensions, and "virtues" of Erikson's developmental schema.

For Erikson, it is axiomatic that each stage must be successfully negotiated. No step can be skipped. No "virtue" accrues until and unless each stage is successfully negotiated. Failing that, an individual will encounter difficulty in subsequent stages. When this happens, an individual must reengage the previous stage to mine its coping powers and incorporate them into his or her repertoire. A critically important aspect of Erikson's schema is that the tensions and "virtues" he identified are heavily oriented toward the affective. Because of this, they have much to do with values. They reflect, perhaps unknowingly, the values, beliefs, and predispositions of one's cultural identity. In short, a child's development takes place on a plane in which the affective side is preeminent. These virtues are acquired gradually, generally without any overt signals to mark their acquisition.

Erikson's theories are well accepted among developmental psychologists, but it should be noted that we do not know for sure that these virtues or skills hold

Table 1   Erikson's Stages of Human Development

Between These Approximate Ages	These Tensions	Produce These Virtues
0–2 yrs.	Trust vs. Mistrust	Hope
2–3 yrs.	Autonomy vs. Shame & Doubt	Willpower
3–4 yrs.	Initiative vs. Guilt	Purpose
4–11 yrs.	Industry vs. Inferiority	Competence
12–20 yrs.	Identity vs. Role Confusion	Fidelity
Young Adulthood	Intimacy vs. Isolation	Love
Adulthood	Generativity vs. Stagnation	Care
Maturity	Ego Integrity vs. Despair	Wisdom

Source: Synopsis of Erikson's stages, adapted from various writings over the course of his career.

true across all cultures. It is not known whether peoples in all parts of the world develop the same virtues during the same time frames or whether the tensions that produce them are the same in all or in most cultures. This caveat notwithstanding, Erikson's conceptual model is useful as a way to frame discussions and to suggest how the maturation of virtues or life skills takes place. But are these virtues always benign? If not, when and why do they cease to be virtues and become liabilities?

In the process of socialization and enculturation, the child is led naturally and inexorably to become ethnocentric: to believe that the cultural values, beliefs, and practices of his or her family, community, and other members of his or her identity group are satisfying and satisfactory. This is especially true for children growing up in a monocultural environment in which cultural differences and complications are rare and, as far as children can discern, their needs are satisfied by the culture they have internalized. Children have no reason to reject, distrust, doubt, or feel insecure about their cultural identities—in short, about the way of life of those around them. In this sense, their feeling of pride and comfort is benign. It is a sign that enculturation has been successful and a baseline has been adopted for interpreting the world in ways that are sanctioned by the child's group. It can be argued, therefore, that ethnocentrism is normal and that it is a component of healthy development in the passage from childhood to adulthood.

Most children are well served by a process whose end result is making them into complex, culturebound creatures with a strong group identity derived from their primary identity group. It is not ethnocentrism per se that is detrimental in the broader social context (i.e., outside the matrix group). Within the matrix group, ethnocentrism is a necessary and indispensable ingredient in the transfer of the parents' culture to their children. It may also be a necessary ingredient in cognitive development, as suggested by developmental psychologist Jean Piaget in his analysis of egocentrism, the personal analogue of ethnocentrism.

Among adults, however, and especially in a context of diversity, ethnocentrism is often regarded as negative. There are good indications that while ethnocentrism is necessary in children, it becomes problematic when it is prolonged, unchecked, undisciplined, and without reflection into adulthood. In adulthood, clinging to ethnocentric sentiments and behavior has the danger of infringing into the lives of other groups

because it may lead to overzealousness and excessive pride regarding one's matrix group. Ethnocentric persons may ignore or diminish the worth of identity patterns other than their own. In a group context of great power differences and/or deeply engrained asymmetries of wealth or status, ethnocentric behavior can be the cause of discrimination and prejudice. It raises the possibility of discord, exclusion, and conflict. Therefore, it is possible to think of some manifestations of prejudice as the result of overextended and unhealthy ethnocentrism.

It should be noted, however, that *culture,* with its powerful (anthropological) baggage, may not be the most accurate term with which to encompass and label the full range of differences that exist between groups. In some cases, when nationality and ethnicity are not the primary determiners of *groupness,* we might elect to focus on worldviews, religions, or value and belief systems to describe differences that occur naturally among and between groups. The concept of culture is not sufficiently utilitarian to help us see all factors that help to shape identity, which may not be, strictly speaking, "ethnic" in nature. Regrettably, there is not an alternative term that can serve as a substitute for culture in such cases.

Institutional Ethnocentrism

Ethnocentrism and racist behavior may differ conceptually, but the results of either may not be very different from the point of view of victimized groups. This is most apparent in dealing with institutions and their engrained behaviors. In education, it is often the case that hidden forms of ethnocentrism play a significant a role in making children feel at home in an institution new to them or, conversely, feeling unwanted or unappreciated in that context. In the context of schools, it is not necessary for educators to choose to be ethnocentric to cause unwanted results in children. Schools, like most social institutions, have cultures of their own that value certain behaviors and ways of thinking and frown upon others. Like institutional racism, institutional ethnocentrism can have the unintended consequence of retarding or impeding feelings of acceptance and belonging on the part of cultural and ethnic minority groups.

At the risk of overgeneralization, we may agree that schools in the United States are based on institutional beliefs and practices originating in Western Europe. School people find it quite "normal" to encourage students to be competitive, to work toward personal rewards, to assert individualistic views and beliefs, and to question the validity of the ideas they read and discuss in class. All of these are well within the set of school behaviors that are accepted in American culture. Moreover, the institution itself encourages values and beliefs that are rarely questioned or held up for debate: the adequacy of speaking only one language, collaborating with fellow students only at certain times, and engaging in a variety of school-sponsored activities to remind students that they live in "the greatest country in the world." Such thoughts, values, and predispositions may not appear to exclude anyone. We take them for granted as "normal" in our school culture. Any single item probably does little harm. It is the aggregate of many such culturally loaded items that can have negative effects on the willingness of children to engage in schoolwork if they regard their participation as questionable in their own culture.

Nowhere is this matter more charged with negative potential than in the emphasis we place as a society on the mastery and use of English in school. For many historical reasons, U.S. society and most of its institutions drifted away from the use of multiple languages. Many American children grow up with the ethnocentric belief that English is the only language that matters. They may not do so with the intention of excluding anyone; it is simply the result of living in a monolingual society and of undergoing enculturation into a monolingual mind-set. Even in schools that operate programs of bilingual education, it is sometimes the case that the children who participate in them are regarded as less than full members of the school community until they master English. Under those conditions, it is doubtful that bilingual education alone will make substantial improvements in student gains.

The range of beliefs and assumptions concerning language is important, especially in the ever-increasing context of language diversity. Only a clear and ringing endorsement of the value of speaking more than one language can help alleviate feelings of alienation or exclusion. Minority and nonminority children alike may suffer when these affective aspects of language use are left unexamined and unattended. Language and cultural differences are good material to help majority group youngsters reflect on their ethnocentrism. For minority children, these differences can be helpful in recognizing that their worth and value as human beings is no less than that of classmates.

Finally, because none of this analysis can be done without using language, the chances of reaching more fruitful conclusions are enhanced by the use of more than one language in the transactions involved.

Josué M. González

See also Acculturation; Culturally Competent Teaching; Enculturation; Language Socialization

Further Readings

Erikson, E. (1964). *Childhood and society* (2nd ed.). New York: Norton.
Piaget, J. (1955). *The child's construction of reality*. London: Routledge & Kegan Paul.

EXCEPTIONAL STUDENTS

See GIFTED AND TALENTED BILINGUALS

EXIT CRITERIA FOR ENGLISH LANGUAGE LEARNER PROGRAMS

In accordance with the Elementary and Secondary Education Act of 2001 ("No Child Left Behind"), each state must identify processes and criteria to guide school districts in exiting or removing English language learners (ELLs) from a range of specialized services offered to students previously identified by the school as ELL or limited English proficient. The terms *exit* or *reclassification* (used synonymously) denote the process in which a student who has previously been identified as limited English proficient exits, or is removed from, programs and services for which they are no longer eligible. This includes transitional bilingual education programs but not necessarily dual-language programs.

Most commonly, such students are subsequently placed in a general education setting in which English is the only mode of instruction except, possibly, for foreign-language classes. Students no longer require, or are eligible to receive, services such as transitional bilingual education (TBE) or English as a Second Language (ESL) support. The term *limited English proficient* (LEP) is commonly used in policy to identify and define students for whom English is not their first or native language. LEP-identified students vary in their abilities to speak, read, or write English; some have little or no ability to do so, while others demonstrate a moderate command of English. The term came into the language of schools after the passage of the 1968 federal Bilingual Education Act, which established Title VII categorical funding. Title VII funding streams were used to develop materials for use with LEP-identified students, including entrance and exit criteria instruments. With the *Lau v. Nichols* (1974) case and subsequent 1975 *Lau* Remedies, schools were required to provide compensatory education for ELLs, allowing them to exit their status as LEP students and equally access curricular resources in English in a "reasonable" amount of time.

Exit criteria for ELLs vary across policy contexts at the state, district, and school campus levels. Variability exists in how policy is developed and interpreted according to the orientation toward English language acquisition and programs provided for ELLs. For example, districts or campuses with accomodationist bilingual education or dual-language programs that promote the use of native language in the acquisition of English may choose a different approach toward the use of exit criteria than those districts or schools that reflect more-assimilationist English-first orientations in programming for ELLs, in which the native language is minimally used and English is the primary mode of instruction. Within the United States, TBE models of bilingual education or ESL predominate. These programs tend to focus on English acquisition as the primary goal, rather than maintenance of native language while acquiring English.

Assuming transitional frameworks, each state has different criteria for determining the process of exit or reclassification of LEP students as fluent or proficient English students. While each state is encouraged to develop its own process in accordance with federal statutes, similarities exist across states. The following section reviews and compares the exit criteria and follow-up procedures across five states with the largest population of ELLs: California, Florida, Illinois, New York, and Texas.

Exit Criteria and Follow-Up

All states are required to have an established and consistent process for exiting students from LEP programs. Of primary concern is measuring and advancing students' relative English language proficiency in order to enable students to successfully engage English-only curricula in general education classrooms.

In California, students are exited from LEP programs when they are reclassified as fluent English proficient (FEP). The process for reclassification of a LEP student as a FEP student in California involves four stages. The first stage into the reclassification process is determined by the students' results on the most current California Standardized Test (CST) in English language arts. The cut scores (the scores that delineate one stage from another) are determined by local districts and typically fall between "basic" and midpoint of "basic." If the results are at or above the cut scores, then the student enters the process for reclassification. Next, results from the annual California English Language Development Test (CELDT) are considered. To continue in the reclassification process, students must have an overall score that is classified as "early advanced" or higher on the CELDT and score at an intermediate or higher level on each skill area—listening, speaking, reading, and writing. A student may also qualify to continue in the process if an overall score in the upper end of the intermediate level on the CELDT and other measures indicate a likelihood of English proficiency. The third stage considers teacher evaluation of academic performance indicators as set by the local school district. Typically, it is a review of the student's grades. The final stage is parent opinion and consultation, in which parents and/or guardians are notified and encouraged to participate in the reclassification, and a face-to-face meeting is set up to encourage participation.

If a student does not meet the criteria at any stage in the process, the student remains classified an English learner, or LEP student. For those students in first and second grade, the first stage does not apply, and the state does not recommended that students in kindergarten who have been identified as LEP exit from services. Once exited from LEP programs, students are monitored for 2 years to ensure success within the general education curriculum. Monitoring does not include CELDT scores, but rather academic performance indicators to ensure adequate yearly progress.

In Illinois, there is no standard procedure for exit, as individual districts are given discretion to set policy and procedures. The transitional bilingual education policy (CR Part 228) states that no child shall be exited from services prior to his or her third year of enrollment in services, unless the student performs at or above grade level for English language skills. However, with the recent adoption of the World-Class Instructional Design and Assessment (WIDA) system, a large-scale test called Assessing Comprehension and Communication in English State-to-State (ACCESS for ELLs), procedures for exit are expected to be clarified in accordance with measured results on this annual assessment.

In New York State, if a student scores at or above the proficient level on the New York State English as a Second Language Achievement Test (NYSESLAT), the student is reclassified as non-LEP and exited from services to enter the general education program. Unlike the other states, New York does not specify a follow-up period, as deference is made to the follow-up procedure set by No Child Left Behind legislation, which is to monitor students for 1 year after exit from LEP services.

In Texas, students are exited from LEP services if the Language Proficiency Assessment Committee (LPAC) determines that the student meets the exit criteria. One exit criteria is a score at or above the 40th percentile on a norm-referenced standardized achievement test for reading and language arts in English, such as the Iowa Test of Basic Skills (ITBS). Students may also be exited if they meet the state performance standards on the reading and writing portions of the accountability examination, the Texas Assessment of Knowledge and Skills (TAKS) in English. Students who are classified as LEP in prekindergarten through first grade are not eligible for exit from services. If the student has been enrolled in a bilingual program, the student's native-language proficiency must be assessed for oral and written skills. Students exited from LEP programs must be monitored for 2 years by the LPAC to determine academic success in the general education curriculum.

In Florida, there are different sets of exit criteria for students in kindergarten through 3rd grade than for those in the 4th through 12th grades. Students in kindergarten through 3rd grade are considered for exit if they score above the LEP range on a state-approved aural/oral proficiency test. Once the student is determined to be a full or fluent English speaker, the LEP committee meets to determine whether the student is eligible for exit on the basis of comparable assessments, procedures, and standards used to qualify the student as LEP. Those criteria include at least two of the following: (a) student interview regarding prior educational and social experiences; (b) written recommendation and observation from current and previous educational staff; (c) level of mastery of basic competencies or skill in English according to local, state, and or national criterion-referenced standards; and (d) grades from current or past years. Other test results may be used; however, these tests must be district or state approved. Students in Grades 4 through 12, in addition to the above criteria, must score at or above the 33rd percentile in both reading and writing on any one of the state-approved assessments. Unlike the other states reviewed, Florida does not have one statewide assessment measure, but rather provides a list of state-approved tests that can be used for both language proficiency and to assess the content area skills. Students in Grades 4 through 12 are not required to take an aural/oral English language proficiency test if the other criteria are met to qualify for exit from LEP services.

In Florida, the academic performance of students who are exited from LEP programs must be monitored for 2 years through periodic reviews of academic performance. In the first year, the student is reviewed twice, and in the second year, the student is reviewed only at the end of the year. If any consistent decline in academic performance is noted, the LEP committee convenes with the parents to determine whether additional English instruction or other services are needed.

Conclusion

Exit policies set forth processes and guidelines that assist school personnel in reclassifying ELLs as general education students. The term *exit* is somewhat misleading since a student is considered to exit only in the sense that he or she moves from one program category to another. While much variation exists across different state contexts, each state's criteria for reclassification or exit from LEP services employ a transitional model that seeks to measure English language growth annually and to promote students' relatively rapid acquisition of English proficiency in schools. The focus on English language acquisition is consistent with the spirit and language of the No Child Left Behind Act and the U.S. Department of Education's Office of English Language Acquisition programs. With some exceptions, these policies are not designed to focus attention on the role native language plays in the acquisition of the English language or measuring and promoting content area skills students learn and demonstrate in another language. This variation in exit criteria reflects the state- and district-level contexts of policy creation and implementation, as well as an unresolved and historically situated tension between accommodationist versus assimilationist orientations toward the education of ELLS.

Barbara J. Dray and William Black

See also Affirmative Steps to English; Designation and Redesignation of English Language Learners

Further Readings

California Department of Education. (2004). *State Board of Education Code Section 313(d)—Reclassification Section 306 English learners.* Retrieved from http://www.cde.ca.gov/sp/el

Florida Department of Education. (2005). *State Board of Education Consent Decree—LULAC.* Office of Multicultural Student Language Education. Retrieved from http://www.firn.edu/doe/aala

Hamayan, E., & Freeman, R. (2006). *English language learners at school: A guide for administrators.* Philadelphia: Caslon.

Illinois State Board of Education. (n.d.). *Transitional bilingual education,* Title 23, Subtitle A, Chapter I, Subchapter F Part 228. Illinois Advisory Council on Bilingual Education. Retrieved from http://www.isbe.state.il.us/bilingual/htmls/iacbe.htm

New York State Bilingual and ESL Network. (n.d.). *Education Department Regulations,* CR Part 117 and CR Part 154. Retrieved from http://www.emsc.nysed.gov/biling/info.shtml

Texas Education Agency. (n.d.). *Commissioner's rules concerning state plan for educating limited English proficient students.* Chapter 89. Adaptations for Special Populations Subchapter BB. Retrieved from http://www.tea.state.tx.us/curriculum/biling

F

FEDERAL COURT DECISIONS AND LEGISLATION

The history of bilingual language policy in education in the United States can be examined through various lenses. This entry focuses on court decisions and selected legislation that have shaped the principle of educational opportunity for all students and specifically for English language learners (ELLs). These legal and legislative milestones include the 1896 Supreme Court case of *Plessy v. Ferguson,* which established the legality of "separate but equal" treatment; the Fourteenth Amendment of 1868, which provides for equal protection under the law; the 1923 *Meyer v. Nebraska* case, which overturned the state of Nebraska's prohibition against the teaching of foreign languages; the 1954 *Brown v. Board of Education* decision, which struck down the constitutionality of "separate but equal"; Title VI of the Civil Rights Act of 1964, which added a ban on discrimination based on language; the 1974 Supreme Court ruling on the landmark case of *Lau v. Nichols,* which requires a meaningful education for all students, regardless of language background; and the 1981 *Castañeda v. Pickard* federal decision that formulated a set of basic standards to determine school district compliance with the Equal Educational Opportunity Act (EEOA) of 1974. This review of litigation includes 15 of the most important federal court decision that have helped to formulate linguistically responsive language policies in public schools for ELLs.

Language Policy and Rights

Language policy plays a significant role in our school communities throughout the nation and directly affects social policy. Although language policy affects the spoken language, its ramifications are complex and extensive. Language policy is not a debate about grammar or syntax. It is about power, points of view, and ideology. Attitudes, values, and beliefs about language are a reflection of social issues such as nationalism and cultural identity. The role of language in a society is built into its structures to such a degree that it is a fundamental variable in that society. Thus, the system of language policy establishes a linguistic preference that underlies the organization of human society and its most important institutions.

Language policy in education is associated with legal cases that have established the thresholds for educational legal compliance. As such, the close relationship between language policy, power, and privilege are at the core of the struggle for equity. In the case of bilingual education in the United States, legal court cases serve to underscore the struggles for language rights by Americans who speak languages in addition to English.

The concept and practice of bilingual education has its roots deep in the history of the United States. Colin Baker suggests four distinct periods of tendencies in language policy: permissive (1700s–1880), restrictive (1880s–1960), opportunistic (1960s–1980), and dismissive (1980s–present). The four periods are important because they point to periods of conflict and tolerance toward the development of a second language and biliteracy. In the permissive period, tolerance or benign neglect existed toward the many languages represented in the new society, especially those of northern Europe. In the restrictive period, linguistic isolationist policies and repressive policies appeared toward Native American languages and embodied anti-German sentiments. A push for all immigrants to be assimilated into one cultural and linguistic mold was the prevailing policy. During the opportunistic period, support for equal access and equal benefits was the driving policy. The 1974 *Lau* decision legitimized services to students who did not speak English and raised the nation's consciousness of the need for bilingual education. Finally, during the dismissive period, a change in government brought a different focus for ELLs and the focus of equal educational access and benefits changed to reduce bilingual program development and research activity. The current focus has been to allow each state to define its approach toward services for ELLs.

Federal Court Cases Affecting Bilingual Education

With the passage of the Fourteenth Amendment of the Constitution in 1868, the constitutional basis for the educational rights of all students was established. This amendment guaranteed that no state can make or enforce any law abridging the privileges or immunities of citizens; nor deprive any person of life, liberty, or property without due process of law; nor deny equal protection of the laws. Between 1886 and 1896, the principle of equal educational opportunity was tested. Under *Plessy v. Ferguson,* the Supreme Court decision of 1896 established the legality of separate but equal. This policy gave impetus to segregation, discrimination, and separate educational services for African Americans and language minority communities.

By 1923, as Heinz Kloss documents, the legislatures of 34 states had dictated English-only instruction in all private and public primary schools. Schooling in any language other than English was forbidden and outlawed. Until *Lau,* the predominant approach to educating language minority students was the undifferentiated method, sometimes called *submersion* because of its sink-or-swim orientation. Although the restrictive period emphasized monolingual English instruction in public schools, the debate about the role of non-English mother-tongue instruction continued. In 1923, in the case of *Meyer v. Nebraska,* the Supreme Court declared Nebraska's prohibition against teaching

foreign languages in elementary schools to be unconstitutional on the basis of the Fourteenth Amendment due process clause. Although the Court accepted that the state may have justification in fostering unity among the populace by means of its education policies, it ruled that this particular attempt reached too far into the liberties of parents to teach what they want to their children. Although educational practices continued to be provided under segregated conditions, the impetus for equal educational opportunity continued. In 1946, *Méndez v. Westminster* helped pave the way for *Brown v. Board of Education* by challenging the institutional nature of segregation "for the cause of Americanization" as did as challenges by Latino parents on behalf of their children. In *Méndez,* the court declared unconstitutional the segregation of Mexican Americans in separate classrooms within "integrated" schools.

By 1954, the separate but equal doctrine established under *Plessy* was challenged in the Supreme Court case of *Brown v. Board of Education.* This case reversed the decision in *Plessy v. Ferguson* of 1896 that permitted separate but equal education for children of color in general. *Brown* declared the separation of African American and White students to be unconstitutional and ordered desegregation of schools. This decision established the principle of equal educational opportunity for all students. With the launching of the Soviet Union's Sputnik satellite into earth's orbit, scientific activity provoked federal policies that supported foreign languages, mathematics, and science, and created the National Defense Education Act in 1958. Although foreign-language instruction was encouraged for English monolinguals, no educational program supported children from non-English language backgrounds. As a result of the civil rights movement, Title VI of the Civil Rights Act of 1964, the creation of the Office for Civil Rights, and changes in immigration laws that terminated the 1924 national origin quota system, the right to equal educational access began to be actualized.

In Florida, subsequent to the Cuban Revolution of 1959, many middle- and upper-income exiled Cubans arrived in Florida and wanted their children to retain their language and culture, and in 1963, two-way bilingual education programs were launched in Dade County, Florida. The Immigration and Nationality Act of 1965 allowed large numbers of Asians and Latin Americans to enter the country, and the need for some type of bilingual instruction became paramount for many schools. To aid and monitor the education of ELLs through mother tongue and English education, the federal government enacted the Bilingual Education Act (Title VII of the Elementary and Secondary Education Act) in 1968. Although the Bilingual Education Act was ambiguous, it moved away from the sink-or-swim educational practices of the 1880s through the 1960s. Language minority students' ancestral languages and cultures were recognized in the curriculum of schools. Although controversial, bilingual education became a household term in the educational community as school districts began to receive federal funds with which to improve incipient programs. To meet federal compliance standards, school districts were obligated to address the needs of ELLs. The Bilingual Education Act began to challenge the English-only instruction laws that were still on the books in many states. As an outcome of the Bilingual Education Act and the Civil Rights Act of 1964, many elementary and some secondary bilingual and English as a Second Language (ESL) programs were implemented throughout the United States. These programs had the objective of addressing the academic, linguistic, and sociocultural needs of students from linguistically diverse backgrounds.

Also important was the Department of Health, Education, and Welfare (DHEW) Office for Civil Rights May 25, 1970, Memorandum, which outlined school districts' responsibility to provide equal educational opportunity to national origin minority group children considered deficient in English language skills. Four years later, enactment of the EEOA of 1974 codified the findings of the *Lau v. Nichols* decision and required specific action by schools and states to prevent the denial of equal educational opportunity. Among the practices ruled illegal by the EEOA was the failure by an educational agency to take appropriate action to overcome language barriers that impede equal participation by students in an instructional program.

Although it did not require bilingual education per se, the 1974 Supreme Court case of *Lau v. Nichols* gave great impetus to bilingual education across the country. The *Lau* decision was the result of a class action suit representing 1,800 Chinese students who alleged discrimination on the grounds that they could not achieve academically because they did not understand their English-speaking teachers. The U.S. Supreme Court concluded that equal treatment of English speaking and non-English-speaking students did not constitute equal educational opportunity and,

therefore, violated non-English-speaking students' civil rights. The *Lau* verdict put aside the sink-or-swim practices of the past. Although the *Lau* decision did not prescribe a specific curricular content or methodology, a broad range of programs with diverse philosophical underpinnings could satisfy the spirit of the law. The San Francisco Unified School District, the defendant in *Lau,* chose a bilingual education program to meet the mandate of the decision.

The *Lau* decision had an enormous affect on the development of bilingual education in the United States. That decision gave impetus to the movement for equal educational opportunity for students who did not speak English, raised the nation's consciousness of the need for bilingual education, and encouraged supportive legislation at the state level. The unanimous decision by the Court emphasizes that the Court in *Lau* was not concerned with the intentions or motivations of the school district. Regardless of how much good faith a school district might be exercising in trying to meet the problem, the only relevant factor is whether the child receives a "meaningful" and "comprehensible" education and "effective participation in the educational program." Thus, under the *Lau v. Nichols* decision, Supreme Court affirmed the authority of the executive branch of government to require affirmative remedial efforts to give special attention to linguistically diverse students.

From 1975 to the early 1980s, school districts developed educational master plans to comply with the *Lau* decision. In 1975, DHEW provided guidelines known as the *Lau* Remedies. To comply with these remedies, a *Lau* plan was required to meet the minimal requirements of the decision and of Title VI of the Civil Rights Act, the legislation under which the case was decided. A *Lau* plan was a working document that was revisited frequently. Essential components of a *Lau* plan include the legal foundation, student assessments, an instructional plan, parental involvement, qualified personnel, a coordination plan, a budget, support services, and other considerations unique to the district in question.

From 1974 to 1982, several court cases addressed the educational language rights of ELLs with respect to assessment, appropriate and well-implemented programs, staffing, and evaluation of program quality. In the 1974 case of *Serna v. Portales Municipal Schools,* the court ascertained that Spanish-surnamed individuals did not reach the same achievement levels as non-Spanish-surnamed peers. The court ordered Portales

Municipal Schools, in New Mexico, to implement a bilingual/bicultural curriculum, revise procedures for assessing achievement, and hire bilingual school personnel. This was the first court to specify bilingual education as a remedy since the *Lau* decision. The court stated that a student who does not understand English and is not provided with bilingual education is therefore precluded from any meaningful education. In 1975, the case of *Otero v. Mesa County Valley School District No. 51* involved a class action complaint on behalf of Mexican American parents and school-aged children residing in a Colorado rural town. The suit alleged that the school district's educational program and hiring practices discriminated against Chicanos. Plaintiffs requested that the court institute a comprehensive bilingual/bicultural curriculum and require affirmative action hirings. In *Otero,* the court entered judgment for the defendants on all counts; however, the Colorado legislature passed a broad bilingual/bicultural program. An important outcome of this lawsuit was notice to educators that schools have to consider the academic aspirations of Latino/Hispanic students.

Regarding program quality, in the 1978 case of *Ríos v. Read,* the federal district court for the eastern district of New York found that the Patchogue-Medford School District's transitional bilingual program was basically a course in English and that students were denied an equal educational opportunity by not receiving academic instruction in Spanish. The court further declared that a denial of educational opportunities to a child in the first years of schooling is not justified by demonstrating that the educational program employed will teach the child English sooner than will a program comprising more extensive Spanish instruction. In the 1978 *Cintrón v. Brentwood Union Free School District* case, the federal district court for the eastern district of New York rejected the Brentwood School District's proposed bilingual program on the grounds that it would violate *Lau* Remedies by unnecessarily segregating Spanish-speaking students from their English-speaking peers in music and art. The court also objected to the program's failure to provide for exiting students whose English language proficiency was sufficient for them to understand mainstream English instruction. This case set the standard for the courts in examining programs for ELLs. Basically, districts must have the following: a pedagogically sound plan for ELL students, sufficient qualified staff to implement the plan, and a system established to evaluate the program.

In contrast to *Cintrón* and *Ríos,* in 1978, the Ninth Circuit Court in *Guadalupe Organization, Inc. v. Tempe Elementary School District* found no right to bilingual/bicultural education. Using the EEOA to reach its decision in favor of the school system, the court found it inappropriate to rule on the adequacy of a bilingual program that was already being implemented by the school board. The court found that by providing a remedial English language program, the school system had met its requirement to provide "appropriate action" to overcome language barriers. Beyond ruling that bilingual/bicultural education was not required; the *Guadalupe* court provided no specific criteria for evaluating whether an educational agency has met its obligation under EEOA. However, in *Castañeda v. Pickard,* the Appeals Court for the Fifth Circuit was proactive and provided such criteria. In *Castañeda,* Mexican American children sued the Raymondville, Texas, school district, claiming that the district's failure to provide an adequate bilingual education program resulted in discrimination. The court delineated a three-pronged test to establish the program's appropriateness, namely, school districts must demonstrate (1) *theory:* a program is based on an educational theory recognized as sound or, at least, as a legitimate experimental strategy; (2) *practice:* the program is actually implemented with instructional practices, resources, and personnel necessary to transfer theory to reality; and (3) *results:* the program must not persist if it fails to produce results.

Subsequent court cases have consistently used the three-pronged test to determine compliance with EEOA. In another important court case in 1981, the federal court ordered the state of Texas to address the needs of ELLs. In *United States v. Texas,* the case requested the court for supplemental relief to require that the state of Texas monitor, enforce, and supervise programs for ELL students in the Texas public schools to ensure that those students receive appropriate educational programs and equal educational opportunities. The U.S. District Court for the eastern district of Texas, Tyler division, instructed the Texas Education Agency to phase in mandatory bilingual education in Grades K–12. This decision outlined specific requirements including 3-year monitoring cycles, identification of ELL students, and a language survey for students entering school, and it established the need for exit criteria. In a similar state context in 1981, the *Idaho Migrant Council v. Board of Education* case effectively mandated that state education agencies be required to supervise local districts to ensure compliance. The court ruled in favor of the Idaho Migrant Council, which was representing the ELLs from Idaho public schools. The Migrant Council argued that the Department of Education and State Board of Education failed to exercise their supervisory power over local school districts to ensure that appellants receive equal education. This case established the legal responsibility of the State Department of Education to monitor implementation of programs for ELL students.

As previously noted, the beginning of the 1980s marked the dismissive period of bilingual programs. With the change to a more conservative government led by President Ronald Reagan, school districts challenged the federal government to be more flexible. The federal government instituted the policies of deregulation and decentralization that led to the use of the *Castañeda v. Pickard* set of basic standards to determine school district compliance with EEOA. The "*Castañeda* test" has been used since 1981 as the predominant criteria for meeting federal language guidelines in determining if equal educational access is provided to ELLs. Today, the *Castañeda* test is used to monitor programs that are attempting to respond to the Civil Rights Act as well as to cases brought under the EEOA.

A court case that tested the *Castañeda* test was *Keyes v. School District No. 1, Denver, CO* in 1983. This case centered on desegregation and, as part of its remedy, supported the use of bilingual education. This option allowed students who were non-English speakers to receive instruction in academic areas in their native language until they could compete effectively in English. A U.S. district court found that a Denver public school district had failed to adequately implement a plan for language minority students—the second element of the *Castañeda* test. The finding in *Keyes* was important because it placed the burden of proof on the school districts, rather than on the students and their families.

Another court case testing the responsibility of a state to ELLs involved *Gómez v. Illinois State Board of Education*, in 1987. In this court case, the Seventh Circuit Court of Appeals ruled that state education agencies are also required, under the EEOA of 1974, to ensure that language minority student's educational needs are met. Under this federal court case, the court ruled that the State Education Agencies must also comply with the three-pronged test established in *Castañeda v. Pickard*.

Challenges Facing School Districts and School Communities

In the state with the greatest linguistic diversity, California voters approved Proposition 187 (1994), a ballot initiative designed to sharply curb illegal immigration through strong restrictions on social and educational services for undocumented persons. Moreover, in November 1996, Proposition 209 was passed, calling for the elimination of affirmative action programs. In June 1998, the passage of Proposition 227 by California voters established that English should be the primary medium of instruction for language minority students, and as a result, ELLs receive less help than before in their native languages. At the federal level, the push against better services to ELLs led to the restructure of bilingual education in 2001 under President George W. Bush's administration's program of "No Child Left Behind." In 1999, under President Bill Clinton, funding cutbacks for bilingual education were restored, but under Title IV of No Child Left Behind (NCLB), the focus of the program under the Bush administration became English language development.

During this period, we have seen increasing resentment toward massive immigration from developing countries, particularly from Asia and Latin America, and highly visible and active anti-immigrant initiatives that call for no support to anything that resembles bilingual instruction. The overview of salient federal court cases affecting bilingual education points to basic orientations toward language and its function in society. Richard Ruiz suggests three orientations: language-as-problem, language-as-right, and language-as-resource. All three orientations link language with politics, economics, society, culture, and opportunity. In the language-as-a-problem domain, maintaining or promoting other languages creates problems of non-assimilation, lack of national cohesiveness, regional disunity, and potential for intergroup conflict. Another perspective of this premise is that the speakers of the nonmajority language belong to an underclass in society, and their low socioeconomic status and underachievement because they do not speak the politically accepted language. In the language-as-right paradigm, an individual or group's language is viewed as a basic human right, on an equal par with freedom of religion, or freedom of movement. The language-as-resource orientation is a pragmatic view of language. Given the need for communication between and among diverse linguistic groups and cultures, it seems that developing and maintaining languages is in everyone's best interests. Certainly the potential for commerce and trade, in both real terms and in ideas and concepts, would be enhanced if languages were treated as resources. In this paradigm, language diversity does not promote national disintegration, and language diversity and unity are not considered mutually exclusive.

Alberto M. Ochoa

See also *Castañeda* Three-Part Test; Civil Rights Act of 1964; Equal Educational Opportunity Act of 1974; *Lau v. Nichols*, Enforcement Documents; *Méndez v. Westminster;* Views of Language Difference

Further Readings

Baker, C. (2006). *Foundations of bilingual education and bilingualism* (4th ed). Clevedon, UK: Multilingual Matters.

Bilingual Education Act, Pub. L. No. 90–247, 81 Stat. 816 (1968).

Brisk, M. E. (2006). *Bilingual education: From compensatory to quality schooling* (2nd ed.). Mahwah, NJ: Lawrence Erlbaum.

Brown v. Board of Education, 347 U.S. 483 (1954).

Castañeda v. Pickard, 648 F.2d 989 (5th Cir. 1981).

Cintrón v. Brentwood Union Free School District, 455 F. Supp. 57 (EDNY 1978).

Civil Rights Act of 1964, 42 U.S.C. Sec. 200d (1964).

Crawford, J. W. (1999). *Bilingual education: History, politics, theory and practice* (4th ed.) Trenton, NJ: Crane.

Department of Health, Education, and Welfare (DHEW) May 25, 1970 Memorandum, 35 Fed. Reg. 11595.

Equal Educational Opportunity Act of 1974, 20 U.S.C. § 1703.

Gómez v. Illinois State Board of Education, 811 F.2d 1030 (7th Cir. 1987).

Guadalupe Organization, Inc. v. Tempe Elementary School District, 578 F.2d 1022, 1027 (9th Cir. 1978).

Idaho Migrant Council v. Board of Education, 647 F.2d. 69 (9th Cir. 1981).

Immigration and Nationality Act of 1965, Pub. L. No. 89-236, 79 Stat. 911 (1965)

Keyes v. School District No. 1, Denver, CO, 576 F. Supp. 503 (D. Colorado, 1983).

Kloss, H. (1966). German American language maintenance efforts. In J. Fishman (Ed.), *Language loyalty in the United States: The maintenance and perpetuation of non-English tongues by American ethnic and religious groups* (pp. 206–252). The Hague, Netherlands: Mouton.

Lau v. Nichols, 414 U.S. 563 (1974).

Méndez v. Westminster, 64 F. Supp. 544 (S.D. Cal. 1946).

Meyer v. Nebraska, 262 U.S. 390 (1923).

National Defense Education Act of 1958, Pub. L. 85–864, Sept. 2, 1958, 72 Stat. 1580 (20 U.S.C. 401 et seq.)

No Child Left Behind Act of 2001, Pub. L. No. 107–110 (2002).

Otero v. Mesa County Valley School District No. 51, 408 F. Supp. 162 (1975).

Plessy v. Ferguson, 163 U.S. 537 (1896).

Ríos v. Read, 480 F. Supp. (1978).

Ruiz, R. (1984). Orientations in language planning. *NABE Journal, 8*(2), 15–34.

San Miguel, G., Jr. (2004). *Contested policy: The rise and fall of federal bilingual education in the United States 1960–2001*. Denton: University of North Texas Press.

Serna v. Portales Municipal Schools, 499 F.2d. 1147, 1154 (10th Cir. 1974).

Title VI of the Civil Rights Act of 1964, 42 U.S.C. 2000(d).

Tollefson, J. W. (1991). *Planning language, planning inequality: Language policy in the community*. New York: Longman.

United States v. State of Texas, 506 F. Supp. 405 (E.D. Tex. 1981).

FERNÁNDEZ, RICARDO (1940–)

Ricardo R. Fernández is president of Lehman College, a 4-year public liberal arts college located in the Bronx. Lehman is part of the City University of New York, the nation's largest urban university. Before assuming this position (on September 1, 1990), he was affiliated with the University of Wisconsin–Milwaukee from 1970 to 1990, where he served as assistant vice chancellor for academic affairs (1988–90) and professor of educational policy and community studies.

Born and raised in Puerto Rico, Fernández received a bachelor's degree in philosophy and a master's degree in Spanish literature from Marquette University, as well as an MA and PhD in romance languages and literatures from Princeton University. He also attended the Harvard Institute for Educational Management in 1992, and was an American Council on Education Fellow in Academic Administration in 1981 to 1982 and a senior fellow of the U.S.–Mexico Solidarity Foundation in 1996. This entry describes Fernández's career and contributions to education.

Fernández began his career at Marquette University in 1968 as an instructor and became an assistant professor of Spanish in 1970. In his first administrative appointment at the University of Wisconsin, Fernández was director of its Spanish Speaking Outreach Institute from 1970 to 1971. He later directed the Midwest

National Origin Desegregation Assistance Center from 1977 to 1987, which was responsible for helping districts in 10 midwestern states to implement education plans to serve English language learners. From 1976 to 1977, he was coordinator of the Governor's Council on Hispanic Affairs (on partial leave from UW–Milwaukee) in the Wisconsin Department of Industry, Labor and Human Relations. From 1986 to 1987, he was a research fellow at the National Center for Effective Secondary Schools at the University of Wisconsin–Madison, where he worked on a book about at-risk students.

During more than three and a half decades in education, Fernández has focused on ways to improve educational outcomes, especially the preparation and encouragement of minority students to graduate from high school and to enter and succeed in college. His books, articles, and research reports deal with the causes of Hispanic school dropout, the desegregation of Hispanic students in the nation's public schools, and bilingual education policy. At Lehman, he has fostered extensive collaboration between the college and local schools in such areas as technology, the arts, professional development, and curriculum development and enrichment. Building on community resources, the college developed a multilingual journalism department that publishes a newspaper in several languages, which is available to the college community and to schools in the area. During his tenure, the college has steadily increased the level of its grant-funded research and the variety and reach of its programs, while becoming a major resource for the borough's economic, cultural, and educational development.

Fernández has been recognized nationally for his leadership. He is past president of the National Association for Bilingual Education, and past chair of the Board of the American Association of Higher Education, the Governing Board of the Hispanic Association of Colleges and Universities (HACU), and the Hispanic Educational Telecommunication System (HETS), an international distance education consortium of colleges and universities. In 2006, he was elected vice chair of the board of directors of the American Council on Education (ACE). In 2006, he joined the boards of directors of the Intercultural Development Research Association in Texas and the Multicultural Education Training and Advocacy (META), which has offices in California and Massachusetts. Other positions include serving on the New York State Commissioner of Education's Advisory Council on Higher Education, the New York–based National Hispanic Business Group's Advisory Board, and the Frito-Lay (North America) Latino/Hispanic Advisory Board. In addition, Fernández has given expert testimony in support of the Minority–Serving Institution Digital and Wireless Network Technology Opportunity Act of 2003 in Washington DC.

Fernández has received extensive recognition for his contributions to education. He received the Comité Noviembre Educational Excellence Award and the National Society of Hispanic MBAs Award in 2002, the P. Gus Cárdenas Award from the Hispanic Association of Colleges and Universities in 2000, the Promesa Community Service Award in 1992, the Interfaith Brotherhood Award of the Riverdale Jewish Community Council in 1991, the National Puerto Rican Coalition's Lifetime Achievement Award in Education in 1990, and the University of Wisconsin–Milwaukee's Faculty Distinguished Service Award in 1984. In 2004, he was selected by Crain's *New York Business* as one of New York City's Top 100 Minority Business Leaders.

Fernández and his wife, Patricia, an attorney, have five children and three grandchildren.

Marietta Saravia-Shore

See also Multicultural Education, Training, and Advocacy (META); National Association for Bilingual Education

Further Readings

H.R. 2183: The Minority-Serving Institution Digital and Wireless Network Technology Opportunity Act of 2003: *Hearings before the House Subcommittee on Research, Committee on Science, House of Representatives*, 108th Cong., 105 (2003). Retrieved February 11, 2008, from http://frwebgate.access.gpo.gov/cgi-bin/getdoc.cgi?dbname=108_house_hearings&docid=f:88165.wais

President Fernández named one of "The 100 most influential Hispanics." (2007, October 9). *Lehman E-News*. Retrieved February 11, 2008, from http://www.lehman.edu/lehman/enews/2007_10_09/feat_fernandez.html

First-Language Acquisition

Considering that language is the primary vehicle through which thoughts are expressed and cultural identity is developed and transmitted, the ability to use language is one of the most essential qualities of human beings. Although it has been proven that other (nonhuman) animals also use a set of language-like communicative skills, as explained by linguist Steve Pinker, the generative nature of human speech is truly unique. To fully appreciate the profound intricacy of language use, the process through which humans acquire the set of skills necessary to communicate must be understood. How, and when, do humans develop the ability to distinguish between words like *play* and *pay?* What prompts children to consistently produce utterances with correct word orders (e.g., subject-verb-object versus verb-subject-object)? At what point do people learn that such phrases as *It's hot in here* can either be a statement or an indirect request (e.g., to open a window)? How is meaning assigned to different tenses (*eat, ate*) and aspects (*is eating, has eaten*)? These examples typify the breadth of language use, and they emphasize the complex nature of how humans acquire such abilities.

The acquisition of language is a combination of biological, environmental, and cognitive influences. The ideas presented here concern the processes involved in acquiring language as a concept rather than any one specific language. To best understand the process of acquisition, language must be viewed from multiple vantage points. The sounds (phonology), grammar (syntax), meaning (semantics), vocabulary (lexicon), and social norms (pragmatics) of language are all intertwined and play equally important roles in the development of a child's capacity to effectively communicate.

Because of the important role that language plays in social construction and cultural maintenance, the process of language acquisition has received much attention from cognitive scientists and linguists, among others. Historically, language acquisition has been one of the most theoretically contested and mysterious biological processes of human beings. Such a complex topic has produced various subfields of interest. Researchers are interested in neurological, semantic, cultural, phonological, pragmatic, and syntactic issues that surround the process of language acquisition. The aim of this entry is to provide an overview of the different topics surrounding first-language (L1) acquisition and examine important ideas connected with this process, but many of the factors outlined here can be extended to the area of second-language (L2) acquisition.

Stages of Acquisition

First, *all* languages are equally complex, and any human being capable of acquiring language can acquire any particular language. As human beings, we are not biologically predisposed to learn any one specific language more easily than another. Though specific features might differ in complexity across languages, children find all languages equally simple to acquire. Furthermore, the following stages of development should be understood as applicable to language in general, taking into consideration that there might be variability between equivalent features of different languages.

Babies are exposed to language even before they are born. Invariably, babies' comprehension of language develops much faster than does their production of it. Actually, the asymmetry between comprehension and production spans adulthood; think of how many dialects a person can understand but cannot easily produce. While learning to decipher the meaning of the language being used around them, babies are concurrently developing the capacity for developing sound systems, vocabulary, and a grammar program.

Around their first birthday, babies usually begin to produce their own words. However, studies conducted by Vivian Cook and Eve Clark show that infants as young as 4 days old can distinguish between different phonemes when spoken to. By monitoring the rate at which a baby sucks on a pacifier, researchers were able to determine that infants detect the difference between words like *par* and *bar* in English and different click sounds in Zulu. Although some sounds tend to develop later than others (e.g., the English "r" and "th" sounds), most children flawlessly acquire the entire phonological inventory of the given language generally by the age of 5.

At about 6 months of age, children begin babbling by repeating a series of identical syllables (e.g., ba-ba-ba), as reported by Edward Finegan. As their vocal apparatus matures in the following months, they begin to expand their babbling to include more complex syllables (e.g., bab-bab-bab). Around the 1-year mark, children begin their single-word (holophrastic) stage. They typically start by producing words for familiar objects (e.g., food, household items, and people) and simple actions (e.g., open, eat, and go). Moreover, simple words like *dada* are used to express a range of thoughts and communicative ends (e.g., There's Daddy! This is Daddy's shirt. Where is Daddy? Come here, Daddy!). Pinker explains that the holophrastic stage can last from 2 months to 1 year. At 18 months, children usually begin to produce two-word sentence structures. These sentences usually comprise two types of words: pivot class words and open class words, as reported by Nancy Parrot Hickerson. Pivot class words are fewer in number and are added more slowly. These are words like *more, see, all-gone,* and *other.* Open class words are quickly acquired and consist of things like family member names, toys, food items, and so on. The two-word productions often are a combination of one word from each class (e.g., more cookie, see doggie). Pinker mentions that children will begin to learn words at a rate of 1 every 2 waking hours (a pattern that typically continues until adolescence).

Even though the two-word stage might seem simplistic, children are displaying definite patterns of grammatical word order. Cook mentions that although their production might not appear complex, the two- and three-word productions reflect the prominent syntactic characteristics of the language. When asked simple questions using subject-verb-object structures, young children can differentiate between different subject-object combinations. In one example, Pinker describes a situation where babies that were still in their one-word stage were able to identify the difference between *Big Bird is tickling Cookie Monster* and *Cookie Monster is tickling Big Bird.*

By the time children are able to produce three-word phrases, definite word order is apparent (e.g., subject-verb-object, verb-subject-object). Usually by the age of three, children are able to have full conversations. At this time, the children are involved in multiple conversations where they are exposed to, and attempt to, produce more complex structures (e.g., embedded clauses and Wh-movement). Children also begin to acquire more detailed inflections and complex grammatical structures (e.g., third person auxiliaries, irregular past-tense forms). Though there may be slight variations from child to child, morphemes and grammatical structures are generally acquired in a set order. Psychologist Roger Brown found that English-speaking children tend to acquire grammatical morphemes in the following order, as cited by Finegan:

1. Present progressive verb (with or without the auxiliary): *(is) playing, (was) singing;*

2–3. Prepositions *in* and *on;*

4. Regular noun plural: *toys, cats, dishes;*

5. Irregular past-tense verbs: *came, fell, saw, hurt;*

6. Possessive noun: *Daddy's, doggie's;*

7. Uncontractible copula: *Here I am, Who is it?;*

8. Articles: *a* and *the;*

9. Regular past-tense verbs: *played, washed, wanted;*

10. Regular third-person singular present-tense verbs: *sees, wants, washes;*

11. Irregular third-person singular present-tense verbs: *does, has;*

12. Uncontractible auxiliary: *She isn't crying, He was eating;*

13. Contractible copula: *That's mine, What's that?;*

14. Contractible auxiliary: *He's crying.*

The pattern of acquiring these types of structures differs across languages. For example, a child learning English might quickly acquire the "s" ending for plural nouns. Other languages might have multiple plural markers depending on the gender of the noun (e.g., masculine, feminine, or neuter), the shape of the object (e.g., flat, round, long), or the relative quantity of the noun being described (e.g., 2 versus 10 versus 100). In such cases, acquiring the ability to accurately mark plurality would be much more complex than in English, and therefore take longer to master.

Considering the development of a child's lexicon, it has been found that children form conceptual categories, as noted by George Lakoff and Clark. Whereas a baby might quickly acquire the word *dog* (or *doggie*), it takes a while before the child can produce words for different types of dogs (e.g., a poodle versus a greyhound). Furthermore, the term *dog* might initially be used to describe all animals. Also, the terms for dog traits are easily used to describe traits of other animals (e.g., using *paws* to describe a duck's feet). Through embodied experiences, children expand their conceptual categories and develop more distinct ways of describing their world, as Lakoff points out. This concept of embodiment is inextricably related to the context of language acquisition.

Context of Language Acquisition

The goal of language acquisition is to become a member of a specific community of speakers. That children learn words and word associations leads to the question of how they form categories and associations between entities. The ways in which a child learns to use a language depends on the community in which he or she is raised. Speech communities share specific linguistic characteristics (syntactic, phonological, semantic, and pragmatic) that are derived from their shared experiences and traditions. Sociolinguist Dell Hymes describes an individual's ability to communicate fluently within a specific sociocultural context as *communicative competence*. Hymes's description of competence encompasses an individual's knowledge of whether something is formally possible within a distinct cultural environment. Communicative competence also entails being able to distinguish whether something is appropriate in relation to a context in which it is used and evaluated.

A combination of cognitive linguistics and sociocultural approaches is necessary to understand the breadth of linguistic grounding and cognitive perception in a first-language acquisition context. This view is echoed in the *use-based* theory of language acquisition, explained further by Michael Tomasello and Clark. According to this view of language, children acquire language by being contextually involved within a speech community. Children create novel utterances and then proceed to modify their speech according to feedback and further observation. As interesting as the use-based theory sounds, other studies have shown that some children are not spoken to, only about, and they still develop fully competent linguistic skills, as found in research by Shirley Brice Heath. Aside from syntactic acquisition, the context of acquisition does determine issues of socialization and enculturation into a speech community.

Noam Chomsky and Universal Grammar

Although *functionalist* views emphasize the importance of pragmatics and semantics in the process of language acquisition, Noam Chomsky's formalist approach posits an underlying cognitive structure that is used in the process of language development. Chomsky believes that the uniformity and efficiency of language acquisition can be attributed to a biologically endowed innate language faculty in the brain that provides children with a set of genetically transmitted formulae for developing the grammar via the exposure to language, as explained by William Ritchie and Tej Bhatia. Chomsky's view holds that our biologically endowed language faculty, also called the language acquisition device (LAD), filters outside linguistic stimuli and detects syntactic patterns

that apply to specific languages. Through ample exposure to native speech, individuals develop a template for producing generative syntactic structures.

The processes involved in first-language acquisition are specifically defined by Chomsky's theory of universal grammar (UG). Chomsky's notion of UG states that certain universal *principles* govern human language. In this theory, all speakers possess an innate mental faculty that consists of syntactic, phonological, and morphological principles that are common to all languages. Every language is derived from the same original set of principles. A specific example of a UG principle is the *structure dependence principle,* which specifies that all grammatical operations are sensitive to the grammatical structure of the sentences to which they apply. Furthermore, these types of principles help a child lay the groundwork for the more detailed nuances of the specific language that they are acquiring. The language-specific characteristics are referred to as *parameters*. All structural learning will be limited to the parameters of the given language. For example, the *pro-drop* parameter tells speakers of Spanish that they may omit the subject in most situations. Simply through their exposure to language, children are able to grasp the UG principles and parameters of their language and quickly begin to produce their own speech.

It has been suggested that the existence of a *poverty of stimulus* in a child's input supports Chomsky's theory of UG. Poverty of stimulus means that spontaneous speech is full of mistakes, repairs, and pauses. This would prove that children's language is not a result of behavioral reinforcement and repetition. Instead, the language acquisition device is processing the information as a uniform structured pattern to set the parameters of the language. Other researchers such as Pinker have stated that caretaker-baby speech (sometimes referred to as *motherese*) is actually methodical and clear in comparison with adult-adult discourse. Although Chomsky's views have made a significant impact on our understanding of language acquisition, they have been contested and extended by such scholars as Ritchie and Bhatia.

The Biology of Language Acquisition

Although there is a lot of discrepancy regarding an exact description of a definable period of language acquisition, many researchers, such as David Birdsong, posit that children *acquire* a language easier than adults do, especially in the area of phonology. Whether this is because of a reduced metabolic rate or the loss of synaptic processes, it has been claimed the onset of puberty produces certain biological changes in the way people can acquire language; this window of linguistic opportunity is referred to as the *critical period*. The sensitive period of language acquisition is highly contested, and ample research argues against it, such as work conducted by Barry McLaughlin, Ellen Bialystok, and Christo Moskovsky.

The atrophy of language-acquisition abilities is widely considered as biologically rooted. During the critical period, neurons have the ability to make more connections than they do later in an individual's life. More specifically, the ability of cortical neurons in the relative cognitive area to form new connections is based on peripheral or outside stimuli versus predetermined genetic connections. The plasticity of the brain during the first 4 years of life apparently allows children to acquire language effortlessly. By the time a child is born, all of her or his neurons have already been formed. The cerebral cortex, where the synapses occur, continues to increase rapidly during the first year. Synapses continue to develop usually until the child has reached 2 years old, at which point, there are 50% more than in an adult brain. Pinker argues that language acquisition demands a high number of synapses, myelinization of brain cells, and a certain elevated level of metabolic activity in the brain. Therefore, the age of immersion or exposure to a given language has been posited as the best predictive variable for the person's ultimate linguistic proficiency, as stated by Birdsong.

Advocates of the critical period hypothesis claim that, once a child reaches puberty, the level of fluency that can be attained in either first- or second-language acquisition is limited. The closure of this critical period results in a loss of access to the innate mental faculty (or latent language structure) for language acquisition that allows children to organize language input into syntactic structures. Variations in language acquisition that are associated with the critical period of language acquisition (i.e., changes in the brain) are also attributed, however, to the accumulation of cultural experiences. Tomasello contends that the mental organization of new cultural knowledge structures and language patterns fossilize over time. Once a concept has been embedded cognitively, acquiring another language system to express the same concept

becomes more difficult than was the case with the first language.

Usually, the critical period hypothesis is used to explain the lack of ability to acquire language in two main areas: syntax and phonology. Though this is especially applicable to the study of second-language acquisition, some studies have looked at individuals who started their first-language acquisition process after puberty. The most famous case is that of Genie, who from the age of 1 year and 8 months to 13 years and 7 months was locked in a closet and deprived of any communication. After Genie was rescued, her linguistic acclimation was closely studied, as reported by Susan Curtiss. Even after years of training and exposure to language, Genie was unable to produce syntactically fluent speech. She failed to acquire three aspects of language: pronominal forms, movement rules, and the English auxiliary system. As interesting (and tragic) a case as Genie's situation has proven to be, it is not a good model to exemplify the late onset of a first-language acquisition. Because of the extreme psychological abuse suffered during the first 13 years of her life, it is not possible to tell whether her language deficiencies are solely the result of biolinguistic processes.

The main argument against the sensitive period of acquisition may not focus directly on the fact that children achieve native-like levels of language fluency more often than adult learners do but, rather, that it is *not* completely impossible for adults to achieve native-like levels of fluency—especially in cases of second-language acquisition, as scholars such as Bialystok argue. Another intriguing argument against the critical period hypothesis concerns phonological production and acquisition. James Flege and Theo Bongaerts conclude that, with proper training and exposure to the target language, adults can achieve near-native levels in pronunciation if properly trained. Advocates of this stance admit that children acquire phonological traits of a language flawlessly, but they maintain that puberty is not an absolute barrier for acquiring a native accent.

The concept that humans have only a certain window of opportunity to acquire a language is hard to ignore, yet it is even more difficult to prove. The idea of depriving individuals of linguistic interaction to better understand such a theory is unthinkable. Therefore, most of the research done on the critical period is based on second-language acquisition. Whereas all humans are innately endowed with a language faculty to flawlessly acquire a first language, attaining a high level of second-language competency depends on numerous other factors.

Eric Johnson

See also Baby Talk; Critical Period Hypothesis; Language Acquisition Device; Language and Thought; Language Defined; Language Learning in Children and Adults; Linguistics, an Overview; Second-Language Acquisition

Further Readings

Bialystok, E. (1997). The structure of age: In search of barriers to second language acquisition. *Second Language Research, 13*(2), 116–137.

Birdsong, D. (1999). *Second language acquisition and the critical period hypothesis.* Mahwah, NJ: Lawrence Erlbaum.

Bongaerts, T. (1999). Ultimate attainment in L2 pronunciation: The case of advanced late L2 learners. In D. Birdsong (Ed.), *Second language acquisition and the critical period hypothesis* (pp. 133–159). Mahwah, NJ: Lawrence Erlbaum.

Chomsky, N. (1965). *Aspects of the theory of syntax.* Cambridge: MIT Press.

Chomsky, N. (1986). *Knowledge of language: Its nature, origins, and use.* New York: Praeger.

Clark, E. (2003). *First language acquisition.* Cambridge, UK: Cambridge University Press.

Cook, V. (1997). *Inside language.* New York: Arnold.

Curtiss, S. (1977). *Genie: A psycholinguistic study of a modern-day "wild-child."* New York: Academic Press.

Finegan, E. (1999). *Language: Its structure and use* (3rd ed). Orlando, FL: Harcourt Brace Jovanovich.

Flege, J. E. (1999). Age of learning and second language speech. In D. Birdsong (Ed.), *Second language acquisition and the critical period hypothesis* (pp. 101–132). Mahwah, NJ: Lawrence Erlbaum.

Heath, S. B. (1996). What no bedtime story means: Narrative skills at home and school. In D. M. Brenneis, Ronald K. S. (Eds.), *The matrix of language: Contemporary linguistic anthropology* (pp. 12–38). Boulder, CO: Westview Press.

Hymes, D. (1977). *Foundations in sociolinguistics: An ethnographic approach.* London: Tavistock.

Lakoff, G. (1987). *Women, fire, and dangerous things.* Chicago: University of Chicago.

McLaughlin, B. (1992). *Myths and misconceptions about second language learning: What every teacher needs to know.* Santa Cruz, CA: National Center for Research on Cultural Diversity and Second Language Learning.

Moskovsky, C. (2001). *The critical period hypothesis revisited.* Proceedings of the Conference of the Australian Linguistic Society. Available from http://au.geocities.com/austlingsoc/proceedings/als2001/moskovsky.pdf

Parrot Hickerson, N. (2000). *Linguistic anthropology.* New York: Harcourt College.

Pinker, S. (1995). Language acquisition. In L. R. Gleitman, M. Liberman, & D. N. Osherson (Eds.), *An invitation to cognitive science* (Vol. 1., pp. 135–182). Cambridge: MIT Press.

Ritchie, W. C., & Bhatia, T. K. (Eds.). (1999). *Handbook of child language acquisition.* San Diego, CA: Academic Press.

Tomasello, M. (2000). First steps toward a usage-based theory of language acquisition. *Cognitive Linguistics, 11,* 61–82.

FISHMAN, JOSHUA A. (1926–)

Joshua A. Fishman's contributions to the field of bilingual education span more than half a century. His own personal and scholarly experience with bilingual education might have spurred Fishman's intellectual creativity as the founder of what has become the field of sociology of language, or Fishmanian sociolinguistics. A review of his roles in bilingual education marks him clearly as a visionary linguist: a supporter of bilingual education as enrichment for one and all, an advocate for the Bilingual Education Act, a critic of Title VII ideology, and a scholar interested in the role that bilingual education plays throughout the world in supporting minority languages and communities. This entry describes some of Fishman's contributions to bilingual education

Born and raised in Philadelphia, Joshua A. Fishman attended the Yiddish Workmen's Circle Schools, supplementary Yiddish schools that had a linguistic and secular function. These schools armed him with a commitment to the development of minority languages, especially Yiddish, and a pro-proletariat activism. He went on to teach in elementary and secondary Jewish secular schools while pursuing his doctorate in social psychology and education at Columbia University. It is not surprising, therefore, that his first book in English was titled *Bilingualism in a Yiddish School: Some Correlates and Non-Correlates.*

Fishman's first major book, *Language Loyalty in the United States: The Maintenance and Perpetuation of non-English Mother Tongues by American Ethnic and Religious Groups* (published in 1966), includes a chapter on what he calls ethnic-mother-tongue schools; these are bilingual education day and supplementary schools run by ethnolinguistic communities—groups of a particular ethnicity, usually regarded also as linguistic minorities. The influence of his work on the passage of the Bilingual Education Act in 1968 was paramount. He testified in the hearings, and his work was frequently cited. Fishman proposed the word *transitional* to substitute for *compensatory,* a term that has since been adopted by policymakers and scholars alike. After the passage of the Bilingual Education Act in 1968, Fishman devoted a great deal of personal and scholarly attention to the topic. In the early 1970s, he and his wife, Gella Schweid Fishman, served as consultants for a Title VII Bilingual Education Curriculum Center at the New York City Board of Education. Between 1970 and 1985, he published 15 important articles on bilingual education as well as three significant books—*Bilingual Education: An International Sociological Perspective* (1976); *Bilingual Education: Current Perspectives, Volume 1: Social Science* (1977); and *Bilingual Education for Hispanic Students in the United States.*

In his 1976 book, Fishman proposed four of the principles of bilingual education that summarize his ideology on the topic:

1. Bilingual education is good for the majority group.

2. Bilingual education is good for the minority group.

3. Bilingual education is good for education.

4. Bilingual education is good for language learning and language teaching.

His insistence that "poor little rich kids" need bilingual education most leads him to promote enrichment bilingual education for all, proposing what we know today as two-way dual-language education. Fishman warned of its limitations by asserting the following:

If both types of children can ultimately wind up in the same classroom . . . , an optimal *modus vivendi* will have been attained. . . . However, if an enrichment language policy is limited or restricted to the schools alone, it will fail as surely as either transitional or maintenance policies when similarly restricted. (1989, p. 414)

Fishman believes that bilingual education is good for several reasons: It provides for multiple memberships and for multiple loyalties in an integrative fashion. It equalizes the children of marked- and unmarked-language backgrounds. Bilingual education can also afford economic possibilities to bilinguals. He has predicted the growth of bilingual education in the future, as local languages are given increased educational recognition, and world languages, especially English, are gaining wider currency.

Although Fishman was a strong supporter of enacting the Bilingual Education Act, he soon became a critic, calling it an act "for the Anglification of non-English speakers and not an act for Bilingualism" (1989, p. 405). He conceptualizes transitional bilingual education as a vaccine with a "little bit of deadened mother tongue, introduced in slow stages in the classroom environment" (1976, p. 34) to cure children who do not speak English of their disease.

Fishman is responsible for the most popular typology of bilingual education in the United States, that of programs being transitional, maintenance, or enrichment. In 1970, with John Lovas, Fishman further proposed four types of bilingual education, thinking about all the bilingual situations in the world:

Type I. Transitional Bilingual Education: The child's home language is used in the early grades.

Type II. Monoliterate Bilingual Education: Literacy skills are developed only in the dominant language.

Type III. Partial Bilingual Education: A form of partial bilingualism, where both languages are used for different subject matter.

Type IV. Biliterate Bilingual Education: Full bilingualism, with both languages used for all subjects, and literacy skills developed in both as well.

Fishman and Lovas point out that although full biliterate-bilingual programs seem to be desirable, they may not be grounded in societal reality, where it is difficult to continue to use two languages if they are functionally redundant. Thus, they suggest that a partial biliterate bilingual program may be sufficient.

In recent years, Fishman's attention has turned to reversing the language shift of threatened languages and the potential of bilingual schools in that enterprise (see, for example, his books *Reversing Language Shift: Theoretical and Empirical Foundations of Assistance to Threatened Languages* and *Can Threatened Languages Be Saved?*). Blending his interest in bilingual education and particularly the ethnic-mother-tongue schools, Fishman has coauthored with Guadalupe Valdés the book *Developing Minority Language Resources: Spanish for Native Speakers in California.*

Fishman's contributions to the development of bilingual education theoretical perspectives, practices, and research throughout the world have been unparalleled. His monumental work of more than 1,000 items has supported the efforts of many ethnolinguistic minority groups, large and small, in different parts of the world, in the development of bilingual schools.

Ofelia García

See also Bilingual Education as Language Policy; Bilingualism Stages; Dual-Language Programs; Language Revival and Renewal; Language Shift and Language Loss; Social Bilingualism; Title VII, Elementary and Secondary Education Act, Key Historical Marker; Transitional Bilingual Educational Programs

Further Readings

Fishman, J. A. (1949). *Bilingualism in a Yiddish school: Some correlates and non-correlates.* Unpublished manuscript. Yiddish Scientific Institute.

Fishman, J. A. (1976). *Bilingual education: An international sociological perspective.* Rowley, MA: Newbury House.

Fishman, J. A. (1977). The social science perspective. In *Bilingual education: Current perspectives* (Vol. 1, pp. 1–49). Arlington, VA: Center for Applied Linguistics.

Fishman, J. A. (1989). *Language and ethnicity in minority sociolinguistic perspective.* Clevedon, UK: Multilingual Matters.

Fishman, J. A. (1991). *Reversing language shift: Theoretical and empirical foundations of assistance to threatened languages.* Clevedon, UK: Multilingual Matters.

Fishman, J. A. (2001). *Can threatened languages be saved? Reversing language shift, revisited, a 21st century perspective.* Clevedon, UK: Multilingual Matters.

Fishman, J. A., & Keller, G. D. (Eds.). (1982). *Bilingual education for Hispanic students in the United States.* New York: Teachers College Press.

Fishman, J. A., & Lovas, J. (1970). Bilingual education in sociolinguistic perspective. *TESOL Quarterly, 4,* 215–222.

Fishman, J. A., Warshauer, V. E., Hofman, J. E., & Hayden, R. G. (1966). *Language loyalty in the United States: The maintenance and perpetuation of non-English mother tongues by American ethnic and religious groups.* The Hague: Mouton.

García, O., Peltz, R., & Schiffman, H. (2006). *Language loyalty, continuity and change: Joshua A. Fishman's contributions to international sociolinguistics.* Clevedon, UK: Multilingual Matters.

Valdés, G., Fishman, J. A., Chávez, R., & Pérez, W. (2006). *Developing minority language resources: Spanish for native speakers in California.* Clevedon, UK: Multilingual Matters.

FLORES V. STATE OF ARIZONA

In Arizona, approximately 15% of students attending public school are English language learners (ELLs), according to the Office of English Language Acquisition. Beginning in 2006, all high school students must pass an achievement test to graduate from high school. In spring 2004, more than 80% of ELLs in high school were still failing the Arizona Instrument to Measure Standards (AIMS) test compared with 26% of the entire high school population, as reported by the Arizona Department of Education.

The struggle for adequate funding for English language learner programs in Arizona's public schools has been going on since 1992. That's when *Flores v. State of Arizona* was filed, alleging that the state was violating federal law by failing to adequately fund ELL programs. That judgment was issued in favor of the plaintiffs in January 2000, but the state has yet to comply with the judgment. As a result, ELL students in Arizona are still not receiving the equal education to which they are entitled under federal law.

The Case

This case was filed as a class action suit in 1992 on behalf of parents and students in the Nogales and Douglas Unified School Districts in Arizona. Originally, the class representative was identified as Evangeline Miranda on behalf of her children and other parents and children similarly situated. Miranda was eventually dismissed, and Miriam Flores was substituted in her place as the named class representative.

The complaint filed in 1992 generally alleged that the state was violating the Equal Education Opportunity Act of 1974 (EEOA). The EEOA requires that local education agencies including the state take "appropriate action" to help non-English-speaking students overcome their language barriers so that they can participate to the same extent as other students in public education. The *Castañeda v. Pickard* case provides the analytical framework for determining whether the EEOA has been violated.

The decision in *Castañeda* established a three-prong test for determining compliance with the EEOA. First, the state must have a recognized educational methodology in place for delivering language acquisition services. At the time the *Flores* case was filed, Arizona had authorized four different methodologies for use by school districts; none of these was challenged by the plaintiffs in *Flores*. Second, the state must allocate appropriate resources to effectively implement the educational methodology that has been approved; the plaintiffs challenged this prong of the test in *Flores*. And, third, even with a recognized methodology and adequate resources to implement it, the program must work. That is, it must produce results indicating that the language barriers confronting students are actually being overcome.

In 1996, the plaintiffs amended their complaint to include an additional claim. That year, the state adopted the AIMS test and established successful completion of the test as a graduation requirement. The additional claim asserted by the plaintiffs in *Flores* was that the AIMS test would have a disparate impact on minority students in violation of Title VI of the Civil Rights Act of 1964.

U.S. District Court Judge Alfredo Marquez established a trial date of August 16, 1999. The plaintiffs and defendants agreed that only the funding issues would be tried to the court and that the programmatic issues in the case would be settled by agreement of the parties and become the subject of a consent order approved by the court. The court heard three days of testimony concerning the state's funding for ELL programs. The court issued its judgment on January 24, 2000.

Judgment's Ruling on EEOA Claim

Judge Marquez ruled in favor of the plaintiffs on their EEOA claim. The judge's decision began with a description of the Arizona school finance system and the manner in which ELL programs are funded through that system. In general, a base level amount of funding is made available to each school district on a per student basis. The state's finance formula increases the base funding amount by weighing certain factors such as the type of student, the experience of the teaching faculty, and the size and type of the school district. The weighting factor for ELL students was established by the state in 1989 to 1990 and was based on a cost study performed in 1987 to 1988. That cost study showed that, on average, school districts were actually spending $450 extra per ELL student.

The state's witness at trial testified that the cost study did not reflect the actual cost of operating a successful language acquisition program for numerous reasons. At the time of trial, the state had not updated or revised the 1987–1988 cost study. In 1989 to 1990, the weight applied to base level funding for ELL students was .02, meaning that schools received approximately $50 more for each ELL student. In 1991 to 1992, the state legislature increased the weight to .06, which resulted in approximately $150 more being apportioned for each ELL student.

After describing the state's school financing scheme, the court extensively summarized the testimony of the director of Bilingual Education and Curriculum for Nogales Unified School District (NUSD). By the time of trial, the plaintiff class had been limited to ELL students and their parents in the NUSD. The class action allegations on behalf of students and parents in Douglas Unified School District had been decertified by the court. The director of Bilingual Education and Curriculum for NUSD testified about the programs NUSD had in place for ELL students and testified that the U.S. Department of Education Office of Civil Rights had conducted a compliance review of NUSD in 1992, and that the district had entered into a compliance agreement to remedy certain problems. She also testified about problems that continued to persist in the district in the operation of ELL programs. Those problems included the need for qualified faculty, additional classroom space, materials, teacher training, parent training, and transportation. The director testified that NUSD lacked the resources to address these inadequacies.

The court held that the state's $150 appropriation per ELL student, in combination with the state's property based financing scheme, was inadequate and resulted in ELL program deficiencies. The court identified the deficiencies as (a) too many students in a classroom, (b) not enough classrooms, (c) not enough qualified teachers including teachers to teach ESL and bilingual teachers to teach content area studies, (d) not enough teacher aides, (e) an inadequate tutoring program, and (f) insufficient teaching materials for both ESL classes and content area courses.

Additionally, the court determined that the state's $150 appropriation per ELL student was based on the state's cost study, which the state conceded was unreliable and which the state had failed to update. Consequently, the court ruled that the ELL program cost on which the state's minimum $150 appropriation was based was arbitrary and capricious.

Judgment's Ruling on the Title VI Claim

The court rejected the plaintiffs' claim that the AIMS test violated Title VI's implementing regulations, which prohibit a recipient of federal funding from using criteria or methods of administration that have the effect of subjecting individuals to discrimination because of their race, color, or national origin (34 C.F.R. §100.3[b][2]). The court held that demonstrating discriminatory effect suffices to establish a violation of the regulations but held that the plaintiffs had failed to make the necessary showing.

The court said that to establish a prima facie case of disparate impact, the plaintiffs had to establish that the AIMS test would have a disproportionate and adverse impact on minority students in NUSD, that the AIMS graduation test causes the disparity, and the disparity falls on the plaintiffs because they are members of a protected group based on race, color, or national origin. The court held that the plaintiffs' evidence failed to establish the necessary causal link between the disparate impact of the test and the plaintiffs' minority status. That was particularly so because there was a correlation in NUSD between low-income, at-risk students and ELL students that eliminated any race-based inferences that might otherwise be drawn. Therefore, the students in NUSD might fail the test because they are low-income, at-risk students who are not legally protected from discriminatory treatment rather than members of a protected group to whom such protections are available.

The Consent Order

Following issuance of the judgment, the plaintiffs and defendants continued to negotiate resolution of the programmatic issues in the case. Those negotiations resulted in a proposed Consent Order that was presented to the court. The court approved the Consent Order on July 31, 2000. With the court's approval, the Consent Order acquired the same force and effect as a judgment and became judicially enforceable.

The Consent Order addresses numerous programmatic issues regarding the delivery of ELL programs in Arizona. Among other issues, the Consent Order requires the following:

1. The Superintendent of Public Instruction selects tests and scores to determine English proficiency.

2. The State Board of Education amends its rules to require that a student exited from an ELL program be reassessed in the two years following exit to determine whether the student is making academic progress. Exited students who do not perform satisfactorily on the reassessment tests shall be re-enrolled in an ELL program or given compensatory instruction aimed at curing the skill or knowledge deficits revealed by the reassessment results.

3. The State Board is also required to amend its rules to require that English language instruction shall be appropriate to the level of English proficiency and shall include listening and speaking skills, reading and writing skills, and cognitive and academic development in English. Additionally, the rules shall require daily instruction in basic subject areas that is understandable and appropriate to the level of academic achievement of the ELL student.

4. The State Board is also required to enact rules to provide that ELL students who are not progressing toward achieving proficiency of the Board's academic standards shall be provided additional compensatory instruction to help them achieve those standards.

5. The Superintendent is required to monitor school districts for compliance with state and federal laws including the Consent Order.

Enforcement Proceedings

Immediately after the court issued its judgment on January 24, 2000, counsel for the plaintiffs delivered a letter to each Arizona legislator and the governor informing them of the judgment and their responsibility to comply with it. By the time the legislative session concluded in May, no legislative action had been taken.

Plaintiffs' First Motion for Injunctive Relief

Given the legislature's failure to take any action during the 2000 legislative session to comply with the judgment in *Flores,* the plaintiffs filed their first motion for injunctive relief in May 2000. They requested that the court order the defendants to perform a cost study upon which legislative action could be based to comply with the funding provisions of the judgment. On October 12, 2000, the court granted the plaintiffs' motion and ordered that a cost study be conducted to determine appropriate funding levels for ELL programs. The court further ordered that the study be completed in sufficient time for the legislature to act during the legislative session that would begin in January 2001.

Plaintiffs' Second Motion for Injunctive Relief

Two legislative sessions passed without any action being taken to comply with the judgment. The plaintiffs then filed another motion asking the court to establish a deadline for compliance.

The court granted that motion and ordered the defendants to comply with the judgment and provide adequate funding for ELL programs by January 31, 2002, or the conclusion of any earlier special session of the legislature that had been called for any other purpose. As it turns out, the governor called the legislature into special session in December 2001 for a purpose unrelated to *Flores.* Rather than face sanctions from the court, the legislature enacted legislation that addressed the judgment in *Flores* but only on an interim basis.

The interim legislation, House Bill 2010, was premised on the notion that the state still did not have reliable cost data to establish appropriate funding levels for ELL programs. In total, House Bill 2010 increased annual funding for ELL programs by more than $40 million. Additionally, the legislation commissioned a comprehensive cost study and required that it be distributed by August 2004.

Plaintiff's Third Motion for Injunctive Relief

The state contracted with the National Conference of State Legislatures (NCSL) to conduct the cost study required by House Bill 2010. By August 2004,

only an executive summary of the study had been published. The plaintiffs determined that prospects for any legislative action in the session beginning January 2005 were becoming unlikely. As a result, they filed a third motion for injunctive relief requesting that the court establish a deadline for compliance with the judgment by the end of the legislative session. In January 2005, the court granted that motion and ordered that the state "constitutionally and adequately fund" programs for English language learners consistent with the court's judgment in previous orders.

Legislation was not introduced to address the *Flores* judgment until the last week of the session. The legislation was sponsored by the majority leadership in the legislature and generally predicated on their belief that the draft NCSL cost study failed to provide them sufficient information from which to accurately assess and fund the cost of ELL programs. In the intent section of the legislation, the legislature declared,

> It has grave concerns regarding the validity and reliability of the cost study performed by the National Conference of State Legislatures . . . the cost study used what it referred to as the "professional judgment approach" to determine the incremental costs for English language learners, yet acknowledged that this kind of approach "depends on the judgment of educational professionals in identifying strategies rather than research that actually shows a linkage between the strategy and student performance." (House Bill 2718, § 17[A])

Instead of relying upon the cost study, the legislation required the development of research-based models of structured English immersion. Once the models were developed, the legislation allowed school districts to apply for additional funding associated with the incremental costs of the research-based models that are in addition to the normal costs of conducting programs for English-proficient students.

House Bill 2718 provided a temporary increase in the funding formula weight for ELL students that amounted to approximately $75 per student. After one year of funding the weight at that level, House Bill 2718 eliminated the weight all together, finding that classification of a pupil as an ELL is "fundamentally different than the classification of the pupil as qualified for any other . . . category" (House Bill 2718, § 17[B]).

The legislation declared that the costs of implementing the new ELL programs could not be determined until the research-based models were developed. Thus, more than five years after the judgment had been issued in the *Flores* case, the legislature had not yet identified the cost of providing ELL programs as required by the court. This was a major defect of the legislation, causing the plaintiffs to oppose it.

In mid-June 2005, the governor released her own legislative proposal relying on the NCSL cost study to establish appropriate funding levels. The governor's proposal provided for phased-in funding over a 4-year period. Like the legislature's proposal, the governor's proposal eliminated the ELL weight and substituted a separate funding mechanism for ELL students that required that the funding be spent solely for ELL purposes. In contrast, the weighted funding system allows school districts to budget ELL funds for any purpose and does not restrict the expenditure of funds to ELLs.

After the 4-year phase-in, the governor's proposal established funding at a level of $1,289 per ELL student. This amount was within the range identified by the NCSL cost study, after total incremental costs were offset by monies that school districts had historically spent on ELL programs from other sources, including federal and locally generated funding. The governor's proposal also included strict accountability provisions for the expenditure of the funds.

The legislative majority's reaction to the governor's proposal was instantaneous. The speaker of the House declared that Arizona would become "Mexico's best school district north of the border." Other legislators denied that the state had any responsibility for educating noncitizens and insisted that children born in the United States to parents who had immigrated illegally were not citizens despite the U.S. Constitution's explicit language to the contrary. One legislator suggested that the children "should be deported, along with their parents."

Subsequent Motions

Given the legislative majority's reaction to the governor's proposal, the plaintiffs determined that they could wait no longer for the executive and legislative branches to discuss, much less agree, on a proposal that would comply with the court's judgment and orders. In late July and early August, the plaintiffs filed two motions seeking further relief from the court: a motion to enjoin the AIMS Test as a graduation requirement on July 28, 2005, and a motion for sanctions against the defendants, on August 2, 2005.

The latter motion requested that the court provide the state with 30 days in which to comply with the court's judgment but if the state fails to take action within that period, the court should enjoin Arizona from receiving federal highway funds.

In December 2005, the district court granted the motion to enjoin the AIMS test as a graduation requirement. Instead of enjoining Arizona from receiving federal highway funds, the district court chose to impose a schedule of fines that would begin 15 days after the legislative session convened in January 2006, if there was no compliance by the date. In late January, fines of $500,000 per day began to be assessed against the state, and by the time the fines were finally terminated, they totaled $21 million. In the meantime, the Arizona legislature had intervened in the case and requested that the Ninth Circuit Court of Appeals stay the distribution of the fines pending the legislature's appeal of the district court's order.

The superintendent and the legislature's appeals were expedited by the Ninth Circuit Court of Appeals. On July 23, 2006, the court of appeals issued a memorandum decision vacating the district court's orders and remanding the case to the district court to conduct an evidentiary hearing, the purpose of which was to provide the legislature and the superintendent an opportunity to show that changed circumstances that had occurred since the judgment was entered in 2000 justified dissolution or a modification of the court's original judgment. Among the changes asserted by the legislature and the superintendent was legislation enacted in 2006 as the fines were accumulating. That legislation established an English Language Learner Task Force to develop models of instruction for adoption by school districts. The models were to include at least 4 hours of daily English language development for first-year ELLs. School districts were then permitted to submit budget requests to recover the incremental costs of implementing the models. However, the amount of the budget request submitted by a school district was to be offset by proportionate shares of federal funds and desegregation funding. Additionally, funding under the legislation would only be provided for any ELL for 2 years.

On remand to the district court, an evidentiary hearing was held in January 2007. The court heard eight days of evidence from the parties and issued an order on March 23, 2007, holding that the superintendent and the legislature had failed to demonstrate changed circumstances that would justify dissolution or modification of the judgment. The district court also held that House Bill 2064, the legislation enacted the previous year, violated federal law by deducting federal funds from the amount of state aid for ELL programs and by terminating funding for ELL students after 2 years. The evidence at the hearing demonstrated that it takes ELLs 3 to 4 years to become English proficient and that the legislation's termination of funding after 2 years violated the EEOA.

The superintendent and the legislature have appealed the district court's decision to the Ninth Circuit Court of Appeals. The court of appeals has not yet set a hearing on the matter.

Implications

The *Flores* case is significant in several respects. First, it is the only reported court decision finding that a state has failed to comply with the EEOA. Other decisions have involved school districts, but a state has not been ordered by a federal court to increase funding for ELL programs before. Second, there have been many school finance decisions across the country in which state courts have determined that school finance systems are unconstitutional under the terms of a state's constitutional provisions. Those questions almost always raise separation of powers issues regarding the state court's ability to mandate legislative compliance with varying results. However, the *Flores* case is one of the few cases in which a federal court has mandated legislative compliance with funding provisions. Although questions regarding separation of powers are not a barrier to judicial enforcement, the integrity of the federal-state relationship poses similar problems. The *Flores* case will test the federal judiciary's ability to enforce federal law against an uncooperative and unwilling state.

From an educational prospective, *Flores* represents a case in which the judiciary has been willing to use state or federal law as a basis for imposing limitations on legislative funding decisions. Those funding decisions have historically been reserved to the sole and exclusive discretion of the legislature. During the past 30 years, however, courts have shown a willingness to review those legislative decisions under either state constitutional provisions or, as in the *Flores* case, federal law.

The judicial trend is toward requiring legislative decisions that have some relationship to the costs of providing an adequate education. Where legislative funding decisions in the educational arena had been politically driven in the past, states are being required in many instances to establish some rational cost basis for their decisions.

That is not to say that states must simply perform a cost study and then provide funding at the recommended level. If that were true, then there would be no need for state legislatures. Instead, the evolving legal standard seems to require an inquiry into the costs of adequately educating students and using that inquiry at least in part as a basis for funding decisions.

Cases like *Flores* are not a panacea for inadequate educational funding. Ultimately, funding decisions are committed to the sound discretion of legislative and executive officials who have been elected to make those decisions. However, cases such as *Flores* established the principle that such discretion is not unlimited and requires consideration of the costs associated with funding inadequate education.

Timothy Hogan

Editor's Note: This entry is a shortened but updated version of a previous report on this legislation prepared by the same author. The original article can be accessed at http://www.nsba.org/site/docs/39500/39473.pdf

See also Costs of Bilingual Education; Equal Educational Opportunity Act of 1974; Federal Court Decisions and Legislation

Further Readings

Arizona Department of Education (2004). *AIMS Report Wizard.* Retrieved from http://www.ade.az.gov/profile/publicview

Castañeda v. Pickard, 648 F.2d 989 (5th Cir. 1981).

Equal Education Opportunities Act, 20 U.S.C. § 1703(f) (1974).

Flores v. State of Arizona, 172 F. Supp. 2d 1225 (D. Ariz. 2000).

Office of English Language Acquisition. (2005). Arizona: Rate of LEP growth 1994/1995–2004/2005. Retrieved from http://www.ncela.gwu.edu/stats/3_bystate.htm

Title VI of the Civil Rights Act of 1964, 42 U.S.C. § 2000.

FLUENCY

See PROFICIENCY, FLUENCY, AND MASTERY

FOREIGN TEACHERS, IMPORTING

See CREDENTIALING FOREIGN-TRAINED TEACHERS

FOUR-SKILLS LANGUAGE LEARNING THEORY

In language learning theory, the *four-skills sequence* refers to a belief that language learners go through a specific sequence in learning a language, any language. According to this theory, we first learn to understand an utterance or an idea, then learn to say it, then read it, and finally write it. Although the theory is somewhat dated because of its simplistic basis, many language teachers still believe that the sequence accounts for a substantial portion of the work involved in teaching a language. In the extreme, the practice means that students are not asked to write what they do not yet read and are not asked to speak utterances they do not yet understand.

The four skills in question are listening, speaking, reading, and writing, and according to structural linguistic theory, language learning is best facilitated by structuring instruction so that language learners progress through the four skills in that sequence. One listens first, and then speaks, which is followed by reading, and writing is the last skill developed. Colin Baker speaks of listening, speaking, reading, and writing as language *abilities;* he believes language skills have measurable and observable components, such as handwriting and pronunciation. Carlos Ovando, Virginia P. Collier, and Mary Carol Combs use the term *language mode* when referring to the four skills. Some purists in the science of linguistics argue that the written form of a language is not part of their science because they consider language to be the spoken phenomenon and the marks we make on paper as merely a representation of the latter. This entry describes the theory and uses the terms *language abilities, language skills,* and *language modes* interchangeably when referring to the four skills: listening, speaking, reading, and writing.

Audio-Lingual Method

The four-skills sequence of language learning was embraced by the audio-lingualists, whose language teaching methods are based on the structural linguistic theoretical perspective. In their practice, audio-lingualist teachers first model dialogues to which beginning language learners listen and then repeat. Then the teacher prompts the students to recombine utterances from the dialogues with different vocabulary, different verb tenses, or additional modifiers, such as adverbs and adjectives. As learners progress through the sequence of dialogues, the amount and complexity of language used increases, and practice to develop additional language abilities is introduced. In most cases, the students would have experienced all phrases or sentences that he or she was asked to incorporate into a learning dialogue.

After some time, learners are introduced to short reading passages related to the topic of the dialogue and integrating previously introduced vocabulary and grammatical structures. After students have sufficient practice with reading, they then start to write short sentences in response to questions about the reading passage. The writing assignments grow more complex over time, until learners are able to write more extended passages on topics of their choosing with the scope of vocabulary and structures to which they were already introduced and familiar.

Ovando et al. point out that the four language modes fit into two dimensions: receptive and productive skills. Listening and reading are receptive skills, and speaking and writing are productive skills. Further, listening and speaking are components of *oracy,* language skills that do not depend on written language. Reading and writing are components of *literacy,* skills that depend on written language. Baker points out that in understanding relationships between the four abilities, receptive and productive skills, and oracy and literacy, one can also understand better the subtleties of what it means to be bilingual and how to arrange instruction for bilingual students.

Sequential Versus Integrated Approach

To classify people as bilinguals or monolinguals is too simplistic because some can understand more than one spoken language and may not be able to speak it, or they may be able to read, but not write in more than one language or in either. This is often the case with immigrant children who come to the United States from preliterate environments such as refugee camps. Further, within the abilities, gradations exist. Some language learners may be more or less fluent speakers than others; others may listen with understanding while shopping but not when listening to an academic lecture. There are also skills within skills, such as pronunciation, extent of vocabulary, correctness of grammar, and so on.

Thus, bilingualism is not the black- and-white phenomenon that many paint it to be, and the four-skills sequence where each type of ability is developed separately from the others is not practicable as a consistent teaching or learning approach. Each ability flows naturally into the next, which makes it difficult to explore any in isolation from the rest. For this reason, using an integrated approach to developing the four language abilities is preferable to a sequential one. An integrated approach to developing all four abilities also allows for a more balanced development in oracy and literacy because both are attended to throughout the language learning process. In an audio-lingual approach where abilities are introduced and developed sequentially, a learner requiring practice in developing literacy but not oracy has to wade through an unnecessary oracy development process that may prove to be too long, or perhaps boring.

Stephen Krashen echoes this concern. First, the effects of skills-based instruction on developing language proficiency are weak. For instance, studies claiming to show a positive effect for grammar study on language learning show only a limited contribution of grammar study to language proficiency. Grammar, spelling, vocabulary, and so on are too complex to be learned consciously. Second, numerous cases exist of people who have achieved high levels of proficiency without skill-based instruction. The skill-building hypothesis, according to Krashen, is an "output" hypothesis. It presupposes that students produce language to acquire it. This contradicts the structural perspective that generally maintains that students first acquire language to produce it. Output, in this context, serves two functions: (1) to expose errors for correction and to lead to better understanding of the existence of rules governing the target language and (2) to solidify learners' knowledge and application of these rules. Krashen maintains that the amount of output that language learners produce in this way is often too small to be a meaningful tool for learning.

Critical Literacy Approach

Baker points out that a four-skills approach results in functional literacy, a low-level literacy, which may be an admirable goal but which is not the optimal literacy goal for language learners. Baker espouses literacy approaches that focus on both meaning and structure and are intertwined with knowledge and inquiry. In the latter instance, language proficiency is means toward a greater end; in the former case, language is an end in itself. Developing literacy skills through the examination of and interaction with authentic, meaningful texts equips students to demonstrate proficiency in the four skills without having to analyze the underlying linguistic structures themselves. In a critical literacy-oriented learning environment, authentic language is modeled and language learners develop implicit language-governing rules that will stand the test of time because learners will use them again and again toward a greater end of producing original ideas and creating new knowledge. This approach contrasts with a four-skills approach that conditions students to manipulate others' ideas in the name of drill and practice focused solely on language structures.

Many bilingual education teachers recognize the complementary advantages of a number of methods and approaches and will mix them to serve specific pedagogical purposes for particular students. The field of language teaching offers many opportunities to study how second-language learners employ various language learning strategies to develop higher levels of proficiency in a second language. Also, rich opportunities exist for further research on relationships between home language skills and proficiency and second-language skills and proficiency, especially with reference to the transferability of skills from the first to the second language.

Elsie M. Szecsy

See also Audio-Lingual Method; Comprehensible Input; Continua of Biliteracy; Linguistics, an Overview; Literacy and Biliteracy; Literacy Instruction, First and Second Language

Further Readings

Baker, C. (2001). *Foundations of bilingual education and bilingualism* (3rd ed.). Clevedon, UK: Multilingual Matters.

Krashen, S. (2004). Why support a delayed-gratification approach to language education? *Language Teacher, 28*(7), 3–7.

Ovando, C., Collier, V. P., & Combs, M. C. (2003). *Bilingual and ESL classrooms: Teaching in multicultural contexts* (3rd ed.). Boston: McGraw-Hill.

GARCÍA, EUGENE E. (1946–)

Eugene E. García was director of the Office of Bilingual Education and Minority Languages Affairs (OBEMLA)—currently known as the Office of English Language Acquisition (OELA)—of the U.S. Department of Education from 1993 to 1995. García was born on June 3, 1946, in a small town on the western slope of Colorado named Grand Junction. His parents were migrant farm workers from the "Four Corners" area—the border region of Arizona, Colorado, New Mexico, and Utah—who worked in seasonal crops, harvesting sugar beets, cherries, apricots, peaches, apples, and pears.

Although neither of his parents attended school on a regular basis, Eugene's family deeply valued education. From young childhood, he was taught in his native Spanish language to value education as an important resource. To all of his children, Eugene's father would often say, *"Nunca te pueden quitar la educación"* ("They can never take your education away"). Although his parents could not offer their children traditional schooling—literacy, mathematics, and science skills—the education Eugene and his siblings received from their parents were respect for family, respect for elders, respect for others, hard work, persistence, patience, the importance of spirituality, and so on.

After completing a BS in psychology at the University of Utah in 1968, García attended graduate school at the University of Kansas, where he received an MS in child development in 1970 and a PhD in human development in 1972. He also completed postdoctoral work at Harvard University, and was a postdoctoral fellow at the National Research Council and the Kellogg Foundation.

García's professional career has been marked by an ongoing commitment to academia, research, administration, and other scholarly activities. He has served as professor, researcher, mentor, and administrator, often concurrently. From 1980 to 1987, he served as director of the Center for Bilingual Education and Research at Arizona State University; from 1990 to 1993, he was chair of the Department of Education and dean of the Division of Social Sciences at University of California, Santa Cruz; during this period, he was also director of the National Research Center for Research on Cultural Diversity and Second Language Learning. From 1993 to 1995, he was director of OBEMLA during President Bill Clinton's administration; from 1995 to 2001, he served as dean of the Graduate School of Education at the University of California, Berkeley, during which time he was a special advisor to the university chancellor. Subsequently, he served as dean of the Mary Lou Fuller College of Education at Arizona State University from 2002 until 2006. In 2003, García was appointed vice president of School-University Partnerships at Arizona State University and is the current chair of the National Task Force on Early Childhood Education for Hispanics.

Even though he has had extensive administrative experience, his fundamental function and identity continues to be that of a professor and researcher. In collaboration with colleagues and grant-issuing bodies nationwide, García has earned more than $13 million in research funding during the past 30 years, serving as principal investigator or coinvestigator, to increase the scientific and practical knowledge-base concerning issues of language development, early education, cognition, bilingualism, culture, curriculum and instruction, and effective schooling practices for language minority and Hispanic children. He has been a professor in the psychology and education departments at several universities, including the University of Utah, the University of California–Santa Barbara, Arizona State University, the University of California–Santa Cruz, and the University of California–Berkeley. Since 2002, he has been a professor in curriculum and instruction at Arizona State University.

García is the recipient of many awards. He was named U.S. Hispanic educator of the year in 1986 by the League of United Latin American Citizens, given the Senior Research Award by the American Education Research Association in 1991, named one of the 100 most influential Hispanics in 2001 by *Hispanic Business* magazine, and was given the Outstanding Support of Hispanic Issues in Higher Education Award in 2005 by the Hispanic Caucus of the American Association of Higher Education. He also has authored or coauthored more than 150 articles and book chapters and has written several books—his most recent authored volumes include *Hispanic Education in the United States: Raíces y Alas* (2001), *Student Cultural Diversity: Understanding and Meeting the Challenge* (2001), and *Teaching and Learning in Two Languages: Bilingualism and Schooling in the United States* (2005).

García is married and has two children and two grandchildren.

Bryant T. Jensen

See also Improving America's Schools Act of 1994; Office of Bilingual Education and Minority Languages Affairs

Further Readings

García, E. (2001). *Hispanic education in the United States: Raíces y alas.* Boulder, CO: Rowman & Littlefield.

García, E. (2001). *Student cultural diversity: Understanding and meeting the challenge* (3rd. ed.). Boston: Houghton Mifflin.

García, E. (2005). *Teaching and learning in two languages: Bilingualism and schooling in the United States.* New York: Teachers College Press.

GERMAN LANGUAGE EDUCATION

The use of various languages in American education occurs in cycles. No single language remains preeminent forever. Spanish occupies an important place today, but at another point in our history, German occupied second place only to English in the schools. Unlike German as a foreign language, in which students learn German as a subject, instruction in and through German uses the language as a tool for teaching other subjects. Proponents of the use of German for instruction were also interested in preserving the language and culture of that group among the young.

The history of bilingual education for children of German immigrants in the United States falls roughly into three periods: (1) the colonial to early Republican period (1683–1800), (2) the early 19th century through the Civil War period (1800–1865), and (3) the post–Civil War period through World War II (1865–1950). In each of these eras, bilingual education in German and English served different groups. The German settlers of the colonial era and the early republic sought refuge from religious oppression, whereas the German immigrants of the 19th century were mainly political refugees. German immigrants and Americans of German heritage in the first half of the 20th century lived, at times, in an environment of anti-German sentiment. During this period of international tensions and wars, those of German heritage were regarded as a threat to U.S. security because it was feared they might be German spies or sympathizers. Such fears find an echo today in concerns about Mexican immigration, which often clouds discussions of bilingual education. This entry describes German-language education in the United States.

Colonial Through Early Republic Period (1683–1800)

The first German settlers arrived in the Pennsylvania colony in 1683, where they founded Germantown, near Philadelphia. Immigrants from German-speaking regions in Europe grew into an influential presence during the colonial period, especially in Pennsylvania and Ohio, and through the birth of the new nation. During this era and into the beginning of the 19th century, German immigrants in the United States aroused little hostility. They had proven themselves to be good patriots as early as the Revolutionary War, and they were well represented at the Philadelphia convention of 1774 and 1775 and in the Continental Army. The Continental Congress even printed German versions of a number of documents, including the Articles of Confederation. Not unexpectedly, many German families during the Colonial era requested that German be included along with English in the curriculum of the schools their children attended. The first bilingual schools, which opened before 1800, were parochial institutions, as was the norm for education in general during this period. Clergy were commonly the teachers. However, some schools were technically not bilingual—German was the only language of instruction in these cases. In other instances, schools were bilingual and included German and English and a variety of balances between German and English as language of instruction, depending on local preferences. Either German or English might be the exclusive language of instruction, with one or the other taught as a subject, or both might be the language of instruction at different times of the day.

Nineteenth Century Through the Civil War (1800–1865)

The number of German immigrants increased during the 19th century. Unlike those arriving in the United States during the 18th century, these immigrants—called 30ers (they arrived in the 1830s)—fled political repression stemming from religious and philosophical differences. Given their history in Germany, these immigrants favored active civic involvement in their new communities in America. This group worked for equal status of the German language with English—and not to the exclusion of English—in those states with strong German presence.

In 1850, Germans were the only important immigrant group in the United States. Of 900,000 immigrants in the United States, only 100,000 claimed English as a native language, and 584,000 were from Germany. In 1880, half a million of the 3.9 million population claimed English as a native language. Two million of the remaining 3.4 million were from Germany. In 1850, 15% of foreign-born people in the United States spoke German; in 1880, 60% of foreign-born people spoke German.

Because German immigrants settled in relatively unpopulated frontier areas of the country where land

was readily available and inexpensive (i.e., Indiana, Illinois, Ohio, Wisconsin, Minnesota, Michigan, Iowa, and Missouri), and they were concentrated in those areas, the German presence went relatively unnoticed elsewhere. German immigrants were in the majority in the regions they inhabited, and many of the frontier areas they settled achieved statehood after their arrival. German immigrants were already a strong presence in rural and urban Texas before 1845, when Texas was an independent republic. In both the upper Midwest frontier and the Lone Star Republic, German immigrant children learned in bilingual schools. Their English-speaking counterparts were the minority population, giving the German element a unique political and social advantage.

In these rural areas, Germans initially had no teachers familiar with English, and there was little need for English language proficiency in this environment during the early years of settlement. The question of language of instruction was rarely raised, and when it was raised, the "30ers" brought political pressure to bear in preserving German by using it as the language of instruction.

The Germans in Ohio, for example, who had first settled the region more than 25 years before Ohio achieved statehood, supported the Democrats in the 1836 election. Charging not only that they had paid taxes for public school support but also that the Democratic party owed them some recognition, the Germans sought to influence the course of study in the public schools in the state. They did not want English to be excluded, but they asked that German be taught as well. In response, the Ohio legislature passed a law by which the German language could be taught in the public schools in districts with large German populations. In the elections of 1839, pledges were taken from the candidates that the wording of the law would be changed to prevent any loopholes. Accordingly, the law was revised in 1840—the date of the introduction of German-English public schools in Ohio. Ohio became the first state to adopt a bilingual education law that authorized German-English instruction at the request of parents.

In Pennsylvania, a law was passed in 1837 permitting German schools to be acknowledged on equal basis with English language schools. Pennsylvania was the only state where such language equality in the public school system was asked for or obtained. In one Wisconsin district, one third of the textbook funds were specified to be spent for German textbooks; in others, school boards could hire only German-speaking teachers, and local school district records were often maintained in German. In Wisconsin, whenever a newly created school district contained a large German population, it was not unusual that instruction was conducted either exclusively in German or in both German and English.

The patriotism Germans demonstrated during the 19th century helped create a receptive climate for bilingual education in the schools. Beginning with the War of 1812 and ending with the Spanish War, Germans were represented in large numbers in the American armies. However, a rise in anti-Catholic sentiment against Irish Catholics in Massachusetts, Maryland, and Connecticut resulted in English literacy tests designed to disenfranchise Irish Catholics; these circumstances also threatened the status of Germans, because many of them were also Roman Catholic. The Civil War broke up the politically powerful Know-Nothing movement that nourished this wave of religious bigotry, thus sparing German immigrants. Unfortunately, this was followed by the formation of the American Protective Association (APA), which marked the end of leniency for the German community.

Post–Civil War to Mid-20th Century (1865–1950)

The teaching of German in the public schools came under attack in the 1880s, and the use of German was discontinued in St. Louis, Missouri; Louisville, Kentucky; St. Paul, Minnesota; and San Francisco, California. Restriction of non-English language instruction was not rationalized on technical and educational grounds. Instead, language restrictionist measures were based on political and economic considerations that caused German immigrants to be regarded as a threat.

The remedy developed by the Germans to preserve the German language on par with English was the use of private and parochial schools for instruction in German because legislation against German-language instruction was limited to public schools. In many districts, Lutheran or Roman Catholic parochial schools displaced the public schools as schools of choice for German immigrants. The remedy was not well received by its opponents. Legislation was proposed in 1889 to force the use of English-only instruction in private and parochial schools. Germans were opposed to the laws on the basis of language and because they regarded these laws as attacks on their religion, culture, and personal liberty.

Perhaps the most heated controversy about the use of English in private and parochial schools took place in the German-populated states of Illinois and Wisconsin. The Edwards Law in Illinois and the Bennett Law in Wisconsin, passed in 1889, required that parochial as well as public schools teach elementary subjects in the English language. These laws were opposed by both Roman Catholic and Lutheran Germans as a violation of freedom of conscience. Other Protestant denominations did not oppose these laws. The Edwards and Bennett laws were repealed in 1893. They were replaced with compulsory attendance laws that did not specify preferences in language of instruction.

Enrollment surveys at the turn of the 20th century reported at least 600,000 primary school students (public and parochial) were receiving part or all of their instruction in German. This number represented approximately 4% of all American children in elementary grades, a larger proportion than is currently involved in bilingual education. As late as 1940, persons of German heritage in the United States were a strong political force by virtue of their relatively large numbers. Of the nearly 5 million persons of German heritage in the United States in 1940, 32.1% were foreign-born; 49.2% were American-born of one or more foreign-born parents; 18.7% were American-born of American-born parents.

The political winds for German immigrants and Americans of German descent shifted during the World War I era. Fears about the loyalty of non-English speakers in general, and of German Americans in particular, prompted many states to enact English-only instruction laws designed to "Americanize" these groups. Some went as far as to ban the study of foreign languages in the elementary grades altogether. This ban was struck down as unconstitutional in 1923, although anti-German laws remained on the books for decades. As late as 1972, Hispanic advocates for bilingual education in Texas had to rescind the Texas version of this law before they could enact legislation to support Spanish-English bilingual education.

At the onset of World War I, state officials maintained the right of private schools to conduct instruction in German provided that this did not violate laws or interfere with war efforts. As anti-German feelings grew, efforts to prohibit the use of German in public and private also grew. For example, the Victoria County Council of Defense in Texas urged the abandonment of the use of German in 1918. In Findlay, Ohio, the town council levied a fine of $25 for the use of the German language in public. At the beginning of the 20th century, legal provisions for using the German language in public and private were permissive, but by 1923, such provisions had turned against German. By 1923, the statutorily required language of instruction in Ohio and other states was English.

The Ohio and similar laws against German-language instruction were subsequently declared unconstitutional by the Supreme Court because these prohibitions were a violation of due process. Importantly, the Court also declared that statutory requirements of English instruction in public and private schools were permitted.

After World War I, Ohio, Nebraska, and Iowa passed statutes inhibiting the teaching of languages other than English, even as a subject, before the eighth grade. German Lutherans contested the statute, which was declared unconstitutional in the *Bohning v. Ohio*, *Meyer v. Nebraska*, and *Bartels v. Iowa* cases in 1923. Though the Court opinion acknowledged the importance of a common tongue among all people in the United States, it also pointed out that the Constitution prohibited laws that single out a particular language. In theory, although perhaps not in practice, this decision placed the United States far ahead of most countries in the New World. The decision permitted immigrant groups to cultivate their languages as a school subject in private elementary schools. No single nationality was put into a lesser or greater position through preferential treatment of its language.

Anti-German activity was harsh, and the road back was slow after World War I. World War II further complicated efforts to encourage the study of German in schools, both in bilingual education and foreign-language programs.

German Bilingual Education Since 1950

Although German foreign-language enrollments expanded during the 1950s and early 1960s as a result of the National Defense Education Act of 1958, it appears that bilingual education in German and English may now be a thing of the past in the United States, except for a few schools scattered across the country. Contemporary examples of private bilingual schools are the Deutsche Schule New York, located in White Plains, which was founded in 1980, and the German International School of Boston, founded in 2001. In these two instances, the curriculum complies with local educational standards for state accreditation, and students can earn a diploma recognized by the state. In addition, the curriculum includes components originating in Germany so that students have the option of earning a German diploma as well. The private schools normally rely on partnerships with German corporate, cultural, and government entities for support, including local German Consulate offices. The students include German nationals and U.S. residents interested in developing German/English bilingualism and biliteracy in their children.

Two public bilingual schools are the German Immersion School in Milwaukee, Wisconsin, and the Twin Cities German Immersion School in Minnesota. The Milwaukee German Immersion School is a magnet elementary school that was founded in 1977, and the Twin Cities German Immersion School is a charter elementary school that began operation in September 2005. The Milwaukee German Immersion School articulates its program with Milwaukee's School of Languages, affording students the opportunity to continue the immersion experience through high school. These public language immersion schools rely on partnerships with local universities for program research and development efforts and also partner with various German cultural, corporate, and government institutions. Today's student pool is predominantly students with no prior background experience with the German language. In the early grades, instruction is totally in German, and English is introduced later, normally in the second or third grade. English instruction is gradually increased during the later elementary grades. Students in these schools must comply with local graduation requirements as well as those of the state.

Similarities exist in the historical trajectory of German bilingual education and the current situation of other language groups. In German bilingual education, public policy and educational practice was a product of the educational, economic, and political circumstances of the time. German speakers negotiated bilingual education for their children through the political process and were successful in their efforts when their patriotism was recognized. When Germans were perceived to be a potential threat to U.S. security, as was the case during World War I, German lost its status as an important language in education. It has never recovered that status. More recent efforts to promote bilingualism in German and English have tended to adopt an international focus in contrast to the previous focus on language and cultural preservation.

Elsie M. Szecsy

See also Americanization by Schooling; Bilingual Education as Language Policy; Early Bilingual Programs, 1960s; German Language in U.S. History;

Further Readings

Bartels v. Iowa, 262 U.S. 404 (1923).

Blanton, C. K. (2004). Tejanos, Germans, and Czechs in the making of the bilingual tradition, 1850–1900. In C. K. Blanton (Ed.), *The strange career of bilingual education in Texas, 1836–1981* (pp. 24–41). College Station: Texas A & M University Press.

Bohning v. Ohio, 262 U.S. 404 (1923).

Kloss, H. (1997/1977). *American bilingual tradition.* McHenry, IL: Delta Systems.

Leibowitz, A. H. (1978). Language policy in the United States. In H. Lafontaine, B. Persky, & L. Golubchick (Eds.), *Educación bilingüe* (pp. 3–13). Wayne, NJ: Avery.

Meyer v. Nebraska, 262 U.S. 390 (1923).

National Association for Bilingual Education. (1998, Spring). History of bilingual education. *Rethinking schools, 12*(3). Retrieved from http://www.rethinkingschools.org/archive/12_03/langhst.shtml

Toth, C. R. (1990). *German-English bilingual schools in America: The Cincinnati tradition in historical context.* New York: Lang.

Wiley, T. (1998). The imposition of World War I era English-only policies and the fate of German in North America. In T. Ricento and B. Burnaby (Eds.), *Language and politics in the United States and Canada* (pp. 211–241). Mahwah, NJ: Lawrence Erlbaum.

German Language in U.S. History

The strong presence of a single language other than English in the United States is hardly a new phenomenon. In the 18th and 19th centuries, German speakers were numerous and influential in the political process in ways similar to today's Spanish speakers. Legend has it that German would have become the official language of the land, were it not for a tie-breaking, dissenting vote. This entry attempts to set the record straight about the legend of German as the official language in the United States, a legend that has roots at two levels of government—the federal level and at the state level in Pennsylvania.

Karl Arndt traced the earliest written account about the status of German to an 1813 article by the Rev. Justus H. C. Helmuth of Philadelphia, who had also been trustee and a professor of German at the University of Pennsylvania. This account predates Franz von Löhrer's 1847 report that is the generally accepted, definitive source on German language policy in early U.S. history. Helmuth reported on recommendations to handle court cases of German speakers in German and to publish the laws of the land in German in places where there were many German-speaking people. Helmuth's vision was for German to be a natural official language in a number of states, but not to be imposed on all states, and certainly not to supplant English. Some aspects of his vision were never realized.

Helmuth also reported on a 1794 petition to the House of Representatives by several Germans who lived in Virginia. The petitioners outlined the language-related obstacles to civic engagement to which German-speakers were subjected; they requested that U.S. laws be made available in German in places where there were many German speakers. The petition was referred to a committee consisting of Francis Preston of Virginia, Daniel Heister of Pennsylvania, and Peter Muhlenberg of Pennsylvania, who was also brother of then Speaker of the House Friedrich A. C. Muhlenberg. In April 1794, the committee passed the bill, but it was never brought to the floor because of political pressures on the speaker of the House, a German American who did not want to appear to be pro-German in an English-dominant political environment. The bill was sidetracked or tabled repeatedly in 1794 and 1795. Though official records include much of the debate on this issue, no official record exists of speeches made by Peter Muhlenberg or Heister in favor of printing U.S. laws in German. Arndt claims that some pro-German comments or speeches were deliberately suppressed to prevent German speakers from pushing for even greater recognition of their language. Thus, it appears that from its beginnings, the United States has been a markedly pro-English nation where there has been little room for other languages in the political arena.

At the state level, specifically in Pennsylvania, Arndt refers to an 1828 article published anonymously in Stuttgart that was corroborated by several other articles in circulation in Europe and the United States at the time. The article reported that German nearly achieved official status in Pennsylvania because of the unified efforts of German speakers in that state. A second article, *Mittheilungen aus Nordamerika* [Reports from North America] by Dr. Ernst Ludwig Brauns, appeared in Braunschweig in 1829. Brauns affirmed Helmuth and repeated the call for German to be coequal with English in places in the United States where there were large numbers of German speakers. Brauns also referred to a motion made in Pennsylvania to elevate German to coequal status with English that failed by one vote.

In a little-known 1817 letter, Thomas Jefferson declared it a government policy to discourage foreigners from settling together in large masses, citing the poor track record of the Germans to assimilate quickly. Though on the surface, this letter may appear tangential, it does provide additional insight into the political context of the time. One can assume in this context that the policy was to ensure that similar language "problems" would not be repeated in the future.

Arndt could not verify claims that German failed to achieve official status by one vote with the bills and resolutions reported and printed for the Pennsylvania House and Senate. He did not accept that lack of verification implied untrue claims. Instead, he argued for unproven claims because of gaps in the official records of the Pennsylvania State Library and the Pennsylvania Legislative Reference Bureau for the period in question. Where records could be found, Arndt found references to bills and resolutions pertaining to the printing of laws in German, but he found none proposing to make German either *the* or *an* official language in the state of Pennsylvania.

Arndt summed up the evidence as follows: (a) At the federal level, German American citizens from Virginia did present a petition to the Third Congress to have the laws of the United States printed in German. One committee in the first session and another in the second session recommended that the petition be granted, but the proposal was defeated through parliamentary chicanery. (b) In the state of Pennsylvania, reports were circulated stating that a proposal to make German an official language of Pennsylvania was defeated by one vote. The official records of Pennsylvania neither prove nor disprove this claim.

Although it may appear that we are left with little certainty with regard to whether German missed official status by one vote, perhaps we miss the real point if we dwell on this disputed factoid. The story of German as an official language resonates with those of many others who have arrived in the United States since then. Each generation of speakers of languages other than English has encountered similar obstacles and used different avenues to turn obstacles into opportunity in their adopted homeland, to encourage civic participation in the United States using a language other than English. No historical evidence indicates that any of these groups attempted to substitute another language for English. Consistently, English speakers have blocked these attempts, no matter what their motivation is. Subsequent attempts at translating policy into practice were contentious for late 18th- and 19th-century German speakers, just as subsequent attempts by other groups in similar efforts have also met with strong obstacles. The decision to use English or German was not only a controversy for the English-speaking U.S. and state governments; it was also a bone of contention within the German-speaking community itself, just as it is among today's Spanish speakers in the United States, for example. Comparative approaches to investigating language policy problems may illuminate not only contemporary language policy but also improve our understanding of the past.

Elsie M. Szecsy

See also Bilingual Education as Language Policy; Ethnocentrism; Language Policy and Social Control; Languages and Power; Languages in Colonial Schools, Eastern; Official Language Designation

Further Readings

Arndt, K. J. R. (1976). German as the official language of the United States of America? *Monatshefte, 68*(2), 129–150.

Brauns, E. L. (1829). *Mittheilungen aus Nordamerika, die höheren Lehranstalten und die Englisirung der dortigen Deutschen betreffend* [Reports from North America, higher education institutions and the Anglicization of Germans in North America]. Braunschweig.

Hagedorn, R. (1942). German, the national language. *American Notes and Queries, 2,* 23.

Helmuth, J. H. C. (1813). Zurufe an die Deutschen in Amerika [Acclamations to the Germans in America].

Evangelisches Magazin, 2, 175–176 (published in Philadelphia).

Lohr, O. (1931). Deutsch als "Landessprache" der Vereinigten Staaten [German as "official language" of the United States]. *Mitteilungen der deutschen Akademie [Reports of the German academy], 4,* 283–290.

Löhrer, F. (1847). *Geschichte und Zustände der Deutschen in Amerika [History and circumstances of the Germans in America].* Cincinnati, OH: Vertag von Eggers und Wulkop and Leipzig: K. F. Kohler.

Werner, W. L. (1942). The "official German Language" legend. *American Speech, 17,* 246.

GIFTED AND TALENTED BILINGUALS

Although it is widely accepted that levels of intelligence and aptitude vary among individuals, giftedness is still somewhat controversial in the field of education and educational research. Despite this, there is still a small but growing body of research about giftedness and bilingualism. Generally, a verbally gifted person has an aptitude for both learning languages and learning about languages; however, verbal giftedness does not necessarily lead to bilingualism and being bilingual is not an automatic indication of verbal giftedness. As with most types of intelligence, verbal intelligence is usually determined by a standardized assessment, such as the Wechsler Intelligence Scale for Children (WISC) or the Scholastic Aptitude Test—Verbal (SAT-V), reflecting a focus on academic skills. Standardized assessments are not catchalls and generally do not adequately identify culturally and linguistically diverse children who are gifted. Additionally, verbally gifted bilinguals may not display their talents in traditionally expected ways, thus highlighting the need to find alternate forms of assessment and identification. Finally, gifted bilingual and English language learner (ELL) students are generally underrepresented in all types of gifted education programs, regardless of what area these children excel in.

Generally, although *verbal intelligence, verbal giftedness,* and *linguistic intelligence* may be used interchangeably, *verbal aptitude* refers to the potential for giftedness or intelligence. Also, some researchers distinguish between verbal intelligence/giftedness and linguistic intelligence. For these researchers, verbal intelligence and verbal giftedness may include verbal reasoning skills or literacy skills, whereas linguistic intelligence suggests knowledge of and about languages.

This entry discusses linguistic intelligence, identifying and testing for verbal giftedness, and language minority children and giftedness.

Linguistic Intelligence

Currently, giftedness is defined as high capability in one or more of the following areas: general or specific intellectual ability, creativity, leadership, visual and performing arts, and psychomotor ability. Children who are verbally gifted excel in their language ability, though linguistic intelligence is also highly correlated with general intelligence. Howard Gardner was one of the first people to study linguistic intelligence, and his theory of multiple intelligences was one of the first to separate linguistic intelligence from general intelligence. Gardner's research has shown that linguistic intelligence can exist relatively independently of other intelligences; however, multiple intelligences, such as logical intelligence and interpersonal intelligence, may be needed in addition to linguistic intelligence to become proficient in other languages or excel in a language arts curriculum. Additionally, it has been shown through ACT scores that a person may be verbally gifted, but only average in other areas.

Characteristics of Verbally Gifted Children

Most of what is known about linguistic intelligence in school-aged children is based on studies of verbally precocious youth enrolled in talent search programs throughout the country. These programs, administered by a number of U.S. universities, are designed to identify, educate, counsel, and study verbally precocious and mathematically precocious youth. Through these programs, it has been possible to better understand and characterize linguistic intelligence.

Children who have high levels of linguistic intelligence have extraordinary verbal ability. For instance, roughly one third of the sixth and seventh graders in the talent search programs score as well or better than the average college-bound senior on the SAT, and their vocabulary and knowledge of written English surpasses that of many college students. Additionally, verbally gifted children have a better memory for words, and those words are more compactly represented in their memories. Verbally gifted children often start reading early and continue to read well, although being an early reader is not an absolute indication of linguistic intelligence. Generally, verbally gifted children also utter their first words between 8 and 10 months of age, much earlier than the typical 12-month milestone, and produce sentences at an earlier age. However, some verbally gifted children start word and sentence production much later than other children, but they rapidly surpass the abilities of children their age once they do start speaking.

Current Research

Oddly, most research in verbal giftedness has been done in monolingual educational settings, and few studies have looked at the relationship between giftedness and bilingualism. For instance, there have been few studies of verbally precocious students in foreign-language classes, but researchers have found that verbally gifted middle school students participating in accelerated German or Latin classes can learn the complete grammar of an introductory course in two-thirds the time that it takes for college students to learn the same material. This indicates that verbally gifted students learn languages well in a classroom setting, but the focus of most previous research has been on monolingual, English-speaking children, ignoring the experiences of verbally gifted bilingual and ELL children both in and out of the classroom.

Identification and Testing of Verbal Giftedness and Aptitude

In understanding how gifted children are tested and identified, it is important to revisit the distinction between *giftedness/intelligence* and *aptitude*. Giftedness and intelligence refer to abilities that already exist, and assessment of verbal giftedness will focus on abilities such as reading comprehension, vocabulary, and analogies. Aptitude differs from giftedness and intelligence in that it encompasses the probability for high ability. Measures of verbal aptitude are generally predictive and include perceiving and learning new sounds, relating sounds to symbols such as letters and words, and identifying patterns in sentences. Although there is much overlap in language aptitude and general ability, language aptitude and verbal giftedness assessments often focus on academic skills, as seen in the assessment items mentioned. This focus means that those children who have higher academic abilities demonstrate higher verbal aptitude on standardized assessments and are generally more readily identified as gifted. These assessments also focus on

vocabulary and grammar, and are not designed to assess language abilities acquired outside of the classroom, nor do they look at communicative ability. For these reasons, parents and teachers are much more reliable for identifying gifted language minority children than are standardized assessments.

Language Minority Children and Giftedness

As mentioned earlier, littlie is known about an entire category of linguistically gifted youth, bilingual and ELL children. These students are often overlooked by schools and talent search programs, because despite their bilingualism or rapid acquisition of English, they may not be identified by tests of verbal ability that are normed for native English speakers. This is a reflection of the broadly accepted assumption in the U.S. education system that English monolingualism is normal and that speaking a language other than English is a deficiency that should be overcome.

Similarly, the length of time required to learn English has been repeatedly distorted by educational legislation. For instance, Arizona's Proposition 203 suggests that 1 year is sufficient for learning English, despite a large body of research that indicates it takes much longer. This type of policy could be devastating for the verbally gifted ELL student who does learn English within one academic year. Instead of standing out for identification as gifted, the child is seen as "normal" under the requirements of Proposition 203, and is reclassified as English proficient rather than gifted.

Additionally, bilingual children may not display classroom characteristics of verbal intelligence, especially if they are still learning English. Verbally gifted children typically have large vocabularies, although this may not be evident in a bilingual child, especially if they are assessed in the language they are learning rather than in both languages. The same follows for the high reading, writing, and speaking abilities usually associated with verbally gifted children in the classroom. Furthermore, English language ability may hinder identification of gifted bilinguals and ELL students because English is the medium of assessment and the tests are generally normed for monolingual native English speakers.

A handful of researchers in bilingual education have pushed for further research in understanding the relationship between giftedness and bilingualism.

Guadalupe Valdés has argued for expanding gifted-ness to include children who interpret for their parents and community. These bilingual, school-aged children are called *language brokers,* and generally have no training in interpreting. Despite their lack of training, language brokers are able to understand and relay information beyond what they learn in school, concerning, for instance, medical and dental problems, school issues, utility bills, and so on. Similarly, language brokers are frequently asked to assume the role of the teacher in classrooms and to instruct other monolingual students. Language brokers understand how to relay this variety of information and are able to assume adult-like roles in conversation, indicating that they know how adults speak in different situations. Furthermore, interpreting requires more than just the ability to speak two languages; interpreters must also have an increased speed of comprehension and production, increased memory capacity, a high learning curve, broad general knowledge, and the ability to foresee and prevent misunderstandings. Given current definitions of giftedness, Valdés argues, these children should also be identified as gifted.

Furthermore, bilingual and ELL children may be gifted in other areas and not at all in language. Ernesto Bernal has been one of the few researchers to focus specifically on bilingual children in gifted education, noting that bilingual and ELL children are underrepresented in gifted education programs. He lists several factors that contribute to this, including a reliance on standardized testing and delaying gifted education until after the student has become fully proficient in English. As mentioned, standardized testing often shortchanges gifted bilingual and ELL students because the tests are administered in English, which may be the student's weaker language, and are normed for monolingual English students. More pervasive, though, is the notion that a student needs to be proficient in English before he or she can benefit from gifted education. This notion is rooted in a deficit-based understanding of bilingualism. Bernal argues that gifted bilingual children benefit the most from early identification and access to a rigorous bilingual gifted education program. Finally, minority teachers are also underrepresented in gifted education, and Bernal suggests that increasing the number of minority gifted education teachers will help increase identification and enrollment of minority students in gifted education programs.

Lastly, a person does not have to be verbally gifted to become bilingual or multilingual. Most of the world's population speaks more than one language, and the standards of normal distribution tell us that it is not possible for all of those bilingual people to be verbally gifted. Many factors affect language acquisition and bilingualism, such as motivation, age, and community. Verbal aptitude and intelligence are also not the only cognitive factors associated with language acquisition. What distinguishes the verbally gifted learner from the average language learner is the speed of acquisition. Verbally gifted learners seem to pick up languages effortlessly, both in formal classroom contexts and out in the street, but an average person may take many years to become proficient or near-proficient.

Kara T. McAlister

See also Bilingual Special Education; Cognitive Benefits of Bilingualism; Deficit-Based Education Theory; English, How Long to Learn; First-Language Acquisition; No Child Left Behind Act of 2001, Testing Requirements; Second-Language Acquisition

Further Readings

Baker, C., & Jones, S. P. (Eds.). (1998). *Encyclopedia of bilingualism and bilingual education.* Clevedon, UK: Multilingual Matters.

Bernal, E. (1994, April). *Finding and cultivating minority gifted/talented students.* Paper presented at the National Conference on Alternative Teacher Certification, Washington, DC.

García, E. E., & Flores, B. (Eds.) (1986). *Language and literacy research in bilingual education.* Tempe: Center for Bilingual Education, Arizona State University.

Gardner, H. (1983). *Frames of mind: The theory of multiple intelligences.* New York: Basic Books.

Olszewski-Kubilius, P., & Whalen, S. P. (2001). The education and development of verbally talented students. In K. Heller, F. Monks, & R. Subotnik (Eds.), *International handbook of giftedness and talent.* London: Pergamon.

Thompson, M. C., & Thompson, M. B. (1996). Reflections on foreign language study of highly able learners. In J. VanTassel-Baska, D. Johnson, & L. Boyce (Eds.), *Developing verbal talent: Ideas and strategies for teachers of elementary and middle school students* (pp. 174–188). Boston: Allyn & Bacon.

Valdés, G. (2003). *Expanding definitions of giftedness: The case of young interpreters from immigrant communities.* Mahwah, NJ: Lawrence Erlbaum.

GÓMEZ, JOEL (1945–)

Joel Gómez was born on February 24, 1945, in a rural area of the lower Rio Grande Valley of Texas. The oldest of five children, Gómez was guided as a child by his grandmother. He was a helpful son who assisted his father at an early age on the family farm. As a non-English-speaking student of Mexican descent, Gómez's primary education began in Catholic school, learning the idiosyncrasies of the English language, later graduating from Brownsville, Texas, public schools in 1963. His pastimes included playing football, participating in Boy Scouts of America, spelunking in Mexico, and other activities, all while keeping up with farm chores. Following high school graduation, he attended the local community college and later transferred to the University of Texas at Austin, earning a BA in Spanish and history and an MA in Latin American studies. This entry describes his career.

Gómez's educational career began in South Texas public schools, teaching sixth grade in a self-contained elementary classroom. He later worked as a teaching assistant at the University of Texas at Austin and served as a lecturer at the Department of Romance Languages at Pan American College in Edinburg, Texas (now University of Texas, Pan American). These experiences allowed Gómez to build on, use, and apply in new contexts the knowledge and skills gained over the years.

Before assuming the directorship of the National Clearinghouse for Bilingual Education, Gómez was hired by Education Service Center, Region XIII (ESC, XIII) in Austin, Texas. He worked on various projects during his tenure at ESC, XIII, developing the leadership and managerial skills that served him in future positions. One of these projects included coordinating a regional Spanish-language materials pilot-test project in Texas, Arizona, and New Mexico for the Spanish Curriculum Development Center (SCDC), administered from Miami, Florida. Reading materials tested by Gómez and other colleagues across the nation paved the way for the development of Spanish-language textbooks used in U.S. bilingual education programs. Other projects during his tenure included directing the Regional Technical Assistance Center, the National Dissemination and Assessment Center, and the Bilingual/Migrant Education Project. While in Austin, Gómez spearheaded the development of a test for use with migrant students for the Texas Education Agency and completed doctoral coursework in Applied Linguistics/Foreign Language Studies at the University of Texas. He also completed an EdD in Higher Education Administration from George Washington University in Washington, D.C.

With varied experiences and numerous accomplishments to his credit within the bilingual education community, Gómez is recognized for being the first director of the National Clearinghouse for Bilingual Education (NCBE) from 1977 to 1984 and from 1990 to 2000, and for successfully operating the Clearinghouse with funding totaling more than $24 million, under both Democratic and Republican administrations.

As NCBE director, Gómez was instrumental in introducing the bilingual education community to the technological changes the educational field now takes for granted. In this way, it was possible to meet the information needs of teachers and administrators serving the educational requirements of English language learners (ELLs) across the nation in the most expeditious manner. His enthusiastic style and high energy guided an initial staff of five in Roslyn, Virginia, during the first year of the Clearinghouse, with little more than unbridled enthusiasm and an 800 telephone number. Gómez is responsible for taking a start-up project with minimal funding, turning it into a highly recognized, comprehensive, and respected repository of information on the education of non-English-speaking students, and establishing an information delivery system on which millions of people in the United States and other countries rely on a daily basis.

Throughout his career, Gómez has maintained an interest and experienced success in competing for federal funds; working with and on an international education project; publishing; serving on local, national, and international advisory boards and commissions; presenting at conferences and meetings; consulting; and providing technical assistance in his areas of expertise. In all of these positions, Gómez has commanded respect from his colleagues and is frequently recognized publicly by George Washington University for his abilities in procuring a number of federally sponsored projects. The NCBE is housed at the George Washington University, now the National Clearinghouse for English Language Acquisition and Language Instruction Educational Programs (NCELA).

Gómez, the father of two daughters and one son, now serves as interim associate dean for research in the Graduate School for Education and Human Development at George Washington University, where he is also an associate professor of Educational Leadership, director of the Institute for Education Studies, and principal investigator and coprincipal investigator for numerous and varied projects, including the NCELA.

Minerva Gorena

See also National Clearinghouse for Bilingual Education

Further Readings

Futrell, M. H., Gómez, J., & Bedden, D. (2003). Teaching the children of a new America: The challenge of diversity. *Phi Delta Kappan, 84*(5), 381–385.

Gómez, J. (1998). *An analysis of federally funded bilingual education personnel preparation programs: The perception of higher education administrators on the ability of faculty to prepare teachers to work with language minority students.* Unpublished paper, George Washington University, Washington DC.

Web Sites

National Clearinghouse for English Language Acquisition and Language Instruction Educational Programs: http://www.ncela.gwu.edu

GÓMEZ, SEVERO (1924–2006)

Severo Gómez, a descendant of Plácido Benavides, the "Paul Revere" of the Texas War for Independence, was born on January 18, 1924, the seventh of nine children, to Severo and Paula Hinojosa Gómez in Woodsboro, Refugio County, Texas.

The younger Severo Gómez had a long history in education in Texas. He graduated as salutatorian in the class of 1942 at Woodsboro High School and entered the school of education at Texas College of Arts and Industries (Texas A & I) in Kingsville (now Texas A & M University) the fall of that year. His college education was interrupted by World War II when he entered the army. He served from 1943 to 1946 in the European Theater. Upon discharge, he returned to Texas A&I

and graduated in 1948 with a bachelor of science degree in chemistry and mathematics. In 1955, he completed a master of science degree. He taught science and math in the Benavides and Rio Grande City High Schools in Texas from 1948 until 1959. This entry describes his career.

In 1960, Gómez began an administrative career at the Texas Education Agency (TEA) in Austin and enrolled at the University of Texas at Austin, earning a PhD in educational administration in 1963. His tenure at the state department of education included serving as a consultant, assistant director of guidance and supervision, program director for science, director of the Division of Program Approvals, and state coordinator for International Education, and culminated with his 1967 appointment as the first Mexican American assistant commissioner of education, and the first head of the International and Bilingual Education department, until his retirement in 1975.

As a member of the Committee on Latin American Affairs of the Southern Association of Colleges and Schools, Gómez traveled extensively in Latin America, conducting programs in bilingual/binational schools in Brazil, Ecuador, Chile, Mexico, Costa Rica, El Salvador, Colombia, and Guatemala.

An advocate for bilingual education internationally, Gómez was largely responsible for planning, organizing, and serving as executive director of the first National Conference on Bilingual Education, held April 14 and 15, 1972, at the University of Texas at Austin. The conference, to the goal of which was the implementation and continued development of bilingual programs throughout the nation, was sponsored by the TEA, in cooperation with Education Service Center, Region XIII, and the U.S. Department of Education. The conference's closing remarks by Gómez gave a succinct summary of the state of understanding of the concept of bilingual education at that early point in its history. Gómez noted that several components mentioned during the conference should become the foundation for bilingual education programs. These included initiating children into school with instruction in their home language, providing language development and instruction of subject matter in their first and second languages, and paying attention to children forming a positive identity with respect to their cultural background. These components, as Gómez called them, served, with only minor modification, as the underpinnings of transitional bilingual education for many years to come.

Gómez's professional association memberships included the National Science Teachers Association, National Educational Association, Texas Academy of Science, Texas State Teachers Association, Phi Delta Kappa, and the International Good Neighbor Council. He was also a member of the Knights of Columbus and volunteered as a Confraternity of Christian Doctrine (CCD) teacher of Catholic teens and counselor to the Columbian Squires, the youth arm of the Knights of Columbus. He died on October 17, 2006, in Albuquerque, New Mexico, and is buried in the Texas State Cemetery in Austin.

Minerva Gorena

See also National Education Association Tucson Symposium

Further Readings

Texas Education Agency, Education Service Center Region XIII, & U.S. Office of Education. (1972). *Proceedings of the National Conference on Bilingual Education, April 14–15, 1972.* Austin, TX: Dissemination Center for Bilingual Bicultural Education—BE#001310

Web Sites

National Clearinghouse for English Language Acquisition and Language Instruction Educational Programs: http://www.ncela.gwu.edu

GONZÁLEZ, HENRY B. (1916–2000)

Congressman Henry Barbosa González was a larger-than-life personality and Democratic Representative from the state of Texas who became the unofficial, and controversial, spokesperson for Mexican Americans in Texas during a pivotal period for that population in American history. González's tenure as a public servant was marked by a passionate, and sometimes tumultuous, advocacy for the rights of minorities and the downtrodden, as described in this entry.

Born in San Antonio, Texas, to recent Mexican immigrants on May 3, 1916, Henry González attended public schools in his hometown, eventually attending both the University of Texas at Austin and San Antonio College during his undergraduate years. He later earned a law degree at St. Mary's University School of Law. Following graduation, González taught English to immigrant workers, developed a Spanish-English translation service with his father, served as a public relations officer for an insurance company, and worked as a civilian cable and radio censor for military intelligence during World War II. From 1946 to 1950, González worked as a probation officer, rising to chief officer of the Bexar County Juvenile Court by the end of his tenure.

In 1950, González entered the political arena and ran for a seat in the Texas House of Representatives. He narrowly lost the election, but won a seat on the San Antonio City Council 3 years later. During his time on the council, González proposed and passed an ordinance ending segregation in the city's public facilities. In 1956, he left for a seat in the Texas state senate, the first Mexican American elected to that body since the mid-1800s. In the senate, González gained notoriety as an outspoken opponent of racist legislation and an ardent supporter of minority rights and the poor. González also began to solidify his reputation as a sometimes irascible and obstinate legislator, and was among the most popular political figures in Texas. Perhaps a sign of things to come, in 1957 González, along with Senator Abraham Kazen, attracted national attention by leading the longest filibuster in Texas senate history, 35 hours, to defeat several racist segregation bills aimed at circumventing *Brown v. Board of Education.*

González continued his political journey in 1961, winning a special election to fill the U.S. House of Representatives vacancy caused by the resignation of Paul J. Kilday (D-Tex.), thereby becoming the first Mexican American from Texas ever to be elected to a national office. González overwhelmingly won all subsequent elections to the House, sometimes receiving as much as 90% of the votes cast or running unopposed.

Like his tenure in the Texas legislature, González's time in Washington was noted for his efforts on behalf of the rights of the disadvantaged. As a member of several committees and subcommittees—including the Subcommittee on Housing and Community Development, the Subcommittee on International Development Institutions and Finance, and the House Small Business Committee, González sponsored and supported numerous bills targeting equal economic opportunities, improved education and public housing programs, higher minimum wages, protection of benefits for workers, and expanded industry for San Antonio. He was also a member, and after 1988 chairman, of the House Banking, Finance, and Urban Affairs Committee, a position he used to impose tighter controls over the savings and loan industry, increase accessibility to credit to small businesses, strengthen anti-money-laundering laws, and make the Federal Reserve more publicly accountable.

Though he never ran on a Hispanic platform, González was actively involved in many Hispanic causes. He was national cochairman of the Viva Kennedy Clubs in 1960 and took an active role in the Viva Johnson movement 4 years later. In 1964, he helped end the Mexican *bracero* program, an agricultural guest worker program, believing it held down U.S. agricultural wages and created poor working conditions. He attended the annual Mexico–U.S. Interparliamentary Conference and served as special liaison representative on Latin American affairs on the House Banking, Finance, and Urban Affairs Committee. González also supported legislation that led to the 1968 Bilingual Education Act and its subsequent reauthorizations, though he urged for expansion of the act to provide for children whose native language was not Spanish. He also helped form the Congressional Hispanic Caucus in 1976, but later dropped out because he did not want to be identified solely by his ethnicity.

Representative González was no stranger to controversy while in Congress. He sometimes took to the House floor for lengthy harangues on abuses by the federal government, sought the impeachments of Presidents Ronald Reagan and George H. W. Bush, and feuded with Reagan administration Secretary of Housing and Urban Development Samuel R. Pierce Jr. over increasing low-cost housing. González also abruptly resigned his chairmanship of the House Select Committee on Assassinations, complaining its work was tied to organized crime. But though he was a hero to many Mexican Americans, González also was criticized during the Chicano Movement in the 1960s and 1970s by groups—particularly the Mexican American Youth Organization in Texas and its offspring, La Raza Unida Party—that thought he had rejected his heritage and was too conservative for their interests.

In 1988, González, age 82, retired from the U.S. House of Representatives for health reasons. Not the typical congressman—González avoided the social scene and eschewed the usual Washington garb for polyester suits and florid ties—his remarkable 37-year career in Congress is remembered for his colorful disposition, inexorable legislating, and ardent defending of equal rights for the disadvantaged. "Henry B" as he was known to friend and foe alike died on November 29, 2000.

Gregory Pearson

See also Bilingual Education as Language Policy; Latino Civil Rights Movement; Appendix D

Further Readings

Brown v. Board of Education, 347 U.S. 483 (1954).

Library of Congress, *Hispanic Americans in Congress, 1822–1995: Henry B. González.* Retrieved from http://www.loc.gov/rr/hispanic/congress/gonzalez.html

Marquis, C. (2000, November 29). Henry González, 84; Served 37 years in House. *New York Times,* p. A33.

Meier, M. S., & Gutiérrez, M. (2003). *The Mexican American experience: An encyclopedia.* Westport, CT: Greenwood.

Meier, M. S., Serri, C. F., & García, R A. (1997). *Notable Latino Americans: A biographical dictionary.* Westport, CT: Greenwood.

U.S. Government Printing Office. (1967). *Hearings before the special subcommittee on bilingual education of the committee on labor and public welfare, ninetieth congress, first session on s.428, part 2.* Washington, DC: Author.

GONZÁLEZ, JOSUÉ M. (1941–)

Josué M. González was born in a small town in the lower Rio Grande Valley of Texas, where his family had been established for several generations. As he put it:

> We were never immigrants; it was the border that moved over to make us Americans. We've been here so long I even had a great-grandfather who fought for the Union Army during the Civil War. But the accent marks are still on my name.

There are interesting parallels between the professional career of Josué M. González and bilingual education. He earned his BA degree from Texas A&I

(now A&M) University in 1963, just about the time the first bilingual education program was starting in Dade County, Florida. In 1967, he was being awarded his master's degree from the same institution at about the time the Senate hearings leading to the Bilingual Education Act were being held. In May 1974, shortly after the *Lau v. Nichols* decision was announced, he received his EdD in educational leadership from the University of Massachusetts at Amherst. Today, after more than 40 years in education, González is the general editor of this encyclopedia and professor of educational leadership and policy studies at Arizona State University.

Bilingual education has figured prominently in González's life and career, as described in this entry. Born and raised within walking distance of the Mexican border, he claims that as a child he always assumed bilingualism was the norm, rather than the exception. He learned to read in Spanish before he entered first grade. As a consequence, he was allowed to skip "Primary," an extra year that was automatically added to the school career of most Latinos in Texas at the time. Long before bilingual education became the core content for his career in education, he had the privilege of having Spanish-speaking teachers and principals in his nearly all-Hispanic hometown in South Texas.

González started his formal career as a high school teacher of French, English, and Spanish, but he taught only a few years before heading off to help develop and promote bilingual education. "Every program was a new battle," he recalls, "but the continuing litany of obstacles we faced only helped to cement ever more firmly the sense that we were doing the right thing." In 1969, when most of the Mexican American high school students in Crystal City, Texas, walked out of school in early December because of discriminatory practices by teachers, González mobilized friends and colleagues in San Antonio to spend their holidays in Crystal City tutoring youngsters who were concerned about missing school. "We taught classes that the high school didn't even have," he remembers, "like using the slide rule, which is now a museum piece, but at that time a slide rule swinging from your belt and a trigonometry book under your arm meant you were on your way to becoming an engineer, and many Chicano youngsters wanted to do that. I think we helped them see that this was possible even though their school had no trigonometry teacher at the time."

As the student walkout drew to a close in January, the school board was adamant that the students could not return to school without losing a letter grade for the semester. Outraged, the students produced a list of the courses and instructors they had worked with during the break, including distinguished professors in several fields. The school board relented. "It was a spiritual experience," recalls González. "The families knew they were doing something important and so did the volunteer teachers. It was a Christmas like none I have experienced before or since."

The Crystal City walkout and the role of the visiting teachers from around the area were a watershed in Texas education. In the spring of 1970, the all-White school board was voted out of office and young Chicanos, led by José Angel Gutiérrez, assumed control of their local schools. The students who had participated in the walkout went on to college in unprecedented numbers. Most chose careers in education, social work, and politics. Although the Texas walkout did not receive as much national attention as the Los Angeles walkout, its impact was enormous. The Crystal City schools soon hired a dynamic Chicano superintendent, and bilingual education became a permanent part of the curriculum. Inspired by the Crystal City example, many communities followed suit, assuming greater control over school boards throughout the state. Today, Texas has more Latino school board members than any other state, and bilingual education flourishes.

González was the first Mexican American teacher ever hired in the first school district in which he taught. Later, he became the first Chicano professor ever tenured at Southern Methodist University. When the U.S. Department of Education was organized by President Jimmy Carter, González became the first director of the Office of Bilingual Education and Minority Languages Affairs (OBEMLA). From this experience, he recalls,

Arguments with fellow bureaucrats over the purposes of bilingual education helped to sharpen my argumentation skills. They would insist that its purpose was to teach English and nothing more. I would counter that to ignore the child's home language and not nurture it creates unnecessary barriers between those children and their parents and grandparents. I argued that government had no business doing that to its people. I guess I was advocating for dual-language immersion programs even before we invented a name for them.

During his tenure at OBEMLA, González is especially proud of having created the Deans' Grant Program, a program through which universities could hire tenure-track young professors and get funding support from Title VII of the Elementary and Secondary Education Act (ESEA) with which to help them do it. "We were creating leadership people," he claims, "many of whom are still around today." Among the leadership positions he has held in his career of more than 40 years, he has been president of the National Association for Bilingual Education and has served on several advisory committees and commissions. He has received numerous awards and recognitions for this work. After his Washington experience, he served as associate superintendent of schools for the Chicago Public Schools, and subsequently, as vice chancellor for Planning, Development and Research for the City Colleges of Chicago, the city's community college system. In addition to teaching appointments at Southern Methodist University in Dallas and Chicago State University, he has taught at Teachers College, Columbia University in New York City. González was one of the founders of the Mexican and American Solidarity Foundation, a binational operating foundation.

González currently teaches at Arizona State University, where he directs the Southwest Center for Education Equity and Language Diversity. He is active in a number of binational education projects between the United States and Mexico. "Ten percent of all Mexicans now live in the United States," he says. "It makes no sense to leave that country out of the equation when it comes to finding educational opportunities for Mexican youngsters. Binational people are a new phenomenon, and they differ from traditional immigrants. No country can afford to ignore the 10% of their population with the best education and the greatest economic power. We need to work with Mexican institutions to create optimum ways of helping them adjust to living in two countries."

Coni Batlle

See also Hispanic Population Growth; Office of Bilingual Education and Minority Languages Affairs; Transnational Students

Further Readings

Lau v. Nichols, 414 U.S. 563 (1974).

González, J. M. (1993). School meanings and cultural bias. *Education and Urban Society, 25*(3), 254–269.

González, J. M. (1994). Bilingual education: A review of policy and ideologies. In R. Rodríguez, N. J. Ramos, & J. A. Ruiz-Escalante (Eds.), *Compendium of readings in bilingual education: Issues and practice*s (pp. 3–13). San Antonio: Texas Association for Bilingual Education.

González, J. M. (1994). Spanish as a second language: Adding language to the discourse of multicultural education. In F. Rivera (Ed.), *Reinventing urban education: Multiculturalism and the social context of schooling* (pp. 257–277). New York: Institute for Urban and Minority Education.

González, J. M. (2006). Urge educar a los mexicanos que se van, no só̱lo a los que se quedan [It is urgent to educate Mexicans who leave, not only those who stay]. In D. González-Casanova (Ed.), *Los mexicanos de aquí y allá: Problemas comunes. Memoria del Segundo Foro de Reflexión Binacional* [Mexicans from here and there: Common issues. Proceedings of the Second Forum of Binational Reflection] (Vol. 1, pp. 125–135). México: Senado de la República, Fundación Solidaridad Mexicano-Americana.

González, J. M., & Darling-Hammond, L. (1997). *New concepts for new challenges: Professional development for teachers of immigrant youth*. Washington, DC: Center for Applied Linguistics.

GRAMMAR-TRANSLATION METHOD

The grammar-translation method is a language teaching method developed during the 18th and 19th centuries in Germany. It is sometimes called the *classical method* because its basic framework was adopted from the traditional method for teaching the classical languages, Latin and Greek. Generally, the classical languages were taught by reading and translating texts extracted from classical literature, and the grammar-translation method was not much different from that, notwithstanding some unique features discussed later in this entry.

For centuries, Latin was a dominant language in many areas such as religion, education, commerce, and so on; thus, it was widely studied. Even after modern European languages such as French, Italian, and English replaced Latin in those areas and Latin ceased to be spoken, learning Latin and Greek was still considered valuable and prestigious, with the justification that the analysis of its grammar and rhetoric was beneficial to mental discipline and intellectual development. The grammar-translation method was used to teach these classical languages, and it was later extended to include modern languages as well. This entry describes the grammar-translation method's development, approaches, and use in the classroom

Origin and Development

According to Anthony Howatt, the grammar-translation method was developed to teach classical languages to secondary schoolchildren at Prussian *Gymnasien,* in Germany, or, more accurately, in Prussia; hence, *Prussian method* is another name for this methodology. The classical method was not considered appropriate for young children because it was a scholastic approach to language learning for highly educated individuals who were trained to read foreign-language texts by applying grammar rules to their reading. However, because people were familiar with this traditional method, it became the basic framework of the grammar-translation method, with some slight modifications. One such modification is that the literature texts used in teaching classical languages were replaced with sentences containing grammar rules that were the focus of each lesson. Inevitably, some sentences were made up artificially and became less meaningful, which became one of the drawbacks of the method.

In England, a change in the educational system enhanced the distribution of the grammar-translation Method. In the mid-19th century, a public examination system was created and justified as a way to maintain the educational standards of the middle class and the universities that controlled the system. As local schools introduced modern European languages into their curriculum, they had to demonstrate that learning those languages was as demanding and mentally beneficial as learning Latin or Greek. This pressure forced language teachers and textbook writers to follow the methods for the classical languages, and this meant that the grammar rules became thoroughly listed; accuracy in the rules of grammar was emphasized, and oral skills were not a focus in the teaching of a foreign language.

Howatt explained that the earliest textbook of the grammar-translation method was a French series for German speakers, written by Johann Valentin Meidinger, whose work became a model for the foreign-language textbooks published during the 19th and early 20th centuries. Some characteristics of this book were the inclusion of several exercises at the sentence level, translating into and out of the foreign language. Sample sentences with grammar rules were presented, and it was thought that the language learners understood the grammar rules in a clearer way in this format. Also, the grammar points were presented one by one, in a sequential, systematic order. Although Meidinger's framework was altered by successive textbook writers for teaching various languages, the general framework of those books in the grammar-translation method were the following: (a) one or two grammar rules per lesson, (b) an explicit explanation of the rules, (c) a vocabulary list from the sentences used in the lessons, and (d) phrases and sentences for practicing translation by applying the grammar rules in the lesson.

New Approaches to Language Learning

During the 19th century, new developments in transportation allowed closer access to European countries, and people were able to travel from one continent to another with greater ease. For example, many Europeans migrated to the United States. This created a demand for learning languages for the purpose of communicating rather than for reading and appreciating literary texts. In addition, during the late 19th century, industrialization created a new class of language learners who did not have academic training for language learning, but had a need for oral proficiency in languages other than their own. The grammar-translation method was not an effective tool for meeting their needs. In the mid- and late 19th century, as the grammar-translation method was questioned and rejected, textbook writers and language teachers had to look for new approaches to language teaching. Some of the new ideas about how to teach a language were the following:

- Spoken language should be primary; listening and speaking should come earlier than reading and writing.
- Grammar can be taught better through an inductive approach, which means that students should practice the grammar rules in context before the teacher explains it explicitly.
- Translating the text from the target language to the native language should not be encouraged because students learn a language better when they associate new meanings within the target language.

These ideas led to the development of naturalistic approaches to language learning. Learning a foreign language was considered the same as acquiring a first language, and the natural method and the direct method developed out of that principle.

Grammar-Translation Method in Language Classrooms

In a language classroom setting, the following steps would be taken using a grammar-translation methodology. First, the chapter or lesson begins with the presentation of grammatical points. Then a text is read, in which some sentences contain the grammar rules of the lesson focus. After every paragraph or each page of the text, simple comprehensive questions are listed to determine whether students understand the text. The teacher may ask a student to read the text aloud and either the student or the teacher translates the text as they read it. New words or phrases from the reading are listed with their equivalent in the students' native language next to or below the text. Accurate pronunciation and intonation are not important. Students are supposed to memorize and be able to explain the grammar rules of the target language. Many of the sentences used for exercises where students apply the grammar rules of the lesson can be so artificial that native speakers of the target language would never produce those sentences. The native language is used mostly for instruction. Usually only some activities such as reading the text aloud, reading vocabulary lists, or dictation time will ask students to use the spoken target language.

The grammar-translation method places a heavy bias on written work and excludes oral production. It includes little or no spoken communication or listening comprehension. This method emphasizes the rote memorization of vocabulary words and study of the explicit rules of grammar. According to Jack Richards and Theodore Rodgers, it is a method without a theory in areas such as linguistics, psychology, or education. However, the method is still used in many parts of the world today, with a greater or lesser modification from that of the 19th century, particularly in contexts where understanding the literary texts is deemed more important than speaking and listening in the target language, and where people do not have much contact with the speakers of the target language. Richards and Rodgers also attribute its popularity to the fact that the grammar-translation method does not require great skill by teachers. Despite the emergence and use of new methodologies, the historical foundations of the grammar-translation method provide valuable insights to situate and understand current practices in language instruction.

Hye Jong Kim

See also Audio-Lingual Method; Natural Approach; Whole Language

Further Readings

Howatt, A. P. R. (1984). *A history of English language teaching.* Oxford, UK: Oxford University Press.

Kelly, L. (1969). *25 Centuries of language teaching.* Rowley, MA: Newbury House.

Larsen-Freeman, D. (1986). *Techniques and principles of language teaching.* Oxford, UK: Oxford University Press.

Richards, J., & Rodgers, T. (2001). *Approaches and methods in language teaching* (2nd ed.). Cambridge, UK: Cambridge University Press.

Rivers, W. M. (1981). *Teaching foreign-language skills* (2nd ed.). Chicago: University of Chicago Press.

GUERRERO, ADALBERTO (1929–)

Adalberto "Beto" Guerrero was a member of a small group of educators in Tucson, Arizona, in the 1950s and 1960s who have been called "pioneers of bilingual education" because of their influence on the passage of the federal Bilingual Education Act in 1968. Other members of the group were Paul Allen, Rosita Cota, Martina García Durán-Cerda, Henry "Hank" Oyama, Paul Streif, and María Urquides. Guerrero's life and career are described in this entry.

Guerrero was born on December 11, 1929, in Bisbee, Arizona, one of seven children of Ramón Quiñones Guerrero and Guadalupe Méndez Guerrero. Ramón Guerrero was an underground miner who survived the Depression by augmenting his income from sporadic mining work by selling scrap metals, bricklaying, grave digging, selling door to door, and storekeeping. When war threatened in Europe in the 1930s, full-time underground employment was ensured. Subsequently, because of persistent inequities and racial discrimination, he became deeply involved in the union movement, a legacy of which Beto Guerrero is extremely proud. Guadalupe and Ramón instilled in their seven children a love of reading through her graphic narrations of stories and novels, fairy and folk tales, historical anecdotes, riddles, and games, as Beto Guerrero later recalled.

Guerrero dropped out of high school in 1944, his freshman year, to work at Fort Huachuca. He returned in 1945 but quit for good after completing one year, to follow "the only life for a real man, working underground." He married his wife, Ana, in November 1950, and was inducted into the army in January 1951. After his discharge in 1953, he returned to mining. At the urging of his father and his wife, Guerrero applied for and was granted admission to the University of Arizona without a high school diploma. Working nights at Hughes Aircraft, and studying days, like many other married University of Arizona students, Guerrero received a bachelor's degree in education in 1957 and began teaching at Pueblo High School in 1958.

At the time, Pueblo had only one additional full-time Spanish teacher who became a mentor and friend to the novice teacher. Although approximately 50% of the school's students were native speakers of Spanish, they were systematically placed, with disastrous results, Guerrero recalled, in classes designed for students learning Spanish as a second language. Consequently, with the encouragement and guidance of his mentor, Guerrero initiated a 4-year program of Spanish for Spanish speakers. He believed that if he could instill in the students pride about their linguistic and cultural origins, they would visualize themselves as succeeding in other subjects as well.

As a young man in Bisbee, Guerrero had noticed that the most fulfilled and successful people were those who were aware of and comfortable with their Mexican cultural and linguistic roots. In contrast, those who were embarrassed about being Mexican and speaking Spanish, and who had abandoned their culture and language to assimilate, ironically, were still rejected by the Anglo-Saxon work world, as Patricia Preciado Martin explains in her historical account of bilingual education in Tucson. Guerrero felt that his own cultural identity was strengthened through the academic study of Spanish, Mexican, and Latin American literature. He wanted to give his Pueblo High School students the same feeling of security by studying and learning the cultures and languages of Mexico and the United States.

The new program at Pueblo was so successful that enrollment by Spanish speakers increased dramatically. Indeed, Guerrero and his colleagues at the high school soon saw that the graduates of the Spanish Honors classes were excelling in their other classes as well, including English and history.

In 1962, because of his success at Pueblo High School, Guerrero was asked to teach a methods course for teachers of advanced Spanish at the University of Arizona National Defense Education Act (NDEA) Summer Institute in Guadalajara, Mexico. In 1963, he was invited to teach full time at the university, dividing his time between the Romance Languages Department and the College of Education. He maintained his connections to Pueblo, however, and continued to develop the curriculum for the Spanish for Spanish speakers course at the school. He left Pueblo High in 1969.

In 1965, several coincidental events set in motion a national dialogue about the need for federal bilingual education funds. First, the Pueblo High School course was used as the model for the first NDEA Bilingual Education Institute for teachers of English as a Second Language (ESL), and for teachers of Spanish to native speakers. Second, Pueblo received the "Pace Maker" Award from the National Education Association's (NEA) *Parade Magazine* because of the academic success of many of its minority students. Finally, Monroe Sweetland, NEA's West Coast legislative consultant, learned about the Spanish classes from Urquides and suggested forming a group to explore and publicize other innovative programs for Spanish-speaking students in the Southwest. As a result, the Tucson-NEA Survey on the Teaching of Spanish to the Spanish-speaking was created. The group's goal was to search out successful programs such as the one at Pueblo; the group divided into teams and began to visit exemplary programs in the five southwestern states that combined special instruction in Spanish and English. Initial contacts for the visits had been made that summer in the University of Arizona's first Institute for Bilingual Education, in which some of the Tucson teachers had participated. Consequently, the Tucson-NEA Survey educators began to visit the programs of colleagues they had met at the institute.

Although the team visited programs similar to the Spanish Honors program at Pueblo High School, it soon became clear that there were successful bilingual programs for much younger learners in which instruction was in Spanish, with English introduced gradually. Team members realized they needed to publicize these programs as well. When the group members reassembled, they wrote an account of their visits. Their report, published in June 1966, was called *The Invisible Minority*. All of the survey members— Guerrero, Urquides, Oyama, Cota, Durán-Cerda, and Streif—contributed equally to the report.

Shortly thereafter, Sweetland asked Urquides to represent the group at a press conference called by the NEA in Washington, D.C., for the release of the report. Urquides insisted that Guerrero attend in her place because she wanted him to be exposed to experiences such as she had enjoyed. The press event lasted almost 2 hours, during which more than 20 reporters asked questions about Mexican American students. Guerrero recalled that most of the reporters seemed unaware that Native Americans were not the only minority group in the western United States.

Because of the severe lack of information that most people—including congressional officials—had about Mexican Americans, a national symposium was organized in October of that year. The symposium focused on the educational condition of Spanish-speaking students in the Southwest, and potential solutions to academic underachievement. Teachers from schools the group had visited throughout the Southwest came to Tucson. The strong consensus emerging from the symposium was the need for bilingual education programs for this population.

Also attending the Tucson Symposium were Senators Ralph Yarborough (D-Tex.) and Joseph Montoya (D-N.M.) and Congressman Morris Udall (D-Ariz.). In 1967, largely as a result of having attended the conference in Tucson, Yarborough sponsored Congressional hearings on the need for federal attention to Mexican American students; Guerrero testified before the Special Subcommittee on Bilingual Education in support of Senate Bill 428, which became Title VII or The Bilingual Education Act, of the Elementary and Secondary Education Act. The bill became law on January 4, 1968.

Although many people participated and were active in the passage of the bill, Guerrero credits Sweetland as the individual most responsible for the enactment of the Bilingual Education Act. Sweetland's immensely important role was finally recognized in 2004 at the National Association for Bilingual Education annual conference in Albuquerque, New Mexico. In 1970, Guerrero received the NEA's Human Rights Award for his work at Pueblo High School, his contribution to the NEA-Tucson Survey, and his Congressional testimony (delivered partly in Spanish). After a brief period at Pima Community College where he helped develop the bilingual education program, he returned to the University of Arizona to continue teaching. From 1973 to 1975, Guerrero served as the first Chicano assistant dean of students, a critical time when university attitudes were changing about minority students in general and Spanish-speaking students in particular. At the time, the relationship between the Tucson Chicano community and the university was often contentious, but Guerrero's work as assistant dean of students established the foundations for the current University of Arizona Office of Chicano/Hispano Student Affairs.

For the next 2 years, Guerrero served as chair of the Mexican American Studies Committee, which evolved into the Mexican American Studies and Research Center. He resigned in 1977, citing inadequate support and funding from the university administration. He returned to the Romance Languages Department to resume his teaching career as a lecturer, a position he held until his retirement in 1994.

Guerrero has been the recipient of many awards throughout his long career, including the U.S. Commission on Civil Rights Award in 1975, Outstanding Faculty Contributor to Minority Student Education (University of Arizona) in 1986, and the National Association for Bilingual Education Pioneer Award in 1990. Guerrero was further honored in 2002 when the Adalberto Guerrero Middle School, in Tucson, was named after him. He remains active at the Guerrero School, and in the Tucson community at large. In addition to his contributions to the Bilingual Education Act, he is proud of the Spanish for Native Speakers courses he established at Pueblo High School and the Spanish for bilingual educators and Children's literature in Spanish courses at the University of Arizona.

Mary Carol Combs

See also National Education Association Tucson Symposium; Oyama, Henry; Title VII Elementary and Secondary Education Act, Key Historical Marker; Title VII, Elementary and Secondary Education Act, 1967 Senate Hearings; Urquides, María

Further Readings

Guerrero, A., Oyama, H., & Urquides, M. (n.d.). *Letter of endorsement for the Tucson Unified School District (TUSD) comprehensive plan for alternate language.* Retrieved from http://tusdstats.tusd.k12.az.us/planning/biled/biledplan.htm

Guerrero, A., Saldate, M., & Baldanegro, S. (1999). Chicano: The term and its meanings. *Arizona Association of*

Chicanos for Higher Education Conference Newsletter. Retrieved from http://www.aache.org/news0999.htm

Jones, M. (2000, November 3). UA student affairs groups argues against Prop. 203. *Arizona Daily Wildcat.* Retrieved from http://wc.arizona.edu/papers/94/54

National Education Association. (1966). *The invisible minority . . . pero no vencibles.* Washington, DC: Author.

Preciado Martin, P. (1995). *Con mucho corazón: An oral history of 25 years of nurturing bilingual/multicultural education in TUSD.* Tucson, AZ: Tucson Unified School District.

Smith, P. H. (2001). Community language resources in dual language schooling. *Bilingual Research Journal, 25*(3), 375–405.

Smith, P. H. (2002). "Ni a pocha va a llegar": Minority language loss and dual language schooling in the U.S.–Mexico borderlands. *Southwest Journal of Linguistics, 21,* 165–183.

H

Hakuta, Kenji (1952–)

Kenji Hakuta, an experimental psycholinguist, is a scholar recognized internationally for his work in the areas of psycholinguistics, bilingualism, and English language acquisition by immigrant populations. This entry describes his research contributions to these fields.

Hakuta was born in Kamakura (Kanagawa Prefecture), Japan, on December 19, 1952. He received a bachelor of arts, magna cum laude in psychology and social relations, and earned his doctorate in experimental psychology, both from Harvard University. He has held academic positions at Yale University, the University of California at Santa Cruz, and Stanford University. He was the Founding Dean of the School of Sciences, Humanities and Arts at University of California, erced, from 2003 to 2006, and is currently a professor of education at Stanford University. He has received more than 21 grants to fund his areas of research from 1979 to the present.

Hakuta has concentrated much of his research in the areas of bilingualism, bilingual education policy, and second-language acquisition, and currently focuses on affirmative action in higher education. In his book *Mirror of Language,* he explores the history of bilingualism and on the process of obtaining a second language on both the child and adult levels. Though the book was written 20 years ago, Hakuta sheds light on the real, literal meaning of bilingualism: how the bilingual mind works in the context of thinking, speaking, and learning with a bilingual brain. He posits that strong appropriate bilingual programs can aid students in developing fluency in their own home or native language and master a second language as well.

Another worthy contribution to the literature of second-language acquisition is the book he coauthored with Bialystok, *In Other Words: The Science and Psychology of Second Language Acquisition,* in 1994. Hakuta and Bialystok examine the process of second-language acquisition with a particular focus on why it may be easier for some individuals to learn a second language, but others find it more difficult. The authors present a thorough review of the theoretical literature, from which they identify five aspects that influence second-language acquisition: brain, language, mind, self, and culture. The aspect of culture is addressed from the standpoint of language diversity in the schools and the implications it has for instruction, curriculum development, and policy making.

Hakuta's most recent interest is affirmative action and university access. In 2003, he coedited *Compelling Interest: Examining the Evidence on Racial Dynamics in Colleges and Universities,* with Mitchell J. Chang, Daria Witt, and James Jones. *Compelling Interest* was cited in the U.S. Supreme Court decision *Grutter v. Bollinger* (2003), a case regarding issues of race in admissions policy at the University of Michigan Law School. The text examines the complex issues involved in university access and presents stimulating discourse for the support and protection of affirmative action in university admissions. The authors posit that supporting inclusive admissions practices results in building diverse student populations in institutions of learning.

Hakuta's commitment to the education of language minorities is reflected in his research and advocacy activities for this student population. He served as an expert witness in court cases such as *Teresa P. v. Berkeley Unified School District* (1989), on behalf of the plaintiffs and the Multicultural Education Training and Advocacy, Inc. He also led the creation of the Stanford Working Group on Federal Education Programs for Limited English Proficient Students, along with Diane August in 1992. Goals of this group included the incorporation of up-to-date research in bilingual education in educational reform.

Throughout his career, Hakuta's work has been recognized with multiple honors and awards. He was named Distinguished Scholar by the Committee on the Role and Status of Minorities in Education Research and Development of the American Educational Research Association in 1993. He has been a member of the National Academy of Education since 1996, and served in the Spencer Postdoctoral Fellow Selection Committee from 1996–1999.

Nancy Sebastian Maldonado

See also Critical Period Hypothesis; Second-Language Acquisition; Stanford Working Group

Further Readings

August, D., & Hakuta, K. (1997). *Improving schooling for language-minority children.* Washington, DC: National Academy Press.

Bialystok, E., & Hakuta, K. (1994). *In other words: The science and psychology of second language acquisition.* New York: Basic Books.

Grutter v. Bollinger, 539 U.S. 306 (2003).

Hakuta, K. (1986). *Mirror of language: The debate on bilingualism.* New York: Basic Books.

Hakuta, K. (1990). Language and cognition in bilingual children. In A. Padilla, C. Valdez, & H. Fairchild (Eds.), *Bilingual education: Issues and strategies* (pp. 47–59). Newbury Park, CA: Sage.

Hakuta, K. (1993). Second-language acquisition, bilingual education, and prospects for a language-rich nation. In Council of Chief State School Officers (Eds.), *Restructuring learning: 1990 summer institute papers and recommendations* (pp. 123–131). Washington, DC: Council of Chief State School Officers.

Hakuta, K. (1995). Language minority students: Challenges and promises. In M. Higginbotham (Ed.), *What governors need to know about education reform.* Washington, DC: National Governors' Association.

Hakuta, K. (2001). A critical period for second language acquisition? In D. Bailey, J. Bruer, F. Symons, & J. Lichtman (Eds.), *Critical thinking about critical periods* (pp. 193–205). Baltimore: Paul Brookes.

Hakuta, K., Bialystok, E., & Wiley, E. (2003). Critical evidence: A test of the critical period hypothesis for second language acquisition. *Psychological Science, 14,* 31–38.

Hakuta, K., Chang, M., Witt, D., & Jones, J. (Eds.). (2003). *Compelling interest: Examining the evidence on racial dynamics in Colleges and Universities.* Stanford, CA: Stanford University Press.

Hakuta, K., & Feldman Mostafapour, E. (1996). Perspectives from the history and politics of bilingualism and bilingual education in the United States. In I. Parasnis (Ed.), *Cultural and language diversity and the deaf experience* (pp. 38–50). New York: Cambridge University Press.

Hakuta, K., Ferdman, B. M., & Díaz, R. M. (1987). Bilingualism and cognitive development: Three perspectives. In S. Rosenberg (Ed.), *Advances in applied psycholinguistics, Vol. 2: Reading, writing, and language learning* (pp. 284–319). Cambridge, UK: Cambridge University Press.

Teresa P. v. Berkeley Unified School District, 724 F. Supp. 698, 713 (N.D. Cal. 1989).

HAUGEN, EINAR (1906–1994)

Einar Ingvald Haugen was born in Sioux City, Iowa, April 19, 1906, to parents who had emigrated from Oppdal, South Trondelag, Norway, in 1899. Later, Haugen attended Morningside College in Sioux City, Iowa, for 3 years, then transferred to St. Olaf College in Northfield, Minnesota, in 1928, where he received his BA degree. In 1931, he received his PhD from the University of Illinois. A bilingual himself, he was one of the earliest scholars of bilingualism in the United States. Haugen might have taught the first known course on bilingualism in the United States at the 1949 Linguistic Institute in Ann Arbor, Michigan. There, a graduate student, Uriel Weinreich, contacted him to ask for a copy of his bibliography. The two of them, Haugen and Weinreich, can be credited with developing the academic field of bilingualism and language contact in the United States. This entry describes Haugen's research.

In 1953, Haugen published *The Norwegian Language in America: A Study in Bilingual Behavior,* the same year as Weinreich published *Languages in Contact.* Haugen's attention to Norwegian in the United States, an immigrant language, led him to study bilingualism more broadly. Haugen's 1956 work, *Bilingualism in the Americas,* established him as the reigning expert on U.S. bilingualism. The book was a survey research guide for bilingual study and included works on education, politics, psychology, and sociology in North and South America to 1970. In this book, he included a section on the education of bilingual children in the United States. His sources were mostly from the American Southwest, and the literature he surveyed focused mostly on education strategies to overcome the "language handicap" of bilingual children. Haugen, however, provided other explanations for the bilingual children's failure, including their low socioeconomic status, the inadequate schools they attended, and the shortcomings of their teachers. In this work, Haugen also supported the use of mother-tongue instruction in teaching immigrant children.

As a linguist, Haugen did much to develop the field of *language contact,* where linguistic items of one language are used in the context of another. Basing his observations on those of Leonard Bloomfield, Haugen describes different kinds of borrowings and distinguishes between *loan words,* where both the form and the meaning of the word is borrowed, as in U.S. Spanish *bildin* (for *edificio* in Spanish, "building" in English), and *loanshifts,* where only the meaning is borrowed, for example; the word *registrar* in Spanish used with the meaning of "to register," although its Spanish meaning is "to search."

Haugen's interest in the bilingual community, beyond the bilingual individual, led him to pioneer two fields that are highly relevant for bilingual education in the 21st century: that of language planning and policy, and that of ecolinguistics. The term *language planning* is usually attributed to Haugen in describing the organized efforts to prepare a normative orthography, grammar, and dictionary that could be used as a guide for people writing and speaking in a heterogeneous speech community. His 1966 book *Language Conflict and Language Planning: The Case of Modern Norwegian,* described the organized efforts to provide

a single officially authorized language norm for Norway. In 1983, Haugen proposed an overall model of the language planning process that is still useful today. Bilingual education clearly has a role in language planning, for its use in school raises the status of a language, and results in an increase in its number of users. This has been the case of, for example, the Basque Autonomous Community, where bilingual education has clearly helped stabilize Euskara (Basque) in relationship to Spanish.

In 1972, *The Ecology of Language: Essays by Einar Haugen* was published. In this work, Haugen underlines the need to study a language in its environment, in its speech community, and in its ecological context. Consequently, Haugen can be credited with pioneering a new field later called ecolinguistics. According to this view, language diversity is essential for a healthy ecosystem because local variations in languages encode local ecological knowledge. This view has supported efforts by educators to revitalize languages that are threatened. This is the case, for example, of the growing language nest schools, an example of which is the *Kohanga Reo* for Māori revitalization in New Zealand.

Haugen never focused on bilingual education itself, but his theoretical contributions to language contact, language planning, and language ecology have deeply influenced how educators think about bilingualism of children in classrooms, plan their bilingualism in teaching, and project their bilingualism in the linguistic ecosystem that surrounds them. His constructs have also helped U.S. scholars frame issues and research agendas in this field.

Ofelia García

See also Bilingualism Stages; Cognates, True and False; Continua of Biliteracy; Language Revival and Renewal; Native American Languages, Legal Support for; Social Bilingualism; Spanish Loan Words in U.S. English

Further Readings

Harris, J., Simon, E., Watkins, C., & Mitchell, S. (2001, May 24). Einar Haugen: Faculty of Arts and Sciences: Memorial Minute. *Harvard University Gazette.* Retrieved from http://www.news.harvard.edu/gazette/2001/05.24/16-haugen.html

Haugen, E. (1953). *The Norwegian language in America: A study in bilingual behavior.* Bloomington: Indiana University Press.

Haugen, E. (1956). *Bilingualism in the Americas: A bibliography and research guide.* Tuscaloosa: University of Alabama Press.

Haugen, E. (1966). *Language conflict and language planning: The case of modern Norwegian.* Cambridge, MA: Harvard University Press.

Haugen, E. (1972). *The ecology of language: Essays by Einar Haugen.* Stanford, CA: Stanford University Press.

Weinreich, U. (1953). *Languages in contact: Findings and problems.* New York: Linguistic Circle of New York.

HAYAKAWA, S. I. (1906–1992)

Samuel Ichiye Hayakawa was a professor of English semantics who was elected to the U.S. Senate for the state of California in 1976. He is known for having written the first amendment proposing the establishment of English as the official language of the United States. This entry describes Hayakawa's life and career.

Hayakawa was born on July 18, 1906, in Vancouver, Canada. His parents were Japanese immigrants who eventually returned to Japan. By his own admission, Hayakawa did not speak Japanese. Hayakawa completed a bachelor's degree at the University of Manitoba in Winnipeg in 1927. He later pursued a master's degree in English literature at McGill University in Montreal, which he obtained in 1928. Awarded a graduate fellowship for doctoral studies at the University of Wisconsin, Madison, he moved to the United States in 1929 and received his PhD in American literature in 1935. Upon graduation, he was hired as a full-time instructor by the University of Wisconsin.

In 1939, Hayakawa and his wife, Margedant Peters, moved to Chicago, where he worked as an associate professor of English at the Illinois Institute of Technology. In Chicago, he became acquainted with Alfred Korzybski, founder of the Institute of General Semantics. Hayakawa attended Korzybski's seminars and regarded Korzybski as an important influence in his own career. Hayakawa wrote a textbook with the purpose of making Korzybski's ideas accessible to the general public: *Language in Action* was first published in 1941, and

it became the Book-of-the-Month Club selection. He published a revised edition in 1949, *Language in Thought and Action.* One of the key points in his work was the emphasis on the role of a common language in the unification of a society for conducting shared work and common goals. His career as a semanticist also included a position as the first editor of the journal *ETC: A Review of General Semantics.*

In 1952, Hayakawa was granted U.S. citizenship. Shortly after, he was invited to teach at San Francisco State College. He moved with his family to California in 1955, and later became president of the college in 1968, in the midst of student strikes with demands of equity for minority groups. He attracted public attention in this position, where he established a reputation for strict leadership and a determined attitude.

After he retired from the presidency of San Francisco State in 1973, Hayakawa joined the Republican party. In 1976, he was elected to the U.S. Senate from California at the age of 70. He sponsored the first version of the English Language Amendment in 1981, which stated that English should become the official language of the United States. Although his proposed amendment never passed, in his speeches and publications Hayakawa made a case for his belief in the dangers of multilingualism for national unity. As he had stated in his publications as a semanticist, he strongly believed in the power of language to bind together individuals from different countries. He cited as alarming the cases of countries like Sri Lanka, India, and Belgium, nations divided owing to what he regarded as language riots, cultural differences unable to be resolved because individuals could not understand each other. He also tapped on the case of his native country, Canada, in the province of Québec, where the French-speaking majority was still in conflict with the English-speaking minority. He argued that unless the mastery of one common language was achieved by all groups in the society, common understanding and agreement could not be possible.

Hayakawa also addressed the role of bilingual education. He asserted that instruction in a child's native language was acceptable as long as it was transitional and geared toward the full mastery of English. It was the taxpayer's sole responsibility, he claimed, to contribute to the education of children exclusively in English, regardless of their origin. Bilingualism could lead to "binationalism," which in his view, was to be prevented at all cost. He believed it was insulting and deleterious for minority groups to be prevented from learning English.

Following the end of his term in the Senate, in 1983, Hayakawa founded the U.S. English organization, in which he served as honorary chairman. This organization continues to seek the passing of legislation making English the only official language of the United States.

Hayakawa retired to his home in Mill Valley, San Francisco, and continued writing in the field of semantics—he cowrote the fifth edition of *Language in Thought and Action* with his son, Alan. He died on February 27, 1992.

*Silvia Nogueró*n

See also Assimilation; Early Immigrants and English Language Learning; English for the Children Campaign; English-Only Organizations; Melting-Pot Theory; Official English Legislation, Favored; Official English Legislation, Position of English Teachers on; Appendix E

Further Readings

Crawford, J. (Ed.). (1992). *Language loyalties.* Chicago: University of Chicago Press.

Fox, R. (1991). A conversation with the Hayakawas. *English Journal, 80*(2), 36–40.

Hayakawa, S. I. (1949). *Language in thought and action.* New York: Harcourt.

Hayakawa, S. I. (1987). Make English official: One common language makes our nation work. *Executive Educator, 9*(1), 29, 36.

Hayakawa, S. I. (1987). Why the English language amendment? *English Journal, 76*(8), 14–16.

Hayakawa, S. I., & Hayakawa, A. R. (1990). *Language in thought and action* (5th ed.). San Diego: Harcourt Brace Jovanovich.

Heron, D. (1998). Hayakawa, Samuel Ichiye. In K. T. Jackson, K. Markoe, & A. Markoe (Eds.), *The Scribner encyclopedia of American lives* (Vol. 3, pp. 250–252). New York: Scribner's.

U.S. English. (2006). *Legislative history: Sen. Hayakawa's speech.* Retrieved from http://www.usenglish.org/inc/legislation/history/speech.asp

HERITAGE LANGUAGE EDUCATION

In the political and educational spheres, heritage language education has emerged during the past decade as an important component of language education formats in the United States. Better said, the concept has reemerged, for it has been present in American education for a long time under other names. This new attention to heritage language education reflects a series of developments in society at large, as well as within the education profession itself. Driving this reappearance are important demographic shifts in the United States, especially the rising proportion of students in the K–12 system who speak languages other than English or who come from homes with such languages in active use. The social and linguistic needs of these students, both with respect to acquiring English and maintaining their home language, have led to a reassessment of long-held assumptions about the process of second-language acquisition and best practices in teaching language. This entry reviews, in a general way, the basic elements of the concept of heritage language education and its place among other aspects of language teaching and learning.

Immigrant families with access to voice over Internet protocol telephony (VOIP), the Internet, Univision, *Al Jazeera*, and other international media no longer feel the need to abandon ancestral languages to become "good Americans." Finally, a range of scholars and government analysts, discussed further later, has begun to focus on the uses of heritage languages and their speakers as resources for promoting U.S. economic, diplomatic, and defense interests around the world.

Within the field of bilingual education, the focus on heritage languages offers a critical opportunity to break through the fossilized debate between the extremes of bilingual education versus English-only programming, Hispanic versus Anglo, and immigrant versus native-born. The discourse of heritage languages presents gentler, less abrasive positions than those that have characterized that debate. Despite—or perhaps because of—the renewed attention currently paid to heritage language education from such disparate academic and practitioner communities, important differences have emerged: They range from fundamental definitions to the issues that should drive a research agenda that can advance heritage language education in the nation.

Definitions and Debates

Debates about heritage language education in the United States and the potential it represents begin with the name of the field. Terrence Wiley cites the specific concern that Colin Baker and Sylvia Prys Jones voiced regarding the term *heritage:* This term may be too focused on the past, on ancient and remote cultures and traditions, rather than recognizing the contemporary use and future growth of modern languages in the United States. Wiley prefers the term *community language,* the analogous term used in Europe and Australia. He argues it is a more appropriate way to designate and understand the vast linguistic resources in the United States today. Ofelia García underscores the point by quoting a 17-year old Dominican student living in New York City: "*¿Lengua de mi herencia? . . . Como algo viejo, mi bisabuela.*" A rough translation: "My heritage language? . . . that sounds like something really old . . . like my great grandmother." García stresses that, in most instances, what is referred to with the term *heritage language* are living, thriving community languages.

Although no consensus has been reached regarding the most appropriate terminology, researchers widely agree that the concept of heritage languages incorporates indigenous, colonial, and immigrant languages in the United States. Spanish represents a useful case with which to elaborate this typology. Spanish was first introduced to the Americas as the colonial language of the Spanish empire. As the United States expanded, fought wars, and bought and annexed territories, Spanish-speaking citizens of Mexico suddenly found themselves living on land that now belonged to the United States. Half a century later, Puerto Rico, another Spanish-speaking country, was also annexed as booty of the Spanish American War. In this sense, then, Spanish is also an indigenous language in the United States, as speakers of the language predate the annexation of their territory to this country. More recently, of course, Spanish has become the largest immigrant language in the United States, in addition to becoming one of the three contenders for the designation of "world language," a distinction shared with Chinese and English. Josué M. González, a language policy analyst, believes that given its ranking as the fourth largest Spanish-speaking nation in the Western Hemisphere, the United States could rightly be considered a Latin American nation.

Because of the number of speakers, Spanish is a unique case. Researchers widely recognize that the term *heritage language* cannot apply in a "one-size-fits-all" way, given that the educational and linguistic needs of each of the language types, discussed earlier, vary greatly. For instance, as many indigenous languages succumb to generations of English-only policies, and in some cases face extinction, the resources and efforts needed for their revitalization are quite distinct from the maintenance needs of such languages as Spanish or Mandarin, languages that are better positioned to resist the pressures of English with increased immigration. Both of these language scenarios are different still from the educational and linguistic challenges presented by what are known as Truly Less Commonly Taught Languages, such as Armenian or Pashto, with far fewer heritage language speakers and a limited tradition of instruction in U.S. educational institutions.

Another important distinction in the field of heritage language education concerns who counts as a heritage language speaker. The question as framed by works edited by Joy Kreeft Peyton, Donald Ranard, and Scott McGinnis is largely around whether greater importance lies with one's affiliation to a particular ethnolinguistic group, or whether one has some level of proficiency in the heritage language itself. A common example used to tease out the distinction is that of African American students studying the language of their ancestors from western Africa. Even though the direct connection to the ancestral language is long past, does the students' membership and identity in this specific ethnolinguistic group qualify them as heritage language students?

The importance of this question is not just one of identity, ethnic consciousness, or pride. Guadalupe Valdés argues that the central question here is one of language acquisition. Although a student may be a member of a given ethnolinguistic group, without any knowledge of the heritage language, the student's process of learning the language will closely mirror that of any other monolingual student learning the same language. Valdés would limit the definition of "heritage speaker" to a student who is raised in a home where a language other than English is spoken and who therefore is bilingual to some degree in the heritage language and English. Including proficiency in the definition of heritage speaker is important in acknowledging that heritage speakers acquire (or reacquire) the language differently than do their monolingual peers in the land that was formerly the homeland of both. This position is supported by linguists such as Stephen Krashen, who argue that the first language is *acquired* whereas subsequent languages are *learned,* and that the processes involved differ markedly.

Scope of the Field

The increasing awareness of heritage language learners and their specific social and linguistic needs is leading the field of language education to a fundamental rethinking of many assumptions we have held about how people learn multiple languages. Two scholars in particular have taken the lead in elaborating a research agenda on the language acquisition process of heritage language speakers. Lourdes Ortega argues for applying an "ethical lens" to our research to ensure that it is socially useful and that it foregrounds the social and linguistic needs of heritage language communities on whose behalf the research is conducted. Valdés has outlined a thorough research agenda that reflects the immense diversity of social and linguistic circumstances in which heritage language speakers find themselves in the United States. Central to this research scheme is recognizing that the traditional model of second-language acquisition (i.e., of monolingual speakers) engaging in a "foreign" language) does not apply to heritage language speakers, who have some level of receptive language skills in the heritage language. Additionally, Valdés's research program challenges many of the language related ideas of traditional foreign-language curricula in privileging an idealized standard variety of the target language. Against this tradition, Valdés reminds us that many heritage language speakers are often proficient in stigmatized varieties of the heritage language (for example, urban varieties of Spanish spoken in Latin American countries versus rural varieties or Castilian Spanish from Spain). She insists that future research on heritage language acquisition must examine how heritage speakers (re-)acquire various dialects and registers of the target language, as well as considering which varieties of the heritage language are the most appropriate for instruction under what circumstances.

In addition to greater knowledge of how heritage speakers acquire and maintain their language, a second major strand of research on heritage language education concerns the programs and policies that are most effective. Wiley reminds us that language education policies that neither include nor foreground the needs of the affected community are rarely successful. One indicator of this is the long-standing mismatch between "foreign" languages taught in school and the actual languages spoken in the country. Additionally, many heritage language programs in the United States have historically existed outside the formal K–12 education system, based instead in community schools, religious institutions, or private organizations. Much of that could easily be considered part of the heritage language agenda. Therefore, researchers and practitioners intent on expanding heritage language education in this country need to begin with the community members themselves, how they use the heritage language, and how they envision the maintenance or expansion of their language.

Richard Brecht and William Rivers recount the 60-year history of federal policies promoting language instruction at the higher education level. They argue that such policies (e.g., Title VI of the Higher Education Act and the Fulbright-Hays Act) have been instrumental in ensuring the existence of programs in less commonly taught languages. More recently, the National Security Language Initiative continues that mode of dealing with less common heritage languages. Although they call for greater funding of such programs, including expansion into the K–12 system, Brecht and Rivers base their advocacy on perceived national language needs rather than on the social and language needs of the heritage language communities themselves.

Finally, heritage language education is intimately entangled in powerful ideological debates about language and language learning in the United States. The debate about the merits of bilingual education has increasingly been overwhelmed by English-only campaigns, such as Propositions 227 in California and 203 in Arizona. These highly racialized efforts at the electoral and ideological level have painted bilingual education as a threat to national unity and to academic success for language minority students, charges that remain unsubstantiated in the research literature. Many advocates of heritage language education—for example, those who have contributed to the works edited by Peyton, Ranard, and McGinnis; Heidi Byrnes; and most recently Robert Blake and Claire Kramsch—see an opportunity to harness heritage language issues to counter such campaigns by recognizing the rich linguistic diversity that exists (and has always existed) in the nation, and by framing this diversity as a question of resource conservation and management.

The second ideological aspect to heritage language education defines this resource, however, in specific ways. In the wake of the events of September 11, 2001, some scholars, such as Brecht and Rivers, and government analysts, including Secretary of Education Margaret Spellings and President George W. Bush, have defined heritage languages, and to a lesser degree their speakers, as vital resources to the United States in meeting its political, economic, and defense needs. A series of new federal policies has emerged, ranging from the recently enacted National Security Language Initiative, which appropriated $114 million for the study of "critical" languages such as Mandarin and Arabic across the K–16 spectrum, to the proposed 21st Century National Defense Education Act and the National Security Education Act. Scholars acknowledge that federal monies are needed to help expand heritage language education, but recent writings reflect growing concerns in the language education community about the consequences of narrowing the definition of linguistic resource solely to the rubric of national security.

Despite these ideological challenges, the renewed attention paid to heritage language education represents a vital opportunity to recognize, honor, and expand the vast linguistic diversity in the United States and simultaneously rethink the scope and process of language education to help develop a more deeply multilingual society.

Donald Jeffrey Bale

See also Benefits of Bilingualism and Heritage Languages; Chinese in the United States; Indigenous Language Revitalization; Japanese Language in Hawai'i; Language Revival and Renewal; Spanish, the Second National Language

Further Readings

Brecht, R. D., & Rivers, W. P. (2001). *Language and national security: The federal role in building language capacity in the U.S.* National Foreign Language Center, University of Maryland.

Blake, R., & Kramsch, C. (2007). Guest editors' introduction. *Modern Language Journal, 91,* 247–249.

Byrnes, H. (2005). Perspectives. *Modern Language Journal, 89,* 583–585.

Crawford, J. (1999). Heritage languages in America: Tapping a "hidden" resource. Retrieved from http://ourworld .compuserve.com/homepages/jwcrawford/hl.htm

García, O. (2005). Positioning heritage languages in the United States. *Modern Language Journal, 89,* 601–605.

González, J. M. (1994). Spanish as a second school language: Adding language to the discourse of multicultural education. In F. Rivera-Batiz (Ed.), *Reinventing urban education* (pp. 257–275). New York: Institute for Urban and Minority Education, Teachers College, Columbia University.

Joint National Committee for Languages & the National Council for Languages and International Studies. (n.d.). Language legislation. Retrieved from http://languagepolicy .org/legislation/index.html

Krashen, S. (1982). *Principles and practices of language acquisition.* New York: Pergamon Press.

Ortega, L. (2005). For what and for whom is our research? The ethical as transformative lens in instructed SLA. *Modern Language Journal, 89,* 427–443.

Peyton, J. K., Ranard, D. A., & McGinnis, S. (Eds.). *Heritage languages in America: Preserving a national resource.* McHenry, IL: Center for Applied Linguistics and Delta Systems.

Schmidt, R. (2007, April). *SLA and U.S. national foreign language education policy.* Paper presented at the American Association for Applied Linguistics 2007 Annual Conference, Costa Mesa, CA.

U.S. Department of Education. (2006, November 21). *Education news parents can use* [Television broadcast]. Washington, DC: Author.

Valdés, G. (2005). Bilingualism, heritage language learners, and SLA research: Opportunities lost or seized? *Modern Language Journal 89*(3), 410–426.

Valdés, G., Fishman, J. A., Chávez, R., & Pérez, W. (2006). *Developing minority language resources: The case of Spanish in California.* Clevedon, UK: Multilingual Matters.

Valdés, G., & Wiley, T. G. (2000). Editors' introduction. Heritage language instruction in the United States: A time for renewal. *Bilingual Research Journal, 24*(4), i–v.

Wiley, T. G. (2005). The reemergence of heritage and community language policy in the U.S. national spotlight. *Modern Language Journal, 89,* 594–601.

Wiley, T. G. (2007). The foreign language "crisis" in the U.S.: Are heritage and community languages the remedy? *Critical Inquiry in Language Studies, 4*(2–3), 179–205.

HERITAGE LANGUAGES IN FAMILIES

Strong families are a vital element for healthy individuals and societies. For millions of immigrant families, intergenerational tensions and cultural conflicts often pose problems between the children, who are quickly embracing the new linguistic and cultural ways of the host country, and their parents, who tend to retain their native ways longer. These tensions can be exacerbated by other communication barriers for dominant heritage language-speaking parents and their English-dominant children. An often overlooked resource is the home or *heritage* language, which can be a wonderful support and bridge between such families as they navigate acculturation in different ways and at different rates, as described in this entry.

A review of research on the characteristics of healthy families conducted by W. Robert Beavers in 1977 and Ted Bowman in 1983 reveals that strong families share the following nine important traits: caring and appreciation, time together, encouragement, commitment, communication, ability to cope with change, spirituality, community and family ties, and clear roles. Individuals from strong families also have greater family pride, supporting the development of self-identity, self-esteem, and self-confidence. Importantly, all the factors that contribute to the formation and support of a strong family are in one way or another related with the ability to communicate. According to Michal Tannenbaum and Pauline Howie, three language patterns emerge among immigrant families in the United States: (1) Both parents and children speak English, (2) the parents speak the heritage language and the children speak in English, or (3) both parents and children speak the heritage language. Although the second is the more frequently observed pattern among immigrant families, Lily Wong Fillmore has found that it leads to great limitations in the range and depth of communication between parents and their children. The third pattern is the ideal for immigrant parents and children to develop to strengthen and reinforce strong resilient families.

The use of heritage languages serves a critical role in enabling family communication and enhancing the quality of family relationships and support for children. Proficiency in the heritage language among children of immigrants sustains and enhances communication with parents and with grandparents, who may be the primary caregivers while the parents work. When children do not have the heritage language skills to adequately communicate with their parents, they often experience a sense of frustration and are less likely to seek parental advice. This frustration and emotional distance tend to increase as children reach adolescence and develop a greater need for parental guidance. Without the ability to communicate with their parents, children do not have a means to gain guidance on issues of sex and career trajectories, for example. A lack of home support can result in increased teenage pregnancies and participation in youth gangs as young people seek acceptance outside the family circle.

When family members do not talk to each other beyond routine daily matters, the parent's guiding role can be minimized and even lost. The child-parent relationship may be reversed, and the parental authority may dwindle, all leading to the widening of the generation gap and an increase in family conflict. On the other hand, when grandparents/parents and children continue to speak the heritage language together, they are likely to spend more time together. Studies by Tannenbaum and Marina Berkovich show that time together creates opportunities for sharing meaningful experiences, fashioning family relationships and forming emotional bonds between grandparents/parents and children. By communicating together in the heritage language, parents and children engage in questioning, answering, negotiation, problem solving, exchanging information, showing love and affection, coming together in times of crisis, developing trust, and lending support. These processes are central for opening channels of communication between parents and children to discuss academic, moral, and social issues.

Wong Fillmore emphasizes that when teachers encourage immigrant parents to use English at home to facilitate English language development for their children, they may be doing a disservice to immigrant families. She explains that the limited range of interactions that are possible for immigrant parents and children with limited English skills can negatively affect their cognitive development, and deny access to the rich cultural resources available at home. Thus, it is essential that children use the heritage language in the home and continue to enhance their heritage language skills.

Heritage language maintenance also nurtures family pride. Families who share spiritual and cultural values and discuss family history pave the way for children to develop a better understanding and appreciation for who they are, that is, their group identity. Inquiries by Jean Phinney, Irma Romero, Monica Nava, and David Huang show a strong relationship between ethnic identity, self-esteem, and academic achievement; Phinney and colleagues found that positive ethnic identity is a significant predictor for high self-esteem and greater academic performance. This makes sense because the more pride and comfort one has about one's origins and family background, the stronger basis exists for social and academic achievement. According to Rubén Rumbaut, immigrant children often experience feelings of embarrassment toward their culture, parents, and home language during adolescence because they symbolize markers that prevent them from being able to fully assimilate with their mainstream peers. Thus, if left unattended, embarrassment in one's family is likely to lead to a distancing from their family and their home culture. Jean Mills points out that limited use of the heritage language can cause parents to be seen as irrelevant or invisible in their children's lives, whereas continued use of the heritage language in the home contributes to a child's sense of family belonging, cultural identity, and ethnic pride. According to Joshua A. Fishman, the encouragement of ethnic pride, which is intricately tied to one's attitudes toward the heritage language, is a critical element in the lives of children of immigrants.

Finally, heritage language and its maintenance are significant for strengthening family cohesion and community ties, which also contribute to the development of healthy family life. Research by Phinney, Anthony Ong, and Tanya Madden has shown that the loss of the child's heritage language skills and the concomitant emphasis on English-only use is detrimental to a family's cohesion. Shiow-Huey Luo and Richard Wiseman found that in families where parents do not have strong English language proficiency, limited use of the heritage language between parents and children, or the absence of the heritage language, creates fragile families, who are more likely to experience emotional distance, tenuous relationships, and greater intergenerational conflict. The heritage language enables families to share cultural and spiritual values and beliefs and thus, create stronger familial ties. The sharing of the heritage language supports the learning in the home.

Many immigrant families are nested within heritage communities and social networks. The strengthening of families also depends on how well an individual is able to and willing to interact and accept the values of the community. Further studies by Alejandro Portes and Richard Schauffler specify that the heritage language is critical for participation in ethnic communities. For example, many immigrant families attend ethnic religious institutions where the knowledge of the heritage language is necessary to participate in the religious services. Because of a lack of heritage language proficiency, children are often forced to attend separate services conducted in English, creating a divide between the community elders and the youth groups. Such divides limit access for the younger generation to access the social and cultural capital that is available through the family and ethnic networks. According to Grace Cho, without the heritage language, studies have found that individuals experience cultural isolation from the ethnic community that limits their access to the social and cultural capital of the family. Much can be gained in cultural and social resources through home and community interactions. Such connections between the child, parent, and community help encourage ethnic pride, develop a more stable sense of identity, counteract a one-dimensional view of parents, preserve respect for parents, and reinforce family values.

Researchers such as David López and Ricardo D. Stanton-Salazar have shown that a stable and supportive family environment is a necessary component for academic, personal, and social success, but children from dysfunctional families experience greater economic and social difficulties in adulthood. Furthermore, studies by Alejandro Portes and Lingxin Hao show that increased familial problems were found in families where parents and children speak only English together, as well as in families where children used English while their parents were dominant in a language other than English, but not in families where the child is bilingual. The evidence suggests that fluent bilingualism is preferable to either English monolingualism or limited bilingualism.

The positive relationship between heritage language use and strong families is clear. But the benefits will only hold over time if the child's language skills grow along with his or her emotional and intellectual growth and maturity. In sum, heritage languages strengthen families by creating the possibilities for a solid foundation in the home and a close parent-child relationship. This can only lead to greater well-being for children, families, and the society in which they live.

Jin Sook Lee and Debra Suárez

See also Benefits of Bilingualism and Heritage Languages; Heritage Language Education; Home Language and Self-Esteem; Home/School Relations

Further Readings

Beavers, W. R. (1977). *Psychotherapy and growth: A family systems perspective.* New York: Brunner/Mazel.

Bowman, T. W. (1983). Promoting family wellness: Implications and issues. In D. Mace (Ed.), *Prevention in family service approaches to family wellness* (pp. 39–48). Newbury Park, CA: Sage.

Cho, G. (2000). The role of heritage language in social interactions and relationships: Reflections from a language minority. *Bilingual Research Journal, 24*(4), 369–384.

Fishman, J. A. (Ed.). (1999). *Handbook of language and ethnic identity.* New York: Oxford University Press.

López, D., & Stanton-Salazar, R. D. (2001). Mexican Americans: A second generation at risk. In R. G. Rumbaut & A. Portes (Eds.), *Ethnicities: Children of immigrants in America* (pp. 57–90). Berkeley: University of California Press.

Luo, S.-H., & Wiseman, R. L. (2000). Ethnic language maintenance among Chinese immigrant children in the United States. *International Journal of Intercultural Relations, 24,* 307–324.

Mills, J. (2001). Being bilingual: Perspective of third generation Asian children. *International Journal of Bilingual Education, 4*(6), 383–402.

Phinney, J., Ong, A., & Madden, T. (2000). Cultural values and intergenerational value discrepancies in immigrant and non-immigrant families. *Child Development, 71,* 528–539.

Phinney, J., Romero, I., Nava, M., & Huang, D. (2001). The role of language, parents, and peers in ethnic identity among adolescents in immigrant families. *Journal of Youth and Adolescence, 30,* 135–153.

Portes, A., & Hao, L. (2002). The price of uniformity: language, family and personality adjustment in the immigrant second generation. *Ethnic and Racial Studies, 25*(6), 889–912.

Portes, A., & Schauffler, R. (1994). Language and the second generation: Bilingualism yesterday and today. *International Migration Review, 28*(4), 640–661.

Rumbaut, R. (2005). Children of immigrants and their achievement: The role of family acculturation, social class, gender, ethnicity, and school contexts. In R. D. Taylor (Ed.), *Addressing the achievement gap: Findings and applications* (pp. 23–59). Greenwich, CT: IAP-Information Age.

Tannenbaum, M., & Berkovich, M. (2005). Family relations and language maintenance: Implications for language educational policies. *Language Policy, 4*(3), 287–309.

Tannenbaum, M., & Howie, P. (2002). The association between language maintenance and family relations: Chinese immigrant children in Australia. *Journal of Multilingual and Multicultural Development, 23*(5), 408–424.

Wong Fillmore, L. (2000). Loss of family languages: Should educators be concerned? *Theory into Practice, 39*(4), 203–210.

Hidden Curriculum

Depending on the level of analysis used, several factors mediate the interactions between English-speaking school personnel and students who enter their classrooms speaking another language. Some of these factors are as obvious as the linguistic mismatch between teacher and learner when the teacher does not speak the child's language, the prime focus of bilingual education. Others are more subtle and difficult to detect, and still others are almost totally overlooked by even the most well-meaning teacher or school leader. Arguably, the most important factors in the latter group are those associated with the hidden curriculum of the schools, the many things that schools teach but are almost always unspoken and unwritten, although they are present in most lessons and classrooms. Students of the hidden curriculum hold that schools do more than simply transmit knowledge, as contained in the official curriculum guides used by schools. By promoting a narrow view of what it means to be a serious student and demonstrate good behavior, schools "teach" important lessons that are rarely examined because they are so deeply engrained in the culture of schools and society. The hidden curriculum is as important as the proclaimed curriculum in defining what it means to teach.

The concept of a hidden curriculum has been addressed by scholars from several distinct points of view, which are summarized briefly in this entry.

The Hidden Curriculum and the Issue of Equity

The phrase *hidden curriculum* is often attributed to Phillip Jackson; in the mid-1960s, Jackson promoted the view that schooling (education) is part of the socialization process by which society recreates itself in the next generation. Benson Snyder used the same phrase to explain why college students often reject what formal education offers them. Snyder believes that campus conflict and students' personal problems may be caused by a generalized but poorly understood angst created by ill-fitting academic and social norms that thwart the students' ability to develop independently or think creatively.

More recent thinking concerning the hidden curriculum has focused on the harmful effects that the unexamined impact of the hidden curriculum can have on minority youngsters, who are even less prepared to question what the schools demand of them. Scholars concerned with this particular set of issues believe that the hidden curriculum can inflict damage even when the schools do not intend to do so. Perhaps the first appearance of this issue before the general public occurred in 1954 in the U.S. Supreme Court finding in the *Brown v. Board of Education* decision. In its famous "Footnote 11," the Supreme Court relied on research presented by a pair of psychologists, Kenneth Clark and Mamie Clark. Their study showed that when given black and white dolls from which to choose during playtime, Black children disproportionately chose white dolls. The implication of this impressed the justices, who became convinced that a segregated education sent out to Black children the message that black skin was inferior to white even when the curriculum never said so explicitly. The message was part of the hidden curriculum.

Other research, by Samuel Bowles and Herbert Gintis, found that similar messages abound in the way schools are organized and how teachers teach. Competition is favored over cooperation, a fact that disadvantages cultures in which competition may be frowned upon by youngsters. In other cases, communication styles—passive versus active, boisterous versus calm, or volunteered versus withheld—are additional examples in which feelings of preferred versus unpopular styles are exhibited by teachers who favor one cultural way of communication over all others. In sum, it can be argued that the much flaunted "meritocracy" of which American schools are an integral part is, in effect, not culture-free or culture-fair. Children emerge from the meritocratic machine that is the schools as successful when the value system of their homes is synchronous with the beliefs in which meritocracy itself is embedded.

Anthropology and Critical Theory

Educational anthropologists and critical theorists began to analyze the hidden aspects of school curricula through essays and descriptive studies attempting to assess the importance of power relations, especially asymmetrical power between schools and students, in the persistent lack of success of students from disenfranchised groups. Much of this early writing occurred in the late 1960s and 1970s as the broader values and tendencies of American society were also being questioned by its youth.

Internationally, the most influential of these writings were those of Pierre Bourdieu, Michel Foucault, and Paulo Freire. These authors focused on power relations in school settings where teachers belonged to high-power groups and students belonged to less powerful groups. These authors—chiefly Freire— also promoted the idea that education should be structured to function as a strong support for democracy. According to Freire, schooling that numbs the learner into being a passive recipient of cultural values, promoted by the schools, results in the mere transmission of societal norms and values rather than in helping to shape individuals who are interested in social justice and who question the way things are, rather than working toward things as they should be. In short, these students question the purpose of education and seek to change values and mores that have gone unquestioned in the past. When their efforts are ignored or frustrated, dissatisfaction and disengagement often result.

The Iconoclastic or Populist View

More recently, a more iconoclastic voice emerged, that of John Taylor Gatto, a New York City public schoolteacher whose acerbic critiques of school life, policies, and procedures stung education leaders. Gatto's populist views challenged the system of public education and "government schools" perhaps because his was the voice of a public schoolteacher who was highly critical of the schools in which he himself worked and which had bestowed on him important awards such as the New York City Teacher of the Year in 3 different years, and New York State Teacher of the Year. In 1991, Gatto resigned his teaching position in the New York City schools to devote himself entirely to writing and speaking out against the hidden curriculum and purposes of the schools. Gatto, whose critiques are somewhat jumbled and poorly organized in writing, are replete with harsh rhetoric. This may explain why his views have not received as much attention as they deserve from mainstream education thinkers and researchers. His critique of what the schools teach and the harm they may inflict remain largely unexamined by education practitioners.

Gatto argues that the institutionalization of public education into cookie-cutter socializing centers that are excessively regimented and rules-driven is a disservice to society, if not a crime. He argues that American public education is a system of governmental institutions designed, from the outset, to be instruments for the management and control of a large population. According to this view, schools are intended to produce through the application of formulae, formulaic human beings whose behavior can be predicted and controlled. This is facilitated by compulsory attendance laws that force young people to attend these schools from ages 5 to 16 in most states. This form of education, according to Gatto, deprives young people of the freewheeling methods of inquiry that lead children and youth to explore ideas and fresh, self-created frames for a useful, ordered, and creative life that is well lived and enjoyed even when it is lived outside the predominant patterns of society. This option tends to be available only to students who attend expensive private schools.

A view similar to Gatto's view that regards the schools as sorting machines to organize and manage the populace was advanced by Bowles and Gintis in their seminal book, *Schooling in Capitalist America.* These authors advanced the idea that the purpose of American education was to sort and organize men and women and prepare them both in knowledge and orientation, for their predestined roles in life. This theory is still widely debated, even though the book that presented it was first published in 1976.

Language in the Hidden Curriculum

In discussing bilingual education, perhaps the most germane aspect is the effect of the hidden curriculum on the role and status of English in American schools. In this and other respects, the schools reflect the society's valuing of the English language to the exclusion of most others. It is part of our accumulated professional wisdom that a comprehensive and powerful command of the English language is needed and must be demonstrated by children and youth at various points in their journey through the schools. In this view, English is a school subject that is deemed most important. Accordingly, the schools' role in promoting

and teaching it is primordial. Until the Supreme Court decision in *Lau v. Nichols,* many people believed that the teaching and learning of English was primarily a family issue that was the primary responsibility of parents rather than the schools. *Lau* put that issue to rest at least from a legal perspective. But the vital nature of English and the zeal with which it must be taught has led many schools and even the federal government to give a high precedence to English, even if it means pushing other school subjects off the curriculum for lack of time and space. Attitudes concerning the importance of mastering the English language—and specifically, a standard variety of English—may not be emphasized daily in classrooms, but indeed transmitted to students, who learn to recognize which language variety is valuable in schools, and which are not.

Josué M. González

See also Critical Literacy; Cultural Deficit and Cultural Mismatch Theories; Culturally Competent Teaching; Social Class and School Success

Further Readings

Bourdieu, P. (1977). Cultural reproduction and social reproduction. In J. Karabel & A. H. Halsey (Eds.), *Power and ideology in education* (pp. 487–511). New York: Oxford University Press.

Bowles, S., & Gintis, H. (1976). *Schooling in capitalist America: Educational reforms and the contradictions of economic life.* New York: Basic Books.

Brown v. Board of Education, 347 U.S. 483 (1954).

Foucault, M. (1981). *Power/knowledge: Selected interviews and other writings.* New York: Pantheon.

Freire, P. (1970). *Pedagogy of the oppressed.* New York: Seabury.

Gatto, J. T. (1992). *Dumbing us down: The hidden curriculum of compulsory schooling.* Philadelphia: New Society.

Gatto, J. T. (2001). *The underground history of American education: An intimate investigation into the prison of modern schooling.* New York: Oxford Village Press.

González, J. M. (1993). School meanings and cultural bias. *Education and Urban Society, 25*(3), 254–269.

Jackson, P. (1968). *Life in classrooms.* New York: Holt, Rinehart and Winston.

John Taylor Gatto Biography. (2003). Retrieved from http://www.johntaylorgatto.com/aboutus/john.htm

Lau v. Nichols, 414 U.S. 563 (1974).

Snyder, B. (1970). *The hidden curriculum.* New York: Knopf.

HIGH-STAKES TESTING

Around the world, a single test score is often used to make a wide range of decisions, from determining citizenship status to grade promotion and graduation in school. When a test is attached to serious consequences in this way, it is considered to be high stakes. This sort of testing usually serves a gatekeeping role and can offer a door to opportunities or bar access to advancement. Language minority students in the United States typically live in households where a language other than English is spoken. Language minority students in need of language support services to succeed in English-medium classrooms are referred to as English language learners (ELLs) among practitioners, and as limited-English-proficient students (LEP) among many policymakers. These students have historically been particularly vulnerable to high-stakes testing, a pattern from the past being repeated in U.S. public schools today.

The primary issue with the use of high-stakes testing for ELLs is that the tests used are often the same ones administered to native-English speakers. They are given in the students' second language, English, even when the test takers do not enjoy a high command of the language. ELLs are often required by school or government authorities to take high-stakes tests, and historically this has happened without sufficient recognition for the effect that language and culture will have on the scores an ELL receives. ELLs typically do not perform as well as native-English speakers and, when the stakes of the test are high, the students are punished for not passing. When ELLs must take high-stakes tests, the students and their teachers are under great pressure to prepare, which results in many changes to teaching and learning. This entry explores the effects of high-stakes testing on immigrant students in school, especially those who speak a language other than English at home.

Historical Perspective

The testing movement originated in the United States with a focus on mental measurement in the form of intelligence quotient (IQ) testing, and has spread globally since World War I. This movement has historically been associated with immigrants and language minorities, as IQ testing began at the turn of the 20th century when immigration to the United States was dramatically increasing. Psychologist Alfred Binet is credited with establishing the IQ test in 1904, at the request of the French government, for identifying children who were learning delayed to be placed into special education programs. The IQ test was then translated into English in 1917 and used to test immigrants to the United States who arrived through Ellis Island. At that time, Henry H. Goddard concluded that 25 of 30 Jews tested were unintelligent; such findings have since been recognized as dubious because of the failure to acknowledge the role of cultural differences and language proficiency in test performance among an immigrant population.

IQ tests were similarly employed by Carl Brigham to two million World War I draftees in the United States as a tool to understand why recent immigrants did not perform as well as those who had been in the United States for 20 years or more. Brigham found that Blacks were inferior to Whites; and within the other racial strands he used—"Nordic, Alpine, and Mediterranean races"—that the Nordic race outperformed all the others. IQ tests were also used in schools with high stakes because they determined student placement; thus, IQ tests became a means of justifying school segregation by race in the 20th century. All these findings have subsequently been proven to be false and the result of biases in the tests or an inability of the test takers to read them.

Brigham later founded the Scholastic Achievement Test (SAT), which was and continues to be used to determine qualification for college entrance. Brigham is believed to have influenced Congress to pass an act restricting immigration by "non-Nordics." English literacy thereby became a way to deny immigrants entrance to the United States and to keep African Americans from voting, and in this way the early years of the testing movement were prejudicial on the basis of race and language proficiency. Although tests are presented as scientific, neutral, and unbiased, from the beginning they have disproportionately penalized poor and minority students, and language minorities in particular.

Current Context

More immigrants arrived in the United States in the 1990s than in any previous decade, and during this time, the population of language minority speakers increased by 40%. In 2001, the U.S. Congress passed the No Child Left Behind Act (NCLB), legislation characterized by an increase in the federal role in education through a greater emphasis on accountability. The law mandates that ELLs participate in English language proficiency and academic content assessments to ensure that these students are making "adequate yearly progress." Most states have interpreted the federal legislation by implementing statewide standardized tests that are used both to meet the requirements of NCLB and to determine high school graduation, grade promotion, or placement into tracked programs. Since NCLB, tests have become increasingly high stakes.

A major issue that has arisen in the implementation of high-stakes testing with immigrant student populations is that, as in the past, most of the tests being used are in English. Even a test of math will be greatly affected by the student's level of English language proficiency if it is only given in English, especially if it involves written explanations or word problems, as modern tests usually do. In this way, the tests are primarily measures of language proficiency rather than content knowledge. In addition to being linguistically complex, test items are also culturally complex in ways that interfere with valid and reliable measurement. One example is a state exam that was implemented in a New York City classroom with students who had recently arrived from West Africa. The test referred to "shopping malls" and the game "Twister" in test items. However, the students did not know these terms because shopping malls are uncommon in their countries as well as in New York City, and because Twister is an American game they had neither heard of nor played. Challenges such as these have yet to be addressed when using the tests for high-stakes decision making.

In addition, ELLs are now frequently being required to pass the same English language-arts exams that native-English speakers take to determine readiness for high school graduation or grade promotion. For instance, 20 states used high school exit exams in 2006 to meet the high school requirements of NCLB as well, and it is predicted that nationally 87% of English language learners will have to pass high school exit exams in coming years.

Researchers are challenging the validity, reliability, and fairness of such practices. The problem is that ELLs typically perform worse than other students on standardized tests of language arts as well as an academic content, and this has serious consequences for them. As of 2006, a wide achievement gap exists between ELLs and other students on statewide assessments, ranging from 20 to 40 percentage points.

Although many states use test accommodations or modifications to lessen the interference of language, few of these successfully reduce the achievement gap between ELLs and non-ELLs, and states are least likely to permit the usage of those that do. For example, an accommodation that most states permit is extended time for ELLs to complete the test. However, if an ELL who has just arrived from China is required to read a passage from the Gettysburg Address and write an essay, or answer a word problem on a math exam about a car and a truck going up an incline at different speeds, extra time may help somewhat, but it will not be sufficient to make this student's test score equivalent to that attained by a native-English speaker—even if this child is extremely knowledgeable in the areas of U.S. history and math. The same test translated into Chinese might be more helpful to measure the student's content knowledge, but translations are rarely permitted. Despite these problems, most states and school districts continue to make major educational decisions for individual students on the basis of a single test score. In this way, we are repeating what happened more than a century ago with the use of IQ tests to evaluate immigrants, without regard for the harsh consequences of the scores they received.

Effects of High-Stakes Testing on ELLs

Opponents note a number of negative consequences of high-stakes testing for ELLs, such as the placement of these students into low-track remedial education programs, increased grade retention and drop-out rates, and higher rates of youths taking the Graduate Equivalency Diploma (GED) exams instead of pursuing a traditional diploma. In addition, opponents find that efforts to improve schoolwide performance on high-stakes tests have resulted in low-performing students being encouraged to leave school by officials, being retained in grade before pivotal testing years, and being suspended or expelled before testing days. Some find that testing reduces the quality of education offered, and a major critique of test-based accountability systems increasingly visible in the literature is that the tests fail poor and minority students and serve as an effective sorting mechanism to ensure that they remain at the bottom of the social hierarchy.

Several scholars have criticized the practice of using high school exit exams as the single criterion for deciding high school graduation because of how it negatively affects ELLs. For example, ELLs fail some of the more demanding statewide graduation tests at a rate of 60 to 90%, and these rates would likely be higher if the students who had already dropped out were included in these tests. These findings further the claim that high-stakes tests result in "disparate impact" on ELLs, disproportionately penalizing this student population in comparison with other groups, and thereby contributing to the reproduction of educational inequalities. In addition, high-stakes testing creates a disincentive for schools to serve low-performing students because schools are pressured to have high overall passing rates, and these students become a downward drag on schoolwide scores.

On the other side of the testing debate, however, supporters of high-stakes testing state that NCLB is critical for doing exactly the opposite and is actually closing the achievement gap among students according to race, class, and ethnicity. Educators talk about the progress they are seeing as a result of the new accountability, by ensuring that students from low-income families, racial minorities, and immigrant students are expected to be taught to high levels. Supporters argue that the law has brought the needs of low-performing students into the public spotlight, causing greater attention to be paid to these students than before. The rationale is that highlighting the wide achievement gap will improve the quality of education these students receive.

Effects of High-Stakes Testing on Instruction and Language Policy

High-stakes testing has a significant effect on teaching and learning, and research indicates that the higher the stakes of tests, the more likely teachers are to report effects on their instruction and curriculum. These effects include pressure to have their students do well, emphasis on test preparation, and time devoted to test content.

There exists a body of literature in what is called testing "washback," which refers to the effects of tests on language teaching and learning. Researchers in this area argue that testing can and should influence teaching and learning, though they often find that the actual effects are unintended. For example, many researchers report "teaching to the test" as a primary washback effect, whereby exams drive education, and curriculum is narrowed to the subjects on the test. Researchers report finding less focus on subjects that are not tested, such as art, music, and social studies. Studies in the United States in the past decade are finding widespread instances of teachers limiting instruction to only those things that are sure to be tested, emphasizing rote memorization of facts, and drilling students on test-taking strategies.

Language policy in education is policy that determines which language(s) will be taught and learned in school. Analyzing the effects of high-stakes testing on teaching and learning, researchers have recently begun to explore the connections between testing and language policy, finding that testing policy strongly affects language policy. Several researchers have argued that embedded within NCLB is implicit English-only policy, and that English-only testing creates an incidental English-only policy. It becomes difficult for educators, even teachers in bilingual education programs, to use a language other than English in instruction when the sole measure of accountability is performance on a state test that is offered only in English. This is particularly evident in those states that have passed antibilingual education legislation. For example, although bilingual teachers in California continued native-language instruction immediately after the passage of Proposition 227 (an English-only law passed in 1998) in that state, teachers report feeling compelled to teach more English because of the English-only state assessments. In states with high-stakes tests provided only in English, bilingual teachers are increasing the amount of English they use, even in dual-language programs in which instruction is meant to be equally in English and another language.

Conclusion

Both testing opponents and supporters alike have recommended that policymakers recognize the role language plays in test performance, and that they avoid those policies that have the most deleterious consequences. Particularly criticized has been the recent policy to use a single test score to determine grade retention, placement of students into low-track classes, and graduation. Instead, many promote the use of multiple measures of student progress as an alternative, such as portfolios that include class assignments and diverse samples of student work, grades in school, teacher assessment, and projects. Until new tests are developed that manage to remove the impact of language and culture or until the stakes of testing are lowered, large numbers of English language learners will continue to be penalized in the next decade for failing high-stakes tests.

Kate Menken

See also Designation and Redesignation of English Language Learners; Language Policy and Social Control; Measuring Language Proficiency; No Child Left Behind Act of 2001, Testing Requirements; Proficiency, Fluency, and Mastery; Proposition 227 (California)

Further Readings

Abedi, J., Hofstetter, C., & Lord, C. (2004). Assessment accommodations for English language learners: Implications for policy-based empirical research. *Review of Educational Research, 74*(1), 1–28.

Amrein, A., & Berliner, D. (2002). *An analysis of some unintended and negative consequences of high-stakes testing.* Tempe: Education Policy Research Unit, Arizona State University. Retrieved from http://www.asu.edu/educ/epsl/EPRU/epru_2002_Research_Writing.htm

Brigham, C. (1923). *A study of American intelligence.* Princeton, NJ: Princeton University Press.

Cheng, L., & Watanabe, Y. (Eds.), with Curtis, A. (Ed.). (2004). *Washback in language testing: Research contexts and methods.* Mahwah, NJ: Lawrence Erlbaum.

Clapham, C., & Corson, D. (Eds.). (1997). Language testing and assessment. In C. Clapham & D. Corson, *Encyclopedia of language and education, Vol. 7: Language testing and assessment.* Dordrecht, Netherlands: Kluwer Academic.

Crawford, J. (2004). *No child left behind: Misguided approach to school accountability for English language learners.* Paper for the Forum on ideas to improve the NCLB accountability provisions for students with disabilities and English language learners. Washington, DC: Center on Education Policy & National Association for Bilingual Education.

Evans, B., & Hornberger, N. H. (2005). No Child Left Behind: Repealing and unpeeling federal language education policy in the United States. *Language Policy, 4,* 87–106.

Goddard, H. (1917). Mental tests and the immigrant. *Journal of Delinquency, 2,* 243–277.

Hakuta, K. (1986). *The mirror of language: The debate on bilingualism.* New York: Basic Books.

Heubert, J., & Hauser, R. (Eds.). (1999). *High stakes testing for tracking, promotion, and graduation.* Washington, DC: National Academy Press.

Menken, K. (2005). *When the test is what counts: How high-stakes testing affects language policy and the education of English language learners in high school.* Unpublished doctoral dissertation. Teachers College, Columbia University.

Menken, K. (2006). Teaching to the test: How standardized testing promoted by *No Child Left Behind* impacts language policy, curriculum, and instruction for English language learners. *Bilingual Research Journal, 30*(2), 521–546.

Mensh, E., & Mensh, H. (1991). *The IQ mythology: Class, race, gender, and inequality.* Carbondale: Southern Illinois University Press.

Rivera, C., & Collum, E. (Eds.). (2006). *State assessment policy and practice for English language learners: A national perspective.* Mahwah, NJ: Lawrence Erlbaum.

Shohamy, E. (2001). *The power of tests: A critical perspective on the uses of language tests.* London: Longman/Pearson Education.

Shohamy, E., & Hornberger, N. H. (Eds.). (2007). *Encyclopedia of language and education, Vol. 7: Language testing and assessment* (2nd ed.). Dordrecht, Netherlands: Kluwer Academic.

Spolsky, B. (1995). *Measured words: The development of objective language testing.* Oxford, UK: Oxford University Press.

Sullivan, P., Yeager, M., Chudowsky, N., Kober, N., O'Brien, E., & Gayler, K. (2005). *State high school exit exams: States try harder, but gaps persist.* Washington, DC: Center on Education Policy.

Valenzuela, A. (Ed.). (2005). *Leaving children behind: How "Texas-style" accountability fails Latino youth.* Albany: State University of New York Press.

Wiley, T., & Wright, W. (2004). Against the undertow: Language-minority education policy and politics in the "age of accountability." *Educational Policy, 18*(1), 142–168.

HISPANIC POPULATION GROWTH

Pressures to adopt bilingual education occurred during a period in which the growth of the Latino or Hispanic population had begun to accelerate markedly. The growing influence of Latino political and civil rights leaders was influential both in the passage of the Bilingual Education Act in 1968 and in subsequent reauthorizations of that legislation. Hispanic influence was also felt in the many state laws favoring bilingual education that were enacted in the 1970s. This entry traces the growth of the Latino population during this period and reviews the education challenges faced by this population.

In 1960, the first time the U.S. Census produced a credible count, the documented Hispanic population of the United States numbered approximately 3.8 million as explained by Herschel T. Manuel. In 2001, the U.S. Census Bureau reported that in 2000, 35,305,818 Hispanics (or Latinos) lived in the United States. According to more recent statistics from the Pew Hispanic Center from 2006, the Hispanic population of the United States increased from 8.5 million in 1966–1967 to 44.7 million in 2006.

Historical Background

During the past four decades, the Hispanic population has accounted for 36% of the 100 million people added to the population of the United States. This is the highest increase of any racial or ethnic group during this period. The rise of this unique linguistic community parallels, in great part, the rise of bilingual education in the country, along with strong demands for civil rights protection in education and other fields. Hispanic demographics deserve attention to understand how bilingual education and the American Hispanic community emerged and developed during the last quarter of the 20th century.

Major factors for expansion of the Hispanic population are immigration from Mexico and Latin America, and the high fertility rates of Latinas as reported by the Pew Hispanic Center in 2006. Before 1960, immigration by Hispanics (particularly from Mexico), to the United States was minuscule by today's standards. Manuel reported that in the decades since 1861, immigration from Mexico was as shown in Table 1.

Table 1   Immigration to the United States from Mexico

Decade	Number	Decade	Number
1861–1870	2,191	1921–1930	459,287
1871–1880	5,162	1931–1940	22,319
1881–1900	Records incomplete	1941–1950	60,589
1901–1910	49,642	1951–1960	299,811
1911–1920	219,001		

Source: Manuel, H. (1965). *Spanish-speaking children of the Southwest: their education and the public welfare.* Austin: University of Texas Press (p. 18).

The Hispanic population is the oldest White and mestizo population to have settled in the American Southwest. The earliest Latinos came primarily from Spain through Mexico and settled in Santa Fe, New Mexico, as early as 1609—fully 11 years before the founding of Plymouth Colony in 1620. By 1680, there were more than 2,500 Spanish-speaking settlers in New Mexico alone, as John Burma explains. Herschel Manuel reports that there were 23,000 Spanish-speaking people in the southwestern United States by 1790. These numbers remind us that the English- and German-speaking colonists of the East Coast were not alone in seeking a foothold in what is now the United States.

Not long after the 13 colonies gained their independence, English speakers began moving west into what was then Mexican land. Americans were primarily coming into central Texas. Initially anxious to see this territory settled, Mexico had invited English-speaking settlers to be a part of Mexico provided they learned Spanish and became Catholic. Texas was at the heart of the U.S.–Mexican disputes over land. As a way to justify their presence there, the U.S. government under President James Polk promoted the idea of a manifest destiny that gave the United States its conception of reaching from the Atlantic to the Pacific.

Concerned about the rising tide of U.S. settlers coming to Texas, Mexican president Antonio López de Santa Anna attempted to curtail the tide. He abolished slavery and enforced customs taxes on the new settlers. However, the new settlers quickly outnumbered the Mexican citizens and soon claimed their independence by revolting. Although the reasons for the Texas revolt were more complex, this revolution eventually led to Mexico losing approximately one half of its lands north of the new Texas border. California, Arizona, New Mexico, Colorado, and Utah, as well as parts of Wyoming and Nevada were also ceded to the United States as a result of the Mexican-American War that ended in 1848. These figures show the long-standing presence of Hispanics in the U.S. Southwest. Estimates of the number of Mexicans that became American by not immigrating—they lived in the ceded territories—vary from a low of 30,000 to more than 100,000.

Since Mexico lost its northern lands to the United States after the Mexican-American War, immigration has played a continuous role in the increase of the Hispanic population in the United States. During the next hundred years, these increases in immigration were aided by significant occurrences in both the United States and Mexico. These included the agricultural development of the American Southwest, the building of the railroads and the subsequent need for labor, the Mexican Revolution of 1910, and the labor shortages caused by World War I and World War II in the United States, as explained by Richard Schaefer.

During the Depression of the 1930s, more than one-half million people were deported to Mexico when they could not prove their citizenship. Most of these were Chicanos or Mexican Americans, Schaefer explains. After the Depression, however, Mexican labor was once again in demand, and the two governments agreed to a new program known as the bracero program. Under this agreement, Mexican laborers were allowed to enter the United States legally to work in the agricultural fields as contracted guest laborers. This program lasted until 1964. Many of these immigrants remained in the United States after their work permits had expired, thus adding to the flow of immigrants from Mexico.

Between 14 million and 16 million immigrants entered the United States during the 1990s. In the 1980s, the immigrant rate was 10 million, and in the 1970s, it was 7 million as reported by Randy Capps and colleagues. Concern about unrestricted illegal immigration led the U.S. Congress to pass the Immigration Reform and Control Act (IRCA) of 1986 that sanctioned U.S. employers who hired illegal aliens (as explained by Gordon Hanson and Antonio Spilimbergo). One of the provisions of this legislation was to provide legal amnesty to several million illegal workers already in the United States.

There has always been considerable debate about how to classify people of "Hispanic" origins. Many favor the term *Latino* whereas others prefer *Hispanic*. Still others prefer a method of disaggregating such data to show the kind of Hispanic or Latino a person is—Mexican, Mexican American, Chicano, Cuban, Puerto Rican, Central American, Spanish, South American, and so on. According to Darryl Fears, the federal Ad Hoc Committee on Racial and Ethnic Definitions of 1975 was responsible for the term *Hispanic* being chosen to designate such individuals for the 1980 census. For the 2000 census, questions on race were changed from those asked on the 1990 census questionnaire. The federal government considered race and Hispanic origin to be two separate and distinct concepts; according to Roberto Ramírez,

Hispanic or Latino was defined in the Census 2000 as "a person of Cuban, Mexican, Puerto Rican, South or Central American, or other Spanish culture or origin regardless of race" (p. 1).

The American Community–Hispanic report for 2004 (U.S. Census Bureau, 2007), reported 40,459,196 Hispanics or Latinos in the United States. This report also disaggregated the total to show that 64% were of Mexican background, 9.6% were of Puerto Rican descent, 3.6% were of Cuban background, with other Central and South American and Caribbean groups constituting the rest. These 40.5 million persons lived in all 50 states and for the first time were described as a heterogeneous aggregation rather than as a single group.

Furthermore, this report also concluded that the majority of Hispanics were born in the United States and that most of them spoke English. In 2004, the percentage of the overall Hispanic population that lived in California and Texas alone was just over 50%. Overall, approximately 80% of Hispanics live in nine states: California, Texas, Florida, New York, Illinois, Arizona, New Jersey, Colorado, and New Mexico. This report also noted that Hispanics in 2004 had a larger proportion of a younger population, and less of an elder population, in comparison with the White, Non-Hispanic group.

Hispanic Student Population Growth

According to Sam Dillon's report in the *New York Times,* in 1972 Hispanic students accounted for a mere 6% of the U.S. population of school-age children. By 2005, the number of Hispanic children attending U.S. schools rose to 20% of all students. During the same period, the White school-age population dropped from 78% in 1972 to 58% in 2005, Dillon explained. Richard Fry found that Hispanics accounted for 64% of the enrollment growth between 1993–1994 and 2002–2003, one of the most concentrated growth periods for American schools. The rapid rise in the number of Hispanic students has put pressure on schools across the country to attend to their language and culture needs.

In contrast to the immigration rates of the 1990s, births have overtaken immigration in ensuing decades as the largest source of Hispanic growth. These new census figures demonstrate that young people will dominate the Hispanic population (as described by

Ana M. Martínez Alemán). Half of this current population is younger than age 27. By comparison, half of non-Hispanic Whites are older than 40. Hispanics have the fastest growth rate among the nation's major racial and ethnic groups, as Martínez Alemán explains. In the 1990s, Hispanics accounted for almost 40% of the country's population increase. From 2000 to 2004, that figure grew to 49%, as D'Vera Cohn reported in the *Washington Post*.

In a study of limited-English-proficient (LEP) children in U.S. schools, Paul Hopstock and Todd Stephenson found that more than 350 languages were listed by school personnel as being spoken by children who could be considered LEP. Spanish was the native language of 76.9% of all LEP children. Hopstock and Stephenson also reported that no other language exceeded more than 3% of the LEP population. Even if many of these children were successful in school and were able to join the English-speaking mainstream, there would still be several million Hispanic children and adults who would retain their Spanish-speaking ability.

Challenges in the Education of Hispanic Students

One of the issues in the education of Hispanic children has historically centered on language. The failure of American educational systems to succeed with Hispanic children has often been referred to as educational neglect because of its persistence. The growth in numbers of Hispanic children since the 1960s has complicated efforts to educate them in the traditional sense. Hispanics grew at a rate of 55% during the 40-year period between 1966 and 2006, as reported by the Pew Hispanic Center in 2006. This growth was also reflected in the Hispanic school-age population. Perhaps no other area stands out among Hispanic demographics as much as that of their growth in the number of Hispanic school-age children during the past two decades.

The growing numbers of Hispanic children also affect the issue of immigrant children's education. Because many non-English-speaking children were being instructed through bilingual education programs, this method of teaching English language learners has recently come under fire by those who feel that English should be the only language used in public schools. California (Proposition 227 in 1998), Arizona (Proposition 203 in 2000), and Massachusetts

(Question 2 in 2002) all have state laws making bilingual instruction illegal in those states.

There were 5,119, 561 LEP students identified during the 2004–2005 school year (as reported by the National Clearinghouse for English Language Acquisition in 2006). Hopstock and Stephenson identified nearly three million Hispanic students as LEP in 2001–2002. Although many of these Spanish-speaking English language learners are being served by a variety of programs such as bilingual education, English as a Second Language (ESL), dual-language programs, and sheltered immersion programs, the overall effect of the antibilingual measures has not yet been assessed. Educators worry that these antibilingual education laws will result in a large underclass of ill-prepared students who will not be proficient in the academic English necessary for success in the American school system. James Crawford explains that the English-only movement and laws are feared to also have a negative effect on the Hispanic population overall.

Another issue that becomes important in the growth of the U.S. Hispanic population is that of poverty. Because many Hispanic children come directly from Mexico and other Latin American countries, poverty often is a main reason for their parents' immigration from the home country. According to Martínez Alemán, Latinos are more likely to live in poverty than other groups. Thus, many Hispanic immigrants arrive in this country in a weak economic condition. In addition, many immigrant families have not had the benefit of a formal education in Spanish in their countries of origin, thus denying the children the added benefit of parental literacy. School—any school in any language—is a new and foreboding experience for such youngsters. Because the parents on average have lower incomes do than their U.S. counterparts, immigrant children have a higher rate of poverty (as reported by Jane Reardon-Anderson, Randy Capps, and Michael Fix). The Texas Education Agency (TEA) reported in 2006 that 55.6% of its school-age population could be considered economically disadvantaged. TEA further reported an overall "at-risk" population of 48.7%. Texas is a recent majority-minority state and many of these children are Hispanic, so it is not difficult to surmise that the poverty rate among many Hispanic children (and therefore, Hispanic families) is quite high.

Other issues that perhaps would be affected by large numbers of Hispanics in the U.S. population are

(a) voting and voting patterns, (b) their impact on the U.S. economy, and (c) the impact Hispanics would have on the overall social fabric of the United States. As mentioned earlier, Hispanics lived in all 50 states with more than 26 million concentrated in California, Texas, Florida, and New York as of 2004. Most of these people were born in the United States, so the potential voting power could be large.

How will these people with a non-English language and different cultures affect how the United States looks and acts in the future? This important question will be examined closely in the decades to come. Whereas the impact of Hispanics in American demographics has been well documented, it has not always been acknowledged or validated in our institutions or schools as well as our overall historical memory, as pointed out by Midobuche, Benavides, Marietta Espinosa-Herold, and Sonia Nieto. With the U.S. Hispanic population currently at greater than 44 million, and expected to reach 102.6 million by 2050—as projected by the U.S. Census Bureau, reported in the 2007 Hispanic Heritage month report—it will remain interesting to see if this will change the American landscape in any significant manner, especially the schools.

Eva Midobuche and
Alfredo H. Benavides

See also Dual-Language Programs; English for the Children Campaign; Latino Civil Rights Movement

Further Readings

Burma, J. H. (Ed.). (1970). *Mexican Americans in the United States*. Cambridge, MA: Schenkman.

Capps, R., Fix, M., Murray, J., Ost, J., Passel, J., & Herwantoro, S. (2005). *The new demography of America's schools: Immigration and the No Child Left Behind Act*. The Urban Institute. Available from http://www.urban.org/UploadedPDF/311230_new_demography.pdf

Cohn, D. (2005). Hispanics growth surge fueled by births in the United States. *Washington Post*. Retrieved from http://www.washingtonpost.com/wp-dyn/content/article/2005/06/08/AR2005060802381.html

Crawford. J. (2004). *Educating English learners* (5th ed.). Los Angeles: Bilingual Educational Services.

Dillon, S. (2007). U.S. data show rapid minority growth in school rolls. *New York Times*. Available from http://www.nytimes.com

Espinosa, P. (1999). PBS, *The border: Struggle over Texan independence, text timeline*. Retrieved from http://www.pbs.org/kpbs/theborder/history/index.html

Fears, D., (2003, October 15). The roots of "Hispanic." *Washington Post*. Available from http://azbilingualed.orgAABE%20Site/AABE%20NEWS%202003/roots_of.htm

Fry, R. (2006). *The changing landscape of American public education: New students, new schools*. Pew Hispanic Center Research Report. Available from http://www.ecs.org

Hanson, G., & Spilimbergo, A. (1999). Illegal immigration, border enforcement, and relative wages: Evidence from apprehensions at the U.S.–Mexico border. *American Economic Review, 89*(5), 1357–1378.

Hopstock, P. J., & Stephenson, T. G. (2003, September 15). *Descriptive study of services to LEP students and LEP students with disabilities, special topic report #1, native languages of LEP students*. Washington, DC: U.S. Department of Education, Office of English Language Acquisition, Language Enhancement and Academic Achievement of LEP Students (OELA). Available from http://www.ncela.gwu.edu/resabout/research/descriptivestudyfiles/native_languages1.pdf

Manuel, H. T. (1965). *Spanish-speaking children of the Southwest: Their education and the public welfare*. Austin: University of Texas Press.

Martínez Alemán, A. M. M. (2006). Latino demographics, democratic individuality, and educational accountability: A pragmatist's view. *Educational Researcher, 35*(7), 25–31.

National Clearinghouse of English Language Acquisition. (2006). *The growing numbers of limited English proficient students: 1994/95—2004/05*. Washington, DC: Office of English Language Acquisition. Available from http://www.ncela.gwu.edu./policy/states/reports/statedata/2004LEP/GrowingLEP_0405_Nov06.pdf

Pew Hispanic Center. (2006, October 10). *From 200 million to 300 million: The numbers behind population growth*. Available from http://pewhispanic.org/files/factsheets/25.pdf

Ramírez, R. (2004, December). *Census 2000 Special Reports: We the people: Hispanics in the United States*. Washington, DC: U.S. Census Bureau. Available from http://www.census.gov/prod/2004pubs/censr-18.pdf

Reardon-Anderson, J., Capps, R., & Fix, M. (2002). The health and well-being of children in immigrant families. *Assessing the New Federalism Policy Brief B-52*. Washington, DC: Urban Institute.

Schaefer, R. T. (1988). *Racial and ethnic groups*. Glenview, IL: Scott Foresman.

Texas Education Agency. (2006). *AEIS Report.* Retrieved June 30, 2007, from http://www.tea.state.tx.us/perfreport/aeis/2006/state.html

U.S. Census Bureau. (2007, July 16). Hispanic heritage month: Sept. 15–Oct. 15. Retrieved from http://www.census.gov/Press-Release/www/releases/archives/facts_for_features_special_editions/010327.html

U.S. Census Bureau; U.S. Department of Commerce Economics and Statistics Administration. (2007, February). *The American community—Hispanics: 2004 American community survey reports.* Available from http://www.census.gov/prod/2007pubs/acs-03.pdf

HOGAN, TIMOTHY M. (1951–)

Timothy M. Hogan was born October 8, 1951. He received his undergraduate degree from Arizona State University and his law degree from the University of Notre Dame Law School. Before joining the Arizona Center for Law in the Public Interest, he was chief counsel for the Arizona Corporation Commission. He also served as Arizona's assistant attorney general in the Civil Rights and Financial Fraud Divisions, and as program director of the Phoenix Program at Community Legal Services. Hogan has argued cases before the Supreme Court of Arizona and the United States District Court of Appeals for the Ninth Circuit. This entry discusses Hogan's advocacy efforts, and his work in the landmark court case *Flores v. State of Arizona.*

The impact of Hogan's legal advocacy on the education of English language learners may not be well known to many outside of the state of Arizona. But within the state, he is widely viewed as the most effective and dedicated legal advocate for the educational rights of English language learners in public schools. As executive director of the Arizona Center for Law in the Public Interest since 1991, Hogan is one of the leading civil rights attorneys in the state. He has been a consistent and tireless legal advocate for the educational rights of linguistic minority students. At the center, Hogan's work focuses primarily on issues relating to public school finance, especially, the ongoing and contentious battle with the Arizona state legislature for equitable school funding for the education of English language learners.

Hogan was cocounsel on the landmark federal court case known as *Flores v. State of Arizona,* filed in 1992 and decided in 2000, in which the state was ordered to increase the amount of funding it allocated to districts serving English language learners. The court also ordered the state to implement new procedures for the reassessment of English language learner (ELL) students and to monitor school district compliance with the law more stringently.

Despite the court order, the state legislature refused to comply, even after the state was charged with contempt for failing to meet its funding obligations. In one of Hogan's numerous court appearances since the case was decided, he asked a federal judge to withhold $500 million in highway funds until the legislature fulfilled its mandate. This request was daring and politically unpopular, and Hogan was vilified by angry legislators in the press and in conservative opinion editorials. Nonetheless, the legislature's unwillingness to obey the *Flores* mandate for ELL funding resulted in an unprecedented court sanction against the state—fines of as much as two million dollars a day until the legislature lived up to its obligations.

The Republican-controlled Arizona state legislature addressed the accruing fines ($21 million by April 2006) by submitting four ELL funding measures: The first three were vetoed by Democratic Governor Janet Napolitano as unacceptable. The fourth measure was ruled inadequate by the same judge who had imposed the fines because, among other problematic issues, the measure added only an additional $76 to the state allocation of $350 per English learner (the latter figure itself is inadequate, considering that in an earlier study to determine the cost of educating English language learners, the state arrived at a much higher figure).

The impact of Hogan's legal advocacy on the education of English language learners is widely acknowledged by detractors and supporters alike. The former view him as audacious, the latter as dedicated and courageous. Because of his vigilance in reminding the legislature of its responsibilities, he has been vilified in the press by angry legislators and in conservative opinion editorials. Nonetheless, Hogan persists. In January 2006, the National Association for Bilingual Education honored him with its Citizen of the Year Award.

Mary Carol Combs

See also Civil Rights Act of 1964; Equal Educational Opportunity Act of 1974; *Flores v. State of Arizona*

Further Readings

Flores v. Arizona, 48 F. Supp. 2d 937 (D. Ariz. 1992).

Flores v. Arizona, Order "WO," December 15, 2005.

Flores v. State of Arizona, 172 F. Supp. 2d 1225 (D. Ariz. 2000).

Web Sites

Arizona Center for Law in the Public Interest: http://www.aclpi.org

HOME LANGUAGE AND SELF-ESTEEM

During the past half century, researchers in the fields of psychology and education have repeatedly demonstrated the importance of self-esteem for learning. Self-esteem is generally defined as the personal judgments that humans make of their own worthiness, capability, significance, and performance. These judgments convey the individual's attitude of approval or disapproval of the self, and may be expressed to others in either word or behavior.

Although such judgments are made by individuals themselves, individuals create their senses of self in society, and to a considerable extent, society shapes their psychological existence, as described in this entry. From the beginning, a child's self-concept is built up bit by bit through interpersonal interaction. Because family and community culture provide the context, models, language, and values by which interactions and experiences can be understood, they play a vital role in a child's self-development. Through their interactions with and around the child, family and immediate community members provide the basic components every individual needs for secure and competent functioning. These include a sense of belonging; an understanding of one's social identity and origins; knowledge of one's connectedness to self, family, and others; knowledge of how to get along with other individuals; and the means to manage adversity.

Self and Culture

Gradually, after children begin school, and through adolescence and adulthood, the predominant importance of family relationships is mitigated by the growing influence of a wider group, which includes other community members, schoolteachers, and peers. When conflict inevitably arises amid these influences and the various forms of evaluative feedback received from each one of them, children will struggle within the self and without, to recreate and maintain a positive sense of self in view of the new challenges. Ideally, families and schools collaborate to guide and assist children and adolescents through the negotiation of a broadening and maturing sense of self.

As the selves of children are socialized through their home languages, children are also apprenticed to become users of those languages. Children develop competence in interpersonal interaction, and their general senses of self-esteem through their home languages. More than a mere communication tool, each language is an index of the culture of the people who use it. Within the grammatical and discourse features of the language of each community, information is encoded about the social organization, rules, expectations, and beliefs of the social group. In learning the home language, children learn to become competent child members of their own cultural communities. As such, children generally enter school with a sense of themselves as competent individuals.

Every child, arriving at school, is most primed and ready to learn in his home language. This is the language in which children are able to ask questions, understand responses, express opinions, indicate what they do not yet understand, and make connections between what they know and what they are learning. Children are able to indicate what they know for the purposes of assessment in their home languages. Schooling children in their home languages offers them the best opportunity to make use of their prior experiences, knowledge, and skills for learning in the new context. Children who achieve strong literacy and content development in their home language are most able to achieve strong literacy and content development in a second language.

Pervasive in pedagogical texts, teaching manuals, and teacher preparation is the underlying principle that students who believe in their self-worth and their abilities to complete tasks are much more likely to be successful. Research has shown that learners with high self-esteem exhibit greater motivation for learning and are more likely to put forth adequate effort, including persistence in the face of initial failure at a learning task. At a minimum, at all education levels—early childhood, elementary, and secondary—the research shows that students' senses of self-worth and competence grow in school contexts in which they feel secure and accepted, where they feel supported in their learning, and where their participation is valued.

Education Policy and Student Self-Esteem

Teachers' individual efforts to support students' self-esteem at the microlevel of specific learning tasks or subjects are significant in their own right. Unfortunately, teachers' effectiveness is limited if macrolevel policy requirements about language of instruction, pedagogy, testing, and curricula prevent them from teaching in ways that support healthy student self-esteem.

Such policies are common in diverse societies in which one group sharing an ethnic and linguistic background is politically and economically dominant, and sets educational policy for the children of all other groups. Because children are prepared for school differently by the various cultural and ethnolinguistic groups from which they come, the degree to which they will function in school with positive self-esteem will depend on the manner in which schools respond to these differences.

Educational policies that place social value only on the achievement in the language of the dominant majority also implicitly ascribe higher value and status to that language, as well as to its speakers. Their language will match the expectations of the teachers, materials, performance standards, and assessment. Considering native language alone, children of the dominant majority, therefore, will tend to be treated as well-prepared for schooling when compared with other children. These children are most likely to feel secure, accepted, supported, and valued in such school environments.

No matter how proficient in their home languages, to the extent that children of other language groups lack native proficiency in the dominant language, children in schools controlled by these macrolevel policies will be viewed as lower status because of their language designation, and as unprepared for school by their parents. Instructed and assessed in a language they do not know well, these children will be designated as low-performing and linguistically deficient—at least for the 7 to 10 years that are required on average for students with little or no home language support to achieve competency in a majority language. Regardless of teachers' microlevel efforts in the classroom to motivate or encourage language minority students in this situation, their self-esteem will suffer at the hands of such policies.

School programs offered to language minority speakers have not often incorporated significant use of the home language for instructional purposes. Rather, the usual educational goal has been to "subtract" or replace the home language as the language of learning. This may be accomplished by simply ignoring students' proficiency status, and placing them in mainstream classrooms to compete with native speakers of the majority language. In another approach known as structured immersion programs, language minority students may be grouped with others who are learning the majority language. In this approach, as in mainstream classrooms, all instruction and testing is conducted in the target language, however, and the home language is ignored.

In programs that view students' minority languages as "handicaps" rather than as educational, psychological, or social resources, students are urged, through subtle and unsubtle messages, to abandon their native languages. For the most part, students respond to these messages by learning the majority language as soon as possible. Socially constructed by the school program as "handicapped," students' self-esteem suffers further assault, as they must struggle to learn and progress academically without adequate proficiency and grounding in the language of instruction. In the meantime, their ability to participate in age-appropriate forms of their home language atrophies as well.

In general, lowered self-esteem follows from negative distinctiveness, and in the school contexts described, many language minority students internalize the belief that their language group is negatively different and may seek to distance themselves from overt ties with their group. For example, they may abandon use of the home language, reject some teachings or practices of the family, withdraw from friendships with members of their own group, or even seek acceptance as a majority-language group member. The rejection of the home language and culture may create a crisis of parental authority and damage the relationships necessary for parents to guide children through adolescence.

Often, this rejection of one's group results in lowered self-esteem. Some students, however, accept the stereotypes of their group as low status, but enjoy positive self-esteem while maintaining the home language and ties to their groups. Study of these groups of students has led researchers to distinguish between group self-esteem (the individual's evaluation of his or her ethnic group) and personal self-esteem (the individual's evaluation of self).

Not surprisingly, parents from ethnic or cultural groups that have been subjected to stigmatizing or discriminatory language policies and practices face difficult choices in raising their children and in deciding what the home language should be. The heritage language best connects children to their history and ancestors, and often to their grandparents and parents as well. Its transmission may provide the most secure and comfortable foundation for growing up in the home culture. However, in the sociopolitical context described earlier, the ability to speak a nonmajority language may subject children to discrimination and resentment, especially in school.

Despite strong ties to their heritage group, many minority language parents, hoping to protect their children, decide not to teach their home language to the children, or to teach it only in limited fashion. Other parents begin with the intention of raising children in the home language. Over time and as children become comfortable using the majority language, parents may find themselves unable or unwilling to insist that the heritage language be used in the home. The danger for parents, especially for those who themselves are not proficient in the majority language, is that they may not be fully able to share themselves and their guidance with their children through the majority language.

Children may certainly be raised successfully at home or in their communities in two languages. The key issue is for parents or primary adults in the child's life to use the language(s) in which they are fluent, and completely capable of raising a child. When language minority parents attempt to raise their children in a majority language that they have not mastered, children's language proficiency suffers in both languages; their school achievement suffers, as does the security of the attachment with the family. Each of these situations affects the child's self-esteem negatively.

Home language maintenance for language minority students can act as a buffer against academic failure. For example, young children whose families provide native-language home environments are more often high achievers at school, compared with children from language minority homes where parents do not provide such an environment. Among high school language minority students, fluent bilinguals are much less likely to drop out of school than are those whose home language fluency is limited.

In some cases, school programs maintain and develop the home language before or alongside the majority language. Such bilingual programs are "additive" in approach because the goal is to develop and maintain children's literate command of the home language while adding and developing the majority language. Research has repeatedly shown that in late-exit or dual-immersion bilingual education programs—which provide continuous and significant home language literacy and content instruction for at least 5 years—language minority children achieve in the majority language at a comparable or higher level than majority language-speaking counterparts. Language minority children educated in these programs also exhibit high levels of self-esteem. Such high self-esteem appears to be socially as well as psychologically constructed. Children experience themselves as competent at school because they are successful and because their language and cultural knowledge is respected as an appropriate basis for learning.

Most bilingual education programs are of the "transitional" variety and do not seek to maintain or develop the home language. In these programs, instruction through the home language is offered only for the first 1 to 3 years of schooling. Children do not achieve strong literacy in their home languages and are moved into majority language instruction, though still functioning academically at relatively low levels in that language. Although this temporary home-language use may ease the transition between home and school, a premature shift into the majority language mainstream classroom brings lower performance and a decline in academic self-confidence. As with programs that make no use of the home language, transitional programs force children to leave their home languages aside, and continue their education in the majority language. This approach is in keeping with older approaches that deal with the home language, implicitly, as being of lower status. Transitional bilingual programs ultimately lead to children's decline in proficiency in that language.

Scholars generally agree that self-esteem has a key role in identity formation and language choices, and the understanding of its complexities has been deepened through its measure and incorporation in cross-disciplinary research. Yet, research also suggests that important cultural differences exist in self-esteem formation, and additionally, that other psychological and contextual factors may also be important. These complexities, inherent in any psychological construct, must temper the confidence with which we view the results of efforts to ascertain the self-esteem of any individuals or groups.

Carol Evans

See also Cultural Deficit and Cultural Mismatch Theories; Designation and Redesignation of English Language Learners; Dual-Language Programs; English Immersion; Language and Identity; Language Educational Policy in Global Perspective; Languages and Power

Further Readings

Bougie, E., Wright, S. C., & Taylor, D. M. (2003). Early heritage-language education and the abrupt shift to a dominant-language classroom: Impact on the personal and collective esteem of Inuit children in arctic Québec. *International Journal of Bilingual Education and Bilingualism, 6*(5), 349–373.

Nieto, S. (2002). *Language, culture, and teaching: Critical perspectives for a new century.* Mahwah, NJ: Lawrence Erlbaum.

Schiefflein, B., & Ochs, E. (1986). *Language socialization across cultures.* Cambridge, UK: Cambridge University Press.

Wong Fillmore, L. (2000). Loss of family languages: Should educators be concerned? *Theory into Practice, 39*(4), 203–210.

Wright, S. C., & Taylor, D. M. (1995). Identity and the language in the classroom: Investigating the impact of heritage versus second-language instruction on personal and collective self-esteem. *Journal of Educational Psychology, 87,* 241–252.

HOME LANGUAGE SURVEY

The *home language survey,* also known as the *primary or home language other than English survey* (PHLOTE), is a federally sanctioned assessment and placement procedure. It has been adopted by most states as part of their processes for identifying incoming students who do not have sufficient proficiency in English to receive instruction solely in that language. The PHLOTE survey is usually a simple form used to determine and document the child's home language. Its only function is to trigger further analysis by the school of the language commonly used in the child's family for everyday communication. This entry describes the uses of the home language survey.

Presumably, the home language survey is a culturally neutral nonpunitive identification measure for collecting minimal language information needed by the school to bring its programs into legal compliance. In school districts in states such as Arizona, California, Illinois, and New York, which experience some of the largest stream of immigrant students, administrators and educators rely on the home language survey to collect information that can help them evaluate each student's level of English proficiency.

Following federal guidelines, the parents or guardians of the newly enrolled children are asked to respond to a home language survey—a form that solicits information about language practices used at home and other related demographic data. To ensure that parents or legal guardians understand the content of the home language survey, education departments in the various states provide school districts with home language surveys in the parents' or guardians' native language. Some school districts, as in California, have provisions requiring parents or legal guardians to submit the completed home language survey 30 days after the student enrolls in a public school in the state.

Although the questions on the home language survey may vary from school district to school district or from state to state, they typically serve the same purpose: soliciting demographic data and information about language practices at home. For example, the California Department of Education provides four questions related to (1) the first language acquired by the child, (2) the language most frequently used by the child to communicate at home, (3) the language the parent uses most frequently to communicate with the child, and (4) the language used most frequently by adults in the home setting. In Massachusetts, home language surveys have often been expanded to include as many as 10 questions, reaching beyond the language used during parent-child interactions to include sibling and family communications, and even interactions with friends in the neighborhood. Seven of these questions focus explicitly on the child's language, whether it relates to a child's oral interactions with individuals in the immediate social surrounding or to the child's literacy skills.

Regardless of the number of questions on each survey, if the parents or legal guardians report any language other than English in any of the questions, then the child is required to undergo further oral or written tests intended to evaluate that child's English proficiency. For example, Mary Ann Zehr has pointed out that if the parents of Navajo children report the use of an indigenous language by a grandparent, then it will be mandatory for their children's English proficiency to be further assessed. Even in cases where parents clearly indicate that neither they nor their child have any form of proficiency in that language, the child still has to undergo further testing. Children who do not perform as anticipated on the test are considered an English language learner, even though English might be their primary language.

Second-language teachers and administrators who support the use of a home language survey argue that it is a good first step in identifying a need for instructional interventions that consider the child's special language needs. The term *home* is crucial in this context. It allows education practitioners to inquire and obtain information about the language(s) children and parents use at home in their various exchanges with each other. Educators often argue that in the classroom setting, they can promote actual concrete learning only if they first identify the students' pragmatic linguistic needs (i.e., students' need to use language in various academic and in social contexts) and devise material and instructional techniques that will best meet those needs.

Despite the benefits the home language survey offers, concerns have been raised about its limitations as a decision-making tool. Mari B. Rasmussen, a critic of the PHLOTE survey, has argued that the home language survey is minimalist. It only informs educators about a child's native language(s) used at home, but the data does not provide much information on the child's actual proficiency in English or in the primary language(s). Teachers and school administrators still have to follow certain formal procedures to assess each student's English proficiency after the survey. Further, as Zehr has indicated, in the case of Navajo children in Arizona, parents are well aware that if they were to affirm that English is the primary language used at home, their children's English language proficiency would not be assessed, and hence, their children could not be considered for participation in programs that allow for the further development of their ancestral language. In addition, if children whose native language is

English reside with family members who are proficient in other languages or if children are bilingual, it does not necessarily mean that their level of proficiency in English is more limited than that of children raised in a monolingual English setting. Hence, critics say, these students' English proficiency should not be assessed just because they are exposed to, or speak, two or more languages at home.

Stella K. Hadjistassou

See also Affirmative Steps to English; Measuring Language Proficiency; Office for Civil Rights, U.S. Department of Education; Proficiency, Fluency, and Mastery

Further Readings

Burnett G. (1993). *The assessment and placement of language minority students.* ERIC Clearinghouse on Urban Education, New York, NY. (ERIC Document Reproduction Service No. ED357131) Retrieved from http://www.ericdigests.org/1993/placement.htm

Home Language Survey. (n.d.). Retrieved from http://multilingual.fresno.k12.ca.us/assmctr/HLS/lanindex.htm

Home Language Survey. (n.d.). Mississippi Department of Education. Retrieved from http://www.mde.k12.ms.us/ACAD/ID/page4.html

Massachusetts Department of Education. (2004). How to identify new LEP students upon their enrollment in a School District. *Office of Language Acquisition and Academic Achievement (OLAAA).* Retrieved from http://www.doe.mass.edu/ell/sei/identify_lep.html

Rossell, C. H. (2000). The federal bilingual education program. *Brookings Papers on Education Policy 2000:* 215–243. Available from http://muse.jhu.edu/journals/bookings_papers_on_education_policy/v2000/2000.1rossell.html

Zehr, M. (2007). Learning the language: What is a home-language survey? *Edweek.org.* Retrieved from http://blogs.edweek.org/edweek/learning-the language/2007/02/whats_in_a_homelanguage_survey_1.html

HOME/SCHOOL RELATIONS

Parental involvement is well established as being correlated with student academic achievement. Five-year summaries of research in this area are available on the Web site of the National Network of Partnership Schools (NNPS), located at Johns Hopkins University.

These research studies corroborate that the involvement of family in a child's schooling contributes to positive results for students, including better school attendance, more responsible class preparation, more course credits earned, and higher achievement even through the high school years. As described in this entry, areas in which parental involvement is significant for student achievement are language development, homework, television supervision, and support to pursue a higher education.

Parent-guided children's visits to informal educational institutions in the community such as natural history museums, botanical gardens, zoos, and cultural institutions such as art museums and libraries can also support a child's education. For families with a single parent or two working parents, community-based organizations (CBOs) are important in helping continue the educational process after school. Organized programs may include the supervision of homework, the opportunity to learn other skills, and assisting with the development of talent in such areas as the arts, sports, and leadership.

For teachers and active parent associations who want to strengthen home/school relations, the NNPS is an established resource that provides materials to assist with parent involvement in schools. In addition, the NNPS Web site provides summaries of research studies on effective family involvement. Currently, more than 1,000 schools, 100 districts, and 17 state departments of education are working with NNPS to use research-based approaches to establish and strengthen their programs of school, family, and community partnerships. One study by NNPS reported a hierarchical linear modeling analysis showing that ongoing parental involvement in high school ameliorated low math achievement test scores of high school students in neighborhoods with high concentrations of poverty. This study also confirmed that it was not too late to initiate parent and community involvement programs, even at the high school level, as benefits accrued through 12th grade.

Research by Joyce Epstein found that the more specific and clear were the instructions for parents to help with homework, the greater the gain in student achievement. Her report also determined that the strongest results in student achievement occurred when the goals as well as the instructions were clear, and the homework help was well designed. Epstein documented that when teachers require parent-child interactions in completing math homework, and provide math materials for families to take home, the percentage of students who achieved math proficiency increased from the previous year to the next. Similarly, an increase in student reading skills was obtained when teachers involved families in subject-specific interventions in reading and related language arts. In the area of science, NNPS studies found family involvement in homework led to significant results for homework completion and for the improvement of students' science report card grades.

Parental Support of Language Development

Programs in family literacy help parents acquire or strengthen their own literacy skills, thus making them better able to assist their children's development of literacy. The National Center for Family Literacy, headquartered in Louisville, Kentucky, is a leader in this effort. Techniques such as the use of recorded books allow adults and children to acquire reading skills together. Children are encouraged to read when they see their parents read and to have their parents read to them. Reading for fun encourages more reading.

The more interaction and communication children have with their parents, the more they learn. Children can learn the importance of language in expressing ideas, feelings, and requests when parents respond to them and validate their thoughts. Children need guidance in learning patterns of communication that will be necessary in the classroom, including how to make a request, ask a question, and respond to questions. Parents can encourage language development by taking time to talk with their children about activities they are doing together, such as having dinner or visiting with relatives. Parents can also model the kinds of communication patterns children use in school by asking them questions about how one activity relates to another, asking how they feel about the activity, or asking them to predict what may happen next while watching television together. By providing this interaction with their children, parents are encouraging language development and reinforcing their children's self-esteem.

Parents can further help their children by providing a home environment that is conducive to learning by designating a space for children to do homework, by supervising their homework, and by communicating the importance parents place on education. In addition, it is important for parents to limit the time their children spend watching television.

Parents are a child's first teachers; children learn language or languages from their parents. Parents and guardians are not always aware, however, of the ways in which they shape their children's language development and communication skills. Parents who are literate in a language other than English may not know that their children can benefit if they support the speaking and reading of their native language at home. Reading to a child in the home language tends to encourage reading for pleasure and helps children begin to make the connection between oral language and reading.

Reading to children at an early age in their native language can also clarify the purpose of reading because the words that can be pointed to on the page become familiar and comprehensible to children. Those who speak Spanish have an advantage in learning to read because they can sound out words in Spanish more readily and the sounds of the vowels is consistent. Parents who take their children to the library to borrow illustrated children's books, selected by their children, demonstrate to their children the importance of literacy.

Incorporating the Home Culture

Cross-culture research by Edward Hall and reported by Marietta Saravia-Shore and Steven Arvizu has shown that the influence of religious and cultural institutions in communities where children live can have enormous impact on how children's values, attitudes, dispositions, and skills develop. Because culture and learning are connected, the experiences and principles of a person's culture can affect the expectations of the learning process. The norms and values of the families' culture need to be respected; parents can work with teachers to help them understand the students' home and community culture to better comprehend those characteristics that may be different from mainstream U.S. culture. For example, some cultures have taboos about touching a student's head. In some cultures, students are taught to remain quiet and listen to the teacher. In other cultures, children are not expected to look directly at adults. These behaviors are not found in the prevailing culture in most U.S. middle and high school classrooms, where teachers encourage students to participate in discussions and expect them to maintain "eye contact." To learn about the culture of the children in their classroom, teachers can ask students to interview their parents about their lives as children, their schooling, the stories they remember, favorite poems, and family recipes. The results of these interviews can be made into booklets and, subsequently, become reading materials for the entire class to help classmates understand the unique practices of their culture.

Teachers need to communicate with parents to understand the reasons for culturally based parent behavior and develop respect for the many different ways parents express concern about the education of their children. For example, Margaret Gibson reported that Punjabi immigrant parents in California often both work and do not attend school functions. They believe it is the teacher's duty to educate children and that parents should not be involved in what goes on at school. Punjabi parents therefore, support their children's education in other ways; for example, they require and supervise homework, ensure that their youngsters do not "hang out" with other American students, and ensure their children apply themselves to schoolwork. These parents also support their children in other ways; for instance, when necessary, parents will work two jobs to prevent their children from working outside the home so that their children have time for homework. As a result, Punjabi students as a group have higher rates of graduation and college acceptance than do other immigrant groups.

Teachers can act as "culture brokers" by interacting and talking with immigrant parents to (a) emphasize the key role parents play in their children's education, (b) clarify the expectations of the school, and (c) suggest ways in which parents might talk more often with their children to prepare them for communication in the classroom.

Students who learn to interact, respect, and work collaboratively with classmates from various cultures will be better prepared for the global world they will face in the 21st century. Teaching and learning strategies which draw on the social history and the everyday lives of students and their cultures assist the learning process. According to Roland Tharp and colleagues, teaching and learning are furthered when they are joint productive activities that involve both peers and teachers. Learning is enhanced when there are instructional conversations, that is, dialogues between teachers and learners about their common, shared learning activities. Teaching and learning are more effective when they are contextualized in the experiences, skills, and values of the community.

Community Resources

Teachers play an important role in referring parents to community resources such as museums and CBOs that can provide help with homework and other activities such as arts and sports programs. Referring parents to CBOs where their children will be safe in structured, supervised, after-school activities, as well as develop their talents furthers children's educational opportunities. Milbury McLaughlin and her colleagues have reported that adolescents who participate regularly in community-based youth development programs have better academic and social outcomes, as well as higher educational and career aspirations than do otherwise similar teens.

Extended families are also a resource. Being part of a social network of relatives enhances the opportunity for multiple alternatives for academic support. Students whose parents have not attended college can be helped by relatives who have attended college and can be guided by through the application procedures and the federal and state financial assistance application process.

Schools, Languages, and Parental Involvement

Communication between the school and parents is crucial. This is critical for parents who speak a language other than English; thus, the communication needs to be in the parents' native language. To reach parents who are not literate, some schools provide automated telephone messages in the languages of the community. These messages are updated week-to-week and inform parents about workshops and school events. To further reach parents, schools can post information to a Web site and send e-mail messages to grade listservs. Some schools, such as those in New York City, have paid full-time parent coordinators, who serve as advocates, answer parents' questions, and help refer parents to community resources. Some parent coordinators have "yellow pages" for parents that include local health, social service, and cultural and educational resources. Other parent coordinators hold or arrange workshops for parents on diverse issues such as parenting skills and school policies. Parents who attend these workshops can learn literacy skills and other activities that enhance their own abilities to support their children's learning of these skills. Some schools provide math, science, and other programs on DVDs or videotapes so parents can view these with their children. These materials are more accessible because they are visual and spoken rather than written.

According to the Children's Defense Fund, in 2000, 7 of 10 children, ages 6 to 13, had either both parents working or lived in a single-parent household. To increase attendance at meetings, parent-teacher organizations can hold meetings after work hours for working parents and can provide translators for those who do not speak English. Teachers can use individual parent-teacher meetings as times to discuss students' progress and homework, and to discuss community resources. If space is available, a room in the school can be set aside for parents to meet and discuss issues concerning their children's education or the school community.

Parents who are welcomed in schools, in ways that are culturally appropriate, become more accessible both as resources and as learners. Music performances, plays, or cultural celebrations may be better attended by parents who work during the school day if they are held in the early evening or on weekends. Parents can be asked to volunteer to provide refreshments or contribute to a potluck lunch after a school production on a Saturday. This increases the opportunities for parents to meet each other and the teachers informally. When students see that the school respects their parents, there may be less conflict between home and school cultures that cause breakdowns of discipline within the family.

Community schools serve as great resources for families because they are open after hours and into the evening to provide space for CBOs that continue learning opportunities for students and families. Some organizations provide prekindergarten and day care facilities. Students can receive help with homework, later use the gym for sports, and use the classrooms for dramatics, art, or music. Parents may also attend evening classes in English language learning, prepare for the GED, or develop their computer skills. Some community schools have on-site clinics where students are treated for ongoing conditions and thus miss less school. Others have on-site dental clinics. Community schools can provide materials about community resources for families in multiple languages. When the schools partner with community organizations, families are able to access resources more easily.

When parents, teachers, and schools collaborate to meet students' educational needs, this leads to strong home/school relationships. These informal partnerships give parents a voice in the education of their children, ensure that teachers create curricula that focuses on students' strengths, create positive school relationships for students and their parents, and provide an environment conducive to learning that contributes to the overall academic success of children. Bilingual education, because it makes use of the home language for instructional purposes, makes it much easier for immigrant parents to become involved in the education of their children.

Marietta Saravia-Shore

See also Heritage Languages in Families; Multicultural Education

Further Readings

Epstein, J. L. (2005). *Developing and sustaining research-based programs of school, family and community partnerships: Summary of five years of NNPS research.* Available from http://www.csos.jhu.edu/p2000/pdf/Research%20Summary.pdf

Gibson, M. A. (1983). *Home-school-community linkages: A study of educational opportunity for Punjabi youth.* Final Report. Stockton, CA: South Asian American Education Association.

Hall, E. T. (1959). *The silent language.* Garden City, NY: Doubleday.

McLaughlin, M., Irby, M. A., & Langman, J. (1994). *Urban sanctuaries: Neighborhood organizations in the lives and futures of inner-city youth.* San Francisco: Jossey-Bass.

Olsen, G., & Fuller, M. L. (2007). *Home-school relations: Working successfully with parents and families* (3rd ed.). Boston: Allyn & Bacon.

Saravia-Shore, M., & Arvizu, S. F. (1992). *Cross-cultural literacy: Ethnographies of communication in multiethnic classrooms.* New York: Garland.

Tharp, R. G., Estrada, P., Dalton, S. S., & Yamaguchi, L. (2000). *Teaching transformed: Achieving excellence, fairness, inclusion and harmony.* Boulder, CO: Westview Press.

HORNBERGER, NANCY (1951–)

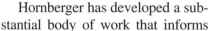

Nancy Hornberger is a renowned professor and the director of the Educational Linguistics Program at the University of Pennsylvania. She was born in Kentfield, California, on December 1, 1951, and completed her undergraduate education at Harvard University. In 1973, she earned an MA in bilingual education from

New York University. Hornberger was awarded her doctorate in 1985 from the University of Wisconsin–Madison, where she studied the use of Quechua and Spanish in schools in areas in the Andes. This entry describes her research and career.

Hornberger has developed a substantial body of work that informs studies in bilingualism, biliteracy, language minority education, language policies, indigenous language revitalization, ethnographic research in education, sociolinguistics, and language teaching. Her meticulous research has earned her an international and national reputation. She has contributed greatly to the field of bilingual education in national and international landscapes through her extensive publications in her areas of expertise. From an ethnographic perspective, she explores the development of biliteracy in bilingual contexts and the implications for planning and implementing language policies.

Hornberger has written more than a hundred scholarly chapters, articles, and book reviews; she has also coedited an international book series on bilingualism and bilingual education. She is the general editor of a 10-volume *Encyclopedia of Language and Education,* now in its second edition, and serves on several prestigious editorial boards including the Executive Committee of the American Association for Applied Linguistics, the Spindler Award Committee of the Council on Anthropology, the Education Committee of the American Anthropological Association, and as Division G program cochair of the American Educational Research Association, among others. Since 2000, Hornberger has served as the convener for the annual Ethnography Forum at the University of Pennsylvania. The forum invites a wide range of scholars, teachers, and administrators from urban areas and gives them an opportunity to examine learning, teaching, and administrative relationships between academic and public interests.

Hornberger's research studies draw from anthropology, sociolinguistics, language policies, and bilingualism. Her work provides a critical lens for schools and educators to better understand the complex nature of bilingualism, bilingual education, and language policies in multilingual societies. She examines the power relations between bilingual speakers of majority and minority languages and explores how language policies may influence the education of language minority populations.

Since 1989, she has studied the interrelationships between biliteracy in context, biliteracy in the individual, and biliteracy media. In the early work "Continua of Biliteracy," published in the *Review of Educational Research*, she explains and defines the continua or the framework as relationships and intersecting variables that may influence the development of biliteracy by focusing on the role of the bilingual as an individual, classroom, community, or society. In 1992, she contrasted the "continua of biliterate contexts," and the "continua of biliterate media," studying Puerto Rican and Cambodian students in two programs in Philadelphia. In a later article, Hornberger and Ellen Skilton-Sylvester maintained that teaching biliteracy cannot occur without considering the relationship between the different aspects described in the continua model: for example, the intersection between languages and literacies with diverse linguistic structures, and different context influences at the micro or macro social levels. Hornberger has engaged other researchers and collaborators both in the United States and abroad to investigate the complexities of developing biliteracy.

A leading authority in the study of bilingualism, bilingual education, language policies, and language rights at the national and international levels, Hornberger is a significant voice for bilingual educators both in the United States and abroad.

Olga Gloria Rubio

See also Bilingual Education as Language Policy; Continua of Biliteracy; Language Education Policy in Global Perspective; Language Policy and Social Control; Literacy and Biliteracy

Further Readings

García, O., Skutnabb-Kangas, T., & Torres-Guzmán, M. E. (Eds.). (2006). *Imagining multilingual schools: Languages in education and glocalization.* Clevedon, UK: Multilingual Matters.

Hornberger, N. H. (1989). Continua of biliteracy. *Review of Educational Research 59*(3), 271–296.

Hornberger, N. H. (2000). Revisiting the continua of biliteracy: International and critical perspectives. *Language and Education, 14*(2), 96–122.

Hornberger, N. H. (Ed.). (2003). *Continua of biliteracy: An ecological framework for educational policy, research, and practice in multilingual settings.* Clevedon, UK: Multilingual Matters.

Hornberger, N. H. (Ed.). (2008). *Encyclopedia of language and education* (2nd ed.). Cambridge, MA: Springer.

Hornberger, N. H., & Skilton-Sylvester, E. (2003). Revisiting the continua of biliteracy: International and critical perspectives. In N. H. Hornberger (Ed.), *Continua of biliteracy: An ecological framework for educational policy, research, and practice in multilingual settings* (pp. 35–67). Clevedon, UK: Multilingual Matters.

Mercado, C. (2003). Biliteracy development among Latino youth in New York City communities: An unexplained potential. In N. H. Hornberger (Ed.), *Continua of biliteracy: An ecological framework for educational policy, research, and practice in multilingual settings* (pp. 166–187). Clevedon, UK: Multilingual Matters.

Ruiz, R. (1984). Orientations in language planning. *NABE Journal, 8*(2), 15–34.

Torres-Guzmán, M. E. (2002). Dual language programs: Key features and results. *Directions in Language and Education, 14,* 1–16.

I

IMMIGRANT ELL EDUCATION

Historically, the experience of immigrating to the United States has varied greatly according to immigrants' countries of origin, ethnicity, gender, first language, educational and literacy levels, and other factors. In his 1990 book, *Coming to America*, Roger Daniels contends that one third of the American population (100 million) have ancestors who emigrated from various countries in southern and eastern Europe. These were the first wave of English language learners (ELLs), who entered the United States through Ellis Island from the late 1800s until the mid-20th century. Between the 1950s and the 1970s, European immigration to the United States nearly stopped, and the descendants of previous waves of eastern and southern European immigrants completed their assimilation into mainstream American society. A second wave, however, from the 1980s to the present, made up chiefly of Hispanic and Asian immigrants, has radically changed the face of America, with the introduction of multiple racial/ethnic and cultural/language backgrounds. This second wave of immigration has allowed a larger number of Americans to trace their ancestries to multiple non-Anglo-Saxon cultural/linguistic backgrounds. In addition, the current ease of mobility between countries has given this new wave of immigrants the flexibility to maintain their cultural heritage and language backgrounds.

Although immigrant groups from both earlier and more recent periods hold the experience of immigration in common, there are major differences in the sociohistorical contexts within which those experiences occurred. This entry traces the historical similarities and differences between the two waves of immigration and the socioeconomic changes that transformed U.S. society, with the shift from a largely industrial to a technology-based economy. This shift has lent urgency to the need for bilingual education for contemporary ELL immigrants. Research evidence suggests that bilingual education is capable of providing better educational opportunities for all ELL immigrant children.

Socioeconomic Historical Changes

Although Ellis Island and contemporary ELL immigrants shared similar demographic characteristics—such as being poor, illiterate, coming from rural backgrounds, and having little access to education—sociohistorical contexts made a difference in their social adaptation in America. Moreover, industrial society allowed Ellis Island descendants to use public schools as social institutions for upward mobility and integration into White mainstream America.

Ellis Island immigrants were capable of making a living as blue-collar workers in the manufacturing industry, without having first-language (L1) literacy skills or achieving English language proficiency. In addition, during the industrial period, society allowed immigrants to earn a living for two or three generations prior to entering middle-class America. In contrast, to enter middle-class America within a single generation, contemporary ELL immigrants need equal access to educational opportunities.

The current technological society, unlike the society of the industrial era, does not allow contemporary ELL immigrants two or three generations of adaptation prior to entering middle-class America. Wider economic gaps and high poverty levels among contemporary ELL immigrants place them at high risk for a low-quality education, poor sociocultural adaptation, underachievement, and high drop-out rates. Presently, equal educational opportunities leading to upward socioeconomic mobility can be possible for ELL contemporary immigrants only if they have access to a high-quality K–12 program and an opportunity for a higher education.

The Ellis Island years ended during the 1950s, a decade that marked changes in the social value of a formal education. Throughout the 1950s until the 1970s, a high school diploma represented a value asset for finding a better job and career opportunity. James Banks points out that in contrast, during the 1980s and 1990s, the technological revolution changed the labor market's demands. Presently, to find a menial job and to have access to postsecondary training, young adults need a high school diploma, but competing for better jobs in global markets requires higher education. Adult immigrants who are illiterate in their L1 and do not speak English will be unable to enter the U.S. labor market. In addition, their children, both foreign- and U.S.-born, will be able to earn a living in the current technological society only if they do not drop out of school.

Recent Demographic Changes in America

A 1998 report prepared by the National Center for Education Statistics showed that from the early 1970s to the mid-1990s, national drop-out numbers for students of all races Grades 10 to 12 ranged between 10% to 17% for low-income families (i.e., families in the lowest 20% income distribution). The data also indicated that Hispanics were more likely than other ethnic groups to leave school. Jennifer Laird, Matthew DeBell, and Chris Chapman point out that the drop-out rate for Hispanic students born outside the United States and between the age of 16 and 24 was much higher than for the general population.

Frank Hobbs and Nicole Stoops report that although the U.S. population increased during the 1990s to 2000, minority groups grew at a higher rate than Whites due to immigration trends and higher fertility rates. During the 20th century, other minority groups had a higher average annual growth rate than Whites. Interestingly, the White population had a higher growth rate than most minority groups during the first half of the 20th century. In contrast, the White population grew more slowly than any other race in the second half of the 20th century and for the century as a whole. According to Hobbs and Stoops, the minority population grew 11 times faster than the White, non-Hispanic population between 1980 and 2000. Contemporary immigration trends also dramatically increased the number of ELL students in U.S. public schools, hence affecting the demographics for culturally and linguistically diverse students.

Poverty Among Minority Groups

According to Bruce Webster and Alemayehu Bishaw, as of 1999, 13.8% of families of all races with children under 18 years of age had incomes below the poverty level. They also reported that this percentage was lower for White families but increased dramatically for minority families. According to the American Community Survey of 2005, 20.5% of Hispanic families were well below the poverty level compared with other minorities. In addition, according to the U.S. Census Bureau, in 2005, most families below the poverty level for all races had households with members who had less than a high school education and more than five children in the home. In contrast, the U.S. Census Bureau reported that only 7.5% of White families were below the poverty level, even though White individuals made up 75.1% of the population in the year 2000.

The effects of poverty on the quality of children's home environments are complex, with an interaction of multiple external factors (e.g., quality of communities and public services, stressors, homelessness, use of illegal drugs, etc.) and internal factors (e.g., children's characteristics and developmental/maturational patterns). Mediating factors, such as a high-quality bilingual education, can prevent minority children from underachieving and dropping out of school, provide access to a higher education, and help students to attain middle-class status. Furthermore, partnerships between educators and minority communities and families are needed to develop and support ELL students' academic achievement. Educators need to become mentors and advocates of ELL students and their families and support their efforts to successfully negotiate and adapt the mainstream school culture to their socioeconomic and educational needs. In addition, the training models for teachers in higher education need to be modified; this is necessary in response to demographic changes in socioeconomic and educational needs of these students and their families.

Advantages of Bilingual Education Programs

The U.S. Census Bureau reported that in 2000, 17.9% of the population 5 years old and over spoke a language other than English at home. According to information provided by David Meyer, David Madden, and Daniel McGrath, the number of ELL students in public schools increased from approximately 2 million in the 1993–1994 school year to 3 million in the 1999–2000 school year. According to the National Center for Education Statistics in 2006, in the 2003–2004 school year, services to ELLs were provided to 3.8 million students, with California and Texas reporting the largest number of students. These figures indicate that the ethnic diversity of students within the public schools increased dramatically during the 1990s and will continue to increase during the first decade of the 21st century.

The education system is the product of socioeconomic factors, and, consequently, the academic achievement gap between mainstream and minority ELL students has been widening since the 1980s. Impoverished neighborhoods have public schools with fewer economic resources; in addition, poor communities expose children to home and environmental stressors. Offering a high-quality bilingual program becomes a key external factor for mediating the negative effects of poverty on children who are learning English. Pushing for high-stakes national standards and reducing the academic achievement gap between mainstream and ELL students can happen only if high-quality bilingual education accelerates their attainment of English proficiency and sociocultural adaptation. As a social institution, public schools can be used as an opportunity for upward mobility to children from minority and low-income families.

It has been shown that the use of a student's L1 as a method of instruction accelerates their English language acquisition, overall development, literacy skills, and steady progress in content areas. A series of research studies, cited by Virginia Collier and Wayne Thomas, have demonstrated that additive bilingualism, maintenance of the L1 while developing the L2, results in positive cognitive, socioemotional growth, such as transfer of skills from L1 to L2, and ultimately prevents dropping out and reduces psychological distance between mainstream and minority groups.

Bilingual education can help ELLs and at-risk immigrant children to finish high school and give them equal access to higher education and higher-socioeconomic status. As advocates have pointed out, ethnically diverse children can enrich this nation and successfully adapt socially and culturally by maintaining their bicultural/bilingual and multicultural/multilingual heritage to move between two worlds. This approach supports *transculturation* as a successful sociocultural adaptation, in which ELL immigrants become English language proficient and socially adapt to mainstream America, while maintaining their L1 and cultural heritage as part of their identities.

Virginia Gonzalez

See also Americanization by Schooling; Hispanic Population Growth; Immigration and Language Policy

Further Readings

Banks, J. A. (2008). *Introduction to multicultural education.* Boston: Allyn & Bacon.

Collier, V., & Thomas, W. (2004). The astounding effectiveness of dual language education for all. *NABE Journal of Research & Practice, 2*(1), 1–19.

Daniels, R. (1990). *Coming to America: A history of immigrants and ethnicity in American life.* New York: HarperCollins.

Hobbs, F., & Stoops, N. (2002). *U.S. Census Bureau, Census 2000 special reports, demographic trends in the 20th century* (CENSR-4). Washington, DC: Government Printing Office.

Hoffman, L., & Sable, J. (2006). *Public elementary and secondary students, staff, schools, and school districts: School year 2003–04* (NCES 2006–307). Washington, DC: National Center for Education Statistics.

Laird, J., DeBell, M., & Chapman, C. (2006). *National assessment of educational progress* (NCES 2007024). Washington, DC: Government Printing Office.

Meyer, D., Madden, D., & McGrath, D. (2004). *English language learner students in U.S. public schools: 1994 and 2000* (NCES 2004035). Washington, DC: Government Printing Office.

National Center for Education Statistics. (1998). *The condition of education: 1998* (NCES 98013). Washington, DC: Government Printing Office. Retrieved from http://nces.ed.gov/pubsearch/pubsinfo.asp?pubid=98013

U.S. Census Bureau. (2000). *Census 2000 summary file 3, language, school enrollment, and educational attainment* (SF 3). Washington, DC: Government Printing Office.

U.S. Census Bureau. (2005). *American community survey: Characteristics of people who speak a language other then English at home* (S1603). Washington, DC: Government Printing Office.

U.S. Census Bureau. (2005). *American community survey: Poverty status in the past 12 months of families* (S1702). Washington, DC: Government Printing Office.

Webster, B. H., & Bishaw, A. (2005). *Income, earnings, and poverty data from the 2005 American community survey* (ACS-02). Washington, DC: Government Printing Office.

IMMIGRATION AND LANGUAGE POLICY

The junctures between demographic shifts and formal social institutions are often characterized by tension and contradiction based on the policies and practices of a given society or government. This is because the psychology, culture, habits, and customs of newcomers do not always coincide with the psychology, culture, habits, and customs of those who maintain those social institutions, including formal organizations of government and public service. These frictions can be understood by evaluating institutional policies and the demographic characteristics of the population that institutions are intended to serve. This entry interprets the historical developments of language and bilingual education policy in the United States in the proportional representation of immigrants throughout the United States, from the 1880s until the present day.

During the past 140 years, language and bilingual education policies have been more restrictive when the proportional representation of immigrants in this country is relatively high and on the rise (see Figure 1). Although several grand theories have been presented to explain this scenario, there is no consensus that any one of these theories can account for the historical shifts in language ideology and policy within public schools. Given the rapid growth of immigration rates during the past few decades and a current emphasis on developing accountability systems to overcome achievement gaps (between racial and ethnic groups, children in poverty, special education students, and English language learners), the extent to which language policies will continue to restrain non-English native languages in public schools is uncertain.

The historical development of language policies in U.S. schools has been discussed by Colin Baker and Sylvia P. Jones in terms of four periods, each characterized by developing ideologies toward language diversity and changing demographic conditions in these schools. Carlos Ovando elaborated on these historical periods by identifying some of the changing political, social, and economic forces that shaped and continue to shape language policies within each period, and discussed the shortcomings of several grand theories presented to account for changes in language ideologies and policies. The first period put forward by Baker and Jones—the permissive period (1700s–1880s)—is not treated here because it largely preceded the common school movement, which by 1870 provided some sort of free elementary schooling to much of the general population. Along with a brief chronology of language policies, social, economic, and political histories, these periods are discussed in terms of the proportional representation and other attributes of the foreign-born population—as well as the population of immigrant children (first and second generation) in schools from 1970 to 2000.

The Restrictive Period (1880s–1960s)

During a 30-year period, from 1880 until 1910, the United States experienced an 83% total population growth—from 50.2 to 92 million people. More than 16% of this growth was directly attributable to newcomers—first-generation immigrants. In 1910, the overall proportion of the foreign-born population was at its peak, 14.7%: the highest percentage since independence from Britain. Most of the immigrants arriving during this time were from Germany and Ireland, and many came from the United Kingdom, Italy, Canada, and Scandinavian countries. Some also arrived from China and other areas of Europe.

Several restrictive language policies emerged toward the end of the 19th century as the common school movement gained momentum. For Native Americans, restrictive language policies were instituted as a part of a comprehensive campaign toward assimilation. For German immigrants, who in 1880 represented nearly one third of all foreign-born individuals in the country, restrictive language policies were associated with growing religious tensions between Catholics and Protestants. In 1889, Illinois and Wisconsin embraced English-only laws, and in 1894, the Immigration Restriction League was founded to educate the population on the immigration system, to gain support for immigration restriction, and to lobby for restrictive legislation. The league remained active for nearly 20 years.

Following measures launched to limit immigration flows—such as the Naturalization Act of 1906, which

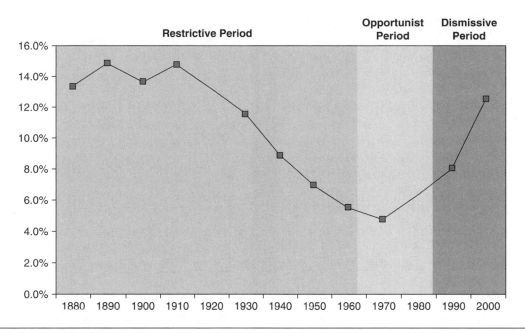

Figure 1   Foreign-Born Percentage of Total U.S. Population: 1880–2000

Source: U.S. Census Bureau (2007).

required immigrants be able to speak English to become naturalized citizens, and the Dillingham Commission—the percentage of overall foreign-born in the United States began to decline. Early 20th-century initiatives were concerned about clashes among the various traditions and languages from Southern, Eastern, and Central Europe. Such initiatives intensified during and after World War I, which resulted in a push toward monolingualism and the elimination of German as part of the curriculum of many schools. Immediately after the war, the Bureau of Naturalization and the Bureau of Education sponsored bills to increase federal aid to teach English to nonnative speakers and to American Indians. By 1923, the legislatures of 34 states had imposed English-only instruction in all private and public schools. Soon thereafter, the ruling of *Meyer v. Nebraska* (1923) allowed non-English instruction to continue in private schools, but had little effect on language of instruction in public schools.

Although the first half of the 20th century experienced a steady decrease in the overall percentage of foreign-born, the pool of newcomers from 1910 to 1960 was more diverse, representing more nations, cultures, languages, and traditions. By 1930, the immigrant landscape included more Latin American and Asian populations than before, even when

measures had been passed to contain flows of people arriving from Mexico, Japan, and China. However, 83% of immigrants were still European—mostly (in order of population size) from Italy, Germany, the United Kingdom, Poland, the Soviet Union, Ireland, Sweden, and Czechoslovakia; 9% were from Canada. By 1960, of the roughly 10.5 million first-generation immigrants, 75% were from Europe, 5% from Asia, and 9% from Latin America and Canada, respectively. A growing portion also represented Africa and Oceania.

As the immigrant pool began to diversify (see Figure 2), the push for American homogenization continued, reflected in English-only policies and practices in schools. Many factors contributed to this phenomenon, including the infrastructural establishment of urban schools, the drive for unity following World War I and during World War II, and the devaluation of immigrant cultures and languages. Little pressure was placed on schools for the educational success of immigrant children, and, as such, the responsibility of making the necessary linguistic, cultural, and cognitive modifications to adjust was largely left to immigrant students and their families. Educators and policymakers, in general, blamed their failure to succeed in school on their lack of assimilation of linguistic and cultural practices.

The Opportunist Period (1960s–1980s)

Following the Soviet Union's successful launch in 1957 of *Sputnik*, the world's first artificial satellite, the United States began to seriously question federal policies associated with the country's educational development. In particular, the National Defense Education Act was passed by Congress in 1958 to stimulate the advancement of education primarily in areas of science, mathematics, and modern foreign languages. This also came at a time when the overall percentage of immigrants in the country was the lowest it had been since the mid-19th century. An increased investment in elementary and secondary education, coupled with a relatively low level of immigration, allowed for the expansion of foreign-language study in U.S schools. However, this did not change the language of instruction for children of immigrants, who continued to be denied the opportunity to learn in their native languages.

During the 1940s and 1950s, immigration laws were passed to more closely monitor immigrants; in 1952, the modern-day U.S. immigration system was established. In the early 1960s, the immigration problem was seemingly contained. Annual quotas for the number of immigrants allowed in were met each year, and immigrant flows were under control. The advent of the civil rights movement and the Civil Rights Act of 1964 gave new impetus to discussions regarding non-English native-language instruction in schools. In addition, a revocation of the national origin quota system allowed more Asians and Latin Americans to enter the country. This occurred while the Cuban exile community, which had fled the island after the Revolution of 1959, was establishing dual-language (Spanish-English) schools in Miami. These schools were supported by funding from the federal government's Cuban Refugee Act, by Cuban parents, and the availability of several well-trained Cuban teachers.

By 1970, bilingual schools in South Florida were doing well, and the overall percentage of immigrants in the country was at the lowest point of the 20th century (4.7% foreign-born; see Figure 1). Because of an increased flow of Mexican immigrants and Cuban refugees, the number of newcomers of Latin American descent doubled from 1960 to 1970. Moreover, in the spirit of the civil rights movement and the federal government's efforts to eradicate poverty, the Bilingual Education Act was passed by Congress in 1968 to help language minority students (particularly Hispanics) perform better in schools. Federal funds were used to support dual-language educational programs, train teachers, develop and distribute curricula, and encourage parental involvement. This represented a turning point in U.S. policy on several fronts. First, it placed a greater responsibility

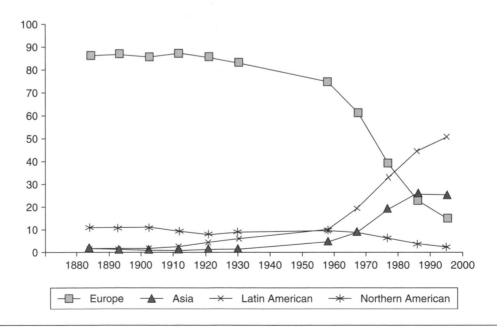

Figure 2   Immigrant Percentage of Total U.S. Foreign-Born, by Region: 1880–2000

Source: U.S. Census Bureau (2007).

on schools for the educational success of immigrant children, moving away from the sink-or-swim ideology that had prevailed before. Second, it gave rise to a greater recognition and appreciation for diverse languages and cultures. Third, it began to undermine English-only policies that were then still current in many states. Finally, it gave rise to community activism, which led to an increase of bilingual instruction throughout the country, and litigations for the educational needs of language minority students who had been neglected. In one of the first of these cases, *Lau v. Nichols* (1974), a class-action lawsuit representing 1,800 Chinese students who alleged discrimination for not receiving adequate instruction in English, the Supreme Court concluded that equal treatment of students did not equate to equal educational opportunity.

By the mid-1970s, the overall proportion of foreign-born in the United States was on the rise for the first time since the turn of the century. Bilingual education had gained momentum, and the National Association for Bilingual Education was established in 1975. The Office of Civil Rights developed guidelines, known as the *Lau* Remedies, for schools that had at least 20 language minority students with the same linguistic background. The *Lau* Remedies included pedagogical strategies and professional standards for bilingual teachers, and were focused on developing biliterate students. Such guidelines served as an impetus for additional litigation. The ruling in *Castañeda v. Pickard* (1981), for example, gave the public a three-step test for determining whether school districts were taking appropriate action to serve language minority students. Although these court rulings provided the opportunity for bilingual education programs to grow in number, the quality and types of programs that emerged varied greatly, and reputable research on best practices for these programs, in student outcomes, was limited.

The Dismissive Period (1980s–Present)

By 1980, the overall proportion of the foreign-born population was steadily rising, and the changing face of America's growing immigrant population could be sensed. In a matter of 20 years, the percentage of European immigrants within the foreign-born population fell from 75 to 39% while immigrants from Asia and Latin America increased from 5.1 to 19.3% and 9.4 to 33.1%, respectively (see Figure 2). In K–12 public schools, 1 in 10 children had at least one parent who was born outside the country (Figure 3), and conflicts regarding language policy in schools were stirring within the federal government.

Through the 1980s, fewer federal dollars were devoted to bilingual programs, and the *Lau* Remedies, which were scheduled for publication in the Federal Register, were never published as official regulations. Beyond Washington, several English-only movements were brewing. These movements became widely visible by the early 1990s when the foreign-born population surpassed 8% of the total U.S. population and the population of children of immigrants in schools surpassed 14% of the total K–12 student enrollment (Figure 4). Policy initiatives to counter immigration and non-English languages were most visible in California, where in 1990 approximately one third of the nation's overall foreign-born population resided. In 1994, California voters approved Proposition 187, a ballot initiative intended to curtail illegal immigration by imposing restrictions on social and educational services. In 1998, as debates heated regarding the effectiveness of bilingual education programs, California voters passed Proposition 227, which stated English should be the primary means of instruction for language minority students. Other state later followed California's lead in adopting or attempting to adopt state laws similar to those of California.

By 2000, the overall percentage of immigrants in the United States was the highest it had been in more than 70 years. By then, more than 12% of the country's total population was born outside the country, and one in five school-aged children (5–17 years old) had an immigrant parent (see Figure 4). More than half of immigrants were from Latin America, and approximately 30% of all immigrants were of Mexican origin. Moreover, between 1990 and 2000, immigrants dispersed to areas of the country that previously had low percentages of foreign-born populations. The South experienced the most rapid growth rate (88%) from 1990 to 2000. North Carolina and Georgia witnessed increases in their immigrant populations of 274 and 233%, respectively. The arrival of the new millennium also brought about sweeping changes in federal education policy. With bipartisan support, the No Child Left Behind Act (NCLB) was passed in 2001. This law called for higher academic standards and accountability, made government funding contingent upon student performance, and gave states the freedom to designate and implement the best methods (and language) of instruction to reach

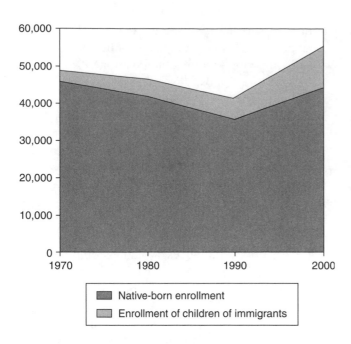

Figure 3   Enrollment of Native-Born and Children of
Immigrant Enrollment in K–12 Public
Schools: 1970–2000

Sources: Fix & Passel (2003); Van Hook & Fix (2000).

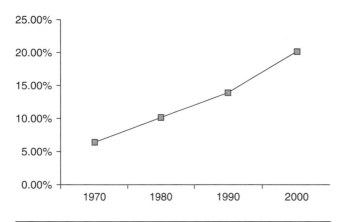

Figure 4   Overall Percentage of Children of
Immigrants of the Total K–12 Student
Population: 1970–2000

Sources: Fix & Passel (2003); Van Hook & Fix (2000).

student achievement goals. Although it did not stipulate, per se, the best program models for language minority students, NCLB eliminated the Bilingual Education Act, replacing it with "Title III, Language

Instruction for Limited English Proficient and Immigrant Students." This new legislation emphasized English acquisition and achievement, rather than the development of bilingualism and biliteracy.

Demographers project that by 2010, the total foreign-born population in the United States will surpass 40 million, about 18% more than the total population of Canada. At least one in four school-aged children will have an immigrant parent. As research evidence continues to build, supporting the value of native-language instruction, especially during the early and elementary school years to optimize the achievement of language minority students, it is unclear how language and bilingual education policies will unfold. The Coachella Valley Unified School District, 10 school districts in Southern California (case number CPF-05–505334 filed in June 2005) are currently suing the State of California for failing to test English language learners in a valid and reliable manner. This lawsuit rests on an NCLB provision stating that student assessments should be "in the language and form most likely to yield accurate data." This lawsuit highlights fundamental friction between federal laws demanding accurate evaluation and increased student achievement, and state laws restricting the language of instruction and assessment. The outcome of this case, akin to other California laws in the past, will likely influence language and education policies throughout the country.

Conclusion

Language ideologies and policies since the common school movement have been inconsistent and are characterized by contradiction. These laws have tended to be more restraining of non-English languages when the overall proportion of immigrants in the United States was and continues to be relatively high and rising. Several restrictive laws were passed before the beginning of the 20th century, mostly in reaction to the cultural and linguistic threat posed by the large corpus of German immigrants. As immigrant percentages decreased through the latter half of the 20th century, so did the polemics of the official status of English and immigration quotas. Following World War II, and an increased investment in public K–12 education, opportunities for bilingual education programs emerged. By the early 1980s, the percent of the foreign-born population was rising quickly. Federal support for bilingual education programs began to wane, and English-only initiatives were reemerging.

With California as their model, at the beginning of the 21st century, voters in Arizona, Colorado, Washington, and Massachusetts passed laws restricting non-English instruction in schools, and limiting public benefits for undocumented immigrants.

Although several grand theories have been proposed to explain historical shifts in language policy in the United States, no consensus exists. Many of the theories posit that shifts depend on certain characteristics of immigrant populations. Some conclude that language policies are based on immigrants' country of origin, meaning that policies have been less restraining of European languages. Others suggest that restrictive policies are race-based. That is, policies have become more restrictive as the pool of immigrants is increasingly non-White. Some suggest the language policies are class-based; the libertarian view conceives language policies as a function of the government's increasing control. Although each of these theories presents supportable arguments, they undermine the social, political, and economic contexts within which language policy has evolved. What can be said, however, is that these laws have tended to be more restraining of immigrants' languages when the overall proportion of the foreign-born in the United States was relatively high and still rising. Conflicts between state and federal policies in public education may challenge this trend.

Bryant T. Jensen

See also Bilingual Education as Language Policy; Early Immigrants and English Language Learning; German Language Education; Language Policy and Social Control; Language Rights in Education; Title VII, Elementary and Secondary Education Act Becomes Title III, No Child Left Behind Act of 2001

Further Readings

Baker, C., & Jones, S. P. (1998). *Encyclopedia of bilingualism and bilingual education.* Clevedon, UK: Multilingual Matters.

Bilingual Education Act, Pub. L. No. 90–247, 81 Stat. 816 (1968).

Capps, R., Fix, M., Murray, J., Ost, J., Passel, J. S., & Herwantoro, S. (2005). *The new demography of America's schools: Immigration and the No Child Left Behind Act.* Washington, DC: Urban Institute.

Castañeda v. Pickard, 648 F.2d 989 (5th Cir. 1981).

Civil Rights Act of 1964, Pub. L. No. 88-352, 78 Stat. 241 (1964).

Cuban Adjustment Act (CAA), Pub. L. 89-732 (1966).

Fix, M., & Passel, J. (2003). *U.S. immigration: Trends and implications for schools.* Washington, DC: Urban Institute.

Larsen, L. J. (2004). *The foreign-born population in the United States: 2003.* Washington, DC: U.S. Government Printing Office, U.S. Census Bureau.

Lau v. Nichols, 414 U.S. 563 (1974).

Meyer v. Nebraska, 262 U.S. 390 (1923).

Naturalization Act of 1906, 34 Stat. [348 U.S. 528, 532] 596 (1906).

No Child Left Behind Act of 2001, Pub. L. No. 107–110 (2002).

Ovando, C. (2003). Bilingual education in the United States: Historical development and current issues. *Bilingual Research Journal, 27*(1), 1–24.

Schimley, A. D. (2001). *Profile of the foreign-born population in the United States: 2000.* Washington, DC: U.S. Government Printing Office, U.S. Census Bureau.

U.S. Census Bureau. (2007). *United States foreign-born population.* Washington, DC: Author. Available from http://www.census.gov/population/www/socdemo/foreign.html

Van Hook, J., & Fix, M. (2000). A profile of the immigrant student population. In J. R. DeVelasco, M. Fix, & T. Clewell (Eds.), *Overlooked and underserved: Immigrant children in U.S. secondary schools.* Washington, DC: Urban Institute.

IMPROVING AMERICA'S SCHOOLS ACT OF 1994

A Historical Essay

Editor's Note: *The last reauthorization of Title VII of the Elementary and Secondary Education Act (the Bilingual Education Act) occurred in 1994. For most of its legislative life, Title VII was beleaguered, and advocates found it difficult to maintain a consistent policy framework for the program. The political winds swayed the law in various directions beginning in 1968 and ending in 2001. Ostensibly, Title VII was merged into the No Child Left Behind Act of 2001 (NCLB) at that point. The author was a lead player in the last reauthorization of Title VII, which was part of an omnibus bill known as Improving America's Schools Act, the predecessor to NCLB. This essay is an insider's view of the dynamics the author encountered in helping the U.S. Department of Education in this effort. In an important sense, the version of Title VII that emerged from this activity led into a darker period in the history of bilingual education, one in which antibilingual education sentiment was stronger than ever. Hence, this entry describes bilingual education legislation, arguably, at its best.*

The author of this entry was invited to submit an article reflecting a mix of information and expert opinion. We acknowledge that parts of it could be disputed or given an alternative interpretation. In several instances, the editors found this approach helpful in more realistically portraying the history and current status of bilingual education in the United States.

The ethnic and linguistic diversity of U.S. schools has grown significantly in the past three decades. This diversity has provided distinct new challenges for schooling efforts. New policy and federal programs, particularly exemplified in Title VII of the 1994 reauthorization of the Elementary and Secondary Education Act (ESEA), attempted to address this challenge. This act called for integrated and comprehensive programming based on a new empirical and conceptual knowledge base, which had emerged over several decades. This essay addresses the demographic circumstances of student diversity, the emerging knowledge base, and the related federal educational reform policy changes that I worked on during the reauthorization of the ESEA in 1993–1994. That reauthorization was signed into law in fall 1994 under the legislative title Improving America's Schools Act, often referred to as the All Children Can Learn Act (the predecessor to the present No Child Left Behind Act of 2001).

The summons to change educational practices in the face of continued language minority student underachievement were not to be ignored, as I came to Washington in September of 1993 as director of the Office of Bilingual Education and Minority Languages Affairs (OBEMLA), a senior officer in the U.S. Department of Education. I was immediately called upon to translate such calls for educational improvement related to language minority and immigrant students into program features that might be helpful to policymakers, educators, and the general public. I was committed to this task for several reasons. I will address two of them here because they are important as context for the policy work that I entered into, as I took on this new facet of my career in education. The first rationale was put simply by my eldest daughter, Marisol, around a dinner table as I discussed, with my two daughters and my wife, the invitation to join the Clinton administration in the U.S. Department of Education: "You are always complaining about policy, why don't you go and do something about it?," she said. At the time, I was a full professor of education and psychology at the

University of California, Santa Cruz, and had been serving as dean of the College of Social Sciences at that university. I had built a solid professional career as a researcher and scholar, primarily investigating the early and later schooling of students like me, students who came to school speaking a primary language other than English. Much of that work did in fact provide a critique of educational practices related to these students. However, I had also spent time researching "effective schools"—schools that served these students well. I was concerned at the time that educational establishments were ignoring and even reluctant to utilize these findings, but I certainly did not see myself as a policymaker. Like anyone who has been trained to be primarily a researcher and academic, and has had some success at it, it was difficult to positively perceive a role change that would take me into the highly politicized policy making world, but as Marisol indicated, now supported by my wife and youngest daughter, "Why not give it a whirl?"

The second reason for this "new beginning" was equally personal, and it went hand in hand with my research and academic background related to trying to "make a difference." My sister told me a story when I was a teenager that made a deep impression on me, and on what I moved forward doing educationally and professionally. She tells of looking forward to a significant new beginning: her first day at school. Her older brothers and sisters reminded her that morning, as usual, that school was important even though they went to their farm work, while my mother accompanied her. It was a small, one-room schoolhouse, and the teacher was held in high esteem, by both the farm and ranch owners and laborers of the local rural Colorado community. Although her siblings had picked up some English in school, my mother—as all my family and my sister—spoke primarily Spanish. Our European and indigenous ancestors, dating back before the arrival of the Pilgrims on Plymouth Rock, decided to stay in the territory ceded to the United States by Mexico in the Treaty of Guadalupe Hidalgo in 1848. Spanish had been the language of this part of the country for many years—English was the language of the new arriving immigrants, largely undocumented, from other parts of the United States.

As teachers have asked and will continue to ask throughout time, the phrase "What is your name?" greeted my sister on her first day of school. "Ciprianita," she happily answered. The teacher tried to pronounce the name and then respectfully requested, "Can I call you Elsie—it is my favorite name." In that one instant, my sister's linguistic and cultural heritage was politely and unintentionally challenged, and in my mother's presence, her child's "*raíces*" or "roots" were metaphorically severed. Ciprianita had developed her social and linguistic roots in her Spanish-speaking family. The teacher mostly likely meant no harm. Her intent was seemingly positive: to translate Ciprianita's unfamiliar name to one with which the teacher felt comfortable and familiar. It probably did not seem like a significant incident to the teacher because such moments of replacing students' home names were common then and common today. But still, my sister will never forget that first day of school—for to her it represented the moment when she was asked to leave her full self at home.

As the saying goes, "This is not the end of the story." Two years later, as my cousin, Rícela, was heading off to her first day at school with her cousin (Ciprianita–now-Elsie) and her older brothers (Pedro-now-Pete and Leandro-now-Leo), she asked them what she should say to the teacher because she did not know much English. Her oldest brother Pete indicated that she would have to give the teacher a name. Leo immediately suggested she tell the teacher her name was "Katy"—it was Leo's favorite name. And at that moment, Rícela became Katy. No longer was it necessary for the teacher to directly influence the ongoing linguistic and cultural identity of these children—the process had taken on a life of its own among those youngsters. By the way, much like Elsie, Pete, Leo, and Katy left school as soon as they could go to work full time in the fields. Such incidents represent an important school stance learned by her and other children who come to school not speaking the school language, English: One's full home self, and in particular the non-English-speaking self at home, is to be checked at the door.

In the most positive interpretation of such ordinary translations by educators, changing students' names, when they enter school, could signify the general educational philosophy that who you are—poor, rich, Anglo, Latino, and so on—does not matter in school. It could signify that despite the individual or group-based differences embodied in names, everyone will be treated as equals, and that changing a name really is not that important.

In the most negative interpretation, a change in a name may signal an unwillingness to respect a student's cultural and linguistic background, and set the stage for

still other instructional and institutional practices that do the same—such as ignoring the child's family history of immigration, or solely using literature with which students cannot identify. Lastly, it might also suggest to the student and the family that they themselves may not belong in the school—because the deepest marker of the home self, one's given name, itself does not belong. Our family was left with a sense of uncertainty about responding, positively or negatively, to a new name thrust into our family.

As I have shared this story with immigrant family members in other regions of the country, heads begin to nod, suggesting, "That happened to me or my family members." It is far too common a reaction. Although they are in many ways the same "under" their names, these children and families also live different lives, in many ways that demand educators' attention and respect. Any overt signal of disrespect for one's home life, from an individual in authority, indicates to those receiving the message that they are not wanted and do not belong in school in general. I entered the work of national policy believing that it need not be that way. Intended or not, the message of rejection or marginality comes through, and language carries the message.

Education Reform for Language Minority Children Through "Improving America's Schools" Act

In the overall educational reform put forward by the U.S. Department of Education, it was important to highlight the distinct population comprising students who, because of particular circumstances in their homes before entering school, were not familiar with the culture of schooling in general. Many come to school with little formal education, few experiences of success in their families, and lack the necessary language and frame of reference required for successful learning in American schools. The term *language minority* is not a monolithic population. As one searches for a comprehensive definition of the language minority student, a continuum of possibilities unfolds. At one end of the continuum were general definitions such as "students who come from homes in which a language other than English is spoken." At the other end of that continuum were highly operational definitions—"students who scored in the first quartile on a standardized test of English language proficiency." Regardless of the definition used, these students come in a variety of linguistic shapes and sizes.

The language minority population in the United States was, then, and continues to be linguistically heterogeneous. More than 140 distinct language groups have been identified in the United States today. Even in the largest language group, those from Spanish-speaking backgrounds, some are monolingual Spanish speakers whereas others are to some degree bilingual. Other non-English-speaking minority groups in the United States are similarly heterogeneous. Describing the "typical" language minority student was and continues to be highly problematic. However, one might agree that this student is one who (a) is characterized by substantive participation in a non-English-speaking social environment, (b) has acquired the normal communication abilities of that social environment, (c) is exposed to a substantive English-speaking environment, more than likely for the first time, during the schooling process, and (d) tests poorly on verbal English language tests.

Need for a New National Education Policy

From this broader context, what specific changes in policy did we address? Typical rationales for changes in national policy are often related to crisis intervention: There is a problem and it must be addressed quickly, usually with more political and philosophical rhetoric than action or new resources. The national policy for serving linguistically and culturally diverse students and their families was driven to a large extent by this "crisis" rationale. Accordingly, crisis policies in this arena have been shortsighted, inflexible, and minimally cohesive and integrated; they are not always informed by a strong knowledge base—conceptual, empirical, or related to the wisdom of practice. Title I and Title VII of the Elementary and Secondary Education Act (ESEA), both prime examples of the crisis-intervention approach (of a remedial-compensatory nature), have suffered from these disadvantages.

New policies that emerged under the reauthorization of ESEA during my service in Washington, although recognizing the acute need to serve this student population, also recognized the following factors in developing new policy:

1. The new knowledge base, both conceptual and empirical, must be central to any proposed changes.

2. Consultation with the field was critical to capitalize on the wisdom of existent policy, administration, curriculum, and instructional practice.

3. Policies and programs must be cohesive, to effectively integrate services that are to be provided—this cohesiveness reflecting the partnership between national, state, and local education policies and programs.

4. The demographic and budgetary realities that are present today and would be operative throughout this decade, and continuing to influence new directions, must be acknowledged.

New policy directions, primarily those related to Title VII (also known as the Bilingual Education Act), were implemented in line with these presuppositions.

Better Knowledge Base

Recent findings from research had redefined the nature of the educational vulnerability of linguistically and culturally diverse students. This research has destroyed common stereotypes and myths and laid a foundation on which to reconceptualize educational practices and launch new initiatives. This foundation recognized the homogeneity/heterogeneity within and between diverse student populations. No single set of descriptions or prescriptions will suffice. However, a set of commonalities deserved particular attention. The foundation that established these findings had documented effective educational practices related to linguistically and culturally diverse students throughout the United States. These descriptive studies identified specific schools and classrooms serving "minority" students that are academically successful. The case-study approach adopted by these studies included examinations of preschool, elementary, and high school classrooms. Teachers, principals, parents, and students were interviewed and specific classroom observations were conducted that assessed the "dynamics" of the instructional process.

The results of these studies provide important insights with regard to general instructional organization, literacy development, academic achievement in content areas (such as math and science), and the views of the students, teachers, administrators, and parents. Interviews with classroom teachers, principals, and parents revealed an interesting set of perspectives regarding the education of the students in these schools.

Classroom teachers who are highly committed to the educational success of their students; perceived themselves as instructional innovators using new learning theories and instructional philosophies to guide their practice; continued to be involved in professional development activities, including participation in small-group support networks; had a strong, demonstrated commitment to student-home communication (several teachers were using a weekly parent interaction format); and felt that they had the autonomy to create or change the instruction and curriculum in their classrooms, even if it did not meet exact district guidelines. They had high academic expectations for all their students (with comments such as "everyone will learn to read in my classroom") and served as advocates for their students. They rejected any conclusion that their students were intellectually or academically disadvantaged.

In summary, effective curriculum, instructional strategies, and teaching staffs recognized that academic learning had its roots in sharing expertise and experiences through multiple avenues of communication. Effective curricula provided abundant and diverse opportunities for speaking, listening, reading, and writing, along with scaffolding to help guide students through the learning process. Further, effective schools for diverse students encouraged them to take risks, construct meaning, and seek reinterpretations of knowledge within compatible social contexts. Under this knowledge-driven curriculum, skills are tools for acquiring knowledge, not ends in themselves. The curriculum recognized that any attempt to address the needs of these students in a deficit or "subtractive" mode was counterproductive. Instead, this new knowledge base recognized, conceptually, that educators must be "additive" in their approach to these students, that is, adding to the rich lore of intellectual, linguistic, academic, and cultural skills they bring to the classroom.

Wisdom of Practice

Too often in the heat of legislation and the political process, policy development is highly centralized in the domains of various interest groups and professional policymakers. In this reauthorization of Title VII, the policy initiatives were crafted in consultation with diverse constituencies. For linguistically and culturally diverse communities, the usual players were consulted. These included the National Association for Bilingual Education (NABE), the Mexican American Legal Defense and Education Fund (MALDEF), which has made specific legislative recommendations of major proportion, and other educational groups, which have made recommendations related to their own interests and expertise. Of particular significance was the work of the Stanford Working Group. This group, funded by the Carnegie Corporation of New York, began almost 2 years before to consult widely with various individuals representing a broad spectrum of theoretical, practical, and policy significant expertise. In published reports and in various forums, they put forward a comprehensive analysis and articulated precise recommendations for policy and legislation related to linguistically and culturally diverse populations. Thus, new policy was shaped in consultation with others. To do otherwise would have negated the importance of shared wisdom from various established perspectives. Moreover, it was understood that any proposed changes, if they were to be effective, must be embraced by those individuals and organizations presently in the field.

Cohesiveness

The proposed policy directions also attempted to view the provision of services to students in a comprehensive and integrated manner. Through the introduction of new major legislation in Goals 2000: Educate America Act, the U.S. Department of Education had set the stage for the formal development and implementation of national goals and standards. Then, with the introduction of the Educate America Act and the reauthorization of the ESEA, an alignment of the goals and standards initiatives with specific resource-allocation policies were accomplished. This alignment recognized that integration of federal, state, and local agency efforts must occur to enhance effectiveness and efficiency. Moreover, the federal role must allow flexibility at the state and local levels while requiring that all children achieve at the highest levels.

The Title VII reauthorization, addressing services to limited-English-proficient (LEP) students as a component of the ESEA, was highly congruent with the alignment principle. As such, Title VII was not seen as yet another intervention aimed at meeting an educational crisis. Instead, it was regarded as a key component of the integrated effort to effectively address the educational needs of students. Specifically, Title VII continued to provide leadership and national, state, and local capacity building, with regard to educational services, professional development, and research related to culturally and linguistically diverse populations. However, other programs, particularly Title I, were important and were intended more directly to increase the services needed by all students in poverty, including those with limited English proficiency.

Demographic and Budgetary Realities

For several decades, large increases in the number of LEP students in our schools have occurred. There was no reason then or now to believe that this trend will subside. It was important then as it is today to recognize that the national presence and the diversity of this population are substantial. In the past three decades, 35 states have been added to the count of those states with more than 10% of their student population identified as LEP or English language learners (ELLs). In 1993, 20 states could be counted in such a column, half of these states having student populations that varied between 10 and 25%. Moreover, the aggregated population of non-English language students served is itself quite diverse with more than 100 language groups represented in programs funded under Title VII at that time.

Unfortunately, the fiscal resources that could be consolidated to meet the growing and diverse demands of this population were not likely to be increased in any significant way. National, state, and local funding for these populations had not grown in proportion to their increase nor was there the political will to enhance those funds. This has not changed. Although new proposals regarding the disposition of Title I funds to high-poverty areas should bring more resources to those students, such funds would still be limited. This meant then as it means today that resources must be used more efficiently.

Specific Changes to Title VII

The final reauthorization of Title VII in 1994 represented a coming of age for that legislation and for those who relied on it to support effective instructional programs. Practitioners had worked during the past 20 years to make such education a necessary and accepted component of public schools, and these efforts have paid off. The 1994 Title VII legislation as well as other legislation under the Elementary and Secondary Education Act was intended to go far in

meeting the needs of millions of linguistically and culturally diverse children in the schools.

In 1994, it was not known how long Title VII would continue to serve as the backbone of services to LEP students in our schools. All the major activities of previous reauthorizations were retained and strengthened. The improvements to Title VII were based on several developments over the years.

First, a newly expanded, robust knowledge base had redefined the nature of our linguistically and culturally diverse students' educational experience. Research and emerging theory documented the educationally effective practices with regard to general organization, literacy development, academic achievement in content areas, and teacher preparation for these students. These new concepts were embedded in the legislation.

The proposed Title VII legislation was part of a cohesive policy direction from the U.S. Department of Education. Title VII continued to serve the missions of leadership and capacity-building with regard to educational services, professional development, and research related to these populations. However, services for LEP students were packaged in a more comprehensive and integrated manner, one that recognized the significance of GOALS 2000, Title I and other ESEA programs, and state and local education efforts. The needs of linguistically and culturally diverse children were recognized and were directly responded to in the new federal legislation. Title I legislation, for example, was opened in a deliberate manner to serve as a major source of federal educational programming for LEP students. This had been a major recommendation of the Stanford Working Group; this resulted in making available expanded funding for bilingual education programs across the country.

Within this framework, several changes were present in Title VII. Direct assistance to local and state education agencies had been the core of federal services to LEP children in our nation's schools. Under the changes contained in the new law, existing programs would be replaced by new programs: development and enhancement grants, comprehensive school grants, and comprehensive district grants. This new configuration recognized the complexity of educational responses for LEP students, as well as the necessity for locally designed and integrated programs. State review of proposals reinforced the implementation of state plans for LEP students.

Other changes under research, evaluation, and dissemination were responsive to input from the field.

Research activities were to be developed by the Office of Bilingual Education and Minority Language Affairs with required consultation from the field, and enhanced coordination with other Department of Education research activities. Program evaluation requirements were simplified to be more "user-friendly" and directed at program improvement and dissemination. To showcase the successes achieved by existing Title VII programs, added emphasis was placed on Academic Excellence Programs—programs with proven effectiveness that disseminate their expertise locally, regionally, and nationally. The work of the Multifunctional Resource Centers and the Evaluation Assistance Centers were merged with new Department of Education technical assistance and professional development efforts. The goal of this refocusing effort was to have more integrated delivery of services to schools on a more economical basis.

After some 20 years of efforts to develop a teaching force prepared to meet the needs of LEP students, this area remained a major challenge. Professional development programs place renewed emphasis and resources on professional development, including a new career-ladder program. To assist institutions of higher education in improving teacher preparation programs, national training institutes for institutions of higher education faculty and administrators were emphasized. In addition to these continuing efforts to prepare teachers, opportunities for professional development through doctoral fellowships remained in place. To continue the development of a strong research and theoretical base, opportunities for postdoctoral studies were created.

These changes were framed by a commitment to the value of bilingualism and the belief that all children can achieve to high standards. The new policy attempted directly to strengthen bilingual education programs and promote their implementation not only through Title VII, but also through Title I and related K–12 education funding, thus opening the possibility of several million additional dollars in funding to meet the great need for services to these students.

This policy effort was intended to ensure that all linguistically and culturally diverse children and their families benefit from educational reform. Most persons involved in the new reauthorization process felt it was time that the children served by our educational system be included in reform efforts from the start and at every level. Systemic reform activities that ignored the needs of these children were considered neither systemic nor genuinely reform-minded.

Aftermath: From Bilingual Education to English-Only Instruction

Regarding LEP students, the 2001 reauthorization of the ESEA was a complete reversal from the reauthorization of 1994 described earlier. Table 1 provides a summary of key differences in how the 1994 and the 2001 reauthorizations of the ESEA address the education of LEP students.

Whereas the 1994 version of the Bilingual Education Act included among its goals "developing the English skills and to the extent possible, the native-language skills" of LEP students, the new law, No Child Left Behind (NCLB), focuses only on attaining "English proficiency." In fact, the word *bilingual* has been completely eliminated from the law and any government office affiliated with the law. A new federal office has been created to replace OBEMLA and oversee the administration of the new law. It is now the Office of English Language Acquisition, Language Enhancement, and Academic Achievement for Limited-English-Proficient Students (OELALEAALEPS or, as it is commonly referred to, OELA). What was formerly known as the National Clearinghouse for Bilingual Education (NCBE) is now known as the National Clearinghouse for English Language Acquisition and Language Instruction Educational Programs (referred to as NCELA). For reasons that are unclear, bilingual education has been totally extirpated from the vernacular of the federal government.

Through Title III of NCLB, federal funds to serve bilingual students will no longer be federally administered via competitive grants designed to ensure equity and promote quality programs; programs that served as good examples to the rest of the nation. Instead, resources were to be allocated primarily through a state formula program for Language Instruction Educational Programs (LIEPs) that are "based on scientifically based research." LIEPs are defined as an instruction course in which LEP students are placed for the purpose of developing and attaining English proficiency, although meeting challenging state and academic content, and student academic achievement standards. A LIEP may make use of both English and a child's native language to enable the child to develop and attain English proficiency. In practice, however, bilingual approaches are discouraged in many states, especially states where bilingual education has been subjected to voter acceptance or rejection.

Table 1   Significant Differences in the 1994 and 2000 Reauthorizations of the ESEA

Issue	1994 Title VII: Bilingual Education Act	2001 Title III: Language Instruction, Limited English Proficient, and Immigrant Students
Eligible Populations	Limited English proficient students Recent immigrants that have not been attending one or more schools in any one or more states for more than 3 full years. (7102(7)) Native Americans, Native Alaskans, Native Hawaiians, Native American Pacific Islanders	Limited English proficient students Immigrant children and youth: 3–21 years of age, not born in any state, have not been attending one or more schools in any one or more states for more than 3 full academic years. (3301(6)) Native Americans, Native Alaskans, Native Hawaiians, Native American Pacific Islanders
Purpose	(A) To help such children and youth develop proficiency in English, and to the extent possible, their native language; and (B) meet the same challenging state content standards and challenging state student performance standards expected of all children. (7111(2)) The use of a child or youth's native language and culture in classroom instruction can promote self-esteem and contribute to academic achievement and learning English by limited English proficient children and youth. (7102(14)) Native Americans and Native American languages . . . have a unique status under Federal law that requires special policies within the broad purposes of this Act to serve the education needs of language minority students in the United States. (7102(6))	To help ensure that children who are limited English proficient, including immigrant children and youth, attain English proficiency, develop high levels of academic attainment in English, and meet the same challenging state academic content and student academic achievement standards as all children are expected to meet. (3102(1)) Programs for Native Americans: To develop English proficiency and, to the extent possible, proficiency in their native language. (3211(2)) To streamline language instruction educational programs into a program carried out through formula grants to state educational agencies and local educational agencies. (3102(7))
Programs	Competitive grants to local education agencies (schools, districts). State education agencies approve the grant application before submission but play no official role in the grants' implementation. Quality bilingual education programs enable children and youth to learn English and meet high academic standards including proficiency in more than one language. (7102(9)) Priority is given to programs that provide for development of bilingual proficiency both in English and another language for all participating students. (7116 (i)(1))	To implement language instruction educational programs based on scientifically based research on teaching limited English proficient children. (3102(9))
Allocation of Funds	Cap of 25% of funds for SAIPs can be lifted if an applicant has demonstrated that developing and implementing a bilingual education programs is not feasible.	95% of funds must be used for grants at the local level to teach limited English proficient children.

Formula grants are distributed to each state based on their enrollments of LEP and immigrant students. Each state must then allocate 95% of the funds to individual local education agencies (LEAs) to fund programs—the LIEPs. The argument for the formula grants claims that the previous system of competitive grants merely benefited a small percentage of LEP students in relatively few schools. Actually, under the new process inherent in NCLB, resources will be spread more thinly than before—among more states, more programs, and more students. Through competitive grants, Title VII support for instructional programs previously served about 500,000 "eligible" students out of an estimated 3.5 million nationwide. Under NCLB, districts automatically receive funding based on the enrollments of LEP and immigrant students. However, the impact of federal dollars would be reduced. For example, before the new process, about $360 was spent per student in Title VII–supported instructional programs. Despite the overall increase in appropriations, under the new process, Title III provided less than $135 per student. Funding for all other purposes—including teacher-training, research, and support services—was restricted to 6.5% of the total budget. That amounted to about $43 million, which reflected a decrease for the first year. Before this, funding was $100 million for professional development alone to address the critical shortage of teachers qualified to meet the needs of bilingual students.

In summary, federal policies now emphasize the teaching and learning of English with little regard for the development of academic bilingual competency, for students coming to school speaking a language other than English. It is unclear whether this reflects only a temporary swing in policy direction or if it will "stay the course" in a political climate that is likely to become harsher as the immigrant populations increase. For now, state policies have begun to mirror this shift in at least three states.

Reflection on the Effort

It is difficult to assess the contribution made by the U.S. Department of Education in formulating and shepherding the legislation through the Congress. It appears, given the provisions of NCLB, that it may have been short lived. Further, anti-immigrant sentiment and antibilingual education initiatives have all worsened since the previous experiences, occurring in 1994. Technically, bilingual education is now illegal in three important states: Arizona, California, and Massachusetts. From a strict national policy perspective, I am not sure that the "new" Ciprianitas and Rícelas will not have some of the same experiences in today's U.S. schools that my sister and cousin had in their day. It is unfortunate for them and the country as students like them increase daily in our classrooms. The country has a long way to go in constructing national programs that can be more supportive of what we know can assist these students in the way they should be educated.

However, the present state of theory, research, and practice was influenced greatly by the actions taken during my time in Washington. The formal launching of specific funding for dual-language programs throughout the United States can be directly traced to the Title VII initiatives of 1994. Those programs have been growing substantially, and the evidence for their effectiveness is solid: They assist ELLs to acquire English and achieve at higher levels while integrated with a broad array of students, and they provide the opportunity for English-speaking students to acquire a second language. These programs particularly attend to the linguistic resources students bring to school and add the important development of schooling goals.

In addition, the increased funding for teacher development and professional development in the Title VII reauthorization of 1994 made it clear that investments in teacher preparation are key to enhancing student achievement. Today, we can directly trace the increased numbers of professionals trained to serve specific ELLs to the enhanced support provided by Title VII. The same can be said about the development of professionals at the doctoral level. I cannot keep track of the times an individual approaches me to thank me for supporting his or her continued education attainment at the doctoral level. Of course it was not me, but the enhancement of the doctoral fellowship program in the 1994 reauthorization that deserves the credit. The field is greatly enriched with this critical augmentation of high-level professionals.

Taken as a whole, the experience, the effort, and the results have been valuable at the individual level and the professional level. The road to educational equity for ELLs remains difficult, and we have much distance yet to cover. But it is a road worth taking for the sake of the students and ultimately for the future of our families, communities, and nation.

Eugene E. García

See also Additive and Subtractive Programs; Maintenance Policy Denied; National Clearinghouse for Bilingual Education; Office of Bilingual Education and Minority Languages Affairs; Title VII, Elementary and Secondary Education Act Becomes Title III, No Child Left Behind Act of 2001

Further Readings

Bilingual Education Act, Pub. L. No. 90–247, 81 Stat. 816 (1968).

Elementary and Secondary Education Act of 1965, 20 U.S.C. §§ 6301 et seq.

García, E. (2001). *Hispanic education in the United States: Raíces y alas.* Boulder, CO: Rowman & Littlefield.

García, E. (2001). *Understanding and meeting the challenge of student diversity* (3rd ed.). Boston: Houghton Mifflin.

García, E. (2005). *Teaching and learning in two languages: Bilingualism and schooling in the United States.* New York: Teachers College Press.

García, E., & Palmer, D. K. (2001). Voices from the field: Bilingual educators speak candidly about Proposition 227. *Bilingual Research Journal, 24*(1 & 2), 169–178.

García, E., & Stritikus, T. (2001). Education of limited English proficient students in California schools: An assessment of the influence of Proposition 227 on selected teachers and classrooms. *Bilingual Research Journal, 24*(1 & 2), 75–86.

García, E., & Wiese, A-M. (2001). The Bilingual Education Act: Language minority students and U.S. federal educational policy. *International Journal of Bilingual Education and Bilingualism, 4*(4), 229–248.

Goals 2000: Educate America Act, Pub. L. No. 103–227 (1994).

Improving America's Schools Act, Pub. L. No. 103–382 (1994).

No Child Left Behind Act of 2001, Pub. L. No. 107–110 (2002).

INDIGENOUS LANGUAGE REVITALIZATION

Language revitalization, described in this entry, is an area of study and a social movement that emerged in response to the endangered status of indigenous and minority languages. Language revitalization is one component of *language regenesis*—activities designed to recover, restore, and strengthen the use of endangered languages. The linguist Christina Paulston divides those activities into three categories:

- *Language revival,* the restoration of oral or written uses for a language that is no longer spoken or for which little or no tradition of print literacy exists. For example, Massachusett, an Algonquian language once spoken by peoples indigenous to what is now the northeastern United States, is being revived using the 1663 Eliot Bible, the first bible published in an indigenous language in the Western Hemisphere.

- *Reversing Language Shift (RLS),* a concept developed by the sociolinguist Joshua. A. Fishman, which entails restoring intergenerational language transmission, primarily in the family and community spheres.

- *Language revitalization,* efforts to engender new vigor in a language still spoken but falling from daily use. Language revitalization activities may target several domains, including family, community, and school.

In practice, language revival, revitalization, and RLS intersect and overlap. Before discussing these processes in detail, it is important to understand their genesis and rationale in the Native American context.

Status of Native American Languages Today

Of 300 to 500 languages indigenous to what is now the United States and Canada, 210 are still spoken. According to the linguist Michael Krauss, this includes 175 Native American languages spoken in the United States alone. These languages represent more than 60 language families, and scores of subfamilies, many of which are no less distinct from each other than are English and Mandarin.

All Native American languages are seriously endangered. In the 2000 U.S. Census, 72% of Native Americans 5 years of age or older reported speaking only English at home. Krauss classifies the present status of Native American languages as follows:

Class A, the 20 languages still spoken by all generations

Class B, the 30 languages spoken only by the parent generation and older

Class C, the 70 languages spoken only by the grandparent generation and older

Class D, the 55 languages spoken only by the very elderly, often less than a dozen people

This means that 155 (80%) of all Native American languages have no new speakers to pass them on. Even Class A languages face an uncertain future, for, unlike immigrant languages, there is no external pool of

Native American language speakers to refresh the speaker pool. Language loss is proceeding at such a rapid rate, Krauss warns, that more native American languages stand to be lost in the next 60 years than have been lost since the first contacts between native peoples and Anglo-Europeans more than 500 years ago.

Why Native American Languages Are Endangered

The fate of a language is intimately tied to that of its speakers and, thus, to power relations among groups. Languages do not fall silent of their own accord. Rather, covert and overt social practices and policies diminish the status and utility of some languages while elevating that of others. Sociolinguist Tove Skutnabb-Kangas refers to this as linguistic genocide or "linguicide." According to some projections, 90% of the world's 6,700 languages are likely to be displaced by dominant languages within the next 90 years. Most of these will be indigenous languages.

For Native Americans, the causes of language shift include a history of physical genocide, territorial dislocation, and explicit federal policies intended to eradicate indigenous languages and lifeways. Following the American Revolution, the new federal government turned its attention to pacifying and "civilizing" native peoples. The primary vehicles for this were military aggression and compulsory federally controlled schooling. In the late 19th century, federal boarding schools were established on and off native lands, often in former army forts that had served as staging areas for military campaigns against tribes just a few years before. Accounts abound of children being forcibly removed from their families to the boarding schools, where they were routinely subjected to physical and emotional abuse for speaking their mother tongues.

Some schools did not come under local, indigenous control until the 1960s civil rights movement and a concurrent movement for Native American self-determination. By this time, the federal schooling system had left a legacy of widespread academic failure and had sown the seeds of language decline.

Tribal Sovereignty and Linguistic Rights

The distinguishing characteristic of Native Americans as a group is their status as First Peoples and internally sovereign nations. Tsianina Lomawaima and Teresa McCarty define *tribal sovereignty* as the right to self-government, self-education, and self-determination, including the right to linguistic and cultural expression according to local languages and norms. From their first encounters, native peoples and Europeans interacted on a government-to-government basis. That relationship has been formalized in federal legislation, treaties, judicial decisions, and various federal agencies charged with overseeing Indian Affairs. The federal government has a legally binding *trust responsibility* to honor these legal commitments and the sovereign status of native nations. No other ethnolinguistic group shares this unique legal and political relationship with the federal government.

Over the years, the trust relationship has been severely tested, and tribal and federal powers have frequently been at odds. In the 1960s and 1970s, tribal leaders, educators, political activists, and scholars pushed for tribal sovereignty in several arenas, including education. Those efforts led to important legislative victories that continue to undergird Native American language revitalization: the 1972 Indian Education Act, which authorizes funding and programs for Native American bilingual/bicultural education; the 1975 Indian Self-Determination and Educational Assistance Act, which provides the legal and financial basis for tribally run schools; the 1978 Tribally Controlled Colleges Act, which provides for tribally operated colleges; and the 1992 Native American Languages Act (NALA), which authorizes programs for language planning, revitalization, and maintenance. In 2006, the Esther Martinez Native American Languages Preservation Act was passed, authorizing native-language survival schools, teacher preparation, and instructional materials development. All these policies recognize the right of tribes to determine their children's education: its content, teachers, leadership, and medium of instruction.

How Native American Languages Are Revitalized

Even as more Native American children enter school speaking English as a primary (or only) language, they continue to be stigmatized as limited-English-proficient (LEP) and tracked into remedial programs. As many as 40% of these children will not graduate from high school. This situation, and the imminent threat of native language loss, have led many Native American communities to implement innovative forms of bilingual education with the dual goals of language revitalization and academic excellence, including high levels of proficiency in the native language and English. Some programs have been implemented in schools; others focus on family- and community-based language learning. All stress the important links between language, culture, and identity. A primary instructional strategy is indigenous-language immersion, in which all or most content is delivered in the native language. This section highlights some of these programs.

Navajo Language Revitalization

The Navajo Nation is the second most populous tribe in the United States, with a population of 298,000. The Navajo reservation, the largest in the United States, stretches over portions of three Southwestern states. Navajo claims the largest number of Native American speakers—approximately 178,000. In Krauss's framework, Navajo is a Class A language. Navajo is nonetheless on the decline, with recent studies indicating that less than half of all Navajo kindergartners are fluent Navajo speakers.

In 1986, a Navajo immersion program was launched at a public elementary school in Fort Defiance, Arizona, near the Arizona–New Mexico border. At the time, most Fort Defiance kindergartners had little or no proficiency in Navajo; at the same time, they did not test well in English, and most were identified as LEP. According to program cofounders Marie Arviso and Wayne Holm, a Navajo immersion program was the only option with some chance of success. The original curriculum included initial literacy in Navajo, math in both languages, and other subjects introduced as content for speaking or writing. In the lower grades, all instruction took place in Navajo; in the second and third grades, students received a half-day of Navajo and a half-day of English instruction. Fourth graders received Navajo instruction for an hour each day. Participation in immersion classes was voluntary, but once children were enrolled, parents' active involvement in the program was required.

After 7 years, program evaluations showed that Navajo immersion students consistently performed as well as or better than their non-immersion peers on local tests of English reading and writing. Immersion students were well ahead of their non-immersion peers in mathematics; on standardized tests of English reading, immersion students were slightly behind but catching up—exactly what the wider literature on second-language acquisition predicts. These students had experienced "additive" bilingualism, performing on par with or better than their non-immersion peers in the mainstream curriculum, while acquiring a second language as well. In comparison, non-immersion students experienced "subtractive" bilingualism, losing all or most of the Navajo-language proficiency they possessed when they entered school.

The Fort Defiance program has evolved into a full-immersion primary/intermediate school called Tséhootsooí Diné Bi'ólta', The Navajo School at the Meadow Between the Rocks. The school continues to emphasize Navajo language revitalization and to demonstrate noteworthy academic success.

Keres and Karuk Language Revitalization

The Pueblos of New Mexico and Arizona are among the most enduring native communities in North America, retaining strong theocratic governments and indigenous religious systems while participating vigorously in the global economy. At the Keres-speaking Pueblos of Cochiti and Acoma in northern New Mexico, language surveys in the mid-1990s showed that intergenerational transmission of Keres had virtually stopped. According to Keres educators Mary Eunice Romero-Little and Christine Sims, this was a serious community concern because Keres is essential for sustaining tribal values, government, and religious life.

Cochiti and Acoma subsequently launched community-based language revitalization programs. Romero-Little, who directed the Cochiti program, describes the pairing of small groups of language learners with teams of fluent speakers who modeled natural dialogue. The focus in both Pueblos has been on oral language rather than print; as Sims points out, the function of tribal languages historically has been their use as the foundation of primarily oral societies. For these Pueblo communities, the most important program outcomes are the growing evidence of native language use in the community and the fact that children have gained conversational proficiency in Keres.

Sims reports on similar efforts among the Karuk of California, where 50 indigenous languages are spoken by youngsters, none as a first language. With more than 2,300 tribal members, only a dozen elderly Karuk speakers remain. For the Karuk and other California tribes, a primary-language revitalization strategy has been the master-apprentice program in which older native speakers and younger language learners team over months or years, carrying out everyday tasks in the native language. Like the Keres programs, the emphasis is on communication-based oral language acquisition with the goal of conversational proficiency for apprentices after 3 years. Communitywide Karuk language camps also involve children, parents, and elders in interactive language learning embedded in daily life. According to Sims, the program has enabled children to learn Karuk at a rapid rate and to transfer their learning to other communicative contexts. Leanne Hinton, a linguistic anthropologist who has worked with California master-apprentice teams for many years, notes that these programs have the added benefit of cultivating positive new relationships between younger and older generations.

Hawaiian-Medium Education

After being banned in public schools for much of the 20th century, the Hawaiian language and culture were nearly decimated. In the 1970s, a "Hawaiian Renaissance" movement took root, with a strong emphasis on language revitalization. In 1978, Hawaiian was designated as co-official with English in Hawai'i, and in 1983, a group of parents and educators established Hawaiian-medium preschools called 'Aha Pūnana Leo ("language nest gathering"). According to program cofounders William Wilson and Kauanoe Kamanā, the Hawaiian-immersion preschools aim to create an environment in which Hawaiian language and culture are conveyed as they were in the home in earlier generations. By 2005, Hawaiian-medium education served more than 2,000 students in a coordinated group of schools, beginning with the preschools and moving through full Hawaiian-medium elementary and secondary schools. As many as 15,000 Hawaiians now use or understand Hawaiian, Wilson reports. Although the original concept of 'Aha Pūnana Leo was not academic achievement for its own sake, Hawaiian immersion students have demonstrated considerable academic success. For example, at the Nāwahīokalani'ōpu Laboratory School (called Nāwahī for short), a full-immersion, early childhood through high school curriculum includes college preparatory courses with an explicit Hawaiian-language revitalization focus. Nāwahī students, many of whom come from poor and working-class backgrounds, surpass their non-immersion peers on English standardized tests. The school has a 100% high school graduation rate and a college attendance rate of 80%. Wilson and Kamanā attribute these successes

to an academically challenging curriculum that applies knowledge to daily life and is rooted in Hawaiian identity and culture.

A community-based Hawaiian language and culture program also promotes native language learning among adults. Called Ke A'a Mākālei (The Root of the Mākālei Tree), the program focuses on sports activities that attract individuals who are unlikely to enroll in Western-style language classes. Ke A'a Mākālei promotes intergenerational use of Hawaiian language and culture in Hawaiian families with children enrolled in immersion preschools. According to Native Hawaiian educator Sam No'eau Warner, the program provides a practical model for indigenous language revitalization that reflects Native Hawaiian values and goals.

Challenges and Future Directions

Less than a decade after passing NALA, Congress passed the No Child Left Behind (NCLB) Act of 2001. Several national studies indicate that NCLB's emphasis on high-stakes testing in English, scripted reading programs, and lack of attention to school funding inequities have widened rather than helped close the achievement gap. A 2005 study published by the National Indian Education Association, for example, found that NCLB has resulted in overattention to standardized testing at the expense of pedagogically sound, linguistically and culturally relevant instruction. Coupled with state initiatives by voters banning bilingual education in two states with large numbers of Native American students, California and Arizona, this federal policy creates new threats to school-based language revitalization efforts.

In this political environment, Native American language revitalization efforts must wedge open new windows of opportunity to survive and grow. New Mexico's 24 native nations, for instance, have developed memoranda-of-agreement with the state to ensure equitable and quality education for Native American children, including instruction in the native language where this is desired by tribes. In Alaska, the Assembly of Alaska Native Educators has developed parallel standards for culturally responsive schools, including guidelines for strengthening indigenous languages. Hawai'i also has Native Hawaiian cultural standards. In California, the Breath of Life workshops have helped native Californians locate archival materials on their languages and to use those materials for language revitalization. Other native communities have looked to charter schools as a means of promoting native-language revitalization. These efforts have yet to be well evaluated.

On the national level, the annual Stabilizing Indigenous Languages Conference brings together educators, community members, linguists, and tribal leaders to share strategies and materials for revitalizing indigenous languages. Organizations such as the Indigenous Language Institute and the American Indian Language Development Institute are actively engaged in research, teacher preparation, materials development, and other language revitalization activities.

A significant and growing body of research demonstrates that well-designed indigenous-language immersion programs can strengthen native languages while promoting children's academic achievement and ethnic pride. By their very nature, these programs involve parents, elders, and communities—a factor widely associated with enhanced academic success. These efforts demonstrate how families, communities, and educators can work together to ensure that Native American children have the tools to succeed both locally and globally by developing high levels of proficiency in the native language and English.

Teresa L. McCarty

See also Boarding Schools and Native Languages; Indigenous Languages, Current Status; Language Socialization of Indigenous Children

Further Readings

Arviso, M., & Holm, W. (2001). Tséhootsooídi Ólta'gi Diné bizaad bíhoo'aah: A Navajo immersion program at Fort Defiance, Arizona. In L. Hinton & K. Hale (Eds.), *The green book of language revitalization in practice* (pp. 203–215). San Diego, CA: Academic Press.

Assembly of Alaska Native Educators. (2001). *Guidelines for strengthening indigenous languages*. Anchorage: Alaska Native Knowledge Network.

Fishman, J. A. (1991). *Reversing language shift: Theoretical and empirical foundations of assistance to threatened languages*. Clevedon, UK: Multilingual Matters.

Hinton, L. (1996). *Flutes of fire: Essays on California Indian languages*. Berkeley, CA: Heyday Books.

Hinton, L., & Hale, K. (Eds.). (2001). *The green book of language revitalization in practice*. San Diego, CA: Academic Press.

Indigenous Language Institute. (2004). *Handbook 1: Awakening our languages: An introduction*. Santa Fe, NM: Indigenous Language Institute.

Krauss, M. (1998). The condition of Native North American languages: The need for realistic assessment and action. *International Journal of the Sociology of Language, 132,* 9–21.

Lomawaima, K. T., & McCarty, T. L. (2006). *"To remain an Indian": Lessons in democracy from a century of Native American education.* New York: Teachers College Press.

McCarty, T. L. (2003). Revitalising indigenous languages in homogenizing times. *Comparative Education, 39,* 147–163.

McCarty, T. L., & Zepeda, O. (Guest Eds.). (1998). *Indigenous language use and change in the Americas.* Theme issue, *International Journal of the Sociology of Language, 132* (entire).

McCarty, T. L., & Zepeda, O. (Eds.). (2006). *One voice, many voices: Recreating indigenous language communities.* Tempe: Arizona State University Center for Indian Education.

Paulston, C. B. (1993). Language regenesis: A conceptual overview of language revival, revitalization and reversal. *Journal of Multilingual and Multicultural Development, 14,* 275–286.

Romero-Little, M. E., & McCarty, T. L. (2006). Language planning challenges and prospects in Native American communities and schools. Tempe: Arizona State University Education Policy Studies Laboratory. Retrieved from http://epsl.asu.edu/epru/documents/EPSL-0602-105-LPRU.pdf

Sims, C. P. (1998). Community-based efforts to preserve native languages: A descriptive study of the Karuk tribe of Northern California. *International Journal of the Sociology of Language, 132,* 95–113.

Sims, C. P. (2001). Native language planning: A pilot process in the Acoma Pueblo community. In L. Hinton & K. Hale (Eds.), *The green book of language revitalization in practice* (pp. 63–73). San Diego, CA: Academic Press.

Sims, C. P. (2005). Tribal languages and the challenges of revitalization. *Anthropology and Education Quarterly, 36,* 104–106.

Skutnabb-Kangas, T. (2000). *Linguistic genocide in education—Or worldwide diversity and human rights?* Mahwah, NJ: Lawrence Erlbaum.

Warner, S. N. (1999). Hawaiian language regenesis: Planning for intergenerational use of Hawaiian beyond the school. In T. Huebner & K. Davis (Eds.), *Sociopolitical perspectives on language policy and planning in the USA* (pp. 313–332). Amsterdam: John Benjamins.

Wilson, W. H., & Kamanā, K. (2001). *"Mai loko mai o ka 'I'ni:* Proceeding from a dream." The 'Aha Pūnana Leo connection in Hawaiian language revitalization. In L. Hinton & K. Hale (Eds.), *The green book of language revitalization in practice* (pp. 147–176). San Diego, CA: Academic Press.

INDIGENOUS LANGUAGES, CURRENT STATUS

When the first English colony was established at Jamestown in 1607, some 350 indigenous languages were spoken on the North American continent. The effects of settler encroachment on Native American lands, forced relocation of entire tribal groups from one area of the country to another, overt efforts to eliminate native-language use in boarding schools, and now mass media and technology have all taken a great toll on indigenous North American languages, as described in this entry. The number still actively spoken is now about 155.

Clarence Wesley, then chairman of the San Carlos Apache Tribe in Arizona, wrote the opening article, "Indian Education," in the inaugural edition of the *Journal of American Indian Education* published in June 1961. He highlighted a need for more effective English language programs particularly in situations where children do not come from English-speaking homes, and where a different culture is the dominant factor.

A generation later, indigenous communities across the country have experienced a dramatic language shift toward English language dominance, at the expense of ancestral languages. This is especially true where it concerns children. The situation in 2007 is now the reverse of what Wesley described in 1961. Native children are now more likely to speak English and know only a few words of their ancestral languages. Native communities have become alarmed by this development, and now federal law and statutes enacted in various states support vigorous campaigns by many American Indian, Alaska Native, and Native Hawaiian groups to preserve, restore, and retain their heritage languages.

Michael Krauss estimates that 87% of the Native American languages still spoken in the United States are moribund, which is evidenced when native children are not learning and using their heritage languages and instead speak English. Krauss further predicts that if the present rate of language loss continues unabated, 105 of the currently viable 155 American Indian/Alaska Native languages will be extinct by 2025, and 135 by 2050, leaving only 20 highly endangered languages.

James Crawford characterizes native languages as an *endangered species* requiring urgent measures to preserve them. Crawford considers Native American languages to be in a state of crisis and threatened with extinction. He further maintains that as many as one-third of these languages, along with the last people who speak them, will vanish unless something is done to stop the trend.

The most recent figures available with respect to the status of American Indian and Alaska Native languages in the United States is reported in the 2000 U.S. Census. The census questionnaire inquired about languages spoken in the home by persons 5 years of age and older. It also asked respondents to identify those languages.

The U.S. Census Bureau's publication, *Characteristics of American Indians and Alaska Natives by Tribe and Language: 2000* lists 2,447,989 individuals who reported their ethnicity as American Indian or Alaska Native. A small subset of that number—115,000—reported their ethnicity as Hispanic American Indian, originating in language groups from Mexico, Central and South America, and the Caribbean. Of the total American Indian/Alaskan Native population, 353,340 individuals—28% over the age of 5 years—reported that a native language was spoken in the home, indicating that the English language seems to have become the dominant language among most American Indians and Alaska Natives. The group with the largest number of active native language speakers is the Navajo; the census indicated that 173,800 persons over the age of 5 years reported speaking it in the home. Conversely, speakers of the Miami language number only 5 individuals. Most of the languages reported have less than 500 speakers and more than one third are spoken only by elders. Populations of American Indians and Alaska Natives are concentrated in the western states where, accordingly, the largest numbers of native language speakers are found: 242,038 across the mountain and desert states and 41,591 in the Pacific region, including Hawai'i and Alaska.

Table 1, extracted from language status data originally compiled by the Summer Institute of Linguistics International Ethnologue in 1996, with a recent version by Raymond Gordon, lists an approximate number of speakers of each of the 155 remaining viable American Indian, Native Alaskan and Hawaiian languages, as well as the states in which the speakers are located.

Though about 500 tribes are federally recognized in the 50 states, in large groups such as the 55,000-member Lumbee Tribe of North Carolina, the ancestral

Table 1   Native Languages Currently Spoken in the United States

Number of Speakers	Language Group	Location
20	Abenaki-Penobscot	Maine
10	Achumawi	California
21	Ahtena	Alaska
*281	Alabama	Texas
*926	Aleut	Alaska
*662	Apache, Jicarilla	New Mexico
18	Apache, Kiowa	Oklahoma
10	Apache, Lipan	New Mexico
1,800	Apache, Mescalero-Chiricahua	New Mexico
12,693	Apache, Western	Arizona
*1,122	Arapaho	Wyoming, Oklahoma
90	Arikara	North Dakota
150	Assiniboine	Montana
4	Atsugewi	California
*1,352	Blackfoot	Montana
141	Caddo	Oklahoma
35	Cahuilla	California
5	Chehalis, Lower	Washington
2	Chehalis, Upper	Washington
*12,009	Cherokee	Oklahoma, North Carolina
5	Chetco	Oregon
*2,075	Cheyenne	Montana
1,000	Chickasaw	Oklahoma
17	Chinook Wawa	Oregon
*9,272	Choctaw	Oklahoma
5	Clallam	Washington
321	Cocopa	Arizona
40	Coeur D'Alene	Idaho
39	Columbia-Wenatchi	Washington
*762	Comanche	Oklahoma
1	Coos	Oregon
2	Cowlitz	Washington
*1,102	Cree, Western	Montana
*4,149	Crow	Montana
9	Cupeño	California
*17,466	Dakota	Nebraska, Minnesota, North Dakota, South Dakota, Montana
40	Degexit'an	Alaska

Number of Speakers	Language Group	Location
1	Eyak	Alaska
10	Gros Ventre	Montana
365	Gwich'in	Alaska
138	Haida	Alaska
7	Han	Alaska
*1,536	Havasupai-Walapai-Yavapai	Arizona
1,000	Hawaiian	Hawai'i
*571	Hidatsa	North Dakota
250	Hocak/Winnebago	Nebraska
12	Holikachuk	Alaska
*5,120	Hopi	Arizona, Utah, New Mexico
*163	Hupa	California
3,500	Inuktitut, North Alaskan	Alaska
4,000	Inuktitut, Northwest Alaskan	Alaska
1,301	Jemez	New Mexico
1	Kalapuya	Oregon
200	Kalispel-Pend Dóreille	Montana
19	Kansa	Oklahoma
*166	Karok	California
50	Kashaya	California
10	Kato	California
10	Kawaiisu	California
4,580	Keres, Eastern	New Mexico
3,390	Keres, Western	New Mexico
*795	Kikapoo	Kansas, Oklahoma, Texas
*1,014	Kiowa	Oklahoma
*131	Klamath-Modoc	Oregon
*245	Koasati	Louisiana, Texas
*100	Koyukon	Alaska
97	Kumiai	California
40	Kuskokwim, Upper	Alaska
*359	Kutenai	Idaho, Montana
6,000	Lakota	Nebraska, Minnesota, North Dakota, South Dakota, Montana
43	Luiseño	California
60	Lushootseed	Washington
10	Maidu, Northwest	California
*143	Makah	Washington
887	Malecite-Passamaquoddy	Maine

(Continued)

Table 1 (Continued)

Number of Speakers	Language Group	Location
*32	Mandan	North Dakota
181	Maricopa	Arizona
*649	Menomini	Wisconsin
800	Mesquakie	Iowa, Oklahoma, Kansas, Nebraska
2,100	Micmac	Boston, New York City
*380	Mikasuki	Florida
5	Miwok, Central Sierra	California
1	Miwok, Coast	California
8	Miwok, Lake	California
10	Miwok, Northern Sierra	California
1	Miwok, Plains	California
10	Miwok, Southern Sierra	California
*183	Mohave	Arizona
*1,163	Mohawk	New York
20	Mono	California
*5,009	Muskogee	Oklahoma, Alabama, Florida
*173,800	Navajo	Arizona, Utah, New Mexico
*555	Nez Perce	Idaho
12	Nisenan	California
8,000	Ojibwa, Eastern	Michigan
35,000	Ojibwa, Western	Montana, Lake Superior, North Dakota
*125	Okangan	Washington
*500	Omaha-Ponca	Nebraska; Oklahoma
*553	Oneida	New York, Wisconsin
15	Onondaga	New York
*159	Osage	Oklahoma
*9,220	O'odham-Pima	Arizona
*1,369	Paiute, Northern	Nevada, Oregon, California, Idaho
20	Panamint	California
4	Pawnee	Oklahoma
40	Pomo, Central	California
1	Pomo, Northeastern	California
10	Pomo, Southeastern	California
40	Pomo, Southern	California
*499	Potawatomi	Michigan, Wisconsin, Kansas, Oklahoma
15	Quapaw	Oklahoma
343	Quechan	California
6	Quinault	Washington
*151	Salish, Southern Puget Sound	Washington
30	Salish, Straits	Washington

Number of Speakers	Language Group	Location
*705	Seneca	New York, Oklahoma
1	Serrano	California
12	Shasta	California
*308	Shawnee	Oklahoma
*2,724	Shoshoni	Nevada, Idaho, Wyoming
100	Skagit	Washington
10	Snohomish	Washington
50	Spokane	Washington
65	Tanacross	Alaska
75	Tanaina	Alaska
30	Tanana, Lower	Alaska
115	Tanana, Upper	Alaska
200	Tenino	Oregon
*3,736	Tewa	New Mexico; Arizona
927	Tiwa, Northern	New Mexico
1,631	Tiwa, Southern	New Mexico
775	Tlingit	Alaska
5	Tolowa	Oregon
*137	Tsimshian	Alaska
6	Tubatulabal	California
10	Tututni	Oregon
50	Umatilla	Oregon
5	Unami	Oklahoma, New Jersey, Delaware
1,984	Ute–Southern Paiute	Colorado, Utah, Arizona, Nevada, California
100	Walla Walla	Oregon
69	Wasco-Wishram	Oregon, Washington
*218	Washo	California, Nevada
10	Wichita	Oklahoma
10	Wintu	California
3,000	Yakima	Washington
*469	Yaqui	Arizona
78	Yokuts	California
12	Yuchi	Oklahoma
6	Yuki	California
10,000	Yupik, Central	Alaska
1,100	Yupik, Central Siberian	Alaska
400	Yupik, Pacific Gulf	Alaska
*231	Yurok	California
*6,903	Zuni	New Mexico

Source: Adapted from Estes (2002).

Note: An asterisk indicates data from the U.S. Census 2000.

language is virtually extinct. In other larger tribal groups, such as the Cherokee and Creek Nations, 90% or more members speak only English.

In some instances where the ancestral languages have all but disappeared, unique English dialect variations have replaced them. The Lumbees, who were among the first to have significant and prolonged contact with European colonizers, are noted for their unique dialect, which Walt Wolfram describes as a little bit Appalachian, a little bit Outer Banks, all Southern; he adds that studying Lumbee English has provided evidence of its features as a strong and distinctive dialect, which contains characteristics of a community-based culture. Wolfram mentions that this language shift exemplifies adaptability, resiliency, and vitality in the Lumbee language community. Similarly, William Leap has written extensively about "Red English," the Native American–influenced English dialects common among many American Indian and Alaska Native populations, which replaced ancestral languages and now serve as a source of common native identity, as well as a communication medium.

In assessing the current status of American Indian and Alaska Native languages, Krauss indicates five classes of language vitality and viability. He applied a criterion based on whether children of the language group are acquiring the native language in a traditional manner, specifically learning from their parents and elders. Class A, the smallest of the categories, includes roughly 20 tribal groups—about 11% of the total number of native languages—where children are actively learning in the traditional way. Class B is the second smallest category and includes 30 tribal groups where parents speak the language among themselves but generally communicate with their children in English. Class C consists of about 40% of native languages where the language is spoken only by older adults and elders, but there is no generational involvement of children and youth. Class D consists of native languages that are almost extinct and barely used, and where only a few, mostly elderly, people recall it. Classes C and D are the largest of all of the four categories, and constitute most of the languages listed in Table 1. Class E includes those languages with no remaining speakers.

A number of past and ongoing efforts have been made at the national level to foster the preservation and revitalization of native languages. The Bilingual Education Act of 1968, also known as Title VII of the Elementary and Secondary Education Act (ESEA), made funding available for programs designed to help English language learners master English. However, the Office of Bilingual Education and Minority Languages Affairs (OBEMLA) that administered Title VII of ESEA no longer exists. Its successor, Title III of the No Child Left Behind Act, does not fund Native American language restoration programs. The Administration for Native Americans in the U.S. Department of Health and Human Services also supports large-scale language preservation and revitalization programs. A final report of the U.S. Secretary of Education's *Indian Nations at Risk Task Force* in 1991, developed with substantial community input, identified the maintenance of native languages and cultures as one of its 10 primary goals.

Native-language maintenance and revitalization has received its greatest impetus from the passage of the Native American Languages Act, Title I, in 1990, recently amended by the Esther Martinez Native American Languages Preservation Act of 2006. Through its passage, Congress declared, "The status of the cultures and languages of Native Americans is unique and the United States has the responsibility to work together with Native Americans to ensure the survival of these unique cultures and languages." The act recognizes the right of Indian tribes and other Native American governing bodies to use their ancestral languages as a medium of instruction in all schools funded by the Secretary of the Interior reflecting the policy to "preserve, protect, and promote the rights and freedom of Native Americans to use, practice, and develop" indigenous languages. Furthermore, the act declares "the right of Native Americans to express themselves through Native American languages shall not be restricted in any public proceeding, including publicly supported education programs."

In response to the threat of losing hundreds of native languages within the next 50 years, many tribes, tribal schools, and native organizations throughout Alaska, Hawai'i, and the mainland United States presently operate their own language revitalization or maintenance programs, many depending on their own resources. Although many native languages have already been relegated to linguistic texts with no living speakers, there is now more commitment and action than ever before to protect and maintain in living use those that have survived. Still, the future of most Native American languages is uncertain.

Enactment of protectionist measures by the federal government cannot ensure the survival of any language. As more Native Americans become urban dwellers, the likelihood that they will adopt English as their everyday language increases. If historical patterns of language shift and language loss hold true, the utilitarian value of ancestral languages will also diminish.

Denis Viri

See also Boarding Schools and Native Languages; Language Socialization of Indigenous Children; Native American Languages, Legal Support for

Further Readings

Crawford, J. (1998). *Endangered Native American languages: What is to be done, and why?* Retrieved from http://ourworld.compuserve.com/homepages/jwcrawford/brj.htm

Estes, J. (2002). *How many indigenous American languages are spoken in the United States? By how many speakers?* Retrieved from http://www.ncela.gwu.edu/expert/faq/20natlang.html

Esther Martinez Native American Languages Preservation Act of 2006, H. R. 4766, 109th Congress (2006).

Gordon, R. G., Jr. (Ed.). 2005. *Ethnologue: Languages of the world* (15th ed.). Dallas, TX: SIL International. Available from http://www.ethnologue.com

Indian Nations at Risk Task Force. (1991, October). *Indian Nations at risk: An educational strategy for action.* Washington, DC: U.S. Department of Education.

Krauss, M. (1992). Statement of Mr. Michael Krauss, representing the Linguistic Society of America. In U.S. Senate, *Native American Languages Act of 1991: Hearing before the Select Committee on Indian Affairs* (pp. 18–22). Washington, DC: U.S. Government Printing Office.

Leap, W. L. (1993). *American Indian English.* Salt Lake City: University of Utah Press.

Native American Languages Act, Pub. L. No. 101–477 (1990).

U.S. Census Bureau. (2000). *Characteristics of American Indians and Alaska Natives by tribe and language: 2000.* Washington, DC. Retrieved from http://www.census.gov/census2000/pubs/phc-5.html

Wesley, C. (1961). Indian education. *Journal of American Indian Education, 1,* 4–7. Retrieved from http://jaie.asu.edu/v1/V1S1indi.htm

Wolfram, W, Dannenberg, C., Knick, S., & Oxendine, L. (2002). *Fine in the world: Lumbee language in time and place.* Pembroke: Museum of the Native American Resource Center, University of North Carolina–Pembroke.

INDIGENOUS LANGUAGES AS SECOND LANGUAGES

Since the conception of American Indian education, school language policies have focused on assimilative and subtractive education: stressing the learning of English at the expense of ancestral languages. For indigenous families and communities, this has meant the suppression and loss of the mother tongue and a situation in which speaking an indigenous mother tongue in early childhood has become a rarity. Consequently, an increasing number of indigenous children *and* adults are learning their heritage languages as second languages, which in many ways is similar to learning other languages, such as Spanish, French, or English, as second languages (L2s). Yet, distinct differences distinguish them from other languages for purposes of learning. For example, unlike other languages, mother-tongue literacy is a recent tradition for most indigenous societies. In fact, many indigenous societies, even those that have developed a written language, have retained their oral traditions and wish to develop revitalization interventions that will strengthen them. Thus, in creating conditions that are conducive for learning indigenous languages, it is important to keep in mind that "preservation" of a language (such as in dictionaries, grammar books, and so forth), is distinctly different than "revitalizing" a language; the latter aims at creating actual speakers with the ultimate goal of reestablishing the indigenous language as home and community languages. In light of this, careful consideration must be given to the means by which indigenous languages are learned and, equally important, intervention initiatives should not compromise the integrity of the oral traditions of communities that have chosen oral-based rather than literacy-based interventions (or a combination of the approaches).

This entry considers several components critical for understanding the dynamic process of indigenous second language (hereafter referred to as IL2) learning. The entry considers the contemporary context of indigenous peoples and their languages, including language intervention initiatives, research, and pedagogy for IL2 learning and concludes with a brief discussion of language policies that can detract or contribute to the reclamation of indigenous languages.

Indigenous Peoples and Languages

During the next century, it is estimated that the linguistic diversity in the world will be drastically reduced from 6,000 languages to less than half of this figure, as reported by Kenneth Hale. A significant number of these threatened languages are spoken by indigenous people, who represent 4% of the world's population (reported by Daniel Nettle and Suzanne Romaine). As of 2001, in the United States, indigenous peoples—Native Americans, Native Hawaiians, and Alaska Natives—represent 1.5% of the total population and more than 560 native nations, each with its own historical, political, governance, economic, cultural, sociolinguistic context. Within this diversity, a deep concern of all native nations is the maintenance of ancestral or mother tongues. Among the indigenous languages still spoken in the United States, only 20 are still being naturally acquired by children as a first language. Having no child speakers of a language is one of the most telling signs that a language is threatened with extinction. To address this situation, a number of language reclamation initiatives have emerged in indigenous communities and schools during the past three decades. Taken together, they constitute a new indigenous language education paradigm reflective of the linguistic and sociocultural context, goals, and desires of indigenous peoples.

Indigenous Language Intervention and Research

Although approaches and methods differ in each indigenous speech community because of a number of critical factors, such as the vitality of the language (e.g., the number and ages of speakers), the existence or extent of mother-tongue literacy, and the sociocultural nature of the community, a central aim of all of the initiatives is the creation of new generations of speakers of these languages. Thus, their primary revitalization goals are oral fluency, communicative competence, and the reestablishment of the indigenous language as a viable daily language.

Much of what is known and understood about IL2 learning comes from the unprecedented worldwide research in indigenous mother-tongue maintenance and reclamation. The successes and failures of this work have been well documented by researchers, scholars, and practitioners such as Leanne Hinton, Joshua A. Fishman, Christine Sims, Teresa McCarty,

and Ofelia Zepeda. One of the most successful and influential models in the world of indigenous language education, *Te Kohanga Reo* (Language Nest), has been developed by the Māori people of Aeotearoa, New Zealand. *Te Kohanga Reo* is a total Māori immersion program in which infants and young children are cared for by Māori-speaking elders. This program was replicated in 1983 by the Hawaiians, who established *'Aha Pūnana Leo,* a Hawaiian immersion preschool. Key in each of these efforts was the development of language teaching methods that were congruent with indigenous culture. In many cases, immersion methods—the teaching of language through the target language—proved to be the most promising for creating new speakers. Originating in Canada, immersion methods were designed to teach a minority language to language majority students using distinct techniques and strategies promoting social interaction in the new or second language. In the case of indigenous languages, this meant teaching a minority language to a minority population.

In the mid-1980s, when the Hawaiian immersion effort began, only 2,000 Hawaiian natives spoke their mother tongue, including 30 children. The language was headed for oblivion. William Wilson and Kauanoe Kamanā report that after two decades of comprehensive and intense grassroots work, almost 10,000 persons now speak Hawaiian. In both the Māori and Hawaiian cases, the children who entered these language immersion programs speaking only English became the first new native speakers in generations.

The Master-Apprentice Approach developed by California indigenous language activists has also served as a model for indigenous language reclamation. This approach was particularly pertinent for languages that have few adult, often elder, which is the case with California indigenous languages. In this one-to-one approach, an indigenous speaker is teamed with a younger member of the community to interact in the target language through practical everyday activities and lessons. The major challenge for the Master-Apprentice teams was finding ways to get the extended periods of exposure to the native language without the use of English. "Leaving English behind" is one of a number of critical principles emerging from the Master-Apprentice approach (as well as the previously mentioned cases) that have proven to be fundamental to successful IL2 learning. Today, the Master-Apprentice teams can be found across the U.S. and beyond including Haida teams in Hydaburg and Kasaan, Alaska, Comanche Nation teams in Oklahoma, and "community language teams" in Australia—the latter teams emerged naturally without knowledge of the U.S. example.

Along with these concerted efforts in New Zealand, Hawai'i, and California are the important lessons learned from researchers and practitioners in the international arenas of linguistics, immersion, bilingual, foreign, and second-language education, including English as a Second Language (ESL). Albeit the purpose and goals of the respective disciplines are different, all have contributed in some way to a deeper understanding of the process of L2 learning in general and of IL2 learning in particular.

Role of L1 and L2 Theories in IL2 learning

Central to all these initiatives are first- and second-language acquisition theories. Although each of these theories—behaviorism, innatism, and social interactionism—all examine how children naturally acquire a first language and what they learn in their early language development, they do so with various lenses. From first-language acquisition studies, for instance, we know that children from across cultures and languages progress through various predictable developmental sequences or stages as they acquire and discover language. In the early weeks of life, prevocal infants are able to hear subtle differences in the sounds of human languages. They can, for example, distinguish the difference between "ba" and "pa." By the end of their first year, young children understand a good number of words and by 2 years of age begin to combine these words into telegraphic sentences—a demonstration, contend Patsy Lightbrown and Nina Spada, that they are connecting words together for meaningful communication. By age 5, most children have mastered the sound system and basic structures of the language(s) spoken to them on a daily basis. Research and practice have demonstrated that IL2 learners progress through similar stages of second-language development as other language learners. Yet, due to less than ideal learning conditions, IL2 learning can be challenging, but not impossible. For instance, like first-language learners, IL2 learners experience a comparable "silent period" (or receptive period), during which they are absorbing the sounds and nuances of the target language, but are not yet ready to speak it. Depending on a number of factors such as frequency and consistency

of exposure to the second language, age and personality of the learner, the patience and support of the target speaker(s), and so on, the silent period in IL2 learning can last considerably longer than in first-language learning. Teachers and learners of LL2s who are aware of and understand these developmental stages are likely to be more effective language teachers and learners—and, in many ways, they can make IL2 learning a more enjoyable and fulfilling endeavor.

Collectively, L1 and L2 theories and the grassroots efforts such as those mentioned earlier have all contributed to our understanding of the IL2 learning process, including what is fundamental in the development of culturally appropriate avenues and effective teaching techniques and strategies for IL2 learning, as well as for reinvigorating and sustaining indigenous languages.

Indigenous L2s

This section examines L2 learning and teaching from a practical, social, and indigenous perspective. In particular, it examines teaching pedagogy and methods, namely what one needs to know at the individual and community levels to effectively and successfully teach and learn an indigenous language as a L2.

Conditions for IL2 Learning

When conditions are ideal, all children, under normal circumstances, learn a primary language—whichever one(s) their caretakers use in interacting with them. Amazingly, children acquire language successfully, seemingly without much effort. As earlier mentioned, in IL2 learning, the conditions for language learning are often less than ideal and much more complex. Just as when one is learning a first language, IL2 learners need *access* to the target language for successful learning. Namely, learners must be in a context where the primary means of communication is in the indigenous language. In this context, the goal is communicative competence, which includes the ability to think and effectively communicate in the heritage language. Lily Wong Fillmore explains that through the IL2 learning process, learners actively apply several cognitive strategies and analytical skills, such as memory, association, inference, and social knowledge to make sense of what other people are saying, and to figure out relationships linguistic forms, functions, and meanings.

Fundamentally, in relation to the cognitive process, IL2 learners need to hear the indigenous language, therefore the speakers must *speak it.* Unfortunately, unlike the conditions surrounding the learning of English as a second language, access to the target indigenous language is often limited or nonexistent because of language loss and shift in homes and the speech community, even where a sufficient number of speakers remain. This is because many speakers today have stopped speaking their mother language and replaced it with the dominant language—English. Thus, in many indigenous language intervention efforts, such as those mentioned earlier, deliberate and well-planned efforts must be made to bring the native speakers to speaking it again. This requires an understanding of linguistic attitudes and sociolinguistic behaviors of both the speakers and learners of a target language. Evangeline Parsons-Yazzie, for example, examined the psycholinguistic interactions between adult Navajo speakers and children and found that when parents, grandparents, aunts, and uncles initiated a conversation with a child in Navajo and the child responded in English, the conversation frequently shifted to English. In each case, the child was the one who decided what language was spoken. She attributes this linguistic behavior to the power children have to control the language of communication with their adult caretakers. This example illuminates a common trend among adult speakers of indigenous languages, which is to unconsciously convert to English when they speak to children, youth, or adult learners. This trend gradually leads to the weakening of intergenerational language transmission, which, in turn, limits the critical access that is essential for IL2 learning.

Being aware of the social dynamics that contribute to a shift from the indigenous language and in favor of the majority language is a beginning step toward understanding what needs to happen on both an individual and community level for successful IL2 learning. This was an initial and critical step in the development of the Dakota Language Preschool at Pezihutazizi of the Upper Sioux Community in Minnesota, detailed by Waziyatawin Angela Wilson and Bill Johnston. The program entailed the training of Dakota language teachers, including creating a consciousness among them of their own linguistic behaviors. The Dakota language teachers, all elder speakers who rarely spoke the language on a daily basis, had become accustomed to speaking primarily English, even to one another. Lack of use (or speaking) of Dakota had, in turn, led to loss of vocabulary and self-confidence. The training, consequently, included extended periods of practice in speaking only the Dakota language.

In addition to the training of speakers to "respeak" the indigenous language, another step in the Dakota revitalization initiative was the development of an effective and culturally relevant pedagogy, including learning what approaches and strategies are conducive and not conducive to IL2 learning for *their* situation. One of their guiding principles was that learners must have meaningful experiences in the language—real interactions and a real engagement with speakers of the language—to successfully and effectively learn the language; consequently, they stressed the creation of a learning environment that promoted a supportive environment, in which students felt welcomed and were not criticized in their efforts. The program also promoted the use of techniques and strategies such as props, manipulatives, and Total Physical Response (TPR), an interactive teaching strategy that introduces language through gestures, expressions, and visuals. This view is contrary to conventional, grammar-based approaches to language instruction in schools, which in many cases focus almost exclusively on translation: learning vocabulary lists or numbers, passively listening to a speaker talking in the language, explaining grammar and reciting, memorizing, or excessive writing. These approaches may not give learners sufficient opportunities to talk in the target language and to connect speech to real communication. The end result often is what is reflected in the following recollection of a graduate student who learned Cherokee as a second language: "I learned to read and write Cherokee very well, so well that every Sunday I was asked to read from the Cherokee bible. I guess I read it correctly. . . . But the interesting thing about this is that I didn't understand what I was reading and I can't speak it." In retrospect, this Cherokee L2 learner realized that her instruction focused primarily on mother tongue literacy, specifically the phonology and grammar of the Cherokee language, with little emphasis on conversational competence. This is not to say that mother-tongue literacy is unimportant but, rather, to make the point that knowing the grammatical rules of the language is not the same as being able to use the language in socially and culturally appropriate ways.

Equally important in the Dakota Language Preschool initiative was the development of teaching materials and lessons reflecting of the nature and distinct structural features of the Dakota language and Dakota beliefs and values. This relates to both the inseparable connection between language and culture, and the ways in which languages can create meaning for and form the basis of understanding, including a people's worldview and cultural practices. For IL2 learners, learning the native language is a means for learning the native culture and practices. The Master-Apprentice teams, for example, learn the vocabulary embedded in traditional ways of life by participating in traditional activities, such as ceremonies, making native tools or dress, gathering and cooking native foods, and so forth. Similarly, a core part of Cochiti Pueblo's (located in New Mexico) "curriculum guide" for developing language lessons is the annual traditional calendar. Second-language learners of Cochiti-Keres, for example, learn the appropriate language and cultural protocol needed for participation in an upcoming communal event. In this way, both language and culture are simultaneously strengthened.

Conclusion

Teachers and learners of IL2s who are aware of and understand the similarities among L1 and L2 learning are likely to be more effective language teachers and learners. As well, knowing and understanding indigenous languages and what distinguishes them from other languages for purposes of learning, such as the varying views of the role of literacy in IL2 and the intimate connection between language and culture, can contribute to a deeper understanding of what is involved in teaching as well as learning an indigenous language as a second language and how to best support an indigenous people's (or person's) IL2 in the home, community, or school contexts. Particularly in schools, where literacy plays a central role in English-dominant classrooms (including indigenous language and culture classrooms), the indigenous language and the best practices for learning it frequently take a backseat to mainstream orientation of teaching, academic subjects and goals, and standardized assessment.

In an era of reclaiming culture, self-determination, and maintaining and revitalizing indigenous languages, changes in local, state, and national policies must coincide with today's dynamic indigenous language movements. In particular, language policy needs to change to support bilingualism (and multilingualism) for all its citizens, including its indigenous citizens. This will require a reexamination of the language education paradigm for the learning of indigenous languages as second languages, with the learning of a mother tongue naturally in infancy and early childhood as the ultimate goal.

Mary Eunice Romero-Little

See also Language and Identity; Language Shift and Language Loss; Language Socialization; Native American Languages, Legal Support for

Further Readings

Benjamin, R., Pecos, R., & Romero, M. E. (1996). Language revitalization efforts in the Pueblo de Cochiti: Becoming "literate" in an oral society. In N. H. Hornberger (Ed.), *Indigenous literacies in the Americas: Language planning from the bottom up* (pp. 115–136). Berlin: Mouton de Gruyter.

Berlin, L. (1999). Indigenous language education and second language acquisition: Are they compatible? In T. L. McCarty & O. Zepeda (Eds.), *One voice, many voices: Recreating indigenous language communities* (pp. 251–273). Tempe: Arizona State University Center for Indian Education.

Crawford, J. (1997). Seven hypotheses on language loss causes and cures. In G. Cantoni (Ed.), *Stabilizing indigenous languages* (pp. 51–68). Flagstaff, AZ: Center for Excellence in Education.

Fishman, J. A. (1991). *Reversing language shift: Theoretical and empirical foundations of assistance to threatened languages.* Clevedon, UK: Multilingual Matters.

Fishman, J. A. (2001). *Can threatened languages be saved?* Clevedon, UK: Multilingual Matters.

Hale, K. (1992). Language endangerment and the human value of linguistic diversity. *Language, 68*(1), 1–42.

Hinton, L. (2002). *How to keep your language alive: A commonsense approach to one-to-one language learning.* Berkeley, CA: Heyday Books.

Hinton, L., & Hale, K. (2001). *The green book of language revitalization in practice.* San Diego, CA: Academic Press.

Lightbrown, P., & Spada, N. (2006). *How languages are learned* (3rd ed.). Oxford, UK: Oxford University Press.

McCarty, T. L., & Zepeda, O. (Eds.). (2006). *One voice, many voices: Recreating indigenous language communities.* Tempe: Arizona State University Center for Indian Education.

Nettle, D., & Romaine, S. (2000). *Vanishing voices.* Oxford, UK: Oxford University Press.

Parsons-Yazzie, E. (1995). Navajo-speaking parents' perceptions for reasons for Navajo language attrition. *Journal of Navajo Education, 8*(1), 29–38.

Peregoy, S., & Boyle, O. (2005). *Reading, writing and learning in ESL: A resource for K–12 teachers* (4th ed.). Boston: Pearson.

Scarcella, R., & Oxford, R. (1992). *The tapestry of language learning: The individual in the communicative classroom.* Boston: Heinle & Heinle.

Sims, C. P. (2004). Tribal languages and the challenges of revitalization. Commentary included in *Anthropology and Education Quarterly, 36*(1), 104–106.

Wilson, W. A., & Johnston, B. (1999). Community-based immersion programming: Establishing a Dakota language preschool at Pezihutazizi. In T. L. McCarty & O. Zepeda (Eds.), *One voice, many voices: Recreating indigenous language communities* (pp. 87–112). Tempe: Arizona State University Center for Indian Education.

Wilson, W., & Kamanā, K. (2001). "Mai Loko Mai O Ka 'I'ini: Proceeding from a dream," The 'Aha Pūnana Leo connection in Hawaiian language revitalization. In L. Hinton & K. Hale (Eds.), *The green book of language revitalization in practice* (pp. 147–176). San Diego, CA: Academic Press.

Wong Fillmore, L. (1991). Second-language learning in children: A model of language learning in social context. In E. Bialystok (Ed.), *Language processing by bilingual children* (pp. 49–69). Cambridge, MA: Cambridge University Press.

Wong Fillmore, L. (2002, June). *Language learning in real world settings: Thoughts for teachers and learners.* Paper presented at the American Indian Language Development Institute, University of Arizona, Tempe.

INDO-EUROPEAN LANGUAGES

An extragalactic visitor examining the languages of the world today would be quickly struck by the many close similarities in grammar and vocabulary among French, Spanish, Portuguese, Italian, and Romanian—sufficient for speakers of one language to understand, with some difficulty, the others—and might wonder how that situation came about. Armed with a knowledge of history, we could tell our visitor that the areas in which these languages are spoken were originally settled by speakers of Latin as the Roman Empire expanded, and we can trace, through historical documents, the gradual emergence of regional differences that led from Latin to the modern languages. Although Latin is often considered to be a "dead" language, it is anything but dead, for all of these languages are in fact just local varieties of living Latin as it is still spoken after 2,000 years.

As described in this entry, this picture of the history of Latin and the documentation of the slow changes that led to the present-day regional differences provide us with a *model* for understanding the nature of language change. From this we recognize the following:

1. Change is natural and inevitable in language.

2. All languages are constantly undergoing change.

3. Languages do not deteriorate or improve in the process of change.

4. No language is better or worse, or more logical, than another.

5. No "pure" language exists.

Thus, classical Latin was no more logical or precise than the modern languages, nor are they less logical or precise than Latin. They are simply different.

Linguists have most often used the *family tree* model as a way of illustrating the development of regional varieties from an earlier stage of a language. Thus, we could depict the descent of the Romance languages from Latin in a family tree format (omitting Romanian) (see figure below).

Although such a diagram provides a useful picture of relationships, it distorts reality by omitting all the intermediate local varieties, and in treating each of the named entities as if it were a uniform reality. What we think of as a "language" is actually a collection of more or less mutually intelligible varieties, some of which are more socially and politically privileged than others. When we closely examine language situations such as this one in geographic context, we find that a boundary cannot be drawn between any of these languages. Rather, there is a continuum of local varieties on which political borders have been arbitrarily imposed, frequently by war. For this reason, it is often said that a "language" is really only a socially prestigious regional variety with an army.

Latin in turn was originally just one of several local varieties known from historical records to have been spoken on the Italian peninsula (including Oscan and Umbrian), which we can assume were all

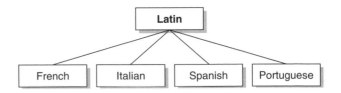

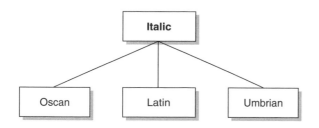

descended from a common ancestor, dubbed Italic (see figure above).

This model of change provided by Latin and the modern Romance languages can be applied to enable us to reconstruct languages for which we have no written record. For example, comparing English, Dutch, German, Norwegian, Swedish, Danish, and the extinct language Gothic, we see numerous similarities in vocabulary and grammar. On this basis, we can classify these into a "language family," usually called *Germanic,* and we can reconstruct many of the features of what we presume to have been the original parent language.

A crucial assumption made in the process of reconstructing earlier languages is the principle of *uniformitarianism:* We assume that events have happened uniformly in the past in the same way they occur today, so that unobserved past events can be understood on the basis of observing present-day phenomena. To take a geological example: The formation of the Grand Canyon can be explained by assuming that it is the result of the same processes of erosion that can be seen on any bare hillside after a rainstorm, operating over millions of years. Just so, we can assume that about 2,500 years ago, there must have been an original Germanic language, which underwent gradual changes over time, producing the modern languages. It helps that for many of the languages, we have more than 1,000 years of written documents, so that we can trace the history of each back to that point. The older the documents, the more similar we find the languages to be, reinforcing our hypothesis that they descended from a single original language.

In 1786, the scholarly world was electrified when Sir William Jones, an English jurist who had been posted to India, announced that he had found systematic resemblances between Sanskrit, the holy language of India, and Greek and Latin, which could only be explained by assuming that they descended from the same original language. This language, which came to be called *Indo-European* for its geographic distribution, must have been spoken before the dawn of recorded history. Its speakers spread from their original homeland on the steppes of southern

Russia, both toward the east into Persia and India and toward the West throughout most of Europe, driving out or absorbing the speakers of other languages they found there. Only one original European language survives today, Basque.

Based on their degree of resemblance, languages may be classified into various groupings and subgroupings. Thus, within Germanic, Swedish, Danish, Norwegian, and Icelandic are grouped as North Germanic; German, Dutch, and English are placed together in West Germanic; and Gothic is the only member of East Germanic. Similarly, other groupings can be made and compared, and their relationship to other groupings of languages can be determined. As a result of this process, 11 subfamilies are now recognized within the Indo-European family (see figure on p. 404).

Some of these subfamilies have only one member, namely Greek, Armenian, Albanian, and Tocharian. The largest subfamily is Indo-Iranian, which has two major branches, Indic (including Sanskrit and its descendents, which include most of the modern languages of northern India) and Iranian (including Persian and other languages of Afghanistan and Pakistan).

As the Indo-Europeans began to expand territorially, the inexorable processes of change began to affect their language, so that different changes occurred in different areas, some spreading to adjacent groups, some not. Thus were born the branches of the Indo-European language family, each of which in turn further ramified, becoming the ancestors of some 450 languages and distinctive varieties spoken today from Ireland to Bangladesh. All of these languages are in a real sense still just regional varieties of one language, projected over the 6,000 years since the original community began to split up. Thus, consider two sentences such as these:

My mother is young.

Mi madre es joven.

Though we label one as "English" and the other as "Spanish," these may be seen as actually being in the same language because everything in them goes back to Indo-European.

The saga of Indo-European is vast and instructive, and linguistics provides us with a window into its history beyond the reach of written records. Understanding something of the history of Indo-European enables us to realize how our own language(s) came to be and

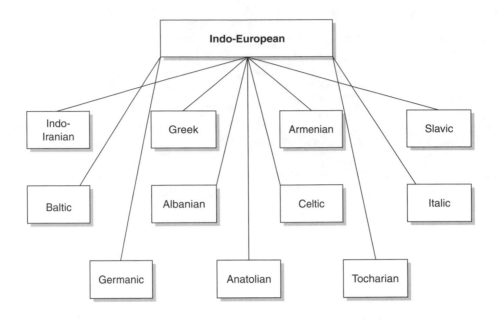

helps us to recognize and appreciate the processes of language change constantly going on around us. Ultimately, all human languages must go back to a single original language, spoken perhaps 80,000 years ago, and language, more than anything, made our ancestors human. For anyone concerned with bilingual education, the conclusion to be recognized is that all languages and varieties are equally valid means for thought and expression, though for reasons of history, some may currently have more economic value or social prestige than others. Thus, all languages, prestigious or not, standard or nonstandard, are equally deserving of respect, and can serve as effective vehicles for instruction and learning.

Rudolph C. Troike

See also Contrastive Analysis; Ebonics; Languages and Power; Spanish Loan Words in U.S. English; World Englishes

Further Readings

Mallory, J. P., & Adams, D. Q. (2006). *The Oxford introduction to proto-Indo-European and the proto-Indo-European world.* Oxford, UK: Oxford University Press.

University of Texas at Austin (2006). *Indo-European Documentation Center.* Retrieved from http://www.utexas.edu/cola/centers/lrc/iedocctr/ie.html

Watkins, C. (2000). Indo-European and the Indo-Europeans. *American dictionary of the English Language* (4th ed.). Retrieved from http://www.bartleby.com/61/8.html

INTERLANGUAGE

Interlanguage is the temporary linguistic system a person develops while learning a second language. A learner's interlanguage is an approximation of the second language being learned, called the *target language* or L2. However, an interlanguage is an intermediate or developmental system that contains features both of the second language (L2) and of the learner's first language (L1), as well as some features that belong to neither. As a learner becomes more proficient in the second language, his or her interlanguage moves closer to the target forms, that is, his or her interlanguage comes to match more closely the linguistic system of a native speaker of the target language. So, interlanguage development can be visualized as a continuum: On one end is the learner's first language, and at the other is the target language, and the learner's interlanguage will be at some point along the continuum, according to the proficiency the learner has achieved in the second language. This entry describes this term and its implications for second-language acquisition.

Although the term *interlanguage* has been used to describe adult language learners' emerging system, it is less clear how the notion of interlanguage applies to younger learners. That is, the interlanguage phenomenon fits well data generated by *sequential bilinguals,* whose L1 is fully formed, but it may less adequately explain *simultaneous bilingualism,* especially those for young children in multilingual settings who are concurrently developing competence in two or more languages. Nevertheless, the processes involved in creating an interlanguage (the combination of grammatical rules from various sources) do mirror the way children make sense of grammar when learning their first language.

Interlanguage and the Study of Second-Language Acquisition

The term *interlanguage* was coined by Larry Selinker in 1972. Selinker stressed that one of the main features of interlanguage is that it is an autonomous or independent language system. Previously, the assumption was that most of L2 learners' errors were caused by interference from the L1, that is, where the grammar of the L1 differs from that of the L2. This approach is called *error analysis.* Thus, Spanish speakers who produced "the book new" in English were applying Spanish word order. However, by studying examples of sentences produced by L2 learners, researchers noted that some of what they produced had grammatical structures that were not found in either the learner's native language or the target language. Therefore, they deduced that learners must have some independent grammar that they relied on to produce such sentences.

Early interlanguage researchers were intrigued by these examples of an independent grammar at work in L2 learners' emerging systems and pointed to them as evidence of Noam Chomsky's claims of "universal grammar," and of a person's innate language faculty. Selinker claimed that the proof that interlanguage exists—the evidence of a learner's separate linguistic system—also pointed to the existence of a latent psychological structure that is activated when one begins learning a second language. During the 1970s and 1980s, interlanguage became the object of research for the newly emerging field of second-language acquisition (SLA) studies, a branch of psycholinguistics. The interest of SLA researchers is focused on the cognitive processes involved when a person who has already acquired his or her first language attempts to acquire a second language, and by taking interlanguage as their theoretical starting point, researchers were able to generate empirical evidence about the internal mental processes of second-language learning.

The Basic Processes of Interlanguage

The interlanguage of an L2 learner can be studied by comparing what the learner produces with what a native speaker who was saying the "same" thing would produce. For example, the interlanguage of L2 learners of English whose native language is Spanish can be studied by comparing what they say in a particular situation with how a native English speaker might convey the same meaning. We can expect that some of the differences between the English learner's and the native speaker's sentences can be explained by the influence of Spanish on what the learner has produced. However, we can expect that there will be some features of the language learner's sentence that belong to neither English (the learner's L2) or Spanish (the learner's L1).

The learner's particular variety of the L2 is not only derived from knowledge of the target language. According to Selinker's original formulation, an interlanguage is created from five cognitive processes: language transfer, transfer of training, strategies of L2 learning, communication strategies, and overgeneralization of L2 rules. *Language transfer* is the effect of mapping L1 structures onto the L2. In the case of positive transfer, where the L1 maps well onto the L2, first-language knowledge helps learners produce correct grammatical structures in the L2. On the other hand, negative transfer occurs when the structures do not map correctly; this has also been referred to as "interference" or "interlingual" errors. The importance of the role of language transfer in interlanguage development has long been debated by SLA researchers, and in particular the question of how to explain individual differences—known as variability of transfer—remains unanswered. *Transfer of training* refers to the instruction the learner has received, and the types of second-language materials and approaches the learner has been exposed to. *Strategies of second-language learning* describe the particular ways learners approach their own learning. *Second-language communication strategies* explain how the learner attempts to resolve the challenges that arise in naturally occurring communicative situations. Finally, *overgeneralization of target-language rules* refers to how the L2 learner tries to hypothesize structures based on partial knowledge of the grammatical system. For example, an L2 learner who knows that *ed* is used to form the past tense will quite often overgeneralize this rule, and produce forms such as *I goed*.

The Interlanguage Continuum and Fossilization

In early research, Stephen Pit Corder termed the learner's intermediate language stage "transitional competence," to capture the idea that interlanguage is evolving and progressing toward the target forms. As mentioned earlier, this process can be visualized as a language-learning continuum, where complete mastery of the L2 is the ending point.

However, most people who have attempted to learn a second or foreign language know that only a small percentage of learners ever gain "complete mastery" in the L2. In fact, some scholars have suggested that one flaw of interlanguage theory is that it presupposes an endpoint of L2 acquisition that only a few L2 learners can ever obtain. Vivian Cook, for example, suggests that the term *multi-competence* may be a more adequate way of conceptualizing the psychological structures of second-language acquisition because the term recognizes the all L2 users have some types of language competence, and their knowledge of the L2 should not be defined only in terms of an idealized native speaker of the target language.

For many SLA theorists, however, one important element of interlanguage is that a terminal point of L2 acquisition stops before nativelike mastery has been achieved. For many learners, errors tend to be repeated, and in a sense become "impervious" to correction. When a particular structure is acquired incorrectly and cannot be remedied, it is said to have become *fossilized*. Hence, fossilization describes the phenomenon where the learner's interlanguage is no longer a dynamic, evolving system but, rather, has become stuck at some point along interlanguage continuum, and further progress in the L2 is unlikely. For bilingual education teachers who experience, on a daily basis, examples of interlanguage, a thorough understanding of that phenomenon should prove useful.

Peter Sayer

See also Critical Period Hypothesis; Language Acquisition Device; Language Learning in Children and Adults; Social Bilingualism

Further Readings

Cook, V. J. (1992). Evidence for multi-competence. *Language Learning, 42*(4), 557–591.

Corder, S. P. (1967). The significance of learners' errors. *International Review of Applied Linguistics (IRAL), 5,* 161–170.

Selinker, L. (1972). Interlanguage. *International Review of Applied Linguistics (IRAL), 10*(3), 209–231.

Selinker, L. (1992). *Rediscovering interlanguage.* London: Longman.

J

Japanese Language in Hawai'i

The story of the use and study of Japanese in Hawai'i is framed by the history of Japanese immigrants to the islands. The development of Japanese-language schools in Hawai'i was greatly influenced by the social and political events that took place around Japanese immigrants and second-generation Japanese Americans known as *Nisei*. Because of the massive immigration of Japanese farmers to Hawai'i in the late 19th century, Japanese-language schools became an important part of these farmers' lives life in Hawai'i. Although the schools faced unparalleled anti-Japanese sentiment during the 1920s, the number of Japanese-language schools increased until the end of World War I. The schools quietly flourished until World War II began, when all Japanese-language schools were forced to shut down because of the prevailing sentiment that considered the maintenance of Japanese language and culture a symbol of disloyalty. That sentiment has now changed, and currently the Japanese language is one of the most studied languages in Hawai'i.

According to the U.S. Census report issued in 2005, Japanese Americans constitute the largest Asian American group in Hawai'i, and many students have acquired Japanese as their heritage language. The state of Hawai'i does not provide bilingual education programs in Japanese and English; nevertheless, there are diverse opportunities to learn the language through Japanese-language schools, Japanese as a second language courses in public schools, and Saturday schools. This entry summarizes the work of Japanese-language schools in Hawai'i, and presents a discussion of the historical experience of Japanese immigrants.

History of Japanese-Language Schools

The history of Japanese language education in Hawai'i starts with the arrival of Japanese immigrants from 1885 through 1924. In 1885, a mighty famine occurred in Japan, and Japanese farmers became genuinely distressed. During this period, Hawai'i recruited a great number of farm laborers for its thriving sugar cane plantations. For Japanese farmers, working in Hawai'i was a highly attractive prospect because the wages in the United States were better than they were in Japan. These Japanese immigrants were a highly selected and educated population. Because immigration was competitive, the Japanese government used educational attainment as a prerequisite condition for emigration. As a result, most of the early emigrants, both men and women, were literate and had 2 to 6 years of basic education. The Japanese government also imposed strict health examinations for prospective emigrants; therefore, rural farmers in poor physical condition were excluded. A large proportion of these immigrant workers were in their 20s. Meyer Weinberg mentions that in the early 1900s, 39% of the population in Hawai'i consisted of Japanese immigrants.

Eileen Tamura explains that the first Japanese-language school opened soon after the first group of Japanese immigrants arrived in Hawai'i in 1892. Most of the early Japanese immigrants did not intend to teach their children English or American culture because the Japanese government ruled that Japanese citizens must return to Japan within 3 years. Weinberg explains that Japanese immigrants felt the need to maintain proper Japanese language and culture because they considered themselves to be temporary workers rather than immigrants.

To accommodate the educational needs of young Japanese children, Japanese-language schools were built almost immediately upon arrival. Another incentive to create Japanese-language schools was that there were no public schools available in the plantation areas where the Japanese worked. As Weinberg stresses, even if such schools had existed, plantation managers would not have allowed the children of Japanese workers to attend the public schools. Hidehiko Ushijima reports that although the first Japanese-language school started with only 30 students, the number of schools increased rapidly. Weinberg and Kimi Kondo recount that by 1939, at their peak, there were 163 schools with 38,000 students. According to Kondo, until 1917, Japanese-language schools in Hawai'i were under the control of the Japanese Ministry of Education. The Japanese government made efforts to develop Japanese citizens with Japanese values and "virtues" through these schools. The schools were required to use the textbooks and teaching materials that were mandated for use in public schools in Japan. After 1917, the Japanese government lost control of the Japanese-language schools because of pressure from the U.S government. However, Japanese-language schools continued to play a significant role as cultural centers in Japanese communities.

Tamura narrates that during World War I, the United States had a slogan, "one nation, one flag, one language"; hence, to unite the country, the Japanese-language schools became the targets of pressure and even hostilities, along with German and other foreign languages. In 1919, Japanese Americans in Hawai'i split over the language education and identity issue. Some Japanese Americans wanted their children to grow up as Americans with perfect command of English, whereas some wanted their children to maintain their language and identity. Weinberg describes that in the 1920s, many Nisei fought for U.S. citizenship and civil rights. When the Japanese ministry of education passed its control of Japanese-language schools to the U.S. government, the Japanese-language schools changed their focus. Their new aim was to develop Japanese Americans and Japanese immigrants with loyalty to America. Kondo states that this became

as important as maintaining the Japanese language and values. Weinberg mentions that reflecting the increasing anti-Japanese sentiment, the Japanese-language schools were restricted to operating only 1 hour a day, after the close of public schools, and to no more than 6 hours a week in 1920. In addition, U.S. government officials began censoring their administrators, teaching materials, and curriculum.

The various manifestations of anti-Japanese sentiment caused internal conflicts among Japanese Americans during this time. According to Tamura, most Japanese schools fought the anti-Japanese measures through the courts; the courts, however, abolished the Japanese-language schools in Hawai'i as part of the prevailing nativist agenda. Although the percentage of Japanese students who attended Japanese schools decreased to 70% because of a series of anti-Japanese laws and other restrictions in the 1920s, Tamura reports that the percentage of enrollment in Japanese-language schools reverted to 87% in the 1930s. This increase in enrollment suggests that Japanese Americans must have had a strong determination to maintain the Japanese culture and language through the schools.

When the Japanese schools were first created, their primary purpose was language instruction; however, other purposes came into play, such as developing close connections between students and their parents outside the schools. Koichi Harada reported that as more and more Japanese Americans attended the Japanese-language schools, training for American citizenship was included in the function of the school as well. Harada wrote that stress was placed on raising American citizens who would be able to pass on American culture, but who could also rely on a strong Japanese background. When the school enrollment greatly decreased because of anti-Japanese sentiment, the Japanese-language schools provided day care services in English. Alan Shoho reports that because the financial support was primarily based on student tuition, day care services were provided as a means to maintain and regain student enrollment. Other sources of finances included charitable contributions and support by churches.

Shoho details how the Japanese-language schools during the 1930s were open 6 days a week for an hour a day on weekdays, and for a half day on Saturday mornings. During weekdays, the classes were held after public schools let out. On Saturdays, classes started in the morning and finished at noon. Classes were divided into two levels: elementary (1st to 8th grades) and secondary (9th to 12th grades). Between 1929 and 1930, 41,151 Japanese American students attended public schools, as reported by the Department of Public Instruction in 1931. Of this total, 93% (38,162 students) also attended Japanese-language schools after public school. In the Japanese-language schools, students learned Japanese and ethics, which taught several values, attributed to the Japanese culture: respect for elders, perseverance, frugality, and loyalty to the country one comes from. One Japanese American student reported in Shoho's work that they felt they became better American citizens through the study of ethics in Japanese-language school.

Japan's aggression in Asia, particularly the war between China and Japan in 1937, was regarded as threatening by the U.S. government and society. The U.S. attitude toward Japanese Americans and Japanese-language schools became suspicion. Tamura reports that a ritual of reciting the pledge of allegiance before an American flag was performed daily in the Japanese-language schools in the 1940s to affirm Japanese American loyalty to the United States and to avert criticism. Japanese textbooks that promoted Japanese nationalism with emperor worship became inappropriate for Japanese Americans born in Hawai'i. To respond to this situation, the Hawai'i Japanese Education Society was formed and developed less nationalistic textbooks for use in Hawai'i. With the outbreak of World War II, all Japanese-language schools were closed in 1942.

Current Status of Japanese in Hawai'i

As mentioned, Japanese Americans are the largest Asian group in Hawai'i. Moreover, Japanese is the most commonly used language at home by non-English Hawaiian residents, Kondo reports. These circumstances may indicate that many Japanese language users study Japanese language as their heritage language. Kondo further mentions that at the University of Hawai'i at Manoa, 46.5% of students enrolled in primary-level Japanese language courses in the fall of 1996 were of Japanese ancestry. Interestingly, Kondo indicates that the state of Hawai'i does not provide a formal bilingual language education program aimed at maintaining the Japanese heritage language among its students, even for those who already speak that language at home.

Japanese-language schools, Japanese courses in public schools, and supplemental schools are still available and accessible. Both the Hawai'i Department of Education and Kondo report that approximately 9,000 students at 51 public primary schools, and 8,000 students at 46 public secondary schools studied the Japanese language as a foreign language in Hawai'i in the academic years 1993 to 1994. This makes Japanese the most commonly taught foreign language at public schools in Hawai'i. Kondo reports that in the public schools, Japanese courses are taught during schooltime, but the contents, duration, and teaching materials vary. No common curriculum or standard exists for the teaching of Japanese. In addition to Japanese courses in public schools, Kondo explains that Japanese-language schools contribute to maintain the linguistic and cultural heritage of Japanese Americans, as well as helping English-speaking Americans who want to study the language.

Currently, 12 Japanese-language schools remain on Oahu Island. Many Japanese-language schools are having financial problems as the number of students who attend declines, Kondo reports. As Japanese-language schools have gone into decline, Japanese supplement schools have begun to make their appearance. Factors such as financial support, curriculum, and instruction are similar between the two types of schools. The difference is that Japanese supplement schools began by targeting the descendents of Japanese immigrants who planned to stay in Hawai'i temporarily and intended to return to Japan. By the late 1990s, however, many Japanese students attending these schools planned to stay in Hawai'i permanently. Supplement schools are considered, by Japanese children, to be more difficult than the former language schools. This makes them less popular and may ultimately influence their survival as optional sites for learning and maintaining Japanese language and culture.

Conclusion

Although Japanese as a foreign language gained popularity in Hawai'i in the 1980s and early 1990s, enrollments in recent years have declined. Kondo claims that although Japanese language enrollments at the university doubled between 1990 and 1994, the growth is currently steady. Two possible causes for this situation are (1) the complexity of the language and (2) problems with the Japanese economy. At the postsecondary level, Eleanor Jorden and Richard Lambert point out that many students of Japanese as a foreign language discontinue their study before they master functional proficiency. According to Kondo, most students at the University of Hawai'i at Manoa usually stop taking Japanese-language courses after completing the language requirement of 2 years. Kondo argues that many students confronted with the use of *kanji* (Chinese characters used in Japanese) and *keigo* (honorific expressions and language use in Japanese) at the intermediate level simply give up because the difficulties in learning the language escalate with these features. Because of its complexity and a heavy memorization load, students tend to give up at a lower level of proficiency. In addition, a long-term decline in the Japanese economy diminishes the students' motivation to learn Japanese as a language of business and commerce. Interest in Asian languages has shifted toward the languages of growing economic powers, such as Chinese and Korean.

Miku Watanabe

See also Benefits of Bingualism and Heritage Languages; Heritage Language Education; Language Education Policy in Global Perspective

Further Readings

Department of Public Instruction. (1931). *Biennial report of the Department of Public Instruction of the Territory of Hawaii: 1929–1930.* Honolulu, HI: Department of Public Instruction.

Haas, M. (1992). *Institutional racism: The case of Hawaii.* Westport, CT: Praeger.

Harada, K. G. (1934). *A survey of the Japanese-language schools in Hawaii.* Unpublished master's thesis, University of Hawai'i.

Hawai'i Department of Education. (1995). *Elementary and secondary AEPL (Asian, European and Pacific Languages) data, 1993–1994.* Unpublished manuscript, Honolulu: Office of Instructional Services/Asian, European and Pacific Languages.

Jorden, E. H., & Lambert, R. D. (1991). *Japanese language instruction in the United States: Resources, practice, and investment strategy.* Washington, DC: National Foreign Language Center Monograph Series.

Kondo, K. (1998). The paradox of U.S. language policy and Japanese language education in Hawaii. *International Journal of Bilingual Education and Bilingualism, 1*(1), 47–64.

Leibowitz, A. H. (1971). *Educational policy and political acceptance: The imposition of English as the language of instruction in American schools.* ERIC No. ED 047 321

Morimoto, T. (1997). *Japanese Americans and cultural continuity: Maintaining language and heritage.* New York: Garland.

Shoho, A. R. (1990). *Americanization through public education of Japanese Americans in Hawaii: 1930–1941.* (Doctoral dissertation, Arizona State University). *Dissertation Abstracts International, 51*(8), 403.

Tamura, E. (1994). *Americanization, acculturation, and ethnic identity: The nisei generation in Hawaii.* Urbana: University of Illinois Press.

U.S. Census Bureau. (2005). *Hawaii: General demographic characteristic.* 2005 American Community Survey. Available from http://factfinder.census.gov

Ushijima, H. (1989). *Ikooka Meriken Kaerooka Japan; Hawaii Imin no Hyakunen [Going to America returning Japan: 100 years of immigrants in Hawai'i].* Tokyo: Kodansha.

Weinberg, M. (1997). *Asian-American education, historical background and current realities.* Mahwah, NJ: Lawrence Erlbaum.

K

KLOSS, HEINZ (1904–1987)

Heinz Kloss is one of the most acclaimed authorities on the history of language policy and language minority rights in the United States. Kloss's scholarly work spans nearly six decades, beginning in 1929, with his last publication posthumously in 1987. Kloss began his work in his native Germany, but in the 1930s early in his career, he made successive trips to the United States and Canada, where he served as director of the Centre international de rècherche sur le bilinguisme of Laval University in Québec. This entry discusses the significance of his scholarly work.

Among Kloss's more important German-language works were *Das Volksgruppenrecht in den Vereinigten Staaten,* Vols. 1–2 (The rights of ethnic groups in the United States), published in 1940; *Das Nationalitätenrecht der Vereinigten Staaten* (The rights of national minorities in the United States), published in 1963; studies on language maintenance among German American immigrants published in 1966; and *The American Bilingual Tradition,* first published in 1977 and republished in 1998. Kloss is best known in the United States for this latter work. Many U.S. language policy scholars have relied on that publication because of its thorough analysis of language laws, territorial language policies, and typology for classifying different types of language policies (*promotion-oriented, tolerance-oriented,* and *restrictive*).

Kloss's work has received widespread acclaim from persons interested in the history of bilingualism in the United States and North America. Researcher Shirley Brice Heath praised *The American Bilingual Tradition* for its use of primary sources and thorough discussion of legal decisions, policies, and legislation dealing with languages other than English in America. Similarly, Carolyn Toth, who has done substantial work on the history of German in the United States, referred to Kloss as an expert on U.S. history of bilingual education. Kloss's work is now becoming dated; nevertheless, given the dearth of subsequent historical work, Kloss's contributions remain foundational for studies for historical analyses of language policy, language discrimination, and linguistic rights.

Kloss's scholarship has been criticized from several directions. Most troublesome is the political context for Kloss's early work, which has been seriously questioned. Christopher Hutton's *Linguistics and the Third Reich,* for example, raises a number of significant issues. Kloss's early work began in the Weimar Republic (the government of Germany from 1919 to 1933) when there was extensive political and cultural debate regarding the German diaspora in Eastern Europe, Italy, and parts of Western Europe. When the National Socialists came to power, they took particular interest reuniting the German diaspora in North and South America. Hutton finds the ideological orientation of Kloss's work written during this period and Kloss's statements regarding racial and ethnic minorities particularly troubling. Did Kloss manage to sufficiently change some of his earlier biased sentiments, as the thrust of his later scholarship in support of more liberal agendas would seem to suggest? This is an important question for those who only read his later work.

Hutton contends that some Fascist-influenced tendencies in Kloss's writings were not exclusively confined to the National Socialism period. He notes that for Kloss, Germans played a prominent role among immigrant groups he studied in *Das Volksgruppenrecht in den Vereinigten Staaten,* which dealt with Germans in the United States. Kloss characterized them as being more analogous to a "people" (*Volk*) than an ethnic group (*Volksgruppe*). Kloss explained German language loss in the United States as resulting from different German "tribes" (*Stämme*) that emigrated from Germany with different dialects, which made German difficult to preserve. Kloss further attributed the loss of German to a lack of intellectual leadership and deterioration in the German immigrant pool after 1850, as well as to the ideological influence of world citizenship and atheism.

This earlier work is important in the assessment of Kloss's later work because he relied heavily on it. In the introduction to *The American Bilingual Tradition,* however, Kloss tried to distance himself from German nationalist sentiments by emphasizing his "European" identity. As a European, Kloss maintained that he was able to view the maintenance of language as a natural thing but saw language shift as the exception. Kloss then advanced his central thesis, which he called the "American Bilingual Tradition." He contended that it was not the dominant tradition but an important minority tradition nevertheless.

Kloss argued that, with the exception of the World War I period, tolerance-oriented policies have held sway in U.S. tradition and most language minorities have shifted to English because of the ability of U.S. society to assimilate language minorities, rather than as a result of coercion or prejudicial policies. As a scholarly resource, the strength of *The American Bilingual Tradition* is its cataloguing of various types of formal policies related to language. A weakness, however, is Kloss's compartmentalization of race and language and his failure to see a connection between racial discrimination and linguistic intolerance. For example, although he noted cases of discrimination against Mexican Americans, he concluded that discrimination against Mexican Americans resulted from racial rather than linguistic prejudice.

Others, however, who have relied on Kloss's work, have reached exactly the opposite conclusion. Arnold Leibowitz, for example, surmised that restrictions against the use of minority languages and the attempt to impose English literacy requirements is based directly on the degree of hostility of the majority toward the language minority group, attributing it to differences in race, color, or religion. In other words, language differences often function as a surrogate for racial/ethnic differences. For Kloss, however, the problems that racial minority groups and foreign-language groups had were very different, even opposite to each other. Thus, whereas Kloss concluded discrimination against language minorities was generally racial, rather than linguistic, others, such as Leibowitz, have understood that linguistic discrimination is *always* connected to race, class, religious, or other forms of social discrimination.

In explaining reasons for minority language maintenance and loss in the United States, Kloss placed greater emphasis on the efforts of language minority groups themselves rather than on that of official language policies. He contended official language policies had been aimed at eliminating non-English languages on only a few occasions. Kloss gave more significance to the influence of individuals, teachers, and community groups and their ability to exert moral pressure of unofficial nature on minority groups' members to maintain their languages.

Kloss, nevertheless, concluded *The American Bilingual Tradition* by locating the movement for language rights as being among the major contemporary emancipatory movements for racial and gender equality. He concluded that the position of Spanish, as the major second language in the United States, was analogous to the position of German during the World War I era.

Given the overall contributions of Kloss to the scholarship on the history of policies toward bilingualism in the United States, and given the scarcity of work on the history of language minority rights in the United States, his scholarly work remains important. No subsequent work has demonstrated such an extensive use of primary sources and analyses of official documents. Nonetheless, because of the ideological context in which Kloss's earlier scholarship was conducted and his subsequent reliance on it, Kloss's work must be used carefully and critically.

Terrence G. Wiley

See also German-Language Education; Language Education Policy in Global Perspective; Language Policy and Social Control

Further Readings

Heath, S. B. (1981). English in our language heritage. In C. A. Ferguson & S. B. Heath (Eds.), *Language in the USA* (pp. 6–20). Cambridge, UK: Cambridge University Press.

Hutton, C. M. (1999). *Linguistics and the Third Reich: Mother-tongue Fascism, race and the science of language.* London: Routledge.

Kloss, H. (1940–1942). *Das Volksgruppenrecht in den Vereinigten Staaten von Amerika.* (Vols. 1–2). Essner: Verlagsanstalt, Essen.

Kloss, H. (1963). *Das Nationalitätenrecht der Vereinigten Staaten von Amerika.* Vienna: Braumuller.

Kloss, H. (1966). German American language maintenance efforts. In J. A. Fishman (Ed.), *Language loyalty in the United States* (pp. 206–252). The Hague: Mouton.

Kloss, H. (1977). *The American bilingual tradition.* Rowley, MA: Newbury House.

Leibowitz, A. H. (1969). English literacy: Legal sanction for discrimination. *Notre Dame Lawyer, 45*(7), 7–67.

Leibowitz, A. H. (1971). *Educational policy and political acceptance: The imposition of English as the language of instruction in American schools.* Eric No. ED 047 321.

Macías, R. F., & Wiley, T. G. (1998). Introduction. In H. Kloss, *The American Bilingual Tradition* (pp. vii–xi). Washington, DC: Center for Applied Linguistics and Delta Systems.

Toth, C. R. (1990). *German-English bilingual schools in America: The Cincinnati tradition in historical context.* New York: Peter Lang.

Wiley, T. G. (2002). Heinz Kloss revisited: National Socialist ideologue or advocate for linguistic human rights? *International Journal of the Sociology of Language, 154,* 83–97.

Krashen, Stephen D. (1941–)

Stephen D. Krashen, noted linguist and education researcher, was born in Chicago in 1941. After spending 2 years in the Peace Corps in Ethiopia, where he taught eighth-grade English and science, Krashen pursued a PhD in linguistics at the University of California, Los Angeles (UCLA), culminated by his 1972 dissertation *Language and the Left Hemisphere.* Krashen accepted a position as a postdoctoral fellow at the UCLA Neuropsychiatric Institute, then went on to serve as professor of linguistics at the City University of New York (CUNY) Graduate Center in New York, and the Linguistics Department of the University of Southern California (USC). In 1994, Krashen joined the USC School of Education, where he currently serves as emeritus professor. He has published more than 350 papers and books and has presented numerous addresses audiences of teachers and scholars both nationally and internationally. This entry describes his research.

Krashen is best known for his work in establishing a general theory of second-language acquisition, commonly called the monitor theory, as the cofounder (with Tracy Terrell) of the natural approach to second-language teaching, and as the inventor of sheltered instruction. A central element of Krashen's approach to second-language acquisition is the view that it occurs naturally, just like first-language acquisition, under appropriate conditions. This view constituted a dramatic shift from an earlier position in Krashen's published work reflecting a commitment to direct instruction and consistent error correction. In a seminar in 1975, Krashen and his students sought to make sense of data pertaining to a fixed pattern of acquisition of grammatical morphemes from second-language speakers. During the seminar, Krashen came up with the idea that two systems, an acquired one and a learned one, must be posited to explain the data.

Krashen's general approach to second-language acquisition evolved to include five interrelated hypotheses, including the natural order hypothesis (the idea that human beings acquire the rules of language in a predictable order); the acquisition/learning hypothesis, which states that adults have two distinctive ways of developing competences in second languages (acquisition—a system that develops from natural language use—and learning—a system that comprises overt knowledge of language rules); the monitor hypothesis (conscious learning can only be used to monitor or edit our language); the input hypothesis (humans acquire language by understanding messages); and the affective filter hypothesis (a mental block, caused by affective factors, prevents input from reaching the language acquisition system in the brain). Krashen has also contributed extensively to an approach in reading known as whole language, which similarly posits that children learn to read by reading and that reading develops naturally under appropriate conditions.

Krashen maintained that bilingual education fills a contextual space against which input may be effectively and efficiently processed by learners. Hence, he maintained that bilingual education was an important component of an immigrant child's educational program, simultaneously providing academic content knowledge in the child's native language and background knowledge facilitating the processing of English language input.

As Krashen believed that education policy in his home state of California became increasingly regressive, he responded with research critical of the new policies, public speaking engagements, and with letters written to newspaper editors. During the campaign to enact an antibilingual education law in California in 1998, known as Proposition 227, Krashen campaigned in public forums and media talk shows and conducted many interviews with journalists on the subject. After other antibilingual education campaigns surfaced around the country, Krashen estimated that, by 2006, he had submitted more than 1,000 letters to editors. Leading by example and in his writings, Krashen has been an advocate for a more activist role by researchers in combating the public's misconceptions about bilingual education.

Jeff MacSwan

See also Affective Filter; Comprehensible Input; Languages, Learned or Acquired; Monitor Model; Second-Language Acquisition

Further Readings

Fromkin, V., Krashen, S., Curtiss, S., Rigler, D., & Rigler, M. (1974). The development of language in Genie: A case of language acquisition beyond the "critical period." *Brain and Language, 1,* 83–107.

Krashen, S. (1972). Language and the left hemisphere. *Dissertation Abstracts International A* 33/08, 82.

Krashen, S. (1985). *The input hypothesis.* Beverly Hills, CA: Laredo.

Krashen, S. (1999). *Condemned without a trial: Bogus arguments against bilingual education.* Portsmouth, NH: Heinemann.

Krashen, S. (2003). *Explorations in language acquisition and use: The Taipei lectures.* Portsmouth, NH: Heinemann.

Krashen, S. (2004). *The power of reading: Insights from the research* (2nd ed.). Portsmouth, NH: Heinemann.

Krashen, S. (2005). Let's tell the public the truth about bilingual education. In V. Gonzales & J. Tinajero (Eds.), *Review of Research and Practice, 3,* 165–173.

Krashen, S., & Seliger, H. (1975). The essential contributions of formal instruction. *TESOL Quarterly, 9,* 173–183.

Krashen, S., & Terrell, T. (1983). *The natural approach: Language acquisition in the classroom.* New York: Prentice Hall.

L

LABELING BILINGUAL EDUCATION CLIENTS: LESA, LEP, AND ELL

Part of the story of the evolving definition of the clients of bilingual education is reflected in the labels used to describe them—more specifically, changes in the labels used to describe their linguistic condition: a less-than-adequate command of English. This entry reviews three of the principal labels and how they changed during three decades of practice.

Limited-English-Speaking Ability (LESA)

Until the mid-1960s, there was no commonly accepted term to describe the children who were to become the primary beneficiaries of bilingual education, English as a Second Language (ESL), or their variations. These children were simply described in phrases alluding to their linguistic condition: "children who do not speak English natively," "children with a poor command of English," "children who speak languages other than English," "children with a language handicap," and so on.

As early programs emerged in the 1960s, and federal funding became available, advocates settled on a term they felt would be appropriate to the situation and useful in managing instructional programs to serve them. Children of *limited-English-speaking ability,* sometimes simply LESA, came into wide use. It was an appropriate term for a historical moment in which filling unmet social needs by the federal government was the role most politicians could support. The terms used to describe the language situation of these students tended to follow the notion of disadvantage-ness, sometimes *cultural disadvantage* that was popularized by Title I of Elementary and Secondary Education Act (ESEA) and Head Start, the two major funding programs of the federal government for poor children. Consistently, the terminology most often used emphasized the negative aspect of their condition, whether social, economic, or linguistic.

LESA, the term that became most associated with the children to be served by bilingual education, continued to emphasize the deficiency of the client group. Neither the term nor the advocacy modalities used made mention of the advantage inherent in speaking other languages. For the times, LESA appeared to be adequately descriptive of the condition these programs sought to resolve: lack of speaking abilities in English. LESA focused attention on children's productive language, a limited ability to use the English language in the spoken form. LESA did not include reading and writing skills. Hence, during the first years of Title VII programming, the inability to speak English made children eligible for bilingual education without regard to their ability to read or write in English or any other language. The educational assumption that went along with the term was that oral production was the best marker of a child's linguistic abilities, a narrow interpretation of language skills. The initial authorization of Title VII, ESEA, also included a poverty requirement. Only *poor children* who did not speak English well were regarded as proper clients of programs funded through that source.

The concept of disadvantage, and the deficit-based remedial approaches so firmly rooted in Title I and Head Start carried over into Title VII and bilingual education in general.

Limited English Proficiency (LEP)

By the time the original authorization of Title VII, ESEA, ended, advocates of bilingual education saw a need to change the eligibility criterion of LESA to include reading and writing, two critically important skill sets for all students. Dialogue on the limitations of the term *LESA* began during the hearings for the1974 reauthorization of Title VII. This led to the adoption of the broader concept of limited proficiency in English, including the written forms of the language. First used in the 1978 amendments to Title VII, *limited English proficiency,* often stated as LEP, replaced LESA as the eligibility marker for Title VII participation. State and local programs readily adopted the same concept as the eligibility marker for those programs although the concept of limited proficiency remained open to interpretation. The poverty criterion in the original legislation was also removed in 1974.

For the last quarter of the century and most of its legislative life, Title VII continued to rely on the concept of limited English proficiency to identify potential client students. Efforts were made during subsequent reauthorizations to include an acknowledgment in Title VII that knowledge of another language and the use of that language for instruction were an important part of the concept of bilingual education. But early critics of the program, beginning with Noel Epstein, undermined this idea. Epstein alleged that bilingual advocates were less interested in educational equity and more interested in *affirmative ethnicity,* the idea that the schools should support programs to restore and maintain language and nationality identities. Other critics such as Linda Chavez and Rosalie Pedalino Porter argued that the push for bilingual education was part of a strategy by ethnic politicians to control blocks of ethnic voters through the publicly supported maintenance of their languages of origin.

English Language Learners (ELLs)

By the 1980s, congressional supporters of Title VII had become increasingly skittish of proposed changes in Title VII that might be interpreted in these ways. With appropriations approaching $200 million annually, Title VII was no longer a small and regionally oriented program. It had become controversial, and a strong push was made to ensure that its purpose was the teaching of English above all else.

Political exigencies and the need to accept compromises to keep the legislation alive attended every reauthorization. This forced advocates of bilingual education to accept far less than full support for the use and maintenance of home languages other than English. Biliteracy was never embraced by Title VII as a program goal. Thus, the advocacy role of organizations such as the National Association for Bilingual Education was more defensive than proactive. Their efforts succeeded in reauthorizing the critically important Title VII legislation. The price, however, was a decline in the use of true bilingual instruction and, instead, the use of a watered-down form called *home-language* or *primary-language support,* a less robust form of the program.

The adoption of *English language learners* (ELLs) as a preferred term to *LEP* in the literature of bilingual education took place in the mid-1990s, and ELL was widely used by the end of that decade. That finally made the point that students who spoke languages other than English were students, like everyone else, who are in the process of learning. This avoids using a term that stresses the negative condition of being *limited* in English. In a 1994 article, Mark LaCelle-Peterson and Charlene Rivera made a case for the new term in the *Harvard Educational Review.* They pointed out that the term *English language learners*

> . . . follows conventional educational usage in that it focuses on what students are accomplishing, rather than on any temporary "limitation" they face prior to having done so, just as we refer to advanced teacher candidates as "student teachers" rather than "limited teaching proficient individuals," and to college students who concentrate their studies in physics as "physics majors" rather than as "students with limited physics proficiency." (p. 75)

Another factor that promoted the use of the term *ELL,* rather than LEP, came with the passage of Propositions 227 in California and 203 in Arizona, which sought to end bilingual education programs and replace them with English immersion. Both propositions used the term *English learners*. Today, only legal and government documents continue to use LEP in print because the term underlies important legal decisions and any change could challenge the bases for those decisions.

In three decades, three different terms were used to describe the children who were the original clients for bilingual education. Arguably, the shift from LESA to LEP to ELLs was helpful although it did not change the perspective of disadvantage that was the legacy of government funded programs, chiefly Title I, ESEA, and Head Start. At no point in the life of Title VII, ESEA, was it a strong policy goal of the federal government to recognize the value of students' home language as a resource that should continue to be developed by the schools. With every successive reauthorization, learning English and a quick exit from bilingual education became the single-minded objectives. *Dual-language programs* and *heritage language education* appeared shortly thereafter. These terms highlighted the broader goal of parallel mastery of the home language along with English.

Josué M. González

See also Deficit-Based Education Theory; Designation and Redesignation of English Language Learners; Dual-Language Programs; Epstein, Noel; Literacy and Biliteracy; Maintenance Policy Denied; National Association for Bilingual Education; Title VII, Elementary and Secondary Education Act, Key Historical Marker

Further Readings

Arizona Secretary of State. (2000). *Proposition 203: English language education for children in public schools.* Retrieved from http://www.azsos.gov/election/2000/info/PubPamphlet/english/prop203.htm

Bilingual Education Act, Pub. L. No. 90–247, 81 Stat. 816 (1968).

California Secretary of State. (1998). *Proposition 227: English language in public schools.* Retrieved from http://primary98.sos.ca.gov/VoterGuide/Propositions/227.htm

Chavez, L. (1991). *Out of the barrio: Toward a new politics of Hispanic assimilation.* New York: Basic Books.

Crawford, J. (1999). *Bilingual Education: History, politics, theory and practice* (4th ed.). Los Angeles: Bilingual Education Services.

Education Amendments of 1978, 20 U.S.C. 2701 (1978).

Epstein, N. (1977). *Language, ethnicity and the schools: Policy alternatives for bilingual-bicultural education.* Washington, DC: Institute for Educational Leadership, George Washington University.

LaCelle-Peterson, M., & Rivera, C. (1994). Is it real for all kids? A framework for equitable assessment policies for ELLs. *Harvard Educational Review, 64*(1), 55–75.

Porter, R. P. (1996). *Forked tongue: The politics of bilingual education* (2nd ed.). New Brunswick, NJ: Transaction.

Schneider, S. G. (1976). *Revolution, reaction or reform: The 1974 Bilingual Education Act.* New York: Las America Publishing.

LaFontaine, Hernán (1934–)

Hernán LaFontaine, one of the founders of the National Association for Bilingual Education, is a native New Yorker whose parents came from Puerto Rico. He was born and raised in East Harlem, popularly known as "El Barrio." He attended public schools and earned his BS and MA degrees in science from the City College of New York. After serving 2 years in the army, he worked as a chemist with a pharmaceutical firm. His involvement with the community and his interest in young people prompted him to change careers and enter the teaching profession. This entry describes his career.

LaFontaine taught science and mathematics in New York City at the junior high and high school levels and then became an assistant principal. In 1968, while enrolled in the doctoral program at Fordham University, he was appointed principal of P.S. 25 in the Bronx, the first completely bilingual school in New York City. Working with the South Bronx community, he planned and directed the establishment of the school, developing a theoretical framework to implement an elementary school curriculum incorporating bilingual education, and this innovative educational program flourished. He obtained federal funding to support the program through Title VII and actively disseminated information about it. During this time, he also developed the first complete program of courses leading to a master of arts in bilingual education at New York University. Addressing educational issues for English language learners became a major focus of his professional life.

In 1972, LaFontaine was tapped to direct the newly established Office of Bilingual Education in the New York City Board of Education, assisting schools in implementing bilingual programs for 75,000 students. Among his responsibilities was the distribution and monitoring of funds specifically allocated for bilingual programs. He worked closely with the city's Commission on Bilingual Education and other community groups to develop recommendations for implementing a consent decree reached between ASPIRA of New York and the Board of Education, as well as policies to meet requirements related to the Supreme Court's *Lau v. Nichols* decision.

During this time, LaFontaine's pioneering work in bilingual education earned him national and international recognition as an educational leader. In addition to his work in the Office of Bilingual Education, he was actively involved in the establishment of local, state, and national professional organizations including the Puerto Rican Educators' Association of New York City, the New York State Association for Bilingual Education, and the National Association for Bilingual Education (NABE). In 1976, he was elected president of NABE, and served with distinction to lay the foundation for the growth of the organization.

In 1979, LaFontaine was appointed superintendent of the Hartford, Connecticut, school system. He continued in that position until his retirement in 1991, the longest tenure of any superintendent in the history of the Hartford public schools. Under his leadership, considerable progress was made in improving student achievement, revising and standardizing the academic curriculum, and establishing computer-based education. Bilingual education was a strong component of the schooling offered to the city's English language learners. LaFontaine also continued his active communication with parents, community members, and businesses, to involve them in the education of Hartford's students.

Following his retirement as superintendent, LaFontaine was invited to join the faculty of Southern Connecticut State University, where he served as professor of educational leadership in the Graduate School of Education and coordinated the superintendent preparation program. His contributions to the department and university earned him election to the status of professor emeritus at his second retirement in 1999.

Not one to move into quiet retirement, LaFontaine further demonstrated his lifelong commitment to public service by standing for election to the Hartford City Council. He was first elected to the council in 2001 and reelected in 2003. He became president of the city council until his third retirement in 2006. During his tenure, he continued his advocacy for improvement of education as well as focusing on public safety, employment, economic development, and affordable housing.

Throughout his career, LaFontaine has been active in consulting, writing, and speaking to share his expertise and knowledge with others. His publications related to bilingual education included an edited volume on *Perspectives in Bilingual Education* and a *TESOL Quarterly* article on the role of paraprofessionals. He has provided expert testimony on state and federal policy issues, including appearances before the Secretary of Education's Hispanic Task Force on Education (1990), National Advisory Council on Bilingual Education (1985), and the Connecticut State Legislature (1989).

In recognition of his many contributions to bilingual education, LaFontaine has received numerous awards from groups including the Association of Puerto Rican Educators, the Haitian Bilingual Education Association, Hispanic Educators Association of the Bronx, National Puerto Rican Coalition, and NABE. He has also received honorary doctorates from the University of Hartford and Briarwood College.

Donna Christian

See also Aspira Consent Decree; Early Bilingual Programs, 1960s; National Association for Bilingual Education

Further Readings

LaFontaine, H. (1968). *A theoretical model for the implementation of the elementary school curriculum through bilingual education.* New York: Author.

LaFontaine, H. (1971). Para professionals: Their role in E.S.O.L. and bilingual education. *TESOL Quarterly,* December 1971.

LaFontaine, H. (1988). Educational challenges and opportunities in serving limited English proficient students. In Council of Chief State School Officers, *School success for students at risk: Analysis and recommendations of the Council of Chief State School Officers* (pp. 120–133). Orlando, FL: Harcourt Brace Jovanovich. .

LaFontaine, H., Golubchick, L., & Persky, B. (1977). *Perspectives in bilingual education.* Plainfield, NJ: Avery.

Lau v. Nichols, 414 U.S. 563 (1974).

LANGUAGE ACQUISITION DEVICE

How children learn to speak and understand a language has long intrigued linguists and psychologists. Many different theories of this process, called *first-language acquisition,* have been proposed, often in response to existing theories. These theories can generally be grouped under four broad headings: behavioralism, innatism, developmental psychology, and interactionism. The innatist approach to first-language acquisition posits that language learning is an internal process and that children are biologically endowed with the innate ability to learn language. The concept of a language acquisition device (LAD) is largely responsible for this process and is a part of the brain specifically designed for language learning. This entry describes the historical context for LAD, how it works, its role in second-language acquisition, and criticisms of this concept.

Historical Context

Noam Chomsky originally proposed the existence of the (virtual, not physical) LAD in developing his theories of syntax and universal grammar (UG) during the late 1950s and early 1960s. Chomsky was working in response to B. F. Skinner's behavioralist theories of language acquisition, which assumed that language was learned through imitation, habit formation, and reinforcement. In behavioralism, language learning is a process external to the child where the environment provides everything necessary for language acquisition. In contrast to this, Chomsky asserted that humans are biologically endowed with an innate mechanism for learning language, and that the environment provides language as input to the language-learning process. The child, using the LAD, processes that input and gradually acquires adult-like knowledge of a language. This process is largely subconscious and is automatic, much like learning to walk.

Chomsky's use of *language* refers to the syntax, or structure, of a language, rather than to its functions and social uses. Similarly, *grammar* is the set of rules for a language that allow any and all sentences in that language to be produced and understood, rather than the traditional prescriptive grammar learned in school (e.g., "ain't" is bad English).

How the LAD Works

The LAD is frequently referred to as an *organ,* although it resides in and is an inseparable part of the human brain. This reflects a modular understanding of both language learning and the mind, indicating that language learning is different from other types of learning (e.g., learning to add and subtract) and that the LAD is only used for language acquisition. The LAD contains the cognitive tools necessary for learning a language as a child, which include UG, and is the primary means of analyzing language input.

Universal Grammar (UG)

UG is the set of *principles* and *parameters* that constrain the possibilities of the language(s) being learned. These principles and parameters are universal to all languages (hence, Universal Grammar) and are innate. Principles are fundamental characteristics of language and grammar, for instance that language is rule-governed, whereas parameters are options for particular features of language. Parameters serve almost as templates, which are used to analyze language input to determine whether the language being learned allows certain features. A parameter can be understood as a toggle switch that starts off in the neutral central position and then gets flipped to the appropriate up or down position based on language evidence. One example of a parameter would be whether a language allows what is called a "null subject." Some languages, such as Spanish and Italian, allow both *Marla speaks French* and *[she] speaks French,* where the *[she]* is understood but not spoken (*Habla francés* with no explicit subject would be understood and accepted as a grammatical Spanish sentence). English only allows *Marla speaks French,* and *[she] speaks French,* where the *[she]* is null, is immediately recognizable as an ungrammatical English sentence (*Speaks French,* omitting the subject, is not recognized as a full sentence). Accordingly, a child learning English would flip the null subject parameter to "no," making it easier for her LAD to remember that English does not allow null subjects.

Principles and parameters facilitate language acquisition in that they limit the range of possibilities that a child must surmount in learning a language, and simultaneously reduce the number of potential mistakes, although those mistakes still occur. Principles and parameters are not language specific, but represent language universals. This means that the same principles and parameters available to a child learning English are also available to a child learning Arabic. Similarly, a child being raised bilingually will use the same principles and parameters for both languages being learned. According to the LAD theory, these principles and parameters are innate and universal to all humans.

The LAD in Language Learning

The innate knowledge contained in the LAD is used to analyze language input from parents, caretakers, and others in the community, whether it is Appalachian English or Parisian French, to create a series of grammars. Each grammar contains a set of hypotheses about the language being learned and is subsequently refined until the grammar reaches its final state, which is that of an adult grammar. For example, a 3-year-old might first say, "I went to the store," having learned *went* as a word without understanding its grammatical nature. A few months later, that same 3-year-old might say, "I goed to the store," hypothesizing that the *–ed* past tense ending works for all verbs, despite having never heard this form. In this instance, what first appears as a regression in learning English is actually a step forward. It signals that the child is refining the past tense patterns of that language. A subsequent grammar will eventually reflect that some verbs have irregular past tense forms. When that occurs, "goed" will become "went" in a fairly seamless manner.

The existence of the LAD can account for a number of problematic phenomena in first-language acquisition. For example, all children tend to learn certain aspects of a language in a relatively similar order, despite learning different languages. Also, children make mistakes that are not evident in the language input, as in the *goed* versus *went* example, and could never be learned by imitating others. Correspondingly, children eventually achieve adult-like language despite the relative lack of corrective feedback from parents and others. Indeed, different children learning the same language reach the same grammar, despite variations in the language input. Finally, children know much more about the grammar of a language than is evident during daily interactions. For instance, children are able to identify ungrammatical sentences and are able to understand sentences that clash with real-world knowledge (e.g., *the book*

reads the dictionary). These phenomena point to the existence of an innate human ability to learn language, driven by universal knowledge and separate from other types of learning, such as accounted for by the LAD.

The LAD in Second-Language Acquisition

Whether the LAD is available beyond first-language acquisition is currently still being debated. It is unclear what role the LAD may play in the critical period hypothesis, and few researchers believe that the LAD is active beyond puberty. However, many of the phenomena mentioned also occur in second-language acquisition and can be just as problematic. For this reason, some researchers argue that at least UG is available in some form during second-language acquisition, if not the LAD. Whatever the outcome of this polemic, it has implications for teachers in bilingual education and English as a Second Language (ESL).

Krashen's Monitor Model

Stephen Krashen's model of second-language learning, the monitor model, does posit the existence of a LAD-like mechanism for second-language acquisition (SLA). Similar to Chomsky, Krashen developed the monitor model during the 1970s and early 1980s as an answer to behavioralist approaches to second-language learning and teaching. According to Krashen, the LAD is responsible for language that is acquired subconsciously during second-language acquisition, compared with language that is consciously learned as in a classroom. Although Krashen does not give much detail about the nature of the LAD itself, he does argue about the type of input the LAD can process (i + 1) and what can affect the availability of input (the affective filter). In this context, i + 1 refers to a corollary concept dubbed *comprehensible input*.

Criticisms

Current interactionist and developmental theories of language learning argue against the existence of the LAD. These theories hold that language learning is part of the larger innate learning ability of children rather than the result of some language-specific innate knowledge or device, such as the LAD. Language acquisition is seen as closely tied to other types of learning and knowledge and is fed by thousands of interactions with other speakers, such as parents or caretakers. Jean Piaget was a Swiss psychologist who focused on the cognitive development of children. He and Chomsky famously debated these issues at Royaumount Abbey in October 1975. Lev Vygotsky, a Russian psychologist interested in the social interactions of children, is another researcher frequently cited in arguments against the existence of the LAD.

Kara T. McAlister

See also Critical Period Hypothesis; First-Language Acquisition; Krashen, Stephen D.; Learning a Language, Best Age; Monitor Model; Second-Language Acquisition; Vygotsky and Language Learning

Further Readings

Chomsky, N. (1959). Review of *Verbal Behavior* by B. F. Skinner. *Language, 35*(1), 26–58.

Chomsky, N. (1986). *Knowledge of language: Its nature, origin, and use.* New York: Praeger.

Crain, S., & Lillo-Martin, D. (1999). *An introduction to linguistic theory and language acquisition.* Oxford, UK: Blackwell.

Gardner, H. (1982). *Art, mind, and brain: A cognitive approach to creativity.* New York: Basic Books.

Krashen, S. (1985). *The input hypothesis: Issues and implications.* London: Longman.

Lightbown, P. M., & Spada, N. (2006). *How languages are learned* (3rd. ed.). Oxford, UK: Oxford University Press.

LANGUAGE AND IDENTITY

Much has been written on language and identity and the influence each has on the other. Academic journals such as *TESOL Quarterly* and *Linguistics and Education* have published special issues exploring the themes of language and identity. The purpose of this entry is to examine selected perspectives regarding the topic of language and identity and possible implications for classroom teachers. The entry begins with some commonly discussed categories of identity and how identity is constructed or negotiated. Following is a discussion of language, identity, and their reciprocal influence. The entry concludes with a brief discussion of implications for pedagogy and language instruction.

Defining Identity

Traditionally an individual's identity was looked upon as singular and stable—perhaps permanent—and over which one had little control. If a person was a carpenter by occupation, that was how everyone viewed him, and how he viewed himself. However, over time, this view has progressively changed. Current literature on the topic holds that individuals have multiple identities, which are constantly changing and being negotiated depending on the time and context of the situation. That is to say, an individual has numerous facets of the self (e.g., man/woman, spouse, parent, boss), all of which together form the individual's multiple identities. These multiple facets or ways of looking at oneself in relation to the world are socially constructed. That is, identities are not biologically preprogrammed but are directly influenced by our social environment. For example, the term *husband* has different meanings depending on the society in which one lives. In some cultures, husbands are allowed numerous wives, whereas in Western society, the law permits only one wife. The concept of husband, therefore, is a socially constructed concept. It can be argued, therefore, that this facet of identity—being a husband—is only one of a person's multiple identities.

Michel Foucault postulates about the individual in a temporal sense: that an individual doesn't "become," but instead continually "transforms." "Becoming" implies that people reach an end in the construction of their identities; "transform" implies that their identities are never finished forming and that people are never finished constructing their identities. In other words, individuals are constantly changing, and thus, their identities change too. This is again a direct challenge to, or a contradiction of, how identities were thought of in the past. A person may have the job title of a carpenter, but depending on the context, he may look at his identity as a carpenter from different perspectives. If he just made an enormous error that will force the crew to restart a project in constructing something, he may have negative thoughts regarding his self-perception of being a carpenter. However, likewise, if he just completed a beautiful, intricately designed, built-in entertainment center in someone's family room, he will be proud to be a carpenter. Hence, his identity as a carpenter is never stagnant, but is always changing and dynamic.

According to Aneta Pavlenko and Adrian Blackledge, identity is placed in three different categories: imposed identities, assumed identities, and negotiable identities. *Imposed identities* can be described as those that cannot be negotiated in a particular time and place. For example, in Nazi Germany, numerous individuals were forced to accept a certain identity, that of being Jewish, which had numerous life-threatening implications. People may have disagreed with being identified as being Jewish, perhaps because they did not practice Judaism or identify themselves as Jews; however, that was irrelevant. There was no negotiation of identity permitted within that specific context. For a less dire example, immigrant children have historically been misplaced in special education programs on the basis of their lack of English language proficiency. These students therefore were identified as "special education students" instead of being rightly diagnosed as second-language learners. These students' identities were thus imposed on them, without them having a say in the matter. Not knowing that the identity imposed on them was possibly harmful to their development, some students may have grown up believing that they belonged in that category.

The second type or category of identity is *assumed identities*. These types of identities can be applied to those who are comfortable with and not willing to contest their identities. Having assumed identities is frequently valued and legitimatized by the dominant group within a given society. An example of this type of identity is the heterosexual White middle-class male in the United States. Although not all heterosexual White middle-class males in the United States feel comfortable with this identity, it is typically not contested. Interestingly, people who have this identity frequently do not consider themselves as "having a culture," but instead will look at others, especially minorities and immigrants, as having a culture. A common phrase from this population is, "I don't have a culture. I am just American." They thus conceptualize culture in a narrow way, such as race (other than Caucasian) or of some display of a stereotyped feature or tradition from a group different from their own.

The third category of identity is *negotiable identities*. Negotiable identities pertain to all identity options that can be, and are, contested or resisted by particular individuals and groups. Take, for example, immigrants to the United States. In today's society, immigrants are expected to assimilate into the mainstream culture and take on U.S. norms, thereby substantially diminishing or losing their culture and self-identification of being from their home country. Even with this formidable

pressure from the dominant culture, immigrants now have a greater choice whether to lose their language, culture, and ways of life from the home country or to continue their own in keeping with their comfort levels, needs, and desires. Numerous immigrants are choosing to maintain their language, culture, and ways of being brought from their home country, thereby contesting the identity of a fully assimilated immigrant to the United States. They choose to be selective in what facets of American life they will appropriate into their identities (following work hours, going to the gym, learning English, etc.).

James Gee believes that in addition to having these various facets of ourselves to use or call upon, if an attribute is not recognized as defining someone as a particular kind of person, then it cannot serve as an identity of any sort. In other words, people construct their identities by the recognition that others give them. Take immigrant students from Mexico, for example, who may try to become members of the dominant society, which in this case is White English-speaking America. However, if they, for whatever reason, are not accepted as members of White English-speaking America by White English-speaking Americans, immigrants from Mexico will never truly appropriate the identity befitting of a member of that community.

To understand identities, it is important to recognize that identities are always constructed in a social context through discourse (language and context). The definitions of the different types of identity described earlier all use some form of positioning. Two specific types of positioning are interactive positioning and reflective positioning. *Interactive positioning* assumes one individual positioning the other. In Germany under Nazi rule, the Nazis positioned others with identities as persons of the Jewish faith. In another previous example, the school or testing structure positioned immigrant students within the special education program. The positioning was done via the interaction between two individuals or groups of individuals.

The second type of positioning is *reflective positioning*. Although how individuals view themselves is heavily influenced by those surrounding them, reflective positioning occurs when individuals actively position themselves. An example of this is when immigrant students in the classroom do not participate in the mainstream English classroom because they believe that their English is not good enough for them to participate. Even though the others within that classroom may or may not agree with these immigrant students' estimation of their English ability, they continue to be passive members of that classroom community, thus literally and figuratively positioning themselves at the margins of that community.

Language and Identity Related

The foregoing brief descriptions of the various types of identity raise the question of what identity has to do with language. An individual negotiates a sense of self within and across different contexts at different times through language. In other words, languages are used to legitimize, challenge, and negotiate particular identities. Another look at the three different types of identities described earlier in the context of language—imposed, assumed, and negotiable—will help to explain this concept.

Imposed identities are those that have been imposed on an individual (e.g., the language learner wrongly being labeled a special education student). To understand how imposition occurs in the context of language, imagine two people having a conversation. When they begin speaking, language is the first thing that the other person is going to hear. They both will be listening not only to intonation, stress, and other speech factors, but also to the word choice (semantics), grammatical structures (syntax), and the manner in which the words are being used (pragmatics). These three factors say a lot about us as members of society. If one were speaking grammatically incorrectly, one may be perceived as an uneducated person. If one were using certain slang terms associated with a younger population, one could be perceived as either a member of that group or perhaps immature for trying to use those terms. If one were using erudite words wrongly or out of context, one may be viewed as trying to impress someone with pedantic language. The language used is like opening a book for others to see inside the speaker.

Because language has this open-book effect, people will position or impose a certain identity on others whether or not it is accurate. Frequently, immigrant children who speak a language other than English as their first language may be looked upon by their teachers and peers as not as bright as they truly are. This is not because they are lacking in intelligence, but because they do not yet have the English-speaking skills to adequately express themselves and negotiate their identity in the school context. Interestingly, after numerous experiences interacting with others who think of these children as unintelligent, these children

may begin to think of themselves as unintelligent as well, which may lead to other negative outcomes in school such as absenteeism, misbehavior in class, and eventually dropping out. Although this may sound oversimplified and perhaps even exaggerated, it is actually a daily occurrence for thousands of immigrant children across the United States. Thus, imposed identities can have a detrimental effect on immigrant students and their futures in school.

Assumed identities are those identities that typically are held by the dominant group within a society. Individuals who have these types of identities are typically not willing to contest these identities. In other words, they understandably like being members of the dominant group within the society and do not typically want to be placed in another position within the social structure of a given society. With the identity as a member of the dominant group comes the belief of having certain rights and privileges (communication is always in the dominant language, all road and business signs are written in the dominant language, school is taught in the dominant language, most movies are in the dominant language, etc.). Although often unknown to members of the dominant language group, these beliefs create a direct positioning of others who do not speak or speak the dominant language with limited proficiency.

The influence that society (the dominant group, or other minority groups) has over an individual's self-perception or identity is powerful. Take again, for example, immigrant children who speak Spanish as their native language at home. When they are home and speaking with their parents in Spanish, they are typically proud to speak to their parents in that language, and their identity as Spanish speakers is strong and confident. However, researchers such as James Cummins, Marcelo Suárez-Orozco and Carola Suárez-Orozco, and Stephen Krashen have demonstrated that after being exposed to "English-only" instruction in school, these same children begin to understand that English is the language whose speakers have the power and control in this society. Simultaneously, they see that Spanish is not a high-status language here. This dichotomy provides the children with a dilemma: Which language should I speak? Popular culture in the United States pressures immigrant children to speak English and forget Spanish, despite losing communication with their parents. Researchers in the fields of immigration and global studies and bilingual education, along with most advocates of bilingual education, many teachers, and families, say that they should learn both languages. Unless that happens, children who were once proud Spanish speakers will consciously attempt to stop speaking Spanish with their parents, family, and friends. Their goal is to speak only English and eradicate Spanish from their lives to avoid a negative ascribed identity. The positioning, whether directly or indirectly, positive or negative, by the dominant language group leaves a profound mark on the individual's identity. This occurrence is not only common, but happens to a large proportion of immigrants in the United States as well as many Native Americans who have lived here for centuries. This phenomenon is partly why linguists for years have been calling the United States a language graveyard: Languages other than English do not prosper here.

To add to the discussion, it is believed that simply by the dominant group members' unawareness that they are indeed the dominant group, or by the dominant group's insistence on keeping itself in the status as the dominant group (proposing English as the official language, English-only education in schools), dominant group members are creating an environment within which their assumed identities are positioning all other members of society as the "other," thereby greatly adding to the social phenomenon of language minority children's relative lack of success in school.

The third category, negotiable identities, refers to all identity options that can be, and are, contested and resisted by individuals and groups. The description of this category of identity mentioned that recent immigrants have the right to choose what aspects of the new culture of their new homeland they can appropriate. With this right, immigrants are opting to raise their children bilingually, understanding the importance of the heritage language as well as the importance of learning English, and instilling a pride in their heritage language as well as in English. When children maintain a pride in their affiliation with their homeland (language and culture), they have a strong identity associated with their heritage language and culture. Research has shown (see, e.g., work conducted by María Eugenia Matute-Bianchi) that such children frequently are more successful academically than when they assimilate to the new culture. This has been mainly shown in Mexican and other Spanish-speaking immigrant populations and in various Asian and South Asian immigrant populations as well (Korean, Indian, and Chinese).

Pedagogical Implications

Language and identity are important facets of a student's life. Because of their reciprocal role, some researchers, such as Krashen and Cummins, believe that the use of English-only policies in school, both in the classroom and on the playground, in effect takes the voice away from nonnative-English-speaking students. Allowing students to speak in their native languages can be looked at as a positive technique that reinforces students' self-perceptions. Teachers can build upon this wealth of knowledge that children have and provide a venue in which they can thrive and learn in their classrooms. It is believed that if teachers and administrators understood the interconnection between language and identity, they would naturally promote diversity and the richness it brings to a classroom. Luis Moll and his colleagues have proposed the idea of "funds of knowledge"—everything that children bring with them (their experiences, understandings of the world, and language)—and using this knowledge as a base from which to continue to build their students' knowledge of the world. Rather than looking at the students from the deficit perspective, according to which they are simply recipients of information that the teachers provide, or empty vessels needing to be filled, students are instead individuals who talk, have perspectives on their past experiences, and have a genuine interest in their futures. Thus, students become individuals who should be conferred with, talked with, and worked with. A review of the literature regarding the mutual influence of language and identity may help teachers and administrators make their own informed decisions on how to best educate language minority students.

James Cohen

See also Additive and Subtractive Programs; Affective Filter; Benefits of Bilingualism and Heritage Languages; Languages and Power; Multicultural Education; Second-Language Acquisition

Further Readings

Cummins, J. (1986). Empowering minority students: A framework for intervention. *Harvard Educational Review, 56*(1), 18–36.

Foucault, M. (1991). Politics and the study of discourse. In G. Buchell, C. Gordon, & P. Vuller (Eds.), *The Foucault effect.* Chicago: University of Chicago Press.

Gee, J. P. (2000). Identity as an analytic lens for research in education. In W. Secada (Ed.), *Review of research in education* (Vol. 25, pp. 99–125). Washington, DC: American Educational Research Association.

Krashen, S. (1996). *The case against bilingual education.* Culver City, CA: Language Education Associates.

Martin-Jones, M., & Heller, M. (Eds.). (1996). Education in multilingual settings: Discourse, identities and power [Special issue]. *Linguistics and Education, 8*(1–2).

Matute-Bianchi, M. E. (1991). Situational ethnicity and patterns of school performance among immigrant and nonimmigrant Mexican-descent students. In M. Gibson & J. Ogbu (Eds.), *Minority Status and Schooling: A comparative study of immigrants and involuntary minorities* (pp. 205–247). New York: Garland Press.

Moll, L. C., & González, N. (2003). Engaging life: A funds-of-knowledge approach to multicultural education. In J. A. Banks & C. A. M. Banks (Eds.), *Handbook on multicultural education* (2nd ed.). San Francisco: Jossey-Bass.

Norton, B. (Ed.). (1997). Language and identity [Special issue]. *TESOL Quarterly, 31*(3).

Pavlenko, A., & Blackledge, A. (Eds.). (2004). *Negotiation of identities in multilingual contexts.* Clevedon, UK: Multilingual Matters.

Suárez-Orozco, C., & Qin-Hillard, D. (2003). Formulating identity in a globalized world. In M. M. Suárez-Orozco & D. Qin-Hillard (Eds.), *Globalization: Culture & education in the new millennium.* Berkeley: University of California Press & Ross Institute.

Suárez-Orozco, C., & Suárez-Orozco, M. M. (2001). *Children of immigration.* Cambridge, MA: Harvard University Press.

LANGUAGE AND THOUGHT

Do Yupik speakers, from western Alaska, think of snow differently than non-Yupik speakers because they have so many more adjectives to describe its texture and density? Do English and Spanish speakers experience reality differently because Spanish has two verb forms for the single English verb *to be?* Whereas an English speaker would say "I am thin" to describe either a change in condition or a permanent condition, someone speaking Spanish would have two options: *"Estoy flaco"* suggests that the person is newly thin because of lost weight, and *"soy flaco"* implies that the person is thin by nature. In short, every time Spanish speakers say they are thin or fat they are expressing a perception of their condition as permanent or temporary depending on the verb form chosen

to express it. Similarly, does the use of the subjunctive voice to express less than 100% certainty make certain languages more appropriate for diplomacy than for engineering? This entry discusses the relationship between language and thought.

In short, does this mean that words are "microcosms to human consciousness," as the Russian psychologist Lev Semenovich Vygotsky would suggest? This interrelation of language and thought was explored by Edward Sapir and Benjamin Lee Whorf, in what is known as the Sapir-Whorf hypothesis. The "strong" version of this hypothesis (also known as linguistic deterministic hypothesis) posits that the way we think is determined by the language we speak; on the other hand, the "weak" version (also known as linguistic relativity hypothesis) simply suggests that different languages are associated with different types of thinking, but do not de facto cause the difference. Not surprisingly, the interrelationship of language, thought, and culture has piqued the curiosity of developmental psychologists, linguistic anthropologists, psycholinguists, philosophers, theologians, cognitive scientists, and bilingual education scholars and practitioners throughout the ages.

Today, considerable research evidence supports the intuitive notion that a powerful symbiotic relationship exists between language, thought, and culture, and that the way people make meaning of the world is socially constructed. According to cognitive scholars Vera John-Steiner and Ellen Souberman, in the afterword of *Mind in Society,* Vygotsky looks at the individual–society relation as a dialectical process, and compares this process to the image of a river and its tributaries, which combine and separate, in the same way elements in human life do. This view challenges the notion of static polarities. Linking this dialectical notion to thought and speech, psychologist John B. Carroll says that for Vygotsky, thought and speech have natures independent of each other, each with its own life and growth. Yet, they have some form of interaction when it comes to development; sometimes language development is ahead of cognitive development, but sometimes these positions are reversed. There is a point, however, at which both processes coincide, and they influence each other: Thought becomes verbal and speech becomes rational.

Likewise, Masahiko Minami, who specializes in English-Japanese children's stories, concludes from his own research that language and thought are inseparable. That is, the particular language that children speak and read determines how they perceive and think about the world. Although most studies so far support the interrelationship between language, thought, and culture, not all researchers agree with the linguistic relativity hypothesis (the "weak" version mentioned earlier), which states that as human languages differ so do the ways their speakers think. Some researchers have questioned it, but others have marshaled evidence to challenge it. They believe that a rock is a rock no matter what it is called in whatever language and cultural context, and that we can communicate via written and visual symbols across cultures to some degree, even if we do not speak each other's language. Matters tend to get more complicated, however if we substitute *democracy* or *justice* in place of "a rock."

Language is a system that enables us to communicate—to express our thoughts—within and across cognitive, academic, linguistic, and cultural borders. Under normal conditions, we employ a sound system, words, and grammar patterns. Beyond the technical aspects of language, communicative competence entails subtle and culture-specific components and domains of language, such as (a) appropriate adjustment to conversations and social situations (e.g., understanding when it is appropriate to interrupt or enter into a conversation, knowing the appropriate way to listen); (b) mastery of abstract language needed for academic purposes in such courses as math, science, technology, and social studies; (c) the ability to gauge nonverbal aspects of language such as body language; and (d) an understanding of vocabulary, written, and visual symbols.

Thus, as an integral aspect of culture, language is a vehicle through which we function as bearers of thought and culture, as well as makers of culture and thought. Although there is considerable disagreement about the meaning of culture, the social anthropologist Edward T. Hall concludes that all social scientists are in agreement about several points, which are the following: (a) Culture is not innate, but learned, (b) culture is shared and has an important role in defining the social boundaries of different groups, and (c) the various facets of culture are interrelated.

In brief, we can think of language in different ways. As a physical phenomenon, language can be seen as a system of sounds and movements made by humans and interpreted by those on the receiving end. Anthropologically, culture is inseparable from cultural and cognitive processes. Culture is not genetically encoded but is learned and shared; it is constantly changing and borrowing from other languages and cultures. The folk singer Pete Seeger quotes his father as having said, "plagiarism is basic to all culture." Cognitively, language is a vehicle for the thought process; according to the semiotician Sebastian Shaumyan, it can be viewed as a system of symbols that have acquired sociocultural significance.

With respect to bilingual education, it is important to keep in mind the dynamic and complex links among language, thought, and cultural relativistic processes because these follow independent and dependent paths in school and society. Given the impact that language has on the way we think and communicate with each other and the way we experience reality, the linguistic/cultural relativity hypothesis challenges bilingual educators to explore deeply and in myriad ways the background variables that can affect the link between language, thought, and cultural processes. In the words of anthropologist David Bidney, cultural relativism can imply that no universal norms exist that work to judge all cultural groups in the same way.

Bilingual education teachers report that they are sometimes asked how they know what language their students are thinking in. Their collective responses vary, but they tend to cluster around a single theme: that the language students are using is not important; what is important is that they are thinking. Indeed, questions dealing with the relationship between language and thought are interesting, perhaps because they raise our hopes. The possibility that a close relationship exists between the two is most intriguing if we could be more certain that close links exist and that thoughts are mediated by language. In this scenario, a bilingual child might be said to bring greater mental flexibility to classroom problems. Regrettably, although we cannot deny this possibility at least in some circumstances, the research has yet to become definitive on this point. As research continues, however, we are now closer to answering a more general question, namely, What is the strength of the relationship between language and cognition, and how can we use our understanding of that relationship to improve student performance?

Carlos J. Ovando

See also Acculturation; Cognitive Benefits of Bilingualism; Enculturation; Metalinguistic Awareness; Vygotsky and Language Learning

Further Readings

Bidney, D. (1968). Cultural relativism. In D. L. Sills (Ed.), *International encyclopedia of the social sciences* (Vol. 3, pp. 543–47). New York: Macmillan.

Bloom, A. H. (1981). *The linguistic shaping of thought: A study in the impact of language on thinking in China and the West.* Hillsdale, NJ: Lawrence Erlbaum.

Carroll, J. B. (1991). Review of *Thought and Language* by Lev Semenovich Vygotsky. In M. Minami & B. P. Kennedy (Eds.), *Language issues in literacy and bilingual/multicultural education.* Cambridge, MA: Harvard Educational Review.

Chomsky, N. (1972). *Language and mind.* New York: Harcourt Brace Jovanovich.

Cole, M., John-Steiner, V., Scribner, S., & Souberman, E. (Eds.). (1978). *L. S. Vygotsky:* Mind in society: *The development of higher psychological processes.* Cambridge, MA: Harvard University Press.

Gumperz, J. J., & Levinson, S. C. (Eds.). (1996). *Rethinking linguistic relativity.* Cambridge, MA: Cambridge University Press.

Hall, E. T. (1976). *Beyond culture.* New York: Doubleday.

Minami, M. (2007). Use of verb forms in narratives told by English-Japanese bilingual children. In M. Minami (Ed.), *Applying theory and research to learning Japanese as a foreign language.* Newcastle-upon-Tyne, UK: Cambridge Scholars.

Minami, M., & Ovando, C. J. (2004). Language issues in multicultural contexts. In J. Banks & C. Banks (Eds.), *Handbook of research on multicultural education,* (2nd ed., pp. 567–588). San Francisco: Jossey-Bass.

Ovando, C. J. (2004). Language diversity and education. In J. A. Banks & C. A. M. Banks (Eds.), *Multicultural education: Issues and perspectives* (5th ed.). Boston: Wiley.

Ovando, C. J., Combs, M. C., & Collier, V. P. (2006). *Bilingual and ESL classrooms: Teaching in multicultural contexts* (4th ed.). Boston: McGraw-Hill.

Sapir, E. (D. Mandelbaum, Ed.). (1956). *Culture, language and personality: Selected essays.* Berkeley: University of California Press.

Shaumyan, S. (1987). *A semiotic theory of language.* Bloomington: Indiana University Press.

Vygotsky, L. S. (1962). *Thought and language* (E. Hanfmann & G. Vakar, Trans.). Cambridge: MIT Press.

Vygotsky, L. S. (M. Cole, V. John-Steiner & E. Souberman, Eds.) (1978). *Mind in Society: The development of higher psychological processes.* Cambridge, MA: Harvard University Press.

Wertch, J. V. (1985). *Vygotsky and the social formation of mind.* Cambridge, MA: Harvard University Press.

Whorf, B. L. (J. B. Carroll, Ed.). (1956). *Language, thought, and reality: Selected writings.* Cambridge: MIT Press.

LANGUAGE BROKERING

Language brokering refers to the act of translating (written language) or interpreting (oral language), usually for adult immigrants who are not yet proficient in the dominant language of the society. Language brokers are translators or interpreters without formal training. Unlike professional translators or interpreters who focus on delivering the information accurately as it is and do not get involved personally, language brokers take a role of mediators and usually have a part in decision making for, or with, the persons they serve.

In the context of bilingual education, language brokers are usually bilingual schoolchildren who mediate between their parents and English-speaking mainstream personnel in institutions that provide public services, as described in this entry. Although scant, current research on language brokering suggests it is a prevalent practice among bilingual children. Lucy Tse reported in her study with Chinese, Vietnamese, and Latin American adolescents that most of them had participated in language brokering on behalf of their families. Specifically, 90% of Chinese- and Vietnamese-descent adolescents and 100% of Latino adolescents reported to have brokered. Some students started to take a role, as a language broker, as early as within 1 year to 5 years of their arrival in the United States. The starting age of brokering was between 8 and 12.

Usually, the oldest child of the family takes the role of a language broker. Girls brokered more often and said that they had more positive feelings about brokering than boys did. Alejandro Morales and William E. Hanson found that language brokers are usually confident, extroverted, good-natured, friendly, sociable, and good listeners. They are also able to provide great detail, and emphasize emotions when translating.

Most of the tasks children take on as language brokers are higher than their cognitive and linguistic developmental levels. They often translate notes and letters between school and parents. They also translate bank and credit card statements, rental agreements, immigration forms, and job applications. Additionally, they are often asked to interpret for parent-teacher conferences, financial agencies, government institutions, and consultations at the doctor's office. They are exposed to various real-world situations, engaging in tasks often above their developmental levels.

Some controversies exist concerning children's role as language brokers. One of them addresses parent-child relationships and how these can be affected by language brokering. Some studies have reported positive effects within families; these effects include stronger bonds, children's commitment to parents, and greater concern about family issues. In some cases, children become advocates of their parents' rights, in scenarios where they get legal assistance for their parents or help them avoid potentially embarrassing and humiliating situations. Others have suggested that children's views of their parents can be negative, as a result of language brokering, because of an unhealthy role reversal. Children's function of authority can cause them to lose respect for their parents.

An additional danger of language brokering is that children sometimes are put into awkward situations where they are required to translate something about themselves that they would not normally hear, know, or care to divulge. They take on more mature roles while they are still children. Some contents of conversations or social situations are cognitively challenging and developmentally inappropriate; other tasks are stressful, intimate, and sensitive such as information given to or received from medical doctors. Even though language brokers are proficient in English at their age levels, they are sometimes unable to accurately interpret some words because the vocabulary level may be too difficult for them. Children also might experience stress or perceive pressure to interpret when they are reluctant to do so.

Researchers report mixed results regarding children's feelings about their role as language broker of the family. Some children reported that they perceive the role as normal and natural. Some reported enjoying the role, having pride in performing it, and appreciating the way it helped them develop their first and second language and culture. On the other hand, some reported feeling frustrated, embarrassed, and pressured to translate accurately. Others said that they do not find it helpful or enjoyable and do not feel good about translating or interpreting.

Lucy Tse and Jeff McQuillan reported that language brokering positively affects children's cognitive and linguistic development. Their second language will gain in development because of the increased input, and by continuously using their first language, they will be able to maintain it. More than 50% of the participants of Tse's study responded that language brokering helped them develop their second language. It was also reported that language brokering develops higher-order decision-making strategies, in addition to communicative competence.

Marguerite Malakoff and Kenji Hakuta also determined that bilingual children in their study translated with high accuracy, which evidences high levels of cognitive and linguistic ability. Malakoff and Hakuta viewed translation as metalinguistic awareness in bilingual children, which refers to the awareness of the nature of underlying linguistic processes, which are not usually noticed when people use language for less consequential purposes. Guadalupe Valdés, a well-known Stanford University scholar, suggests using a linguistic and cultural lens to view giftedness. She believes that immigrant children's functioning as language brokers should be viewed as an indicator of being gifted.

Despite the high performance capacity of child language brokers, studies of the effects of language brokering on academic performance varied in their findings regarding whether these indicated negative or positive consequences or no relation at all. Tse's study showed no relationship; she inferred that these results were because tests fail to accurately measure students' performance. Most of the tests are developed for monolingual English speakers, and thus, their results are not accurate for bilingual populations. Positive responses by the school to this important social function can be a way to improve these students' educational environment. Recognition of the high-order language skills involved in brokering, paired with participation in sensitive and responsive programs, may nurture these students' abilities to their full potential.

Chanyoung Park

See also Benefits of Bilingualism and Heritage Languages; Code Switching; Home Language and Self-Esteem

Further Readings

Malakoff, M., & Hakuta, K. (1991). Translation skill and metalinguistic awareness in bilinguals. In E. Bialystok (Ed.), *Language processing in bilingual children* (pp. 141–166). Cambridge, UK: Cambridge University Press.

McQuillan, J., & Tse, L. (1995). Child language brokering in linguistic minority communities: Effects on cultural interaction, cognition, and literacy. *Language and Education, 9*(3), 195–215.

Morales, A., & Hanson, W. E. (2005). Language brokering: An integrative review of the literature. *Hispanic Journal of Behavioral Sciences, 27*(4), 471–503.

Tse, L. (1995). Language brokering among Latino adolescents: Prevalence, attitudes, and school performance. *Hispanic Journal of Behavioral Sciences, 17*(2), 180–193.

Tse, L. (1995). When students translate for parents: Effects of language brokering. *CABE Newsletter, 17*(4), 16–17.

Tse, L. (1996). Language brokering in linguistic minority communities: The case of Chinese- and Vietnamese-American students. *Bilingual Research Journal, 20*(3&4), 485–498.

Valdés, G. (2003). *Expanding definitions of giftedness: The case of young interpreters from immigrant communities.* Mahwah, NJ: Lawrence Erlbaum.

LANGUAGE DEFINED

To define *language* is complicated because the definition considers what language does as well as what language is. It is the conduit through which one finds answers to questions about people's identities and experiences. Through language, we find out about the individual and about the current and historical context in which the individual is situated. A definition of language is more than simply describing a communication system. This entry considers this aspect of language first because it is arguably the most common.

Language is a system of communication that one group of people shares. Pidgins, Creoles, and dialects are not languages according to this definition but are language variations used to connect two or more groups or connect subgroups within a larger language community. Language is often governed by a grammar that is applied to verbal communication. Some disagree with this understanding of the relationship of grammar with language and maintain that language is a system that includes various media of transmission (speech, writing, or sign). In this view, language is the product of the interaction of transmission medium, grammar, and meaning to communicate ideas, notions, or other content among those sharing this system. Either of these definitions applies to all sorts of languages, including natural human languages and artificial languages and programming languages that organize the operation of computers.

Though one can understand language as a system to serve technical purposes—such as those related to computer programming languages—this entry confines itself to discussion of seven general features of language in the domain of natural human language.

First, each language has always served a number of functions among those who share it. It is used in social interaction to express emotion, to persuade, and to explain. It is also used in individual reflection to organize one's thoughts. Language is the tool whereby one communicates what is important, valued, beautiful, or sacred among its speakers. All languages are equal. However, the speakers of each language often believe that their language is the one best language.

Second, in the history of humankind, language has always been an indicator of status because people believe that some languages are more useful than others for particular purposes. Some believe that some languages are primitive especially when they do not have a written form. Others believe that some languages are superior to others in a general way. Classical Latin and Greek were considered superior because of the literature and thought that they expressed. Classical Arabic has been identified with the Muslim religion as the language of the Qur'an. Similar claims have been made for Sanskrit and Classical Hebrew, and German was once considered superior because of beliefs that German is especially useful in expressing scientific thoughts. An interesting twist on German is the notion that early speakers of that language did not participate in the building of the Tower of Babel. Certain beliefs and today's controversies surrounding the supremacy of English are misconceptions or simple assumptions that the language of the sole remaining super power in the world must surely be a super language too.

Third, language is intimately intertwined with identity in every sense of this term. The language one speaks conveys what group one belongs to, one's social status, personality type, intellectual ability, role, and context in which one is situated. How one speaks a language can reveal the speaker's age or gender status. It reveals geographic, ethnic, and national identity. The way one speaks the language reflects social position or level of education. One's role in society governs the language variety that one uses.

Fourth, as much as language binds, it also separates speakers within groups by their respective roles in the group. When one assumes a role, one also uses a language variety related to that role. Changing language or language variety signals distancing from one group and embracing another voluntarily or involuntarily. One uses a language variety in a court of law or church that is different from the variety used in dinner parties, job interviews, business meetings, and other occasions.

Fifth, we do not know definitively how language originated. Earlier theories about the origin of language related spoken language to sounds in the environment, human emotions, human interaction with the environment, and the human need to collaborate and express oneself. All of these theories have been disproved and are not commonly accepted. More recently, glossogenetics (i.e., the study of the formation and development of human language) has attempted to shed light on the origin of language through modern scientific method. Contributing sciences to glossogenetics are sociobiology, anthropology, psychology, semiotics, neurology, primatology, and linguistics.

Sixth, the world's thousands of languages are organized into families, and each family is descended from a parent language. For instance, Romance languages are descendants of Classical Latin and share similarities in grammars and lexicons. Classical Latin is an offspring of Proto-Indo-European, and its sister languages are Celtic, Germanic, Italic, Balto-Slavic, Albanian, Greek, Armenian, Indo-Iranian, and Tocharian. Other language families include Uralic languages (i.e., ancestors of Finnish, Hungarian, and others in present-day northern Russia), Caucasian languages rooted in Georgia and Southern Russia, Palaeosiberian, Altaic, Dravidian, Austro-Asiatic, Thai, Sino-Tibetan, Chinese languages, African languages, Austronesian languages (also known as Malayo-Polynesian), Indo-Pacific family (including Tasmanian, Māori, Tahitian, Samoan, and Javanese), indigenous languages in the Americas, and indigenous languages in Australia.

Finally, language is constantly changing. As a language's speakers come into contact with speakers of other languages, they use words and other features from each other's languages. Few languages are pure or static. All languages change over time, or die if their speakers remain in isolation and do not reproduce themselves to ensure transmission of the language to a following generation. Languages can also die if political factors place their speakers in a disadvantageous position. In some cases, changes are moderated through academies that monitor and standardize grammatical and lexical changes to the language, with the intent of maintaining the purity of the language and the integrity of the culture that it reflects. This is the case today with the Spanish Royal Academy of the Language and a similar group in France.

Language is a tool for preserving traditions from one generation to the next, and a medium for remembering the past, regardless of differences in social, economic, or political circumstances of its speakers from one generation to the next. In short, language is an important, pervasive, and essential part of life.

Elsie M. Szecsy

See also Code Switching; First-Language Acquisition; Indo-European Languages; Language and Identity; Linguistics, an Overview

Further Readings

Crystal, D. (1997). *The Cambridge encyclopedia of language* (2nd ed.). New York: Cambridge University Press.

LANGUAGE DOMINANCE

Language dominance is often understood to refer to either one's current preference for a language, or the skill or amount of practice one has in a language. No single definition of dominance in language research exists, so many researchers propose their own, depending on their experiences, research purpose, or the population they are working with.

The concept of dominance, as discussed in this entry, is closely linked to the notion of proficiency, or how well one can speak and understand a language, although many agree that these two concepts are not the same. *Language proficiency* is often defined as the overall level of achievement and the competency of language use. It is the ability of a speaker to use the language in various situations. When a person speaks two languages with equal proficiency, the language skills are said to be balanced across the two languages and the person is a balanced bilingual. When skills in one language are stronger or the person is more proficient in using one language than another, this language is referred to as the dominant one. However, that is the extent of the agreement among language researchers. Even the idea of balance is debated because it is nearly impossible to make judgments concerning balance between two languages in every arena of life (e.g., family life, work, worship, dreams, intimate conversations).

On a more technical issue of what constitutes a dominant language, researchers and practitioners have many different views. Some believe that dominance is limited only to the exhibition of certain grammatical features while mixing languages. For example, if a child speaks English and Spanish, when mixing the two languages in a phrase with an article (or adjective) and a noun, they might unconsciously use a Spanish article and an English noun. That is because Spanish articles reflect gender and number and in this are more descriptive than are English articles. Scientists who believe in that view of dominance limit their view to certain grammatical features of the language and agree that a person can be proficient in both languages, but dominant in one only when using this particular grammatical feature.

Another view of dominance is that a language is dominant if and when its pace of development is faster than other languages one might speak. This happens if a person speaks one language more than another, as is often the case in immigrant communities where the emphasis is on English rather than on the native language.

The third view of dominance is that of relative proficiency. That means that language use depends on the situation and circumstance, on how and when the language is used. Scholars who hold this view may not label a language as dominant at all but, rather, talk about the ability of using languages in different circumstances. The proponents of this view would argue that bilingual speakers use their two languages for various purposes, in different circumstances and with different people. Because of that, dominance would depend on the relative use of language in an area. Those who hold this view argue that although a person is proficient in English when talking about her job, that does not mean that her English is dominant when she talks about other topics or matters such as politics or religion.

Finally, some believe that dominance is a multifaceted concept and cannot be restricted to grammar use only. Researchers who hold this view think that proficiency is only one aspect of dominance. Other aspects may include, but are not limited to, pronunciation, grammar, and appropriate cultural use of a language.

No matter what view the researchers hold, they generally agree that dominance is linked to the amount of practice a person has in a language and that dominance can change over time. Thus, if a person becomes exposed to another language later in life and stops using his native language, over time, the native language could lose dominance and the second language might become dominant instead. This often happens with immigrant children who come to use a new language. If they do not have anyone to help them sustain and nourish their native language, eventually the language they acquire in their new country becomes dominant.

Language Dominance and Education

Although linguists and psychologists are concerned with language dominance in an effort to understand the dynamics of language development, educators and policymakers have attempted to use this construct to answer practical questions concerning the placement of students in programs and services such as English as a Second Language (ESL), transitional bilingual education, or two-way language immersion programs.

These types of programs stem from various state and federal legal mandates, the most prominent being *Lau v. Nichols,* decided by the Supreme Court in 1974. This case was brought by the Lau family on behalf of many Chinese-speaking students against the San Francisco Unified School District. The case argued that Chinese-speaking students did not get the same education as their English-speaking peers because Chinese-speaking students did not understand the language of instruction (English). It was further argued that this was in violation of the constitutional right for equal education for all. *Lau v. Nichols* clearly stated that providing equal access to education is not enough if the access to knowledge is given in a language a child does not understand. This means that for education to be meaningful and for the students to become successful learners, students need to be taught in the language they are comfortable with and can comprehend. Although the Supreme Court did not specifically rule for bilingual education, it indicated that students who do not speak English well enough to receive instruction in English must be provided with alternative ways to access the same curriculum. Some experts and advocates interpreted the ruling as a question of language dominance, although the high court did not use this phrase.

As a result of this ruling, in 1975 the Department of Health, Education and Welfare developed a document known as the *Lau* Remedies, a set of guidelines for schools to follow to comply with the ruling. The *Lau* Remedies give authority to school districts to provide appropriate instruction to non-English speakers. The document recommended, where practical, the use of bilingual instruction for such children on the assumption that children learn best when instruction is provided in their dominant language.

At about the same time, another legal case, this time in the state of New York, was also decided. In the case of *Aspira of New York, Inc. v. Board of Education, City of New York,* which was settled through a consent decree, the court issued an order that involved testing Hispanic-origin students to determine their English language proficiency. Those who received low scores on such tests were eligible to receive bilingual instruction. To comply with these and other court rulings, students whose primary language is not English have to be tested to find out whether their English skills are good enough for them to be educated in English.

Since the *Lau* Remedies were introduced, school districts have had to find ways to systematically and accurately identify those who need bilingual instruction. The obvious way to do so seemed to be to test for language dominance and, on the basis of that, decide on the most appropriate language of instruction. The assumption was that instruction should be given in the language in which the student is dominant. Since the mid-1970s when these cases were decided, major changes have taken place in the compliance procedures required of school districts. The question of dominance has become even more complex as new light is shed on that concept by research. Massive testing programs of all language minority students were contested on the grounds that it would be prohibitively expensive.

Measuring Dominance

Over the years, many different measures or tests to identify language dominance have been proposed, depending on the view that researchers and policymakers held at the time. Some of the measures or tests are well known. They are designed by testing companies and used widely across the nation. One example of such a test is the Peabody Picture Vocabulary test, which is available in English and Spanish and is used widely in research and practical settings. Other tests are created for use by local school boards and are known only in those localities where they are used. For example, El Paso Public Schools in Texas developed its own language proficiency measure for use with the bilingual population that resides there.

Regardless of whether the test is widely known or not, these tests tend to measure only one or two aspects of a language such as grammar or vocabulary. Generally, these measures can be broken down into four broad categories: (1) questionnaires and surveys, (2) vocabulary tests, (3) grammar tests, and (4) test batteries.

Questionnaires and Surveys

One of the easiest but perhaps least effective ways to assess dominance in bilinguals is to ask them which language they feel is stronger. The questionnaires and surveys are designed to do just that. When assessing children's language using questionnaires, often parents or teachers are asked to rate the languages children speak, and sometimes the language environment. An example of such a measure is the Language Background Questionnaire for the Bilingual Child, designed to probe the linguistic environment of a child's home. For adults, self-rating questionnaires are available. The positive aspect of this approach is that surveys and questionnaires are usually easy to conduct and score. The drawback in using this method of assessment is that it can be biased because subjective opinions are expressed. Another drawback is that these questionnaires often depend on the good use of English and are thus open to various problems of comprehension and interpretation.

Lexical Tests

In 1961, Susan Ervin-Tripp designed a test to assess dominance in speakers of English and Italian. This test consisted of many pictures of nameable objects. The participants were asked to name half of them in English and then switch and name the rest in Italian. Then the procedure was repeated in the reversed order of languages. The time it took each participant to respond in each language was recorded, and those pictures the participants could not name were flagged. The difference in response times was said to be the measure of relative dominance.

This test is just one of many that rely on someone's knowledge of vocabulary in the two languages to measure which language is stronger or dominant. As with the surveys, such tests are usually easy to administer and score. The drawback of such measures is that they measure only one aspect of language—lexicon. Many researchers and practitioners, however, question whether measuring this aspect of a language is a true indicator of one's language dominance.

Grammar Measures

Some researchers agree that measuring grammar when assessing dominance may be better than assessing vocabulary, pronunciation, or semantics because grammar is a more stable language trait that does not change drastically in dialects. An example of a test that focuses on the use of grammar to assess dominance is the Bilingual Syntax Measure. The test is designed to measure oral language with respect to proficient use of various syntactical structures. The positive side of such tests is that they do not require structured responses. A child can say anything, whether a word, a phrase, a sentence, or a story. Another positive feature of such tests is that they are usually quick to administer. Scoring these tests, however, may be a lengthy process. Another drawback is that those who administer and score this type of test require a good command of grammar in all languages being tested. Finally, as with vocabulary tests that measure dominance, such tests only focus on one aspect of language—grammar.

Another method used under the grammar approach is calculating the mean length of utterance (MLU). The MLU is calculated by dividing the total number of utterances into the total number of morphemes, or the smallest units of meaning in a word within a given period. Roger Brown, who proposed the MLU measure in 1973, stated that it is an easy and simple measure of grammatical development because most of new language knowledge increases the length of an utterance. To calculate the MLU, Brown proposed a set of rules that take into account child language development and basic rules of English grammar. The argument in favor of the use of MLU is that it is easy to calculate. The proponents of MLU also agree that it provides the necessary mechanism of grouping children for research purposes. Even though MLU is used widely, especially in research settings, many view it as a poor indicator of a person's language dominance. This is especially true in cross-linguistic studies because MLU was created as a specific

English measure and may not work well in other languages with different grammatical structures.

Batteries of Measures

An important aspect to consider when looking for a test on language dominance is that such tests often provide a single score of dominance. Many researchers and practitioners see that as a problem because a single score may not be accurate in capturing a person's real language capacity. An answer to a concern that a test gives a single score only is to use a test battery. Test batteries try to cover as many language aspects as possible. The researchers who work with bilingual children, for example, often use a set of tests to understand in which language a child is stronger.

This type of test includes MLU measures in each language, the length of the longest utterance in a speech sample, number of unique word types in 100 utterances; number of unique verb types in the same 100 utterances, and number of utterances in a 30-minute speech sample. These are used to ensure that dominance is evaluated on multiple scales (lexicon, syntax, and volubility). When using these five measures, researchers label a language that has higher scores in four or five measures as dominant. If participants score higher only on two or three measures, then they are labeled balanced with a slight dominance in the language where three measures had higher scores.

Although using a set of measures instead of a single test may be time-consuming to administer and to score, using the test batteries solves the problem of unidimensionality of individual tests. Using multiple tests also provides a range of scores that allows teachers, administrators, and speech professionals to understand the language of the child more fully and more objectively than a single score would allow. The drawback of such test batteries is that these tests do not tap into the knowledge of culture and appropriate cultural use of language, an essential element of dominance.

Change in Direction

Policymakers and practitioners soon realized that the concept they chose to emphasize as a focus in deciding the way to offer instruction was problematic. These tests pointed out that the concept of dominance is much more elusive for even a battery of tests to figure out because it consists of a great many aspects such as pronunciation, lexicon, and grammar as well as cultural awareness and use of language in appropriate cultural situations. This led to the realization that no matter what tests are used, the scores produced are not necessarily indicative of one's true language dominance even in a single context of use, as in classroom language. Moreover, some argued that a person does not have to be dominant in a language to receive instruction in it; it is enough to be comfortable learning in English. These arguments and the realization that the costly tests were not doing their jobs prompted researchers and practitioners to seek an alternative way of looking to what constitutes language knowledge and at what point a person is ready to receive instruction in English.

In the late 1980s and early 1990s, there was a national movement to set academic content standards for what students should learn and be able to do. This reform resulted in creating a set of criteria, or subject-matter benchmarks, to measure academic achievement for students. The goal of English as a Second Language (ESL) instruction, according to the ESL standards, was to lead students to eventual English proficiency. This effectively changed the focus of educators and policymakers from the notion of language dominance to the notion of language proficiency.

Although the notion of proficiency is related to that of language dominance, they are not identical. The general view among researchers is that one does not have to be dominant in a language to be a proficient user of that language. The four areas of proficiency as defined for the purpose of standards-based education, were speaking, reading, writing, and listening.

In 2001, the reauthorization of the Elementary and Secondary School Act, better known as the No Child Left Behind Act, mandated that the assessments used for the purposes of identifying English language learners must be based on national educational standards. As a part of the identification procedure, students must be assessed in all four areas mentioned previously to understand their proficiency levels in English.

Implications for Future Policy Directions

Determining which language is dominant is important in education because it helps determine the language of instruction that would be most beneficial for the child. The use of dominance and proficiency measures may be different in education settings because educators are trying to understand what children are capable of in any language(s) they might speak at a given moment. This is done so that instruction is tailored to ensure learning. Two approaches are usually taken in education settings to understand where a child is in relation to the language knowledge, ability, and proficiency of his/her peers.

One approach is cross-linguistic. A child is asked to complete a variety of language tasks in each of the two languages, and then the results are compared. Another approach is to compare the performance of a bilingual child, on a variety of tasks, with the performance of a monolingual child on the same tasks. The advantage of such tests is that they are usually quick and easy to administer and do not take long to score. However, these tests are only a one-time measurement of what children can do with either of their languages, and such abilities can and do change quickly. Educators must keep in mind that a contrary assumption underlies this approach—that dominance is stable and does not change with time and across various contexts.

Regardless of the approach taken to assess language dominance and proficiency, children's language is still developing at the time of assessment, and children's development of both languages is an ongoing process. Thus, although children might have significant abilities in both languages, the tests might not recognize this because they are often designed to measure only the sort of language used in academic or laboratory settings.

Educators must also remember that knowing one language can be helpful when learning another because we draw on our language experience to understand how another language works. Thus, in the situations where a child is acquiring a second language that is the language of schooling, it is often important not to shun the native language but, rather, to use it as an aide in learning.

Finally, educators should remember that being dominant in a language does not necessarily mean that a person is proficient in using the language in all aspects of language use. The language of instruction is often dominant in instructional settings only, and for certain periods. It may not necessarily reflect the language used at home, with peers, and in the community at large. Ultimately, achieving proficiency in both languages is the ideal eventual outcome.

Ellina Chernobilsky

See also Compound and Coordinate Bilingualism; Measuring Language Proficiency; Proficiency, Fluency, and Mastery

Further Readings

Arnberg, L. (1987). *Raising children bilingually: The pre-school years.* Clevedon, UK: Multilingual Matters.

Aspira of New York, Inc. v. Board of Education, City of New York, 72 Civ. 4002 (SDNY Aug. 29, 1974).

Bialystok, E. (2001). *Bilingualism in AA development: Language, literacy and cognition.* Cambridge, UK: Cambridge University Press.

Bialystok, E., & Hakuta, K. (1994). *In other words: The science and psychology of second-language acquisition.* New York: Basic Books.

Grosjean, F. (1982). *Life with two languages: An introduction to bilingualism.* Cambridge, MA: Harvard University Press.

Hakuta, K. (2001). *Key policy milestones and directions in the education of English language learners.* Paper presented at the Rockefeller Foundation Symposium Leveraging Change: An Emerging Framework for Educational Equity, Washington, DC. Retrieved from http://www.stanford.edu/~hakuta/www/docs/rockefeller/index.html

Hamers, J. F., & Blanc, M. H. A. (1989). *Bilinguality and bilingualism.* Cambridge, UK: Cambridge University Press.

Lau v. Nichols, 414 U.S. 563 (1974).

Shohamy, E. (1994). The role of language tests in the construction and validation of second-language acquisition theories. In E. E. Tarone, S. M. Gass, & A. D. Cohen (Eds.), *Research methodology in language acquisition* (pp. 133–142). Hillsdale, NJ: Lawrence Erlbaum.

LANGUAGE EDUCATION POLICY IN GLOBAL PERSPECTIVE

Bilingual education, even in the United States, has developed as a result of explicit and implicit language policies that are carried out sometimes by nation-states, other times by ethnolinguistic groups and families, and yet other times by educators themselves. Sometimes the language education policy has to do with enrichment, or the *addition* of a second language, as in elite forms of bilingual education for majority children. Other language policies have to do with the *maintenance* of a minority language or even the *revitalization* of a language that has been lost, as in the case of the Māori Kōhanga Reo "language nest" programs for preschoolers. At yet other times, the language education policy is about ensuring that language minority children *shift* as quickly as possible to a dominant language. This is the case with transitional bilingual education programs in the United States for immigrant children and in many African countries for children speaking languages other than those used in the educational system.

Scholars such as Robert Kaplan and Richard Baldauf distinguish between "language planning," which is about activities to promote linguistic change including beliefs, practices, and laws and regulations, and "language policy," which consists of the laws and regulations themselves. But Bernard Spolsky uses the term *language policy* for the entire enterprise, distinguishing between practices, beliefs, or ideology, and what he calls management (the laws and regulations, which for others is planning). This entry uses this broader definition of language policy, referring then to the field, as Sue Wright and Thomas Ricento have done before, as *language policy and language planning* (LPLP).

Bilingual education is perhaps the most important instrument of LPLP. It is directly related to what has been called *acquisition planning* because the implementation of bilingual education programs creates new language learners and new users of a language. Also, by giving a language a prestigious domain in which to function such as the school, bilingual education is also a means of *status planning,* that is, modifying the prestige of a language. Finally, because of the school's emphasis on literacy, bilingual education is an important means of *corpus planning,* standardizing the language forms, and developing new terms for academic functions.

Three stages of their geopolitical climate, epistemological paradigms (concerning the nature of knowledge), and research paradigms are identified and described later. These three stages have influenced the views of language held, the models of LPLP pursued, and the corresponding bilingual education models developed throughout the world. Although this discussion has been simplified by referring to stages in practice and as dependent on societal circumstance, the views of language, models of LPLP used, and bilingual education models extend throughout time. Thus, language ideologies, LPLP activities, and bilingual education practices that were prevalent in the early 1970s are equally valuable today in some contexts, although not all. This entry explains the different models of bilingual education that have resulted from different views of language and different LPLP models in global contexts.

Stage I

After World War II, the newly independent countries in Asia and Africa pursued social cohesion as stepping-stones to statehood. Modernization theory posited that the development of an independent and modern nation-state depends on urbanization, secularization, and the citizens' transformation from a traditional to a "modern" disposition. The emergence of LPLP as an academic discipline was an attempt to engineer social change through linguistic means. In its infancy, the research surrounding LPLP was driven by the imperative to solve what was perceived as the emergent states' "language problem," their multilingualism, with bilingual education seen as a possible means to alleviate what was perceived to be a threat to social cohesion. Bilingual and multilingual education became instruments, in some cases, of improving the teaching of the language chosen for modernization, and in others, of linguistically assimilating all people in the shared space that aspired to nationhood.

In 1953, the United Nations Educational, Scientific and Cultural Organization (UNESCO), responding to the educational failure of children in colonial situations, issued an important resolution declaring that it was axiomatic that a child be taught to read in the home language. The resolution stated that the use of the native language should be extended as much as possible; it advised for students to begin academic instruction through their native language. Because this is the language children understand best, this practice was thought to help bridge the gap between the home and school contexts.

Efforts to use the children's language in education, especially in the early grades, gained strength, leading to the first uses of what has since been termed *transitional bilingual education,* that is, the use of the child's heritage language in the early grades and *only* until the child is fluent in the majority or politically dominant language. In the United States, this period corresponded to the awakening of ethnic sentiment and the era of civil rights. The Bilingual Education Act of 1968 and its ensuing amendments was, in some measure, an example of language education policy and planning, endorsing in 1974 the transitional bilingual education model to ensure the children's shift to English. The development of contemporary bilingual education within a civil rights ideology meant that, especially at first, Chicano and Puerto Rican activists develop many *maintenance* bilingual education programs that used both English and Spanish in instruction throughout the children's education, asserting a bicultural identity and dreams of self-determination.

In the Canadian province of Québec, where French is the numerically majority language and was increasingly coming into power, some Anglophone parents, considered the powerful majority, demanded a way of making their children fully bilingual through school. Immersion bilingual education came into being, planned by scholars from McGill University, notably Wallace Lambert. In these programs, children are taught initially in the language they are learning, and by the second or third year, half of the instruction is through their home language and the other half through the language of immersion.

Stage II

The worldwide economic downturn in the 1970s and the ensuing widening of social inequities led to the questioning of bilingual education policies in transforming citizens and societies, espoused by theories of modernization. The role of sociohistorical processes in shaping particular forms of bilingual education, and in particular the role of class, ethnicity, race, language and gender in such shaping, was given increased attention. Specific forms of bilingual education, especially transitional bilingual education, were increasingly criticized, as indigenous peoples and autochthonous minorities claimed their language rights in education. They sought to develop their own forms of bilingual education, with language development goals they could support as communities with shared interests.

Developmental bilingual education programs—that is, programs that use the children's home language in addition to a second language throughout the child's education—spread throughout the world. In the United States, these developmental bilingual education programs are also known as late-exit bilingual education. The goal of these programs is to develop two languages, one being the majority language, the other being the language of autochthonous minorities or indigenous peoples. This was the case, for example, of the bilingual education programs in Wales in the rural Welsh heartland. In these traditional or "natural" bilingual schools, children are taught in Welsh initially, and from the age of 7, they study English, with both languages used as media of instruction throughout primary years. There are also designated schools *(immersion programs* for Anglophone children).

Some peoples, especially indigenous ones, have experienced such devastating language loss that they have had to develop bilingual education programs for their children in an effort to revitalize their languages. For example, after passage of the Māori Language Act of 1987, New Zealanders started a type of immersion revitalization bilingual education as a desperate attempt to get elderly grandparents to pass on the language to their grandchildren. The *Kōhanga Reo* programs, or "language nest" as they were called, involved preschool children under the age of 5 in centers where the *whanau,* extended family, impart Māori spiritual values, language, and culture. In Hawai'i the 'Aha Pūnana Leo preschools were modeled after those of Māoris in New Zealand to revitalize the Hawaiian language. In the United States, Navajo and other Native American groups attempted similar programs with varying degrees of success.

Stage III

The end of the cold war, the collapse of the former Soviet Union, pandemic globalization, and the increasing role of international organizations have accelerated the movement of peoples and challenged the sovereignty of the state in the 21st century. With increasing awareness of other languages and the dominance especially of English, but also of Chinese, Spanish, and Arabic throughout the world, bilingual education has taken yet another turn; this time, growing often without the direct intervention of the state, and including forms that respond to a much more dynamic language use. The newer forms of bilingual education, based on a more ecological approach, prepare language communities to balance their own linguistic ecologies, enabling them to go back and forth freely in their overlapping languages and literacies.

Nowhere is this more visible than in the European Union's newly designed educational programs, where a second language is used to teach nonlinguistic content matter. Called *Content and language integrated learning/Enseignement d'une matière intégrée à une langue étrangère* (or CLIL/EMILE), these programs take on varied forms. However, their goal is to develop plurilingualism. Plurilingualism is defined by the Language Policy Division of the Council of Europe as having proficiency, of varying degrees, in several languages and experience of several cultures.

In the United States, the effort to develop two-way bilingual education programs for language majority and language minority children can also be considered a shift in ideological orientation. Although these programs have been around at least since the Coral Way School in the early 1960s, these programs gained popularity in the past decade, as bilingualism has been accepted as a resource by some parents. Yet increasingly, the U.S. official bilingual education policies have swung the other way, often even resisting the transitional bilingual education model of the 1970s. For example, transitional bilingual education was abolished in California in 1998, in Arizona in 2000, and in Massachusetts in 2002. Only immersion in English, and only for a year, is legal in those states.

Although some bilingual education policies are explicit, others are implicit. For example, in Spain's Basque Autonomous Region, there are three models of bilingual instruction and parents have a choice— Model A in which instruction is carried out in Spanish, and Euskara (Basque) is taught as a subject; Model B, in which instruction is 50% in Spanish and 50% in Euskara; and Model D, in which instruction is in Euskara and Spanish is taught as a subject. In the United States, however, there is no mandate for bilingual education per se. Even Title VII of the Elementary and Secondary Education Act, which became known as the Bilingual Education Act, was only a funding source for different kinds of bilingual programs. Its substitute as of 2002, Title III of No Child Left Behind (NCLB), Public Law 107–110, is also not as explicit regarding a bilingual or even nonbilingual education stance. Although it substitutes the "Language Instruction for Limited English Proficient and Immigrant Students" for the older "Bilingual Education Act," thus silencing the word *bilingual,* it offers no explicit language education policy. However, it outlines an explicit assessment policy, requiring the annual testing of all English language learners, and focuses on standard written English as the only valid measure of knowledge. It can then be said that this assessment policy is in itself a language education policy, privileging monolingual education over bilingual education in the United States. The consequence of Title III of the NCLB, that is, monolingualism, exists in tension with the spirit of the worldwide ecological model of

LPLP, which celebrates linguistic diversity and asserts bilingualism as a resource.

Ofelia García and Pei Ju Tsai

See also Bilingual Education as Language Policy; Bilingualism Stages; Language Policy and Social Control; Maintenance Policy Denied

Further Readings

Kaplan, R., & Baldauf, R. (1997). *Language planning: From practice to theory.* Clevedon, UK: Multilingual Matters.

Language Policy Division. (n.d.). Retrieved from http://www.coe.int/t/dg4/linguistic/default_en.asp

Ricento, T. (Ed.). (2006). *An introduction to language policy: Theory and method.* Malden, MA: Blackwell.

Spolsky, B. (2004). *Language policy.* Cambridge, UK: Cambridge University Press.

Wright, S. (2004). *Language policy and language planning: From nationalism to globalization.* New York: Palgrave Macmillan.

LANGUAGE EXPERIENCE APPROACH TO READING

It is Friday morning in the village of Supai in Havasu Canyon, a branch of the Grand Canyon. Supai is the home of the Havasupai people, one of more than 30 American Indian nations in the state of Arizona. A popular tourist destination, Supai is home to several hundred Havasupai, and an elementary school serves the children of the village from kindergarten through eighth grade. On Thursday evenings, the cafeteria in the elementary school becomes a theater, as the community gathers for movies. The movie this Thursday has been a horror show, and the children in the primary grade classroom are full of conversation about it.

After opening exercises, a teacher gathers the young children around her and asks them about the movie that they saw: What was the movie about? What did they think about it? She calls on individual children to share their opinions and feelings. Then she brings out a sheet of chart paper and tells the children that together they are going to create a story about the movie they saw. She asks the children to think carefully about what they want to say, and she tells them that she will call on them one by one and write down what they say. She calls on one child who says, "Last night we seed a movie." The teacher repeats the sentence and then pronounces each word slowly as she writes, "Last night we seed a movie." The teacher then asks for another child to volunteer a sentence. A young girl says, "It was about a monster." The teacher repeats the sentence and then writes it out word by word, articulating each word as she writes. This procedure continues until the group generates a story that reads

Last night we seed a movie.

It was about a monster.

He was scary.

And kill people.

He die.

I like it.

After the teacher has written the children's sentences, she asks the children to listen carefully as she reads the story one more time. The teacher repeats what is on the chart, running her hand under the words in each sentence as she reads them. The teacher asks the children to read the story along with her, and she leads them in a choral reading of what they have created. The teacher then returns to the beginning of the story and asks if there is an individual child who wants to read one of the sentences. Individuals volunteer to read each sentence, after which the group rereads the entire story. The teacher announces that she is going to place the story in a particular place in the classroom, and during the day, when children have free time, they can walk over to the chart and read it for themselves.

Over the next several days, the teacher will use this chart to focus on particular aspects of written language. For example, she may use the words *movie* and *monster* to focus on the sound that the letter *m* makes, writing *movie* and *monster* on the board, asking the children to read the words with her, and then asking the children to share other words that begin with "mmmm" as do *movie* and *monster.* She may point out that the word *was* occurs two times in this story and in other stories as well. *Was* is a word that we use frequently when we talk, read, and write. She may point out that each sentence in the story begins with a word whose first letter is a capital letter, and each sentence in this story ends with a period. In these ways, the teacher moves from the whole experience of the story to parts of the language, such as high-frequency words and sound-letter correspondences that students will need to use as they become independent readers and writers.

Foundations

The vignette you have just read exemplifies one way of engaging young children in reading, which is described in this entry. It has been termed the *language experience approach* (LEA) to reading, and it is based in the idea that experiences that children have become the basis for charts created through dictations to the teacher. These experience charts then form reading materials for the learners. Denise Nessel and Margaret Jones describe the basic steps in the creation of a language experience chart as the following:

Step 1: Teacher and children converse about the topic for the dictation.

Step 2: The children dictate an account to the teacher, and the teacher records their statements.

Step 3: Teacher and children read the story several times, until the story becomes familiar to the children.

Step 4: The teacher designs activities to help the children attend to individual words and other aspects of reading such as sounds and letters and punctuation.

Step 5: Students move from reading their own dictation to reading material written by other authors as they develop confidence and skill as readers.

In 1943, Lillian Lamoreaux and Dorris Lee first detailed the use of language experience charts in their book *Learning to Read Through Experience*. In 1963, Lee collaborated with Roach Van Allen to produce the second edition of this book. Allen, who began his career in the San Diego County public schools, became linked closely with this way of teaching young children to read, and he is credited with relating the language experience approach to young children's development of critical understandings regarding print. In particular, Allen asserted that using experience charts would facilitate children's coming to understand that

Anything a child thinks about can be talked about.

What a child talks about can be expressed in writing (or in painting or in some other expressive form).

What a child writes can be read.

Children can read what they write and what others write as well.

Allen went on to explain that, through the experience of creating charts and through teachers' subsequent use of these charts to focus on particular aspects of written language, children come to understand concepts such as written words, high-frequency words in texts, letters and sounds and how they are related, spacing between words, and punctuation. Most importantly, children come to understand reading as a process of developing meaning from patterns of symbols and meaning as coming from the individual experiences of the reader.

Group Charts

The creation of class experience charts, such as the one whose development is described previously, forms one of the central features of the language experience approach to reading. But other instructional engagements are important as well. One of these is the use of a wide variety of classroom charts that serve multiple purposes. For example, classrooms may display classroom rules and jobs, attendance counts, and lunch menus and counts on charts. Teacher and children may create the News of the Day, or the Child of the Week. Other charts may be related to content under study. Before beginning a unit of study on insects, for example, using a KWL chart format, the children may share what they already know about insects (K) and what they want to learn (W). As the unit progresses, they will dictate what they have learned (L). Charts may be used to outline procedures that learners have followed as they engaged with content; charts may be kept to keep a record of favorite songs or books that have been read aloud or sung. All of these provide demonstrations of a variety of purposes for writing and reading, and all of the charts provide opportunities for the teacher to work with the children on particular features of written language.

Key Words

A second engagement advocated by many LEA educators is that of key words or key vocabulary. Key word use is a strategy developed in the 1940s and 1950s by New Zealand educator Sylvia Ashton-Warner, when she worked with Māori children. The

Māori are a Polynesian people who arrived in what is now New Zealand about a thousand years ago. They were well established in what they called Aotearoa when European explorers and later British settlers came to their land. The young Māori children that Ashton-Warner taught spoke the Māori language and a dialect of English called Māori English. The language of the schools was English, but because Ashton-Warner had learned to speak Māori, she used Māori as well as English in her classroom.

Ashton-Warner became critical of the readers provided to her to teach her young students to read because the readers did not reflect the life experiences and the culture of the Māori children. She believed that children's first reading needed to be with words and stories that held intense meaning for them. So she devoted instructional time each day to asking her students what words were most important to them, what words they most wanted to have written down for them on the tag board, so that they could share these words with others. In her book, *Teacher,* she shares details of her teaching practice. The words the children chose were ones that held power for them, words such as *kiss, ghost, jet, bomb,* or *tigers.* Each time that Ashton-Warner wrote a word on a tag board card, she gave the word to the child, with instructions that the child take the word home to read it to his or her family. The children also read their words to each other in the classroom. Over several months, each child accumulated a pile of key words, words that could be read by the individual and shown to others.

Ashton-Warner also selected a word each day from the children's key words and used that word to invite the children to converse. One day, for example, she picked the word *frightened.* When she read that word to the children, they began immediately to talk about what frightened them. These conversations both expanded the children's oral language and provided the basis for experience stories. The publication of *Teacher* in the United States in 1963 influenced many who had been advocates of experience charts to expand their understanding of language experience to include key vocabulary.

Personal Charts

A third strategy in the language experience approach involves the creation of personal rather than group or class experience charts. Most often, this engagement begins with child-created artwork followed by individual dictation to the teacher. Thus, for example, if the class is studying insects, children might be asked to draw an insect of particular interest to them and to decide what they want to share about the insect chosen. As they complete their pictures, the teacher circulates, converses with each child about his or her picture, and elicits and writes one or two sentences on each child's creation. The individual charts are then shared with the class. All of these strategies focus on using children's own lives, in and out of school, as a source for some of their reading experiences, and all of them serve as demonstrations of the connections between spoken and written language.

LEA and Bilingual Education

The earliest proponents of the language experience approach to reading did not address specifically using this way of teaching with bilingual children or children in second-language situations. However, the classroom examples provided earlier in this entry make it clear that educators working in bilingual and second-language contexts found the approach compelling, and began to use it and advocate for it. LEA has resonated among literacy educators working in bilingual education because it creates a place for children's lives, cultures, and language(s) in the classroom. As Ashton-Warner and many others since have pointed out, commercial textbooks created to teach reading often do not reflect the lives and realities, the cultural and experiential frameworks, of the schoolchildren who use them. Language experience charts do reflect these realities because it is the children's lives and happenings that are especially meaningful to them that become the content of the stories. Additionally, community and individual language patterns, ways of using both a native and additional languages, often do not appear in commercial reading materials. In contrast, in language experience charts, teachers write down children's contributions to a narration in the language that they actually use. Thus, learners see their own cultures and language varieties in the stories that they read. LEA instructional strategies also are powerful because teachers provide demonstrations of taking ideas from spoken to written form. This demonstration of writing can help second-language learners who are reluctant to write to understand that their early writing experiences can be based in talk that is written down.

One concern for many teachers of English as a Second Language (ESL) is the provision of quality reading experiences for learners at varying English proficiency levels. Because LEA integrates the language processes of listening, speaking, reading, and writing, the creation of key word banks and experience charts may be based on oral language and content units of study that are a part of the school curriculum. Teachers may adapt LEA strategies according to the language abilities and needs of the learners. Beginning level ESL students involved in a study of insects, for example, may be able to participate in key vocabulary engagements by sharing the name of an insect they want to have in writing. If learners are not able to articulate complete sentences, the teacher may choose to use pattern sentences such as "Butterflies have ____" and ask individual children to fill in the last word to create an experience chart such as

Butterflies have wings.

Butterflies have a head.

Butterflies have eyes.

Butterflies have feelers.

When learners become more comfortable in speaking English, their narrations, whether done individually or with others, will be more extensive. Some ESL educators suggest using wordless picture books (picture books whose illustrations are particularly clear in a story sequence) for learners of intermediate and more advanced oral language. Learners are able to create stories using the pictures. At any level of English development, comprehension is not an issue because the narrations come from the learners.

A concern often expressed by ESL teachers who are using language experience dictation is the acceptance of English sentences that are not grammatically correct according to adult, native-English-speaking standards (in the first example earlier, children used the word "seed" instead of "saw"). Teachers worry about reinforcing incorrect habits and that students will never learn correct grammar if they are allowed to read sentences that do not reflect standard usage. This fear is not well founded, according to experts in LEA. Internationally known ESL educator Pat Rigg argues that it is important to accept and write out whatever language the learners use (as we saw in the Havasupai story) to validate what the learners are able to articulate. She notes that a generation of research in second-language learning has made it clear that

language learning is not a process of habit formation and stimulus-response learning. Rather learners, over time, construct the language they are learning, making mistakes as they do so, and gradually coming ever closer to what could be called the standard. Thus, their ways of expressing themselves at a given time do not remain static. Rather than the teacher correcting the students' grammar, Rigg suggests saving language experience charts from earlier in a school year, and returning to them later in the year for editing, to reflect students' growing command of English. She has demonstrated that when the teacher rereads a chart and asks the learners if they want to make any changes, frequently the students are able to comment on how they expressed themselves earlier and make corrections. Additionally, the teacher may be able to call students' attention to particular issues of usage.

More than 60 years have passed since Lamoreaux and Lee proposed that teachers use language experience charts as a central feature of reading instruction for young children. Since its introduction, LEA has been used in elementary, secondary, and even adult education classrooms. Recently, educators (for example, Linda Labbo, Jonathan Eakle, and Kristiina Montero) have adapted LEA into literacy instruction that uses technological innovations such as computers and digital cameras. For numerous learners around the world, experience charts scribed by a teacher have provided learners the support and demonstrations they need to begin to see themselves as readers and writers.

Sarah Hudelson

See also Academic English; Communicative Approach; Continua of Biliteracy; Culturally Competent Teaching; Four-Skills Language Learning Theory; Literacy and Biliteracy; Phonics in Bilingual Education

Further Readings

Allen, R. V., & Allen, C. (1976). *Language experience activities.* Boston: Houghton Mifflin.

Ashton-Warner, S. (1963). *Teacher.* New York: Simon & Schuster.

Dixon, C., & Nessel, D. (1983). *Language experience approach to reading and writing: LEA for ESL.* Hayward, CA: Alemany.

Labbo, L. D., Eakle, A. J., & Montero, M. K. (2002, May). Digital language experience approach: Using digital photographs and software as a language experience approach innovation. *Reading Online, 5*(8), 24–43.

Retrieved from http://www.readingonline.org/electronic/ elec_index.asp?HREF=/electronic/labbo2/index.html

Lamoreaux, L., & Lee, D. (1943). *Learning to read through experience.* New York: Appleton-Century.

Lee, D., & Allen, R. V. (1963). *Learning to read through experience* (2nd ed.). New York: Appleton-Century Crofts.

Nessel, D., & Jones, M. B. (1981). *The language experience approach to reading: A handbook for teachers.* New York: Teachers College Press.

Rigg, P. (1989). *When they don't all speak English: Integrating the ESL student into the regular classroom.* Urbana, IL: National Council of Teachers of English.

Veatch, J., Sawicki, F., Elliott, G., Flake, E., & Blakey, J. (1979). *Key words to reading: The language experience approach begins.* Columbus, OH: Charles Merrill.

LANGUAGE LEARNING IN CHILDREN AND ADULTS

Bilingualism has always been a part of the human experience. Many groups of people worldwide need to be proficient in more than one language to carry out the tasks they have to perform in their daily lives. Moreover, the interconnected world we live in through the Internet and the migrations of many peoples have made it increasingly important to communicate in more than one language. In linguistic communities such as Switzerland or South Africa, children acquire more than one language concurrently; in other linguistic environments, children learn the second language sequentially, when they already have established their first language. Many people choose to, or have to, learn a second language during adulthood.

Acquiring language is an experience so close to all human beings that we all have opinions about how and when we best acquire it. One popular belief is that whereas children acquire languages quickly, easily, and effortlessly, adults need more time and effort to learn a second language. There is a widely held belief that regardless of their commitment and interest, adults cannot attain the level of mastery of a second language that children achieve so readily and almost without fail. Paradoxically, another popular assumption is that it is problematic to have young children learn more than one language at a time because they may get confused and be unable to master either of the two languages well. These assumptions are probably based on observations of children and adults learning languages, but they do not consider the complexity of languages, the different ways children and adults learn languages, and variations in the linguistic input learners receive. Not surprisingly, these popular viewpoints raise many questions and are far from being accepted by experts and language researchers, who see language acquisition as an extremely complex phenomenon that still requires much investigation to be understood.

Evaluating these popular beliefs requires answers to several questions that researchers have been struggling with for years. These questions include the following: How do human beings acquire their first language? How do we acquire second or additional languages? Are there differences in the way children and adults learn a second language? If differences exist, at what age do they become apparent? What level of proficiency is required for an individual to be considered bilingual? This entry reviews some of the current knowledge on the differences between children and adult ways of learning language.

Language Components and Language Acquisition

Acquiring language involves mastering the following interrelated components of language: *phonology,* the sounds or phonological structure of the language; *morphology,* the way sound units are organized into words; *syntax,* the order of the words in sentences; and *semantics,* the meaning of the words. The main goal of mastering a language is being able to use the language (pragmatics) to communicate. However, communicating effectively necessitates linguistic knowledge and knowledge of the socially established rules of interaction followed in specific places and by specific linguistic groups. Regardless of the daunting task of attaining mastery of a given language, almost all children follow a certain order in acquiring certain aspects of a specific language, have a tendency to make the same mistakes, and by 5 years of age are confident and competent speakers of their first language.

How do children accomplish this complicated task of integrating all the aspects of learning a language, or even more than one language? No one universal theory explains how and why human beings are able to acquire language; many theories end up only partially explaining how languages are acquired in childhood. All theories acknowledge the importance of the learner, the environment, and the linguistic principles to explain language development, and bilingualism in particular. Ellen Bialystok, in her book *Bilingualism in Development: Language, Literacy, & Cognition,* considered simultaneous and sequential bilingualism in childhood in light of two different sets of theories that addressed the issues outlined.

Formal Theory

For formal theorists such as Noam Chomsky and Steven Pinker, the most important ingredient in explaining language acquisition is the human being's innate capacity to learn language. This language ability is separate from other cognitive abilities, and it manifests itself in abstract linguistic rules. For the formal theorists, the linguistic input provided in social and communicative contexts is needed, but is less important than the innate ability. According to this theory, there are no qualitative differences between learning one or two languages either simultaneously or sequentially. The innate language ability will activate regardless of the number of languages once the child is in contact with more than one language.

Some followers of this theory, however, stress the importance of age in learning language. Eric Lenneberg affirms that the innate linguistic ability activates during a specific time in life, known as a critical period, in which language is easily acquired. Depending on the experts, the critical period is between 2 and 9 or 2 and 12 years of age. Eric Lenneberg argued that there is a biological reason for the child to be able to acquire language easily in a specific age range: Before age 2 the child's brain is not yet prepared, and after age 9 or 12, the human brain loses the plasticity needed to learn language. This claim is supported because children speak the language or languages they learn without accent, from exposure to the language in the environment, but many adults never lose the accent they form in their second or other languages and need formal instruction in the language.

Functional Theory

For functional theorists, including Charles Fillmore and Robert Van Valin, the language ability of human beings is part of a more general human cognitive ability and the determinant factor in acquiring language is the linguistic input provided in a specific social context that allows the learner to infer the linguistic rules. Learning one or more languages simultaneously or sequentially is qualitatively different for these theorists. They claim that knowing a language certainly influences the cognitive structures of the learner. Furthermore, the linguistic input provided—for example in who, when, and for what purposes language is used to communicate—is different for monolingual and bilingual children and therefore qualitatively affects the learning process.

Other Theories and Recent Research

Bialystok points out that each of these theories explains the role of some of the components of language in language development—the formalists focus on syntax and phonology and the functional theorists on semantics and pragmatics—but no theory explains how all the interdependent components of language work together. Moreover, although all experts agree that certain abilities that the learner brings to the task, as well as to the environment, have an important role in acquiring a language, no theory fully explains the role of each. According to Bialystok, the research available is not conclusive regarding the existence of a critical period to learn language; it may be that a critical period exists for certain components of language (e.g., phonology) but not for others.

The controversial questions regarding the existence of qualitative differences in the way children and adults learn a second language are well presented in Barry McLaughlin's two volumes on *Second Language Acquisition in Childhood;* however, the research available is inconclusive. Experts such as Lenneberg and Michael Long claim the existence of a critical period during which it is easier to learn language, and therefore, qualitative differences exist in the way children and adults learn language. According to these theorists, children and adults process language differently: Children bring to the learning process a linguistic ability distinctively available to process language, whereas adults process language through a more general cognitive ability. Furthermore, Hans Stern claimed that learning a language creates cognitive and linguistic structures that interfere or assist in learning a second language, depending on how similar or different the first and second languages are, making the paths to bilingualism for young children and adults necessarily different.

In contrast, Susan Ervin-Tripp and Kenji Hakuta argue that learning a second language in childhood or adulthood involves the same cognitive processes. To understand the apparent differences in the ways children and adults learn a second language, these researchers focus on the cognitive characteristics of the learners, affective factors, and the linguistic and sociocultural contexts as well. The idea that children attain bilingualism fast and easily may arise because the demands on a bilingual child and a bilingual adult are different in the vocabulary and the length and structure of sentences expected of each. In several studies cited by Yugo Butler and Hakuta, adults outperformed children; in another study, 12- to 15-year-olds and adults (in that order) do better than children in rate of acquisition when controls for the amount of linguistic input are used.

Learning language is a difficult task for children and adults alike. Children and adults learn language only after intensive and extensive exposure to the language or languages. In the case of young children, they may learn the second language by being immersed in a natural and playful linguistic environment with other children, or by watching television, which make us think of the experience as effort-free. Adults, on the other hand, may not get the necessary linguistic input from being immersed in a natural environment and need to be formally taught the second language. Older children, however, may also receive formal support in learning the second language in school.

Research on second-language acquisition in adults conducted by Robert Gardner and Wallace Lambert highlights the role of affective factors such as attitude toward the language, motivation, anxiety, and self-confidence in accounting for the variation in outcomes in acquiring the second language. These factors may influence the success of children as well. In general, children are motivated to interact with their peers to be able to play; adults may be motivated for economic reasons, to communicate with other adults, or to be part of the new culture. Adults, however, may fear losing the identity they convey through their first language and are often afraid of making mistakes and feeling ridiculous, which can prevent them from practicing the new language.

These affective factors cannot be understood without analyzing the specific linguistic and sociocultural contexts in which they develop. The following factors contribute both to creating positive or negative attitudes and motivation toward a second language and to the success in acquiring it: (a) the prestige of the second language relative to the native language, (b) the

possibility of acquiring a new language without risking the loss of the first language, (c) the socioeconomic status of the learner, (d) the quality of the linguistic input, and (e) the nature of the learning situation.

Conclusion

The research available addressing language learning in children and adults is inconclusive. Although some experts, such as Long, affirm that learning a second language in childhood involves different processes than does learning it in adulthood, others, including Hakuta and Stephen Krashen, claim that there are differences only in the style that children and adults use to learn a second language. Most researchers agree, however, that acquiring more than one language in childhood does not necessarily negatively affect the proficiency attained in both languages. To sum up the dilemma, the difficulty in understanding how human beings acquire one or more languages stems from the complexity of the linguistic experience, which necessarily involves individuals with different educational, cognitive, and affective characteristics (such as attitude and motivation), living in different linguistic and sociocultural contexts—all variables that affect language acquisition.

M. Victoria Rodríguez

See also Affective Filter; Bilingualism Stages; Comprehensive Input; Critical Period Hypothesis; First-Language Acquisition; Language Acquisition Device; Learning a Language, Best Age; Second-Language Acquisition

Further Readings

Bialystok, E. (2001). *Bilingualism in development: Language, literacy, & cognition.* Cambridge, UK: Cambridge University Press.

Butler, Y. G., & Hakuta, K. (2006). Bilingualism and second language acquisition. In T. J. Bhatia & W. C. Ritchie (Eds.), *The handbook of bilingualism* (pp. 114–138). Malden, MA: Blackwell.

Chomsky, N. (1965). *Aspects of the theory of syntax.* Cambridge: MIT Press.

Ervin-Tripp, S. (1981). Social process in first- and second-language learning. In H. Winitz (Ed.), *Native language and foreign language acquisition* (pp. 33–58). New York: New York Academy of Sciences.

Fillmore, C. (1988). The mechanisms of construction grammar. In S. Axmaker, A. Jaisser, & H. Signmaster

(Eds.), *Proceedings of the 14th annual meeting of the Berkeley Linguistics Society* (pp. 35–55). Berkeley, CA: Berkeley Linguistics Society.

Gardner, R. C. (1985). *Psychology and second language learning. The role of attitudes and motivation.* London: Edward Arnold.

Gardner, R. C., & Lambert, W. E. (1972). *Attitudes and motivation in second-language learning.* Rowley, MA: Newbury House.

Hakuta, K. (1986). *Mirror of language.* New York: Basic Books.

Krashen, S. D. (1982). *Principles and practice in second language acquisition.* New York: Pergamon Press.

Lenneberg, E. (1967). *Biological foundations of language.* New York: Wiley.

Long, M. (1990). Maturational constraints on language development. *Studies in second language acquisition, 12,* 251–285.

McLaughlin, B. (1984). *Second-language acquisition in childhood: Vol. 1. Preschool children.* Hillsdale, NJ: Lawrence Erlbaum.

McLaughlin, B. (1984). *Second-language acquisition in childhood: Vol. 2. School-age children.* Hillsdale, NJ: Lawrence Erlbaum.

Pinker, S. (1994). *The language instinct.* New York: Morrow.

Stern, H. (1970). *Perspectives in second language teaching.* Toronto: Ontario Institute for Studies in Education.

Van Valin, R. D. (2005). *Exploring the syntax-semantic interface.* Cambridge, UK: Cambridge University Press.

LANGUAGE LOYALTY

To be loyal to one's language is generally evidenced by a desire to retain an identity that is articulated through the use of that language, and to adhere to cultural practices associated with that language. Language loyalty leads people to work toward maintaining the language in question even under adverse conditions. Language maintenance consists of strategies that groups use to keep the language to which they are loyal alive; language persistence is the result. Through religious and educational institutions, social organizations, the popular press, and the political process, persons loyal to their language work to maintain the language by using it to worship, educating their young in it so that the next generation uses it, and using it in interaction with one another socially and through print and broadcast media and the political process.

This entry reviews what is known about the complex phenomenon of language loyalty, exploring the following questions: Under what circumstances does a person or group demonstrate loyalty to one's language? Is being loyal to a language something that all people do, or is it particular to certain groups of people or circumstances? Are some more loyal to their language than others? What are the motivations for language loyalty? Is it possible to be loyal to more than one language?

Types of Language Loyalty in U.S. History

Joshua A. Fishman, who wrote the first major work on language loyalty in the United States, asserts that various types of language loyalty played a major role during the last five centuries of European history. Each of these loyalty types is related in different ways to nationhood. The earliest immigrants came to North America from Europe because they were disconnected from the nation building process by virtue of their peasant status and had no stake in staying in Europe. Another group came because of a concern that the European nation was corrupting the language and culture and the belief the New World provided for the preservation of their language and culture. A third group came out of fear that the language and culture were being obliterated by outside political forces in their nation, and the New World provided the place to be at liberty to live the language and culture of the Old Country.

In the colonial era and early national U.S. history, language loyalty was associated with a tension between nation building and ethnic identity. Though language loyalty was important to the nation building that was an outgrowth of the Renaissance, early immigrants arrived in the U.S. colonies and the newly established nation having meager familiarity with European events and movements to which language loyalty was related. The early immigrants were not among the European intelligentsia, middle class, and working class who stayed behind in Europe. Those who remained in Europe considered language loyalty and the maintenance of ethnic languages and cultures important to the building of European nations. Generally, those who ventured forth to the American colonies did not consider language loyalty an important factor in nation building in the New World.

Thus, as Fishman states, though the United States was born during a period when European nationalism was extremely important, and though the United States was a reaction to that nationalism, millions of immigrant people to the United States paid little attention to language loyalty as a nationalistic concern. What was more important to successive waves of immigrants throughout U.S. history appears to have been ethnicity of a traditional, particularistic, and nonideological character. Ethnicity, with its associated language and perhaps religion, has been the general rule among immigrants rather than language as a symbol of nationalism. Languages spoken and to which immigrants have been loyal in early U.S. history were related more to everyday life than to causes or ideologies.

Though immigrants may leave their homelands without much thought about their language and ethnicity, it is generally accepted that only after arrival in the new country does loyalty to one's language become a conscious concern. Fishman asserts that in some instances, many immigrants only became aware of their *groupness* in America—their common origin, their common past, and problems shared with their group related to their current situation. Thus, we can assume, for purposes of this analysis, that only after immigration does language loyalty become a conscious concern among newcomers to any country, including the United States because it is in the comfort zone of shared language as an everyday, particularistic, and nonideological nature that group members can celebrate their common origin and understand their common past. In this same zone, they can also work together to solve problems and learn to live according to the customs in the new country.

After arrival in the new country and as their old ways of life appeared to fade, successive immigrant groups to the United States have turned to their language to protect the way of life that they came with. They have established voluntary organizations, schools, and communications media unheard of in the Old Country. These tools were expressions of their language loyalty; they were also shaped by people who would have had little prior experience in building these mechanisms had they remained in the homeland. The organizations, schools, and media worked both to preserve people's loyalty to the language, ethnic costumes, foods, and celebrations and to facilitate group members' entry into new customs of their newly adopted country. In this respect, language loyalty comes to play in a context of social change where immigrants simultaneously grasp for continuity and extend themselves into new ways of living.

A second type of language loyalty came with later immigrants who came with the express purpose of preserving a language and culture that they feared was not possible in newly established European nations. Fishman reported that many immigrants, including those in the early German sects in the United States, considered themselves as saviors of their respective languages and cultures. They came to the New World with a language loyalty for the purpose of preserving what they feared was being lost in the nationalistic European context in the 17th, 18th, and 19th centuries and could only be preserved by relocating to the New World. At times, members of these groups practiced separatist and nonparticipatory philosophies. In others, intellectualized concepts of nationalism and pluralistic rationales were evident. In these instances, language loyalty was expressed via political groups, schools, children's camps, choral groups, and literary and scholarly associations. Members of these groups published at an appreciably higher level than did the mass immigrant press or the mass English language press. These social and political institutions were an expression of language loyalty. Their purpose was to maintain their language and ethnic culture. Though members of this type of group have been more numerous and more influential since World War II, the preservationists have been among the many waves of immigrant groups to U.S. shores throughout U.S. history.

A third type of language loyalty is reflected in more recent waves of European immigrants, especially those from Eastern Europe who arrived following World War II—asylum-seekers who came seeking a place to preserve their language and culture threatened by outside forces. These immigrants are distinguished by their formal education in their mother tongue. More of these than those of earlier immigrant groups came with a knowledge of the national history of their homeland, and they were more likely to have what Fishman calls a diaspora consciousness that carries with it a language loyalistic and retentivistic orientation. These immigrants left homelands that were under antireligious and antinationalistic control. Upon arrival in the United States, they considered themselves the only ones who could preserve their language and culture during a period of domination by outside control in their homelands.

Examples of Language Loyalty in U.S. History

Throughout U.S. history, immigrant speakers of languages other than English have demonstrated versions of these types of loyalty to their languages of origin. Until the mid-20th century, most newcomers were loyal to European languages. Some European immigrant languages were of higher status than others. The three of longest standing and perhaps of highest status are French, German, and Spanish.

French immigrants from Canada settled first in New England in the 19th century. They came for economic reasons to textile mill towns, and they sent remittances to their families who remained in Québec. For this group, language loyalty was intimately intertwined with their religious heritage in the Roman Catholic Church. In this tradition, language was the bond among all, regardless of social or economic station in life. Loss of language meant loss of faith, and loss of faith meant loss of eternity. Language maintenance efforts expressive of this loyalty included French-language worship, French-language parochial schools, French societies, and a French-language press that reported on French parochial schools and the need for French-speaking clergy.

Language loyalty among Franco-Americans was a family affair. Societies supported the Church, the school, and the family in remaining loyal to French and maintaining the language. Perhaps because of the egalitarian and closed nature of Franco-American community and families and their limitations in identifying loyalist leaders, the preservation of French in New England was limited because no one was available to transform concepts to concrete language maintenance efforts that would keep the French language alive in future generations. Franco-Americans hinged their language loyalty and maintenance hopes on an amorphous elite interested in French language and ethnic values. As the younger generation failed to take on leadership in preserving the language and culture, over time there was no French language to which to be loyal in the community. Today, with the exception of northern Maine, the daily use of French in New England is rare.

Immigrant speakers of German, especially those in Pennsylvania, arrived as early as the late 1600s, and came in the largest numbers in the 1800s. German immigrants considered themselves partners and equals to others in establishing the new republic. Like the French, their language loyalty was expressed in church and in elementary school. Unlike the French, language loyalty leadership was not as markedly egalitarian an enterprise within the group. Fishman reports that although 95% came for economic reasons, their outlook was shaped by a better-educated 5% who came for ideological reasons, be they religious or political. These 5% were represented in four categories: Roman Catholics, Orthodox Lutherans, other Protestants, and Liberals.

For the most part, rural Germans were *Kirchendeutsche* (Church Germans) of the first three categories; and urbanites were *Vereinsdeutsche* (Club Germans) of the fourth category. The main dividing line among them was between Roman Catholics and Orthodox Lutherans on the one hand, and other Protestants and Liberals on the other. As the public schools started offering German as a subject, other Protestants and Liberals abandoned their German-language schools. Because Roman Catholics and Orthodox Lutherans had always stressed bilingualism, they remained loyal to the German language and continued and expanded their language maintenance efforts through German-language schools.

Some of the German immigrants who arrived between the two world wars in the 20th century were ambivalent about the German language. They arrived at a time when nativist tendencies made language loyalty of any kind, but especially German, an unpopular enterprise among German immigrants in the United States. This ambivalence drove many Germans to dampen their urge to preserve the language among their children and to ease their acceptance into the society by allowing them to become monolingual English speakers.

The Case of Spanish

Immigrants loyal to the Spanish language also have a long history in the United States. What sets them apart from the French and Germans is that most came not from Europe, but from Latin America, primarily Mexico and the Caribbean. Also confounding our understanding of language loyalty among Spanish-speaking people in the United States is that many of them are technically not immigrants at all. Many have lived in the U.S. Southwest for generations and were already there when the territory belonged to Spain and subsequently to Mexico. The border moved as a result of political struggles between Mexico and the early United States that culminated in the Gadsden Purchase and the Treaty of Guadalupe Hidalgo in the 1800s. U.S. citizenship was conferred on those who remained in the territory. However, some argue that equal treatment did not necessarily follow.

Other Spanish speakers came to many East Coast cities, including Philadelphia and New York, from the Commonwealth of Puerto Rico. They came with a history of attempts by the United States—beginning in 1898—to colonize their homeland and to impose the English language on its inhabitants. A third major Spanish-speaking group came to the United States, primarily to Miami, Florida, from Cuba following the 1959 revolution there. A second wave of Cuban immigrants arrived in 1980 in the *Mariel* boatlift. Unlike the earlier German immigrant waves in Pennsylvania, the first Cuban arrivals to the United States were among Cuba's intelligentsia. The later wave was less educated. As with their predecessors, church, school, societies, and the political process were incubators of loyalty to the Spanish language wherever Spanish speakers from Mexico, Puerto Rico, and Cuba settled. Also similar were the struggles between Spanish-speakers whose loyalty to the Spanish language and culture prompted them to educate their children to carry on the language and culture through bilingualism in church, school, social organizations, and the press. In recent decades, these early Hispanic Americans have been augmented by hundreds of thousands of immigrants from Central and South America and the Dominican Republic. Because these groups have moved into communities that are already predominantly Latino, they have not experienced great difficulty maintaining their Spanish, at least as long as they live in those communities.

The case of Spanish is perhaps the best context in which to remind the reader that loyalty to one language does not preclude loyalty to English, the lingua franca of the nation. All of the research with respect to this topic reveals that this is the case with Spanish speakers.

Conclusion

The experiences of French, German, and Spanish speakers have been repeated as many times as the number of languages represented by newcomers to the United States who speak languages other than English. However, the most recent newcomers are coming not only from the European continent. Many emigrate from Asia and Latin America, along with refugees from a number of African nations. All bring with them a particular language and culture to which they are loyal to varying degrees and for different reasons. As with their predecessors throughout U.S.

history, language loyalty offers both continuity between old and new and community with others who share the same language, culture, and problems adapting to their new environment.

U.S. history and current sociological studies seem to suggest that it is inevitable that as those loyal to the home language grow older and the next generations mature, the language of the Old Country gives way to the language of the new, English. Appearances can deceive, because what may have been expedient for immigrants throughout the past in the United States may not be the best option for the future. Appearances can also deceive because the history may have been told in the past through an American ethnocentric lens. Perhaps today's immigrants' present experience, as we understand it, is closer to the truth of previous waves of immigrants than the history books describe. Perhaps we are all still too close to the present experience to see the similarity between these groups' loyalties to their languages and those of previous newcomers. Time will tell.

What is also not clear but worthy of continued study is the degree to which it is possible to have multiple language loyalties and consequently become multilingual in a global economy where nationalism is giving way to transnationalism and where proficiency in more than one language places one at an advantage socially, economically, politically. Also worthy of clarification is the possibility that additional reasons exist for language loyalty than those explained by Fishman some 40 years ago because global sociopolitical and geopolitical circumstances have changed since then. New patterns of relationships between language communities have emerged throughout the world. The definitive study on language loyalty for the 21st century may tell a different story from that of the 20th century.

Elsie M. Szecsy

See also Ethnocentrism; German Language Education; Japanese Language in Hawai'i; Languages in Colonial Schools, Eastern; Languages in Colonial Schools, Western; Latino Attitudes Toward English; Melting-Pot Theory; Transnational Students

Further Readings

Crawford, J. (Ed.). (1992). *Language loyalties: A source book on the official English controversy.* Chicago: University of Chicago Press.

Fishman, J. A. (1966). *Language loyalty in the United States: The maintenance and perpetuation of non-English mother tongues by American ethnic and religious groups.* The Hague, the Netherlands: Mouton.

Schmid, C. (2001). *The politics of language: Conflict, identity and cultural pluralism in comparative perspective.* New York: Oxford University Press.

Schmidt, R. (2000). *Language policy and identity politics in the United States.* Philadelphia: Temple University Press.

Tse, L. (2001). *Why don't they learn English: Separating fact from fallacy in the U.S. language debate.* New York: Teachers College Press.

LANGUAGE PERSISTENCE

This entry addresses the issue of language persistence, the ability of a language to survive and thrive in a society. Language persistence depends on a number of ambient conditions and other influential factors. Issues that influence language persistence include the historical period or era in question, those who use the language, the reasons that the language is used, and the importance of that language. All of these factors determine the degree to which the overall societal environment is accepting of that language. In most cases, it is not the mere existence of a single condition—such as a large base of timeless literature—that allows a language to exist but the intersection of internal and external pressures that have the greatest effect and influence on whether the language persistence will be supported or rejected. Because each of these factors is constantly changing, the conditions faced by any given language are always in flux, as is the language's likelihood to persist.

Historical Influences

A language will persist depending on conditions during the era and how that period intersects with issues that produce favorable conditions for that language. Conditions can be a product of an era's level of encouragement for language diversity and intolerance for language extinction and can be contingent on other factors, such as the place where the language exists, the language's linguistic characteristics, and the language's use. indigenous languages in the United States present a good example of languages that are either extinct or in decline. Following the Civil War, the

U.S. government began a process of systematic forced assimilation by removing Native American children from their families and tribes. The ultimate objective of this assimilation was to "improve" their way of life and make them more American. This included eliminating their home language and teaching them English. These strategies played a part in the eradication or near extinction of many indigenous languages. Today, public sentiment will not tolerate the open and willful eradication of native languages in this way. The knowledge that these languages are endangered has allowed public and private funding to help indigenous people revive their languages. This interest, in some cases, has helped reverse the decline, and several native languages are now experiencing a promising revitalization. The critical difference is the historical period in which one or the other outcome could be expected to gain traction.

The era can largely determine the modes of communication used in a specific area; for example, how the language is able to adapt to those communicative uses determines the language's likelihood to survive. Period-specific modes of communication such as the printed press, Internet, and television have had, and continue to have, a profound effect on languages. These technologies illustrate the importance a historical era or period will have on languages. We can imagine then, that in the future, most languages in existence will continue because of interpretive technology, but that would be overly simplistic. We also know that other factors will be at play. Nevertheless, the time window for gaining a foothold on the Internet era is closing. And a language without an active Internet presence, and the existence of numerous Web sites, risks a lack of persistence into the 22nd century. European linguists believe that the Czech language is a good example of conditions that affect language. With only 10 million active speakers, a shrinking population, and young people actively surfing the Web in English, it is difficult to imagine the emergence of Czech as one of the dominant languages of Europe. Similar fears have been expressed about the Italian language because it exists in an area populated by older people and in a society that lags behind other nations with respect to technology.

Where the Language Exists

A language's chance to persist partly depends on where it exists. The coexistence of other languages in the location where a language exists, for example, can reduce or enhance a language's chance to persist, depending on the language's standing among other languages spoken in the same region. Other factors that affect a language's survival include the area's proximity to or association with political entities where that language is prevalent or predominates, the stability of the area where the language exists, and the perceived level of threat or existing power structures posed by persons who use the language. Each of these factors can reduce or enhance a language's chance to persist depending on the relationship with other factors that produce conditions favorable to the language. A language's standing can be measured in several ways, among these the total number of speakers; number of speakers from the political, social, or economic elite; and benefits of speaking the language such as economic returns or fending off social or economic control by outside forces.

The former Yugoslavia is a textbook example of how the place where a language exists affects a language's chance to persist. In Yugoslavia, the place-where-the-language-exists factor interconnected greatly with the historical-era factor to create different environments for the multiple languages of the region. For instance, during the rule of Josip Broz Tito from 1953 until his death in 1980, language pluralism dominated Yugoslavia. Language maintenance, bilingualism, and language variety were widely and strongly supported during the Tito regime and languages enjoyed powerful legal protections. Pluralism was tied to the ideologies of national unity and linguistic equality. The likelihood that languages in the region would persist was good.

Following Tito's death and until Slovenia declared independence in 1990, the Serbs, who constituted the largest nationality group in Yugoslavia, imposed Serbian-based centralist policy and did away with pluralism. Chances that several languages in the region would persist alongside a dominant Serbian language now seem relatively weak. Interestingly, with the break-up of Yugoslavia, the likelihood that languages of the region would persist again turned promising. Slovenia, for example, adopted pluralism and protected the minority languages of Italian and Hungarian in its new constitution. Language was given human rights protection along with such characteristics as race, sex, and religion.

In an unexpected turn of events, Slovenia's openness to other languages and its stronger ties to Western Europe have worked against the Slovene language, which has suffered losses to English and German languages in important domains. As a result, the Slovene language's chance to persist has diminished.

Speakers of the Language

A language's speakers do much for the conditions faced by a language. Increases in the number of speakers, for example through a high birth rate or through immigration, affect its likelihood of persisting, although not always positively depending on the intersection with other factors. Increases in the number of low-status immigrants who speak a different language or dialect have been met with backlash when persons and institutions of power over sociocultural, religious, and economic entities feel that their power is threatened by a surge of speakers entering "their" society.

Illustrations of backlash toward non-English speakers can be seen in the United States. Large increases in the number of Spanish speakers in several states has spurred the emergence of language restrictionist measures in those states aimed at curbing the use of Spanish and raising fears among the general public about its effect on the society. In Arizona, the Spanish-speaking population grew from 14% in 1990 to 20% in 2000. Concurrently, a drive against bilingual education led to a voter initiative to eliminate bilingual education in the public schools. The voter initiative against bilingual education was not coincidental. Other propositions followed to restrict Spanish-language use in the state, including a restriction against the use of Spanish by public employees in the exercise of their duties. Policy changes ending the practice of providing drivers' license examinations in other languages have taken effect in several states. Hence, the persistence of Spanish in an otherwise positive environment of growth has been stymied by negative public policies rooted in the same conditions. In this instance, the factor of political power made a difference. Although the Hispanic population grew rapidly, its political power did not. Rapid population growth without a parallel increase in political power led to retaliatory public policies against the language.

A backlash can also occur with increases in the social status of a language's speakers. Increased social status is generally thought to increase a language's likelihood to persist, but increased social status of the language's speakers can also lead to retaliation against a language or languages depending on the intersection with other factors. Press reports in California showed that more persons who speak Asian languages were getting into medical schools than before and were subsequently increasing the proportion of Asian medical doctors in the state. This led to calls to raise English language proficiency requirements for admission to medical school. The long-term effect of these dynamics is likely to be a decision by many Asian families to reduce the use of Asian languages in the home and focus on English as the family language of choice.

Unless they are driven by strong nationalistic sentiment, most humans are practical when it comes to language. They often take the well-worn course of least resistance. Speakers of a language must see the benefits and advantages of a given language's persistence if they are to join in supporting the effort. Such benefits may be tied to identity, culture, economics, tradition, relationships, or other such contexts. But benefits will generally trump disadvantages when it comes to language use. Clearly observable benefits are among the strongest factors that contribute to conditions for language persistence. Language often becomes an identity marker within a given historical period. Often, it is not a difficult choice for young people to seek to identify with the persons with the more positive identity and to move away from those who are in some way stigmatized as speakers of a less prestigious language.

Language Use and Persistence

A language's use has a significant influence on its persistence. If a language is one used by educational institutions and education increases the chances to succeed, then persons will value that language provided they have access to educational institutions that use that language. But the reverse can also be true. If use of the language by educational institutions serves the function of limiting access to educational services, then the quality of educational services that accrue to this population will be poor, and the language involved may not persist within that population. The case of Arizona is once again illustrative, specifically the state's policy intended to curb the use of Spanish. Although there is little proof of the policy's effect on the use of Spanish in Arizona, the effect on access to quality education for the state's Spanish speakers has been documented. Language

policy can become, whether by design or not, the interests of the state, the media, or a multitude of other players, a gatekeeping mechanism to deny or grant access to services in education.

Whereas changes can be slow and unremarkable, what constitutes a particular language is constantly changing even when the language is mature and somewhat standardized. For example, words may be added or dropped, borrowed from other languages, or mutate in meaning. Although limited flexibility to accommodate its users helps a language's survival, excessive tolerance for change does not ensure that the language will persist. If a language mutates rapidly to the point of becoming unrecognizable in a few generations, it ceases to be classified as that language and runs the risk of being lost or becoming a low status dialect. The combined factors of ease of accommodation and speed of acceptance of foreign elements act against its persistence. English, for example, holds on to an arcane system of spelling that could benefit from simplification. But there is no movement to simplify the spelling of English words. The reasons for this are probably complex, but one factor contributing to that is fear that it would subsequently appear to be less whole, more childlike, or that it may lose its literary history and prestige. How the linguistic characteristics of a language intersect with other factors that affect persistence can determine, at least in part, the language's chances for survival—for example, how a language intersects with current modes of communication and how the language is positioned on multiple scales in a given area. Among these are degrees of prestige, prevalence, and prominence. All of these affect the language's chance for survival.

Mario J. Castro

See also English for the Children Campaign; Languages in Colonial Schools, Eastern; Languages in Colonial Schools, Western; Social Bilingualism

Further Readings

Baker, C. (2006). *Foundations of bilingual education and bilingualism.* Clevedon, UK: Multilingual Matters.

Castro, M., & Wiley, T. G. (2008). Adult biliteracy and language diversity: How well do national data inform policy? In K. M. Rivera & A. Huerta-Macías (Eds.), *Adult biliteracy: Sociocultural and programmatic responses.* Mahwah, NJ: Lawrence Erlbaum.

Crawford, J. (1996). *Endangered Native American languages: What is to be done, and why?* Retrieved February 1, 2007, from http://www.ncela.gwu.edu/pubs/crawford/endangered.htm

English Language Education for Children in Public Schools, Arizona Revised Statues (A.R.S.) §§ 15–751 *et seq.* (2004).

McKay, S. L., & Hornberger, N. H. (Eds.). (1996). *Sociolinguistics and language teaching.* New York: Cambridge University Press.

Ricento, T. (Ed.). (2000). *Ideology, politics, and language policies: Focus on English.* Philadelphia: John Benjamins.

Skutnabb-Kangas, T. (2000). *Linguistic genocide in education, or worldwide diversity and human rights?* Mahwah, NJ: Lawrence Erlbaum.

Tollefson, J. W. (Ed.). (2002). *Language policies in education: Critical issues.* Mahwah, NJ: Lawrence Erlbaum.

U.S. Census Bureau. (1990). Table 1. Language use and English ability, persons 5 years and over, by state: 1990 Census. *1990 census of population,* CPHL-96. Washington, DC: Author.

U.S. Census Bureau. (2003). Table 1. Language use, English ability, and linguistic isolation for the population 5 years and over by state: 2000. *Census 2000,* Summary File 3, Tables P19, PCT13, and PCT14. Internet release date: February 25, 2003. Washington, DC: Author.

Wiley, T. G. (2005). *Literacy and language diversity in the United States* (2nd ed.). Washington, DC: Center for Applied Linguistics and Delta Systems.

LANGUAGE POLICY AND SOCIAL CONTROL

Language policy refers to official or quasi-official efforts to manage or regulate the use or form of a language within a community. Language policy encompasses the range of decisions that people make about language. The decision to make English the official language of India offers one example of language policy, and another is a decision for instruction to be in Tagalog at a local elementary school in the Philippines. The use of one language rather than others within a community establishes and maintains the high status of that language and its speakers, positioning others lower in the hierarchy, and contributing to the loss or maintenance of a language.

Language policy is directly linked to social control and the privileging of one group of people over others using language as a vehicle to do so. Though the loss of a language from the world's linguistic landscape is typically seen as a natural, evolutionary process over time, it is often a direct result of choices that people in power have made. The reality is that language policies are often concerted, politically motivated efforts to assert the power of one group of speakers over another.

Knowledge of the high-status language offers certain advantages to the people who speak it, such as easier access to school curricula or more lucrative jobs. History offers countless examples of the use of language policies to assert power and dominance, most obviously by governments in their efforts to create and enforce a national identity, as this entry describes.

Language Policies in Conquest, Colonization, and Nationalism

Throughout time, language has played a central role in conquest, colonization, and the formation of nations, as speakers of different languages are brought into contact amid power struggles, usually resulting in language spread. The spread of Latin during the Roman Empire, Arabic during Islamic expansion, and French during the 17th century offer instances of groups using language to promote their economic, political, or religious missions. Language has often been used to advance the goals of colonial leadership and, as a result, English has been promoted in East Africa, Russian in the former Soviet Union, and Japanese in Korea. Newly democratized or independent nations such as South Africa, Estonia, and Bangladesh have also relied on language policy to symbolize a reenvisioned national identity.

The colonization of the African continent offers many illustrations of the central role of language policy in wide-scale efforts to gain social control. French colonization in West Africa was characterized by efforts to assimilate Africans into French culture and thereby "civilize" them, and by a belief in the superiority of the French language. The exclusive use of standard French was formalized in the Brazzaville Conference of 1944, when a recommendation was made to designate it as the exclusive language of schools, and any use of local languages was forbidden. As a result, many local languages were lost.

Under apartheid, the official languages of South Africa were English and Afrikaans. In 1974, the government issued a decree that made Afrikaans, seen as the language of the oppressors, as a medium of instruction for 50% of subjects from the last year of primary school to the last year of high school. The enforcement of this policy spawned the student uprising of 1976 in Soweto, to which the government responded violently. To reverse exclusive apartheid policies after the end of apartheid, a new constitution was formally adopted in 1996 that recognized 9 local languages in addition to English and Afrikaans. This has created a unique context in South Africa, which now has 11 official languages.

Not all new nations adopt multilingual policies, however, and most follow the one-nation, one-language ideology that took root in the early nationalist period. In the case of Israel, Zionist ideology actively and effectively promoted Hebrew monolingualism, upholding the symbolic, political connection between Hebrew and national identity. Historically, it was expected that immigrants to Israel would quickly learn Hebrew because it was necessary for their everyday lives and for their absorption and assimilation into Zionist culture. Normalization of Hebrew that revitalized the language from a primarily religious, written form into a modern, spoken language was essentially completed by 1914. By the time the state of Israel declared independence in 1948, 80% of the Jewish population claimed to know Hebrew, and more than 50% claimed to use it as their sole language. This language revitalization and subsequent shift to Hebrew took place within 50 years. With regard to social control, though this monolingual policy was viewed as essential for the state's unification, it has resulted in the marginalization of Arabic, as well as the loss of minority Jewish languages such as Yiddish and Ladino.

There have been other examples and evidence of the connection between language policy and social control; the 1976 Soweto uprising was not the only time that language policy has been a touch point for violence and resistance to domination. When Pakistan gained independence in 1947, and the national government established Urdu as the national language, Bangla speakers in the eastern part of the country resisted. The police responded violently to a strike in 1952, killing several students. This led to greater resistance and, ultimately, when the first constitution of Pakistan came into effect in 1956, it recognized Bangla as a state language. Bangladesh became independent from Pakistan in 1973 and declared Bangla its official language.

The struggles described previously are about far more than just language. They are also about how society manages diversity, culture, power, identity, and mainly, how it treats the people who are the speakers of different languages.

Language Policy and Gatekeeping

The power of language policy as a mechanism for social control stems from the fact that language policy often functions as gatekeeper, giving access to some and denying others, in arenas such as civic participation, economic mobility, and educational opportunity. In civic affairs, language choices can be used to constrain the ability of people who do not speak the dominant language(s) to take part in elections and political discourse in general, and in some places, citizenship is only granted to speakers of the dominant language. For example, Estonia gained independence in 1991 after 50 years of Soviet rule, and established Estonian as the official language. In a backlash against the preceding "Russification" period and Russian speakers who had entered the country during that time, a law passed in 1992 requires knowledge of Estonian to gain citizenship.

In the United States, English literacy testing has historically provided a legal means for discrimination in civic participation and citizenship. Although it has been illegal since 1870 to prohibit male citizens over the age of 21 from voting, southern states adopted literacy tests as a way to bar Blacks from participation. This practice was ongoing until the passage of the Voting Rights Act of 1965. Although this law banned literacy tests for voting, literacy testing has remained a requirement for naturalization as a U.S. citizen since 1917.

Although the government initially accepted literacy in any language for citizenship, this changed in 1950 when federal law established literacy in English as a condition of naturalization. Language policies such as these bar certain groups from civic participation and citizenship, illustrating how language policies and practices can be used for social control.

With regard to economic mobility, knowledge of high-status languages is directly correlated with income and socioeconomic status. Most jobs require knowledge of the dominant language, and in some workplaces, speaking a minority language is even forbidden. In an example of a workplace language policy, Rose Associates, a building company in New York City, sent out a memo in 2007 forbidding building workers from speaking languages other than

English in all public areas as well as on the radio as a company policy and common courtesy. This policy demotes languages other than English to lesser status and curtails the opportunities for workers with limited knowledge of English to advance professionally.

In Pakistan, English provides access to jobs within the government bureaucracy and the major industrial and business sectors. However, only students of the elite private and public schools have the opportunity to learn English. Likewise, in Israel, both Hebrew and English proficiency are directly correlated with socioeconomic status. For example, knowledge of both is necessary to pass the Bagrut, a higher education matriculation exam, and for most White-collar employment. This disadvantages Arabic speakers, who speak Hebrew as a second language and English as a third language after Hebrew. Results of the national achievement exams consistently show that Jewish students outperform students in the Arab sector in English. Given that both Hebrew and English are necessary for higher education and extremely beneficial in the job market, Arab students are being systematically denied equal access to opportunity.

As evident from these examples, education has historically been a primary way that powers around the world have implemented their language policies. In schools, language policies can contribute to minority language loss or, correspondingly, academic disparities because of language; in this way, schools often participate in the marginalization of minority language speakers. The Chinese government requires Han Chinese culture and language in Tibetan schools as a form of domination, which places Tibetan students at a disadvantage and limits their ability to access the curriculum. In Kazakhstan, Soviet language education policy led to dramatic language loss, and the "Russification" of schools under Soviet rule created the situation in the mid-1980s whereby 40% of Kazakh youth were unable to read their native language. New language policy is reversing that trend by strongly emphasizing the Kazakh language in education; however, now this new language policy poses an equal threat to Russian in today's Kazakhstan.

As a result of the imposition of English-only policies in public schools in the United States, the languages of immigrant families are typically lost by the second or third generation and replaced with English. Decisions to impose English as the only language of instruction have reflected popular attitudes toward particular ethnic groups and the relationship between the United States and the students' country of origin, as in the case of Japanese Americans just after World War II or the treatment of Puerto Rican Americans. The extreme losses of Hawaiian and Native American languages in the United States resulted from intentional education policies, which actively sought to replace these minority languages with English as part of wider efforts to Americanize and control these groups. Perhaps the most egregious language policy in the United States was a state law in Louisiana that made it illegal for slaves to use their native languages while they worked. The same law also forbade the teaching of English to slaves.

Although nations typically use language policies to promote one language at the expense of others, as evident in these examples, many countries now have policies designed to protect and promote regional and ethnic languages, which will preserve the vitality of these languages over time. South Africa exemplifies this—by raising nine local languages to official status in its new constitution, the government contributes to maintaining these languages. Language policies can be adopted that conserve minority languages and offer opportunities to the people who speak them. As postapartheid South Africa shows, linguistic diversity need not be viewed as a threat to national identity, but can instead be seen as a national resource. Likewise, more accepting language policies can enable and encourage civic participation and can contribute to equalizing economic and educational opportunities for all people. For this reason, language policy research in recent years has primarily advocated the adoption of language policies that create opportunities and are inclusive rather than exclusive.

Kate Menken

See also Language Dominance; Language Education Policy in Global Perspective; Languages and Power; Language Shift and Language Loss; Languages in Colonial Schools, Eastern; Languages in Colonial Schools, Western

Further Readings

Baker, C. (2006). *Foundations of bilingual education and bilingualism* (4th ed.). Clevedon, UK: Multilingual Matters.

Bartlett, L., Menken, K., Seghers, M., & Adely, F. (2003). *Human development and language policy.* New York: United Nations Development Programme.

Heugh, K. (1999). Languages, development and reconstructing education in South Africa. *International Journal of Educational Development, 19*(1999), 301–313.

Kaplan, R. & Baldauf, R. (1997). *Language planning: From practice to theory.* Clevedon, UK: Multilingual Matters.

Liebowitz, A. (1969). English literacy: Legal sanction for discrimination. *Notre Dame Lawyer, 45*(1, Fall), 7–67.

Leibowitz, A. (1971). *Educational policy and political acceptance: The imposition of English as the language of instruction in American schools.* Washington, DC: ERIC Reports.

Shohamy, E. (2006). *Language policy: Hidden agendas and new approaches.* London: Routledge.

Skutnabb-Kangas, T. (2000). *Linguistic genocide in education—Or worldwide diversity and human rights?* Mahwah, NJ: Lawrence Erlbaum.

Spolsky, B. (2004). *Language policy.* Cambridge, UK: Cambridge University Press.

Spolsky, B., & Shohamy, E. (1999). *The languages of Israel: Policy, ideology, and practice.* Clevedon, UK: Multilingual Matters.

Tollefson, J. (1991). *Planning language, planning inequality: Language policy in the community.* London: Longman.

LANGUAGE REGISTERS

Users of most languages alter the way they address others according to social backgrounds, intentions, geography, gender, and age. Other factors, such as occupation, may also influence register. When we speak, we sometimes shift registers to communicate effectively and appropriately with others. When we speak of *language registers,* we are generally referring to the variations that speakers or writers use in their language when addressing interlocutors other than in the expected mode or level of formality. Register shifts may be horizontal or vertical. *Horizontal shift* implies language variations used within the same group as the speaker's. *Vertical shift* relates to the degree of formality, ranging from frozen to intimate. Register is a broad concept; it may imply variations in all aspects of language, including phonology, morphology, semantics, syntax, and pragmatics. Shifts may involve both verbal and nonverbal elements. This entry describes why people shift language registers, theories of language registers, variations in language use, and implications for second-language users.

Why We Shift Language Registers

When we use language, we must consider a number of factors: who we are, who we are speaking to, the relationship between us and the other person or people, the context we find ourselves in, the purpose of our communication, and the rules for communication in that specific context. Based on our analysis of these, and other factors, we make choices relative to vocabulary, pronunciation, intonation, velocity of speech, gestures and posture, syntax, proximity, and eye contact. We consider whether to tell a joke and even how we should appear physically—type of clothing and accessories, perfumes or colognes, makeup, or hairstyle.

In short, we shift language registers in appropriate ways to follow the social rules, relate to others in some way, and make sure that we accomplish our purpose as communicators. We may want to get a job, invite someone out on a date, share a secret with a friend, explain a lesson to a group of students, write a short story, show that we are part of a group, share findings of a research project at a conference, give a guided scripted tour at a local park, or write a polite letter of complaint to a service provider. If we do not communicate in the right way, our message may not come across correctly, we may offend the person or people we are addressing, or we may detract from our message because the listener focuses attention on our inappropriateness. When language users do not know how and when to shift, they will face communication difficulties that could, in turn, lead to other types of problems—issues with relationships, work-related problems, or poor grades, among other things.

Theories of Language Registers

As with most language phenomena, *language register* is defined in different ways by different people. Thomas Bertram Reid, in 1956, is credited with the first use of the term, which then became more commonly used in the 1960s by linguists who wanted to speak or write about variations in language according to user and related to the interaction of different variables. Michael Halliday has written about user selection of language variations according to the setting. He defines three variables that influence the variation selected: field (subject matter), tenor (relationships), and mode (type of communication being spoken or written). Rodney Quirk and colleagues distribute register shifts across a formality scale that includes very formal and frozen, formal, neutral, informal and casual or familiar. Martin Joos speaks of five styles: frozen, formal, consultative, casual, and intimate (a commonly used model).

Register shifts can be placed on a continuum. It would be difficult to place language usage neatly into one particular style at any time because users tend to overlap in their style usage, or there are modes in between, for example, intimate and casual or frozen and formal. As language users, we each operate with our own *idiolect,* a personal way of speaking and writing that lets others recognize us, and within dialects (according to age, occupation, gender, or region). Each of these adds another variable when considering register shifts. Each language user has a particular style and way of operating within the registers. People who are adept at "reading" interlocutors sometimes shift between or among registers during an initial conversation. These people observe the effect that each register type has on the other person and quickly move to whatever register seems to work best given the purpose of the exchange. Users also have varying degrees of experience within registers, which will influence how and when they use that variation. For example, a user may have little experience with frozen registers (a young child, for example) or with casual registers (someone who has few contacts with others and is mostly in a professional or formal setting). Registers also change with time. Expressions or gestures, for example, that are "in" one day may be "out" the next day, therefore marking a change in the casual register. Failure to keep up with widespread register changes can have the result of labeling the speaker as outdated or old fashioned. Individuals change and so do the times, and with these changes, language adapts and appropriateness is redefined.

Variations in Language Use

Language register may imply shifts in phonology, morphology, syntax, semantics, pragmatics, and paralinguistics. Examples of phonology shifts would be the use of abbreviated or reduced forms, like "did´ja," or "could´ja" in casual settings. A language user in a more formal setting would use "did you" or "could you" and avoid reduced forms. In an informal mode involving mother and baby, a mother might say "wabbit" instead of "rabbit" when playing with her child, as a strategy of endearment or imitation. In terms of morphology, depending on social class or geographical region, a speaker might violate rules—for example, using "sheeps" or "oxes" to represent the plural instead of "sheep" and "oxen," although language evolves with time, and usage patterns produce changes such as the acceptance of "fishes" instead of "fish" for the plural form because of common usage. An example of syntax shifting could be, "Are you interested in reading the report?" rather than "Wanna read the report?" In the case of semantics, the examples are many. Perhaps the area that has most adjustments in register shifting is that of word choice. In a more formal setting, for example, we might call a gathering of people to talk a "planning session" or a "roundtable discussion" but in casual terms, we might call it a "jam session" or a session to "chew the fat." A problem might more formally be called "an incident," "an inconvenience," or "an area of opportunity," but in more casual terms, it might be "a pain in the neck," "a glitch," or "a mess-up." Pragmatically, we shift to follow social rules, to modify our style to fit the purpose. This might relate to how much information we give or how we represent an issue. For example, a politician or spokesperson at the White House might give telegraphic, nondescript information about an international incident, but a reporter would spill all the details she had available to her editor to facilitate a decision by the editor concerning the same story. In an interview, should the interviewee ask questions or challenge the interviewers? Is it all right to ask the panel to repeat or paraphrase the question?

Paralinguistically, people make decisions on issues such as clothing, jewelry, scents, makeup, body language, and gestures. When going for a job interview, should a woman wear a suit (pants or a skirt, what color, what style?) or a dress (is the look too feminine, not "power-oriented")? Should she use jewelry or avoid it? Perhaps, if the interview is for a teaching position, the look might be a bit more conservative, as a possible partner in a law firm would look more "business oriented," but if the position is for a cosmetic salesperson, a feminine use of clothing and makeup might be key. Should the interviewee shake everyone's hand, sit down before being asked to sit, or hand out materials that he has brought even though they were not requested by the interviewers? When a language user opens his mouth to speak or sits down at the computer and starts to write, he makes important decisions about how he will deliver his message. What will he say and not say, and how will he say it within that particular setting? Written and spoken language have variations between them. Commonly, young students write the way they speak, very informally, even in their own language. They do not perceive the difference between the two. In writing, just as in speaking, the user will need to decide which register or style to use. The selection of style depends on the function of the document and how we will judge the relative success of the communication. A friendly letter, a memo, a technical report, a poem, a contract, a television script, a short story that includes regional dialogues, a prayer, and a speech are all different and require different types of language.

Implications for Second-Language Learners

To function successfully in a society as a language user, English language learners (ELLs) must be able to effectively maneuver through the maze of decisions associated with register, to ensure that they are getting their messages across in a way that is appropriate according to the context in which they find themselves. A second-language learner who finds himself or herself in an English-speaking country with the task of learning how to use English appropriately must deal with many linguistic and cultural issues. Usually learners, by definition, do not dominate the language 100%, nor do they know the cultural or social rules completely. They have a competing set of linguistic and cultural rules that they have operated with all of their lives. These rules may be similar to or different from the rules in their new location, even when the language is the same. Under these circumstances, ELLs are faced with a completely new palette of words, expressions, gestures, and social relationships. Perhaps in a given country, one does not sit until invited to do so, women do not speak directly to men, children are not involved in adult conversations, certain subjects are taboo in business settings, or one must deal with social niceties before getting down to business. The learner does not know whether certain words are formal or informal and, hence, cannot judge whether they are appropriate. Should titles be used? Who can take the lead in a conversation? Should the person who approached first be the leader? All of these questions relate to facility in the selection and use of appropriate registers.

In second-language learning situations, the issue of register, especially in the case of teenagers and adults—and maybe even more so when dealing with English for special purposes—must be dealt with concretely. Learners should be familiar with the concept of register shifting and should be able to move across registers as needed when they interact with others. This familiarity and practice can occur through role plays, reading, talking about films, or interacting in real-life situations of various types. Language learners need to have experience with observing and acting upon different types of social contexts. A demonstrated ability to maneuver within registers will facilitate entrée into, and success within, the English-speaking world. Uncertainty in handling register changes may come across as an uncertainty concerning the purpose of the exchange or the sincerity of the speaker.

Kathryn Singh

See also Attitudes Toward Language Diversity; Linguistics, an Overview; Status Differences Among Languages

Further Readings

Halliday, M. A. K. (1978). *Language as social semiotic: The social interpretation of language and meaning.* London: Edward Arnold.

Joos, M. (1961). *The five clocks.* New York: Harcourt, Brace and World.

Quirk, R., Greenbaum, S., Leech, G., & Svartuik, J. (1985). *A comprehensive grammar of the English language.* London: Longman.

Reid, T. B. (1956). Linguistics, structuralism, philology. *Archivum Linguisticum, 8,* 28–37.

Trudgill, P. (1992). *Introducing language and society.* London: Penguin.

LANGUAGE RESTRICTIONISM

In the context of U.S. bilingual education, *language restrictionism* is defined as systematic efforts to stop a linguistic or ethnic group of people from speaking, learning, or maintaining their native or home language. In the United States, language restrictionism has been justified under the banner of promoting national unity, ensuring the homogeneity of the citizenry, or as a means of "Americanizing" immigrants or native peoples. Learning and using the English language is usually considered the defining characteristic of "Americanism."

Many scholars agree that a restrictive period of language policy lasted from the 1880s through the 1960s. James Crawford, in his book *Educating English Learners,* provides what may be the most comprehensive overview of the history of language restrictionism in the United States, as expressed in attitudes and policies restricting bilingual education. This entry draws from his work and that of others who have looked into this peculiarly American idea.

Although the founding fathers never selected an official language for the new nation, restricting the use of languages in public places, especially in schooling, is documented as early as the mid-17th century. Benjamin Franklin was perhaps the most notable personality who promoted language restrictionism. He opened an English-only parochial school for native German-speaking children in the 1750s. When parents realized that the school's emphasis was imposing a language shift away from German, they removed their children and withdrew political support for Franklin. In 1780, John Adams also proposed opening an English-only school, but his request was ignored by the Continental Congress, probably because the support of German-speaking colonists was vital to the nation-building effort that lay ahead.

Terrence Wiley, in a book chapter titled "Accessing Language Rights in Education," provides a history of educational language policy in the United States. In it, he identifies the groups against whom language restrictionism has been aimed historically: immigrants, including refugees, enslaved peoples, and indigenous peoples. He and others have argued that language restrictions targeting minority populations are directly and indirectly associated with social, political, economic, and educational policy debates. Further, presumed social hostility against certain populations resonates in the degree of restrictiveness against a language and the impact of restrictions on that population.

Enslaved Peoples

Often language restrictionism results in the emergence of new or altered languages as speakers resist restrictions on their native languages, chiefly the inability to study the conventional form of their languages in school. Language restrictionism, on the one hand, and powerlessness on the other are part of the explanation for how plantation owners exerted dominance over large slave populations in places where African slaves outnumbered Whites. Linguists such as John Baugh have presented the theory that African American Vernacular English (AAVE, sometimes called "Black English" or Ebonics) emerged because (a) slaves from different language backgrounds were forced to find means of communication, and (b) educational apartheid in the United States denied access to English language and literacy development for African Americans. In the case of language restrictionism aimed at African American slaves, compulsory ignorance laws barred access to literacy until 1865. *Compulsory ignorance* refers to the practice whereby slaves were prevented from speaking their own tongues, but also prevented from learning English. In some slaveholding states, Whites were punished if they were found teaching slaves to read and write. Even after the last laws against compulsory ignorance were voided in 1918, however, equal access to education for African Americans was not provided. In 1896, *Plessy v. Ferguson* upheld the "separate but equal" doctrine that further restricted access to schooling and to the language of schooling for 50 years, until it was overturned by *Brown v. Board of Education* in 1954. Baugh and others have documented anecdotal recollections that point to the gatekeeping structures that limit access to native speakers.

Indigenous Peoples

Evidence of attempts by White Americans to restrict the use of indigenous languages appears as early as 1674, as noted by Richard Bailey in his book chapter "American English: Its Origins and History." He reports the Superintendent of the Indians in Massachusetts writing a proposal to stop attempts at teaching indigenous literacy and replacing them with how to speak, read, and write English. Beyond this early example, little documentation of language restriction exists until much later. In 1819, the Civilization Fund Act was passed to advance English education and practical skills for Native Americans, including English and Anglo values, thus restricting the maintenance of indigenous language and culture.

By the mid-19th century, language restrictionism expanded in scope tremendously and was aimed at "civilizing" Native Americans. Directly after his election as president in 1830, Andrew Jackson pushed a law through Congress called the Indian Removal Act, which required indigenous peoples to move west of the Mississippi River. This occurred largely through coercion and force. The best-known result of the Removal Act is the historical event referred to as the Trail of Tears. Cherokees who refused to leave their land were forced westward by U.S. troops; en route, nearly 4,000 died of cold, hunger, and disease. Once resettled, tribes instituted bilingual and Cherokee medium of instruction schools, resulting in the spread of native language and literacy (an oral language, it was assigned a syllabic writing system by Sequoyah and adopted by the Cherokee nation in 1821). Ultimately, the Cherokee achieved 90% literacy levels among their people, far beyond that of White Americans of the time. One governmental response was an attack on indigenous peoples' language and culture. Crawford notes that in 1868 the Indian Peace Commission stated, "In the difference of language to-day lies two thirds of our trouble. . . . Schools should be established, which children should be required to attend; their barbarous dialects should be blotted out and the English language substituted" (p. 48). To enforce this concept, off-reservation boarding schools were created where Native American children were forcibly Anglicized and Americanized. In 1877, Congress began appropriating funding for Native American schooling, appropriating $20,000 the first year. Restricting indigenous language use was a key objective in the new program initiatives. The superintendent of Indian Schools announced in 1887 that a native's "inability to speak another language than his own renders his companionship with civilized man impossible," and J. D. C. Atkins, Commissioner of Indian Affairs, lauded English in arguing, "This language, which is good enough for a White man and a Black man, ought to be good enough for the red man" (p. 51). In his book *Language Loyalties,* Crawford refers to the following excerpt taken from Atkins's annual report on Indian Affairs:

> The object of greatest solicitude should be to break down the prejudices of tribe among the Indians; to blot the boundary lines which divide them into distinct nations, and fuse them into one homogeneous mass. Uniformity of language will do this—nothing else will. (p. 48)

In response to these calls, a "No Indian" rule was instated at boarding schools in 1890, meaning students were never permitted to speak their native languages—all communication was to be in English. In implementing this policy, most schools punished children for speaking native languages. Adult Navajos have reported having been assigned chores, having hands slapped with rulers, and mouths washed out with soap for disobeying the English-only rules while in dormitory living spaces. Among the most successful boarding schools at teaching English was Carlisle Academy in Pennsylvania, where some teachers claimed students could attain oralcy and literacy in English as quickly as in 6 to 9 weeks. Indian boarding schools exist today in a different light, as settings for students to revitalize native language and culture, but the older model of boarding schools lasted through the mid-20th century along with language restrictionism.

Immigrants

The most obvious and persistent efforts toward language restrictionism in the United States have been the promotion of a single language for immigrants. This was among the purposes of Noah Webster's dictionary. Webster intended to craft a language that reflected American culture and values and distinguished American English from British English. As noted by its publisher in 1806, Webster's was "A Compendious Dictionary of the English Language," the only truly American dictionary of its time. It was the first to document uniquely American words. Often, he changed the spelling of words so that they would reflect a distinctly American usage.

Although Webster's work may reflect early and well-meaning civic contributions to the society, often language restrictionism itself is covert, or hidden, by claims of promoting a unifying national language—English—over the languages of smaller groups that are deemed less important. Language restriction can also be overt, however, as was the case when in 1812, Thomas Jefferson considered an English-only law following the acquisition of lands from the Louisiana Purchase and Louisiana's entry into the Union. He ultimately conceded to the French-speaking majority because of near-rebellion from New Orleans residents. As noted by Crawford, from 1790 to 1830, fewer immigrants to the United States resulted in the weakening of languages other than English, until a great wave of immigrants from Germany arrived, causing German and German-English bilingual schools to gain strongholds in certain areas of the country. Bilingual schooling in German-English and other languages was widely accepted until the 1880s, when a second wave of immigration from southern and eastern Europe

(Russia, Poland, Hungary, Slovenia, Lithuania, and Italy) spread, causing renewed anti-immigrant sentiment across the country. These "new immigrants" were from a variety of different countries and their linguistic, ethnic, religious, and cultural backgrounds were less familiar to Americans than were those of their predecessors from Northern Europe (Germany, England, Scandinavia, and Ireland).

In 1889, English-only schooling laws aimed at German Catholics were passed in Illinois (Edward Law) and Wisconsin (Bennett Law). Although both were repealed in 1893, these legislative efforts reflect resistance against and distrust of languages other than English. Several years later, in 1906, Congress passed a law requiring English proficiency for naturalization.

Attempts at assimilating these new immigrants by defining or redefining American identity partly as English speakers meant promoting the idea that immigrants' native language use should occur only in the home. According to historian Ezri Atzmon, the Bureau of Naturalization of the Immigration and Naturalization Service adopted the goal of implementing English language and citizenship classes for immigrants across the country between 1914 and 1920. In 1916, the agency invited more than 200,000 naturalization applicants to join such classes. This sort of "social support" reflected a move away from the acceptance and integration of the languages and cultures brought by immigrants to the United States and a new emphasis on "Americanization" through the imposition of English.

After the United States entered World War I in 1917, the move for Americanizing "the other" gained even more momentum as xenophobia set in, particularly against the substantial number of German immigrants who had arrived in the United States in earlier decades. As noted by Bernard Spolsky, a massive reaction against anything resembling Germany took hold, especially regarding language, an obvious marker. Thirty states passed laws requiring nonnative English speakers to attend English language classes, and 34 states passed English-only schooling laws. According to Aneta Pavlenko, a Nebraska Congressman's words illustrate popularly held notions of anti-immigrant and anti-immigrant's language, "If these people are Americans, let them speak our language. If they don't know it, let them learn it. If they don't like it, let them move" (p. 178). Restrictions against the use of German were widespread, and those heard speaking German were perceived as unpatriotic and as suspect. Wiley notes that in Jefferson County, Nebraska, local council members

ordered telephone operators to cut off those who publicly spoke German over open lines. Movie theaters were closed, bans on German music ensued, German Americans were encouraged to cancel subscriptions to materials printed in German, and ultimately instruction in foreign languages was deemed un-American. Pavlenko identifies two discourses that were adopted in pursuit of language restrictionism: (1) the positive cognitive and linguistic influences of learning English, and (2) devaluing multilingualism, foreign-language teaching, and native-language maintenance among immigrant populations. In 1919, Theodore Roosevelt, addressing the American Defense Society, called for restrictions on languages other than English, stating, "We have room for but one language here, and that is the English language, for we intend to see that the crucible turns our people out as Americans, of American nationality, and not as dwellers in a polyglot boarding house; and we have room for but one sole loyalty, and that is the loyalty to the American people." Americanization efforts, largely manifested as language restrictionism in the form of antibilingual education and antiforeign-language instruction continued through the 1920s, and in 1924, the National Origins Act identified quotas based on immigrants' national origins, which reduced incoming immigration until the 1960s.

Despite this period of restrictiveness, there were advocates for German Americans and supporters of rights to native language use and maintenance. These attitudes, although shared by far fewer Americans, are evident in such cases as *Meyer v. Nebraska* in 1923, which overturned an earlier case that prohibited German-language instruction, and *Farrington v. Tokushige* in 1927, in which the Supreme Court ordered that a ban on heritage language instruction in Japanese, Korean, and Chinese offered outside of public schooling was unconstitutional. The restrictions on language of this period were eventually overturned in policies that grew out of the civil rights movements of the 1960s but have since been reinstated, evidenced, for example, by English-only medium of instruction laws enacted in Arizona, California, and Massachusetts. This last wave of restrictionism has been specifically aimed against bilingual education and is the greatest single policy threat at the moment. As of this writing, there has been no move to reverse them.

Sarah Catherine Moore

See also Americanization by Schooling; Ebonics; English for the Children Campaign; German Language Education; Language Rights in Education; Languages in Colonial

Schools, Eastern; Native American Languages, Legal Support for

Further Readings

Atzmon, E. (1958, Spring). The educational programs for immigrants in the United States. *History of Education Journal, 9*(3), 75–80.

Bailey, R. (2004). American English: Its origins and history. In E. Finegan & J. Rickford (Eds.), *Language in the USA* (pp. 3–18). Cambridge, UK: Cambridge University Press.

Baugh, J. (2000). *Beyond Ebonics: Linguistic pride and racial prejudice.* Oxford, UK: Oxford University Press.

Brown v. Board of Education, 347 U.S. 483 (1954).

Crawford, J. (Ed.). (1992). *Language loyalties: A source book on the official English controversy.* Chicago: University of Chicago Press.

Crawford, J. (2005). *Educating English learners: Language diversity in the classroom.* Los Angeles: Bilingual Education Services.

Farrington v. Tokushige, 273 U.S. 284 (1927).

Meyer v. Nebraska, 262 U.S. 390 (1923).

Ovando, C. J. (2003). Bilingual education in the United States: Historical development and critical issues. *Bilingual Research Journal, 27,* 1–24.

Pavlenko, A. (2002). "We have room for but one language here": Language and national identity in the U.S. at the turn of the 20th century, *Multilingua, 21,* 163–196.

Plessy v. Ferguson, 163 U.S. 537 (1896).

Roosevelt, T. (1926, Memorial edition). *Works of Theodore Roosevelt* (Vol. 24). New York: Scribner's.

Spolsky, B. (2004). *Language policy: Key topics in socio-linguistics.* Cambridge, UK: Cambridge University Press.

Wilcy, T. G. (2002). Accessing language rights in education: A brief history of the U.S. context. In J. W. Tollefson (Ed.), *Language policies in education: Critical issues.* Mahwah, NJ: Lawrence Erlbaum.

LANGUAGE RESTRICTIONISM IN EDUCATION

See ENGLISH FOR THE CHILDREN CAMPAIGN

LANGUAGE REVIVAL AND RENEWAL

Half of the 6,000 to 7,000 languages worldwide are considered "endangered," as parental transmission loses out to other influences and power languages take over the task of global communications. Of these, more than 500 are considered "moribund" or nearly extinct, with only a few elderly speakers still living, according to the language resource *Ethnologue.* In the United States, 68 indigenous languages are in this category. The process by which languages become extinct is known as language loss, language obsolescence, language death, or extinction. On the other side of the language coin, efforts to instill vitality in a language that is either extinct or in the process of becoming so are referred to as *language maintenance, language revival, language renewal,* and more generally, as *language revitalization.* This entry discusses those efforts.

Languages and the sociocultural contexts in which they function have never been static, and language loss is not a new phenomenon. The nature, scale, and scope of the current pattern of linguistic change is unprecedented and distinct from what occurred before the colonial projects starting in the 16th century and the formation of large nation-states in the 18th and 19th centuries. Since then, languages have been lost at an unprecedented pace. This replacement of thousands of languages by a few languages represents a loss of cultural and intellectual diversity to the world. From an individual perspective, language loss represents a shift in identity; from a community perspective, it represents the loss of cultural values, beliefs, traditions, and knowledge that arc closely tied to the languages in question. Many scholars, including Joshua A. Fishman, David Crystal, and Leanne Hinton, agree that cultures cannot long survive without the languages that are used to express their more nuanced feelings, emotions, and ideas.

Besides the loss of important linguistic resources to the world, maintaining a community language is nowadays considered a basic linguistic human right to be protected. Around the world, local and indigenous communities have become aware of this problem and are taking action to reverse the course of language loss. Patterns of language loss and extinction are nearly always tied to political, military, or economic takeover or decline. They may be either slow and steady or abrupt, happening within a single generation. In the 20th century, developments in communication and universal education contributed to the decrease in the domains in which local and indigenous language may be used. Today, the phenomenon of globalization is also contributing to the decline in use of local and indigenous languages. Languages of wider communication, such as English, Spanish, and Chinese, are considered instrumental in conducting business and communicating on a global scale. According to the Endangered Language Fund, if the current patterns of language shift and language loss continue, half of the current languages in the world will be extinct by the year 2100.

Language revival and *renewal* are two of the terms applied in the literature to efforts by communities and advocates to maintain local and indigenous languages in use and halt the process of language loss and extinction. These terms, together with the more general *language revitalization,* are not always defined consistently; although some authors make clear distinctions among them, others choose to use them interchangeably. *Language revival,* in its most strict definition, applies to efforts to revive a language that is no longer in use by any native speakers. In a broader sense, this refers to the process by which members of a speech community try to revive fluency, strengthen existing competence, and expand the language's uses by adding new domains of use. *Language renewal* is referred to as efforts by adult community members to ensure that at least some of them will continue to use and promote a traditional language that has experienced decline in use. An example of this is the Master-Apprentice Language Program in California, in which elderly speakers of native languages act as mentors to adult members of the community, teaching them the language so they in turn help the community in revitalizing the language.

A related term, *language revitalization,* is used to refer to efforts to impart vigor and restore vitality to a language that is experiencing a decline in use. Reinstatement of the transmission of a language across generations may not necessarily be the primary or essential goal of these efforts; they involve increasing the number of users and promoting new uses of the language, by expanding its domains and instituting learning programs. The goals of these efforts usually depend on the particular situation of a language and the community that speaks it. Although the process of language loss and extinction is seldom planned, language revival and renewal efforts usually require deliberate actions by the community, known as language planning.

Factors in Language Revival and Renewal

Endangered languages may still be spoken by all age groups in a community, but there may be a decline in the proportion of children learning the language at home or a decline in the domains in which the language is used. There may be cases where a language is no longer being learned by children in the homes, with either the parent or grandparent generation as the last fluent speakers of the language. A language may have only a few individuals, or elders, who still know the language and may or may not have a chance to speak it. Or, a language may have lost all its speakers. The United Nations Educational, Scientific and Cultural Organization (UNESCO) the expert group on endangered languages identifies nine factors for assessing the vitality of a language, including the following: (1) intergenerational language transmission, or whether the language is still in use by all generations, (2) absolute number of speakers, (3) proportion of speakers within the total population, (4) trends in existing language domains, or whether the language is used in all domains and for all functions, (5) response to new domains and the media, (6) availability and promotion of materials for language education and literacy, (7) governmental and institutional language attitudes and policies including official status and use, ranging from equal support to prohibition, (8) community members' attitudes toward their own language, ranging from all members valuing and supporting the language to no one caring if the language is lost, and (9) amount and quality of documentation, ranging from comprehensive to inadequate.

Although language communities are complex and diverse and a single factor is not sufficient to determine the need for documentation for a particular language, these guidelines taken together may be useful in assessing a language's situation in a society, and helping determine what types of efforts are necessary in the maintenance, revitalization, revival, or renewal of the language.

Another set of factors that may contribute to revival and renewal efforts are offered by David Crystal, in his book *Language Death.* He argues that languages may improve their chances of being maintained if their speakers (a) increase their prestige within the dominant community, (b) increase their wealth, (c) increase their legitimate power in the eyes of the dominant community, (d) have a strong presence in the education system, (e) can write the language down, and (f) can make use of electronic technology. The role of literacy and the media in language revival and renewal is controversial, and one that has been extensively argued. Although some consider literacy as an important, even crucial factor in the revival efforts of a language, others see it as detrimental to a community's oral tradition. The role of the media is also controversial because it exposes formerly isolated communities to the influence of a globalized economy and the pressures to acquire dominant languages. At the same time, the media can function as a powerful tool in aiding the efforts of communities to maintain their community connected and the language in use. The Internet in particular has been reported as useful in both documenting languages and connecting communities and their languages.

Stage-Based Approaches to Language Revival and Renewal

In an effort to conceptualize a course of action to reinstate intergenerational transmission, Joshua Fishman offers a typology and rationale for Reversing Language Shift (RLS) in eight sequential stages through which this can be accomplished, referred to as the Graded Intergenerational Disruption Scale (GIDS). This scale consists of a continuum of eight stages of language loss in which eight is closest to extinction and one closest to dynamic continued use. Fishman proposes GIDS as an assessment tool to establish the language's situation and, at the same time, as guidelines to determine what course of action is needed to restore the language to the vitality needed for intergenerational transmission. *Stage eight* refers to "nearly extinct" languages with only a few isolated elders who speak the language. At this stage, possible courses of action include documentation through recordings and transcription, master-apprentice programs in which adults learn from the elders, and getting elders connected via telephone and digital media. *Stage seven* happens when only adults beyond childbearing age speak the language. Possible courses of action at this stage include grandparents teaching their grandchildren the language, and the establishment of immersion preschools or "language nests" where these speakers team up with teachers to expose young children to the language. *Stage six* refers to the reappearance of intergenerational oral transmission of the language. Fishman notes that this is a difficult and crucial stage because most languages survive at this level without the need to go to subsequent stages. Courses of action at this stage include developing places in the community where the language is promoted and used, and encouraging families to speak the language at home with and around their children.

Stage five includes the use of literacy in home, school, and community, but without necessarily being present in formal institutions. Courses of action at this stage might include promoting literacy in the language through voluntary programs in schools and other institutions to increase prestige and use. *Stage four* involves the required use of the language in elementary education. At this stage, courses of action include the improvement of instructional methods, developing dual-language programs where children outside the community learn the language, and developing textbooks and literature in the language for content and literacy instruction. This is the first step that may require regular contact and cooperation outside the speech community. *Stage three* involves the use of the language outside the community in places of business and some work environments. Actions that may be taken at this stage are the promotion of the language as the language of work throughout the community and developing vocabulary so that the language can be used in all work environments. *Stage two* is achieved when the language is used by local government and local mass media. Actions at this stage include promoting the use of the written form in government and business, as well as promoting periodicals, radio, and television in the language. *Stage one* refers to the use of the language in higher education, government, and the media (without political independence). Fishman cautions that achieving this stage does not mean the end of problems despite the advantage of reaching this level; rather, problems become more politicized and aggravated. Actions at this stage include teaching a variety of subjects in the language in higher education, promoting publication of literature and public performances (i.e., theater, concerts) in the language, as well as creating awards to promote these efforts. Fishman's model has been adopted and adapted extensively; however, the situation of endangered languages is usually complex, involving several of the stages at the same time, which makes the linear application of his model either difficult or impossible. Further, in some instances, achieving intergenerational transmission is no longer possible but maintaining the language in different domains is.

Leanne Hinton, in the introduction to *The Green Book of Language Revitalization in Practice,* offers an adaptation of Fishman's model that provides steps toward language revitalization. She notes that these steps may happen simultaneously and may begin even before the language planning first step takes place. In Hinton's model, *step one* involves language assessment and planning. *Step two* involves reconstruction of the language in cases where there are no speakers left, and *step three* involves documentation when only a few elder speakers remain. *Step four* involves developing second-language learning programs for adults who will become instrumental in later steps. *Step five* involves redeveloping and enhancing cultural practices that promote the use of the endangered language at home and in public. *Step six* involves an intensive language-learning program for children, and *step seven* involves the use of the language in the homes as the primary means of communication. *Step eight* involves expanding the use of the language to different domains within the community, and *step nine* involves doing the same outside the community. Hinton stresses that some of these steps may be outside the desired goals of small communities, though some of the early steps may not be necessary for some communities.

Hinton also describes different approaches used in language revitalization efforts, which include (a) school-based programs, (b) children's programs outside of school, (c) adult language programs, (d) documentation and materials development, and (e) home-based programs. School-based programs include the teaching of the endangered language as a subject, bilingual education, immersion schools and classrooms, and culture programs. Children's programs outside of school include after-school programs and summer intensive language and culture camps. Adult programs include evening classes for adults and their families, community recreation programs, and master-apprentice programs. Documentation efforts are particularly important in the case of seriously endangered languages and they must be carried in conjunction with other measures. Some languages are better documented than others, and having more documentation is always better. Modern audiovisual and digital technology may prove valuable in carrying out these efforts, especially in relation to how people actually use the language. Home-based programs are aimed at establishing transmission across generations, and involve both the parent and the grandparent generations carrying out daily tasks as well as traditional activities in the language. Depending on the language community, some of these efforts will take precedence over others, but all scholars and advocates in this field agree that a combination of measures is most effective in revitalizing a language.

The most famous case of language revival is that of Hebrew, which went from being a liturgical language to a spoken vernacular with the advent of the state of Israel. Other known cases of language revival and renewal around the world include Catalan and Basque in Spain, Irish in Ireland, Māori in New Zealand, Sami in Norway, Quechua in the Andean countries, and Hawaiian in the United States. Official status granted to many of these languages was one of the measures taken, but this alone is not enough as a combination of official governmental measures and community-driven actions are often necessary to achieve the goals of revitalizing a language. This is especially important given the social nature of language that needs its speakers more than official documents. In many instances, efforts to revitalize these languages achieved no more than halting the decline in the number of speakers, or adding new domains to the language. However, had these measures not been taken, the state of these languages might be different today.

Valentina Canese

See also Language Education Policy in Global Perspective; Language Persistence; Language Socialization of Indigenous Children; Views of Language Difference

Further Readings

Crystal, D. (2000). *Language death.* Cambridge, UK: Cambridge University Press.

Fishman, J. A. (1991). *Reversing language shift: Theoretical and empirical foundations of assistance to threatened languages.* Clevedon, UK: Multilingual Matters.

Gordon, R. G., Jr. (Ed.). (2005). *Ethnologue: Languages of the World* (15th ed.). Dallas, TX: SIL International. Available from http://www.ethnologue.com

Hinton, L., & Hale, K. (Eds.). (2001). *The green book of language revitalization in practice.* San Diego, CA: Academic Press.

Reyner, J., Cantoni, G., St. Clair, R. N., & Yazzie, E. P. (1999). *Revitalizing indigenous languages.* Flagstaff: Center for Excellence in Education, Northern Arizona University. Retrieved from http://jan.ucc.nau.edu/~jar/RIL_Contents.html

UNESCO Ad Hoc Expert Group on Endangered Languages. (2003, March 10–12). *Language vitality and endangerment.* International Expert Meeting on the UNESCO Programme *Safeguarding of Endangered Language,* Paris, France.

Web Sites

Endangered Language Fund: http://www.endangeredlanguagefund.org

LANGUAGE RIGHTS IN EDUCATION

In dealing with educational language rights in the United States, it is useful to make a distinction between the *right to access* education and the *right to an education in one's mother tongue(s)*. For language minority students, both rights are important for participation in the broader society and staying connected with their home/community language. According to Reynaldo Macías, two basic rights exist: (1) the right to freedom *from* discrimination on the basis of language, and (2) the right to use one's language in the activities of communal life. There is no legally protected right to choice of language except as it flows from these two rights in combination with other rights, such as due process, equal enforcement of the laws, and so on.

In the United States and other Western countries, rights are usually located in the individual rather than in groups, explains Macías. In international law, all the existing rights are individual rights and freedoms, although their manifestations may involve more than one individual, according to Fernand de Varennes. The idea of language rights generally means something different than freedom of speech. Language rights around the world frequently are ignored in the formulation of educational policies. Unfortunately, even though organizations such as the United Nations have passed resolutions supporting the right of children to instruction in their native languages, member nations, including the United States, do not act on them because these resolutions are not binding, clarifies Tove Skutnabb-Kangas.

In the United States, language rights are largely derived from their association with other constitutional protections, which are also linked to race, religion, and national origin. Bill Piatt argues that some accommodations for the use of minority languages have been made in some legal cases dealing with educational, economic, and political access; the recognition of language rights generally and linguistic accommodations, therefore are on a tenuous legal foundation. This entry describes the orientations and implications of language policies, their historical context, and key court decisions relating to educational language policies.

Policy Orientations and Their Implications

Language policies have a direct effect on language rights. In considering policies, it is useful to note their functions in either promoting or restricting rights. Traditionally, many scholars—such as Heinz Kloss, for example—limited their analyses to formal policies, or explicit language laws. Language rights in practice are also shaped by *implicit/covert* policies as well as by *informal* practices that can have the same or even greater force than official policies. *Implicit* policies include those that overtly start out to be language policies but have the effect of policy. Arnold Leibowitz explains that *covert* policies, as the word implies, are more menacing because they use English language or literacy requirements as a means of barring someone from social, political, educational, or economic participation.

Promotion-oriented policies are those that use the resources of the government to advance a language. Historically, by the 1920s, English had been officially designated as the language of schooling in the majority of states. Even before the official designation of English, most language resources have flowed primarily into English instruction. The federal and state governments have rarely tried to promote languages other than English in education, except for purposes of strategic national self-interest or defense. A recent exception has been the Native American Languages Preservation Act of 2006 (H. R. 4766, 109th Congress), which has authorized funds for the promotion of threatened languages. More typically, governmental educational policies of the past several decades only have sought to assist in communicating with non-English-speaking populations through *expediency-oriented accommodations*. These are also used when, as Kloss notes, the government/state sees a need to communicate with speakers of minority languages to provide a bridge between minority populations.

Historical Context

In the United States, much of the focus on language rights and schooling has centered on immigrant language minorities. Immigration certainly has been an important source of language diversity. Nevertheless, other sources are also important. Historically, the major types of language minorities have been *immigrants; refugees; enslaved peoples,* who were forcibly brought here; and *indigenous peoples.* Meyer Weinberg explains that enslaved Africans were among the early recipients of attention and experienced the brunt of early restrictions on their language rights and educational rights, and Native Americans were targeted during the latter

19th century with policies designed to eradicate their languages.

Leibowitz reports that in 1790, approximately 23,000 Spanish-speaking people inhabited areas on the North American continent that would later become part of the southwestern United States. Macías has argued that the notion of indigenous peoples should be extended to include (a) those Spanish-speaking peoples who inhabited an area that later became part of the United States, before its national expansion into the region they occupied, and (b) groups that have a historical or cultural bond to the Americas before European colonization. A similar case could be made for those who spoke French or Russian at the time of their incorporation. Thus, for many, language shift to English resulted not from the choice to assimilate, but as a result of involuntary immigration and enslavement, or annexation and conquest. Territorial expansion and forced assimilation aside, immigration was the major source of language diversity in the 19th and 20th centuries.

During the first 130-plus years of U.S. history, a *tolerance-orientated* policy climate prevailed toward speakers of most European languages. Although the federal and state governments did not promote these languages, attempts to restrict them were rare. During the early republic, education among European-origin peoples was largely supported through private and sectarian means. During this period of relative tolerance, German Americans provided support for instruction in German or bilingual instruction in German and English. Some states, such as Ohio and Pennsylvania, with large German-origin populations during the 19th century allowed public-supported education in German and German/English. Terrence Wiley reports that nevertheless, for the most part, local and private stakeholders provided support for instruction in languages other than English as well as bilingual education. African-origin peoples, however, had a different experience given that *restrictive* literacy policies appeared in slave codes in the 1740s. Slaveholders saw literacy as a direct threat to their ability to control those enslaved. The last of the *compulsory illiteracy* laws, which made it illegal to teach literacy, remained on the books until 1865. During the 1880s, Native American children were forcibly wrenched away from their families and required to attend military-style boarding schools where only English was permitted, as Weinberg explains. Attitudes and policies toward speakers of European languages began to change during the World War I era, however, as speakers of German, the second most populous linguistic group at that time, suddenly found

themselves stigmatized and forced to use English, alleges Wiley. During the 1920s and 1930s, Chinese and Japanese community-based schools operated, often meeting resistance from territorial authorities in Hawai'i and state authorities in California.

School-based language requirements and standards have been used covertly as surrogates for racial discrimination. In Hawai'i during the 1920s, for example, so-called English Standard Schools were implemented. Placement in these schools was determined by performance on Standard English tests. Students were sorted into "standard," "nonstandard," and "feebleminded" educational tracks. Michael Hass claims that without resorting to overt racially based segregation, language proficiency became the means by which a system of racially segregated schooling was established wherein English language proficiency generally correlated with race or ethnicity.

Educational Language Policies in Societal Context

A number of scholars contend that educational language policies are best understood in their relationship to broader societal policies, dominant beliefs, and power relationships between groups. In this regard, Leibowitz concluded that language policies have been used as instruments of *social control*. He argued that official language policies in education are related to larger problems in society, and language was one of many responses. He noted, for example, that although English was used as the official language for specific functions (e.g., instruction at school, and voting), its use was paired with limitations for the use of languages other than English. In addition, legislation and practices in other areas were discriminatory in nature toward linguistic minority groups; this included undisclosed humiliations. Leibowitz highlights how these situations did not relate only to language, but rather to broader issues. He contends that English-only policies imposed on German, Japanese, and Chinese immigrants as well as on Native Americans, Mexican Americans, and Puerto Ricans corresponded to the general level of *hostility* of the dominant group toward various language minority groups.

Key Court Decisions

The belief that all children deserve the right to educational opportunity in public education received support only gradually. A legal basis for their language backgrounds being accommodated is much more recent. During the 19th century, the notion that children have a right to publicly supported education gradually gained favor. Even as it did, however, the right to equal educational opportunity was withheld from many children of color, many of whom were also language minorities, as Joel Spring and Weinberg explain. The 1896 Supreme Court decision *Plessy v. Ferguson* (163 U.S. 537) affirmed the dogma of segregated, *separate but equal* education, which was not overturned until 1954 in *Brown v. Board of Education* (347 U.S. 483). In *Brown,* race was the singular focus, but some language scholars such as Skutnabb-Kangas have made a similar case for the importance of language rights, though this position has found little support in U.S. law.

Meyer v. Nebraska

Following the antiforeignism of World War I, many states passed laws prohibiting children from studying a foreign language until Grade 6 or Grade 8. Nebraska similarly passed a law prohibiting foreign-language instruction. The intent of these measures was to make foreign languages inaccessible during those ages when children would have the best opportunity for learning and retaining them. By 1923, several appeals challenging these prohibitions had been filed with the Supreme Court, as Piatt explains. The critical case was *Meyer v. Nebraska* (262 U.S. 390 [1923]). Meyer was a parochial schoolteacher who was convicted and fined for breaking the Nebraska law prohibiting foreign-language teaching. He appealed to the Nebraska Supreme Court and lost. The Nebraska court took the position that teaching German to children of immigrants was a threat to national safety and self-interest. However, in 1923, the Supreme Court overturned the Nebraska decision based on the reasoning that in peacetime such an extreme restriction on foreign-language teachers or parents who wanted their children to learn foreign languages. By a 7–2 vote, the Nebraska law was held to be an infringement of the Due Process Clause of the Fourteenth Amendment (as described by I. N. Edwards, Paul Murphy, Piatt, and Wiley).

Murphy explains that although the *Meyer* case ruled that unduly restrictive educational language policies were unconstitutional, it failed to establish little more than a weak precedent for educational rights because the court accepted the view that all citizens of the United States should be required to speak a common tongue. *Meyer* also affirmed the "power of the state to compel attendance at some school and to make reasonable regulations for all schools. The requirement that they give instruction in English was not questioned . . ." (as cited in Jill Norgren & Serena Nanda, 1988, p. 188). Thus, a major outcome of *Meyer* was to affirm the official status of English language instruction.

Farrington v. Tokushige

A few years after *Meyer,* in a related decision, *Farrington v. Tokushige* (273 U.S. 284 [1927]), the Supreme Court, following *Meyer,* ruled against the territorial governor of Hawai'i who had attempted to impose restrictions on private or community-based Japanese, Korean, and Chinese foreign-language schools. *Farrington* was important because a large number of such schools had been established in Hawai'i and in California, as reported by Leibowitz and by Robert Bell. Many of these schools thrived during the 1920s and 1930s, just as similar schools do today. These heritage language schools provided supplemental instruction in native languages to the English-only instruction provided in public schools. During World War II, however, *Farrington* had no impact when the federal government prohibited Japanese instruction in the federal internment camps in which Japanese Americans were imprisoned, as illustrated in U.S. Senate documents from 1943 to 1974.

Lau v. Nichols *and Related Cases*

The most significant legal case with implications for language minority students' educational rights since *Meyer* was *Lau v. Nichols.* The case was filed in San Francisco. California, like many other states, had a prior history of discriminating against language minorities. During the late 19th century, segregation of Asian-origin students was legal, and as late as 1943, the California constitution had affirmed legal segregation of schoolchildren of Indian, Chinese, Japanese, or "Mongolian" parentage. This stipulation was not overturned until 1947.

As in many educational discrimination cases, *Lau* was brought as a lawsuit only after failed efforts by parents and community language rights activists to receive appropriate educational programs for language minority children. Li-Ching Wang, a community leader involved in the 4-year litigation, noted that the Chinese American community had held meetings with the San Francisco school administrators over a 3-year period. They did several studies demonstrating what children who did not speak English needed and developed proposals of several ways to approach these issues and staged demonstrations in protest of district inaction. As a last resort, Chinese American parents and community leaders filed a lawsuit offering as evidence that of 2,856 Chinese-speaking student who needed help, 1,790 of them did not receive any help or special instruction; only 260 of 1,066 of this student population who received special instruction in English had bilingual Chinese-speaking teachers, as Edward De Avila, Edward Steinman, and Wang further explain.

Despite these inequities, the circuit court of appeals sided with the school district concluding,

> *The discrimination suffered by these children* is not the result of laws passed by the state of California, presently or historically, but *is the result of deficiencies created by the children themselves* in failing to know and learn the English language. (Cited in De Avila, Steinman, & Wang, 1994, p. 16; emphases added)

In 1974, the Supreme Court, however, ruled in favor of the plaintiffs. In writing for the majority, Justice William O. Douglas noted the connections between language and race, ethnicity, and national origin as he concluded,

> The failure of the San Francisco school system to provide English language instruction to approximately 1,800 students of Chinese ancestry who do not speak English, or to provide them with other adequate instructional procedures, denies them a meaningful opportunity to participate in the public educational program and thus violates § 601 of the Civil Rights Act of 1964, which bans discrimination based on "the ground of race, color, or national origin," in "any program or activity receiving financial assistance. . . ." (*Lau v. Nichols*, 414 U.S. 563 [1974])

Focusing on the issue of the importance of language for educational access, Douglas chided the lower court and school district for implying that schools are not "legally or morally obligated to teach English," as he concluded,

> Basic English skills are at the very core of what these public schools teach. Imposition of a requirement

that, *before a child can effectively participate in the educational program, he must already have acquired those basic skills is to make a mockery of public education.* We know that those who do not understand English are certain to find their classroom experiences wholly incomprehensible and in no way meaningful. . . . (*Lau v. Nichols*, 414 U.S. 563 [1974] emphasis added)

The significance of *Lau* is that it required schools to accommodate children who do not speak English. It did not, however as is sometimes thought, require bilingual education or any other specific educational remedy. Douglas noted, "Teaching English to the students of Chinese ancestry is one choice. Giving instructions to this group in Chinese is another."

In the mid- to later 1970s, federal authorities did attempt to outline what approaches could be used to accommodate language minority children. These came to be known as the *Lau* Remedies. These were subsequently withdrawn by the Reagan administration (see work by James Crawford). Nevertheless, using *transitional* bilingual education as a remedy was prescribed in several district court cases, the first of which was *Serna v. Portales Municipal Schools* (499 F.2d. 1147, 1154 [10th Cir. 1974]). Other important district court cases that prescribed transitional bilingual education include *United States v. Texas* (506 F. Supp. 405 [E.D. Texas 1981]) and *Ríos v. Reed* (480 F. Supp. 1978). Significantly, however, neither *Lau* nor related cases such as *Serna* addressed the constitutional issue of equal protection under the Fourteenth Amendment. This means that language access in education issues have been largely based on legislative protections against discrimination under the Civil Rights Act of 1964, rather than directly on the Constitution.

According to Martha Jiménez, the question of determining whether the school districts have complied with *Lau* was left to federal courts to resolve. The significant case in addressing this issue was *Castañeda v. Pickard* (648 F.2d 989 [5th Cir. 1981]). The importance of *Castañeda* is that it laid out criteria known as the three-part test by which "'appropriate actions'" by school districts "'to overcome language barriers'" could be assessed. These criteria required that any educational remedy for language minority children must (1) be based on sound educational theory; (2) it must have a reasonable plan for implementation, including the hiring of appropriate personnel; and (3) it must produce positive educational results.

In returning to the distinction between the right to access education and the right to an education in one's mother tongue(s), court decisions in the United States have upheld the former within the context of accommodating language minorities. This is essentially a right of access. To date, the courts have largely sidestepped the issue of the right to education in one's home or community language through public schools. Language minority parents and communities can, however, do so through private and community-based efforts without restriction based on the *Meyer* and *Farrington* decisions.

Terrence G. Wiley

Editor's Note: This entry is based, in part, on Wiley, T. G. (2002). Accessing language rights in education: A brief history of the U.S. context. In J. Tollefson (Ed.), *Language policies in education: Critical readings* (pp. 39–64). Mahwah, NJ: Lawrence Erlbaum.

See also Bilingual Education as Language Policy; Federal Court Decisions and Legislation

Further Readings

Bell, R. (1935/1974). Japanese language schools in California. Public school education of second generation Japanese in California. In *Educational-Psychology, Vol. 1* (pp. 20–23). Stanford University Publications. Reprinted in S. Cohen (Ed.), *Education in the United States: A documentary history* (Vol. 5, pp. 2974–2976). New York: McGraw-Hill.

Crawford, J. (1992). The question of minority language rights. In J. Crawford (Ed.), *Language loyalties: A source book on the official English controversy* (pp. 225–228). Chicago: University of Chicago Press.

De Avila, E. A., Steinman, E., & Wang, L. C. (1994). Historical overview. In Art, Research and Curriculum Associates (ARC), *Revisiting the Lau Decision: 20 years after.* Symposium Proceedings (November 3–4, 1994, pp. 13–21). San Francisco: ARC.

De Varennes, F. (1999). The existing rights of minorities in international law. In M Kontra, R. Phillipson, T. Skutnabb-Kangas & T. Várady (Eds.), *Language: A right and a resource approach to linguistic human rights* (pp. 117–146). Budapest, Hungary: Central European University Press.

Edwards, I. N. (1923). The legal status of foreign languages in the schools. *Elementary School Journal, 24*(December), 270–278.

Jiménez, M. (1992). The educational rights of language minority children. In J. Crawford (Ed.), *Language loyalties* (pp. 243–251). Chicago: University of Chicago Press.

Kloss, H. (1998). *The American bilingual tradition.* Washington, DC: Center for Applied Linguistics & Delta Systems.

Leibowitz, A. H. (1971). *Educational policy and political acceptance: The imposition of English as the Language of Instruction in American Schools.* Eric No. ED 047 321.

Leibowitz, A. H. (1974, August). *Language as a means of social control.* Paper presented at the VIII World Congress of Sociology, University of Toronto, Toronto, Canada.

Macías, R. F. (1979). Choice of language as a human right—Public policy implications in the United States. In R. V. Padilla (Ed.), *Bilingual education and pubic policy in the United States* (pp. 39–75). Ypsilanti: Eastern Michigan University.

Macías, R. F. (1999). Language policies and the sociolinguistics historiography of Spanish in the United States. In J. K. Peyton, P. Griffin, & R. Fasold (Eds.), *Language in Action* (pp. 52–83). Creskill, NJ: Hampton Press.

Murphy, P. L. (1992). *Meyer v. Nebraska.* In K. L. Hall (Ed.), *The Oxford companion to the Supreme Court of the United States* (pp. 543–544). New York: Oxford University Press.

Norgren, J., & Nanda, S. (1988). *American cultural pluralism and the law.* New York: Praeger.

Piatt, B. (1992). The confusing state of minority language rights. In J. Crawford (Ed.), *Language loyalties* (pp. 229–234). Chicago: University of Chicago Press.

Skutnabb-Kangas, T. (1999). Linguistic diversity, human rights, and the "free" market. In M. Kontra, R. Phillipson, T. Skutnabb-Kangas, & T. Várady (Eds.), *Language: A right and a resource approaches to linguistic human rights* (pp. 187–222) Budapest, Hungary: Central European University Press.

Spring, J. (1994). *Deculturation and the struggle for equality: A brief history of the education of dominated cultures in the United States.* New York: McGraw-Hill.

U.S. Senate. (1943–1974). Description of education in the internment camps. From Miscellaneous Documents, 1–142, 78th Cong. 1st Sess. Document No. 96. Segregation of loyal and disloyal Japanese (1943), p. 11. Reprinted in S. Cohen (Ed.), *Education in the United States: A documentary history, Vol. 2* (p. 2977). New York: McGraw-Hill.

Wang, L. (1976). *Lau v. Nichols:* History of a struggle for equal and quality education. In E. Gee (Ed.), *Counterpoint* (pp. 240–259). Los Angeles: Regents of the University of California/The UCLA Asian American Studies Center.

Weinberg, M. (1995). *A chance to learn: A history of race and education in the United States* (2nd ed.). Long Beach: California State University Press, Long Beach.

Wiley, T. G. (1999). Comparative historical analysis of U.S. language policy and language planning: Extending the foundations. In T. Huebner & K. A. Davis (Eds.), *Sociopolitical perspectives on language policy and planning in the USA* (pp. 17–37). Amsterdam: John Benjamins.

LANGUAGES, LEARNED OR ACQUIRED

As this entry describes, a common debate in language teaching and in linguistics centers on the question of whether languages are learned or acquired. Stephen Krashen used the term *learning* to refer to a conscious process of language development that occurs as a result of direct teaching. In contrast, *acquisition* is a subconscious process of language development that occurs as the result of exposure to meaningful messages in a language. Even though some researchers have argued that there is a continuum moving from acquisition to learning rather than a clear distinction, the two terms are widely used in the research literature, and the distinction seems to be a useful one.

Most researchers agree that many aspects of a child's first language are acquired. Children seem to acquire the phonology of a language. Within a fairly short time, they can understand and produce messages in a language their parents or other caregivers use to communicate with them. In addition to the sounds of the language, children acquire the syntax. Experiments with young children brought up by English-speaking parents show that they understand the difference between "Big Bird is washing Cookie Monster" and "Cookie Monster is washing Big Bird." This research demonstrates that the children recognize that there is a link between the order of the words and the meaning, and that in English, the first noun phrase is the subject or actor whereas the second is the object of the sentence.

Although phonology and syntax appear to be acquired rather than learned, other aspects of a first language, such as the vocabulary, may be learned. However, there is more debate about whether additional languages can be acquired. Similarly, some would argue that written language is learned, but others hold that literacy is acquired in the same way that oral language is. The debate is not simply academic because the position one holds has clear implications for teaching in bilingual classes.

First-Language Acquisition

Support for the claim that first languages are acquired comes from Noam Chomsky's theories of linguistics. Chomsky, the foremost linguist in the United States, developed a theory referred to as *generative linguistics*. Chomsky was interested in describing language as a set of rules that could be applied to generate all the sentences of a particular language. No limit exists on the number of different sentences that can be expressed in any language, so there must be a finite set of rules capable of generating an infinite number of sentences. For this description, to reflect psychological reality, the number of rules must be relatively small. Otherwise, humans couldn't acquire them.

Chomsky's answer to the question of how children acquire language is that children have an innate capacity for language, which he at first called a *language acquisition device*. This language acquisition device is a specialized area of the brain designed for language. According to Chomsky, humans do not simply have a special cognitive capacity for figuring out language. Rather, humans are born with the basic structures of all human languages already present in the brain. Chomsky calls this innate knowledge of language *Universal Grammar.* Children are not born with knowledge of English or Japanese or any other human language. Instead, they are born with knowledge of those elements that are common to all human languages.

As a result, the task facing the child is not to learn how language works, starting from scratch. Instead, because children are born with an implicit knowledge of language in general, and they have to figure out how the particular language (or languages) they hear functions. For example, all languages have something like prepositions, words that show relationships among things (The book is *on* the table). In such languages as English, these words that show position come in front of the noun, so they are called *pre*positions. In other languages, these words follow the noun, so in those languages, a child would encounter sentences with this pattern (e.g., The book is the table *on*). In such languages, these words are called *post*positions because they come after (post), not before (pre).

Children are born with the built-in knowledge that the language they hear will have a word to show position. What children must figure out is whether the position word precedes the noun or follows it. This is a much easier task than starting without any knowledge and having to learn that there are some words that show position and having to learn where those words go in the sentence.

If children have a Universal Grammar, this hard-wired knowledge, then it is not surprising that most children acquire the language that surrounds them. Not all of language, however, is innate. Certainly, children have to learn individual words. Vocabulary can't be built in because it is not completely systematic and predictable. There is no regular connection between sounds of words and their meanings. Even though there are patterns within vocabulary that enable children (and adults) to develop vocabulary knowledge fairly rapidly, learning vocabulary is different from acquiring the phonology or syntax of a language. However, Chomsky's claim is that most of language is innate. He and other linguists base this claim on certain facts: (a) Most children acquire a first language rapidly and without formal instruction, (b) they do this with only a limited amount of evidence, and (c) they do it with only limited feedback.

Second and Written Languages

Stephen Krashen bases his theory of second-language acquisition on Chomsky's theory of linguistics. Krashen claims that the same process the enables a child to acquire a first language applies to a child or an adult acquiring a second language or learning to read and write. Evidence for Krashen's position comes from the fact that most students who attempt to learn a second language in school fail to reach high levels of proficiency and quickly lose their ability to speak the language if they do not continue to use it. Conversely, people who live in an environment where communication takes place in a second language seem to be able to pick up the language naturally and to retain it. In this context, the second language is acquired, not learned. In addition to his acquisition/learning hypothesis, Krashen developed several other hypotheses to account for how second languages are acquired. These include the Natural Order Hypothesis, the Monitor Hypothesis, the Input Hypothesis, and the Affective Filter Hypothesis.

The Natural Order Hypothesis

Krashen reviews research that shows that language, both first and second, is acquired in a natural order. Simply put, some aspects of language appear in the speech of language learners before other features. For example, babies acquiring English first produce sounds with vowels (usually the low, back "ah" sound) and later add consonants beginning with consonants formed with the lips like *p* or *m*. This helps explain why the first word of many infants is something like *mama* or *papa,* much to the delight of a parent. Sounds like *r* come later. That's why young children might say, like Elmer Fudd, *wabbit* instead of *rabbit.* Other parts of language also appear in a natural order. Statements come before questions. Positive statements come before negatives, and so on.

Researchers in second language found the same phenomenon. The natural order of second-language acquisition differs slightly from that of first language, but there is a definite order. Heidi Dulay and Marina Burt studied Spanish and Chinese speakers acquiring English and looked at the order in which certain morphemes appeared. Dulay and Burt noted that the plural *s* in a word such as *toys* showed up in children's speech earlier than the third person *s* of present tense verbs in sentences like "He plays." Whether researchers look at the acquisition of sounds, word parts, or sentence patterns, they find an order of acquisition that is the same even for children whose first languages are different. The order seems to come from the language being acquired, rather than a transfer of features from the first language.

The Monitor Hypothesis

This hypothesis helps explain the role of learning in the process of language acquisition. Acquired language forms the basis for the ability to understand and produce the language. The phonology, morphology, and syntax are acquired. Acquisition is what enables native English speakers to tell what "sounds right" in the language. They may not be able to explain why "He is married to her" sounds better than "He is married with her," but because native speakers have acquired the language, they can make these kinds of judgments.

Learned knowledge also plays a role in language competence. The rules that people learn can be used to monitor spoken or written output. In other words, people can use these rules to check what they say or write. For monitor use to be effective, language users must have time, they must focus on language form, and they must know the rules. Even in the first language, most people monitor their speech in formal situations such as giving a speech to a large group of people. To use the monitor effectively, one must have learned the rules. Is it *different from* or *different than?* Unless the speaker has learned the right answer, he or she can't monitor the output well.

Spoken language is difficult to monitor using learned rules because if we start focusing on form, we cannot also focus on meaning. However, editing during the writing process represents an ideal situation to apply the monitor because there is time, and one can focus specifically on the correctness of the language, learned knowledge, to be sure that sentences are complete and words are spelled right. On the other hand, when writers are drafting, they may depend more on their acquired knowledge because too much focus on form may interrupt the flow of their ideas.

The Input Hypothesis

How does acquisition take place? According to Krashen, the key is comprehensible input, messages, either oral or written, that students understand. Not all input leads to acquisition. Krashen says that students acquire language when they receive input that is slightly beyond their current level. He refers to this as $i + 1$ (input plus one). If students receive input that is below or at their current level ($i + 0$), there is nothing new to acquire. However, if the input is too much beyond their current level ($i + 10$, for example), it no longer is comprehensible.

Providing comprehensible input is not an exact science. Teachers can't possibly ensure that everything they say or write will be exactly at the $i + 1$ level for every student. The students in a class are all at different levels of proficiency. Nevertheless, as long as students understand most of what they hear or read in a new language, they will acquire the language. Different students will acquire different parts of the language depending on their current level. Krashen is an especially strong advocate of reading for language acquisition. He cites research showing that reading provides excellent comprehensible input and is the source of one's knowledge of vocabulary, grammar, and spelling.

The Affective Filter Hypothesis

How do affective factors such as nervousness, boredom, or anxiety influence language acquisition? If language is acquired when a person receives comprehensible input, that input has to reach the part of the brain that processes language. That part of the brain is what Chomsky calls the language acquisition device. Boredom or anxiety are affective factors that can serve as a kind of filter to block out incoming messages and prevent them from reaching the language acquisition device. As a result, even though a teacher may present a comprehensible lesson, some students may not acquire the language of the presentation because their affective filter operates to block the input. Students cannot acquire language that never reaches the language acquisition device. On the other hand, when the filter is open, when students are relaxed and engaged in a lesson, even messages that are not easy to comprehend will trigger the acquisition process.

In sum, Krashen argues that both second and written languages are acquired, not learned, and that the process is the same as for first-language acquisition. Acquisition occurs in a natural order when people receive comprehensible input and their affective filter is low. Rules that people learn can be used to monitor the output, either speech or writing. Although other theorists have pointed to the importance of output and interaction in the process of developing a second language or learning to read and write, most researchers agree that all forms of language are largely acquired rather than learned.

David E. Freeman and Yvonne S. Freeman

See also BICS/CALP Theory; Compound and Coordinate Bilingualism; First-Language Acquisition; Linguistics, an Overview; Second-Language Acquisition

Further Readings

Chomsky, N. (1975). *Reflections on language.* New York: Pantheon.

Dulay, H. & Burt, M. (1974). Natural sequences in child second language acquisition. *Language Learning, 24*(1), 37–53.

Krashen, S. (1982). *Principles and practices of language acquisition.* New York: Pergamon.

Krashen, S. (2003). *Explorations in language acquisition and use.* Portsmouth, NH: Heinemann.

Pinker, S. (1994). *The language instinct: How the mind creates language.* New York: Morrow.

LANGUAGES AND POWER

Max Weber, a German sociologist and political economist, defined power as the capability of a person or group of persons to impose their will on others, even against the wishes of those others. Other scholars have noted that power can be manifested in different ways; it can be exercised physically and forcibly or more subtly to sustain oppression and coercion. In many cases, language plays a role as an instrument and as a symbol of power, dominance, and control. Michel Foucault, a French philosopher and social scientist, explains that language reflects the way in which power relations in the social structure function between institutions and sociocultural groups. He believes that those in power have access to special knowledge, and that they use language policies as a means to remain in power. Paraphrasing Weber, the relationship between language and power can be understood as the ability of a person or group to impose their will on others and against the resistance of others. This can be based on a variety of factors, but one of them is the ability of the more powerful group to establish the uses and status of one or more languages. This entry discusses language and power, particularly relative to bilingual education.

Language and Power in Society

An important distinction exists between the notion of the power of a language and the notion of power relations surrounding a language; the former is related to the communicative function that a language carries, and the latter can be related to the symbolic value that speakers give to a language in a community. In the social structure of the United States, power dynamics are most clearly reflected in the unequal value ascribed to one language above all others. In schools, students of minority groups who speak another language are viewed by members of the mainstream group as deficient, incompetent, and members of a lower class. Members of the majority group, even when they are monolingual, are considered more normative because they speak English, the language of power and influence. Spanish is viewed as inferior and less prestigious, as is African American Vernacular English, also known as Ebonics or Black English. Black English is regarded as a substandard version of mainstream English and an impediment to learning.

In every society, the prestigious languages are those spoken by the mainstream group and are usually used in government, official, religious, and economic functions; these languages are usually learned at school.

Less prestigious languages are commonly used for less formal functions and to communicate with family and friends; these languages are usually learned at home. Language and culture are closely linked. Both are an important part of life and identity. In most societies, one language tends to be used as a sorting mechanism of power. That language determines which individuals will have access to benefits, opportunities, education, and other resources commonly available to speakers of the mainstream language. A language can be used to coerce those who speak another language to oblige them to follow the rules established by the group in power. Historically, there have been cases where the uses of languages other than English have been viewed as a symbol of resistance and lack of patriotism as well as a symbol of lack of interest in assimilation to mainstream culture. In some cases, language interacts with the factor of race to create important hierarchies and to act as screens to equal participation. Arguably, this kind of categorizing and sorting led the country to appoint a German American general to lead the Allied Forces in Europe during World War II, while collecting Japanese Americans in internment camps.

Throughout the history of the United States, social science researchers have applied different approaches to explore the power and status that a language might have in society. A technique that has proven useful for this task is documenting the public's attitudes toward a particular language. John Attinasi and James Bradac have concluded that the attitudes people have toward a language will, if such patterns persist over time, influence the status of a given language. Attitudes and assumptions about language may be expanded to determine how people feel about the social, cultural, political, and economic standing of a certain group or culture; these attitudes have influential implications for language policy.

During the 1950s and before, many schools in Texas and California demanded the acquisition of English for Spanish-speaking students as a mechanism of assimilation; students were not allowed to speak Spanish in the classrooms, at lunchtime, or on playgrounds and were often punished for doing so. The story of Native American languages is another example of the power of one language group to oppress others. In the 1800s, Native American boarding schools engaged in physical force and coercion as disciplinary measures to oblige students to speak English and abandon their ancestral languages.

Language and Power Relations in Bilingual Education

How the speakers of the majority language feel about the value of languages is likely to affect the support or lack of support for programs such as bilingual education for language minority youngsters. In the United States, it is not merely the use of two languages that is disdained; it is the *continued use* of two languages by people who learned the "other language" at home rather than at school. Although it is not strongly encouraged, no stigma is attached to having children of the majority group study languages as school subjects.

Attitudes toward the use of more than one language at school have varied throughout the history of the country. More often than not, the nature of these changes has been related to public attitudes toward immigration and the resultant policies on the subject. Other factors such as commerce, globalization, transnationalism, multicultural awareness, and democratization have become important in recent history.

In much of the world, the use of two or more languages is the norm rather than the exception. Many European countries accept and tolerate cultural and linguistic diversity. In the United States, however, the use of a standard form of English in society and education has become a symbol of an immigrant's willingness to undergo assimilation. Standard English is understood as the use of a homogenized language—vocabulary, grammar, spelling, and pronunciation—and avoidance of regional "accents." Standard English is also regarded by many as a symbol of a good and proper education.

Today, all school systems in the United States, whether public or private, demand the acquisition of English as mandatory for the integration and adaptation of students to the school context. This type of policy is not universal. In many countries, families can choose what language to use in the education of their children according to their choice of schools conducted in particular languages. Once again, the issue of power is played out in a practice that has become so ingrained in the country that it is hardly recognized as a matter of social control. Whether or not schools value, respect, and provide opportunities for students to learn through other languages underscores how the society regards diversity. Schools that uniformly deny this aspect of education are, in effect, making decisions about the relative importance of languages in society and in human development. The almost complete absence of schools conducted in other languages makes linguistic choice impossible. Even in schools that employ bilingual education, especially *transitional* bilingual education, minority students who are learning English can be seen as disadvantaged. Spanish-speaking students who are learning English are more likely to be regarded by the dominant group as having a deficit, but native English speakers who study Spanish as a *foreign language* are not viewed in the same way.

With respect to the study of languages, the future may hold different patterns of student participation. Changing demographics, employment trends, globalization, and transnational ties are encouraging parents from mainstream groups to enroll their children in foreign-language immersion programs. Evidence of this is the creation of Chinese, German, French, and Spanish immersion and dual-language programs across the country. These programs begin as early as kindergarten, and students may learn to read and write in their second language before they learn in English. Their purpose is to help young students develop communicative skills in other modern languages and enable them to compete better in the global marketplace. Although this trend may appear benign, it may not be entirely so from the perspective of power relationships and the question of who benefits from such programs and policies. Some scholars suggest that the emphasis on training native English speakers in foreign-language programs does not empower language minority students. Although there are negative views and negative attitudes toward bilingual minorities, bilingual members of majority groups are viewed in a positive and nondiscriminatory way. Language policy researchers Tove Skutnabb-Kangas and Robert Phillipson are critical of dual-language programs for the mainstream students; their view is that when the students of an English-speaking majority background learn other languages, this group will be favored over other speakers when competing for jobs that require bilingual skills. Other scholars believe it is too early in the history of these programs and efforts to reach a definitive conclusion.

Language, Power, and Public Policy

According to Richard Ruiz, the use of language can be seen from three different perspectives: as a problem, as a right, or as a resource. The definition of what is a problem, a right, or a resource is usually made by those who have the power to enact these ideas into practice. In American society, when language is viewed as a problem, it is often connected to problems of poverty, underachievement in school, and lack of integration to mainstream culture. When language is viewed as a right, it means that people have the freedom to choose the language they want to use to communicate with others in society. When this view prevails and is supported by those in power, language discrimination may be viewed as analogous to racial or religious discrimination. Language as a resource means that language is used to close the gap that exists among different cultures and groups. In this case, additive approaches to bilingual education are supported because the additional language is viewed as a resource instead of being a problem.

If policies in the United States were to recognize the languages of language minority students as a resource, this could improve the status of those languages and those who speak them. In the United States, current global and transnational trends promote the education of foreign languages among majority groups, but the use of foreign languages within minority groups is devalued. Guadalupe San Miguel, a scholar in the field, considers this orientation to be a major inconsistency and a paradoxical point of view in the United States. Although it may be paradoxical, the views and policies connected with these sentiments underscore the need of those who hold power to maintain it. Hence, the paradox might be explained by some degree of threat that is experienced by members of the cultural and linguistic majority. It appears to be related to issues of immigration control and a felt need to control more effectively who will enter the country and under what conditions. It may also involve fear of the influence that new immigrants may come to exert on other aspects of the society: cultural identity, social economic standing, and access to the resources of the society. In the United States, context language has been used as a tool to create social distinctions between groups. The trepidation of the majority society to support widespread dual-language education may originate in the fear, pure and simple, that the English language may change in unacceptable ways because of heavy immigration. The point has not been lost: The more power, status, and prestige the speakers of a language have, the higher status their language will have in that society.

Luis Xavier Rangel-Ortiz

See also Cultural Deficit and Cultural Mismatch Theories; Ebonics; Heritage Language Education; Language Policy and Social Control; Spanish-Language Enrollments; Status Differences Among Languages; Views of Language Difference

Further Readings

Acuña, R. (1988). *Occupied America: A history of Chicanos.* New York: HarperCollins.

Akkari, A. (1998). Bilingual education: Beyond linguistic instrumentalization. *Bilingual Research Journal, 22*(2, 3, 4), 103–125.

Attinasi, J. J. (1983). Language attitudes and working class ideology in a Puerto Rican barrio in New York. *Ethnic Groups, 5,* 55–78.

Beebe, L. M. (1988). Five sociolinguistic approaches to second language acquisition. In L. M. Beebe (Ed.), *Issues in second language acquisition: Multiple perspectives* (pp. 41–77). New York: Newbury House.

Bourdieu, P. (1991). *Language and symbolic power.* Cambridge, MA: Harvard University Press.

Bradac, J. J. (1990). Language in social relations: language attitudes and impression formation. In H. Giles & P. Robinson (Eds.), *Handbook of language and social psychology* (pp. 387–412). New York: Wiley.

Cummins, J. (2000). *Language, power and pedagogy: Bilingual children in the crossfire.* Clevedon, UK: Multilingual Matters.

Fairclough, N. (2001). *Language and power* (2nd ed.). London: Longman.

Foucault, M. (1971). *The discourse in language.* Paris: Gallimard.

Giles, H. (1992). *Current and future directions in sociolinguistics: A social psychological contribution.* In K. Bolton & H. Kwok (Eds.), *Sociolinguistics today: International perspectives* (pp. 361–368). London: Routledge.

Lippi-Green, R. (1997). English with an accent: Language, ideology, and discrimination in the United States. New York: Routledge.

Macgregor-Mendoza, P. (2000). Aquí no se habla Español: Stories of linguistic repression in Southwest schools. *Bilingual Research Journal, 24*(4), 355–368.

Portes, A., & Rumbault, R. G. (1996). *Immigrant America.* Berkeley: University of California Press.

Ruiz, R. (1984). Orientations in language planning. *NABE Journal, 8*(2), 15–34.

San Miguel, G. (2004). *Contested policy. The rise and fall of federal bilingual education in the United States 1960–2001.* Denton: University of North Texas Press.

Skutnabb-Kangas, T., & Phillipson, R (1995). *Linguistic human rights: Overcoming discrimination.* Berlin: Mouton de Gruyter.

Van Dijk, T. A. (1993). Principles of critical discourse analysis. *Discourse and Society, 4*(2), 249–283.

Van Dijk, T. A. (1997). The study of discourse. In T. A. Van Dijk (Ed.), *Discourse as structure and process* (pp. 1–34). London: Sage.

Weber, M. (1978). *Economy and society: An outline of interpretive sociology.* Berkeley: University of California Press.

Zentella, A. C. (1997). *Growing up bilingual: Puerto Rican children in New York.* Malden, MA: Blackwell.

Language Shift and Language Loss

Every year, all over the planet, languages die. Most of us are unaware of this even when it occurs in our own country. This entry reviews and summarizes two important concepts in the study of language survival and disappearance: language shift and language loss. Language death is often the ultimate result of this progression. Because of its obvious meaning, it will be discussed only briefly. Definitions of *language shift* and *language loss* will be followed by more extensive discussion, including efforts to stop or retard language loss.

Language shift can occur in an individual or within a community. For an individual, *language shift* can generally be defined as a loss in language proficiency or a decreasing use of that language for different purposes. This leads, in turn, to a linguistic atrophy caused by the non-use of a language. For a community, the term refers to a change from one language to another (e.g., immigrants in the United States tend to shift from the use of another language to English). As the shift becomes permanent, fluency in and mastery of the first-acquired language—Spanish, Chinese, Korean, or other—usually declines.

Language shift is usually talked about concomitantly with *language loss,* which is the process of losing proficiency—either limited or completely—in a language whether by an individual or a language community. A total and irreversible language loss may be described as language death.

Language death is total language loss—when there are no longer any speakers of that language. When the last native speaker of the language has died or the language is no longer used as a medium of communication, the language is considered "dead." Language death generally occurs when the older generation stops passing the language on to its children, the children refuse to speak the ancestral language, or when the speakers shift to using another language. In the United States, language death is usually linked to indigenous language minority communities such as Native Americans and Native Alaskans. In Alaska, of the 20 native languages still spoken, only 2 are being taught to the next generation. Since the arrival of the Europeans, hundreds of Native American languages have disappeared. Linguist Michael Krauss forecast that 45 Native American languages would lose their last native speakers by the year 2000, 125 by 2025, and 155 by 2050.

Many scholars and linguists are working actively to record languages before the languages die, whereas others are trying to revive endangered languages by creating language immersion schools for them, and encouraging parents and grandparents to pass the language onto their children and grandchildren. According to James Crawford, 90% of existing languages worldwide are likely to become extinct in the next century; only 10% of languages (approximately 600 languages) have a secure future. These dire predictions are echoed by the two most important scholars who advocate for language revival and language rights today: Joshua Fishman and Tove Skutnabb-Kangas.

Language Maintenance

Language maintenance also can take place within an individual or a community. Language maintenance occurs when language shift is staved off. It exists when speakers of a language (both adults and children) maintain proficiency in a language and retain the use of the language in various domains. A good sign of language maintenance is when older generations continue passing the language on to their children.

Many factors can influence whether a language is maintained or lost. Colin Baker, an authority on the subject, believes that 10 critical factors explain why some languages are kept and others lost: (1) number and density of speakers, (2) supply and resupply through immigration, (3) proximity to homeland and communication with homeland, (4) attitude toward homeland and rate of return, (5) stability of immigrant community (growth/decay), (6) economic stability of the group, (7) social mobility of the group, (8) economic utility of the mother tongue (native language), (9) level of education in the mother tongue, and (10) intensity of group identity with the mother tongue in the face of negative forces, such as discrimination or linguistic restrictionism.

Going further, Baker argues that other factors that affect language maintenance or loss of native or heritage languages are the following: (a) the presence or absence of *mother tongue* (MT) institutions (e.g., media, schools, community organizations, leisure activities); (b) the strength of cultural and religious activities in the MT; (c) the extent to which the MT is a recognized language of the homeland; (d) the salience of the MT as a marker of ethnic, family, or community identity; (e) the importance of the MT as a language for instruction; and (f) the degree of acceptance of the majority language in instruction.

Other research on heritage language maintenance has looked at variables such as gender, language attitudes, birth order, and speaker social networks as factors explaining why some maintain their heritage language but others lose it. Most of the important factors, however, are those identified by Baker.

Language Shift in the United States

Given Baker's emphasis on various factors why some languages are kept and others lost and his six factors that affect this process, it is natural to wonder if some immigrant groups are better at maintaining their native or heritage language than others are, or if maintenance is facilitated by the dominant society, for some language groups but not for others.

Based on Baker's list of factors, one might assume that Spanish speakers in the United States are better able to maintain their native or heritage language because there is a large number and density of speakers, a continual supply or resupply of immigrants, and close proximity between Mexico and the United States; this is a different scenario than that of Vietnamese speakers, who are much fewer in number and density of speakers, there is no continual supply or resupply of immigrants from Vietnam, and the distance between Vietnam and the United States is great. Russell Young and MyLuong Tran, researching a Vietnamese American group in California in 1999, found that a three-generation model of language shift holds true, even though an overwhelming majority of the parents surveyed reported that Vietnamese was the only language spoken at home. Although the children communicate with their parents in Vietnamese, a definite shift could be seen. More than half of the parents reported

that the children were using either English only, or a combination of Vietnamese and English in their interactions with their peers.

Interestingly, in 2006, researchers Ruben Rumbaut and Frank Bean at the University of California–Irvine, and Douglas Massey at Princeton University, found that Spanish speakers in southern California also follow the three-generation model of language shift and loss, and that by the third generation, most Hispanics speak English only. The researchers state that this pattern of language shift and loss holds true for other immigrant groups in the United States, such as Europeans and Chinese. Thus, despite the differences in the strength of factors as cited by Baker that may help some groups maintain their languages, the bulk of literature and research suggests that all language minority groups in the United States are continuing to follow a three-generation model language shift and loss process. This suggests that the maintenance of languages other-than-English is not propitiated; instead, cultural pressures actively discourage it. Evidence indicates that language maintenance in the United States is openly discouraged by social and educational policies of linguistic restrictionism.

Calvin Veltman, an American sociologist, demographer, and sociolinguist, asserts that one key misperception by many in the United States is that today's immigrants, unlike immigrants of yesteryear—especially Spanish speakers—are successfully resisting assimilation into American culture, not learning English, and holding onto their native languages. Some have even argued that immigrants are so good at maintaining their native languages that the dominance of the English language is threatened in the United States. This fear may stem from seeing and hearing the use of Spanish on billboards, on television, in automated phone messages, at grocery stores and other establishments, and in government documents (e.g., voter registration, driver's license applications). Veltman argues that no rejection of the English language is involved. Instead, the open use of Spanish does not mean that today's immigrants are better at maintaining their native languages than immigrants of previous generations but, rather, indicates that a large, continuous stream of Spanish-speaking immigrants is coming to the United States.

Overall, the literature regarding heritage language maintenance among immigrant groups reveals a three-generation model, with the first generation being dominant in the heritage language and slowly acquiring

English, the second generation speaking English in the school and other public domains and speaking the heritage language at home with family members, and the third generation becoming dominant in English with little, if any, proficiency in the heritage language. Thus, many grandchildren of immigrants become English monolinguals and are not able to speak with their grandparents who speak only the ancestral language. Many immigrants experience language shift and loss before the third generation, and it is not rare to find that this can happen to some immigrant children within one generation.

Consequences of Language Shift and Loss

That some children can lose their native or heritage language within one generation is particularly noteworthy because some immigrant parents may lose the ability to communicate effectively with their children. In a study by Lily Wong Fillmore and colleagues, more than 1,000 immigrant and American Indian families were interviewed to determine the extent to which family language patterns were affected by their children's early learning of English in preschool programs. The study found that as immigrant children learned English, the patterns of language use changed in their homes and that the younger the children were when they learned English, the greater the effect. An important aspect of this study is that immigrant children who attended Head Start programs became the change agents who determined what language would be spoken at home. The study also found that even though many of the parents were not fluent in English, if the children wanted to speak English at home, the parents would accommodate them by speaking English—even if the parents were not comfortable in that language. Young children, it appears, are powerful actors in the linguistic choices that go on in their communities.

Some public policies have unintended linguistic consequences. Evidence from the Wong Fillmore study suggests that as young children learn English, they lose their heritage languages. Some may argue that the Head Start program has been successful because it achieved its goal of helping the students get a "head start" by teaching them English so that they would not fall behind their peers. Persons concerned with language loss may argue, however, that the Head Start program contributes to the shift and eventual loss of immigrant languages, when it does not include

a language-maintenance component. It is not clear that a government-funded program such as Head Start should be responsible for the language cleavage that develops when children are no longer able to speak to their parents or grandparents. It can certainly be argued strongly that this is a parental prerogative. An interesting aspect of this research is that when parents were asked, "Are you worried about your children losing their heritage language?," many were not concerned about heritage language loss until after their children had stopped speaking their heritage language. By then, of course, it may have been too late for the families involved.

There are many arguments for language maintenance. One of the benefits of language maintenance is to prevent such consequences of language shift and loss as increased friction and conflict between immigrant parents and their children because parents are no longer able to pass on wisdom because of language and cultural barriers. The relationship between ethnic identity and heritage language learning was studied by Kiyomi Chinen and Richard Tucker. In a sample of Japanese American students, Chinen and Tucker assessed students' perception of their language skills in Japanese and their ethnic identity. The study findings revealed that both variables were strongly related.

Some scholars have used the ecological model argument (the beauty of linguistic diversity), whereas others give more pragmatic reasons such as that we are living in an increasingly global world and that speaking more than one language gives us a competitive edge in business. Others have argued that language maintenance and bilingualism are good because the United States needs people who can speak foreign languages for military purposes, and others argue for bilingualism because of its cognitive benefits.

Currently, immigration has been a hot topic in politics and legislation. Topics such as stricter enforcement of the U.S.–Mexico border, building a wall along the U.S.–Mexico border, and President George W. Bush's proposed guest worker program all have implications for language shift and language loss with respect to Spanish. Given a growing nativism in the United States, it is not surprising that legislation such as California's Proposition 227, Arizona's Proposition 203, and Massachusetts' Question 2 were passed; their effect has been, in essence, to restrict bilingual education programs in these states. By reducing the use of other languages and bilingual education programs, these measures have a powerful effect on the shift and loss of important languages. Indigenous language groups have not been the targets of this spate of legislation. They have been able to develop their own language immersion programs such as the Navajo Immersion Program at Ft. Defiance Elementary School in Arizona and the Ayaprun Elitnaurviat Immersion School in Alaska.

Some immigrant groups do not depend on the public schools to teach their heritage languages. Instead these groups (e.g., Chinese, Koreans, and Vietnamese) have organized weekend heritage language schools in their local communities to teach both the heritage language and culture. In particular, the Chinese and Korean communities have been particularly effective in creating weekend and after-school heritage language schools for their children. Many of these heritage language schools are organized in conjunction with local churches, temples, and community organizations.

Educators and community leaders now recognize that the phenomena of language shift and language loss are real and dramatically affect the lives of immigrant children and the future of their families. Various groups are attempting to address this need by creating resources such as John Webb and Barbara Miller's book *Teaching Heritage Language Learners: Voices from the Classroom* to help language teachers understand the different needs of heritage language learners, compared with those learning a language as a foreign language. The University of California, Los Angeles, has created the National Heritage Language Resource Center, whose focus is the development of effective pedagogical approaches to teaching heritage language learners by creating a research base and developing curriculum, materials, and teacher education resources. These institutional efforts provide useful resources to address issues of language shift and language loss in the United States. All are fairly recent; it remains to be seen how useful these will be in helping language communities restore their respective languages.

Ha Lam

See also Baker, Colin; Benefits of Bilingualism and Heritage Languages; Crawford, James; English for the Children Campaign; Fishman, Joshua A.; Krashen, Stephen D.

Further Readings

Baker, C. (2001). Languages in society. In C. Baker (Ed.), *Foundations of bilingual education and bilingualism* (3rd ed.). Clevedon, UK: Multilingual Matters.

Chinen, K., & Tucker, R. G. (2005). Heritage language development: Understanding the roles of ethnic identity and Saturday school participation. *Heritage Language Journal, 3*(1), 27–59.

Crawford, J. (2000). *At war with diversity: U.S. language policy in an age of anxiety.* Clevedon, UK: Multilingual Matters.

Fishman, J. A. (1972). *The sociology of language.* Rowley, MA: Newbury.

Hinton, L., & Hale, K. (Eds.) (2001). *The green book on language revitalization in practice.* New York: Academic Press.

Kouritzin, S. G. (1999). *Face(t)s of first language loss.* Mahwah, NJ: Lawrence Erlbaum.

Krauss, M. (1992). Statement of Mr. Michael Krauss representing the Linguistic Society of America. In U.S. Senate, Native American Languages Act of 1991: Hearing before the Select Committee on Indian Affairs (pp. 18–22).

Portes, A., & Rumbaut, R. G. (2006). *Immigrant America: A portrait* (3rd ed.). Los Angeles: University of California Press.

Rumbaut, R., Massey, D., & Bean, F. (2006). Linguistic life expectancies: Immigrant language retention in southern California. *Population and Development Review, 32*(3), 447–460.

Skutnabb-Kangas, T. (2000). *Linguistic genocide in education—or worldwide diversity and human rights?* Mahwah, NJ: Lawrence Erlbaum.

Veltman, C. (1983). *Language shift in the United States.* Berlin: Mouton de Gruyter.

Webb, J. B., & Miller, B. L. (Eds.) (2000). *Teaching heritage language learners: Voices from the classroom.* Yonkers, NY: American Council on the Teaching of Foreign Languages.

Wong Fillmore, L. (1991). When learning a second language means losing the first. *Early Childhood Research Quarterly, 6*, 323–346.

Young, R., & Tran, M. (1999). Vietnamese parent attitudes toward bilingual education. *Bilingual Research Journal, 23*(2–3), 225–234.

LANGUAGES IN COLONIAL SCHOOLS, EASTERN

In the history of education in the eastern United States, we find a tradition of cultural and linguistic diversity that predated the arrival of English-speaking settlers. Nearly 2,000 languages were spoken in the Western Hemisphere when the first European explorers arrived. Though the English language was important for participation in community life as part of a family, a congregation, and in the marketplace, other languages, including Dutch, German, Scandinavian languages, and indigenous languages were also common and important. This entry reviews a complex dialectic tension between English and other languages in education in selected Atlantic Coast colonies from the late 1500s to the birth of the nation in the late 1700s.

Virginia and New England

The original purpose of the colonization by English speakers of what is now roughly equivalent to Virginia in the late 1500s was economic gain. Only after work had begun on developing the land and infrastructure and learning how to survive in this new environment did women and tenants follow and families form to create a need for formal education in Roanoke and in a second settlement, Jamestown, also in Virginia. Over time, the purpose shifted from a search for gold to providing food for survival, and there was no clear understanding of a relationship between education and either of these purposes.

In the Virginia colonies, the trappings of community life—including families, government, and religion—contributed to a vision of using education to convert the children of Indians and settlers to the English language and culture. The vision was not realized, but it indicated recognition of an English colonial experience that would depend on self-sufficient agricultural and trading communities, the planting of families, and the development of English institutions that would educate families.

Intent on learning from the failures of the Virginia colonies, John Winthrop set out to establish a Puritan plantation in New England that would be profitable and of service to the church and the commonwealth. The Pilgrims came in 1620 for religious freedom, to preserve their cultural identity, and to convert others to their way of life. Education was conducted by the family and the churches, rather than by a school or college. Both the Puritans and the Pilgrims came to the colony as a community, but the Puritans also brought with them a vision of a community that modeled Christian charity. Within this mission, the education of the sons played an important role in transmitting an English-speaking intellectual heritage and serving as an agency for the pursuit of an English cultural ideal.

New Amsterdam

In 1624, the Dutch established New Amsterdam in what is now Manhattan, the Hudson River Valley northward to what is now Albany, New York, and western Long Island. New Amsterdam was a commercial trading post, and Dutch-speaking inhabitants were apparently more occupied, at least early on, with survival and building thriving businesses than with educating their children. By 1638, the first elementary school was established, and in 1652, the first formal instruction in the classics was introduced. The Dutch were the most numerous but there were speakers of other languages in that colony, including the English, French-speaking Belgians, Swedes, Finns, French, Portuguese, and Africans. Though government, education, architecture, and churches were characteristically Dutch, official communication was normally in more than one language.

Eventually, the English captured New Amsterdam, and the inhabitants continued using their languages and practicing their cultural traditions. Language instruction fell to the church, but in New Amsterdam, language instruction was multilingual. It happened in many different languages. Where there were Dutch schools, instruction continued in Dutch, even after the English conquest in 1674. During the first 30 years of English rule, education was relatively open. Though the colony was governed in English, there was a willingness to permit diversity of belief, worship, instruction, and language.

New Sweden

The Swedes, with Dutch support, founded New Sweden in 1638 as a commercial trading center in the territory where Wilmington, Delaware, southeastern Pennsylvania, and southern New Jersey now are. The project failed after 17 years, and the Dutch took over in 1655, followed by the English a decade later. Although the Swedes attempted to preserve their language and culture under English domination, they gradually took on English language and ways.

Like neighboring Pennsylvania, New Sweden was a colony without an established church. Most young people in New Sweden received their vocational education via apprenticeships. The Bible and the catechism were the only frequently read books, and book learning in Swedish, or any of the other languages represented in the colony, was generally left to the religious authorities. Young Swedes learned to read the Bible and catechism in Swedish. The language of instruction was Swedish to ensure its preservation in the colony. Instruction and literacy in Swedish was of lower priority, though, than was ensuring enough provisions to survive the winter.

Some assert that respect for education was slow in coming. As the need for education shifted from religious and cultural goals toward commercial ones, the Swedes began to take on the English language ways. Under English domination, older Swedes resisted assimilation into the English way of life. However, younger Swedes grew so accustomed to the English language that they became reluctant to express themselves in Swedish. Israel Acrelius, provost of the Swedish churches in America, saw this language confusion as a symptom of a more basic conflict of culture between the Swedish and the English during the colonial period.

As early as 1654, the Scotch-Irish began to establish themselves in New Sweden. However, their first academies were more noted for their students' enthusiasm than their academic achievement. Later, the academies focused more deeply on reason and theological knowledge based in Presbyterianism. English- and Welsh-speaking Quakers also established schools so that their sons and daughters learned reading, writing, and arithmetic. As the settlers improved their economic conditions, they saw to it that their children received an elementary education. In some cases, teachers were purchased as indentured servants, an arrangement reflecting the low status of people in the teaching profession. Over time, teachers opened their own schools. Vocational education, including professions such as law and medicine, was provided within the family or by apprenticeship. The first Swedish-language school in the colony was opened before 1700 in the Old Swedes' Church. During the last half of the 18th century, the leading educational institution was the Wilmington Academy, which was built in 1765. Before 1791, no provision was made for free schools. In Delaware's state constitution of 1791, provision was made for establishing schools, and in 1796, an act was passed by the legislature applying all moneys received from marriage and tavern licenses to a school fund, paving the way for a public school system.

Pennsylvania

Pennsylvania was founded in 1681 by the English as a holy experiment. English- and Welsh-speaking Quakers and German Protestants organized their own communities within Pennsylvania in which they preserved their respective languages and cultures. The first German arrivals were predominantly Mennonite and Amish and were joined later by Lutherans and Reformed and other Protestant sects. Presbyterian Scotch-Irish followed in the early 1700s. In 1756, an estimated third of the population was English- or Welsh-speaking Quaker, another third German, and among the rest were speakers of English, Scottish, Scotch-Irish, French, Celtic Irish, Dutch, and Swedish.

In 1683, a Pennsylvania ordinance provided that all children be instructed in reading and writing until age 12. Thereafter, they should be taught a trade or skill so that they become self-sufficient adults. However, this apparently straightforward requirement would be a challenge because of the linguistic diversity of the colony. Of all the immigrant groups, the most challenging to the English in Pennsylvania were the Germans because, of all the non-English-speaking groups, the Germans were the most numerous. Because of a fear that the English would be Germanized instead of the Germans Anglicized, various measures to control Germans were recommended, but not implemented, including the prohibition of German-language publications, the establishment of English language schools, the introduction of an English language literacy requirement, and encouragement of intermarriage of English and Germans. This fear was also instrumental in the establishment of charity schools that provided for the cultural Anglicization of the Germans.

Money to support the establishment of these schools was raised by the English in Holland and Scotland. Some maintain that the most important impact on the Germans of these efforts was the stimulation of their own effort to preserve the German language and culture. Though the Germans maintained separate schools and churches and a college to train their own religious and civic leaders to preserve the German language and culture, they eventually recognized the necessity to read, write, and speak English.

Within Diversity, English Predominates

A number of language and cultural dynamics bear on colonial education. First, education was a family enterprise for which the family looked to the church for assistance. Clergy provided children instruction in the home language, and the Scriptures and catechism were the primary texts. Second, in some cases, everyone in the colony spoke the same language. In other cases, many different languages were used. Third, the purpose of education was to transmit the language and culture. Its purpose was not to educate for vocation. Fourth, public schools as we know them were not commonplace, and where something like a public school did exist, its purpose was to Anglicize rather than preserve indigenous or other languages and cultures. Fifth, the early settlers did not take financial responsibility for establishing public schools. Sixth, the northern colonists' primary motivation for coming to the New World was to escape religious persecution, and the southern colonists' primary motivation was generally to achieve economic well-being. The middle colonists' motivation reflected varying degrees of both. In Pennsylvania, especially, the English invited oppressed Europeans with the promise of a better life, but there were pressures to live that better life in English. Seventh, although education was considered important in the northern colonies to preserve the English language and religious culture, it was of lesser importance in the middle colonies and of least importance in the southern colonies. In short, although the English speakers were not ardent promoters of their language, they apparently outdid everyone else, who seemed not to notice that their own languages were slowly eroding in favor of English.

Finally, the settlers depended on continuing financial support from their homelands to support educational activities designed to preserve their languages and cultures. The English also relied on the homeland for financial support to Anglicize other settlers. Perhaps the English sources of support were more generous. Rarely was an effort made to learn the language of the indigenous people, though on occasion such attempts were made.

Just as it is important to consider what was today's immigrants' prior history in their countries of origin, it is also important to consider the social context of the early settlers. The English shared a common heritage with the Dutch, the Spanish, the French, and others on the European continent. Notwithstanding the rivalries of royal families, the concept of the nation-state had not yet hardened into the strict lines of demarcation that came about in the 18th and 19th centuries accompanied by nationalistic fervor. Upper-class English read the Bible and the literature of great thinkers from Ancient Greece and Rome, and the peasant class was beginning to enjoy secular pursuits, including

Shakespeare's dramas. The English also embraced the ideas of contemporaries such as Erasmus (a Dutchman) and Montaigne (a Frenchman), among other continental Europeans. Also, the English culture itself was changing. For example, there were struggles between Protestant and Catholic, Anglican and Puritan, scientist and humanist, among others, in England. These struggles played themselves out to a certain extent in the New World as well and merit consideration when pondering language and education policies and practices in the eastern colonies.

Particularly pertinent is the struggle between medieval and Renaissance thinking that was taking place in Europe at the time of the North American explorations. Though Renaissance thinking may have motivated the settlers to make the journey to the New World, medieval thinking still operated strongly in their worldviews. Lawrence Cremin reports that the English, above all in Europe, were the earliest to capitalize on the great information and communications technology of the age: the printing press. The printing press was possibly the most important invention in ushering in the Renaissance era in northern Europe. Though a German invention, there was no German state organized to harness the power of the press. The European English were better organized to produce and use print materials to facilitate the transformation of their citizenry to critical thinkers, learners, and leaders. They were also better organized to support the development of print media to Anglicize others in the New World. An interesting parallel today is the prevalence of English on the Internet where, once again, the technology comes with English thrown in, free of charge.

New situations encountered in the New World required a rethinking of the medieval worldview. Edward Gray and Norman Fiering assert that the prevailing explanation in Europe at that time regarding language diversity involved the Biblical account of the Tower of Babel: With the fall of the Tower of Babel, 72 mutually unintelligible languages arose. When the settlers encountered many more indigenous languages in the New World, they needed new ways to align the Biblical story with the new reality. When they found an abundance of languages and cultures in non-Christian North America, the European settlers interpreted the language diversity that they found as an indication of social decay. European settlers learned Native American languages and with the indigenous people developed pidgins such as Pidgin

Delaware as tools more geared to Anglicization of Native American peoples than to mutual understanding. Another purpose served by learning indigenous languages and pidgins was to satisfy the settlers' real need to know more about their new environment by learning about it from the indigenous peoples who had already experienced it. With this knowledge, they would be better prepared to survive the cold, harsh winters. In neither case was the indigenous peoples' concept of well-being a primary consideration. Learning and using indigenous languages was not a school-based activity. Where it did occur, it usually happened in the harsher environments of the receding frontier as the settlers moved west.

Some might argue that the English used their resourcefulness heavy-handedly in new social and physical situations they encountered in the New World. For instance, in the early days of the new nation, African slaves were denied access to education in any language because of fear that they would be able to read the abolition literature, thus threatening the economic balance in the South. Though linguistic and cultural diversity existed in the colonies, a linguistic and cultural pluralism that placed English and other languages at parity with each other never took root in institutional educational settings. The education historian Joel Spring goes one step further. He argues that educational practices during the colonial period paved the way for using schools to impose English language and culture on others throughout U.S. history.

Elsie M. Szecsy

See also German Language Education; Languages in Colonial Schools, Western

Further Readings

Acrelius, I. (1966/1874). *A history of New Sweden.* Ann Arbor, MI: University Microfilms.

Axtell, J. (2000). Babel of tongues: Communicating with the Indians in eastern North America. In E. G. Gray & N. Fiering (Eds.), *The language encounter in the Americas, 1492–1800: A collection of essays* (pp. 15–60). New York: Berghahn Books.

Cremin, L. A. (1970). *American education: The colonial experience.* New York: Harper & Row.

Goddard, I. (2000). The use of pidgins and jargons on the East Coast of North America. In E. G. Gray & N. Fiering (Eds.), *The language encounter in the Americas,*

1492–1800: A collection of essays (pp. 61–78). New York: Berghahn Books.

Gray, E. G. (1999). *New World babel: Languages & nations in Early America.* Princeton, NJ: Princeton University Press.

Gray, E. G. & Fiering, N. (2000). *The language encounter in the Americas, 1492–1800: A collection of essays.* New York: Berghahn Books.

Munroe, J. A. (1978). *Colonial Delaware: A history.* Millwood, NY: KTO Press.

Spring, J. (2005). *The American school: 1642–2000* (6th ed.). New York: McGraw-Hill.

LANGUAGES IN COLONIAL SCHOOLS, WESTERN

From the arrival of Hernán Cortés in Mexico in 1519 to 1821 when Mexico won independence from colonial rule, Spain actively sought to Christianize and "Castilianize" native populations. The Spanish sought to expand the Spanish empire and culture, including their language, to the farthest reaches of the New World. In this version of colonial education, bilingual instruction in mission schools was used much more than in the English colonies and their Native American neighbors. This entry examines that phenomenon in brief fashion.

To achieve their colonizing goals, the Spaniards brought Catholic missionaries to conduct the work of Christianization. Every military excursion also brought missionaries; the sword and the cross traveled together. Spanish missionaries established chains of missions throughout the Americas that defined colonial life for 300 years. The mission system became the single most powerful vehicle for achieving control of the landscape of New Spain. Language, religion, education, culture, law, social customs, economy, and even clothing all flowed from the missions. Little wonder that they played such a key role in establishing Spanish as the lingua franca in New Spain, and in creating an enduring Mexican presence in the American territories.

With the signing of the Treaty of Guadalupe Hidalgo in 1848, the United States took possession of the southwestern states. Under the new English-speaking nation, *mestizos*—the term used to describe the offspring of Spanish and Indians—experienced a fleeting tolerance for their culture and language for several decades, but the advent of mandatory school attendance laws ultimately ended non-English languages from the schools. The push for Americanization ushered in deep-seated prejudices. In an ironic twist of fate, the language of the Spanish conquerors would become a primary identity marker for *mestizos,* later known as Mexicans, Hispanics, and Latinos. The Spanish language would serve as the unifying force for the steady influx of other Spanish speakers migrating to the United States. The tenacity of these groups in retaining Spanish would remain a symbol of resistance to total assimilation into the American mainstream.

Background

Spain was among the most powerful nations in the world in the late 15th century. With the expulsion of the Moors and Jews from Spain, it garnered special favor from Pope Alexander I, who granted the Spanish crown authority over the Catholic Church under its domain. In 1493, a year after Columbus's first voyage to the Americas, the pope divided the unexplored territories in the Western Hemisphere, ceding to Spain North America, Central America and a large portion of South America, including the islands of the Caribbean. A steady stream of Spanish explorers fanned out into the New World, laying claim to the new frontier in the name of Spain. Cortés and his men arrived in Mexico City in 1519. In the name of Christianity, they destroyed the indigenous civilization in the valley of Mexico and implanted Spanish colonial control in what would be known as the "New Spain."

Genesis of the Mission Model in Mexico

After settling in Tenochtitlán (the Aztec capital), Cortés petitioned King Carlos V for missionaries, soldiers, masons, carpenters, and other skilled workers to help establish more permanent settlements in Mexico. The Flemish Franciscan Brother Peter Van der Moere of Ghent (known in New Spain as Pedro de Gante) spent the first few years in Texcoco, second largest city after Tenochtitlán, before moving to the latter to establish a school.

Gante found a hostile climate in Tenochtitlán, where Cortés wanted the school. The bloody and violent overthrow of the capital had left the Aztecs distrustful of the conquerors. Despite Spanish power at his disposal, Pedro de Gante realized that teaching the Aztecs would be a monumental challenge. Further, he understood that changing the culture and customs of an entire nation required a more organic approach. This meant that it was more essential to educate the masses than the privileged classes. Teaching the common man had potential for uplifting cultural values from the ground up and changing the oppressive treatment of women and children. Convinced that his educational plan was sound, he agreed to open a school in 1527.

Eager to make Gante's school endeavor successful, Cortés overreached. He ordered his men to round up all the young boys they could find and hold them within the mission enclosure. Parents objected vehemently, and the boys rebelled in anger. Teaching religion to more than a thousand boys held against their will was an unsatisfying and frustrating situation. Gante was nearly overcome with frustration and was tempted to return to Flanders. His vow of obedience, however, obliged him to ponder his plight carefully.

Fusion of Spanish and Native Cultures

After futile attempts to teach the defiant students and after much reflection, Gante arrived at an important insight: He needed to integrate Aztec culture as a link to the boys' lived experiences to pique their interest in learning. Having lived in the region of Texcoco for 3 years, he had observed Aztec enthusiasm for music, dance, and performance. Wasting little time, he began with singing and dancing lessons. To the boys' surprise and delight, Gante himself participated in the dancing and singing. Demonstrating respect for their culture earned him the boys' trust. As a way to manage the large group, Gante selected 20 of the brightest students to assist with the teaching. They received special instruction before Gante's introduction of the lesson to the whole class. In this way, he was able to manage the large group of students. The student leaders' fluency in Nahuatl, the language of the Aztecs, and their intimate knowledge of Aztec cultural traditions contributed to their own conversion.

Without conceding basic tenets of Catholic doctrine, Gante incorporated culture and art in his instruction, allowing an outlet for creative expression. His approach proved effective in maintaining student interest. Centuries later, in the context of the United States, the idea of adapting instruction to native cultures would become a prime tenet of bilingual and multicultural pedagogy.

Treatment of Indigenous Languages

Communication with indigenous people was daunting. But, unlike English-speaking settlers in the United States who worked at eradicating Indian languages, Spanish missionaries embraced the native languages of their converts as tools for teaching. For those early clerics, it was self-evident that success in converting the natives required two basic principles: First, learn the native language, and second, use the native language for instruction. Imposing Spanish would have been viewed as a sign of arrogance and disrespect, inciting greater resistance to conversion. Aside from its pedagogical merit, dealing with natives in their mother tongue reflected a sign of good will and served as a method of self-preservation for the friars who worked in hostile surroundings. Gante had studied Nahuatl in Texcoco where he also started recording the Nahuatl sounds using the Latin alphabet. In this way, he developed a written alphabet for Nahuatl that he later used to write a book on Catholic doctrine.

Breadth and Scope of the Missions

The typical mission structure was designed as a quadrangle. It included a church, a private residence for the priests, a mission school, a dormitory on one side for boys, another on the opposite side for girls, a kitchen, infirmary, and several workrooms. In the expansive American frontier, missions also functioned as garrisons, providing shelter, food, and protection for the Christianized Indians against the abuses of soldiers and civilians, warring tribes, and other European settlers. Missions were made possible by royal land grants situated in prime, strategic locations. Spanish monarchs and wealthy lay patrons paid for the creation and operation of the mission schools in an early form of school-community partnerships. Viceroys in the various regions of New Spain exercised authority over church and state matters, paying missionary salaries, setting administrative policies, providing military protection, and enforcing colonial law.

Organization of Mission Life

The missionaries' long-term goal was to establish independent Christian towns where property, resources, and labor served the common good and operated under their absolute control. Although missions were not militarized, nor were natives (with few exceptions) physically forced to convert, but once baptized, converts were required to live in the mission complex. They were forbidden to leave or have contact with outsiders. Mission Indians lived under constant supervision, following a strict monastic-like lifestyle that included prayer, catechism, academic instruction, work, chores, meals, and recreation. Boys were taught agricultural and industrial skills; girls were taught sewing, cooking, quilting, weaving, spinning, and other domestic skills considered essential for marriage. Catholic holidays and liturgical celebrations broke the monotony of everyday life.

Missionaries raised horses, cattle, and other domestic farm animals brought from Spain. Neophytes were taught farming, cattle raising, ranching, and whatever agricultural and industrial skills were needed for the day-to-day operation of the mission complex. Missionaries also planted indigenous crops and myriad European vegetables, herbs, and fruits. In time, the missions became profitable enterprises, raising a substantial number of cattle and producing an abundance of vegetables, grains, and fruit for themselves as well as for sale to the locals.

Academic Curriculum

Along with the practical skills necessary for the operation of the mission, students were taught counting, reading, and writing in Nahuatl. Latin and Spanish as foreign languages were added later. Because of the clergy's strong tradition and talent in music, song, and musical instruments, these fine arts were also incorporated in the early curricula of the mission schools. In effect, each mission became a microcosm of Spanish civilization. This organization of Spanish missions in Mexico proved so successful that elements of it were incorporated into the state laws of California, Texas, New Mexico, Louisiana, Arizona, Florida, Georgia, and the Carolinas. Even today, several of these states retain elements of Spanish law side-by-side with English common law that prevailed on the Atlantic seaboard.

The power and influence of the Franciscan missionaries over the early colonial settlements and emerging towns became a source of envy among the increasing Spanish population and secular clergy that ministered to persons outside the missions. Missionary priests had a monopoly over the missions. Under pain of excommunication, no one could interfere in their work—not even secular priests charged with the spiritual ministry of civilians. Autonomy over the operation of the missions allowed missionaries to exert great power and influence. As each mission became self-sufficient, colonial authorities petitioned the king for secularization of the missions. Secularization entailed transferring control of the missions to civilian authorities and secular clergy. Lacking the educational background, discipline, organizational skills, goals, and earned respect of the missionary priests, civilians failed to keep the missions prosperous and intact. Ultimately, most of the missions declined and fell into dysfunctional remnants of their former glory.

Duplicating the Mission Model in the United States

As the French and English competed for territories in the American frontier, the Spanish moved quickly to establish missions in those regions as a way to retain the land for Spain. Jesuit and Franciscan missionaries moved into Florida, Georgia, the Carolinas, Texas, New Mexico, Arizona, and California. There, they emulated the mission model they had developed in Mexico and the state of Baja California. Frontier missions, however, were difficult to sustain because they were located in isolated areas and far from Mexico's protection. Missionaries lived in hostile surroundings and suffered extreme hardships trying to make them prosper. Many missions were destroyed or razed, but others, notably those in California, endured and still exist, albeit with different goals. They serve as a reminder of the singular, most powerful vehicle for the transmission of Spanish/Mexican culture.

Florida, Georgia, and the Carolinas

Juan Ponce de León landed in the southeast territory of the United States in April 1513. He named it *la Pascua Florida,* commemorating Easter Sunday, the day of his arrival. The territory of *La Florida* extended from present-day Florida north to the Chesapeake Bay. De León explored the territory up to the Carolinas and attempted to establish a colony in what is now Charlotte Harbor in 1521, but the Calusa Indians attacked his party, seriously wounding him, and forcing him to retreat to Cuba, where he later died. Jesuit missionaries established a mission in St. Augustine, Florida. From there, they proceeded north, building missions among the Apalachees in Georgia and the Carolinas. Missionary efforts to convert the natives, however, met with limited success because of adverse conditions, Indian resistance, and difficulty in confining Indians to the missions. Positioned on the Atlantic coast, *La Florida* was a dangerous front line because the area served as a primary entry into mainland territory for the steady influx of European explorers. Missions in Florida doubled as forts, providing a modicum of safety for missionaries, their converts, and Spanish civilians against English and French invaders.

In 1573, Franciscan missionaries replaced the Jesuits in Florida, and although, they, too, faced great challenges, they were more successful in establishing enduring missions. They organized a school for the children of the soldiers in the local garrison. As they had done elsewhere, missionaries planted crops and raised livestock, providing essential food staples. Few details exist concerning the inner workings of mission schools in *La Florida,* but recent archeological discoveries of Indian-language Bibles and catechisms written with Spanish phonetics are proof that the missionaries provided Catholic doctrine in at least some of the indigenous languages of the region. Although those languages became extinct, the Indian-language books survived.

More than one hundred Spanish missions were established from 1526 to 1702 in what are now the states of Florida, Georgia, and the Carolinas. At various intervals, however, each mission was abandoned because of inadequate resources, inability to protect themselves, epidemics, Indian resistance, and annihilation of the friars. English colonists wrestling for control of Florida also pillaged and destroyed a number of missions in this area. The English and their Indian allies committed atrocities against the Spanish Apalachees in Georgia and the Carolinas, killing the missionaries and capturing Hispanicized Indians as slaves for the thriving plantations in South Carolina. The city of St. Augustine, founded in 1565, holds the distinction of being the oldest town in the United States. Franciscans maintained a mission at St. Augustine that later evolved into the first school for Whites. This school existed one year before the arrival of the English in Jamestown and operated 30 years before an English language school was established in North America.

New Mexico, Texas, and Louisiana Territories

During this Spanish/Mexican era, New Mexico, Texas, and western Louisiana were part of a sprawling territory that explorer Juan de Oñate called "the Kingdom of Saint Francis of the New Mexico." In 1540, Francisco Vasquez de Coronado explored the territory north of New Spain in the area now known as West Texas. Eight Franciscan missionaries who accompanied him chose to stay behind to begin the conversion of the natives, but failed to establish permanent settlements in Texas. In 1558, Oñate led another group of Franciscans to New Mexico, where they founded the first permanent settlement, Mission San Gabriel, in what is now San Juan Pueblo. They worked among the Pueblo Indians. For more than a decade, this settlement served as the capital of New Mexico before the capital was moved to Santa Fe. By 1598, Franciscans had operated mission schools for 75 years.

In Taos, Pecos, and Santa Fe, missionaries set up more schools where they taught catechism, reading, writing, and music, including agricultural and industrial arts. Pueblo Indians in Santa Fe and nearby pueblos learned new techniques for their various crafts. It is difficult to determine the exact number of mission schools opened in the territory of New Mexico, but according to archives, there were at least 59 friaries with each friary housing one or more schools.

Franciscans converted and taught a large number of natives in the New Mexican territory, but faced ongoing resistance. Even as the Franciscans reached their "golden era" of mission work, the Indian pueblos rebelled against Spanish colonization, killing 21 Franciscans and 400 civilians and soldiers. As a result, the missionaries moved to Albuquerque, where they established other mission schools. In Albuquerque, the friars introduced horses, cattle, and sheep, teaching the Indians to breed and care for the animals. The friars also introduced Indians to improved methods of spinning and weaving. Hostile Indian tribes eventually destroyed the missions and pushed the Catholic friars to present-day El Paso, Texas. In small towns and villages within the current Texas border, the friars established 26 missions and outposts. The semi-nomadic lives of Texas Indians worked against the cloistered life required of converts. Indians rebelled, and the Spaniards failed to establish enduring settlements throughout the vast territory of Texas, with the exception of El Paso, San Antonio, and the Rio Grande Valley.

Texas missions did not flourish as well as those in California but were instrumental in creating the foundation for the strong presence of Spanish and Mexican culture that exists today. By the late 1700s, a large number of Indians in Texas were fully assimilated into the Spanish and Indian culture of the towns, becoming devout, Spanish-speaking Catholics. With their Spanish names given to them by the missionaries, they were indistinguishable from other mestizos of the region. A testament of Pedro de Gante's philosophy of education and the staying power of Spanish was evident as late as 1890 to 1898 in the El Paso public schools' requirement that English-speaking teachers pass a Spanish exam to teach the large number of Spanish speaking students.

California

Father Junípero Serra led a team of Franciscan missionaries into present-day California in 1769. They founded a chain of 21 missions along the west coast of California, from present-day San Diego near the Mexican border to San Francisco. Each mission was located one day's horseback ride from the other, along a trail named *La Calle Real* (the Royal Highway). In California, as elsewhere, missionaries were not all saintly, equally kind, or above reproach. Those who demonstrated genuine concern for the physical, spiritual, and intellectual welfare of the Indians, however, quickly earned their trust and cooperation. Other missionaries who took more authoritarian approaches, resorting to force and exploitation, faced Indian resistance, retaliation, and revolts.

Teaching took place in various Indian languages, but proved a constant challenge. In some cases, there was a different language every 10 to 15 miles. Records indicate that at Mission San Francisco, the friars taught in five different native languages. For the most part, California mission schools followed a traditional curriculum similar to the one designed in Mexico. As the neophytes became more fluent in Spanish, the missionaries used both the native language and Spanish in their instruction. Indian converts attended schools in the missions where they were confined for the duration of their schooling. Girls were required to reside in the monastery. At night, they were locked inside the *monjerío* (nunnery), which served as their living quarters, and were supervised by a *maestra* (female teacher). A misnomer, the *monjerío* was not a convent. The girls were neither preparing to become nuns, nor did they remain there for life. Alongside mission schools, colonial towns across the Spanish/ Mexican territories had secular clerics and Catholic nuns who ran private Catholic schools for the children of Spaniards and Creoles in the community. Instruction in those schools was in Spanish.

All missions were completely secularized in the late 18th century. Along with secularization, a royal decree required that all schools in the empire abandon the use of native languages and institute Spanish as the official language. Many Franciscan missionaries throughout the Spanish settlements in U.S. territories ignored the new policy and quietly continued using the native languages. Some missionaries in Texas welcomed the new directives, arguing that Hispanicization was so complete in some towns that there was little need for Indian languages. California missions were among the largest in the Spanish empire. San Luis Rey Mission, for example, sprawled across 90,000 acres of land. In the mid-1830s, it owned 50,500 head of cattle, approximately 29,000 sheep, 5,000 horses, and an enormous number of pigs, goats, and other domestic animals. Franciscan missionaries wielded so much economic power over the Indians and Catholic laity, and the missions had accumulated so much wealth that those two factors alone intensified the push for total secularization. Most California missions still exist in their original or restored condition, and although they were secularized, many continue to operate as viable Catholic churches. An excellent example of this longevity and continued service is the church at San Luis Rey near present-day San Diego.

Arizona

Franciscan missionaries arrived in Hopi land in 1630. They endeavored to establish the Mexican mission model in there too, beginning with *la doctrina* (Catholic doctrine) and following with basic reading and writing skills. Instruction was reserved for Christian converts; others were not included. Brighter students were taught Latin and Spanish in addition to the basic curriculum. The task of evangelization was not easy; missionaries faced great obstacles. In due time, however, they built a monastery in the center of Hopi territory. The isolation of the missions made them easy targets for Indian raids. Fearing this constant danger, the Franciscans ordered Spanish soldiers to build a garrison for their protection and the protection of their wards. Hopi Indians objected to their militarized encroachment and stormed the construction site, killing the priests and their converts, and destroying the monastery.

Southern Arizona missions were originally founded by Jesuit missionaries who worked in the northern part of Mexico in the area of present-day Mexican states of Sonora, Durango, Chihuahua, and Sinaloa, but their missions extended into a portion of Arizona. On the Mexican side, the Jesuits founded mission schools and colleges. Indian resistance was generally the rule. Many had witnessed multiple atrocities against their people, so they fought back, ultimately killing all the Jesuit missionaries.

Despite their losses and constant attacks from the Tarahumara and Yaqui Indians, the Jesuits persisted. By 1691, Father Eusebio Francisco Kino stretched the missionary work into the territory of the Pima Indians along the Gila River in Arizona. Father Kino brought another cleric and a team of Sonora Indians to help with the construction of the mission and instruction of the natives in this region. Pleased with the initial response, he took hundreds of head of cattle from Sonora to help support the mission. Father Kino specialized in teaching adult Indians. His genuine affection for Indians was known throughout the territory. In his youth, the Pueblo Indians referred to him affectionately as El Padre Negro. Later they nicknamed him *el viejito* (the old one) and sat around for hours listening to his stories and teachings. Kino used visual aids to teach his converts until he mastered their languages. He also organized a children's school. The Jesuits remained in Arizona for 100 years before the pope expelled them from all the territories. Franciscan missionaries took over their work in southern Arizona.

Conclusion

The Spanish established hundreds of missions throughout the vast territories of New Spain. Those missions operated schools and churches that served as effective tools for social reproduction of Spanish culture, solidifying and expanding the Spanish empire, and spreading the Spanish language among indigenous peoples. Many mission settlements became large profitable enterprises, giving missionaries tremendous influence and control over the lives of people within the mission and the surrounding areas. The Spanish were successful in establishing Christian towns and colonizing millions of indigenous peoples. Mestizos became the majority in Mexico and a large segment of the population in the expanding American colonies. When the U.S. Declaration of Independence was signed in 1776, most people within what is now the United States were probably Spanish speakers—from the Californios on the West Coast to the Spanish-speaking Apalachees in Georgia and the criollos of Florida.

Unlike the English, who intentionally worked at eradicating indigenous languages and cultures, and rejected the notion of mixed racial unions, the Spanish were interested in saving their souls. Catholic doctrine and royal policies dictated that indigenous peoples were human beings with rights, deserving protection by the Spanish crown and its representatives. This dictate was not always obeyed; abuses abounded throughout the empire. Three centuries of mounting resistance from Creoles and Mexican elite against Spanish exploitation erupted in 1810 with Father Miguel Hidalgo's call for independence from Spain. Although mestizos outnumbered the Spanish 10 to one, the bloody battle for independence lasted 11 years, ending in 1821. The new Republic of Mexico, however, was unable to retain possession of the huge expanses of land in what is now the U.S. Southwest. With the signing of the Treaty of Guadalupe Hidalgo in 1848, Mexico lost those territories to the United States. Despite this loss, missions were instrumental in building an enduring Mexican cultural presence. Today, the missions that are still standing are chiefly museums and historical points of interest throughout the Southwest.

In Mexico, secularization also changed the role and function of the missions. Secularization brought with it the end of Indian schooling by the Spanish. The Spanish crown had ordered colonial schools throughout the empire to serve exclusively for Spanish-speaking children. The king's directive was not closely followed in the frontier colonies, but pressure to shift the academic curriculum for Indians to an industrial curriculum began to mount. Often, the deep-seated prejudices of the Spanish and, later, of the Mexican elite began to question whether advanced studies for Indians (and the lower classes) were essential when they were unlikely to use such knowledge. Furthermore, the elites argued that Indians were better suited for agricultural and industrial skills. In many communities, those colonial attitudes are still evident in the public education system in Mexico,

which serves the poor and rural descendents of the early residents of the Spanish missions.

Maria de la Luz Reyes

See also Languages in Colonial Schools, Eastern; Language Socialization of Indigenous Children; Native American Languages, Legal Support for; Spanish, the Second National Language; Spanish Loan Words in U.S. English

Further Readings

Blanton, C. K. (2004). *The strange career of bilingual education in Texas, 1836–1981.* Kingsville: Texas A&M University Press.

Cardenas, M. L. (1984). *Legacy of Mexico to the philosophy of American education.* Unpublished PhD Dissertation, Arizona State University, Tempe.

Heath, S. B. (1972). *Telling tongues: Language policy in Mexico, colony to nation.* New York: Teachers College Press.

Palfrey, D. H. (1998). *Mexico's colonial era, Part II: Religion & Society in New Spain.* Retrieved from http://mex connect.com/mex_/travel/dpalfrey/dpcolonial2.html

Weber, D. J. (1992). *The Spanish frontier in North America.* New Haven, CT: Yale University Press.

Wright, R. (2001). Spanish missions. In *The handbook of Texas online.* Retrieved from http://www.tsha.utexas.edu/handbook/online/articles/SS/its2.html

LANGUAGE SOCIALIZATION

Language socialization refers to the process by which individuals acquire the knowledge and practices that enable them to participate effectively in a language community. Based on concepts related to language acquisition and anthropology, language socialization theory is a theory of language learning that argues that one learns language and culture simultaneously. In other words, when someone learns a language, by definition that person is also learning culture. From a language socialization perspective, language and culture are inseparable; that is, one is simultaneously learning language (linguistic knowledge) and acquiring sociocultural knowledge (how to use language in context).

Language socialization theory differs from other theories of socialization in that it argues that language is the primary symbolic medium through which cultural knowledge is communicated, and therefore reproduced. Specifically, language socialization theory developed as a response to other theories of first-language acquisition prevalent in the 1960s and 1970s that did not consider the sociocultural context, and instead focused on the internal, cognitive aspects of language learning.

Initially, language socialization theory was developed as an explanation for infants' and young children's development of their first language. Early scholars and the main architects of this theory, Elinor Ochs and Bambi Schieffelin, examined the process of first-language acquisition in a cultural context through detailed ethnographic studies of small, often isolated monolingual societies. From these studies, a view emerged explaining that the process of learning a language is a social activity that relies on the building up of routines of interactions. This early work, although not directly focused on issues of bilingualism and bilingual education, paved the way for other studies that directly addressed the issue of how language socialization in the home could differentially affect the experiences of children when they attend school.

Beginning in the 1990s, a second generation of studies in language socialization broadened the scope of research to look explicitly at the processes of socialization in cultural contexts other than the home environment. These studies focused on understanding the processes of language socialization in bilingual and multilingual contexts. This entry describes the development of language socialization theory.

Roots of Language Socialization Theory

Language socialization theory portrays a developmental process through which children learn how to speak like adults do, and therefore, they learn to become adults. Ochs and Schieffelin, drawing on the work of linguistic anthropologists Dell Hymes and John Gumperz, characterized societies as having a fairly fixed and predetermined set of norms, values, and rules for behavior, which children acquire through their interactions with adults in the process of everyday life. Through participation in everyday social interactions, children engage in and internalize the practices of the society. Over time, through practice in routines and regular activities, children become more and more skilled in the social practices considered appropriate in their communities. For example, through their participation, children learn when it is

appropriate to speak or be silent, when it is appropriate to tell jokes or be serious, and when it is appropriate to talk about certain topics and not others. In addition to "when" children also learned "how" to speak, joke, and be serious. In other words, as young children interact with their caregivers, they simultaneously acquire the necessary social and language skills needed to develop a specific cultural view of the world that shows them how to behave appropriately in their society or community.

Although the initial conceptualization of language socialization theory rested on the analysis of isolated communities, an early work by Shirley Brice Heath showed the importance of language socialization theory for bilingual education in the United States. In her ethnographic study titled *Ways With Words,* Heath compares the language socialization practices in three communities and extends the study of language socialization from the home to the school. In this study, Heath demonstrates the ways in which children in two different working-class communities are socialized into "ways with words," ways of using language that form the heart of what it means to be a competent member of their home communities. Heath then moves on to show how these "ways with words" are incompatible with the sets of expectations of schoolteachers in elementary schools. Particularly, because these expectations derive from schoolteachers' own home "mainstream," middle-class ways of using words to accomplish or carry out social interactions.

This and other works view the concept of "home-school differences" as an important explanation for the lack of success in school by nonmainstream students, including bilingual and English language learners. Associated with the concept of home-school differences was also a clear call for working with teachers, so that they might become aware of the sociocultural differences between children. This knowledge may help teachers change their attitudes toward minority children and adjust their classroom practices to reduce the disadvantages children from different sociocultural backgrounds face when they attend school.

Second-Generation Language Socialization Theory

In more recent years, language socialization research has broadened to encompass studies of second-language socialization and bilingual language socialization, thus making a more direct link to issues of bilingualism and bilingual education. Some of the insights presented here have emerged through the analysis of bilingual and multilingual communities. This is because communities in which two or more codes (be they languages or language varieties) exist together for whatever reason, they do so inevitably with issues of difference, dominance, or conflict that surround the languages and the speakers of those languages. By examining language socialization in contexts where different social practices come into contact or conflict with one another, these studies highlight the focus on social practice that is the hallmark of language socialization research. A review by Robert Bayley and Sandra Schecter provides an overview of a wide-range study on language socialization in bilingual and multilingual contexts. This work addresses some concerns with the early model of language socialization and offers a variety of extensions.

The first extension of this research, exemplified by Heath, was an extension of the focus of studies on larger, less isolated communities, concerned with studying language socialization practices beyond the scope of the home community, in cases where two or more codes come in contact with one another. This is precisely what happens in the case of language minority children entering language majority schools.

Another extension of the research was to examine the process of socialization not only in childhood, but also as an ongoing process throughout the life span. Adolescence, in this extension, takes on a particular importance because this is when individuals in modern societies find themselves at the intersection between childhood and adulthood. In this period, social identity formation becomes central; hence, extending the scope of socialization beyond childhood entails a shift from seeing socialization as a developmental process to one that sees socialization as practice.

From this perspective, individuals engage in social practices that reflect their identity in age-appropriate ways throughout the life cycle, and in response to the social environment in which they find themselves. In essence, this extension suggests that language socialization is not simply a developmental process leading to adulthood, but rather a component of what it means to be human, namely to be a member of a group. For instance, the practices required to be a "good 5-year-old" are not the same as those required for an adolescent, a young adult, or a senior citizen. The extension suggests that a variety of factors related to identity

help shape what particular behaviors are appropriate for which members of a society. For boys and girls to be considered competent boys and girls, they must behave in quite different ways; likewise, teenagers and senior citizens engage in different behaviors appropriate to their identities and positions in a community. All of those shifts in social practices, in routines of behavior, over time are examples of the language socialization processes. Studies of language socialization also extend to examine the process by which individuals learn the language and the sociocultural practices needed to become competent tool-and-die operators, folk dancers, middle-school students, university professors, meat packers, baseball players, and so on.

An additional extension of recent work in language socialization is the view that cultural norms and practices of communities are far from static or predictable. Rather, communities are indeed always changing to some degree because the individuals who are their members are capable of change. The source of such change can come from broad macrolevel social historical processes at the level of the society and even transnational influences; or it can also come from local level shifts in practices that may permeate a community from the inside. Hence, the process of language socialization is considerably more complex because individuals not only engage in routine practices but must also be aware of how they are changing over time. One example of this research is Don Kulick's *Language Shift and Cultural Reproduction: Socialization, Self and Syncretism in a Papua New Guinean Village.* Kulick examines how macrosociological processes influence language choice, and how the shift to monolingualism in Tok Pisin among children in Papua, New Guinea, occurs.

An additional extension of language socialization research, one drawn particularly from research in bilingual and multilingual settings, shows how the norms and values that dictate and define the language and other social practices also shift over time from one small community to another. *Language as Cultural Practice: Mexicanos en el norte,* by Schecter and Bayley, examines the different ways in which Mexican American families practice and define their culture, and the ways in which both monolingual and bilingual Spanish and English practices form part of that culture. Individuals at different stages of their lives, to be considered members of a community, engage in different practices; along with them, communities change over time. This social practice view of language socialization allows a more fluid and multifaceted conception of socialization and those social identities associated with it.

Finally, second-language socialization studies have examined cases where language socialization does not occur. These studies employ the same methods for examining social groups, and the same underlying concepts of how it is through social practice that individuals can be in a position to negotiate, challenge, contest, reject, or transform existing social practices in contexts that they find themselves in. Patricia Duff addressed this topic in a research study that is particularly relevant to bilingual and second-language education. Duff examined behaviors of resistance to school-imposed norms and social practices that fail to incorporate or value the language and social practices of language minority youth.

In sum, language socialization theory outlines a view of language learning as embedded in the social practices in which language is used. Through the close examination of everyday routines and practices of individuals in various contexts and communities in which they find themselves, we can learn how and when, in the case of bilingual populations, individuals use the various language codes at their disposal. By extending the scope of research to the broader social processes in which these everyday activities and practices occur, we can also provide explanations for the maintenance and shift of languages in bilingual contexts, as well as the ways in which languages map onto, or construct different social identities, including ethnic and linguistic identities.

Juliet Langman

See also Communities of Practice; First-Language Acquisition; Home/School Relations; Language and Identity; Language Learning in Children and Adults; Languages and Power; Language Socialization of Indigenous Children; Second-Language Acquisition

Further Readings

Bayley, R., & S. Schecter (Eds.). (2003). *Language socialization in bilingual and multilingual societies.* Clevedon, UK: Multilingual Matters.

Canagarajah, A. S. (1993). Critical ethnography of a Sri Lankan classroom: Ambiguities in student opposition to reproduction through ESOL. *TESOL Quarterly, 28,* 601–626.

Crago, M. B. (1992). Communicative interaction and second language acquisition: An Inuit example. *TESOL Quarterly, 26,* 487–505.

Crago, M. B., Genesee, F., & Allen, S. M. (1998). Power and difference: Bilingual decision making in Inuit homes. *Journal for a Just and Caring Education, 4,* 78–95.

Duff, P. (1996). Different languages, different practices: Socialization of discourse competence in dual-language school classrooms in Hungary. In K. Bailey & D. Nunan (Eds.), *Voices from the language classroom: Qualitative research in second language education* (pp. 407–433). New York: Cambridge University Press.

Duff, P. (2003). New directions in second language socialization research. *Korean Journal of English language and Linguistics, 3,* 309–339.

Eckert, P. (2000). *Linguistic variation as social practice: The linguistic construction of identity in Belten High.* Oxford, UK: Blackwell.

Garrett, P., & Baquedano-Lopez, P. (2002). Language socialization: Reproduction and continuity, transformation and change. *Annual Review of Anthropology, 31,* 339–361.

Heath, S. B. (1983). *Ways with words: Language, life, and work in communities and classrooms.* New York: Cambridge University Press.

Hymes, D. (1972). On communicative competence. In J. B. Pride & J. Holmes (Eds.), *Sociolinguistics: Selected readings* (pp. 269–293). Harmondsworth, UK: Penguin Books.

Kulick, D. (1992). *Language shift and cultural reproduction: Socialization, self and syncretism in a Papua New Guinean village.* Cambridge, UK: Cambridge University Press.

Ochs, E. (1988). *Culture and language development: Language acquisition and socialization in a Samoan village.* New York: Cambridge University Press.

Ochs, E. (1993). Constructing social identity: A language socialization perspective. *Research on Language and Social Interaction, 26,* 287–306.

Ochs, E., & B. Schieffelin. (1984). Language acquisition and socialization: Three developmental stories and their implications. In R. Schweder & R. LeVine (Eds.), *Culture theory: Essays in mind, self and emotion* (pp. 276–320). New York: Cambridge University Press.

Schecter, S. R., & Bayley, R. (2002). *Language as cultural Practice: Mexicanos en el norte.* Mahwah, NJ: Lawrence Erlbaum.

Schieffelin, B. B. (1990). *The give and take of everyday life.* Cambridge, UK: Cambridge University Press.

Schieffelin, B. B., & Ochs, E. (1986). Language socialization. *Annual Review of Anthropology, 15,* 163–191.

Schieffelin, B. B., & Ochs E. (Eds.). (1986). *Language socialization across cultures.* Cambridge, UK: Cambridge University Press.

Watson-Gegeo, K. (2004). Mind, language, and epistemology: Toward a language socialization paradigm for SLA. *The Modern Language Journal, 88,* 331–350.

LANGUAGE SOCIALIZATION OF INDIGENOUS CHILDREN

The acquisition of language is a universal and fascinating aspect of human development. Language socialization research shows that when acquiring a first language, children are simultaneously acquiring the cultural and social knowledge necessary for becoming competent members of their respective families and communities. From an indigenous perspective, the mother language serves as a basic and fundamental source of identity, sacredness, and strength of an individual, family, and community. This entry begins with a general overview of indigenous peoples, their languages and their cultures, and outlines some of the ways that indigenous children of the United States, Native Americans (also known as American Indians), Alaska Natives, and Native Hawaiians are socialized into their homes and cultures.

Indigenous Peoples, Languages, and Cultures

Indigenous peoples around the world and in the United States differ in a number of striking ways, such as governance, culture (i.e., dress, art, and ceremony), genesis theories, acculturation, and languages. Presently indigenous peoples constitute 4% of the world's population; they also speak an estimated 4,000 to 5,000 of the 6,000 world's languages (as reported by Daniel Nettle and Suzanne Romaine). In the United States, indigenous peoples equal 4.3 million or 1.5% of the total population and represent more than 560 autonomous indigenous nations, including Chippewa, Lakota, Jemez Pueblo (Walatowa), Diné (Navajo Nation), Inuit, Eastern and Western Cherokee, Tohono O'odham, Caddo, Eastern Pequot, Seminole, and Oneida. There are 175 U.S. indigenous languages, which range in various degrees of vitality from a handful of elderly speakers of Pii Paash, a Yuman language, also known as Maricopa (Arizona), to more than 178,000 speakers of Navajo, an Athabaskan language, whose use stretches from the sub-Arctic to the U.S. border with Mexico.

Equally important to understand about indigenous languages is that most of them predominately remain oral languages with cultural knowledge and traditions being orally transmitted among generations; however, language vitality in each community (and family) varies. For most communities that have a written language, mother-tongue literacy is reserved primarily for schools. For example, Zuni is a language isolated in New Mexico, which is spoken by 90% of the 10,000 Zuni members; however, only an estimated 5% of the population is able to read and write the language. Similarly, mother-tongue literacy has existed for nearly 100 years among the Navajo and is currently taught in model language education programs reservation-wide, yet their distinct child socialization practices and patterns remain primarily oral. This is not to say that mother-tongue literacy is not important but, rather, that the socialization of children essentially remains an oral process in indigenous cultures.

Language Socialization Research

Language socialization research is, in general, influenced by the fields of anthropology, sociolinguistics, psychology, and sociology—all of which critically examine human development and human nature, including language acquisition and language and cognitive development. This entry takes a sociolinguistic perspective, strongly influenced by the work of Russian psychologist Lev Vygotsky. In this theoretical view, through various interactions with adults and other cultural experts, young children tacitly, yet actively, absorb social knowledge; they internalize what they acquire from these external activities to make it their own. Vygotsky referred to this sociocognitive process as *internalization,* where an external interaction is transformed into internal mental functioning. In his view, through their verbal and nonverbal sociolinguistic interactions with experts (adults), children come to know who they are in relation to others in their world. In other words, they are acquiring a self-identity in a world of social meaning.

According to Elinor Ochs and Bambi Schieffelin, language socialization research is concerned with how children and other novices are socialized through language and how they learn to use it in their homes and communities. Thus, language socialization research provides insight into the sociolinguistic and cultural world of children before they enter school. This research is critical because it can assist educators who may be unaware of the language and cultural resources that ethnic and linguistic minority children bring from home, including Native American children. Because these children do not behave linguistically and socially as mainstream English-speaking children do, educators can mistakenly perceive them as having learning difficulties, or may underestimate their abilities to understand when they are actually learning and using language in culturally appropriate ways. Susan Phillips's classic study, for example, illustrated how disparities between the Anglo teacher discourse and the Warm Spring Native students' discourse negatively affected the learning and achievement of culturally and linguistically diverse children. As critical as this sociolinguistic research was, there continues to be a dire need for additional contemporary studies of language socialization of indigenous children.

Language Socialization in Home and Community

Populations around the world have found ways to socialize their children according to their realities and the logic of their languages. Through these socialization practices, a group's youngest members acquire the means to carry this cultural knowledge into the next generation. Experts assume that when children are socialized, they will eventually acquire the home language as well as the beliefs, values, and precepts embedded in it, the means with which to communicate with family members, to function successfully in the world of the home and family first, and eventually the social world of the larger community, including school. What do indigenous socializers (caretakers) believe indigenous children should learn? How do they believe children acquire this "local knowledge?" Do they need to be taught, and if so, who teaches them? People will be able to answer these questions from their own linguistic and cultural experiences and from their perceptions and beliefs about the nature of children, their abilities, and their roles in the cultural world; this is where the discussion now turns.

Beliefs and Perceptions of Children

A renowned native speaker of the Lakota language, Beatrice Medicine, explained that the Lakota word for children, *wakanyeia,* is derived from "wakan," meaning sacred, and reflects the Lakota belief of the sacredness of children. She further explained that Lakotas socialized in the Lakota language and culture believe that an unborn child is a highly intellectual spiritual being, preparing to enter the physical world and that before being born, the child has preselected his or her parents and caretakers. Simultaneously or respectively, children are considered sacred blessings by parents and family members, and therefore, young children are respected and treated as capable of understanding both the physical and spiritual nature of life. Similar perceptions of children are held by the Pueblo people of New Mexico. A Pueblo grandfather, when asked about his views of children, replied, "Every child is sacred because we don't know what is destined for this child; therefore, we treat every child with equal value" (as reported in research conducted by Mary Eunice Romero-Little). This epistemology of human existence frames the Lakota, the Pueblo, and other indigenous societies and guides them throughout their lives, including how they carry out their "sacred trust" for children. In other words, how they care for, nurture, and value their youngest members.

Becoming Indigenous: Cultural Plans for Socializing Children

Across indigenous cultures and communities, a number of common threads are interwoven to create the cultural plans that guide the socialization of children. One core thread prevalent throughout most indigenous societies is the belief and value of "respect"—respect for the human interconnections with land, water, sky and, one's relations. Respect is reflected in many forms through language and ways of speaking, as indicated by sociolinguist Dell Hymes, and as Leanne Hinton has shown among the Wintu Indians of California:

> Many of the verbs that express coercion in our language—such as to take a baby to (the shade), or to change the baby—are formed in a way that they express a cooperative effort instead. For example, the Wintu would say, "I *went with* the baby," instead of, "I *took* the baby." . . . They never say, and in fact they cannot say, as we do, "I have a sister," or a "son" or a "husband." Instead, they say, "I am sistered" or "I live with my sister." To *live with* is the usual way in which they express what we call possession, and they use this term for everything that they respect. (p. 62)

Culture and socialization practices influence the way children behave linguistically and socially, how they express their feelings and emotions, and how they understand their world. For example, greetings—whether in English or in the native language—are the means for showing respect to others and acknowledging one's interconnectedness with others. This is illustrated in the following vignette of a young Pueblo girl learning through Keres, the communal language, the important forms of greetings and acknowledgments and the proper way of interacting with others:

> A four-year-old girl and her mother enter the house. The mother greets the adults (several women and a couple of men) inside the house. Immediately, at the sight of the youngster, the adults in the house give special attention to her. They greet the young girl with smiles and expressions of verbal delight. The shy young girl does not smile or respond; she clings on to her mother and hides behind her dress. The mother continues to greet the women with her daughter clinging on to her leg. She appears not to mind her clinging child. After greeting each person, the mother sits down on a bench across from several women who are busy rolling out dough for pie-crust bottoms. The mother whispers in her daughter's ear as one of the women smiles at the young girl and says in Keres, "How are you, my little one? Do you want to help?" The young girl hugs her mother and does not respond. Her mother gives her daughter a little push and instructs her, "Go say hello to your aunt." The young girl refuses to go or to respond. The mother then takes her daughter by her hand and walks her over to the women working at the table. Together they approach each of the women. The mother models for the daughter the proper verbal greeting and the proper nonverbal gestures (a hug or a handshake). Gradually, with a hesitant smile, the young girl holds out her hand to each of the women and with the assistance of her mother, greets everyone present in the house. The women are delighted and tell the young girl in Keres, "Come help us. Here's some dough." (Romero-Little, p. 175)

As this young girl grows older, through guided practice and numerous opportunities for peripheral participation, as characterized in the model proposed by Jean Lave and Etienne Wenger in the home and communal context, she will learn appropriate social and linguistic practices.

For indigenous children, who, from birth—and in some indigenous cultures, *before* birth—grow up with many familial and community caretakers throughout their lives, special cultural events and daily sociocultural activities (such as illustrated in the previous vignette) collectively contribute to the development of their self and communal identities. Language plays a central role in shaping their perspectives of themselves and kinship (another common thread in the socialization of indigenous children), namely how one is related to others and how to properly acknowledge and interact with them. "Knowing the people" is identified by a young Pueblo parent as being vital to her daughter's development of a sense of self and communal identity: "I want her to know the people. I want the people to know her. And, of course, I want her to learn the language. But I think that those relationships are really going to help that part out. So, we try and teach her who people are" (as reported in Romero's study). Likewise, David Sing, Alapa Hunter, and Manu Meyer report that Native Hawaiian children are instilled with the *ohana* (family) and community when they participate in practices in the "Hawaiian way," such as learning hula, making rope out of *hau* or carving stones for *ulumaika,* chanting, and through storytelling or "talking story"—all of which are embedded with life lessons and traditions.

Through their intrapersonal and interpersonal sociolinguistic interactions with their caretakers, children acquire the knowledge of relationships, in particular the prominent role carried out by the extended family and grandparents. For instance, in the Kiowa society, a Plains Indian nation of Oklahoma, young children learn to use language in ways that acknowledge the various extended relations, especially their connections with elders, which constitute the core (or circle) of their social and cognitive worlds, as illustrated in the following story told by a Kiowa man who was asked who his most important childhood caretakers were:

> As a young boy growing up, I became excited and charmed by my grandfather . . . I can remember feeling attached to this powerful man and proud to be part of his family—his circle. My other relatives were also important in my care and upbringing. I can still remember with fondness as my mother or grandparents would introduce me to an older woman at a powwow or church and say, "this is your grandma." It was not until the eighth grade that I came to the realization I only had one set of biological grandparents. The images and cohesiveness of this extended

circle played a powerful role in my development. (Rogers, n.d.)

In many indigenous societies, one is related to many individuals in many ways that extend beyond one's blood relations. Children must learn this tapestry of social, cultural, and religious relationships early in their lives.

Patricia García contends that one way that parents socialize a child on the importance of language and other cultural practices is through attitudes toward language and practices that may not be overtly taught; they are often displayed in daily interaction or communication. This is exemplified in the socialization of Alaska Native children, as reported by the Alaska Native Language Center. In Alaska Native villages, daily life and much of the daily learning of both children and adults evolve around essential seasonal subsistence activities such as hunting, fishing, berry picking, and so on. Each summer, for instance, children accompany their families to fish camps for months at a time. While at the fish camps, children are integral contributors to the myriad tasks for preparing fish for the winter food supply. From morning to dusk, the entire family is busy catching, cutting, cleaning, and drying the fish. Young children, if not directly engaged in a task, are silent participants. They listen, observe, and quietly internalize the daily activities of others. In this way, they learn the important things they will need to know when it is their turn to take on these responsibilities and to pass them on to the next generation.

Conclusion

Children, including indigenous children, come to school with well-established ways of communicating, and particular forms of knowing and learning that are framed through their languages, cultures, and socialization experiences. In this socialization process, which is part of a culture and begins well before children enter school, are found methods for imparting what a community truly believes children ought to learn and may not resemble the language and literacy practices of schools. This is not to say that indigenous families do not value and promote the knowledge and skills taught in mainstream schools. Quite the opposite, they value them as much as mainstream families do. As witnessed in this entry, however, what is taught in school is only a small part of what indigenous

children must learn if they are to be successful in and beyond their own community. First, these children must learn how to relate to others in their own cultural world and become skilled at carrying out their duties and responsibilities as members of their cultural community; they must also acquire the cultural literacy to do this. For this reason, indigenous peoples faithfully carry out cultural plans for their children. Thus, in a deep sense, the language socialization process is key to an indigenous people's cultural and linguistic survival. The family and community goals for indigenous children reach far beyond the form of literacy shaped and promoted by formal schooling. Although their early socialization may differ from those of mainstream children, indigenous children are provided with many rich and meaningful opportunities to acquire the cultural symbols and intellectual traditions, which according to Rebecca Benjamin, Regis Pecos, and Romero, are important and vital for the development of their personal and collective identities and, equally important, for ensuring their bilingual and bicultural competence and successes beyond their cultural worlds, in mainstream schools.

Mary Eunice Romero-Little

See also Acculturation; Enculturation; Home/School Relations; Language and Identity; Language Socialization; Native American Languages, Legal Support for

Further Readings

Alaska Native Language Center. (2002). *Alaska Native ways: What the elders have taught us.* Portland, OR: Graphic Arts Center.

Benjamin, R., Pecos, R., & Romero, M. E. (1997). Language revitalization efforts in the Pueblo de Pueblo: Becoming "literate" in an oral society. In N. H. Hornberger (Ed.), *Indigenous literacies in the Americas: Language planning from the bottom up* (pp. 115–136). Berlin: Mouton de Gruyter.

García, P. (2005). Case study parental language attitudes and practices to socialize children in a diglossic society. *International Journal of Bilingual Education and Bilingualism, 8*(4), 328–344.

Hinton, L. (1994). *Flute of fire.* Berkeley, CA: Heyday Books.

Hymes, D. (1974). *Foundations in sociolinguistics: An ethnographic approach.* Philadelphia: University of Pennsylvania Press.

Lave, J., & Wenger, E. (1991). *Situated learning: Legitimate peripheral participation.* New York: Cambridge University Press.

Ludescher, S. L. (2000, April 21). Zunis stress native tongue, *Gallup Independent.* Retrieved from http://www.gallupindependent.com/1999-2001/4-21-00.html#anchor3

Medicine, B. (1985). Child socialization among Native Americans: The Lakota (Sioux) in cultural context. *Wicazo Sa Review, 1*(2), 23–28.

Nettle, D., & Romaine, S. (2000). *Vanishing voices: The extinction of the world's languages.* New York: Oxford University Press.

Ochs, E., & Schieffelin, B. B. (1984). Language acquisition and socialization: Three developmental stories. In R. Shweder & R. LeVine (Eds.), *Culture theory: Essays on mind, self and emotion* (pp. 276–320). New York: Cambridge University Press.

Park, E., & King, K. (2003). *Cultural diversity and language socialization in the early years.* ERIC Digest, Washington, DC: Center for Applied Linguistics. EDO-FL-03–13.

Phillips, S. (1983). *The invisible culture: Communication in classroom and community on the Warm Springs Indian Reservation.* Prospects Heights, IL: Waveland.

Rogers, B. (n.d.). *A path of healing and wellness for native families.* Your Native Resource for Quality Training. Accessed January 16, 2007, from http://www.nativewellness.com/article.htm

Romero-Little, M. E. (2003). *Perpetuating the Pueblo way of life: language socialization and language shift in a Pueblo community.* Unpublished doctoral dissertation, Department of Education, Language, Literacy, and Culture, University of California at Berkeley.

Sing, D., Hunter, A., & Meyer, M. A. (1999). Native Hawaiian education: Talking story with three Hawaiian educators, *Journal of American Indian Education, 39*(1), 4–13.

Vygotsky, L. (1978*). Mind in society: The development of higher psychological processes.* Cambridge, MA: Harvard University Press.

Wertsch, J. (1985). *Vygotsky and the social formation of mind.* Cambridge, MA: Harvard University Press.

Wong Fillmore, L. (2000). The loss of family languages: Should educators be concerned? *Theory into Practice, 39*(4), 203–210.

Zentella, A. C. (1997). *Growing up bilingual.* Oxford, UK: Blackwell.

LANGUAGE STUDY TODAY

Although the United States is a nation of diverse languages and populations, foreign-language study has had a checkered history in the nation's schools and colleges. Foreign-language enrollments during the 20th century at the high school and university levels rose and fell consistently with societal ideologies that affected our collective outlook on cultural and language diversity. Interest in foreign-language study has sometimes coincided with policies associated with national defense. More often, however, opposition to immigration and perceived threats to a national American identity have contributed to devaluing the study of certain foreign languages in schools. The see-saw effects of less-than-decisive policies and public sentiment have had a negative affect on foreign-language study. This entry examines some of these changes during the last half of the 20th century, the period that parallels the contemporary history of bilingual education.

By the end of the 20th century, only 60% of post-secondary institutions had foreign-language requirements for graduation. The United States is one of the few countries in the world, perhaps the only one, where it is possible to receive a university education without any foreign-language requirement. Historical data illustrate the worsening of this situation over time.

Language Enrollments in Schools in the 20th Century

Estimates for foreign-language enrollments from 1900 to 1920 indicate that most students were enrolled in foreign languages, primarily Latin, followed by German, French, and Spanish. Latin was often a requirement for admissions to liberal arts colleges. After World War I, German language enrollment fell dramatically, although it experienced a comeback in the 1930s. During this period, there was also a shift from colleges primarily offering courses in Latin to "modern language instruction" that eventually outpaced the classical languages. From the 1920s to the 1950s, foreign-language instruction overall fell in the United States as the country became more isolated and xenophobic. In addition, an increasing number of students turned to fields of study other than languages.

The launch of the world's first artificial satellite, *Sputnik,* by the Soviet Union in 1957 resulted in a renewed, albeit short-lived interest in foreign-language studies, especially at the federal level. The National Defense Education Act (NDEA) was passed in 1958 to encourage the advancement of education in science, mathematics, and modern foreign languages. One purpose of NDEA was to encourage the teaching of languages designated as "critical" or "strategic" by government entities and the Modern Language Association (MLA). The immediate purpose, however, was to move the United States ahead of the Soviet Union during the space race through better education. This had a direct impact on foreign-language enrollments, and by 1960, 86% of postsecondary institutions had foreign-language requirements. Although language enrollments continued to rise throughout the 1960s, enrollment fell off in the 1970s as a result of many colleges removing their foreign-language requirements for reasons that are not altogether clear.

In 1978, President Jimmy Carter created the President's Commission on Foreign Language and International Studies to investigate whether the United States was maintaining its commitment to the 1975 Helsinki Accords on foreign-language study and also address the concerns of the State Department and National Security Council regarding the nation's capability in foreign-language training and research. The commission discovered persistent problems at all levels of foreign-language instruction, including inadequate training of teachers, insufficient administrative support, a lack of imaginative curricula, poor coordination, and a lack of sound criteria for measuring progress in these fields. The commission made 65 recommendations; however, by the end of the 20th century, few of those recommendations had been implemented. Despite national reports detailing the need for Americans to be competent in languages and cultures other than their own, only a handful of states had mandated foreign language be taught in schools and only 60% of postsecondary institutions had a foreign-language requirement.

Enrollment Numbers in Universities and High Schools

Since 1958, the MLA has conducted surveys every 4 years to track foreign-language enrollment in postsecondary institutions. The last survey conducted in the 20th century was in 1998. In the 1960s, foreign-language enrollment was at an all time high with 17% of students enrolled in a foreign language (Table 1). The top five languages that accounted for 95% of the foreign-language enrollment were French, Spanish, German, Russian, and Latin (see Table 2). Since the 1960s, the choice of which foreign language to study has shifted significantly. Although French was the most popular foreign language in 1960, its enrollments experienced a steady

Table 1   Modern Foreign-Language (MFL) Enrollments Compared With Higher Education Enrollments, 1960–1998

Year	College Enrollments	MFL Enrollments	%
1960	3,789,000	642,896	17.0
1965	5,920,864	1,034,877	17.5
1968	7,513,091	1,125,594	15.0
1970	8,580,887	1,101,659	12.8
1972	9,214,820	1,002,030	10.9
1977	11,285,787	933,468	8.3
1980	12,096,895	924,372	7.6
1983	12,464,661	966,013	7.8
1986	12,503,511	1,003,234	8.0
1990	13,818,637	1,184,489	8.6
1995	14,261,781	1,138,772	8.0
1998	14,507,000	1,194,648	8.2

Source: Draper & Hicks (2002).

decline. German and Russian, along with French, also saw a steady decline in enrollment numbers (Table 3). Although still a popular foreign language, by the end of the 20th century, French was far outpaced by Spanish (see Table 2). In 1998, Spanish accounted for more than half of all foreign-language enrollments. Foreign languages such as Chinese, Japanese, Arabic, and Korean also saw major increases in enrollment (see Table 3). In 1998, Japanese became the fifth most commonly taught language, and Chinese the sixth.

Although the actual number of foreign-language enrollment is currently at an all-time high, the past 40 years have demonstrated the waxing and waning interest in foreign-language study in the United States. Throughout the 1960s, enrollment remained on a steady incline, reaching more than a million students by 1965. Then, during the 1970s, enrollment declined before increasing again in the 1980s and 1990s. This growth in foreign-language enrollment numbers, though, has not been consistent with the total growth of college enrollments. College enrollments have outpaced foreign-language enrollments. Since the mid-1980s, foreign-language enrollments have stayed at approximately 8% of total college enrollments compared with 16% 40 years ago.

Foreign-language study at the high school level also shifted throughout the 20th century. Beginning

Table 2 Enrollments in the Leading Foreign Languages by Decade

	1960	%	1970	%	1980	%	1990	%	1998	%
Spanish	178,689	27.8	389,150	35.3	379,379	41.6	533,944	45.7	656,590	56.0
French	228,813	35.6	359,313	32.6	248,361	27.3	272,472	23.3	199,064	17.0
German	146,116	22.7	202,569	18.4	126,910	13.9	133,348	11.4	89,020	7.6
Italian	11,142	1.7	34,244	3.1	34,791	3.8	49,699	4.3	49,287	4.2
Japanese	1,746	0.3	6,620	0.6	11,506	1.3	45,717	3.9	43,141	3.7
Chinese	1,844	0.3	6,238	0.6	11,366	1.2	19,490	1.7	28,456	2.4
Latin	25,700	4.0	27,591	2.5	25,035	2.7	28,178	2.4	26,145	2.2
Russian	30,570	4.8	36,189	3.3	23,987	2.6	44,626	3.8	23,791	2.0
Ancient Greek	12700	2.0	16,679	1.5	22,111	2.4	16,401	1.4	16,402	1.4
Hebrew	3,834	0.6	16,567	1.5	19,429	2.1	12,995	1.1	15,833	1.4
ASL	0	0.0	0	0.0	0	0.0	1,602	0.1	11,938	1.0
Portuguese	1,033	0.2	5,065	0.5	4,894	0.5	6,211	0.5	6,926	0.6
Arabic	541	0.1	1,333	0.1	3,466	0.4	3,475	0.3	5,505	0.5
Total	642,728		1,101,558		911,235		1,168,158		1,172,098	

Source: Draper & Hicks (2002).

Table 3 Change in Enrollments in Leading Foreign Languages

	1960	1998	% Change
Spanish	178,689	656,607	267.5
French	228,813	199,370	−12.9
German	146,116	89,537	−38.7
Italian	11,142	48,947	339.3
Japanese	1,746	42,978	2361.5
Chinese	1,844	28,652	1453.8
Russian	30,570	23,877	−21.9
Hebrew	3,834	15,520	304.8
Arabic	541	5,969	1003.4
Korean	168	4,775	2742.5

Source: Draper & Hicks (2002).

Table 4 Top Five Foreign-Language Enrollments in U.S. Public High Schools, 1900–2000

Year	High School Enrollment	Language Enrollment	%
1900	519,251	377,517	73
1910	915,061	762,273	83
1922	2,230,000	1,224,275	55
1934	5,620,626	1,995,322	35
1948	5,399,452	1,169,974	22
1960	8,649,495	2,342,028	27
1970	13,301,883	3,779,346	28
1982	12,879,254	2,909,778	23
1990	11,099,648	4,256,925	38
2000	13,457,780	5,898,138	44

Source: Draper & Hicks (2002).

in 1958, the MLA began tracking high school foreign-language enrollment. Eventually, the American Council on the Teaching of Foreign Languages, a division of the MLA, assumed data collection. In the early part of the 20th century, foreign-language enrollment was at an all-time high with 83% of students learning Latin, French, German, or Spanish (Table 4). Foreign-language enrollments reached an all-time low after World War II but have increased since then. Although enrollment numbers steadily declined, during the 1900s and until the middle of the century, Latin was the foreign language of choice. As the popularity of Latin declined, Spanish quickly became the most popular foreign language. Spanish now accounts for almost 70% of all foreign-language classes being taught in high school. In 2000, 43% of students were enrolled in a foreign language. Spanish, French, German, Italian, and Latin account for 96% of all foreign-language enrollments (Table 5).

Table 5   High School Enrollments in the Top Foreign Languages

Year	Spanish	%	French	%	German	%	Latin	%	Italian	%
1900	0	0	40,503	11	74,252	20	262,752	70	0	0
1910	6,406	1	90,591	12	216,869	28	448,383	59	0	0
1922	252,000	21	345,650	28	13,385	1	613,250	50	0	0
1934	348,479	17	612,648	31	134,897	7	899,300	45	0	0
1948	442,755	38	253,781	22	43,195	4	429,174	37	0	0
1960	933,409	40	744,404	32	150,764	6	654,670	28	20,026	1
1970	1,810,775	48	1,230,686	33	410,535	11	265,293	7	27,321	1
1982	1,562,789	54	857,984	29	266,901	9	169,580	6	44,114	2
1990	2,611,367	61	1,089,355	26	295,398	7	163,923	4	40,402	1
2000	4,057,608	69	1,075,421	18	283,301	5	177,477	3	64,098	1

Source: Draper & Hicks (2002).

Language Organizations

Various organizations are dedicated to the study and teaching of modern languages in schools in the United States. These include the MLA, the American Council on the Teaching of Foreign Languages (ACTFL), and the Center for Applied Linguistics (CAL). Throughout the 20th century and continuing in the 21st century, these organizations have been dedicated to the study and promotion of foreign languages and language issues in the United States.

Founded in 1883, the MLA is a scholarly organization that provides opportunities to share findings and teaching experiences as well as discuss trends in the study of languages. The ACTFL was founded in 1967 by the MLA and remains the only national organization dedicated to the improvement and expansion of the teaching and learning of all languages. This organization has been involved in developing proficiency guidelines and national standards for foreign languages. CAL was established in 1959 as a private nonprofit organization working to improve communication through better understanding of language and culture. CAL is also involved in the National K–12 Foreign Language Resource Center. The resource center was established in 1994 as a collaborative effort between CAL and Iowa State University and funded by a grant from the U.S. Department of Education. The center seeks to improve foreign-language education in Grades K–12 through professional development of K–12 foreign-language teachers.

Conclusion

Despite the support of organizations devoted to foreign-language instruction and the rising numbers of enrollments in foreign languages, language study in the United States overall remains inadequate. Research shows immersion programs to be the best method of language learning, yet those programs remain scarce, and most schools only require a minimum of foreign-language study that limits proficiency to beginning levels. Because of the autonomy of schools in choice of instructional program, both at the secondary and postsecondary levels, foreign-language learning is often disjointed and precludes any meaningful competence. The assumption of most language programmers in schools is that languages are best taught in classrooms three to five times a week in the same way as are all other subjects. There is no research to show that this is actually the optimum arrangement for teaching and learning languages. This is coupled with the consistent problems of funding shortages, inadequate in-service training and lack of quality materials for language instruction.

Foreign-language study in schools in the 20th and 21st centuries has been greatly affected by the lack of commitment to language diversity at the local, state, and national levels. Despite the advent of globalization at the end of the 20th century, the United States embraced a monolingual English-only language policy for schools and society.

Current foreign-language enrollments document how many students are enrolled at a particular time.

Although only 8% might be enrolled when the survey is given, it does not mean that only 8% of students have received foreign-language instruction. Currently, 60% of universities have a foreign-language requirement, meaning that at least 60% of students will graduate with some foreign-language study.

Larisa Warhol

See also Audio-Lingual Method; Center for Applied Linguistics, Initial Focus; Center for Applied Linguistics, Recent Focus; Communicative Approach; Defense Language Institute; National Defense Education Act of 1958; President's Commission on Foreign Language and International Studies

Further Readings

Draper, J., & Hicks, J. (2002). *Foreign language enrollments in public secondary schools, Fall 2000.* Available from the American Council on the Teaching of Foreign Languages Website, http://eric.ed.gov

Plottel, J. (1960). Foreign language entrance and degree requirements for the BA degree in accredited colleges and universities. *PMLA, 75, 4, Part 2: Supplement.* 14–28.

Welles, E. B. (2002). Foreign language enrollment numbers: Some (mis)interpretations explained. *Modern Language Journal, 86,* 253–255.

Welles, E. B. (2004). *Foreign language enrollments in United States institutions of higher education, Fall 2002.* Retrieved March 15, 2007, from http://www.mla.org/adfl/bulletin/v35n2/35

LATINO ATTITUDES TOWARD ENGLISH

The U.S. Bureau of the Census reported that, in the last official census, the number of persons who speak Spanish at home rose from 10.2 million in 1980 to 24.7 million in 2000. This growth has sparked concerns among some critics of bilingual education who fear that Spanish has become pervasive and that some proportion of Latino students will not learn English if they are permitted to participate in bilingual education for a protracted time. The assumption of these critics is that bilingual education detracts from the immigrants' desire to learn English, particularly in the case of Latinos, by far the largest of the immigrant groups. Research with

Spanish speakers, however, challenges the myth that Spanish-speaking immigrants, their children, and their grandchildren resist learning English. This entry reviews what is known about Latino attitudes toward English, and possible reasons for beliefs held by some that Latinos in the United States do not want to learn English.

The Importance of Language Attitudes

Attitudes are difficult to measure because unlike other attributes, such as height and weight, they cannot be observed directly. An attitude represents internal thoughts, feelings, and behavioral tendencies that vary with time and context. An attitude can be a predisposing factor, and it can also be an outcome. Those with positive attitudes toward learning a language before they start learning it may succeed in their studies. Also possible is that through language study, language learners will develop a positive attitude toward the language they are learning. Conversely, a learner with a negative attitude about a language may experience more than the usual problems learning that language.

Colin Baker describes various types of language attitudes. According to Baker, some may be loyal to their own language and hold a less generous attitude toward a minority or immigrant language. Others may have favorable attitudes to both their own and another language. They may also have particular attitudes to a language variation, dialect, or speech style. Other attitudinal targets include strategies of language instruction and the notion of learning a new language in itself. These differences color people's identity with respect to the society in which they are situated. Attitudes associated with these differences, have myriad implications for how people of varying language backgrounds, abilities, and motivations accommodate each other when interacting with one another in a given language.

Josiane Hamers and Michael Blanc suggest that attitudes appear to be associated with the speakers' desired future for themselves and their group within a given society. Immigrants who opt for the identity of their adopted homeland may favor quick assimilation. Those who opt for preserving their ethnic identity may favor a cultural pluralism that permits them to maintain their cultural heritage. These differences have implications for bilingualism. Baker also mentions research indicating that people may also have integrative or instrumental attitudes toward a language other than their own. Those with positive integrative attitudes may want to learn the second language because they want to identify with its speakers, participate in their cultural activities, and form new friendships. Persons with positive instrumental language attitudes may want to learn the second language for utilitarian purposes, such as finding a better job, improving their career prospects, passing exams, performing well on the job, or helping their children with schoolwork. The same person might also have instrumental language attitudes in some circumstances and integrative language attitudes in others.

Baker further emphasizes the importance of situating the study of language attitudes in its parent discipline, the social psychology of attitudes. To neglect to do so would place language attitudinal studies at risk of reaching poorly defined, naïve conclusions, which might place researchers and consumers of research at risk of replicating previous mistakes. To do so could place us in danger of overgeneralizing apparently similar language attitudes experienced by others earlier in history, and applying conclusions that might have been poorly conceived to current situations. One such potentially harmful conclusion is the assumption that Latino people who are loyal to Spanish have poor attitudes toward English.

Research on Latino Attitudes Toward English

Recent research about Latino attitudes toward English using direct means such as attitude questionnaires is limited. Baker asserts that certain attitudinal instruments, such as attitude-to-bilingualism questionnaires, can fail to reveal subconscious or socially undesirable attitudes. Another weakness has been the implicit assumption in some designs that a favorable attitude toward one language excludes the possibility of a simultaneous favorable attitude toward another language.

Given the difficulties associated with using direct means to research attitudes, researchers typically rely on indirect methods. One generally accepted indirect research strategy is the *matched guise technique,* where respondents listen to the same person read the same passage in different languages or with different accents or styles within a language.

Respondents do not know that the same person is reading and are asked to make judgments about the speaker. The matched guise technique has proven useful in identifying listeners' attitudes about the speaker according to three dimensions: the speaker's competence, his or her personal integrity, and his or her social attractiveness.

Another indirect research method is surveys. Despite their weaknesses, surveys can provide insights into community thoughts, beliefs, and preferences about their own and other languages. Especially pertinent research about Latino attitudes toward English are the following survey results: Calvin Veltman's work, published Sin 1988 by the Hispanic Policy Development Project; the 1991 Gallup Study of Attitudes toward English as the Official Language commissioned by the U.S. English organization; the Southwest Voter Research Institute 1996 *Latino Issues Survey;* and two surveys conducted by the Pew Hispanic Center in 2002 and 2004.

Veltman reported that by the time Latino immigrants have been in the United States for 15 years, three-quarters of them reported using English on a regular basis. His research also pointed out regional differences with respect to the speed of language shift from Spanish to English. In Texas and New Mexico, Latinos "migrated" from Spanish to English more slowly, and in Colorado, Latinos "migrated" more quickly. Age also made a difference. Not surprisingly, immigrants who arrived at an older age migrated to English at slower rates than did younger Latino immigrants.

In the 1991 Gallup study, 42% of Latino respondents responded in favor of making English the official language, but 78% of non-Latino respondents favored this option as well. Only 34% of Latinos reported in favor of limiting bilingual education to the period when children are learning English, but 54% of non-Latinos did. Forty-five percent (45%) of Latino respondents reported a belief that maintaining immigrant languages and cultures should be a private concern, and 71% of non-Latinos reported similarly. Some might conclude from these statistics that Latinos as a group think differently from non-Latinos, but such a conclusion may overgeneralize other factors associated with these statistics, such as the age of the Latino respondents, the length of time of residence in the United States, and citizenship status. Carol Schmid reported that the small sample of Latinos in this study makes it difficult to analyze the data and reach defensible conclusions.

Table 1 Hispanic Attitudes Toward English Language in the United States

	Citizens	Noncitizens
Percentage that support . . .		
Making English the official language of the U.S.	37.1	23.2
Eliminating bilingual education	12.2	7.5
Eliminating ballots in Spanish	10.1	9.2
Eliminating the use of Spanish in government	8.7	5.4
Percentage that will use a ballot in English	83.5	54.7

Source: Schmid, C. (2001). *The politics of language: Conflict, identity and cultural pluralism in comparative perspective.* New York: Oxford University Press.

Schmid also reports that Latino respondents to the *Latino Issues Survey,* though generally in opposition to making English the official language of the United States, did not have unanimous opinions on this matter. When asked if they would use a ballot in Spanish or in English to vote, 83.5% of U.S. citizen Latinos and 54.7% of noncitizen Latinos reported a preference for an English language ballot.

The Pew Hispanic Center surveyed Latino opinion on education and civic engagement and included questions about attitudes toward English. Respondents were asked whether they thought immigrants have to speak English to assert they are part of American society. They were also asked whether teaching English to immigrant children is very important, somewhat important, not too important, or not important at all.

Latino respondents reported that immigrants have to speak English to be a part of American society and that English should be taught to the children of immigrants. The endorsement of the English language, both for immigrants and for their children, was strong among Hispanics of all backgrounds in socioeconomic status, party affiliation, fluency in English, or length of residence in the United States. How long Latinos had been in the United States, however, did make a slight difference in their attitudes. Latino immigrants are slightly more likely to say that immigrants have to learn English than are native-born Latinos. Most Latinos—across socioeconomic status

and levels of education—viewed it essential that immigrants learn English.

Latino and other respondents also reported that it is important that English be taught to children of immigrant families. Latinos held stronger views than either non-Latino Whites or Blacks. This support was equally high regardless of party affiliation, income level, or language ability. Foreign-born Latinos were stronger in their opinion that English be taught to immigrant children than were U.S.-born Hispanics. The Pew survey also reported another telling statistic: Among Latinos, only 2% held the view that teaching English to immigrant children was not important, whereas 27% of non-Latinos held this view.

Evidence from the Pew Hispanic Center's 2002 survey about civic engagement suggests that Latinos who speak both Spanish and English prefer to use English. Although many native-born Latinos can speak Spanish, few reported strong reading capacities in Spanish. In nearly all job settings, bilingual Latinos use English. Fewer than 10% of all

Table 2 Percentages of Responses to the Question, "Do immigrants have to speak English to say they are part of American society, or not?"

Total of Latino Respondents[a]	Answer	
	Yes	No
Nativity		
Foreign born	57	41
U.S. native born	52	46
Primary language		
English	55	43
Bilingual	52	46
Spanish	56	40
Party affiliation		
Democrat	52	33
Independent	58	28
Republican	64	16

Source: From Pew Hispanic Center/Kaiser Family Foundation (2006). *Hispanic attitudes toward learning English.* Conducted April 21–June 9, 2004. Retrieved from http://pewhispanic.org/factsheets/factsheet.php?FactsheetID=20

Notes: [a]N = 2,288 Latino Adults Nationwide; Margin of Error = +/–2.83; Island-born Puerto Ricans are identified as Foreign Born.

Table 3 Percentage of Responses to the Question, "How important is the goal of teaching English to the children of immigrant families? Is it…?"

Total Sample[a]

	Race/Ethnicity			Party Affiliation		
Answer	Total	Latinos	Whites	Blacks	Democrat	Independent	Republican
Very Important	87	92	87	83	86	90	89

Total Latinos[b]

	Nativity		Primary Language			Party Affiliation		
Answer	Foreign Born	Native Born	English	Bilingual	Spanish	Democrat	Independent	Republican
Very Important	96	88	88	92	96	92	92	91

Source: Pew Hispanic Center/Kaiser Family Foundation. (2004). *National Survey of Latinos: Education.* Conducted August 7–October 15, 2003. Retrieved from http://pewhispanic.org/reports/report.php?ReportID=25

Notes: [a]N = 3,421 Adults Nationwide, Margin of Error = +/–2.43.

[b]N = 1,508 Latinos, Margin of Error = +/–3.03, Island-born Puerto Ricans are identified as Foreign Born.

bilingual Latinos obtained news information solely in Spanish, and fewer than 20% used Spanish exclusively at home. Because the home is considered the ultimate domain for imparting language ability from one generation to the next, it was not clear in 2002 whether English-Spanish bilingualism will remain prevalent in future generations of native-born Latinos. This finding reconfirmed what Veltman reported in 1988.

On a related topic, respondents also commented on the importance of assimilating into a dominant culture. Seventy-three percent of Latinos surveyed reported it somewhat or very important for Latinos to change so that they blend into the larger society, as for example, in the image of the melting pot of cultures. Fifty-five percent reported that an immigrant has to speak English to say they are a part of American society. Fifty-four percent felt that one must be a U.S. citizen, 65% indicated that one must vote in U.S. elections, and 79% reported that one must believe in the U.S. Constitution to demonstrate that they are part of American society. However, among all Latinos, 87% reported it very, or somewhat, important to maintain their distinct cultures, and 93% reported it very,

or somewhat, important that future generations of Latinos living in the United States speak Spanish.

Conclusion

The research suggests positive language attitudes among Latinos toward English. What the evidence does not show are the reasons for these positive attitudes. There are insufficient data to suggest which factors are at play within the Latino community in encouraging these attitudes. The data are also insufficient to suggest which contextual factors outside of the Latino community, such as inaccurate understandings of non-Latino people, influence these attitudes and people's perspectives on them.

Given historical accounts of immigrant speakers of languages other than English in the United States, some may conclude that today's Latino experience follows a different trajectory from that of previous immigrant groups. However, historical accounts about other immigrant groups' experiences in the United States may be incomplete. Accounts of our non-English-speaking European ancestors' struggles with English may have failed to adequately capture the unobservable and therefore not reportable, which is now so vividly articulated simply through prolonged, immediate contact with today's Latino community in everyday life.

Also absent from historical records are comprehensive studies such as Veltman's and the Pew Hispanic Center's. Perhaps a previously held, implicit expectation that newcomers would learn English and relinquish their native languages precluded surveying immigrant opinion on the matter. Factors such as the nativist attitudes that surfaced at various times in U.S. history among those already in the United States when the newcomers arrived sometimes go unnoticed. Also, many of us grew up in an era when immigration to the United States was at its low point. This era was not the norm that we might tend to believe. Amnesia about these realities may have colored our understanding of the past and its similarity to the present. Today's Latinos' positive attitudes toward English and Spanish remind us that one can have positive attitudes about more than one language, and more accurate recollections of our past might lead us to conclude that our ancestors may have felt the same way although scientific research was not conducted to help us find this out. With this realization, the question becomes less of a question, and the evidence becomes less of a surprise.

Elsie M. Szecsy

See also Accommodation Theory, Second-Language; Acculturation; Assimilation; Language Loyalty; Second-Language Acquisition; Social Bilingualism

Further Readings

Baker, C. (1992). *Attitudes and language.* Philadelphia: Multilingual Matters.

Baker, C., & Jones, S. P. (1998). *Encyclopedia of bilingualism and bilingual education.* Philadelphia: Multilingual Matters.

Hamers, J. F., & Blanc, M. H. A. (2003). *Bilinguality and bilingualism* (2nd ed.) New York: Cambridge University Press.

Pew Hispanic Center/Kaiser Family Foundation. (2004). *National Survey of Latinos: Education.* Conducted August 7–October 15, 2003. Retrieved from http://pewhispanic.org/reports/report.php?ReportID=25

Pew Hispanic Center/Kaiser Family Foundation. (2006). *Hispanic attitudes toward learning English.* Conducted April 21–June 9, 2004. Retrieved from http://pewhispanic.org/factsheets/factsheet.php?FactsheetID=20

Schmid, C. (2001). *The politics of language: Conflict, identity, and cultural pluralism in comparative perspective.* New York: Oxford University Press.

Southwest Voter Research Institute. (1996). *Latino issues survey.* San Antonio, TX: Author.

U.S. English/Gallup Opinion Poll. (1991). *A Gallup study of attitudes toward English as the official language of the U.S. Government.* Princeton, NJ: Gallup Organization.

Veltman, C. (1988). *The future of the Spanish language in the United States.* New York: Hispanic Policy Development Project.

Wyman, M. (1992). *Round-trip to America: The immigrants return to Europe, 1880–1930.* Ithaca, NY: Cornell University Press.

LATINO CIVIL RIGHTS MOVEMENT

Historically, much of the civil rights struggle in the United States has concerned the constitutional rights, legal status, and treatment of minority groups that are marked off from the majority by race, religion, or national origin. For the Latino population, civil rights struggles emerged in the mid-1800s over constitutional rights to property, citizenship, treatment, and the very meaning of their community. By the early 1900s, however, a shift began to take place in matters of economic, educational, and political equality. Mexican Americans—the largest group within the Latino population in the United States at the time, with a long history of discrimination, segregation, and second-class citizenship since the end of the Mexican-American War of 1846–1848—led the struggle. To understand and appreciate the struggle for civil rights by Mexicans and other Latinos, one must consider the historical relationship of this community to the majority group in power. Although the term *Latino* is used widely today in conjunction with the civil rights movement, the primary reference group and examples in this article are drawn mainly from the Mexican American community. This entry briefly reviews early struggles by Mexican Americans in education and how these struggles helped pave the way for the Latino civil rights movement of the 1960s and 1970s. Particular attention is given to the relationship between the movement and the emergence of bilingual education. It is important to note, however, that Puerto Ricans, Cuban Americans, and others also played important roles in promoting bilingual instruction.

Historical Antecedents and Early Education Struggles

The Mexican American community gained a more visible legal status in the United States after the Mexican American War ended in 1848. As a result of the war, Mexico ceded more than half of its territory to the United States. The vast territory lost by Mexico to the United States and known in U.S. history books as the "ceded territories" comprises what are now the states of New Mexico, Colorado, Arizona, California, Nevada, and parts of Utah. The Treaty of Guadalupe Hidalgo, which ended the war, made certain assurances to the Mexican population living in the conquered land. The treaty set forth the terms by which the former Mexican citizens and their property would be incorporated into the United States. Former Mexican citizens had as long as a year to choose their preference for citizenship—Mexico or the United States. Staying in the United States meant accepting U.S. nationality and citizenship. Most chose to remain on the land where they had settled and consequently became citizens of the United States. Their property was supposed to be respected as covered in Articles VII and IX of the Treaty, but many violations of these assurances occurred, and property was lost or stolen. Legal battles to recover property continue. Some Chicano scholars argue that the Treaty of Guadalupe Hidalgo, a legal document between two sovereign nations, guaranteed the civil rights, language, and religious freedom of the Mexican population who became United States citizens. The relevance of this argument surfaced in at least one desegregation school case in the 1940s and will be discussed in the next section.

Following the Mexican American War, the integration of Mexican Americans into the U.S. society between 1848 and 1915 has been characterized by political historians as one of a "politics of resistance." Mexicano struggles throughout the Southwest centered on maintaining control of their property as well as efforts to maintain a cohesive and culturally distinctive communal identity. The tradition of bilingual instruction, prevalent at the time in California and New Mexico, contributed to the maintenance of community. But public sentiment toward bilingual schooling began to turn in the late 1800s. In Texas, for example, arguments for English-only pedagogy emerged, although, as Carlos Kevin Blanton documented, legislation with criminal punishments did not take hold until after World War I in the context of American nativism fed by the war and increased immigration. Some of the antibilingual sentiment was directed at Mexican Americans. But as hostility increased toward Germany, German became as unpopular as Spanish in state laws and in the public schools.

The first major wave of Mexican immigration that significantly increased the Mexican population in the United States occurred at the turn of the 20th century, pushed by the Mexican Revolution of 1910 and pulled by the economic expansion of the agricultural and industrial sectors in the United States. Children of these immigrants started attending school in large numbers, and by World War II, many of them became soldiers; of these, many fought and died in Europe.

After the enactment of mandatory school attendance laws in the 1920s and 1930s, the public schools emerged as the primary institutions charged with the task of preparing students for productive adult roles in society, including the inculcation of American values and the ability to speak English. Unfortunately, opportunities to pursue long-term schooling were limited for most Mexican students. The predominant policy of segregation and Americanization initiated differential treatment and discrimination based on race, ethnicity, and national origin.

The legal precedent for separate but equal facilities upholding racial segregation was decided by the Supreme Court case *Plessy v. Ferguson* in 1896. The interpretation of this decision was extended to racial segregation in schools and applied to African American, Mexican American, and Native American students. During the first half of the 20th century, Mexican American children were subjected to the practice of segregation into either "Mexican classrooms" or into separate "Mexican schools." Chicano historian Ruben Donato estimates that by 1930, 85% of Mexican children in the Southwest were attending either separate classrooms or entirely separate schools. Anglo community and education leaders believed that the practice of segregating Mexican children from their White counterparts was best to train them for their expected station in life, Americanize them, and teach them English. Many Mexican parents engaged in struggles protesting segregation and discriminatory educational practices. Among the practices used to discriminate against Mexican American children was punishing them for speaking Spanish on the school grounds at any time and for any reason. As late as 1968, when the U.S. Commission on Civil Rights held hearings in Texas relative to these practices, one of the witnesses produced a "Spanish Detention Slip," which he explained was used in his child's school to document that the child was being punished for speaking Spanish. This was the same year that the Bilingual Education Act was passed in Congress as Title VII of the Elementary and Secondary Education Act (ESEA).

Desegregation Cases in Texas and California

Some political scientists argue that from 1915 to the 1950s, the Mexican American community pursued accommodation as a strategy to integrate into U.S. society. Given the nativist sentiments against German Americans and Mexican Americans deriving from World War I and the Mexican Revolution, many Mexican Americans did seek greater assimilation and cultural integration. This period saw the rise of the (hyphenated) Mexican-American generation and the birth of civic organizations such as the League of United Latin American Citizens (LULAC) and the American GI Forum. Note that at least in the case of these organizations, the word *Mexican* did not appear in their names. The Mexican-American generation sought to integrate by practicing their patriotism, serving in the armed forces, adopting American ideals, acculturating, and working within the system. Working within the political system meant standing up for their civil rights. Examples of these struggles are provided by several desegregation court cases, three of which will be discussed here.

The first milestone case was the 1930 *Independent School District v. Salvatierra* in Del Rio, Texas. A group of Mexican American parents sued the Del Rio Independent School District for illegal racial segregation. Attorneys for LULAC represented the parents in court. School officials reasoned that because Mexican Americans spoke Spanish, it was pedagogically necessary to segregate them, especially in the first three grades to teach them English. The judge hearing the case ruled in favor of the school district, noting that if the existing pedagogical segregation was limited to the first three grades, it was not inherent racial discrimination. In essence, the judge found de jure segregation illegal, yet in practice *Salvatierra* maintained pedagogical segregation as a legal loophole for de facto racial segregation.

The second historic case—*Alvarez v. Lemon Grove*—took place in California and was also decided in 1931. Mexican parents sued the school district of Lemon Grove for illegal racial segregation. School officials made a similar argument, claiming that it was necessary to segregate Mexican American students to facilitate their English language development and Americanization. In this instance, the court ruled in favor of the Mexican community on the grounds that separate facilities for Mexican American students were not beneficial to Americanization or to their English language development.

The third landmark case, *Méndez v. Westminster School District,* was decided in a California federal court in 1947. The court ruled that the school had illegally segregated Mexican American students from Whites, yet they were not legally classified as separate races. Moreover, the judge who heard the case found no statute or congressional mandate that permitted school boards to segregate Mexican American students and stated that the Fourteenth Amendment and the ratification of the Treaty of Guadalupe Hidalgo had guaranteed Mexican Americans equal rights. The *Méndez* case provided renewed inspiration to terminate segregation, especially in Texas where LULAC and the American GI Forum led the effort challenging the legality of pedagogical segregation. New cases were filed in 1948 (*Delgado v. Bastrop Independent School District*) and 1957 (*Hernandez v. Driscoll*). Attorneys for the NAACP Legal Defense Fund were carefully following these cases because they all contributed in some way to the epic Supreme Court decision in *Brown v. Board of Education.* The Court found the schools guilty of de jure segregation in Texas, however, many school districts resisted changing the practice of pedagogical segregation well into the 1960s, arguing that they were justified on pedagogical grounds because of students' limited English proficiency. The language question did not become a central civil rights issue until the 1960s and 1970s.

Shifting Sentiments Toward Native-Language Instruction

The decade of the 1960s ushered in an important change not only in the methods of teaching non-English-speaking children through use of the native language, but also in the type of leadership emerging from Latino communities, which differed significantly from the accommodationist politics of previous generations of Mexican Americans. After the enactment of Title VII of ESEA and the successful experiment of refugee Cuban children in bilingual schools in Florida, the Office of Education in the Department of Health, Education and Welfare began to fund programs experimenting with bilingualism and native-language instruction. Other factors that entered into this different mind-set included increased immigration from Asia and Latin America, and a gradual rethinking of assimilation and ethnicity. This political and cultural context influenced some leaders and language scholars to shift their thinking away from an exclusive English-only pedagogy to the emergent technique of English as a Second Language (ESL), which was more sympathetic to native languages. Early experimentation and research with native-language instruction and ESL in New York and Florida illustrated the promise of this new approach. Bilingual education followed close behind and eventually became the program of choice among Mexican American civil rights activists.

New York and other northeastern cities had experienced an influx of Puerto Rican workers and families since the 1930s. Puerto Rican children attending public schools encountered the same English-only pedagogy as did Mexican Americans in the Southwest. This schooling practice contributed to low educational attainment and high drop-out levels among Puerto Rican youth. In the late 1950s, concerned Puerto Rican community leaders and professionals in New York began to organize to address discrimination and push for educational equity. As a result of these efforts, the civic organization ASPIRA was founded in 1961 to address the high drop-out rate and push for the empowerment of the Puerto Rican community. The increased number of Puerto Rican children in New York City schools coupled with the reported failure of English-only instruction, and pressure from ASPIRA prompted school officials to initiate native-language instruction programs. In 1963, the superintendent of schools, Calvin Gross, advocated native-language instruction to help develop the bilingual and bicultural capabilities of Puerto Rican children to the benefit of the city, nation, and a multicultural world.

South Florida provided a different example regarding the incorporation and instruction of Latinos into American society and its educational system. Miami and Dade County Public Schools experienced an influx of Cuban refugees following the 1959 Cuban Revolution. The arrival of thousands of Spanish-speaking Cuban exiles prompted the national and local government and school officials to act. The state of Florida had no constitutional obligation to provide political refugees with services in education and other areas as it would for its citizens. Yet on political and moral grounds, the state accepted them as a group and provided all or some of the rights they had enjoyed in Cuba, including education in their native language. The sympathetic reception by Florida toward the Cuban refugees combined with the advocacy of Cuban refugee leaders prompted the federal government to provide aid to facilitate their settlement and assimilation. In 1961, the Cuban Refugee Program was established through the U.S. Department of Health, Education and Welfare. Through this program, incoming refugees were registered and a determination made of their eligibility for support and services. Various forms of assistance were provided, among them providing Spanish and English instruction to refugee children in Dade County schools, as well as vocational training to adults. From the start, a concerted effort was made by the school district to train teachers in English language instruction techniques and in developing appropriate materials for teaching English language arts to Spanish-speaking students. In 1963, the Dade County School Board approved the funding and implementation of a bilingual education project to serve both Cuban and American children. Based on the willingness of school administrators and teachers and the support from the Cuban American and Anglo American communities, the bilingual education project grew into a broader concept of two-way bilingual education for both Spanish-speaking and English-speaking students. English-speaking children learned Spanish and Spanish-speaking children learned English. The Mexican American experience with bilingual schooling, however, was different in style and substance.

Emergence of *Movimiento* Leadership

In the 1960s, educational attainment for Mexican Americans in the Southwest ranked among the lowest of all ethnic groups. Moreover, the practice of punishing students for speaking Spanish on school grounds continued. This practice went hand-in-hand with English-only pedagogy and was meant to shame the speaker into speaking English. The prevailing belief among educators in the Southwest was that if students learned English, abandoning their native language and culture, they would assimilate into American society faster and more effectively. The Mexican-American generation had embraced aspects of this conviction as an avenue to assimilation and social mobility. However, evidence showed that even after having learned English and given up Spanish, Mexican Americans continued to suffer the effects of years of segregation, discrimination, poverty, and powerlessness, without much hope of improvement. Furthermore, leaders saw that African American and other groups were getting more response from the federal government than Mexican Americans were. Inspired by the confrontational politics of the civil rights and antiwar movements, a new generation of Mexican American leaders began to change their politics. The new leadership drew much of its energy from Mexican American students and youth who had grown disenchanted with the traditional Mexican American political groups and organizations that had pursued the politics of accommodation. The leadership of this new Chicano generation espoused a greater sense of ethnic pride and cultural distinctiveness and preferred to self-identify as *Chicano* instead of the hyphenated *Mexican-American*. They also felt that Spanish was integral to their cultural distinctiveness and sought to have it recognized more openly and used more widely in schools. The preferred self-identification term *Chicano* served as a statement of the politics of identity and as a statement of self-affirmation and community empowerment. In rejecting the accommodationist style of their parents' generation, the style of the Chicano generation was more confrontational, grounded in activism and action, and formed the basis of their philosophical outlook, designated by the term *chicanismo*. The philosophy held that to be a Chicano or Chicana meant someone who fought for the rights of the Mexican American community and against Anglo-American bigotry, not merely seeking to integrate themselves into the society as their parents had done. Chicanismo was also concerned with the loss of Spanish and with cultural erosion, the lack of economic and social mobility, discrimination, and lack of educational equity.

In 1966, following a walkout by Chicano leaders from an Equal Employment Opportunity Commission conference in Albuquerque, New Mexico, and a call for more direct intervention, President Lyndon B. Johnson created the Inter-Agency Committee on Opportunities for the Spanish Speaking and named Vicente Ximenez to head the cabinet-level agency. Ximenez coordinated another conference in El Paso in 1967 that focused on Mexican American issues. Mexican Americans presented papers at the conference advocating the inclusion of Mexican American culture and language in schools on an equal basis with Anglo culture. Some of the young leaders who participated in these events grew disaffected with what they saw as all talk and no action. This group of alienated Chicano leaders organized their own *Raza* (literally meaning "the people") unity conference in El Paso and called for more self-determined efforts. A series of other *Raza* unity conferences were held in Texas and the Southwest, which brought members of different Chicano organizations and regions together to exchange ideas and strategies for addressing the problems facing Mexican Americans.

Among the central concerns discussed at these gatherings were political mobilization, cultural nationalism, the plight of Chicano education, and the need for bilingual education. Chicano leaders sought to gain representation at all levels of political life and called for governmental action on behalf of their group in education, health, housing, and employment. Fearful of the crumbling Hispanic support, the Johnson administration responded to the pressure from the different wings of the civil rights movement with programs under the banner of the Great Society and the War on Poverty. The passage of Title VII, known as the Bilingual Education Act (BEA) of 1968, was a component of the Great Society's antipoverty efforts through education. Although it was poorly funded, initially, supporters of Title VII believed that it was not just a linguistic tool in the education of non-English speakers but also a mechanism of empowerment and integration for language minorities into the mainstream. For Mexican Americans and other Latinos, the passage of the Bilingual Education Act created the potential of "additive" practices of bilingual education, which countered the Americanization and English-only "subtractive" approach extant since the late 1800s. Although the full promise of the Bilingual Education Act did not materialize, bilingual education supported by Title VII was a significant step forward in making possible a more meaningful relationship between schools and Latino communities. This noninstructional aspect of bilingual education has yet to be evaluated.

Armando L. Trujillo

See also Americanization and Its Critics; Early Bilingual Programs, 1960s; Languages in Colonial Schools, Western; *Méndez v. Westminster;* Title VII, Elementary and Secondary Education Act, Key Historical Marker

Further Readings

Alvarez v. Lemon Grove, Superior Court, San Diego County, No. 66625 (1931).

Delgado et al. v. Bastrop Independent School District of Bastrop County et al., No. 338 (W. D. Tex., 1948).

Beebe, V. N., & Mackey, W. F. (1990). *Bilingual schooling and the Miami experience.* Coral Gables, FL: Institute of Interamerican Studies, Graduate School of International Studies, University of Miami.

Blanton, C. K. (2004). *The strange career of bilingual education in Texas, 1836–1982.* College Station: Texas A&M University Press.

Brown v. Board of Education, 347 U.S. 483 (1954).

Donato, R. (1997). *The other struggle for equal schools: Mexican Americans during the civil rights era.* Albany: State University of New York Press.

Garcia, I. M. (1997). *Chicanismo: The forging of a militant ethos among Mexican Americans.* Tucson: University of Arizona Press.

Griswold del Castillo, R. (1990). *The treaty of Guadalupe Hidalgo: A legacy of conflict.* Norman: University of Oklahoma Press.

Hernandez v. Driscoll CISD, Civ. A 1384, U.S. District Court, (S.D. Tex., 1957).

Independent School District v. Salvatierra, 33 S.W.2d 790, 791 (Tex. Civ. App. 1930).

Jenkins, M. (1971). *Bilingual education in New York City.* New York: New York City Board of Education.

Konvitz, M. R. (1961). *A century of civil rights.* New York: Columbia University Press.

Méndez v. Westminster School District, 64 F. Supp. 544 (S.D. Cal. 1946), aff'd 161 F.2d 774 (1947).

Plessy v. Ferguson, 163 U.S. 537 (1896).

Trujillo, A. L. (1998). *Chicano empowerment and bilingual education: Movimiento politics in Crystal City, Texas.* New York: Garland.

U.S. Commission on Civil Rights. (1970). *Stranger in one's land.* U.S. Commission on Civil Rights Clearing House Publication No. 19. Washington, DC: U.S. Government Printing Office.

Lau v. Nichols, Enforcement Documents

Lau v. Nichols was a landmark federal court case filed in 1970 by parents of native Chinese-speaking students in San Francisco. The families argued that a lack of special support services for learning English violated their children's rights to an equal educational opportunity. In 1974, the Supreme Court found unanimously for the plaintiffs, finding that students who do not speak English are entitled to special accommodations under Title VI of the Civil Rights Act of 1964. An important antecedent document in the case was a May 25, 1970, memorandum sent by the Office of Civil Rights (OCR) in the then-Department of Health, Education and Welfare (now the Department of Education) to school districts around the nation. That memorandum anticipated the ruling in *Lau* by several years. It outlined the special responsibilities of public schools toward these students. The "May 25th Memorandum," as it is generally known, was not actually part of the *Lau* decision, but it was given higher visibility and status by that ruling.

The *Lau* decision and its effect on education policy have been much discussed among educators and school policymakers for more than 30 years. Important changes have taken place in the last 20 years, if not to the letter of the law in *Lau,* certainly to the tenor and vigor of enforcement efforts by the federal government. To fully understand the actual and potential impact of the *Lau* decision, it is useful to examine a number of supporting documents that trace the history of enforcement of the *Lau* ruling by the OCR. This entry reviews each of these documents briefly and relates them to the evolving interpretation and enforcement of *Lau.* Readers should be mindful that new rulings of the U.S. Supreme Court or actions by the Congress can affect the status of these policy documents later.

In chronological order, the pertinent documents to be reviewed here are the following:

1. The "*Lau* Remedies" issued by the OCR in 1975

2. The proposed *Lau* enforcement regulations published in the Federal Register in August 1980, as a Notice of Proposed Rulemaking

3. Guidance and policy memorandum by the director of OCR issued in 1985

4. Policy Update on Schools' Obligations Toward National Origin Minority Students With Limited-English Proficiency, issued in 1991

The *Lau* Remedies, 1975

Following the *Lau v. Nichols* decision, the *Lau* Remedies were published in 1975 under the title "Task-Force Findings Specifying Remedies Available for Eliminating Past Educational Practices Ruled Unlawful Under *Lau v. Nichols.*" This document gave districts guidance regarding how to identify English language learners (ELLs), which types of programs ELLs should be placed in; existing criteria, and standards for teacher qualifications. Moreover, the Remedies stated that when students' civil rights were violated, bilingual education should be implemented (they did not, however, require bilingual education in all cases). The Remedies found three types of programs suitable for ELLs: (1) bilingual/bicultural, (2) multilingual/multicultural, and (3) transitional bilingual education (TBE).

The Remedies are organized into nine sections: (1) Identification of Student's Primary or Home Language, (2) Diagnostic/Prescriptive Approach (identify the nature and extent of each student's educational needs and then prescribe an educational program utilizing the most effective teaching style), (3) Educational Program Selection, (4) Required and Elective Courses (must show that required and elective courses are not designed to have a discriminatory effect), (5) Instructional Personnel Requirements (instructional personnel must be linguistically/culturally familiar with the backgrounds of the students to be affected), (6) Racial/Ethnic Isolation or Identifiability of Schools and Classes (not educationally necessary nor legally permissible to create racially/ethnically identifiable schools to respond to student language characteristics), (7) Notification to Parents of Students Whose Primary or Home Language Is Other Than English (districts have the responsibility to notify parents of students identified as ELLs), (8) Evaluation (plans must include both a product result; and process evaluation-periodic evaluation throughout implementation), and (9) Bilingual/Bicultural Program (a program which utilizes the student's native language and cultural factors in instructing, maintaining, and further developing all the necessary skills in the student's native language and culture while introducing, maintaining, and developing all the necessary skills in the second language, English).

As noted by researcher Kenji Hakuta, the federal government emphasized a policy of implementing transitional bilingual education throughout the 1970s and moved away from English immersion toward the maintenance of native language and culture. The OCR largely used the *Lau* Remedies as a vehicle for this shift in program implementation. During this period, the number of bilingual education programs in the country grew substantially. James Crawford asserts that although schools in Alhambra, California, for instance, had no bilingual programs in 1977, OCR

citations for civil rights violations resulted in the district's implementation of 120 bilingual programs by 1987. These included instruction in Spanish, Vietnamese, Cantonese, and Mandarin at various levels. Although the *Lau* Remedies recommended native-language instruction, these programs had never been regulated by the OCR. Rather, complaints about violations of *Lau* were resolved based on recommendations to schools and districts, rather than requirements.

Notice of Proposed *Lau* Regulations, 1980

In August 1980, the Department of Education under Education Secretary Shirley Hufstedler published a Notice of Proposed Rulemaking (NPRM) titled "Nondiscrimination Under Programs Receiving Federal Assistance Through the Department of Education, Effectuation of Title VI of the Civil Rights Act of 1964." This would have replaced the *Lau* Remedies with more stringent requirements for schools educating ELLs. The changes would have mandated that all schools serving a certain number of ELLs from the same language background provide bilingual education as the program of choice for such children. When President Ronald Reagan took office, however, these proposed regulations were withdrawn. James Crawford cites Education Secretary Terrel Bell, who called the proposed regulations "harsh, inflexible, burdensome, unworkable, and incredibly costly . . . an intrusion on state and local responsibility." The Reagan administration promised to issue new, less intrusive regulations in the near future, but never published such rules in the Federal Register for public comment.

Since 1981, bilingual education programs have endured considerable scrutiny and opposition in policy making, with several judicial decisions as key exceptions. Today, OCR compliance issues are addressed on a case-by-case basis, although the process for filing complaints and recommendations is still viable and available. The May 25, 1970, Memorandum affirmed in the *Lau* decision and Title VI are still referenced in nearly all investigations decades later.

Guidance and Policy Memo, 1985

A memorandum titled "Policy Regarding the Treatment of National Origin Minority Students Who Are Limited English Proficient," initially published December 3, 1985, by the Assistant Secretary for Civil

Rights updated the May 25, 1970, OCR memorandum mentioned at the beginning of this entry. This document outlines the procedures OCR followed, during the mid 1980s in applying the standards affirmed by the Supreme Court in the *Lau* case, and in Title VI compliance reviews. The memo provides the background information presented in this entry and further reviews OCR's current procedures for conducting compliance investigations. It states that districts may use any method or program that has proven successful for educating language minority students, but that districts are expected to evaluate and modify programs that do not meet expectations. The memo lists two general areas in determining Title VI compliance: (1) whether an alternative program is needed for language minority students, and (2) whether the alternative program is likely to be effective in meeting the needs of language minority students. If English language learners are not able to participate effectively in the instructional program, an alternative should be implemented. The memo references the factors that influence the success of various approaches and pedagogies, including student characteristics, such as age and previous schooling, and school characteristics, such as the number of students from shared language backgrounds. In determining Title VI compliance, the OCR set forth an analytic framework including (a) whether an alternative program is necessary, and (b) whether the alternative program is likely to be effective.

Need for an Alternative

Determining whether students are served by programs may be based on a number of factors. Exiting criteria for placement in programs based on English proficiency levels may permit placement in regular instructional programs, and past academic records may be predictors of the assistance provided in alternative programs. Information for screening may include language assessment instruments, information from parents, or interviews. These methods may vary based on the number of students from shared language backgrounds, ages of students, size of school district, or availability of assessment tools. Districts may show that students placed in regular instructional programs do not need alternative programs for assistance, or that students can be transferred to alternative programs for a portion of the school day if necessary, for additional educational support. Although OCR may find schools that do not provide alternative programs to be

in violation of Title VI, the absence of formal identification, assessment, and a formal program may not constitute violations. For example, schools with low numbers of language minority students or in which a recent influx of ELLs has occurred may not be expected to have formal procedures or programs in place.

Whether the Alternative Is Effective

Within this second portion of the analytic framework, the memo outlines three questions: (1) Is the alternative program based on a sound design? (2) Is the alternative program being carried out in such a way to ensure the effective participation of the language minority students as soon as reasonably possible? and (3) Is the alternative program being evaluated by the district and are modifications made in the program when the district's evaluation indicates they are needed? For the first question, the OCR avoids making educational judgments about decisions made by local educational agencies. Factors that would be considered by OCR in compliance reviews include (a) whether at least some experts deem the program based on sound educational theory (an expert is an individual qualified for judgment based on experience, training, and objectivity), (b) whether there is an explanation for how the program meets the needs of language minority students (including a description of the program's components and activities and a rationale explaining how the program expects to meet students' needs), and (c) whether the district has implemented a plan approved by OCR (previously accepted plans remain valid).

Regarding how the program is being carried out, districts in compliance must have appropriate staff in place (training, qualifications, and experience should be consistent with the program) and adequate resources (timely availability of equipment and instruction material but limited finances do not constitute Title VI violations). Districts faced with such challenges as teacher shortages will not be penalized because the OCR will not place unrealistic expectations on districts. For program evaluation, districts are in compliance with Title VI when students are taught English and mainstreamed into regular instructional settings within a reasonable period. OCR approaches compliance concerns with caution, given the expertise of local education agencies in ensuring the efficacy of alternative programs. There are no regulations for data collection regarding alternative programs for districts. The 1985 memo stated that OCR expects districts to maintain accurate information about program implementation and effectiveness based on student progress.

In closing, the 1985 memo specifically states that OCR does not require a particular educational approach for compliance with Title VI. Legally, programs are deemed adequate if strategies have worked or promise to work based on the recommendations of experts. This memorandum was reissued without change on April 6, 1990.

Policy Update, 1991

In 1991, the OCR published the "Policy Update on Schools' Obligations Toward National Origin Minority Students with Limited-English Proficiency" memorandum, which represents the most comprehensive recent formal extension of the *Lau* Remedies. This document cites two equally important memoranda, May 1970 and December 1985; the three of them were "designed for use in conducting *Lau* compliance reviews." The memo cites *Lau* and the *Lau* Remedies as well as the court cases *Castañeda v. Pickard, Keyes v. School District No. 1, Teresa P. v. Berkeley Unified School District,* and a handful of less well-known cases in its guidance.

Notably, much of the document references the *Castañeda* case's standard, which is a three-pronged test for ensuring adequate educational support for language minority students (see below). This test requires that the program meet three standards: (1) It must be based on a sound educational approach, (2) the approach must be implemented effectively, and (3) adequately trained staff must be provided for the program within a reasonable amount of time. For the first prong, the policy update lists the following approaches as acceptable: transitional and developmental bilingual education, bilingual/bicultural education, structured immersion, and English as a Second Language (ESL). Addressing proper implementation (second prong), the document reads, "A recipient must either hire formally qualified teachers for LEP [limited English proficient] students or require that teachers already on staff work toward attaining those formal qualifications." Minimum qualifications for bilingual staff include ability to speak, read, and write in both languages and instruction in bilingual methods. Teachers in programs other than bilingual must complete training and demonstrate mastery of methods for this program. Districts should "use validated evaluative instruments—that is, tests that have been shown to accurately measure the skills in question." Also reviewed under implementation requirements are exit criteria for language minority and LEP students, special education programs, gifted/talented programs, and other specialized programs. For program evaluation (the third prong), the memo again references *Castañeda,* requiring that schools modify programs if they are unsuccessful and that programs are evaluated regularly to ensure student improvement. Formal programs should set achievement goals or demonstrate that students are overcoming language barriers. Further, programs are permitted to segregate ELLs from the mainstream population, but they must do so in the least segregative manner possible. Finally, the document states that the OCR will continue to use the *Castañeda* standard in reviewing complaints against schools' obligation to ensure educational equity for ELLs.

Educators, families, and researchers in the field have raised concerns regarding the English-only movement given the *Lau* and *Castañeda* cases. In 1998, the OCR published "Questions That May Be Raised by Proposition 227" regarding California's English-only initiative. This document repeatedly references the *Lau* decision, Title VI of the Civil Rights Act, and the May 25, 1970, Memorandum and states that placing ELLs in mainstream classes without additional assistance is a violation of *Lau.* The list of questions includes whether the Department of Justice or Department of Education will play a role in litigation challenging Proposition 227; the reply ensures that both will continue to monitor the implementation of program models post-227 and "whether children with limited English proficiency are provided realistic opportunities to succeed academically, consistent with federal civil rights requirements." Citing *Lau,* the document states that districts cannot limit special support for ELLs to one year and that if parents opt out of a program, districts must ensure that students have an equal opportunity to meet their needs relevant to learning English. This clarification notwithstanding, issues of *Lau* compliance in the context of the voter initiatives in Arizona, California, and Massachusetts are far from settled. In the years immediately after passage of the initiatives, OCR has given great latitude to these states to seek forms of compliance that they themselves design and allowed time for these to be tested.

Sarah Catherine Moore

See also Affirmative Steps to English; *Castañeda* Three-Part Test; Civil Rights Act of 1964; *Lau v. Nichols,* the Ruling; Appendix C

Further Readings

August, D., & Hakuta, K. (1997). *Improving schooling for language-minority children: A research agenda.* Washington, DC: National Academy Press.

Baker, C., & de Kanter, A. (Eds.). (1983). *Bilingual education: A reappraisal of federal policy.* Lexington, MA: Lexington Books.

Castañeda v. Pickard, 648 F.2d 989 (5th Cir. 1981).

Crawford, J. (2004). *Educating English learners: Language diversity in the classroom* (5th ed). Los Angeles: Bilingual Education Services.

Hakuta, K. (n.d.). *Lau site map.* Retrieved from http://www.stanford.edu/~kenro/LAU/LAUsitemap.htm

Keyes v. School District No. 1, Denver, CO, 413 U.S. 189 (1973).

Lau v. Nichols, 414 U.S. 563 (1974).

Nondiscrimination under programs receiving federal assistance through the department of education, effectuation of Title VI of the Civil Rights. Act of 1964 (Notice of Proposed Rulemaking). Fed. Reg. 45, 152 (Aug. 5, 1980).

Office for Civil Rights (1970). *Identification of discrimination and denial of services on the basis of national origin* (May 25th Memorandum). Retrieved from http://www.ed.gov/about/offices/list/ocr/docs/lau1970.html

Office for Civil Rights. (1975). *Task-force findings specifying remedies available for eliminating past educational practices ruled unlawful under* Lau v. Nichols (Lau *Remedies*). Retrieved from http://www.stanford.edu/~kenro/LAU/LauRemedies.htm

Office for Civil Rights. (1985). *Policy regarding the treatment of national origin minority students who are limited English proficient.* Retrieved from http://www.ed.gov/about/offices/list/ocr/docs/lau1990_and_1985.html

Office for Civil Rights. (1991). *Policy update on schools' obligations toward national origin minority students with limited-English proficiency.* Retrieved from http://www.ed.gov/about/offices/list/ocr/docs/lau1991.html

Teresa P. v. Berkeley Unified School District, 724 F. Supp. 698, 713 (N.D. Cal. 1989).

U.S. Department of Education. (2005). *Limited English proficient resources.* Retrieved from http://www.ed.gov/about/offices/list/ocr/ellresources.html

LAU V. NICHOLS, SAN FRANCISCO UNIFIED SCHOOL DISTRICT'S RESPONSE

The January 1974 U.S. Supreme Court decision in *Lau v. Nichols* was instrumental in guaranteeing linguistic minority students an education that is equal in quality to that of their English-speaking peers and has become synonymous with education rights in the United States. This entry describes the *Lau v. Nichols* case and the manner in which the San Francisco Unified School district (SFUSD), defendant in the case, responded to the legal mandate imposed on it by the U.S. Supreme Court, and subsequently, on remand, by the U.S. District Court in San Francisco.

The *Lau* decision was the outcome of a case brought against the SFUSD by a group of community members and parents of Chinese-speaking children. The parents claimed their children could not gain the same benefit from instruction in English as their native-English-speaking peers, and on this basis took legal action against the SFUSD for its failure to provide those students with an equal access to the district's instructional program. This was a class action suit. That is, parents and community members who brought the suit did so not only on behalf of their own children, but also on behalf of all children who might be suffering the same lack of access for the same reason. The plaintiffs did not seek a specific solution to the problem. Instead, they asked that the Board of Education of the SFUSD be directed to rectify the situation by the best means possible.

The original case, filed in federal district court, relied on the Equal Protection Clause of the Fourteenth Amendment to the U.S. Constitution and the Civil Rights Act of 1974. The latter excludes recipients of aid that discriminate against racial groups from participation in federal financial assistance. The parents claimed that these children, who were attending school in a district that received a significant amount of federal financial assistance, were being denied equal protection under the law because of their national origin. This case demonstrates the complicated and unpredictable nature of the pursuit of language and other rights through the courts.

Although *Lau* is perhaps the most pivotal of all language rights cases, it followed an unusual course through the judicial system and had a somewhat unlikely outcome. The original claims made by the parents (who were the plaintiffs in this case) were rejected by two lower courts. Neither the district court nor the court of appeals found the school district to be in violation of the students' rights. The Supreme Court's seldom-granted agreement to review the court of appeals decision led to the landmark nature of the case.

The court of appeal's argument in denying the parents' claim was that the school district was not responsible for the preexisting condition of lack of knowledge of English. It reasoned, "Every student brings to the starting line of his educational career different advantages and disadvantages caused in part by social, economic and cultural background, created and continued completely apart from any contribution by the school system" (*Lau v. Nichols,* 1973). The parents bringing this case were not satisfied with this outcome and continued to pursue a solution to the problem. Although a case that is lost in the court of appeals cannot be appealed directly, plaintiffs who lose a case at that level can request that the Supreme Court review the decision by filing a petition for writ of certiorari. This petition presents arguments about why the Court should grant the writ; that is, why it should review the case. These petitions are usually denied. In this case, however, the Court decided to grant the petition because of "the public importance of the question presented" (*Lau v. Nichols,* 1974).

After reviewing the case, the Supreme Court found in favor of the plaintiffs and returned the case to the U.S. District Court for the Northern District of California (a process known as "remand"), directing that court to fashion an appropriate solution, by directing the San Francisco Board of Education to "apply its expertise to the problem and rectify the situation" (*Lau v. Nichols,* 1974). The agreement between the SFUSD and the court, known as the consent decree, was the district's plan to provide all students access to a meaningful education. It became, and remains, pivotal to how schools provide students who do not speak or understand English with a meaningful education.

To craft an appropriate plan for the education of English language learners, the district contracted with the Center for Applied Linguistics, a group of educators and researchers with significant expertise in the area of English learner education. The Center for Applied Linguistics and a group of parents and community members recruited by the district called the Citizen's Task Force worked together to develop a "Master Plan for Bilingual-Bicultural Education in the San Francisco Unified School District." This detailed plan took more than a year to prepare and consisted of four volumes when it was finally submitted to the court in May 1975.

The plan detailed in this consent decree became the blueprint for the education of English language learners not only in the SFUSD but also in much of the United States. Kenji Hakuta points out in a timeline titled *Evolution of Important Events in California* that the California Legislature passed the Chacón-Moscone Bilingual-Bicultural Education Act in 1976,

which was the first state legislative act that mandated school districts provide language minority students with equal educational opportunities, despite their limited proficiency in English. Unlike federal legislation, which left decision making regarding how to ensure equal educational opportunity to district discretion, the California legislature asserted the right of English language learners to bilingual education.

Following is a summary of the plan, developed by the Citizen's Task Force in collaboration with the Center for Applied Linguistics and described in the consent decree between the plaintiffs and the San Francisco Unified School District.

The Master Plan

The consent decree stipulated that the SFUSD would implement a master plan for bilingual-bicultural education for the major language groups in the district—Chinese, Filipino, and Spanish—and established a formula for defining a "major" language group. The decree also stated that students from all such groups would be provided a bilingual education program to correct the problems identified in the proceedings. The decree further stated that the district would provide English as a Second Language (ESL) and other special programs for students from other language groups and would provide bilingual instruction for students from the less common language groups whenever feasible.

The plan provided detailed descriptions and definitions of the various program aspects, including instructional alternatives and techniques that could be used along with sample schedules and descriptions of how classroom organization and teacher and instructional aide time might be allocated. The plan also included criteria for choosing among different instructional options in different situations and provided a similar level of detail with regard to choosing appropriate instruments for assessing students' English and primary-language skills and for the preparation and certification of teachers for bilingual-bicultural education.

The master plan included a detailed timeline for implementation of each aspect of the program and specified that information about the progress of this implementation would be submitted to the court. Finally, the consent decree stipulated that the district would gather and report detailed information about the program to the court on an annual basis. This information-gathering and accountability for what the district would do to remedy the situation for linguistic minority students, how it would do this, and the way it would report progress of implementation of the solution were key aspects of the agreement. The specific information required of the district included the following:

1. Information about program participation and nonparticipation for students who speak a language other than English at home, as well as the numbers of these students and a description of the process for identifying them

2. A detailed description of these programs, how students are recruited for and assigned to them, identification of the school sites that maintain "model bilingual programs" for the major language groups, and those school sites that have other types of bilingual classes described in the master plan

3. Information about language skills and professional preparation of teaching and other staff and about their assignment to bilingual or other types of classes

This information-gathering became the model for data collected by the federal government and by many states. In addition, the consent decree required that the school board appoint a group of individuals from the community, the community council, including parents of both program participant and nonparticipant children, to serve as advisors regarding the plan and to assist in monitoring its implementation. The decree also stipulated that the district would provide assistance to and cooperation with the activities of the community council. Finally, the consent decree established a process for parents and others to express any objections to how the district was implementing the plan, for the district to respond to these objections, and for resolving disagreements between the two.

Conclusion

Although it has been somewhat eroded by recent interpretations of applicable law, the *Lau* case remains a key language-rights decision. With this case, the judicial system debated the question of whether schools must address the unique education needs of children who do not speak or understand English. The Supreme Court was unequivocal in affirming the rights of these children to have these needs addressed and school districts' legal obligation to do so. Moreover, the Court's finding that treating all children the same does not constitute an equal education for students who do not speak or understand English was an important precedent with regard to

educating English language learners in the nation's public schools. At the same time, the case's nonprescriptive approach shifted the policy and political debate about how to address the needs of these students and set a precedent for allowing school districts to determine how they will address this issue at the local level. Agreement by the school district to use chiefly a bilingual education approach further helped establish the preferred instructional modality for serving these children.

Julie Renee Maxwell-Jolly

See also Affirmative Steps to English; Center for Applied Linguistics, Initial Focus; Chacón-Moscone Legislation; Designation and Redesignation of English Language Learners; *Lau v. Nichols,* the Ruling

Further Readings

Center for Applied Linguistics and Citizen's Task Force on Bilingual Education. (1975, February 25). *A masterplan for bilingual-bicultural education in the San Francisco Unified School District in response to the Supreme Court decision in the case of* Lau v. Nichols, (Parts 1–4). Arlington, VA: Center for Applied Linguistics.

Center for Applied Linguistics and Citizen's Task Force on Bilingual Education. (1975). *A master plan for bilingual-bicultural education in the San Francisco Unified School District,* (Part 4), Appendix A. Arlington, VA: Center for Applied Linguistics.

Center for Applied Linguistics and Citizen's Task Force on Bilingual Education. (1975). *A master plan for bilingual-bicultural education in the San Francisco Unified School District,* (Part 4). Appendix D. Arlington, VA: Center for Applied Linguistics.

Chacón-Moscone Bilingual-Bicultural Education Act, California AB 1329 (1976).

Civil Rights Act of 1964, Pub. L. No. 88–352, July 2, 1964, 78 Stat. 241 (Title 28, Sec. 1447; Title 42, Sec. 1971, 1975a-1975d, 2000a *et seq*).

Del Valle, S. (2003). *Language rights and the law in the United States: Finding our voices.* In Bilingual Education and Bilingualism Series. Clevedon, UK: Multilingual Matters:

Hakuta, K. (n.d.). *Evolution of Important Events in California Bilingual Education Policy.* Retrieved from http://faculty.ucmerced.edu/khakuta/policy/ELL/timeline.html

Lau v. Nichols, 483 F.2d 791 (9th Cir. 1973).

Lau v. Nichols, 414 U.S. 563 (1974).

Tech Law Journal. (2007). *Online Glossary definition for certiorari.* Retrieved from http://www.techlawjournal.com/glossary/legal/certiorari.htm

LAU V. NICHOLS, THE RULING

Editor's Note: *This entry summarizes the ruling of the U.S. Supreme Court in* Lau v. Nichols. *This case is multifaceted. For a more complete explanation of the impact and significance of the case, please consult the entries listed under "See Also . . ." and the text of* Lau v. Nichols *reproduced in Appendix C.*

In 1974, the U.S. Supreme Court handed down a landmark decision in *Lau v. Nichols.* The Court ruled that Chinese-speaking students in San Francisco had a right to a better education than they were currently receiving, that the San Francisco Unified School District was responsible for providing them a more "meaningful" education, and that the Office for Civil Rights (OCR) of the U.S. Department of Education had the authority to compel the San Francisco Unified School District to provide such a program. More than 30 years after this historic decision, it continues to be widely discussed by experts and stakeholders, many of whom believe that the promise of the *Lau* decision has not yet been fulfilled.

The U.S. Supreme Court has dealt only infrequently with issues of language and language policy. In its history, only a handful of cases involving language have been decided by the Court. This is hardly surprising given the overwhelming prevalence of English in U.S. society. With the exception of Spanish, which is spoken by more than 30 million Americans, few languages are likely to have a continuing effect on as many cities and regions of the country during this century. The language group involved in the *Lau* case was a group of Chinese-speaking students attending the San Francisco schools. At the beginning of the 21st century, Chinese is the second-largest language community in the United States, second only to Spanish.

This entry describes fundamental concepts and issues of the ruling, the significance of the case, and recent developments regarding the case.

Fundamental Concepts and Issues

The decision by the Supreme Court to hear *Lau v. Nichols* on appeal from the Ninth Circuit Court in San Francisco was not made to resolve a language policy issue but, rather, a civil rights issue. During its 30-year history, the *Lau* case has come to be viewed as an important statement of equity for millions of public school students who come to school speaking languages

other than English. The case was not intended to be dispositive on the question of whether bilingual education is preferable to English as a Second Language (ESL) or vice versa, even though the case became inextricably embroiled in that debate. The *Lau* case was concerned with civil rights rather than language rights. The ruling made it abundantly clear that school leaders and policymakers are required to operate school programs with due cognizance of the requirements of Title VI of the Civil Rights Act of 1964, a measure that has now undergone modification by the more conservative justices who were subsequently appointed to that Court.

Several legal concepts are important for a full understanding of the current and future status of *Lau,* Title VI of the Civil Rights Act (CRA) of 1964, and related topics. Among the most important of these are "disparate impact," "private right of action," "coextensiveness," and "intent to discriminate" under the Equal Protection Clause. The future of civil rights protection under *Lau* and Title VI of the CRA will continue to evolve because of the impact of these terms and others. Interested readers are urged to consult legal sources to remain abreast of developments in this area.

Two fundamental issues went before the Supreme Court in *Lau.* The first of these was whether the Department of Health, Education and Welfare (now the U.S. Department of Education) has the authority to regulate the services offered by schools receiving federal assistance with respect to services to non-English-speaking students. Title VII of the Elementary and Secondary Education Act of 1965, as amended in 1968, provided funding for the creation and operation of bilingual education programs based on proposals submitted by school districts. Title VII of Elementary and Secondary Education Act was the proverbial carrot and Title VI of the CRA was the stick. The Court reviewed the legislative history of Section 602 of the 1964 CRA, which imposed on all federal agencies the responsibility for ensuring nondiscrimination in programs and activities involving federal financial assistance. The second and equally important issue was whether the educational program of the San Francisco Unified School District, at the time, violated Section 601 of the 1964 CRA. This issue was also decided in favor of the plaintiffs. Upon reviewing the findings of the lower courts, the Supreme Court reversed the lower court rulings and remanded the case back to the federal district court to fashion an appropriate remedy. The remedy that eventually issued from a citizen's advisory committee was bilingual education.

The San Francisco Unified School District adopted that recommendation.

Significance of the Decision

Perhaps the most important aspect of *Lau* was the ringing endorsement it provided for the idea that children who have language characteristics different from those of the mainstream population must be educated with proper cognizance of those differences. The Supreme Court asserted that it is not enough to provide the same education to children who are different; opportunity for one group may mean a denial of opportunity for another. In much of the litigation brought by African American children against the schools after *Brown v. Board of Education* in 1954, plaintiffs sought access to school programs already available to majority group students. In the main, desegregation cases sought access by Black students to the same curriculum and school activities available to White students. In *Lau,* the opposite was true; a remedy could only be said to exist if differentiated instruction were made available. *Lau v. Nichols* made clear that equality is not synonymous with sameness. What is good for one group of children may be inappropriate for another. In the language of the decision,

> There is no equality of treatment merely by providing students with the same facilities, textbooks, teachers, and curriculum; for students who do not understand English are effectively foreclosed from any meaningful education. . . . We know that those who do not understand English are certain to find their classroom experiences wholly incomprehensible and in no way meaningful.

Another important message in *Lau* was that schools have a responsibility to teach those academic skills they require of their students before they can graduate from high school. At the time of *Lau,* high-stakes graduation tests were not as common as they are today. California, however, required that high school students must demonstrate a strong command of the English language to graduate. The Supreme Court did not question California's right to require this:

> § 8573 of the [California] Education Code provides that no pupil shall receive a diploma of graduation from grade 12 who has not met the standards of proficiency in "English," as well as other prescribed subjects. Moreover, by § 12101 of the Education Code (Supp. 1973) children between the ages of six and 16 years are (with exceptions not material here) subject to compulsory full-time education.

Elsewhere, the opinion stated,

> This is a public school system of California, and § 71 of the California Education Code states that "English shall be the basic language of instruction in all schools." That section permits a school district to determine "when and under what circumstances instruction may be given bilingually."

Having noted the available options, the Court went no further. It mandated the district to ensure that schools teach English effectively to students who speak other home languages. The Court was explicit on this point:

> Basic English skills are at the very core of what these public schools teach. Imposition of a requirement that, before a child can effectively participate in the educational program, he must already have acquired those basic skills is to make a mockery of public education.

This posture by the Supreme Court supports conceptions of school accountability that have currency today. We can only speculate whether the use of high-stakes testing in English for graduation would be viewed in the same way today by the courts, if that requirement were to be challenged on the grounds that it violated the spirit of *Lau* absent an effective instructional program for teaching English. To our knowledge, no such case has yet been brought. Under the current interpretation of the No Child Left Behind (NCLB) 2001 legislation, the requirement of passing a test in English and other subjects appears to sit squarely on the shoulders of students rather than serve as a test of the viability of the instructional program and its promise to facilitate a good command of English. As the requirements of NCLB continue to evolve, it is possible that a legal challenge of this type could take place. In addition, considerable controversy exists concerning the degree to which children who do not yet have a command of English should be tested only in that language merely to satisfy the testing requirements of NCLB.

Among scholars and long-term observers of the decision who tend to view it in a wider context of educational change, some are concerned about the focus on English embodied in *Lau.* Richard Ruiz, an expert on language policy and politics, asserts that the emphasis on language barriers and on the primacy of English over all other subjects underscores the widespread popular view concerning the overarching importance of English. Ruiz believes that suggesting that young people are, in some sense, less than complete until and unless they learn English is an ethnocentric and narrow view of education. Furthermore, because the Supreme Court referred to this single aspect of education—teaching the *lingua franca*— and to no other, the decision gives no support to a broad mandate for making schools more sensitive to other needs of language minority children.

On the question of bilingual instruction, *Lau* was not the final word. The Court noted that there may be several ways of meeting the needs of these children:

> No specific remedy is urged upon us. Teaching English to the students of Chinese ancestry who do not speak the language is one choice. Giving instructions to this group in Chinese is another. There may be others. Petitioners ask only that the Board of Education be directed to apply its expertise to the problem and rectify the situation.

With respect to what remedy is most appropriate, the Court invoked the well-established principle of judicial restraint: A court should not answer questions that have not been brought to it for adjudication. Having acknowledged that several remedies are available, the Court disposed of the matter by noting that, in this case, "a remedy is not urged upon us." It reiterated that responsibility for policy remedies rests with the executive branch, in this case with the U.S. Department of Education and its OCR.

Lau recognized the right and legal responsibility of enforcement agencies in the executive branch to clarify, expand, and enforce the judgments of courts in accordance with Title VI of the Civil Rights Act of 1964, the legal basis on which the case rests. By so doing, the Court accepted one of the requirements promulgated by the OCR (of the then-Department of Health, Education and Welfare) in a now-famous memorandum called the May 25, 1970, Memorandum, signed by J. Stanley Pottinger, the then-director of the OCR. By affirming previous enforcement efforts by the OCR, the Supreme Court, in effect, adopted an important provision of the

May 25, 1970, Memorandum: the requirement that in cases where parents do not speak English, communications sent by the school to the home should be in the parents' language. To our knowledge, that requirement has never been challenged in other litigation, although few schools may be doing it. Many experts and stakeholders believe that because of the Supreme Court's acknowledgment, the May 25, 1970, Memorandum is entitled to great weight in planning school programs. Even in states that have passed antibilingual education measures, it can be assumed that the mandate for school-home communications in the child's home language remains valid and enforceable because school-home communications were not a school practice that was abolished by antibilingual initiatives in those states.

Furthermore, the Supreme Court affirmed the responsibility of the OCR to provide operational definitions and interpretations to the schools. As an example, the Court noted the May 25, 1970, Memorandum that had been sent to school districts by OCR. The Supreme Court seemed to approve of that policy and quoted two specific points from the memorandum in its ruling:

> 1. Where inability to speak and understand the English language excludes national origin-minority group children from effective participation in the educational program offered by a school district, the district must take affirmative steps to rectify the language deficiency to open its instructional program to these students.

> 2. Any ability grouping or tracking system employed by the school system to deal with the special language skill needs of national origin-minority group children must be designed to meet such language skill needs as soon as possible and must not operate as an educational dead-end or permanent track. (May 25, 1970, Memorandum)

Hence, although the Supreme Court avoided opining on the merits of bilingual instruction, it validated OCR's prescription on the use of other-than-English languages for communications between school personnel and non-English-speaking families.

The Court went on to reiterate,

> Respondent school district contractually agreed to comply with Title VI of the Civil Rights Act of 1964 . . . and all requirements imposed by or pursuant to

the Regulation of DHEW which are "issued pursuant to that title . . ." and also immediately to "take any measures necessary to effectuate this agreement." The Federal Government has power to fix the terms on which its money allotments to the States shall be disbursed. Whatever the limits of that power, they have not been reached here.

Recent Developments

Powerful and clear as the language of the *Lau* decision was, serious challenges to the continued viability of the decision and its reliance on the CRA have arisen post-*Lau*. The Supreme Court became more conservative after 1980, which has eroded the importance of Title VI of the CRA. The CRA was designed to enhance the Equal Protection Clause of the Fourteenth Amendment of the Constitution. The difference is that the Equal Protection Clause requires that plaintiffs show that the agency in question intended to discriminate against the person or group involved. Under the CRA, plaintiffs did not need to prove intent to discriminate, merely to document the negative impact of the school district's policies and practices. This difference has been slowly but surely eroded under the theory that Title VI of the CRA, and the Equal Protection Clause are coextensive; in short, that they are parallel laws with the same purpose. Further, that whatever requirement of intent to discriminate attaches to the Equal Protection Clause also applies to suits brought under CRA. This means that if *Lau* were to be tried under today's interpretation of CRA, the Supreme Court would probably reach different conclusions. Finally, because of another change imposed on Title VI of the CRA in recent years, individuals can no longer bring suits under the CRA. Only a federal agency may use CRA to seek relief against a government entity on behalf of an aggrieved individual. In legal parlance, Title VI no longer allows private right of action. Today, therefore, individuals must rely on another law to bring an action against a public body, the Equal Educational Opportunity Act of 1974, a measure that codified the findings in *Lau* explicitly.

Ha Lam and Josué M. González

See also Bilingual Education as Language Policy; *Castañeda* Three-Part Test; Civil Rights Act of 1964; Equal Educational Opportunity Act of 1974; *Lau v. Nichols,* Enforcement Documents; Appendix C

Further Readings

Brown v. Board of Education, 347 U.S. 483 (1954).
Lau v. Nichols, 414 U.S. 563 (1974).
Office for Civil Rights. (1970). *Identification of discrimination and denial of services on the basis of national origin* (May 25th Memorandum). Retrieved from http://www.ed.gov/about/offices/list/ocr/docs/lau1970.html

LAU V. NICHOLS AND RELATED DOCUMENTS

See APPENDIX C

LEARNING A LANGUAGE, BEST AGE

A controversial topic among linguists and researchers is the critical period hypothesis (CPH) and research studies that pertain to the best age in which to learn a language. CPH was first proposed by neurologist Wilder Penfield and coauthor Lamar Roberts in 1959. CPH claims that the presentation of adequate stimuli during the first few years of life are critical for individuals to acquire a first language, According to the theory, if language input does not occur during this period, the individual will never achieve a full command of the language—especially the grammatical systems. CPH was popularized in 1967 by Eric H. Lenneberg, with the introduction of his book *Biological Foundations of Language.*

Lenneberg's theory has extended to include a critical period for second-language acquisition (SLA) and has influenced research in the field, which is evidenced by studies including those supportive and unsupportive of CPH. Generally, researchers in the field of SLA have explored the following questions:

1. Does age affect how fast we can learn or acquire a second language over a reasonable period?

2. Does the type of exposure to the second language relate to age?

3. Does the age at which we begin learning a second language affect how fluent we can become in that language after a long time?

4. Do all these effects hold for all levels or types of linguistic knowledge?

This entry considers studies that have tried to look at both early-stage performance and ultimate attainment of those language learners studied. Results of studies in second-language acquisition indicate researchers are divided in their positions regarding CPH. Some researchers support CPH and insist that a critical period for learning a language does exist. For example, Mark Patkowski conducted a study about the likelihood of a critical period for learning a second language that found that learners younger than age 15 achieved a higher syntactic proficiency than did those who were older than age 15 at the onset of exposure. Among all factors Patkowski examined, age was the factor that had the most significant impact for success in learning a second language.

Results of some studies are mixed. For example, Stephen D. Krashen found in a 1973 study that adult learners proceeded through the early stages of syntactic and morphological development faster than children did, and that older children acquired this growth faster than younger children who were in the early stages of language development. Similarly, Anna K. Fathman and Lois Precup, in their 1983 study of immigrants acquiring English as a second language in the United States, reported that those who had immigrated at a younger age achieved higher levels of phonetic/ phonological proficiency than later arrivals. However, an opposing pattern was found in respect to morphosyntactic proficiency. A similar example is the 1999 study by Ellen Bialystok and Brenda A. Miller; they replicated the 1989 study of Jacqueline Johnson and Elissa Newport, and found differences in the performance on a grammar judgment test between native speakers of Chinese and Spanish acquiring English, before the age of 15. Although the younger Spanish-English bilinguals showed an advantage in performance over the older participants, the same pattern did not apply to Chinese-English bilinguals. They conclude that their results do not provide enough evidence to support the critical period hypothesis when acquiring a second language.

Results in some studies contradict what proponents of CPH claim. For example, Theo Bongaerts, Brigitte Planken, and Erik Schills have provided evidence that the groups of English language learners involved in their 1995 study were indistinguishable from the group of native speakers of English with respect to their pronunciation and thus passed themselves off as native speakers. These findings are contrary to the widely accepted belief proposed by Lenneberg that a

second language is learned only through extensive conscious effort and that an accent cannot be overcome easily. Thus, researchers, in summarizing phonological studies over the years, note that age may be central to ultimate attainment, but that no evidence has as yet been provided for the claim that second-language speech will automatically be accent-free if it is learned before the age of six and that it will definitely be foreign-accented if learned after puberty.

The inconsistency of results from research studies has provoked questions from researchers about whether the difference between young learners and adults must be the result of the critical period. For example, three misconceptions about age and second-language learning were recognized through a study conducted by Stefka H. Marinova-Todd, D. Bradford Marshall, and Catherine Snow in 2000. The first is the misinterpretation of observations of differences between children and adult learners, which may suggest that children are faster and more efficient at picking up a second language. Marinova-Todd, Marshall, and Snow admit that most adult second-language learners do end up with lower-than-native-like levels of proficiency, a failure often caused by a lack of engagement in the task and sufficient motivation. However, hard data make it clear that children learn a new language slowly, and with less speed, and with more effort than do adolescents or adults. The second misconception is the misattribution of conclusions about language proficiency to facts about brain functions. Marinova-Todd, Marshall, and Snow hold that the connection between brain functioning and language performance will no doubt be confirmed, but the exact nature cannot be guessed from the data available on brain function in early versus late bilinguals. The third misconception is based on poor adult learners, and the less emphasis placed on adults who master a second language at native-like levels. Marinova-Todd, Marshall, and Snow point out that sufficient motivation, commitment of time and energy, and support from the environment are the factors that have been overlooked by researchers, thereby seeming to lend support to the myths that children learn more quickly than adults, and that adults are incapable of achieving native-like second-language proficiency.

Researchers such as Bialystok and Kenji Hakuta have examined the role of linguistic and cognitive factors and explored how age might interact with these. Their research found both younger and older learners made more mistakes on items containing grammatical features that were different between their first and second languages, than on items that were similar in both, a phenomenon that cannot be explained by the linguistic theory of Universal Grammar, proposed by Noam Chomsky. Their study provides evidence that cognitive factors such as different instructional formats, the literacy difference of the learners, the availability of written texts, and the opportunity for instruction may lead to differences in proficiency levels.

David Singleton raised the issue from a different perspective, concerning diverse proposals or variations of CPH. He points out that the variety of ways CPH is understood affects the implications for second-language instruction. For example, Herbert W. Seliger suggests an earlier start of the phonetic/phonological acquisition of language by 12-year-olds is not consistent with that proposed by Lenneberg. Karl C. Diller, on the other hand, asserts that second-language accents can be avoided only if phonetic/phonological acquisition takes place by the ages of 6 to 8. Though Thomas Scovel asserts that the critical period, generally, ends progressively over a number of years beginning around ages 6 or 7; this is then followed by a second maturational phase, from 7 years to puberty. Michael H. Long proposes that a prerequisite for the acquisition of the second-language morphology and syntax to native level should be exposure to the second language before age 15.

The range of the critical period proposed so far extends from 1 year of age to adolescence, and the difference in between casts doubt on the credibility of CPH. This also confirms the well-founded comment made by researchers that the end of CPH for language in humans has proven difficult to find. In addition, the "fuzzy boundaries" used in language acquisition such as early child first language and second language, late child second language, adolescent second language, and adult second language have also caused problems. The divisions, all based on puberty, were not supported because researchers, in their studies of SLA, actually do not evaluate for age or whether a child has reached puberty.

Even though CPH has drawn many controversies and criticisms, its implications for second-language instruction cannot be overlooked. Research topics in the field of SLA also include how and to what extent the CPH concept can be applied to second-language instruction in school settings. For example, the idea of "younger equals better" by Penfield and the neurological evidence were the driving forces of movements advocating foreign-language education in elementary schools in the 1950s and 1960s. These arguments find support in CPH literature that claims biological and maturational factors constrain language learning beyond a certain age.

The influence of CPH, on the debate over the best age to learn a language, continues in the domain of SLA. Although the complexity of the behavioral systems to CPH concepts, which are applied to young children make it difficult, if not impossible, to identify the boundaries of sensitive periods with great specificity, it is imperative that educators consider all factors that lead to the success of second-language learners other than age alone. For example, linguistic, cognitive, and social factors, most of which have not been considered by previous studies on CPH may all play a part in the learner's language acquisition.

Li Jia

See also Critical Period Hypothesis; Language Learning in Children and Adults; Linguistics, an Overview

Further Readings

Bialystok, E., & Hakuta, K. (1994). *In other words: The science and psychology of second language acquisition.* New York: Basic Books.

Bialystok, E., & Miller, B. (1999). The problem of age in second language acquisition: Influences from language, structure and task. *Bilingualism: Language and cognition,* 2(2), 127–25.

Bongaerts, T., Planken, B., & Schills, E. (1995). Can late starters attain a native accent in a foreign language: A test of the Critical Period Hypothesis. In D. Singleton and Z. Lengyel (Eds.), *The age factor in second language acquisition* (pp. 30–50). Clevedon, UK: Multilingual Matters.

Diller, K. (1981). "Natural methods" of foreign language teaching: Can they exist? What criteria must they meet? In H. Winnitz (Ed.), *Native language and foreign language acquisition* (pp. 75–91). New York: New York Academy of Sciences.

Fathman, A., & Precup, L. (1983). Influences of age and setting on second language oral proficiency. In K. M. Bailey, M. H. Long, S. Peck (Eds.), *Second language acquisition studies* (pp. 151–161). Rowley, MA: Newbury House.

Johnson, S. J., & Newport, L. E. (1989). Critical period effects in second language learning: The influence of maturational state on the acquisition of ESL. *Cognitive Psychology, 21(*1), 60–99.

Krashen, S. D. (1973). Lateralization, language learning and the critical period: Some new evidence. *Language Learning, 23*(1), 63–74.

Lenneberg, E. H. (1967). *Biological foundations of language.* New York: Wiley.

Long, M. H. (1990). Maturational constraints on language development. *Studies in Second Language Acquisition, 12*(3), 251–285.

Marinova-Todd, S., Marshall, D., & Snow, C. (2000). Three misconceptions about age and L2 Learning. *TESOL Quarterly, 34,* 9–34.

Patkowski, M. S. (1980). The sensitive period for the acquisition of syntax in a second language. *Language Learning, 30,* 449–472.

Penfield, W., & Roberts, L. (1959). *Speech and brain mechanisms.* Princeton, NJ: Princeton University Press.

Scovel, T. (1988). *A Time to speak: A psycholinguistic inquiry into the critical period for human language.* Rowley, MA: Newbury House.

Seliger, H. W. (1978). Implications of a multiple critical periods hypothesis for second language learning. In W. Ritchie (Ed.), *Second language acquisition research: Issues and implications* (pp. 11–19). New York: Academic Press.

Singleton, D. (2005). The Critical Period Hypothesis: A coat of many colors. *International Review of Applied Linguistics, 43,* 269–285.

Singleton, D., & Lengyel, Z. (Eds.). (1995). *The age factor in second language acquisition.* Clevedon, UK: Multilingual Matters.

LINGUISTIC MATURITY THEORY

See LEARNING A LANGUAGE, BEST AGE

LINGUISTICS, AN OVERVIEW

One of the central academic disciplines underlying the collective knowledge base of bilingual education is that of linguistics. *Linguistics* can be defined, in the broadest terms, as the scientific description of human language. Tony Howatt explains in the introduction to the *Linguistics Encyclopedia* (2nd ed.) that serious study of the human capacity for language is presumed to have begun in the first literate human societies (e.g., Mesopotamia, Northern India, China, and Egypt). However, the roots of Western linguistics as a specific area of scientific study date back to the 19th century. Two central questions have shaped the field since that time: First, what is the nature of human language; and second, what is involved in the study of human language? This entry addresses those two questions by way of providing an overview of the science of linguistics.

Nature of Language

It is difficult to capture, succinctly, the myriad ways in which different traditions of linguistic study conceive of the nature of human language. As discussed later in this entry, there are substantive debates about language that prevent such a brief summary. Ralph Fasold and Jeff Connor-Linton have attempted to provide an overview of certain features that they maintain most linguists would accept as universal to humans' capacity for language.

The first of these features is the *modularity* of language. Language is composed of distinct and discrete units, or modules. Each module has a particular role to play, but they function together in a coordinated way to allow humans to produce and understand language. Related to modularity is the principle of *constituency*. Languages are organized in constituent parts such that more complex constituents may be used to take the place of simpler forms. An example of the principle of constituency might be, "*They* argued heatedly about the new work assignment." The simple constituent *They* can be replaced by a more complicated one, for example, "*The manager and her employee* argued heatedly about the new work assignment," or even "*The new manager and her employee who had worked there for many years* argued heatedly about the new work assignment." The principle of constituency describes how like constituents of varying degrees of complexity may be exchanged for one another. However, this principle does not mean that language is random. On the contrary, "*heatedly and her new employee* argued about the new work assignment" is not a possible construction, because "heatedly" and "they" or "the manager and her employee" are not like constituents.

The principle of constituency is particularly important in that it allows for an infinite number of utterances, even though languages are composed of a finite number of units. This phenomenon of language is known as *recursion*. The ability to construct an infinite number of utterances from a finite number of constituent parts has an enormous impact on our understanding of language. Above all, it means that humans do not acquire language by memorizing each word in a language. Instead, there must be some other explanation for how humans are able to learn language such that we can produce and understand an infinite number of sentences. We will return to this issue later.

The linguistic property of *discreteness* manifests itself in two particular ways. The first has to do with the sounds that humans are capable of producing. Imagine the sounds a violin makes as its player tunes the instrument. As the string becomes more taut, the pitch rises. In much of Western music, that spectrum of sound has been broken into incremental steps of a scale, the smallest unit of which is a half step between, as an example, C and C sharp. In most cases, those who play and compose Western music have socially agreed to divide the full spectrum of sound in this way. But when we are exposed to music from other parts of the world, we discover various ways in which to divide the spectrum of sound that incorporate discrete units much smaller than a half step. Languages function in much the same way. Within each language community, a social contract of sorts is in effect that agrees about how to distinguish the spectrum of possible sounds into discrete, intelligible units. In English, we differentiate a long i sound, as in *eye,* from a long e sound, as in *bee.* That distinction allows us to know when someone is talking about bites or beats, for example. But not every language brackets sound in the same way. This means that the distinction between long i and long e, which comes naturally to native speakers of English, may be entirely indistinguishable to speakers of languages that do not compartmentalize sound in the same way.

Discreteness in language is shown, as well, in how humans understand the world around them. For example, different languages divide time in different ways. Even languages that share the concepts of year, month, day, hour, and so on often reflect different distinctions in time. English terms such as *morning, afternoon, evening,* and *night,* for instance, do not fully equate to Spanish terms such as *mañana, tarde, noche,* and *madrugada.* Thus, natural phenomena experienced by all humans, such as time, are captured in unique ways in each language. Nonetheless, in borderland regions such as that between the United States and Mexico, bilingual speakers often minimize the subtleties and end up equating terms to facilitate communication. This occurs as well in bilingual classrooms. The net

effect is the adaptation of both languages to each other. In those circumstances, a fully fluent bilingual individual can detect the borrowing of grammatical or lexical features from one language to the other.

The principle of *productivity* is demonstrated by every language being capable of creating new words to better understand changes in the world around us. Think of the many words that have emerged in the United States to refer to a car (e.g., hatchback, coupe, SUV, RV, compact, pickup, wagon, etc.). Similarly, all languages are able to create new words in an instance. If this new word fits the sound and word patterns in the language—and if the wider social community of that language accepts and begins to use that word— then it can become part of that language system. A prime example would be the term *Spanglish.* Whatever our opinions may be of the linguistic phenomenon to which the term refers, this term was coined to refer to a language variety that is distinct from standard varieties of English and Spanish. The word follows sound and word patterns in English (but not in Spanish) and has been widely accepted in the greater speech community as a word.

The final three universal aspects of human language are perhaps the most critical. The first of these is the acknowledgment that the words we coin, the sounds we bracket within the spectrum of sound, and so forth, reflect completely arbitrary decisions. The *arbitrariness* of language implies that there is nothing about the sounds /t/-/ej/-/b/-/1/ or its standard English spelling "table" that has any systematic or innate connection to a flat, hard surface (usually) held up by four rods. Instead, it has been socially agreed upon and transmitted across generations that this collection of sounds, and this manner of representing those sounds graphically, will refer to such an object. Likewise, such words as *mesa* or *Tisch* (in Spanish and German, respectively) are not any more connected to this object than "table" is in English. However, the arbitrary nature of the correlation between sound and object does not mean language is random. Instead, how languages combine sounds, words, and phrases is governed by distinct patterns that allow in English for the /b/ and /1/ sounds to combine as they do in the word "table," but not so in a word like "lbate."

Moreover, human language reflects *duality* in its structure. Every language is composed of discrete units that on their own have little or no meaning. The sounds /d/, /i/, and /g/ alone, for example, have no meaning to native speakers of English. Yet, when we combine these three sounds together, we get a larger unit of language, "dig," that assumes various meanings in English. Linguistic duality underscores the importance of context in communication; individual units of any language are meaningful only inasmuch as we understand them in relation to other linguistic units. The importance of context can be seen more clearly with larger units of language (e.g., at the word or sentence level). Consider the many English language arts teachers who work tirelessly to help their students know when to write "to," "too," or "two." The problem here stems from the principle of duality. Each word on its own has little meaning. When placed in the context of a phrase or sentence, however, each word takes on specific meaning, and the listener is able to know at once which word is meant.

The final universal property of language is its *variability*. We see this feature in several other properties of language discussed earlier, for example, how different languages divvy up the sound spectrum, or the ability to create new words based on existing sound and word systems. But another aspect of linguistic variability is that humans change their language to reflect who they are, and where and with whom they are interacting. A simple example is how we choose to address a group of people at once. Whether we say "you guys," "y'all," "you's" or "you's guys," or just simply "you" says a lot about where we come from, how formal or not the situation is, our age, and so on. The words we choose, the way we pronounce them, what we do not say at all—all of these linguistic moments reflect our identities and our understanding of the social context around us. Another aspect of linguistic variability concerns the varieties of language that emerge when different language systems are in contact; examples of these include Spanglish in the United States or the varieties of English that are native to postcolonial societies such as India or Nigeria.

Linguistic Traditions and Domains of Study

As suggested earlier, the tradition of linguistics in the West dates back to the 19th century. Known then as *philology*, the primary focus of research was the historical and comparative study of language. Howatt outlines the factors that influenced philology. First, linguistic studies found important models for research in the natural sciences. The work of Carl Linnaeus in the 18th century, for example, in classifying the plant

world served as a guide for classifying human languages. Charles Darwin's development of the theory of evolution also provided an important model to 19th-century philologists in identifying language families that have evolved over time. A second important influence on philology were the projects of nation-building taking place in the Western world at this time. Romantic notions of the nation-state being composed of one people and one language required a history of that people and its language that reached back far into time. Colonialism brought Western philologists into contact with long-standing linguistic traditions, especially that of the ancient Indian language Sanskrit, as they sought to find Western linguistic and national roots in ancient civilizations.

Structuralism

Although he emerged from this intellectual environment, Ferdinand de Saussure fundamentally altered the landscape of linguistic study. His greatest contributions to linguistics were made in a series of lectures published posthumously in 1916 as *Cours de linguistique générale*. In his lectures, Saussure differentiated historical study of language, *diachrony*, from nonhistorical study, *synchrony*. For him, the latter envisions language as a living whole, existing at a particular moment in time. The goal for linguists should be, so Saussure stated, to understand a language in its current state before engaging in a historical study of its development.

Saussure's most famous contribution to the study of language is his tripartite conception of human language. His notions of *langage, langue,* and *parole* would later become the foundation of *structuralism*. Saussure named the overall human capacity for language *langage*. Within this capacity, he distinguished between separate language systems, or *langue*, and the manifestations of those systems as actual speech, or *parole*. He argued that the primary focus of linguistic study should be to better understand the nature of each individual language system, *langue*. For Saussure, *langue* is a social phenomenon, a system that has been socially agreed upon within a linguistic community. Saussure first identified the arbitrary nature of language with his distinction between signifier and signified. Although no inherent connection exists between a given sound (the signifier) and its meaning (the signified), each linguistic community must agree to a convention of matching the two for communication to occur and be effective. However, signifiers in language systems have meaning only in relation to other signs. For example, the English word "house" has meaning only inasmuch as we contrast it with apartment, cabin, shanty, or mansion to identify various housing structures.

Saussure made an additional distinction about the nature of language that draws from his notion of signifiers and signified. Each language system organizes the signs it employs in two particular ways. Saussure conceived of this as two intersecting axes. The horizontal axis represents a *syntagmatic* organization of signs, in which different signs are linked together into utterances. The vertical axis represents a *paradigmatic* organization of signs, which represents different categories of signs (e.g., things, actions, descriptions) that are more or less constrained by the structure of each language system.

In the United States, the structuralist tradition stems in large part from the field of anthropology. Howatt describes the insights into linguistic study offered by Franz Boas in his *Handbook of American Indian Linguistics.* The first of these, the phoneme principle, establishes that each language has a limited and distinct set of sounds from which to construct utterances. The primary job of linguistics, then, is to describe those sounds as accurately as possible, and from there derive any generalizations about the language. Additionally, Boas further argued that all languages are distinct; that each language must be understood on its own terms, not by projecting a model of one language onto another; and that the basic unit of linguistic study should be the spoken sentence.

Another anthropologist, Edward Sapir, built on Boas's ideas and formally introduced the concept of specific patterns, or structures, in language in his 1921 work, *Language.* Sapir took a holistic approach to understanding culture, language, and social life as an integrated whole. He is perhaps best known for his notion, developed together with his student and colleague, Benjamin Whorf, of the relationship between the constraints of language systems and cognition, known as the *Sapir-Whorf hypothesis.* Howatt defines the extreme version of this hypothesis, which argues that humans are limited by the structure of their language system as they conceive of, or understand, the world around them. Although such a deterministic view of language and cognition has long been debated, weaker versions of the Sapir-Whorf hypothesis support the notion that different languages capture different worldviews, making each human language distinct and intrinsically valuable.

Generativism

Generativism, the second major tradition in linguistics, is most closely associated with the work of Noam Chomsky, although his work in transformational-generative grammar is only one trajectory of generativist scholarship. Chomsky's work represents a break with structuralists' focus on patterns. For structuralists, the aim of linguistic study was to describe spoken language as accurately as possible, to allow for inductive generalizations about patterns in a given language system. For Chomsky and his notion of transformational grammar, the focus of study was on identifying a series of rules underlying the construction of phrases and sentences. He made a distinction between the *surface structure* of word order, that is, how an actual sentence was ordered, and the *deep structure* that governed its construction. The example he began with was active and passive sentences. Although at the surface level, each type of sentence appears to be different, an underlying grammar is the same in determining how each sentence will be structured.

Whereas Chomsky's original work focused on word order, a central concern of his scholarship has been to explain how humans acquire language at all. He has posited a series of controversial theories to explain this universal characteristic of humans. Chomsky has argued that humans are genetically endowed with the ability to acquire language. The acquisition process is directed by a *language acquisition device,* a specific area in the brain that enables children to induce and acquire the rules of the particular language system in which they are immersed. Chomsky adds to this the notion of *Universal Grammar,* which acts as a set of parameters for language that all humans are endowed with genetically. Within the parameters set by Universal Grammar, each language system develops its own settings that children acquire naturally.

Stemming from this concept of Universal Grammar is a distinction made by Chomsky that relates in certain ways to Saussure's differentiation of *langue* and *parole.* Chomsky distinguishes between linguistic competence (i.e., tacit knowledge) of a given language system based in Universal Grammar, and linguistic performance (i.e., how we demonstrate that competence in social communication). Although Saussure's notion of *langue* is rooted in the language system unique to a particular linguistic community, competence for Chomsky is rooted in the genetic ability for humans to acquire language. This definition of competence and its focus on cognition has been criticized for relying too much on idealized native speakers and listeners of a given language and their linguistic competence, while disregarding actual speech in real-world social contexts.

Functionalism

The third major tradition in linguistic study, *functionalism,* concerns itself precisely with real-world language use. This perspective on language study focuses on the social functions of language as a system of signs that humans develop to meet complex social, cultural, and communicative needs. The form that a given language takes still matters, but the study of the relationships between various forms (i.e., their function) is particularly important.

Michael Halliday's contributions to functionalist linguistics have been enormous. His conception of language as a social semiotic understands language as a system of signs that humans create to act upon the environment and to interact with one another. He outlined various *metafunctions* of language that allow humans to do this. According to this researcher and theorist, *ideational functions* of language allow individuals to interact with their environment, to understand it, and act upon it. *Interpersonal functions* of language allow groups of individuals to interact with one another in specific social contexts. The central aim of linguistic study should be, then, to engage in systematic analysis of why people make the choices they do within the framework of specific linguistic systems, and the metafunctions at play within them.

Connections to the Study of Bilingualism

In addition to the three theoretical traditions of linguistics, the United States has a rich history of interdisciplinary approaches to language study. It is impossible to name and summarize each approach here, but among the most important is *applied linguistics.* As the name suggests, applied linguistics aims to link theoretical linguistic study with practical questions about language, especially second- and foreign-language learning, language pedagogy, translation studies, language policy and planning, and other educational fields.

Sociolinguistics focuses on the interaction between a language variety and the structure and functioning of the society in which it is located. Finally, *psycholinguistics* concentrates on the impact of specific psychological processes, such as attention and memory, on linguistic behavior. In each case, these fields emerged in the 1960s and have grown, along with many others, to become major traditions of linguistic inquiry in their own right.

Each of the various interdisciplinary approaches has produced important scholarship on the nature of bilingualism. Many foundational concepts in bilingualism and how children acquire second languages have derived from the intersection of psychology and language study. An early example is the work of William Lambert and his distinction between *additive* and *subtractive bilingualism.* Yet another major theoretical insight on the connection between cognition and language acquisition is James Cummins's *Thresholds Theory.* Neither this theory, nor further theoretical developments that grow out of it (e.g., Cummins's distinction between social and academic language) has gone without controversy (see critique by Jeff MacSwan and Kellie Rolstad and by Terrence Wiley). Nevertheless, they remain foundational notions in the development of scholarship on bilingualism and language acquisition.

Stephen Krashen's contributions to the field of bilingualism have also been invaluable, both at the theoretical and advocacy levels. His conception of second-language acquisition is composed of five distinct but related hypotheses. The acquisition-learning hypothesis distinguishes the natural acquisition process, which occurs subconsciously as second-language learners engage in meaningful interaction in the target language, from the conscious knowledge about the second language that results from explicit instruction. His monitor hypothesis speculates about the relationship between acquisition and learning; namely, that learned knowledge about the second language acts as a monitor that edits the utterances produced by acquired knowledge. Krashen's natural order hypothesis posits that elements of the second language are acquired in a predictable order. However, the order of acquisition is language specific and not tied to the language learner's age, first language, or amount of instruction. His input hypothesis focuses on acquisition, rather than learning, of the second language and argues that input in the target language must be comprehensible, that is, at a degree of difficulty just above what the learner already can understand, for the language to be acquired. Finally, Krashen developed the affective filter hypothesis to account for the role of emotional, motivational, and other related factors in the second-language acquisition process.

The field of sociolinguistics has produced a fundamentally different approach to understanding bilingualism and how people acquire additional languages. Most prominent in this tradition of scholarship is Joshua Fishman. His early work on multilingualism challenged psychological approaches to the study of bilingualism that investigated language learning only at the level of the individual, leading to the idealized notion of the "balanced bilingual." For Fishman, multilingualism is a social phenomenon that reflects social patterns of rights, obligations, and interactions. His work is driven by what he calls "partisanship" in supporting linguistic minorities and trying to understand language use from their insider perspective. This commitment has led to several decades of groundbreaking scholarship on questions of bilingualism, including the following: refinement of the notions of domain, and diglossia as a way to understand language use within a given community; exhaustive study of language shift among linguistic minorities in the United States; a theory of reversing language shift, including the Graded Intergenerational Disruption Scale as a tool for identifying various stages of language shift or language maintenance; and compelling theories of the relationship between language use and ethnic consciousness.

Major Themes

Despite the great diversity in linguistic inquiry, two major themes have dominated the debates about the nature of language and the most appropriate way to study it. On the one hand is the basic distinction between language systems and language-in-use. This distinction surfaces in various ways, be it Saussure's langue/parole, Chomsky's competence/performance, or the form and function divide in functionalism. Although there are important differences among these traditions, each represents theoretical distinctions that have important consequences for the methodology of linguistic study and for the applications that flow from the knowledge thus acquired. On the other hand are questions about the diversity versus the universality of language. From the descriptivist traditions that recognize the uniqueness of each language, to strong versions of the Sapir-Whorf

hypothesis that state we can only understand the world inasmuch as we have linguistic categories with which to do so, a long tradition exists in linguistics of attempting to understand each language as a unique system. Still, there has also been the recognition that language—a system of sounds and signs that humans employ in creative ways to interact—is a defining characteristic of our species. The recognition of this universality led to the study of the principles at the start of this entry, as well as to notions of genetic endowments and universal systems of grammar that govern language-in-use.

Donald Jeffrey Bale

See also BICS/CALP Theory; First-Language Acquisition; Language Acquisition Device; Language and Thought; Language Defined; Second-Language Acquisition

Further Readings

Chomsky, N. (1965). *Aspects of the theory of syntax.* Cambridge: MIT Press.

Chomsky, N. (1975). *The logical structure of linguistic theory.* New York: Plenum.

Chomsky, N. (1995). *The minimalist program.* Cambridge: MIT Press.

Crystal, D. (1985). *Linguistics* (2nd ed.). Harmondsworth, UK: Penguin.

Cummins, J. (1979). Linguistic interdependence and the educational development of bilingual children. *Review of Educational Research, 49,* 221–251.

Cummins, J. (1980). The cross-linguistic dimensions of language proficiency: Implications for bilingual education and the optimal age issue. *TESOL Quarterly, 14*(3), 175–187.

Cummins, J. A. (1981). The role of primary language development in promoting educational success for language minority students. In C. Leyba (Ed.), *Schooling and language minority students: A theoretical framework.* Sacramento: California State Department of Education.

Fasold, R. E., & Connor-Linton, J. (Eds.). (2006). *An introduction to language and linguistics.* Cambridge, UK: Cambridge University Press.

Fishman, J. A. (1991). *Reversing language shift.* Clevedon, U.K. Multilingual Matters.

Halliday, M. A. K. (1978). *Language as social semiotic.* London: Edward Arnold.

Halliday, M. A. K. (1994). *An introduction to functional grammar* (2nd ed.). London: Edward Arnold.

Howatt, T. (2002). Introduction. In K. Malmkjær (Ed.), *Linguistics encyclopedia* (2nd ed.). London: Routledge.

Krashen, S. (1981). *Second language acquisition and second language learning.* New York: Pergamon.

Krashen, S. (1982). *Principles and practice in second language acquisition.* New York: Pergamon.

Lambert, W. E. (1975). Culture and language as factors in learning and education. In A. Wolfgang (Ed.), *Education of immigrant children.* Toronto: Ontario Institute for Studies in Education.

MacSwan, J., & Rolstad, K. (2003). Linguistic diversity, schooling and social class: Rethinking our conception of language proficiency in language minority education. In C. B. Paulston & G. R. Tucker (Eds.), *Sociolinguistics: The essential readings.* Oxford, UK: Blackwell.

Sapir, E. (1939/1921). *Language: An introduction to the study of speech.* New York: Harcourt, Brace.

Saussure, F. de. (1959). *Course in general linguistics.* New York: Philosophical Library.

Wiley, T. G. (1996). *Literacy and language diversity in the United States.* McHenry, IL: Center for Applied Linguistics and Delta Systems.

LITERACY AND BILITERACY

Among both lay people and experts, everyone seems to agree that literacy is important. Nevertheless, there has been little consensus regarding what it means to be literate or regarding what all the purported benefits of literacy are to both individuals and to the larger society. Ever since the 1950s in the United States, sensationalist headlines have drawn national attention to an alleged literacy crisis. Implicit within the captions is an assumption that literacy equates to literacy in English. Literacy in other languages is generally ignored. Even a 2006 high-profile report by Diane August and Timothy Shanahan on developing literacy among second-language learners focuses on English literacy almost exclusively. Perhaps because of negative language politics, knowledgeable professionals tend to ignore the fact that bilingual learners are well positioned to acquire some level of literacy in English and another language—that is, to become biliterate. This entry discusses beliefs about literacy, defines *literacy,* compares bilingualism and literacy, and discusses approaches to literacy and limitations of assessments of literacy.

Beliefs About Literacy

Most discussions about the importance of literacy in society tend to reflect several basic metaphors or beliefs about literacy. Sylvia Scribner identified these as literacy as adaptation, literacy as power, and literacy as a state of grace. Literacy as adaptation sees literacy as essential for social and economic functioning. Certainly literacy is necessary for access to most jobs and for participation in society, so this view has been influential in framing most popular discussions about literacy. Literacy has also been portrayed as power or as a transformative means to empowerment. This position was most notably popularized by Paulo Freire's influential *Pedagogy of the Oppressed.* This work emphasized the importance of using literacy for breaking cultures of silence among those not literate. English literacy has been seen as necessary in the United States, but several adult education specialists, drawing on Freire, have argued that native-language literacy provides the most direct and efficient means for empowering many adult language minority immigrants who have previously lacked opportunities for formal education. Surely, the issue of promoting literacy does not need to be framed as English literacy versus native-language literacy—as some pundits would try to have us believe—because the latter can also facilitate the acquisition of the former.

According to Scribner, the most popular metaphor has been to see literacy as a state of grace, wherein literacy is positioned as a kind of salvation in which literate people are seen to have special virtues; hence, the traditional notion of the literati.

Defining Literacy

Regardless of what beliefs people have about literacy, unless literacy is clearly defined, it cannot be measured and assessed. There is little consensus regarding what it means to be literate; however, the ability to interpret or produce meaning using written text is common to most definitions. One of the reasons literacy has been difficult to define is that expectations regarding what it means to be literate do not remain stable over time. Throughout much of history, given the demands of time and effort needed to produce or gather food, literacy was only accessible to elites who had the leisure time to acquire it. As a result, literacy came to be a powerful tool for the control of specialized knowledge, whether it was in the ability to recite or decipher sacred texts or interpret laws. In many traditions, literacy has involved the ability to read and or write in classical scripts that are not commonly spoken, or that may correspond to common vernaculars.

In these cases, literacy has often involved some degree of bilingualism.

In the United States, it has been common to focus on literacy as discrete individual skills that can be tested. Many scholars, such as Shirley Heath and Brian Street, focus on literacy as socially constructed practices involving print. From this perspective, literacy practices are embedded within social contexts and involve shared knowledge within social networks. Specialized knowledge can be accessed within a network in which all members have equal knowledge or skills, as long as one knows who has the knowledge and ability to access that knowledge.

As Terrence Wiley explained, despite the lack of consensus, the following list tends to be representative of some of the influential definitions of literacy:

Minimal literacy refers to the ability to read or write at any level. Minimal reading ability became one of the requirements for entry into the United States during the World War I era when immigrants were required to read a short passage from the Bible—whether or not they were Christian—in their native language. Interestingly, at that time, for purposes of immigration, literacy in languages other than English was recognized. Subsequently, this requirement has been replaced by an English-only literacy requirement.

Conventional literacy refers to the ability to read, write, and comprehend familiar texts. In many language-minority communities in the United States, familiar texts would include those in their native languages rather than English.

Basic literacy refers to the attainment of literacy that allows for ongoing, self-sustained development. A major debate in the United States has centered on whether language minority children and adults, who have not yet acquired literacy in their native languages, should receive instruction in English or their native languages first. Many bilingual theorists and researchers, Virginia Collier and Wayne Thomas, for example, stress the importance of the latter, even though educational policies have imposed the former in some states.

Functional literacy refers to the ability to use print to achieve personal goals and the demands of society, while effectively being employed and functioning as a consumer, voter, and everyday problem solver. Functional literacy has preoccupied much of the national debate about literacy in the United States. Functional literacy presumes basic literacy and the ability to read, write, and comprehend familiar text, but it extends the definition to include the ability to use reading and writing to fulfill an economic or social purpose. Although English literacy is often assumed to be necessary to function successfully in this country, many families are able to negotiate the literacy demands of their environments in their native languages to meet their basic needs. They are able to do this without always being literate in English because literacy involves more than just their individual knowledge. It also involves the ability to access a social network, in which others have knowledge that they share within this network.

Restricted literacy refers to literacy activities that are only available to a minority of people without the aid of state-supported school literacy. There have been some language communities where a script has been developed and informally taught outside state and federal policy. Scribner and Michael Cole conducted research with the Vai people in West Africa, who developed a script for their own social and commercial purposes. Restricted literacies tend to be informally taught based on local, practical needs. They do not necessarily compete with dominant societal language of literacy taught through state-supported public schools; nevertheless, they can offer rich possibilities for enhancing communication within local communities.

Vernacular literacies are those that are generated through popular and local practices. They often challenge or conflict with the conventions of standardized or dominant modes of literacy. Vernacular literacies such as those that have developed around rap and hip-hop cultures blur the distinction between oral and literate communication because oral styles may also be represented in writing. These literacies may also involve the use of nonstandard varieties of language.

Elite literacy refers to knowledge and skills certified by academic credentials acquired in school. Degrees, diplomas, and other forms of literacy certification are taken as evidence of mastery without their holders having to continue demonstrating the literacy skills that were needed to attain them. Thus, these skills become markers of literacy status. Although an elite education often includes instruction in languages other than English, reading and writing knowledge of a language other than English does not necessarily count unless one has acquired it through formal education.

Multiliteracies refer to knowledge and skills specifically related to particular types of literacy skills related to, for example, so-called cultural literacy, computer literacy, mathematical literacy or numeracy, or critical literacy. During the 1990s, the National

Adult Literacy Survey (NALS) prepared by Irwin Kirsch, Ann Jungeblut, Lynn Jenkins, and Andrew Kolstad attempted to assess three domains of literacy: document, prose, and quantitative. These were generally conceived as subsets of functional literacy, but only in English.

One common element of these definitions, as applied in the United States, is that they can—but frequently do not—reference literacy in languages other than English because of the ideological dominance of the English language.

Bilingualism Versus Biliteracy

Literacy is often assumed to correspond with spoken languages as speech written down. There are theoretical and technical problems with this view, but the notion persists. From a school perspective, language is typically conceived as four skills: speaking, listening, reading, and writing. The notion of four skills, therefore, presumes literacy. There are, however, approximately 6,000 to 7,000 spoken languages in the world, many of which do have writing systems or systems that are commonly used. As a result, there are fewer languages of literacy than spoken languages, and fewer yet that are languages of literacy used in formal schooling. Thus, bilingualism and multilingualism are not necessarily associated with literacy.

The widespread school's eye view that language involves four skills also leads to the assumption that there can be so-called balanced bilinguals, or people with equal abilities in speaking, listening, reading, and writing of two languages. Increasingly, however, the idea that there can be fully balanced bilinguals has been criticized. Guadalupe Valdés refers to them as "mythological" bilinguals, because, although it is possible in theory, it is not frequent that people obtain the exact same access to both languages in identical contexts or that they use language for the same functions and persons they interact with. Thus, finding fully balanced biliterates is equally unlikely. Nevertheless, many people do achieve a high degree of biliteracy when provided with the opportunity.

In highly multilingual countries such as India, children who have access to schooling are expected to receive education in the national language, Hindi, as well as in English and in the dominant language of their local state. These options may, or may not, however, correspond to the language(s) of their family and community. In the United States, immigrant language minority students have no inherent right to native language-instruction, and only a small number have access to it. Thus, a potential resource for developing some degree of biliteracy through schooling is underused.

Approaches to Estimating Literacy

Regardless of whether we are interested in English literacy, biliteracy, or native-language literacy in languages other than English, literacy is measured or estimated in only three major ways. These involve direct assessments, literacy surrogates or equivalencies, or self-reports. Direct assessments of literacy involve tests or demonstrations of literacy. If we attempt to determine national literacy rates, direct measures are not feasible for the entire population. Thus, there have been attempts to gather representative samples of the adult population. To date, most attempts at national assessment have been limited to English literacy. Such was the focus of the National Adult Literacy Survey and subsequent surveys that have sought to assess three major types of literacy skills and knowledge, related to texts involving prose, documents, or mathematical computation.

Surrogate indicators of literacy are sometimes used to provide crude measures of literacy when direct measures are not feasible. The most common are based on years of schooling. Six or 8 years of schooling, for example, have been taken as equivalent to basic or functional literacy. Most surveys, such as the U.S. Census, rely on self-reported information; thus, surrogate and self-reported indicators may work in tandem. Direct measures are certainly preferable to either, but even these are subject to scrutiny regarding their authenticity. Testing one's skills in quantitative literacy related to a problem about shopping is not as authentic as actually studying how people manage their money in actual shopping. Despite their limitations, surrogate and self-reported measures of literacy abilities, nevertheless, can provide some useful information, particularly about literacy in languages other than English.

Limitations of Assessments That Focus Only on English

For the past several decades, the United States has seen a major increase in language diversity, largely through immigration; according to Ofelia García, the United States now has the fifth largest Spanish-speaking population in the world. By ignoring literacy in

Spanish and other languages, the literacy picture of the United States is both incomplete and distorted. Failure to account for literacy in languages other than English increases the perception of a "literacy crisis" and stigmatizes those people who are literate in other languages as if they were "illiterate."

A related problem involves confusing literacy with spoken language abilities. National demographic surveys have tended to place more emphasis on English-speaking ability than on English literacy. Similarly, adult education programs for language minority populations often emphasize the acquisition of oral English or sustained English literacy development.

Other problems have related to biases in sampling. Reynaldo Macías notes that significant problems were found in the 1990 U.S. Census data of specific groups, whose reported figures were lower than what they were supposed to be. Thus, reported data tend to be more accurate in characterizations of the general population than of linguistic minorities. Macías stresses that because most of the surveys had been designed for the assessment of English literacy, the samples might

have excluded those who had limited or no proficiency in English. Macías further cautions that the representation of language diversity in the census samples does not necessarily include those subjects who had a limited ability in the English language from selection or analysis. A final area of concern in national literacy profiles relates to ambiguity in linguistic, ethnic, and racial identification. Macías also warns that there has been extensive indistinctness in how labels are used in studies of literacy wherein ethnic identifiers often are treated as surrogates for language background.

Regardless of how literacy is defined, if literacy in languages other than English is excluded, the perception of a literacy crisis will be inflated. In recent years, there has been a slight improvement in the attempt to gather more information on literacy in languages other than English. Although the 1993 National Adult Literacy Survey, for example, only attempted to directly assess, or test, literacy abilities in English, the survey did include some self-reported data on literacy in other languages. If we focus on literacy among the U.S. Hispanic population, the importance of including a focus on native-language literacy and biliteracy becomes apparent. Based

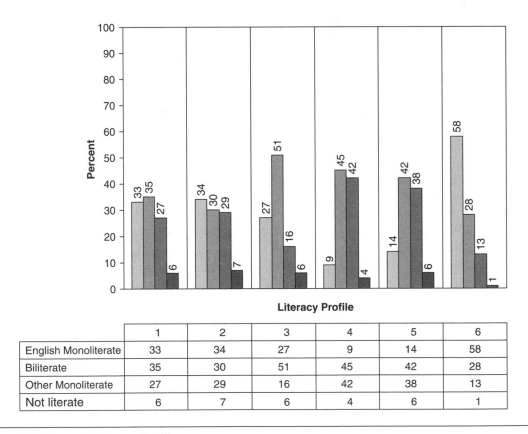

	1	2	3	4	5	6
English Monoliterate	33	34	27	9	14	58
Biliterate	35	30	51	45	42	28
Other Monoliterate	27	29	16	42	38	13
Not literate	6	7	6	4	6	1

Figure 1   U.S. Hispanic Literacy Profile

Source: Adapted from Greenberg et al. (2001), Table 2.4, p. 32.

on self-reported literacy data, 94% of all adult Hispanics were literate. If literacy and Spanish and other languages were excluded, however, only 68% of the sample would have been considered literate. When Latino subgroups such as Cuban Americans are considered (see Figure 1), only 54% would have been considered literate if Spanish and other languages had been excluded, compared with an overall rate of 96% when they are included. There is also a substantial degree of biliteracy among all Hispanics (35%) and particularly among Puerto Rican Americans (51%).

These data indicate that a focus on only English literacy inflates the perception of the purported "literacy crisis." Designing national literacy assessments that incorporate estimates of English literacy and literacy in languages other than English will provide a more accurate picture of literacy in the United States. There is equally a need to assess the kinds of literacy needs and interests of the populations being surveyed. This requires more ethnographic study of literacy practices among various linguistic communities.

Terrence G. Wiley

Editor's Note: Portions of this entry are based on the author's more detailed treatment of the subject in Wiley (2005).

See also Continua of Biliteracy; Literacy Instruction, First and Second Language

Further Readings

August, D., & Shanahan, T. (Eds.) (2006). *Developing literacy in second-language learners: Report of the national literacy panel on language-minority children and youth.* Mahwah, NJ: Lawrence Erlbaum.

Collier, V. P., & Thomas, W. P. (1998). *Language minority student achievement and program effectiveness: Research summary of ongoing study.* Fairfax, VA: George Mason University.

Freire, P. (1970). *Pedagogy of the oppressed.* New York: Seabury Press.

García, O. (2005). Positioning heritage languages in the United States. *Modern Language Journal, 89,* 601–605.

Greenberg, E., Macías, R. F., Rhodes, D., & Chan, T. (2001). *English literacy and language minorities in the United States.* Washington, DC: Center for Educational Statistics, U.S. Department of Education.

Heath, S. B. (1993). *Ways with words: Language, life, and work in communities and classrooms.* New York: Cambridge University Press.

Kirsch, I. S., Jungeblut, A., Jenkins, L., & Kolstad, A. (1993). *Adult literacy in America: A first look at the results of the National Adult Literacy Survey.* Washington, DC: U.S. Department of Education, Office of Educational Research and Improvement.

Macías, R. F. (1994). Inheriting sins while seeking absolution: Language diversity and national statistical data sets. In D. Spener (Ed.), *Adult biliteracy in the United States* (pp. 15–45). Washington, DC: Center for Applied Linguistics and Delta Systems.

Scribner, S. (1988). Literacy in three metaphors. In E. R. Kintgen, B. M. Kroll, & M. Rose (Eds.), *Perspectives on literacy* (pp. 71–81). Carbondale: Southern Illinois University Press.

Scribner, S., & Cole, M. (1981). *The psychology of literacy.* Cambridge, MA: Harvard University Press.

Street, B. (1984). *Literacy in theory and practice.* Cambridge, UK: Cambridge University Press.

Valdés, G. (2001). Heritage language students: Profiles and possibilities. In J. K. Peyton, D. A. Ranard, & S. McGinnis (Eds.), *Heritage languages in America: Preserving a national resource* (pp. 37–80). Washington, DC: Center for Applied Linguistics and Delta Systems.

Wiley, T. G. (2005). *Literacy and language diversity in the United States* (2nd ed.). Washington, DC: Center for Applied Linguistics and Delta Systems.

LITERACY INSTRUCTION, FIRST AND SECOND LANGUAGE

Imagine you have a 5-year-old daughter going off to her first day of kindergarten in a U.S. public school. Your child is fluent in your family's mother tongue (which, let's imagine, is not English). Perhaps you have read children's books to her every night before bed. Perhaps she can recognize some words in environmental print or, depending on the richness of her literacy environment, can read and write some letters or words in her mother tongue. Now, however, on her first day of school, her teacher is speaking to her in a language she does not understand. Your child is not alone. Millions of primary-age children enter U.S. classrooms fluent in a language other than English. If you can imagine this child's anxiety on her first day in school, in a classroom in which she does not understand anything her teacher says, consider her situation in the next few weeks, as she begins to receive reading instruction in a language she does not speak or comprehend.

On the basis of this scenario, you may recognize intuitively how little sense it makes to teach children how to read in a second language before they can read in their mother tongue. Research is clear on this matter: It is better to help children become literate in their mother tongue before attempting to foster literacy in a second or additional language, a language that they are still acquiring. It is not possible (in some states not even legal), however, to provide literacy instruction to children in their mother tongue (other than English) first in many U.S. classrooms. Our classrooms are growing in diversity such that it is possible to have multiple languages represented in a single classroom. It is not likely that classroom teachers will be literate in all of the languages in their classroom to the extent that they can facilitate literacy in each student's native language. Further, some states, such as California, Arizona, and Massachusetts, have passed legislation that severely limits the accessibility of bilingual classrooms, even in schools that have somewhat homogeneous student populations (e.g., schools with large numbers of Latino students). Therefore, what is theoretically best is not always practically feasible in the classroom. However, classroom teachers can support native-language literacy in classrooms in many ways, even when they are not literate in their students' native languages. This entry describes native-language-literacy research and its effects in and beyond the classroom.

Research on Native-Language Literacy

Research by Steve Krashen, Jim Cummins, Jeff McQuillan, and others shows that children who first learn to read in their native language become literate in a target language faster than if they are expected to learn to read in a second language. Further, several studies (see work by Stephen Krashen) have shown a correlation of ability level in native-language literacy compared with target-language literacy. In other words, the higher the reading ability level in English was, the higher it was in the native language.

Native-language literacy helps support target-language literacy for several reasons. One is that it is easier to learn to read in a language one already speaks. Another is that once someone learns to read in one language, their reading skills may transfer to other languages (especially when those languages share alphabetic similarities, such as Spanish and English).

A slightly more technical look at the reasoning behind supporting native-language literacy first involves the process of reading itself. Reading requires the use of multiple cueing systems so the reader can construct meaning from a text. Readers use schemas (as explained by Richard Anderson, Rand Spiro, and M. C. Anderson), which are existing knowledge structures within each reader, to make meaning as they read. Schemas are both experiential and linguistic. Thus, it is easier for readers to make predictions based on schemas if they have experiences and language in common with the text. The three basic cueing systems are syntactic, semantic, and graphophonic, as Kenneth Goodman explains. *Syntactic cues* refer to grammar and language structure, such as word order. *Semantic cues* are the context cues a reader uses to predict meaning. *Graphophonic cues* are letter-sound correspondences the reader uses to predict specific words. Proficient readers use all three cues simultaneously.

It is easier for readers to use all three cueing systems in a language they already speak. Native speakers of most languages have already acquired the sounds and structures of the language that they need to predict meaning as they read. Take, for example, the following sentence:

I have a *pink* pig.

Native speakers of English already have syntactic knowledge that would allow them to predict the word *pink* because their experience with English would inform them that in English, adjectives generally precede the nouns they modify. Further, these readers would likely have schemas for the word *pink*. It would be easier for native speakers of English to make syntactic and semantic predictions about this sentence because of the linguistic and experiential knowledge that they have in English. The same is true for any native speaker of any language. Once readers have learned how to use schemas, language cues, and reading strategies to construct meaning from text in their native language, they can use the same skills to construct meaning from texts in their second language. Even if the native language is nonalphabetic, or runs from right to left, such as Mandarin (which is character-based) or Farsi, schemas, context, reading strategies, and language cues (other than graphophonic cues, in the case of character-based languages) are involved in constructing meaning from text, and these skills transfer such that readers can draw from them, as they construct meaning from text in their second language.

Bringing this discussion back to the child in our example, it will be much easier for her to learn to read in the language in which she has already established schemas, including experiences and language structures that will allow her to use prediction skills to construct meaning from text. Her affective experiences will also be much more positive, which will contribute to her sense of confidence as a reader and writer. Confidence is a key component of success in literacy.

Native-Language Literacy in the Classroom

Teachers can support native-language literacy in the classroom in many ways, even if they do not speak the language. Researchers (see for example the work by McQuillan) cite the importance of the availability of native-language materials in the classroom. High-quality children's literature, including predictable books, picture books, or big books, that are in the native language of students are vital to supporting native-language and target-language literacy. Bilingual books as well as books in English that reflect the schemas of students in our classrooms should also be a part of our classroom libraries. Such materials can be found in public libraries, online book ordering companies, and local bookstores, as well as from specialty publishers.

In addition, community members are great resources for native-language literature, including children's books, poetry, and stories passed down by oral tradition. Parents and community members can be invited into the classroom to provide support in workshop settings in which students engage in reading aloud, storytelling, shared readings, and the like.

Children can be allowed to read and write in their native language. Sociopsycholinguistic theories maintain that children learn to read by reading and they learn to write by writing, as explained by Kenneth and Yetta Goodman. Children can be encouraged and supported by well-trained teachers to engage in meaningful literacy experiences in their native language. For example, children can write in their native language—even as emerging writers use scribble writing, prephonemic writing, or invented spellings in English, they can do the same in the native language. Journal writing activities, shared writing (in which the teacher and students write a common text, discussing writing decisions explicitly), and write-aloud activities (in which the teacher or a speaker of the native language from the community think aloud as they are demonstrating writing and the decision making that goes into it), and process writing (taking writing through the process of rough draft, revision, editing, and publishing/sharing) can all use the students' native languages.

The benefits of native-language literacy for target-language literacy have been well documented by scientific research, including that cited previously. Thus, it behooves teachers to find as many means as possible to support native-language literacy. This will require resourcefulness, creativity, and the support of beyond-school communities, but it is worthwhile. Imagine the best-case scenario: Our child walking into a classroom in which a welcoming adult speaks her language—someone who can tell her where to hang her coat, where to find the restroom, where to get a drink of water; someone who, beyond those basic needs, can help her find her way to the world of literacy. Imagine our child finding stories and books that reflect who she is culturally and linguistically. These needs are fundamental, and every child has the right to have them met in the classroom, one way or another.

Native-Language Literacy Beyond the Classroom

Native-language literacy is not only a means to an end, it is also an end in itself. As our growing students expand their knowledge, they also explore their sense of identity. The goal, in short, is biliteracy. Thus empowered, students can continue to read in their native language, to write in their native language, and to become bilingual, biliterate, unique individuals who have access to multiple worlds of literature.

Cathy A. Coulter

See also Acculturation; Affective Filter; Biculturalism; Bilingualism Stages; Native American Languages, Legal Support for; Phonics in Bilingual Education; Threshold Hypothesis; Whole Language

Further Readings

Anderson, R. C., Spiro, R. J., & Anderson, M. C. (1977). *Schemata as scaffolding for the representation of meaning in connected discourse.* (Tech, Rep. no. 24.) Urbana, IL: Center for the Study of Reading (ERIC): (ED 136–236).

Cummins, J. (2000). *Language, power and pedagogy: Bilingual children in the crossfire.* Buffalo, NY: Multilingual Matters.

Freeman, Y., & Freeman, D. (1997). *Teaching reading and writing in Spanish in the Bilingual Classroom.* Portsmouth, NH: Heinemann.

García, G. G. (Ed.). (2005). *English learners: Reaching the highest level of English literacy.* Upper Saddle River, NJ: Pearson Merrill Prentice Hall.

Goodman, K. S. (1965). A linguistic study of cues and miscues in reading. *Elementary English, 42,* 639–643.

Goodman, K. S., & Goodman, Y. M. (1979). Learning to read is natural. In L. B. Resnic & P. A. Weaver (Eds.), *Theory and practice of early reading* (Vol. 1, pp. 137–154). Hillsdale, NJ: Lawrence Erlbaum.

Krashen, S. (2002). Does transition really happen? Some case histories. *The multilingual educator, 3*(1), 50–54.

Krashen, S. (2005). Three roles for reading for minority-language children. In G. G. Garcia (Ed.), *English learners: Reaching the highest level of English literacy* (pp. 55–70). Upper Saddle River, NJ: Pearson Merrill Prentice Hall.

McQuillan, J. (1998). *The literacy crisis: False claims, real solutions.* Portsmouth, NH: Heinemann.

Lyons, James J. (1947–)

James John Lyons was a respected senior adviser and specialist on civil rights for a decade before becoming the executive director and legislative counsel of the National Association for Bilingual Education (NABE). Jim, as he is known to countless bilingual educators across the country, held that highly visible position for 9 years before stepping down in 1998. An attorney father who was committed to helping those in social disfavor and psychologist Kenneth B. Clark, who played a central role in the desegregation of American schools, were major influences in shaping Lyons's personal and professional life. During his tenure at NABE, Lyons gained the support and respect of a broad-based constituency nationwide that admired his tireless championing of bilingual education, his gifts as an orator, and his Capitol Hill savvy, as he led NABE through what were arguably its greatest years as an organization.

Lyons was born and raised in Omaha, Nebraska. While in high school, he earned statewide recognition for his debating skills. His abilities as a debater earned him a 4-year scholarship to George Washington University (GWU), where he received a BA degree in American thought and civilization in 1969. While attending law school at GWU, he was hired by Clark and his wife Mamie Phipps Clark as a staff member with the Washington, D.C., Office of the Metropolitan Applied Research Center. The Clarks had gained national prominence for their testimony as expert witnesses in *Briggs v. Elliott,* a case that was later merged into *Brown v. Board of Education,* which officially overturned racial segregation in public education. Lyons and Dr. Clark remained friends and colleagues until Clark's death in 2005. Clark, a supporter of bilingual education for all children, had urged Lyons to apply discipline, research, and reason to help society overcome inequality and discrimination. That ideology guided Lyons through the early stages of a newly found passion: bilingual education.

In 1980, Lyons was appointed senior adviser to the assistant secretary for legislation within the newly created U.S. Department of Education. In August of that year, President Jimmy Carter's administration published a Notice of Proposed Rulemaking (NPRM) to clarify the legal responsibilities of school districts serving limited-English-proficient students. The NPRM, although much needed and long overdue, ignited a firestorm of political controversy hotter than even previous conflagrations over "forced busing." As the Carter administration's chief firefighter on Capitol Hill on this issue, Lyons was able to contain the damage. Following the election of Ronald Reagan in November, Lyons was asked by Reagan's new education secretary, Terrel Bell, to stay on to help develop a new *Lau* enforcement program that would protect the rights of language minority students but would not create unnecessary furor. Conservatives within and outside the Reagan administration pushed for a total renunciation of *Lau v. Nichols;* Lyons countered their ideological arguments with cogent legal analysis, and in the end, Secretary Bell promulgated the results-oriented set of *Lau* enforcement guidelines Lyons had developed. Having accomplished the vital objective, Lyons resigned his position in the department and turned his full attention to bilingual education.

After leaving the U.S. Department of Education, Lyons assumed the position of legislative counsel for NABE. His strategy was to increase awareness and knowledge about the value of bilingual education for all students. He accomplished this by building coalitions with respected organizations that represented American Indian, Latino, and Asian communities. In 1983, congressional representatives Baltasar Corrada (D-PR) and Dale Kildee (D-MI) asked Lyons to rewrite legislation revamping Title VII of the Elementary and Secondary Education Act. Lyons worked closely with Lori Orum of the National Council of La Raza, and they rewrote the existing law and accomplished a significant strengthening of the act. As Lyons later noted, "The legislation recast bilingual education as a vital language enrichment program rather than a remedial teaching program." In 1984, President Reagan signed that bill into law.

The executive board of NABE asked Lyons in 1989 to become both the executive director and legislative counsel. The challenges he faced were considerable; NABE was in organizational disarray. Working closely with various executive boards, presidents, and staff, he led the effort to transform NABE into a viable and visible organization. As Nancy Zelasko, founding director of the National Clearinghouse for English Language Acquisition and former deputy director of NABE, asserted, Lyons was instrumental in the transformation of the organization regarding its national recognition, stability, and influence.

Lyons resigned from NABE in 1998. Even though he is no longer directly involved with NABE, he is still considered by many in the field as one of the most important and influential leaders in the progression of bilingual education in the United States. Bilingual education remains a part of Lyons's life and, as he recently commented, "If the current generation of our nation's leaders had received quality bilingual bicultural education, our society would be better and stronger, and our reputation in the world community would be better and safer."

Paul E. Martínez

See also National Association for Bilingual Education; Title VII, Elementary and Secondary Education Act, Key Historical Marker; Title VII, Elementary and Secondary Education Act, Subsequent Amendments; Zelasko, Nancy

Further Readings

Briggs v. Elliott, 342 U.S. 350 (1952).

Brown v. Board of Education, 347 U.S. 483 (1954).

Lau v. Nichols, 414 U.S. 563 (1974).

Lyons, J. J. (1990). The past and future directions of federal bilingual-education policy. *The ANNALS of the American Academy of Political and Social Science, 508,* 66–80.

Medina, L. (2003). Introduction. In L. Medina (Ed.), *At issue: Bilingual education.* San Diego: Greenhaven Press. Retrieved from http://www.enotes.com/bilingual-education-article/38841